Arvo

urbit/pkg/arvo/sys/

West Martian Limited Company
2nd Edition, November 2023

Content from urbit/urbit is available under the MIT license at https://github.org/urbit/urbit.
First printing 2023
Second printing 2023
The publisher can be contacted at westmartian.com
ISBN-13: 979-8-218-30955-8 Paperback

Contents

Arvo

Arvo

Arvo 237K

```
 1  =>   ..ride  =>
 2  !:
 3  |%
 4  +|   %global
 5  ::
 6  ++   arvo   %237
 7  ::
 8  ::    $arch: node identity
 9  ::    $axal: fundamental node, recursive (trie)
10  ::    $axil: fundamental node
11  ::    $beak: global context
12  ::    $beam: global name
13  ::    $bone: opaque duct handle
14  ::    $case: global version
15  ::    $cage: marked vase
16  ::    +cask: marked data builder
17  ::    $desk: local workspace
18  ::    $dock: message target
19  ::    $gang: infinite set of peers
20  ::    $mark: symbolic content type
21  ::    $mien: orientation
22  ::    $page: untyped cage
23  ::    $omen: fully-qualified namespace path
24  ::    $ship: network identity
25  ::    $sink: subscription
26  ::
27  +$   arch   (axil @uvI)
28  ++   axal
29    |$  [item]
30    [fil=(unit item) dir=(map @ta $)]
31  ++   axil
32    |$  [item]
33    [fil=(unit item) dir=(map @ta ~)]
34  ::
35  +$   beak   (trel ship desk case)
36  +$   beam   [beak s=path]
37  +$   bone   @ud
38  +$   case
39    $%  ::  %da:  date
40        ::  %tas: label
41        ::  %ud:  sequence
42        ::  %uv:  hash
43        ::
44      [%da p=@da]
45      [%tas p=@tas]
46      [%ud p=@ud]
47      [%uv p=@uv]
48    ==
49  +$   cage   (cask vase)
50  ++   cask   |$  [a]   (pair mark a)
51  +$   desk   @tas
52  +$   dock   (pair @p term)
53  +$   gang   (unit (set ship))
54  +$   mark   @tas
55  +$   mien   [our=ship now=@da eny=@uvJ]
```

```
56  +$   page   (cask)
57  +$   omen   [vis=view bem=beam]
58  +$   ship   @p
59  +$   sink   (trel bone ship path)
60  ::
61  +|   %meta
62  ::
63  ::   +hypo: type-associated builder
64  ::   $meta: meta-vase
65  ::   $maze: vase, or meta-vase
66  ::
67  ++   hypo
68    |$  [a]
69    (pair type a)
70  +$   meta   (pair)
71  +$   maze   (each vase meta)
72  ::
73  +|   %interface
74  ::
75  ::   $ball: dynamic kernel action
76  ::   $card: tagged, untyped event
77  ::   $duct: causal history
78  ::   +hobo: %soft task builder
79  ::   $goof: crash label and trace XX fail/ruin/crud/flaw/lack/miss
80  ::   $mass: memory usage
81  ::   $move: cause and action
82  ::   $ovum: card with cause
83  ::   $roof: namespace
84  ::   $rook: meta-namespace (super advanced)
85  ::   +room: generic namespace
86  ::   +roon: partial namespace
87  ::   $root: raw namespace
88  ::   $view: namespace perspective
89  ::   +wind: kernel action builder
90  ::   $wire: event pretext
91  ::   +wite: kernel action/error builder
92  ::
93  +$   ball   (wite [vane=term task=maze] maze)
94  +$   card   (cask)
95  +$   duct   (list wire)
96  ++   hobo
97    |$  [a]
98    $?  $%  [%soft p=*]
99        ==
100         a
101    ==
102  +$   goof   [mote=term =tang]
103  +$   mass   $~   $+|+~
104              (pair cord (each * (list mass)))
105  +$   move   [=duct =ball]
106  +$   ovum   [=wire =card]
107  ::
108  +$   roof   (room vase)                              ::  namespace
109  +$   rook   (room meta)                              ::  meta-namespace
110  ++   room                                            ::  either namespace
111    |$  [a]
112    $~   =>(~ |~(* ~))
113    $-   $:  lyc=gang                                  ::  leakset
```

```
114          pov=path                                      ::  provenance
115          omen                                          ::  perspective, path
116        ==                                              ::
117    %-  unit                                            ::  ~: unknown
118    %-  unit                                            ::  ~ ~: invalid
119    (cask a)                                            ::
120  +$  roon                                              ::  partial namespace
121    $~  =>(~ |~(* ~))
122    $-  [lyc=gang pov=path car=term bem=beam]
123    (unit (unit cage))
124  +$  root   $-(^ (unit (unit)))
125  +$  view   $@(term [way=term car=term])               ::  perspective
126  ::
127  ++  wind
128    |$  ::  a: forward
129        ::  b: reverse
130        ::
131        [a b]
132    $%  ::  %pass: advance
133        ::  %slip: lateral
134        ::  %give: retreat
135        ::
136        [%pass p=path q=a]
137        [%slip p=a]
138        [%give p=b]
139    ==
140  +$  wire   path
141  ++  wite
142    |$  ::  note: a routed $task
143        ::  gift: a reverse action
144        ::
145        ::    NB:  task: a forward action
146        ::         sign: a sourced $gift
147        ::
148        [note gift]
149    $%  ::  %hurl: action failed
150        ::  %pass: advance
151        ::  %slip: lateral
152        ::  %give: retreat
153        ::
154        [%hurl =goof wite=$;($>(?(%pass %give) $))]
155        [%pass =wire =note]
156        [%slip =note]
157        [%give =gift]
158    ==
159  ::
160  +|  %implementation
161  ::
162  ::  $debt: ephemeral state
163  ::  $grub: persistent state, larval stage
164  ::  $germ: worklist source and bar stack
165  ::  $heir: upgradeable state
166  ::  $plan: worklist
167  ::  $soul: persistent state
168  ::  $vane: kernel module
169  ::  $vere: runtime version
170  ::  $vile: reflexive constants
171  ::  $waif: arvo task, from anywhere
```

```
172  ::   $wasp: arvo task, from Outside
173  ::   $weft: kelvin version, tag and number
174  ::   $worm: compiler cache
175  ::   $wisp: arvo task, larval stage
176  ::   $wynn: kelvin stack
177  ::
178  +$  debt
179    $:  ::  run: list of worklists
180        ::  out: pending output
181        ::  kel: kernel files
182        ::  fil: pending files
183        ::
184        run=(list plan)
185        out=(list ovum)
186        kel=(list (pair path (cask)))
187        fil=(list (pair path (cask)))
188    ==
189  +$  germ   [vane=term bars=(list duct)]
190  +$  grub
191    $:  ::  who: identity once we know it
192        ::  eny: entropy once we learn it
193        ::  lac: laconicity as we want it
194        ::  ver: the Outside as we see it
195        ::  fat: source when we attain it
196        ::  lul: %lull when we acquire it
197        ::  zus: %zuse once we receive it
198        ::  van: vanes while we desire it
199        ::
200        who=(unit ship)
201        eny=(unit @)
202        lac=?
203        ver=(unit vere)
204        fat=(unit (axal (cask)))
205        lul=(unit (trap vase))
206        zus=(unit (trap vase))
207        van=(map term (trap vase))
208    ==
209  +$  heir
210    $%  $:  %grub
211            $%  [?(%240 %239 %238 %237) =grub]
212        ==  ==
213        [?(%240 %239 %238 %237) =debt =soul]
214    ==
215  +$  plan  (pair germ (list move))
216  +$  soul
217    $:  ::  identity, time, entropy
218        ::  fad: configuration
219        ::  zen: Outside knowledge
220        ::  mod: internal modules
221        ::
222        mien
223        $=  fad
224        $:  ::  lac: not verbose
225            ::
226            lac=?
227        ==
228        $=  zen
229        $:  ::  ver: runtime version
```

```
230            ::  lag: upgrade blocked
231            ::
232            ver=vere
233            lag=_|
234        ==
235      $=  mod
236      $:  ::  fat: filesystem
237          ::  lul: %lull
238          ::  zus: %zuse
239          ::  van: vanes
240          ::
241          fat=(axal (cask))
242          lul=vase
243          zus=vase
244          van=(map term vane)
245        ==
246    ==
247  +$  vane  [=vase =worm]
248  +$  vere  [[non=@ta rev=path] kel=wynn]
249  +$  vile
250    $:  typ=type    ::  -:!>(*type)
251        duc=type    ::  -:!>(*duct)
252        wir=type    ::  -:!>(*wire)
253        dud=type    ::  -:!>(*(unit goof))
254    ==
255  ::
256  +$  waif
257    ::  %trim: trim state, spam to all
258    ::  %what: update from files
259    ::  %whey: produce $mass                    ::  XX remove, scry
260    ::  %verb: toggle laconicity
261    ::  %whiz: prime vane caches
262    ::
263    $%  [%trim p=@ud]
264        [%what p=(list (pair path (cask)))]
265        [%whey ~]
266        [%verb p=(unit ?)]
267        [%whiz ~]
268    ==
269  +$  wasp
270    ::  %crud: reroute $ovum with $goof
271    ::  %wack: iterate entropy
272    ::  %wyrd: check/record runtime kelvin stack
273    ::
274    $%  [%crud =goof =ovum]
275        [%wack p=@uvJ]
276        [%wyrd p=vere]
277    ==
278  +$  weft  [lal=@tas num=@ud]
279  +$  worm
280    $:  ::  +nest, +play, and +mint
281        ::
282        nes=(set ^)
283        pay=(map (pair type hoon) type)
284        mit=(map (pair type hoon) (pair type nock))
285    ==
286  +$  wisp
287    $%  $>(?(%verb %what) waif)
```

```
288       $>(?(%wack %wyrd) wasp)
289         [%whom p=ship]
290    ==
291 +$  wynn  (list weft)
292 --  =>
293 ::
294 ~%  %hex  ..ut  ~
295 |%
296 ::::::::::::::::::::::::::::::::::::::::::::::::::::::::::::::
297 ::                  section 3bE, Arvo core              ::
298 ::
299 ++  en-beam
300   |=(b=beam =*(s scot `path`[(s %p p.b) q.b (s r.b) s.b]))
301 ::
302 ++  de-beam
303   ~/  %de-beam
304   |=  p=path
305   ^-  (unit beam)
306   ?.  ?=([@ @ @ *] p)  ~
307   ?~  who=(slaw %p i.p)  ~
308   ?~  des=?~(i.t.p (some %$) (slaw %tas i.t.p))  ~  :: XX +sym ;~(pose low (easy %$))
309   ?~  ved=(de-case i.t.t.p)  ~
310   `[[`ship`u.who `desk`u.des u.ved] t.t.t.p]
311 ::
312 ++  de-case
313   ~/  %de-case
314   |=  =knot
315   ^-  (unit case)
316   ?^  num=(slaw %ud knot)  `[%ud u.num]
317   ?^  wen=(slaw %da knot)  `[%da u.wen]
318   ?^  hax=(slaw %uv knot)  `[%uv u.hax]
319   ?~  lab=(slaw %tas knot)  ~
320   `[%tas u.lab]
321 ::
322 ++  en-omen
323   |=  omen
324   ^-  path
325   :_  (en-beam bem)
326   ?@  vis  vis
327   ~(rent co [%many $/tas/way.vis $/tas/car.vis ~])
328 ::
329 ++  de-omen
330   ~/  %de-omen
331   |=  pax=path
332   ^-  (unit omen)
333   ?~  pax  ~
334   ?~  bem=(de-beam t.pax)  ~
335   ?:  ((sane %tas) i.pax)
336     `[i.pax u.bem]
337   =/  lot=(unit coin)  (rush i.pax ;~(pfix dot perd:so))
338   ?.  ?&  ?=(^ lot)
339           ?=([%many [%$ %tas @] [%$ %tas @] ~] u.lot)
340       ==
341     ~
342   `[[q.p.i q.p.i.t]:p.u.lot u.bem]
343 ::
344 ++  look
345   ~/  %look
```

```
346    |=  [rof=roof lyc=gang pov=path]
347    ^-  root
348    ~/  %in
349    |=  [ref=* raw=*]
350    ?~  pax=((soft path) raw)  ~
351    ?~  mon=(de-omen u.pax)  ~
352    ?~  dat=(rof lyc pov u.mon)  ~
353    ?~  u.dat  [~ ~]
354    =*  vax  q.u.u.dat
355    ?.  ?&  ?=(^ ref)
356            =(hoon-version -.ref)
357            -:(~(nets wa *worm) +.ref p.vax)
358        ==
359      ~>(%slog.[0 leaf+"arvo: scry-lost"] ~)
360    [~ ~ q.vax]
361  ::  |wyrd: kelvin negotiation
362  ::
363  ::    specified but unimplemented:
364  ::    arvo should produce a [wend/wynn] effect
365  ::    to signal downgrade
366  ::
367  ++  wyrd
368    |%
369    ::  +sane: kelvin stack for validity
370    ::
371    ++  sane
372      |=  kel=wynn
373      ^-  ?
374      ?:  =(~ kel)  &
375      =^  las=weft  kel  kel
376      |-  ^-  ?
377      ?~  kel  &
378      ?&  (gte num.las num.i.kel)
379          $(las i.kel, kel t.kel)
380      ==
381    ::  +need: require kelvins
382    ::
383    ++  need
384      |=  [run=wynn hav=wynn]
385      ::  wyr: ~: runtime supports all required kelvins
386      ::       ^: runtime support is missing or lagging
387      ::
388      =;  wyr  !.
389        ?~  wyr
390          same
391        ~&  wyrd=wyr
392        ~_  :+  %rose
393               [" " ~ ~]
394             :~  =+  p.u.wyr
395                 leaf/"%{(trip lal)} %{(scow %ud num)} required;"
396                 ?~  q.u.wyr
397                   leaf/"runtime missing support"
398                 leaf/"runtime only supports %{(scow %ud u.q.u.wyr)}"
399             ==
400        ~>  %mean.'arvo: upgrade blocked'
401        ~>  %mean.'wyrd'
402        !!
403      ::
```

```
404        |-  ^-  (unit (pair weft (unit @ud)))
405        ?~  hav   ~
406        ::
407        ::  fel: %&: runtime kelvin for [i.hav]
408        ::         %|: no specified runtime support
409        ::
410        =/  fel
411          |-  ^-  (each @ud weft)
412          ?~  run  |/i.hav
413          ?:(=(lal.i.hav lal.i.run) &/num.i.run $(run t.run))
414        ::
415        ?-  -.fel
416          %|  `[p.fel ~]
417          %&  ?.((lte p.fel num.i.hav) `[i.hav `p.fel] $(hav t.hav))
418        ==
419      --
420    ::
421    ::  |of: axal engine
422    ::
423    ++  of
424      =|  fat=(axal)
425      |@
426      ++  del
427        |=  pax=path
428        ^+  fat
429        ?~  pax  [~ dir.fat]
430        =/  kid  (~(get by dir.fat) i.pax)
431        ?~  kid  fat
432        fat(dir (~(put by dir.fat) i.pax $(fat u.kid, pax t.pax)))
433        ::  Descend to the axal at this path
434        ::
435      ++  dip
436        |=  pax=path
437        ^+  fat
438        ?~  pax  fat
439        =/  kid  (~(get by dir.fat) i.pax)
440        ?~  kid  [~ ~]
441        $(fat u.kid, pax t.pax)
442        ::
443      ++  gas
444        |=  lit=(list (pair path _?>(?=(^ fil.fat) u.fil.fat)))
445        ^+  fat
446        ?~  lit  fat
447        $(fat (put p.i.lit q.i.lit), lit t.lit)
448        ::
449      ++  get
450        |=  pax=path
451        fil:(dip pax)
452        ::  Fetch file at longest existing prefix of the path
453        ::
454      ++  fit
455        |=  pax=path
456        ^+  [pax fil.fat]
457        ?~  pax  [~ fil.fat]
458        =/  kid  (~(get by dir.fat) i.pax)
459        ?~  kid  [pax fil.fat]
460        =/  low  $(fat u.kid, pax t.pax)
461        ?~  +.low
```

```
462        [pax fil.fat]
463      low
464    ::
465    ++  has
466      |=  pax=path
467      !=(~ (get pax))
468    ::  Delete subtree
469    ::
470    ++  lop
471      |=  pax=path
472      ^+  fat
473      ?~  pax  fat
474      |-
475      ?~  t.pax  fat(dir (~(del by dir.fat) i.pax))
476      =/  kid  (~(get by dir.fat) i.pax)
477      ?~  kid  fat
478      fat(dir (~(put by dir.fat) i.pax $(fat u.kid, pax t.pax)))
479    ::
480    ++  put
481      |*  [pax=path dat=*]
482      =>  .(dat `_?>(?=(^ fil.fat) u.fil.fat)`dat, pax `path`pax)
483      |-  ^+  fat
484      ?~  pax  fat(fil `dat)
485      =/  kid  (~(gut by dir.fat) i.pax ^+(fat [~ ~]))
486      fat(dir (~(put by dir.fat) i.pax $(fat kid, pax t.pax)))
487    ::
488    ++  tap
489      =|  pax=path
490      =|  out=(list (pair path _?>(?=(^ fil.fat) u.fil.fat)))
491      |-  ^+  out
492      =?  out  ?=(^ fil.fat)  :_(out [pax u.fil.fat])
493      =/  dir  ~(tap by dir.fat)
494      |-  ^+  out
495      ?~  dir  out
496      %=  $
497        dir  t.dir
498        out  ^$(pax (weld pax /[p.i.dir]), fat q.i.dir)
499      ==
500    ::  Serialize to map
501    ::
502    ++  tar
503      (~(gas by *(map path _?>(?=(^ fil.fat) u.fil.fat))) tap)
504    --
505  ::
506  ++  wa                                        ::  cached compile
507    |_  worm
508    ++  nell  |=(ref=type (nest [%cell %noun %noun] ref))  ::  nest in cell
509    ++  nest                                    ::  nest:ut, cached
510      |=  [sut=type ref=type]
511      ^-  [? worm]
512      ?:  (~(has in nes) [sut ref])  [& +>+<]
513      ?.  (~(nest ut sut) | ref)
514        ~&  %nest-failed
515        =+  foo=(skol ref)
516        =+  bar=(skol sut)
517        ~&  %nest-need
518        ~>  %slog.[0 bar]
519        ~&  %nest-have
```

```
520      ~>  %slog.[0 foo]
521      [| +>+<.$]
522    [& +>+<(nes (~(put in nes) [sut ref]))]
523  ::
524  ++  call                                        ::  call gate
525    |=  [vax=vase nam=term som=(each vase ^)]
526    ^-  [vase worm]
527    =^  duf  +>+<.$  (open vax nam som)
528    (slap duf [%limb %$])
529  ::
530  ++  open                                        ::  assemble door
531    |=  [vax=vase nam=term som=(each vase ^)]
532    ^-  [vase worm]
533    =*  key  [%cncb [[%& 2] ~] [[[%& 6] ~] [%$ 3]] ~]
534    =^  dor  +>+<.$  (slap vax [%limb nam])
535    =^  mes  +>+<.$  (slot 6 dor)
536    =^  hip  +>+<.$
537      ?-  -.som
538        %&  (nest p.mes p.p.som)
539        %|  (nets p.mes -.p.som)
540      ==
541    ?>  hip
542    [[p.dor q.dor(+6 +7.som)] +>+<.$]
543  ::
544  ++  neat                                        ::  type compliance
545    |=  [typ=type som=(each vase ^)]
546    ^-  worm
547    =^  hip  +>+<.$
548      ?-  -.som
549        %&  (nest typ p.p.som)
550        %|  (nets typ -.p.som)
551      ==
552    ?>  hip
553    +>+<.$
554  ::
555  ++  nets                                        ::  typeless nest
556    |=  [sut=* ref=*]
557    ^-  [? worm]
558    ?:  (~(has in nes) [sut ref])  [& +>+<]
559    =+  gat=|=([a=type b=type] (~(nest ut a) | b))
560    ?.  (? (slum gat [sut ref]))
561      ~&  %nets-failed
562      =+  tag=`*`skol
563      =+  foo=(tank (slum tag ref))
564      =+  bar=(tank (slum tag sut))
565      ~&  %nets-need
566      ~>  %slog.[0 bar]
567      ~&  %nets-have
568      ~>  %slog.[0 foo]
569      [| +>+<.$]
570    [& +>+<.$(nes (~(put in nes) [sut ref]))]
571  ::  +play: +play:ut, cached
572  ::
573  ++  play
574    |=  [sut=type gen=hoon]
575    ^-  [type worm]
576    =+  old=(~(get by pay) [sut gen])
577    ?^  old  [u.old +>+<.$]
```

```
578    =+  new=(~(play ut sut) gen)
579    [new +>+<.$(pay (~(put by pay) [sut gen] new))]
580  ::  +mint: +mint:ut to noun, cached
581  ::
582  ++  mint
583    |=  [sut=type gen=hoon]
584    ^-  [(pair type nock) worm]
585    =+  old=(~(get by mit) [sut gen])
586    ?^  old  [u.old +>+<.$]
587    =+  new=(~(mint ut sut) %noun gen)
588    [new +>+<.$(mit (~(put by mit) [sut gen] new))]
589  ::  +slam: +slam:ut, cached
590  ::
591  ++  slam
592    |=  [gat=vase sam=vase]
593    =/  sut=type  [%cell p.gat p.sam]
594    =/  gen=hoon  [%cnsg [%$ ~] [%$ 2] [%$ 3] ~]
595    =^  new=type  +>+<.$  (play sut gen)
596    [[new (slum q.gat q.sam)] +>+<.$]
597  ::  +slap: +slap:ut, cached
598  ::
599  ++  slap
600    |=  [vax=vase gen=hoon]
601    ^-  [vase worm]
602    =^  gun  +>+<  (mint p.vax gen)
603    [[p.gun .*(q.vax q.gun)] +>+<.$]
604  ::  +slot: +slot:ut, cached
605  ::
606  ++  slot
607    |=  [axe=@ vax=vase]
608    ^-  [vase worm]
609    =^  gun  +>+<  (mint p.vax [%$ axe])
610    [[p.gun .*(q.vax [0 axe])] +>+<.$]
611  ::
612  ::  +slur: slam a vase with a maze
613  ::
614  ++  slur
615    |=  [gat=vase sam=maze]
616    ^-  [vase worm]
617    =^  cur  +>+<.$  (slot 6 gat)
618    =.  +>+<.$  (neat p.cur sam)
619    (slym gat q.p.sam)
620  ::  +slym: +slym:ut, cached
621  ::
622  ++  slym
623    |=  [gat=vase sam=*]
624    ^-  [vase worm]
625    (slap gat(+<.q sam) [%limb %$])
626  ::
627  ++  sped                                          ::  specialize vase
628    |=  vax=vase
629    ^-  [vase worm]
630    =+  ^=  gen  ^-  hoon
631      ?@  q.vax    [%wtts [%base [%atom %$]] [%& 1]~]
632      ?@  -.q.vax  [%wtts [%leaf %tas -.q.vax] [%& 2]~]
633      [%wtts [%base %cell] [%& 1]~]
634    =^  typ  +>+<.$  (play p.vax [%wtgr gen [%$ 1]])
635    [[typ q.vax] +>+<.$]
```

```
636      ::
637      ++   spot                                       ::  slot then sped
638        |=  [axe=@ vax=vase]
639        ^-  [vase worm]
640        =^  xav  +>+<  (slot axe vax)
641        (sped xav)
642      ::
643      ++   stop                                       ::  sped then slot
644        |=  [axe=@ vax=vase]
645        ^-  [vase worm]
646        =^  xav  +>+<  (sped vax)
647        (slot axe xav)
648      --
649    ::
650    ::  |part: arvo structures and engines
651    ::
652    ++   part
653      =>  |%
654          ::  $card: tagged, untyped event
655          ::  $ovum: card with cause
656          ::  $news: collated updates
657          ::  $oped: module updates
658          ::  $seed: next kernel source
659          ::
660          +$  news
661              $:  ::  sys: installs + replacements
662                  ::  use: non-system files
663                  ::
664                  sys=(map path (cask))
665                  use=(map path (cask))
666              ==
667          +$  oped
668            $:  lul=(unit cord)
669                zus=(unit cord)
670                van=(list (cask cord))
671            ==
672          +$  seed  [hun=(unit cord) arv=cord]
673          --
674      ::
675      ~%  %part  ..part  ~
676      |%
677      ::
678      +|  %engines
679      ::
680      ::  |eden: lifecycle and bootstrap formula generators
681      ::
682      ::    while unused by arvo itself, these nock formulas
683      ::    bootstrap arvo and define its lifecycle.
684      ::
685      ::    we're creating an event series E whose lifecycle can be computed
686      ::    with the urbit lifecycle formula L, `[2 [0 3] [0 2]]`. that is:
687      ::    if E is the list of events processed by a computer in its life,
688      ::    its final state is S, where S is nock(E L).
689      ::
690      ::    in practice, the first five nouns in E are: two boot formulas,
691      ::    a hoon compiler as a nock formula, the same compiler as source,
692      ::    and the arvo kernel as source.
693      ::
```

```
694  ::    after the first five special events, we enter an iterative
695  ::    sequence of regular events which continues for the rest of the
696  ::    computer's life.  during this sequence, each state is a function
697  ::    that, passed the next event, produces the next state.
698  ::
699  ::    a regular event is an $ovum, or `[date wire type data]` tuple, where
700  ::    `date` is a 128-bit Urbit date; `wire` is an opaque path which
701  ::    output can match to track causality; `type` is a symbol describing
702  ::    the type of input; and `data` is input data specific to `type`.
703  ::
704  ::    in real life we don't actually run the lifecycle loop,
705  ::    since real life is updated incrementally and also cares
706  ::    about things like output.  we couple to the internal
707  ::    structure of the state machine and work directly with
708  ::    the underlying arvo engine.
709  ::
710  ::    this arvo core, which is at `+7` (Lisp `cddr`) of the state
711  ::    function (see its public interface in `sys/arvo`), gives us
712  ::    extra features, like output, which are relevant to running
713  ::    a real-life urbit vm, but don't affect the formal definition.
714  ::
715  ::    so a real-life urbit interpreter is coupled to the shape of
716  ::    the arvo core.  it becomes very hard to change this shape.
717  ::    fortunately, it is not a very complex interface.
718  ::
719  ++  eden
720    |%
721    ::  +aeon: arvo lifecycle loop
722    ::
723    ::      the first event in a ship's log,
724    ::      computing the final state from the rest of log
725    ::      when invoked via the lifecycle formula: [%2 [%0 3] %0 2]
726    ::
727    ::      the formal urbit state is always just a gate (function)
728    ::      which, passed the next event, produces the next state.
729    ::
730    ++  aeon
731      ^-  *
732      =>  ::  boot: kernel bootstrap, event 2
733          ::  tale: events 3-n
734          ::
735          *log=[boot=* tale=*]
736      !=  ::  arvo: bootstrapped kernel
737          ::  epic: remainder of the log
738          ::
739      =+  [arvo epic]=.*(tale.log boot.log)
740      |-  ^-  *
741      ?@  epic  arvo
742      %=  $
743        epic  +.epic
744        arvo  .*([arvo -.epic] [%9 2 %10 [6 %0 3] %0 2])
745      ==
746    ::
747    ::  +boot: event 2: bootstrap a kernel from source
748    ::
749    ++  boot
750      ^-  *
751      ::
```

```
752    ::    event 2 is the startup formula, which verifies the compiler
753    ::    and starts the main lifecycle.
754    ::
755    =>    ::    fate: event 3: a nock formula producing the hoon bootstrap compiler
756          ::    hoon: event 4: compiler source
757          ::    arvo: event 5: kernel source
758          ::    epic: event 6-n
759          ::
760          *log=[fate=* hoon=@ arvo=@ epic=*]
761    !=
762    ::
763    ::    activate the compiler gate.  the product of this formula
764    ::    is smaller than the formula.  so you might think we should
765    ::    save the gate itself rather than the formula producing it.
766    ::    but we have to run the formula at runtime, to register jets.
767    ::
768    ::    as always, we have to use raw nock as we have no type.
769    ::    the gate is in fact ++ride.
770    ::
771    ~>    %slog.[0 leaf+"1-b"]
772    =/    compiler-gate  .*(0 fate.log)
773    ::
774    ::    compile the compiler source, producing (pair span nock).
775    ::    the compiler ignores its input so we use a trivial span.
776    ::
777    ~>    %slog.[0 leaf+"1-c (compiling compiler, wait a few minutes)"]
778    =/    compiler-tool
779      ~>    %bout
780      .*([compiler-gate noun/hoon.log] [%9 2 %10 [6 %0 3] %0 2])
781    ::
782    ::    switch to the second-generation compiler.  we want to be
783    ::    able to generate matching reflection nouns even if the
784    ::    language changes -- the first-generation formula will
785    ::    generate last-generation spans for `!>`, etc.
786    ::
787    ~>    %slog.[0 leaf+"1-d"]
788    =.    compiler-gate  ~>(%bout .*(0 +.compiler-tool))
789    ::
790    ::    get the span (type) of the kernel core, which is the context
791    ::    of the compiler gate.  we just compiled the compiler,
792    ::    so we know the span (type) of the compiler gate.  its
793    ::    context is at tree address `+>` (ie, `+7` or Lisp `cddr`).
794    ::    we use the compiler again to infer this trivial program.
795    ::
796    ~>    %slog.[0 leaf+"1-e"]
797    =/    kernel-span
798      ~>    %bout
799      -:.*([compiler-gate -.compiler-tool '+>'] [%9 2 %10 [6 %0 3] %0 2])
800    ::
801    ::    compile the arvo source against the kernel core.
802    ::
803    ~>    %slog.[0 leaf+"1-f"]
804    =/    kernel-tool
805      ~>    %bout
806      .*([compiler-gate kernel-span arvo.log] [%9 2 %10 [6 %0 3] %0 2])
807    ::
808    ::    create the arvo kernel, whose subject is the kernel core.
809    ::
```

```
810        ~>  %slog.[0 leaf+"1-g"]
811        ~>  %bout
812      [.*(+>.compiler-gate +.kernel-tool) epic.log]
813      --
814    ::
815    ::  |adapt
816    ::
817    ++  adapt
818      =>  |%
819          ::  deep file as source
820          ::
821          ++  sole  |=(a=(cask) `cord`?>(?=([%hoon @t] a) q.a))
822          --
823      |_  fat=(axal (cask))
824      ::
825      ::  +group: collate changes
826      ::
827      ++  group
828        |=  fal=(list (pair path (cask)))
829        =|  del=news
830        |-  ^+  del
831        ?~  fal  del
832        ::  classify files, ignoring unchanged
833        ::
834        =*  pax  p.i.fal
835        =*  dat  q.i.fal
836        =/  hav  (~(get of fat) pax)
837        =?  del  |(?=(~ hav) !=(u.hav dat))
838          ?:  ?=([%sys *] pax)
839            del(sys (~(put by sys.del) pax dat))
840          del(use (~(put by use.del) pax dat))
841        $(fal t.fal)
842      ::  +usurp: consider self-replacement
843      ::
844      ++  usurp
845        |=  del=news
846        ^-  (unit (pair seed (list (pair path (cask)))))
847        =/  hun  (~(get by sys.del) /sys/hoon)
848        =/  arv  (~(get by sys.del) /sys/arvo)
849        ?~  hun
850          ?~  arv  ~
851          `[`(sole u.arv) [/sys/arvo u.arv] ~]
852        =/  rav
853          ~|  %usurp-hoon-no-arvo
854          ((bond |.((need (~(get of fat) /sys/arvo)))) arv)
855        ~!  rav
856        :+  ~
857          [`(sole u.hun) (sole rav)]
858        [[/sys/arvo rav] [/sys/hoon u.hun] ~]
859      ::  +adorn: augment capabilities
860      ::
861      ++  adorn
862        |=  [del=news all=?]
863        ^-  (pair oped _fat)
864        ::  lull: shared structures
865        ::
866        =^  lul  fat
867          ?^  hav=(~(get by sys.del) /sys/lull)
```

```
868        :-  `(sole u.hav)
869        (~(put of fat) /sys/lull u.hav)
870      :_  fat
871      ~|  %adorn-no-lull
872      ?.(all ~ `(sole (need (~(get of fat) /sys/lull))))
873    ::  zuse: shared library
874    ::
875    ::    %lull is the subject of %zuse; force all if we have a new %lull
876    ::
877    =.  all  |(all ?=(^ lul))
878    =^  zus    fat
879      ?^  hav=(~(get by sys.del) /sys/zuse)
880        :-  `(sole u.hav)
881        (~(put of fat) /sys/zuse u.hav)
882      :_  fat
883      ~|  %adorn-no-zuse
884      ?.(all ~ `(sole (need (~(get of fat) /sys/zuse))))
885    ::  kernel modules
886    ::
887    ::    %zuse is the subject of the vanes; force all if we have a new %zuse
888    ::
889    =.  all  |(all ?=(^ zus))
890    =|  nav=(map term cord)
891    =?  nav  all
892      %-  ~(gas by nav)
893      %+  turn
894        ~(tap by dir:(~(dip of fat) /sys/vane))
895      |=([name=@ta _fat] [`@tas`name (sole (need fil))])
896    ::
897    =^  new  fat
898      %^    spin
899          %+  skim  ~(tap by sys.del)
900          |=([p=path *] ?=([%sys %vane @tas ~] p))
901        fat
902      |=  [[p=path q=(cask)] taf=_fat]
903      ^-  (pair (cask cord) _fat)
904      ?>  ?=([%sys %vane @tas ~] p)
905      =*  nam  i.t.t.p
906      ?>  ((sane %tas) nam)
907      [[`@tas`nam (sole q)] (~(put of taf) p q)]
908    ::
909    =;  van
910      [[lul zus van] fat]
911    %+  sort  ~(tap by (~(gas by nav) new))
912    |=([[a=@tas *] [b=@tas *]] (aor a b))
913  --  :: adapt
914  ::
915  ::  |me: dynamic analysis
916  ::
917  ++  me
918    ~/  %me
919    |_  ::  sac: compiler cache
920        ::  pyt: cached types
921        ::
922        [sac=worm vil=vile]
923    ::  +refine-moves: move list from vase
924    ::
925    ++  refine-moves
```

```
926      |=  vax=vase
927      ^-  (pair (list move) worm)
928      ?:  =(~ q.vax)  [~ sac]
929      =^  hed  sac  (~(slot wa sac) 2 vax)
930      =^  tal  sac  (~(slot wa sac) 3 vax)
931      =^  mov  sac  (refine-move hed)
932      =^  moz  sac  $(vax tal)
933      [[mov moz] sac]
934    ::  +refine-move: move from vase
935    ::
936    ++  refine-move
937      |=  vax=vase
938      ^-  (pair move worm)
939      ~>  %mean.'bad-move'
940      =^  hip  sac  (~(nell wa sac) p.vax)
941      ?.  hip
942        ~>(%mean.'not-cell' !!)
943      =/  duc
944        ~>  %mean.'bad-duct'
945        ;;(duct -.q.vax)
946      ::
947      ::  yat: specialized ball vase
948      ::
949      =^  yat  sac  (~(spot wa sac) 3 vax)
950      =^  del  sac  (refine-ball yat)
951      [[duc del] sac]
952    ::  +refine-ball: ball from vase
953    ::
954    ++  refine-ball
955      |=  vax=vase
956      ^-  (pair ball worm)
957      ?+    q.vax
958          ~>  %mean.'bad-ball'
959          ~_  (sell vax)
960          !!
961      ::
962          [%give card]
963        ::  yed: vase containing card
964        ::  hil: card as maze
965        ::
966        =^  yed  sac  (~(spot wa sac) 3 vax)
967        =^  hil  sac  (refine-card yed)
968        [[%give hil] sac]
969      ::
970          [%pass wire=* vane=term card]
971        =/  =wire
972          ~>  %mean.'bad-wire'
973          ;;(wire wire.q.vax)
974        =/  vane
975          ~>  %mean.'bad-vane-label'
976          ?>  ((sane %tas) vane.q.vax)
977          vane.q.vax
978        ::
979        ::  yed: vase containing card
980        ::  hil: card as maze
981        ::
982        =^  xav  sac  (~(spot wa sac) 7 vax)
983        =^  yed  sac  (~(spot wa sac) 3 xav)
```

```
984        =^  hil  sac  (refine-card yed)
985        [[%pass wire vane hil] sac]
986      ::
987          [%slip vane=term card]
988        =/  vane
989         ~>  %mean.'bad-vane-label'
990         ?>  ((sane %tas) vane.q.vax)
991         vane.q.vax
992        ::
993        ::  yed: vase containing card
994        ::  hil: card as maze
995        ::
996        =^  xav  sac  (~(spot wa sac) 3 vax)
997        =^  yed  sac  (~(spot wa sac) 3 xav)
998        =^  hil  sac  (refine-card yed)
999        [[%slip vane hil] sac]
1000     ::
1001         [%hurl goof=^ ball=*]
1002       =/  =goof
1003        =/  mote  -.goof.q.vax
1004        ?>  ?&  ?=(@ mote)
1005                ((sane %tas) mote)
1006            ==
1007        [mote ;;(tang +.goof.q.vax)]
1008       ::
1009       =^  bal  sac
1010        =^  lab  sac  (~(spot wa sac) 7 vax)
1011        $(vax lab)
1012       ::
1013       ?>  ?=(?(%pass %give) -.p.bal)
1014       [[%hurl goof p.bal] sac]
1015       ==
1016   ::  +refine-card: card from vase
1017   ::
1018   ++  refine-card
1019     |=  vax=vase
1020     ^-  (pair maze worm)
1021     ~>  %mean.'bad-card'
1022     =^  hip  sac  (~(nell wa sac) p.vax)
1023     ?>  hip
1024     ?.  ?=(%meta -.q.vax)
1025       ::
1026       ::  for a non-meta card, the maze is the vase
1027       ::
1028       [[%& vax] sac]
1029     ~>  %mean.'bad-meta'
1030     ::
1031     ::  tiv: vase of vase of card
1032     ::  typ: vase of span
1033     ::
1034     =^  tiv  sac  (~(slot wa sac) 3 vax)
1035     =^  hip  sac  (~(nell wa sac) p.tiv)
1036     ?>  hip
1037     =^  typ  sac  (~(slot wa sac) 2 tiv)
1038     =.  sac  (~(neat wa sac) typ.vil [%& typ])
1039     ::
1040     ::  support for meta-meta-cards has been removed
1041     ::
```

```
1042        ?>   ?=(meta q.tiv)
1043        [[%| q.tiv] sac]
1044      --
1045    ::
1046    ::   |va: vane engine
1047    ::
1048    ++   va
1049     =>   ~%   %va-ctx  ..va  ~
1050          |%
1051          +$   vane-sample  [now=@da eny=@uvJ rof=rook]
1052          ::
1053          ++   smit
1054          |=  [cap=tape sub=vase pax=path txt=@t]
1055          ^-  vase
1056          ~>  %slog.[0 leaf/"{cap}: {(scow uv+(mug txt))}"]
1057          ~>  %bout
1058          %-  road  |.
1059          ~_  leaf/"{cap}: build failed"
1060          (slap sub (rain pax txt))
1061          ::
1062          ++   create
1063          ~/  %create
1064          |=  [our=ship zus=vase lal=term pax=path txt=@t]
1065          ^-  vase
1066          =/  cap  "vane: %{(trip lal)}"
1067          (slym (smit cap zus pax txt) our)
1068          ::
1069          ++   settle
1070          ~/  %settle
1071          |=  van=vase
1072          ^-  (pair vase worm)
1073          =|  sac=worm
1074          =^  rig=vase  sac  (~(slym wa sac) van *vane-sample)
1075          =^  gat=vase  sac  (~(slap wa sac) rig [%limb %scry])
1076          =^  pro=vase  sac  (~(slap wa sac) gat [%limb %$])
1077          [van +:(~(mint wa sac) p.pro [%$ 7])]
1078          ::
1079          ::   XX pass identity to preserve behavior?
1080          ::
1081          ++   update
1082          ~/  %update
1083          |=  [las=vase nex=vase]
1084          ^-  vase
1085          =/  sam=vase  (slap (slym las *vane-sample) [%limb %stay])
1086          =/  gat=vase  (slap (slym nex *vane-sample) [%limb %load])
1087          (slam gat sam)
1088          --
1089    ::
1090    ~%   %va  ..va  ~
1091    |_  [vil=vile vax=vase sac=worm]
1092    ::
1093    ::   |plow:va: operate in time and space
1094    ::
1095    ++   plow
1096     ~/  %plow
1097     |=  [now=@da rok=rook]
1098     ~%  %plow-core  +  ~
1099     |%
```

```
1100        ::    +peek:plow:va: read from a local namespace
1101        ::
1102        ++  peek
1103          ~/  %peek
1104          ^-  rook
1105          |=  [lyc=gang pov=path omen]
1106          ^-  (unit (unit (cask meta)))
1107          ::  namespace reads receive no entropy
1108          ::
1109          =/  sam=vane-sample  [now *@uvJ rok]
1110          =^  rig  sac
1111            ~>  %mean.'peek: activation failed'
1112            (~(slym wa sac) vax sam)
1113          =^  gat  sac
1114            ~>  %mean.'peek: pull failed'
1115            (~(slap wa sac) rig [%limb %scry])
1116          ::
1117          =/  mas=[gang path view beam]  [lyc pov vis bem]
1118          ::
1119          =^  pro  sac
1120            ~>  %mean.'peek: call failed'
1121            (~(slym wa sac) gat mas)
1122          ?~  q.pro  ~
1123          ?~  +.q.pro  [~ ~]
1124          =^  dat  sac  (~(slot wa sac) 7 pro)
1125          ``[(,mark -.q.dat) (,^ +.q.dat)]
1126        ::
1127        ::  |spin:plow:va: move statefully
1128        ::
1129        ++  spin
1130          |=  [hen=duct eny=@uvJ dud=(unit goof)]
1131          =*  duc  [duc.vil hen]
1132          =*  err  [dud.vil dud]
1133          =/  sam=vane-sample  [now eny rok]
1134          =^  rig  sac
1135            ~>  %mean.'spin: activation failed'
1136            (~(slym wa sac) vax sam)
1137          ::
1138          =>  |%
1139              ::    +slid: cons a vase onto a maze
1140              ::
1141              ++  slid
1142                |=  [hed=vase tal=maze]
1143                ^-  maze
1144                ?-  -.tal
1145                  %&  [%& (slop hed p.tal)]
1146                  %|  [%| [%cell p.hed p.p.tal] [q.hed q.p.tal]]
1147                ==
1148              --
1149          |%
1150        ::    +peel:spin:plow:va: extract products, finalize vane
1151        ::
1152        ++  peel
1153          |=  pro=vase
1154          ^-  (pair [vase vase] worm)
1155          =^  moz  sac  (~(slot wa sac) 2 pro)
1156          =^  vem  sac  (~(slot wa sac) 3 pro)
1157          ::  replace vane sample with default to plug leak
```

```
1158          ::
1159          =.  +<.q.vem  *vane-sample
1160          [[moz vem] sac]
1161      ::  +call:spin:plow:va: advance statefully
1162      ::
1163      ++  call
1164        |=  task=maze
1165        ^-  (pair [vase vase] worm)
1166        ~>  %mean.'call: failed'
1167        =^  gat  sac
1168          (~(slap wa sac) rig [%limb %call])
1169        ::
1170        ::  sample is [duct (unit goof) (hobo task)]
1171        ::
1172        =/  sam=maze
1173          (slid duc (slid err task))
1174        =^  pro  sac  (~(slur wa sac) gat sam)
1175        (peel pro)
1176      ::  +take:spin:plow:va: retreat statefully
1177      ::
1178      ++  take
1179        |=  [=wire from=term gift=maze]
1180        ^-  (pair [vase vase] worm)
1181        ~>  %mean.'take: failed'
1182        =^  gat  sac
1183          (~(slap wa sac) rig [%limb %take])
1184        =/  src=vase
1185          [[%atom %tas `from] from]
1186        ::
1187        ::  sample is [wire duct (unit goof) sign=[term gift]]
1188        ::
1189        =/  sam=maze
1190          =*  tea  [wir.vil wire]
1191          (slid tea (slid duc (slid err (slid src gift))))
1192        =^  pro  sac  (~(slur wa sac) gat sam)
1193        (peel pro)
1194        --
1195    --
1196  --
1197  ::
1198  ::  |le: arvo event-loop engine
1199  ::
1200  ++  le
1201    ~%  %le  ..le  ~
1202    =|  $:  ::  run: list of worklists
1203            ::  out: pending output
1204            ::  gem: worklist metadata
1205            ::  dud: propagate error
1206            ::  but: reboot signal
1207            ::
1208            ::
1209            run=(list plan)
1210            out=(list ovum)
1211            gem=germ
1212            dud=(unit goof)
1213            $=  but  %-  unit
1214                $:  gat=$-(heir (trap ^))
1215                    kel=(list (pair path (cask)))
```

```
1216                        fil=(list (pair path (cask)))
1217                   ==
1218          ==
1219    ::
1220    |_  [[pit=vase vil=vile] soul]
1221    +*  this  .
1222        sol   +<+
1223    ::
1224    ::  +abet: finalize loop
1225    ::
1226    ++  abet
1227      ^-  (each (pair (list ovum) soul) (trap ^))
1228      ?~  but
1229        ^-  [%& (pair (list ovum) soul)]
1230        &/[(flop out) sol]
1231      |/(gat.u.but [arvo [run out [kel fil]:u.but] sol])
1232    ::  +poke: prepare a worklist-of-one from outside
1233    ::
1234    ++  poke
1235      |=  =ovum
1236      ^+  this
1237      ~>  %mean.'arvo: poke crashed'
1238      ~?  !lac.fad  ["" %unix p.card.ovum wire.ovum now]
1239      (poke:pith ovum)
1240    ::
1241    ++  jump
1242      |=  =debt
1243      ^+  this
1244      =:  run  run.debt
1245          out  out.debt
1246        ==
1247      ::  apply remaining update
1248      ::
1249      =.  ..this  (~(lod what:pith fil.debt) kel.debt)
1250      ::  send upgrade notifications
1251      ::
1252      =+  [wir car]=[/arvo vega/~]
1253      =.  ..this  (xeno:pith $/wir car)
1254      (emit $/~ (spam:pith wir !>(car)))
1255    ::  +emit: enqueue a worklist with source
1256    ::
1257    ++  emit
1258      |=  pan=plan
1259      this(run [pan run])
1260    ::  +loop: until done
1261    ::
1262    ++  loop
1263      ^+  abet
1264      ?:  ?|  ?=(~ run)
1265              ?=(^ but)
1266          ==
1267        abet
1268      ?:  =(~ q.i.run)      :: XX TMI
1269        loop(run t.run)
1270      =.  dud   ~
1271      =.  gem  p.i.run
1272      =^  mov=move  q.i.run  q.i.run
1273      loop:(step mov)
```

```
1274    ::  +step: advance the loop one step by routing a move
1275    ::
1276    ++  step
1277    |=  =move
1278    ^+  this
1279    ::
1280    ~?  &(!lac.fad ?=(^ dud))  %goof
1281    ::
1282    ?-  -.ball.move
1283    ::
1284    ::  %pass: forward move
1285    ::
1286        %pass
1287    =*  wire  wire.ball.move
1288    =*  duct  duct.move
1289    =*  vane  vane.note.ball.move
1290    =*  task  task.note.ball.move
1291    ::
1292    ~?  &(!lac.fad !=(%$ vane.gem))
1293      :-  (runt [(lent bars.gem) '|'] "")
1294      :^  %pass  [vane.gem vane]
1295        ?:  ?=(?(%deal %deal-gall) +>-.task)
1296          :-  :-  +>-.task
1297            ;;([[ship ship path] term term] [+>+< +>+>- +>+>+<]:task)
1298          wire
1299        [(symp +>-.task) wire]
1300      duct
1301    ::
1302    ::  cons source onto wire, and wire onto duct
1303    ::
1304    (call [[vane.gem wire] duct] vane task)
1305    ::
1306    ::  %slip: lateral move
1307    ::
1308        %slip
1309    =*  duct  duct.move
1310    =*  vane  vane.note.ball.move
1311    =*  task  task.note.ball.move
1312    ::
1313    ~?  !lac.fad
1314      :-  (runt [(lent bars.gem) '|'] "")
1315      [%slip [vane.gem vane] (symp +>-.task) duct]
1316    ::
1317    (call duct vane task)
1318    ::
1319    ::  %give: return move
1320    ::
1321        %give
1322    ?.  ?=(^ duct.move)
1323      ~>(%mean.'give-no-duct' !!)
1324    ::
1325    =/  wire  i.duct.move
1326    =/  duct  t.duct.move
1327    =*  gift  gift.ball.move
1328    ::
1329    =^  way=term  wire
1330      ~|  [%give duct.move (symp -.q.p.gift)]
1331      ?>(?=(^ wire) wire)
```

```
          ::
          ~?  &(!lac.fad !=(%$ way) |(!=(%blit +>-.gift) !=(%d vane.gem)))
              :-  (runt [(lent bars.gem) '|'] "")
              :^  %give   vane.gem
                ?:  ?=(%unto +>-.gift)
                  [+>-.gift (symp +>+<.gift)]
                (symp +>-.gift)
              duct.move
          ::
        (take duct wire way gift)
      ::
      ::  %hurl: action with error
      ::
          %hurl
      %=  $
        dud         `goof.ball.move
        ball.move   wite.ball.move
      ==
    ==
  ::  +whey: measure memory usage
  ::
  ++  whey
    ^-  mass
    =;  sam=(list mass)
      :+  %arvo  %|
      :~  :+  %hoon  %|
          :~  one+&+..bloq
              two+&+..turn
              tri+&+..year
              qua+&+..sane
              pen+&+..ride
          ==
          hex+&+..part
          pit+&+pit
          lull+|+[dot+&+q typ+&+p ~]:lul.mod
          zuse+|+[dot+&+q typ+&+p ~]:zus.mod
          vane+|+sam
      ==
    ::
    %+  turn
      (sort ~(tap by van.mod) |=([[a=@tas *] [b=@tas *]] (aor a b)))
    =/  bem=beam  [[our %$ da+now] //whey]
    |=  [nam=term =vane]
    =;  mas=(list mass)
      nam^|+(welp mas [dot+&+q.vase typ+&+p.vase sac+&+worm ~]:vane)
    ?~  met=(peek [~ ~] / [nam %x] bem)  ~
    ?~  u.met  ~
    ~|  mass+nam
    ;;((list mass) q.q.u.u.met)
  ::  +peek: read from the entire namespace
  ::
  ++  peek
    ^-  rook
    |=  [lyc=gang pov=path omen]
    ^-  (unit (unit (cask meta)))
    ::  vane and care may be concatenated
    ::
    =/  [way=term car=term]
```

```
1390        ?^  vis  vis
1391        ?.  =(2 (met 3 vis))
1392          [vis %$]
1393        [(end 3 vis) (rsh 3 vis)]
1394      ::
1395      ?:  ?=(%$ way)
1396        (peek:pith lyc pov car bem)
1397      ::
1398      =.  way  (grow way)
1399      ?~  van=(~(get by van.mod) way)
1400        ~
1401      %.  [lyc pov car bem]
1402      peek:spin:(~(plow va [vil u.van]) now peek)
1403    ::  +call: advance to target
1404    ::
1405    ++  call
1406      |=  [=duct way=term task=maze]
1407      ^+  this
1408      ?:  ?=(%$ way)
1409        ~>  %mean.'arvo: call:pith failed'
1410        %-  call:pith
1411        ~>  %mean.'call: bad waif'
1412        ;;(waif q.p.task)
1413      ::
1414      =.  way  (grow way)
1415      %+  push  [way duct bars.gem]
1416      ~|  bar-stack=`(list ^duct)`[duct bars.gem]
1417      %.  task
1418      call:(spin:(plow way) duct eny dud)
1419    ::  +take: retreat along call-stack
1420    ::
1421    ++  take
1422      |=  [=duct =wire way=term gift=maze]
1423      ^+  this
1424      ?:  ?=(%$ way)
1425        ::
1426        ::   the caller was Outside
1427        ::
1428        ?>  ?=(~ duct)
1429        (xeno:pith wire ;;(card q.p.gift))
1430      ::  the caller was a vane
1431      ::
1432      =.  way  (grow way)
1433      %+  push  [way duct bars.gem]
1434      ::
1435      ::  cons source onto .gift to make a $sign
1436      ::
1437      ~|  wire=wire
1438      ~|  bar-stack=`(list ^duct)`[duct bars.gem]
1439      %.  [wire [vane.gem gift]]
1440      take:(spin:(plow way) duct eny dud)
1441    ::  +push: finalize an individual step
1442    ::
1443    ++  push
1444      |=  [gum=germ [zom=vase vax=vaso] sac=worm]
1445      ^+  this
1446      =^  moz  sac
1447        (~(refine-moves me sac vil) zom)
```

```
1448      =.  van.mod  (~(put by van.mod) vane.gum [vax sac])
1449      (emit `plan`[`germ`gum `(list move)`moz])
1450    ::  +plow: operate on a vane, in time and space
1451    ::
1452    ++  plow
1453      |=  way=term
1454      ~|  [%plow-failed way]
1455      =/  =vane
1456        ~|  [%missing-vane way]
1457        (~(got by van.mod) way)
1458      (~(plow va [vil vane]) now peek)
1459    ::
1460    ::  |pith: operate on arvo internals
1461    ::
1462    ++  pith
1463      |%
1464      ++  gest
1465        |=  =ovum
1466        ^-  $>(%pass ball)
1467        =^  way=term  wire.ovum  wire.ovum
1468        ::
1469        ::  %$: default, routed to arvo-proper as trivial vase
1470        ::  @:  route to vane as $hobo
1471        ::
1472        =/  =vase
1473          ?-  way
1474            %$  noun/card.ovum
1475            @   [cell/[atom/tas/`%soft %noun] soft/card.ovum]
1476          ==
1477        [%pass wire.ovum way &/vase]
1478      ::
1479      ::  |what: update engine
1480      ::
1481      ::    +kel: (maybe) initiate a kernel update
1482      ::    +lod: continue with update after kernel +load
1483      ::    +mod: update the modules of the kernel
1484      ::
1485      ++  what
1486        |_  fil=(list (pair path (cask)))
1487        ::
1488        ++  kel
1489          ^+  ..pith
1490          =/  del  (~(group adapt fat.mod.sol) fil)
1491          =/  tub  (~(usurp adapt fat.mod.sol) del)
1492          ?~  tub
1493            (mod del |)
1494          =/  gat  (boot kel.ver.zen [hun arv]:p.u.tub)
1495          ..pith(but `[gat q.u.tub fil])
1496        ::
1497        ++  lod
1498          |=  kel=(list (pair path (cask)))
1499          ^+  ..pith
1500          =.  fat.mod.sol  (~(gas of fat.mod.sol) kel)
1501          %+  mod
1502            (~(group adapt fat.mod.sol) fil)
1503          %+  lien  kel
1504          |=  [p=path *]
1505          ?=(([%sys ?(%arvo %hoon) *] p)
```

```
1506        ::
1507     ++  mod
1508       |=  [del=news all=?]
1509       ^+  ..pith
1510       =^  job=oped  fat.mod.sol  (~(adorn adapt fat.mod.sol) del all)
1511       =?  lul.mod.sol  ?=(^ lul.job)
1512         (smit:va "lull" pit /sys/lull/hoon u.lul.job)
1513       =?  zus.mod.sol  ?=(^ zus.job)
1514         (smit:va "zuse" lul.mod.sol /sys/zuse/hoon u.zus.job)
1515       %-  %+  need:wyrd   kel.ver.zen
1516           :~  lull/;;(@ud q:(slap lul.mod.sol limb/%lull))
1517               zuse/;;(@ud q:(slap zus.mod.sol limb/%zuse))
1518           ==
1519       %=      ..pith
1520           van.mod
1521         %+  roll  van.job
1522         |=  [[nam=term txt=cord] van=_van.mod.sol]
1523         ^+  van
1524         =/  nex  (create:va our zus.mod.sol nam /sys/vane/[nam]/hoon txt)
1525         =/  nav  (~(get by van) nam)
1526         =?  nex  ?=(^ nav)  (update:va vase.u.nav nex)
1527         (~(put by van) nam (settle:va nex))
1528       ==
1529     --
1530     ::
1531   ++  call
1532     |=  =waif
1533     ^+  ..pith
1534     ?^  dud  ~>(%mean.'pith: goof' !!)
1535     ?-  -.waif
1536       ::
1537       ::  %trim: clear state
1538       ::
1539       ::    clears compiler caches if high-priority
1540       ::    XX add separate $wasp if this should happen last
1541       ::
1542       %trim  =?  van.mod  =(0 p.waif)
1543                (~(run by van.mod) |=(=vane vane(worm *worm)))
1544              (emit $/~ (spam /arvo !>(waif)))
1545       ::
1546       %verb  ..pith(lac.fad ?~(p.waif !lac.fad u.p.waif))
1547       %what  ~(kel what p.waif)
1548       %whey  ..pith(out [[//arvo mass/whey] out])
1549       ::
1550         %whiz
1551       ..pith(van.mod (~(run by van.mod) |=(vane (settle:va:part vase))))
1552     ==
1553     ::
1554   ++  peek
1555     ^-  roon
1556     |=  [lyc=gang pov=path car=term bem=beam]
1557     ^-  (unit (unit cage))
1558     ?.  ?&  =(our p.bem)
1559             ?=(%$ q.bem)
1560             =([%da now] r.bem)
1561         ==
1562       ~
1563     ?+  s.bem  ~
```

```
1564        [%whey ~]        ``mass/!>(whey)
1565        [%fad %lac ~]    ``noun/!>(lac.fad)
1566        [%zen %lag ~]    ``noun/!>(lag.zen)
1567        [%zen %ver ~]    ``noun/!>(ver.zen)
1568        [%mod %fat *]    ``noun/!>((~(dip of fat.mod) t.t.s.bem))
1569      ==
1570    ::
1571    ++  poke
1572      |=  =ovum
1573      ^+  ..pith
1574      ?~  wire.ovum
1575        ~>(%mean.'pith: bad wire' !!)
1576      ::
1577      ?.  ?=(?(%crud %wack %wyrd) p.card.ovum)
1578        (emit $/~ [*duct (gest ovum)] ~)
1579      ::
1580      =/  buz  ~>  %mean.'pith: bad wasp'
1581                ;;(wasp card.ovum)
1582      ?-  -.buz
1583      ::
1584      ::  %crud: forward error notification
1585      ::
1586        %crud  =?  lag.zen  ?&  ?=(%exit mote.goof.buz)
1587                               ?=(^  tang.goof.buz)
1588                               ?=([%leaf *] i.tang.goof.buz)
1589                               ?=(%wyrd (crip p.i.tang.goof.buz))
1590                           ==
1591               ~&(%lagging &)
1592             (emit $/~ [*duct hurl/[goof.buz (gest ovum.buz)]] ~)
1593      ::
1594      ::  XX review
1595      ::
1596        %wack  ..pith(eny (shaz (cat 3 eny p.buz)))
1597      ::
1598      ::  %wyrd: check for runtime kelvin compatibility
1599      ::
1600        %wyrd  ?.  (sane:wyrd kel.p.buz)
1601                 ~>(%mean.'wyrd: insane' !!)
1602             %-  %+  need:wyrd  kel.p.buz
1603                 ^-  wynn
1604                 :~  hoon/hoon-version
1605                     arvo/arvo
1606                     lull/;;(@ud q:(slap lul.mod limb/%lull))
1607                     zuse/;;(@ud q:(slap zus.mod limb/%zuse))
1608                 ==
1609             =?  lag.zen  !=(rev.ver.zen rev.p.buz)  ~&(%unlagging |)
1610             ..pith(ver.zen p.buz)
1611      ==
1612    ::
1613    ++  spam
1614      |=  [=wire =vase]
1615      ^-  (list move)
1616      %+  turn
1617        %+  sort  ~(tap by van.mod)
1618        |=([[a=@tas *] [b=@tas *]] (aor a b))
1619      |=([way=term *] `move`[*duct %pass wire way `maze`&/vase])
1620    ::
1621    ++  xeno
```

```
1622        |=  =ovum
1623        ^+  ..pith
1624        ..pith(out [ovum out])
1625          --
1626        --
1627      --
1628  ::
1629  ++  symp                                              ::  symbol or empty
1630    |=  a=*  ^-  @tas
1631    ?.(&(?=(@ a) ((sane %tas) a)) %$ a)
1632  ::
1633  ++  boot
1634    |=  [kel=wynn hun=(unit @t) van=@t]
1635    ^-  $-(heir (trap ^))
1636    ~>  %mean.'arvo: upgrade failed'
1637    ~>  %slog.[0 'arvo: beginning upgrade']
1638    ?~  hun
1639      =/  gat
1640        ~>  %slog.[0 'arvo: compiling next arvo']
1641        ~>  %bout
1642        %-  road  |.
1643        (slap !>(..ride) (rain /sys/arvo/hoon van))
1644      =/  lod
1645        (slap (slot 7 gat) [%limb %load])
1646      |=  =heir
1647      |.  ~>  %slog.[0 'arvo: +load next']
1648      ;;(^ q:(slam lod !>(heir)))
1649    ::
1650    ::  hyp: hoon core type
1651    ::  hoc: hoon core
1652    ::  cop: compiler gate
1653    ::
1654    =/  [hyp=* hoc=* cop=*]
1655      ::  compile new hoon.hoon source with the current compiler
1656      ::
1657      =/  raw
1658        ~>  %slog.[0 'arvo: compiling hoon']
1659        ~>  %bout
1660        (road |.((ride %noun u.hun)))
1661      ::  activate the new compiler gate, producing +ride
1662      ::
1663      =/  cop  .*(0 +.raw)
1664      ::  find the kelvin version number of the new compiler
1665      ::
1666      =/  nex
1667        ;;(@ .*(cop q:(~(mint ut p.raw) %noun [%limb %hoon-version])))
1668      ::  require single-step upgrade
1669      ::
1670      ?.  |(=(nex hoon-version) =(+(nex) hoon-version))
1671        =*  ud  |=(a=@ (scow %ud a))
1672        ~_  leaf/"cannot upgrade to hoon %{(ud nex)} from %{(ud hoon-version)}"
1673        !!
1674      ::  require runtime compatibility
1675      ::
1676      %-  (need:wyrd kel [hoon/nex ~])
1677      ::
1678      ::  if we're upgrading language versions, recompile the compiler
1679      ::
```

```
1680      =^  hot=*  cop
1681        ?:  =(nex hoon-version)
1682          [raw cop]
1683        =/  hot
1684          ~>  %slog.[0 leaf/"arvo: recompiling hoon %{(scow %ud nex)}"]
1685          ~>  %bout
1686          (road |.((slum cop [%noun u.hun])))
1687        [hot .*(0 +.hot)]
1688      ::  extract the hoon core from the outer gate (+ride)
1689      ::
1690      =/  hoc  .*(cop [%0 7])
1691      ::  compute the type of the hoon.hoon core
1692      ::
1693      =/  hyp  -:(slum cop [-.hot '+>'])
1694      ::
1695      [hyp hoc cop]
1696    ::
1697    ::  compile arvo
1698    ::
1699    =/  rav
1700      ~>  %slog.[0 'arvo: compiling next arvo']
1701      ~>  %bout
1702      (road |.((slum cop [hyp van])))
1703    ::  activate arvo and extract the arvo core from the outer gate
1704    ::
1705    =/  voc  .*(hoc [%7 +.rav %0 7])
1706    ::
1707    ::  extract the upgrade gate +load
1708    ::
1709    =/  lod
1710      ::  vip: type of the arvo.hoon core
1711      ::  fol: formula for the +load gate
1712      ::
1713      =/  vip  -:(slum cop [-.rav '+>'])
1714      =/  fol  +:(slum cop [vip 'load'])
1715      ::  produce the upgrade gate
1716      ::
1717      .*(voc fol)
1718    ::
1719    |=  =heir
1720    |.  ~>  %slog.[1 'arvo: +load next']
1721    ;;(^ (slum lod heir))
1722  ::
1723  ++  viol                                    ::  vane tools
1724    |=  but=type
1725    ^-  vile
1726    =+  pal=|=(a=@t ^-(type (~(play ut but) (vice a))))
1727    :*  typ=(pal '$:type')
1728        duc=(pal '$:duct')
1729        wir=(pal '$:wire')
1730        dud=(pal '=<($ (unit goof))')  ::  XX misparse
1731    ==
1732  ::
1733  ++  grow
1734    |=  way=term
1735    ?+  way  way
1736      %a  %ames
1737      %b  %behn
```

```
1738        %c    %clay
1739        %d    %dill
1740        %e    %eyre
1741        %g    %gall
1742        %i    %iris
1743        %j    %jael
1744        %k    %khan
1745        %l    %lick
1746      ==
1747  --  =>
1748  ::
1749  ::    cached reflexives
1750  ::
1751  =/  pit=vase  !>(..part)
1752  =/  vil=vile  (viol p.pit)
1753  ::
1754  ::    arvo state, as a discriminable sample
1755  ::
1756  =|  [_arvo soul]
1757  =*  sol  ->
1758  |%
1759  ::    +load: upgrade from previous state
1760  ::
1761  ++  load                                              ::    +4
1762    |=  hir=$<(%grub heir)
1763    ^-  ^
1764    ~|  %load
1765    ::    store persistent state
1766    ::
1767    =.  sol
1768      ?-  -.hir
1769        ?(%240 %239 %238 %237)  soul.hir
1770      ==
1771    ::    clear compiler caches
1772    ::
1773    =.  van.mod  (~(run by van.mod) |=(=vane vane(worm *worm)))
1774    ::
1775    %-  %+  need:wyrd  kel.ver.zen
1776        ^-  wynn
1777        :~  hoon/hoon-version
1778            arvo/arvo
1779            lull/;;(@ud q:(slap lul.mod limb/%lull))
1780            zuse/;;(@ud q:(slap zus.mod limb/%zuse))
1781        ==
1782    ::    restore working state and resume
1783    ::
1784    =/  zef=(each (pair (list ovum) soul) (trap ^))
1785      loop:(~(jump le:part [pit vil] sol) debt.hir)
1786    ?-  -.zef
1787      %&  [p.p.zef ..load(sol q.p.zef)]
1788      %|  $:p.zef
1789    ==
1790  ::
1791  ::    +peek: external inspect
1792  ::
1793  ++  peek                                              ::    +22
1794    |=  $:  lyc=gang
1795            $=  nom
```

```
1796            %+  each  path
1797            $%  [%once vis=view syd=desk tyl=spur]
1798                [%beam omen]  :: XX unfortunate naming
1799            ==
1800        ==
1801    ^-  (unit (cask))
1802    =/  hap=(unit [pat=? omen])
1803      ?-  nom
1804        [%& *]          ?~(mon=(de-omen p.nom) ~ `[| u.mon])
1805        [%| %beam *]  `[| vis bem]:p.nom
1806        [%| %once *]  `[& vis.p.nom [our syd.p.nom da/now] tyl.p.nom]
1807      ==
1808    ::
1809    ?~  hap  ~
1810    =/  pro  (~(peek le:part [pit vil] sol) lyc / [vis bem]:u.hap)
1811    ?:  |(?=(~ pro) ?=(~ u.pro))  ~
1812    =/  dat=(cask)  [p q.q]:u.u.pro
1813    ?.  pat.u.hap  `dat
1814    `[%omen (en-omen [vis bem]:u.hap) dat]
1815  ::
1816  ::  +poke: external apply
1817  ::
1818  ++  poke                                        ::  +23
1819    |=  [now=@da ovo=ovum]
1820    ^-  ^
1821    ::  this assertion is not yet viable, as vere's timestamps
1822    ::  are too unreliable. sad!
1823    ::
1824    ::  ?.  (gth now now.sol)
1825    ::    ~|  poke/[now=now last=now.sol wire.ovo p.card.ovo]
1826    ::    ~>(%mean.'time-marches-on' !!)
1827    ::
1828    =:  eny.sol  (shaz (cat 3 eny now))  ::  XX review
1829        now.sol  now
1830      ==
1831    ::
1832    ~|  poke/p.card.ovo
1833    =/  zef=(each (pair (list ovum) soul) (trap ^))
1834    loop:(~(poke le:part [pit vil] sol) ovo)
1835    ?-  -.zef
1836      %&  [p.p.zef ..poke(sol q.p.zef)]
1837      %|  $:p.zef
1838    ==
1839  ::
1840  ::  +wish: external compute
1841  ::
1842  ++  wish                                        ::  +10
1843    |=  txt=@
1844    q:(slap zus.mod (ream txt))
1845  --  =>
1846  ::
1847  ::  larval stage
1848  ::
1849  ::    The true Arvo kernel knows who it is. It should not *maybe*
1850  ::    have an identity, nor should it contain multitudes. This outer
1851  ::    kernel exists to accumulate identity, entropy, and the
1852  ::    standard library. Upon having done so, it upgrades itself into
1853  ::    the true Arvo kernel. Subsequent upgrades will fall through
```

```
1854  ::    the larval stage directly into the actual kernel.
1855  ::
1856  ::    For convenience, this larval stage also supports hoon compilation
1857  ::    with +wish and vane installation with the %veer event.
1858  ::
1859  =>   |%
1860  ++   molt
1861       |=  [now=@da grub]
1862       ^-  (unit $>(_arvo heir))
1863       ?.  &(?=(^ who) ?=(^ eny) ?=(^ ver) ?=(^ fat) ?=(^ lul) ?=(^ zus))
1864         ~
1865       =/  lul  $:u.lul
1866       =/  zus  $:u.zus
1867       %-  %+  need:wyrd  kel.u.ver
1868           ^-  wynn
1869           :~  hoon/hoon-version
1870               arvo/arvo
1871               lull/;;(@ud q:(slap lul limb/%lull))
1872               zuse/;;(@ud q:(slap zus limb/%zuse))
1873           ==
1874       =/  nav  %-  ~(run by van)
1875                |=(a=(trap vase) (settle:va:part (slym $:a u.who)))
1876       :^  ~  arvo  *debt
1877       [[u.who now u.eny] [lac] [u.ver |] u.fat lul zus nav]
1878       ::
1879  ++   what
1880       =>  |%
1881       ++  smit
1882           |=  [cap=tape sub=(trap vase) pax=path txt=@t]
1883           ^-  (trap vase)
1884           ~>  %slog.[0 leaf/"{cap}: {(scow uv+(mug txt))}"]
1885           %-  road  |.
1886           ~_  leaf/"{cap}: build failed"
1887           (swat sub (rain pax txt))
1888       --
1889       ::
1890       |=  [grub fil-(list (pair path (cask)))]
1891       ^-  grub
1892       =*  gub  +<-
1893       =/  taf  (fall fat *(axal (cask)))
1894       =/  del  (~(group adapt:part taf) fil)
1895       =/  tub  (~(usurp adapt:part taf) del)
1896       ?:  &(?=(^ dir.taf) ?=(^ tub))
1897         ~>(%mean.'arvo: larval reboot' !!)     :: XX support
1898       ::
1899       :: require, and unconditionally adopt, initial kernel source
1900       ::
1901       =?  taf  =(~ dir.taf)      :: XX TMI
1902         ~|  %larval-need-kernel
1903         ?>  &(?=(^ tub) ?=(^ hun.p.u.tub))
1904         (~(gas of taf) q.u.tub)
1905       ::
1906       =^  job=oped:part  taf  (~(adorn adapt:part taf) del |)
1907       =?  lul  ?=(^ lul.job)
1908         `(smit "lull" |.(pit) /sys/lull/hoon u.lul.job)
1909       =?  zus  ?=(^ zus.job)
1910         ?.  ?=(^ lul)
1911           ~|(%larval-need-lull !!)
```

```
1912        `(smit "zuse" u.lul /sys/zuse/hoon u.zus.job)
1913      =?  van  !=(~ van.job)      ::  XX TMI
1914      ?.  ?=(^ zus)
1915        ~|(%larval-need-zuse !!)
1916      %+  roll  van.job
1917      |=  [[nam=term txt=cord] =_van]
1918      ^+  van
1919      %+  ~(put by van)  nam
1920      (smit "vane: %{(trip nam)}" u.zus /sys/vane/[nam]/hoon txt)
1921    gub(fat `taf)
1922    --
1923  ::
1924  ::  larval state, as a discriminable sample
1925  ::
1926  =|  [%grub _arvo grub]
1927  =*  gub  ->+
1928  ::
1929  |%
1930  ++  load                                    ::    +4
1931    |=  hir=heir
1932    ?:  ?=(%grub -.hir)
1933      ~>(%mean.'arvo: larval reboot' !!)     ::  XX support
1934    (^load hir)
1935  ::
1936  ++  peek  _~                                ::   +22
1937  ++  poke                                    ::   +23
1938    |=  [now=@da ovo=ovum]
1939    ^-  ^
1940    ~|  poke/p.card.ovo
1941    =/  wip
1942      ~>  %mean.'arvo: bad wisp'
1943      ;;(wisp card.ovo)
1944    ::
1945    =.  ..poke
1946      ?-    -.wip
1947        %verb  ..poke(lac ?~(p.wip !lac u.p.wip))
1948        %wack  ..poke(eny `p.wip)
1949        %what  ..poke(gub (what gub p.wip))
1950        %whom  ..poke(who ~|(%whom-once ?>(?=(~ who) `p.wip)))
1951      ::
1952        %wyrd  ?.  (sane:wyrd kel.p.wip)
1953                   ~>(%mean.'wyrd: insane' !!)
1954          %-  %+  need:wyrd  kel.p.wip
1955              ^-  wynn
1956              :*  hoon/hoon-version
1957                  arvo/arvo
1958                  ?~  lul  ~
1959                  :-  lull/;;(@ud q:(slap $:u.lul limb/%lull))
1960                  ?~  zus  ~
1961                  [zuse/;;(@ud q:(slap $:u.zus limb/%zuse)) ~]
1962              ==
1963          ..poke(ver `p.wip)
1964      ==
1965    ::
1966    ::  upgrade once we've accumulated necessary state
1967    ::
1968    ?~  hir=(molt now gub)
1969      [~ ..poke]
```

```
1970      ~>  %slog.[0 leaf+"arvo: metamorphosis"]
1971    (load u.hir)
1972  ::
1973  ++  wish                                              ::    +10
1974    |=  txt=*
1975    q:(slap ?~(zus pit $:u.zus) (ream ;;(@t txt)))
1976  --
1977  ::
1978  ::  Arvo formal interface
1979  ::
1980  ::    this lifecycle wrapper makes the arvo door (multi-armed core)
1981  ::    look like a gate (function or single-armed core), to fit
1982  ::    urbit's formal lifecycle function (see aeon:eden:part).
1983  ::    a practical interpreter can and will ignore it.
1984  ::
1985  |=  [now=@da ovo=ovum]
1986  ^-  *
1987  .(+> +:(poke now ovo))
```

Hoon 139K

```
1  ::
2  :::::      /sys/hoon                                      ::
3    ::                                                       ::
4  =<  ride
5  =>  %139  =>
6  ::                                                         ::
7  :::::      0: version stub                                 ::
8    ::                                                       ::
9  ~%  %k.139  ~  ~                                           ::
10 |%
11 ++  hoon-version  +
12 --  =>
13 ~%  %one  +  ~
14 ::    layer-1
15 ::
16 ::  basic mathematical operations
17 |%
18 ::    unsigned arithmetic
19 +|  %math
20 ++  add
21   ~/  %add
22   ::    unsigned addition
23   ::
24   ::  a: augend
25   ::  b: addend
26   |=  [a=@ b=@]
27   ::  sum
28   ^-  @
29   ?:  =(0 a)  b
30   $(a (dec a), b +(b))
31 ::
32 ++  dec
33   ~/  %dec
34   ::    unsigned decrement by one.
35   |=  a=@
36   ~_  leaf+"decrement-underflow"
37   ?<  =(0 a)
38   =+  b=0
39   ::  decremented integer
40   |-  ^-  @
41   ?:  =(a +(b))  b
42   $(b +(b))
43 ::
44 ++  div
45   ~/  %div
46   ::    unsigned divide
47   ::
48   ::  a: dividend
49   ::  b: divisor
50   |:  [a=`@`1 b=`@`1]
51   ::  quotient
52   ^-  @
53   -:(dvr a b)
54 ::
55 ++  dvr
56   ~/  %dvr
```

```
57    ::      unsigned divide with remainder
58    ::
59    ::   a: dividend
60    ::   b: divisor
61    |:   [a=`@`1 b=`@`1]
62    ::   p: quotient
63    ::   q: remainder
64    ^-   [p=@ q=@]
65    ~_   leaf+"divide-by-zero"
66    ?<   =(0 b)
67    =+   c=0
68    |-
69    ?:   (lth a b)  [c a]
70    $(a (sub a b), c +(c))
71  ::
72  ++  gte
73    ~/  %gte
74    ::      unsigned greater than or equals
75    ::
76    ::   returns whether {a >= b}.
77    ::
78    ::   a: left hand operand (todo: name)
79    ::   b: right hand operand
80    |=   [a=@ b=@]
81    ::   greater than or equal to?
82    ^-   ?
83    !(lth a b)
84  ::
85  ++  gth
86    ~/  %gth
87    ::      unsigned greater than
88    ::
89    ::   returns whether {a > b}
90    ::
91    ::   a: left hand operand (todo: name)
92    ::   b: right hand operand
93    |=   [a=@ b=@]
94    ::   greater than?
95    ^-   ?
96    !(lte a b)
97  ::
98  ++  lte
99    ~/  %lte
100   ::      unsigned less than or equals
101   ::
102   ::   returns whether {a >= b}.
103   ::
104   ::   a: left hand operand (todo: name)
105   ::   b: right hand operand
106   |=   [a=@ b=@]
107   ::   less than or equal to?
108   |(=(a b) (lth a b))
109 ::
110 ++  lth
111   ~/  %lth
112   ::      unsigned less than
113   ::
114   ::   a: left hand operand (todo: name)
```

```
115    ::   b: right hand operand
116    |=   [a=@ b=@]
117    ::   less than?
118    ^-   ?
119    ?&   !=(a b)
120         |-
121         ?|   =(0 a)
122              ?&   !=(0 b)
123                   $(a (dec a), b (dec b))
124    ==   ==   ==
125  ::
126  ++   max
127    ~/   %max
128    ::       unsigned maximum
129    |=   [a=@ b=@]
130    ::   the maximum
131    ^-   @
132    ?:   (gth a b)   a
133    b
134  ::
135  ++   min
136    ~/   %min
137    ::       unsigned minimum
138    |=   [a=@ b=@]
139    ::   the minimum
140    ^-   @
141    ?:   (lth a b)   a
142    b
143  ::
144  ++   mod
145    ~/   %mod
146    ::       unsigned modulus
147    ::
148    ::   a: dividend
149    ::   b: divisor
150    |:   [a=`@`1 b=`@`1]
151    ::   the remainder
152    ^-   @
153    +:(dvr a b)
154  ::
155  ++   mul
156    ~/   %mul
157    ::       unsigned multiplication
158    ::
159    ::   a: multiplicand
160    ::   b: multiplier
161    |:   [a=`@`1 b=`@`1]
162    ::   product
163    ^-   @
164    =+   c=0
165    |-
166    ?:   =(0 a)   c
167    $(a (dec a), c (add b c))
168  ::
169  ++   sub
170    ~/   %sub
171    ::       unsigned subtraction
172    ::
```

```
173    ::  a: minuend
174    ::  b: subtrahend
175    |=  [a=@ b=@]
176    ~_  leaf+"subtract-underflow"
177    ::  difference
178    ^-  @
179    ?:  =(0 b)  a
180    $(a (dec a), b (dec b))
181  ::
182  ::    tree addressing
183  +|  %tree
184  ++  cap
185    ~/  %cap
186    ::    tree head
187    ::
188    ::  tests whether an `a` is in the head or tail of a noun. produces %2 if it
189    ::  is within the head, or %3 if it is within the tail.
190    |=  a=@
191    ^-  ?(%2 %3)
192    ?-  a
193      %2        %2
194      %3        %3
195      ?(%0 %1)  !!
196      *         $(a (div a 2))
197    ==
198  ::
199  ++  mas
200    ~/  %mas
201    ::    axis within head/tail
202    ::
203    ::  computes the axis of `a` within either the head or tail of a noun
204    ::  (depends whether `a` lies within the the head or tail).
205    |=  a=@
206    ^-  @
207    ?-  a
208      ?(%2 %3)  1
209      ?(%0 %1)  !!
210      *         (add (mod a 2) (mul $(a (div a 2)) 2))
211    ==
212  ::
213  ++  peg
214    ~/  %peg
215    ::    axis within axis
216    ::
217    ::  computes the axis of {b} within axis {a}.
218    |=  [a=@ b=@]
219    ?<  =(0 a)
220    ::  a composed axis
221    ^-  @
222    ?-  b
223      %1  a
224      %2  (mul a 2)
225      %3  +((mul a 2))
226      *   (add (mod b 2) (mul $(b (div b 2)) 2))
227    ==
228  ::
229  ::  # %containers
230  ::
```

```
231  ::     the most basic of data types
232  +|    %containers
233  ::
234  +$  bite
235  ::      atom slice specifier
236  ::
237  $@(bloq [=bloq =step])
238  ::
239  +$  bloq
240  ::      blocksize
241  ::
242  ::  a blocksize is the power of 2 size of an atom. ie, 3 is a byte as 2^3 is
243  ::  8 bits.
244  @
245  ::
246  ++  each
247  |$  [this that]
248  ::      either {a} or {b}, defaulting to {a}.
249  ::
250  ::  mold generator: produces a discriminated fork between two types,
251  ::  defaulting to {a}.
252  ::
253  $%  [%| p=that]
254      [%& p=this]
255  ==
256  ::
257  +$  gate
258  ::      function
259  ::
260  ::  a core with one arm, `$`--the empty name--which transforms a sample noun
261  ::  into a product noun. If used dryly as a type, the subject must have a
262  ::  sample type of `*`.
263  $-(* *)
264  ::
265  ++  list
266  |$  [item]
267  ::      null-terminated list
268  ::
269  ::  mold generator: produces a mold of a null-terminated list of the
270  ::  homogeneous type {a}.
271  ::
272  $@(~ [i=item t=(list item)])
273  ::
274  ++  lone
275  |$  [item]
276  ::      single item tuple
277  ::
278  ::  mold generator: puts the face of `p` on the passed in mold.
279  ::
280  p=item
281  ::
282  ++  lest
283  |$  [item]
284  ::      null-terminated non-empty list
285  ::
286  ::  mold generator: produces a mold of a null-terminated list of the
287  ::  homogeneous type {a} with at least one element.
288  [i=item t=(list item)]
```

```
289  ::
290  +$  mold
291      ::      normalizing gate
292      ::
293      ::  a gate that accepts any noun, and validates its shape, producing the
294      ::  input if it fits or a default value if it doesn't.
295      ::
296      ::  examples: * @ud  ,[p=time q=?(%a %b)]
297  $~(* $-(* *))
298  ::
299  ++  pair
300  |$  [head tail]
301      ::      dual tuple
302      ::
303      ::  mold generator: produces a tuple of the two types passed in.
304      ::
305      ::  a: first type, labeled {p}
306      ::  b: second type, labeled {q}
307      ::
308  [p=head q=tail]
309  ::
310  ++  pole
311  |$  [item]
312      ::      faceless list
313      ::
314      ::  like ++list, but without the faces {i} and {t}.
315      ::
316  $@(~ [item (pole item)])
317  ::
318  ++  qual
319  |$  [first second third fourth]
320      ::      quadruple tuple
321      ::
322      ::  mold generator: produces a tuple of the four types passed in.
323      ::
324  [p=first q=second r=third s=fourth]
325  ::
326  ++  quip
327  |$  [item state]
328      ::      pair of list of first and second
329      ::
330      ::  a common pattern in hoon code is to return a ++list of changes, along with
331      ::  a new state.
332      ::
333      ::  a: type of list item
334      ::  b: type of returned state
335      ::
336  [(list item) state]
337  ::
338  ++  step
339      ::      atom size or offset, in bloqs
340      ::
341  _`@u`1
342  ::
343  ++  trap
344  |$  [product]
345      ::      a core with one arm `$`
346      ::
```

```
347    _|?($:product)
348  ::
349  ++  tree
350    |$  [node]
351    ::    tree mold generator
352    ::
353    ::  a `++tree` can be empty, or contain a node of a type and
354    ::  left/right sub `++tree` of the same type. pretty-printed with `{}`.
355    ::
356    $@(~ [n=node l=(tree node) r=(tree node)])
357  ::
358  ++  trel
359    |$  [first second third]
360    ::    triple tuple
361    ::
362    ::  mold generator: produces a tuple of the three types passed in.
363    ::
364    [p=first q=second r=third]
365  ::
366  ++  unit
367    |$  [item]
368    ::    maybe
369    ::
370    ::  mold generator: either `~` or `[~ u=a]` where `a` is the
371    ::  type that was passed in.
372    ::
373    $@(~ [~ u=item])
374  --  =>
375  ::
376  ~%  %two  +  ~
377  ::    layer-2
378  ::
379  |%
380  ::    2a: unit logic
381  +|  %unit-logc
382  ::
383  ++  biff                                    ::  apply
384    |*  [a=(unit) b=$-(* (unit))]
385    ?~  a  ~
386    (b u.a)
387  ::
388  ++  bind                                    ::  argue
389    |*  [a=(unit) b=gate]
390    ?~  a  ~
391    [~ u=(b u.a)]
392  ::
393  ++  bond                                    ::  replace
394    |*  a=(trap)
395    |*  b=(unit)
396    ?~  b  $:a
397    u.b
398  ::
399  ++  both                                    ::  all the above
400    |*  [a=(unit) b=(unit)]
401    ?~  a  ~
402    ?~  b  ~
403    [~ u=[u.a u.b]]
404  ::
```

```
405  ++    clap                                                    ::  combine
406    |*    [a=(unit) b=(unit) c=_=>(~ |=(^ +<-))]
407    ?~    a    b
408    ?~    b    a
409    [~ u=(c u.a u.b)]
410  ::
411  ++    clef                                                    ::  compose
412    |*    [a=(unit) b=(unit) c=_=>(~ |=(^ `+<-))]
413    ?~    a    ~
414    ?~    b    ~
415    (c u.a u.b)
416  ::
417  ++    drop                                                    ::  enlist
418    |*    a=(unit)
419    ?~    a    ~
420    [i=u.a t=~]
421  ::
422  ++    fall                                                    ::  default
423    |*    [a=(unit) b=*]
424    ?~(a b u.a)
425  ::
426  ++    flit                                                    ::  make filter
427    |*    a=$-(* ?)
428    |*    b=*
429    ?.((a b) ~ [~ u=b])
430  ::
431  ++    hunt                                                    ::  first of units
432    |*    [ord=$-(^ ?) a=(unit) b=(unit)]
433    ^-    %-  unit
434        $?    _?>(?=(^ a) u.a)
435              _?>(?=(^ b) u.b)
436        ==
437    ?~    a    b
438    ?~    b    a
439    ?:((ord u.a u.b) a b)
440  ::
441  ++    lift                                                    ::  lift mold (fmap)
442    |*    a=mold                                                ::  flipped
443    |*    b=(unit)                                              ::  curried
444    (bind b a)                                                  ::  bind
445  ::
446  ++    mate                                                    ::  choose
447    |*    [a=(unit) b=(unit)]
448    ?~    b    a
449    ?~    a    b
450    ?.(=(u.a u.b) ~>(%mean.'mate' !!) a)
451  ::
452  ++    need                                                    ::  demand
453    ~/  %need
454    |*    a=(unit)
455    ?~    a    ~>(%mean.'need' !!)
456    u.a
457  ::
458  ++    some                                                    ::  lift (pure)
459    |*    a=*
460    [~ u=a]
461  ::
462  ::      2b: list logic
```

```
463  +|   %list-logic
464  ::   +snoc: append an element to the end of a list
465  ::
466  ++   snoc
467    |*   [a=(list) b=*]
468    (weld a ^+(a [b]~))
469  ::
470  ::   +lure: List pURE
471  ++   lure
472    |*   a=*
473    [i=a t=~]
474  ::
475  ++   fand                                      ::  all indices
476    ~/   %fand
477    |=   [nedl=(list) hstk=(list)]
478    =|   i=@ud
479    =|   fnd=(list @ud)
480    |-   ^+  fnd
481    =+   [n=nedl h=hstk]
482    |-
483    ?:   |(?=(~ n) ?=(~ h))
484     (flop fnd)
485    ?:   =(i.n i.h)
486     ?~  t.n
487       ^$(i +(i), hstk +.hstk, fnd [i fnd])
488     $(n t.n, h t.h)
489    ^$(i +(i), hstk +.hstk)
490  ::
491  ++   find                                      ::  first index
492    ~/   %find
493    |=   [nedl=(list) hstk=(list)]
494    =|   i=@ud
495    |-   ^-  (unit @ud)
496    =+   [n=nedl h=hstk]
497    |-
498    ?:   |(?=(~ n) ?=(~ h))
499         ~
500    ?:   =(i.n i.h)
501     ?~  t.n
502       `i
503     $(n t.n, h t.h)
504    ^$(i +(i), hstk +.hstk)
505  ::
506  ++   flop                                      ::  reverse
507    ~/   %flop
508    |*   a=(list)
509    =>   .(a (homo a))
510    ^+   a
511    =+   b=`_a`~
512    |-
513    ?~   a  b
514    $(a t.a, b [i.a b])
515  ::
516  ++   gulf                                      ::  range inclusive
517    |=   [a=@ b=@]
518    ?>   (lte a b)
519    |-   ^-  (list @)
520    ?:(=(a +(b)) ~ [a $(a +(a))])
```

```
521  ::
522  ++  homo                                              ::  homogenize
523    |*  a=(list)
524    ^+  =<  $
525      |@  ++  $  ?:(*? ~ [i=(snag 0 a) t=$])
526      --
527    a
528  ::  +join: construct a new list, placing .sep between every pair in .lit
529  ::
530  ++  join
531    |*  [sep=* lit=(list)]
532    =.  sep  `_?>(?=(^ lit) i.lit)`sep
533    ?~  lit  ~
534    =|  out=(list _?>(?=(^ lit) i.lit))
535    |-  ^+  out
536    ?~  t.lit
537      (flop [i.lit out])
538    $(out [sep i.lit out], lit t.lit)
539  ::
540  ::  +bake: convert wet gate to dry gate by specifying argument mold
541  ::
542  ++  bake
543    |*  [f=gate a=mold]
544    |=  arg=a
545    (f arg)
546  ::
547  ++  lent                                              ::  length
548    ~/  %lent
549    |=  a=(list)
550    ^-  @
551    =+  b=0
552    |-
553    ?~  a  b
554    $(a t.a, b +(b))
555  ::
556  ++  levy                                              ::  all of
557    ~/  %levy
558    |*  [a=(list) b=$-(* ?)]
559    |-  ^-  ?
560    ?~  a  &
561    ?.  (b i.a)  |
562    $(a t.a)
563  ::
564  ++  lien                                              ::  some of
565    ~/  %lien
566    |*  [a=(list) b=$-(* ?)]
567    |-  ^-  ?
568    ?~  a  |
569    ?:  (b i.a)  &
570    $(a t.a)
571  ::
572  ++  limo                                              ::  listify
573    |*  a=*
574    ^+  =<  $
575      |@  ++  $  ?~(a ~ ?:(*? [i=-.a t=$] $(a +.a)))
576      --
577    a
578  ::
```

```
579  ++   murn                                              ::  maybe transform
580   ~/   %murn
581   |*   [a=(list) b=$-(* (unit))]
582   =>   .(a (homo a))
583   |-   ^-  (list _?>(?=(^ a) (need (b i.a))))
584   ?~   a   ~
585   =/   c  (b i.a)
586   ?~   c  $(a t.a)
587   [+.c $(a t.a)]
588  ::
589  ++   oust                                              ::  remove
590   ~/   %oust
591   |*   [[a=@ b=@] c=(list)]
592   (weld (scag +<-< c) (slag (add +<-< +<->) c))
593  ::
594  ++   reap                                              ::  replicate
595   ~/   %reap
596   |*   [a=@ b=*]
597   |-   ^-  (list _b)
598   ?~   a   ~
599   [b $(a (dec a))]
600  ::
601  ++   rear                                              ::  last item of list
602   ~/   %rear
603   |*   a=(list)
604   ^-   _?>(?=(^ a) i.a)
605   ?>   ?=(^ a)
606   ?:   =(~ t.a)  i.a  ::NOTE  avoiding tmi
607   $(a t.a)
608  ::
609  ++   reel                                              ::  right fold
610   ~/   %reel
611   |*   [a=(list) b=_=>(~ |=([* *] +<+))]
612   |-   ^+  ,.+<+.b
613   ?~   a
614        +<+,b
615   (b i.a $(a t.a))
616  ::
617  ++   roll                                              ::  left fold
618   ~/   %roll
619   |*   [a=(list) b=_=>(~ |=([* *] +<+))]
620   |-   ^+  ,.+<+.b
621   ?~   a
622        +<+.b
623   $(a t.a, b b(+<+ (b i.a +<+.b)))
624  ::
625  ++   scag                                              ::  prefix
626   ~/   %scag
627   |*   [a=@ b=(list)]
628   |-   ^+  b
629   ?:   |(?=(~ b) =(0 a))  ~
630   [i.b $(b t.b, a (dec a))]
631  ::
632  ++   skid                                              ::  separate
633   ~/   %skid
634   |*   [a=(list) b=$-(* ?)]
635   |-   ^+  [p=a q=a]
636   ?~   a  [~ ~]
```

```
637     =+  c=$(a t.a)
638     ?:((b i.a) [[i.a p.c] q.c] [p.c [i.a q.c]])
639   ::
640   ++  skim                                        ::  only
641     ~/  %skim
642     |*  [a=(list) b=$-(* ?)]
643     |-
644     ^+  a
645     ?~  a  ~
646     ?:((b i.a) [i.a $(a t.a)] $(a t.a))
647   ::
648   ++  skip                                        ::  except
649     ~/  %skip
650     |*  [a=(list) b=$-(* ?)]
651     |-
652     ^+  a
653     ?~  a  ~
654     ?:((b i.a) $(a t.a) [i.a $(a t.a)])
655   ::
656   ++  slag                                        ::  suffix
657     ~/  %slag
658     |*  [a=@ b=(list)]
659     |-  ^+  b
660     ?:  =(0 a)  b
661     ?~  b  ~
662     $(b t.b, a (dec a))
663   ::
664   ++  snag                                        ::  index
665     ~/  %snag
666     |*  [a=@ b=(list)]
667     |-  ^+  ?>(?=(^ b) i.b)
668     ?~  b
669       ~_  leaf+"snag-fail"
670       !!
671     ?:  =(0 a)  i.b
672     $(b t.b, a (dec a))
673   ::
674   ++  snip                                        ::  drop tail off list
675     ~/  %snip
676     |*  a=(list)
677     ^+  a
678     ?~  a  ~
679     ?:  =(~ t.a)  ~
680     [i.a $(a t.a)]
681   ::
682   ++  sort  !.                                     ::  quicksort
683     ~/  %sort
684     |*  [a=(list) b=$-([* *] ?)]
685     =>  .(a ^.(homo a))
686     |-  ^+  a
687     ?~  a  ~
688     =+  s=(skid t.a |:(c=i.a (b c i.a)))
689     %+  weld
690       $(a p.s)
691     ^+  t.a
692     [i.a $(a q.s)]
693   ::
694   ++  spin                                        ::  stateful turn
```

```
695    ::
696    ::    a: list
697    ::    b: state
698    ::    c: gate from list-item and state to product and new state
699    ~/  %spin
700    |*  [a=(list) b=* c=_|=(^ [** +<+])]
701    =>  .(c `$-([_?>(?=(^ a) i.a) _b] [_-:(c) _b])`c)
702    =/  acc=(list _-:(c))  ~
703    ::    transformed list and updated state
704    |-  ^-  (pair _acc _b)
705    ?~  a
706      [(flop acc) b]
707    =^  res  b  (c i.a b)
708    $(acc [res acc], a t.a)
709    ::
710  ++  spun                                          ::  internal spin
711    ::
712    ::    a: list
713    ::    b: gate from list-item and state to product and new state
714    ~/  %spun
715    |*  [a=(list) b=_|=(^ [** +<+])]
716    ::    transformed list
717    p:(spin a +<+.b b)
718    ::
719  ++  swag                                          ::  slice
720    |*  [[a=@ b=@] c=(list)]
721    (scag +<-> (slag +<-< c))
722    ::  +turn: transform each value of list :a using the function :b
723    ::
724  ++  turn
725    ~/  %turn
726    |*  [a=(list) b=gate]
727    =>  .(a (homo a))
728    ^-  (list _?>(?=(^ a) (b i.a)))
729    |-
730    ?~  a  ~
731    [i=(b i.a) t=$(a t.a)]
732    ::
733  ++  weld                                          ::  concatenate
734    ~/  %weld
735    |*  [a=(list) b=(list)]
736    =>  .(a ^.(homo a), b ^.(homo b))
737    |-  ^+  b
738    ?~  a  b
739    [i.a $(a t.a)]
740    ::
741  ++  snap                                          ::  replace item
742    ~/  %snap
743    |*  [a=(list) b=@ c=*]
744    ^+  a
745    (weld (scag b a) [c (slag +(b) a)])
746    ::
747  ++  into                                          ::  insert item
748    ~/  %into
749    |*  [a=(list) b=@ c=*]
750    ^+  a
751    (weld (scag b a) [c (slag b a)])
752    ::
```

```
753  ++  welp                                          ::  faceless weld
754    ~/  %welp
755    |*  [* *]
756    ?~  +<-
757      +<-(. +<+)
758    +<-(+ $(+<- +<->))
759  ::
760  ++  zing                                          ::  promote
761    ~/  %zing
762    |*  *
763    ?~  +<
764      +<
765    (welp +<- $(+< +<+))
766  ::
767  ::    2c: bit arithmetic
768  +|  %bit-arithmetic
769  ::
770  ++  bex                                            ::  binary exponent
771    ~/  %bex
772    |=  a=bloq
773    ^-  @
774    ?:  =(0 a)  1
775    (mul 2 $(a (dec a)))
776  ::
777  ++  can                                            ::  assemble
778    ~/  %can
779    |=  [a=bloq b=(list [p=step q=@])]
780    ^-  @
781    ?~  b  0
782    (add (end [a p.i.b] q.i.b) (lsh [a p.i.b] $(b t.b)))
783  ::
784  ++  cat                                            ::  concatenate
785    ~/  %cat
786    |=  [a=bloq b=@ c=@]
787    (add (lsh [a (met a b)] c) b)
788  ::
789  ++  cut                                            ::  slice
790    ~/  %cut
791    |=  [a=bloq [b=step c=step] d=@]
792    (end [a c] (rsh [a b] d))
793  ::
794  ++  end                                            ::  tail
795    ~/  %end
796    |=  [a=bite b=@]
797    =/  [=bloq =step]  ?^(a a [a *step])
798    (mod b (bex (mul (bex bloq) step)))
799  ::
800  ++  fil                                            ::  fill bloqstream
801    ~/  %fil
802    |=  [a=bloq b=step c=@]
803    =|  n=@ud
804    =.  c  (end a c)
805    =/  d  c
806    |-  ^-  @
807    ?:  =(n b)
808      (rsh a d)
809    $(d (add c (lsh a d)), n +(n))
810  ::
```

```
811  ++  lsh                                             ::  left-shift
812    ~/  %lsh
813    |=  [a=bite b=@]
814    =/  [=bloq =step]  ?^(a a [a *step])
815    (mul b (bex (mul (bex bloq) step)))
816  ::
817  ++  met                                             ::  measure
818    ~/  %met
819    |=  [a=bloq b=@]
820    ^-  @
821    =+  c=0
822    |-
823    ?:  =(0 b)  c
824    $(b (rsh a b), c +(c))
825  ::
826  ++  rap                                             ::  assemble variable
827    ~/  %rap
828    |=  [a=bloq b=(list @)]
829    ^-  @
830    ?~  b  0
831    (cat a i.b $(b t.b))
832  ::
833  ++  rep                                             ::  assemble fixed
834    ~/  %rep
835    |=  [a=bite b=(list @)]
836    =/  [=bloq =step]  ?^(a a [a *step])
837    =|  i=@ud
838    |-  ^-  @
839    ?~  b  0
840    %+  add  $(i +(i), b t.b)
841    (lsh [bloq (mul step i)] (end [bloq step] i.b))
842  ::
843  ++  rev
844    ::    reverses block order, accounting for leading zeroes
845    ::
846    ::  boz: block size
847    ::  len: size of dat, in boz
848    ::  dat: data to flip
849    ~/  %rev
850    |=  [boz=bloq len=@ud dat=@]
851    ^-  @
852    =.  dat  (end [boz len] dat)
853    %+  lsh
854      [boz (sub len (met boz dat))]
855    (swp boz dat)
856  ::
857  ++  rip                                             ::  disassemble
858    ~/  %rip
859    |=  [a=bite b=@]
860    ^-  (list @)
861    ?:  =(0 b)  ~
862    [(end a b) $(b (rsh a b))]
863  ::
864  ++  rsh                                             ::  right-shift
865    ~/  %rsh
866    |=  [a=bite b=@]
867    =/  [=bloq =step]  ?^(a a [a *step])
868    (div b (bex (mul (bex bloq) step)))
```

```
869  ::
870  ++  run                                           ::  +turn into atom
871  ~/  %run
872  |=  [a=bite b=@ c=$-(@ @)]
873  (rep a (turn (rip a b) c))
874  ::
875  ++  rut                                           ::  +turn into list
876  ~/  %rut
877  |*  [a=bite b=@ c=$-(@ *)]
878  (turn (rip a b) c)
879  ::
880  ++  sew                                           ::  stitch into
881  ~/  %sew
882  |=  [a=bloq [b=step c=step d=@] e=@]
883  ^-  @
884  %+  add
885    (can a b^e c^d ~)
886  =/  f  [a (add b c)]
887  (lsh f (rsh f e))
888  ::
889  ++  swp                                           ::  naive rev bloq order
890  ~/  %swp
891  |=  [a=bloq b=@]
892  (rep a (flop (rip a b)))
893  ::
894  ++  xeb                                           ::  binary logarithm
895  ~/  %xeb
896  |=  a=@
897  ^-  @
898  (met 0 a)
899  ::
900  ++  fe                                            ::  modulo bloq
901  |_  a=bloq
902  ++  dif                                           ::  difference
903    |=([b=@ c=@] (sit (sub (add out (sit b)) (sit c))))
904  ++  inv  |=(b=@ (sub (dec out) (sit b)))           ::  inverse
905  ++  net  |=  b=@  ^-  @                            ::  flip byte endianness
906          =>  .(b (sit b))
907          ?:  (lte a 3)
908            b
909          =+  c=(dec a)
910          %+  con
911            (lsh c $(a c, b (cut c [0 1] b)))
912          $(a c, b (cut c [1 1] b))
913  ++  out  (bex (bex a))                            ::  mod value
914  ++  rol  |=  [b=bloq c=@ d=@]  ^-  @              ::  roll left
915          =+  e=(sit d)
916          =+  f=(bex (sub a b))
917          =+  g=(mod c f)
918          (sit (con (lsh [b g] e) (rsh [b (sub f g)] e)))
919  ++  ror  |=  [b=bloq c=@ d=@]  ^-  @              ::  roll right
920          =+  e=(sit d)
921          =+  f=(bex (sub a b))
922          =+  g=(mod c f)
923          (sit (con (rsh [b g] e) (lsh [b (sub f g)] e)))
924  ++  sum  |=([b=@ c=@] (sit (add b c)))            ::  wrapping add
925  ++  sit  |=(b=@ (end a b))                        ::  enforce modulo
926  --
```

```
927  ::
928  ::      2d: bit logic
929  +|    %bit-logic
930  ::
931  ++  con                                              :: binary or
932    ~/  %con
933    |=  [a=@ b=@]
934    =+  [c=0 d=0]
935    |-  ^-  @
936    ?:  ?&(=(0 a) =(0 b))  d
937    %=  $
938      a   (rsh 0 a)
939      b   (rsh 0 b)
940      c   +(c)
941      d   %+  add  d
942          %+  lsh  [0 c]
943          ?&  =(0 (end 0 a))
944              =(0 (end 0 b))
945          ==
946    ==
947  ::
948  ++  dis                                              :: binary and
949    ~/  %dis
950    |=  [a=@ b=@]
951    =|  [c=@ d=@]
952    |-  ^-  @
953    ?:  ?|(=(0 a) =(0 b))  d
954    %=  $
955      a   (rsh 0 a)
956      b   (rsh 0 b)
957      c   +(c)
958      d   %+  add  d
959          %+  lsh  [0 c]
960          ?|  =(0 (end 0 a))
961              =(0 (end 0 b))
962          ==
963    ==
964  ::
965  ++  mix                                              :: binary xor
966    ~/  %mix
967    |=  [a=@ b=@]
968    ^-  @
969    =+  [c=0 d=0]
970    |-
971    ?:  ?&(=(0 a) =(0 b))  d
972    %=  $
973      a   (rsh 0 a)
974      b   (rsh 0 b)
975      c   +(c)
976      d   (add d (lsh [0 c] =((end 0 a) (end 0 b))))
977    ==
978  ::
979  ++  not  |=  [a=bloq b=@ c=@]                         :: binary not (sized)
980    (mix c (dec (bex (mul b (bex a)))))
981  ::
982  ::      2e: insecure hashing
983  +|    %insecure-hashing
984  ::
```

```
985  ++  muk                                                  ::  standard murmur3
986  ~%  %muk  ..muk  ~
987  =+  ~(. fe 5)
988  |=  [syd=@ len=@ key=@]
989  =.  syd      (end 5 syd)
990  =/  pad      (sub len (met 3 key))
991  =/  data     (weld (rip 3 key) (reap pad 0))
992  =/  nblocks  (div len 4)  ::  intentionally off-by-one
993  =/  h1  syd
994  =+  [c1=0xcc9e.2d51 c2=0x1b87.3593]
995  =/  blocks  (rip 5 key)
996  =/  i  nblocks
997  =.  h1  =/  hi  h1  |-
998    ?:  =(0 i)  hi
999    =/  k1  (snag (sub nblocks i) blocks)  ::  negative array index
1000   =.  k1  (sit (mul k1 c1))
1001   =.  k1  (rol 0 15 k1)
1002   =.  k1  (sit (mul k1 c2))
1003   =.  hi  (mix hi k1)
1004   =.  hi  (rol 0 13 hi)
1005   =.  hi  (sum (sit (mul hi 5)) 0xe654.6b64)
1006   $(i (dec i))
1007 =/  tail  (slag (mul 4 nblocks) data)
1008 =/  k1    0
1009 =/  tlen  (dis len 3)
1010 =.  h1
1011   ?+  tlen  h1  ::  fallthrough switch
1012     %3  =.  k1  (mix k1 (lsh [0 16] (snag 2 tail)))
1013         =.  k1  (mix k1 (lsh [0 8] (snag 1 tail)))
1014         =.  k1  (mix k1 (snag 0 tail))
1015         =.  k1  (sit (mul k1 c1))
1016         =.  k1  (rol 0 15 k1)
1017         =.  k1  (sit (mul k1 c2))
1018         (mix h1 k1)
1019     %2  =.  k1  (mix k1 (lsh [0 8] (snag 1 tail)))
1020         =.  k1  (mix k1 (snag 0 tail))
1021         =.  k1  (sit (mul k1 c1))
1022         =.  k1  (rol 0 15 k1)
1023         =.  k1  (sit (mul k1 c2))
1024         (mix h1 k1)
1025     %1  =.  k1  (mix k1 (snag 0 tail))
1026         =.  k1  (sit (mul k1 c1))
1027         =.  k1  (rol 0 15 k1)
1028         =.  k1  (sit (mul k1 c2))
1029         (mix h1 k1)
1030   ==
1031 =.  h1  (mix h1 len)
1032 |^  (fmix32 h1)
1033 ++  fmix32
1034   |=  h=@
1035   =.  h  (mix h (rsh [0 16] h))
1036   =.  h  (sit (mul h 0x85eb.ca6b))
1037   =.  h  (mix h (rsh [0 13] h))
1038   =.  h  (sit (mul h 0xc2b2.ae35))
1039   =.  h  (mix h (rsh [0 16] h))
1040   h
1041 --
1042 ::
```

```
1043  ++    mug                                                    ::  mug with murmur3
1044    ~/   %mug
1045    |=   a=*
1046    |^   ?@   a  (mum 0xcafe.babe 0x7fff a)
1047         =/   b  (cat 5 $(a -.a) $(a +.a))
1048         (mum 0xdead.beef 0xfffe b)
1049    ::
1050    ++   mum
1051    |=   [syd=@uxF fal=@F key=@]
1052    =/   wyd  (met 3 key)
1053    =|   i=@ud
1054    |-   ^-   @F
1055    ?:   =(8 i)   fal
1056    =/   haz=@F  (muk syd wyd key)
1057    =/   ham=@F  (mix (rsh [0 31] haz) (end [0 31] haz))
1058    ?.(=(0 ham) ham $(i +(i), syd +(syd)))
1059    --
1060  ::                                                           ::
1061  ::    2f: noun ordering
1062  +|    %noun-ordering
1063  ::
1064  ::    +aor: alphabetical order
1065  ::
1066  ::    Orders atoms before cells, and atoms in ascending LSB order.
1067  ::
1068  ++    aor
1069    ~/   %aor
1070    |=   [a=* b=*]
1071    ^-   ?
1072    ?:   =(a b)   &
1073    ?.   ?=(@ a)
1074      ?:   ?=(@ b)   |
1075      ?:   =(-.a -.b)
1076        $(a +.a, b +.b)
1077      $(a -.a, b -.b)
1078    ?.   ?=(@ b)   &
1079    |-
1080    =+   [c=(end 3 a) d=(end 3 b)]
1081    ?:   =(c d)
1082      $(a (rsh 3 a), b (rsh 3 b))
1083    (lth c d)
1084  ::    +dor: depth order
1085  ::
1086  ::    Orders in ascending tree depth.
1087  ::
1088  ++    dor
1089    ~/   %dor
1090    |=   [a=* b=*]
1091    ^-   ?
1092    ?:   =(a b)   &
1093    ?.   ?=(@ a)
1094      ?:   ?=(@ b)   |
1095      ?:   =(-.a -.b)
1096        $(a +.a, b +.b)
1097      $(a -.a, b -.b)
1098    ?.   ?=(@ b)   &
1099    (lth a b)
1100  ::    +gor: mug order
```

```
1101  ::
1102  ::      Orders in ascending +mug hash order, collisions fall back to +dor.
1103  ::
1104  ++  gor
1105    ~/  %gor
1106    |=  [a=* b=*]
1107    ^-  ?
1108    =+  [c=(mug a) d=(mug b)]
1109    ?:  =(c d)
1110      (dor a b)
1111    (lth c d)
1112  ::  +mor: (more) mug order
1113  ::
1114  ::      Orders in ascending double +mug hash order, collisions fall back to +dor.
1115  ::
1116  ++  mor
1117    ~/  %mor
1118    |=  [a=* b=*]
1119    ^-  ?
1120    =+  [c=(mug (mug a)) d=(mug (mug b))]
1121    ?:  =(c d)
1122      (dor a b)
1123    (lth c d)
1124  ::
1125  ::      2g: unsigned powers
1126  +|  %unsigned-powers
1127  ::
1128  ++  pow                                         ::  unsigned exponent
1129    ~/  %pow
1130    |=  [a=@ b=@]
1131    ?:  =(b 0)  1
1132    |-  ?:  =(b 1)  a
1133    =+  c=$(b (div b 2))
1134    =+  d=(mul c c)
1135    ?~  (dis b 1)  d  (mul d a)
1136  ::
1137  ++  sqt                                         ::  unsigned sqrt/rem
1138    ~/  %sqt
1139    |=  a=@  ^-  [p=@ q=@]
1140    ?~  a  [0 0]
1141    =+  [q=(div (dec (xeb a)) 2) r=0]
1142    =-  [-.b (sub a +.b)]
1143    ^=  b  |-
1144    =+  s=(add r (bex q))
1145    =+  t=(mul s s)
1146    ?:  =(q 0)
1147      ?:((lte t a) [s t] [r (mul r r)])
1148    ?:  (lte t a)
1149      $(r s, q (dec q))
1150    $(q (dec q))
1151  ::
1152  ::      2h: set logic
1153  +|  %set-logic
1154  ::
1155  ++  in                                          ::  set engine
1156    ~/  %in
1157    =|  a=(tree)  ::  (set)
1158    |@
```

```
1159  ++  all                                    ::  logical AND
1160    ~/  %all
1161    |*  b=$-(* ?)
1162    |-  ^-  ?
1163    ?~  a
1164      &
1165    ?&((b n.a) $(a l.a) $(a r.a))
1166  ::
1167  ++  any                                    ::  logical OR
1168    ~/  %any
1169    |*  b=$-(* ?)
1170    |-  ^-  ?
1171    ?~  a
1172      |
1173    ?|((b n.a) $(a l.a) $(a r.a))
1174  ::
1175  ++  apt                                    ::  check correctness
1176    =<  $
1177    ~/  %apt
1178    =|  [l=(unit) r=(unit)]
1179    |.  ^-  ?
1180    ?~  a  &
1181    ?&  ?~(l & &((gor n.a u.l) !=(n.a u.l)))
1182        ?~(r & &((gor u.r n.a) !=(u.r n.a)))
1183        ?~(l.a & ?&((mor n.a n.l.a) !=(n.a n.l.a) $(a l.a, l `n.a)))
1184        ?~(r.a & ?&((mor n.a n.r.a) !=(n.a n.r.a) $(a r.a, r `n.a)))
1185    ==
1186  ::
1187  ++  bif                                    ::  splits a by b
1188    ~/  %bif
1189    |*  b=*
1190    ^+  [l=a r=a]
1191    =<  +
1192    |-  ^+  a
1193    ?~  a
1194      [b ~ ~]
1195    ?:  =(b n.a)
1196      a
1197    ?:  (gor b n.a)
1198      =+  c=$(a l.a)
1199      ?>  ?=(^ c)
1200      c(r a(l r.c))
1201    =+  c=$(a r.a)
1202    ?>  ?=(^ c)
1203    c(l a(r l.c))
1204  ::
1205  ++  del                                    ::  b without any a
1206    ~/  %del
1207    |*  b=*
1208    |-  ^+  a
1209    ?~  a
1210      ~
1211    ?.  =(b n.a)
1212      ?:  (gor b n.a)
1213        a(l $(a l.a))
1214      a(r $(a r.a))
1215    |-  ^-  [$?(~ _a)]
1216    ?~  l.a  r.a
```

```
1217      ?~  r.a  l.a
1218      ?:  (mor n.l.a n.r.a)
1219        l.a(r $(l.a r.l.a))
1220      r.a(l $(r.a l.r.a))
1221    ::
1222    ++  dif                                      ::  difference
1223      ~/  %dif
1224      |*  b=_a
1225      |-  ^+  a
1226      ?~  b
1227        a
1228      =+  c=(bif n.b)
1229      ?>  ?=(^ c)
1230      =+  d=$(a l.c, b l.b)
1231      =+  e=$(a r.c, b r.b)
1232      |-  ^-  [$?(~ _a)]
1233      ?~  d  e
1234      ?~  e  d
1235      ?:  (mor n.d n.e)
1236        d(r $(d r.d))
1237      e(l $(e l.e))
1238    ::
1239    ++  dig                                      ::  axis of a in b
1240      |=  b=*
1241      =+  c=1
1242      |-  ^-  (unit @)
1243      ?~  a  ~
1244      ?:  =(b n.a)  [~ u=(peg c 2)]
1245      ?:  (gor b n.a)
1246        $(a l.a, c (peg c 6))
1247      $(a r.a, c (peg c 7))
1248    ::
1249    ++  gas                                      ::  concatenate
1250      ~/  %gas
1251      |=  b=(list _?>(?=(^ a) n.a))
1252      |-  ^+  a
1253      ?~  b
1254        a
1255      $(b t.b, a (put i.b))
1256    ::  +has: does :b exist in :a?
1257    ::
1258    ++  has
1259      ~/  %has
1260      |*  b=*
1261      ^-  ?
1262      ::    wrap extracted item type in a unit because bunting fails
1263      ::
1264      ::  If we used the real item type of _?^(a n.a !!) as the sample type,
1265      ::  then hoon would bunt it to create the default sample for the gate.
1266      ::
1267      ::  However, bunting that expression fails if :a is ~. If we wrap it
1268      ::  in a unit, the bunted unit doesn't include the bunted item type.
1269      ::
1270      ::  This way we can ensure type safety of :b without needing to perform
1271      ::  this failing bunt. It's a hack.
1272      ::
1273      %.  [~ b]
1274      |=  b=(unit _?>(?=(^ a) n.a))
```

```
1275      =>   .(b ?>(?=(^ b) u.b))
1276      |-   ^-   ?
1277      ?~   a
1278        |
1279      ?:   =(b n.a)
1280        &
1281      ?:   (gor b n.a)
1282        $(a l.a)
1283      $(a r.a)
1284    ::
1285    ++  int                                    ::  intersection
1286    ~/  %int
1287    |*  b=_a
1288    |-  ^+  a
1289    ?~  b
1290      ~
1291    ?~  a
1292      ~
1293    ?.  (mor n.a n.b)
1294      $(a b, b a)
1295    ?:  =(n.b n.a)
1296      a(l $(a l.a, b l.b), r $(a r.a, b r.b))
1297    ?:  (gor n.b n.a)
1298      %-  uni(a $(a l.a, r.b ~))  $(b r.b)
1299    %-  uni(a $(a r.a, l.b ~))  $(b l.b)
1300    ::
1301    ++  put                                     ::  puts b in a, sorted
1302    ~/  %put
1303    |*  b=*
1304    |-  ^+  a
1305    ?~  a
1306      [b ~ ~]
1307    ?:  =(b n.a)
1308      a
1309    ?:  (gor b n.a)
1310      =+  c=$(a l.a)
1311      ?>  ?=(^ c)
1312      ?:  (mor n.a n.c)
1313        a(l c)
1314      c(r a(l r.c))
1315    =+  c=$(a r.a)
1316    ?>  ?=(^ c)
1317    ?:  (mor n.a n.c)
1318      a(r c)
1319    c(l a(r l.c))
1320    ::
1321    ++  rep                                     ::  reduce to product
1322    ~/  %rep
1323    |*  b=_=>(~ |=([* *] +<+))
1324    |-
1325    ?~  a  +<+.b
1326    $(a r.a, +<+.b $(a l.a, +<+.b (b n.a +<+.b)))
1327    ::
1328    ++  run                                     ::  apply gate to values
1329    ~/  %run
1330    |*  b=gate
1331    =+  c=`(set _?>(?=(^ a) (b n.a)))`~
1332    |-  ?~  a  c
```

```
1333      =.   c   (~(put in c) (b n.a))
1334      =.   c   $(a l.a, c c)
1335      $(a r.a, c c)
1336    ::
1337    ++  tap                                          ::  convert to list
1338      =<  $
1339      ~/  %tap
1340      =+  b=`(list _?>(?=(^ a) n.a))`~
1341      |.  ^+  b
1342      ?~  a
1343        b
1344      $(a r.a, b [n.a $(a l.a)])
1345    ::
1346    ++  uni                                          ::  union
1347      ~/  %uni
1348      |*  b=_a
1349      ?:  =(a b)  a
1350      |-  ^+  a
1351      ?~  b
1352        a
1353      ?~  a
1354        b
1355      ?:  =(n.b n.a)
1356        b(l $(a l.a, b l.b), r $(a r.a, b r.b))
1357      ?:  (mor n.a n.b)
1358        ?:  (gor n.b n.a)
1359          $(l.a $(a l.a, r.b ~), b r.b)
1360        $(r.a $(a r.a, l.b ~), b l.b)
1361      ?:  (gor n.a n.b)
1362        $(l.b $(b l.b, r.a ~), a r.a)
1363      $(r.b $(b r.b, l.a ~), a l.a)
1364    ::
1365    ++  wyt                                          ::  size of set
1366      =<  $
1367      ~%  %wyt  +  ~
1368      |.  ^-  @
1369      ?~(a 0 +((add $(a l.a) $(a r.a))))
1370      --
1371  ::
1372  ::    2i: map logic
1373  +|  %map-logic
1374  ::
1375  ++  by                                             ::  map engine
1376    ~/  %by
1377    =|  a=(tree (pair))  ::  (map)
1378    |@
1379    ++  all                                          ::  logical AND
1380      ~/  %all
1381      |*  b=$-(* ?)
1382      |-  ^-  ?
1383      ?~  a
1384        &
1385      ?&((b q.n.a) $(a l.a) $(a r.a))
1386    ::
1387    ++  any                                          ::  logical OR
1388      ~/  %any
1389      |*  b=$-(* ?)
1390      |-  ^-  ?
```

```
1391      ?~  a
1392        |
1393      ?|((b q.n.a) $(a l.a) $(a r.a))
1394    ::
1395    ++  bif                                      ::  splits a by b
1396      ~/  %bif
1397      |*  [b=* c=*]
1398      ^+  [l=a r=a]
1399      =<  +
1400      |-  ^+  a
1401      ?~  a
1402        [[b c] ~ ~]
1403      ?:  =(b p.n.a)
1404        ?:  =(c q.n.a)
1405          a
1406        a(n [b c])
1407      ?:  (gor b p.n.a)
1408        =+  d=$(a l.a)
1409        ?>  ?=(^ d)
1410        d(r a(l r.d))
1411      =+  d=$(a r.a)
1412      ?>  ?=(^ d)
1413      d(l a(r l.d))
1414    ::
1415    ++  del                                      ::  delete at key b
1416      ~/  %del
1417      |*  b=*
1418      |-  ^+  a
1419      ?~  a
1420        ~
1421      ?.  =(b p.n.a)
1422        ?:  (gor b p.n.a)
1423          a(l $(a l.a))
1424        a(r $(a r.a))
1425      |-  ^-  [$?(~ _a)]
1426      ?~  l.a  r.a
1427      ?~  r.a  l.a
1428      ?:  (mor p.n.l.a p.n.r.a)
1429        l.a(r $(l.a r.l.a))
1430      r.a(l $(r.a l.r.a))
1431    ::
1432    ++  dif                                      ::  difference
1433      ~/  %dif
1434      |*  b=_a
1435      |-  ^+  a
1436      ?~  b
1437        a
1438      =+  c=(bif p.n.b q.n.b)
1439      ?>  ?=(^ c)
1440      =+  d=$(a l.c, b l.b)
1441      =+  e=$(a r.c, b r.b)
1442      |-  ^-  [$?(~ _a)]
1443      ?~  d  e
1444      ?~  e  d
1445      ?:  (mor p.n.d p.n.e)
1446        d(r $(d r.d))
1447      e(l $(e l.e))
1448    ::
```

```
1449    ++  dig                                              :: axis of b key
1450      |=  b=*
1451      =+  c=1
1452      |-  ^-  (unit @)
1453      ?~  a  ~
1454      ?:  =(b p.n.a)  [~ u=(peg c 2)]
1455      ?:  (gor b p.n.a)
1456        $(a l.a, c (peg c 6))
1457      $(a r.a, c (peg c 7))
1458    ::
1459    ++  apt                                              :: check correctness
1460      =<  $
1461      ~/  %apt
1462      =|  [l=(unit) r=(unit)]
1463      |.  ^-  ?
1464      ?~  a  &
1465      ?&  ?~(l & &((gor p.n.a u.l) !=(p.n.a u.l)))
1466          ?~(r & &((gor u.r p.n.a) !=(u.r p.n.a)))
1467          ?~  l.a  &
1468          &((mor p.n.a p.n.l.a) !=(p.n.a p.n.l.a) $(a l.a, l `p.n.a))
1469          ?~  r.a  &
1470          &((mor p.n.a p.n.r.a) !=(p.n.a p.n.r.a) $(a r.a, r `p.n.a))
1471      ==
1472    ::
1473    ++  gas                                               :: concatenate
1474      ~/  %gas
1475      |*  b=(list [p=* q=*])
1476      =>  .(b `(list _?>(?=(^ a) n.a))`b)
1477      |-  ^+  a
1478      ?~  b
1479        a
1480      $(b t.b, a (put p.i.b q.i.b))
1481    ::
1482    ++  get                                               :: grab value by key
1483      ~/  %get
1484      |*  b=*
1485      =>  .(b `_?>(?=(^ a) p.n.a)`b)
1486      |-  ^-  (unit _?>(?=(^ a) q.n.a))
1487      ?~  a
1488        ~
1489      ?:  =(b p.n.a)
1490        (some q.n.a)
1491      ?:  (gor b p.n.a)
1492        $(a l.a)
1493      $(a r.a)
1494    ::
1495    ++  got                                               :: need value by key
1496      |*  b=*
1497      (need (get b))
1498    ::
1499    ++  gut                                               :: fall value by key
1500      |*  [b=* c=*]
1501      (fall (get b) c)
1502    ::
1503    ++  has                                               :: key existence check
1504      ~/  %has
1505      |*  b=*
1506      !=(~ (get b))
```

```
1507      ::
1508      ++  int                                          ::  intersection
1509       ~/  %int
1510       |*  b=_a
1511       |-  ^+  a
1512       ?~  b
1513         ~
1514       ?~  a
1515         ~
1516       ?:  (mor p.n.a p.n.b)
1517         ?:  =(p.n.b p.n.a)
1518           b(l $(a l.a, b l.b), r $(a r.a, b r.b))
1519         ?:  (gor p.n.b p.n.a)
1520           %-  uni(a $(a l.a, r.b ~))  $(b r.b)
1521         %-  uni(a $(a r.a, l.b ~))  $(b l.b)
1522       ?:  =(p.n.a p.n.b)
1523         b(l $(b l.b, a l.a), r $(b r.b, a r.a))
1524       ?:  (gor p.n.a p.n.b)
1525         %-  uni(a $(b l.b, r.a ~))  $(a r.a)
1526       %-  uni(a $(b r.b, l.a ~))  $(a l.a)
1527      ::
1528      ++  jab
1529       ~/  %jab
1530       |*  [key=_?>(?=(^ a) p.n.a) fun=$-(_?>(?=(^ a) q.n.a) _?>(?=(^ a) q.n.a))]
1531       ^+  a
1532       ::
1533       ?~  a  !!
1534       ::
1535       ?:  =(key p.n.a)
1536         a(q.n (fun q.n.a))
1537       ::
1538       ?:  (gor key p.n.a)
1539         a(l $(a l.a))
1540       ::
1541       a(r $(a r.a))
1542      ::
1543      ++  mar                                          ::  add with validation
1544       |*  [b=* c=(unit *)]
1545       ?~  c
1546         (del b)
1547       (put b u.c)
1548      ::
1549      ++  put                                          ::  adds key-value pair
1550       ~/  %put
1551       |*  [b=* c=*]
1552       |-  ^+  a
1553       ?~  a
1554         [[b c] ~ ~]
1555       ?:  =(b p.n.a)
1556         ?:  =(c q.n.a)
1557           a
1558         a(n [b c])
1559       ?:  (gor b p.n.a)
1560         =+  d=$(a l.a)
1561         ?>  ?=(^ d)
1562         ?:  (mor p.n.a p.n.d)
1563           a(l d)
1564         d(r a(l r.d))
```

```
1565      =+  d=$(a r.a)
1566      ?>  ?=(^ d)
1567      ?:  (mor p.n.a p.n.d)
1568        a(r d)
1569      d(l a(r l.d))
1570    ::
1571    ++  rep                                 ::  reduce to product
1572      ~/  %rep
1573      |*  b=_=>(~ |=([* *] +<+))
1574      |-
1575      ?~  a  +<+.b
1576      $(a r.a, +<+.b $(a l.a, +<+.b (b n.a +<+.b)))
1577    ::
1578    ++  rib                                 ::  transform + product
1579      |*  [b=* c=gate]
1580      |-  ^+  [b a]
1581      ?~  a  [b ~]
1582      =+  d=(c n.a b)
1583      =.  n.a  +.d
1584      =+  e=$(a l.a, b -.d)
1585      =+  f=$(a r.a, b -.e)
1586      [-.f a(l +.e, r +.f)]
1587    ::
1588    ++  run                                 ::  apply gate to values
1589      ~/  %run
1590      |*  b=gate
1591      |-
1592      ?~  a  a
1593      [n=[p=p.n.a q=(b q.n.a)] l=$(a l.a) r=$(a r.a)]
1594    ::
1595    ++  rut                                 ::  apply gate to nodes
1596      |*  b=gate
1597      |-
1598      ?~  a  a
1599      [n=[p=p.n.a q=(b p.n.a q.n.a)] l=$(a l.a) r=$(a r.a)]
1600    ::
1601    ++  tap                                 ::  listify pairs
1602      =<  $
1603      ~/  %tap
1604      =+  b=`(list _?>(?=(^ a) n.a))`~
1605      |.  ^+  b
1606      ?~  a
1607        b
1608      $(a r.a, b [n.a $(a l.a)])
1609    ::
1610    ++  uni                                 ::  union, merge
1611      ~/  %uni
1612      |*  b=_a
1613      |-  ^+  a
1614      ?~  b
1615        a
1616      ?~  a
1617        b
1618      ?:  =(p.n.b p.n.a)
1619        b(l $(a l.a, b l.b), r $(a r.a, b r.b))
1620      ?:  (mor p.n.a p.n.b)
1621        ?:  (gor p.n.b p.n.a)
1622          $(l.a $(a l.a, r.b ~), b r.b)
```

```
1623        $(r.a $(a r.a, l.b ~), b l.b)
1624      ?:  (gor p.n.a p.n.b)
1625        $(l.b $(b l.b, r.a ~), a r.a)
1626      $(r.b $(b r.b, l.a ~), a l.a)
1627    ::
1628    ++  uno                                     ::  general union
1629    |*  b=_a
1630    |*  meg=$-([* * *] *)
1631    |-  ^+  a
1632    ?~  b
1633      a
1634    ?~  a
1635      b
1636    ?:  =(p.n.b p.n.a)
1637      :+  [p.n.a `_?>(?=(^ a) q.n.a)`(meg p.n.a q.n.a q.n.b)]
1638        $(b l.b, a l.a)
1639      $(b r.b, a r.a)
1640    ?:  (mor p.n.a p.n.b)
1641      ?:  (gor p.n.b p.n.a)
1642        $(l.a $(a l.a, r.b ~), b r.b)
1643      $(r.a $(a r.a, l.b ~), b l.b)
1644    ?:  (gor p.n.a p.n.b)
1645      $(l.b $(b l.b, r.a ~), a r.a)
1646    $(r.b $(b r.b, l.a ~), a l.a)
1647    ::
1648    ++  urn                                     ::  apply gate to nodes
1649    ~/  %urn
1650    |*  b=$-([* *] *)
1651    |-
1652    ?~  a  ~
1653    a(n n.a(q (b p.n.a q.n.a)), l $(a l.a), r $(a r.a))
1654    ::
1655    ++  wyt                                     ::  depth of map
1656    =<  $
1657    ~%  %wyt  +  ~
1658    |.  ^-  @
1659    ?~(a 0 +((add $(a l.a) $(a r.a))))
1660    ::
1661    ++  key                                     ::  set of keys
1662    =<  $
1663    ~/  %key
1664    =+  b=`(set _?>(?=(^ a) p.n.a))`~
1665    |.  ^+  b
1666    ?~  a  b
1667    $(a r.a, b $(a l.a, b (~(put in b) p.n.a)))
1668    ::
1669    ++  val                                     ::  list of vals
1670    =+  b=`(list _?>(?=(^ a) q.n.a))`~
1671    |-  ^+  b
1672    ?~  a  b
1673    $(a r.a, b [q.n.a $(a l.a)])
1674    --
1675    ::
1676    ::    2j: jar and jug logic
1677    +|  %jar-and-jug-logic
1678    ++  ja                                      ::  jar engine
1679    =|  a=(tree (pair * (list)))  ::  (jar)
1680    |@
```

```
1681  ++  get                                      ::  gets list by key
1682    |*  b=*
1683    =+  c=(~(get by a) b)
1684    ?~(c ~ u.c)
1685    ::
1686  ++  add                                      ::  adds key-list pair
1687    |*  [b=* c=*]
1688    =+  d=(get b)
1689    (~(put by a) b [c d])
1690    --
1691  ++  ju                                       ::  jug engine
1692    =|  a=(tree (pair * (tree)))  ::  (jug)
1693    |@
1694  ++  del                                      ::  del key-set pair
1695    |*  [b=* c=*]
1696    ^+  a
1697    =+  d=(get b)
1698    =+  e=(~(del in d) c)
1699    ?~  e
1700      (~(del by a) b)
1701    (~(put by a) b e)
1702    ::
1703  ++  gas                                      ::  concatenate
1704    |*  b=(list [p=* q=*])
1705    =>  .(b `(list _?>(?=([[* ^] ^] a) [p=p q=n.q]:n.a))`b)
1706    |-  ^+  a
1707    ?~  b
1708      a
1709    $(b t.b, a (put p.i.b q.i.b))
1710    ::
1711  ++  get                                      ::  gets set by key
1712    |*  b=*
1713    =+  c=(~(get by a) b)
1714    ?~(c ~ u.c)
1715    ::
1716  ++  has                                      ::  existence check
1717    |*  [b=* c=*]
1718    ^-  ?
1719    (~(has in (get b)) c)
1720    ::
1721  ++  put                                      ::  add key-set pair
1722    |*  [b=* c=*]
1723    ^+  a
1724    =+  d=(get b)
1725    (~(put by a) b (~(put in d) c))
1726    --
1727  ::
1728  ::    2k: queue logic
1729  +|  %queue-logic
1730  ::
1731  ++  to                                       ::  queue engine
1732    =|  a=(tree)  ::  (qeu)
1733    |@
1734  ++  apt                                      ::  check correctness
1735    |-  ^-  ?
1736    ?~  a  &
1737    ?&  ?~(l.a & ?&((mor n.a n.l.a) $(a l.a)))
1738        ?~(r.a & ?&((mor n.a n.r.a) $(a r.a)))
```

```
1739          ==
1740      ::
1741      ++  bal
1742        |-  ^+  a
1743      ?~  a  ~
1744      ?.  |(?=(~ l.a) (mor n.a n.l.a))
1745        $(a l.a(r $(a a(l r.l.a))))
1746      ?.  |(?=(~ r.a) (mor n.a n.r.a))
1747        $(a r.a(l $(a a(r l.r.a))))
1748      a
1749      ::
1750      ++  dep                                  ::  max depth of queue
1751        |-  ^-  @
1752      ?~  a  0
1753      +((max $(a l.a) $(a r.a)))
1754      ::
1755      ++  gas                                  ::  insert list to que
1756        |=  b=(list _?>(?=(^ a) n.a))
1757        |-  ^+  a
1758      ?~(b a $(b t.b, a (put i.b)))
1759      ::
1760      ++  get                                  ::  head-rest pair
1761        |-  ^+  ?>(?=(^ a) [p=n.a q=*(tree _n.a)])
1762      ?~  a
1763        !!
1764      ?~  r.a
1765        [n.a l.a]
1766      =+  b=$(a r.a)
1767      :-  p.b
1768      ?:  |(?=(~ q.b) (mor n.a n.q.b))
1769        a(r q.b)
1770      a(n n.q.b, l a(r l.q.b), r r.q.b)
1771      ::
1772      ++  nip                                  ::  removes root
1773        |-  ^+  a
1774      ?~  a  ~
1775      ?~  l.a  r.a
1776      ?~  r.a  l.a
1777      ?:  (mor n.l.a n.r.a)
1778        l.a(r $(l.a r.l.a))
1779      r.a(l $(r.a l.r.a))
1780      ::
1781      ++  nap                                  ::  removes root
1782      ?>  ?=(^ a)
1783      ?:  =(~ l.a)  r.a
1784      =+  b=get(a l.a)
1785      bal(n.a p.b, l.a q.b)
1786      ::
1787      ++  put                                  ::  insert new tail
1788        |*  b=*
1789        |-  ^+  a
1790      ?~  a
1791        [b ~ ~]
1792      bal(l.a $(a l.a))
1793      ::
1794      ++  tap                                  ::  adds list to end
1795      =+  b=`(list _?>(?=(^ a) n.a))`~
1796        |-  ^+  b
```

```
1797      =+  0                                     ::  hack for jet match
1798      ?~  a
1799        b
1800      $(a r.a, b [n.a $(a l.a)])
1801    ::
1802    ++  top                                     ::  produces head
1803    |-  ^-  (unit _?>(?=(^ a) n.a))
1804    ?~  a  ~
1805    ?~(r.a [~ n.a] $(a r.a))
1806    --
1807    ::
1808    ::      21: container from container
1809    +|  %container-from-container
1810    ::
1811    ++  malt                                    ::  map from list
1812    |*  a=(list)
1813    (molt `(list [p=_-<.a q=_->.a])`a)
1814    ::
1815    ++  molt                                    ::  map from pair list
1816    |*  a=(list (pair))  ::  ^-  =,(i.-.a (map _p _q))
1817    (~(gas by `(tree [p=_p.i.-.a q=_q.i.-.a])`~) a)
1818    ::
1819    ++  silt                                    ::  set from list
1820    |*  a=(list)  ::  ^-  (set _i.-.a)
1821    =+  b=*(tree _?>(?=(^ a) i.a))
1822    (~(gas in b) a)
1823    ::
1824    ::      2m: container from noun
1825    +|  %container-from-noun
1826    ::
1827    ++  ly                                      ::  list from raw noun
1828    le:nl
1829    ::
1830    ++  my                                      ::  map from raw noun
1831    my:nl
1832    ::
1833    ++  sy                                      ::  set from raw noun
1834    si:nl
1835    ::
1836    ++  nl
1837    |%
1838    ::                                          ::
1839    ++  le                                      ::  construct list
1840    |*  a=(list)
1841    ^+  =<  $
1842    |@  ++  $  ?:(*? ~ [i=(snag 0 a) t=$])
1843    --
1844    a
1845    ::                                          ::
1846    ++  my                                      ::  construct map
1847    |*  a=(list (pair))
1848    =>  .(a ^+((le a) a))
1849    (~(gas by `(map _p.i.-.a _q.i.-.a)`~) a)
1850    ::                                          ::
1851    ++  si                                      ::  construct set
1852    |*  a=(list)
1853    =>  .(a ^+((le a) a))
1854    (~(gas in `(set _i.-.a)`~) a)
```

```
1855      ::                                              ::
1856      ++  snag                                        ::  index
1857        |*  [a=@ b=(list)]
1858        ?~  b
1859          ~_  leaf+"snag-fail"
1860          !!
1861        ?:  =(0 a)  i.b
1862        $(b t.b, a (dec a))
1863      ::                                              ::
1864      ++  weld                                        ::  concatenate
1865        |*  [a=(list) b=(list)]
1866        =>  .(a ^+((le a) a), b ^+((le b) b))
1867        =+  42
1868        |-
1869        ?~  a  b
1870        [i=i.a t=$(a t.a)]
1871      --
1872  ::    2n: functional hacks
1873  +|  %functional-hacks
1874  ::
1875  ++  aftr  |*(a=$-(* *) |*(b=$-(* *) (pair b a)))    ::  pair after
1876  ++  cork  |*([a=$-(* *) b=$-(* *)] (corl b a))      ::  compose forward
1877  ++  corl                                            ::  compose backwards
1878    |*  [a=$-(* *) b=$-(* *)]
1879    =<  +:|.((a (b)))          ::  type check
1880    |*  c=_+<.b
1881    (a (b c))
1882  ::
1883  ++  cury                                            ::  curry left
1884    |*  [a=$-(^ *) b=*]
1885    |*  c=_+<+.a
1886    (a b c)
1887  ::
1888  ++  curr                                            ::  curry right
1889    |*  [a=$-(^ *) c=*]
1890    |*  b=_+<+.a
1891    (a b c)
1892  ::
1893  ++  fore  |*(a=$-(* *) |*(b=$-(* *) (pair a b)))    ::  pair before
1894  ::
1895  ++  head  |*(^ ,:+<-)                               ::  get head
1896  ++  same  |*(* +<)                                  ::  identity
1897  ::
1898  ++  succ  |=(@ +(+<))                               ::  successor
1899  ::
1900  ++  tail  |*(^ ,:+<+)                               ::  get tail
1901  ++  test  |=(^ =(+<- +<+))                          ::  equality
1902  ::
1903  ++  lead  |*(* |*(* [+>+< +<]))                     ::  put head
1904  ++  late  |*(* |*(* [+< +>+<]))                     ::  put tail
1905  ::
1906  ::    2o: containers
1907  +|  %containers
1908  ++  jar  |$  [key value]  (map key (list value))   ::  map of lists
1909  ++  jug  |$  [key value]  (map key (set value))    ::  map of sets
1910  ::
1911  ++  map                                             ::  table
1912    |$  [key value]
```

```
1913      $|  (tree (pair key value))
1914      |=(a=(tree (pair)) ?:(=(~ a) & ~(apt by a)))
1915    ::
1916    ++  qeu
1917      |$  [item]                                          ::  queue
1918      $|  (tree item)
1919      |=(a=(tree) ?:(=(~ a) & ~(apt to a)))
1920    ::
1921    ++  set
1922      |$  [item]                                          ::  set
1923      $|  (tree item)
1924      |=(a=(tree) ?:(=(~ a) & ~(apt in a)))
1925    ::
1926    ::    2p: serialization
1927    +|  %serialization
1928    ::
1929    ++  cue                                                ::  unpack
1930      ~/  %cue
1931      |=  a=@
1932      ^-  *
1933      =+  b=0
1934      =+  m=`(map @ *)`~
1935      =<  q
1936      |-  ^-  [p=@ q=* r=(map @ *)]
1937      ?:  =(0 (cut 0 [b 1] a))
1938        =+  c=(rub +(b) a)
1939        [+(p.c) q.c (~(put by m) b q.c)]
1940      =+  c=(add 2 b)
1941      ?:  =(0 (cut 0 [+(b) 1] a))
1942        =+  u=$(b c)
1943        =+  v=$(b (add p.u c), m r.u)
1944        =+  w=[q.u q.v]
1945        [(add 2 (add p.u p.v)) w (~(put by r.v) b w)]
1946      =+  d=(rub c a)
1947      [(add 2 p.d) (need (~(get by m) q.d)) m]
1948    ::
1949    ++  jam                                                ::  pack
1950      ~/  %jam
1951      |=  a=*
1952      ^-  @
1953      =+  b=0
1954      =+  m=`(map * @)`~
1955      =<  q
1956      |-  ^-  [p=@ q=@ r=(map * @)]
1957      =+  c=(~(get by m) a)
1958      ?~  c
1959        =>  .(m (~(put by m) a b))
1960        ?:  ?=(@ a)
1961          =+  d=(mat a)
1962          [(add 1 p.d) (lsh 0 q.d) m]
1963        =>  .(b (add 2 b))
1964        =+  d=$(a -.a)
1965        =+  e=$(a +.a, b (add b p.d), m r.d)
1966        [(add 2 (add p.d p.e)) (mix 1 (lsh [0 2] (cat 0 q.d q.e))) r.e]
1967      ?:  ?&(?=(@ a) (lte (met 0 a) (met 0 u.c)))
1968        =+  d=(mat a)
1969        [(add 1 p.d) (lsh 0 q.d) m]
1970      =+  d=(mat u.c)
```

```
1971      [(add 2 p.d) (mix 3 (lsh [0 2] q.d)) m]
1972  ::
1973  ++   mat                                              ::   length-encode
1974   ~/   %mat
1975   |=   a=@
1976   ^-   [p=@ q=@]
1977   ?:  =(0 a)
1978     [1 1]
1979   =+  b=(met 0 a)
1980   =+  c=(met 0 b)
1981   :-  (add (add c c) b)
1982   (cat 0 (bex c) (mix (end [0 (dec c)] b) (lsh [0 (dec c)] a)))
1983  ::
1984  ++   rub                                              ::   length-decode
1985   ~/   %rub
1986   |=   [a=@ b=@]
1987   ^-   [p=@ q=@]
1988   =+   ^=  c
1989       =+  [c=0 m=(met 0 b)]
1990       |-  ?<  (gth c m)
1991       ?.  =(0 (cut 0 [(add a c) 1] b))
1992         c
1993       $(c +(c))
1994   ?:  =(0 c)
1995     [1 0]
1996   =+  d=(add a +(c))
1997   =+  e=(add (bex (dec c)) (cut 0 [d (dec c)] b))
1998   [(add (add c c) e) (cut 0 [(add d (dec c)) e] b)]
1999  ::
2000  ++   fn  ::    float, infinity, or NaN
2001          ::
2002          ::  s=sign, e=exponent, a=arithmetic form
2003          ::  (-1)^s * a * 2^e
2004      $%  [%f s=? e=@s a=@u]
2005          [%i s=?]
2006          [%n ~]
2007      ==
2008  ::
2009  ++   dn  ::    decimal float, infinity, or NaN
2010          ::
2011          ::  (-1)^s * a * 10^e
2012      $%  [%d s=? e=@s a=@u]
2013          [%i s=?]
2014          [%n ~]
2015      ==
2016  ::
2017  ++   rn  ::    parsed decimal float
2018          ::
2019      $%  [%d a=? b=[c=@ [d=@ e=@] f=? i=@]]
2020          [%i a=?]
2021          [%n ~]
2022      ==
2023  ::
2024  ::    2q: molds and mold builders
2025  +|   %molds-and-mold-builders
2026  ::
2027  +$   axis  @                                          ::  tree address
2028  +$   bean  ?                                          ::  0=&=yes, 1=|=no
```

```
2029 +$  flag  ?
2030 +$  char  @t                                            ::  UTF8 byte
2031 +$  cord  @t                                            ::  UTF8, LSB first
2032 +$  byts  [wid=@ud dat=@]                               ::  bytes, MSB first
2033 +$  date  [[a=? y=@ud] m=@ud t=tarp]                    ::  parsed date
2034 +$  knot  @ta                                           ::  ASCII text
2035 +$  noun  *                                             ::  any noun
2036 +$  path  (list knot)                                   ::  like unix path
2037 +$  pith  (list iota)                                   ::  typed urbit path
2038 +$  stud                                                ::  standard name
2039          $@  mark=@tas                                  ::  auth=urbit
2040          $:  auth=@tas                                  ::  standards authority
2041              type=path                                 ::  standard label
2042          ==                                            ::
2043 +$  tang  (list tank)                                   ::  bottom-first error
2044 ::                                                      ::
2045 +$  iota                                                ::  typed path segment
2046   $~  [%n ~]
2047   $@  @tas
2048   $%  [%ub @ub]   [%uc @uc]   [%ud @ud]   [%ui @ui]
2049       [%ux @ux]   [%uv @uv]   [%uw @uw]
2050       [%sb @sb]   [%sc @sc]   [%sd @sd]   [%si @si]
2051       [%sx @sx]   [%sv @sv]   [%sw @sw]
2052       [%da @da]   [%dr @dr]
2053       [%f ?]      [%n ~]
2054       [%if @if]   [%is @is]
2055       [%t @t]     [%ta @ta]   ::  @tas
2056       [%p @p]     [%q @q]
2057       [%rs @rs]   [%rd @rd]   [%rh @rh]   [%rq @rq]
2058   ==
2059 ::
2060 ::  $tank: formatted print tree
2061 ::
2062 ::    just a cord, or
2063 ::    %leaf: just a tape
2064 ::    %palm: backstep list
2065 ::           flat-mid, open, flat-open, flat-close
2066 ::    %rose: flat list
2067 ::           flat-mid, open, close
2068 ::
2069 +$  tank
2070   $~  leaf/~
2071   $@  cord
2072   $%  [%leaf p=tape]
2073       [%palm p=(qual tape tape tape tape) q=(list tank)]
2074       [%rose p=(trel tape tape tape) q=(list tank)]
2075   ==
2076 ::
2077 +$  tape  (list @tD)                                     ::  utf8 string as list
2078 +$  tour  (list @c)                                      ::  utf32 clusters
2079 +$  tarp  [d=@ud h=@ud m=@ud s=@ud f=(list @ux)]         ::  parsed time
2080 +$  term  @tas                                           ::  ascii symbol
2081 +$  wain  (list cord)                                    ::  text lines
2082 +$  wall  (list tape)                                    ::  text lines
2083 ::
2084 --  =>
2085 ::                                                      ::
2086 ~%  %tri  +
```

```
2087    ==
2088      %year   year
2089      %yore   yore
2090      %ob     ob
2091    ==
2092  ::    layer-3
2093  ::
2094  |%
2095  ::    3a: signed and modular ints
2096  +|  %signed-and-modular-ints
2097  ::
2098  ++  egcd                                          ::  schneier's egcd
2099    |=  [a=@ b=@]
2100    =+  si
2101    =+  [c=(sun a) d=(sun b)]
2102    =+  [u=[c=(sun 1) d=--0] v=[c=--0 d=(sun 1)]]
2103    |-  ^-  [d=@ u=@s v=@s]
2104    ?:  =(--0 c)
2105      [(abs d) d.u d.v]
2106    ::  ?>  ?&  =(c (sum (pro (sun a) c.u) (pro (sun b) c.v)))
2107    ::          =(d (sum (pro (sun a) d.u) (pro (sun b) d.v)))
2108    ::      ==
2109    =+  q=(fra d c)
2110    %=  $
2111      c  (dif d (pro q c))
2112      d  c
2113      u  [(dif d.u (pro q c.u)) c.u]
2114      v  [(dif d.v (pro q c.v)) c.v]
2115    ==
2116  ::
2117  ++  fo                                            ::  modulo prime
2118    ^|
2119    |_  a=@
2120    ++  dif
2121      |=  [b=@ c=@]
2122      (sit (sub (add a b) (sit c)))
2123    ::
2124    ++  exp
2125      |=  [b=@ c=@]
2126      ?:  =(0 b)
2127        1
2128      =+  d=$(b (rsh 0 b))
2129      =+  e=(pro d d)
2130      ?:(=(0 (end 0 b)) e (pro c e))
2131    ::
2132    ++  fra
2133      |=  [b=@ c=@]
2134      (pro b (inv c))
2135    ::
2136    ++  inv
2137      |=  b=@
2138      =+  c=(dul:si u:(egcd b a) a)
2139      c
2140    ::
2141    ++  pro
2142      |=  [b=@ c=@]
2143      (sit (mul b c))
2144    ::
```

```
2145    ++  sit
2146      |=  b=@
2147      (mod b a)
2148    ::
2149    ++  sum
2150      |=  [b=@ c=@]
2151      (sit (add b c))
2152    --
2153  ::
2154  ++  si                                            ::  signed integer
2155    ^?
2156    |%
2157    ++  abs  |=(a=@s (add (end 0 a) (rsh 0 a)))      ::  absolute value
2158    ++  dif  |=  [a=@s b=@s]                          ::  subtraction
2159             (sum a (new !(syn b) (abs b)))
2160    ++  dul  |=  [a=@s b=@]                           ::  modulus
2161             =+(c=(old a) ?:(-.c (mod +.c b) (sub b +.c)))
2162    ++  fra  |=  [a=@s b=@s]                          ::  divide
2163             (new =(0 (mix (syn a) (syn b))) (div (abs a) (abs b)))
2164    ++  new  |=  [a=? b=@]                            ::  [sign value] to @s
2165             `@s`?:(a (mul 2 b) ?:(=(0 b) 0 +((mul 2 (dec b)))))
2166    ++  old  |=(a=@s [(syn a) (abs a)])              ::  [sign value]
2167    ++  pro  |=  [a=@s b=@s]                          ::  multiplication
2168             (new =(0 (mix (syn a) (syn b))) (mul (abs a) (abs b)))
2169    ++  rem  |=([a=@s b=@s] (dif a (pro b (fra a b))))   ::  remainder
2170    ++  sum  |=  [a=@s b=@s]                          ::  addition
2171             =+  [c=(old a) d=(old b)]
2172             ?:  -.c
2173               ?:  -.d
2174                 (new & (add +.c +.d))
2175               ?:  (gte +.c +.d)
2176                 (new & (sub +.c +.d))
2177               (new | (sub +.d +.c))
2178             ?:  -.d
2179               ?:  (gte +.c +.d)
2180                 (new | (sub +.c +.d))
2181               (new & (sub +.d +.c))
2182             (new | (add +.c +.d))
2183    ++  sun  |=(a=@u (mul 2 a))                      ::  @u to @s
2184    ++  syn  |=(a=@s =(0 (end 0 a)))                 ::  sign test
2185    ++  cmp  |=  [a=@s b=@s]                          ::  compare
2186             ^-  @s
2187             ?:  =(a b)
2188               --0
2189             ?:  (syn a)
2190               ?:  (syn b)
2191                 ?:  (gth a b)
2192                   --1
2193                 -1
2194               --1
2195             ?:  (syn b)
2196               -1
2197             ?:  (gth a b)
2198               -1
2199             --1
2200    --
2201  ::
2202  ::      3b: floating point
```

```
+|  %floating-point
::
++  fl                                                   ::  arb. precision fp
  =/  [[p=@u v=@s w=@u] r=$?(%n %u %d %z %a) d=$?(%d %f %i)]
      [[113 -16.494 32.765] %n %d]
  ::  p=precision:     number of bits in arithmetic form; must be at least 2
  ::  v=min exponent:  minimum value of e
  ::  w=width:         max - min value of e, 0 is fixed point
  ::  r=rounding mode: nearest (ties to even), up, down, to zero, away from zero
  ::  d=behavior:      return denormals, flush denormals to zero,
  ::                   infinite exponent range
  =>
    ~%  %cofl  +>  ~
    ::    cofl
    ::
    ::  internal functions; mostly operating on [e=@s a=@u], in other words
    ::  positive numbers. many of these error out if a=0.
    |%
    ++  rou
      |=  [a=[e=@s a=@u]]  ^-  fn  (rau a &)
    ::
    ++  rau
      |=  [a=[e=@s a=@u] t=?]  ^-  fn
      ?-  r
        %z  (lug %fl a t)  %d  (lug %fl a t)
        %a  (lug %ce a t)  %u  (lug %ce a t)
        %n  (lug %ne a t)
      ==
    ::
    ++  add                                              ::  add; exact if e
      |=  [a=[e=@s a=@u] b=[e=@s a=@u] e=?]  ^-  fn
      =+  q=(dif:si e.a e.b)
      |-  ?.  (syn:si q)  $(b a, a b, q +(q))            ::  a has larger exp
      ?:  e
        [%f & e.b (^add (lsh [0 (abs:si q)] a.a) a.b)]
      =+  [ma=(met 0 a.a) mb=(met 0 a.b)]
      =+  ^=  w  %+  dif:si  e.a  %-  sun:si              ::  expanded exp of a
        ?:  (gth prc ma)  (^sub prc ma)  0
      =+  ^=  x  %+  sum:si  e.b  (sun:si mb)             ::  highest exp for b
      ?:  =((cmp:si w x) --1)                             ::  don't need to add
        ?-  r
          %z  (lug %fl a &)  %d  (lug %fl a &)
          %a  (lug %lg a &)  %u  (lug %lg a &)
          %n  (lug %na a &)
        ==
      (rou [e.b (^add (lsh [0 (abs:si q)] a.a) a.b)])
    ::
    ++  sub                                              ::  subtract; exact if e
      |=  [a=[e=@s a=@u] b=[e=@s a=@u] e=?]  ^-  fn
      =+  q=(dif:si e.a e.b)
      |-  ?.  (syn:si q)
        (fli $(b a, a b, q +(q), r swr))
      =+  [ma=(met 0 a.a) mb=(met 0 a.b)]
      =+  ^=  w  %+  dif:si  e.a  %-  sun:si
        ?:  (gth prc ma)  (^sub prc ma)  0
      =+  ^=  x  %+  sum:si  e.b  (sun:si +(mb))
      ?:  &(!e =((cmp:si w x) --1))
        ?-  r
```

```
2261        %z  (lug %sm a &)   %d  (lug %sm a &)
2262        %a  (lug %ce a &)   %u  (lug %ce a &)
2263        %n  (lug %nt a &)
2264        ==
2265      =+  j=(lsh [0 (abs:si q)] a.a)
2266      |-  ?.  (gte j a.b)
2267        (fli $(a.b j, j a.b, r swr))
2268      =+  i=(^sub j a.b)
2269      ?~  i [%f & zer]
2270      ?:  e [%f & e.b i]  (rou [e.b i])
2271    ::
2272    ++  mul                               ::  multiply
2273      |=  [a=[e=@s a=@u] b=[e=@s a=@u]]  ^-  fn
2274      (rou (sum:si e.a e.b) (^mul a.a a.b))
2275    ::
2276    ++  div                               ::  divide
2277      |=  [a=[e=@s a=@u] b=[e=@s a=@u]]   ^-  fn
2278      =+  [ma=(met 0 a.a) mb=(met 0 a.b)]
2279      =+  v=(dif:si (sun:si ma) (sun:si +((^add mb prc))))
2280      =.  a ?:  (syn:si v)  a
2281      a(e (sum:si v e.a), a (lsh [0 (abs:si v)] a.a))
2282      =+  [j=(dif:si e.a e.b) q=(dvr a.a a.b)]
2283      (rau [j p.q] =(q.q 0))
2284    ::
2285    ++  sqt                               ::  square root
2286      |=  [a=[e=@s a=@u]]  ^-  fn
2287      =.  a
2288        =+  [w=(met 0 a.a) x=(^mul +(prc) 2)]
2289        =+  ?:((^lth w x) (^sub x w) 0)
2290        =+  ?:  =((dis - 1) (dis (abs:si e.a) 1))  -
2291          (^add - 1)
2292        a(e (dif:si e.a (sun:si -)), a (lsh [0 -] a.a))
2293      =+  [y=(^sqt a.a) z=(fra:si e.a --2)]
2294      (rau [z p.y] =(q.y 0))
2295    ::
2296    ++  lth                               ::  less-than
2297      |=  [a=[e=@s a=@u] b=[e=@s a=@u]]  ^-  ?
2298      ?:  =(e.a e.b)  (^lth a.a a.b)
2299      =+  c=(cmp:si (ibl a) (ibl b))
2300      ?:  =(c -1)  &  ?:  =(c --1)  |
2301      ?:  =((cmp:si e.a e.b) -1)
2302        (^lth (rsh [0 (abs:si (dif:si e.a e.b))] a.a) a.b)
2303      (^lth (lsh [0 (abs:si (dif:si e.a e.b))] a.a) a.b)
2304    ::
2305    ++  equ                               ::  equals
2306      |=  [a=[e=@s a=@u] b=[e=@s a=@u]]  ^-  ?
2307      ?.  =((ibl a) (ibl b))  |
2308      ?:  =((cmp:si e.a e.b) -1)
2309        =((lsh [0 (abs:si (dif:si e.a e.b))] a.b) a.a)
2310      =((lsh [0 (abs:si (dif:si e.a e.b))] a.a) a.b)
2311    ::
2312    ::    integer binary logarithm: 2^ibl(a) <= |a| < 2^(ibl(a)+1)
2313    ++  ibl
2314      |=  [a=[e=@s a=@u]]  ^-  @s
2315      (sum:si (sun:si (dec (met 0 a.a))) e.a)
2316    ::
2317    ::  +uni
2318    ::
```

```
2319    ::      change to a representation where a.a is odd
2320    ::      every fn has a unique representation of this kind
2321    ++  uni
2322      |=  [a=[e=@s a=@u]]
2323      |-  ?:  =((end 0 a.a) 1)  a
2324      $(a.a (rsh 0 a.a), e.a (sum:si e.a --1))
2325    ::
2326    ::  +xpd: expands to either full precision or to denormalized
2327    ++  xpd
2328      |=  [a=[e=@s a=@u]]
2329      =+  ma=(met 0 a.a)
2330      ?:  (gte ma prc)  a
2331      =+  ?:  =(den %i)  (^sub prc ma)
2332          =+  ^=  q
2333            =+  w=(dif:si e.a emn)
2334            ?:  (syn:si w)  (abs:si w)  0
2335          (min q (^sub prc ma))
2336      a(e (dif:si e.a (sun:si -)), a (lsh [0 -] a.a))
2337    ::
2338    ::  +lug: central rounding mechanism
2339    ::
2340    ::      can perform: floor, ceiling, smaller, larger,
2341    ::                   nearest (round ties to: even, away from 0, toward 0)
2342    ::      s is sticky bit: represents a value less than ulp(a) = 2^(e.a)
2343    ::
2344    ++  lug
2345      ~/  %lug
2346      |=  [t=$?(%fl %ce %sm %lg %ne %na %nt) a=[e=@s a=@u] s=?]  ^-  fn
2347      ?<  =(a.a 0)
2348      =-
2349        ?.  =(den %f)  -                           :: flush denormals
2350        ?.  ?=([%f *] -)  -
2351        ?:  =((met 0 ->+>) prc)  -  [%f & zer]
2352      ::
2353      =+  m=(met 0 a.a)
2354      ?>  |(s (gth m prc))                         :: require precision
2355      =+  ^=  q  %+  max
2356          ?:  (gth m prc)  (^sub m prc)  0         :: reduce precision
2357        %-  abs:si  ?:  =(den %i)  --0             :: enforce min. exp
2358        ?:  =((cmp:si e.a emn) -1)  (dif:si emn e.a)  --0
2359      =^  b  a  :-  (end [0 q] a.a)
2360        a(e (sum:si e.a (sun:si q)), a (rsh [0 q] a.a))
2361      ::
2362      ?~  a.a
2363        ?<  =(den %i)
2364        ?-  t
2365          %fl  [%f & zer]
2366          %sm  [%f & zer]
2367          %ce  [%f & spd]
2368          %lg  [%f & spd]
2369          %ne  ?:  s  [%f & ?:((lte b (bex (dec q))) zer spd)]
2370               [%f & ?:((^lth b (bex (dec q))) zer spd)]
2371          %nt  ?:  s  [%f & ?:((lte b (bex (dec q))) zer spd)]
2372               [%f & ?:((^lth b (bex (dec q))) zer spd)]
2373          %na  [%f & ?:((^lth b (bex (dec q))) zer spd)]
2374        ==
2375      ::
2376      =.  a  (xpd a)
```

```
2377            ::
2378            =.  a
2379              ?-  t
2380                %fl  a
2381                %lg  a(a +(a.a))
2382                %sm  ?.  &(=(b 0) s)  a
2383                     ?:  &(=(e.a emn) !=(den %i))  a(a (dec a.a))
2384                     =+  y=(dec (^mul a.a 2))
2385                     ?.  (lte (met 0 y) prc)  a(a (dec a.a))
2386                     [(dif:si e.a --1) y]
2387                %ce  ?:  &(=(b 0) s)  a  a(a +(a.a))
2388                %ne  ?~  b  a
2389                     =+  y=(bex (dec q))
2390                     ?:  &(=(b y) s)                    ::  round halfs to even
2391                       ?~  (dis a.a 1)  a  a(a +(a.a))
2392                     ?:  (^lth b y)  a  a(a +(a.a))
2393                %na  ?~  b  a
2394                     =+  y=(bex (dec q))
2395                     ?:  (^lth b y)  a  a(a +(a.a))
2396                %nt  ?~  b  a
2397                     =+  y=(bex (dec q))
2398                     ?:  =(b y)  ?:  s  a  a(a +(a.a))
2399                     ?:  (^lth b y)  a  a(a +(a.a))
2400              ==
2401            ::
2402            =.  a  ?.  =((met 0 a.a) +(prc))  a
2403              a(a (rsh 0 a.a), e (sum:si e.a --1))
2404            ?~  a.a  [%f & zer]
2405            ::
2406            ?:  =(den %i)  [%f & a]
2407            ?:  =((cmp:si emx e.a) -1)  [%i &]  [%f & a]   ::  enforce max. exp
2408          ::
2409          ++  drg                                    ::  dragon4; get
2410            ~/  %drg                                 ::  printable decimal;
2411            |=  [a=[e=@s a=@u]]  ^-  [@s @u]         ::  guaranteed accurate
2412            ?<  =(a.a 0)                             ::  for rounded floats
2413            =.  a  (xpd a)
2414            =+  r=(lsh [0 ?:((syn:si e.a) (abs:si e.a) 0)] a.a)
2415            =+  s=(lsh [0 ?.((syn:si e.a) (abs:si e.a) 0)] 1)
2416            =+  mn=(lsh [0 ?:((syn:si e.a) (abs:si e.a) 0)] 1)
2417            =+  mp=mn
2418            =>  ?.
2419                  ?&  =(a.a (bex (dec prc)))             ::  if next smallest
2420                    |(!=(e.a emn) =(den %i))             ::  float is half ULP,
2421                  ==                                     ::  tighten lower bound
2422                .
2423              %=  .
2424                mp  (lsh 0 mp)
2425                r   (lsh 0 r)
2426                s   (lsh 0 s)
2427              ==
2428            =+  [k=--0 q=(^div (^add s 9) 10)]
2429            |-  ?:  (^lth r q)
2430              %=  $
2431                k   (dif:si k --1)
2432                r   (^mul r 10)
2433                mn  (^mul mn 10)
2434                mp  (^mul mp 10)
```

```
2435            ==
2436    |-  ?:  (gte (^add (^mul r 2) mp) (^mul s 2))
2437      $(s (^mul s 10), k (sum:si k --1))
2438    =+  [u=0 o=0]
2439    |-                                              ::  r/s+o = a*10^-k
2440    =+  v=(dvr (^mul r 10) s)
2441    =>  %=  .
2442        k   (dif:si k --1)
2443        u   p.v
2444        r   q.v
2445        mn  (^mul mn 10)
2446        mp  (^mul mp 10)
2447        ==
2448    =+  l=(^lth (^mul r 2) mn)                       ::  in lower bound
2449    =+  ^=  h                                        ::  in upper bound
2450      ?|  (^lth (^mul s 2) mp)
2451          (gth (^mul r 2) (^sub (^mul s 2) mp))
2452          ==
2453    ?:  &(!l !h)
2454      $(o (^add (^mul o 10) u))
2455    =+  q=&(h |(!l (gth (^mul r 2) s)))
2456    =.  o  (^add (^mul o 10) ?:(q +(u) u))
2457    [k o]
2458    ::
2459    ++  toj                                          ::  round to integer
2460    |=  [a=[e=@s a=@u]]  ^-  fn
2461    ?.  =((cmp:si e.a --0) -1)  [%f & a]
2462    =+  x=(abs:si e.a)
2463    =+  y=(rsh [0 x] a.a)
2464    ?:  |(=(r %d) =(r %z))  [%f & --0 y]
2465    =+  z=(end [0 x] a.a)
2466    ?:  |(=(r %u) =(r %a))  [%f & --0 ?~(z y +(y))]
2467    =+  i=(bex (dec x))
2468    ?:  &(=(z i) =((dis y 1) 0))  [%f & --0 y]
2469    ?:  (^lth z i)  [%f & --0 y]  [%f & --0 +(y)]
2470    ::
2471    ++  ned                                          ::  require ?=([%f *] a)
2472    |=  [a=fn]  ^-  [%f s=? e=@s a=@u]
2473    ?:  ?=([%f *] a)  a
2474    ~_  leaf+"need-float"
2475    !!
2476    ::
2477    ++  shf                                          ::  a * 2^b; no rounding
2478    |=  [a=fn b=@s]
2479    ?:  |(?=([%n *] a) ?=([%i *] a))  a
2480    a(e (sum:si e.a b))
2481    ::
2482    ++  fli                                          ::  flip sign
2483    |=  [a=fn]  ^-  fn
2484    ?-(-.a %f a(s !s.a), %i a(s !s.a), %n a)
2485    ::
2486    ++  swr  ?+(r r %d %u, %u %d)                     ::  flipped rounding
2487    ++  prc  ?>((gth p 1) p)                          ::  force >= 2 precision
2488    ++  den  d                                        ::  denorm+flush+inf exp
2489    ++  emn  v                                        ::  minimum exponent
2490    ++  emx  (sum:si emn (sun:si w))                  ::  maximum exponent
2491    ++  spd  [e=emn a=1]                              ::  smallest denormal
2492    ++  spn  [e=emn a=(bex (dec prc))]                ::  smallest normal
```

```
2493    ++   lfn   [e=emx a=(fil 0 prc 1)]                      ::  largest
2494    ++   lfe   (sum:si emx (sun:si prc))                    ::  2^lfe is > than all
2495    ++   zer   [e=--0 a=0]
2496    --
2497    |%
2498    ++   rou                                                ::  round
2499    |=  [a=fn]   ^-  fn
2500    ?.  ?=([%f *] a)   a
2501    ?~  a.a  [%f s.a zer]
2502    ?:  s.a   (^rou +>.a)
2503    =.(r swr (fli (^rou +>.a)))
2504    ::
2505    ++   syn                                                ::  get sign
2506    |=  [a=fn]   ^-  ?
2507    ?-(-.a %f s.a, %i s.a, %n &)
2508    ::
2509    ++   abs                                                ::  absolute value
2510    |=  [a=fn]   ^-  fn
2511    ?:  ?=([%f *] a)   [%f & e.a a.a]
2512    ?:  ?=([%i *] a)   [%i &]   [%n ~]
2513    ::
2514    ++   add                                                ::  add
2515    |=  [a=fn b=fn]   ^-  fn
2516    ?:  |(?=([%n *] a) ?=([%n *] b))   [%n ~]
2517    ?:  |(?=([%i *] a) ?=([%i *] b))
2518      ?:  &(?=([%i *] a) ?=([%i *] b))
2519        ?:  =(a b)   a  [%n ~]
2520      ?:  ?=([%i *] a)   a  b
2521    ?:  |(=(a.a 0) =(a.b 0))
2522      ?.  &(=(a.a 0) =(a.b 0))   %-  rou  ?~(a.a b a)
2523      [%f ?:(=(r %d) &(s.a s.b) |(s.a s.b)) zer]
2524    %-  |=  [a=fn]
2525        ?.  ?=([%f *] a)   a
2526        ?.  =(a.a 0)   a
2527        [%f !=(r %d) zer]
2528    ?:  =(s.a s.b)
2529      ?:  s.a   (^add +>.a +>.b |)
2530      =.(r swr (fli (^add +>.a +>.b |)))
2531    ?:  s.a   (^sub +>.a +>.b |)
2532    (^sub +>.b +>.a |)
2533    ::
2534    ++   ead                                                ::  exact add
2535    |=  [a=fn b=fn]   ^-  fn
2536    ?:  |(?=([%n *] a) ?=([%n *] b))   [%n ~]
2537    ?:  |(?=([%i *] a) ?=([%i *] b))
2538      ?:  &(?=([%i *] a) ?=([%i *] b))
2539        ?:  =(a b)   a  [%n ~]
2540      ?:  ?=([%i *] a)   a  b
2541    ?:  |(=(a.a 0) =(a.b 0))
2542      ?.  &(=(a.a 0) =(a.b 0))   ?~(a.a b a)
2543      [%f ?:(=(r %d) &(s.a s.b) |(s.a s.b)) zer]
2544    %-  |=  [a=fn]
2545        ?.  ?=([%f *] a)   a
2546        ?.  =(a.a 0)   a
2547        [%f !=(r %d) zer]
2548    ?:  =(s.a s.b)
2549      ?:  s.a   (^add +>.a +>.b &)
2550      (fli (^add +>.a +>.b &))
```

```
2551    ?:  s.a  (^sub +>.a +>.b &)
2552    (^sub +>.b +>.a &)
2553    ::
2554  ++  sub                                           ::  subtract
2555    |=  [a=fn b=fn]   ^-  fn  (add a (fli b))
2556    ::
2557  ++  mul                                           ::  multiply
2558    |=  [a=fn b=fn]   ^-  fn
2559    ?:  |(?=([%n *] a) ?=([%n *] b))   [%n ~]
2560    ?:  ?=([%i *] a)
2561      ?:  ?=([%i *] b)
2562      [%i =(s.a s.b)]
2563    ?:  =(a.b 0)  [%n ~]  [%i =(s.a s.b)]
2564    ?:  ?=([%i *] b)
2565      ?:  =(a.a 0)   [%n ~]  [%i =(s.a s.b)]
2566    ?:  |(=(a.a 0) =(a.b 0))  [%f =(s.a s.b) zer]
2567    ?:  =(s.a s.b)  (^mul +>.a +>.b)
2568    =.(r swr (fli (^mul +>.a +>.b)))
2569    ::
2570  ++  emu                                           ::  exact multiply
2571    |=  [a=fn b=fn]   ^-  fn
2572    ?:  |(?=([%n *] a) ?=([%n *] b))   [%n ~]
2573    ?:  ?=([%i *] a)
2574      ?:  ?=([%i *] b)
2575      [%i =(s.a s.b)]
2576    ?:  =(a.b 0)  [%n ~]  [%i =(s.a s.b)]
2577    ?:  ?=([%i *] b)
2578      ?:  =(a.a 0)  [%n ~]  [%i =(s.a s.b)]
2579    ?:  |(=(a.a 0) =(a.b 0))  [%f =(s.a s.b) zer]
2580    [%f =(s.a s.b) (sum:si e.a e.b) (^^mul a.a a.b)]
2581    ::
2582  ++  div                                           ::  divide
2583    |=  [a=fn b=fn]   ^-  fn
2584    ?:  |(?=([%n *] a) ?=([%n *] b))   [%n ~]
2585    ?:  ?=([%i *] a)
2586      ?:  ?=([%i *] b)  [%n ~]  [%i =(s.a s.b)]
2587    ?:  ?=([%i *] b)  [%f =(s.a s.b) zer]
2588    ?:  =(a.a 0)  ?:  =(a.b 0)  [%n ~]  [%f =(s.a s.b) zer]
2589    ?:  =(a.b 0)  [%i =(s.a s.b)]
2590    ?:  =(s.a s.b)  (^div +>.a +>.b)
2591    =.(r swr (fli (^div +>.a +>.b)))
2592    ::
2593  ++  fma                                           ::  fused multiply-add
2594    |=  [a=fn b=fn c=fn]   ^-  fn                    ::  (a * b) + c
2595    (add (emu a b) c)
2596    ::
2597  ++  sqt                                           ::  square root
2598    |=  [a=fn]   ^-  fn
2599    ?:  ?=([%n *] a)  [%n ~]
2600    ?:  ?=([%i *] a)  ?:(s.a a [%n ~])
2601    ?~  a.a  [%f s.a zer]
2602    ?:  s.a  (^sqt +>.a)  [%n ~]
2603    ::
2604  ++  inv                                           ::  inverse
2605    |=  [a=fn]   ^-  fn
2606    (div [%f & --0 1] a)
2607    ::
2608  ++  sun                                           ::  uns integer to float
```

```
2609      |=  [a=@u]   ^-  fn
2610      (rou [%f & --0 a])
2611    ::
2612    ++  san                                    ::  sgn integer to float
2613      |=  [a=@s]   ^-  fn
2614      =+  b=(old:si a)
2615      (rou [%f -.b --0 +.b])
2616    ::
2617    ++  lth                                    ::  less-than
2618      ::    comparisons return ~ in the event of a NaN
2619      |=  [a=fn b=fn]   ^-  (unit ?)
2620      ?:  |(?=([%n *] a) ?=([%n *] b))   ~   :-   ~
2621      ?:  =(a b)   |
2622      ?:  ?=([%i *] a)   !s.a   ?:   ?=([%i *] b)   s.b
2623      ?:  |(=(a.a 0) =(a.b 0))
2624        ?:  &(=(a.a 0) =(a.b 0))   |
2625        ?:  =(a.a 0)   s.b   !s.a
2626      ?:  !=(s.a s.b)   s.b
2627      ?:  s.a   (^lth +>.a +>.b)   (^lth +>.b +>.a)
2628    ::
2629    ++  lte                                    ::  less-equal
2630      |=  [a=fn b=fn]   ^-  (unit ?)
2631      %+  bind  (lth b a)   |=  a=?   !a
2632    ::
2633    ++  equ                                    ::  equal
2634      |=  [a=fn b=fn]   ^-  (unit ?)
2635      ?:  |(?=([%n *] a) ?=([%n *] b))   ~   :-   ~
2636      ?:  =(a b)   &
2637      ?:  |(?=([%i *] a) ?=([%i *] b))   |
2638      ?:  |(=(a.a 0) =(a.b 0))
2639        ?:  &(=(a.a 0) =(a.b 0))   &   |
2640      ?:  |(=(e.a e.b) !=(s.a s.b))   |
2641      (^equ +>.a +>.b)
2642    ::
2643    ++  gte                                    ::  greater-equal
2644      |=  [a=fn b=fn]   ^-  (unit ?)   (lte b a)
2645    ::
2646    ++  gth                                    ::  greater-than
2647      |=  [a=fn b=fn]   ^-  (unit ?)   (lth b a)
2648    ::
2649    ++  drg                                    ::  float to decimal
2650      |=  [a=fn]   ^-  dn
2651      ?:  ?=([%n *] a)   [%n ~]
2652      ?:  ?=([%i *] a)   [%i s.a]
2653      ?~  a.a   [%d s.a --0 0]
2654      [%d s.a (^drg +>.a)]
2655    ::
2656    ++  grd                                    ::  decimal to float
2657      |=  [a=dn]   ^-  fn
2658      ?:  ?=([%n *] a)   [%n ~]
2659      ?:  ?=([%i *] a)   [%i s.a]
2660      =>  .(r %n)
2661      =+  q=(abs:si e.a)
2662      ?:  (syn:si e.a)
2663      (mul [%f s.a --0 a.a] [%f & e.a (pow 5 q)])
2664      (div [%f s.a --0 a.a] [%f & (sun:si q) (pow 5 q)])
2665    ::
2666    ++  toi                                    ::  round to integer @s
```

```
2667      |=  [a=fn]  ^-  (unit @s)
2668      =+  b=(toj a)
2669      ?.  ?=([%f *] b)  ~  :-  ~
2670      =+  c=(^^mul (bex (abs:si e.b)) a.b)
2671      (new:si s.b c)
2672   ::
2673   ++  toj                                    ::  round to integer fn
2674      |=  [a=fn]  ^-  fn
2675      ?.  ?=([%f *] a)  a
2676      ?~  a.a  [%f s.a zer]
2677      ?:  s.a  (^toj +>.a)
2678      =.(r swr (fli (^toj +>.a)))
2679      --
2680   ::     +ff
2681   ::
2682   ::  this core has no use outside of the functionality
2683   ::  provided to ++rd, ++rs, ++rq, and ++rh
2684   ::
2685   ::  w=width:          bits in exponent field
2686   ::  p=precision:      bits in fraction field
2687   ::  b=bias:           added to exponent when storing
2688   ::  r=rounding mode: same as in ++fl
2689   ++  ff                                      ::  ieee 754 format fp
2690      |_  [[w=@u p=@u b=@s] r=$?(%n %u %d %z %a)]
2691      ::
2692      ++  sb  (bex (^add w p))                 ::  sign bit
2693      ++  me  (dif:si (dif:si --1 b) (sun:si p)) ::  minimum exponent
2694      ::
2695      ++  pa
2696      %*(. fl p +(p), v me, w (^sub (bex w) 3), d %d, r r)
2697      ::
2698      ++  sea                                  ::  @r to fn
2699      |=  [a=@r]  ^-  fn
2700      =+  [f=(cut 0 [0 p] a) e=(cut 0 [p w] a)]
2701      =+  s=(sig a)
2702      ?:  =(e 0)
2703        ?:  =(f 0)  [%f s --0 0]  [%f s me f]
2704      ?:  =(e (fil 0 w 1))
2705        ?:  =(f 0)  [%i s]  [%n ~]
2706      =+  q=:(sum:si (sun:si e) me -1)
2707      =+  r=(^add f (bex p))
2708      [%f s q r]
2709      ::
2710      ++  bit  |=  [a=fn]  (bif (rou:pa a))    ::  fn to @r w+ rounding
2711      ::
2712      ++  bif                                  ::  fn to @r no rounding
2713      |=  [a=fn]  ^-  @r
2714      ?:  ?=([%i *] a)
2715        =+  q=(lsh [0 p] (fil 0 w 1))
2716        ?:  s.a  q  (^add q sb)
2717      ?:  ?=([%n *] a)  (lsh [0 (dec p)] (fil 0 +(w) 1))
2718      ?~  a.a  ?:  s.a  `@r`0  sb
2719      =+  ma=(met 0 a.a)
2720      ?.  =(ma +(p))
2721        ?>  =(e.a me)
2722        ?>  (^lth ma +(p))
2723        ?:  s.a  `@r`a.a  (^add a.a sb)
2724      =+  q=(sum:si (dif:si e.a me) --1)
```

```
2725        =+  r=(^add (lsh [0 p] (abs:si q)) (end [0 p] a.a))
2726        ?:  s.a  r  (^add r sb)
2727      ::
2728      ++  sig                                    :: get sign
2729        |=  [a=@r]  ^-  ?
2730        =(0 (cut 0 [(^add p w) 1] a))
2731      ::
2732      ++  exp                                    :: get exponent
2733        |=  [a=@r]  ^-  @s
2734        (dif:si (sun:si (cut 0 [p w] a)) b)
2735      ::
2736      ++  add                                    :: add
2737        |=  [a=@r b=@r]
2738        (bif (add:pa (sea a) (sea b)))
2739      ::
2740      ++  sub                                    :: subtract
2741        |=  [a=@r b=@r]
2742        (bif (sub:pa (sea a) (sea b)))
2743      ::
2744      ++  mul                                    :: multiply
2745        |=  [a=@r b=@r]
2746        (bif (mul:pa (sea a) (sea b)))
2747      ::
2748      ++  div                                    :: divide
2749        |=  [a=@r b=@r]
2750        (bif (div:pa (sea a) (sea b)))
2751      ::
2752      ++  fma                                    :: fused multiply-add
2753        |=  [a=@r b=@r c=@r]
2754        (bif (fma:pa (sea a) (sea b) (sea c)))
2755      ::
2756      ++  sqt                                    :: square root
2757        |=  [a=@r]
2758        (bif (sqt:pa (sea a)))
2759      ::
2760      ++  lth                                    :: less-than
2761        |=  [a=@r b=@r]  (fall (lth:pa (sea a) (sea b)) |)
2762      ++  lte                                    :: less-equals
2763        |=  [a=@r b=@r]  (fall (lte:pa (sea a) (sea b)) |)
2764      ++  equ                                    :: equals
2765        |=  [a=@r b=@r]  (fall (equ:pa (sea a) (sea b)) |)
2766      ++  gte                                    :: greater-equals
2767        |=  [a=@r b=@r]  (fall (gte:pa (sea a) (sea b)) |)
2768      ++  gth                                    :: greater-than
2769        |=  [a=@r b=@r]  (fall (gth:pa (sea a) (sea b)) |)
2770      ++  sun                                    :: uns integer to @r
2771        |=  [a=@u]  (bit [%f & --0 a])
2772      ++  san                                    :: signed integer to @r
2773        |=  [a=@s]  (bit [%f (syn:si a) --0 (abs:si a)])
2774      ++  toi                                    :: round to integer
2775        |=  [a=@r]  (toi:pa (sea a))
2776      ++  drg                                    :: @r to decimal float
2777        |=  [a=@r]  (drg:pa (sea a))
2778      ++  grd                                    :: decimal float to @r
2779        |=  [a=dn]  (bif (grd:pa a))
2780      --
2781    ::
2782  ++  rlyd  |=  a=@rd  ^-  dn  (drg:rd a)         :: prep @rd for print
```

```
2783  ++  rlys  |=  a=@rs  ^-  dn  (drg:rs a)           :: prep @rs for print
2784  ++  rlyh  |=  a=@rh  ^-  dn  (drg:rh a)           :: prep @rh for print
2785  ++  rlyq  |=  a=@rq  ^-  dn  (drg:rq a)           :: prep @rq for print
2786  ++  ryld  |=  a=dn  ^-  @rd  (grd:rd a)           :: finish parsing @rd
2787  ++  ryls  |=  a=dn  ^-  @rs  (grd:rs a)           :: finish parsing @rs
2788  ++  rylh  |=  a=dn  ^-  @rh  (grd:rh a)           :: finish parsing @rh
2789  ++  rylq  |=  a=dn  ^-  @rq  (grd:rq a)           :: finish parsing @rq
2790  ::
2791  ++  rd                                            :: double precision fp
2792   ^|
2793  ~%  %rd  +>  ~
2794  |_  r=$?(%n %u %d %z)
2795  ::  round to nearest, round up, round down, round to zero
2796  ::
2797  ++  ma
2798   %*(. ff w 11, p 52, b --1.023, r r)
2799  ::
2800  ++  sea                                           :: @rd to fn
2801   |=  [a=@rd]  (sea:ma a)
2802  ::
2803  ++  bit                                           :: fn to @rd
2804   |=  [a=fn]  ^-  @rd  (bit:ma a)
2805  ::
2806  ++  add  ~/  %add                                 :: add
2807   |=  [a=@rd b=@rd]  ^-  @rd
2808   ~_  leaf+"rd-fail"
2809   (add:ma a b)
2810  ::
2811  ++  sub  ~/  %sub                                 :: subtract
2812   |=  [a=@rd b=@rd]  ^-  @rd
2813   ~_  leaf+"rd-fail"
2814   (sub:ma a b)
2815  ::
2816  ++  mul  ~/  %mul                                 :: multiply
2817   |=  [a=@rd b=@rd]  ^-  @rd
2818   ~_  leaf+"rd-fail"
2819   (mul:ma a b)
2820  ::
2821  ++  div  ~/  %div                                 :: divide
2822   |=  [a=@rd b=@rd]  ^-  @rd
2823   ~_  leaf+"rd-fail"
2824   (div:ma a b)
2825  ::
2826  ++  fma  ~/  %fma                                 :: fused multiply-add
2827   |=  [a=@rd b=@rd c=@rd]  ^-  @rd
2828   ~_  leaf+"rd-fail"
2829   (fma:ma a b c)
2830  ::
2831  ++  sqt  ~/  %sqt                                 :: square root
2832   |=  [a=@rd]  ^-  @rd  ~_  leaf+"rd-fail"
2833   (sqt:ma a)
2834  ::
2835  ++  lth  ~/  %lth                                 :: less-than
2836   |=  [a=@rd b=@rd]
2837   ~_  leaf+"rd-fail"
2838   (lth:ma a b)
2839  ::
2840  ++  lte  ~/  %lte                                 :: less-equals
```

```
2841        |=  [a=@rd b=@rd]
2842        ~_  leaf+"rd-fail"
2843        (lte:ma a b)
2844      ::
2845    ++  equ  ~/  %equ                              ::  equals
2846        |=  [a=@rd b=@rd]
2847        ~_  leaf+"rd-fail"
2848        (equ:ma a b)
2849      ::
2850    ++  gte  ~/  %gte                              ::  greater-equals
2851        |=  [a=@rd b=@rd]
2852        ~_  leaf+"rd-fail"
2853        (gte:ma a b)
2854      ::
2855    ++  gth  ~/  %gth                              ::  greater-than
2856        |=  [a=@rd b=@rd]
2857        ~_  leaf+"rd-fail"
2858        (gth:ma a b)
2859      ::
2860    ++  sun  |=  [a=@u]   ^-  @rd  (sun:ma a)      ::  uns integer to @rd
2861    ++  san  |=  [a=@s]   ^-  @rd  (san:ma a)      ::  sgn integer to @rd
2862    ++  sig  |=  [a=@rd]  ^-  ?  (sig:ma a)        ::  get sign
2863    ++  exp  |=  [a=@rd]  ^-  @s  (exp:ma a)       ::  get exponent
2864    ++  toi  |=  [a=@rd]  ^-  (unit @s)  (toi:ma a) ::  round to integer
2865    ++  drg  |=  [a=@rd]  ^-  dn  (drg:ma a)       ::  @rd to decimal float
2866    ++  grd  |=  [a=dn]   ^-  @rd  (grd:ma a)      ::  decimal float to @rd
2867      --
2868  ::
2869  ++  rs                                          ::  single precision fp
2870    ~%  %rs  +>  ~
2871    ^|
2872    ::   round to nearest, round up, round down, round to zero
2873    |_  r=$?(%n %u %d %z)
2874    ::
2875    ++  ma
2876      %*(. ff w 8, p 23, b --127, r r)
2877      ::
2878    ++  sea                                        ::  @rs to fn
2879        |=  [a=@rs]  (sea:ma a)
2880      ::
2881    ++  bit                                        ::  fn to @rs
2882        |=  [a=fn]  ^-  @rs  (bit:ma a)
2883      ::
2884    ++  add  ~/  %add                              ::  add
2885        |=  [a=@rs b=@rs]  ^-  @rs
2886        ~_  leaf+"rs-fail"
2887        (add:ma a b)
2888      ::
2889    ++  sub  ~/  %sub                              ::  subtract
2890        |=  [a=@rs b=@rs]  ^-  @rs
2891        ~_  leaf+"rs-fail"
2892        (sub:ma a b)
2893      ::
2894    ++  mul  ~/  %mul                              ::  multiply
2895        |=  [a=@rs b=@rs]  ^-  @rs
2896        ~_  leaf+"rs-fail"
2897        (mul:ma a b)
2898      ::
```

```
2899    ++  div   ~/  %div                                  ::  divide
2900    |=  [a=@rs b=@rs]   ^-  @rs
2901    ~_  leaf+"rs-fail"
2902    (div:ma a b)
2903    ::
2904    ++  fma   ~/  %fma                                  ::  fused multiply-add
2905    |=  [a=@rs b=@rs c=@rs]   ^-  @rs
2906    ~_  leaf+"rs-fail"
2907    (fma:ma a b c)
2908    ::
2909    ++  sqt   ~/  %sqt                                  ::  square root
2910    |=  [a=@rs]   ^-  @rs
2911    ~_  leaf+"rs-fail"
2912    (sqt:ma a)
2913    ::
2914    ++  lth   ~/  %lth                                  ::  less-than
2915    |=  [a=@rs b=@rs]
2916    ~_  leaf+"rs-fail"
2917    (lth:ma a b)
2918    ::
2919    ++  lte   ~/  %lte                                  ::  less-equals
2920    |=  [a=@rs b=@rs]
2921    ~_  leaf+"rs-fail"
2922    (lte:ma a b)
2923    ::
2924    ++  equ   ~/  %equ                                  ::  equals
2925    |=  [a=@rs b=@rs]
2926    ~_  leaf+"rs-fail"
2927    (equ:ma a b)
2928    ::
2929    ++  gte   ~/  %gte                                  ::  greater-equals
2930    |=  [a=@rs b=@rs]
2931    ~_  leaf+"rs-fail"
2932    (gte:ma a b)
2933    ::
2934    ++  gth   ~/  %gth                                  ::  greater-than
2935    |=  [a=@rs b=@rs]
2936    ~_  leaf+"rs-fail"
2937    (gth:ma a b)
2938    ::
2939    ++  sun  |=  [a=@u]   ^-  @rs  (sun:ma a)           ::  uns integer to @rs
2940    ++  san  |=  [a=@s]   ^-  @rs  (san:ma a)           ::  sgn integer to @rs
2941    ++  sig  |=  [a=@rs]  ^-  ?  (sig:ma a)             ::  get sign
2942    ++  exp  |=  [a=@rs]  ^-  @s  (exp:ma a)            ::  get exponent
2943    ++  toi  |=  [a=@rs]  ^-  (unit @s)  (toi:ma a)     ::  round to integer
2944    ++  drg  |=  [a=@rs]  ^-  dn  (drg:ma a)            ::  @rs to decimal float
2945    ++  grd  |=  [a=dn]   ^-  @rs  (grd:ma a)           ::  decimal float to @rs
2946    --
2947  ::
2948  ++  rq                                               ::  quad precision fp
2949    ~%  %rq  +>  ~
2950    ^|
2951    ::  round to nearest, round up, round down, round to zero
2952    |_  r=$?(%n %u %d %z)
2953    ::
2954    ++  ma
2955    %*(. ff w 15, p 112, b --16.383, r r)
2956    ::
```

```
2957  ++  sea                                          ::  @rq to fn
2958    |=  [a=@rq]  (sea:ma a)
2959  ::
2960  ++  bit                                          ::  fn to @rq
2961    |=  [a=fn]  ^-  @rq  (bit:ma a)
2962  ::
2963  ++  add  ~/  %add                                ::  add
2964    |=  [a=@rq b=@rq]  ^-  @rq
2965    ~_  leaf+"rq-fail"
2966    (add:ma a b)
2967  ::
2968  ++  sub  ~/  %sub                                ::  subtract
2969    |=  [a=@rq b=@rq]  ^-  @rq
2970    ~_  leaf+"rq-fail"
2971    (sub:ma a b)
2972  ::
2973  ++  mul  ~/  %mul                                ::  multiply
2974    |=  [a=@rq b=@rq]  ^-  @rq
2975    ~_  leaf+"rq-fail"
2976    (mul:ma a b)
2977  ::
2978  ++  div  ~/  %div                                ::  divide
2979    |=  [a=@rq b=@rq]  ^-  @rq
2980    ~_  leaf+"rq-fail"
2981    (div:ma a b)
2982  ::
2983  ++  fma  ~/  %fma                                ::  fused multiply-add
2984    |=  [a=@rq b=@rq c=@rq]  ^-  @rq
2985    ~_  leaf+"rq-fail"
2986    (fma:ma a b c)
2987  ::
2988  ++  sqt  ~/  %sqt                                ::  square root
2989    |=  [a=@rq]  ^-  @rq
2990    ~_  leaf+"rq-fail"
2991    (sqt:ma a)
2992  ::
2993  ++  lth  ~/  %lth                                ::  less-than
2994    |=  [a=@rq b=@rq]
2995    ~_  leaf+"rq-fail"
2996    (lth:ma a b)
2997  ::
2998  ++  lte  ~/  %lte                                ::  less-equals
2999    |=  [a=@rq b=@rq]
3000    ~_  leaf+"rq-fail"
3001    (lte:ma a b)
3002  ::
3003  ++  equ  ~/  %equ                                ::  equals
3004    |=  [a=@rq b=@rq]
3005    ~_  leaf+"rq-fail"
3006    (equ:ma a b)
3007  ::
3008  ++  gte  ~/  %gte                                ::  greater-equals
3009    |=  [a=@rq b=@rq]
3010    ~_  leaf+"rq-fail"
3011    (gte:ma a b)
3012  ::
3013  ++  gth  ~/  %gth                                ::  greater-than
3014    |=  [a=@rq b=@rq]
```

```
3015        ~_  leaf+"rq-fail"
3016      (gth:ma a b)
3017    ::
3018    ++  sun  |=  [a=@u]   ^-  @rq  (sun:ma a)          ::  uns integer to @rq
3019    ++  san  |=  [a=@s]   ^-  @rq  (san:ma a)          ::  sgn integer to @rq
3020    ++  sig  |=  [a=@rq]  ^-  ?    (sig:ma a)          ::  get sign
3021    ++  exp  |=  [a=@rq]  ^-  @s   (exp:ma a)          ::  get exponent
3022    ++  toi  |=  [a=@rq]  ^-  (unit @s)  (toi:ma a)    ::  round to integer
3023    ++  drg  |=  [a=@rq]  ^-  dn   (drg:ma a)          ::  @rq to decimal float
3024    ++  grd  |=  [a=dn]   ^-  @rq  (grd:ma a)          ::  decimal float to @rq
3025    --
3026  ::
3027  ++  rh                                              ::  half precision fp
3028    ~%  %rh  +>  ~
3029    ^|
3030    ::     round to nearest, round up, round down, round to zero
3031    |_  r=$?(%n %u %d %z)
3032    ::
3033    ++  ma
3034      %*(. ff w 5, p 10, b --15, r r)
3035    ::
3036    ++  sea                                            ::  @rh to fn
3037      |=  [a=@rh]  (sea:ma a)
3038    ::
3039    ++  bit                                            ::  fn to @rh
3040      |=  [a=fn]  ^-  @rh  (bit:ma a)
3041    ::
3042    ++  add  ~/  %add                                  ::  add
3043      |=  [a=@rh b=@rh]  ^-  @rh
3044      ~_  leaf+"rh-fail"
3045      (add:ma a b)
3046    ::
3047    ++  sub  ~/  %sub                                  ::  subtract
3048      |=  [a=@rh b=@rh]  ^-  @rh
3049      ~_  leaf+"rh-fail"
3050      (sub:ma a b)
3051    ::
3052    ++  mul  ~/  %mul                                  ::  multiply
3053      |=  [a=@rh b=@rh]  ^-  @rh
3054      ~_  leaf+"rh-fail"
3055      (mul:ma a b)
3056    ::
3057    ++  div  ~/  %div                                  ::  divide
3058      |=  [a=@rh b=@rh]  ^-  @rh
3059      ~_  leaf+"rh-fail"
3060      (div:ma a b)
3061    ::
3062    ++  fma  ~/  %fma                                  ::  fused multiply-add
3063      |=  [a=@rh b=@rh c=@rh]  ^-  @rh
3064      ~_  leaf+"rh-fail"
3065      (fma:ma a b c)
3066    ::
3067    ++  sqt  ~/  %sqt                                  ::  square root
3068      |=  [a=@rh]  ^-  @rh
3069      ~_  leaf+"rh-fail"
3070      (sqt:ma a)
3071    ::
3072    ++  lth  ~/  %lth                                  ::  less-than
```

```
3073        |=  [a=@rh b=@rh]
3074        ~_  leaf+"rh-fail"
3075        (lth:ma a b)
3076      ::
3077    ++  lte  ~/  %lte                                ::  less-equals
3078        |=  [a=@rh b=@rh]
3079        ~_  leaf+"rh-fail"
3080        (lte:ma a b)
3081      ::
3082    ++  equ  ~/  %equ                                ::  equals
3083        |=  [a=@rh b=@rh]
3084        ~_  leaf+"rh-fail"
3085        (equ:ma a b)
3086      ::
3087    ++  gte  ~/  %gte                                ::  greater-equals
3088        |=  [a=@rh b=@rh]
3089        ~_  leaf+"rh-fail"
3090        (gte:ma a b)
3091      ::
3092    ++  gth  ~/  %gth                                ::  greater-than
3093        |=  [a=@rh b=@rh]
3094        ~_  leaf+"rh-fail"
3095        (gth:ma a b)
3096      ::
3097    ++  tos                                          ::  @rh to @rs
3098        |=  [a=@rh]  (bit:rs (sea a))
3099      ::
3100    ++  fos                                          ::  @rs to @rh
3101        |=  [a=@rs]  (bit (sea:rs a))
3102      ::
3103    ++  sun  |=  [a=@u]   ^-  @rh  (sun:ma a)         ::  uns integer to @rh
3104    ++  san  |=  [a=@s]   ^-  @rh  (san:ma a)         ::  sgn integer to @rh
3105    ++  sig  |=  [a=@rh]  ^-  ?  (sig:ma a)           ::  get sign
3106    ++  exp  |=  [a=@rh]  ^-  @s  (exp:ma a)          ::  get exponent
3107    ++  toi  |=  [a=@rh]  ^-  (unit @s)  (toi:ma a)   ::  round to integer
3108    ++  drg  |=  [a=@rh]  ^-  dn  (drg:ma a)          ::  @rh to decimal float
3109    ++  grd  |=  [a=dn]   ^-  @rh  (grd:ma a)         ::  decimal float to @rh
3110    --
3111  ::
3112  ::    3c: urbit time
3113  +|  %urbit-time
3114  ::
3115  ++  year                                           ::  date to @d
3116      |=  det=date
3117      ^-  @da
3118      =+  ^=  yer
3119        ?:  a.det
3120          (add 292.277.024.400 y.det)
3121        (sub 292.277.024.400 (dec y.det))
3122      =+  day=(yawn yer m.det d.t.det)
3123      (yule day h.t.det m.t.det s.t.det f.t.det)
3124  ::
3125  ++  yore                                           ::  @d to date
3126      |=  now=@da
3127      ^-  date
3128      =+  rip=(yell now)
3129      =+  ger=(yall d.rip)
3130      :-  ?:  (gth y.ger 292.277.024.400)
```

```
3131        [a=& y=(sub y.ger 292.277.024.400)]
3132        [a=| y=+((sub 292.277.024.400 y.ger))]
3133      [m.ger d.ger h.rip m.rip s.rip f.rip]
3134    ::
3135    ++  yell                                          ::  tarp from @d
3136    |=  now=@d
3137    ^-  tarp
3138    =+  sec=(rsh 6 now)
3139    =+  ^=  fan
3140        =+  [muc=4 raw=(end 6 now)]
3141        |-  ^-  (list @ux)
3142        ?:  |(=(0 raw) =(0 muc))
3143            ~
3144        =>  .(muc (dec muc))
3145        [(cut 4 [muc 1] raw) $(raw (end [4 muc] raw))]
3146    =+  day=(div sec day:yo)
3147    =>  .(sec (mod sec day:yo))
3148    =+  hor=(div sec hor:yo)
3149    =>  .(sec (mod sec hor:yo))
3150    =+  mit=(div sec mit:yo)
3151    =>  .(sec (mod sec mit:yo))
3152    [day hor mit sec fan]
3153    ::
3154    ++  yule                                          ::  time atom
3155    |=  rip=tarp
3156    ^-  @d
3157    =+  ^=  sec   ;:  add
3158                 (mul d.rip day:yo)
3159                 (mul h.rip hor:yo)
3160                 (mul m.rip mit:yo)
3161                 s.rip
3162             ==
3163    =+  ^=  fac  =+  muc=4
3164                |-  ^-  @
3165                ?~  f.rip
3166                  0
3167                =>  .(muc (dec muc))
3168                (add (lsh [4 muc] i.f.rip) $(f.rip t.f.rip))
3169    (con (lsh 6 sec) fac)
3170    ::
3171    ++  yall                                          ::  day / to day of year
3172    |=  day=@ud
3173    ^-  [y=@ud m=@ud d=@ud]
3174    =+  [era=0 cet=0 lep=*?]
3175    =>  .(era (div day era:yo), day (mod day era:yo))
3176    =>  ^+  .
3177        ?:  (lth day +(cet:yo))
3178          .(lep &, cet 0)
3179        =>  .(lep |, cet 1, day (sub day +(cet:yo)))
3180        .(cet (add cet (div day cet:yo)), day (mod day cet:yo))
3181    =+  yer=(add (mul 400 era) (mul 100 cet))
3182    |-  ^-  [y=@ud m=@ud d=@ud]
3183    =+  dis=?:(lep 366 365)
3184    ?.  (lth day dis)
3185      =+  ner=+(yer)
3186      $(yer ner, day (sub day dis), lep =(0 (end [0 2] ner)))
3187    |-  ^-  [y=@ud m=@ud d=@ud]
3188    =+  [mot=0 cah=?:(lep moy:yo moh:yo)]
```

```
3189    |-  ^-  [y=@ud m=@ud d=@ud]
3190    =+  zis=(snag mot cah)
3191    ?:  (lth day zis)
3192      [yer +(mot) +(day)]
3193    $(mot +(mot), day (sub day zis))
3194  ::
3195  ++  yawn                                    ::  days since Jesus
3196    |=  [yer=@ud mot=@ud day=@ud]
3197    ^-  @ud
3198    =>  .(mot (dec mot), day (dec day))
3199    =>  ^+  .
3200      %=  .
3201          day
3202        =+  cah=?:((yelp yer) moy:yo moh:yo)
3203        |-  ^-  @ud
3204        ?:  =(0 mot)
3205          day
3206        $(mot (dec mot), cah (slag 1 cah), day (add day (snag 0 cah)))
3207      ==
3208    |-  ^-  @ud
3209    ?.  =(0 (mod yer 4))
3210      =+  ney=(dec yer)
3211      $(yer ney, day (add day ?:((yelp ney) 366 365)))
3212    ?.  =(0 (mod yer 100))
3213      =+  nef=(sub yer 4)
3214      $(yer nef, day (add day ?:((yelp nef) 1.461 1.460)))
3215    ?.  =(0 (mod yer 400))
3216      =+  nec=(sub yer 100)
3217      $(yer nec, day (add day ?:((yelp nec) 36.525 36.524)))
3218    (add day (mul (div yer 400) (add 1 (mul 4 36.524))))
3219  ::
3220  ++  yelp                                    ::  leap year
3221    |=  yer=@ud  ^-  ?
3222    &(=(0 (mod yer 4)) |(!=(0 (mod yer 100)) =(0 (mod yer 400))))
3223  ::
3224  ++  yo                                       ::  time constants
3225    |%  ++  cet  36.524              ::  (add 24 (mul 100 365))
3226        ++  day  86.400             ::  (mul 24 hor)
3227        ++  era  146.097            ::  (add 1 (mul 4 cet))
3228        ++  hor  3.600              ::  (mul 60 mit)
3229        ++  jes  106.751.991.084.417  ::  (mul 730.692.561 era)
3230        ++  mit  60
3231        ++  moh  `(list @ud)`[31 28 31 30 31 30 31 31 30 31 30 31 ~]
3232        ++  moy  `(list @ud)`[31 29 31 30 31 30 31 31 30 31 30 31 ~]
3233        ++  qad  126.144.001        ::  (add 1 (mul 4 yer))
3234        ++  yer  31.536.000         ::  (mul 365 day)
3235    --
3236  ::
3237  ::    3d: SHA hash family
3238  +|  %sha-hash-family
3239  ::
3240  ++  shad  |=(ruz=@ (shax (shax ruz)))       ::  double sha-256
3241  ++  shaf                                     ::  half sha-256
3242    |=  [sal=@ ruz=@]
3243    =+  haz=(shas sal ruz)
3244    (mix (end 7 haz) (rsh 7 haz))
3245  ::
3246  ++  sham                                     ::  128bit noun hash
```

```
3247      |=  yux=*  ^-  @uvH  ^-  @
3248      ?@  yux
3249        (shaf %mash yux)
3250      (shaf %sham (jam yux))
3251    ::
3252    ++  shas                                        ::  salted hash
3253    ~/  %shas
3254    |=  [sal=@ ruz=@]
3255    (shax (mix sal (shax ruz)))
3256    ::
3257    ++  shax                                        ::  sha-256
3258    ~/  %shax
3259    |=  ruz=@  ^-  @
3260    (shay [(met 3 ruz) ruz])
3261    ::
3262    ++  shay                                        ::  sha-256 with length
3263    ~/  %shay
3264    |=  [len=@u ruz=@]  ^-  @
3265    =>  .(ruz (cut 3 [0 len] ruz))
3266    =+  [few==>(fe .(a 5)) wac=|=([a=@ b=@] (cut 5 [a 1] b))]
3267    =+  [sum=sum.few ror=ror.few net=net.few inv=inv.few]
3268    =+  ral=(lsh [0 3] len)
3269    =+  ^=  ful
3270        %+  can  0
3271        :~  [ral ruz]
3272            [8 128]
3273            [(mod (sub 960 (mod (add 8 ral) 512)) 512) 0]
3274            [64 (~(net fe 6) ral)]
3275        ==
3276    =+  lex=(met 9 ful)
3277    =+  ^=  kbx  0xc671.78f2.bef9.a3f7.a450.6ceb.90be.fffa.
3278                  8cc7.0208.84c8.7814.78a5.636f.748f.82ee.
3279                  682e.6ff3.5b9c.ca4f.4ed8.aa4a.391c.0cb3.
3280                  34b0.bcb5.2748.774c.1e37.6c08.19a4.c116.
3281                  106a.a070.f40e.3585.d699.0624.d192.e819.
3282                  c76c.51a3.c24b.8b70.a81a.664b.a2bf.e8a1.
3283                  9272.2c85.81c2.c92e.766a.0abb.650a.7354.
3284                  5338.0d13.4d2c.6dfc.2e1b.2138.27b7.0a85.
3285                  1429.2967.06ca.6351.d5a7.9147.c6e0.0bf3.
3286                  bf59.7fc7.b003.27c8.a831.c66d.983e.5152.
3287                  76f9.88da.5cb0.a9dc.4a74.84aa.2de9.2c6f.
3288                  240c.a1cc.0fc1.9dc6.efbe.4786.e49b.69c1.
3289                  c19b.f174.9bdc.06a7.80de.b1fe.72be.5d74.
3290                  550c.7dc3.2431.85be.1283.5b01.d807.aa98.
3291                  ab1c.5ed5.923f.82a4.59f1.11f1.3956.c25b.
3292                  e9b5.dba5.b5c0.fbcf.7137.4491.428a.2f98
3293    =+  ^=  hax  0x5be0.cd19.1f83.d9ab.9b05.688c.510e.527f.
3294                  a54f.f53a.3c6e.f372.bb67.ae85.6a09.e667
3295    =+  i=0
3296    |-  ^-  @
3297    ?:  =(i lex)
3298      (run 5 hax net)
3299    =+  ^=  wox
3300        =+  dux=(cut 9 [i 1] ful)
3301        =+  wox=(run 5 dux net)
3302        =+  j=16
3303        |-  ^-  @
3304        ?:  =(64 j)
```

```
3305            wox
3306       =+  :*  l=(wac (sub j 15) wox)
3307               m=(wac (sub j 2) wox)
3308               n=(wac (sub j 16) wox)
3309               o=(wac (sub j 7) wox)
3310           ==
3311       =+  x=:(mix (ror 0 7 l) (ror 0 18 l) (rsh [0 3] l))
3312       =+  y=:(mix (ror 0 17 m) (ror 0 19 m) (rsh [0 10] m))
3313       =+  z=:(sum n x o y)
3314       $(wox (con (lsh [5 j] z) wox), j +(j))
3315     =+  j=0
3316     =+  :*  a=(wac 0 hax)
3317             b=(wac 1 hax)
3318             c=(wac 2 hax)
3319             d=(wac 3 hax)
3320             e=(wac 4 hax)
3321             f=(wac 5 hax)
3322             g=(wac 6 hax)
3323             h=(wac 7 hax)
3324         ==
3325     |-  ^-  @
3326     ?:  =(64 j)
3327       %=  ^$
3328       i  +(i)
3329       hax  %+  rep  5
3330            :~  (sum a (wac 0 hax))
3331                (sum b (wac 1 hax))
3332                (sum c (wac 2 hax))
3333                (sum d (wac 3 hax))
3334                (sum e (wac 4 hax))
3335                (sum f (wac 5 hax))
3336                (sum g (wac 6 hax))
3337                (sum h (wac 7 hax))
3338            ==
3339     ==
3340     =+  l=:(mix (ror 0 2 a) (ror 0 13 a) (ror 0 22 a))      :: s0
3341     =+  m=:(mix (dis a b) (dis a c) (dis b c))              :: maj
3342     =+  n=(sum l m)                                         :: t2
3343     =+  o=:(mix (ror 0 6 e) (ror 0 11 e) (ror 0 25 e))      :: s1
3344     =+  p=:(mix (dis e f) (dis (inv e) g))                  :: ch
3345     =+  q=:(sum h o p (wac j kbx) (wac j wox))              :: t1
3346     $(j +(j), a (sum q n), b a, c b, d c, e (sum d q), f e, g f, h g)
3347   ::
3348  ++  shaw                                       :: hash to nbits
3349    |=  [sal=@ len=@ ruz=@]
3350    (~(raw og (shas sal (mix len ruz))) len)
3351  ::
3352  ++  shaz                                                :: sha-512
3353    |=  ruz=@  ^-  @
3354    (shal [(met 3 ruz) ruz])
3355  ::
3356  ++  shal                                       :: sha-512 with length
3357    ~/  %shal
3358    |=  [len=@ ruz=@]  ^-  @
3359    =>  .(ruz (cut 3 [0 len] ruz))
3360    =+  [few==>(fe .(a 6)) wac=|=([a=@ b=@] (cut 6 [a 1] b))]
3361    =+  [sum=sum.few ror=ror.few net=net.few inv=inv.few]
3362    =+  ral=(lsh [0 3] len)
```

```
3363    =+  ^=  ful
3364        %+  can  0
3365        :~  [ral ruz]
3366            [8 128]
3367            [(mod (sub 1.920 (mod (add 8 ral) 1.024)) 1.024) 0]
3368            [128 (~(net fe 7) ral)]
3369        ==
3370    =+  lex=(met 10 ful)
3371    =+  ^=  kbx  0x6c44.198c.4a47.5817.5fcb.6fab.3ad6.faec.
3372                    597f.299c.fc65.7e2a.4cc5.d4be.cb3e.42b6.
3373                    431d.67c4.9c10.0d4c.3c9e.be0a.15c9.bebc.
3374                    32ca.ab7b.40c7.2493.28db.77f5.2304.7d84.
3375                    1b71.0b35.131c.471b.113f.9804.bef9.0dae.
3376                    0a63.7dc5.a2c8.98a6.06f0.67aa.7217.6fba.
3377                    f57d.4f7f.ee6e.d178.eada.7dd6.cde0.eb1e.
3378                    d186.b8c7.21c0.c207.ca27.3ece.ea26.619c.
3379                    c671.78f2.e372.532b.bef9.a3f7.b2c6.7915.
3380                    a450.6ceb.de82.bde9.90be.fffa.2363.1e28.
3381                    8cc7.0208.1a64.39ec.84c8.7814.a1f0.ab72.
3382                    78a5.636f.4317.2f60.748f.82ee.5def.b2fc.
3383                    682e.6ff3.d6b2.b8a3.5b9c.ca4f.7763.e373.
3384                    4ed8.aa4a.e341.8acb.391c.0cb3.c5c9.5a63.
3385                    34b0.bcb5.e19b.48a8.2748.774c.df8e.eb99.
3386                    1e37.6c08.5141.ab53.19a4.c116.b8d2.d0c8.
3387                    106a.a070.32bb.d1b8.f40e.3585.5771.202a.
3388                    d699.0624.5565.a910.d192.e819.d6ef.5218.
3389                    c76c.51a3.0654.be30.c24b.8b70.d0f8.9791.
3390                    a81a.664b.bc42.3001.a2bf.e8a1.4cf1.0364.
3391                    9272.2c85.1482.353b.81c2.c92e.47ed.aee6.
3392                    766a.0abb.3c77.b2a8.650a.7354.8baf.63de.
3393                    5338.0d13.9d95.b3df.4d2c.6dfc.5ac4.2aed.
3394                    2e1b.2138.5c26.c926.27b7.0a85.46d2.2ffc.
3395                    1429.2967.0a0e.6e70.06ca.6351.e003.826f.
3396                    d5a7.9147.930a.a725.c6e0.0bf3.3da8.8fc2.
3397                    bf59.7fc7.beef.0ee4.b003.27c8.98fb.213f.
3398                    a831.c66d.2db4.3210.983e.51b2.ee66.dfab.
3399                    76f9.88da.8311.53b5.5cb0.a9dc.bd41.fbd4.
3400                    4a74.84aa.6ea6.e483.2de9.2c6f.592b.0275.
3401                    240c.a1cc.77ac.9c65.0fc1.9dc6.8b8c.d5b5.
3402                    efbe.4786.384f.25e3.e49b.69c1.9ef1.4ad2.
3403                    c19b.f174.cf69.2694.9bdc.06a7.25c7.1235.
3404                    80de.b1fe.3b16.96b1.72be.5d74.f27b.896f.
3405                    550c.7dc3.d5ff.b4e2.2431.85be.4ee4.b28c.
3406                    1283.5b01.4570.6fbe.d807.aa98.a303.0242.
3407                    ab1c.5ed5.da6d.8118.923f.82a4.af19.4f9b.
3408                    59f1.11f1.b605.d019.3956.c25b.f348.b538.
3409                    e9b5.dba5.8189.dbbc.b5c0.fbcf.ec4d.3b2f.
3410                    7137.4491.23ef.65cd.428a.2f98.d728.ae22
3411    =+  ^=  hax  0x5be0.cd19.137e.2179.1f83.d9ab.fb41.bd6b.
3412                    9b05.688c.2b3e.6c1f.510e.527f.ade6.82d1.
3413                    a54f.f53a.5f1d.36f1.3c6e.f372.fe94.f82b.
3414                    bb67.ae85.84ca.a73b.6a09.e667.f3bc.c908
3415    =+  i=0
3416    |-  ^-  @
3417    ?:  =(i lex)
3418      (run 6 hax net)
3419    =+  ^=  wox
3420        =+  dux=(cut 10 [i 1] ful)
```

```
3421        =+    wox=(run 6 dux net)
3422        =+    j=16
3423        |-    ^-    @
3424        ?:    =(80 j)
3425            wox
3426        =+    :*  l=(wac (sub j 15) wox)
3427                 m=(wac (sub j 2) wox)
3428                 n=(wac (sub j 16) wox)
3429                 o=(wac (sub j 7) wox)
3430             ==
3431        =+    x=:(mix (ror 0 1 l) (ror 0 8 l) (rsh [0 7] l))
3432        =+    y=:(mix (ror 0 19 m) (ror 0 61 m) (rsh [0 6] m))
3433        =+    z=:(sum n x o y)
3434        $(wox (con (lsh [6 j] z) wox), j +(j))
3435    =+  j=0
3436    =+  :*  a=(wac 0 hax)
3437            b=(wac 1 hax)
3438            c=(wac 2 hax)
3439            d=(wac 3 hax)
3440            e=(wac 4 hax)
3441            f=(wac 5 hax)
3442            g=(wac 6 hax)
3443            h=(wac 7 hax)
3444        ==
3445    |-    ^-    @
3446    ?:    =(80 j)
3447      %=    ^$
3448        i    +(i)
3449        hax   %+  rep  6
3450            :~  (sum a (wac 0 hax))
3451                (sum b (wac 1 hax))
3452                (sum c (wac 2 hax))
3453                (sum d (wac 3 hax))
3454                (sum e (wac 4 hax))
3455                (sum f (wac 5 hax))
3456                (sum g (wac 6 hax))
3457                (sum h (wac 7 hax))
3458            ==
3459      ==
3460    =+  l=:(mix (ror 0 28 a) (ror 0 34 a) (ror 0 39 a))    :: S0
3461    =+  m=:(mix (dis a b) (dis a c) (dis b c))             :: maj
3462    =+  n=(sum l m)                                        :: t2
3463    =+  o=:(mix (ror 0 14 e) (ror 0 18 e) (ror 0 41 e))    :: S1
3464    =+  p=(mix (dis e f) (dis (inv e) g))                  :: ch
3465    =+  q=:(sum h o p (wac j kbx) (wac j wox))             :: t1
3466    $(j +(j), a (sum q n), b a, c b, d c, e (sum d q), f e, g f, h g)
3467    ::
3468    ++  shan                                      ::  sha-1 (deprecated)
3469      |=  ruz=@
3470      =+  [few==>(fe .(a 5)) wac=|=([a=@ b=@] (cut 5 [a 1] b))]
3471      =+  [sum=sum.few ror=ror.few rol=rol.few net=net.few inv=inv.few]
3472      =+  ral=(lsh [0 3] (met 3 ruz))
3473      =+  ^=  ful
3474        %+  can  0
3475        :~  [ral ruz]
3476            [8 128]
3477            [(mod (sub 960 (mod (add 8 ral) 512)) 512) 0]
3478            [64 (~(net fe 6) ral)]
```

```
3479        ==
3480    =+  lex=(met 9 ful)
3481    =+  kbx=0xca62.c1d6.8f1b.bcdc.6ed9.eba1.5a82.7999
3482    =+  hax=0xc3d2.e1f0.1032.5476.98ba.dcfe.efcd.ab89.6745.2301
3483    =+  i=0
3484    |-
3485    ?:  =(i lex)
3486      (rep 5 (flop (rip 5 hax)))
3487    =+  ^=  wox
3488        =+  dux=(cut 9 [i 1] ful)
3489        =+  wox=(rep 5 (turn (rip 5 dux) net))
3490        =+  j=16
3491        |-  ^-  @
3492        ?:  =(80 j)
3493          wox
3494        =+  :*  l=(wac (sub j 3) wox)
3495                m=(wac (sub j 8) wox)
3496                n=(wac (sub j 14) wox)
3497                o=(wac (sub j 16) wox)
3498            ==
3499        =+  z=(rol 0 1 :(mix l m n o))
3500        $(wox (con (lsh [5 j] z) wox), j +(j))
3501    =+  j=0
3502    =+  :*  a=(wac 0 hax)
3503            b=(wac 1 hax)
3504            c=(wac 2 hax)
3505            d=(wac 3 hax)
3506            e=(wac 4 hax)
3507        ==
3508    |-  ^-  @
3509    ?:  =(80 j)
3510      %=  ^$
3511        i  +(i)
3512        hax  %+  rep  5
3513             :~
3514                  (sum a (wac 0 hax))
3515                  (sum b (wac 1 hax))
3516                  (sum c (wac 2 hax))
3517                  (sum d (wac 3 hax))
3518                  (sum e (wac 4 hax))
3519             ==
3520      ==
3521    =+  fx=(con (dis b c) (dis (not 5 1 b) d))
3522    =+  fy=:(mix b c d)
3523    =+  fz=:(con (dis b c) (dis b d) (dis c d))
3524    =+  ^=  tem
3525        ?:  &((gte j 0) (lte j 19))
3526          :(sum (rol 0 5 a) fx e (wac 0 kbx) (wac j wox))
3527        ?:  &((gte j 20) (lte j 39))
3528          :(sum (rol 0 5 a) fy e (wac 1 kbx) (wac j wox))
3529        ?:  &((gte j 40) (lte j 59))
3530          :(sum (rol 0 5 a) fz e (wac 2 kbx) (wac j wox))
3531        :(sum (rol 0 5 a) fy e (wac 3 kbx) (wac j wox))
3532    $(j +(j), a tem, b a, c (rol 0 30 b), d c, e d)
3533    ::
3534    ++  og                                              ::  shax-powered rng
3535      ~/  %og
3536      |_  a=@
```

```
3537  ++  rad                                      ::  random in range
3538    |=  b=@   ^-   @
3539    ~_  leaf+"rad-zero"
3540    ?<  =(0 b)
3541    =+  c=(raw (met 0 b))
3542    ?:((lth c b) c $(a +(a)))
3543  ::
3544  ++  rads                                     ::  random continuation
3545    |=  b=@
3546    =+  r=(rad b)
3547    [r +>.$(a (shas %og-s (mix a r)))]
3548  ::
3549  ++  raw                                      ::  random bits
3550    ~/  %raw
3551    |=  b=@   ^-   @
3552    %+  can
3553        0
3554    =+  c=(shas %og-a (mix b a))
3555    |-  ^-  (list [@ @])
3556    ?:  =(0 b)
3557        ~
3558    =+  d=(shas %og-b (mix b (mix a c)))
3559    ?:  (lth b 256)
3560      [[b (end [0 b] d)] ~]
3561    [[256 d] $(c d, b (sub b 256))]
3562  ::
3563  ++  raws                                     ::  random bits
3564    |=  b=@                                     ::  continuation
3565    =+  r=(raw b)
3566    [r +>.$(a (shas %og-s (mix a r)))]
3567  --
3568  ::
3569 ++  sha                                       ::  correct byte-order
3570  ~%  %sha  ..sha  ~
3571  =>  |%
3572      ++  flin  |=(a=@ (swp 3 a))              ::  flip input
3573      ++  flim  |=(byts [wid (rev 3 wid dat)]) ::  flip input w= length
3574      ++  flip  |=(w=@u (cury (cury rev 3) w)) ::  flip output of size
3575      ++  meet  |=(a=@ [(met 3 a) a])          ::  measure input size
3576      --
3577  |%
3578  ::
3579  ::  use with @
3580  ::
3581  ++  sha-1     (cork meet sha-1l)
3582  ++  sha-256  :(cork flin shax (flip 32))
3583  ++  sha-512  :(cork flin shaz (flip 64))
3584  ::
3585  ::  use with byts
3586  ::
3587  ++  sha-256l  :(cork flim shay (flip 32))
3588  ++  sha-512l  :(cork flim shal (flip 64))
3589  ::
3590  ++  sha-1l
3591    ~/  %sha1
3592    |=  byts
3593    ^-  @
3594    =+  [few==>(fe .(a 5)) wac=|=([a=@ b=@] (cut 5 [a 1] b))]
```

```
3595    =+    [sum=sum.few ror=ror.few rol=rol.few net=net.few inv=inv.few]
3596    =+    ral=(lsh [0 3] wid)
3597    =+    ^=    ful
3598          %+    can   0
3599          :~    [ral (rev 3 wid dat)]
3600                [8 128]
3601                [(mod (sub 960 (mod (add 8 ral) 512)) 512) 0]
3602                [64 (~(net fe 6) ral)]
3603          ==
3604    =+    lex=(met 9 ful)
3605    =+    kbx=0xca62.c1d6.8f1b.bcdc.6ed9.eba1.5a82.7999
3606    =+    hax=0xc3d2.e1f0.1032.5476.98ba.dcfe.efcd.ab89.6745.2301
3607    =+    i=0
3608    |-
3609    ?:    =(i lex)
3610      (rep 5 (flop (rip 5 hax)))
3611    =+    ^=    wox
3612          =+    dux=(cut 9 [i 1] ful)
3613          =+    wox=(rep 5 (turn (rip 5 dux) net))
3614          =+    j=16
3615          |-    ^-    @
3616          ?:    =(80 j)
3617             wox
3618          =+    :*  l=(wac (sub j 3) wox)
3619                    m=(wac (sub j 8) wox)
3620                    n=(wac (sub j 14) wox)
3621                    o=(wac (sub j 16) wox)
3622                ==
3623          =+    z=(rol 0 1 :(mix l m n o))
3624          $(wox (con (lsh [5 j] z) wox), j +(j))
3625    =+    j=0
3626    =+    :*  a=(wac 0 hax)
3627            b=(wac 1 hax)
3628            c=(wac 2 hax)
3629            d=(wac 3 hax)
3630            e=(wac 4 hax)
3631        ==
3632    |-    ^-    @
3633    ?:    =(80 j)
3634      %=    ^$
3635        i   +(i)
3636        hax   %+  rep  5
3637              :~
3638                    (sum a (wac 0 hax))
3639                    (sum b (wac 1 hax))
3640                    (sum c (wac 2 hax))
3641                    (sum d (wac 3 hax))
3642                    (sum e (wac 4 hax))
3643              ==
3644      ==
3645    =+    fx=(con (dis b c) (dis (not 5 1 b) d))
3646    =+    fy=:(mix b c d)
3647    =+    fz=:(con (dis b c) (dis b d) (dis c d))
3648    =+    ^=    tem
3649          ?:    &((gte j 0) (lte j 19))
3650            :(sum (rol 0 5 a) fx e (wac 0 kbx) (wac j wox))
3651          ?:    &((gte j 20) (lte j 39))
3652            :(sum (rol 0 5 a) fy e (wac 1 kbx) (wac j wox))
```

```
3653        ?:  &((gte j 40) (lte j 59))
3654          :(sum (rol 0 5 a) fz e (wac 2 kbx) (wac j wox))
3655          :(sum (rol 0 5 a) fy e (wac 3 kbx) (wac j wox))
3656      $(j +(j), a tem, b a, c (rol 0 30 b), d c, e d)
3657      --
3658  ::    3f: scrambling
3659  +|  %scrambling
3660  ::
3661  ++  un                                          ::  =(x (wred (wren x)))
3662    |%
3663    ++  wren                                      ::  conceal structure
3664    |=  pyn=@  ^-  @
3665    =+  len=(met 3 pyn)
3666    ?:  =(0 len)
3667        0
3668    =>  .(len (dec len))
3669    =+  mig=(zaft (xafo len (cut 3 [len 1] pyn)))
3670    %+  can  3
3671    %-  flop  ^-  (list [@ @])
3672    :-  [1 mig]
3673    |-  ^-  (list [@ @])
3674    ?:  =(0 len)
3675        ~
3676    =>  .(len (dec len))
3677    =+  mog=(zyft :(mix mig (end 3 len) (cut 3 [len 1] pyn)))
3678    [[1 mog] $(mig mog)]
3679    ::
3680    ++  wred                                      ::  restore structure
3681    |=  cry=@  ^-  @
3682    =+  len=(met 3 cry)
3683    ?:  =(0 len)
3684        0
3685    =>  .(len (dec len))
3686    =+  mig=(cut 3 [len 1] cry)
3687    %+  can  3
3688    %-  flop  ^-  (list [@ @])
3689    :-  [1 (xaro len (zart mig))]
3690    |-  ^-  (list [@ @])
3691    ?:  =(0 len)
3692        ~
3693    =>  .(len (dec len))
3694    =+  mog=(cut 3 [len 1] cry)
3695    [[1 :(mix mig (end 3 len) (zyrt mog))] $(mig mog)]
3696    ::
3697    ++  xafo  |=([a=@ b=@] +((mod (add (dec b) a) 255)))
3698    ++  xaro  |=([a=@ b=@] +((mod (add (dec b) (sub 255 (mod a 255))) 255)))
3699    ::
3700    ++  zaft                                       ::  forward 255-sbox
3701    |=  a=@D
3702    =+  ^=  b
3703        0xcc.75bc.86c8.2fb1.9a42.f0b3.79a0.92ca.21f6.1e41.cde5.fcc0.
3704        7e85.51ae.1005.c72d.1246.07e8.7c64.a914.8d69.d9f4.59c2.8038.
3705        1f4a.dca2.6fdf.66f9.f561.a12e.5a16.f7b0.a39f.364e.cb70.7318.
3706        1de1.ad31.63d1.abd4.db68.6a33.134d.a760.edee.5434.493a.e323.
3707        930d.8f3d.3562.bb81.0b24.43cf.bea5.a6eb.52b4.0229.06b2.6704.
3708        78c9.45ec.d75e.58af.c577.b7b9.c40e.017d.90c3.87f8.96fa.1153.
3709        0372.7f30.1c32.ac83.ff17.c6e4.d36d.6b55.e2ce.8c71.8a5b.b6f3.
3710        9d4b.eab5.8b3c.e7f2.a8fe.9574.5de0.bf20.3f15.9784.9939.5f9c.
```

```
      e609.564f.d8a4.b825.9819.94aa.2c08.8e4c.9b22.477a.2840.3ed6.
      3750.6ef1.44dd.89ef.6576.d00a.fbda.9ed2.3b6c.7b0c.bde9.2ade.
      5c88.c182.481a.1b0f.2bfd.d591.2726.57ba
  (cut 3 [(dec a) 1] b)
  ::
  ++  zart                                        ::  reverse 255-sbox
    |=  a=@D
    =+  ^=  b
        0x68.4f07.ea1c.73c9.75c2.efc8.d559.5125.f621.a7a8.8591.5613.
        dd52.40eb.65a2.60b7.4bcb.1123.ceb0.1bd6.3c84.2906.b164.19b3.
        1e95.5fec.ffbc.f187.fbe2.6680.7c77.d30e.e94a.9414.fd9a.017d.
        3a7e.5a55.8ff5.8bf9.c181.e5b6.6ab2.35da.50aa.9293.3bc0.cdc6.
        f3bf.1a58.4130.f844.3846.744e.36a0.f205.789e.32d8.5e54.5c22.
        0f76.fce7.4569.0d99.d26e.e879.dc16.2df4.887f.1ffe.4dba.6f5d.
        bbcc.2663.1762.aed7.af8a.ca20.dbb4.9bc7.a942.834c.105b.c4d4.
        8202.3e61.a671.90e6.273d.bdab.3157.cfa4.0c2e.df86.2496.f7ed.
        2b48.2a9d.5318.a343.d128.be9c.a5ad.6bb5.6dfa.c5e1.3408.128d.
        2c04.0339.97a1.2ff0.49d0.eeb8.6c0a.0b37.b967.c347.d9ac.e072.
        e409.7b9f.1598.1d3f.33de.8ce3.8970.8e7a
  (cut 3 [(dec a) 1] b)
  ::
  ++  zyft                                        ::  forward 256-sbox
    |=  a=@D
    =+  ^=  b
        0xbb49.b71f.b881.b402.17e4.6b86.69b5.1647.115f.dddb.7ca5.
        8371.4bd5.19a9.b092.605d.0d9b.e030.a0cc.78ba.5706.4d2d.
        986a.768c.f8e8.c4c7.2f1c.effe.3cae.01c0.253e.65d3.3872.
        ce0e.7a74.8ac6.daac.7e5c.6479.44ec.4143.3d20.4af0.ee6c.
        c828.deca.0377.249f.ffcd.7b4f.eb7d.66f2.8951.042e.595a.
        8e13.f9c3.a79a.f788.6199.9391.7fab.6200.4ce5.0758.e2f1.
        7594.c945.d218.4248.afa1.e61a.54fb.1482.bea4.96a2.3473.
        63c2.e7cb.155b.120a.4ed7.bfd8.b31b.4008.f329.fca3.5380.
        9556.0cb2.8722.2bea.e96e.3ac5.d1bc.10e3.2c52.a62a.b1d6.
        35aa.d05e.f6a8.0f3b.31ed.559d.09ad.f585.6d21.fd1d.8d67.
        370b.26f4.70c1.b923.4684.6fbd.cf8b.5036.0539.9cdc.d93f.
        9068.1edf.8f33.b632.d427.97fa.9ee1
  (cut 3 [a 1] b)
  ::
  ++  zyrt                                        ::  reverse 256-sbox
    |=  a=@D
    =+  ^=  b
        0x9fc8.2753.6e02.8fcf.8b35.2b20.5598.7caa.c9a9.30b0.9b48.
        47ce.6371.80f6.407d.00dd.0aa5.ed10.ecb7.0f5a.5c3a.e605.
        c077.4337.17bd.9eda.62a4.79a7.ccb8.44cd.8e64.1ec4.5b6b.
        1842.ffd8.1dfb.fd07.f2f9.594c.3be3.73c6.2cb6.8438.e434.
        8d3d.ea6a.5268.72db.a001.2e11.de8c.88d3.0369.4f7a.87e2.
        860d.0991.25d0.16b9.978a.4bf4.2a1a.e96c.fa50.85b5.9aeb.
        9dbb.b2d9.a2d1.7bba.66be.e81f.1946.29a8.f5d2.f30c.2499.
        c1b3.6583.89e1.ee36.e0b4.6092.937e.d74e.2f6f.513e.9615.
        9c5d.d581.e7ab.fe74.f01b.78b1.ae75.af57.0ec2.adc7.3245.
        12bf.2314.3967.0806.31dc.cb94.d43f.493c.54a6.0421.c3a1.
        1c4a.28ac.fc0b.26ca.5870.e576.f7f1.616d.905f.ef41.33bc.
        df4d.225e.2d56.7fd6.1395.a3f8.c582
  (cut 3 [a 1] b)
  --
  ::
++  ob
  ~%  %ob  ..ob
```

```
3769        ==
3770          %fein  fein
3771          %fynd  fynd
3772        ==
3773    |%
3774    ::
3775    ::  +fein: conceal structure, v3.
3776    ::
3777    ::      +fein conceals planet-sized atoms.  The idea is that it should not be
3778    ::      trivial to tell which planet a star has spawned under.
3779    ::
3780    ++  fein
3781      ~/  %fein
3782      |=  pyn=@  ^-  @
3783      ?:  &((gte pyn 0x1.0000) (lte pyn 0xffff.ffff))
3784        (add 0x1.0000 (feis (sub pyn 0x1.0000)))
3785      ?:  &((gte pyn 0x1.0000.0000) (lte pyn 0xffff.ffff.ffff.ffff))
3786        =/  lo  (dis pyn 0xffff.ffff)
3787        =/  hi  (dis pyn 0xffff.ffff.0000.0000)
3788        %+  con  hi
3789        $(pyn lo)
3790      pyn
3791    ::
3792    ::  +fynd: restore structure, v3.
3793    ::
3794    ::      Restores obfuscated values that have been enciphered with +fein.
3795    ::
3796    ++  fynd
3797      ~/  %fynd
3798      |=  cry=@  ^-  @
3799      ?:  &((gte cry 0x1.0000) (lte cry 0xffff.ffff))
3800        (add 0x1.0000 (tail (sub cry 0x1.0000)))
3801      ?:  &((gte cry 0x1.0000.0000) (lte cry 0xffff.ffff.ffff.ffff))
3802        =/  lo  (dis cry 0xffff.ffff)
3803        =/  hi  (dis cry 0xffff.ffff.0000.0000)
3804        %+  con  hi
3805        $(cry lo)
3806      cry
3807    ::  +feis: a four-round generalised Feistel cipher over the domain
3808    ::         [0, 2^32 - 2^16 - 1].
3809    ::
3810    ::      See: Black & Rogaway (2002), Ciphers for arbitrary finite domains.
3811    ::
3812    ++  feis
3813      |=  m=@
3814      ^-  @
3815      (fee 4 0xffff 0x1.0000 (mul 0xffff 0x1.0000) eff m)
3816    ::
3817    ::  +tail: reverse +feis.
3818    ::
3819    ++  tail
3820      |=  m=@
3821      ^-  @
3822      (feen 4 0xffff 0x1.0000 (mul 0xffff 0x1.0000) eff m)
3823    ::
3824    ::  +fee: "Fe" in B&R (2002).
3825    ::
3826    ::      A Feistel cipher given the following parameters:
```

```
3827    ::
3828    ::      r:      number of Feistel rounds
3829    ::      a, b: parameters such that ab >= k
3830    ::      k:      value such that the domain of the cipher is [0, k - 1]
3831    ::      prf: a gate denoting a family of pseudorandom functions indexed by
3832    ::              its first argument and taking its second argument as input
3833    ::      m:      an input value in the domain [0, k - 1]
3834    ::
3835    ++  fee
3836      |=  [r=@ a=@ b=@ k=@ prf=$-([j=@ r=@] @) m=@]
3837      ^-  @
3838      =/  c  (fe r a b prf m)
3839      ?:  (lth c k)
3840        c
3841      (fe r a b prf c)
3842    ::
3843    ::  +feen: "Fe^-1" in B&R (2002).
3844    ::
3845    ::      Reverses a Feistel cipher constructed with parameters as described in
3846    ::      +fee.
3847    ::
3848    ++  feen
3849      |=  [r=@ a=@ b=@ k=@ prf=$-([j=@ r=@] @) m=@]
3850      ^-  @
3851      =/  c  (fen r a b prf m)
3852      ?:  (lth c k)
3853        c
3854      (fen r a b prf c)
3855    ::
3856    ::  +fe: "fe" in B&R (2002).
3857    ::
3858    ::      An internal function to +fee.
3859    ::
3860    ::      Note that this implementation differs slightly from the reference paper
3861    ::      to support some legacy behaviour.  See urbit/arvo#1105.
3862    ::
3863    ++  fe
3864      |=  [r=@ a=@ b=@ prf=$-([j=@ r=@] @) m=@]
3865      =/  j  1
3866      =/  ell  (mod m a)
3867      =/  arr  (div m a)
3868      |-  ^-  @
3869      ::
3870      ?:  (gth j r)
3871        ?.  =((mod r 2) 0)
3872        (add (mul arr a) ell)
3873        ::
3874        :: Note that +fe differs from B&R (2002)'s "fe" below, as a previous
3875        :: implementation of this cipher contained a bug such that certain inputs
3876        :: could encipher to the same output.
3877        ::
3878        :: To correct these problem cases while also preserving the cipher's
3879        :: legacy behaviour on most inputs, we check for a problem case (which
3880        :: occurs when 'arr' is equal to 'a') and, if detected, use an alternate
3881        :: permutation instead.
3882        ::
3883        ?:  =(arr a)
3884        (add (mul arr a) ell)
```

```
3885        (add (mul ell a) arr)
3886      ::
3887      =/  f  (prf (sub j 1) arr)
3888      ::
3889      =/  tmp
3890        ?.  =((mod j 2) 0)
3891          (mod (add f ell) a)
3892        (mod (add f ell) b)
3893      ::
3894      $(j +(j), ell arr, arr tmp)
3895    ::
3896    ::  +fen:  "fe^-1" in B&R (2002).
3897    ::
3898    ::    Note that this implementation differs slightly from the reference paper
3899    ::    to support some legacy behaviour.  See urbit/arvo#1105.
3900    ::
3901    ++  fen
3902      |=  [r=@ a=@ b=@ prf=$-([j=@ r=@] @) m=@]
3903      =/  j  r
3904      ::
3905      =/  ahh
3906        ?.  =((mod r 2) 0)
3907          (div m a)
3908        (mod m a)
3909      ::
3910      =/  ale
3911        ?.  =((mod r 2) 0)
3912          (mod m a)
3913        (div m a)
3914      ::
3915      :: Similar to the comment in +fe, +fen differs from B&R (2002)'s "fe^-1"
3916      :: here in order to preserve the legacy cipher's behaviour on most inputs.
3917      ::
3918      :: Here problem cases can be identified by 'ahh' equating with 'a'; we
3919      :: correct those cases by swapping the values of 'ahh' and 'ale'.
3920      ::
3921      =/  ell
3922        ?:  =(ale a)
3923          ahh
3924        ale
3925      ::
3926      =/  arr
3927        ?:  =(ale a)
3928          ale
3929        ahh
3930      ::
3931      |-  ^-  @
3932      ?:  (lth j 1)
3933        (add (mul arr a) ell)
3934      =/  f  (prf (sub j 1) ell)
3935      ::
3936      :: Note that there is a slight deviation here to avoid dealing with
3937      :: negative values.  We add 'a' or 'b' to arr as appropriate and reduce
3938      :: 'f' modulo the same number before performing subtraction.
3939      ::
3940      =/  tmp
3941        ?.  =((mod j 2) 0)
3942          (mod (sub (add arr a) (mod f a)) a)
```

```
3943      (mod (sub (add arr b) (mod f b)) b)
3944    ::
3945    $(j (sub j 1), ell tmp, arr ell)
3946  ::
3947  ::    +eff: a murmur3-based pseudorandom function.  'F' in B&R (2002).
3948  ::
3949  ++  eff
3950    |=  [j=@ r=@]
3951    ^-  @
3952    (muk (snag j raku) 2 r)
3953  ::
3954  ::    +raku: seeds for eff.
3955  ::
3956  ++  raku
3957    ^-  (list @ux)
3958    :~  0xb76d.5eed
3959        0xee28.1300
3960        0x85bc.ae01
3961        0x4b38.7af7
3962    ==
3963  ::
3964  --
3965  ::
3966  ::    3g: molds and mold builders
3967  +|  %molds-and-mold-builders
3968  ::
3969  +$  coin  $~  [%$ %ud 0]                             ::  print format
3970            $%  [%$ p=dime]                            ::
3971                [%blob p=*]                            ::
3972                [%many p=(list coin)]                 ::
3973            ==                                        ::
3974  +$  dime  [p=@ta q=@]                                ::
3975  +$  edge  [p=hair q=(unit [p=* q=nail])]            ::  parsing output
3976  +$  hair  [p=@ud q=@ud]                              ::  parsing trace
3977  ++  like  |*  a=$-(* *)                              ::  generic edge
3978            |:  b=`*`[(hair) ~]                        ::
3979            :-  p=(hair -.b)                           ::
3980            ^=  q                                     ::
3981            ?@  +.b  ~                                 ::
3982            :-  ~                                     ::
3983            u=[p=(a +>-.b) q=[p=(hair -.b) q=(tape +.b)]]  ::
3984  +$  nail  [p=hair q=tape]                            ::  parsing input
3985  +$  pint  [p=[p=@ q=@] q=[p=@ q=@]]                 ::  line+column range
3986  +$  rule  _|:($:nail $:edge)                         ::  parsing rule
3987  +$  spot  [p=path q=pint]                            ::  range in file
3988  +$  tone  $%  [%0 product=*]                         ::  success
3989                [%1 block=*]                          ::  single block
3990                [%2 trace=(list [@ta *])]             ::  error report
3991            ==                                        ::
3992  +$  toon  $%  [%0 p=*]                               ::  success
3993                [%1 p=*]                              ::  block
3994                [%2 p=(list tank)]                    ::  stack trace
3995            ==                                        ::
3996  ++  wonk  |*  veq=_$:edge                            ::  product from edge
3997            ?~(q.veq !! p.u.q.veq)                     ::
3998  --  =>                                              ::
3999  ::
4000  ~%    %qua
```

```
4001        +
4002      ==
4003      %mure   mure
4004      %mute   mute
4005      %show   show
4006      ==
4007  ::      layer-4
4008  ::
4009  |%
4010  ::
4011  ::      4a: exotic bases
4012  +|  %exotic-bases
4013  ::
4014  ++  po                                              ::  phonetic base
4015    ~/  %po
4016    =+  :-  ^=  sis                                   ::  prefix syllables
4017        'dozmarbinwansamlitsighidfidlissogdirwacsabwissib\
4018        /rigsoldopmodfoglidhopdardorlorhodfolrintogsilmir\
4019        /holpaslacrovlivdalsatlibtabhanticpidtorbolfosdot\
4020        /losdilforpilramtirwintadbicdifrocwidbisdasmidlop\
4021        /rilnardapmolsanlocnovsitnidtipsicropwitnatpanmin\
4022        /ritpodmottamtolsavposnapnopsomfinfonbanmorworsip\
4023        /ronnorbotwicsocwatdolmagpicdavbidbaltimtasmallig\
4024        /sivtagpadsaldivdactansidfabtarmonranniswolmispal\
4025        /lasdismaprabtobrollatlonnodnavfignomnibpagsopral\
4026        /bilhaddocridmocpacravripfaltodtiltinhapmicfanpat\
4027        /taclabmogsimsonpinlomrictapfirhasbosbatpochactid\
4028        /havsaplindibhosdabbitbarracparloddosbortochilmac\
4029        /tomdigfilfasmithobharmighinradmashalraglagfadtop\
4030        /mophabnilnosmilfopfamdatnoldinhatnacrisfotribhoc\
4031        /nimlarfitwalrapsarnalmoslandondanladdovrivbacpol\
4032        /laptalpitnambonrostonfodponsovnocsorlavmatmipfip'
4033        ^=  dex                                       ::  suffix syllables
4034        'zodnecbudwessevpersutletfulpensytdurwepserwylsun\
4035        /rypsyxdyrnuphebpeglupdepdysputlughecryttyvsydnex\
4036        /lunmeplutseppesdelsulpedtemledtulmetwenbynhexfeb\
4037        /pyldulhetmevruttylwydtepbesdexsefwycburderneppur\
4038        /rysrebdennutsubpetrulsynregtydsupsemwynrecmegnet\
4039        /secmulnymtevwebsummutnyxrextebfushepbenmuswyxsym\
4040        /selrucdecwexsyrwetdylmynmesdetbetbeltuxtugmyrpel\
4041        /syptermebsetdutdegtexsurfeltudnuxruxrenwytnubmed\
4042        /lytdusnebrumtynseglyxpunresredfunrevrefmectedrus\
4043        /bexlebduxrynnumpyxrygryxfeptyrtustyclegnemfermer\
4044        /tenlusnussyltecmexpubrymtucfyllepdebbermughuttun\
4045        /bylsudpemdevlurdefbusbeprunmelpexdytbyttyplevmyl\
4046        /wedducfurfexnulluclennerlexrupnedlecrydlydfenwel\
4047        /nydhusrelrudneshesfetdesretdunlernyrsebhulryllud\
4048        /remlysfynwerrycsugnysnyllyndyndemluxfedsedbecmun\
4049        /lyrtesmudnytbyrsenwegfyrmurtelreptegpecnelnevfes'
4050    |%
4051  ++  ins  ~/  %ins                                   ::  parse prefix
4052           |=  a=@tas
4053           =+  b=0
4054           |-  ^-  (unit @)
4055           ?:(=(256 b) ~ ?:(=(a (tos b)) [~ b] $(b +(b))))
4056  ++  ind  ~/  %ind                                   ::  parse suffix
4057           |=  a=@tas
4058           =+  b=0
```

```
4059          |-  ^-  (unit @)
4060          ?:(=(256 b) ~ ?:(=(a (tod b)) [~ b] $(b +(b))))
4061  ++  tos  ~/  %tos                                    :: fetch prefix
4062          |=(a=@ ?>((lth a 256) (cut 3 [(mul 3 a) 3] sis)))
4063  ++  tod  ~/  %tod                                    :: fetch suffix
4064          |=(a=@ ?>((lth a 256) (cut 3 [(mul 3 a) 3] dex)))
4065  --
4066  ::
4067  ++  fa                                               :: base58check
4068    =+  key='123456789ABCDEFGHJKLMNPQRSTUVWXYZabcdefghijkmnopqrstuvwxyz'
4069    =/  yek=@ux  ~+
4070      =-  yek:(roll (rip 3 key) -)
4071      =+  [a=*char b=*@ yek=`@ux`(fil 3 256 0xff)]
4072      |.
4073      [+(b) (mix yek (lsh [3 `@u`a] (~(inv fe 3) b)))]
4074    |%
4075    ++  cha  |=(a=char `(unit @uF)`=+(b=(cut 3 [`@`a 1] yek) ?:(=(b 0xff) ~ `b)))
4076    ++  tok
4077      |=  a=@ux  ^-  @ux
4078      =+  b=(pad a)
4079      =-  (~(net fe 5) (end [3 4] (shay 32 -)))
4080      (shay (add b (met 3 a)) (lsh [3 b] (swp 3 a)))
4081    ::
4082    ++  pad  |=(a=@ =+(b=(met 3 a) ?:((gte b 21) 0 (sub 21 b))))
4083    ++  enc  |=(a=@ux `@ux`(mix (lsh [3 4] a) (tok a)))
4084    ++  den
4085      |=  a=@ux  ^-  (unit @ux)
4086      =+  b=(rsh [3 4] a)
4087      ?.  =((tok b) (end [3 4] a))
4088        ~
4089      `b
4090    --
4091  ::    4b: text processing
4092  +|  %text-processing
4093  ::
4094  ++  at                                               :: basic printing
4095    |_  a=@
4096    ++  r
4097      ?:  ?&  (gte (met 3 a) 2)
4098              |-
4099              ?:  =(0 a)
4100                &
4101              =+  vis=(end 3 a)
4102              ?&  ?|(=('-' vis) ?&((gte vis 'a') (lte vis 'z')))
4103                  $(a (rsh 3 a))
4104              ==
4105        rtam
4106      ?:  (lte (met 3 a) 2)
4107        rud
4108      rux
4109    ::
4110    ++  rf    `tape`[?-(a %& '&', %| '|', * !!) ~]
4111    ++  rn    `tape`[?>(=(0 a) '~') ~]
4112    ++  rt    `tape`['\'' (weld (mesc (trip a)) `tape`['\'' ~])]
4113    ++  rta   rt
4114    ++  rtam  `tape`['%' (trip a)]
4115    ++  rub   `tape`['0' 'b' (rum 2 ~ |=(b=@ (add '0' b)))]
```

```
4117    ++  rud    (rum 10 ~ |=(b=@ (add '0' b)))
4118    ++  rum
4119      |=  [b=@ c=tape d=$-(@ @)]
4120      ^-  tape
4121      ?:  =(0 a)
4122        [(d 0) c]
4123      =+  e=0
4124      |-  ^-  tape
4125      ?:  =(0 a)
4126        c
4127      =+  f=&(!=(0 e) =(0 (mod e ?:(=(10 b) 3 4))))
4128      %=  $
4129        a  (div a b)
4130        c  [(d (mod a b)) ?:(f [?:(=(10 b) ',' '-') c] c)]
4131        e  +(e)
4132      ==
4133    ::
4134    ++  rup
4135      =+  b=(met 3 a)
4136      ^-  tape
4137      :-  '-'
4138      |-  ^-  tape
4139      ?:  (gth (met 5 a) 1)
4140        %+  weld
4141          $(a (rsh 5 a), b (sub b 4))
4142        `tape`['-' '-' $(a (end 5 a), b 4)]
4143      ?:  =(0 b)
4144        ['~' ~]
4145      ?:  (lte b 1)
4146        (trip (tos:po a))
4147      |-  ^-  tape
4148      ?:  =(2 b)
4149        =+  c=(rsh 3 a)
4150        =+  d=(end 3 a)
4151        (weld (trip (tod:po c)) (trip (tos:po (mix c d))))
4152      =+  c=(rsh [3 2] a)
4153      =+  d=(end [3 2] a)
4154      (weld ^$(a c, b (met 3 c)) `tape`['-' $(a (mix c d), b 2)])
4155    ::
4156    ++  ruv
4157      ^-  tape
4158      :+  '0'
4159        'v'
4160      %^    rum
4161          64
4162        ~
4163      |=  b=@
4164      ?:  =(63 b)
4165        '+'
4166      ?:  =(62 b)
4167        '-'
4168      ?:((lth b 26) (add 65 b) ?:((lth b 52) (add 71 b) (sub b 4)))
4169    ::
4170    ++  rux  `tape`['0' 'x' (rum 16 ~ |=(b=@ (add b ?:((lth b 10) 48 87))))]
4171    --
4172  ++  cass                                          ::  lowercase
4173    |=  vib=tape
4174    ^-  tape
```

```
4175    (turn vib |=(a=@ ?.(&((gte a 'A') (lte a 'Z')) a (add 32 a))))
4176  ::
4177  ++  cuss                                         ::  uppercase
4178    |=  vib=tape
4179    ^-  tape
4180    (turn vib |=(a=@ ?.(&((gte a 'a') (lte a 'z')) a (sub a 32))))
4181  ::
4182  ++  crip  |=(a=tape `@t`(rap 3 a))               ::  tape to cord
4183  ::
4184  ++  mesc                                         ::  ctrl code escape
4185    |=  vib=tape
4186    ^-  tape
4187    ?~  vib
4188      ~
4189    ?:  =('\\' i.vib)
4190      ['\\' '\\' $(vib t.vib)]
4191    ?:  ?|((gth i.vib 126) (lth i.vib 32) =(`@`39 i.vib))
4192      ['\\' (welp ~(rux at i.vib) '/' $(vib t.vib))]
4193    [i.vib $(vib t.vib)]
4194  ::
4195  ++  runt                                         ::  prepend repeatedly
4196    |=  [[a=@ b=@] c=tape]
4197    ^-  tape
4198    ?:  =(0 a)
4199      c
4200    [b $(a (dec a))]
4201  ::
4202  ++  sand                                         ::  atom sanity
4203    |=  a=@ta
4204    (flit (sane a))
4205  ::
4206  ++  sane                                         ::  atom sanity
4207    |=  a=@ta
4208    |=  b=@  ^-  ?
4209    ?.  =(%t (end 3 a))
4210      ::  XX more and better sanity
4211      ::
4212      &
4213    =+  [inx=0 len=(met 3 b)]
4214    ?:  =(%tas a)
4215      |-  ^-  ?
4216      ?:  =(inx len)  &
4217      =+  cur=(cut 3 [inx 1] b)
4218      ?&  ?|  &((gte cur 'a') (lte cur 'z'))
4219              &(=('-' cur) !=(0 inx) !=(len inx))
4220              &(&((gte cur '0') (lte cur '9')) !=(0 inx))
4221          ==
4222          $(inx +(inx))
4223      ==
4224    ?:  =(%ta a)
4225      |-  ^-  ?
4226      ?:  =(inx len)  &
4227      =+  cur=(cut 3 [inx 1] b)
4228      ?&  ?|  &((gte cur 'a') (lte cur 'z'))
4229              &((gte cur '0') (lte cur '9'))
4230              |(=('-' cur) =('~' cur) =('_' cur) =('.' cur))
4231          ==
4232          $(inx +(inx))
```

```
4233        ==
4234    |-  ^-  ?
4235    ?:  =(inx len)  &
4236    =+  cur=(cut 3 [inx 1] b)
4237    ?:  &((lth cur 32) !=(10 cur))  |
4238    =+  tef=(teff cur)
4239    ?&  ?|  =(1 tef)
4240            =+  i=1
4241            |-  ^-  ?
4242            ?|  =(i tef)
4243                ?&  (gte (cut 3 [(add i inx) 1] b) 128)
4244                    $(i +(i))
4245        ==  ==  ==
4246        $(inx (add inx tef))
4247    ==
4248  ::
4249  ++  ruth                                 ::  biblical sanity
4250    |=  [a=@ta b=*]
4251    ^-  @
4252    ?^  b  !!
4253    ::  ?.  ((sane a) b)  !!
4254    b
4255  ::
4256  ++  trim                                 ::  tape split
4257    |=  [a=@ b=tape]
4258    ^-  [p=tape q=tape]
4259    ?~  b
4260      [~ ~]
4261    ?:  =(0 a)
4262      [~ b]
4263    =+  c=$(a (dec a), b t.b)
4264    [[i.b p.c] q.c]
4265  ::
4266  ++  trip                                 ::  cord to tape
4267    ~/  %trip
4268    |=  a=@  ^-  tape
4269    ?:  =(0 (met 3 a))
4270      ~
4271    [^-(@ta (end 3 a)) $(a (rsh 3 a))]
4272  ::
4273  ++  teff                                 ::  length utf8
4274    |=  a=@t  ^-  @
4275    =+  b=(end 3 a)
4276    ?:  =(0 b)
4277      ?>(=(`@`0 a) 0)
4278    ?>  |((gte b 32) =(10 b))
4279    ?:((lte b 127) 1 ?:((lte b 223) 2 ?:((lte b 239) 3 4)))
4280  ::
4281  ++  taft                                 ::  utf8 to utf32
4282    |=  a=@t
4283    ^-  @c
4284    %+  rap  5
4285    |-  ^-  (list @c)
4286    =+  b=(teff a)
4287    ?:  =(0 b)  ~
4288    =+  ^=  c
4289        %+  can  0
4290        %+  turn
```

```
4291        ^-  (list [p=@ q=@])
4292        ?+  b  !!
4293          %1  [[0 7] ~]
4294          %2  [[8 6] [0 5] ~]
4295          %3  [[16 6] [8 6] [0 4] ~]
4296          %4  [[24 6] [16 6] [8 6] [0 3] ~]
4297          ==
4298        |=([p=@ q=@] [q (cut 0 [p q] a)])
4299      ?>  =((tuft c) (end [3 b] a))
4300      [c $(a (rsh [3 b] a))]
4301  ::
4302  ++  tuba                                      ::  utf8 to utf32 tape
4303    |=  a=tape
4304    ^-  (list @c)
4305    (rip 5 (taft (rap 3 a)))                     ::  XX horrible
4306  ::
4307  ++  tufa                                      ::  utf32 to utf8 tape
4308    |=  a=(list @c)
4309    ^-  tape
4310    ?~  a  ""
4311    (weld (rip 3 (tuft i.a)) $(a t.a))
4312  ::
4313  ++  tuft                                      ::  utf32 to utf8 text
4314    |=  a=@c
4315    ^-  @t
4316    %+  rap  3
4317    |-  ^-  (list @)
4318    ?:  =(`@`0 a)
4319      ~
4320    =+  b=(end 5 a)
4321    =+  c=$(a (rsh 5 a))
4322    ?:  (lte b 0x7f)
4323      [b c]
4324    ?:  (lte b 0x7ff)
4325      :*  (mix 0b1100.0000 (cut 0 [6 5] b))
4326          (mix 0b1000.0000 (end [0 6] b))
4327          c
4328      ==
4329    ?:  (lte b 0xffff)
4330      :*  (mix 0b1110.0000 (cut 0 [12 4] b))
4331          (mix 0b1000.0000 (cut 0 [6 6] b))
4332          (mix 0b1000.0000 (end [0 6] b))
4333          c
4334      ==
4335    :*  (mix 0b1111.0000 (cut 0 [18 3] b))
4336        (mix 0b1000.0000 (cut 0 [12 6] b))
4337        (mix 0b1000.0000 (cut 0 [6 6] b))
4338        (mix 0b1000.0000 (end [0 6] b))
4339        c
4340    ==
4341  ::
4342  ++  wack                                      ::  knot escape
4343    |=  a=@ta
4344    ^-  @ta
4345    =+  b=(rip 3 a)
4346    %+  rap  3
4347    |-  ^-  tape
4348    ?~  b
```

```
4349          ~
4350    ?:  =('~' i.b)  ['~' '~' $(b t.b)]
4351    ?:  =('_' i.b)  ['~' '-' $(b t.b)]
4352    [i.b $(b t.b)]
4353  ::
4354  ++  wick                                        ::  knot unescape
4355    |=  a=@
4356    ^-  (unit @ta)
4357    =+  b=(rip 3 a)
4358    =-  ?^(b ~ (some (rap 3 (flop c))))
4359    =|  c=tape
4360    |-  ^-  [b=tape c=tape]
4361    ?~  b  [~ c]
4362    ?.  =('~' i.b)
4363      $(b t.b, c [i.b c])
4364    ?~  t.b  [b ~]
4365    ?-  i.t.b
4366      %'~'  $(b t.t.b, c ['~' c])
4367      %'-'  $(b t.t.b, c ['_' c])
4368      @     [b ~]
4369    ==
4370  ::
4371  ++  woad                                        ::  cord unescape
4372    |=  a=@ta
4373    ^-  @t
4374    %+  rap  3
4375    |-  ^-  (list @)
4376    ?:  =(`@`0 a)
4377      ~
4378    =+  b=(end 3 a)
4379    =+  c=(rsh 3 a)
4380    ?:  =('.' b)
4381      [' ' $(a c)]
4382    ?.  =('~' b)
4383      [b $(a c)]
4384    =>  .(b (end 3 c), c (rsh 3 c))
4385    ?+  b  =-  (weld (rip 3 (tuft p.d)) $(a q.d))
4386            ^=  d
4387            =+  d=0
4388            |-  ^-  [p=@ q=@]
4389            ?:  =('.' b)
4390              [d c]
4391            ?<  =(0 c)
4392            %=    $
4393              b  (end 3 c)
4394              c  (rsh 3 c)
4395              d  %+  add  (mul 16 d)
4396                 %+  sub  b
4397                 ?:  &((gte b '0') (lte b '9'))  48
4398                 ?>(&((gte b 'a') (lte b 'z')) 87)
4399            ==
4400      %'.'  ['.' $(a c)]
4401      %'~'  ['~' $(a c)]
4402    ==
4403  ::
4404  ++  wood                                        ::  cord escape
4405    |=  a=@t
4406    ^-  @ta
```

```
4407    %+  rap  3
4408    |-  ^-  (list @)
4409    ?:  =(`@`0 a)
4410      ~
4411    =+  b=(teff a)
4412    =+  c=(taft (end [3 b] a))
4413    =+  d=$(a (rsh [3 b] a))
4414    ?:  ?|  &((gte c 'a') (lte c 'z'))
4415            &((gte c '0') (lte c '9'))
4416            =(`@`'-' c)
4417        ==
4418    [c d]
4419    ?+  c
4420      :-  '~'
4421      =+  e=(met 2 c)
4422      |-  ^-  tape
4423      ?:  =(0 e)
4424        ['.' d]
4425      =.  e  (dec e)
4426      =+  f=(rsh [2 e] c)
4427      [(add ?:((lte f 9) 48 87) f) $(c (end [2 e] c))]
4428      ::
4429      %' '  ['.' d]
4430      %'.'  ['~' '.' d]
4431      %'~'  ['~' '~' d]
4432    ==
4433    ::
4434    ::  4c: tank printer
4435    +|  %tank-printer
4436    ::
4437    ++  wash                                        ::  render tank at width
4438    |=  [[tab=@ edg=@] tac=tank]  ^-  wall
4439    (~(win re tac) tab edg)
4440    ::
4441    ::  +re: tank renderer
4442    ::
4443    ++  re
4444    |_  tac=tank
4445    ::  +ram: render a tank to one line (flat)
4446    ::
4447    ++  ram
4448      ^-  tape
4449      ?@  tac
4450        (trip tac)
4451      ?-    -.tac
4452          %leaf  p.tac
4453      ::
4454      ::  flat %palm rendered as %rose with welded openers
4455      ::
4456          %palm
4457        =*  mid  p.p.tac
4458        =*  for  (weld q.p.tac r.p.tac)
4459        =*  end  s.p.tac
4460      ram(tac [%rose [mid for end] q.tac])
4461      ::
4462      ::  flat %rose rendered with open/mid/close
4463      ::
4464          %rose
```

```
4465        =*  mid  p.p.tac
4466        =*  for  q.p.tac
4467        =*  end  r.p.tac
4468        =*  lit  q.tac
4469        %+  weld
4470          for
4471        |-  ^-  tape
4472        ?~  lit
4473          end
4474        %+  weld
4475          ram(tac i.lit)
4476        =*  voz  $(lit t.lit)
4477        ?~(t.lit voz (weld mid voz))
4478      ==
4479    ::  +win: render a tank to multiple lines (tall)
4480    ::
4481    ::      indented by .tab, soft-wrapped at .edg
4482    ::
4483    ++  win
4484      |=  [tab=@ud edg=@ud]
4485      ::  output stack
4486      ::
4487      =|  lug=wall
4488      |^  ^-  wall
4489        ?@  tac
4490          (rig (trip tac))
4491        ?-    -.tac
4492            %leaf  (rig p.tac)
4493          ::
4494            %palm
4495          =/  hom  ram
4496          ?:  (lte (lent hom) (sub edg tab))
4497            (rig hom)
4498          ::
4499          =*  for  q.p.tac
4500          =*  lit  q.tac
4501          ?~  lit
4502            (rig for)
4503          ?~  t.lit
4504            =:  tab  (add 2 tab)
4505                lug  $(tac i.lit)
4506              ==
4507            (rig for)
4508          ::
4509          =>  .(lit `(list tank)`lit)
4510          =/  lyn  (mul 2 (lent lit))
4511          =.  lug
4512            |-  ^-  wall
4513            ?~  lit
4514              lug
4515            =/  nyl  (sub lyn 2)
4516            %=  ^$
4517              tac  i.lit
4518              tab  (add tab nyl)
4519              lug  $(lit t.lit, lyn nyl)
4520            ==
4521          (wig for)
4522        ::
```

```
4523            %rose
4524            =/  hom  ram
4525            ?:  (lte (lent hom) (sub edg tab))
4526              (rig hom)
4527            ::
4528            =*  for  q.p.tac
4529            =*  end  r.p.tac
4530            =*  lit  q.tac
4531            =.  lug
4532              |-  ^-  wall
4533            ?~  lit
4534              ?~(end lug (rig end))
4535            %=  ^$
4536              tac  i.lit
4537              tab  (mod (add 2 tab) (mul 2 (div edg 3)))
4538              lug  $(lit t.lit)
4539            ==
4540          ?~(for lug (wig for))
4541        ==
4542      ::  +rig: indent tape and cons with output stack
4543      ::
4544      ++  rig
4545        |=  hom=tape
4546        ^-  wall
4547        [(runt [tab ' '] hom) lug]
4548      ::  +wig: indent tape and cons with output stack
4549      ::
4550      ::      joined with the top line if whitespace/indentation allow
4551      ::
4552      ++  wig
4553        |=  hom=tape
4554        ^-  wall
4555        ?~  lug
4556          (rig hom)
4557        =/  wug  :(add 1 tab (lent hom))
4558        ?.  =+  mir=i.lug
4559            |-  ^-  ?
4560            ?~  mir  |
4561            ?|  =(0 wug)
4562                ?&(=(' ' i.mir) $(mir t.mir, wug (dec wug)))
4563            ==
4564          (rig hom)        :: ^ XX regular form?
4565        :_  t.lug
4566        %+  runt  [tab ' ']
4567        (weld hom `tape`['  ' (slag wug i.lug)])
4568      --
4569
4570  ++  show                                    ::  XX deprecated!
4571    |=  vem=*
4572    |^  ^-  tank
4573    ?:  ?=(@ vem)
4574      [%leaf (mesc (trip vem))]
4575    ?-    vem
4576      [s=~  c=*]
4577      [%leaf '\'' (weld (mesc (tape +.vem)) `tape`['\'' ~])]
4578    ::
4579      [s=%a c=@]        [%leaf (mesc (trip c.vem))]
4580      [s=%b c=*]        (shop c.vem |=(a=@ ~(rub at a)))
```

```
            [s=[%c p=@] c=*]
      :+  %palm
        [['.' ~] ['-' ~] ~ ~]
      [[%leaf (mesc (trip p.s.vem))] $(vem c.vem) ~]
    ::
        [s=%d c=*]          (shop c.vem |=(a=@ ~(rud at a)))
        [s=%k c=*]          (tank c.vem)
        [s=%h c=*]
      :+  %rose
        [['/' ~] ['/' ~] ~]
      =+  yol=((list @ta) c.vem)
      (turn yol |=(a=@ta [%leaf (trip a)])))
    ::
        [s=%l c=*]          (shol c.vem)
        [s=%o c=*]
      %=    $
          vem
        :-  [%m '%h::[%d %d].[%d %d]>']
        [-.c.vem +<-.c.vem +<+.c.vem +>-.c.vem +>+.c.vem ~]
      ==
    ::
        [s=%p c=*]          (shop c.vem |=(a=@ ~(rup at a)))
        [s=%q c=*]          (shop c.vem |=(a=@ ~(r at a)))
        [s=%r c=*]          $(vem [[%r ' ' '{' '}'] c.vem])
        [s=%t c=*]          (shop c.vem |=(a=@ ~(rt at a)))
        [s=%v c=*]          (shop c.vem |=(a=@ ~(ruv at a)))
        [s=%x c=*]          (shop c.vem |=(a=@ ~(rux at a)))
        [s=[%m p=@] c=*]    (shep p.s.vem c.vem)
        [s=[%r p=@] c=*]
      $(vem [[%r ' ' (cut 3 [0 1] p.s.vem) (cut 3 [1 1] p.s.vem)] c.vem])
    ::
        [s=[%r p=@ q=@ r=@] c=*]
      :+  %rose
        :*  p=(mesc (trip p.s.vem))
            q=(mesc (trip q.s.vem))
            r=(mesc (trip r.s.vem))
        ==
      |-  ^-  (list tank)
      ?@  c.vem
        ~
      [^$(vem -.c.vem) $(c.vem +.c.vem)]
    ::
        [s=%z c=*]          $(vem [[%r %$ %$ %$] c.vem])
        *                   !!
      ==
++  shep
  |=  [fom=@ gar=*]
  ^-  tank
  =+  l=(met 3 fom)
  =+  i=0
  :-  %leaf
  |-  ^-  tape
  ?:  (gte i l)
    ~
  =+  c=(cut 3 [i 1] fom)
  ?.  =(37 c)
    (weld (mesc [c ~]) $(i +(i)))
  =+  d=(cut 3 [+(i) 1] fom)
```

```
4639      ?.   .?(gar)
4640       ['\\' '#' $(i (add 2 i))]
4641      (weld ~(ram re (show d -.gar)) $(i (add 2 i), gar +.gar))
4642    ::
4643    ++  shop
4644      |=  [aug=* vel=$-(a=@ tape)]
4645      ^-  tank
4646      ?:  ?=(@ aug)
4647        [%leaf (vel aug)]
4648      :+  %rose
4649        [[' ' ~] ['[' ~] [']' ~]]
4650      =>  .(aug `*`aug)
4651      |-  ^-  (list tank)
4652      ?:  ?=(@ aug)
4653        [^$ ~]
4654      [^$(aug -.aug) $(aug +.aug)]
4655    ::
4656    ++  shol
4657      |=  lim=*
4658      :+  %rose
4659        [['.' ~] ~ ~]
4660      |-    ^-  (list tank)
4661      ?:  ?=(@ lim)  ~
4662      :_  $(lim +.lim)
4663      ?+  -.lim  (show '#')
4664        ~   (show '$')
4665        c=@  (show c.lim)
4666        [%& %1]  (show '.')
4667        [%& c=@]
4668      [%leaf '+' ~(rud at c.lim)]
4669      ::
4670        [%| @ ~]  (show ',')
4671        [%| n=@ ~ c=@]
4672      [%leaf (weld (reap n.lim '^') ?~(c.lim "$" (trip c.lim)))]
4673      ==
4674    --
4675  ::
4676  ::    4d: parsing (tracing)
4677  +|  %parsing-tracing
4678  ::
4679  ++  last  |=  [zyc=hair naz=hair]                ::  farther trace
4680           ^-  hair
4681           ?:  =(p.zyc p.naz)
4682             ?:((gth q.zyc q.naz) zyc naz)
4683           ?:((gth p.zyc p.naz) zyc naz)
4684  ::
4685  ++  lust  |=  [weq=char naz=hair]                ::  detect newline
4686           ^-  hair
4687           ?:(=(`@`10 weq) [+(p.naz) 1] [p.naz +(q.naz)])
4688  ::
4689  ::    4e: parsing (combinators)
4690  +|  %parsing-combinators
4691  ::
4692  ++  bend                                         ::  conditional comp
4693    ~/  %bend
4694    |*  raq=_|*([a=* b=*] [~ u=[a b]])
4695    ~/  %fun
4696    |*  [vex=edge sab=rule]
```

```
4697      ?~  q.vex
4698        vex
4699      =+  yit=(sab q.u.q.vex)
4700      =+  yur=(last p.vex p.yit)
4701      ?~  q.yit
4702        [p=yur q=q.vex]
4703      =+  vux=(raq p.u.q.vex p.u.q.yit)
4704      ?~  vux
4705        [p=yur q=q.vex]
4706      [p=yur q=[~ u=[p=u.vux q=q.u.q.yit]]]
4707    ::
4708    ++  comp
4709      ~/  %comp
4710      |*  raq=_|*([a=* b=*] [a b])                    ::  arbitrary compose
4711      ~/  %fun
4712      |*  [vex=edge sab=rule]
4713      ~!  +<
4714      ?~  q.vex
4715        vex
4716      =+  yit=(sab q.u.q.vex)
4717      =+  yur=(last p.vex p.yit)
4718      ?~  q.yit
4719        [p=yur q=q.yit]
4720      [p=yur q=[~ u=[p=(raq p.u.q.vex p.u.q.yit) q=q.u.q.yit]]]
4721    ::
4722    ++  fail  |=(tub=nail [p=p.tub q=~])              ::  never parse
4723    ++  glue                                          ::  add rule
4724      ~/  %glue
4725      |*  bus=rule
4726      ~/  %fun
4727      |*  [vex=edge sab=rule]
4728      (plug vex ;~(pfix bus sab))
4729    ::
4730    ++  less                                          ::  no first and second
4731      |*  [vex=edge sab=rule]
4732      ?~  q.vex
4733        =+  roq=(sab)
4734        [p=(last p.vex p.roq) q=q.roq]
4735      (fail +<.sab)
4736    ::
4737    ++  pfix                                          ::  discard first rule
4738      ~/  %pfix
4739      |*  sam=[vex=edge sab=rule]
4740      %.  sam
4741      (comp |*([a=* b=*] b))
4742    ::
4743    ++  plug                                          ::  first then second
4744      ~/  %plug
4745      |*  [vex=edge sab=rule]
4746      ?~  q.vex
4747        vex
4748      =+  yit=(sab q.u.q.vex)
4749      =+  yur=(last p.vex p.yit)
4750      ?~  q.yit
4751        [p=yur q=q.yit]
4752      [p=yur q=[~ u=[p=[p.u.q.vex p.u.q.yit] q=q.u.q.yit]]]
4753    ::
4754    ++  pose                                          ::  first or second
```

```
4755    ~/  %pose
4756    |*  [vex=edge sab=rule]
4757    ?~  q.vex
4758      =+  roq=(sab)
4759      [p=(last p.vex p.roq) q=q.roq]
4760    vex
4761    ::
4762    ++  simu                                    ::  first and second
4763    |*  [vex=edge sab=rule]
4764    ?~  q.vex
4765      vex
4766    =+  roq=(sab)
4767    roq
4768    ::
4769    ++  sfix                                     ::  discard second rule
4770    ~/  %sfix
4771    |*  sam=[vex=edge sab=rule]
4772    %.  sam
4773    (comp |*([a=* b=*] a))
4774    ::
4775    ::    4f: parsing (rule builders)
4776    +|  %parsing-rule-builders
4777    ::
4778    ++  bass                                     ::  leftmost base
4779    |*  [wuc=@ tyd=rule]
4780    %+  cook
4781      |=  waq=(list @)
4782      %+  roll
4783        waq
4784      =|([p=@ q=@] |.((add p (mul wuc q))))
4785    tyd
4786    ::
4787    ++  boss                                     ::  rightmost base
4788    |*  [wuc=@ tyd=rule]
4789    %+  cook
4790      |=  waq=(list @)
4791      %+  reel
4792        waq
4793      =|([p=@ q=@] |.((add p (mul wuc q))))
4794    tyd
4795    ::
4796    ++  cold                                     ::  replace w+ constant
4797    ~/  %cold
4798    |*  [cus=* sef=rule]
4799    ~/  %fun
4800    |=  tub=nail
4801    =+  vex=(sef tub)
4802    ?~  q.vex
4803      vex
4804    [p=p.vex q=[~ u=[p=cus q=q.u.q.vex]]]
4805    ::
4806    ++  cook                                     ::  apply gate
4807    ~/  %cook
4808    |*  [poq=gate sef=rule]
4809    ~/  %fun
4810    |=  tub=nail
4811    =+  vex=(sef tub)
4812    ?~  q.vex
```

```
4813        vex
4814      [p=p.vex q=[~ u=[p=(poq p.u.q.vex) q=q.u.q.vex]]]
4815    ::
4816    ++  easy                                              ::  always parse
4817      ~/  %easy
4818      |*  huf=*
4819      ~/  %fun
4820      |=  tub=nail
4821      ^-  (like _huf)
4822      [p=p.tub q=[~ u=[p=huf q=tub]]]
4823    ::
4824    ++  fuss
4825      |=  [sic=@t non=@t]
4826      ;~(pose (cold %& (jest sic)) (cold %| (jest non)))
4827    ::
4828    ++  full                                              ::  has to fully parse
4829      |*  sef=rule
4830      |=  tub=nail
4831      =+  vex=(sef tub)
4832      ?~(q.vex vex ?:(=(~ q.q.u.q.vex) vex [p=p.vex q=~]))
4833    ::
4834    ++  funk                                              ::  add to tape first
4835      |*  [pre=tape sef=rule]
4836      |=  tub=nail
4837      (sef p.tub (weld pre q.tub))
4838    ::
4839    ++  here                                              ::  place-based apply
4840      ~/  %here
4841      |*  [hez=_|=([a=pint b=*] [a b]) sef=rule]
4842      ~/  %fun
4843      |=  tub=nail
4844      =+  vex=(sef tub)
4845      ?~  q.vex
4846        vex
4847      [p=p.vex q=[~ u=[p=(hez [p.tub p.q.u.q.vex] p.u.q.vex) q=q.u.q.vex]]]
4848    ::
4849    ++  inde  |*  sef=rule                                ::  indentation block
4850      |=  nail  ^+  (sef)
4851      =+  [har tap]=[p q]:+<
4852      =+  lev=(fil 3 (dec q.har) ' ')
4853      =+  eol=(just `@t`10)
4854      =+  =-  roq=((star ;~(pose prn ;~(sfix eol (jest lev)) -)) har tap)
4855          ;~(simu ;~(plug eol eol) eol)
4856      ?~  q.roq  roq
4857      =+  vex=(sef har(q 1) p.u.q.roq)
4858      =+  fur=p.vex(q (add (dec q.har) q.p.vex))
4859      ?~  q.vex  vex(p fur)
4860      =-  vex(p fur, u.q -)
4861      :+  &3.vex
4862        &4.vex(q.p (add (dec q.har) q.p.&4.vex))
4863      =+  res=|4.vex
4864      |-  ?~  res  |4.roq
4865      ?.  =(10 -.res)  [-.res $(res +.res)]
4866      (welp [`@t`10 (trip lev)] $(res +.res))
4867    ::
4868    ++  ifix
4869      |*  [fel=[rule rule] hof=rule]
4870      ~!  +<
```

```
4871    ~!  +<:-.fel
4872    ~!  +<:+.fel
4873    ;~(pfix -.fel ;~(sfix hof +.fel))
4874  ::
4875  ++  jest                                        ::  match a cord
4876    |=  daf=@t
4877    |=  tub=nail
4878    =+  fad=daf
4879    |-  ^-  (like @t)
4880    ?:  =(`@`0 daf)
4881      [p=p.tub q=[~ u=[p=fad q=tub]]]
4882    ?:  |(?=(~ q.tub) !=((end 3 daf) i.q.tub))
4883      (fail tub)
4884    $(p.tub (lust i.q.tub p.tub), q.tub t.q.tub, daf (rsh 3 daf))
4885  ::
4886  ++  just                                        ::  XX redundant, jest
4887    ~/  %just                                      ::  match a char
4888    |=  daf=char
4889    ~/  %fun
4890    |=  tub=nail
4891    ^-  (like char)
4892    ?~  q.tub
4893      (fail tub)
4894    ?.  =(daf i.q.tub)
4895      (fail tub)
4896    (next tub)
4897  ::
4898  ++  knee                                         ::  callbacks
4899    |*  [gar=* sef=_|.(*rule)]
4900    |=  tub=nail
4901    ^-  (like _gar)
4902    ((sef) tub)
4903  ::
4904  ++  mask                                         ::  match char in set
4905    ~/  %mask
4906    |=  bud=(list char)
4907    ~/  %fun
4908    |=  tub=nail
4909    ^-  (like char)
4910    ?~  q.tub
4911      (fail tub)
4912    ?.  (lien bud |=(a=char =(i.q.tub a)))
4913      (fail tub)
4914    (next tub)
4915  ::
4916  ++  more                                         ::  separated, *
4917    |*  [bus=rule fel=rule]
4918    ;~(pose (most bus fel) (easy ~))
4919  ::
4920  ++  most                                         ::  separated, +
4921    |*  [bus=rule fel=rule]
4922    ;~(plug fel (star ;~(pfix bus fel)))
4923  ::
4924  ++  next                                         ::  consume a char
4925    |=  tub=nail
4926    ^-  (like char)
4927    ?~  q.tub
4928      (fail tub)
```

```
4929    =+  zac=(lust i.q.tub p.tub)
4930    [zac [~ i.q.tub [zac t.q.tub]]]
4931  ::
4932  ++  perk                                    ::  parse cube fork
4933    |*  a=(pole @tas)
4934    ?~  a  fail
4935    ;~  pose
4936    (cold -.a (jest -.a))
4937    $(a +.a)
4938    ==
4939  ::
4940  ++  pick                                    ::  rule for ++each
4941    |*  [a=rule b=rule]
4942    ;~  pose
4943    (stag %& a)
4944    (stag %| b)
4945    ==
4946  ++  plus  |*(fel=rule ;~(plug fel (star fel)))    ::
4947  ++  punt  |*([a=rule] ;~(pose (stag ~ a) (easy ~)))    ::
4948  ++  sear                                    ::  conditional cook
4949    |*  [pyq=$-(* (unit)) sef=rule]
4950    |=  tub=nail
4951    =+  vex=(sef tub)
4952    ?~  q.vex
4953    vex
4954    =+  gey=(pyq p.u.q.vex)
4955    ?~  gey
4956    [p=p.vex q=~]
4957    [p=p.vex q=[~ u=[p=u.gey q=q.u.q.vex]]]
4958  ::
4959  ++  shim                                    ::  match char in range
4960    ~/  %shim
4961    |=  [les=@ mos=@]
4962    ~/  %fun
4963    |=  tub=nail
4964    ^-  (like char)
4965    ?~  q.tub
4966    (fail tub)
4967    ?.  ?&((gte i.q.tub les) (lte i.q.tub mos))
4968    (fail tub)
4969    (next tub)
4970  ::
4971  ++  stag                                    ::  add a label
4972    ~/  %stag
4973    |*  [gob=* sef=rule]
4974    ~/  %fun
4975    |=  tub=nail
4976    =+  vex=(sef tub)
4977    ?~  q.vex
4978    vex
4979    [p=p.vex q=[~ u=[p=[gob p.u.q.vex] q=q.u.q.vex]]]
4980  ::
4981  ++  stet                                    ::
4982    |*  leh=(list [?(@ [@ @]) rule])
4983    |-
4984    ?~  leh
4985    ~
4986    [i=[p=-.i.leh q=+.i.leh] t=$(leh t.leh)]
```

```
4987  ::
4988  ++    stew                                               ::  switch by first char
4989    ~/  %stew
4990    |*  leh=(list [p=?(@ [@ @]) q=rule])                   ::  char+range keys
4991    =+  ^=  wor                                            ::  range complete lth
4992        |=  [ort=?(@ [@ @]) wan=?(@ [@ @])]
4993        ?@  ort
4994          ?@(wan (lth ort wan) (lth ort -.wan))
4995        ?@(wan (lth +.ort wan) (lth +.ort -.wan))
4996    =+  ^=  hel                                            ::  build parser map
4997        =+  hel=`(tree _?>(?=(^ leh) i.leh))`~
4998        |-  ^+  hel
4999        ?~  leh
5000          ~
5001        =+  yal=$(leh t.leh)
5002        |-  ^+  hel
5003        ?~  yal
5004          [i.leh ~ ~]
5005        ?:  (wor p.i.leh p.n.yal)
5006          =+  nuc=$(yal l.yal)
5007          ?>  ?=(^ nuc)
5008          ?:  (mor p.n.yal p.n.nuc)
5009            [n.yal nuc r.yal]
5010          [n.nuc l.nuc [n.yal r.nuc r.yal]]
5011        =+  nuc=$(yal r.yal)
5012        ?>  ?=(^ nuc)
5013        ?:  (mor p.n.yal p.n.nuc)
5014          [n.yal l.yal nuc]
5015        [n.nuc [n.yal l.yal l.nuc] r.nuc]
5016    ~%  %fun  ..^$  ~
5017    |=  tub=nail
5018    ?~  q.tub
5019      (fail tub)
5020    |-
5021    ?~  hel
5022      (fail tub)
5023    ?:  ?@  p.n.hel
5024          =(p.n.hel i.q.tub)
5025        ?&((gte i.q.tub -.p.n.hel) (lte i.q.tub +.p.n.hel))
5026      ::  (q.n.hel [(lust i.q.tub p.tub) t.q.tub])
5027      (q.n.hel tub)
5028    ?:  (wor i.q.tub p.n.hel)
5029      $(hel l.hel)
5030    $(hel r.hel)
5031  ::
5032  ++    slug                                               ::
5033    |*  raq=_=>(~ |*([a=* b=*] [a b]))
5034    |*  [bus=rule fel=rule]
5035    ;~((comp raq) fel (stir +<+.raq raq ;~(pfix bus fel)))
5036  ::
5037  ++    star                                               ::  0 or more times
5038    |*  fel=rule
5039    (stir `(list _(wonk *fel))`~ |*([a=* b=*] [a b]) fel)
5040  ::
5041  ++    stir
5042    ~/  %stir
5043    |*  [rud=* raq=_=>(~ |*([a=* b=*] [a b])) fel=rule]
5044    ~/  %fun
```

```
5045      |=  tub=nail
5046      ^-  (like _rud)
5047      ::
5048      ::  lef: successful interim parse results (per .fel)
5049      ::  wag: initial accumulator (.rud in .tub at farthest success)
5050      ::
5051      =+  ^=  [lef wag]
5052        =|  lef=(list _(fel tub))
5053        |-  ^-  [_lef (pair hair [~ u=(pair _rud nail)])]
5054        =+  vex=(fel tub)
5055        ?~  q.vex
5056          :-  lef
5057          [p.vex [~ rud tub]]
5058        $(lef [vex lef], tub q.u.q.vex)
5059      ::
5060      ::  fold .lef into .wag, combining results with .raq
5061      ::
5062      %+  roll  lef
5063      |=  _[vex=(fel tub) wag=wag]  :: q.vex is always (some)
5064      ^+  wag
5065      :-  (last p.vex p.wag)
5066      [~ (raq p.u.+.q.vex p.u.q.wag) q.u.q.wag]
5067    ::
5068    ++  stun                                       ::  parse several times
5069      ~/  %stun
5070      |*  [lig=[@ @] fel=rule]
5071      |=  tub=nail
5072      ^-  (like (list _(wonk (fel))))
5073      ?:  =(0 +.lig)
5074        [p.tub [~ ~ tub]]
5075      =+  vex=(fel tub)
5076      ?~  q.vex
5077        ?:  =(0 -.lig)
5078          [p.vex [~ ~ tub]]
5079        vex
5080      =+  ^=  wag  %=  $
5081                    -.lig  ?:(=(0 -.lig) 0 (dec -.lig))
5082                    +.lig  ?:(=(0 +.lig) 0 (dec +.lig))
5083                    tub  q.u.q.vex
5084                  ==
5085      ?~  q.wag
5086        wag
5087      [p.wag [~ [p.u.q.vex p.u.q.wag] q.u.q.wag]]
5088    ::
5089    ::    4g: parsing (outside caller)
5090    +|  %parsing-outside-caller
5091    ::
5092    ++  rash  |*([naf=@ sab=rule] (scan (trip naf) sab))
5093    ++  rose  |*  [los=tape sab=rule]
5094              =+  vex=(sab [[1 1] los])
5095              =+  len=(lent los)
5096              ?.  =(+(len) q.p.vex)  [%| p=(dec q.p.vex)]
5097              ?~  q.vex
5098                [%& p=~]
5099              [%& p=[~ u=p.u.q.vex]]
5100    ++  rush  |*([naf=@ sab=rule] (rust (trip naf) sab))
5101    ++  rust  |*  [los=tape sab=rule]
5102              =+  vex=((full sab) [[1 1] los])
```

```
5103            ?~(q.vex ~ [~ u=p.u.q.vex])
5104  ++   scan  |*  [los=tape sab=rule]
5105           =+  vex=((full sab) [[1 1] los])
5106           ?~   q.vex
5107            ~_  (show [%m '{%d %d}'] p.p.vex q.p.vex ~)
5108            ~_(leaf+"syntax error" !!)
5109           p.u.q.vex
5110  ::
5111  ::    4h: parsing (ascii glyphs)
5112  +|  %parsing-ascii-glyphs
5113  ::
5114  ++   ace  (just ' ')                          ::  spACE
5115  ++   bar  (just '|')                          ::  vertical BAR
5116  ++   bas  (just '\\')                         ::  Back Slash (escaped)
5117  ++   buc  (just '$')                          ::  dollars BUCks
5118  ++   cab  (just '_')                          ::  CABoose
5119  ++   cen  (just '%')                          ::  perCENt
5120  ++   col  (just ':')                          ::  COLon
5121  ++   com  (just ',')                          ::  COMma
5122  ++   doq  (just '"')                          ::  Double Quote
5123  ++   dot  (just '.')                          ::  dot dot dot ...
5124  ++   fas  (just '/')                          ::  Forward Slash
5125  ++   gal  (just '<')                          ::  Greater Left
5126  ++   gar  (just '>')                          ::  Greater Right
5127  ++   hax  (just '#')                          ::  Hash
5128  ++   hep  (just '-')                          ::  HyPhen
5129  ++   kel  (just '{')                          ::  Curly Left
5130  ++   ker  (just '}')                          ::  Curly Right
5131  ++   ket  (just '^')                          ::  CareT
5132  ++   lus  (just '+')                          ::  pLUS
5133  ++   mic  (just ';')                          ::  seMIColon
5134  ++   pal  (just '(')                          ::  Paren Left
5135  ++   pam  (just '&')                          ::  AMPersand pampersand
5136  ++   par  (just ')')                          ::  Paren Right
5137  ++   pat  (just '@')                          ::  AT pat
5138  ++   sel  (just '[')                          ::  Square Left
5139  ++   ser  (just ']')                          ::  Square Right
5140  ++   sig  (just '~')                          ::  SIGnature squiggle
5141  ++   soq  (just '\'')                         ::  Single Quote
5142  ++   tar  (just '*')                          ::  sTAR
5143  ++   tic  (just '`')                          ::  backTiCk
5144  ++   tis  (just '=')                          ::  'tis tis, it is
5145  ++   wut  (just '?')                          ::  wut, what?
5146  ++   zap  (just '!')                          ::  zap! bang! crash!!
5147  ::
5148  ::    4i: parsing (useful idioms)
5149  +|  %parsing-useful-idioms
5150  ::
5151  ++   alf  ;~(pose low hig)                    ::  alphabetic
5152  ++   aln  ;~(pose low hig nud)                ::  alphanumeric
5153  ++   alp  ;~(pose low hig nud hep)            ::  alphanumeric and -
5154  ++   bet  ;~(pose (cold 2 hep) (cold 3 lus))  ::  axis syntax - +
5155  ++   bin  (bass 2 (most gon but))             ::  binary to atom
5156  ++   but  (cook |=(a=@ (sub a '0')) (shim '0' '1'))  ::  binary digit
5157  ++   cit  (cook |=(a=@ (sub a '0')) (shim '0' '7'))  ::  octal digit
5158  ++   dem  (bass 10 (most gon dit))            ::  decimal to atom
5159  ++   dit  (cook |=(a=@ (sub a '0')) (shim '0' '9'))  ::  decimal digit
5160  ++   dog  ;~(plug dot gay)                    ::  .  number separator
```

```
5161  ++  dof  ;~(plug hep gay)                                  ::  - @q separator
5162  ++  doh  ;~(plug ;~(plug hep hep) gay)                     ::  -- phon separator
5163  ++  dun  (cold ~ ;~(plug hep hep))                         ::  -- (stop) to ~
5164  ++  duz  (cold ~ ;~(plug tis tis))                         ::  == (stet) to ~
5165  ++  gah  (mask [`@`10 ' ' ~])                              ::  newline or ace
5166  ++  gap  (cold ~ ;~(plug gaq (star ;~(pose vul gah))))     ::  plural space
5167  ++  gaq  ;~  pose                                          ::  end of line
5168             (just `@`10)
5169             ;~(plug gah ;~(pose gah vul))
5170             vul
5171         ==
5172  ++  gaw  (cold ~ (star ;~(pose vul gah)))                  ::  classic white
5173  ++  gay  ;~(pose gap (easy ~))                             ::
5174  ++  gon  ;~(pose ;~(plug bas gay fas) (easy ~))            ::  long numbers \ /
5175  ++  gul  ;~(pose (cold 2 gal) (cold 3 gar))                ::  axis syntax < >
5176  ++  hex  (bass 16 (most gon hit))                          ::  hex to atom
5177  ++  hig  (shim 'A' 'Z')                                    ::  uppercase
5178  ++  hit  ;~  pose                                          ::  hex digits
5179             dit
5180             (cook |=(a=char (sub a 87)) (shim 'a' 'f'))
5181             (cook |=(a=char (sub a 55)) (shim 'A' 'F'))
5182         ==
5183  ++  iny                                                    ::  indentation block
5184  |*  sef=rule
5185  |=  nail  ^+  (sef)
5186  =+  [har tap]=[p q]:+<
5187  =+  lev=(fil 3 (dec q.har) ' ')
5188  =+  eol=(just `@t`10)
5189  =+  =-  roq=((star ;~(pose prn ;~(sfix eol (jest lev)) -)) har tap)
5190         ;~(simu ;~(plug eol eol) eol)
5191  ?~  q.roq  roq
5192  =+  vex=(sef har(q 1) p.u.q.roq)
5193  =+  fur=p.vex(q (add (dec q.har) q.p.vex))
5194  ?~  q.vex  vex(p fur)
5195  =-  vex(p fur, u.q -)
5196  :+  &3.vex
5197    &4.vex(q.p (add (dec q.har) q.p.&4.vex))
5198  =+  res=|4.vex
5199  |-  ?~  res  |4.roq
5200  ?.  =(10 -.res)  [-.res $(res +.res)]
5201  (welp [`@t`10 (trip lev)] $(res +.res))
5202  ::
5203  ++  low  (shim 'a' 'z')                                    ::  lowercase
5204  ++  mes  %+  cook                                          ::  hexbyte
5205             |=([a=@ b=@] (add (mul 16 a) b))
5206           ;~(plug hit hit)
5207  ++  nix  (boss 256 (star ;~(pose aln cab)))               ::
5208  ++  nud  (shim '0' '9')                                    ::  numeric
5209  ++  prn  ;~(less (just `@`127) (shim 32 256))             ::  non-control
5210  ++  qat  ;~  pose                                         ::  chars in blockcord
5211             prn
5212             ;~(less ;~(plug (just `@`10) soz) (just `@`10))
5213         ==
5214  ++  qit  ;~  pose                                         ::  chars in a cord
5215             ;~(less bas soq prn)
5216             ;~(pfix bas ;~(pose bas soq mes))              ::  escape chars
5217         ==
5218  ++  qut  ;~  simu  soq                                    ::  cord
```

```
5219                ;~  pose
5220                  ;~  less  soz
5221                    (ifix [soq soq] (boss 256 (more gon qit)))
5222                ==
5223              =+  hed=;~(pose ;~(plug (plus ace) vul) (just '\0a'))
5224              %-  iny  %+  ifix
5225                :-  ;~(plug soz hed)
5226                ;~(plug (just '\0a') soz)
5227              (boss 256 (star qat))
5228          ==
5229      ==
5230  ++  soz  ;~(plug soq soq soq)                          ::  delimiting '''
5231  ++  sym                                                ::  symbol
5232    %+  cook
5233      |=(a=tape (rap 3 ^-((list @) a)))
5234    ;~(plug low (star ;~(pose nud low hep)))
5235  ::
5236  ++  mixed-case-symbol
5237    %+  cook
5238      |=(a=tape (rap 3 ^-((list @) a)))
5239    ;~(plug alf (star alp))
5240  ::
5241  ++  ven   ;~  (comp |=([a=@ b=@] (peg a b)))           ::  +>- axis syntax
5242            bet
5243            =+  hom=`?`|
5244            |=  tub=nail
5245            ^-  (like @)
5246            =+  vex=?:(hom (bet tub) (gul tub))
5247            ?~  q.vex
5248              [p.tub [~ 1 tub]]
5249            =+  wag=$(p.tub p.vex, hom !hom, tub q.u.q.vex)
5250            ?>  ?=(^ q.wag)
5251            [p.wag [~ (peg p.u.q.vex p.u.q.wag) q.u.q.wag]]
5252            ==
5253  ++  vit                                                ::  base64 digit
5254    ;~  pose
5255      (cook |=(a=@ (sub a 65)) (shim 'A' 'Z'))
5256      (cook |=(a=@ (sub a 71)) (shim 'a' 'z'))
5257      (cook |=(a=@ (add a 4)) (shim '0' '9'))
5258      (cold 62 (just '-'))
5259      (cold 63 (just '+'))
5260    ==
5261  ++  vul  %+  cold   ~                                  ::  comments
5262           ;~  plug  col  col
5263           (star prn)
5264           (just `@`10)
5265           ==
5266  ::
5267  ::    4j: parsing (bases and base digits)
5268  +|  %parsing-bases-and-base-digits
5269  ::
5270  ++  ab
5271    |%
5272    ++  bix  (bass 16 (stun [2 2] six))
5273    ++  fem  (sear |=(a=@ (cha:fa a)) aln)
5274    ++  haf  (bass 256 ;~(plug tep tiq (easy ~)))
5275    ++  hef  %+  sear  |=(a=@ ?:(=(a 0) ~ (some a)))
5276            %+  bass  256
```

```
5277                     ;~(plug tip tiq (easy ~))
5278    ++   hif    (bass 256 ;~(plug tip tiq (easy ~)))
5279    ++   hof    (bass 0x1.0000 ;~(plug hef (stun [1 3] ;~(pfix hep hif))))
5280    ++   huf    (bass 0x1.0000 ;~(plug hef (stun [0 3] ;~(pfix hep hif))))
5281    ++   hyf    (bass 0x1.0000 ;~(plug hif (stun [3 3] ;~(pfix hep hif))))
5282    ++   pev    (bass 32 ;~(plug sev (stun [0 4] siv)))
5283    ++   pew    (bass 64 ;~(plug sew (stun [0 4] siw)))
5284    ++   piv    (bass 32 (stun [5 5] siv))
5285    ++   piw    (bass 64 (stun [5 5] siw))
5286    ++   qeb    (bass 2 ;~(plug seb (stun [0 3] sib)))
5287    ++   qex    (bass 16 ;~(plug sex (stun [0 3] hit)))
5288    ++   qib    (bass 2 (stun [4 4] sib))
5289    ++   qix    (bass 16 (stun [4 4] six))
5290    ++   seb    (cold 1 (just '1'))
5291    ++   sed    (cook |=(a=@ (sub a '0')) (shim '1' '9'))
5292    ++   sev    ;~(pose sed sov)
5293    ++   sew    ;~(pose sed sow)
5294    ++   sex    ;~(pose sed sox)
5295    ++   sib    (cook |=(a=@ (sub a '0')) (shim '0' '1'))
5296    ++   sid    (cook |=(a=@ (sub a '0')) (shim '0' '9'))
5297    ++   siv    ;~(pose sid sov)
5298    ++   siw    ;~(pose sid sow)
5299    ++   six    ;~(pose sid sox)
5300    ++   sov    (cook |=(a=@ (sub a 87)) (shim 'a' 'v'))
5301    ++   sow    ;~  pose
5302                    (cook |=(a=@ (sub a 87)) (shim 'a' 'z'))
5303                    (cook |=(a=@ (sub a 29)) (shim 'A' 'Z'))
5304                    (cold 62 (just '-'))
5305                    (cold 63 (just '~'))
5306                ==
5307    ++   sox    (cook |=(a=@ (sub a 87)) (shim 'a' 'f'))
5308    ++   ted    (bass 10 ;~(plug sed (stun [0 2] sid)))
5309    ++   tep    (sear |=(a=@ ?:(=(a 'doz') ~ (ins:po a))) til)
5310    ++   tip    (sear |=(a=@ (ins:po a)) til)
5311    ++   tiq    (sear |=(a=@ (ind:po a)) til)
5312    ++   tid    (bass 10 (stun [3 3] sid))
5313    ++   til    (boss 256 (stun [3 3] low))
5314    ++   urs    %+  cook
5315                    |=(a=tape (rap 3 ^-((list @) a)))
5316                (star ;~(pose nud low hep dot sig cab))
5317    ++   urt    %+  cook
5318                    |=(a=tape (rap 3 ^-((list @) a)))
5319                (star ;~(pose nud low hep dot sig))
5320    ++   urx    %+  cook
5321                    |=(a=tape (rap 3 ^-((list @) a)))
5322                %-  star
5323                ;~  pose
5324                  nud
5325                  low
5326                  hep
5327                  cab
5328                  (cold ' ' dot)
5329                  (cook tuft (ifix [sig dot] hex))
5330                ;~(pfix sig ;~(pose sig dot))
5331                ==
5332    ++   voy    ;~(pfix bas ;~(pose bas soq bix))
5333    --
5334 ++   ag
```

```
5335    |%
5336    ++  ape   |*(fel=rule ;~(pose (cold `@`0 (just '0')) fel))
5337    ++  bay   (ape (bass 16 ;~(plug qeb:ab (star ;~(pfix dog qib:ab)))))
5338    ++  bip   =+  tod=(ape qex:ab)
5339              (bass 0x1.0000 ;~(plug tod (stun [7 7] ;~(pfix dog tod))))
5340    ++  dem   (ape (bass 1.000 ;~(plug ted:ab (star ;~(pfix dog tid:ab)))))
5341    ++  dim   (ape dip)
5342    ++  dip   (bass 10 ;~(plug sed:ab (star sid:ab)))
5343    ++  dum   (bass 10 (plus sid:ab))
5344    ++  fed   %+  cook   fynd:ob
5345              ;~  pose
5346                %+  bass  0x1.0000.0000.0000.0000            ::  oversized
5347                  ;~  plug
5348                    huf:ab
5349                    (plus ;~(pfix doh hyf:ab))
5350                  ==
5351                hof:ab                                       ::  planet or moon
5352                haf:ab                                       ::  star
5353                tiq:ab                                       ::  galaxy
5354              ==
5355    ++  feq   %+  cook   |=(a=(list @) (rep 4 (flop a)))
5356              ;~  plug
5357                ;~(pose hif:ab tiq:ab)
5358                (star ;~(pfix dof hif:ab))
5359              ==
5360    ++  fim   (sear den:fa (bass 58 (plus fem:ab)))
5361    ++  hex   (ape (bass 0x1.0000 ;~(plug qex:ab (star ;~(pfix dog qix:ab)))))
5362    ++  lip   =+  tod=(ape ted:ab)
5363              (bass 256 ;~(plug tod (stun [3 3] ;~(pfix dog tod))))
5364    ++  mot   ;~  pose
5365              ;~  pfix
5366                (just '1')
5367                (cook |=(a=@ (add 10 (sub a '0'))) (shim '0' '2'))
5368              ==
5369              sed:ab
5370              ==
5371    ++  viz   (ape (bass 0x200.0000 ;~(plug pev:ab (star ;~(pfix dog piv:ab)))))
5372    ++  vum   (bass 32 (plus siv:ab))
5373    ++  wiz   (ape (bass 0x4000.0000 ;~(plug pew:ab (star ;~(pfix dog piw:ab)))))
5374    --
5375  ++  mu
5376    |_  [top=@ bot=@]
5377    ++  zag   [p=(end 4 (add top bot)) q=bot]
5378    ++  zig   [p=(end 4 (add top (sub 0x1.0000 bot))) q=bot]
5379    ++  zug   (mix (lsh 4 top) bot)
5380    --
5381  ++  ne
5382    |_  tig=@
5383    ++  c   (cut 3 [tig 1] key:fa)
5384    ++  d   (add tig '0')
5385    ++  x   ?:((gte tig 10) (add tig 87) d)
5386    ++  v   ?:((gte tig 10) (add tig 87) d)
5387    ++  w   ?:(=(tig 63) '~' ?:(=(tig 62) '-' ?:((gte tig 36) (add tig 29) x)))
5388    --
5389  ::
5390  ::    4k: atom printing
5391  +|  %atom-printing
5392  ::
```

```
5393  ++  co
5394    !:
5395    ~%  %co  ..co  ~
5396    =<  |_  lot=coin
5397        ++  rear  |=(rom=tape rend(rep rom))
5398        ++  rent  ~+  `@ta`(rap 3 rend)
5399        ++  rend
5400          ^-  tape
5401          ~+
5402          ?:  ?=(%blob -.lot)
5403            ['~' '0' ((v-co 1) (jam p.lot))]
5404          ?:  ?=(%many -.lot)
5405            :-  '.'
5406            |-  ^-  tape
5407            ?~  p.lot
5408              ['_' '_' rep]
5409            ['_' (weld (trip (wack rent(lot i.p.lot))) $(p.lot t.p.lot))]
5410          =+  [yed=(end 3 p.p.lot) hay=(cut 3 [1 1] p.p.lot)]
5411          |-  ^-  tape
5412          ?+  yed  (z-co q.p.lot)
5413            %c  ['~' '-' (weld (rip 3 (wood (tuft q.p.lot))) rep)]
5414            %d
5415          ?+  hay  (z-co q.p.lot)
5416            %a
5417            =+  yod=(yore q.p.lot)
5418            =?  rep  ?=(^ f.t.yod)  ['.' (s-co f.t.yod)]
5419            =?  rep  !&(?=(~ f) =(0 h) =(0 m) =(0 s)):t.yod
5420              =.  rep  ['.' (y-co s.t.yod)]
5421              =.  rep  ['.' (y-co m.t.yod)]
5422              ['.' '.' (y-co h.t.yod)]
5423            =.  rep  ['.' (a-co d.t.yod)]
5424            =.  rep  ['.' (a-co m.yod)]
5425            =?  rep  !a.yod  ['-' rep]
5426            ['~' (a-co y.yod)]
5427          ::
5428            %r
5429            =+  yug=(yell q.p.lot)
5430            =?  rep  ?=(^ f.yug)  ['.' (s-co f.yug)]
5431            :-  '~'
5432            ?:  &(=(0 d.yug) =(0 m.yug) =(0 h.yug) =(0 s.yug))
5433              ['s' '0' rep]
5434            =?  rep  !=(0 s.yug)  ['.' 's' (a-co s.yug)]
5435            =?  rep  !=(0 m.yug)  ['.' 'm' (a-co m.yug)]
5436            =?  rep  !=(0 h.yug)  ['.' 'h' (a-co h.yug)]
5437            =?  rep  !=(0 d.yug)  ['.' 'd' (a-co d.yug)]
5438            +.rep
5439          ==
5440          ::
5441            %f
5442            ?:  =(& q.p.lot)
5443              ['.' 'y' rep]
5444            ?:(=(| q.p.lot) ['.' 'n' rep] (z-co q.p.lot))
5445          ::
5446            %n  ['~' rep]
5447            %i
5448          ?+  hay  (z-co q.p.lot)
5449            %f  ((ro-co [3 10 4] |=(a=@ ~(d ne a))) q.p.lot)
5450            %s  ((ro-co [4 16 8] |=(a=@ ~(x ne a))) q.p.lot)
```

```
5451        ==
5452      ::
5453          %p
5454      =+  sxz=(fein:ob q.p.lot)
5455      =+  dyx=(met 3 sxz)
5456      :-  '~'
5457      ?:  (lte dyx 1)
5458        (weld (trip (tod:po sxz)) rep)
5459      =+  dyy=(met 4 sxz)
5460      =|  imp=@ud
5461      |-  ^-  tape
5462      ?:  =(imp dyy)
5463        rep
5464      %=  $
5465        imp  +(imp)
5466        rep  =/  log  (cut 4 [imp 1] sxz)
5467              ;:  weld
5468                (trip (tos:po (rsh 3 log)))
5469                (trip (tod:po (end 3 log)))
5470                ?:(=((mod imp 4) 0) ?:(=(imp 0) "" "--") "-")
5471                rep
5472        ==        ==
5473      ::
5474          %q
5475      :+  '.'  '~'
5476      =;  res=(pair ? tape)
5477        (weld q.res rep)
5478      %+  roll
5479        =*  val  q.p.lot
5480        ?:(=(0 val) ~[0] (rip 3 val))
5481      |=  [q=@ s=? r=tape]
5482      :-  !s
5483      %+  weld
5484        (trip ?:(s tod:po tos:po) q))
5485      ?.(&(s !=(r "")) r ['-' r])
5486      ::
5487          %r
5488      ?+  hay  (z-co q.p.lot)
5489        %d  ['.' '~' (r-co (rlyd q.p.lot))]
5490        %h  ['.' '~' '~' (r-co (rlyh q.p.lot))]
5491        %q  ['.' '~' '~' '~' (r-co (rlyq q.p.lot))]
5492        %s  ['.' (r-co (rlys q.p.lot))]
5493      ==
5494      ::
5495          %u
5496      ?:  ?=(%c hay)
5497        %+  welp  ['0' 'c' (reap (pad:fa q.p.lot) '1')]
5498        (c-co (enc:fa q.p.lot))
5499      ::
5500      =;  gam=(pair tape tape)
5501        (weld p.gam ?:(=(0 q.p.lot) `tape`['0' ~] q.gam))
5502      ?+  hay  [~ ((ox-co [10 3] |=(a=@ ~(d ne a))) q.p.lot)]
5503        %b  [['0' 'b' ~] ((ox-co [2 4] |=(a=@ ~(d ne a))) q.p.lot)]
5504        %i  [['0' 'i' ~] ((d-co 1) q.p.lot)]
5505        %x  [['0' 'x' ~] ((ox-co [16 4] |=(a=@ ~(x ne a))) q.p.lot)]
5506        %v  [['0' 'v' ~] ((ox-co [32 5] |=(a=@ ~(x ne a))) q.p.lot)]
5507        %w  [['0' 'w' ~] ((ox-co [64 5] |=(a=@ ~(w ne a))) q.p.lot)]
5508      ==
```

```
5509          ::
5510            %s
5511          %+  weld
5512            ?:((syn:si q.p.lot) "--" "-")
5513          $(yed 'u', q.p.lot (abs:si q.p.lot))
5514          ::
5515            %t
5516        ?:  =('a' hay)
5517          ?:  =('s' (cut 3 [2 1] p.p.lot))
5518          (weld (rip 3 q.p.lot) rep)
5519        ['~' '.' (weld (rip 3 q.p.lot) rep)]
5520        ['~' '~' (weld (rip 3 (wood q.p.lot)) rep)]
5521          ==
5522      --
5523  =|  rep=tape
5524  =<  |%
5525      ::  rendering idioms, output zero-padded to minimum lengths
5526      ::
5527      ::  +a-co: decimal
5528      ::  +c-co: base58check
5529      ::  +d-co: decimal, takes minimum output digits
5530      ::  +r-co: floating point
5531      ::  +s-co: list of '.'-prefixed base16, 4 digit minimum
5532      ::  +v-co: base32, takes minimum output digits
5533      ::  +w-co: base64, takes minimum output digits
5534      ::  +x-co: base16, takes minimum output digits
5535      ::  +y-co: decimal, 2 digit minimum
5536      ::  +z-co: '0x'-prefixed base16
5537      ::
5538      ++  a-co  |=(dat=@ ((d-co 1) dat))
5539      ++  c-co  (em-co [58 1] |=([? b=@ c=tape] [~(c ne b) c]))
5540      ++  d-co  |=(min=@ (em-co [10 min] |=([? b=@ c=tape] [~(d ne b) c])))
5541      ::
5542      ++  r-co
5543      |=  a=dn
5544      ?:  ?=([%i *] a)  (weld ?:(s.a "inf" "-inf") rep)
5545      ?:  ?=([%n *] a)  (weld "nan" rep)
5546      =;  rep  ?:(s.a rep ['-' rep])
5547      =/  f  ((d-co 1) a.a)
5548      =^  e  e.a
5549        =/  e=@s  (sun:si (lent f))
5550        =/  sci  :(sum:si e.a e -1)
5551        ?:  (syn:si (dif:si e.a --3))  [--1 sci]  :: 12000 -> 12e3 e>+2
5552        ?:  !(syn:si (dif:si sci -2))  [--1 sci]  :: 0.001 -> 1e-3 e<-2
5553        [(sum:si sci --1) --0] :: 1.234e2 -> '.'@3 -> 123 .4
5554      =?  rep  !=(--0 e.a)
5555        :(weld ?:((syn:si e.a) "e" "e-") ((d-co 1) (abs:si e.a)))
5556      (weld (ed-co e f) rep)
5557      ::
5558      ++  s-co
5559      |=  esc=(list @)  ^-  tape
5560      ?~  esc  rep
5561      ['.' =>(.(rep $(esc t.esc)) ((x-co 4) i.esc))]
5562      ::
5563      ++  v-co  |=(min=@ (em-co [32 min] |=([? b=@ c=tape] [~(v ne b) c])))
5564      ++  w-co  |=(min=@ (em-co [64 min] |=([? b=@ c=tape] [~(w ne b) c])))
5565      ++  x-co  |=(min=@ (em-co [16 min] |=([? b=@ c=tape] [~(x ne b) c])))
5566      ++  y-co  |=(dat=@ ((d-co 2) dat))
```

```
5567        ++  z-co   |=(dat=@ `tape`['0' 'x' ((x-co 1) dat)])
5568        --
5569    |%
5570    ::  +em-co: format in numeric base
5571    ::
5572    ::    in .bas, format .min digits of .hol with .par
5573    ::
5574    ::    - .hol is processed least-significant digit first
5575    ::    - all available digits in .hol will be processed, but
5576    ::      .min digits can exceed the number available in .hol
5577    ::    - .par handles all accumulated output on each call,
5578    ::      and can edit it, prepend or append digits, &c
5579    ::    - until .hol is exhausted, .par's sample is [| digit output],
5580    ::      subsequently, it's [& 0 output]
5581    ::
5582    ++  em-co
5583      |=  [[bas=@ min=@] par=$-([? @ tape] tape)]
5584      |=  hol=@
5585      ^-  tape
5586      ?:  &(=(0 hol) =(0 min))
5587        rep
5588      =/  [dar=@ rad=@]  (dvr hol bas)
5589      %=  $
5590        min  ?:(=(0 min) 0 (dec min))
5591        hol  dar
5592        rep  (par =(0 dar) rad rep)
5593      ==
5594    ::
5595    ::  +ed-co: format in numeric base, with output length
5596    ::
5597    ::    - like +em-co, but .par's sample will be [| digit output]
5598    ::      on the first call, regardless of the available digits in .hol
5599    ::    - used only for @r* floats
5600    ::
5601    ++  ed-co
5602      |=  [exp=@s int=tape]  ^-  tape
5603      =/  [pos=? dig=@u]  [=(--1 (cmp:si exp --0)) (abs:si exp)]
5604      ?.  pos
5605        (into (weld (reap +(dig) '0') int) 1 '.')
5606      =/  len  (lent int)
5607      ?:  (lth dig len)  (into int dig '.')
5608      (weld int (reap (sub dig len) '0'))
5609    ::
5610    ::  +ox-co: format '.'-separated digit sequences in numeric base
5611    ::
5612    ::    in .bas, format each digit of .hol with .dug,
5613    ::    with '.' separators every .gop digits.
5614    ::
5615    ::    - .hol is processed least-significant digit first
5616    ::    - .dug handles individual digits, output is prepended
5617    ::    - every segment but the last is zero-padded to .gop
5618    ::
5619    ++  ox-co
5620      |=  [[bas=@ gop=@] dug=$-(@ @)]
5621      %+  em-co
5622        [(pow bas gop) 0]
5623      |=  [top=? seg=@ res=tape]
5624      %+  weld
```

```
5625        ?:(top ~ `tape`['.' ~])
5626      %.  seg
5627      %+  em-co(rep res)
5628        [bas ?:(top 0 gop)]
5629      |=([? b=@ c=tape] [(dug b) c])
5630    ::
5631    ::  +ro-co: format '.'-prefixed bloqs in numeric base
5632    ::
5633    ::      in .bas, for .buz bloqs 0 to .dop, format at least one
5634    ::      digit of .hol, prefixed with '.'
5635    ::
5636    ::      - used only for @i* addresses
5637    ::
5638    ++  ro-co
5639      |=  [[buz=@ bas=@ dop=@] dug=$-(@ @)]
5640      |=  hol=@
5641      ^-  tape
5642      ?:  =(0 dop)
5643        rep
5644      :-  '.'
5645      =/  pod  (dec dop)
5646      %.  (cut buz [pod 1] hol)
5647      %+  em-co(rep $(dop pod))
5648        [bas 1]
5649      |=([? b=@ c=tape] [(dug b) c])
5650    --
5651  ::
5652  ::    41: atom parsing
5653  +|  %atom-parsing
5654  ::
5655  ++  so
5656    ~%  %so  +  ~
5657    |%
5658    ++  bisk
5659      ~+
5660      ;~  pose
5661        ;~  pfix  (just '0')
5662          ;~  pose
5663            (stag %ub ;~(pfix (just 'b') bay:ag))
5664            (stag %uc ;~(pfix (just 'c') fim:ag))
5665            (stag %ui ;~(pfix (just 'i') dim:ag))
5666            (stag %ux ;~(pfix (just 'x') hex:ag))
5667            (stag %uv ;~(pfix (just 'v') viz:ag))
5668            (stag %uw ;~(pfix (just 'w') wiz:ag))
5669          ==
5670        ==
5671        (stag %ud dem:ag)
5672      ==
5673    ++  crub
5674      ~+
5675      ;~  pose
5676        (cook |=(det=date `dime`[%da (year det)]) when)
5677        ::
5678        %+  cook
5679          |=  [a=(list [p=?(%d %h %m %s) q=@]) b=(list @)]
5680          =+  rop=`tarp`[0 0 0 0 b]
5681          |-  ^-  dime
5682          ?~  a
```

```
5683          [%dr (yule rop)]
5684        ?-  p.i.a
5685          %d  $(a t.a, d.rop (add q.i.a d.rop))
5686          %h  $(a t.a, h.rop (add q.i.a h.rop))
5687          %m  $(a t.a, m.rop (add q.i.a m.rop))
5688          %s  $(a t.a, s.rop (add q.i.a s.rop))
5689          ==
5690      ;~  plug
5691        %+  most
5692          dot
5693          ;~  pose
5694            ;~(pfix (just 'd') (stag %d dim:ag))
5695            ;~(pfix (just 'h') (stag %h dim:ag))
5696            ;~(pfix (just 'm') (stag %m dim:ag))
5697            ;~(pfix (just 's') (stag %s dim:ag))
5698          ==
5699          ;~(pose ;~(pfix ;~(plug dot dot) (most dot qix:ab)) (easy ~))
5700        ==
5701      ::
5702      (stag %p fed:ag)
5703      ;~(pfix dot (stag %ta urs:ab))
5704      ;~(pfix sig (stag %t urx:ab))
5705      ;~(pfix hep (stag %c (cook taft urx:ab)))
5706      ==
5707  ++  nuck
5708    ~/  %nuck  |=  a=nail  %.  a
5709    %+  knee  *coin  |.  ~+
5710    %-  stew
5711    ^.  stet  ^.  limo
5712    :~  :-  ['a' 'z']  (cook |=(a=@ta [%$ %tas a]) sym)
5713        :-  ['0' '9']  (stag %$ bisk)
5714        :-  '-'        (stag %$ tash)
5715        :-  '.'        ;~(pfix dot perd)
5716        :-  '~'        ;~(pfix sig ;~(pose twid (easy [%$ %n 0])))
5717    ==
5718  ++  nusk
5719    ~+
5720    :(sear |=(a=@ta (rush a nuck)) wick urt:ab)
5721  ++  perd
5722    ~+
5723    ;~  pose
5724      (stag %$ zust)
5725      (stag %many (ifix [cab ;~(plug cab cab)] (more cab nusk)))
5726    ==
5727  ++  royl
5728    ~+
5729    ;~  pose
5730      (stag %rh royl-rh)
5731      (stag %rq royl-rq)
5732      (stag %rd royl-rd)
5733      (stag %rs royl-rs)
5734    ==
5735    ::
5736  ++  royl-rh  (cook rylh ;~(pfix ;~(plug sig sig) (cook royl-cell royl-rn)))
5737  ++  royl-rq  (cook rylq ;~(pfix ;~(plug sig sig sig) (cook royl-cell royl-rn)))
5738  ++  royl-rd  (cook ryld ;~(pfix sig (cook royl-cell royl-rn)))
5739  ++  royl-rs  (cook ryls (cook royl-cell royl-rn))
5740    ::
```

```
5741    ++  royl-rn
5742      =/  moo
5743        |=  a=tape
5744        :-  (lent a)
5745        (scan a (bass 10 (plus sid:ab)))
5746      ;~  pose
5747        ;~  plug
5748          (easy %d)
5749          ;~(pose (cold | hep) (easy &))
5750          ;~  plug  dim:ag
5751            ;~  pose
5752              ;~(pfix dot (cook moo (plus (shim '0' '9'))))
5753              (easy [0 0])
5754            ==
5755            ;~  pose
5756              ;~  pfix
5757                (just 'e')
5758                ;~(plug ;~(pose (cold | hep) (easy &)) dim:ag)
5759              ==
5760              (easy [& 0])
5761            ==
5762          ==
5763        ==
5764        ::
5765        ;~  plug
5766          (easy %i)
5767          ;~  sfix
5768            ;~(pose (cold | hep) (easy &))
5769            (jest 'inf')
5770          ==
5771        ==
5772        ::
5773        ;~  plug
5774          (easy %n)
5775          (cold ~ (jest 'nan'))
5776        ==
5777      ==
5778    ::
5779    ++  royl-cell
5780      |=  rn
5781      ^-  dn
5782      ?.  ?=([%d *] +<)  +<
5783      =+  ^=  h
5784        (dif:si (new:si f.b i.b) (sun:si d.b))
5785      [%d a h (add (mul c.b (pow 10 d.b)) e.b)]
5786    ::
5787    ++  tash
5788      ~+
5789      =+  ^=  neg
5790        |=  [syn=? mol=dime]  ^-  dime
5791        ?>  =('u' (end 3 p.mol))
5792        [(cat 3 's' (rsh 3 p.mol)) (new:si syn q.mol)]
5793      ;~  pfix  hep
5794        ;~  pose
5795          (cook |=(a=dime (neg | a)) bisk)
5796          ;~(pfix hep (cook |=(a=dime (neg & a)) bisk))
5797        ==
5798      ==
```

```
5799    ::
5800    ++  twid
5801      ~+
5802      ;~  pose
5803        %+  stag  %blob
5804        %+  sear  |=(a=@ (mole |.((cue a))))
5805        ;~(pfix (just '0') vum:ag)
5806      ::
5807        (stag %$ crub)
5808      ==
5809    ::
5810    ++  when
5811      ~+
5812      ;~  plug
5813        %+  cook
5814          |=([a=@ b=?] [b a])
5815        ;~(plug dim:ag ;~(pose (cold | hep) (easy &)))
5816        ;~(pfix dot mot:ag)    ::   month
5817        ;~(pfix dot dip:ag)    ::   day
5818        ;~  pose
5819          ;~  pfix
5820            ;~(plug dot dot)
5821            ;~  plug
5822              dum:ag
5823              ;~(pfix dot dum:ag)
5824              ;~(pfix dot dum:ag)
5825              ;~(pose ;~(pfix ;~(plug dot dot) (most dot qix:ab)) (easy ~))
5826          ==
5827        ==
5828        (easy [0 0 0 ~])
5829      ==
5830    ==
5831    ::
5832    ++  zust
5833      ~+
5834      ;~  pose
5835        (stag %is bip:ag)
5836        (stag %if lip:ag)
5837        royl
5838        (stag %f ;~(pose (cold & (just 'y')) (cold | (just 'n'))))
5839        (stag %q ;~(pfix sig feq:ag))
5840      ==
5841    --
5842  ::
5843  ::    4m: formatting functions
5844  +|  %formatting-functions
5845  ++  scot
5846    ~/  %scot
5847    |=(mol=dime ~(rent co %$ mol))
5848  ++  scow
5849    ~/  %scow
5850    |=(mol=dime ~(rend co %$ mol))
5851  ++  slat  |=(mod=@tas |=(txt=@ta (slaw mod txt)))
5852  ++  slav  |=([mod=@tas txt=@ta] (need (slaw mod txt)))
5853  ++  slaw
5854    ~/  %slaw
5855    |=  [mod=@tas txt=@ta]
5856    ^-  (unit @)
```

```
5857    ?+      mod
5858         ::   slow fallback case to the full slay
5859         ::
5860         =+  con=(slay txt)
5861         ?.(&(?=([~ %$ @ @] con) =(p.p.u.con mod)) ~ [~ q.p.u.con])
5862    ::
5863         %da
5864      (rush txt ;~(pfix sig (cook year when:so)))
5865    ::
5866         %p
5867      (rush txt ;~(pfix sig fed:ag))
5868    ::
5869         %ud
5870      (rush txt dem:ag)
5871    ::
5872         %ux
5873      (rush txt ;~(pfix (jest '0x') hex:ag))
5874    ::
5875         %uv
5876      (rush txt ;~(pfix (jest '0v') viz:ag))
5877    ::
5878         %ta
5879      (rush txt ;~(pfix ;~(plug sig dot) urs:ab))
5880    ::
5881         %tas
5882      (rush txt sym)
5883    ==
5884  ::
5885  ++  slay
5886    |=  txt=@ta  ^-  (unit coin)
5887    =+  ^=  vex
5888        ?:  (gth 0x7fff.ffff txt)                        ::  XX   petty cache
5889          ~+  ((full nuck:so) [[1 1] (trip txt)])
5890        ((full nuck:so) [[1 1] (trip txt)])
5891    ?~  q.vex
5892        ~
5893    [~ p.u.q.vex]
5894  ::
5895  ++  smyt                                               ::  pretty print path
5896    |=  bon=path  ^-  tank
5897    :+  %rose  [['/' ~] ['/' ~] ~]
5898    (turn bon |=(a=@ [%leaf (trip a)]))
5899  ::
5900  ++  spat  |=(pax=path (crip (spud pax)))               ::  render path to cord
5901  ++  spud  |=(pax=path ~(ram re (smyt pax)))            ::  render path to tape
5902  ++  stab  |=(zep=@t `path`(rash zep stap))             ::  parse cord to path
5903  ++  stap                                               ::  path parser
5904    %+  sear
5905      |=  p=path
5906      ^-  (unit path)
5907      ?:  ?=([~ ~] p)  `~
5908      ?.  =(~ (rear p))  `p
5909        ~
5910    ;~(pfix fas (most fas urs:ab))
5911  ::
5912  ++  stip                                               ::  typed path parser
5913    =<  swot
5914    |%
```

```
5915  ++  swot  |=(n=nail (;~(pfix fas (more fas spot)) n))
5916  ::
5917  ++  spot
5918    %+  sear  (soft iota)
5919    %-  stew
5920    ^.  stet  ^.  limo
5921    :~  :-  'a'^'z'  (stag %tas sym)
5922        :-  '$'      (cold [%tas %$] buc)
5923        :-  '0'^'9'  bisk:so
5924        :-  '-'      tash:so
5925        :-  '.'      zust:so
5926        :-  '~'      ;~(pfix sig ;~(pose crub:so (easy [%n ~])))
5927        :-  '\''     (stag %t qut)
5928    ==
5929    --
5930  ::
5931  ++  pout
5932    |=  =pith
5933    ^-  path
5934    %+  turn  pith
5935    |=  i=iota
5936    ?@(i i (scot i))
5937  ::
5938  ++  pave
5939    |=  =path
5940    ^-  pith
5941    %+  turn  path
5942    |=  i=@ta
5943    (fall (rush i spot:stip) [%ta i])
5944  ::
5945  ::    4n: virtualization
5946  +|  %virtualization
5947  ::
5948  ::  +mack: untyped, scry-less, unitary virtualization
5949  ::
5950  ++  mack
5951    |=  [sub=* fol=*]
5952    ^-  (unit)
5953    =/  ton  (mink [sub fol] |~(^ ~))
5954    ?.(?=(%0 -.ton) ~ `product.ton)
5955  ::  +mink: raw virtual nock
5956  ::
5957  ++  mink  !.
5958    ~/  %mink
5959    |=  $:  [subject=* formula=*]
5960            scry=$-(^ (unit (unit)))
5961        ==
5962    =|  trace=(list [@ta *])
5963    |^  ^-  tone
5964        ?+  formula  [%2 trace]
5965          [^ *]
5966        =/  head  $(formula -.formula)
5967        ?.  ?=(%0 -.head)  head
5968        =/  tail  $(formula +.formula)
5969        ?.  ?=(%0 -.tail)  tail
5970        [%0 product.head product.tail]
5971    ::
5972          [%0 axis=@]
```

```
5973        =/  part  (frag axis.formula subject)
5974        ?~  part  [%2 trace]
5975        [%0 u.part]
5976      ::
5977          [%1 constant=*]
5978        [%0 constant.formula]
5979      ::
5980          [%2 subject=* formula=*]
5981        =/  subject  $(formula subject.formula)
5982        ?.  ?=(%0 -.subject)  subject
5983        =/  formula  $(formula formula.formula)
5984        ?.  ?=(%0 -.formula)  formula
5985        %=  $
5986          subject  product.subject
5987          formula  product.formula
5988        ==
5989      ::
5990          [%3 argument=*]
5991        =/  argument  $(formula argument.formula)
5992        ?.  ?=(%0 -.argument)  argument
5993        [%0 .?(product.argument)]
5994      ::
5995          [%4 argument=*]
5996        =/  argument  $(formula argument.formula)
5997        ?.  ?=(%0 -.argument)  argument
5998        ?^  product.argument  [%2 trace]
5999        [%0 .+(product.argument)]
6000      ::
6001          [%5 a=* b=*]
6002        =/  a  $(formula a.formula)
6003        ?.  ?=(%0 -.a)  a
6004        =/  b  $(formula b.formula)
6005        ?.  ?=(%0 -.b)  b
6006        [%0 =(product.a product.b)]
6007      ::
6008          [%6 test=* yes=* no=*]
6009        =/  result  $(formula test.formula)
6010        ?.  ?=(%0 -.result)  result
6011        ?+  product.result
6012            [%2 trace]
6013          %&  $(formula yes.formula)
6014          %|  $(formula no.formula)
6015        ==
6016      ::
6017          [%7 subject=* next=*]
6018        =/  subject  $(formula subject.formula)
6019        ?.  ?=(%0 -.subject)  subject
6020        %=  $
6021          subject  product.subject
6022          formula  next.formula
6023        ==
6024      ::
6025          [%8 head=* next=*]
6026        =/  head  $(formula head.formula)
6027        ?.  ?=(%0 -.head)  head
6028        %=  $
6029          subject  [product.head subject]
6030          formula  next.formula
```

```
6031            ==
6032        ::
6033            [%9 axis=@ core=*]
6034        =/  core  $(formula core.formula)
6035        ?.  ?=(%0 -.core)  core
6036        =/  arm  (frag axis.formula product.core)
6037        ?~  arm  [%2 trace]
6038        %=  $
6039          subject  product.core
6040          formula  u.arm
6041        ==
6042        ::
6043            [%10 [axis=@ value=*] target=*]
6044        ?:  =(0 axis.formula)  [%2 trace]
6045        =/  target  $(formula target.formula)
6046        ?.  ?=(%0 -.target)  target
6047        =/  value  $(formula value.formula)
6048        ?.  ?=(%0 -.value)  value
6049        =/  mutant=(unit *)
6050          (edit axis.formula product.target product.value)
6051        ?~  mutant  [%2 trace]
6052        [%0 u.mutant]
6053        ::
6054            [%11 tag=@ next=*]
6055        =/  next  $(formula next.formula)
6056        ?.  ?=(%0 -.next)  next
6057        :-  %0
6058        .*  subject
6059        [11 tag.formula 1 product.next]
6060        ::
6061            [%11 [tag=@ clue=*] next=*]
6062        =/  clue  $(formula clue.formula)
6063        ?.  ?=(%0 -.clue)  clue
6064        =/  next
6065          =?    trace
6066              ?=(?(%hunk %hand %lose %mean %spot) tag.formula)
6067            [[tag.formula product.clue] trace]
6068          $(formula next.formula)
6069        ?.  ?=(%0 -.next)  next
6070        :-  %0
6071        .*  subject
6072        [11 [tag.formula 1 product.clue] 1 product.next]
6073        ::
6074            [%12 ref=* path=*]
6075        =/  ref  $(formula ref.formula)
6076        ?.  ?=(%0 -.ref)  ref
6077        =/  path  $(formula path.formula)
6078        ?.  ?=(%0 -.path)  path
6079        =/  result  (scry product.ref product.path)
6080        ?~  result
6081          [%1 product.path]
6082        ?~  u.result
6083          [%2 [%hunk product.ref product.path] trace]
6084        [%0 u.u.result]
6085        ==
6086    ::
6087    ++  frag
6088      |=  [axis=@ noun=*]
```

```
6089       ^-  (unit)
6090       ?:  =(0 axis)  ~
6091       |-  ^-  (unit)
6092       ?:  =(1 axis)  `noun
6093       ?@  noun  ~
6094       =/  pick  (cap axis)
6095       %=  $
6096         axis  (mas axis)
6097         noun  ?-(pick %2 -.noun, %3 +.noun)
6098       ==
6099    ::
6100    ++  edit
6101      |=  [axis=@ target=* value=*]
6102      ^-  (unit)
6103      ?:  =(1 axis)  `value
6104      ?@  target  ~
6105      =/  pick  (cap axis)
6106      =/  mutant
6107        %=  $
6108          axis    (mas axis)
6109          target  ?-(pick %2 -.target, %3 +.target)
6110        ==
6111      ?~  mutant  ~
6112      ?-  pick
6113        %2  `[u.mutant +.target]
6114        %3  `[-.target u.mutant]
6115      ==
6116    --
6117  ::  +mock: virtual nock
6118  ::
6119  ++  mock
6120    |=  [[sub=* fol=*] gul=$-(^ (unit (unit)))]
6121    (mook (mink [sub fol] gul))
6122  ::  +mook: convert %tone to %toon, rendering stack frames
6123  ::
6124  ++  mook
6125    |=  ton=tone
6126    ^-  toon
6127    ?.  ?=([%2 *] ton)
6128      ton
6129    |^  [%2 (turn skip rend)]
6130    ::
6131    ++  skip
6132      ^+  trace.ton
6133      =/  yel  (lent trace.ton)
6134      ?.  (gth yel 1.024)  trace.ton
6135      %+  weld
6136        (scag 512 trace.ton)
6137      ^+  trace.ton
6138      :_  (slag (sub yel 512) trace.ton)
6139      :-  %lose
6140      (crip "[skipped {(scow %ud (sub yel 1.024))} frames]")
6141    ::
6142    ::  +rend: raw stack frame to tank
6143    ::
6144    ::      $%  [%hunk ref=* path]          ::  failed scry ([~ ~])
6145    ::          [%lose cord]                ::  skipped frames
6146    ::          [%hand *]                   ::  mug any
```

```
6147  ::              [%mean $@(cord (trap tank))]  ::  ~_ et al
6148  ::              [%spot spot]                  ::  source location
6149  ::      ==
6150  ::
6151  ++  rend
6152    |=  [tag=@ta dat=*]
6153    ^-  tank
6154    ?+    tag
6155    ::
6156      leaf+"mook.{(rip 3 tag)}"
6157    ::
6158        %hunk
6159    ?@  dat  leaf+"mook.hunk"
6160    =/  sof=(unit path)  ((soft path) +.dat)
6161    ?~  sof  leaf+"mook.hunk"
6162    (smyt u.sof)
6163    ::
6164        %lose
6165    ?^  dat  leaf+"mook.lose"
6166    leaf+(rip 3 dat)
6167    ::
6168        %hand
6169    leaf+(scow %p (mug dat))
6170    ::
6171        %mean
6172    ?@  dat  leaf+(rip 3 dat)
6173    =/  mac  (mack dat -.dat)
6174    ?~  mac  leaf+"####"
6175    =/  sof  ((soft tank) u.mac)
6176    ?~  sof  leaf+"mook.mean"
6177    u.sof
6178    ::
6179        %spot
6180    =/  sof=(unit spot)  ((soft spot) dat)
6181    ?~  sof  leaf+"mook.spot"
6182    :+  %rose  [":" ~ ~]
6183    :~  (smyt p.u.sof)
6184        =*  l  p.q.u.sof
6185        =*  r  q.q.u.sof
6186        =/  ud  |=(a=@u (scow %ud a))
6187        leaf+"<[{(ud p.l)} {(ud q.l)}].[{(ud p.r)} {(ud q.r)}]>"
6188    ==
6189      ==
6190    --
6191  ::  +mole: typed unitary virtual
6192  ::
6193  ++  mole
6194    ~/  %mole
6195    |*  tap=(trap)
6196    ^-  (unit _$:tap)
6197    =/  mur  (mure tap)
6198    ?~(mur ~ `$:tap)
6199  ::  +mong: virtual slam
6200  ::
6201  ++  mong
6202    |=  [[gat=* sam=*] gul=$-(^ (unit (unit)))]
6203    ^-  toon
6204    ?.  ?=([* ^] gat)  [%2 ~]
```

```
6205    (mock [gat(+< sam) %9 2 %0 1] gul)
6206  ::  +mule: typed virtual
6207  ::
6208  ++  mule
6209    ~/  %mule
6210    |*  tap=(trap)
6211    =/  mud  (mute tap)
6212    ?-  -.mud
6213      %&  [%& p=$:tap]
6214      %|  [%| p=p.mud]
6215    ==
6216  ::  +mure: untyped unitary virtual
6217  ::
6218  ++  mure
6219    |=  tap=(trap)
6220    ^-  (unit)
6221    =/  ton  (mink [tap %9 2 %0 1] |=(a=^ ``.*(a [%12 [%0 2] %0 3])))
6222    ?.(?=(%0 -.ton) ~ `product.ton)
6223  ::  +mute: untyped virtual
6224  ::
6225  ++  mute
6226    |=  tap=(trap)
6227    ^-  (each * (list tank))
6228    =/  ton  (mock [tap %9 2 %0 1] |=(a=^ ``.*(a [%12 [%0 2] %0 3])))
6229    ?-  -.ton
6230      %0  [%& p.ton]
6231    ::
6232      %1  =/  sof=(unit path)  ((soft path) p.ton)
6233          [%| ?~(sof leaf+"mute.hunk" (smyt u.sof)) ~]
6234    ::
6235      %2  [%| p.ton]
6236    ==
6237  ::  +slum: slam a gate on a sample using raw nock, untyped
6238  ::
6239  ++  slum
6240    ~/  %slum
6241    |=  sub=[gat=* sam=*]
6242    .*(sub [%9 2 %10 [6 %0 3] %0 2])
6243  ::  +soft: virtual clam
6244  ::
6245  ++  soft
6246    |*  han=$-(* *)
6247    |=(fud=* (mole |.((han fud))))
6248  ::
6249  ::    4o: molds and mold builders
6250  +|  %molds-and-mold-builders
6251  ::
6252  +$  abel  typo                              ::  original sin: type
6253  +$  alas  (list (pair term hoon))           ::  alias list
6254  +$  atom  @                                 ::  just an atom
6255  +$  aura  @ta                               ::  atom format
6256  +$  base                                    ::  base mold
6257    $@  $?  %noun                             ::  any noun
6258            %cell                             ::  any cell
6259            %flag                             ::  loobean
6260            %null                             ::  ~ == 0
6261            %void                             ::  empty set
6262        ==                                    ::
```

```
6263      [%atom p=aura]                                   ::  atom
6264  ::                                                   ::
6265  +$  woof  $@(@ [~ p=hoon])                           ::  simple embed
6266  +$  chum  $?  lef=term                               ::  jet name
6267            [std=term kel=@]                           ::  kelvin version
6268            [ven=term pro=term kel=@]                  ::  vendor and product
6269            [ven=term pro=term ver=@ kel=@]            ::  all of the above
6270            ==                                         ::
6271  +$  coil  $:  p=garb                                 ::  name, wet=dry, vary
6272            q=type                                     ::  context
6273            r=(pair seminoun (map term tome))          ::  chapters
6274            ==                                         ::
6275  +$  garb  (trel (unit term) poly vair)               ::  core
6276  +$  poly  ?(%wet %dry)                               ::  polarity
6277  +$  foot  $%  [%dry p=hoon]                          ::  dry arm, geometric
6278            [%wet p=hoon]                              ::  wet arm, generic
6279            ==                                         ::
6280  +$  link                                             ::  lexical segment
6281        $%  [%chat p=term]                             ::  |chapter
6282            [%cone p=aura q=atom]                       ::  %constant
6283            [%frag p=term]                             ::  .face
6284            [%funk p=term]                             ::  +arm
6285            [%plan p=term]                             ::  $spec
6286            ==                                         ::
6287  +$  cuff  (list link)                                ::  parsed lex segments
6288  +$  crib  [summary=cord details=(list sect)]         ::
6289  +$  help  [=cuff =crib]                              ::  documentation
6290  +$  limb  $@  term                                   ::  wing element
6291        $%  [%& p=axis]                                ::  by geometry
6292            [%| p=@ud q=(unit term)]                    ::  by name
6293            ==                                         ::
6294            ::  XX more and better sanity              ::
6295            ::                                         ::
6296  +$  null  ~                                          ::  null, nil, etc
6297  +$  onyx  (list (pair type foot))                    ::  arm activation
6298  +$  opal                                             ::  limb match
6299        $%  [%& p=type]                                ::  leg
6300            [%| p=axis q=(set [p=type q=foot])]         ::  arm
6301            ==                                         ::
6302  +$  pica  (pair ? cord)                              ::  & prose, | code
6303  +$  palo  (pair vein opal)                           ::  wing trace, match
6304  +$  pock  (pair axis nock)                           ::  changes
6305  +$  port  (each palo (pair type nock))               ::  successful match
6306  +$  spec                                             ::  structure definition
6307        $~  [%base %null]                              ::
6308        $%  [%base p=base]                             ::  base type
6309            [%dbug p=spot q=spec]                       ::  set debug
6310            [%gist p=[%help p=help] q=spec]             ::  formal comment
6311            [%leaf p=term q=@]                          ::  constant atom
6312            [%like p=wing q=(list wing)]                ::  reference
6313            [%loop p=term]                             ::  hygienic reference
6314            [%made p=(pair term (list term)) q=spec]    ::  annotate synthetic
6315            [%make p=hoon q=(list spec)]                ::  composed spec
6316            [%name p=term q=spec]                       ::  annotate simple
6317            [%over p=wing q=spec]                       ::  relative to subject
6318            ::                                         ::
6319            [%bcgr p=spec q=spec]                       ::  $>, filter: require
6320            [%bcbc p=spec q=(map term spec)]            ::  $$, recursion
```

```
6321              [%bcbr p=spec q=hoon]                    ::  $|, verify
6322              [%bccb p=hoon]                            ::  $_, example
6323              [%bccl p=[i=spec t=(list spec)]]          ::  $:, tuple
6324              [%bccn p=[i=spec t=(list spec)]]          ::  $%, head pick
6325              [%bcdt p=spec q=(map term spec)]          ::  $., read-write core
6326              [%bcgl p=spec q=spec]                     ::  $<, filter: exclude
6327              [%bchp p=spec q=spec]                     ::  $-, function core
6328              [%bckt p=spec q=spec]                     ::  $^, cons pick
6329              [%bcls p=stud q=spec]                     ::  $+, standard
6330              [%bcfs p=spec q=(map term spec)]          ::  $/, write-only core
6331              [%bcmc p=hoon]                            ::  $;, manual
6332              [%bcpm p=spec q=hoon]                     ::  $&, repair
6333              [%bcsg p=hoon q=spec]                     ::  $~, default
6334              [%bctc p=spec q=(map term spec)]          ::  $`, read-only core
6335              [%bcts p=skin q=spec]                     ::  $=, name
6336              [%bcpt p=spec q=spec]                     ::  $@, atom pick
6337              [%bcwt p=[i=spec t=(list spec)]]          ::  $?, full pick
6338              [%bczp p=spec q=(map term spec)]          ::  $!, opaque core
6339          ==                                            ::
6340  +$  tent                                              ::  model builder
6341          $%  [%| p=wing q=tent r=(list spec)]          ::  ~(p q r...)
6342              [%& p=(list wing)]                        ::  a.b:c.d
6343          ==                                            ::
6344  +$  tiki                                              ::  test case
6345          $%  [%& p=(unit term) q=wing]                 ::  simple wing
6346              [%| p=(unit term) q=hoon]                 ::  named wing
6347          ==                                            ::
6348  +$  skin                                              ::  texture
6349          $@  =term                                     ::  name/~[term %none]
6350          $%  [%base =base]                             ::  base match
6351              [%cell =skin =skin]                       ::  pair
6352              [%dbug =spot =skin]                       ::  trace
6353              [%leaf =aura =atom]                       ::  atomic constant
6354              [%help =help =skin]                       ::  describe
6355              [%name =term =skin]                       ::  apply label
6356              [%over =wing =skin]                       ::  relative to
6357              [%spec =spec =skin]                       ::  cast to
6358              [%wash depth=@ud]                         ::  strip faces
6359          ==                                            ::
6360  +$  tome  (pair what (map term hoon))                 ::  core chapter
6361  +$  tope                                              ::  topographic type
6362      $@  $?  %&                                        ::  cell or atom
6363              %|                                        ::  atom
6364          ==                                            ::
6365      (pair tope tope)                                  ::  cell
6366  ++  hoot                                              ::  hoon tools
6367      |%
6368  +$  beer  $@(char [~ p=hoon])                         ::  simple embed
6369  +$  mane  $@(@tas [@tas @tas])                        ::  XML name+space
6370  +$  manx  $~([[%$ ~] ~] [g=marx c=marl])              ::  dynamic XML node
6371  +$  marl  (list tuna)                                 ::  dynamic XML nodes
6372  +$  mart  (list [n=mane v=(list beer)])               ::  dynamic XML attrs
6373  +$  marx  $~([%$ ~] [n=mane a=mart])                  ::  dynamic XML tag
6374  +$  mare  (each manx marl)                            ::  node or nodes
6375  +$  maru  (each tuna marl)                            ::  interp or nodes
6376  +$  tuna                                              ::  maybe interpolation
6377      $~  [[%$ ~] ~]
6378      $^  manx
```

```
6379        $:  ?(%tape %manx %marl %call)
6380            p=hoon
6381        ==
6382    --                                          ::
6383  +$  hoon                                      ::  hoon AST
6384    $~  [%zpzp ~]                               ::
6385    $^  [p=hoon q=hoon]                         ::
6386    $%                                          ::
6387      [%$ p=axis]                               ::  simple leg
6388    ::                                          ::
6389      [%base p=base]                            ::  base spec
6390      [%bust p=base]                            ::  bunt base
6391      [%dbug p=spot q=hoon]                     ::  debug info in trace
6392      [%eror p=tape]                            ::  assembly error
6393      [%hand p=type q=nock]                     ::  premade result
6394      [%note p=note q=hoon]                     ::  annotate
6395      [%fits p=hoon q=wing]                     ::  underlying ?=
6396      [%knit p=(list woof)]                     ::  assemble string
6397      [%leaf p=(pair term @)]                   ::  symbol spec
6398      [%limb p=term]                            ::  take limb
6399      [%lost p=hoon]                            ::  not to be taken
6400      [%rock p=term q=*]                        ::  fixed constant
6401      [%sand p=term q=*]                        ::  unfixed constant
6402      [%tell p=(list hoon)]                     ::  render as tape
6403      [%tune p=$@(term tune)]                   ::  minimal face
6404      [%wing p=wing]                            ::  take wing
6405      [%yell p=(list hoon)]                     ::  render as tank
6406      [%xray p=manx:hoot]                       ::  ;foo; templating
6407    ::                                ::::::  cores
6408      [%brbc sample=(lest term) body=spec]      ::  |$
6409      [%brcb p=spec q=alas r=(map term tome)]   ::  |_
6410      [%brcl p=hoon q=hoon]                     ::  |:
6411      [%brcn p=(unit term) q=(map term tome)]   ::  |%
6412      [%brdt p=hoon]                            ::  |.
6413      [%brkt p=hoon q=(map term tome)]          ::  |^
6414      [%brhp p=hoon]                            ::  |-
6415      [%brsg p=spec q=hoon]                     ::  |~
6416      [%brtr p=spec q=hoon]                     ::  |*
6417      [%brts p=spec q=hoon]                     ::  |=
6418      [%brpt p=(unit term) q=(map term tome)]   ::  |@
6419      [%brwt p=hoon]                            ::  |?
6420    ::                                ::::::  tuples
6421      [%clcb p=hoon q=hoon]                     ::  :_ [q p]
6422      [%clkt p=hoon q=hoon r=hoon s=hoon]       ::  :^ [p q r s]
6423      [%clhp p=hoon q=hoon]                     ::  :- [p q]
6424      [%clls p=hoon q=hoon r=hoon]              ::  :+ [p q r]
6425      [%clsg p=(list hoon)]                     ::  :~ [p ~]
6426      [%cltr p=(list hoon)]                     ::  :* p as a tuple
6427    ::                                ::::::  invocations
6428      [%cncb p=wing q=(list (pair wing hoon))]  ::  %_
6429      [%cndt p=hoon q=hoon]                     ::  %.
6430      [%cnhp p=hoon q=hoon]                     ::  %-
6431      [%cncl p=hoon q=(list hoon)]              ::  %:
6432      [%cntr p=wing q=hoon r=(list (pair wing hoon))]  ::  %*
6433      [%cnkt p=hoon q=hoon r=hoon s=hoon]       ::  %^
6434      [%cnls p=hoon q=hoon r=hoon]              ::  %+
6435      [%cnsg p=wing q=hoon r=(list hoon)]       ::  %~
6436      [%cnts p=wing q=(list (pair wing hoon))]  ::  %=
```

```
6437      ::                                      :::::::  nock
6438      [%dtkt p=spec q=hoon]                   ::  .^  nock 11
6439      [%dtls p=hoon]                          ::  .+  nock 4
6440      [%dttr p=hoon q=hoon]                   ::  .*  nock 2
6441      [%dtts p=hoon q=hoon]                   ::  .=  nock 5
6442      [%dtwt p=hoon]                          ::  .?  nock 3
6443      ::                                      :::::::  type conversion
6444      [%ktbr p=hoon]                          ::  ^|  contravariant
6445      [%ktdt p=hoon q=hoon]                   ::  ^.  self-cast
6446      [%ktls p=hoon q=hoon]                   ::  ^+  expression cast
6447      [%kthp p=spec q=hoon]                   ::  ^-  structure cast
6448      [%ktpm p=hoon]                          ::  ^&  covariant
6449      [%ktsg p=hoon]                          ::  ^~  constant
6450      [%ktts p=skin q=hoon]                   ::  ^=  label
6451      [%ktwt p=hoon]                          ::  ^?  bivariant
6452      [%kttr p=spec]                          ::  ^*  example
6453      [%ktcl p=spec]                          ::  ^:  filter
6454      ::                                      :::::::  hints
6455      [%sgbr p=hoon q=hoon]                   ::  ~|  sell on trace
6456      [%sgcb p=hoon q=hoon]                   ::  ~_  tank on trace
6457      [%sgcn p=chum q=hoon r=tyre s=hoon]     ::  ~%  general jet hint
6458      [%sgfs p=chum q=hoon]                   ::  ~/  function j-hint
6459      [%sggl p=$@(term [p=term q=hoon]) q=hoon]  ::  ~<  backward hint
6460      [%sggr p=$@(term [p=term q=hoon]) q=hoon]  ::  ~>  forward hint
6461      [%sgbc p=term q=hoon]                   ::  ~$  profiler hit
6462      [%sgls p=@ q=hoon]                      ::  ~+  cache=memoize
6463      [%sgpm p=@ud q=hoon r=hoon]             ::  ~&  printf=priority
6464      [%sgts p=hoon q=hoon]                   ::  ~=  don't duplicate
6465      [%sgwt p=@ud q=hoon r=hoon s=hoon]      ::  ~?  tested printf
6466      [%sgzp p=hoon q=hoon]                   ::  ~!  type on trace
6467      ::                                      :::::::  miscellaneous
6468      [%mcts p=marl:hoot]                     ::  ;=  list templating
6469      [%mccl p=hoon q=(list hoon)]            ::  ;:  binary to nary
6470      [%mcfs p=hoon]                          ::  ;/  [%$ [%$ p ~] ~]
6471      [%mcgl p=spec q=hoon r=hoon s=hoon]     ::  ;<  bind
6472      [%mcsg p=hoon q=(list hoon)]            ::  ;~  kleisli arrow
6473      [%mcmc p=spec q=hoon]                   ::  ;;  normalize
6474      ::                                      :::::::  compositions
6475      [%tsbr p=spec q=hoon]                   ::  =|  push bunt
6476      [%tscl p=(list (pair wing hoon)) q=hoon]  ::  =:  q w= p changes
6477      [%tsfs p=skin q=hoon r=hoon]            ::  =/  typed variable
6478      [%tsmc p=skin q=hoon r=hoon]            ::  =;  =/(q p r)
6479      [%tsdt p=wing q=hoon r=hoon]            ::  =.  r with p as q
6480      [%tswt p=wing q=hoon r=hoon s=hoon]     ::  =?  conditional =.
6481      [%tsgl p=hoon q=hoon]                   ::  =<  =>(q p)
6482      [%tshp p=hoon q=hoon]                   ::  =-  =+(q p)
6483      [%tsgr p=hoon q=hoon]                   ::  =>  q w=subject p
6484      [%tskt p=skin q=wing r=hoon s=hoon]     ::  =^  state machine
6485      [%tsls p=hoon q=hoon]                   ::  =+  q w=[p subject]
6486      [%tssg p=(list hoon)]                   ::  =~  hoon stack
6487      [%tstr p=(pair term (unit spec)) q=hoon r=hoon]  ::  =*  new style
6488      [%tscm p=hoon q=hoon]                   ::  =,  overload p in q
6489      ::                                      :::::::  conditionals
6490      [%wtbr p=(list hoon)]                   ::  ?|  loobean or
6491      [%wthp p=wing q=(list (pair spec hoon))]  ::  ?-  pick case in q
6492      [%wtcl p=hoon q=hoon r=hoon]            ::  ?:  if=then=else
6493      [%wtdt p=hoon q=hoon r=hoon]            ::  ?.  ?:(p r q)
6494      [%wtkt p=wing q=hoon r=hoon]            ::  ?^  if p is a cell
```

```
6495       [%wtgl p=hoon q=hoon]                              ::   ?<   ?:(p !! q)
6496       [%wtgr p=hoon q=hoon]                              ::   ?>   ?:(p q !!)
6497       [%wtls p=wing q=hoon r=(list (pair spec hoon))]    ::   ?+   ?-   w=default
6498       [%wtpm p=(list hoon)]                              ::   ?&   loobean and
6499       [%wtpt p=wing q=hoon r=hoon]                       ::   ?@   if p is atom
6500       [%wtsg p=wing q=hoon r=hoon]                       ::   ?~   if p is null
6501       [%wthx p=skin q=wing]                              ::   ?#   if q matches p
6502       [%wtts p=spec q=wing]                              ::   ?=   if q matches p
6503       [%wtzp p=hoon]                                     ::   ?!   loobean not
6504    ::                                          ::::::   special
6505       [%zpcm p=hoon q=hoon]                              ::   !,
6506       [%zpgr p=hoon]                                     ::   !>
6507       [%zpgl p=spec q=hoon]                              ::   !<
6508       [%zpmc p=hoon q=hoon]                              ::   !;
6509       [%zpts p=hoon]                                     ::   !=
6510       [%zppt p=(list wing) q=hoon r=hoon]                ::   !@
6511       [%zpwt p=$@(p=@ [p=@ q=@]) q=hoon]                 ::   !?
6512       [%zpzp ~]                                          ::   !!
6513    ==                                                    ::
6514 +$  tyre  (list [p=term q=hoon])                         ::
6515 +$  tyke  (list (unit hoon))                             ::
6516 ::                                                       ::::::: virtual nock
6517 +$  nock  $^  [p=nock q=nock]                            ::  autocons
6518           $%  [%1 p=*]                                   ::  constant
6519               [%2 p=nock q=nock]                         ::  compose
6520               [%3 p=nock]                                ::  cell test
6521               [%4 p=nock]                                ::  increment
6522               [%5 p=nock q=nock]                         ::  equality test
6523               [%6 p=nock q=nock r=nock]                  ::  if, then, else
6524               [%7 p=nock q=nock]                         ::  serial compose
6525               [%8 p=nock q=nock]                         ::  push onto subject
6526               [%9 p=@ q=nock]                            ::  select arm and fire
6527               [%10 p=[p=@ q=nock] q=nock]                ::  edit
6528               [%11 p=$@(@ [p=@ q=nock]) q=nock]          ::  hint
6529               [%12 p=nock q=nock]                        ::  grab data from sky
6530               [%0 p=@]                                   ::  axis select
6531           ==                                             ::
6532 +$  note                                                 ::  type annotation
6533           $%  [%help p=help]                             ::  documentation
6534               [%know p=stud]                             ::  global standard
6535               [%made p=term q=(unit (list wing))]        ::  structure
6536           ==                                             ::
6537 +$  type  $~  %noun                                      ::
6538           $@  $?  %noun                                  ::  any nouns
6539                   %void                                  ::  no noun
6540               ==                                         ::
6541           $%  [%atom p=term q=(unit @)]                  ::  atom / constant
6542               [%cell p=type q=type]                      ::  ordered pair
6543               [%core p=type q=coil]                      ::  object
6544               [%face p=$@(term tune) q=type]             ::  namespace
6545               [%fork p=(set type)]                       ::  union
6546               [%hint p=(pair type note) q=type]          ::  annotation
6547               [%hold p=type q=hoon]                      ::  lazy evaluation
6548           ==                                             ::
6549 +$  tony                                                 ::  ++tone done right
6550           $%  [%0 p=tine q=*]                            ::  success
6551               [%1 p=(set)]                               ::  blocks
6552               [%2 p=(list [@ta *])]                      ::  error ~_s
```

```
6553              ==                                    ::
6554  +$   tine                                         ::  partial noun
6555              $@   ~                                ::  open
6556              $%   [%& p=tine q=tine]               ::  half-blocked
6557                   [%| p=(set)]                     ::  fully blocked
6558              ==                                    ::
6559  +$   tool  $@(term tune)                          ::  type decoration
6560  +$   tune                                         ::  complex
6561              $~   [~ ~]                             ::
6562              $:   p=(map term (unit hoon))         ::  aliases
6563                   q=(list hoon)                    ::  bridges
6564              ==                                    ::
6565  +$   typo  type                                   ::  old type
6566  +$   vase  [p=type q=*]                           ::  type-value pair
6567  +$   vise  [p=typo q=*]                           ::  old vase
6568  +$   vial  ?(%read %rite %both %free)             ::  co/contra/in/bi
6569  +$   vair  ?(%gold %iron %lead %zinc)             ::  in/contra/bi/co
6570  +$   vein  (list (unit axis))                     ::  search trace
6571  +$   sect  (list pica)                            ::  paragraph
6572  +$   whit                                         ::  prefix docs parse
6573      $:  bat=(map cuff (pair cord (list sect)))    ::  batch comment
6574      ==                                            ::
6575  +$   whiz  cord                                   ::  postfix doc parse
6576  +$   what  (unit (pair cord (list sect)))         ::  help slogan/section
6577  +$   wing  (list limb)                            ::  search path
6578  ::
6579  ::  +block: abstract identity of resource awaited
6580  ::
6581  +$  block
6582    path
6583  ::
6584  ::  +result: internal interpreter result
6585  ::
6586  +$  result
6587    $@(~ seminoun)
6588  ::
6589  ::  +thunk: fragment constructor
6590  ::
6591  +$  thunk
6592    $-(@ud (unit noun))
6593  ::
6594  ::  +seminoun:
6595  ::
6596  +$  seminoun
6597  ::   partial noun; blocked subtrees are ~
6598  ::
6599  $~  [[%full / ~ ~] ~]
6600  [mask=stencil data=noun]
6601  ::
6602  ::  +stencil: noun knowledge map
6603  ::
6604  +$  stencil
6605      $%  ::
6606          ::   %half: noun has partial block substructure
6607          ::
6608          [%half left=stencil rite=stencil]
6609          ::
6610          ::  %full: noun is either fully complete, or fully blocked
```

```
6611        ::
6612        [%full blocks=(set block)]
6613        ::
6614        ::    %lazy: noun can be generated from virtual subtree
6615        ::
6616        [%lazy fragment=axis resolve=thunk]
6617    ==
6618  ::
6619  +$  output
6620    ::  ~: interpreter stopped
6621    ::
6622    %-  unit
6623    $%  ::
6624        ::    %done: output is complete
6625        ::
6626        [%done p=noun]
6627        ::
6628        ::    %wait: output is waiting for resources
6629        ::
6630        [%wait p=(list block)]
6631    ==
6632  :: profiling
6633  +$  doss
6634    $:  mon=moan                                ::  sample count
6635        hit=(map term @ud)                      ::  hit points
6636        cut=(map path hump)                     ::  cut points
6637    ==
6638  +$  moan                                      ::  sample metric
6639    $:  fun=@ud                                 ::  samples in C
6640        noc=@ud                                 ::  samples in nock
6641        glu=@ud                                 ::  samples in glue
6642        mal=@ud                                 ::  samples in alloc
6643        far=@ud                                 ::  samples in frag
6644        coy=@ud                                 ::  samples in copy
6645        euq=@ud                                 ::  samples in equal
6646    ==                                          ::
6647  ::
6648  +$  hump
6649    $:  mon=moan                                ::  sample count
6650        out=(map path @ud)                      ::  calls out of
6651        inn=(map path @ud)                      ::  calls into
6652    ==
6653  --
6654  ::
6655  ~%    %pen
6656      +
6657    ==
6658    %ap     ap
6659    %ut     ut
6660    ==
6661  ::    layer-5
6662  ::
6663  |%
6664  ::
6665  ::    5aa: new partial nock interpreter
6666  +|  %new-partial-nock-interpreter
6667  ::
6668  ++  musk  !.                                  ::  nock with block set
```

```
6669      |%
6670      ++  abet
6671      ::      simplify raw result
6672      ::
6673      |=  $:  ::  noy: raw result
6674              ::
6675              noy=result
6676          ==
6677      ^-  output
6678      ::  propagate stop
6679      ::
6680      ?~  noy  ~
6681      :-  ~
6682      ::  merge all blocking sets
6683      ::
6684      =/  blocks  (squash mask.noy)
6685      ?:  =(~ blocks)
6686        ::  no blocks, data is complete
6687        ::
6688      done/data.noy
6689      ::  reduce block set to block list
6690      ::
6691      wait/~(tap in blocks)
6692      ::
6693      ++  araw
6694      ::      execute nock on partial subject
6695      ::
6696      |=  $:  ::  bus: subject, a partial noun
6697              ::  fol: formula, a complete noun
6698              ::
6699              bus=seminoun
6700              fol=noun
6701          ==
6702      ::  interpreter loop
6703      ::
6704      |-  ^-  result
6705      ?@  fol
6706        ::  bad formula, stop
6707        ::
6708        ~
6709      ?:  ?=(^ -.fol)
6710        ::  hed: interpret head
6711        ::
6712        =+  hed=$(fol -.fol)
6713        ::  propagate stop
6714        ::
6715        ?~  hed  ~
6716        ::  tal: interpret tail
6717        ::
6718        =+  tal=$(fol +.fol)
6719        ::  propagate stop
6720        ::
6721        ?~  tal  ~
6722        ::  combine
6723        ::
6724        (combine hed tal)
6725      ?+    fol
6726        ::  bad formula; stop
```

```
6727    ::
6728          ~
6729    ::  0; fragment
6730    ::
6731        [%0 b=@]
6732    ::  if bad axis, stop
6733    ::
6734    ?:  =(0 b.fol)  ~
6735    ::  reduce to fragment
6736    ::
6737    (fragment b.fol bus)
6738    ::
6739    ::  1; constant
6740    ::
6741        [%1 b=*]
6742    ::  constant is complete
6743    ::
6744    [full/~ b.fol]
6745    ::
6746    ::  2; recursion
6747    ::
6748        [%2 b=* c=*]
6749    ::  require complete formula
6750    ::
6751    %+  require
6752        ::  compute formula with current subject
6753        ::
6754        $(fol c.fol)
6755    |=  ::  ryf: next formula
6756        ::
6757        ryf=noun
6758    ::  lub: next subject
6759    ::
6760    =+  lub=^$(fol b.fol)
6761    ::  propagate stop
6762    ::
6763    ?~  lub  ~
6764    ::  recurse
6765    ::
6766    ^$(fol ryf, bus lub)
6767    ::
6768    ::  3; probe
6769    ::
6770        [%3 b=*]
6771    %+  require
6772        $(fol b.fol)
6773    |=  ::  fig: probe input
6774        ::
6775        fig=noun
6776    ::  yes if cell, no if atom
6777    ::
6778    [full/~ .?(fig)]
6779    ::
6780    ::  4; increment
6781    ::
6782        [%4 b=*]
6783    %+  require
6784        $(fol b.fol)
```

```
6785        |=  ::  fig: increment input
6786            ::
6787            fig=noun
6788        ::  stop for cells, increment for atoms
6789        ::
6790        ?^(fig ~ [full/~ +(fig)])
6791     ::
6792     ::  5; compare
6793     ::
6794        [%5 b=* c=*]
6795      %+  require
6796        $(fol b.fol)
6797      |=  ::  hed: left input
6798          ::
6799          hed=noun
6800      %+  require
6801        ^$(fol c.fol)
6802      |=  ::  tal: right input
6803          ::
6804          tal=noun
6805      [full/~ =(hed tal)]
6806     ::
6807     ::  6; if-then-else
6808     ::
6809        [%6 b=* c=* d=*]
6810        ::  semantic expansion
6811        ::
6812      %+  require
6813        $(fol b.fol)
6814      |=  ::  fig: boolean
6815          ::
6816          fig=noun
6817        ::  apply proper booleans
6818        ::
6819      ?:  =(& fig)  ^$(fol c.fol)
6820      ?:  =(| fig)  ^$(fol d.fol)
6821        ::  stop on bad test
6822        ::
6823        ~
6824     ::
6825     ::  7; composition
6826     ::
6827        [%7 b=* c=*]
6828        ::  one: input
6829        ::
6830      =+  one=$(fol b.fol)
6831        ::  propagate stop
6832        ::
6833      ?~  one  ~
6834        ::  complete composition
6835        ::
6836      $(fol c.fol, bus one)
6837     ::
6838     ::  8; introduction
6839     ::
6840        [%8 b=* c=*]
6841        ::  one: input
6842        ::
```

```
6843      =+   one=$(fol b.fol)
6844      ::   propagate stop
6845      ::
6846      ?~   one   ~
6847      ::   complete introduction
6848      ::
6849      $(fol c.fol, bus (combine one bus))
6850    ::
6851    ::   9; invocation
6852    ::
6853        [%9 b=* c=*]
6854      ::   semantic expansion
6855      ::
6856      ?^   b.fol   ~
6857      ::   one: core
6858      ::
6859      =+   one=$(fol c.fol)
6860      ::   propagate stop
6861      ::
6862      ?~   one   ~
6863      ::   if core is constant
6864      ::
6865      ?:   ?=([[%full ~] *] one)
6866        ::   then call virtual nock directly
6867        ::
6868        =+   (mack data.one [%9 b.fol %0 1])
6869        ::   propagate stop
6870        ::
6871        ?~   -   ~
6872        ::   produce result
6873        ::
6874        [[%full ~] u.-]
6875      ::   else complete call
6876      ::
6877      %+   require
6878        ::   retrieve formula
6879        ::
6880        (fragment b.fol one)
6881      ::   continue
6882      ::
6883      |=(noun ^$(bus one, fol +<))
6884    ::
6885    ::   10; edit
6886    ::
6887        [%10 [b=@ c=*] d=*]
6888      ::   tar:  target of edit
6889      ::
6890      =+   tar=$(fol d.fol)
6891      ::   propagate stop
6892      ::
6893      ?~   tar   ~
6894      ::   inn:  inner value
6895      ::
6896      =+   inn=$(fol c.fol)
6897      ::   propagate stop
6898      ::
6899      ?~   inn   ~
6900      (mutate b.fol inn tar)
```

```
6901      ::
6902      ::  11; static hint
6903      ::
6904          [%11 @ c=*]
6905        ::  ignore hint
6906        ::
6907      $(fol c.fol)
6908      ::
6909      ::  11; dynamic hint
6910      ::
6911          [%11 [b=* c=*] d=*]
6912        ::  noy: dynamic hint
6913        ::
6914      =+  noy=$(fol c.fol)
6915        ::  propagate stop
6916        ::
6917      ?~  noy   ~
6918        ::  if hint is a fully computed trace
6919        ::
6920      ?:  &(?=(%spot b.fol) ?=([[[%full ~] *] noy))
6921        ::  compute within trace
6922        ::
6923        ~_((show %o +.noy) $(fol d.fol))
6924        ::  else ignore hint
6925        ::
6926      $(fol d.fol)
6927    ==
6928    ::
6929  ++  apex
6930    ::    execute nock on partial subject
6931    ::
6932    |=  $:  ::  bus: subject, a partial noun
6933            ::  fol: formula, a complete noun
6934            ::
6935            bus=seminoun
6936            fol=noun
6937        ==
6938    ~+
6939    ^-  output
6940    ::  simplify result
6941    ::
6942    (abet (araw bus fol))
6943    ::
6944  ++  combine
6945    ::    combine a pair of seminouns
6946    ::
6947    |=  $:  ::  hed: head of pair
6948            ::  tal: tail of pair
6949            ::
6950            hed=seminoun
6951            tal=seminoun
6952        ==
6953    ^-  seminoun
6954    ?.  ?&  &(?=(%full -.mask.hed) ?=(%full -.mask.tal))
6955            =(=(~ blocks.mask.hed) =(~ blocks.mask.tal))
6956        ==
6957      ::  default merge
6958      ::
```

```
6959          [half/[mask.hed mask.tal] [data.hed data.tal]]
6960       ::   both sides total
6961       ::
6962       ?:  =(~ blocks.mask.hed)
6963         ::   both sides are complete
6964         ::
6965       [full/~ data.hed data.tal]
6966       ::   both sides are blocked
6967       ::
6968       [full/(~(uni in blocks.mask.hed) blocks.mask.tal) ~]
6969     ::
6970     ++  complete
6971       ::     complete any laziness
6972       ::
6973       |=  bus=seminoun
6974       ^-  seminoun
6975       ?-  -.mask.bus
6976         %full  bus
6977         %lazy  ::  fragment 1 is the whole thing
6978                ::
6979                ?:  =(1 fragment.mask.bus)
6980                  ::  blocked; we can't get fragment 1 while compiling it
6981                  ::
6982                  [[%full [~ ~ ~]] ~]
6983                ::   execute thunk
6984                ::
6985                =+  (resolve.mask.bus fragment.mask.bus)
6986                ::   if product is nil
6987                ::
6988                ?~  -
6989                  ::   then blocked
6990                  ::
6991                  [[%full [~ ~ ~]] ~]
6992                ::   else use value
6993                ::
6994                [[%full ~] u.-]
6995         %half  ::   recursive descent
6996                ::
6997                %+  combine
6998                  $(bus [left.mask.bus -.data.bus])
6999                  $(bus [rite.mask.bus +.data.bus])
7000       ==
7001     ::
7002     ++  fragment
7003       ::     seek to an axis in a seminoun
7004       ::
7005       |=  $:  ::  axe: tree address of subtree
7006               ::  bus: partial noun
7007               ::
7008               axe=axis
7009               bus=seminoun
7010           ==
7011       ^-  result
7012       ::  1 is the root
7013       ::
7014       ?:  =(1 axe)  bus
7015       ::  now: top of axis (2 or 3)
7016       ::  lat: rest of axis
```

```
7017        ::
7018        =+  [now=(cap axe) lat=(mas axe)]
7019        ?-  -.mask.bus
7020          %lazy  ::  propagate laziness
7021                 ::
7022                 bus(fragment.mask (peg fragment.mask.bus axe))
7023        ::
7024          %full  ::  if fully blocked, produce self
7025                 ::
7026                 ?^  blocks.mask.bus  bus
7027                 ::  descending into atom, stop
7028                 ::
7029                 ?@  data.bus  ~
7030                 ::  descend into complete cell
7031                 ::
7032                 $(axe lat, bus [full/~ ?:(=(2 now) -.data.bus +.data.bus)])
7033        ::
7034          %half  ::  descend into partial cell
7035                 ::
7036                 %=  $
7037                   axe   lat
7038                   bus  ?:  =(2 now)
7039                        [left.mask.bus -.data.bus]
7040                        [rite.mask.bus +.data.bus]
7041        ==          ==
7042    ::
7043    ++  mutate
7044    ::      change a single axis in a seminoun
7045    ::
7046    |=  $:  ::  axe: axis within big to change
7047            ::  lit: (little) seminoun to insert within big at axe
7048            ::  big: seminoun to mutate
7049            ::
7050            axe=@
7051            lit=seminoun
7052            big=seminoun
7053        ==
7054    ^-  result
7055    ::  stop on zero axis
7056    ::
7057    ?~  axe  ~
7058    ::  edit root of big means discard it
7059    ::
7060    ?:  =(1 axe)  lit
7061    ::  decompose axis into path of head-tail
7062    ::
7063    |-  ^-  result
7064    ?:  =(2 axe)
7065      ::  mutate head of cell
7066      ::
7067      =+  tal=(fragment 3 big)
7068      ::  propagate stop
7069      ::
7070      ?~  tal  ~
7071      (combine lit tal)
7072    ?:  =(3 axe)
7073      ::  mutate tail of cell
7074      ::
```

```
7075    =+  hed=(fragment 2 big)
7076    ::  propagate stop
7077    ::
7078    ?~  hed   ~
7079    (combine hed lit)
7080    ::  deeper axis: keep one side of big and
7081    ::  recurse into the other with smaller axe
7082    ::
7083    =+  mor=(mas axe)
7084    =+  hed=(fragment 2 big)
7085    ::  propagate stop
7086    ::
7087    ?~  hed   ~
7088    =+  tal=(fragment 3 big)
7089    ::  propagate stop
7090    ::
7091    ?~  tal   ~
7092    ?:  =(2 (cap axe))
7093      ::  recurse into the head
7094      ::
7095      =+  mut=$(big hed, axe mor)
7096      ::  propagate stop
7097      ::
7098      ?~  mut   ~
7099      (combine mut tal)
7100    ::  recurse into the tail
7101    ::
7102    =+  mut=$(big tal, axe mor)
7103    ::  propagate stop
7104    ::
7105    ?~  mut   ~
7106    (combine hed mut)
7107    ::
7108    ++  require
7109      ::    require complete intermediate stop
7110      ::
7111      |=  $:  noy=result
7112              yen=$-(* result)
7113          ==
7114      ^-  result
7115      ::  propagate stop
7116      ::
7117      ?~  noy   ~
7118      ::  suppress laziness
7119      ::
7120      =/  bus=seminoun  (complete noy)
7121      ?<  ?=(%lazy -.mask.bus)
7122      ::  if partial block, squash blocks and stop
7123      ::
7124      ?:  ?=(%half -.mask.bus)  [full/(squash mask.bus) ~]
7125      ::  if full block, propagate block
7126      ::
7127      ?:  ?=(^ blocks.mask.bus)  [mask.bus ~]
7128      ::  otherwise use complete noun
7129      ::
7130      (yen data.bus)
7131    ::
7132    ++  squash
```

```
7133      ::      convert stencil to block set
7134      ::
7135      |=  tyn=stencil
7136      ^-  (set block)
7137      ?-  -.tyn
7138        %lazy  $(tyn -:(complete tyn ~))
7139        %full  blocks.tyn
7140        %half  (~(uni in $(tyn left.tyn)) $(tyn rite.tyn))
7141      ==
7142    --
7143  ::
7144  ::    5a: compiler utilities
7145  +|  %compiler-utilities
7146  ::
7147  ++  bool  `type`(fork [%atom %f `0] [%atom %f `1] ~)    :: make loobean
7148  ++  cell                                                :: make %cell type
7149    ~/  %cell
7150    |=  [hed=type tal=type]
7151    ^-  type
7152    ?:(=(%void hed) %void ?:(=(%void tal) %void [%cell hed tal]))
7153  ::
7154  ++  core                                                :: make %core type
7155    ~/  %core
7156    |=  [pac=type con=coil]
7157    ^-  type
7158    ?:(=(%void pac) %void [%core pac con])
7159  ::
7160  ++  hint
7161    |=  [p=(pair type note) q=type]
7162    ^-  type
7163    ?:  =(%void q)  %void
7164    ?:  =(%noun q)  %noun
7165    [%hint p q]
7166  ::
7167  ++  face                                                :: make %face type
7168    ~/  %face
7169    |=  [giz=$@(term tune) der=type]
7170    ^-  type
7171    ?:  =(%void der)
7172      %void
7173    [%face giz der]
7174  ::
7175  ++  fork                                                :: make %fork type
7176    ~/  %fork
7177    |=  yed=(list type)
7178    =|  lez=(set type)
7179    |-  ^-  type
7180    ?~  yed
7181      ?~  lez  %void
7182      ?:  ?=([* ~ ~] lez)  n.lez
7183      [%fork lez]
7184    %=    $
7185        yed  t.yed
7186        lez
7187      ?:  =(%void i.yed)  lez
7188      ?:  ?=([[%fork *] i.yed)  (~(uni in lez) p.i.yed)
7189      (~(put in lez) i.yed)
7190    ==
```

```
7191  ::
7192  ++  cove                                      ::  extract [0 *] axis
7193    |=  nug=nock
7194    ?-    nug
7195      [%0 *]    p.nug
7196      [%11 *]   $(nug q.nug)
7197      *         ~_(leaf+"cove" !!)
7198    ==
7199  ++  comb                                      ::  combine two formulas
7200    ~/  %comb
7201    |=  [mal=nock buz=nock]
7202    ^-  nock
7203    ?:  ?&(?=([%0 *] mal) !=(0 p.mal))
7204      ?:  ?&(?=([%0 *] buz) !=(0 p.buz))
7205      [%0 (peg p.mal p.buz)]
7206      ?:  ?=([%2 [%0 *] [%0 *]] buz)
7207      [%2 [%0 (peg p.mal p.p.buz)] [%0 (peg p.mal p.q.buz)]]
7208      [%7 mal buz]
7209    ?:  ?=([^ [%0 %1]] mal)
7210      [%8 p.mal buz]
7211    ?:  =([%0 %1] buz)
7212      mal
7213    [%7 mal buz]
7214  ::
7215  ++  cond                                      ::  ?:  compile
7216    ~/  %cond
7217    |=  [pex=nock yom=nock woq=nock]
7218    ^-  nock
7219    ?-  pex
7220      [%1 %0]  yom
7221      [%1 %1]  woq
7222      *        [%6 pex yom woq]
7223    ==
7224  ::
7225  ++  cons                                      ::  make formula cell
7226    ~/  %cons
7227    |=  [vur=nock sed=nock]
7228    ^-  nock
7229    ::  this optimization can remove crashes which are essential
7230    ::
7231    ::  ?:  ?=([[%0 *] [%0 *]] +<)
7232    ::  ?:  ?&(=(+(p.vur) p.sed) =((div p.vur 2) (div p.sed 2)))
7233    ::  [%0 (div p.vur 2)]
7234    ::  [vur sed]
7235    ?:  ?=([[%1 *] [%1 *]] +<)
7236      [%1 p.vur p.sed]
7237    [vur sed]
7238  ::
7239  ++  fitz                                      ::  odor compatibility
7240    ~/  %fitz
7241    |=  [yaz=term wix=term]
7242    =+  ^=  fiz
7243      |=  mot=@ta  ^-  [p=@ q=@ta]
7244      =+  len=(met 3 mot)
7245      ?:  =(0 len)
7246        [0 %$]
7247      =+  tyl=(rsh [3 (dec len)] mot)
7248      ?:  &((gte tyl 'A') (lte tyl 'Z'))
```

```
7249            [(sub tyl 64) (end [3 (dec len)] mot)]
7250          [0 mot]
7251     =+  [yoz=(fiz yaz) wux=(fiz wix)]
7252     ?&  ?|  =(0 p.yoz)
7253             =(0 p.wux)
7254             &(!=(0 p.wux) (lte p.wux p.yoz))
7255         ==
7256         |-  ?|  =(%$ p.yoz)
7257                 =(%$ p.wux)
7258             ?&  =((end 3 p.yoz) (end 3 p.wux))
7259                 $(p.yoz (rsh 3 p.yoz), p.wux (rsh 3 p.wux))
7260             ==
7261         ==
7262     ==
7263 ::
7264 ++  flan                                    ::  loobean  &
7265   ~/  %flan
7266   |=  [bos=nock nif=nock]
7267   ^-  nock
7268   ?:  =(bos nif)  bos
7269   ?:  =([%0 0] bos)  nif
7270   ?:  =([%0 0] nif)  bos
7271   ?-    bos
7272       [%1 %1]   bos
7273       [%1 %0]   nif
7274       *
7275     ?-    nif
7276        [%1 %1]   nif
7277        [%1 %0]   bos
7278        *             [%6 bos nif [%1 1]]
7279     ==
7280   ==
7281 ::
7282 ++  flip                                    ::  loobean negation
7283   ~/  %flip
7284   |=  dyr=nock
7285   ?:  =([%0 0] dyr)  dyr
7286   [%6 dyr [%1 1] [%1 0]]
7287 ::
7288 ++  flor                                    ::  loobean  |
7289   ~/  %flor
7290   |=  [bos=nock nif=nock]
7291   ^-  nock
7292   ?:  =(bos nif)  bos
7293   ?:  =([%0 0] bos)  nif
7294   ?:  =([%0 0] nif)  bos
7295   ?-  bos
7296       [%1 %1]   nif
7297       [%1 %0]   bos
7298       *
7299     ?-  nif
7300        [%1 %1]   bos
7301        [%1 %0]   nif
7302        *             [%6 bos [%1 0] nif]
7303     ==
7304   ==
7305 ::
7306 ++  hike
```

```
7307   ~/   %hike
7308   |=   [a=axis pac=(list (pair axis nock))]
7309   |^   =/   rel=(map axis nock)   (roll pac insert)
7310        =/   ord=(list axis)        (sort ~(tap in ~(key by rel)) gth)
7311        |-   ^-   nock
7312        ?~   ord
7313          [%0 a]
7314        =/   b=axis   i.ord
7315        =/   c=nock   (~(got by rel) b)
7316        =/   d=nock   $(ord t.ord)
7317        [%10 [b c] d]
7318   ::
7319   ++   contains
7320        |=   [container=axis contained=axis]
7321        ^-   ?
7322        =/   big=@     (met 0 container)
7323        =/   small=@   (met 0 contained)
7324        ?:   (lte small big)   |
7325        =/   dif=@   (sub small big)
7326        =(container (rsh [0 dif] contained))
7327   ::
7328   ++   parent
7329        |=   a=axis
7330        `axis`(rsh 0 a)
7331   ::
7332   ++   sibling
7333        |=   a=axis
7334        ^-   axis
7335        ?~   (mod a 2)
7336          +(a)
7337        (dec a)
7338   ::
7339   ++   insert
7340        |=   [e=[axe=axis fol=nock] n=(map axis nock)]
7341        ^-   (map axis nock)
7342        ?:   =/   a=axis   axe.e
7343             |-   ^-   ?
7344             ?:   =(1 a)   |
7345             ?:   (~(has by n) a)
7346               &
7347             $(a (parent a))
7348          ::   parent already in
7349          n
7350        =.   n
7351          ::   remove children
7352          %+   roll   ~(tap by n)
7353          |=   [[axe=axis fol=nock] m=_n]
7354          ?.   (contains axe.e axe)   m
7355          (~(del by m) axe)
7356        =/   sib   (sibling axe.e)
7357        =/   un    (~(get by n) sib)
7358        ?~   un    (~(put by n) axe.e fol.e)
7359        ::   replace sibling with parent
7360        %=   $
7361          n   (~(del by n) sib)
7362          e   :-   (parent sib)
7363              ?:   (gth sib axe.e)
7364                (cons fol.e u.un)
```

```
7365              (cons u.un fol.e)
7366          ==
7367       --
7368  ::
7369  ++  jock
7370    |=  rad=?
7371    |=  lot=coin  ^-  hoon
7372    ?-    -.lot
7373        ~
7374      ?:(rad [%rock p.lot] [%sand p.lot])
7375        ::
7376          %blob
7377      ?:  rad
7378        [%rock %$ p.lot]
7379      ?@(p.lot [%sand %$ p.lot] [$(p.lot -.p.lot) $(p.lot +.p.lot)])
7380        ::
7381          %many
7382        [%cltr (turn p.lot |=(a=coin ^$(lot a)))]
7383      ==
7384  ::
7385  ++  look
7386    ~/  %look
7387    |=  [cog=term dab=(map term hoon)]
7388    =+  axe=1
7389    |-  ^-  (unit [p=axis q=hoon])
7390    ?-  dab
7391        ~  ~
7392      ::
7393        [* ~ ~]
7394      ?:(=(cog p.n.dab) [~ axe q.n.dab] ~)
7395      ::
7396        [* ~ *]
7397      ?:  =(cog p.n.dab)
7398        [~ (peg axe 2) q.n.dab]
7399      ?:  (gor cog p.n.dab)
7400        ~
7401      $(axe (peg axe 3), dab r.dab)
7402      ::
7403        [* * ~]
7404      ?:  =(cog p.n.dab)
7405        [~ (peg axe 2) q.n.dab]
7406      ?:  (gor cog p.n.dab)
7407        $(axe (peg axe 3), dab l.dab)
7408        ~
7409      ::
7410        [* * *]
7411      ?:  =(cog p.n.dab)
7412        [~ (peg axe 2) q.n.dab]
7413      ?:  (gor cog p.n.dab)
7414        $(axe (peg axe 6), dab l.dab)
7415      $(axe (peg axe 7), dab r.dab)
7416      ==
7417  ::
7418  ++  loot
7419    ~/  %loot
7420    |=  [cog=term dom=(map term tome)]
7421    =+  axe=1
7422    |-  ^-  (unit [p=axis q=hoon])
```

```
7423    ?-   dom
7424         ~    ~
7425    ::
7426         [* ~ ~]
7427    %+   bind  (look cog q.q.n.dom)
7428    |=((pair axis hoon) [(peg axe p) q])
7429    ::
7430         [* ~ *]
7431    =+   yep=(look cog q.q.n.dom)
7432    ?^   yep
7433    [~ (peg (peg axe 2) p.u.yep) q.u.yep]
7434    $(axe (peg axe 3), dom r.dom)
7435    ::
7436         [* * ~]
7437    =+   yep=(look cog q.q.n.dom)
7438    ?^   yep
7439    [~ (peg (peg axe 2) p.u.yep) q.u.yep]
7440    $(axe (peg axe 3), dom l.dom)
7441    ::
7442         [* * *]
7443    =+   yep=(look cog q.q.n.dom)
7444    ?^   yep
7445    [~ (peg (peg axe 2) p.u.yep) q.u.yep]
7446    =+   pey=$(axe (peg axe 6), dom l.dom)
7447    ?^   pey  pey
7448    $(axe (peg axe 7), dom r.dom)
7449    ==
7450  ::
7451  ::    5b: macro expansion
7452  +|   %macro-expansions
7453  ::
7454  ++   ah                                        :: tiki engine
7455  |_   tik=tiki
7456  ++   blue
7457  |=   gen=hoon
7458  ^-   hoon
7459  ?.   &(?=(%| -.tik) ?=(~ p.tik))  gen
7460  [%tsgr [%$ 3] gen]
7461  ::
7462  ++   teal
7463  |=   mod=spec
7464  ^-   spec
7465  ?:   ?=(%& -.tik)  mod
7466  [%over [%& 3]~ mod]
7467  ::
7468  ++   tele
7469  |=   syn=skin
7470  ^-   skin
7471  ?:   ?=(%& -.tik)  syn
7472  [%over [%& 3]~ syn]
7473  ::
7474  ++   gray
7475  |=   gen=hoon
7476  ^-   hoon
7477  ?-   -.tik
7478  %&   ?~(p.tik gen [%tstr [u.p.tik ~] [%wing q.tik] gen])
7479  %|   [%tsls ?~(p.tik q.tik [%ktts u.p.tik q.tik]) gen]
7480      ==
```

```
7481    ::
7482    ++  puce
7483      ^-  wing
7484      ?-  -.tik
7485        %&  ?~(p.tik q.tik [u.p.tik ~])
7486        %|  [[%& 2] ~]
7487      ==
7488    ::
7489    ++  wthp  |=  opt=(list (pair spec hoon))
7490              %+  gray  %wthp
7491              [puce (turn opt |=([a=spec b=hoon] [a (blue b)]))]
7492    ++  wtkt  |=([sic=hoon non=hoon] (gray [%wtkt puce (blue sic) (blue non)]))
7493    ++  wtls  |=  [gen=hoon opt=(list (pair spec hoon))]
7494              %+  gray  %wtls
7495              [puce (blue gen) (turn opt |=([a=spec b=hoon] [a (blue b)]))]
7496    ++  wtpt  |=([sic=hoon non=hoon] (gray [%wtpt puce (blue sic) (blue non)]))
7497    ++  wtsg  |=([sic=hoon non=hoon] (gray [%wtsg puce (blue sic) (blue non)]))
7498    ++  wthx  |=(syn=skin (gray [%wthx (tele syn) puce]))
7499    ++  wtts  |=(mod=spec (gray [%wtts (teal mod) puce]))
7500    --
7501  ::
7502  ++  ax
7503    =+  :*  ::  .dom: axis to home
7504            ::  .hay: wing to home
7505            ::  .cox: hygienic context
7506            ::  .bug: debug annotations
7507            ::  .nut: annotations
7508            ::  .def: default expression
7509            ::
7510            dom=`axis`1
7511            hay=*wing
7512            cox=*(map term spec)
7513            bug=*(list spot)
7514            nut=*(unit note)
7515            def=*(unit hoon)
7516        ==
7517    |_  mod=spec
7518    ::
7519    ++  autoname
7520      ::    derive name from spec
7521      ::
7522      |-  ^-  (unit term)
7523      ?-  -.mod
7524        %base  ?.(?=([%atom *] p.mod) ~ ?:(=(%$ p.p.mod) `%atom `p.p.mod))
7525        %dbug  $(mod q.mod)
7526        %gist  $(mod q.mod)
7527        %leaf  `p.mod
7528        %loop  `p.mod
7529        %like  ?~(p.mod ~ ?^(i.p.mod ?:(=(%& -.i.p.mod) ~ q.i.p.mod) `i.p.mod))
7530        %make  ~(name ap p.mod)
7531        %made  $(mod q.mod)
7532        %over  $(mod q.mod)
7533        %name  $(mod q.mod)
7534        ::
7535        %bcbc  $(mod p.mod)
7536        %bcbr  $(mod p.mod)
7537        %bccb  ~(name ap p.mod)
7538        %bccl  $(mod i.p.mod)
```

```
7539      %bccn   $(mod i.p.mod)
7540      %bcdt   ~
7541      %bcgl   $(mod q.mod)
7542      %bcgr   $(mod q.mod)
7543      %bchp   $(mod p.mod)
7544      %bckt   $(mod q.mod)
7545      %bcls   $(mod q.mod)
7546      %bcfs   ~
7547      %bcmc   ~(name ap p.mod)
7548      %bcpm   $(mod p.mod)
7549      %bcsg   $(mod q.mod)
7550      %bctc   ~
7551      %bcts   $(mod q.mod)
7552      %bcpt   $(mod q.mod)
7553      %bcwt   $(mod i.p.mod)
7554      %bczp   ~
7555    ==
7556  ::
7557  ++  function
7558    ::    construct a function example
7559    ::
7560  |=  [fun=spec arg=spec]
7561  ^-  hoon
7562  ::  minimal context as subject
7563  ::
7564  :+  %tsgr
7565    ::  context is example of both specs
7566    ::
7567    [example:clear(mod fun) example:clear(mod arg)]
7568  ::  produce an %iron (contravariant) core
7569  ::
7570  :-  %ktbr
7571  ::  make an actual gate
7572  ::
7573  :+  %brcl
7574    [%$ 2]
7575  [%$ 15]
7576  ::
7577  ++  interface
7578    ::    construct a core example
7579    ::
7580  |=  [variance=vair payload=spec arms=(map term spec)]
7581  ^-  hoon
7582  ::  attach proper variance control
7583  ::
7584  =-  ?-  variance
7585        %gold  -
7586        %lead  [%ktwt -]
7587        %zinc  [%ktpm -]
7588        %iron  [%ktbr -]
7589      ==
7590  ^-  hoon
7591  :+  %tsgr  example:clear(mod payload)
7592  :+  %brcn  ~
7593  =-  [[%$ ~ -] ~ ~]
7594  %-  ~(gas by *(map term hoon))
7595  %+  turn
7596    ~(tap by arms)
```

```
7597      |=  [=term =spec]
7598      ::
7599      ::  note that we *don't* make arm specs in an interface
7600      ::  hygienic -- we leave them in context, to support
7601      ::  maximum programmer flexibility
7602      ::
7603      [term example:clear(mod spec)]
7604    ::
7605    ++  home
7606      ::    express a hoon against the original subject
7607      ::
7608      |=  gen=hoon
7609      ^-  hoon
7610      =/  ,wing
7611          ?:  =(1 dom)
7612            hay
7613          (weld hay `wing`[[%& dom] ~])
7614      ?~  - gen
7615      [%tsgr [%wing -] gen]
7616    ::
7617    ++  clear
7618      ::    clear annotations
7619      ^+  .
7620      .(bug ~, def ~, nut ~)
7621    ::
7622    ++  basal
7623      ::    example base case
7624      ::
7625      |=  bas=base
7626      ?-  bas
7627      ::
7628        [%atom *]
7629      ::  we may want sped
7630      ::
7631        [%sand p.bas ?:(=(%da p.bas) ~2000.1.1 0)]
7632      ::
7633        %noun
7634      ::  raw nock produces noun type
7635      ::
7636      =+([%rock %$ 0] [%ktls [%dttr - - [%rock %$ 1]] -])
7637      ::
7638        %cell
7639      ::  reduce to pair of nouns
7640      ::
7641      =+($(bas %noun) [- -])
7642      ::
7643        %flag
7644      ::  comparison produces boolean type
7645      ::
7646      =+([%rock %$ 0] [%ktls [%dtts - -] -])
7647      ::
7648        %null
7649      [%rock %n 0]
7650      ::
7651        %void
7652      [%zpzp ~]
7653      ==
7654    ::
```

```
7655  ++  unfold
7656      |=  [fun=hoon arg=(list spec)]
7657      ^-  hoon
7658      [%cncl fun (turn arg |=(spec ktcl/+<))]
7659  ::
7660  ++  unreel
7661      |=  [one=wing res=(list wing)]
7662      ^-  hoon
7663      ?~(res [%wing one] [%tsgl [%wing one] $(one i.res, res t.res)])
7664  ::
7665  ++  descend
7666      ::    record an axis to original subject
7667      ::
7668      |=  axe=axis
7669      +>(dom (peg axe dom))
7670  ::
7671  ++  decorate
7672      ::    apply documentation to expression
7673      ::
7674      |=  gen=hoon
7675      ^-  hoon
7676      =-  ?~(nut - [%note u.nut -])
7677      |-
7678      ?~(bug gen [%dbug i.bug $(bug t.bug)])
7679  ::
7680  ++  pieces
7681      ::    enumerate tuple wings
7682      ::
7683      |=  =(list term)
7684      ^-  (^list wing)
7685      (turn list |=(=term `wing`[term ~]))
7686  ::
7687  ++  spore
7688      ::    build default sample
7689      ::
7690      ^-  hoon
7691      ::  sample is always typeless
7692      ::
7693      :+  %ktls
7694        [%bust %noun]
7695      ::  consume debugging context
7696      ::
7697      %-  decorate
7698      ::  use home as subject
7699      ::
7700      %-  home
7701      ::  if default is set, use it
7702      ::
7703      ?^  def  u.def
7704      ::  else map structure to expression
7705      ::
7706      ~+
7707      |-  ^-  hoon
7708      ?-  mod
7709        [%base *]  ?:(=(%void p.mod) [%rock %n 0] (basal p.mod))
7710        [%bcbc *]  ::    track hygienic recursion points lexically
7711                   ::
7712                   %=  $
```

```
7713                         mod  p.mod
7714                         cox  ::   merge lexically and don't forget %$
7715                              ::
7716                              (~(put by ^+(cox (~(uni by cox) q.mod))) %$ p.mod)
7717                         ==
7718         [%dbug *]   [%dbug p.mod $(mod q.mod)]
7719         [%gist *]   $(mod q.mod)
7720         [%leaf *]   [%rock p.mod q.mod]
7721         [%loop *]   ~|([%loop p.mod] $(mod ~(got by cox) p.mod)))
7722         [%like *]   $(mod bcmc/(unreel p.mod q.mod))
7723         [%made *]   $(mod q.mod)
7724         [%make *]   $(mod bcmc/(unfold p.mod q.mod))
7725         [%name *]   $(mod q.mod)
7726         [%over *]   $(hay p.mod, mod q.mod)
7727      ::
7728         [%bcbr *]   $(mod p.mod)
7729         [%bccb *]   [%rock %n 0]
7730         [%bccl *]   |-  ^-  hoon
7731                     ?~  t.p.mod   ^$(mod i.p.mod)
7732                     :-  ^$(mod i.p.mod)
7733                     $(i.p.mod i.t.p.mod, t.p.mod t.t.p.mod)
7734         [%bccn *]   ::  use last entry
7735                     ::
7736                     |-  ^-  hoon
7737                     ?~  t.p.mod   ^$(mod i.p.mod)
7738                     $(i.p.mod i.t.p.mod, t.p.mod t.t.p.mod)
7739         [%bchp *]   ::  see under %bccb
7740                     ::
7741                     [%rock %n 0]
7742         [%bcgl *]   $(mod q.mod)
7743         [%bcgr *]   $(mod q.mod)
7744         [%bckt *]   $(mod q.mod)
7745         [%bcls *]   [%note [%know p.mod] $(mod q.mod)]
7746         [%bcmc *]   ::  borrow sample
7747                     ::
7748                     [%tsgl [%$ 6] p.mod]
7749         [%bcpm *]   $(mod p.mod)
7750         [%bcsg *]   [%kthp q.mod p.mod]
7751         [%bcts *]   [%ktts p.mod $(mod q.mod)]
7752         [%bcpt *]   $(mod p.mod)
7753         [%bcwt *]   ::  use last entry
7754                     ::
7755                     |-  ^-  hoon
7756                     ?~  t.p.mod   ^$(mod i.p.mod)
7757                     $(i.p.mod i.t.p.mod, t.p.mod t.t.p.mod)
7758         [%bcdt *]   [%rock %n 0]
7759         [%bcfs *]   [%rock %n 0]
7760         [%bctc *]   [%rock %n 0]
7761         [%bczp *]   [%rock %n 0]
7762      ==
7763   ::
7764   ++  example
7765     ::   produce a correctly typed default instance
7766     ::
7767     ~+
7768     ^-  hoon
7769     ?+  mod
7770        ::  in the general case, make and analyze a spore
```

```
7771        ::
7772        :+  %tsls
7773          spore
7774        ~(relative analyze:(descend 3) 2)
7775        ::
7776        [%base *]  (decorate (basal p.mod))
7777        [%dbug *]  example(mod q.mod, bug [p.mod bug])
7778        [%gist *]  example(mod q.mod, nut `p.mod)
7779        [%leaf *]  (decorate [%rock p.mod q.mod])
7780        [%like *]  example(mod bcmc/(unreel p.mod q.mod))
7781        [%loop *]  [%limb p.mod]
7782        [%made *]  example(mod q.mod, nut `made/[p.p.mod `(pieces q.p.mod)])
7783        [%make *]  example(mod bcmc/(unfold p.mod q.mod))
7784        [%name *]  example(mod q.mod, nut `made/[p.mod ~])
7785        [%over *]  example(hay p.mod, mod q.mod)
7786        ::
7787        [%bccb *]  (decorate (home p.mod))
7788        [%bccl *]  %-  decorate
7789                   |-  ^-  hoon
7790                   ?~  t.p.mod
7791                     example:clear(mod i.p.mod)
7792                   :-  example:clear(mod i.p.mod)
7793                   example:clear(i.p.mod i.t.p.mod, t.p.mod t.t.p.mod)
7794        [%bchp *]  (decorate (function:clear p.mod q.mod))
7795        [%bcmc *]  (decorate (home [%tsgl [%limb %$] p.mod]))
7796        [%bcsg *]  [%ktls example(mod q.mod) (home p.mod)]
7797        [%bcls *]  (decorate [%note [%know p.mod] example(mod q.mod)])
7798        [%bcts *]  (decorate [%ktts p.mod example:clear(mod q.mod)])
7799        [%bcdt *]  (decorate (home (interface %gold p.mod q.mod)))
7800        [%bcfs *]  (decorate (home (interface %iron p.mod q.mod)))
7801        [%bczp *]  (decorate (home (interface %lead p.mod q.mod)))
7802        [%bctc *]  (decorate (home (interface %zinc p.mod q.mod)))
7803      ==
7804    ::
7805    ++  factory
7806    ::      make a normalizing gate (mold)
7807    ::
7808    ^-  hoon
7809    ::  process annotations outside construct, to catch default
7810    ::
7811    ::TODO: try seeing if putting %gist in here fixes %brbc
7812    ?:  ?=(%dbug -.mod)  factory(mod q.mod, bug [p.mod bug])
7813    ?:  ?=(%bcsg -.mod)  factory(mod q.mod, def `[%kthp q.mod p.mod])
7814    ^-  hoon
7815    ::  if we recognize an indirection
7816    ::
7817    ?:  &(=(~ def) ?=(?(%bcmc %like %loop %make) -.mod))
7818        ::  then short-circuit it
7819        ::
7820    %-  decorate
7821    %-  home
7822    ?-  -.mod
7823      %bcmc  p.mod
7824      %like  (unreel p.mod q.mod)
7825      %loop  [%limb p.mod]
7826      %make  (unfold p.mod q.mod)
7827    ==
7828    ::  else build a gate
```

```
7829        ::
7830        :+  %brcl
7831          [%ktsg spore]
7832        :+  %tsls
7833          ~(relative analyze:(descend 7) 6)
7834        ::  trigger unifying equality
7835        ::
7836        :+  %tsls  [%dtts $/14 $/2]
7837        $/6
7838      ::
7839      ++  analyze
7840        ::    normalize a fragment of the subject
7841        ::
7842        |_  $:  ::  axe: axis to fragment
7843                ::
7844                axe=axis
7845            ==
7846      ++  basic
7847        |=  bas=base
7848        ^-  hoon
7849        ?-  bas
7850          [%atom *]
7851          :+  %ktls  example
7852          ^-  hoon
7853          :^    %zppt
7854            [[[%| 0 `%ruth] ~] ~]
7855            [%cnls [%limb %ruth] [%sand %ta p.bas] fetch]
7856          [%wtpt fetch-wing fetch [%zpzp ~]]
7857        ::
7858          %cell
7859          :+  %ktls  example
7860          =+  fetch-wing
7861          :-  [%wing [[%& %2] ~]]
7862              [%wing [[%& %3] ~]]
7863        ::
7864          %flag
7865          :^    %wtcl
7866            [%dtts [%rock %$ &] [%$ axe]]
7867            [%rock %f &]
7868          :+  %wtgr
7869            [%dtts [%rock %$ |] [%$ axe]]
7870          [%rock %f |]
7871        ::
7872          %noun
7873        fetch
7874        ::
7875          %null
7876          :+  %wtgr
7877            [%dtts [%bust %noun] [%$ axe]]
7878          [%rock %n ~]
7879        :::
7880          %void
7881        [%zpzp ~]
7882        ==
7883      ++  clear
7884        .(..analyze ^clear)
7885      ::
7886      ++  fetch
```

```
7887      ::      load the fragment
7888      ::
7889      ^-  hoon
7890      [%$ axe]
7891    ::
7892    ++  fetch-wing
7893      ::      load, as a wing
7894      ::
7895      ^-  wing
7896      [[%& axe] ~]
7897    ::
7898    ++  choice
7899      ::      match full models, by trying them
7900      ::
7901      |=  $:  ::  one: first option
7902              ::  rep: other options
7903              ::
7904              one=spec
7905              rep=(list spec)
7906          ==
7907      ^-  hoon
7908      ::  if no other choices, construct head
7909      ::
7910      ?~  rep  relative:clear(mod one)
7911      ::  build test
7912      ::
7913      :^    %wtcl
7914          ::  if we fit the type of this choice
7915          ::
7916          [%fits example:clear(mod one) fetch-wing]
7917        ::  build with this choice
7918        ::
7919        relative:clear(mod one)
7920      ::  continue through loop
7921      ::
7922      $(one i.rep, rep t.rep)
7923    ::
7924    ++  switch
7925      |=  $:  ::  one: first format
7926              ::  two: more formats
7927              ::
7928              one=spec
7929              rep=(list spec)
7930          ==
7931      |-  ^-  hoon
7932      ::  if no other choices, construct head
7933      ::
7934      ?~  rep  relative:clear(mod one)
7935      ::  fin: loop completion
7936      ::
7937      =/  fin=hoon  $(one i.rep, rep t.rep)
7938      ::  interrogate this instance
7939      ::
7940      :^    %wtcl
7941          ::  test if the head matches this wing
7942          ::
7943          :+  %fits
7944            [%tsgl [%$ 2] example:clear(mod one)]
```

```
7945        fetch-wing(axe (peg axe 2))
7946        ::  if so, use this form
7947        ::
7948        relative:clear(mod one)
7949      ::  continue in the loop
7950      ::
7951      fin
7952    ::
7953    ++  relative
7954      ::    local constructor
7955      ::
7956      ~+
7957      ^-  hoon
7958      ?-    mod
7959      ::
7960      ::  base
7961      ::
7962          [%base *]
7963        (decorate (basic:clear p.mod))
7964      ::
7965      ::  debug
7966      ::
7967          [%dbug *]
7968        relative(mod q.mod, bug [p.mod bug])
7969      ::
7970      ::  formal comment
7971      ::
7972          [%gist *]
7973        relative(mod q.mod, nut `p.mod)
7974      ::
7975      ::  constant
7976      ::
7977          [%leaf *]
7978      %-  decorate
7979      :+  %wtgr
7980          [%dtts fetch [%rock %$ q.mod]]
7981        [%rock p.mod q.mod]
7982      ::
7983      ::  composite
7984      ::
7985          [%make *]
7986        relative(mod bcmc/(unfold p.mod q.mod))
7987      ::
7988      ::  indirect
7989      ::
7990          [%like *]
7991        relative(mod bcmc/(unreel p.mod q.mod))
7992      ::
7993      ::  loop
7994      ::
7995          [%loop *]
7996        (decorate [%cnhp [%limb p.mod] fetch])
7997      ::
7998      ::  simple named structure
7999      ::
8000          [%name *]
8001        relative(mod q.mod, nut `made/[p.mod ~])
8002      ::
```

```
8003      ::  synthetic named structure
8004      ::
8005          [%made *]
8006        relative(mod q.mod, nut `made/[p.p.mod `(pieces q.p.mod)])
8007      ::
8008      ::  subjective
8009      ::
8010          [%over *]
8011        relative(hay p.mod, mod q.mod)
8012      ::
8013      ::  recursive, $$
8014      ::
8015          [%bcbc *]
8016        ::
8017        ::  apply semantically
8018        ::
8019        :+  %brkt
8020          relative(mod p.mod, dom (peg 3 dom))
8021        =-  [[%$ ~ -] ~ ~]
8022        %-  ~(gas by *(map term hoon))
8023        ^-  (list (pair term hoon))
8024        %+  turn
8025          ~(tap by q.mod)
8026        |=  [=term =spec]
8027        [term relative(mod spec, dom (peg 3 dom))]
8028      ::
8029      ::  normalize, $&
8030      ::
8031          [%bcpm *]
8032        ::  push the raw result
8033        ::
8034        :+  %tsls  relative(mod p.mod)
8035        ::  push repair function
8036        ::
8037        :+  %tsls
8038          [%tsgr $/3 q.mod]
8039        ::  push repaired product
8040        ::
8041        :+  %tsls
8042          [%cnhp $/2 $/6]
8043        ::  sanity-check repaired product
8044        ::
8045        :+  %wtgr
8046          ::  either
8047          ::
8048          :~  %wtbr
8049              ::  the repair did not change anything
8050              ::
8051              [%dtts $/14 $/2]
8052              ::  when we fix it again, it stays fixed
8053              ::
8054              [%dtts $/2 [%cnhp $/6 $/2]]
8055          ==
8056        $/2
8057      ::
8058      ::  verify, $|
8059      ::
8060          [%bcbr *]
```

```
8061        ^-  hoon
8062        ::  push the raw product
8063        ::
8064        :+  %tsls  relative(mod p.mod)
8065        ^-  hoon
8066        ::  assert
8067        ::
8068        :+  %wtgr
8069          ::  run the verifier
8070          ::
8071          [%cnhp [%tsgr $/3 q.mod] $/2]
8072        ::  produce verified product
8073        ::
8074        $/2
8075      ::
8076      ::  special, $_
8077      ::
8078          [%bccb *]
8079        (decorate (home p.mod))
8080      ::
8081      ::  switch, $%
8082      ::
8083          [%bccn *]
8084        (decorate (switch i.p.mod t.p.mod))
8085      ::
8086      ::  tuple, $:
8087      ::
8088          [%bccl *]
8089        %-  decorate
8090        |-  ^-  hoon
8091        ?~  t.p.mod
8092          relative:clear(mod i.p.mod)
8093        :-  relative:clear(mod i.p.mod, axe (peg axe 2))
8094        %=  relative
8095          i.p.mod  i.t.p.mod
8096          t.p.mod  t.t.p.mod
8097          axe      (peg axe 3)
8098        ==
8099      ::
8100      ::  exclude, $<
8101      ::
8102          [%bcgl *]
8103        :+  %tsls
8104          relative:clear(mod q.mod)
8105        :+  %wtgl
8106          [%wtts [%over ~[&/3] p.mod] ~[&/4]]
8107        $/2
8108      ::
8109      ::  require, $>
8110      ::
8111          [%bcgr *]
8112        :+  %tsls
8113          relative:clear(mod q.mod)
8114        :+  %wtgr
8115          [%wtts [%over ~[&/3] p.mod] ~[&/4]]
8116        $/2
8117      ::
8118      ::  function
```

```
8119          ::
8120              [%bchp *]
8121          %-  decorate
8122          =/  fun  (function:clear p.mod q.mod)
8123          ?^  def
8124            [%ktls fun u.def]
8125          fun
8126          ::
8127          ::  bridge, $^
8128          ::
8129              [%bckt *]
8130          %-  decorate
8131          :^    %wtcl
8132            [%dtwt fetch(axe (peg axe 2))]
8133            relative:clear(mod p.mod)
8134          relative:clear(mod q.mod)
8135          ::
8136          ::  synthesis, $;
8137          ::
8138              [%bcmc *]
8139          (decorate [%cncl (home p.mod) fetch ~])
8140          ::
8141          ::  default
8142          ::
8143              [%bcsg *]
8144          relative(mod q.mod, def `[%kthp q.mod p.mod])
8145          ::
8146          ::  choice, $?
8147          ::
8148              [%bcwt *]
8149          (decorate (choice i.p.mod t.p.mod))
8150          ::
8151          ::  name, $=
8152          ::
8153              [%bcts *]
8154          [%ktts p.mod relative(mod q.mod)]
8155          ::
8156          ::  branch, $@
8157          ::
8158              [%bcpt *]
8159          %-  decorate
8160          :^    %wtcl
8161            [%dtwt fetch]
8162            relative:clear(mod q.mod)
8163          relative:clear(mod p.mod)
8164          ::
8165          [%bcls *]  [%note [%know p.mod] relative(mod q.mod)]
8166          [%bcdt *]  (decorate (home (interface %gold p.mod q.mod)))
8167          [%bcfs *]  (decorate (home (interface %iron p.mod q.mod)))
8168          [%bczp *]  (decorate (home (interface %lead p.mod q.mod)))
8169          [%bctc *]  (decorate (home (interface %zinc p.mod q.mod)))
8170        ==
8171      --
8172    --
8173  ::
8174  ++  ap                                              ::  hoon engine
8175    ~%    %ap
8176        +>+
```

```
8177        ==
8178          %open   open
8179          %rake   rake
8180        ==
8181    |_  gen=hoon
8182    ::
8183    ++  grip
8184      |=  =skin
8185      =|  rel=wing
8186      |-  ^-  hoon
8187      ?-    skin
8188            @
8189          [%tsgl [%tune skin] gen]
8190            [%base *]
8191          ?:  ?=(%noun base.skin)
8192            gen
8193          [%kthp skin gen]
8194        ::
8195            [%cell *]
8196          =+  haf=~(half ap gen)
8197          ?^  haf
8198            :-  $(skin skin.skin, gen p.u.haf)
8199            $(skin ^skin.skin, gen q.u.haf)
8200          :+  %tsls
8201            gen
8202          :-  $(skin skin.skin, gen [%$ 4])
8203          $(skin ^skin.skin, gen [%$ 5])
8204        ::
8205            [%dbug *]
8206          [%dbug spot.skin $(skin skin.skin)]
8207        ::
8208            [%leaf *]
8209          [%kthp skin gen]
8210        ::
8211            [%help *]
8212          [%note [%help help.skin] $(skin skin.skin)]
8213        ::
8214            [%name *]
8215          [%tsgl [%tune term.skin] $(skin skin.skin)]
8216        ::
8217            [%over *]
8218          $(skin skin.skin, rel (weld wing.skin rel))
8219        ::
8220            [%spec *]
8221          :+  %kthp
8222            ?~(rel spec.skin [%over rel spec.skin])
8223          $(skin skin.skin)
8224        ::
8225            [%wash *]
8226          :+  %tsgl
8227            :-  %wing
8228            |-  ^-  wing
8229            ?:  =(0 depth.skin)  ~
8230            [[%| 0 ~] $(depth.skin (dec depth.skin))]
8231          gen
8232        ==
8233    ::
8234    ++  name
```

```
8235       |-  ^-  (unit term)
8236       ?+   gen   ~
8237         [%wing *]  ?~  p.gen   ~
8238                    ?^  i.p.gen
8239                      ?:(?=(%& -.i.p.gen) ~ q.i.p.gen)
8240                    `i.p.gen
8241         [%limb *]  `p.gen
8242         [%dbug *]  $(gen ~(open ap gen))
8243         [%tsgl *]  $(gen ~(open ap gen))
8244         [%tsgr *]  $(gen q.gen)
8245       ==
8246     ::
8247     ++  feck
8248       |-  ^-  (unit term)
8249       ?-   gen
8250         [%sand %tas @]   [~ q.gen]
8251         [%dbug *]        $(gen q.gen)
8252         *                ~
8253       ==
8254     ::
8255     ::  not used at present; see comment at %csng in ++open
8256 ::::
8257 ::++  hail
8258 ::   |=  axe=axis
8259 ::   =|  air=(list (pair wing hoon))
8260 ::   |-  ^+  air
8261 ::   =+  hav=half
8262 ::   ?~  hav  [[[[%| 0 ~] [%& axe] ~] gen] air]
8263 ::   $(gen p.u.hav, axe (peg axe 2), air $(gen q.u.hav, axe (peg axe 3)))
8264 ::
8265     ++  half
8266       |-  ^-  (unit (pair hoon hoon))
8267       ?+   gen   ~
8268         [^ *]      `[p.gen q.gen]
8269         [%dbug *]  $(gen q.gen)
8270         [%clcb *]  `[q.gen p.gen]
8271         [%clhp *]  `[p.gen q.gen]
8272         [%clkt *]  `[p.gen %clls q.gen r.gen s.gen]
8273         [%clsg *]  ?~(p.gen ~ `[i.p.gen %clsg t.p.gen])
8274         [%cltr *]  ?~  p.gen   ~
8275                    ?~(t.p.gen $(gen i.p.gen) `[i.p.gen %cltr t.p.gen])
8276       ==
8277 ::::
8278     ::  +flay: hoon to skin
8279     ::
8280     ++  flay
8281       |-  ^-  (unit skin)
8282       ?+     gen
8283       =+(open ?:(=(- gen) ~ $(gen -)))
8284       ::
8285         [^ *]
8286       =+  [$(gen p.gen) $(gen q.gen)]
8287       ?~(-< ~ ?~(-> ~ `[%cell -<+ ->+]))
8288       ::
8289         [%base *]
8290       `gen
8291       ::
8292         [%rock *]
```

```
8293          ?@(q.gen `[%leaf p.gen q.gen] ~)
8294        ::
8295            [%cnts [@ ~] ~]
8296          `i.p.gen
8297        ::
8298            [%tsgr *]
8299        %+  biff   reek(gen p.gen)
8300        |=  =wing
8301        (bind ^$(gen q.gen) |=(=skin [%over wing skin]))
8302        ::
8303            [%limb @]
8304          `p.gen
8305        ::
8306        ::  [%rock *]
8307        ::  [%spec %leaf q.gen q.gen]
8308        ::
8309            [%note [%help *] *]
8310        (bind $(gen q.gen) |=(=skin [%help p.p.gen skin]))
8311        ::
8312            [%wing *]
8313        ?:  ?=([@ ~] p.gen)
8314          `i.p.gen
8315        =/  depth  0
8316        |-  ^-  (unit skin)
8317        ?~  p.gen  `[%wash depth]
8318        ?.  =([%| 0 ~] i.p.gen)  ~
8319        $(p.gen t.p.gen)
8320        ::
8321            [%kttr *]
8322        `[%spec p.gen %base %noun]
8323        ::
8324            [%ktts *]
8325        %+  biff  $(gen q.gen)
8326        |=  =skin
8327        ?@  p.gen  `[%name p.gen skin]
8328        ?.  ?=([%name @ [%base %noun]] p.gen)  ~
8329        `[%name term.p.gen skin]
8330      ==
8331  ::
8332  ::  +open: desugarer
8333  ++  open
8334    ^-  hoon
8335    ?-    gen
8336      [~ *]        [%cnts [[%& p.gen] ~] ~]
8337      ::
8338      [%base *]  ~(factory ax `spec`gen)
8339      [%bust *]  ~(example ax %base p.gen)
8340      [%ktcl *]  ~(factory ax p.gen)
8341      [%dbug *]   q.gen
8342      [%eror *]  ~_((crip p.gen) !!)
8343      ::
8344        [%knit *]                           ::
8345      :+  %tsgr  [%ktts %v %$ 1]            ::  =>  v=.
8346      :-  %brhp                             ::  |-
8347      :+  %ktls                             ::  ^+
8348        :-  %brhp                           ::  |-
8349        :^    %wtcl                         ::  ?:
8350            [%bust %flag]                   ::  ?
```

```
8351              [%bust %null]                        :: ~
8352         :-  [%ktts %i [%sand 'tD' *@]]            :: :-  i=~~
8353         [%ktts %t [%limb %$]]                     :: t=$
8354       |-  ^-  hoon                                ::
8355     ?~  p.gen                                     ::
8356         [%bust %null]                             :: ~
8357     =+  res=$(p.gen t.p.gen)                      ::
8358     ^-  hoon                                      ::
8359     ?@  i.p.gen                                   ::
8360         [[%sand 'tD' i.p.gen] res]                :: [~~{i.p.gen} {res}]
8361       :+  %tsls                                   ::
8362         :-  :+  %ktts                             :: ^=
8363               %a                                  :: a
8364             :+  %ktls                             :: ^+
8365               [%limb %$]                          :: $
8366             [%tsgr [%limb %v] p.i.p.gen]          :: =>(v {p.i.p.gen})
8367         [%ktts %b res]                            :: b=[res]
8368     ^-  hoon                                      ::
8369     :-  %brhp                                     :: |-
8370     :^    %wtpt                                   :: ?@
8371         [%a ~]                                    :: a
8372       [%limb %b]                                  :: b
8373     :-  [%tsgl [%$ 2] [%limb %a]]                 :: :-  -.a
8374     :+  %cnts                                     :: %=
8375       [%$ ~]                                      :: $
8376     [[[%a ~] [%tsgl [%$ 3] [%limb %a]]] ~]        :: a  +.a
8377   ::
8378       [%leaf *]   ~(factory ax `spec`gen)
8379       [%limb *]   [%cnts [p.gen ~] ~]
8380       [%tell *]   [%cncl [%limb %noah] [%zpgr [%cltr p.gen]] ~]
8381       [%wing *]   [%cnts p.gen ~]
8382       [%yell *]   [%cncl [%limb %cain] [%zpgr [%cltr p.gen]] ~]
8383       [%note *]   q.gen
8384   ::
8385   ::TODO: does %gist need to be special cased here?
8386       [%brbc *]   =-  ?~  -  !!
8387                       :+  %brtr
8388                         [%bccl -]
8389                       |-
8390                   ?.  ?=([%gist *] body.gen)
8391                     [%ktcl body.gen]
8392                   [%note p.body.gen $(body.gen q.body.gen)]
8393             %+  turn  `(list term)`sample.gen
8394             |=  =term
8395             ^-  spec
8396             =/  tar  [%base %noun]
8397             [%bcts term [%bcsg tar [%bchp tar tar]]]
8398       [%brcb *]   :+  %tsls  [%kttr p.gen]
8399                   :+  %brcn  ~
8400             %-  ~(run by r.gen)
8401             |=  =tome
8402             :-  p.tome
8403             %-  ~(run by q.tome)
8404             |=  =hoon
8405             ?~  q.gen  hoon
8406             [%tstr [p.i.q.gen ~] q.i.q.gen $(q.gen t.q.gen)]
8407       [%brcl *]   [%tsls p.gen [%brdt q.gen]]
8408       [%brdt *]   :+  %brcn  ~
```

```
8409                        =-  [[%$ ~ -] ~ ~]
8410                        (~(put by *(map term hoon)) %$ p.gen)
8411          [%brkt *]  :+  %tsgl  [%limb %$]
8412                     :+  %brcn  ~
8413                     =+  zil=(~(get by q.gen) %$)
8414                     ?~  zil
8415                       %+  ~(put by q.gen)  %$
8416                       [*what [[%$ p.gen] ~ ~]]
8417                     %+  ~(put by q.gen)  %$
8418                     [p.u.zil (~(put by q.u.zil) %$ p.gen)]
8419          [%brhp *]  [%tsgl [%limb %$] [%brdt p.gen]]
8420          [%brsg *]  [%ktbr [%brts p.gen q.gen]]
8421          [%brtr *]  :+  %tsls  [%kttr p.gen]
8422                     :+  %brpt  ~
8423                     =-  [[%$ ~ -] ~ ~]
8424                     (~(put by *(map term hoon)) %$ q.gen)
8425          [%brts *]  :+  %brcb  p.gen
8426                     =-  [~ [[%$ ~ -] ~ ~]]
8427                     (~(put by *(map term hoon)) %$ q.gen)
8428          [%brwt *]  [%ktwt %brdt p.gen]
8429        ::
8430          [%clkt *]  [p.gen q.gen r.gen s.gen]
8431          [%clls *]  [p.gen q.gen r.gen]
8432          [%clcb *]  [q.gen p.gen]
8433          [%clhp *]  [p.gen q.gen]
8434          [%clsg *]
8435      |-  ^-  hoon
8436      ?~  p.gen
8437        [%rock %n ~]
8438      [i.p.gen $(p.gen t.p.gen)]
8439        ::
8440          [%cltr *]
8441      |-  ^-  hoon
8442      ?~  p.gen
8443        [%zpzp ~]
8444      ?~  t.p.gen
8445        i.p.gen
8446      [i.p.gen $(p.gen t.p.gen)]
8447        ::
8448          [%kttr *]  [%ktsg ~(example ax p.gen)]
8449          [%cncb *]  [%ktls [%wing p.gen] %cnts p.gen q.gen]
8450          [%cndt *]  [%cncl q.gen [p.gen ~]]
8451          [%cnkt *]  [%cncl p.gen q.gen r.gen s.gen ~]
8452          [%cnls *]  [%cncl p.gen q.gen r.gen ~]
8453          [%cnhp *]  [%cncl p.gen q.gen ~]
8454          ::  this probably should work, but doesn't
8455          ::
8456          ::  [%cncl *]  [%cntr [%$ ~] p.gen [[[[%& 6] ~] [%cltr q.gen]] ~]]
8457          [%cncl *]  [%cnsg [%$ ~] p.gen q.gen]
8458          [%cnsg *]
8459      ::  this complex matching system is a leftover from the old
8460      ::  "electroplating" era.  %cnsg should be removed and replaced
8461      ::  with the commented-out %cncl above.  but something is broken.
8462      ::
8463      :^  %cntr  p.gen  q.gen
8464      =+  axe=6
8465      |-  ^-  (list [wing hoon])
8466      ?~  r.gen  ~
```

```
8467        ?~  t.r.gen  [[[[%| 0 ~] [%& axe] ~] i.r.gen] ~]
8468        :-  [[[%| 0 ~] [%& (peg axe 2)] ~] i.r.gen]
8469        $(axe (peg axe 3), r.gen t.r.gen)
8470      ::
8471          [%cntr *]
8472        ?:  =(~ r.gen)
8473        [%tsgr q.gen [%wing p.gen]]
8474        :+  %tsls
8475          q.gen
8476        :+  %cnts
8477          (weld p.gen `wing`[[%& 2] ~])
8478        (turn r.gen |=([p=wing q=hoon] [p [%tsgr [%$ 3] q]]))
8479      ::
8480          [%ktdt *]   [%ktls [%cncl p.gen q.gen ~] q.gen]
8481          [%kthp *]   [%ktls ~(example ax p.gen) q.gen]
8482          [%ktts *]   (grip(gen q.gen) p.gen)
8483      ::
8484          [%sgbr *]
8485        :+  %sggr
8486        :-  %mean
8487        =+  fek=~(feck ap p.gen)
8488        ?^  fek  [%rock %tas u.fek]
8489        [%brdt [%cncl [%limb %cain] [%zpgr [%tsgr [%$ 3] p.gen]] ~]]
8490        q.gen
8491      ::
8492          [%sgcb *]   [%sggr [%mean [%brdt p.gen]] q.gen]
8493          [%sgcn *]
8494        :+  %sggl
8495        :-  %fast
8496        :-  %clls
8497        :+  [%rock %$ p.gen]
8498          [%zpts q.gen]
8499        :-  %clsg
8500        =+  nob=`(list hoon)`~
8501        |-  ^-  (list hoon)
8502        ?~  r.gen
8503          nob
8504        [[[%rock %$ p.i.r.gen] [%zpts q.i.r.gen]] $(r.gen t.r.gen)]
8505        s.gen
8506      ::
8507          [%sgfs *]   [%sgcn p.gen [%$ 7] ~ q.gen]
8508          [%sggl *]   [%tsgl [%sggr p.gen [%$ 1]] q.gen]
8509          [%sgbc *]   [%sggr [%live [%rock %$ p.gen]] q.gen]
8510          [%sgls *]   [%sggr [%memo %rock %$ p.gen] q.gen]
8511          [%sgpm *]
8512        :+  %sggr
8513        [%slog [%sand %$ p.gen] [%cncl [%limb %cain] [%zpgr q.gen] ~]]
8514        r.gen
8515      ::
8516          [%sgts *]   [%sggr [%germ p.gen] q.gen]
8517          [%sgwt *]
8518        :+  %tsls  [%wtdt q.gen [%bust %null] [[%bust %null] r.gen]]
8519        :^  %wtsg  [%& 2]~
8520        [%tsgr [%$ 3] s.gen]
8521        [%sgpm p.gen [%$ 5] [%tsgr [%$ 3] s.gen]]
8522      ::
8523          [%mcts *]
8524        |-
```

```
8525        ?~  p.gen  [%bust %null]
8526        ?-  -.i.p.gen
8527            ^         [[%xray i.p.gen] $(p.gen t.p.gen)]
8528        %manx  [p.i.p.gen $(p.gen t.p.gen)]
8529        %tape  [[%mcfs p.i.p.gen] $(p.gen t.p.gen)]
8530        %call  [%cncl p.i.p.gen [$(p.gen t.p.gen)]~]
8531        %marl  =-  [%cndt [p.i.p.gen $(p.gen t.p.gen)] -]
8532               ^-  hoon
8533               :+  %tsbr  [%base %cell]
8534               :+  %brpt  ~
8535               ^-  (map term tome)
8536               =-  [[%$ ~ -] ~ ~]
8537               ^-  (map term hoon)
8538               :_  [~ ~]
8539               =+  sug=[[%& 12] ~]
8540               :-  %$
8541               :^  %wtsg  sug
8542                 [%cnts sug [[[[%& 1] ~] [%$ 13]] ~]]
8543               [%cnts sug [[[[%& 3] ~] [%cnts [%$ ~] [[sug [%$ 25]] ~]]] ~]]
8544        ==
8545    ::
8546        [%mccl *]
8547      ?-     q.gen
8548             ~         [%zpzp ~]
8549        [* ~]  i.q.gen
8550            ^
8551        :+  %tsls
8552          p.gen
8553        =+  yex=`(list hoon)`q.gen
8554        |-  ^-  hoon
8555        ?-  yex
8556        [* ~]   [%tsgr [%$ 3] i.yex]
8557        [* ^]   [%cncl [%$ 2] [%tsgr [%$ 3] i.yex] $(yex t.yex) ~]
8558          ~          !!
8559        ==
8560    ==
8561    ::
8562        [%mcfs *]  =+(zoy=[%rock %ta %$] [%clsg [zoy [%clsg [zoy p.gen] ~]] ~])
8563        [%mcgl *]  [%cnls [%cnhp q ktcl+p] r [%brts p [%tsgr $+3 s]]]:gen
8564    ::
8565        [%mcsg *]                              ::                    ;~
8566      |-  ^-  hoon                             ::
8567      ?-  q.gen                                ::
8568          ~         ~_(leaf+"open-mcsg" !!)    ::
8569          ^                                    ::
8570        :+  %tsgr  [%ktts %v %$ 1]             ::  => v=.
8571        |-  ^-  hoon                           ::
8572        ?:  ?=(~ t.q.gen)                      ::
8573          [%tsgr [%limb %v] i.q.gen]           ::  =>(v {i.q.gen})
8574        :+  %tsls  [%ktts %a $(q.gen t.q.gen)] ::  =+  ^=  a
8575        :+  %tsls                              ::        {$(q.gen t.q.gen)}
8576          [%ktts %b [%tsgr [%limb %v] i.q.gen]] ::  =+  ^=  b
8577        :+  %tsls                              ::    =>(v {i.q.gen})
8578          :+  %ktts  %c                        ::  =+  c=,.+6.b
8579          :+  %tsgl                            ::
8580            [%wing [%| 0 ~] [%& 6] ~]          ::
8581          [%limb %b]                           ::
8582        :-  %brdt                              ::  |.
```

```
8583    :^    %cnls                                  ::   %+
8584      [%tsgr [%limb %v] p.gen]                   ::      =>(v {p.gen})
8585      [%cncl [%limb %b] [%limb %c] ~]            ::   (b c)
8586    :+  %cnts  [%a ~]                            ::   a(,.+6 c)
8587    [[[[%| 0 ~] [%& 6] ~] [%limb %c]] ~]         ::
8588    ==                                           ::
8589  ::
8590      [%mcmc *]                                  ::                    ;;
8591    [%cnhp ~(factory ax p.gen) q.gen]
8592  ::
8593      [%tsbr *]
8594    [%tsls ~(example ax p.gen) q.gen]
8595  ::
8596      [%tstr *]
8597    :+  %tsgl
8598      r.gen
8599    [%tune [[p.p.gen ~ ?~(q.p.gen q.gen [%kthp u.q.p.gen q.gen])] ~ ~] ~]
8600  ::
8601      [%tscl *]
8602    [%tsgr [%cncb [[%& 1] ~] p.gen] q.gen]
8603  ::
8604      [%tsfs *]
8605    [%tsls [%ktts p.gen q.gen] r.gen]
8606  ::
8607      [%tsmc *]   [%tsfs p.gen r.gen q.gen]
8608      [%tsdt *]
8609    [%tsgr [%cncb [[%& 1] ~] [[p.gen q.gen] ~]] r.gen]
8610      [%tswt *]                                  ::                 =?
8611    [%tsdt p.gen [%wtcl q.gen r.gen [%wing p.gen]] s.gen]
8612  ::
8613      [%tskt *]                                  ::               =^
8614    =+  wuy=(weld q.gen `wing`[%v ~])            ::
8615    :+  %tsgr   [%ktts %v %$ 1]                  ::   =>  v=.
8616    :+  %tsls   [%ktts %a %tsgr [%limb %v] r.gen] ::   =+  a==>(v \r.gen)
8617    :^  %tsdt   wuy  [%tsgl [%$ 3] [%limb %a]]
8618    :+  %tsgr   :-  :+  %ktts  [%over [%v ~] p.gen]
8619                        [%tsgl [%$ 2] [%limb %a]]
8620                [%limb %v]
8621    s.gen
8622  ::
8623      [%tsgl *]   [%tsgr q.gen p.gen]
8624      [%tsls *]   [%tsgr [p.gen [%$ 1]] q.gen]
8625      [%tshp *]   [%tsls q.gen p.gen]
8626      [%tssg *]
8627    |-  ^-  hoon
8628    ?~  p.gen    [%$ 1]
8629    ?~  t.p.gen  i.p.gen
8630    [%tsgr i.p.gen $(p.gen t.p.gen)]
8631  ::
8632      [%wtbr *]
8633    |-
8634    ?~(p.gen [%rock %f 1] [%wtcl i.p.gen [%rock %f 0] $(p.gen t.p.gen)])
8635  ::
8636      [%wtdt *]   [%wtcl p.gen r.gen q.gen]
8637      [%wtgl *]   [%wtcl p.gen [%zpzp ~] q.gen]
8638      [%wtgr *]   [%wtcl p.gen q.gen [%zpzp ~]]
8639      [%wtkt *]   [%wtcl [%wtts [%base %atom %$] p.gen] r.gen q.gen]
8640  ::
```

```
8641          [%wthp *]
8642        |-
8643        ?~  q.gen
8644          [%lost [%wing p.gen]]
8645        :^    %wtcl
8646          [%wtts p.i.q.gen p.gen]
8647        q.i.q.gen
8648        $(q.gen t.q.gen)
8649      ::
8650          [%wtls *]
8651      [%wthp p.gen (weld r.gen `_r.gen`[[[%base %noun] q.gen] ~])]
8652      ::
8653          [%wtpm *]
8654        |-
8655        ?~(p.gen [%rock %f 0] [%wtcl i.p.gen $(p.gen t.p.gen) [%rock %f 1]])
8656      ::
8657          [%xray *]
8658      |^    :-  [(open-mane n.g.p.gen) %clsg (turn a.g.p.gen open-mart)]
8659          [%mcts c.p.gen]
8660      ::
8661      ++  open-mane
8662        |=  a=mane:hoot
8663        ?@(a [%rock %tas a] [[%rock %tas -.a] [%rock %tas +.a]])
8664      ::
8665      ++  open-mart
8666        |=  [n=mane:hoot v=(list beer:hoot)]
8667        [(open-mane n) %knit v]
8668      --
8669      ::
8670          [%wtpt *]    [%wtcl [%wtts [%base %atom %$] p.gen] q.gen r.gen]
8671          [%wtsg *]    [%wtcl [%wtts [%base %null] p.gen] q.gen r.gen]
8672          [%wtts *]    [%fits ~(example ax p.gen) q.gen]
8673          [%wtzp *]    [%wtcl p.gen [%rock %f 1] [%rock %f 0]]
8674          [%zpgr *]
8675      [%cncl [%limb %onan] [%zpmc [%kttr [%bcmc %limb %abel]] p.gen] ~]
8676      ::
8677          [%zpwt *]
8678      ?:  ?:  ?=(@ p.gen)
8679          (lte hoon-version p.gen)
8680        &((lte hoon-version p.p.gen) (gte hoon-version q.p.gen))
8681        q.gen
8682      ~_(leaf+"hoon-version" !!)
8683      ::
8684        *                gen
8685    ==
8686  ::
8687  ++  rake  ~>(%mean.'rake-hoon' (need reek))
8688  ++  reek
8689    ^-  (unit wing)
8690    ?+  gen  ~
8691    [~ *]        `[[%& p.gen] ~]
8692    [%limb *]    `[p.gen ~]
8693    [%wing *]    `p.gen
8694    [%cnts * ~]  `p.gen
8695    [%dbug *]    reek(gen q.gen)
8696    ==
8697  ++  rusk
8698    ^-  term
```

```
8699      =+  wig=rake
8700      ?.  ?=([@ ~] wig)
8701        ~>(%mean.'rusk-hoon' !!)
8702      i.wig
8703    --
8704  ::
8705  ::    5c: compiler backend and prettyprinter
8706  +|  %compiler-backend-and-prettyprinter
8707  ::
8708  ++  ut
8709    ~%    %ut
8710        +>+
8711      ==
8712        %ar    ar
8713        %fan   fan
8714        %rib   rib
8715        %vet   vet
8716        %blow  blow
8717        %burp  burp
8718        %busk  busk
8719        %buss  buss
8720        %crop  crop
8721        %duck  duck
8722        %dune  dune
8723        %dunk  dunk
8724        %epla  epla
8725        %emin  emin
8726        %emul  emul
8727        %feel  feel
8728        %felt  felt
8729        %fine  fine
8730        %fire  fire
8731        %fish  fish
8732        %fond  fond
8733        %fund  fund
8734        %funk  funk
8735        %fuse  fuse
8736        %gain  gain
8737        %lose  lose
8738        %mile  mile
8739        %mine  mine
8740        %mint  mint
8741        %moot  moot
8742        %mull  mull
8743        %nest  nest
8744        %peel  peel
8745        %play  play
8746        %peek  peek
8747        %repo  repo
8748        %rest  rest
8749        %sink  sink
8750        %tack  tack
8751        %toss  toss
8752        %wrap  wrap
8753      ==
8754  =+  :*  fan=*(set [type hoon])
8755          rib=*(set [type type hoon])
8756          vet=`?`&
```

```
8757          ==
8758    =+  sut=`type`%noun
8759    |%
8760    ++  clip
8761      |=  ref=type
8762      ?>  ?|(!vet (nest(sut ref) & sut))
8763      ref
8764    ::
8765    ::  +ar: texture engine
8766    ::
8767    ++  ar  !:
8768      ~%  %ar
8769          +>
8770          ==
8771          %fish   fish
8772          %gain   gain
8773          %lose   lose
8774          ==
8775      |_  [ref=type =skin]
8776      ::
8777      ::  +fish: make a $nock that tests a .ref at .axis for .skin
8778      ::
8779      ++  fish
8780        |=  =axis
8781        ^-  nock
8782        ?@  skin  [%1 &]
8783        ?-    -.skin
8784        ::
8785            %base
8786          ?-  base.skin
8787            %cell       $(skin [%cell [%base %noun] [%base %noun]])
8788            %flag       ?:  (~(nest ut bool) | ref)
8789                          [%1 &]
8790                        %+  flan
8791                          $(skin [%base %atom %$])
8792                        %+  flor
8793                          [%5 [%0 axis] [%1 &]]
8794                        [%5 [%0 axis] [%1 |]]
8795            %noun       [%1 &]
8796            %null       $(skin [%leaf %n ~])
8797            %void       [%1 |]
8798            [%atom *]   ?:  (~(nest ut [%atom %$ ~]) | ref)
8799                          [%1 &]
8800                        ?:  (~(nest ut [%cell %noun %noun]) | ref)
8801                          [%1 |]
8802                        (flip [%3 %0 axis])
8803          ==
8804        ::
8805            %cell
8806          ?:  (~(nest ut [%atom %$ ~]) | ref)  [%1 |]
8807          %+  flan
8808            ?:  (~(nest ut [%cell %noun %noun]) | ref)
8809              [%1 &]
8810            [%3 %0 axis]
8811          %+  flan
8812            $(ref (peek(sut ref) %free 2), skin skin.skin)
8813          $(ref (peek(sut ref) %free 3), skin ^skin.skin)
8814        ::
```

```
8815            %leaf
8816          ?:  (~(nest ut [%atom %$ `atom.skin]) | ref)
8817            [%1 &]
8818          [%5 [%1 atom.skin] [%0 axis]]
8819        ::
8820            %dbug  $(skin skin.skin)
8821            %help  $(skin skin.skin)
8822            %name  $(skin skin.skin)
8823            %over  $(skin skin.skin)
8824            %spec  $(skin skin.skin)
8825            %wash  [%1 1]
8826        ==
8827      ::
8828      ::  +gain: make a $type by restricting .ref to .skin
8829      ::
8830      ++  gain
8831        |-  ^-  type
8832        ?@  skin  [%face skin ref]
8833        ?-    -.skin
8834        ::
8835            %base
8836          ?-    base.skin
8837            %cell      $(skin [%cell [%base %noun] [%base %noun]])
8838            %flag      (fork $(skin [%leaf %f &]) $(skin [%leaf %f |]) ~)
8839            %null      $(skin [%leaf %n ~])
8840            %void      %void
8841            %noun      ?:((~(nest ut %void) | ref) %void ref)
8842            [%atom *]
8843          =|  gil=(set type)
8844          |-  ^-  type
8845          ?-    ref
8846            %void      %void
8847            %noun      [%atom p.base.skin ~]
8848            [%atom *]  ?.  (fitz p.base.skin p.ref)
8849                         ~>(%mean.'atom-mismatch' !!)
8850                       :+  %atom
8851                         (max p.base.skin p.ref)
8852                       q.ref
8853            [%cell *]  %void
8854            [%core *]  %void
8855            [%face *]  (face p.ref $(ref q.ref))
8856            [%fork *]  (fork (turn ~(tap in p.ref) |=(=type ^$(ref type))))
8857            [%hint *]  (hint p.ref $(ref q.ref))
8858            [%hold *]  ?:  (~(has in gil) ref)  %void
8859                       $(gil (~(put in gil) ref), ref repo(sut ref))
8860          ==
8861        ==
8862      ::
8863            %cell
8864          =|  gil=(set type)
8865          |-  ^-  type
8866          ?-    ref
8867            %void      %void
8868            %noun      [%cell %noun %noun]
8869            [%atom *]  %void
8870            [%cell *]  =+  ^$(skin skin.skin, ref p.ref)
8871                       ?:  =(%void -)  %void
8872                       (cell - ^$(skin ^skin.skin, ref q.ref))
```

```
8873              [%core *]  =+  ^$(skin skin.skin, ref p.ref)
8874                         ?:  =(%void -)  %void
8875                         ?.  =(%noun ^skin.skin)
8876                           (cell - ^$(skin ^skin.skin, ref %noun))
8877                         [%core - q.ref]
8878              [%face *]  (face p.ref $(ref q.ref))
8879              [%fork *]  (fork (turn ~(tap in p.ref) |=(=type ^$(ref type))))
8880              [%hint *]  (hint p.ref $(ref q.ref))
8881              [%hold *]  ?:  (~(has in gil) ref)  %void
8882                         $(gil (~(put in gil) ref), ref repo(sut ref))
8883          ==
8884      ::
8885          %leaf
8886      =|  gil=(set type)
8887      |-  ^-  type
8888      ?-  ref
8889        %void      %void
8890        %noun      [%atom aura.skin `atom.skin]
8891        [%atom *]  ?:  &(?=(^ q.ref) !=(atom.skin u.q.ref))
8892                     %void
8893                   ?.  (fitz aura.skin p.ref)
8894                     ~>(%mean.'atom-mismatch' !!)
8895                   :+  %atom
8896                     (max aura.skin p.ref)
8897                   `atom.skin
8898        [%cell *]  %void
8899        [%core *]  %void
8900        [%face *]  (face p.ref $(ref q.ref))
8901        [%fork *]  (fork (turn ~(tap in p.ref) |=(=type ^$(ref type))))
8902        [%hint *]  (hint p.ref $(ref q.ref))
8903        [%hold *]  ?:  (~(has in gil) ref)  %void
8904                   $(gil (~(put in gil) ref), ref repo(sut ref))
8905      ==
8906      ::
8907        %dbug  $(skin skin.skin)
8908        %help  (hint [sut %help help.skin] $(skin skin.skin))
8909        %name  (face term.skin $(skin skin.skin))
8910        %over  $(skin skin.skin, sut (~(play ut sut) %wing wing.skin))
8911        %spec  =/  yon  $(skin skin.skin)
8912               =/  hit  (~(play ut sut) ~(example ax spec.skin))
8913               ?>  (~(nest ut hit) & yon)
8914               hit
8915        %wash  =-  $(ref (~(play ut ref) -))
8916               :-  %wing
8917               |-  ^-  wing
8918               ?:  =(0 depth.skin)  ~
8919               [[%| 0 ~] $(depth.skin (dec depth.skin))]
8920      ==
8921  ::
8922  ::  +lose: make a $type by restricting .ref to exclude .skin
8923  ::
8924  ++  lose
8925    |-  ^-  type
8926    ?@  skin  [%face skin ref]
8927    ?-    -.skin
8928        ::
8929        %base
8930      ?-      base.skin
```

```
8931            %cell       $(skin [%cell [%base %noun] [%base %noun]])
8932            %flag       $(skin [%base %atom %f])
8933            %null       $(skin [%leaf %n ~])
8934            %void       ref
8935            %noun       %void
8936            [%atom *]
8937        =|  gil=(set type)
8938        |-  ^-  type
8939        ?-    ref
8940            %void       %void
8941            %noun       [%cell %noun %noun]
8942            [%atom *]   %void
8943            [%cell *]   ref
8944            [%core *]   ref
8945            [%face *]   (face p.ref $(ref q.ref))
8946            [%fork *]   (fork (turn ~(tap in p.ref) |=(=type ^$(ref type))))
8947            [%hint *]   (hint p.ref $(ref q.ref))
8948            [%hold *]   ?:  (~(has in gil) ref)  %void
8949                        $(gil (~(put in gil) ref), ref repo(sut ref))
8950        ==
8951      ==
8952    ::
8953        %cell
8954    =|  gil=(set type)
8955    |-  ^-  type
8956    ?-    ref
8957        %void       %void
8958        %noun       [%atom %$ ~]
8959        [%atom *]   ref
8960        [%cell *]   =+  ^$(skin skin.skin, ref p.ref)
8961                    ?:  =(%void -)  %void
8962                    (cell - ^$(skin ^skin.skin, ref q.ref))
8963        [%core *]   =+  ^$(skin skin.skin, ref p.ref)
8964                    ?:  =(%void -)  %void
8965                    ?.  =(%noun ^skin.skin)
8966                       (cell - ^$(skin ^skin.skin, ref %noun))
8967                    [%core - q.ref]
8968        [%face *]   (face p.ref $(ref q.ref))
8969        [%fork *]   (fork (turn ~(tap in p.ref) |=(=type ^$(ref type))))
8970        [%hint *]   (hint p.ref $(ref q.ref))
8971        [%hold *]   ?:  (~(has in gil) ref)  %void
8972                    $(gil (~(put in gil) ref), ref repo(sut ref))
8973      ==
8974    ::
8975        %leaf
8976    =|  gil=(set type)
8977    |-  ^-  type
8978    ?-  ref
8979        %void       %void
8980        %noun       %noun
8981        [%atom *]   ?:  =(q.ref `atom.skin)
8982                      %void
8983                    ref
8984        [%cell *]   ref
8985        [%core *]   ref
8986        [%face *]   (face p.ref $(ref q.ref))
8987        [%fork *]   (fork (turn ~(tap in p.ref) |=(=type ^$(ref type))))
8988        [%hint *]   (hint p.ref $(ref q.ref))
```

```
8989          [%hold *]   ?:  (~(has in gil) ref)  %void
8990                      $(gil (~(put in gil) ref), ref repo(sut ref))
8991        ==
8992      ::
8993          %dbug  $(skin skin.skin)
8994          %help  $(skin skin.skin)
8995          %name  $(skin skin.skin)
8996          %over  $(skin skin.skin)
8997          %spec  $(skin skin.skin)
8998          %wash  ref
8999        ==
9000      --
9001    ::
9002    ++  blow
9003    |=  [gol=type gen=hoon]
9004    ^-  [type nock]
9005    =+  pro=(mint gol gen)
9006    =+  jon=(apex:musk bran q.pro)
9007    ?:  |(?=(~ jon) ?=(%wait -.u.jon))
9008      [p.pro q.pro]
9009    [p.pro %1 p.u.jon]
9010    ::
9011    ++  bran
9012    ~+
9013    =+  gil=*(set type)
9014    |-  ~+  ^-  seminoun:musk
9015    ?-    sut
9016      %noun       [full/[~ ~ ~] ~]
9017      %void       [full/[~ ~ ~] ~]
9018      [%atom *]   ?~(q.sut [full/[~ ~ ~] ~] [full/~ u.q.sut])
9019      [%cell *]   (combine:musk $(sut p.sut) $(sut q.sut))
9020      [%core *]   %+  combine:musk
9021                    p.r.q.sut
9022                  $(sut p.sut)
9023      [%face *]   $(sut repo)
9024      [%fork *]   [full/[~ ~ ~] ~]
9025      [%hint *]   $(sut repo)
9026      [%hold *]   ?:  (~(has in gil) sut)
9027                    [full/[~ ~ ~] ~]
9028                  $(sut repo, gil (~(put in gil) sut))
9029    ==
9030    ::
9031    ++  burp
9032    ::      expel undigested seminouns
9033    ::
9034    ^-  type
9035    ~+
9036    =-  ?.(=(sut -) - sut)
9037    ?+  sut        sut
9038      [%cell *]  [%cell burp(sut p.sut) burp(sut q.sut)]
9039      [%core *]  :+  %core
9040                   burp(sut p.sut)
9041                 :*  p.q.sut
9042                   burp(sut q.q.sut)
9043                   :_  q.r.q.sut
9044                   ?:  ?=([[%full ~] *] p.r.q.sut)
9045                     p.r.q.sut
9046                   [[%full ~ ~ ~] ~]
```

```
9047                ==
9048      [%face *]   [%face p.sut burp(sut q.sut)]
9049      [%fork *]   [%fork (~(run in p.sut) |=(type burp(sut +<)))]
9050      [%hint *]   (hint [burp(sut p.p.sut) q.p.sut] burp(sut q.sut))
9051      [%hold *]   [%hold burp(sut p.sut) q.sut]
9052    ==
9053  ::
9054  ++  busk
9055    ~/  %busk
9056    |=  gen=hoon
9057    ^-  type
9058  [%face [~ [gen ~]] sut]
9059  ::
9060  ++  buss
9061    ~/  %buss
9062    |=  [cog=term gen=hoon]
9063    ^-  type
9064  [%face [[[cog ~ gen] ~ ~] ~] sut]
9065  ::
9066  ++  crop
9067    ~/  %crop
9068    |=  ref=type
9069    =+  bix=*(set [type type])
9070    =<  dext
9071    |%
9072    ++  dext
9073      ^-  type
9074      ~_  leaf+"crop"
9075      ::  ~_  (dunk 'dext: sut')
9076      ::  ~_  (dunk(sut ref) 'dext: ref')
9077      ?:  |(=(sut ref) =(%noun ref))
9078        %void
9079      ?:  =(%void ref)
9080        sut
9081      ?-    sut
9082          [%atom *]
9083        ?+  ref        sint
9084          [%atom *]  ?^  q.sut
9085                       ?^(q.ref ?:(=(q.ref q.sut) %void sut) %void)
9086                     ?^(q.ref sut %void)
9087          [%cell *]  sut
9088        ==
9089      ::
9090          [%cell *]
9091        ?+  ref        sint
9092          [%atom *]  sut
9093          [%cell *]  ?.  (nest(sut p.ref) | p.sut)  sut
9094                     (cell p.sut dext(sut q.sut, ref q.ref))
9095        ==
9096      ::
9097          [%core *]  ?:(?=(?([%atom *] [%cell *]) ref) sut sint)
9098          [%face *]  (face p.sut dext(sut q.sut))
9099          [%fork *]  (fork (turn ~(tap in p.sut) |=(type dext(sut +<))))
9100          [%hint *]  (hint p.sut dext(sut q.sut))
9101          [%hold *]  ?<  (~(has in bix) [sut ref])
9102                     dext(sut repo, bix (~(put in bix) [sut ref]))
9103          %noun      dext(sut repo)
9104          %void      %void
```

```
9105          ==
9106      ::
9107      ++  sint
9108        ^-  type
9109        ?+    ref      !!
9110          [%core *]   sut
9111          [%face *]   dext(ref repo(sut ref))
9112          [%fork *]   =+  yed=~(tap in p.ref)
9113                      |-  ^-  type
9114                      ?~  yed  sut
9115                      $(yed t.yed, sut dext(ref i.yed))
9116          [%hint *]   dext(ref repo(sut ref))
9117          [%hold *]   dext(ref repo(sut ref))
9118        ==
9119      --
9120    ::
9121    ++  cool
9122      |=  [pol=? hyp=wing ref=type]
9123      ^-  type
9124      =+  fid=(find %both hyp)
9125      ?-  -.fid
9126        %|  sut
9127        %&  =<  q
9128            %+  take  p.p.fid
9129            |=(a=type ?:(pol (fuse(sut a) ref) (crop(sut a) ref)))
9130      ==
9131    ::
9132    ++  duck  ^-(tank ~(duck us sut))
9133    ++  dune  |.(duck)
9134    ++  dunk
9135      |=  paz=term  ^-  tank
9136      :+  %palm
9137        [['.' ~] ['-' ~] ~ ~]
9138      [[%leaf (mesc (trip paz))] duck ~]
9139    ::
9140    ++  elbo
9141      |=  [lop=palo rig=(list (pair wing hoon))]
9142      ^-  type
9143      ?:  ?=(%& -.q.lop)
9144        |-  ^-  type
9145        ?~  rig
9146          p.q.lop
9147        =+  zil=(play q.i.rig)
9148        =+  dar=(tack(sut p.q.lop) p.i.rig zil)
9149        %=  $
9150          rig      t.rig
9151          p.q.lop  q.dar
9152        ==
9153      =+  hag=~(tap in q.q.lop)
9154      %-  fire
9155      |-  ^+  hag
9156      ?~  rig
9157        hag
9158      =+  zil=(play q.i.rig)
9159      =+  dix=(toss p.i.rig zil hag)
9160      %=  $
9161        rig  t.rig
9162        hag  q.dix
```

```
9163        ==
9164    ::
9165    ++  ergo
9166    |=  [lop=palo rig=(list (pair wing hoon))]
9167    ^-  (pair type nock)
9168    =+  axe=(tend p.lop)
9169    =|  hej=(list (pair axis nock))
9170    ?:  ?=(%& -.q.lop)
9171      =-  [p.- (hike axe q.-)]
9172      |-  ^-  (pair type (list (pair axis nock)))
9173      ?~  rig
9174        [p.q.lop hej]
9175      =+  zil=(mint %noun q.i.rig)
9176      =+  dar=(tack(sut p.q.lop) p.i.rig p.zil)
9177      %=  $
9178        rig       t.rig
9179        p.q.lop   q.dar
9180        hej       [[p.dar q.zil] hej]
9181      ==
9182    =+  hag=~(tap in q.q.lop)
9183    =-  [(fire p.-) [%9 p.q.lop (hike axe q.-)]]
9184    |-  ^-  (pair (list (pair type foot)) (list (pair axis nock)))
9185    ?~  rig
9186      [hag hej]
9187    =+  zil=(mint %noun q.i.rig)
9188    =+  dix=(toss p.i.rig p.zil hag)
9189    %=  $
9190      rig   t.rig
9191      hag   q.dix
9192      hej   [[p.dix q.zil] hej]
9193    ==
9194    ::
9195    ++  endo
9196    |-  [lop=(pair palo palo) dox=type rig=(list (pair wing hoon))]
9197    ^-  (pair type type)
9198    ?:  ?=(%& -.q.p.lop)
9199      ?>  ?=(%& -.q.q.lop)
9200      |-  ^-  (pair type type)
9201      ?~  rig
9202        [p.q.p.lop p.q.q.lop]
9203      =+  zil=(mull %noun dox q.i.rig)
9204      =+  ^=  dar
9205        :-  p=(tack(sut p.q.p.lop) p.i.rig p.zil)
9206            q=(tack(sut p.q.q.lop) p.i.rig q.zil)
9207      ?>  =(p.p.dar p.q.dar)
9208      %=  $
9209        rig         t.rig
9210        p.q.p.lop   q.p.dar
9211        p.q.q.lop   q.q.dar
9212      ==
9213    ?>  ?=(%| -.q.q.lop)
9214    ?>  =(p.q.p.lop p.q.q.lop)
9215    =+  hag=[p=~(tap in q.q.p.lop) q=~(tap in q.q.q.lop)]
9216    =-  [(fire p.-) (fire(vet |) q.-)]
9217    |-  ^-  (pair (list (pair type foot)) (list (pair type foot)))
9218    ?~  rig
9219      hag
9220    =+  zil=(mull %noun dox q.i.rig)
```

```
9221      =+  ^=  dix
9222          :-  p=(toss p.i.rig p.zil p.hag)
9223              q=(toss p.i.rig q.zil q.hag)
9224      ?>  =(p.p.dix p.q.dix)
9225      %=  $
9226        rig  t.rig
9227        hag  [q.p.dix q.q.dix]
9228      ==
9229    ::
9230    ++  et
9231      |_  [hyp=wing rig=(list (pair wing hoon))]
9232      ::
9233      ++  play
9234        ^-  type
9235        =+  lug=(find %read hyp)
9236        ?:  ?=(%| -.lug)  ~>(%mean.'hoon' ?>(?=(~ rig) p.p.lug))
9237        (elbo p.lug rig)
9238      ::
9239      ++  mint
9240        |=  gol=type
9241        ^-  (pair type nock)
9242        =+  lug=(find %read hyp)
9243        ?:  ?=(%| -.lug)  ~>(%mean.'hoon' ?>(?=(~ rig) p.lug))
9244        =-  ?>(?|(!vet (nest(sut gol) & p.-)) -)
9245        (ergo p.lug rig)
9246      ::
9247      ++  mull
9248        |=  [gol=type dox=type]
9249        ^-  [type type]
9250        =+  lug=[p=(find %read hyp) q=(find(sut dox) %read hyp)]
9251        ?:  ?=(%| -.p.lug)
9252          ?>    &(?=(%| -.q.lug) ?=(~ rig))
9253          [p.p.p.lug p.p.q.lug]
9254        ?>  ?=(%& -.q.lug)
9255        =-  ?>(?|(!vet (nest(sut gol) & p.-)) -)
9256        (endo [p.p.lug p.q.lug] dox rig)
9257      --
9258    ::
9259    ++  epla
9260      ~/  %epla
9261      |=  [hyp=wing rig=(list (pair wing hoon))]
9262      ^-  type
9263      ~(play et hyp rig)
9264    ::
9265    ++  emin
9266      ~/  %emin
9267      |=  [gol=type hyp=wing rig=(list (pair wing hoon))]
9268      ^-  (pair type nock)
9269      (~(mint et hyp rig) gol)
9270    ::
9271    ++  emul
9272      ~/  %emul
9273      |=  [gol=type dox=type hyp=wing rig=(list (pair wing hoon))]
9274      ^-  (pair type type)
9275      (~(mull et hyp rig) gol dox)
9276    ::
9277    ++  felt  !!
9278    ::                                                        ::
```

```
9279    ++  feel                                              ::  detect existence
9280      |=  rot=(list wing)
9281      ^-  ?
9282      =.  rot  (flop rot)
9283      |-  ^-  ?
9284      ?~  rot  &
9285      =/  yep  (fond %free i.rot)
9286      ?~  yep  |
9287      ?-    -.yep
9288        %&  %=  $
9289              rot  t.rot
9290              sut  p:(fine %& p.yep)
9291            ==
9292        %|  ?-  -.p.yep
9293              %&  |
9294              %|  %=  $
9295                    rot  t.rot
9296                    sut  p:(fine %| p.p.yep)
9297                  ==
9298      ==      ==
9299    ::
9300    ++  fond
9301      ~/  %fond
9302      |=  [way=vial hyp=wing]
9303      =>  |%
9304          ++  pony                                      ::  raw match
9305                  $@  ~                                ::  void
9306                  %+  each                             ::  natural/abnormal
9307                    palo                               ::  arm or leg
9308                  %+  each                             ::  abnormal
9309                    @ud                                ::  unmatched
9310                  (pair type nock)                     ::  synthetic
9311          --
9312      ^-  pony
9313      ?~  hyp
9314        [%& ~ %& sut]
9315      =+  mor=$(hyp t.hyp)
9316      ?-      -.mor
9317          %|
9318      ?-      -.p.mor
9319          %&  mor
9320          %|
9321      =+  fex=(mint(sut p.p.p.mor) %noun [%wing i.hyp ~])
9322      [%| %| p.fex (comb q.p.p.mor q.fex)]
9323      ==
9324    ::
9325          %&
9326      =.  sut
9327        =*  lap  q.p.mor
9328        ?-  -.lap
9329          %&  p.lap
9330          %|  (fork (turn ~(tap in q.lap) head))
9331        ==
9332      =>  :_  +
9333          :*  axe=`axis`1
9334              lon=p.p.mor
9335              heg=?^(i.hyp i.hyp [%| p=0 q=(some i.hyp)])
9336          ==
```

```
9337    ?:  ?=(%& -.heg)
9338      [%& [`p.heg lon] %& (peek way p.heg)]
9339    =|  gil=(set type)
9340    =<  $
9341    |%  ++   here  ?:  =(0 p.heg)
9342                       [%& [~ `axe lon] %& sut]
9343                       [%| %& (dec p.heg)]
9344        ++  lose  [%| %& p.heg]
9345        ++  stop  ?~(q.heg here lose)
9346        ++  twin  |=  [hax=pony yor=pony]
9347                  ^-  pony
9348                  ~_  leaf+"find-fork"
9349                  ?:  =(hax yor)  hax
9350                  ?~  hax  yor
9351                  ?~  yor  hax
9352                  ?:  ?=(%| -.hax)
9353                    ?>  ?&  ?=(%| -.yor)
9354                            ?=(%| -.p.hax)
9355                            ?=(%| -.p.yor)
9356                            =(q.p.p.hax q.p.p.yor)
9357                        ==
9358                    :+  %|
9359                    %|
9360                    [(fork p.p.p.hax p.p.p.yor ~) q.p.p.hax]
9361                  ?>  ?=(%& -.yor)
9362                  ?>  =(p.p.hax p.p.yor)
9363                  ?:  &(?=(%& -.q.p.hax) ?=(%& -.q.p.yor))
9364                    :+  %&  p.p.hax
9365                    [%& (fork p.q.p.hax p.q.p.yor ~)]
9366                  ?>  &(?=(%| -.q.p.hax) ?=(%| -.q.p.yor))
9367                  ?>  =(p.q.p.hax p.q.p.yor)
9368                  =+  wal=(~(uni in q.q.p.hax) q.q.p.yor)
9369                  :+  %&  p.p.hax
9370                  [%| p.q.p.hax wal]
9371        ++  $
9372          ^-  pony
9373          ?-   sut
9374            %void      ~
9375            %noun      stop
9376            [%atom *]  stop
9377            [%cell *]
9378          ?~  q.heg  here
9379          =+  taf=$(axe (peg axe 2), sut p.sut)
9380          ?~  taf  ~
9381          ?:  |(?=(%& -.taf) ?=(%| -.p.taf))
9382            taf
9383          $(axe (peg axe 3), p.heg p.p.taf, sut q.sut)
9384          ::
9385            [%core *]
9386          ?~  q.heg  here
9387          =^  zem  p.heg
9388            =+  zem=(loot u.q.heg q.r.q.sut)
9389            ?~  zem  [~ p.heg]
9390            ?:(=(0 p.heg) [zem 0] [~ (dec p.heg)])
9391          ?^  zem
9392            :+  %&
9393            [`axe lon]
9394            =/  zut  ^-  foot
```

```
9395        ?-  q.p.q.sut
9396          %wet  [%wet q.u.zem]
9397          %dry  [%dry q.u.zem]
9398          ==
9399      [%| (peg 2 p.u.zem) [[sut zut] ~ ~]]
9400    =+  pec=(peel way r.p.q.sut)
9401    ?.  sam.pec  lose
9402    ?:  con.pec  $(sut p.sut, axe (peg axe 3))
9403    $(sut (peek(sut p.sut) way 2), axe (peg axe 6))
9404  ::
9405      [%hint *]
9406    $(sut repo)
9407  ::
9408      [%face *]
9409    ?:  ?=(~ q.heg)  here(sut q.sut)
9410    =*  zot  p.sut
9411    ?@  zot
9412      ?:(=(u.q.heg zot) here(sut q.sut) lose)
9413    =<  main
9414    |%
9415    ++  main
9416      ^-  pony
9417      =+  tyr=(~(get by p.zot) u.q.heg)
9418      ?~  tyr
9419        next
9420      ?~  u.tyr
9421        $(sut q.sut, lon [~ lon], p.heg +(p.heg))
9422      ?.  =(0 p.heg)
9423        next(p.heg (dec p.heg))
9424      =+  tor=(fund way u.u.tyr)
9425      ?-  -.tor
9426        %&  [%& (weld p.p.tor `vein`[~ `axe lon]) q.p.tor]
9427        %|  [%| %| p.p.tor (comb [%0 axe] q.p.tor)]
9428      ==
9429    ++  next
9430      |-  ^-  pony
9431      ?~  q.zot
9432        ^$(sut q.sut, lon [~ lon])
9433      =+  tiv=(mint(sut q.sut) %noun i.q.zot)
9434      =+  fid=^$(sut p.tiv, lon ~, axe 1, gil ~)
9435      ?~  fid  ~
9436      ?:  ?=([%| %& *] fid)
9437        $(q.zot t.q.zot, p.heg p.p.fid)
9438      =/  vat=(pair type nock)
9439        ?-    -.fid
9440          %&  (fine %& p.fid)
9441          %|  (fine %| p.p.fid)
9442        ==
9443      [%| %| p.vat (comb (comb [%0 axe] q.tiv) q.vat)]
9444    --
9445  ::
9446      [%fork *]
9447    =+  wiz=(turn ~(tap in p.sut) |=(a=type ^$(sut a)))
9448    ?~  wiz  ~
9449    |-  ^-  pony
9450    ?~  t.wiz  i.wiz
9451    (twin i.wiz $(wiz t.wiz))
9452  ::
```

```
9453                    [%hold *]
9454                ?:  (~(has in gil) sut)
9455                  ~
9456                $(gil (~(put in gil) sut), sut repo)
9457            ==
9458        --
9459    ==
9460  ::
9461  ++  find
9462    ~/  %find
9463    |=  [way=vial hyp=wing]
9464    ^-  port
9465    ~_  (show [%c %find] %1 hyp)
9466    =-  ?@  -  !!
9467        ?-    -<
9468        %&  [%& p.-]
9469        %|  ?-  -.p.-
9470              %|  [%| p.p.-]
9471              %&  !!
9472        ==  ==
9473    (fond way hyp)
9474  ::
9475  ++  fund
9476    ~/  %fund
9477    |=  [way=vial gen=hoon]
9478    ^-  port
9479    =+  hup=~(reek ap gen)
9480    ?~  hup
9481      [%| (mint %noun gen)]
9482    (find way u.hup)
9483  ::
9484  ++  fine
9485    ~/  %fine
9486    |=  tor=port
9487    ^-  (pair type nock)
9488    ?-  -.tor
9489      %|  p.tor
9490      %&  =+  axe=(tend p.p.tor)
9491          ?-  -.q.p.tor
9492          %&  [`type`p.q.p.tor %0 axe]
9493          %|  [(fire ~(tap in q.q.p.tor)) [%9 p.q.p.tor %0 axe]]
9494    ==  ==
9495  ::
9496  ++  fire
9497    |=  hag=(list [p=type q=foot])
9498    ^-  type
9499    ?:  ?=([[* [%wet ~ %1]] ~] hag)
9500      p.i.hag
9501    %-  fork
9502    %+  turn
9503      hag.$
9504    |=  [p=type q=foot]
9505    ?.  ?=([%core *] p)
9506      ~_  (dunk %fire-type)
9507      ~_  leaf+"expected-fork-to-be-core"
9508      ~_  (dunk(sut p) %fork-type)
9509      ~>(%mean.'fire-core' !!)
9510    :-  %hold
```

```
9511      =+  dox=[%core q.q.p q.p(r.p %gold)]
9512      ?:  ?=(%dry -.q)
9513        ::  ~_  (dunk(sut [%cell q.q.p p.p]) %fire-dry)
9514        ?>  ?|(!vet (nest(sut q.q.p) & p.p))
9515        [dox p.q]
9516      ?>  ?=(%wet -.q)
9517        ::  ~_  (dunk(sut [%cell q.q.p p.p]) %fire-wet)
9518      =.  p.p  (redo(sut p.p) q.q.p)
9519      ?>  ?|  !vet
9520              (~(has in rib) [sut dox p.q])
9521              !=(** (mull(sut p, rib (~(put in rib) sut dox p.q)) %noun dox p.q))
9522        ==
9523      [p p.q]
9524    ::
9525    ++  fish
9526      ~/  %fish
9527      |=  axe=axis
9528      =+  vot=*(set type)
9529      |-  ^-  nock
9530      ?-  sut
9531        %void       [%1 1]
9532        %noun       [%1 0]
9533        [%atom *]   ?~  q.sut
9534                      (flip [%3 %0 axe])
9535                    [%5 [%1 u.q.sut] [%0 axe]]
9536        [%cell *]
9537      %+  flan
9538        [%3 %0 axe]
9539      (flan $(sut p.sut, axe (peg axe 2)) $(sut q.sut, axe (peg axe 3)))
9540        ::
9541        [%core *]   ~>(%mean.'fish-core' !!)
9542        [%face *]   $(sut q.sut)
9543        [%fork *]   =+  yed=~(tap in p.sut)
9544                    |-  ^-  nock
9545                    ?~(yed [%1 1] (flor ^$(sut i.yed) $(yed t.yed)))
9546        [%hint *]   $(sut q.sut)
9547        [%hold *]
9548      ?:  (~(has in vot) sut)
9549        ~>(%mean.'fish-loop' !!)
9550      =>  %=(. vot (~(put in vot) sut))
9551      $(sut repo)
9552      ==
9553    ::
9554    ++  fuse
9555      ~/  %fuse
9556      |=  ref=type
9557      =+  bix=*(set [type type])
9558      |-  ^-  type
9559      ?:  ?|(=(sut ref) =(%noun ref))
9560        sut
9561      ?-      sut
9562        [%atom *]
9563      ?-      ref
9564        [%atom *]   =+  foc=?:((fitz p.ref p.sut) p.sut p.ref)
9565                    ?^  q.sut
9566                      ?^  q.ref
9567                        ?:  =(q.sut q.ref)
9568                          [%atom foc q.sut]
```

```
9569                                   %void
9570                              [%atom foc q.sut]
9571                              [%atom foc q.ref]
9572            [%cell *]    %void
9573            *               $(sut ref, ref sut)
9574        ==
9575          [%cell *]
9576        ?-  ref
9577          [%cell *]    (cell $(sut p.sut, ref p.ref) $(sut q.sut, ref q.ref))
9578            *               $(sut ref, ref sut)
9579        ==
9580      ::
9581        [%core *]    $(sut repo)
9582        [%face *]    (face p.sut $(sut q.sut))
9583        [%fork *]    (fork (turn ~(tap in p.sut) |=(type ^$(sut +<))))
9584        [%hint *]    (hint p.sut $(sut q.sut))
9585        [%hold *]
9586      ?:  (~(has in bix) [sut ref])
9587        ~>(%mean.'fuse-loop' !!)
9588      $(sut repo, bix (~(put in bix) [sut ref]))
9589      ::
9590        %noun        ref
9591        %void        %void
9592      ==
9593    ::
9594    ++  gain
9595    ~/  %gain
9596    |=  gen=hoon  ^-  type
9597    (chip & gen)
9598    ::
9599    ++  hemp
9600      ::    generate formula from foot
9601      ::
9602    |=  [hud=poly gol=type gen=hoon]
9603    ^-  nock
9604    ~+
9605    =+  %hemp-141
9606    ?-  hud
9607      %dry  q:(mint gol gen)
9608      %wet  q:(mint(vet |) gol gen)
9609    ==
9610    ::
9611    ++  laze
9612      ::    produce lazy core generator for static execution
9613      ::
9614    |=  [nym=(unit term) hud=poly dom=(map term tome)]
9615    ~+
9616    ^-  seminoun
9617    =+  %hemp-141
9618    ::  tal: map from battery axis to foot
9619    ::
9620    =;  tal=(map @ud hoon)
9621      ::  produce lazy battery
9622      ::
9623      :_  ~
9624      :+  %lazy  1
9625      |=  axe=@ud
9626      ^-  (unit noun)
```

```
9627        %+  bind  (~(get by tal) axe)
9628        |=  gen=hoon
9629        %.  [hud %noun gen]
9630        hemp(sut (core sut [nym hud %gold] sut [[%lazy 1 ..^$] ~] dom))
9631      ::
9632      %-  ~(gas by *(map @ud hoon))
9633      =|  yeb=(list (pair @ud hoon))
9634      =+  axe=1
9635      |^  ?-  dom
9636          ~            yeb
9637          [* ~ ~]  (chapter q.q.n.dom)
9638          [* * ~]  %=  $
9639                       dom  l.dom
9640                       axe  (peg axe 3)
9641                       yeb  (chapter(axe (peg axe 2)) q.q.n.dom)
9642                   ==
9643          [* ~ *]  %=  $
9644                       dom  r.dom
9645                       axe  (peg axe 3)
9646                       yeb  (chapter(axe (peg axe 2)) q.q.n.dom)
9647                   ==
9648          [* * *]  %=  $
9649                       dom  r.dom
9650                       axe  (peg axe 7)
9651                       yeb  %=  $
9652                                dom  l.dom
9653                                axe  (peg axe 6)
9654                                yeb  (chapter(axe (peg axe 2)) q.q.n.dom)
9655          ==        ==       ==
9656      ++  chapter
9657      |=  dab=(map term hoon)
9658      ^+  yeb
9659      ?-  dab
9660          ~            yeb
9661          [* ~ ~]  [[axe q.n.dab] yeb]
9662          [* * ~]  %=  $
9663                       dab  l.dab
9664                       axe  (peg axe 3)
9665                       yeb  [[(peg axe 2) q.n.dab] yeb]
9666                   ==
9667          [* ~ *]  %=  $
9668                       dab  r.dab
9669                       axe  (peg axe 3)
9670                       yeb  [[(peg axe 2) q.n.dab] yeb]
9671                   ==
9672          [* * *]  %=  $
9673                       dab  r.dab
9674                       axe  (peg axe 7)
9675                       yeb  %=  $
9676                                dab  l.dab
9677                                axe  (peg axe 6)
9678                                yeb  [[(peg axe 2) q.n.dab] yeb]
9679          ==        ==       ==
9680      --
9681    ::
9682    ++  lose
9683    ~/  %lose
9684    |=  gen=hoon  ^-  type
```

```
9685       (chip | gen)
9686     ::
9687     ++  chip
9688       ~/  %chip
9689       |=  [how=? gen=hoon]   ^-  type
9690       ?:  ?=([%wtts *] gen)
9691         (cool how q.gen (play ~(example ax p.gen)))
9692       ?:  ?=([%wthx *] gen)
9693         =+  (play %wing q.gen)
9694         ~>  %slog.[0 [%leaf "chipping"]]
9695         ?:  how
9696           =-  ~>  %slog.[0 (dunk(sut +<) 'chip: gain: ref')]
9697               ~>  %slog.[0 (dunk(sut -) 'chip: gain: gain')]
9698               -
9699           ~(gain ar - p.gen)
9700         ~(lose ar - p.gen)
9701       ?:  ?&(how ?=([%wtpm *] gen))
9702         |-(?~(p.gen sut $(p.gen t.p.gen, sut ^$(gen i.p.gen))))
9703       ?:  ?&(!how ?=([%wtbr *] gen))
9704         |-(?~(p.gen sut $(p.gen t.p.gen, sut ^$(gen i.p.gen))))
9705       =+  neg=~(open ap gen)
9706       ?:(=(neg gen) sut $(gen neg))
9707     ::
9708     ++  bake
9709       |=  [dox=type hud=poly dab=(map term hoon)]
9710       ^-  *
9711       ?:  ?=(~ dab)
9712         ~
9713       =+  ^=  dov
9714          ::  this seems wrong but it's actually right
9715          ::
9716          ?-  hud
9717            %dry  (mull %noun dox q.n.dab)
9718            %wet  ~
9719          ==
9720       ?-  dab
9721         [* ~ ~]  dov
9722         [* ~ *]  [dov $(dab r.dab)]
9723         [* * ~]  [dov $(dab l.dab)]
9724         [* * *]  [dov $(dab l.dab) $(dab r.dab)]
9725       ==
9726     ::
9727     ++  balk
9728       |=  [dox=type hud=poly dom=(map term tome)]
9729       ^-  *
9730       ?:  ?=(~ dom)
9731         ~
9732       =+  dov=(bake dox hud q.q.n.dom)
9733       ?-     dom
9734         [* ~ ~]  dov
9735         [* ~ *]  [dov $(dom r.dom)]
9736         [* * ~]  [dov $(dom l.dom)]
9737         [* * *]  [dov $(dom l.dom) $(dom r.dom)]
9738       ==
9739     ::
9740     ++  mile
9741       ::     mull all chapters and feet in a core
9742       ::
```

```
9743      |=  [dox=type mel=vair nym=(unit term) hud=poly dom=(map term tome)]
9744      ^-  (pair type type)
9745      =+  yet=(core sut [nym hud %gold] sut (laze nym hud dom) dom)
9746      =+  hum=(core dox [nym hud %gold] dox (laze nym hud dom) dom)
9747      =+  (balk(sut yet) hum hud dom)
9748      [yet hum]
9749      ::
9750    ++  mine
9751      ::    mint all chapters and feet in a core
9752      ::
9753      |=  [gol=type mel=vair nym=(unit term) hud=poly dom=(map term tome)]
9754      ^-  (pair type nock)
9755      |^
9756      =/  log  (chapters-check (core-check gol))
9757      =/  dog  (get-tomes log)
9758      =-  :_  [%1 dez]
9759          (core sut [nym hud mel] sut [[%full ~] dez] dom)
9760      ^=  dez
9761      =.  sut  (core sut [nym hud %gold] sut (laze nym hud dom) dom)
9762      |-  ^-  ?(~ ^)
9763      ?:  ?=(~ dom)
9764        ~
9765      =/  dov=?(~ ^)
9766        =/  dab=(map term hoon)  q.q.n.dom
9767        =/  dag  (arms-check dab (get-arms dog p.n.dom))
9768        |-  ^-  ?(~ ^)
9769        ?:  ?=(~ dab)
9770          ~
9771        =/  gog  (get-arm-type log dag p.n.dab)
9772        =+  vad=(hemp hud gog q.n.dab)
9773        ?-    dab
9774          [* ~ ~]   vad
9775          [* ~ *]   [vad $(dab r.dab)]
9776          [* * ~]   [vad $(dab l.dab)]
9777          [* * *]   [vad $(dab l.dab) $(dab r.dab)]
9778        ==
9779      ?-    dom
9780        [* ~ ~]   dov
9781        [* ~ *]   [dov $(dom r.dom)]
9782        [* * ~]   [dov $(dom l.dom)]
9783        [* * *]   [dov $(dom l.dom) $(dom r.dom)]
9784      ==
9785      ::
9786      ::  all the below arms are used for gol checking and should have no
9787      ::  effect other than giving more specific errors
9788      ::
9789      ::  +gol-type: all the possible types we could be expecting.
9790      ::
9791    +$  gol-type
9792      $~  %noun
9793      $@  %noun
9794      $%  [%cell p=type q=type]
9795          [%core p=type q=coil]
9796          [%fork p=(set gol-type)]
9797      ==
9798      ::  +core-check: check that we're looking for a core
9799      ::
9800    ++  core-check
```

```
9801      |=  log=type
9802      |-  ^-  gol-type
9803      ?+    log  $(log repo(sut log))
9804        %noun        (nice log &)
9805        %void        (nice %noun |)
9806        [%atom *]    (nice %noun |)
9807        [%cell *]    (nice log (nest(sut p.log) & %noun))
9808        [%core *]    (nice log(r.p.q %gold) &)
9809        [%fork *]
9810      =/  tys  ~(tap in p.log)
9811      :-  %fork
9812      |-  ^-  (set gol-type)
9813      ?~  tys
9814          ~
9815      =/  a  ^$(log i.tys)
9816      =/  b  $(tys t.tys)
9817      (~(put in b) a)
9818    ==
9819  ::  +chapters-check: check we have the expected number of chapters
9820  ::
9821  ++  chapters-check
9822    |=  log=gol-type
9823    |-  ^-  gol-type
9824    ?-    log
9825        %noun        (nice log &)
9826        [%cell *]    (nice log &)
9827        [%core *]    ~_  leaf+"core-number-of-chapters"
9828                     (nice log =(~(wyt by dom) ~(wyt by q.r.q.log)))
9829        [%fork *]
9830      =/  tys  ~(tap in p.log)
9831      |-  ^-  gol-type
9832      ?~  tys
9833        log
9834      =/  a  ^$(log i.tys)
9835      =/  b  $(tys t.tys)
9836      log
9837    ==
9838  ::  +get-tomes: get map of tomes if exists
9839  ::
9840  ++  get-tomes
9841    |=  log=gol-type
9842    ^-  (unit (map term tome))
9843    ?-    log
9844        %noun        ~
9845        [%cell *]    ~
9846        [%fork *]    ~  ::  maybe could be more aggressive
9847        [%core *]    `q.r.q.log
9848    ==
9849  ::  +get-arms: get arms in tome
9850  ::
9851  ++  get-arms
9852    |=  [dog=(unit (map term tome)) nam=term]
9853    ^-  (unit (map term hoon))
9854    %+  bind  dog
9855    |=  a=(map term tome)
9856    ~_  leaf+"unexpcted-chapter.{(trip nam)}"
9857    q:(~(got by a) nam)
9858  ::  +arms-check: check we have the expected number of arms
```

```
9859      ::
9860      ++  arms-check
9861        |=  [dab=(map term hoon) dag=(unit (map term hoon))]
9862        ?~  dag
9863          dag
9864        =/  a
9865          =/  exp  ~(wyt by u.dag)
9866          =/  hav  ~(wyt by dab)
9867          ~_  =/  expt  (scow %ud exp)
9868              =/  havt  (scow %ud hav)
9869              leaf+"core-number-of-arms.exp={expt}.hav={havt}"
9870          ~_  =/  missing  ~(tap in (~(dif in ~(key by u.dag)) ~(key by dab)))
9871              leaf+"missing.{<missing>}"
9872          ~_  =/  extra  ~(tap in (~(dif in ~(key by dab)) ~(key by u.dag)))
9873              leaf+"extra.{<extra>}"
9874          ~_  =/  have  ~(tap in ~(key by dab))
9875              leaf+"have.{<have>}"
9876          (nice dag =(exp hav))
9877        a
9878      ::  +get-arm-type: get expected type of this arm
9879      ::
9880      ++  get-arm-type
9881        |=  [log=gol-type dag=(unit (map term hoon)) nam=term]
9882        ^-  type
9883        %-  fall  :_  %noun
9884        %+  bind  dag
9885        |=  a=(map term hoon)
9886        =/  gen=hoon
9887          ~_  leaf+"unexpected-arm.{(trip nam)}"
9888          (~(got by a) nam)
9889        (play(sut log) gen)
9890      ::
9891      ++  nice
9892        |*  [typ=* gud=?]
9893        ?:  gud
9894          typ
9895        ~_  leaf+"core-nice"
9896        !!
9897      --
9898    ::
9899    ++  mint
9900      ~/  %mint
9901      |=  [gol=type gen=hoon]
9902      ^-  [p=type q=nock]
9903      ::~&  %pure-mint
9904      |^  ^-  [p=type q=nock]
9905      ?:  ?&(=(%void sut) !?=([%dbug *] gen))
9906        ?.  |(!vet ?=([%lost *] gen) ?=([%zpzp *] gen))
9907          ~>(%mean.'mint-vain' !!)
9908        [%void %0 0]
9909      ?-    gen
9910      ::
9911          [^ *]
9912        =+  hed=$(gen p.gen, gol %noun)
9913        =+  tal=$(gen q.gen, gol %noun)
9914        [(nice (cell p.hed p.tal)) (cons q.hed q.tal)]
9915      ::
9916          [%brcn *]  (grow %gold p.gen %dry [%$ 1] q.gen)
```

```
9917        [%brpt *]   (grow %gold p.gen %wet [%$ 1] q.gen)
9918    ::
9919        [%cnts *]   (~(mint et p.gen q.gen) gol)
9920    ::
9921        [%dtkt *]
9922    =+  nef=$(gen [%kttr p.gen])
9923    [p.nef [%12 [%1 hoon-version p.nef] q:$(gen q.gen, gol %noun)]]
9924    ::
9925        [%dtls *]   [(nice [%atom %$ ~]) [%4 q:$(gen p.gen, gol [%atom %$ ~])]]
9926        [%sand *]   [(nice (play gen)) [%1 q.gen]]
9927        [%rock *]   [(nice (play gen)) [%1 q.gen]]
9928    ::
9929        [%dttr *]
9930    [(nice %noun) [%2 q:$(gen p.gen, gol %noun) q:$(gen q.gen, gol %noun)]]
9931    ::
9932        [%dtts *]
9933    [(nice bool) [%5 q:$(gen p.gen, gol %noun) q:$(gen q.gen, gol %noun)]]
9934    ::
9935        [%dtwt *]   [(nice bool) [%3 q:$(gen p.gen, gol %noun)]]
9936        [%hand *]   [p.gen q.gen]
9937        [%ktbr *]   =+(vat=$(gen p.gen) [(nice (wrap(sut p.vat) %iron)) q.vat])
9938    ::
9939        [%ktls *]
9940    =+(hif=(nice (play p.gen)) [hif q:$(gen q.gen, gol hif)])
9941    ::
9942        [%ktpm *]   =+(vat=$(gen p.gen) [(nice (wrap(sut p.vat) %zinc)) q.vat])
9943        [%ktsg *]   (blow gol p.gen)
9944        [%tune *]   [(face p.gen sut) [%0 %1]]
9945        [%ktwt *]   =+(vat=$(gen p.gen) [(nice (wrap(sut p.vat) %lead)) q.vat])
9946    ::
9947        [%note *]
9948    =+  hum=$(gen q.gen)
9949    [(hint [sut p.gen] p.hum) q.hum]
9950    ::
9951        [%sgzp *]   ~_(duck(sut (play p.gen)) $(gen q.gen))
9952        [%sggr *]
9953    =+  hum=$(gen q.gen)
9954    :: ?:  &(huz !?=(%|(@ [?(%sgcn %sgls) ^]) p.gen))
9955    ::  hum
9956    :-  p.hum
9957    :+  %11
9958      ?-    p.gen
9959        @   p.gen
9960        ^   [p.p.gen q:$(gen q.p.gen, gol %noun)]
9961      ==
9962    q.hum
9963    ::
9964        [%tsgr *]
9965    =+  fid=$(gen p.gen, gol %noun)
9966    =+  dov=$(sut p.fid, gen q.gen)
9967    [p.dov (comb q.fid q.dov)]
9968    ::
9969        [%tscm *]
9970    $(gen q.gen, sut (busk p.gen))
9971    ::
9972        [%wtcl *]
9973    =+  nor=$(gen p.gen, gol bool)
9974    =+  fex=(gain p.gen)
```

```
9975        =+  wux=(lose p.gen)
9976        =+  ^=  duy
9977          ?:  =(%void fex)
9978           ?:(=(%void wux) [%0 0] [%1 1])
9979          ?:(=(%void wux) [%1 0] q.nor)
9980        =+  hiq=$(sut fex, gen q.gen)
9981        =+  ran=$(sut wux, gen r.gen)
9982        [(fork p.hiq p.ran ~) (cond duy q.hiq q.ran)]
9983    ::
9984        [%wthx *]
9985    :-  (nice bool)
9986    =+  fid=(find %read [[%& 1] q.gen])
9987    ~>  %mean.'mint-fragment'
9988    ?>  &(?=(%& -.fid) ?=(%& -.q.p.fid))
9989    (~(fish ar `type`p.q.p.fid `skin`p.gen) (tend p.p.fid))
9990    ::
9991        [%fits *]
9992    :-  (nice bool)
9993    =+  ref=(play p.gen)
9994    =+  fid=(find %read q.gen)
9995    ~|  [%test q.gen]
9996    |-  ^-  nock
9997    ?-  -.fid
9998      %&  ?-  -.q.p.fid
9999            %&  (fish(sut ref) (tend p.p.fid))
10000           %|  $(fid [%| (fine fid)])
10001          ==
10002      %|  [%7 q.p.fid (fish(sut ref) 1)]
10003    ==
10004    ::
10005        [%dbug *]
10006    ~_  (show %o p.gen)
10007    =+  hum=$(gen q.gen)
10008    [p.hum [%11 [%spot %1 p.gen] q.hum]]
10009    ::
10010        [%zpcm *]    [(nice (play p.gen)) [%1 q.gen]]      ::  XX validate!
10011        [%lost *]
10012    ?:  vet
10013      ~_  (dunk(sut (play p.gen)) 'lost')
10014      ~>(%mean.'mint-lost' !!)
10015    [%void [%0 0]]
10016    ::
10017        [%zpmc *]
10018    =+  vos=$(gol %noun, gen q.gen)
10019    =+  ref=p:$(gol %noun, gen p.gen)
10020    [(nice (cell ref p.vos)) (cons [%1 burp(sut p.vos)] q.vos)]
10021    ::
10022        [%zpgl *]
10023    =/  typ  (nice (play [%kttr p.gen]))
10024    =/  val
10025      =<  q
10026      %_  $
10027        gol  %noun
10028        gen
10029      :^    %wtcl
10030          :+  %cncl  [%limb %levi]
10031          :~  [%tsgr [%zpgr [%kttr p.gen]] [%$ 2]]
10032              [%tsgr q.gen [%$ 2]]
```

```
10033                    ==
10034                  [%tsgr q.gen [%$ 3]]
10035                [%zpzp ~]
10036              ==
10037          [typ val]
10038        ::
10039            [%zpts *]    [(nice %noun) [%1 q:$(vet |, gen p.gen)]]
10040            [%zppt *]    ?:((feel p.gen) $(gen q.gen) $(gen r.gen))
10041        ::
10042            [%zpzp ~]    [%void [%0 0]]
10043            *
10044      =+  doz=~(open ap gen)
10045      ?:  =(doz gen)
10046        ~_  (show [%c 'hoon'] [%q gen])
10047        ~>(%mean.'mint-open' !!)
10048      $(gen doz)
10049      ==
10050      ::
10051    ++  nice
10052      |=  typ=type
10053      ~_  leaf+"mint-nice"
10054      ?>  ?|(!vet (nest(sut gol) & typ))
10055      typ
10056      ::
10057    ++  grow
10058      |=  [mel=vair nym=(unit term) hud=poly ruf=hoon dom=(map term tome)]
10059      ^-  [p=type q=nock]
10060      =+  dan=^$(gen ruf, gol %noun)
10061      =+  pul=(mine gol mel nym hud dom)
10062      [(nice p.pul) (cons q.pul q.dan)]
10063      --
10064    ::
10065    ++  moot
10066      =+  gil=*(set type)
10067      |-  ^-  ?
10068      ?-  sut
10069        [%atom *]  |
10070        [%cell *]  |($(sut p.sut) $(sut q.sut))
10071        [%core *]  $(sut p.sut)
10072        [%face *]  $(sut q.sut)
10073        [%fork *]  (levy ~(tap in p.sut) |=(type ^$(sut +<)))
10074        [%hint *]  $(sut q.sut)
10075        [%hold *]  |((~(has in gil) sut) $(gil (~(put in gil) sut), sut repo))
10076        %noun      |
10077        %void          &
10078      ==
10079    ::
10080    ++  mull
10081      ~/  %mull
10082      |=  [gol=type dox=type gen=hoon]
10083      |^  ^-  [p=type q=type]
10084      ?:  =(%void sut)
10085        ~>(%mean.'mull-none' !!)
10086      ?-    gen
10087        ::
10088          [^ *]
10089        =+  hed=$(gen p.gen, gol %noun)
10090        =+  tal=$(gen q.gen, gol %noun)
```

```
10091        [(nice (cell p.hed p.tal)) (cell q.hed q.tal)]
10092    ::
10093        [%brcn *]   (grow %gold p.gen %dry [%$ 1] q.gen)
10094        [%brpt *]   (grow %gold p.gen %wet [%$ 1] q.gen)
10095        [%cnts *]   (~(mull et p.gen q.gen) gol dox)
10096        [%dtkt *]   =+($(gen q.gen, gol %noun) $(gen [%kttr p.gen]))
10097        [%dtls *]   =+($(gen p.gen, gol [%atom %$ ~]) (beth [%atom %$ ~]))
10098        [%sand *]   (beth (play gen))
10099        [%rock *]   (beth (play gen))
10100    ::
10101        [%dttr *]
10102    =+([$(gen p.gen, gol %noun) $(gen q.gen, gol %noun)] (beth %noun))
10103    ::
10104        [%dtts *]
10105    =+([$(gen p.gen, gol %noun) $(gen q.gen, gol %noun)] (beth bool))
10106    ::
10107        [%dtwt *]   =+($(gen p.gen, gol %noun) (beth bool)) ::   XX   =|
10108        [%hand *]   [p.gen p.gen]
10109        [%ktbr *]
10110    =+(vat=$(gen p.gen) [(wrap(sut p.vat) %iron) (wrap(sut q.vat) %iron)])
10111    ::
10112        [%ktls *]
10113    =+  hif=[p=(nice (play p.gen)) q=(play(sut dox) p.gen)]
10114    =+($(gen q.gen, gol p.hif) hif)
10115    ::
10116        [%ktpm *]
10117    =+(vat=$(gen p.gen) [(wrap(sut p.vat) %zinc) (wrap(sut q.vat) %zinc)])
10118    ::
10119        [%tune *]
10120    [(face p.gen sut) (face p.gen dox)]
10121    ::
10122        [%ktwt *]
10123    =+(vat=$(gen p.gen) [(wrap(sut p.vat) %lead) (wrap(sut q.vat) %lead)])
10124    ::
10125        [%note *]
10126    =+  vat=$(gen q.gen)
10127    [(hint [sut p.gen] p.vat) (hint [dox p.gen] q.vat)]
10128    ::
10129        [%ktsg *]   $(gen p.gen)
10130        [%sgzp *]   ~_(duck(sut (play p.gen)) $(gen q.gen))
10131        [%sggr *]   $(gen q.gen)
10132        [%tsgr *]
10133    =+  lem=$(gen p.gen, gol %noun)
10134    $(gen q.gen, sut p.lem, dox q.lem)
10135    ::
10136        [%tscm *]
10137    =/  boc  (busk p.gen)
10138    =/  nuf  (busk(sut dox) p.gen)
10139    $(gen q.gen, sut boc, dox nuf)
10140    ::
10141        [%wtcl *]
10142    =+  nor=$(gen p.gen, gol bool)
10143    =+  ^=  hiq  ^-  [p=type q=type]
10144        =+  fex=[p=(gain p.gen) q=(gain(sut dox) p.gen)]
10145        ?:  =(%void p.fex)
10146          :-  %void
10147          ?:  =(%void q.fex)
10148            %void
```

```
10149            ~>(%mean.'if-z' (play(sut q.fex) q.gen))
10150          ?:  =(%void q.fex)
10151            ~>(%mean.'mull-bonk-b' !!)
10152          $(sut p.fex, dox q.fex, gen q.gen)
10153    =+  ^=  ran  ^-  [p=type q=type]
10154        =+  wux=[p=(lose p.gen) q=(lose(sut dox) p.gen)]
10155        ?:  =(%void p.wux)
10156          :-  %void
10157          ?:  =(%void q.wux)
10158            %void
10159          ~>(%mean.'if-a' (play(sut q.wux) r.gen))
10160        ?:  =(%void q.wux)
10161          ~>(%mean.'mull-bonk-c' !!)
10162        $(sut p.wux, dox q.wux, gen r.gen)
10163      [(nice (fork p.hiq p.ran ~)) (fork q.hiq q.ran ~)]
10164    ::
10165        [%fits *]
10166    =+  waz=[p=(play p.gen) q=(play(sut dox) p.gen)]
10167    =+  ^=  syx  :-  p=(cove q:(mint %noun [%wing q.gen]))
10168               q=(cove q:(mint(sut dox) %noun [%wing q.gen]))
10169    =+  pov=[p=(fish(sut p.waz) p.syx) q=(fish(sut q.waz) q.syx)]
10170    ?.  &(=(p.syx q.syx) =(p.pov q.pov))
10171      ~>(%mean.'mull-bonk-a' !!)
10172    (beth bool)
10173    ::
10174        [%wthx *]
10175    ~>  %mean.'mull-bonk-x'
10176    =+  :-  =+  (find %read [[%& 1] q.gen])
10177          ?>  &(?=(%& -.-) ?=(%& -.q.p.-))
10178          new=[type=p.q.p.- axis=(tend p.p.-)]
10179      =+  (find(sut dox) %read [%& 1] q.gen)
10180      ?>  &(?=(%& -.-) ?=(%& -.q.p.-))
10181      old=[type=p.q.p.- axis=(tend p.p.-)]
10182    ?>  =(axis.old axis.new)
10183    ?>  (nest(sut type.old) & type.new)
10184    (beth bool)
10185    ::
10186        [%dbug *]  ~_((show %o p.gen) $(gen q.gen))
10187        [%zpcm *]  [(nice (play p.gen)) (play(sut dox) p.gen)]
10188        [%lost *]
10189    ?:  vet
10190      ::  ~_  (dunk(sut (play p.gen)) 'also')
10191      ~>(%mean.'mull-skip' !!)
10192    (beth %void)
10193    ::
10194        [%zpts *]  (beth %noun)
10195    ::
10196        [%zpmc *]
10197    =+  vos=$(gol %noun, gen q.gen)        ::  XX validate!
10198    [(nice (cell (play p.gen) p.vos)) (cell (play(sut dox) p.gen) q.vos)]
10199    ::
10200        [%zpgl *]
10201    ::  XX is this right?
10202    (beth (play [%kttr p.gen]))
10203    ::
10204        [%zppt *]
10205    =+  [(feel p.gen) (feel(sut dox) p.gen)]
10206    ?.  =(-< ->)
```

```
10207        ~>(%mean.'mull-bonk-f' !!)
10208      ?:  -<
10209        $(gen q.gen)
10210      $(gen r.gen)
10211    ::
10212        [%zpzp *]   (beth %void)
10213        *
10214    =+  doz=~(open ap gen)
10215    ?:  =(doz gen)
10216      ~_  (show [%c 'hoon'] [%q gen])
10217      ~>(%mean.'mull-open' !!)
10218    $(gen doz)
10219    ==
10220    ::
10221  ++  beth
10222    |=  typ=type
10223    [(nice typ) typ]
10224    ::
10225  ++  nice
10226    |=  typ=type
10227    ::  ~_  (dunk(sut gol) 'need')
10228    ::  ~_  (dunk(sut typ) 'have')
10229    ~_  leaf+"mull-nice"
10230    ?>  ?|(!vet (nest(sut gol) & typ))
10231    typ
10232    ::
10233  ++  grow
10234    |=  [mel=vair nym=(unit term) hud=poly ruf=hoon dom=(map term tome)]
10235    ::  make al
10236    ~_  leaf+"mull-grow"
10237    ^-  [p=type q=type]
10238    =+  dan=^$(gen ruf, gol %noun)
10239    =+  yaz=(mile(sut p.dan) q.dan mel nym hud dom)
10240    [(nice p.yaz) q.yaz]
10241    --
10242  ++  meet  |=(ref=type &((nest | ref) (nest(sut ref) | sut)))
10243  ::                                               ::
10244  ++  miss                                         ::  nonintersection
10245    |=  $:  ::  ref: symmetric type
10246            ::
10247            ref=type
10248        ==
10249    ::  intersection of sut and ref is empty
10250    ::
10251    ^-  ?
10252    =|  gil=(set (set type))
10253    =<  dext
10254    |%
10255    ++  dext
10256    ^-  ?
10257    ::
10258    ?:  =(ref sut)
10259    (nest(sut %void) | sut)
10260    ?-  sut
10261    %void       &
10262    %noun       (nest(sut %void) | ref)
10263    [%atom *]   sint
10264    [%cell *]   sint
```

```
10265        [%core *]    sint(sut [%cell %noun %noun])
10266        [%fork *]    %+  levy  ~(tap in p.sut)
10267                     |=(type dext(sut +<))
10268        [%face *]    dext(sut q.sut)
10269        [%hint *]    dext(sut q.sut)
10270        [%hold *]    =+  (~(gas in *(set type)) `(list type)`[sut ref ~])
10271                     ?:  (~(has in gil) -)
10272                       &
10273                     %=  dext
10274                       sut   repo
10275                       gil  (~(put in gil) -)
10276     ==              ==
10277   ++  sint
10278     ?+  ref      dext(sut ref, ref sut)
10279       [%atom *]   ?.  ?=([%atom *] sut)  &
10280                   ?&  ?=(^ q.ref)
10281                       ?=(^ q.sut)
10282                       !=(q.ref q.sut)
10283                   ==
10284       [%cell *]   ?.  ?=([%cell *] sut)  &
10285                   ?|  dext(sut p.sut, ref p.ref)
10286                       dext(sut q.sut, ref q.ref)
10287     ==              ==
10288     --
10289   ++  mite  |=(ref=type |((nest | ref) (nest(sut ref) & sut)))
10290   ++  nest
10291     ~/  %nest
10292     |=  [tel=? ref=type]
10293     =|  $:  seg=(set type)                    ::  degenerate sut
10294             reg=(set type)                    ::  degenerate ref
10295             gil=(set [p=type q=type])         ::  assume nest
10296         ==
10297     =<  dext
10298     ~%  %nest-in  ..$  ~
10299     |%
10300     ++  deem
10301       |=  [mel=vair ram=vair]
10302       ^-  ?
10303       ?.  |(=(mel ram) =(%lead mel) =(%gold ram))  |
10304       ?-  mel
10305         %lead  &
10306         %gold  meet
10307         %iron  dext(sut (peek(sut ref) %rite 2), ref (peek %rite 2))
10308         %zinc  dext(sut (peek %read 2), ref (peek(sut ref) %read 2))
10309       ==
10310     ::
10311     ++  deep
10312       |=  $:  dom=(map term tome)
10313               vim=(map term tome)
10314           ==
10315       ^-  ?
10316       ?:  ?=(~ dom)  =(vim ~)
10317       ?:  ?=(~ vim)  |
10318       ?&  =(p.n.dom p.n.vim)
10319           $(dom l.dom, vim l.vim)
10320           $(dom r.dom, vim r.vim)
10321       ::
10322           =+  [dab hem]=[q.q.n.dom q.q.n.vim]
```

```
10323              |-    ^-   ?
10324        ?:    ?=(~ dab)   =(hem ~)
10325        ?:    ?=(~ hem)    |
10326        ?&    =(p.n.dab p.n.hem)
10327              $(dab l.dab, hem l.hem)
10328              $(dab r.dab, hem r.hem)
10329              %=    dext
10330                 sut   (play q.n.dab)
10331                 ref   (play(sut ref) q.n.hem)
10332       ==   ==   ==
10333   ::
10334   ++  dext
10335     =<   $
10336     ~%   %nest-dext   +   ~
10337     |.
10338     ^-   ?
10339     =-   ?:   -   &
10340        ?.  tel  |
10341        ~_  (dunk %need)
10342        ~_  (dunk(sut ref) %have)
10343        ~>  %mean.'nest-fail'
10344        !!
10345     ?:   =(sut ref)   &
10346     ?-   sut
10347       %void       sint
10348       %noun       &
10349       [%atom *]   ?.   ?=([%atom *] ref)   sint
10350                   ?&   (fitz p.sut p.ref)
10351                        |(?=(~ q.sut) =(q.sut q.ref))
10352                   ==
10353       [%cell *]   ?.   ?=([%cell *] ref)   sint
10354                   ?&   dext(sut p.sut, ref p.ref, seg ~, reg ~)
10355                        dext(sut q.sut, ref q.ref, seg ~, reg ~)
10356                   ==
10357       [%core *]   ?.   ?=([%core *] ref)   sint
10358                   ?:   =(q.sut q.ref)   dext(sut p.sut, ref p.ref)
10359                   ?&   =(q.p.q.sut q.p.q.ref)   ::   same wet/dry
10360                        meet(sut q.q.sut, ref p.sut)
10361                        dext(sut q.q.ref, ref p.ref)
10362                        (deem(sut q.q.sut, ref q.q.ref) r.p.q.sut r.p.q.ref)
10363                        ?:   =(%wet q.p.q.sut)   =(q.r.q.sut q.r.q.ref)
10364                        ?|   (~(has in gil) [sut ref])
10365                             %.   [q.r.q.sut q.r.q.ref]
10366                             %=   deep
10367                                gil   (~(put in gil) [sut ref])
10368                                sut   sut(p q.q.sut, r.p.q %gold)
10369                                ref   ref(p q.q.ref, r.p.q %gold)
10370                        ==   ==
10371                   ==
10372       [%face *]   dext(sut q.sut)
10373       [%fork *]   ?.   ?=(?([%atom *] %noun [%cell *] [%core *]) ref)   sint
10374                   (lien ~(tap in p.sut) |=(type dext(tel |, sut +<)))
10375       [%hint *]   dext(sut q.sut)
10376       [%hold *]   ?:   (~(has in seg) sut)   |
10377                   ?:   (~(has in gil) [sut ref])   &
10378                   %=   dext
10379                      sut   repo
10380                      seg   (~(put in seg) sut)
```

```
10381                        gil  (~(put in gil) [sut ref])
10382            ==                    ==
10383      ::
10384      ++  meet  &(dext dext(sut ref, ref sut))
10385      ++  sint
10386        ^-  ?
10387        ?-  ref
10388          %noun        |
10389          %void        &
10390          [%atom *]    |
10391          [%cell *]    |
10392          [%core *]    dext(ref repo(sut ref))
10393          [%face *]    dext(ref q.ref)
10394          [%fork *]    (levy ~(tap in p.ref) |=(type dext(ref +<)))
10395          [%hint *]    dext(ref q.ref)
10396          [%hold *]    ?:  (~(has in reg) ref)  &
10397                       ?:  (~(has in gil) [sut ref])  &
10398                       %=  dext
10399                         ref  repo(sut ref)
10400                         reg  (~(put in reg) ref)
10401                         gil  (~(put in gil) [sut ref])
10402            ==                    ==
10403        --
10404      ::
10405      ++  peek
10406        ~/  %peek
10407        |=  [way=?(%read %rite %both %free) axe=axis]
10408        ^-  type
10409        ?:  =(1 axe)
10410          sut
10411        =+  [now=(cap axe) lat=(mas axe)]
10412        =+  gil=*(set type)
10413        |-  ^-  type
10414        ?-    sut
10415          [%atom *]    %void
10416          [%cell *]    ?:(=(2 now) ^$(sut p.sut, axe lat) ^$(sut q.sut, axe lat))
10417          [%core *]
10418        ?.  =(3 now)  %noun
10419        =+  pec=(peel way r.p.q.sut)
10420        =/  tow
10421          ?:  =(1 lat)  1
10422          (cap lat)
10423        %=    ^$
10424          axe  lat
10425          sut
10426        ?:  ?|  =([& &] pec)
10427                &(sam.pec =(tow 2))
10428                &(con.pec =(tow 3))
10429            ==
10430          p.sut
10431        ~_  leaf+"payload-block"
10432        ?.  =(way %read)  !!
10433        %+  cell
10434          ?.(sam.pec %noun ^$(sut p.sut, axe 2))
10435        ?.(con.pec %noun ^$(sut p.sut, axe 3))
10436        ==
10437      ::
10438          [%fork *]    (fork (turn ~(tap in p.sut) |=(type ^$(sut +<))))
```

```
10439              [%hold *]
10440        ?:  (~(has in gil) sut)
10441          %void
10442        $(gil (~(put in gil) sut), sut repo)
10443      ::
10444        %void          %void
10445        %noun          %noun
10446        *              $(sut repo)
10447      ==
10448    ::
10449    ++  peel
10450    |=  [way=vial met=?(%gold %iron %lead %zinc)]
10451    ^-  [sam=? con=?]
10452    ?:  ?=(%gold met)  [& &]
10453    ?-  way
10454      %both  [| |]
10455      %free  [& &]
10456      %read  [?=(%zinc met) |]
10457      %rite  [?=(%iron met) |]
10458    ==
10459    ::
10460    ++  play
10461    ~/  %play
10462    =>  .(vet |)
10463    |=  gen=hoon
10464    ^-  type
10465    ?-  gen
10466      [^ *]        (cell $(gen p.gen) $(gen q.gen))
10467      [%brcn *]    (core sut [p.gen %dry %gold] sut *seminoun q.gen)
10468      [%brpt *]    (core sut [p.gen %wet %gold] sut *seminoun q.gen)
10469      [%cnts *]    ~(play et p.gen q.gen)
10470      [%dtkt *]    $(gen [%kttr p.gen])
10471      [%dtls *]    [%atom %$ ~]
10472      [%rock *]    |-  ^-  type
10473                   ?@  q.gen  [%atom p.gen `q.gen]
10474                   [%cell $(q.gen -.q.gen) $(q.gen +.q.gen)]
10475      [%sand *]    ?@  q.gen
10476                     ?:  =(%n p.gen)  ?>(=(0 q.gen) [%atom p.gen `q.gen])
10477                     ?:  =(%f p.gen)  ?>((lte q.gen 1) bool)
10478                     [%atom p.gen ~]
10479                   $(-.gen %rock)
10480      [%tune *]    (face p.gen sut)
10481      [%dttr *]    %noun
10482      [%dtts *]    bool
10483      [%dtwt *]    bool
10484      [%hand *]    p.gen
10485      [%ktbr *]    (wrap(sut $(gen p.gen)) %iron)
10486      [%ktls *]    $(gen p.gen)
10487      [%ktpm *]    (wrap(sut $(gen p.gen)) %zinc)
10488      [%ktsg *]    $(gen p.gen)
10489      [%ktwt *]    (wrap(sut $(gen p.gen)) %lead)
10490      [%note *]    (hint [sut p.gen] $(gen q.gen))
10491      [%sgzp *]    ~_(duck(sut ^$(gen p.gen)) $(gen q.gen))
10492      [%sggr *]    $(gen q.gen)
10493      [%tsgr *]    $(gen q.gen, sut $(gen p.gen))
10494      [%tscm *]    $(gen q.gen, sut (busk p.gen))
10495      [%wtcl *]    =+  [fex=(gain p.gen) wux=(lose p.gen)]
10496                   %-  fork  :~
```

```
10497                     ?:(=(%void fex) %void $(sut fex, gen q.gen))
10498                     ?:(=(%void wux) %void $(sut wux, gen r.gen))
10499                   ==
10500      [%fits *]  bool
10501      [%wthx *]  bool
10502      [%dbug *]  ~_((show %o p.gen) $(gen q.gen))
10503      [%zpcm *]  $(gen p.gen)
10504      [%lost *]  %void
10505      [%zpmc *]  (cell $(gen p.gen) $(gen q.gen))
10506      [%zpgl *]  (play [%kttr p.gen])
10507      [%zpts *]  %noun
10508      [%zppt *]  ?:((feel p.gen) $(gen q.gen) $(gen r.gen))
10509      [%zpzp *]  %void
10510      *          =+  doz=~(open ap gen)
10511                 ?:  =(doz gen)
10512                   ~_  (show [%c 'hoon'] [%q gen])
10513                   ~>  %mean.'play-open'
10514                   !!
10515                 $(gen doz)
10516    ==
10517  ::                                             ::
10518  ++  redo                                       ::  refurbish faces
10519    ~/  %redo
10520    |=  $:  ::  ref: raw payload
10521            ::
10522            ref=type
10523        ==
10524    ::  :type: subject refurbished to reference namespace
10525    ::
10526    ^-  type
10527    ::  hos: subject tool stack
10528    ::  wec: reference tool stack set
10529    ::  gil: repetition set
10530    ::
10531    =|  hos=(list tool)
10532    =/  wec=(set (list tool))  [~ ~ ~]
10533    =|  gil=(set (pair type type))
10534    =<  ::  errors imply subject/reference mismatch
10535        ::
10536        ~|  %redo-match
10537        ::  reduce by subject
10538        ::
10539        dext
10540    |%
10541    ::                                           ::
10542    ++  dear                                     ::  resolve tool stack
10543      ::  :(unit (list tool)): unified tool stack
10544      ::
10545      ^-  (unit (list tool))
10546      ::  empty implies void
10547      ::
10548      ?~  wec  `~
10549      ::  any reference faces must be clear
10550      ::
10551      ?.  ?=([* ~ ~] wec)
10552        ~&  [%dear-many wec]
10553        ~
10554      :-  ~
```

```
10555      ::   har: single reference tool stack
10556      ::
10557      =/  har   n.wec
10558      ::   len: lengths of [sut ref] face stacks
10559      ::
10560      =/  len   [p q]=[(lent hos) (lent har)]
10561      ::   lip: length of sut-ref face stack overlap
10562      ::
10563      ::       AB
10564      ::        BC
10565      ::
10566      ::       +lip is (lent B), where +hay is forward AB
10567      ::       and +liv is forward BC (stack BA and CB).
10568      ::
10569      ::       overlap is a weird corner case.  +lip is
10570      ::       almost always 0.  brute force is fine.
10571      ::
10572      =/  lip
10573        =|  lup=(unit @ud)
10574        =|  lip=@ud
10575        |-  ^-  @ud
10576        ?:  |((gth lip p.len) (gth lip q.len))
10577          (fall lup 0)
10578        ::   lep: overlap candidate: suffix of subject face stack
10579        ::
10580        =/  lep   (slag (sub p.len lip) hos)
10581        ::   lap: overlap candidate: prefix of reference face stack
10582        ::
10583        =/  lap   (scag lip har)
10584        ::   save any match and continue
10585        ::
10586        $(lip +(lip), lup ?.(=(lep lap) lup `lip))
10587      ::   ~&  [har+har hos+hos len+len lip+lip]
10588      ::   produce combined face stack (forward ABC, stack CDA)
10589      ::
10590      (weld hos (slag lip har))
10591    ::                                             ::
10592    ++  dext                                       ::  subject traverse
10593      ::   :type: refurbished subject
10594      ::
10595      ^-  type
10596      ::   check for trivial cases
10597      ::
10598      ?:  ?|  =(sut ref)
10599              ?=(?(%noun %void [?(%atom %core) *]) ref)
10600          ==
10601        done
10602      ::   ~_  (dunk 'redo: dext: sut')
10603      ::   ~_  (dunk(sut ref) 'redo: dext: ref')
10604      ?-    sut
10605          ?(%noun %void [?(%atom %core) *])
10606        ::   reduce reference and reassemble leaf
10607        ::
10608        done:(sint &)
10609      ::
10610          [%cell *]
10611        ::   reduce reference to match subject
10612        ::
```

```
10613          =>  (sint &)
10614          ?>  ?=([%cell *] sut)
10615          ::  leaf with possible recursive descent
10616          ::
10617          %=    done
10618             sut
10619          ::  clear face stacks for descent
10620          ::
10621          =:  hos  ~
10622              wec  [~ ~ ~]
10623            ==
10624          ::  descend into cell
10625          ::
10626          :+  %cell
10627            dext(sut p.sut, ref (peek(sut ref) %free 2))
10628          dext(sut q.sut, ref (peek(sut ref) %free 3))
10629        ==
10630      ::
10631          [%face *]
10632        ::  push face on subject stack, and descend
10633        ::
10634        dext(hos [p.sut hos], sut q.sut)
10635      ::
10636          [%hint *]
10637        ::  work through hint
10638        ::
10639        (hint p.sut dext(sut q.sut))
10640      ::
10641          [%fork *]
10642        ::  reconstruct each case in fork
10643        ::
10644        (fork (turn ~(tap in p.sut) |=(type dext(sut +<))))
10645      ::
10646          [%hold *]
10647        ::  reduce to hard
10648        ::
10649        =>  (sint |)
10650        ?>  ?=([%hold *] sut)
10651        ?:  (~(has in fan) [p.sut q.sut])
10652          ::  repo loop; redo depends on its own product
10653          ::
10654          done:(sint &)
10655        ?:  (~(has in gil) [sut ref])
10656          ::  type recursion, stop renaming
10657          ::
10658          done:(sint |)
10659        ::  restore unchanged holds
10660        ::
10661        =+  repo
10662        =-  ?:(=(- +<) sut -)
10663        dext(sut -, gil (~(put in gil) sut ref))
10664      ==
10665      ::                                              ::
10666  ++  done                                            ::  complete assembly
10667    ^-  type
10668    ::  :type: subject refurbished
10669    ::
10670    ::  lov: combined face stack
```

```
10671        ::
10672        =/  lov
10673            =/  lov   dear
10674            ?~  lov
10675              ::  ~_  (dunk 'redo: dear: sut')
10676              ::  ~_  (dunk(sut ref) 'redo: dear: ref')
10677            ~&  [%wec wec]
10678            !!
10679          (need lov)
10680        ::  recompose faces
10681        ::
10682        |-  ^-  type
10683        ?~  lov  sut
10684        $(lov t.lov, sut (face i.lov sut))
10685    ::
10686    ++  sint                                      ::  reduce by reference
10687      |=  $:  ::  hod: expand holds
10688              ::
10689              hod=?
10690          ==
10691      ::  :::.: reference with face/fork/hold reduced
10692      ::
10693      ^+  .
10694      ::  =-  ~>  %slog.[0 (dunk 'sint: sut')]
10695      ::      ~>  %slog.[0 (dunk(sut ref) 'sint: ref')]
10696      ::      ~>  %slog.[0 (dunk(sut =>(- ref)) 'sint: pro')]
10697      ::      -
10698      ?+  ref  .
10699        [%hint *]  $(ref q.ref)
10700        [%face *]
10701      ::  extend all stacks in set
10702      ::
10703      %=  $
10704        ref  q.ref
10705        wec  (~(run in wec) |=((list tool) [p.ref +<]))
10706      ==
10707      ::
10708        [%fork *]
10709      ::  reconstruct all relevant cases
10710      ::
10711      =-  ::  ~>  %slog.[0 (dunk 'fork: sut')]
10712          ::  ~>  %slog.[0 (dunk(sut ref) 'fork: ref')]
10713          ::  ~>  %slog.[0 (dunk(sut (fork ->)) 'fork: pro')]
10714          +(wec -<, ref (fork ->))
10715      =/  moy  ~(tap in p.ref)
10716      |-  ^-  (pair (set (list tool)) (list type))
10717      ?~  moy  [~ ~]
10718      ::  head recurse
10719      ::
10720      =/  mor  $(moy t.moy)
10721      ::  prune reference cases outside subject
10722      ::
10723      ?:  (miss i.moy)  mor
10724      ::  unify all cases
10725      ::
10726      =/  dis  ^$(ref i.moy)
10727      [(~(uni in p.mor) wec.dis) [ref.dis q.mor]]
10728      ::
```

```
10729            [%hold *]
10730          ?.  hod  .
10731            $(ref repo(sut ref))
10732        ==
10733      --
10734    ::
10735    ++  repo
10736      ^-  type
10737      ?-  sut
10738        [%core *]    [%cell %noun p.sut]
10739        [%face *]    q.sut
10740        [%hint *]    q.sut
10741        [%hold *]    (rest [[p.sut q.sut] ~])
10742        %noun        (fork [%atom %$ ~] [%cell %noun %noun] ~)
10743        *            ~>(%mean.'repo-fltt' !!)
10744      ==
10745    ::
10746    ++  rest
10747      ~/  %rest
10748      |=  leg=(list [p=type q=hoon])
10749      ^-  type
10750      ?:  (lien leg |=([p=type q=hoon] (~(has in fan) [p q])))
10751        ~>(%mean.'rest-loop' !!)
10752      =>  .(fan (~(gas in fan) leg))
10753      %-  fork
10754      %~  tap  in
10755      %-  ~(gas in *(set type))
10756      (turn leg |=([p=type q=hoon] (play(sut p) q)))
10757    ::
10758    ++  sink
10759      ~/  %sink
10760      |^  ^-  cord
10761      ?-  sut
10762        %void        'void'
10763        %noun        'noun'
10764        [%atom *]    (rap 3 'atom ' p.sut ' ' ?~(q.sut '~' u.q.sut) ~)
10765        [%cell *]    (rap 3 'cell ' (mup p.sut) ' ' (mup q.sut) ~)
10766        [%face *]    (rap 3 'face ' ?@(p.sut p.sut (mup p.sut)) ' ' (mup q.sut) ~)
10767        [%fork *]    (rap 3 'fork ' (mup p.sut) ~)
10768        [%hint *]    (rap 3 'hint ' (mup p.sut) ' ' (mup q.sut) ~)
10769        [%hold *]    (rap 3 'hold ' (mup p.sut) ' ' (mup q.sut) ~)
10770      ::
10771        [%core *]
10772      %+  rap  3
10773      :~  'core '
10774          (mup p.sut)
10775          ' '
10776          ?~(p.p.q.sut '~' u.p.p.q.sut)
10777          ' '
10778          q.p.q.sut
10779          ' '
10780          r.p.q.sut
10781          ' '
10782          (mup q.q.sut)
10783          ' '
10784          (mup p.r.q.sut)
10785      ==
10786      ==
```

```
10787    ::
10788    ++  mup  |=(* (scot %p (mug +<)))
10789    --
10790  ::
10791  ++  take
10792    |=  [vit=vein duz=$-(type type)]
10793    ^-  (pair axis type)
10794    :-  (tend vit)
10795    =.  vit  (flop vit)
10796    |-  ^-  type
10797    ?~  vit  (duz sut)
10798    ?~  i.vit
10799      |-  ^-  type
10800      ?+  sut        ^$(vit t.vit)
10801      [%face *]  (face p.sut ^$(vit t.vit, sut q.sut))
10802      [%hint *]  (hint p.sut ^$(sut q.sut))
10803      [%fork *]  (fork (turn ~(tap in p.sut) |=(type ^$(sut +<))))
10804      [%hold *]  $(sut repo)
10805      ==
10806    =+  vil=*(set type)
10807    |-  ^-  type
10808    ?:  =(1 u.i.vit)
10809      ^$(vit t.vit)
10810    =+  [now lat]=(cap u.i.vit)^(mas u.i.vit)
10811    ?-  sut
10812      %noun        $(sut [%cell %noun %noun])
10813      %void        %void
10814      [%atom *]    %void
10815      [%cell *]    ?:  =(2 now)
10816                     (cell $(sut p.sut, u.i.vit lat) q.sut)
10817                     (cell p.sut $(sut q.sut, u.i.vit lat))
10818      [%core *]    ?:  =(2 now)
10819                     $(sut repo)
10820                     (core $(sut p.sut, u.i.vit lat) q.sut)
10821      [%face *]    (face p.sut $(sut q.sut))
10822      [%fork *]    (fork (turn ~(tap in p.sut) |=(type ^$(sut +<))))
10823      [%hint *]    (hint p.sut $(sut q.sut))
10824      [%hold *]    ?:  (~(has in vil) sut)
10825                     %void
10826                     $(sut repo, vil (~(put in vil) sut))
10827    ==
10828  ::
10829  ++  tack
10830    |=  [hyp=wing mur=type]
10831    ~_  (show [%c %tack] %l hyp)
10832    =+  fid=(find %rite hyp)
10833    ?>  ?=(%& -.fid)
10834    (take p.p.fid |=(type mur))
10835  ::
10836  ++  tend
10837    |=  vit=vein
10838    ^-  axis
10839    ?~(vit 1 (peg $(vit t.vit) ?~(i.vit 1 u.i.vit)))
10840  ::
10841  ++  toss
10842    ~/  %toss
10843    |=  [hyp=wing mur=type men=(list [p=type q=foot])]
10844    ^-  [p=axis q=(list [p=type q=foot])]
```

```
10845      =-   [(need p.wib) q.wib]
10846      ^=   wib
10847      |-   ^-   [p=(unit axis) q=(list [p=type q=foot])]
10848      ?~   men
10849        [*(unit axis) ~]
10850      =+   geq=(tack(sut p.i.men) hyp mur)
10851      =+   mox=$(men t.men)
10852      [(mate p.mox `_p.mox`[~ p.geq]) [[q.geq q.i.men] q.mox]]
10853      ::
10854    ++  wrap
10855      ~/   %wrap
10856      |=   yoz=?(%lead %iron %zinc)
10857      ~_   leaf+"wrap"
10858      ^-   type
10859      ?+   sut   sut
10860        [%cell *]   (cell $(sut p.sut) $(sut q.sut))
10861        [%core *]   ?>(|(=(%gold r.p.q.sut) =(%lead yoz)) sut(r.p.q yoz))
10862        [%face *]   (face p.sut $(sut q.sut))
10863        [%fork *]   (fork (turn ~(tap in p.sut) |=(type ^$(sut +<))))
10864        [%hint *]   (hint p.sut $(sut q.sut))
10865        [%hold *]   $(sut repo)
10866      ==
10867      --
10868    ++  us                                          ::  prettyprinter
10869      =>   |%
10870        +$   cape   [p=(map @ud wine) q=wine]        ::
10871        +$   wine                                    ::
10872             $@   $?   %noun                         ::
10873                      %path                          ::
10874                      %type                          ::
10875                      %void                          ::
10876                      %wall                          ::
10877                      %wool                          ::
10878                      %yarn                          ::
10879                  ==                                 ::
10880             $%   [%mato p=term]                     ::
10881                  [%core p=(list @ta) q=wine]        ::
10882                  [%face p=term q=wine]              ::
10883                  [%list p=term q=wine]              ::
10884                  [%pear p=term q=@]                 ::
10885                  [%bcwt p=(list wine)]              ::
10886                  [%plot p=(list wine)]              ::
10887                  [%stop p=@ud]                      ::
10888                  [%tree p=term q=wine]              ::
10889                  [%unit p=term q=wine]              ::
10890                  [%name p=stud q=wine]              ::
10891                  ==                                 ::
10892        --
10893      |_   sut=type
10894    ++  dash
10895      |=   [mil=tape lim=char lam=tape]
10896      ^-   tape
10897      =/   esc   (~(gas in *(set @tD)) lam)
10898      :-   lim
10899      |-   ^-   tape
10900      ?~   mil   [lim ~]
10901      ?:   ?|   =(lim i.mil)
10902                =('\\' i.mil)
```

```
10903            (~(has in esc) i.mil)
10904         ==
10905       ['\\' i.mil $(mil t.mil)]
10906     ?:  (lte ' ' i.mil)
10907       [i.mil $(mil t.mil)]
10908     ['\\' ~(x ne (rsh 2 i.mil)) ~(x ne (end 2 i.mil)) $(mil t.mil)]
10909   ::
10910  ++  deal  |=(lum=* (dish dole lum))
10911  ++  dial
10912    |=  ham=cape
10913    =+  gid=*(set @ud)
10914    =<  `tank`-:$
10915    |%
10916    ++  many
10917      |=  haz=(list wine)
10918      ^-  [(list tank) (set @ud)]
10919      ?~  haz  [~ gid]
10920      =^  mor  gid  $(haz t.haz)
10921      =^  dis  gid  ^$(q.ham i.haz)
10922      [[dis mor] gid]
10923    ::
10924    ++  $
10925      ^-  [tank (set @ud)]
10926      ?-    q.ham
10927        %noun      :_(gid [%leaf '*' ~])
10928        %path      :_(gid [%leaf '/' ~])
10929        %type      :_(gid [%leaf '#' 't' ~])
10930        %void      :_(gid [%leaf '#' '!' ~])
10931        %wool      :_(gid [%leaf '*' '"' '"' ~])
10932        %wall      :_(gid [%leaf '*' '\'' '\'' ~])
10933        %yarn      :_(gid [%leaf '"' '"' ~])
10934        [%mato *]  :_(gid [%leaf '@' (trip p.q.ham)])
10935        [%core *]
10936      =^  cox  gid  $(q.ham q.q.ham)
10937      :_  gid
10938      :+  %rose
10939        [[' ' ~] ['<' ~] ['>' ~]]
10940        |-  ^-  (list tank)
10941      ?~  p.q.ham  [cox ~]
10942      [[%leaf (rip 3 i.p.q.ham)] $(p.q.ham t.p.q.ham)]
10943    ::
10944        [%face *]
10945      =^  cox  gid  $(q.ham q.q.ham)
10946      :_(gid [%palm [['=' ~] ~ ~ ~] [%leaf (trip p.q.ham)] cox ~])
10947    ::
10948        [%list *]
10949      =^  cox  gid  $(q.ham q.q.ham)
10950      :_(gid [%rose [" " (weld (trip p.q.ham) "(") ")"] cox ~])
10951    ::
10952        [%bcwt *]
10953      =^  coz  gid  (many p.q.ham)
10954      :_(gid [%rose [[' ' ~] ['?' '(' ~] [')' ~]] coz])
10955    ::
10956        [%plot *]
10957      =^  coz  gid  (many p.q.ham)
10958      :_(gid [%rose [[' ' ~] ['[' ~] [']' ~]] coz])
10959    ::
10960        [%pear *]
```

```
10961        :_(gid [%leaf '%' ~(rend co [%$ p.q.ham q.q.ham])])
10962      ::
10963        [%stop *]
10964      =+  num=~(rend co [%$ %ud p.q.ham])
10965      ?:  (~(has in gid) p.q.ham)
10966        :_(gid [%leaf '#' num])
10967      =^  cox  gid
10968        %=  $
10969          gid    (~(put in gid) p.q.ham)
10970          q.ham  (~(got by p.ham) p.q.ham)
10971        ==
10972      :_(gid [%palm [['.' ~] ~ ~ ~] [%leaf ['^' '#' num]] cox ~])
10973      ::
10974        [%tree *]
10975      =^  cox  gid  $(q.ham q.q.ham)
10976      :_(gid [%rose [" " (weld (trip p.q.ham) "(") ")"] cox ~])
10977      ::
10978        [%unit *]
10979      =^  cox  gid  $(q.ham q.q.ham)
10980      :_(gid [%rose [" " (weld (trip p.q.ham) "(") ")"] cox ~])
10981      ::
10982        [%name *]
10983      :_  gid
10984      ?@  p.q.ham  (cat 3 '#' mark.p.q.ham)
10985      (rap 3 '#' auth.p.q.ham '+' (spat type.p.q.ham) ~)
10986      ==
10987    --
10988  ::
10989  ++  dish  !:
10990    |=  [ham=cape lum=*]  ^-  tank
10991    ~|  [%dish-h ?@(q.ham q.ham -.q.ham)]
10992    ~|  [%lump lum]
10993    ~|  [%ham ham]
10994    %-  need
10995    =|  gil=(set [@ud *])
10996    |-  ^-  (unit tank)
10997    ?-  q.ham
10998        %noun
10999      %=  $
11000        q.ham
11001      ?:  ?=(@ lum)
11002        [%mato %$]
11003      :-  %plot
11004      |-  ^-  (list wine)
11005      [%noun ?:(?=(@ +.lum) [[%mato %$] ~] $(lum +.lum))]
11006      ==
11007    ::
11008        %path
11009      :-  ~
11010      :+  %rose
11011      [['/' ~] ['/' ~] ~]
11012      |-  ^-  (list tank)
11013      ?~  lum  ~
11014      ?@  lum  !!
11015      ?>  ?=(@ -.lum)
11016      [[%leaf (rip 3 -.lum)] $(lum +.lum)]
11017    ::
11018        %type
```

```
11019    =+  tyr=|.((dial dole))
11020    =+  vol=tyr(sut lum)
11021    =+  cis=;;(tank .*(vol [%9 2 %0 1]))
11022    :^  ~    %palm
11023      [~ ~ ~ ~]
11024    [[%leaf '#' 't' '/' ~] cis ~]
11025  ::
11026      %wall
11027    :-  ~
11028    :+  %rose
11029      [[' ' ~] ['<' '|' ~] ['|' '>' ~]]
11030    |-  ^-  (list tank)
11031    ?~  lum   ~
11032    ?@  lum   !!
11033    [[%leaf (trip ;;(@ -.lum))] $(lum +.lum)]
11034  ::
11035      %wool
11036    :-  ~
11037    :+  %rose
11038      [[' ' ~] ['<' '<' ~] ['>' '>' ~]]
11039    |-  ^-  (list tank)
11040    ?~  lum   ~
11041    ?@  lum   !!
11042    [(need ^$(q.ham %yarn, lum -.lum)) $(lum +.lum)]
11043  ::
11044      %yarn
11045    [~ %leaf (dash (tape lum) '"' "\{")]
11046  ::
11047      %void
11048      ~
11049  ::
11050      [%mato *]
11051    ?.  ?=(@ lum)
11052      ~
11053    :+  ~
11054      %leaf
11055    ?+    (rash p.q.ham ;~(sfix (cook crip (star low)) (star hig)))
11056        ~(rend co [%$ p.q.ham lum])
11057      %$    ~(rend co [%$ %ud lum])
11058      %t    (dash (rip 3 lum) '\'' ~)
11059      %tas  ['%' ?.(=(0 lum) (rip 3 lum) ['$' ~])]
11060    ==
11061  ::
11062      [%core *]
11063    ::  XX  needs rethinking for core metal
11064    ::  ?.  ?=(^ lum)   ~
11065    ::  =>  .(lum `*`lum)
11066    ::  =-  ?~(tok ~ [~ %rose [[' ' ~] ['<' ~] ['>' ~]] u.tok])
11067    ::  ^=  tok
11068    ::  |-  ^-  (unit (list tank))
11069    ::  ?~  p.q.ham
11070    ::    =+  den=^$(q.ham q.q.ham)
11071    ::    ?~(den ~ [~ u.den ~])
11072    ::  =+  mur=$(p.q.ham t.p.q.ham, lum +.lum)
11073    ::  ?~(mur ~ [~ [[%leaf (rip 3 i.p.q.ham)] u.mur]])
11074    [~ (dial ham)]
11075  ::
11076      [%face *]
```

```
11077      =+  wal=$(q.ham q.q.ham)
11078      ?~  wal
11079        ~
11080      [~ %palm [['=' ~] ~ ~ ~] [%leaf (trip p.q.ham)] u.wal ~]
11081  ::
11082        [%list *]
11083      ?:  =(~ lum)
11084      [~ %leaf '~' ~]
11085      =-  ?~  tok
11086          ~
11087        [~ %rose [[' ' ~] ['~' '[' ~] [']' ~]] u.tok]
11088      ^=  tok
11089      |-  ^-  (unit (list tank))
11090      ?:  ?=(@ lum)
11091        ?.(=(~ lum) ~ [~ ~])
11092      =+  [for=^$(q.ham q.q.ham, lum -.lum) aft=$(lum +.lum)]
11093      ?.  &(?=(^ for) ?=(^ aft))
11094        ~
11095      [~ u.for u.aft]
11096  ::
11097        [%bcwt *]
11098      |-  ^-  (unit tank)
11099      ?~  p.q.ham
11100        ~
11101      =+  wal=^$(q.ham i.p.q.ham)
11102      ?~  wal
11103        $(p.q.ham t.p.q.ham)
11104      wal
11105  ::
11106        [%plot *]
11107      =-  ?~  tok
11108          ~
11109        [~ %rose [[' ' ~] ['[' ~] [']' ~]] u.tok]
11110      ^=  tok
11111      |-  ^-  (unit (list tank))
11112      ?~  p.q.ham
11113        ~
11114      ?:  ?=([* ~] p.q.ham)
11115        =+  wal=^$(q.ham i.p.q.ham)
11116        ?~(wal ~ [~ [u.wal ~]])
11117      ?@  lum
11118        ~
11119      =+  gim=^$(q.ham i.p.q.ham, lum -.lum)
11120      ?~  gim
11121        ~
11122      =+  myd=$(p.q.ham t.p.q.ham, lum +.lum)
11123      ?~  myd
11124        ~
11125      [~ u.gim u.myd]
11126  ::
11127        [%pear *]
11128      ?.  =(lum q.q.ham)
11129        ~
11130      =.  p.q.ham
11131        (rash p.q.ham ;~(sfix (cook crip (star low)) (star hig)))
11132      =+  fox=$(q.ham [%mato p.q.ham])
11133      ?>  ?=([~ %leaf ^] fox)
11134      ?:  ?=(?(%n %tas) p.q.ham)
```

```
11135          fox
11136        [~ %leaf '%' p.u.fox]
11137    ::
11138        [%stop *]
11139    ?:  (~(has in gil) [p.q.ham lum])   ~
11140    =+  kep=(~(get by p.ham) p.q.ham)
11141    ?~  kep
11142      ~|([%stop-loss p.q.ham] !!)
11143    $(gil (~(put in gil) [p.q.ham lum]), q.ham u.kep)
11144    ::
11145        [%tree *]
11146    =-  ?~  tok
11147          ~
11148        [~ %rose [[' ' ~] ['{' ~] ['}' ~]] u.tok]
11149    ^=  tok
11150    =+  tuk=*(list tank)
11151    |-  ^-  (unit (list tank))
11152    ?:  =(~ lum)
11153      [~ tuk]
11154    ?.  ?=([n=* l=* r=*] lum)
11155          ~
11156    =+  rol=$(lum r.lum)
11157    ?~  rol
11158          ~
11159    =+  tim=^$(q.ham q.q.ham, lum n.lum)
11160    ?~  tim
11161          ~
11162    $(lum l.lum, tuk [u.tim u.rol])
11163    ::
11164        [%unit *]
11165    ?@  lum
11166      ?.(=(~ lum) ~ [~ %leaf '~' ~])
11167    ?.  =(~ -.lum)
11168          ~
11169    =+  wal=$(q.ham q.q.ham, lum +.lum)
11170    ?~  wal
11171          ~
11172    [~ %rose [[' ' ~] ['[' ~] [']' ~]] [%leaf '~' ~] u.wal ~]
11173    ::
11174        [%name *]
11175    $(q.ham q.q.ham)
11176    ==
11177  ::
11178  ++  doge
11179    |=  ham=cape
11180    =-  ?+  woz  woz
11181          [%list * [%mato %'ta']]   %path
11182          [%list * [%mato %'t']]    %wall
11183          [%list * [%mato %'tD']]   %yarn
11184          [%list * %yarn]           %wool
11185        ==
11186    ^=  woz
11187    ^-  wine
11188    ?.  ?=([%stop *] q.ham)
11189      ?:  ?&  ?=  [%bcwt [%pear %n %0] [%plot [%pear %n %0] [%face *] ~] ~]
11190                q.ham
11191              =(1 (met 3 p.i.t.p.i.t.p.q.ham))
11192          ==
```

```
11193          [%unit =<([p q] i.t.p.i.t.p.q.ham)]
11194        q.ham
11195     =+  may=(~(get by p.ham) p.q.ham)
11196     ?~  may
11197        q.ham
11198     =+  nul=[%pear %n 0]
11199     ?.  ?&  ?=([%bcwt *] u.may)
11200             ?=([* * ~] p.u.may)
11201             |(=(nul i.p.u.may) =(nul i.t.p.u.may))
11202         ==
11203        q.ham
11204     =+  din=?:(=(nul i.p.u.may) i.t.p.u.may i.p.u.may)
11205     ?:  ?&  ?=([%plot [%face *] [%face * %stop *] ~] din)
11206             =(p.q.ham p.q.i.t.p.din)
11207             =(1 (met 3 p.i.p.din))
11208             =(1 (met 3 p.i.t.p.din))
11209         ==
11210       :+  %list
11211         (cat 3 p.i.p.din p.i.t.p.din)
11212       q.i.p.din
11213     ?:  ?&  ?=  $:  %plot
11214                     [%face *]
11215                     [%face * %stop *]
11216                     [[%face * %stop *] ~]
11217                 ==
11218               din
11219             =(p.q.ham p.q.i.t.p.din)
11220             =(p.q.ham p.q.i.t.t.p.din)
11221             =(1 (met 3 p.i.p.din))
11222             =(1 (met 3 p.i.t.p.din))
11223             =(1 (met 3 p.i.t.t.p.din))
11224         ==
11225       :+  %tree
11226         %^    cat
11227             3
11228           p.i.p.din
11229         (cat 3 p.i.t.p.din p.i.t.t.p.din)
11230       q.i.p.din
11231     q.ham
11232   ::
11233   ++  dole
11234     ^-  cape
11235     =+  gil=*(set type)
11236     =+  dex=[p=*(map type @) q=*(map @ wine)]
11237     =<  [q.p q]
11238     |-  ^-  [p=[p=(map type @) q=(map @ wine)] q=wine]
11239     =-  [p.tez (doge q.p.tez q.tez)]
11240     ^=  tez
11241     ^-  [p=[p=(map type @) q=(map @ wine)] q=wine]
11242     ?:  (~(meet ut sut) -:!>(*type))
11243     [dex %type]
11244     ?-    sut
11245         %noun      [dex sut]
11246         %void      [dex sut]
11247         [%atom *]  [dex ?~(q.sut [%mato p.sut] [%pear p.sut u.q.sut])]
11248         [%cell *]
11249       =+  hin=$(sut p.sut)
11250       =+  yon=$(dex p.hin, sut q.sut)
```

```
11251        :-  p.yon
11252        :-  %plot
11253        ?:(?=([%plot *] q.yon) [q.hin p.q.yon] [q.hin q.yon ~])
11254      ::
11255          [%core *]
11256        =+  yad=$(sut p.sut)
11257        :-  p.yad
11258        =+  ^=  doy  ^-  [p=(list @ta) q=wine]
11259          ?:  ?=([%core *] q.yad)
11260            [p.q.yad q.q.yad]
11261            [~ q.yad]
11262        :-  %core
11263        :_  q.doy
11264        :_  p.doy
11265      %^  cat  3
11266        %~  rent  co
11267        :+  %$  %ud
11268        %-  ~(rep by (~(run by q.r.q.sut) |=(tome ~(wyt by q.+<))))
11269        |=([[@ a=@u] b=@u] (add a b))
11270      %^  cat  3
11271        ?-(r.p.q.sut %gold '.', %iron '|', %lead '?', %zinc '&')
11272        =+  gum=(mug q.r.q.sut)
11273      %+  can  3
11274        :~  [1 (add 'a' (mod gum 26))]
11275            [1 (add 'a' (mod (div gum 26) 26))]
11276            [1 (add 'a' (mod (div gum 676) 26))]
11277        ==
11278      ::
11279          [%hint *]
11280        =+  yad=$(sut q.sut)
11281        ?.  ?=(%know -.q.p.sut)  yad
11282        [p.yad [%name p.q.p.sut q.yad]]
11283      ::
11284          ⌊%face *⌋
11285        =+  yad=$(sut q.sut)
11286        ?^(p.sut yad [p.yad [%face p.sut q.yad]])
11287      ::
11288          [%fork *]
11289        =+  yed=(sort ~(tap in p.sut) aor)
11290        =-  [p [%bcwt q]]
11291        |-  ^-  [p=[p=(map type @) q=(map @ wine)] q=(list wine)]
11292        ?~  yed
11293          [dex ~]
11294        =+  mor=$(yed t.yed)
11295        =+  dis=^$(dex p.mor, sut i.yed)
11296        [p.dis q.dis q.mor]
11297      ::
11298          [%hold *]
11299        =+  hey=(~(get by p.dex) sut)
11300        ?^  hey
11301        [dex [%stop u.hey]]
11302        ?:  (~(has in gil) sut)
11303          =+  dyr=+(~(wyt by p.dex))
11304          [[(~(put by p.dex) sut dyr) q.dex] [%stop dyr]]
11305        =+  rom=$(gil (~(put in gil) sut), sut ~(repo ut sut))
11306        =+  rey=(~(get by p.p.rom) sut)
11307        ?~  rey
11308          rom
```

```
11309        [[p.p.rom (~(put by q.p.rom) u.rey q.rom)] [%stop u.rey]]
11310      ==
11311    ::
11312    ++  duck  (dial dole)
11313    --
11314  ++  cain  sell                                    ::  $-(vase tank)
11315  ++  noah  text                                    ::  $-(vase tape)
11316  ++  onan  seer                                    ::  $-(vise vase)
11317  ++  levi                                          ::  $-([type type] ?)
11318    |=  [a=type b=type]
11319    (~(nest ut a) & b)
11320  ::
11321  ++  text                                          ::  tape pretty-print
11322    |=  vax=vase  ^-  tape
11323    ~(ram re (sell vax))
11324  ::
11325  ++  seem  |=(toy=typo `type`toy)                  ::  promote typo
11326  ++  seer  |=(vix=vise `vase`vix)                  ::  promote vise
11327  ::
11328  ::  +sell: pretty-print a vase to a tank using +deal.
11329  ::
11330  ++  sell
11331    ~/  %sell
11332    |=  vax=vase
11333    ^-  tank
11334    ~|  %sell
11335    (~(deal us p.vax) q.vax)
11336  ::
11337  ::  +skol: $-(type tank) using duck.
11338  ::
11339  ++  skol
11340    |=  typ=type
11341    ^-  tank
11342    ~(duck ut typ)
11343  ::
11344  ++  slam                                          ::  slam a gate
11345    |=  [gat=vase sam=vase]  ^-  vase
11346    =+  :-  ^=  typ  ^-  type
11347            [%cell p.gat p.sam]
11348        ^=  gen  ^-  hoon
11349        [%cnsg [%$ ~] [%$ 2] [%$ 3] ~]
11350    =+  gun=(~(mint ut typ) %noun gen)
11351    [p.gun (slum q.gat q.sam)]
11352  ::
11353  ::  +slab: states whether you can access an arm in a type.
11354  ::
11355  ::    .way: the access type ($vial): read, write, or read-and-write.
11356  ::    The fourth case of $vial, %free, is not permitted because it would
11357  ::    allow you to discover "private" information about a type,
11358  ::    information which you could not make use of in (law-abiding) hoon anyway.
11359  ::
11360  ++  slab                                          ::  test if contains
11361    |=  [way=?(%read %rite %both) cog=@tas typ=type]
11362    ?=  [%& *]
11363    (~(fond ut typ) way ~[cog])
11364  ::
11365  ++  slap
11366    |=  [vax=vase gen=hoon]  ^-  vase                ::  untyped vase .*
```

```
11367    =+  gun=(~(mint ut p.vax) %noun gen)
11368    [p.gun .*(q.vax q.gun)]
11369  ::
11370  ++  slog                                         ::  deify printf
11371    =|  pri=@                                       ::  priority level
11372    |=  a=tang  ^+  same                            ::  .=  ~&(%a 1)
11373    ?~(a same ~>(%slog.[pri i.a] $(a t.a)))         ::  ((slog ~[>%a<]) 1)
11374  ::                                                ::
11375  ++  mean                                          ::  crash with trace
11376    |=  a=tang
11377    ^+  !!
11378    ?~  a  !!
11379    ~_(i.a $(a t.a))
11380  ::
11381  ++  road
11382    |*  =(trap *)
11383    ^+  $:trap
11384    =/  res  (mule trap)
11385    ?-  -.res
11386      %&  p.res
11387      %|  (mean p.res)
11388    ==
11389  ::
11390  ++  slew                                          ::  get axis in vase
11391    |=  [axe=@ vax=vase]
11392    =/  typ  |.  (~(peek ut p.vax) %free axe)
11393    |-  ^-  (unit vase)
11394    ?:  =(1 axe)  `[$:typ q.vax]
11395    ?@  q.vax    ~
11396    $(axe (mas axe), q.vax ?-((cap axe) %2 -.q.vax, %3 +.q.vax))
11397  ::
11398  ++  slim                                          ::  identical to seer?
11399    |=  old=vise  ^-  vase
11400    old
11401  ::
11402  ++  slit                                          ::  type of slam
11403    |=  [gat=type sam=type]
11404    ?>  (~(nest ut (~(peek ut gat) %free 6)) & sam)
11405    (~(play ut [%cell gat sam]) [%cnsg [%$ ~] [%$ 2] [%$ 3] ~])
11406  ::
11407  ++  slob                                          ::  superficial arm
11408    |=  [cog=@tas typ=type]
11409    ^-  ?
11410    ?+  typ  |
11411      [%hold *]  $(typ ~(repo ut typ))
11412      [%hint *]  $(typ ~(repo ut typ))
11413      [%core *]
11414    |-  ^-  ?
11415    ?~  q.r.q.typ  |
11416    ?|  (~(has by q.q.n.q.r.q.typ) cog)
11417        $(q.r.q.typ l.q.r.q.typ)
11418        $(q.r.q.typ r.q.r.q.typ)
11419    ==
11420    ==
11421  ::
11422  ++  sloe                                          ::  get arms in core
11423    |=  typ=type
11424    ^-  (list term)
```

```
11425    ?+    typ    ~
11426      [%hold *]  $(typ ~(repo ut typ))
11427      [%hint *]  $(typ ~(repo ut typ))
11428      [%core *]
11429    %-  zing
11430    %+  turn  ~(tap by q.r.q.typ)
11431      |=  [* b=tome]
11432    %+  turn  ~(tap by q.b)
11433      |=  [a=term *]
11434      a
11435    ==
11436  ::
11437  ++  slop                                      ::  cons two vases
11438    |=  [hed=vase tal=vase]
11439    ^-  vase
11440    [[%cell p.hed p.tal] [q.hed q.tal]]
11441  ::
11442  ++  slot                                      ::  got axis in vase
11443    |=  [axe=@ vax=vase]  ^-  vase
11444    [(~(peek ut p.vax) %free axe) .*(q.vax [0 axe])]
11445  ::
11446  ++  slym                                      ::  slam w+o sample-type
11447    |=  [gat=vase sam=*]  ^-  vase
11448    (slap gat(+<.q sam) [%limb %$])
11449  ::
11450  ++  sped                                      ::  reconstruct type
11451    |=  vax=vase
11452    ^-  vase
11453    :_  q.vax
11454    ?@  q.vax  (~(fuse ut p.vax) [%atom %$ ~])
11455    ?@  -.q.vax
11456      ^=  typ
11457      %-  ~(play ut p.vax)
11458      [%wtgr [%wtts [%leaf %tas -.q.vax] [%& 2]~] [%$ 1]]
11459    (~(fuse ut p.vax) [%cell %noun %noun])
11460  ::  +swat: deferred +slap
11461  ::
11462  ++  swat
11463    |=  [tap=(trap vase) gen=hoon]
11464    ^-  (trap vase)
11465    =/  gun  (~(mint ut p:$:tap) %noun gen)
11466    |.  ~+
11467    [p.gun .*(q:$:tap q.gun)]
11468  ::
11469  ::    5d: parser
11470  +|  %parser
11471  ::
11472  ::  +vang: set +vast params
11473  ::
11474  ::    bug: debug mode
11475  ::    doc: doccord parsing
11476  ::    wer: where we are
11477  ::
11478  ++  vang
11479    |=  [f=$@(? [bug=? doc=?]) wer=path]
11480    %*(. vast bug ?@(f f bug.f), doc ?@(f & doc.f), wer wer)
11481  ::
11482  ++  vast                                       ::  main parsing core
```

```
11483    =+   [bug=`?`| wer=*path doc=`?`&]
11484    |%
11485    ++   gash  %+  cook                                    ::   parse path
11486               |=  a=(list tyke)  ^-  tyke
11487               ?~(a ~ (weld i.a $(a t.a)))
11488            (more fas limp)
11489    ++   gasp  ;~  pose                                    ::   parse =path= etc.
11490               %+  cook
11491               |=([a=tyke b=tyke c=tyke] :(weld a b c))
11492             ;~  plug
11493               (cook |=(a=(list) (turn a |=(b=* ~))) (star tis))
11494               (cook |=(a=hoon [[~ a] ~]) hasp)
11495               (cook |=(a=(list) (turn a |=(b=* ~))) (star tis))
11496             ==
11497               (cook |=(a=(list) (turn a |=(b=* ~))) (plus tis))
11498             ==
11499    ++   glam  ~+((glue ace))
11500    ++   hasp  ;~  pose                                    ::   path element
11501             (ifix [sel ser] wide)
11502             (stag %cncl (ifix [pal par] (most ace wide)))
11503             (stag %sand (stag %tas (cold %$ buc)))
11504             (stag %sand (stag %t qut))
11505               %+  cook
11506               |=(a=coin [%sand ?:(?=([~ %tas *] a) %tas %ta) ~(rent co a)])
11507               nuck:so
11508             ==
11509    ++   limp  %+  cook
11510               |=  [a=(list) b=tyke]
11511               ?~  a  b
11512               $(a t.a, b [`[%sand %tas %$] b])
11513             ;~(plug (star fas) gasp)
11514    ++   mota  %+  cook
11515               |=([a=tape b=tape] (rap 3 (weld a b)))
11516             ;~(plug (star low) (star hig))
11517    ++   docs
11518      |%
11519      ::   +apex: prefix comment. may contain batch comments.
11520      ::
11521      ::   when a prefix doccord is parsed, it is possible that there is no +gap
11522      ::   afterward to be consumed, so we add an additional newline and
11523      ::   decrement the line number in the `hair` of the parser
11524      ::
11525      ::   the reason for this is that the whitespace parsing under +vast seems
11526      ::   to factor more cleanly this way, at least compared to the variations
11527      ::   tried without the extra newline. this doesn't mean there isn't a
11528      ::   better factorization without it, though.
11529      ++   apex
11530        ?.  doc (easy *whit)
11531        %+  knee *whit |.  ~+
11532        ;~  plug
11533          |=  tub=nail
11534          =/  vex
11535          %.  tub
11536          %-  star
11537          %+  cook  |*([[a=* b=*] c=*] [a b c])
11538          ;~(pfix (punt leap) into ;~(pose larg smol))
11539        ?~  q.vex  vex
11540        :-  p=p.vex
```

```
11541          %-  some
11542          ?~  p.u.q.vex
11543            [p=~ q=q.u.q.vex]
11544          :-  p=(malt p.u.q.vex)
11545          q=`nail`[[(dec p.p.q.u.q.vex) q.p.q.u.q.vex] ['\0a' q.q.u.q.vex]]
11546        ==
11547      ::
11548      :: +apse: postfix comment.
11549      ::
11550      ::    a one line comment at the end of a line (typically starting at column
11551      ::    57) that attaches to the expression starting at the beginning of the
11552      ::    current line. does not use a $link.
11553      ++  apse
11554        ?.  doc  (easy *whiz)
11555        %+  knee  *whiz  |.  ~+
11556        ;~  pose
11557          ;~(less ;~(plug into step en-link col ace) ;~(pfix into step line))
11558          ::
11559          (easy *whiz)
11560        ==
11561      ::
11562      ++  leap                                  ::  whitespace w/o docs
11563        %+  cold  ~
11564        ;~  plug
11565          ;~  pose
11566          (just '\0a')
11567            ;~(plug gah ;~(pose gah skip))
11568            skip
11569          ==
11570          (star ;~(pose skip gah))
11571        ==
11572      ::
11573      :: +smol: 2 aces then summary, 4 aces then paragraphs.
11574      ++  smol
11575        ;~  pfix
11576          step
11577          ;~  plug
11578            ;~  plug
11579            (plus en-link)
11580              ;~  pose
11581              (ifix [;~(plug col ace) (just '\0a')] (cook crip (plus prn)))
11582              (ifix [(star ace) (just '\0a')] (easy *cord))
11583            ==
11584          ==
11585          (rant ;~(pfix step step text))
11586        ==
11587      ==
11588      ::
11589      :: +larg: 4 aces then summary, 2 aces then paragraphs.
11590      ++  larg
11591        ;~  pfix
11592          step step
11593          ;~  plug
11594            ;~  sfix
11595              ;~  plug
11596                ;~  pose
11597                ;~(sfix (plus en-link) col ace)
11598                ;~(less ace (easy *cuff))
```

```
11599              ==
11600            ;~(less ace (cook crip (plus prn)))
11601          ==
11602          (just '\0a')
11603        ==
11604        (rant ;~(pfix step teyt))
11605      ==
11606    ==
11607  ::
11608  ++  rant
11609    |*  sec=rule
11610    %-  star
11611    ;~  pfix
11612      (ifix [into (just '\0a')] (star ace))
11613      (plus (ifix [into (just '\0a')] sec))
11614    ==
11615  ::
11616  ++  skip                                    ::  non-doccord comment
11617    ;~  plug
11618      col  col
11619      ;~(less ;~(pose larg smol) ;~(plug (star prn) (just '\0a')))
11620    ==
11621  ::
11622  ++  null  (cold ~ (star ace))
11623  ++  text  (pick line code)
11624  ++  teyt  (pick line ;~(pfix step code))
11625  ++  line  ;~(less ace (cook crip (star prn)))
11626  ++  code  ;~(pfix step ;~(less ace (cook crip (star prn))))
11627  ++  step  ;~(plug ace ace)
11628  ::
11629  ++  into
11630    ;~(plug (star ace) col col)
11631  ::
11632  ++  en-link
11633    |=  a=nail  %.  a
11634    %+  knee  *link  |.  ~+
11635    %-  stew
11636    ^.  stet  ^.  limo
11637    :~  :-  '|'  ;~(pfix bar (stag %chat sym))
11638        :-  '.'  ;~(pfix dot (stag %frag sym))
11639        :-  '+'  ;~(pfix lus (stag %funk sym))
11640        :-  '$'  ;~(pfix buc (stag %plan sym))
11641        :-  '%'  ;~(pfix cen (stag %cone bisk:so))
11642    ==
11643    --
11644  ::
11645  ++  clad                                     ::  hoon doccords
11646    |*  fel=rule
11647    %+  cook
11648    |=  [a=whit b=hoon c=whiz]
11649    =?  b  !=(c *whiz)
11650      [%note help/`[c]~ b]
11651    =+  docs=~(tap by bat.a)
11652    |-
11653    ?~  docs  b
11654    $(docs t.docs, b [%note help/i.docs b])
11655    (seam fel)
11656  ++  coat                                     ::  spec doccords
```

```
11657      |*  fel=rule
11658      %+  cook
11659        |=  [a=whit b=spec c=whiz]
11660        =?  b  !=(c *whiz)
11661          [%gist help/`[c]~ b]
11662        =+  docs=~(tap by bat.a)
11663        |-
11664        ?~  docs  b
11665        $(docs t.docs, b [%gist help/i.docs b])
11666      (seam fel)
11667    ++  scye                                     ::  with prefix doccords
11668      |*  fel=rule
11669      ;~(pose ;~(plug apex:docs ;~(pfix gap fel)) ;~(plug (easy *whit) fel))
11670    ++  seam                                     ::  with doccords
11671      |*  fel=rule
11672      (scye ;~(plug fel apse:docs))
11673    ::
11674    ++  plex                                     ::  reparse static path
11675      |=  gen=hoon  ^-  (unit path)
11676      ?:  ?=([%dbug *] gen)                      ::  unwrap %dbug
11677        $(gen q.gen)
11678      ?.  ?=([%clsg *] gen)  ~                   ::  require :~ hoon
11679      %+  reel  p.gen                            ::  build using elements
11680      |=  [a=hoon b=_`(unit path)`[~ u=/]]      ::  starting from just /
11681      ?~  b  ~
11682      ?.  ?=([%sand ?(%ta %tas) @] a)  ~         ::  /foo constants
11683      `[q.a u.b]
11684    ::
11685    ++  phax
11686      |=  ruw=(list (list woof))
11687      =+  [yun=*(list hoon) cah=*(list @)]
11688      =+  wod=|=([a=tape b=(list hoon)] ^+(b ?~(a b [[%mcfs %knit (flop a)] b])))
11689      |-  ^+  yun
11690      ?~  ruw
11691        (flop (wod cah yun))
11692      ?~  i.ruw  $(ruw t.ruw)
11693      ?@  i.i.ruw
11694        $(i.ruw t.i.ruw, cah [i.i.ruw cah])
11695      $(i.ruw t.i.ruw, cah ~, yun [p.i.i.ruw (wod cah yun)])
11696    ::
11697    ++  posh
11698      |=  [pre=(unit tyke) pof=(unit [p=@ud q=tyke])]
11699      ^-  (unit (list hoon))
11700      =-  ?^(- - ~&(%posh-fail -))
11701      =+  wom=(poof wer)
11702      %+  biff
11703        ?~  pre  `u=wom
11704        %+  bind  (poon wom u.pre)
11705        |=  moz=(list hoon)
11706        ?~(pof moz (weld moz (slag (lent u.pre) wom)))
11707      |=  yez=(list hoon)
11708      ?~  pof  `yez
11709      =+  zey=(flop yez)
11710      =+  [moz=(scag p.u.pof zey) gul=(slag p.u.pof zey)]
11711      =+  zom=(poon (flop moz) q.u.pof)
11712      ?~(zom ~ `(weld (flop gul) u.zom))
11713    ::
11714    ++  poof                                           ::  path -> (list hoon)
```

```
11715      |=(pax=path ^-((list hoon) (turn pax |=(a=@ta [%sand %ta a])))))
11716      ::
11717      ::   tyke is =foo== as ~[~ `foo ~ ~]
11718      ::   interpolate '=' path components
11719      ++  poon                                        ::  try to replace '='s
11720        |=  [pag=(list hoon) goo=tyke]                ::    default to pag
11721        ^-  (unit (list hoon))                        ::    for null goo's
11722        ?~  goo  `~                                   ::  keep empty goo
11723        %+  both                                      ::  otherwise head comes
11724          ?^(i.goo i.goo ?~(pag ~ `u=i.pag))          ::    from goo or pag
11725        $(goo t.goo, pag ?~(pag ~ t.pag))             ::  recurse on tails
11726      ::
11727      ++  poor
11728        %+  sear  posh
11729        ;~  plug
11730          (stag ~ gash)
11731          ;~(pose (stag ~ ;~(pfix cen porc)) (easy ~))
11732        ==
11733      ::
11734      ++  porc
11735        ;~  plug
11736          (cook |=(a=(list) (lent a)) (star cen))
11737          ;~(pfix fas gash)
11738        ==
11739      ::
11740      ++  rump
11741        %+  sear
11742          |=  [a=wing b=(unit hoon)]  ^-  (unit hoon)
11743          ?~(b [~ %wing a] ?.(?=([@ ~] a) ~ [~ [%rock %tas i.a] u.b]))
11744        ;~(plug rope ;~(pose (stag ~ wede) (easy ~)))
11745      ::
11746      ++  rood
11747        ;~  pfix  fas
11748          (stag %clsg poor)
11749        ==
11750      ::
11751      ++  reed
11752        ;~  pfix  fas
11753          (stag %clsg (more fas stem))
11754        ==
11755      ::
11756      ++  stem
11757        %+  knee  *hoon  |.  ~+
11758        %+  cook
11759          |=  iota=$%([%hoon =hoon] iota)
11760          ?@  iota  [%rock %tas iota]
11761          ?:  ?=(%hoon -.iota)  hoon.iota
11762          [%clhp [%rock %tas -.iota] [%sand iota]]
11763        |^  %-  stew
11764          ^.  stet  ^.  limo
11765          :~  :-  'a'^'z'  ;~  pose
11766                            (spit (stag %cncl (ifix [pal par] (most ace wide))))
11767                            (spit (ifix [sel ser] wide))
11768                            (slot sym)
11769                          ==
11770              :-  '$'      (cold %$ buc)
11771              :-  '0'^'9'  (slot bisk:so)
11772              :-  '-'      (slot tash:so)
```

```
11773        :-  '.'           ;~(pfix dot zust:so)
11774        :-  '~'           (slot ;~(pfix sig ;~(pose crub:so (easy [%n ~]))))
11775        :-  '\''          (stag %t qut)
11776        :-  '['           (slip (ifix [sel ser] wide))
11777        :-  '('           (slip (stag %cncl (ifix [pal par] (most ace wide)))))
11778      ==
11779    ::
11780    ++  slip  |*(r=rule (stag %hoon r))
11781    ++  slot  |*(r=rule (sear (soft iota) r))
11782    ++  spit
11783      |*  r=rule
11784      %+  stag  %hoon
11785      %+  cook
11786        |*([a=term b=*] `hoon`[%clhp [%rock %tas a] b])
11787      ;~((glue lus) sym r)
11788      --
11789    ::
11790    ++  rupl
11791      %+  cook
11792        |=  [a=? b=(list hoon) c=?]
11793        ?:  a
11794          ?:  c
11795            [%clsg [%clsg b] ~]
11796          [%clsg b]
11797        ?:  c
11798          [%clsg [%cltr b] ~]
11799        [%cltr b]
11800      ;~  plug
11801        ;~  pose
11802          (cold | (just '['))
11803          (cold & (jest '~['))
11804        ==
11805        ::
11806        ;~  pose
11807          (ifix [ace gap] (most gap tall))
11808          (most ace wide)
11809        ==
11810        ::
11811        ;~  pose
11812          (cold & (jest ']~'))
11813          (cold | (just ']'))
11814        ==
11815      ==
11816    ::
11817    ::
11818    ++  sail                                        :: xml template
11819      |=  in-tall-form=?  =|  lin=?
11820      |%
11821      ::
11822      ++  apex                                      :: product hoon
11823        %+  cook
11824          |=  tum=(each manx:hoot marl:hoot)  ^-  hoon
11825          ?-  -.tum
11826            %&  [%xray p.tum]
11827            %|  [%mcts p.tum]
11828          ==
11829        top-level
11830      ::
```

```
11831    ++  top-level                                    ::  entry-point
11832      ;~(pfix mic ?:(in-tall-form tall-top wide-top))
11833    ::
11834    ++  inline-embed                                 ::  brace interpolation
11835      %+  cook  |=(a=tuna:hoot a)
11836      ;~  pose
11837        ;~(pfix mic bracketed-elem(in-tall-form |))
11838        ;~(plug tuna-mode sump)
11839        (stag %tape sump)
11840      ==
11841    ::
11842    ++  script-or-style                              ::  script or style
11843      %+  cook  |=(a=marx:hoot a)
11844      ;~  plug
11845        ;~(pose (jest %script) (jest %style))
11846        wide-attrs
11847      ==
11848    ::
11849    ++  tuna-mode                                    ::  xml node(s) kind
11850      ;~  pose
11851        (cold %tape hep)
11852        (cold %manx lus)
11853        (cold %marl tar)
11854        (cold %call cen)
11855      ==
11856    ::
11857    ++  wide-top                                     ::  wide outer top
11858      %+  knee  *(each manx:hoot marl:hoot)  |.  ~+
11859      ;~  pose
11860        (stag %| wide-quote)
11861        (stag %| wide-paren-elems)
11862        (stag %& ;~(plug tag-head wide-tail))
11863      ==
11864    ::
11865    ++  wide-inner-top                               ::  wide inner top
11866      %+  knee  *(each tuna:hoot marl:hoot)  |.  ~+
11867      ;~  pose
11868        wide-top
11869        (stag %& ;~(plug tuna-mode wide))
11870      ==
11871    ::
11872    ++  wide-attrs                                   ::  wide attributes
11873      %+  cook  |=(a=(unit mart:hoot) (fall a ~))
11874      %-  punt
11875      %+  ifix  [pal par]
11876      %+  more  (jest ', ')
11877      ;~((glue ace) a-mane hopefully-quote)
11878    ::
11879    ++  wide-tail                                    ::  wide elements
11880      %+  cook  |=(a=marl:hoot a)
11881      ;~(pose ;~(pfix col wrapped-elems) (cold ~ mic) (easy ~))
11882    ::
11883    ++  wide-elems                                   ::  wide elements
11884      %+  cook  |=(a=marl:hoot a)
11885      %+  cook  join-tops
11886      (star ;~(pfix ace wide-inner-top))
11887    ::
11888    ++  wide-paren-elems                             ::  wide flow
```

```
11889      %+  cook  |=(a=marl:hoot a)
11890      %+  cook  join-tops
11891      (ifix [pal par] (more ace wide-inner-top))
11892    ::
11893    ::+|
11894    ::
11895    ++  drop-top
11896      |=  a=(each tuna:hoot marl:hoot)  ^-  marl:hoot
11897      ?-  -.a
11898        %&  [p.a]~
11899        %|  p.a
11900      ==
11901    ::
11902    ++  join-tops
11903      |=  a=(list (each tuna:hoot marl:hoot))  ^-  marl:hoot
11904      (zing (turn a drop-top))
11905    ::
11906    ::+|
11907    ::
11908    ++  wide-quote                               ::  wide quote
11909      %+  cook  |=(a=marl:hoot a)
11910      ;~  pose
11911        ;~  less  (jest '"""')
11912        (ifix [doq doq] (cook collapse-chars quote-innards))
11913        ==
11914      ::
11915      %-  inde
11916      %+  ifix  [(jest '"""\0a') (jest '\0a"""')]
11917      (cook collapse-chars quote-innards(lin |))
11918      ==
11919    ::
11920    ++  quote-innards                            ::  wide+tall flow
11921      %+  cook  |=(a=(list $@(@ tuna:hoot)) a)
11922      %-  star
11923      ;~  pose
11924        ;~(pfix bas ;~(pose (mask "-+*%;\{") bas doq bix:ab))
11925        inline-embed
11926        ;~(less bas kel ?:(in-tall-form fail doq) prn)
11927        ?:(lin fail ;~(less (jest '\0a"""') (just '\0a')))
11928        ==
11929    ::
11930    ++  bracketed-elem                           ::  bracketed element
11931      %+  ifix  [kel ker]
11932      ;~(plug tag-head wide-elems)
11933    ::
11934    ++  wrapped-elems                            ::  wrapped tuna
11935      %+  cook  |=(a=marl:hoot a)
11936      ;~  pose
11937        wide-paren-elems
11938        (cook |=(@t `marl`[;/((trip +<))]~) qut)
11939        (cook drop-top wide-top)
11940        ==
11941    ::
11942    ++  a-mane                                   ::  mane as hoon
11943      %+  cook
11944        |=  [a=@tas b=(unit @tas)]
11945        ?~(b a [a u.b])
11946      ;~  plug
```

```
11947        mixed-case-symbol
11948        ;~  pose
11949          %+  stag  ~
11950            ;~(pfix cab mixed-case-symbol)
11951          (easy ~)
11952        ==
11953      ==
11954    ::
11955    ++  en-class
11956      |=  a=(list [%class p=term])
11957      ^-  (unit [%class tape])
11958      ?~  a  ~
11959      %-  some
11960      :-  %class
11961      |-
11962      %+  welp  (trip p.i.a)
11963      ?~  t.a  ~
11964      [' ' $(a t.a)]
11965    ::
11966    ++  tag-head                               ::  tag head
11967      %+  cook
11968        |=  [a=mane:hoot b=mart:hoot c=mart:hoot]
11969        ^-  marx:hoot
11970        [a (weld b c)]
11971      ;~  plug
11972        a-mane
11973        ::
11974        %+  cook
11975          |=  a=(list (unit [term (list beer:hoot)]))
11976          ^-  (list [term (list beer:hoot)])
11977          ::  discard nulls
11978          (murn a same)
11979        ;~  plug
11980          (punt ;~(plug (cold %id hax) (cook trip sym)))
11981          (cook en-class (star ;~(plug (cold %class dot) sym)))
11982          (punt ;~(plug ;~(pose (cold %href fas) (cold %src pat)) soil))
11983          (easy ~)
11984        ==
11985      ::
11986        wide-attrs
11987      ==
11988    ::
11989    ++  tall-top                               ::  tall top
11990      %+  knee  *(each manx:hoot marl:hoot)  |.  ~+
11991      ;~  pose
11992        (stag %|  ;~(pfix (plus ace) (cook collapse-chars quote-innards)))
11993        (stag %&  ;~(plug script-or-style script-style-tail))
11994        (stag %&  tall-elem)
11995        (stag %|  wide-quote)
11996        (stag %|  ;~(pfix tis tall-tail))
11997        (stag %&  ;~(pfix gar gap (stag [%div ~] cram)))
11998        (stag %|  ;~(plug ;~((glue gap) tuna-mode tall) (easy ~)))
11999        (easy %|  [;/("\0a")]~)
12000      ==
12001    ::
12002    ++  tall-attrs                             ::  tall attributes
12003      %-  star
12004      ;~  pfix  ;~(plug gap tis)
```

```
12005            ;~((glue gap) a-mane hopefully-quote)
12006          ==
12007        ::
12008        ++  tall-elem                                    ::  tall preface
12009          %+  cook
12010            |=  [a=[p=mane:hoot q=mart:hoot] b=mart:hoot c=marl:hoot]
12011            ^-  manx:hoot
12012            [[p.a (weld q.a b)] c]
12013          ;~(plug tag-head tall-attrs tall-tail)
12014        ::
12015        ::REVIEW is there a better way to do this?
12016        ++  hopefully-quote                              ::  prefer "quote" form
12017          %+  cook  |=(a=(list beer:hoot) a)
12018          %+  cook  |=(a=hoon ?:(?=(%knit -.a) p.a [~ a]~))
12019          wide
12020        ::
12021        ++  script-style-tail                            ::  unescaped tall tail
12022          %+  cook  |=(a=marl:hoot a)
12023          %+  ifix  [gap ;~(plug gap duz)]
12024          %+  most  gap
12025          ;~  pfix  mic
12026            %+  cook  |=(a=tape ;/(a))
12027            ;~  pose
12028              ;~(pfix ace (star prn))
12029              (easy "\0a")
12030            ==
12031          ==
12032        ::
12033        ++  tall-tail                                    ::  tall tail
12034          ?>  in-tall-form
12035          %+  cook  |=(a=marl:hoot a)
12036          ;~  pose
12037            (cold ~ mic)
12038            ;~(pfix col wrapped-elems(in-tall-form |))
12039            ;~(pfix col ace (cook collapse-chars(in-tall-form |) quote-innards))
12040            (ifix [gap ;~(plug gap duz)] tall-kids)
12041          ==
12042        ::
12043        ++  tall-kids                                    ::  child elements
12044          %+  cook  join-tops
12045          ::  look for sail first, or markdown if not
12046          (most gap ;~(pose top-level (stag %| cram)))
12047        ::
12048        ++  collapse-chars                               ::  group consec chars
12049          |=  reb=(list $@(@ tuna:hoot))
12050          ^-  marl:hoot
12051          =|  [sim=(list @) tuz=marl:hoot]
12052          |-  ^-  marl:hoot
12053          ?~  reb
12054            =.  sim
12055              ?.  in-tall-form    sim
12056              [10 |-(?~(sim sim ?:(=(32 i.sim) $(sim t.sim) sim)))]
12057            ?~(sim tuz [;/((flop sim)) tuz])
12058          ?@  i.reb
12059            $(reb t.reb, sim [i.reb sim])
12060          ?~  sim  [i.reb $(reb t.reb, sim ~)]
12061          [;/((flop sim)) i.reb $(reb t.reb, sim ~)]
12062        --
```

```
12063   ++  cram                                      ::  parse unmark
12064     =>  |%
12065         ++  item  (pair mite marl:hoot)          ::  xml node generator
12066         ++  colm  @ud                            ::  column
12067         ++  tarp  marl:hoot                      ::  node or generator
12068         ++  mite                                 ::  context
12069           $?  %down                              ::  outer embed
12070               %lunt                              ::  unordered list
12071               %lime                              ::  list item
12072               %lord                              ::  ordered list
12073               %poem                              ::  verse
12074               %bloc                              ::  blockquote
12075               %head                              ::  heading
12076           ==                                     ::
12077         ++  trig                                 ::  line style
12078           $:  col=@ud                            ::  start column
12079               sty=trig-style                     ::  style
12080           ==                                     ::
12081         ++  trig-style                           ::  type of parsed line
12082           $%  $:  %end                           ::  terminator
12083               $?  %done                          ::  end of input
12084                   %stet                          ::    == end of markdown
12085                   %dent                          ::    outdent
12086               ==  ==                             ::
12087               $:  %one                           ::  leaf node
12088               $?  %rule                          ::    --- horz rule
12089                   %fens                          ::    ``` code fence
12090                   %expr                          ::    ;sail expression
12091               ==  ==                             ::
12092               [%new p=trig-new]                  ::  open container
12093               [%old %text]                       ::  anything else
12094           ==                                     ::
12095         ++  trig-new                             ::  start a
12096           $?  %lite                              ::    + line item
12097               %lint                              ::    - line item
12098               %head                              ::  # heading
12099               %bloc                              ::  > block-quote
12100               %poem                              ::    [ ]{8} poem
12101           ==                                     ::
12102         ++  graf                                 ::  paragraph element
12103           $%  [%bold p=(list graf)]              ::  *bold*
12104               [%talc p=(list graf)]              ::  _italics_
12105               [%quod p=(list graf)]              ::  "double quote"
12106               [%code p=tape]                     ::  code literal
12107               [%text p=tape]                     ::  text symbol
12108               [%link p=(list graf) q=tape]       ::  URL
12109               [%mage p=tape q=tape]              ::  image
12110               [%expr p=tuna:hoot]                ::  interpolated hoon
12111           ==
12112         --
12113     =<  (non-empty:parse |=(nail `(like tarp)`~($ main +<)))
12114     |%
12115     ++  main
12116       ::
12117       ::      state of the parsing loop.
12118       ::
12119       ::  we maintain a construction stack for elements and a line
12120       ::  stack for lines in the current block.  a blank line
```

```
12121     ::  causes the current block to be parsed and thrown in the
12122     ::  current element.  when the indent column retreats, the
12123     ::  element stack rolls up.
12124     ::
12125     ::  .verbose: debug printing enabled
12126     ::  .err: error position
12127     ::  .ind: outer and inner indent level
12128     ::  .hac: stack of items under construction
12129     ::  .cur: current item under construction
12130     ::  .par: current "paragraph" being read in
12131     ::  .[loc txt]: parsing state
12132     ::
12133     =/  verbose  &
12134     =|  err=(unit hair)
12135     =|  ind=[out=@ud inr=@ud]
12136     =|  hac=(list item)
12137     =/  cur=item  [%down ~]
12138     =|  par=(unit (pair hair wall))
12139     |_  [loc=hair txt=tape]
12140     ::
12141     ++  $                                      ::  resolve
12142       ^-  (like tarp)
12143       =>  line
12144       ::
12145       ::  if error position is set, produce error
12146       ?.  =(~ err)
12147         ~&  err+err
12148         [+.err ~]
12149       ::
12150       ::  all data was consumed
12151       =-  [loc `[- [loc txt]]]
12152       =>  close-par
12153       |-  ^-  tarp
12154       ::
12155       ::  fold all the way to top
12156       ?~  hac  cur-to-tarp
12157       $(..^$ close-item)
12158     ::
12159     ::+|
12160     ::
12161     ++  cur-indent
12162       ?-  p.cur
12163         %down  2
12164         %head  0
12165         %lunt  0
12166         %lime  2
12167         %lord  0
12168         %poem  8
12169         %bloc  2
12170       ==
12171     ::
12172     ++  back                                   ::  column retreat
12173       |=  luc=@ud
12174       ^+  +>
12175       ?:  (gte luc inr.ind)  +>
12176       ::
12177       ::  nex: next backward step that terminates this context
12178       =/  nex=@ud  cur-indent  ::  REVIEW code and poem blocks are
```

```
12179                                      :: handled elsewhere
12180          ?:  (gth nex (sub inr.ind luc))
12181            ::
12182            ::  indenting pattern violation
12183            ~?  verbose  indent-pattern-violation+[p.cur nex inr.ind luc]
12184            ..^$(inr.ind luc, err `[p.loc luc])
12185          =.  ..^$  close-item
12186          $(inr.ind (sub inr.ind nex))
12187        ::
12188        ++  cur-to-tarp                          ::  item to tarp
12189          ^-  tarp
12190          ?:  ?=(?(%down %head %expr) p.cur)
12191            (flop q.cur)
12192          =-  [[- ~] (flop q.cur)]~
12193          ?-  p.cur
12194            %lunt  %ul
12195            %lord  %ol
12196            %lime  %li
12197            %poem  %div ::REVIEW actual container element?
12198            %bloc  %blockquote
12199          ==
12200        ::
12201        ++  close-item  ^+  .                     ::  complete and pop
12202          ?~  hac  .
12203          %=  .
12204            hac  t.hac
12205            cur  [p.i.hac (weld cur-to-tarp q.i.hac)]
12206          ==
12207        ::
12208        ++  read-line                             ::  capture raw line
12209          =|  lin=tape
12210          |-  ^+  [[lin *(unit _err)] +<.^$]   :: parsed tape and halt/error
12211          ::
12212          ::  no unterminated lines
12213          ?~  txt
12214            ~?  verbose  %unterminated-line
12215            [[~ ``loc] +<.^$]
12216          ?.  =(`@`10 i.txt)
12217            ?:  (gth inr.ind q.loc)
12218              ?.  =(' ' i.txt)
12219                ~?  verbose  expected-indent+[inr.ind loc txt]
12220                [[~ ``loc] +<.^$]
12221              $(txt t.txt, q.loc +(q.loc))
12222            ::
12223            ::  save byte and repeat
12224            $(txt t.txt, q.loc +(q.loc), lin [i.txt lin])
12225          =.  lin
12226            ::
12227            ::  trim trailing spaces
12228            |-  ^-  tape
12229            ?:  ?=([%' ' *] lin)
12230              $(lin t.lin)
12231            (flop lin)
12232          ::
12233          =/  eat-newline=nail  [[+(p.loc) 1] t.txt]
12234          =/  saw  look(+<.$ eat-newline)
12235          ::
12236          ?:  ?=([~ @ %end ?(%stet %dent)] saw)    ::  stop on == or dedent
```

```
12237            [[lin `~] +<.^$]
12238           [[lin ~] eat-newline]
12239         ::
12240         ++  look                                     ::  inspect line
12241           ^-  (unit trig)
12242           %+  bind  (wonk (look:parse loc txt))
12243           |=  a=trig  ^+  a
12244           ::
12245           ::  treat a non-terminator as a terminator
12246           ::  if it's outdented
12247           ?:  =(%end -.sty.a)  a
12248           ?:  (lth col.a out.ind)
12249             a(sty [%end %dent])
12250           a
12251         ::
12252         ++  close-par                                ::  make block
12253           ^+  .
12254           ::
12255           ::  empty block, no action
12256           ?~  par  .
12257           ::
12258           ::  if block is verse
12259           ?:  ?=(%poem p.cur)
12260             ::
12261             ::  add break between stanzas
12262             =.  q.cur  ?~(q.cur q.cur [[[%br ~] ~] q.cur])
12263             =-  close-item(par ~, q.cur (weld - q.cur), inr.ind (sub inr.ind 8))
12264             %+  turn  q.u.par
12265             |=  tape  ^-  manx
12266             ::
12267             ::  each line is a paragraph
12268             :-  [%p ~]
12269             :_  ~
12270             ;/("{+<}\0a")
12271           ::
12272           ::  yex: block recomposed, with newlines
12273           =/  yex=tape
12274             %-  zing
12275             %+  turn  (flop q.u.par)
12276             |=  a=tape
12277             (runt [(dec inr.ind) ' '] "{a}\0a")
12278           ::
12279           ::  vex: parse of paragraph
12280           =/  vex=(like tarp)
12281             ::
12282             ::  either a one-line header or a paragraph
12283             %.  [p.u.par yex]
12284             ?:  ?=(%head p.cur)
12285               (full head:parse)
12286             (full para:parse)
12287           ::
12288           ::  if error, propagate correctly
12289           ?~  q.vex
12290             ~?  verbose  [%close-par p.cur yex]
12291             ..$(err `p.vex)
12292           ::
12293           ::  finish tag if it's a header
12294           =<  ?:(?=(%head p.cur) close-item ..$)
```

```
12295      ::
12296      ::  save good result, clear buffer
12297      ..$(par ~, q.cur (weld p.u.q.vex q.cur))
12298    ::
12299  ++  line  ^+  .                                    ::  body line loop
12300      ::
12301      ::  abort after first error
12302      ?:  !=(~ err)  .
12303      ::
12304      ::  saw: profile of this line
12305      =/  saw  look
12306      ~?  [debug=|]  [%look ind=ind saw=saw txt=txt]
12307      ::
12308      ::  if line is blank
12309      ?~  saw
12310        ::
12311        ::  break section
12312        =^  a=[tape fin=(unit _err)]  +<.$  read-line
12313        ?^  fin.a
12314          ..$(err u.fin.a)
12315        =>(close-par line)
12316      ::
12317      ::  line is not blank
12318      =>  .(saw u.saw)
12319      ::
12320      ::  if end of input, complete
12321      ?:  ?=(%end -.sty.saw)
12322        ..$(q.loc col.saw)
12323      ::
12324      =.  ind  ?~(out.ind [col.saw col.saw] ind)       ::  init indents
12325      ::
12326      ?:  ?|  ?=(~ par)                            ::  if after a paragraph or
12327              ?&  ?=(?(%down %lime %bloc) p.cur)   ::  unspaced new container
12328                  |(!=(%old -.sty.saw) (gth col.saw inr.ind))
12329          ==  ==
12330        =>  .(..$ close-par)
12331          ::
12332        ::  if column has retreated, adjust stack
12333        =.  ..$  (back col.saw)
12334          ::
12335        =^  col-ok  sty.saw
12336          ?+  (sub col.saw inr.ind)  [| sty.saw]       ::  columns advanced
12337            %0  [& sty.saw]
12338            %8  [& %new %poem]
12339          ==
12340        ?.  col-ok
12341          ~?  verbose  [%columns-advanced col.saw inr.ind]
12342          ..$(err `[p.loc col.saw])
12343      ::
12344      =.  inr.ind  col.saw
12345    ::
12346      ::  unless adding a matching item, close lists
12347      =.  ..$
12348        ?:  ?|  &(?=(%lunt p.cur) !?=(%lint +.sty.saw))
12349                &(?=(%lord p.cur) !?=(%lite +.sty.saw))
12350            ==
12351          close-item
12352        ..$
```

```
12353          ::
12354          =<  line(par `[loc ~])  ^+  ..$            :: continue with para
12355          ?-    -.sty.saw
12356            %one  (read-one +.sty.saw)               :: parse leaves
12357            %new  (open-item p.sty.saw)              :: open containers
12358            %old  ..$                                :: just text
12359          ==
12360          ::
12361          ::
12362          ::- - - foo
12363          ::  detect bad block structure
12364          ?.  ::  first line of container is legal
12365            ?~  q.u.par  &
12366            ?-  p.cur
12367          ::
12368            ::  can't(/directly) contain text
12369            ?(%lord %lunt)  ~|(bad-leaf-container+p.cur !!)
12370          ::
12371            ::  only one line in a header
12372            %head  |
12373          ::
12374            ::  indented literals need to end with a blank line
12375            %poem  (gte col.saw inr.ind)
12376          ::
12377            ::  text tarps must continue aligned
12378            ?(%down %lunt %lime %lord %bloc)  =(col.saw inr.ind)
12379          ==
12380          ~?  verbose  bad-block-structure+[p.cur inr.ind col.saw]
12381          ..$(err `[p.loc col.saw])
12382          ::
12383          ::  accept line and maybe continue
12384          =^  a=[lin=tape fin=(unit _err)]  +<.$  read-line
12385          =.  par  par(q.u [lin.a q.u.par])
12386          ?^  fin.a  ..$(err u.fin.a)
12387          line
12388      ++  parse-block                              :: execute parser
12389        |=  fel=$-(nail (like tarp))  ^+  +>
12390        =/  vex=(like tarp)  (fel loc txt)
12391        ?~  q.vex
12392          ~?  verbose  [%parse-block txt]
12393          +>.$(err `p.vex)
12394        =+  [res loc txt]=u.q.vex
12395        %_  +>.$
12396          loc  loc
12397          txt  txt
12398          q.cur  (weld (flop `tarp`res) q.cur)       :: prepend to the stack
12399        ==
12400      ::
12401      ++  read-one                                 :: read %one item
12402        |=  sty=?(%expr %rule %fens)  ^+  +>
12403        ?-  sty
12404          %expr  (parse-block expr:parse)
12405          %rule  (parse-block hrul:parse)
12406          %fens  (parse-block (fens:parse inr.ind))
12407        ==
12408      ::
12409      ++  open-item                                :: enter list/quote
12410        |=  saw=trig-new
```

```
12411      =<  +>.$:apex
12412      |%
12413      ++  apex  ^+  .                           ::  open container
12414        ?-  saw
12415          %poem  (push %poem)                   ::  verse literal
12416          %head  (push %head)                   ::  heading
12417          %bloc  (entr %bloc)                   ::  blockquote line
12418          %lint  (lent %lunt)                   ::  unordered list
12419          %lite  (lent %lord)                   ::  ordered list
12420        ==
12421      ::
12422      ++  push                                   ::  push context
12423        |=(mite +>(hac [cur hac], cur [+< ~]))
12424      ::
12425      ++  entr                                   ::  enter container
12426        |=  typ=mite
12427        ^+  +>
12428        ::
12429        ::  indent by 2
12430        =.  inr.ind  (add 2 inr.ind)
12431        ::
12432        ::  "parse" marker
12433        =.  txt  (slag (sub inr.ind q.loc) txt)
12434        =.  q.loc  inr.ind
12435        ::
12436        (push typ)
12437      ::
12438      ++  lent                                   ::  list entry
12439        |=  ord=?(%lord %lunt)
12440        ^+  +>
12441        =>  ?:(=(ord p.cur) +>.$ (push ord))     ::  push list if new
12442        (entr %lime)
12443        --
12444      --
12445    ::
12446    ++  parse                                     ::  individual parsers
12447      |%
12448    ++  look                                       ::  classify line
12449    %+  cook  |=(a=(unit trig) a)
12450    ;~  pfix  (star ace)
12451      %+  here                                    ::  report indent
12452        |=([a=pint b=?(~ trig-style)] ?~(b ~ `[q.p.a b]))
12453      ;~  pose
12454        (cold ~ (just `@`10))                     ::  blank line
12455      ::
12456        (full (easy [%end %done]))                ::  end of input
12457        (cold [%end %stet] duz)                   ::  == end of markdown
12458      ::
12459        (cold [%one %rule] ;~(plug hep hep hep))  ::  --- horizontal ruler
12460        (cold [%one %fens] ;~(plug tic tic tic))  ::  ``` code fence
12461        (cold [%one %expr] mic)                   ::  ;sail expression
12462      ::
12463        (cold [%new %head] ;~(plug (star hax) ace)) ::  # heading
12464        (cold [%new %lint] ;~(plug hep ace))      ::  - line item
12465        (cold [%new %lite] ;~(plug lus ace))      ::  + line item
12466        (cold [%new %bloc] ;~(plug gar ace))      ::  > block-quote
12467      ::
12468        (easy [%old %text])                       ::  anything else
```

```
12469            ==
12470          ==
12471        ::
12472        ::
12473        ++  calf                              ::  cash but for tic tic
12474        |*  tem=rule
12475        %-  star
12476        ;~  pose
12477          ;~(pfix bas tem)
12478          ;~(less tem prn)
12479          ==
12480        ++  cash                              ::  escaped fence
12481        |*  tem=rule
12482        %-  echo
12483        %-  star
12484        ;~  pose
12485          whit
12486          ;~(plug bas tem)
12487          ;~(less tem prn)
12488          ==
12489        ::
12490        ++  cool                              ::  reparse
12491        |*  $:  ::  fex: primary parser
12492                ::  sab: secondary parser
12493                ::
12494                fex=rule
12495                sab=rule
12496            ==
12497        |=  [loc=hair txt=tape]
12498        ^+  *sab
12499        ::
12500        ::  vex: fenced span
12501        =/  vex=(like tape)  (fex loc txt)
12502        ?~  q.vex   vex
12503        ::
12504        ::  hav: reparse full fenced text
12505        =/  hav  ((full sab) [loc p.u.q.vex])
12506        ::
12507        ::  reparsed error position is always at start
12508        ?~  q.hav  [loc ~]
12509        ::
12510        ::  the complete type with the main product
12511        :-  p.vex
12512        `[p.u.q.hav q.u.q.vex]
12513      ::
12514      ::REVIEW surely there is a less hacky "first or after space" solution
12515      ++  easy-sol                            ::  parse start of line
12516        |*  a=*
12517        |=  b=nail
12518      ?:  =(1 q.p.b)  ((easy a) b)
12519      (fail b)
12520      ::
12521      ++  echo                                ::  hoon literal
12522        |*  sab=rule
12523        |=  [loc=hair txt=tape]
12524        ^-  (like tape)
12525        ::
12526        ::  vex: result of parsing wide hoon
```

```
12527        =/  vex  (sab loc txt)
12528        ::
12529        ::  use result of expression parser
12530        ?~  q.vex  vex
12531        =-  [p.vex `[- q.u.q.vex]]
12532        ::
12533        ::  but replace payload with bytes consumed
12534        |-  ^-  tape
12535        ?:  =(q.q.u.q.vex txt)  ~
12536        ?~  txt  ~
12537        [i.txt $(txt +.txt)]
12538      ::
12539      ++  non-empty
12540        |*  a=rule
12541        |=  tub=nail  ^+  (a)
12542        =/  vex  (a tub)
12543        ~!  vex
12544        ?~  q.vex  vex
12545        ?.  =(tub q.u.q.vex)  vex
12546        (fail tub)
12547      ::
12548      ::
12549    ++  word                              ::  tarp parser
12550      %+  knee  *(list graf)  |.  ~+
12551      %+  cook
12552        |=  a=$%(graf [%list (list graf)])
12553        ^-  (list graf)
12554        ?:(?=(%list -.a) +.a [a ~])
12555      ;~  pose
12556        ::
12557        ::  ordinary word
12558        ::
12559        %+  stag  %text
12560        ;~(plug ;~(pose low hig) (star ;~(pose nud low hig hep)))
12561        ::
12562        ::  naked \escape
12563        ::
12564        (stag %text ;~(pfix bas (cook trip ;~(less ace prn))))
12565        ::
12566        ::  trailing \ to add <br>
12567        ::
12568        (stag %expr (cold [[%br ~] ~] ;~(plug bas (just '\0a'))))
12569        ::
12570        ::  *bold literal*
12571        ::
12572        (stag %bold (ifix [tar tar] (cool (cash tar) werk)))
12573        ::
12574        ::  _italic literal_
12575        ::
12576        (stag %talc (ifix [cab cab] (cool (cash cab) werk)))
12577        ::
12578        ::  "quoted text"
12579        ::
12580        (stag %quod (ifix [doq doq] (cool (cash doq) werk)))
12581        ::
12582        ::  `classic markdown quote`
12583        ::
12584        (stag %code (ifix [tic tic] (calf tic)))
```

```
12585          ::
12586          ::   ++arm, +$arm, +*arm, ++arm:core, ...
12587          ::
12588        %+  stag  %code
12589        ;~  plug
12590          lus  ;~(pose lus buc tar)
12591          low  (star ;~(pose nud low hep col))
12592        ==
12593        ::
12594        :: [arbitrary *content*](url)
12595        ::
12596        %+  stag  %link
12597        ;~  (glue (punt whit))
12598          (ifix [sel ser] (cool (cash ser) werk))
12599          (ifix [pal par] (cash par))
12600        ==
12601        ::
12602        ::  ![alt text](url)
12603        ::
12604        %+  stag  %mage
12605        ;~  pfix  zap
12606          ;~  (glue (punt whit))
12607            (ifix [sel ser] (cash ser))
12608            (ifix [pal par] (cash par))
12609          ==
12610        ==
12611        ::
12612        ::  #hoon
12613        ::
12614        %+  stag  %list
12615        ;~  plug
12616          (stag %text ;~(pose (cold " " whit) (easy-sol ~)))
12617          (stag %code ;~(pfix hax (echo wide)))
12618          ;~(simu whit (easy ~))
12619        ==
12620        ::
12621        ::  direct hoon constant
12622        ::
12623        %+  stag  %list
12624        ;~  plug
12625          (stag %text ;~(pose (cold " " whit) (easy-sol ~)))
12626          ::
12627          %+  stag  %code
12628          %-  echo
12629          ;~  pose
12630            ::REVIEW just copy in 0x... parsers directly?
12631            ;~(simu ;~(plug (just '0') alp) bisk:so)
12632            ::
12633            tash:so
12634            ;~(pfix dot perd:so)
12635            ;~(pfix sig ;~(pose twid:so (easy [%$ %n 0])))
12636            ;~(pfix cen ;~(pose sym buc pam bar qut nuck:so))
12637          ==
12638          ::
12639          ;~(simu whit (easy ~))
12640        ==
12641        ::
12642        ::  whitespace
```

```
12643          ::
12644            (stag %text (cold " " whit))
12645          ::
12646          ::  {interpolated} sail
12647          ::
12648            (stag %expr inline-embed:(sail |))
12649          ::
12650          ::  just a byte
12651          ::
12652            (stag %text (cook trip ;~(less ace prn)))
12653          ==
12654      ::
12655      ++  werk  (cook zing (star word))               ::  indefinite tarp
12656      ::
12657      ++  down                                        ::  parse inline tarp
12658        %+  knee  *tarp  |.  ~+
12659        =-  (cook - werk)
12660        ::
12661        ::  collect raw tarp into xml tags
12662        |=  gaf=(list graf)
12663        ^-  tarp
12664        =<  main
12665        |%
12666        ++  main
12667          ^-  tarp
12668          ?~  gaf  ~
12669          ?.  ?=(%text -.i.gaf)
12670            (weld (item i.gaf) $(gaf t.gaf))
12671          ::
12672          ::  fip: accumulate text blocks
12673          =/  fip=(list tape)  [p.i.gaf]~
12674          |-  ^-  tarp
12675          ?~  t.gaf  [;/((zing (flop fip))) ~]
12676          ?.  ?=(%text -.i.t.gaf)
12677            [;/((zing (flop fip))) ~$(gaf t.gaf)]
12678          $(gaf t.gaf, fip :_(fip p.i.t.gaf))
12679        ::
12680        ++  item
12681          |=  nex=graf
12682          ^-  tarp  ::CHECK can be tuna:hoot?
12683          ?-  -.nex
12684            %text  !!  ::  handled separately
12685            %expr  [p.nex]~
12686            %bold  [[%b ~]  ^$(gaf p.nex)]~
12687            %talc  [[%i ~]  ^$(gaf p.nex)]~
12688            %code  [[%code ~]  ;/(p.nex) ~]~
12689            %quod  ::
12690                   ::  smart quotes
12691                   %=    ^$
12692                       gaf
12693                     :-  [%text (tufa ~-~201c. ~)]
12694                     %+  weld  p.nex
12695                     `(list graf)`[%text (tufa ~-~201d. ~)]~
12696                   ==
12697            %link  [[%a [%href q.nex] ~]  ^$(gaf p.nex)]~
12698            %mage  [[%img [%src q.nex] ?~(p.nex ~ [%alt p.nex]~)]  ~]~
12699          ==
12700        --
```

```
12701        ::
12702        ++  hrul                                      ::    empty besides fence
12703        %+  cold   [[%hr ~] ~]~
12704        ;~(plug (star ace) hep hep hep (star hep) (just '\0a'))
12705        ::
12706        ++  tics
12707        ;~(plug tic tic tic (just '\0a'))
12708        ::
12709        ++  fens
12710        |=  col=@u  ~+
12711        =/  ind  (stun [(dec col) (dec col)] ace)
12712        =/  ind-tics  ;~(plug ind tics)
12713        %+  cook  |=(txt=tape `tarp`[[%pre ~] ;/(txt) ~]~)
12714        ::
12715        :: leading outdent is ok since container may
12716        :: have already been parsed and consumed
12717        %+  ifix  [;~(plug (star ace) tics) ind-tics]
12718        %^  stir  ""  |=([a=tape b=tape] "{a}\0a{b}")
12719        ;~  pose
12720          %+  ifix  [ind (just '\0a')]
12721          ;~(less tics (star prn))
12722        ::
12723          (cold "" ;~(plug (star ace) (just '\0a')))
12724        ==
12725        ::
12726        ++  para                                      ::    paragraph
12727        %+  cook
12728          |=(a=tarp ?~(a ~ [[%p ~] a]~))
12729        ;~(pfix (punt whit) down)
12730        ::
12731        ++  expr                                      ::    expression
12732        =>  (sail &)                                  ::    tall-form
12733        %+  ifix  [(star ace) ;~(simu gap (easy))]    ::    look-ahead for gap
12734        (cook drop-top top-level)                     ::    list of tags
12735        ::
12736        ::
12737        ++  whit                                      ::    whitespace
12738        (cold ' ' (plus ;~(pose (just ' ') (just '\0a'))))
12739        ::
12740        ++  head                                      ::    parse heading
12741        %+  cook
12742          |=  [haxes=tape kids=tarp]  ^-  tarp
12743          =/  tag  (crip 'h' <(lent haxes)>)          ::    e.g. ### -> %h3
12744          =/  id  (contents-to-id kids)
12745          [[tag [%id id]~] kids]~
12746        ::
12747        ;~(pfix (star ace) ;~((glue whit) (stun [1 6] hax) down))
12748        ::
12749        ++  contents-to-id                            ::    # text into elem id
12750        |=  a=(list tuna:hoot)  ^-  tape
12751        =;  raw=tape
12752          %+  turn  raw
12753          |=  @tD
12754          ^-  @tD
12755          ?:  ?|  &((gte +< 'a') (lte +< 'z'))
12756                  &((gte +< '0') (lte +< '9'))
12757              ==
12758            +<
```

```
12759          ?:  &((gte +< 'A') (lte +< 'Z'))
12760            (add 32 +<)
12761          '-'
12762      ::
12763      ::  collect all text in header tarp
12764      |-  ^-  tape
12765      ?~  a  ~
12766      %+  weld
12767        ^-  tape
12768        ?-    i.a
12769          [[%$ [%$ *] ~] ~]                        ::  text node contents
12770          (murn v.i.a.g.i.a |=(a=beer:hoot ?^(a ~ (some a))))
12771          [^ *]  $(a c.i.a)                        ::  concatenate children
12772          [@ *]  ~                                 ::  ignore interpolation
12773        ==
12774      $(a t.a)
12775      --
12776    --
12777  ::
12778  ++  scad
12779    %+  knee  *spec  |.  ~+
12780    %-  stew
12781    ^.  stet  ^.  limo
12782    :~
12783      :-  '_'
12784        ;~(pfix cab (stag %bccb wide))
12785      :-  ','
12786        ;~(pfix com (stag %bcmc wide))
12787      :-  '$'
12788        (stag %like (most col rope))
12789      :-  '%'
12790        ;~  pose
12791          ;~  pfix  cen
12792            ;~  pose
12793              (stag %leaf (stag %tas (cold %$ buc)))
12794              (stag %leaf (stag %f (cold & pam)))
12795              (stag %leaf (stag %f (cold | bar)))
12796              (stag %leaf (stag %t qut))
12797              (stag %leaf (sear |=(a=coin ?:(?=(%$ -.a) (some +.a) ~)) nuck:so))
12798            ==
12799          ==
12800        ==
12801      :-  '('
12802        %+  cook  |=(spec +<)
12803        %+  stag  %make
12804        %+  ifix  [pal par]
12805        ;~  plug
12806          wide
12807          ;~(pose ;~(pfix ace (most ace wyde)) (easy ~))
12808        ==
12809      :-  '['
12810        (stag %bccl (ifix [sel ser] (most ace wyde)))
12811      :-  '*'
12812        (cold [%base %noun] tar)
12813      :-  '/'
12814        ;~(pfix fas (stag %loop ;~(pose (cold %$ buc) sym)))
12815      :-  '@'
12816        ;~(pfix pat (stag %base (stag %atom mota)))
```

```
12817          :-  '?'
12818            ;~  pose
12819              %+  stag  %bcwt
12820              ;~(pfix wut (ifix [pal par] (most ace wyde)))
12821            ::
12822              (cold [%base %flag] wut)
12823            ==
12824          :-  '~'
12825            (cold [%base %null] sig)
12826          :-  '!'
12827            (cold [%base %void] ;~(plug zap zap))
12828          :-  '^'
12829            ;~  pose
12830            (stag %like (most col rope))
12831            (cold [%base %cell] ket)
12832            ==
12833          :-  '='
12834            ;~  pfix  tis
12835              %+  sear
12836              |=  [=(unit term) =spec]
12837              %+  bind
12838                ~(autoname ax spec)
12839              |=  =term
12840              =*  name  ?~(unit term (cat 3 u.unit (cat 3 '-' term)))
12841              [%bcts name spec]
12842            ;~  pose
12843              ;~(plug (stag ~ ;~(sfix sym tis)) wyde)
12844              (stag ~ wyde)
12845            ==
12846          ==
12847          :-  ['a' 'z']
12848            ;~  pose
12849            (stag %bcts ;~(plug sym ;~(pfix tis wyde)))
12850            (stag %like (most col rope))
12851            ==
12852        ==
12853    ::
12854  ++  scat
12855    %+  knee  *hoon  |.  ~+
12856    %-  stew
12857    ^.  stet  ^.  limo
12858    :~
12859      :-  ','
12860        ;~  pose
12861          (stag %ktcl ;~(pfix com wyde))
12862          (stag %wing rope)
12863        ==
12864      :-  '!'
12865        ;~  pose
12866          (stag %wtzp ;~(pfix zap wide))
12867          (stag %zpzp (cold ~ ;~(plug zap zap)))
12868        ==
12869      :-  '_'
12870        ;~(pfix cab (stag %ktcl (stag %bccb wide)))
12871      :-  '$'
12872        ;~  pose
12873          ;~  pfix  buc
12874            ;~  pose
```

```
12875            ::   XX: these are all obsolete in hoon 142
12876            ::
12877            (stag %leaf (stag %tas (cold %$ buc)))
12878            (stag %leaf (stag %t qut))
12879            (stag %leaf (sear |=(a=coin ?:(?=(%$ -.a) (some +.a) ~)) nuck:so))
12880          ==
12881        ==
12882      rump
12883    ==
12884  :-  '%'
12885    ;~  pfix  cen
12886      ;~  pose
12887        (stag %clsg (sear |~([a=@ud b=tyke] (posh ~ ~ a b)) porc))
12888        (stag %rock (stag %tas (cold %$ buc)))
12889        (stag %rock (stag %f (cold & pam)))
12890        (stag %rock (stag %f (cold | bar)))
12891        (stag %rock (stag %t qut))
12892        (cook (jock &) nuck:so)
12893        (stag %clsg (sear |=(a=(list) (posh ~ ~ (lent a) ~)) (star cen)))
12894      ==
12895    ==
12896  :-  '&'
12897    ;~  pose
12898      (cook |=(a=wing [%cnts a ~]) rope)
12899      (stag %wtpm ;~(pfix pam (ifix [pal par] (most ace wide))))
12900      ;~(plug (stag %rock (stag %f (cold & pam))) wede)
12901      (stag %sand (stag %f (cold & pam)))
12902    ==
12903  :-  '\''
12904    (stag %sand (stag %t qut))
12905  :-  '('
12906    (stag %cncl (ifix [pal par] (most ace wide)))
12907  :-  '*'
12908    ;~  pose
12909      (stag %kttr ;~(pfix tar wyde))
12910      (cold [%base %noun] tar)
12911    ==
12912  :-  '@'
12913    ;~(pfix pat (stag %base (stag %atom mota)))
12914  :-  '+'
12915    ;~  pose
12916      (stag %dtls ;~(pfix lus (ifix [pal par] wide)))
12917      ::
12918      %+  cook
12919        |=  a=(list (list woof))
12920        :-  %mcfs
12921        [%knit |-(^-((list woof) ?~(a ~ (weld i.a $(a t.a)))))]
12922      (most dog ;~(pfix lus soil))
12923      ::
12924      (cook |=(a=wing [%cnts a ~]) rope)
12925    ==
12926  :-  '-'
12927    ;~  pose
12928      (stag %sand tash:so)
12929      ::
12930      %+  cook
12931        |=  a=(list (list woof))
12932        [%clsg (phax a)]
```

```
12933        (most dog ;~(pfix hep soil))
12934      ::
12935        (cook |=(a=wing [%cnts a ~]) rope)
12936      ==
12937    :-  '.'
12938      ;~  pose
12939        (cook (jock |) ;~(pfix dot perd:so))
12940        (cook |=(a=wing [%cnts a ~]) rope)
12941      ==
12942    :-  ['0' '9']
12943      %+  cook
12944        |=  [a=dime b=(unit hoon)]
12945        ?~(b [%sand a] [[%rock a] u.b])
12946      ;~(plug bisk:so (punt wede))
12947    :-  ':'
12948      ;~  pfix  col
12949        ;~  pose
12950          (stag %mccl (ifix [pal par] (most ace wide)))
12951          ;~(pfix fas (stag %mcfs wide))
12952        ==
12953      ==
12954    :-  '='
12955      ;~  pfix  tis
12956        ;~  pose
12957          (stag %dtts (ifix [pal par] ;~(glam wide wide)))
12958        ::
12959          %+  sear
12960            :: mainly used for +skin formation
12961            ::
12962            |=  =spec
12963            ^-  (unit hoon)
12964            %+  bind  ~(autoname ax spec)
12965            |=(=term `hoon`[%ktts term %kttr spec])
12966          wyde
12967        ==
12968      ==
12969    :-  '?'
12970      ;~  pose
12971        %+  stag  %ktcl
12972        (stag %bcwt ;~(pfix wut (ifix [pal par] (most ace wyde))))
12973      ::
12974        (cold [%base %flag] wut)
12975      ==
12976    :-  '['
12977      rupl
12978    :-  '^'
12979      ;~  pose
12980        (stag %wing rope)
12981        (cold [%base %cell] ket)
12982      ==
12983    :-  '`'
12984      ;~  pfix  tic
12985        ;~  pose
12986          %+  cook
12987          |=([a=@ta b=hoon] [%ktls [%sand a 0] [%ktls [%sand %$ 0] b]])
12988          ;~(pfix pat ;~(plug mota ;~(pfix tic wide)))
12989        ;~  pfix  tar
12990          (stag %kthp (stag [%base %noun] ;~(pfix tic wide)))
```

```
12991                 ==
12992               (stag %kthp ;~(plug wyde ;~(pfix tic wide)))
12993               (stag %ktls ;~(pfix lus ;~(plug wide ;~(pfix tic wide))))
12994               (cook |=(a=hoon [[%rock %n ~] a]) wide)
12995             ==
12996           ==
12997       :-  '"'
12998         %+  cook
12999           |=  a=(list (list woof))
13000           [%knit |-(^-((list woof) ?~(a ~ (weld i.a $(a t.a)))))]
13001         (most dog soil)
13002       :-  ['a' 'z']
13003         rump
13004       :-  '|'
13005         ;~  pose
13006           (cook |=(a=wing [%cnts a ~]) rope)
13007           (stag %wtbr ;~(pfix bar (ifix [pal par] (most ace wide))))
13008           ;~(plug (stag %rock (stag %f (cold | bar))) wede)
13009           (stag %sand (stag %f (cold | bar)))
13010         ==
13011       :-  '~'
13012         ;~  pose
13013           rupl
13014           ::
13015           ;~  pfix  sig
13016             ;~  pose
13017               (stag %clsg (ifix [sel ser] (most ace wide)))
13018               ::
13019               %+  stag  %cnsg
13020               %+  ifix
13021                 [pal par]
13022               ;~(glam rope wide (most ace wide))
13023               ::
13024               (cook (jock |) twid:so)
13025               (stag [%bust %null] wede)
13026               (easy [%bust %null])
13027             ==
13028           ==
13029         ==
13030       :-  '/'
13031         rood
13032       :-  '<'
13033         (ifix [gal gar] (stag %tell (most ace wide)))
13034       :-  '>'
13035         (ifix [gar gal] (stag %yell (most ace wide)))
13036       :-  '#'
13037         ;~(pfix hax reed)
13038     ==
13039  ++  soil
13040    ;~  pose
13041      ;~  less  (jest '"""')
13042        %+  ifix  [doq doq]
13043        %-  star
13044        ;~  pose
13045          ;~(pfix bas ;~(pose bas doq kel bix:ab))
13046          ;~(less doq bas kel prn)
13047          (stag ~ sump)
13048        ==
```

```
13049            ==
13050        ::
13051        %-  iny  %+  ifix
13052            [(jest '"""'\0a') (jest '\0a"""')]
13053        %-  star
13054        ;~  pose
13055          ;~(pfix bas ;~(pose bas kel bix:ab))
13056          ;~(less bas kel prn)
13057          ;~(less (jest '\0a"""') (just `@`10))
13058          (stag ~ sump)
13059        ==
13060      ==
13061  ++  sump  (ifix [kel ker] (stag %cltr (most ace wide)))
13062  ++  norm                                          ::  rune regular form
13063    |=  tol=?
13064    |%
13065    ++  structure
13066    %-  stew
13067    ^.  stet  ^.  limo
13068    :~  :-  '$'
13069          ;~  pfix  buc
13070            %-  stew
13071            ^.  stet  ^.  limo
13072            :~  [':' (rune col %bccl exqs)]
13073                ['%' (rune cen %bccn exqs)]
13074                ['<' (rune gal %bcgl exqb)]
13075                ['>' (rune gar %bcgr exqb)]
13076                ['^' (rune ket %bckt exqb)]
13077                ['~' (rune sig %bcsg exqd)]
13078                ['|' (rune bar %bcbr exqc)]
13079                ['&' (rune pam %bcpm exqc)]
13080                ['@' (rune pat %bcpt exqb)]
13081                ['_' (rune cab %bccb expa)]
13082                ['-' (rune hep %bchp exqb)]
13083                ['=' (rune tis %bcts exqg)]
13084                ['?' (rune wut %bcwt exqs)]
13085                [';' (rune mic %bcmc expa)]
13086                ['+' (rune lus %bcls exqg)]
13087            ==
13088        ==
13089        :-  '%'
13090          ;~  pfix  cen
13091            %-  stew
13092            ^.  stet  ^.  limo
13093            :~  :-  '^'
13094              %+  cook
13095                |=  [%cnkt a=hoon b=spec c=spec d=spec]
13096                [%make a b c d ~]
13097              (rune ket %cnkt exqy)
13098            ::
13099              :-  '+'
13100              %+  cook
13101                |=  [%cnls a=hoon b=spec c=spec]
13102                [%make a b c ~]
13103              (rune lus %cnls exqx)
13104            ::
13105              :-  '-'
13106              %+  cook
```

```
13107              |=  [%cnhp a=hoon b=spec]
13108              [%make a b ~]
13109            (rune hep %cnhp exqd)
13110        ::
13111            :-  ':'
13112          %+  cook
13113              |=  [%cncl a=hoon b=(list spec)]
13114              [%make a b]
13115            (rune col %cncl exqz)
13116        ==
13117      ==
13118    :-  '#'
13119      ;~  pfix  hax  fas
13120        %+  stag  %bccl
13121        %+  cook
13122            |=  [[i=spec t=(list spec)] e=spec]
13123            [i (snoc t e)]
13124        ;~  plug
13125          %+  most  ;~(less ;~(plug fas tar) fas)
13126          %-  stew
13127          ^.  stet  ^.  limo
13128          :~  :-  ['a' 'z']
13129              ;~  pose
13130                ::  /name=@aura
13131                ::
13132                %+  cook
13133                  |=  [=term =aura]
13134                  ^-  spec
13135                  :+  %bccl
13136                    [%leaf %tas aura]
13137                  :_  ~
13138                  :+  %bcts  term
13139                  ?+  aura  [%base %atom aura]
13140                    %f  [%base %flag]
13141                    %n  [%base %null]
13142                  ==
13143                ;~(plug sym ;~(pfix tis pat mota))
13144              ::
13145              ::  /constant
13146              ::
13147              (stag %leaf (stag %tas ;~(pose sym (cold %$ buc))))
13148            ==
13149          ::
13150            ::  /@aura
13151            ::
13152            :-  '@'
13153          %+  cook
13154            |=  =aura
13155            ^-  spec
13156            :+  %bccl
13157              [%leaf %tas aura]
13158            [%base %atom aura]~
13159          ;~(pfix pat mota)
13160          ::
13161            ::  /?
13162            ::
13163            :-  '?'
13164          (cold [%bccl [%leaf %tas %f] [%base %flag] ~] wut)
```

```
13165              ::
13166                ::   /~
13167                ::
13168                :-   '~'
13169                (cold [%bccl [%leaf %tas %n] [%base %null] ~] sig)
13170          ==
13171        ::
13172          ::   open-ended or fixed-length
13173          ::
13174          ;~  pose
13175            (cold [%base %noun] ;~(plug fas tar))
13176            (easy %base %null)
13177          ==
13178        ==
13179      ==
13180    ==
13181  ++  expression
13182    %-  stew
13183    ^.  stet  ^.  limo
13184    :~  :-  '|'
13185          ;~  pfix  bar
13186            %-  stew
13187            ^.  stet  ^.  limo
13188            :~  ['_' (rune cab %brcb exqr)]
13189                ['%' (runo cen %brcn ~ expe)]
13190                ['@' (runo pat %brpt ~ expe)]
13191                [':' (rune col %brcl expb)]
13192                ['.' (rune dot %brdt expa)]
13193                ['-' (rune hep %brhp expa)]
13194                ['^' (rune ket %brkt expr)]
13195                ['~' (rune sig %brsg exqc)]
13196                ['*' (rune tar %brtr exqc)]
13197                ['=' (rune tis %brts exqc)]
13198                ['?' (rune wut %brwt expa)]
13199                ['$' (rune buc %brbc exqe)]
13200            ==
13201          ==
13202        :-  '$'
13203          ;~  pfix  buc
13204            %-  stew
13205            ^.  stet  ^.  limo
13206            :~  ['@' (stag %ktcl (rune pat %bcpt exqb))]
13207                ['_' (stag %ktcl (rune cab %bccb expa))]
13208                [':' (stag %ktcl (rune col %bccl exqs))]
13209                ['%' (stag %ktcl (rune cen %bccn exqs))]
13210                ['<' (stag %ktcl (rune gal %bcgl exqb))]
13211                ['>' (stag %ktcl (rune gar %bcgr exqb))]
13212                ['|' (stag %ktcl (rune bar %bcbr exqc))]
13213                ['&' (stag %ktcl (rune pam %bcpm exqc))]
13214                ['^' (stag %ktcl (rune ket %bckt exqb))]
13215                ['~' (stag %ktcl (rune sig %bcsg exqd))]
13216                ['-' (stag %ktcl (rune hep %bchp exqb))]
13217                ['=' (stag %ktcl (rune tis %bcts exqg))]
13218                ['?' (stag %ktcl (rune wut %bcwt exqs))]
13219                ['+' (stag %ktcl (rune lus %bcls exqg))]
13220                ['.' (rune dot %kttr exqa)]
13221                [',' (rune com %ktcl exqa)]
13222            ==
```

```
13223                ==
13224            :-  '%'
13225              ;~  pfix  cen
13226                %-  stew
13227                ^.  stet  ^.  limo
13228                :~  ['_' (rune cab %cncb exph)]
13229                    ['.' (rune dot %cndt expb)]
13230                    ['^' (rune ket %cnkt expd)]
13231                    ['+' (rune lus %cnls expc)]
13232                    ['-' (rune hep %cnhp expb)]
13233                    [':' (rune col %cncl expi)]
13234                    ['~' (rune sig %cnsg expn)]
13235                    ['*' (rune tar %cntr expm)]
13236                    ['=' (rune tis %cnts exph)]
13237                ==
13238              ==
13239            :-  ':'
13240              ;~  pfix  col
13241                %-  stew
13242                ^.  stet  ^.  limo
13243                :~  ['_' (rune cab %clcb expb)]
13244                    ['^' (rune ket %clkt expd)]
13245                    ['+' (rune lus %clls expc)]
13246                    ['-' (rune hep %clhp expb)]
13247                    ['~' (rune sig %clsg exps)]
13248                    ['*' (rune tar %cltr exps)]
13249                ==
13250              ==
13251            :-  '.'
13252              ;~  pfix  dot
13253                %-  stew
13254                ^.  stet  ^.  limo
13255                :~  ['+' (rune lus %dtls expa)]
13256                    ['*' (rune tar %dttr expb)]
13257                    ['=' (rune tis %dtts expb)]
13258                    ['?' (rune wut %dtwt expa)]
13259                    ['^' (rune ket %dtkt exqn)]
13260                ==
13261              ==
13262            :-  '^'
13263              ;~  pfix  ket
13264                %-  stew
13265                ^.  stet  ^.  limo
13266                :~  ['|' (rune bar %ktbr expa)]
13267                    ['.' (rune dot %ktdt expb)]
13268                    ['-' (rune hep %kthp exqc)]
13269                    ['+' (rune lus %ktls expb)]
13270                    ['&' (rune pam %ktpm expa)]
13271                    ['~' (rune sig %ktsg expa)]
13272                    ['=' (rune tis %ktts expj)]
13273                    ['?' (rune wut %ktwt expa)]
13274                    ['*' (rune tar %kttr exqa)]
13275                    [':' (rune col %ktcl exqa)]
13276                ==
13277              ==
13278            :-  '~'
13279              ;~  pfix  sig
13280                %-  stew
```

```
13281              ^.  stet  ^.  limo
13282         :~  ['|' (rune bar %sgbr expb)]
13283             ['$' (rune buc %sgbc expf)]
13284             ['_' (rune cab %sgcb expb)]
13285             ['%' (rune cen %sgcn hind)]
13286             ['/' (rune fas %sgfs hine)]
13287             ['<' (rune gal %sggl hinb)]
13288             ['>' (rune gar %sggr hinb)]
13289             ['+' (rune lus %sgls hinc)]
13290             ['&' (rune pam %sgpm hinf)]
13291             ['?' (rune wut %sgwt hing)]
13292             ['=' (rune tis %sgts expb)]
13293             ['!' (rune zap %sgzp expb)]
13294           ==
13295         ==
13296     :-  ';'
13297       ;~  pfix  mic
13298         %-  stew
13299         ^.  stet  ^.  limo
13300         :~  [':' (rune col %mccl expi)]
13301             ['/' (rune fas %mcfs expa)]
13302             ['<' (rune gal %mcgl expz)]
13303             ['~' (rune sig %mcsg expi)]
13304             [';' (rune mic %mcmc exqc)]
13305           ==
13306         ==
13307     :-  '='
13308       ;~  pfix  tis
13309         %-  stew
13310         ^.  stet  ^.  limo
13311         :~  ['|' (rune bar %tsbr exqc)]
13312             ['.' (rune dot %tsdt expq)]
13313             ['?' (rune wut %tswt expw)]
13314             ['^' (rune ket %tskt expt)]
13315             [':' (rune col %tscl expp)]
13316             ['/' (rune fas %tsfs expo)]
13317             [';' (rune mic %tsmc expo)]
13318             ['<' (rune gal %tsgl expb)]
13319             ['>' (rune gar %tsgr expb)]
13320             ['-' (rune hep %tshp expb)]
13321             ['*' (rune tar %tstr expg)]
13322             [',' (rune com %tscm expb)]
13323             ['+' (rune lus %tsls expb)]
13324             ['~' (rune sig %tssg expi)]
13325           ==
13326         ==
13327     :-  '?'
13328       ;~  pfix  wut
13329         %-  stew
13330         ^.  stet  ^.  limo
13331         :~  ['|' (rune bar %wtbr exps)]
13332             [':' (rune col %wtcl expc)]
13333             ['.' (rune dot %wtdt expc)]
13334             ['<' (rune gal %wtgl expb)]
13335             ['>' (rune gar %wtgr expb)]
13336             ['-' ;~(pfix hep (toad txhp))]
13337             ['^' ;~(pfix ket (toad tkkt))]
13338             ['=' ;~(pfix tis (toad txts))]
```

```
13339              ['#' ;~(pfix hax (toad txhx))]
13340              ['+' ;~(pfix lus (toad txls))]
13341              ['&' (rune pam %wtpm exps)]
13342              ['@' ;~(pfix pat (toad tkvt))]
13343              ['~' ;~(pfix sig (toad tksg))]
13344              ['!' (rune zap %wtzp expa)]
13345            ==
13346          ==
13347        :-  '!'
13348        ;~  pfix  zap
13349          %-  stew
13350          ^.  stet  ^.  limo
13351          :~  [':' ;~(pfix col (toad expy))]
13352              ['.' ;~(pfix dot (toad |.(loaf(bug |))))]
13353              [',' (rune com %zpcm expb)]
13354              [';' (rune mic %zpmc expb)]
13355              ['>' (rune gar %zpgr expa)]
13356              ['<' (rune gal %zpgl exqc)]
13357              ['@' (rune pat %zppt expx)]
13358              ['=' (rune tis %zpts expa)]
13359              ['?' (rune wut %zpwt hinh)]
13360            ==
13361          ==
13362      ==
13363  ::
13364  ++  boog  !:
13365    %+  knee  [p=*whit q=*term r=*help s=*hoon]
13366    |.(~+((scye ;~(pose bola boba))))
13367  ++  bola                                    ::  ++  arms
13368    %+  knee  [q=*term r=*help s=*hoon]  |.  ~+
13369    %+  cook
13370    |=  [q=term r=whiz s=hoon]
13371    ?:  =(r *whiz)
13372      [q *help s]
13373    [q [[%funk q]~ [r]~] s]
13374    ;~  pfix  (jest '++')
13375      ;~  plug
13376        ;~(pfix gap ;~(pose (cold %$ buc) sym))
13377        apse:docs
13378        ;~(pfix jump loaf)
13379      ==
13380    ==
13381  ::TODO consider special casing $%
13382  ++  boba                                    ::  +$  arms
13383    %+  knee  [q=*term r=*help s=*hoon]  |.  ~+
13384    %+  cook
13385    |=  [q=term r=whiz s=spec]
13386    ?:  =(r *whiz)
13387      [q *help [%ktcl %name q s]]
13388    [q [[%plan q]~ [r]~] [%ktcl %name q s]]
13389    ;~  pfix  (jest '+$')
13390      ;~  plug
13391        ;~(pfix gap sym)
13392        apse:docs
13393        ;~(pfix jump loan)
13394      ==
13395    ==
13396  ::
```

```
13397       ::  parses a or [a b c] or a  b  c  ==
13398    ++  lynx
13399      =/  wid  (ifix [sel ser] (most ace sym))
13400      =/  tal
13401        ;~  sfix
13402         (most gap sym)
13403         ;~(plug gap duz)
13404        ==
13405      =/  one
13406       %-  cook  :_  sym
13407       |=  a=term
13408       `(list term)`~[a]
13409      %-  cook
13410      :_  ;~(pose (runq wid tal) one)
13411      ::  lestify
13412      |=  a=(list term)
13413      ?~(a !! a)
13414    ::
13415    ++  whap  !:                                ::  chapter
13416      %+  cook
13417      |=  a=(list (qual whit term help hoon))
13418      ::  separate $helps into their own list to be passed to +glow
13419      =/  [duds=(list help) nude=(list (pair term hoon))]
13420       %+  roll  a
13421       |=  $:  $=  bog
13422               (qual whit term help hoon)
13423             ::
13424               $=  gob
13425               [duds=(list help) nude=(list (pair term hoon))]
13426           ==
13427       =/  [unt=(list help) tag=(list help)]
13428         %+  skid  ~(tap by bat.p.bog)  |=(=help =(~ cuff.help))
13429       :-  ?:  =(*help r.bog)
13430               (weld tag duds.gob)
13431             [r.bog (weld tag duds.gob)]
13432       |-
13433       ?~  unt  [[q.bog s.bog] nude.gob]
13434       =.  s.bog  [%note help/i.unt s.bog]
13435       $(unt t.unt)
13436      ::
13437      %+  glow  duds
13438      |-  ^-  (map term hoon)
13439      ?~  nude  ~
13440      =+  $(nude t.nude)
13441      %+  ~(put by -)
13442        p.i.nude
13443      ?:  (~(has by -) p.i.nude)
13444        [%eror (weld "duplicate arm: +" (trip p.i.nude))]
13445      q.i.nude
13446      ::
13447    (most mush boog)
13448    ::
13449    ::  +glow: moves batch comments to the correct arm
13450    ++  glow
13451      |=  [duds=(list help) nude=(map term hoon)]
13452      ^-  (map term hoon)
13453      |-
13454      ?~  duds  nude
```

```
13455      ::  if there is no link, its not part of a batch comment
13456    ?~  cuff.i.duds
13457      ::  this shouldn't happen yet until we look for cuffs of length >1
13458      ::  but we need to prove that cuff is nonempty anyways
13459    $(duds t.duds)
13460    ::
13461    ::TODO: look past the first link. this probably requires
13462    ::a major rethink on how batch comments work
13463    =/  nom=(unit term)
13464      ?+    i.cuff.i.duds   ~
13465      ::  we only support ++ and +$ batch comments right now
13466      ::
13467          ?([%funk *] [%plan *])
13468        `p.i.cuff.i.duds
13469      ==
13470    %=  $
13471      duds  t.duds
13472      nude  ?~  nom  nude
13473            ?.  (~(has by nude) u.nom)
13474              ::  ~>  %slog.[0 leaf+"glow: unmatched link"]
13475              nude
13476            (~(jab by nude) u.nom |=(a=hoon [%note help+i.duds a]))
13477      ==
13478    ::
13479    ++  whip                                   ::  chapter declare
13480      %+  cook
13481      |=  [[a=whit b=term c=whiz] d=(map term hoon)]
13482      ^-  [whit (pair term (map term hoon))]
13483      ?.  =(*whit a)
13484        [a b d]
13485      ?:  =(*whiz c)
13486        [*whit b d]
13487      [%*(. *whit bat (malt [[%chat b]~ [c]~]~)) b d]
13488      ;~(plug (seam ;~(pfix (jest '+|') gap cen sym)) whap)
13489    ::
13490    ++  wasp                                   ::  $brcb aliases
13491      ;~  pose
13492        %+  ifix
13493          [;~(plug lus tar muck) muck]
13494        (most muck ;~(gunk sym loll))
13495      ::
13496        (easy ~)
13497      ==
13498    ::
13499    ++  wisp  !:                                ::  core tail
13500      ?.  tol  fail
13501      %+  cook
13502      |=  a=(list [wit=whit wap=(pair term (map term hoon))])
13503      ^-  (map term tome)
13504      =<  p
13505      |-  ^-  (pair (map term tome) (map term hoon))
13506      ?~  a  [~ ~]
13507      =/  mor  $(a t.a)
13508      =.  q.wap.i.a
13509        %-  ~(urn by q.wap.i.a)
13510        |=  b=(pair term hoon)  ^+  +.b
13511        ::  tests for duplicate arms between two chapters
13512        ?.  (~(has by q.mor) p.b)  +.b
```

```
13513          [%eror (weld "duplicate arm: +" (trip p.b))]
13514        :_  (~(uni by q.mor) q.wap.i.a)
13515      %+  ~(put by p.mor)
13516        p.wap.i.a
13517      :-  %-  ~(get by bat.wit.i.a)
13518          ?:  (~(has by bat.wit.i.a) [%chat p.wap.i.a]~)
13519            [%chat p.wap.i.a]~
13520          ~
13521        ?.  (~(has by p.mor) p.wap.i.a)
13522          q.wap.i.a
13523        [[%$ [%eror (weld "duplicate chapter: |" (trip p.wap.i.a))]] ~ ~]
13524      ::
13525      ::TODO: allow cores with unnamed chapter as well as named chapters?
13526      ;~  pose
13527      dun
13528        ;~  sfix
13529          ;~  pose
13530            (most mush whip)
13531            ;~(plug (stag *whit (stag %$ whap)) (easy ~))
13532        ==
13533        gap
13534        dun
13535      ==
13536    ==
13537  ::
13538  ::TODO: check parser performance
13539  ++  toad                                    ::  untrap parser expr
13540    |*  har=_expa
13541    =+  dur=(ifix [pal par] $:har(tol |))
13542    ?.  tol
13543      dur
13544    ;~(pose ;~(pfix jump $:har(tol &)) ;~(pfix gap $:har(tol &)) dur)
13545  ::
13546  ++  rune                                    ::  build rune
13547    |*  [dif=rule tuq=* har=_expa]
13548    ;~(pfix dif (stag tuq (toad har)))
13549  ::
13550  ++  runo                                    ::  rune plus
13551    |*  [dif=rule hil=* tuq=* har=_expa]
13552    ;~(pfix dif (stag hil (stag tuq (toad har))))
13553  ::
13554  ++  runq                                    ::  wide or tall if tol
13555    |*  [wid=rule tal=rule]                   ::  else wide
13556    ?.  tol
13557      wid
13558    ;~(pose wid tal)
13559  ::
13560  ++  butt  |*  zor=rule                       ::  closing == if tall
13561            ?:(tol ;~(sfix zor ;~(plug gap duz)) zor)
13562  ++  ulva  |*  zor=rule                       ::  closing -- and tall
13563            ?.(tol fail ;~(sfix zor ;~(plug gap dun)))
13564  ++  glop  ~+((glue mash))                    ::  separated by space
13565  ++  gunk  ~+((glue muck))                    ::  separated list
13566  ++  goop  ~+((glue mush))                    ::  separator list & docs
13567  ++  hank  (most mush loaf)                   ::  gapped hoons
13568  ++  hunk  (most mush loan)                   ::  gapped specs
13569  ++  jump  ;~(pose leap:docs gap)             ::  gap before docs
13570  ++  loaf  ?:(tol tall wide)                  ::  hoon
```

```
13571  ++  loll  ?:(tol tall(doc |) wide(doc |))          ::  hoon without docs
13572  ++  loan  ?:(tol till wyde)                         ::  spec
13573  ++  lore  (sear |=(=hoon ~(flay ap hoon)) loaf)     ::  skin
13574  ++  lomp  ;~(plug sym (punt ;~(pfix tis wyde)))     ::  typeable name
13575  ++  mash  ?:(tol gap ;~(plug com ace))              ::  list separator
13576  ++  muss  ?:(tol jump ;~(plug com ace))             ::  list w/ doccords
13577  ++  muck  ?:(tol gap ace)                           ::  general separator
13578  ++  mush  ?:(tol jump ace)                          ::  separator w/ docs
13579  ++  teak  %+  knee  *tiki  |.  ~+                   ::  wing or hoon
13580        =+  ^=  gub
13581            |=  [a=term b=$%([%& p=wing] [%| p=hoon])]
13582            ^-  tiki
13583        ?-(-.b %& [%& [~ a] p.b], %| [%| [~ a] p.b])
13584        =+  ^=  wyp
13585            ;~  pose
13586              %+  cook  gub
13587              ;~  plug
13588                sym
13589                ;~(pfix tis ;~(pose (stag %& rope) (stag %| wide)))
13590              ==
13591            ::
13592              (stag %& (stag ~ rope))
13593              (stag %| (stag ~ wide))
13594            ==
13595        ?.  tol  wyp
13596        ;~  pose
13597          wyp
13598        ::
13599          ;~  pfix
13600          ;~(plug ket tis gap)
13601          %+  cook  gub
13602          ;~  plug
13603            sym
13604            ;~(pfix gap ;~(pose (stag %& rope) (stag %| tall)))
13605          ==
13606        ==
13607        ::
13608          (stag %| (stag ~ tall))
13609        ==
13610  ++  rack  (most muss ;~(goop loaf loaf))            ::  list [hoon hoon]
13611  ++  ruck  (most muss ;~(goop loan loaf))            ::  list [spec hoon]
13612  ++  rick  (most mash ;~(goop rope loaf))            ::  list [wing hoon]
13613  ::  hoon contents
13614  ::
13615  ++  expa  |.(loaf)                                  ::  one hoon
13616  ++  expb  |.(;~(goop loaf loaf))                    ::  two hoons
13617  ++  expc  |.(;~(goop loaf loaf loaf))               ::  three hoons
13618  ++  expd  |.(;~(goop loaf loaf loaf loaf))          ::  four hoons
13619  ++  expe  |.(wisp)                                  ::  core tail
13620  ++  expf  |.(;~(goop ;~(pfix cen sym) loaf))        ::  %term and hoon
13621  ++  expg  |.(;~(gunk lomp loll loaf))               ::  term/spec, two hoons
13622  ++  exph  |.((butt ;~(gunk rope rick)))             ::  wing, [wing hoon]s
13623  ++  expi  |.((butt ;~(goop loaf hank)))             ::  one or more hoons
13624  ++  expj  |.(;~(goop lore loaf))                    ::  skin and hoon
13625  ::  ++  expk  |.(;~(gunk loaf ;~(plug loaf (easy ~))))::  list of two hoons
13626  ::  ++  expl  |.(;~(gunk sym loaf loaf))            ::  term, two hoons
13627  ++  expm  |.((butt ;~(gunk rope loaf rick)))        ::  several [spec hoon]s
13628  ++  expn  |.  ;~  gunk  rope  loaf                  ::  wing, hoon,
```

```
13629                      ;~(plug loaf (easy ~))                    ::  list of one hoon
13630                 ==                                             ::
13631      ++  expo  |.(;~(goop wise loaf loaf))                    ::  =;
13632      ++  expp  |.(;~(goop (butt rick) loaf))                  ::  [wing hoon]s, hoon
13633      ++  expq  |.(;~(goop rope loaf loaf))                    ::  wing and two hoons
13634      ++  expr  |.(;~(goop loaf wisp))                         ::  hoon and core tail
13635      ++  exps  |.((butt hank))                                ::  closed gapped hoons
13636      ++  expt  |.(;~(gunk wise rope loaf loaf))               ::  =^
13637      ++  expu  |.(;~(gunk rope loaf (butt hank)))             ::  wing, hoon, hoons
13638   :: ++  expv  |.((butt rick))                                ::  just changes
13639      ++  expw  |.(;~(goop rope loaf loaf loaf))               ::  wing and three hoons
13640      ++  expx  |.(;~(goop ropa loaf loaf))                    ::  wings and two hoons
13641      ++  expy  |.(loaf(bug &))                                ::  hoon with tracing
13642      ++  expz  |.(;~(goop loan loaf loaf loaf))               ::  spec and three hoons
13643      ::  spec contents
13644      ::
13645      ++  exqa  |.(loan)                                       ::  one spec
13646      ++  exqb  |.(;~(goop loan loan))                         ::  two specs
13647      ++  exqc  |.(;~(goop loan loaf))                         ::  spec then hoon
13648      ++  exqd  |.(;~(goop loaf loan))                         ::  hoon then spec
13649      ++  exqe  |.(;~(goop lynx loan))                         ::  list of names then spec
13650      ++  exqs  |.((butt hunk))                                ::  closed gapped specs
13651      ++  exqg  |.(;~(goop sym loan))                          ::  term and spec
13652   ::++  exqk  |.(;~(goop loaf ;~(plug loan (easy ~))))::  hoon with one spec
13653      ++  exqn  |.(;~(gunk loan (stag %cltr (butt hank))))::  autoconsed hoons
13654      ++  exqr  |.(;~(gunk loan ;~(plug wasp wisp)))          ::  spec/aliases?/tail
13655   ::++  exqw  |.(;~(goop loaf loan))                         ::  hoon and spec
13656      ++  exqx  |.(;~(goop loaf loan loan))                   ::  hoon, two specs
13657      ++  exqy  |.(;~(goop loaf loan loan loan))              ::  hoon, three specs
13658      ++  exqz  |.(;~(goop loaf (butt hunk)))                 ::  hoon, n specs
13659      ::
13660      ::    tiki expansion for %wt runes
13661      ::
13662      ++  txhp  |.  %+  cook  |=  [a=tiki b=(list (pair spec hoon))]
13663                        (~(wthp ah a) b)
13664                    (butt ;~(gunk teak ruck))
13665      ++  tkkt  |.  %+  cook  |=  [a=tiki b=hoon c=hoon]
13666                        (~(wtkt ah a) b c)
13667                    ;~(gunk teak loaf loaf)
13668      ++  txls  |.  %+  cook  |=  [a=tiki b=hoon c=(list (pair spec hoon))]
13669                        (~(wtls ah a) b c)
13670                    (butt ;~(gunk teak loaf ruck))
13671      ++  tkvt  |.  %+  cook  |=  [a=tiki b=hoon c=hoon]
13672                        (~(wtpt ah a) b c)
13673                    ;~(gunk teak loaf loaf)
13674      ++  tksg  |.  %+  cook  |=  [a=tiki b=hoon c=hoon]
13675                        (~(wtsg ah a) b c)
13676                    ;~(gunk teak loaf loaf)
13677      ++  txts  |.  %+  cook  |=  [a=spec b=tiki]
13678                        (~(wtts ah b) a)
13679                    ;~(gunk loan teak)
13680      ++  txhx  |.  %+  cook  |=  [a=skin b=tiki]
13681                        (~(wthx ah b) a)
13682                    ;~(gunk lore teak)
13683      ::
13684      ::  hint syntax
13685      ::
13686      ++  hinb  |.(;~(goop bont loaf))                         ::  hint and hoon
```

```
13687    ++  hinc  |.                                      ::  optional =en, hoon
13688          ;~(pose ;~(goop bony loaf) (stag ~ loaf)) ::
13689    ++  hind  |.(;~(gunk bonk loaf ;~(goop bonz loaf)))  ::  jet hoon "bon"s hoon
13690    ++  hine  |.(;~(goop bonk loaf))                 ::  jet-hint and hoon
13691    ++  hinf  |.                                      ::  0-3 >s, two hoons
13692      ;~  pose
13693      ;~(goop (cook lent (stun [1 3] gar)) loaf loaf)
13694      (stag 0 ;~(goop loaf loaf))
13695      ==
13696    ++  hing  |.                                      ::  0-3 >s, three hoons
13697      ;~  pose
13698      ;~(goop (cook lent (stun [1 3] gar)) loaf loaf loaf)
13699      (stag 0 ;~(goop loaf loaf loaf))
13700      ==
13701    ++  bonk                                          ::  jet signature
13702      ;~  pfix  cen
13703        ;~  pose
13704          ;~(plug sym ;~(pfix col ;~(plug sym ;~(pfix dot ;~(pfix dot dem)))))
13705          ;~(plug sym ;~(pfix col ;~(plug sym ;~(pfix dot dem))))
13706          ;~(plug sym ;~(pfix dot dem))
13707          sym
13708        ==
13709      ==
13710    ++  hinh  |.                                      ::  1/2 numbers, hoon
13711      ;~  goop
13712        ;~  pose
13713          dem
13714          (ifix [sel ser] ;~(plug dem ;~(pfix ace dem)))
13715        ==
13716        loaf
13717      ==
13718    ++  bont  ;~  (bend)                              ::  term, optional hoon
13719            ;~(pfix cen sym)
13720            ;~(pfix dot ;~(pose wide ;~(pfix muck loaf)))
13721      ==
13722    ++  bony  (cook |=(a=(list) (lent a)) (plus tis))  ::  base 1 =en count
13723    ++  bonz                                          ::  term-labelled hoons
13724      ;~  pose
13725      (cold ~ sig)
13726      %+  ifix
13727        ?:(tol [;~(plug duz gap) ;~(plug gap duz)] [pal par])
13728      (more mash ;~(gunk ;~(pfix cen sym) loaf))
13729      ==
13730    --
13731    ::
13732    ++  lang                                          ::  lung sample
13733    $:  ros=hoon
13734        $=  vil
13735        $%  [%tis p=hoon]
13736            [%col p=hoon]
13737            [%ket p=hoon]
13738            [%lit p=(list (pair wing hoon))]
13739        ==
13740    ==
13741    ::
13742    ++  lung
13743    ~+
13744    %-  bend
```

```
13745      |:  $:lang
13746      ^-  (unit hoon)
13747      ?-    -.vil
13748      %col  ?:(=([%base %flag] ros) ~ [~ %tsgl ros p.vil])
13749      %lit  (bind ~(reek ap ros) |=(hyp=wing [%cnts hyp p.vil]))
13750      %ket  [~ ros p.vil]
13751      %tis  =+  rud=~(flay ap ros)
13752            ?~(rud ~ `[%ktts u.rud p.vil])
13753      ==
13754    ::
13755    ++  long
13756      %+  knee  *hoon  |.  ~+
13757      ;~  lung
13758        scat
13759        ;~  pose
13760          ;~(plug (cold %tis tis) wide)
13761          ;~(plug (cold %col col) wide)
13762          ;~(plug (cold %ket ket) wide)
13763          ;~  plug
13764            (easy %lit)
13765            (ifix [pal par] lobo)
13766          ==
13767        ==
13768      ==
13769    ::
13770    ++  lobo  (most ;~(plug com ace) ;~(glam rope wide))
13771    ++  loon  (most ;~(plug com ace) ;~(glam wide wide))
13772    ++  lute                                         ::  tall [] noun
13773      ~+
13774      %+  cook  |=(hoon +<)
13775      %+  stag  %cltr
13776      %+  ifix
13777        [;~(plug sel gap) ;~(plug gap ser)]
13778      (most gap tall)
13779    ::
13780    ++  ropa  (most col rope)
13781    ++  rope                                         ::  wing form
13782      %+  knee  *wing
13783      |.  ~+
13784      %+  (slug |=([a=limb b=wing] [a b]))
13785        dot
13786      ;~  pose
13787        (cold [%| 0 ~] com)
13788        %+  cook
13789          |=([a=(list) b=term] ?~(a b [%| (lent a) `b]))
13790          ;~(plug (star ket) ;~(pose sym (cold %$ buc)))
13791        ::
13792        %+  cook
13793          |=(a=axis [%& a])
13794        ;~  pose
13795          ;~(pfix lus dim:ag)
13796          ;~(pfix pam (cook |=(a=@ ?:(=(0 a) 0 (mul 2 +($(a (dec a)))))) dim:ag))
13797          ;~(pfix bar (cook |=(a=@ ?:(=(0 a) 1 +((mul 2 $(a (dec a)))))) dim:ag))
13798          ven
13799          (cold 1 dot)
13800        ==
13801      ==
13802    ::
```

```
13803  ++  wise
13804    ;~  pose
13805      ;~  pfix  tis
13806        %+  sear
13807          |=  =spec
13808          ^-  (unit skin)
13809          %+  bind  ~(autoname ax spec)
13810          |=  =term
13811          [%name term %spec spec %base %noun]
13812        wyde
13813      ==
13814    ::
13815      %+  cook
13816        |=  [=term =(unit spec)]
13817        ^-  skin
13818        ?~  unit
13819          term
13820        [%name term %spec u.unit %base %noun]
13821      ;~  plug  sym
13822        (punt ;~(pfix ;~(pose fas tis) wyde))
13823      ==
13824    ::
13825      %+  cook
13826        |=  =spec
13827        ^-  skin
13828        [%spec spec %base %noun]
13829      wyde
13830    ==
13831  ::
13832  ++  tall                                   ::  full tall form
13833    %+  knee  *hoon
13834    |.(~+((wart (clad ;~(pose expression:(norm &) long lute apex:(sail &))))))
13835  ++  till                                   ::  mold tall form
13836    %+  knee  *spec
13837    |.(~+((wert (coat ;~(pose structure:(norm &) scad)))))
13838  ++  wede                                   ::  wide bulb
13839    ::  XX: lus deprecated
13840    ::
13841    ;~(pfix ;~(pose lus fas) wide)
13842  ++  wide                                   ::  full wide form
13843    %+  knee  *hoon
13844    |.(~+((wart ;~(pose expression:(norm |) long apex:(sail |)))))
13845  ++  wyde                                   ::  mold wide form
13846    %+  knee  *spec
13847    |.(~+((wert ;~(pose structure:(norm |) scad))))
13848  ++  wart
13849    |*  zor=rule
13850    %+  here
13851      |=  [a=pint b=hoon]
13852      ?:(bug [%dbug [wer a] b] b)
13853    zor
13854  ++  wert
13855    |*  zor=rule
13856    %+  here
13857      |=  [a=pint b=spec]
13858      ?:(bug [%dbug [wer a] b] b)
13859    zor
13860  --
```

```
13861  ::
13862  ++  vest
13863    ~/  %vest
13864    |=  tub=nail
13865    ^-  (like hoon)
13866    %.  tub
13867    %-  full
13868    (ifix [gay gay] tall:vast)
13869  ::
13870  ++  vice
13871    |=  txt=@ta
13872    ^-  hoon
13873    (rash txt wide:vast)
13874  ::
13875  ++  make                                    ::  compile cord to nock
13876    |=  txt=@
13877    q:(~(mint ut %noun) %noun (ream txt))
13878  ::
13879  ++  rain                                    ::  parse with % path
13880    |=  [bon=path txt=@]
13881    ^-  hoon
13882    =+  vaz=vast
13883    ~|  bon
13884    (scan (trip txt) (full (ifix [gay gay] tall:vaz(wer bon))))
13885  ::
13886  ++  ream                                    ::  parse cord to hoon
13887    |=  txt=@
13888    ^-  hoon
13889    (rash txt vest)
13890  ::
13891  ++  reck                                    ::  parse hoon file
13892    |=  bon=path
13893    (rain bon .^(@t %cx (weld bon `path`[%hoon ~])))
13894  ::
13895  ++  ride                                    ::  end-to-end compiler
13896    |=  [typ=type txt=@]
13897    ^-  (pair type nock)
13898    ~>  %slog.[0 leaf/"ride: parsing"]
13899    =/  gen  (ream txt)
13900    ~>  %slog.[0 leaf/"ride: compiling"]
13901    ~<  %slog.[0 leaf/"ride: compiled"]
13902    (~(mint ut typ) %noun gen)
13903  ::
13904  ::    5e: molds and mold builders
13905  +|  %molds-and-mold-builders
13906  ::
13907  +$  mane  $@(@tas [@tas @tas])              ::  XML name+space
13908  +$  manx  $~([[%$ ~] ~] [g=marx c=marl])    ::  dynamic XML node
13909  +$  marl  (list manx)                       ::  XML node list
13910  +$  mars  [t=[n=%$ a=[i=[n=%$ v=tape] t=~]] c=~]  ::  XML cdata
13911  +$  mart  (list [n=mane v=tape])            ::  XML attributes
13912  +$  marx  $~([%$ ~] [n=mane a=mart])        ::  dynamic XML tag
13913  +$  mite  (list @ta)                        ::  mime type
13914  +$  pass  @                                 ::  public key
13915  +$  ring  @                                 ::  private key
13916  +$  ship  @p                                ::  network identity
13917  +$  shop  (each ship (list @ta))            ::  urbit/dns identity
13918  +$  spur  path                              ::  ship desk case spur
```

```
13919  +$  time  @da                                        ::  galactic time
13920  ::
13921  ::      5f: profiling support (XX move)
13922  +|  %profiling-support
13923  ::
13924  ++  pi-heck
13925    |=  [nam=@tas day=doss]
13926    ^-  doss
13927    =+  lam=(~(get by hit.day) nam)
13928    day(hit (~(put by hit.day) nam ?~(lam 1 +(u.lam))))
13929  ::
13930  ++  pi-noon                                          ::  sample trace
13931    |=  [mot=term paz=(list path) day=doss]
13932    =|  lax=(unit path)
13933    |-  ^-  doss
13934    ?~  paz  day(mon (pi-mope mot mon.day))
13935    %=    $
13936      paz  t.paz
13937      lax  `i.paz
13938      cut.day
13939      %+  ~(put by cut.day)  i.paz
13940      ^-  hump
13941      =+  nax=`(unit path)`?~(t.paz ~ `i.t.paz)
13942      =+  hup=`hump`=+(hup=(~(get by cut.day) i.paz) ?^(hup u.hup [*moan ~ ~]))
13943      :+  (pi-mope mot mon.hup)
13944        ?~  lax  out.hup
13945        =+  hag=(~(get by out.hup) u.lax)
13946        (~(put by out.hup) u.lax ?~(hag 1 +(u.hag)))
13947      ?~  nax  inn.hup
13948      =+  hag=(~(get by inn.hup) u.nax)
13949      (~(put by inn.hup) u.nax ?~(hag 1 +(u.hag)))
13950    ==
13951  ++  pi-mope                                           ::  add sample
13952    |=  [mot=term mon=moan]
13953    ?+  mot  mon
13954      %fun  mon(fun +(fun.mon))
13955      %noc  mon(noc +(noc.mon))
13956      %glu  mon(glu +(glu.mon))
13957      %mal  mon(mal +(mal.mon))
13958      %far  mon(far +(far.mon))
13959      %coy  mon(coy +(coy.mon))
13960      %euq  mon(euq +(euq.mon))
13961    ==
13962  ++  pi-moth                                           ::  count sample
13963    |=  mon=moan  ^-  @ud
13964    :(add fun.mon noc.mon glu.mon mal.mon far.mon coy.mon euq.mon)
13965  ::
13966  ++  pi-mumm                                           ::  print sample
13967    |=  mon=moan  ^-  tape
13968    =+  tot=(pi-moth mon)
13969    ;:  welp
13970      ^-  tape
13971      ?:  =(0 noc.mon)  ~
13972      (welp (scow %ud (div (mul 100 noc.mon) tot)) "n ")
13973    ::
13974      ^-  tape
13975      ?:  =(0 fun.mon)  ~
13976      (welp (scow %ud (div (mul 100 fun.mon) tot)) "c ")
```

```
13977      ::
13978        ^-  tape
13979        ?:  =(0 glu.mon)  ~
13980        (welp (scow %ud (div (mul 100 glu.mon) tot)) "g ")
13981      ::
13982        ^-  tape
13983        ?:  =(0 mal.mon)  ~
13984        (welp (scow %ud (div (mul 100 mal.mon) tot)) "m ")
13985      ::
13986        ^-  tape
13987        ?:  =(0 far.mon)  ~
13988        (welp (scow %ud (div (mul 100 far.mon) tot)) "f ")
13989      ::
13990        ^-  tape
13991        ?:  =(0 coy.mon)  ~
13992        (welp (scow %ud (div (mul 100 coy.mon) tot)) "y ")
13993      ::
13994        ^-  tape
13995        ?:  =(0 euq.mon)  ~
13996        (welp (scow %ud (div (mul 100 euq.mon) tot)) "e ")
13997      ==
13998  ::
13999  ++  pi-tell                                       ::  produce dump
14000    |=  day=doss
14001    ^-  (list tape)
14002    ?:  =(day *doss)  ~
14003    =+  tot=(pi-moth mon.day)
14004    ;:  welp
14005      [(welp "events: " (pi-mumm mon.day)) ~]
14006      ::
14007      %+  turn
14008        %+  sort  ~(tap by hit.day)
14009        |=  [a=[* @] b=[* @]]
14010        (lth +.a +.b)
14011      |=  [nam=term num=@ud]
14012      :(welp (trip nam) ": " (scow %ud num))
14013      ["" ~]
14014      ::
14015      %-  zing
14016      ^-  (list (list tape))
14017      %+  turn
14018        %+  sort  ~(tap by cut.day)
14019        |=  [one=(pair path hump) two=(pair path hump)]
14020        (gth (pi-moth mon.q.one) (pi-moth mon.q.two))
14021      |=  [pax=path hup=hump]
14022      =+  ott=(pi-moth mon.hup)
14023      ;:  welp
14024        [(welp "label: " (spud pax)) ~]
14025        [(welp "price: " (scow %ud (div (mul 100 ott) tot))) ~]
14026        [(welp "shape: " (pi-mumm mon.hup)) ~]
14027        ::
14028        ?:  =(~ out.hup)  ~
14029        :-  "into:"
14030        %+  turn
14031          %+  sort  ~(tap by out.hup)
14032          |=([[* a=@ud] [* b=@ud]] (gth a b))
14033        |=  [pax=path num=@ud]
14034        ^-  tape
```

```
14035        :(welp "  " (spud pax) ": " (scow %ud num))
14036      ::
14037        ?:  =(~ inn.hup)   ~
14038        :-  "from:"
14039        %+  turn
14040          %+  sort  ~(tap by inn.hup)
14041          |=([[* a=@ud] [* b=@ud]] (gth a b))
14042        |=  [pax=path num=@ud]
14043        ^-  tape
14044        :(welp "  " (spud pax) ": " (scow %ud num))
14045      ::
14046        ["" ~]
14047        ~
14048      ==
14049    ==
14050  --
```

Lull 323K

```
1  ::  /sys/lull
2  ::  %lull: arvo structures
3  !:
4  =>  ..part
5  ~%  %lull  ..part  ~
6  |%
7  ++  lull  %323
8  ::                                                          ::  ::
9  ::::                                                        ::  ::  (1) models
10  ::                                                         ::  ::
11  ::  #  %misc
12  ::
13  ::  miscellaneous systems types
14  ::+|
15  ::  +capped-queue: a +qeu with a maximum number of entries
16  ::
17  ++  capped-queue
18    |$  [item-type]
19    $:  queue=(qeu item-type)
20        size=@ud
21        max-size=_64
22    ==
23  ::  +clock: polymorphic cache type for use with the clock replacement algorithm
24  ::
25  ::      The +by-clock core wraps interface arms for manipulating a mapping from
26  ::      :key-type to :val-type. Detailed docs for this type can be found there.
27  ::
28  ++  clock
29    |$  ::  key-type: mold of keys
30        ::  val-type: mold of values
31        ::
32        [key-type val-type]
33    $:  lookup=(map key-type [val=val-type fresh=@ud])
34        queue=(qeu key-type)
35        size=@ud
36        max-size=_2.048
37        depth=_1
38    ==
39  ::  +mop: constructs and validates ordered ordered map based on key,
40  ::  val, and comparator gate
41  ::
42  ++  mop
43    |*  [key=mold value=mold]
44    |=  ord=$-([key key] ?)
45    |=  a=*
46    =/  b  ;;((tree [key=key val=value]) a)
47    ?>  (apt:((on key value) ord) b)
48    b
49  ::
50  ::
51  ++  ordered-map  on
52  ::  +on: treap with user-specified horizontal order, ordered-map
53  ::
54  ::  WARNING: ordered-map will not work properly if two keys can be
55  ::  unequal under noun equality but equal via the compare gate
```

```
56  ::
57  ++  on
58    ~%  %on  ..part  ~
59    |*  [key=mold val=mold]
60    =>  |%
61        +$  item  [key=key val=val]
62        --
63    ::  +compare: item comparator for horizontal order
64    ::
65    ~%  %comp  +>+  ~
66    |=  compare=$-([key key] ?)
67    ~%  %core    +  ~
68    |%
69    ::  +all: apply logical AND boolean test on all values
70    ::
71    ++  all
72      ~/  %all
73      |=  [a=(tree item) b=$-(item ?)]
74      ^-  ?
75      |-
76      ?~  a
77        &
78      ?&((b n.a) $(a l.a) $(a r.a))
79    ::  +any: apply logical OR boolean test on all values
80    ::
81    ++  any
82      ~/  %any
83      |=  [a=(tree item) b=$-(item ?)]
84      |-  ^-  ?
85      ?~  a
86        |
87      ?|((b n.a) $(a l.a) $(a r.a))
88    ::  +apt: verify horizontal and vertical orderings
89    ::
90    ++  apt
91      ~/  %apt
92      |=  a=(tree item)
93      =|  [l=(unit key) r=(unit key)]
94      |-  ^-  ?
95      ::  empty tree is valid
96      ::
97      ?~  a  %.y
98      ::  nonempty trees must maintain several criteria
99      ::
100     ?&  ::  if .n.a is left of .u.l, assert horizontal comparator
101         ::
102         ?~(l %.y (compare key.n.a u.l))
103         ::  if .n.a is right of .u.r, assert horizontal comparator
104         ::
105         ?~(r %.y (compare u.r key.n.a))
106         ::  if .a is not leftmost element, assert vertical order between
107         ::  .l.a and .n.a and recurse to the left with .n.a as right
108         ::  neighbor
109         ::
110         ?~(l.a %.y &((mor key.n.a key.n.l.a) $(a l.a, l `key.n.a)))
111         ::  if .a is not rightmost element, assert vertical order
112         ::  between .r.a and .n.a and recurse to the right with .n.a as
113         ::  left neighbor
```

```
114        ::
115        ?~(r.a %.y &((mor key.n.a key.n.r.a) $(a r.a, r `key.n.a)))
116      ==
117    ::  +bap: convert to list, right to left
118    ::
119    ++  bap
120      ~/  %bap
121      |=  a=(tree item)
122      ^-  (list item)
123      =|  b=(list item)
124      |-  ^+  b
125      ?~  a  b
126      $(a r.a, b [n.a $(a l.a)])
127    ::  +del: delete .key from .a if it exists, producing value iff deleted
128    ::
129    ++  del
130      ~/  %del
131      |=  [a=(tree item) =key]
132      ^-  [(unit val) (tree item)]
133      ?~  a  [~ ~]
134      ::  we found .key at the root; delete and rebalance
135      ::
136      ?:  =(key key.n.a)
137        [`val.n.a (nip a)]
138      ::  recurse left or right to find .key
139      ::
140      ?:  (compare key key.n.a)
141        =+  [found lef]=$(a l.a)
142        [found a(l lef)]
143      =+  [found rig]=$(a r.a)
144      [found a(r rig)]
145    ::  +dip: stateful partial inorder traversal
146    ::
147    ::    Mutates .state on each run of .f.  Starts at .start key, or if
148    ::    .start is ~, starts at the head.  Stops when .f produces .stop=%.y.
149    ::    Traverses from left to right keys.
150    ::    Each run of .f can replace an item's value or delete the item.
151    ::
152    ++  dip
153      ~/  %dip
154      |*  state=mold
155      |=  $:  a=(tree item)
156              =state
157              f=$-([state item] [(unit val) ? state])
158          ==
159      ^+  [state a]
160      ::  acc: accumulator
161      ::
162      ::    .stop: set to %.y by .f when done traversing
163      ::    .state: threaded through each run of .f and produced by +abet
164      ::
165      =/  acc  [stop=`?`%.n state=state]
166      =<  abet  =<  main
167      |%
168      ++  this  .
169      ++  abet  [state.acc a]
170      ::  +main: main recursive loop; performs a partial inorder traversal
171      ::
```

```
172    ++  main
173     ^+  this
174     ::  stop if empty or we've been told to stop
175     ::
176     ?:  =(~ a)  this
177     ?:  stop.acc  this
178     ::  inorder traversal: left -> node -> right, until .f sets .stop
179     ::
180     =.  this  left
181     ?:  stop.acc  this
182     =^  del  this  node
183     =?  this  !stop.acc  right
184     =?  a  del  (nip a)
185     this
186   ::  +node: run .f on .n.a, updating .a, .state, and .stop
187   ::
188    ++  node
189     ^+  [del=*? this]
190     ::  run .f on node, updating .stop.acc and .state.acc
191     ::
192     ?>  ?=(^ a)
193     =^  res  acc  (f state.acc n.a)
194     ?~  res
195       [del=& this]
196     [del=| this(val.n.a u.res)]
197   ::  +left: recurse on left subtree, copying mutant back into .l.a
198   ::
199    ++  left
200     ^+  this
201     ?~  a  this
202     =/  lef  main(a l.a)
203     lef(a a(l a.lef))
204   ::  +right: recurse on right subtree, copying mutant back into .r.a
205   ::
206    ++  right
207     ^+  this
208     ?~  a  this
209     =/  rig  main(a r.a)
210     rig(a a(r a.rig))
211     --
212   ::  +gas: put a list of items
213   ::
214    ++  gas
215     ~/  %gas
216     |=  [a=(tree item) b=(list item)]
217     ^-  (tree item)
218     ?~  b  a
219     $(b t.b, a (put a i.b))
220   ::  +get: get val at key or return ~
221   ::
222    ++  get
223     ~/  %get
224     |=  [a=(tree item) b=key]
225     ^-  (unit val)
226     ?~  a  ~
227     ?:  =(b key.n.a)
228       `val.n.a
229     ?:  (compare b key.n.a)
```

```
230        $(a l.a)
231      $(a r.a)
232    ::  +got: need value at key
233    ::
234    ++  got
235    |=  [a=(tree item) b=key]
236    ^-  val
237    (need (get a b))
238    ::  +has: check for key existence
239    ::
240    ++  has
241    ~/  %has
242    |=  [a=(tree item) b=key]
243    ^-  ?
244    !=(~ (get a b))
245    ::  +lot: take a subset range excluding start and/or end and all elements
246    ::  outside the range
247    ::
248    ++  lot
249    ~/  %lot
250    |=  $:  tre=(tree item)
251            start=(unit key)
252            end=(unit key)
253        ==
254    ^-  (tree item)
255    |^
256    ?:  ?&(?=(~ start) ?=(~ end))
257      tre
258    ?~  start
259    (del-span tre %end end)
260    ?~  end
261    (del-span tre %start start)
262    ?>  (compare u.start u.end)
263    =.  tre  (del-span tre %start start)
264    (del-span tre %end end)
265    ::
266    ++  del-span
267    |=  [a=(tree item) b=?(%start %end) c=(unit key)]
268    ^-  (tree item)
269    ?~  a  a
270    ?~  c  a
271    ?-  b
272      %start
273      ::  found key
274      ?:  =(key.n.a u.c)
275      (nip a(l ~))
276      ::  traverse to find key
277      ?:  (compare key.n.a u.c)
278        ::  found key to the left of start
279        $(a (nip a(l ~)))
280      ::  found key to the right of start
281      a(l $(a l.a))
282    ::
283      %end
284      ::  found key
285      ?:  =(u.c key.n.a)
286      (nip a(r ~))
287      ::  traverse to find key
```

```
288        ?:  (compare key.n.a u.c)
289          :: found key to the left of end
290          a(r $(a r.a))
291          :: found key to the right of end
292          $(a (nip a(r ~)))
293        ==
294      --
295  ::  +nip: remove root; for internal use
296  ::
297  ++  nip
298    ~/  %nip
299    |=  a=(tree item)
300    ^-  (tree item)
301    ?>  ?=(^ a)
302    :: delete .n.a; merge and balance .l.a and .r.a
303    ::
304    |-  ^-  (tree item)
305    ?~  l.a  r.a
306    ?~  r.a  l.a
307    ?:  (mor key.n.l.a key.n.r.a)
308      l.a(r $(l.a r.l.a))
309    r.a(l $(r.a l.r.a))
310  ::
311  ::  +pop: produce .head (leftmost item) and .rest or crash if empty
312  ::
313  ++  pop
314    ~/  %pop
315    |=  a=(tree item)
316    ^-  [head=item rest=(tree item)]
317    ?~  a     !!
318    ?~  l.a  [n.a r.a]
319    =/  l  $(a l.a)
320    :-  head.l
321    :: load .rest.l back into .a and rebalance
322    ::
323    ?:  |(?=(~ rest.l) (mor key.n.a key.n.rest.l))
324      a(l rest.l)
325    rest.l(r a(r r.rest.l))
326  ::  +pry: produce head (leftmost item) or null
327  ::
328  ++  pry
329    ~/  %pry
330    |=  a=(tree item)
331    ^-  (unit item)
332    ?~  a     ~
333    |-
334    ?~  l.a  `n.a
335    $(a l.a)
336  ::  +put: ordered item insert
337  ::
338  ++  put
339    ~/  %put
340    |=  [a=(tree item) =key =val]
341    ^-  (tree item)
342    :: base case: replace null with single-item tree
343    ::
344    ?~  a  [n=[key val] l=~ r=~]
345    :: base case: overwrite existing .key with new .val
```

```
346      ::
347      ?:  =(key.n.a key)  a(val.n val)
348      ::  if item goes on left, recurse left then rebalance vertical order
349      ::
350      ?:  (compare key key.n.a)
351        =/  l  $(a l.a)
352        ?>  ?=(^ l)
353        ?:  (mor key.n.a key.n.l)
354          a(l l)
355        l(r a(l r.l))
356      ::  item goes on right; recurse right then rebalance vertical order
357      ::
358      =/  r  $(a r.a)
359      ?>  ?=(^ r)
360      ?:  (mor key.n.a key.n.r)
361        a(r r)
362      r(l a(r l.r))
363    ::  +ram: produce tail (rightmost item) or null
364    ::
365    ++  ram
366      ~/  %ram
367      |=  a=(tree item)
368      ^-  (unit item)
369      ?~  a    ~
370      |-
371      ?~  r.a  `n.a
372      $(a r.a)
373    ::  +run: apply gate to transform all values in place
374    ::
375    ++  run
376      ~/  %run
377      |*  [a=(tree item) b=$-(val *)]
378      |-
379      ?~  a  a
380      [n=[key.n.a (b val.n.a)] l=$(a l.a) r=$(a r.a)]
381    ::  +tab: tabulate a subset excluding start element with a max count
382    ::
383    ++  tab
384      ~/  %tab
385      |=  [a=(tree item) b=(unit key) c=@]
386      ^-  (list item)
387      |^
388      (flop e:(tabulate (del-span a b) b c))
389      ::
390      ++  tabulate
391        |=  [a=(tree item) b=(unit key) c=@]
392        ^-  [d=@ e=(list item)]
393        ?:  ?&(?=(~ b) =(c 0))
394          [0 ~]
395        =|  f=[d=@ e=(list item)]
396        |-  ^+  f
397        ?:  ?|(?=(~ a) =(d.f c))  f
398        =.  f  $(a l.a)
399        ?:  =(d.f c)  f
400        =.  f  [+(d.f) [n.a e.f]]
401        ?:(=(d.f c) f $(a r.a))
402      ::
403      ++  del-span
```

```
404        |=  [a=(tree item) b=(unit key)]
405        ^-  (tree item)
406        ?~  a  a
407        ?~  b  a
408        ?:  =(key.n.a u.b)
409          r.a
410        ?:  (compare key.n.a u.b)
411          $(a r.a)
412        a(l $(a l.a))
413      --
414    ::  +tap: convert to list, left to right
415    ::
416    ++  tap
417      ~/  %tap
418      |=  a=(tree item)
419      ^-  (list item)
420      =|  b=(list item)
421      |-  ^+  b
422      ?~  a  b
423      $(a l.a, b [n.a $(a r.a)])
424    ::  +uni: unify two ordered maps
425    ::
426    ::      .b takes precedence over .a if keys overlap.
427    ::
428    ++  uni
429      ~/  %uni
430      |=  [a=(tree item) b=(tree item)]
431      ^-  (tree item)
432      ?~  b  a
433      ?~  a  b
434      ?:  =(key.n.a key.n.b)
435        [n=n.b l=$(a l.a, b l.b) r=$(a r.a, b r.b)]
436      ?:  (mor key.n.a key.n.b)
437        ?:  (compare key.n.b key.n.a)
438          $(l.a $(a l.a, r.b ~), b r.b)
439        $(r.a $(a r.a, l.b ~), b l.b)
440      ?:  (compare key.n.a key.n.b)
441        $(l.b $(b l.b, r.a ~), a r.a)
442      $(r.b $(b r.b, l.a ~), a l.a)
443    ::  +wyt: measure size
444    ::
445    ++  wyt
446      ~/  %wyt
447      |=  a=(tree item)
448      ^-  @ud
449      ?~(a 0 +((add $(a l.a) $(a r.a))))
450      --
451  ::
452  +$  deco  ?(~ %bl %br %un)                      ::  text decoration
453  +$  json                                       ::  normal json value
454    $@  ~                                        ::  null
455    $%  [%a p=(list json)]                       ::  array
456        [%b p=?]                                 ::  boolean
457        [%o p=(map @t json)]                     ::  object
458        [%n p=@ta]                               ::  number
459        [%s p=@t]                                ::  string
460    ==                                           ::
461  +$  life  @ud                                  ::  ship key revision
```

```
462  +$   rift   @ud                                          ::  ship continuity
463  +$   mime   (pair mite octs)                             ::  mimetyped data
464  +$   octs   (pair @ud @)                                 ::  octet-stream
465  +$   sock   (pair ship ship)                             ::  outgoing [src dest]
466  +$   sack   (trel ship ship path)                        ::  $sock /w provenance
467  +$   stub   (list (pair stye (list @c)))                 ::  styled unicode
468  +$   stye   (pair (set deco) (pair tint tint))           ::  decos/bg/fg
469  +$   styl   %+  pair  (unit deco)                        ::  cascading style
470            (pair (unit tint) (unit tint))                 ::
471  +$   styx   (list $@(@t (pair styl styx)))               ::  styled text
472  +$   tint   $@   ?(%r %g %b %c %m %y %k %w %~)            ::  text color
473            [r=@uxD g=@uxD b=@uxD]                          ::  24bit true color
474  +$   turf   (list @t)                                    ::  domain, tld first
475  ::                                                       ::::
476  ::::                      ++ethereum-types                 ::  eth surs for jael
477    ::                                                     ::::
478  ++   ethereum-types
479    |%
480    ::  ethereum address, 20 bytes.
481    ::
482    ++  address   @ux
483    ::  event location
484    ::
485    +$  event-id  [block=@ud log=@ud]
486    ::
487    ++  events  (set event-id)
488    --
489  ::                                                       ::::
490  ::::                      ++azimuth-types                  ::  az surs for jael
491    ::                                                     ::::
492  ++   azimuth-types
493    =,  ethereum-types
494    |%
495    ++  point
496     $:   ::  ownership
497          ::
498          $=  own
499          $:  owner=address
500              management-proxy=address
501              voting-proxy=address
502              transfer-proxy=address
503          ==
504        ::
505        ::  networking
506        ::
507        $=  net
508        %-  unit
509        $:  =life
510            =pass
511            continuity-number=@ud
512            sponsor=[has=? who=@p]
513            escape=(unit @p)
514        ==
515        ::
516        ::  spawning
517        ::
518        $=  kid
519        %-  unit
```

```
520          $:   spawn-proxy=address
521               spawned=(set @p)  ::TODO  sparse range, pile, see old jael ++py
522          ==
523      ==
524   ::
525   +$  dnses  [pri=@t sec=@t ter=@t]
526   ::
527   ++  diff-azimuth
528      $%  [%point who=@p dif=diff-point]
529          [%dns dnses]
530      ==
531   ::
532   ++  diff-point
533      $%  [%full new=point]                          ::
534          [%owner new=address]                       ::  OwnerChanged
535          [%activated who=@p]                        ::  Activated
536          [%spawned who=@p]                          ::  Spawned
537          [%keys =life =pass]                        ::  ChangedKeys
538          [%continuity new=@ud]                      ::  BrokeContinuity
539          [%sponsor new=[has=? who=@p]]              ::  EscapeAcc/LostSpons
540          [%escape new=(unit @p)]                    ::  EscapeReq/Can
541          [%management-proxy new=address]            ::  ChangedManagementPro
542          [%voting-proxy new=address]                ::  ChangedVotingProxy
543          [%spawn-proxy new=address]                 ::  ChangedSpawnProxy
544          [%transfer-proxy new=address]              ::  ChangedTransferProxy
545      ==
546   --
547 ::   +vane-task: general tasks shared across vanes
548 ::
549 +$  vane-task
550   $~  [%born ~]
551   $%  ::  i/o device replaced (reset state)
552      ::
553      [%born ~]
554      ::  boot completed (XX legacy)
555      ::
556      [%init ~]
557      ::  trim state (in response to memory pressure)
558      ::
559      [%trim p=@ud]
560      ::  kernel upgraded
561      ::
562      [%vega ~]
563      ::  receive message via %ames
564      ::
565      ::    TODO: move .vane from $plea to here
566      ::
567      [%plea =ship =plea:ames]
568   ==
569 ::                                                   ::::
570 ::::                        ++http                   ::
571   ::                                                 ::::
572 ::  http: shared representations of http concepts
573 ::
574 ++  http  ^?
575   |%
576   ::  +header-list: an ordered list of http headers
577   ::
```

```
578   +$  header-list
579     (list [key=@t value=@t])
580   ::  +method: exhaustive list of http verbs
581   ::
582   +$  method
583     $?  %'CONNECT'
584         %'DELETE'
585         %'GET'
586         %'HEAD'
587         %'OPTIONS'
588         %'PATCH'
589         %'POST'
590         %'PUT'
591         %'TRACE'
592     ==
593   ::  +request: a single http request
594   ::
595   +$  request
596     $:  ::  method: http method
597         ::
598         method=method
599         ::  url: the url requested
600         ::
601         ::      The url is not escaped. There is no escape.
602         ::
603         url=@t
604         ::  header-list: headers to pass with this request
605         ::
606         =header-list
607         ::  body: optionally, data to send with this request
608         ::
609         body=(unit octs)
610     ==
611   ::  +response-header: the status code and header list on an http request
612   ::
613   ::      We separate these away from the body data because we may not wait for
614   ::      the entire body before we send a %progress to the caller.
615   ::
616   +$  response-header
617     $:  ::  status: http status code
618         ::
619         status-code=@ud
620         ::  headers: http headers
621         ::
622         headers=header-list
623     ==
624   ::  +http-event: packetized http
625   ::
626   ::      Urbit treats Earth's HTTP servers as pipes, where Urbit sends or
627   ::      receives one or more %http-events. The first of these will always be a
628   ::      %start or an %error, and the last will always be %cancel or will have
629   ::      :complete set to %.y to finish the connection.
630   ::
631   ::      Calculation of control headers such as 'Content-Length' or
632   ::      'Transfer-Encoding' should be performed at a higher level; this structure
633   ::      is merely for what gets sent to or received from Earth.
634   ::
635   +$  http-event
```

```
636      $%  ::  %start: the first packet in a response
637          ::
638          $:  %start
639              ::  response-header: first event information
640              ::
641              =response-header
642              ::  data: data to pass to the pipe
643              ::
644              data=(unit octs)
645              ::  whether this completes the request
646              ::
647              complete=?
648          ==
649          ::  %continue: every subsequent packet
650          ::
651          $:  %continue
652              ::  data: data to pass to the pipe
653              ::
654              data=(unit octs)
655              ::  complete: whether this completes the request
656              ::
657              complete=?
658          ==
659          ::  %cancel: represents unsuccessful termination
660          ::
661          [%cancel ~]
662      ==
663  ::  +get-header: returns the value for :header, if it exists in :header-list
664  ::
665  ++  get-header
666    |=  [header=@t =header-list]
667    ^-  (unit @t)
668    ::
669    ?~  header-list
670        ~
671    ::
672    ?:  =(key.i.header-list header)
673      `value.i.header-list
674    ::
675    $(header-list t.header-list)
676  ::  +set-header: sets the value of an item in the header list
677  ::
678  ::    This adds to the end if it doesn't exist.
679  ::
680  ++  set-header
681    |=  [header=@t value=@t =header-list]
682    ^-  ^header-list
683    ::
684    ?~  header-list
685      ::  we didn't encounter the value, add it to the end
686      ::
687      [[header value] ~]
688    ::
689    ?:  =(key.i.header-list header)
690      [[header value] t.header-list]
691    ::
692    [i.header-list $(header-list t.header-list)]
693  ::  +delete-header: removes the first instance of a header from the list
```

```
694      ::
695      ++  delete-header
696        |=  [header=@t =header-list]
697        ^-  ^header-list
698        ::
699        ?~  header-list
700          ~
701        ::  if we see it in the list, remove it
702        ::
703        ?:  =(key.i.header-list header)
704          t.header-list
705        ::
706        [i.header-list $(header-list t.header-list)]
707      ::  +unpack-header: parse header field values
708      ::
709      ++  unpack-header
710        |^  |=  value=@t
711            ^-  (unit (list (map @t @t)))
712            (rust (cass (trip value)) values)
713        ::
714        ++  values
715          %+  more
716            (ifix [. .]:(star ;~(pose ace (just '\09'))) com)
717          pairs
718        ::
719        ++  pairs
720          %+  cook
721            ~(gas by *(map @t @t))
722          %+  most  (ifix [. .]:(star ace) mic)
723          ;~(plug token ;~(pose ;~(pfix tis value) (easy '')))
724        ::
725        ++  value
726          ;~(pose token quoted-string)
727        ::
728        ++  token                              ::  7230 token
729          %+  cook  crip
730          ::NOTE  this is ptok:de-purl:html, but can't access that here
731          %-  plus
732          ;~  pose
733            aln  zap  hax  buc  cen  pam  soq  tar  lus
734            hep  dot  ket  cab  tic  bar  sig
735          ==
736        ::
737        ++  quoted-string                      ::  7230 quoted string
738          %+  cook   crip
739          %+  ifix   [. .]:;~(less (jest '\\"') doq)
740          %-  star
741          ;~  pose
742            ;~(pfix bas ;~(pose (just '\09') ace prn))
743            ;~(pose (just '\09') ;~(less (mask "\22\5c\7f") (shim 0x20 0xff)))
744          ==
745        --
746      ::  +simple-payload: a simple, one event response used for generators
747      ::
748      +$  simple-payload
749        $:  ::  response-header: status code, etc
750            ::
751            =response-header
```

```
752        ::  data: the data returned as the body                                    ::::
753        ::                                                                          ::::
754        data=(unit octs)
755      ==
756    --
757  ::                                                                          ::::
758  ::::                        ++ames                              ::  (1a) network
759    ::                                                                        ::::
760  ++  ames  ^?
761    |%
762    ::  $task: job for ames
763    ::
764    ::      Messaging Tasks
765    ::
766    ::      %hear: packet from unix
767    ::      %dear: lane from unix
768    ::      %heed: track peer's responsiveness; gives %clog if slow
769    ::      %jilt: stop tracking peer's responsiveness
770    ::      %cork: request to delete message flow
771    ::      %tame: request to delete route for ship
772    ::      %kroc: request to delete specific message flows, from their bones
773    ::      %plea: request to send message
774    ::      %deep: deferred calls to %ames, from itself
775    ::
776    ::      Remote Scry Tasks
777    ::
778    ::      %keen: peek: [ship /vane/care/case/spur]
779    ::      %yawn: cancel request from arvo
780    ::      %wham: cancels all scry request from any vane
781    ::
782    ::      System and Lifecycle Tasks
783    ::
784    ::      %born: process restart notification
785    ::      %init: vane boot
786    ::      %prod: re-send a packet per flow, to all peers if .ships is ~
787    ::      %sift: limit verbosity to .ships
788    ::      %snub: set packet blocklist to .ships
789    ::      %spew: set verbosity toggles
790    ::      %cong: adjust congestion control parameters
791    ::      %stir: recover from timer desync and assorted debug commands
792    ::      %trim: release memory
793    ::      %vega: kernel reload notification
794    ::
795    +$  task
796      $+  ames-task
797      $%  [%hear =lane =blob]
798          [%dear =ship =lane]
799          [%heed =ship]
800          [%jilt =ship]
801          [%cork =ship]
802          [%tame =ship]
803          [%kroc bones=(list [ship bone])]
804          $>(%plea vane-task)
805          [%deep =deep]
806      ::
807          [%keen spar]
808          [%yawn spar]
809          [%wham spar]
```

```
810      ::
811          $>(%born vane-task)
812          $>(%init vane-task)
813          [%prod ships=(list ship)]
814          [%sift ships=(list ship)]
815          [%snub form=?(%allow %deny) ships=(list ship)]
816          [%spew veb=(list verb)]
817          [%cong msg=@ud mem=@ud]
818          [%stir arg=@t]
819          $>(%trim vane-task)
820          $>(%vega vane-task)
821      ==
822  ::  $gift: effect from ames
823  ::
824  ::    Messaging Gifts
825  ::
826  ::    %boon: response message from remote ship
827  ::    %clog: notify vane that %boon's to peer are backing up locally
828  ::    %done: notify vane that peer (n)acked our message
829  ::    %lost: notify vane that we crashed on %boon
830  ::    %send: packet to unix
831  ::
832  ::    Remote Scry Gifts
833  ::
834  ::    %tune: peek result
835  ::
836  ::    System and Lifecycle Gifts
837  ::
838  ::    %turf: domain report, relayed from jael
839  ::
840  +$  gift
841    $%  [%boon payload=*]
842        [%clog =ship]
843        [%done error=(unit error)]
844        [%lost ~]
845        [%send =lane =blob]
846    ::
847        [%tune spar roar=(unit roar)]
848    ::
849        [%turf turfs=(list turf)]
850    ==
851  ::
852  ::::                                                  ::  (1a2)
853    ::
854  ++  acru  $_  ^?                                      ::  asym cryptosuite
855    |%                                                  ::  opaque object
856    ++  as  ^?                                          ::  asym ops
857      |%  ++  seal  |~([a=pass b=@] *@)                 ::  encrypt to a
858          ++  sign  |~(a=@ *@)                          ::  certify as us
859          ++  sigh  |~(a=@ *@)                          ::  certification only
860          ++  sure  |~(a=@ *(unit @))                   ::  authenticate from us
861          ++  safe  |~([a=@ b=@] *?)                    ::  authentication only
862          ++  tear  |~([a=pass b=@] *(unit @))          ::  accept from a
863      --  ::as                                          ::
864    ++  de  |~([a=@ b=@] *(unit @))                     ::  symmetric de, soft
865    ++  dy  |~([a=@ b=@] *@)                            ::  symmetric de, hard
866    ++  en  |~([a=@ b=@] *@)                            ::  symmetric en
867    ++  ex  ^?                                          ::  export
```

```
868        |%   ++   fig   *@uvH                          ::   fingerprint
869             ++   pac   *@uvG                          ::   default passcode
870             ++   pub   *pass                          ::   public key
871             ++   sec   *ring                          ::   private key
872        --   ::ex                                      ::
873     ++  nu  ^?                                        ::   reconstructors
874        |%   ++   pit   |~([a=@ b=@] ^?(..nu))          ::   from [width seed]
875             ++   nol   |~(a=ring ^?(..nu))             ::   from ring
876             ++   com   |~(a=pass ^?(..nu))             ::   from pass
877        --   ::nu                                       ::
878     --  ::acru                                        ::
879   ::  +protocol-version: current version of the ames wire protocol
880   ::
881   ++  protocol-version  `?(%0 %1 %2 %3 %4 %5 %6 %7)`%0
882   ::  $address: opaque atomic transport address to or from unix
883   ::
884   +$  address   @uxaddress
885   ::  $verb: verbosity flag for ames
886   ::
887   +$  verb  ?(%snd %rcv %odd %msg %ges %for %rot %kay %fin)
888   ::  $blob: raw atom to or from unix, representing a packet
889   ::
890   +$  blob   @uxblob
891   ::  $error: tagged diagnostic trace
892   ::
893   +$  error   [tag=@tas =tang]
894   ::  $lane: ship transport address; either opaque $address or galaxy
895   ::
896   ::    The runtime knows how to look up galaxies, so we don't need to
897   ::    know their transport addresses.
898   ::
899   +$  lane  (each @pC address)
900   ::  $plea: application-level message, as a %pass
901   ::
902   ::    vane: destination vane on remote ship
903   ::    path: internal route on the receiving ship
904   ::    payload: semantic message contents
905   ::
906   +$  plea  [vane=@tas =path payload=*]
907   ::  $spar:  pair of $ship and $path
908   ::
909   ::    Instead of fully qualifying a scry path, ames infers rift and
910   ::    life based on the ship.
911   ::
912   +$  spar  [=ship =path]
913   ::  $deep: deferred %ames call, from self, to keep +abet cores pure
914   ::
915   +$  deep
916     $%  [%nack =ship =nack=bone =message-blob]
917         [%sink =ship =target=bone naxplanation=[=message-num =error]]
918         [%drop =ship =nack=bone =message-num]
919         [%cork =ship =bone]
920         [%kill =ship =bone]
921     ==
922   :: +|  %atomics
923   ::
924   +$  bone            @udbone
925   +$  fragment        @uwfragment
```

```
926  +$   fragment-num      @udfragmentnum
927  +$   message-blob      @udmessageblob
928  +$   message-num       @udmessagenum
929  +$   public-key        @uwpublickey
930  +$   symmetric-key     @uwsymmetrickey
931  ::
932  ::  $hoot: request packet payload
933  ::  $yowl: serialized response packet payload
934  ::  $hunk: a slice of $yowl fragments
935  ::
936  +$   hoot              @uxhoot
937  +$   yowl              @uxyowl
938  +$   hunk              [lop=@ len=@]
939  ::
940  ::  +|  %kinetics
941  ::  $dyad: pair of sender and receiver ships
942  ::
943  +$   dyad    [sndr=ship rcvr=ship]
944  ::  $shot: noun representation of an ames datagram packet
945  ::
946  ::    Roundtrips losslessly through atom encoding and decoding.
947  ::
948  ::    .origin is ~ unless the packet is being forwarded.  If present,
949  ::    it's an atom that encodes a route to another ship, such as an IPv4
950  ::    address.  Routes are opaque to Arvo and only have meaning in the
951  ::    interpreter. This enforces that Ames is transport-agnostic.
952  ::
953  ::    req: is a request
954  ::    sam: is using the ames protocol (not fine or another protocol)
955  ::
956  +$   shot
957    $:  dyad
958        req=?
959        sam=?
960        sndr-tick=@ubC
961        rcvr-tick=@ubC
962        origin=(unit @uxaddress)
963        content=@uxcontent
964    ==
965  ::  $ack: positive ack, nack packet, or nack trace
966  ::
967  +$   ack
968    $%  [%ok ~]
969        [%nack ~]
970        [%naxplanation =error]
971    ==
972  ::
973  ::  +|  %statics
974  ::  $ship-state: all we know about a peer
975  ::
976  ::    %alien: no PKI data, so enqueue actions to perform once we learn it
977  ::    %known: we know their life and public keys, so we have a channel
978  ::
979  +$   ship-state
980    $+  ship-state
981    $%  [%alien alien-agenda]
982        [%known peer-state]
983    ==
```

```
984  ::  $alien-agenda: what to do when we learn a peer's life and keys
985  ::
986  ::    messages: pleas local vanes have asked us to send
987  ::    packets: packets we've tried to send
988  ::    heeds: local tracking requests; passed through into $peer-state
989  ::
990  +$  alien-agenda
991    $+  alien-agenda
992    $:  messages=(list [=duct =plea])
993        packets=(set =blob)
994        heeds=(set duct)
995        keens=(jug path duct)
996    ==
997  ::  $peer-state: state for a peer with known life and keys
998  ::
999  ::    route: transport-layer destination for packets to peer
1000 ::    qos: quality of service; connection status to peer
1001 ::    ossuary: bone<->duct mapper
1002 ::    snd: per-bone message pumps to send messages as fragments
1003 ::    rcv: per-bone message sinks to assemble messages from fragments
1004 ::    nax: unprocessed nacks (negative acknowledgments)
1005 ::        Each value is ~ when we've received the ack packet but not a
1006 ::        nack-trace, or an error when we've received a nack-trace but
1007 ::        not the ack packet.
1008 ::
1009 ::        When we hear a nack packet or an explanation, if there's no
1010 ::        entry in .nax, we make a new entry. Otherwise, if this new
1011 ::        information completes the packet+nack-trace, we remove the
1012 ::        entry and emit a nack to the local vane that asked us to send
1013 ::        the message.
1014 ::    heeds: listeners for %clog notifications
1015 ::    closing: bones closed on the sender side
1016 ::    corked:  bones closed on both sender and receiver
1017 ::
1018 +$  peer-state
1019   $+  peer-state
1020   $:  $:  =symmetric-key
1021           =life
1022           =rift
1023           =public-key
1024           sponsor=ship
1025       ==
1026       route=(unit [direct=? =lane])
1027       =qos
1028       =ossuary
1029       snd=(map bone message-pump-state)
1030       rcv=(map bone message-sink-state)
1031       nax=(set [=bone =message-num])
1032       heeds=(set duct)
1033       closing=(set bone)
1034       corked=(set bone)
1035       keens=(map path keen-state)
1036   ==
1037 +$  keen-state
1038   $+  keen-state
1039   $:  wan=((mop @ud want) lte)   ::  request packets, sent
1040       nex=(list want)            ::  request packets, unsent
1041       hav=(list have)            ::  response packets, backward
```

```
1042            num-fragments=@ud
1043            num-received=@ud
1044            next-wake=(unit @da)
1045            listeners=(set duct)
1046            metrics=pump-metrics
1047        ==
1048    +$  want
1049      $:  fra=@ud
1050          =hoot
1051          packet-state
1052      ==
1053    +$  have
1054      $:  fra=@ud
1055          meow
1056      ==
1057    ::
1058    +$  meow  ::  response fragment
1059      $:  sig=@ux  ::  signature
1060          num=@ud  ::  number of fragments
1061          dat=@ux  ::  contents
1062      ==
1063    ::
1064    +$  peep  ::  fragment request
1065      $:  =path
1066          num=@ud
1067      ==
1068    ::
1069    +$  wail  ::  tagged request fragment
1070      $%  [%0 peep] :: unsigned
1071      ==
1072    ::
1073    +$  roar  ::  response message
1074      (tale:pki:jael (pair path (unit (cask))))
1075    ::
1076    +$  purr  ::  response packet payload
1077      $:  peep
1078          meow
1079      ==
1080    ::
1081    ::  $qos: quality of service; how is our connection to a peer doing?
1082    ::
1083    ::      .last-contact: last time we heard from peer, or if %unborn, when
1084    ::      we first started tracking time
1085    ::
1086    +$  qos
1087      $~  [%unborn *@da]
1088      [?(%live %dead %unborn) last-contact=@da]
1089    ::  $ossuary: bone<->duct bijection and .next-bone to map to a duct
1090    ::
1091    ::      The first bone is 0. They increment by 4, since each flow includes
1092    ::      a bit for each message determining forward vs. backward and a
1093    ::      second bit for whether the message is on the normal flow or the
1094    ::      associated diagnostic flow (for naxplanations).
1095    ::
1096    ::      The least significant bit of a $bone is:
1097    ::      1 if "forward", i.e. we send %plea's on this flow, or
1098    ::      0 if "backward", i.e. we receive %plea's on this flow.
1099    ::
```

```
1100  ::      The second-least significant bit is 1 if the bone is a
1101  ::      naxplanation bone, and 0 otherwise.  Only naxplanation
1102  ::      messages can be sent on a naxplanation bone, as %boon's.
1103  ::
1104  +$  ossuary
1105    $:  =next=bone
1106        by-duct=(map duct bone)
1107        by-bone=(map bone duct)
1108    ==
1109  ::  $message-pump-state: persistent state for |message-pump
1110  ::
1111  ::      Messages queue up in |message-pump's .unsent-messages until they
1112  ::      can be packetized and fed into |packet-pump for sending.  When we
1113  ::      pop a message off .unsent-messages, we push as many fragments as
1114  ::      we can into |packet-pump, which sends every packet it eats.
1115  ::      Packets rejected by |packet-pump are placed in .unsent-fragments.
1116  ::
1117  ::      When we hear a packet ack, we send it to |packet-pump to be
1118  ::      removed from its queue of unacked packets.
1119  ::
1120  ::      When we hear a message ack (positive or negative), we treat that
1121  ::      as though all fragments have been acked.  If this message is not
1122  ::      .current, then this ack is for a future message and .current has
1123  ::      not yet been acked, so we place the ack in .queued-message-acks.
1124  ::
1125  ::      If we hear a message ack before we've sent all the fragments for
1126  ::      that message, clear .unsent-fragments and have |packet-pump delete
1127  ::      all sent fragments from the message. If this early message ack was
1128  ::      positive, print it out because it indicates the peer is not
1129  ::      behaving properly.
1130  ::
1131  ::      If the ack is for the current message, have |packet-pump delete
1132  ::      all packets from the message, give the message ack back
1133  ::      to the client vane, increment .current, and check if this next
1134  ::      message is in .queued-message-acks.  If it is, emit the message
1135  ::      (n)ack, increment .current, and check the next message.  Repeat
1136  ::      until .current is not fully acked.
1137  ::
1138  ::      The following equation is always true:
1139  ::      .next - .current == number of messages in flight
1140  ::
1141  ::      At the end of a task, |message-pump sends a %halt task to
1142  ::      |packet-pump, which can trigger a timer to be set or cleared based
1143  ::      on congestion control calculations. When the timer fires, it will
1144  ::      generally cause a packet to be re-sent.
1145  ::
1146  ::      Message sequence numbers start at 1 so that the first message will
1147  ::      be greater than .last-acked.message-sink-state on the receiver.
1148  ::
1149  ::      current: sequence number of earliest message sent or being sent
1150  ::      next: sequence number of next message to send
1151  ::      unsent-messages: messages to be sent after current message
1152  ::      unsent-fragments: fragments of current message waiting for sending
1153  ::      queued-message-acks: future message acks to be applied after current
1154  ::      packet-pump-state: state of corresponding |packet-pump
1155  ::
1156  +$  message-pump-state
1157    $+  message-pump-state
```

```
1158    $:  current=_`message-num`1
1159        next=_`message-num`1
1160        unsent-messages=(qeu message-blob)
1161        unsent-fragments=(list static-fragment)
1162        queued-message-acks=(map message-num ack)
1163        =packet-pump-state
1164    ==
1165  +$  static-fragment
1166    $:  =message-num
1167        num-fragments=fragment-num
1168        =fragment-num
1169        =fragment
1170    ==
1171  ::  $packet-pump-state: persistent state for |packet-pump
1172  ::
1173  ::    next-wake: last timer we've set, or null
1174  ::    live: packets in flight; sent but not yet acked
1175  ::    metrics: congestion control information
1176  ::
1177  +$  packet-pump-state
1178    $+  packet-pump-state
1179    $:  next-wake=(unit @da)
1180        live=((mop live-packet-key live-packet-val) lte-packets)
1181        metrics=pump-metrics
1182    ==
1183  ::  +lte-packets: yes if a is before b
1184  ::
1185  ++  lte-packets
1186    |=  [a=live-packet-key b=live-packet-key]
1187    ^-  ?
1188    ::
1189    ?:  (lth message-num.a message-num.b)
1190      %.y
1191    ?:  (gth message-num.a message-num.b)
1192      %.n
1193    (lte fragment-num.a fragment-num.b)
1194  ::  $pump-metrics: congestion control state for a |packet-pump
1195  ::
1196  ::    This is an Ames adaptation of TCP's Reno congestion control
1197  ::    algorithm.  The information signals and their responses are
1198  ::    identical to those of the "NewReno" variant of Reno; the
1199  ::    implementation differs because Ames acknowledgments differ from
1200  ::    TCP's, because this code uses functional data structures, and
1201  ::    because TCP's sequence numbers reset when a peer becomes
1202  ::    unresponsive, whereas Ames sequence numbers only change when a
1203  ::    ship breaches.
1204  ::
1205  ::    A deviation from Reno is +fast-resend-after-ack, which re-sends
1206  ::    timed-out packets when a peer starts responding again after a
1207  ::    period of unresponsiveness.
1208  ::
1209  ::    If .skips reaches 3, we perform a fast retransmit and fast
1210  ::    recovery.  This corresponds to Reno's handling of "three duplicate
1211  ::    acks".
1212  ::
1213  ::    rto: retransmission timeout
1214  ::    rtt: roundtrip time estimate, low-passed using EWMA
1215  ::    rttvar: mean deviation of .rtt, also low-passed with EWMA
```

```
1216    ::      ssthresh: slow-start threshold
1217    ::      cwnd: congestion window; max unacked packets
1218    ::
1219    +$  pump-metrics
1220      $:  rto=_~s1
1221          rtt=_~s1
1222          rttvar=_~s1
1223          ssthresh=_10.000
1224          cwnd=_1
1225          counter=@ud
1226      ==
1227    +$  live-packet
1228      $:  key=live-packet-key
1229          val=live-packet-val
1230      ==
1231    +$  live-packet-key
1232      $:  =message-num
1233          =fragment-num
1234      ==
1235    +$  live-packet-val
1236      $:  packet-state
1237          num-fragments=fragment-num
1238          =fragment
1239      ==
1240    +$  packet-state
1241      $:  last-sent=@da
1242          tries=_1
1243          skips=@ud
1244      ==
1245    ::  $message-sink-state: state of |message-sink to assemble messages
1246    ::
1247    ::      last-acked: highest $message-num we've fully acknowledged
1248    ::      last-heard: highest $message-num we've heard all fragments on
1249    ::      pending-vane-ack: heard but not processed by local vane
1250    ::      live-messages: partially received messages
1251    ::
1252    +$  message-sink-state
1253      $+  message-sink-state
1254      $:  last-acked=message-num
1255          last-heard=message-num
1256          pending-vane-ack=(qeu [=message-num message=*])
1257          live-messages=(map message-num partial-rcv-message)
1258          nax=(set message-num)
1259      ==
1260    ::  $partial-rcv-message: message for which we've received some fragments
1261    ::
1262    ::      num-fragments: total number of fragments in this message
1263    ::      num-received: how many fragments we've received so far
1264    ::      fragments: fragments we've received, eventually producing a $message
1265    ::
1266    +$  partial-rcv-message
1267      $:  num-fragments=fragment-num
1268          num-received=fragment-num
1269          fragments=(map fragment-num fragment)
1270      ==
1271    ::  $rank: which kind of ship address, by length
1272    ::
1273    ::      0b0: galaxy or star -- 2  bytes
```

```
1274  ::     0b1:  planet          -- 4  bytes
1275  ::     0b10: moon            -- 8  bytes
1276  ::     0b11: comet           -- 16 bytes
1277  ::
1278  +$  rank  ?(%0b0 %0b1 %0b10 %0b11)
1279  ::
1280  ::  +|  %coding
1281  ::  +sift-ship-size: decode a 2-bit ship type specifier into a byte width
1282  ::
1283  ::     Type 0: galaxy or star -- 2 bytes
1284  ::     Type 1: planet         -- 4 bytes
1285  ::     Type 2: moon           -- 8 bytes
1286  ::     Type 3: comet          -- 16 bytes
1287  ::
1288  ++  sift-ship-size
1289  |=  rank=@ubC
1290  ^-  @
1291  ::
1292  ?+  rank  !!
1293    %0b0   2
1294    %0b1   4
1295    %0b10  8
1296    %0b11  16
1297  ==
1298  ::  +is-valid-rank: does .ship match its stated .size?
1299  ::
1300  ++  is-valid-rank
1301  |=  [=ship size=@ubC]
1302  ^-  ?
1303  .=  size
1304  =/  wid  (met 3 ship)
1305  ?:  (lte wid 1)   2
1306  ?:  =(2 wid)      2
1307  ?:  (lte wid 4)   4
1308  ?:  (lte wid 8)   8
1309  ?>  (lte wid 16)  16
1310  ::  +sift-shot: deserialize packet from bytestream or crash
1311  ::
1312  ++  sift-shot
1313  |=  =blob
1314  ^-  shot
1315  ~|  %sift-shot-fail
1316  ::  first 32 (2^5) bits are header; the rest is body
1317  ::
1318  =/  header  (end 5 blob)
1319  =/  body    (rsh 5 blob)
1320  ::  read header; first two bits are reserved
1321  ::
1322  =/  req  =(& (cut 0 [2 1] header))
1323  =/  sam  =(& (cut 0 [3 1] header))
1324  ::
1325  =/  version  (cut 0 [4 3] header)
1326  ?.  =(protocol-version version)
1327    ~&  [%ames-protocol-version protocol-version version]
1328    ~|  ames-protocol-version+version  !!
1329  ::
1330  =/  sndr-size  (sift-ship-size (cut 0 [7 2] header))
1331  =/  rcvr-size  (sift-ship-size (cut 0 [9 2] header))
```

```
1332      =/  checksum   (cut 0 [11 20] header)
1333      =/  relayed    (cut 0 [31 1] header)
1334      ::  origin, if present, is 6 octets long, at the end of the body
1335      ::
1336      =^  origin=(unit @)  body
1337        ?:  =(| relayed)
1338          [~ body]
1339        =/  len  (sub (met 3 body) 6)
1340        [`(end [3 6] body) (rsh [3 6] body)]
1341      ::  .checksum does not apply to the origin
1342      ::
1343      ?.  =(checksum (end [0 20] (mug body)))
1344        ~&  >>>  %ames-checksum
1345        ~|  %ames-checksum  !!
1346      ::  read fixed-length sndr and rcvr life data from body
1347      ::
1348      ::    These represent the last four bits of the sender and receiver
1349      ::    life fields, to be used for quick dropping of honest packets to
1350      ::    or from the wrong life.
1351      ::
1352      =/  sndr-tick  (cut 0 [0 4] body)
1353      =/  rcvr-tick  (cut 0 [4 4] body)
1354      ::  read variable-length .sndr and .rcvr addresses
1355      ::
1356      =/  off    1
1357      =^  sndr  off  [(cut 3 [off sndr-size] body) (add off sndr-size)]
1358      ?.  (is-valid-rank sndr sndr-size)
1359        ~&  >>>  [%ames-sender-imposter sndr sndr-size]
1360        ~|  ames-sender-impostor+[sndr sndr-size]  !!
1361      ::
1362      =^  rcvr  off  [(cut 3 [off rcvr-size] body) (add off rcvr-size)]
1363      ?.  (is-valid-rank rcvr rcvr-size)
1364        ~&  >>>  [%ames-receiver-imposter rcvr rcvr-size]
1365        ~|  ames-receiver-impostor+[rcvr rcvr-size]  !!
1366      ::  read variable-length .content from the rest of .body
1367      ::
1368      =/  content  (cut 3 [off (sub (met 3 body) off)] body)
1369      [[sndr rcvr] req sam sndr-tick rcvr-tick origin content]
1370    ::
1371    ++  sift-wail
1372      |=  =hoot
1373      ^-  wail
1374      ?>  =(0 (end 3 hoot))
1375      [%0 +:(sift-peep (rsh 3 hoot))]
1376    ::
1377    ++  sift-purr
1378      |=  =hoot
1379      ^-  purr
1380      =+  [wid peep]=(sift-peep hoot)
1381      [peep (sift-meow (rsh [3 wid] hoot))]
1382    ::
1383    ++  sift-peep
1384      |=  =hoot
1385      ^-  [wid=@ =peep]
1386      =+  num=(cut 3 [0 4] hoot)
1387      =+  len=(cut 3 [4 2] hoot)
1388      =+  pat=(cut 3 [6 len] hoot)
1389      ~|  pat=pat
```

```
1390      :-  (add 6 len)
1391      :_  num
1392    (rash pat ;~(pfix fas (most fas (cook crip (star ;~(less fas prn)))))))
1393    ::
1394    ++  sift-meow
1395      |=  =yowl
1396      :*  sig=(cut 3 [0 64] yowl)
1397          num=(cut 3 [64 4] yowl)
1398          dat=(rsh 3^68 yowl)
1399      ==
1400    ::  +etch-shot: serialize a packet into a bytestream
1401    ::
1402    ++  etch-shot
1403      |=  shot
1404      ^-  blob
1405      ::
1406      =/  sndr-meta  (ship-meta sndr)
1407      =/  rcvr-meta  (ship-meta rcvr)
1408      ::
1409      =/  body=@
1410        ;:  mix
1411          sndr-tick
1412          (lsh 2 rcvr-tick)
1413          (lsh 3 sndr)
1414          (lsh [3 +(size.sndr-meta)] rcvr)
1415          (lsh [3 +((add size.sndr-meta size.rcvr-meta))] content)
1416        ==
1417      =/  checksum  (end [0 20] (mug body))
1418      =?  body  ?=(^ origin)  (mix u.origin (lsh [3 6] body))
1419      ::
1420      =/  header=@
1421        %+  can  0
1422        :~  [2 reserved=0]
1423            [1 req]
1424            [1 sam]
1425            [3 protocol-version]
1426            [2 rank.sndr-meta]
1427            [2 rank.rcvr-meta]
1428            [20 checksum]
1429            [1 relayed=.?(origin)]
1430        ==
1431      (mix header (lsh 5 body))
1432    ::
1433    ::  +ship-meta: produce size (in bytes) and address rank for .ship
1434    ::
1435    ::    0: galaxy or star
1436    ::    1: planet
1437    ::    2: moon
1438    ::    3: comet
1439    ::
1440    ++  ship-meta
1441      |=  =ship
1442      ^-  [size=@ =rank]
1443      ::
1444      =/  size=@  (met 3 ship)
1445      ::
1446      ?:  (lte size 2)  [2 %0b0]
1447      ?:  (lte size 4)  [4 %0b1]
```

```
1448        ?:  (lte size 8)  [8 %0b10]
1449        [16 %0b11]
1450      --  ::ames
1451    ::                                                        ::::
1452    ::::                          ++behn                      ::  (1b) timekeeping
1453      ::                                                      ::::
1454  ++  behn  ^?
1455      |%
1456      +$  gift                                               ::  out result <-$
1457        $%  [%doze p=(unit @da)]                             ::  next alarm
1458            [%wake error=(unit tang)]                        ::  wakeup or failed
1459            [%meta p=vase]                                   ::
1460            [%heck syn=sign-arvo]                            ::  response to %huck
1461        ==
1462      +$  task                                               ::  in request ->$
1463        $~  [%vega ~]                                        ::
1464        $%  $>(%born vane-task)                              ::  new unix process
1465            [%rest p=@da]                                    ::  cancel alarm
1466            [%drip p=vase]                                   ::  give in next event
1467            [%huck syn=sign-arvo]                            ::  give back
1468            $>(%trim vane-task)                              ::  trim state
1469            $>(%vega vane-task)                              ::  report upgrade
1470            [%wait p=@da]                                    ::  set alarm
1471            [%wake ~]                                        ::  timer activate
1472        ==
1473      --  ::behn
1474    ::                                                        ::::
1475    ::::                          ++clay                      ::  (1c) versioning
1476      ::                                                      ::::
1477  ++  clay  ^?
1478      |%
1479      +$  gift                                               ::  out result <-$
1480        $%  [%boon payload=*]                                ::  ames response
1481            [%croz rus=(map desk [r=regs w=regs])]           ::  rules for group
1482            [%cruz cez=(map @ta crew)]                       ::  permission groups
1483            [%dirk p=@tas]                                   ::  mark mount dirty
1484            [%ergo p=@tas q=mode]                            ::  version update
1485            [%hill p=(list @tas)]                            ::  mount points
1486            [%done error=(unit error:ames)]                  ::  ames message (n)ack
1487            [%mere p=(each (set path) (pair term tang))]     ::  merge result
1488            [%ogre p=@tas]                                   ::  delete mount point
1489            [%rule red=dict wit=dict]                        ::  node r+w permissions
1490            [%tire p=(each rock:tire wave:tire)]             ::  app state
1491            [%writ p=riot]                                   ::  response
1492            [%wris p=[%da p=@da] q=(set (pair care path))]   ::  many changes
1493        ==                                                   ::
1494      +$  task                                               ::  in request ->$
1495        $~  [%vega ~]                                        ::
1496        $%  [%boat ~]                                        ::  pier rebooted
1497            [%cred nom=@ta cew=crew]                         ::  set permission group
1498            [%crew ~]                                        ::  permission groups
1499            [%crow nom=@ta]                                  ::  group usage
1500            [%drop des=desk]                                 ::  cancel pending merge
1501            [%info des=desk dit=nori]                        ::  internal edit
1502            $>(%init vane-task)                              ::  report install
1503            [%into des=desk all=? fis=mode]                  ::  external edit
1504            $:  %merg                                        ::  merge desks
1505                des=desk                                     ::  target
```

```
1506          her=@p   dem=desk   cas=case          ::  source
1507          how=germ                              ::  method
1508      ==                                        ::
1509    $:  %fuse                                    ::  merge many
1510        des=desk                                ::  target desk
1511        bas=beak                                ::  base desk
1512        con=(list [beak germ])                  ::  merges
1513      ==                                        ::
1514    [%mont pot=term bem=beam]                    ::  mount to unix
1515    [%dirk pot=term]                             ::  mark mount dirty
1516    [%ogre pot=$@(term beam)]                    ::  delete mount point
1517    [%park des=desk yok=yoki ran=rang]           ::  synchronous commit
1518    [%perm des=desk pax=path rit=rite]           ::  change permissions
1519    [%pork ~]                                    ::  resume commit
1520    [%prep lat=(map lobe page)]                  ::  prime clay store
1521    [%rein des=desk ren=rein]                    ::  extra apps
1522    [%stir arg=*]                                ::  debug
1523    [%tire p=(unit ~)]                           ::  app state subscribe
1524    [%tomb =clue]                                ::  tombstone specific
1525    $>(%trim vane-task)                          ::  trim state
1526    $>(%vega vane-task)                          ::  report upgrade
1527    [%warp wer=ship rif=riff]                    ::  internal file req
1528    [%werp who=ship wer=ship rif=riff-any]       ::  external file req
1529    [%wick ~]                                    ::  try upgrade
1530    [%zeal lit=(list [=desk =zest])]             ::  batch zest
1531    [%zest des=desk liv=zest]                    ::  live
1532    $>(%plea vane-task)                          ::  ames request
1533  ==                                            ::
1534  ::                                            ::
1535  ::::                                          ::  (1c2)
1536    ::                                          ::
1537  +$  aeon  @ud                                  ::  version number
1538  +$  beam  [[p=ship q=desk r=case] s=path]      ::  global name
1539  +$  beak  [p=ship q=desk r=case]               ::  path prefix
1540  +$  cable                                      ::  lib/sur/mark ref
1541    $:  face=(unit term)                         ::
1542        file-path=term                           ::
1543      ==                                        ::
1544  +$  care                                       ::  clay submode
1545    $?  %a  %b  %c  %d  %e  %f                   ::
1546        %p  %q  %r  %s  %t  %u                   ::
1547        %v  %w  %x  %y  %z                       ::
1548      ==                                        ::
1549  +$  cash                                       ::  case or tako
1550    $%  [%tako p=tako]                           ::
1551        case                                     ::
1552      ==                                        ::
1553  +$  cass  [ud=@ud da=@da]                       ::  cases for revision
1554  +$  clue                                       ::  murder weapon
1555    $%  [%lobe =lobe]                            ::  specific lobe
1556        [%all ~]                                 ::  all safe targets
1557        [%pick ~]                                ::  collect garbage
1558        [%norm =ship =desk =norm]                ::  set default norm
1559        [%worn =ship =desk =tako =norm]          ::  set commit norm
1560        [%seek =ship =desk =cash]                ::  fetch source blobs
1561      ==                                        ::
1562  +$  cone  (map [ship desk] dome)               ::  domes
1563  ::                                            ::
```

```
1564    ::  Desk state.
1565    ::
1566    ::  Includes a checked-out ankh with current content, most recent version, map
1567    ::  of all version numbers to commit hashes (commits are in hut.rang), and map
1568    ::  of labels to version numbers.
1569    ::
1570    ::  `mim` is a cache of the content in the directories that are mounted
1571    ::  to unix.  Often, we convert to/from mime without anything really
1572    ::  having changed; this lets us short-circuit that in some cases.
1573    ::  Whenever you give an `%ergo`, you must update this.
1574    ::
1575    +$  dome
1576      $:  let=aeon                          ::  top id
1577          hit=(map aeon tako)               ::  versions by id
1578          lab=(map @tas aeon)               ::  labels
1579          tom=(map tako norm)               ::  tomb policies
1580          nor=norm                          ::  default policy
1581          mim=(map path mime)               ::  mime cache
1582          fod=flue                          ::  ford cache
1583          wic=(map weft yoki)               ::  commit-in-waiting
1584          liv=zest                          ::  running agents
1585          ren=rein                          ::  force agents on/off
1586      ==                                    ::
1587    +$  crew  (set ship)                    ::  permissions group
1588    +$  dict  [src=path rul=real]           ::  effective permission
1589    +$  domo                                ::  project state
1590      $:  let=@ud                           ::  top id
1591          hit=(map @ud tako)                ::  changes by id
1592          lab=(map @tas @ud)                ::  labels
1593      ==                                    ::
1594    +$  germ                                ::  merge style
1595      $?  %init                             ::  new desk
1596          %fine                             ::  fast forward
1597          %meet                             ::  orthogonal files
1598          %mate                             ::  orthogonal changes
1599          %meld                             ::  force merge
1600          %only-this                        ::  ours with parents
1601          %only-that                        ::  hers with parents
1602          %take-this                        ::  ours unless absent
1603          %take-that                        ::  hers unless absent
1604          %meet-this                        ::  ours if conflict
1605          %meet-that                        ::  hers if conflict
1606      ==                                    ::
1607    +$  lobe  @uvI                          ::  blob ref
1608    +$  miso                                ::  file delta
1609      $%  [%del ~]                          ::  delete
1610          [%ins p=cage]                     ::  insert
1611          [%dif p=cage]                     ::  mutate from diff
1612          [%mut p=cage]                     ::  mutate from raw
1613      ==                                    ::
1614    +$  misu                                ::  computed delta
1615      $%  [%del ~]                          ::  delete
1616          [%ins p=cage]                     ::  insert
1617          [%dif p=lobe q=cage]              ::  mutate from diff
1618      ==                                    ::
1619    +$  mizu  [p=@u q=(map @ud tako) r=rang]   ::  new state
1620    +$  moar  [p=@ud q=@ud]                 ::  normal change range
1621    +$  moat  [from=case to=case =path]     ::  change range
```

```
1622  +$  mode  (list [path (unit mime)])              ::  external files
1623  +$  mood  [=care =case =path]                     ::  request in desk
1624  +$  mool  [=case paths=(set (pair care path))]    ::  requests in desk
1625  +$  nori                                          ::  repository action
1626      $%  [%& p=soba]                               ::  delta
1627          [%| p=@tas q=(unit aeon)]                 ::  label
1628      ==                                            ::
1629  +$  nuri                                          ::  repository action
1630      $%  [%& p=suba]                               ::  delta
1631          [%| p=@tas]                               ::  label
1632      ==                                            ::
1633  +$  norm  (axal ?)                                ::  tombstone policy
1634  +$  open  $-(path vase)                           ::  get prelude
1635  +$  page  ^page                                   ::  export for compat
1636  +$  pour                                          ::  ford build w/content
1637      $%  [%file =path]
1638          [%nave =mark]
1639          [%dais =mark]
1640          [%cast =mars]
1641          [%tube =mars]
1642          ::  leafs
1643          ::
1644          [%vale =path =lobe]
1645          [%arch =path =(map path lobe)]
1646      ==
1647  +$  rang                                          ::  repository
1648      $+  rang
1649      $:  hut=(map tako yaki)                        ::  changes
1650          lat=(map lobe page)                       ::  data
1651      ==                                            ::
1652  +$  rant                                          ::  response to request
1653      $:  p=[p=care q=case r=desk]                  ::  clade release book
1654          q=path                                    ::  spur
1655          r=cage                                    ::  data
1656      ==                                            ::
1657  +$  rave                                          ::  general request
1658      $%  [%sing =mood]                             ::  single request
1659          [%next =mood]                             ::  await next version
1660          [%mult =mool]                             ::  next version of any
1661          [%many track=? =moat]                     ::  track range
1662      ==                                            ::
1663  +$  real                                          ::  resolved permissions
1664      $:  mod=?(%black %white)                      ::
1665          who=(pair (set ship) (map @ta crew))      ::
1666      ==                                            ::
1667  +$  regs  (map path rule)                         ::  rules for paths
1668  +$  rein  (map dude:gall ?)                       ::  extra apps
1669  +$  riff  [p=desk q=(unit rave)]                  ::  request+desist
1670  +$  riff-any                                      ::
1671      $%  [%1 =riff]                                ::
1672      ==                                            ::
1673  +$  rite                                          ::  new permissions
1674      $%  [%r red=(unit rule)]                      ::  for read
1675          [%w wit=(unit rule)]                      ::  for write
1676          [%rw red=(unit rule) wit=(unit rule)]     ::  for read and write
1677      ==                                            ::
1678  +$  riot  (unit rant)                             ::  response+complete
1679  +$  rule  [mod=?(%black %white) who=(set whom)]   ::  node permission
```

```
1680  +$  rump  [p=care q=case r=@tas s=path]              ::  relative path
1681  +$  saba  [p=ship q=@tas r=moar s=dome]              ::  patch+merge
1682  +$  soak                                             ::  ford result
1683    $%  [%cage =cage]
1684        [%vase =vase]
1685        [%arch dir=(map @ta vase)]
1686        [%dais =dais]
1687        [%tube =tube]
1688    ==
1689  +$  soba  (list [p=path q=miso])                     ::  delta
1690  +$  suba  (list [p=path q=misu])                     ::  delta
1691  +$  tako  @uvI                                       ::  yaki ref
1692  +$  toro  [p=@ta q=nori]                             ::  general change
1693  ++  unce                                             ::  change part
1694    |*  a=mold                                         ::
1695    $%  [%& p=@ud]                                     ::  skip[copy]
1696        [%| p=(list a) q=(list a)]                     ::  p -> q[chunk]
1697    ==                                                 ::
1698  ++  urge  |*(a=mold (list (unce a)))                 ::  list change
1699  +$  waft                                             ::  kelvin range
1700    $^  [[%1 ~] p=(set weft)]                          ::
1701    weft                                               ::
1702  +$  whom  (each ship @ta)                            ::  ship or named crew
1703  +$  yoki  (each yuki yaki)                           ::  commit
1704  +$  yuki                                             ::  proto-commit
1705    $:  p=(list tako)                                  ::  parents
1706        q=(map path (each page lobe))                  ::  namespace
1707    ==                                                 ::
1708  +$  yaki                                             ::  commit
1709    $:  p=(list tako)                                  ::  parents
1710        q=(map path lobe)                              ::  namespace
1711        r=tako                                         ::  self-reference
1712        t=@da                                          ::  date
1713    ==                                                 ::
1714  +$  zest  $~(%dead ?(%dead %live %held))             ::  how live
1715  ::                                                   ::
1716  ++  tire                                             ::  app state
1717    |%                                                 ::
1718  +$  rock  (map desk [=zest wic=(set weft)])          ::
1719  +$  wave                                             ::
1720    $%  [%wait =desk =weft]                            ::  blocked
1721        [%warp =desk =weft]                            ::  unblocked
1722        [%zest =desk =zest]                            ::  running
1723    ==                                                 ::
1724    ::                                                 ::
1725  ++  wash                                             ::  patch
1726    |=  [=rock =wave]
1727    ^+  rock
1728    ?-    -.wave
1729        %wait
1730      =/  got=[=zest wic=(set weft)]
1731      (~(gut by rock) desk.wave *zest ~)
1732      (~(put by rock) desk.wave got(wic (~(put in wic.got) weft.wave)))
1733    ::
1734        %warp
1735      %-  ~(run by rock)
1736      |=  [=zest wic=(set weft)]
1737      [zest (~(del in wic) weft.wave)]
```

```
1738      ::
1739        %zest
1740      ?:  ?=(%dead zest.wave)
1741        (~(del by rock) desk.wave)
1742      =/  got=[=zest wic=(set weft)]
1743        (~(gut by rock) desk.wave *zest ~)
1744      (~(put by rock) desk.wave got(zest zest.wave))
1745      ==
1746    ::
1747    ++  walk                                    ::  diff
1748      |=  [a=rock b=rock]
1749      ^-  (list wave)
1750      =/  adds  (~(dif by b) a)
1751      =/  dels  (~(dif by a) b)
1752      =/  bots  (~(int by a) b)
1753      ;:  welp
1754        ^-  (list wave)
1755        %-  zing
1756        %+  turn  ~(tap by adds)
1757        |=  [=desk =zest wic=(set weft)]
1758        ^-  (list wave)
1759        :-  [%zest desk zest]
1760        %+  turn  ~(tap in wic)
1761        |=  =weft
1762        [%wait desk weft]
1763      ::
1764        ^-  (list wave)
1765        %+  turn  ~(tap by dels)
1766        |=  [=desk =zest wic=(set weft)]
1767        ^-  wave
1768        [%zest desk %dead]
1769      ::
1770        ^-  (list wave)
1771        %-  zing
1772        %+  turn  ~(tap by bots)
1773        |=  [=desk * *]
1774        ^-  (list wave)
1775        =/  aa  (~(got by a) desk)
1776        =/  bb  (~(got by b) desk)
1777        =/  wadds  (~(dif in wic.bb) wic.aa)
1778        =/  wdels  (~(dif in wic.aa) wic.bb)
1779        ;:  welp
1780          ?:  =(zest.aa zest.bb)
1781            ~
1782          [%zest desk zest.bb]~
1783        ::
1784          %+  turn  ~(tap by wadds)
1785          |=  =weft
1786          ^-  wave
1787          [%wait desk weft]
1788        ::
1789          %+  turn  ~(tap by wdels)
1790          |=  =weft
1791          ^-  wave
1792          [%warp desk weft]
1793        ==
1794      ==
1795    --
```

```
1796    ::
1797    ::  +page-to-lobe: hash a page to get a lobe.
1798    ::
1799    ++  page-to-lobe  |=(page (shax (jam +<)))
1800    ::
1801    ++  cord-to-waft
1802      |=  =cord
1803      ^-  waft
1804      =/  wefts=(list weft)
1805        %+  turn  (rash cord (star (ifix [gay gay] tall:vast)))
1806        |=  =hoon
1807        !<(weft (slap !>(~) hoon))
1808      ?:  ?=([* ~] wefts)
1809        i.wefts
1810      [[%1 ~] (sy wefts)]
1811    ::
1812    ++  waft-to-wefts
1813      |=  kal=waft
1814      ^-  (set weft)
1815      ?^  -.kal
1816        p.kal
1817      [kal ~ ~]
1818    ::
1819    ::  +make-yaki: make commit out of a list of parents, content, and date.
1820    ::
1821    ++  make-yaki
1822      |=  [p=(list tako) q=(map path lobe) t=@da]
1823      ^-  yaki
1824      =+  ^=  has
1825        %^  cat  7  (sham [%yaki (roll p add) q t])
1826        (sham [%tako (roll p add) q t])
1827      [p q has t]
1828    ::
1829    ::  $leak: ford cache key
1830    ::
1831    ::    This includes all build inputs, including transitive dependencies,
1832    ::    recursively.
1833    ::
1834    +$  leak
1835      $~  [*pour ~]
1836      $:  =pour
1837          deps=(set leak)
1838      ==
1839    ::
1840    ::  $flow: global ford cache
1841    ::
1842    ::    Refcount includes references from other items in the cache, and
1843    ::    from spills in each desk
1844    ::
1845    ::    This is optimized for minimizing the number of rebuilds, and given
1846    ::    that, minimizing the amount of memory used.  It is relatively slow
1847    ::    to lookup, because generating a cache key can be fairly slow (for
1848    ::    files, it requires parsing; for tubes, it even requires building
1849    ::    the marks).
1850    ::
1851    +$  flow  (map leak [refs=@ud =soak])
1852    ::
1853    ::  Per-desk ford cache
```

```
1854    ::
1855    ::      Spill is the set of "roots" we have into the global ford cache.
1856    ::      We add a root for everything referenced directly or indirectly on
1857    ::      a desk, then invalidate them on commit only if their dependencies
1858    ::      change.
1859    ::
1860    ::      Sprig is a fast-lookup index over the global ford cache.  The only
1861    ::      goal is to make cache hits fast.
1862    ::
1863    +$  flue  [spill=(set leak) sprig=(map mist [=leak =soak])]
1864    ::
1865    ::  Ford build without content.
1866    ::
1867    +$  mist
1868      $%  [%file =path]
1869          [%nave =mark]
1870          [%dais =mark]
1871          [%cast =mars]
1872          [%tube =mars]
1873          [%vale =path]
1874          [%arch =path]
1875      ==
1876    ::
1877    ::  $pile: preprocessed hoon source file
1878    ::
1879    ::      /-  sur-file           ::  surface imports from /sur
1880    ::      /+  lib-file           ::  library imports from /lib
1881    ::      /=  face  /path        ::  imports built hoon file at path
1882    ::      /~  face  type   /path ::  imports built hoon files from directory
1883    ::      /%  face  %mark        ::  imports mark definition from /mar
1884    ::      /$  face  %from  %to   ::  imports mark converter from /mar
1885    ::      /*  face  %mark  /path ::  unbuilt file imports, as mark
1886    ::
1887    +$  pile
1888      $:  sur=(list taut)
1889          lib=(list taut)
1890          raw=(list [face=term =path])
1891          raz=(list [face=term =spec =path])
1892          maz=(list [face=term =mark])
1893          caz=(list [face=term =mars])
1894          bar=(list [face=term =mark =path])
1895          =hoon
1896      ==
1897    ::  $taut: file import from /lib or /sur
1898    ::
1899    +$  taut  [face=(unit term) pax=term]
1900    ::  $mars: mark conversion request
1901    ::  $tube: mark conversion gate
1902    ::  $nave: typed mark core
1903    ::
1904    +$  mars  [a=mark b=mark]
1905    +$  tube  $-(vase vase)
1906    ++  nave
1907      |$  [typ dif]
1908      $_
1909      ^?
1910      |%
1911      ++  diff  |~([old=typ new=typ] *dif)
```

```
1912    ++  form  *mark
1913    ++  join  |~([a=dif b=dif] *(unit (unit dif)))
1914    ++  mash
1915      |~  [a=[ship desk dif] b=[ship desk dif]]
1916    *(unit dif)
1917    ++  pact  |~([typ dif] *typ)
1918    ++  vale  |~(noun *typ)
1919    --
1920  ::  $dais: processed mark core
1921  ::
1922  +$  dais
1923    $_  ^|
1924    |_  sam=vase
1925    ++  diff  |~(new=_sam *vase)
1926    ++  form  *mark
1927    ++  join  |~([a=vase b=vase] *(unit (unit vase)))
1928    ++  mash
1929      |~  [a=[ship desk diff=vase] b=[ship desk diff=vase]]
1930    *(unit vase)
1931    ++  pact  |~(diff=vase sam)
1932    ++  vale  |~(noun sam)
1933    --
1934  ::
1935  ++  get-fit
1936    |=  [bek=beak pre=@tas pax=@tas]
1937    ^-  (unit path)
1938    =/  paz  (segments pax)
1939    |-  ^-  (unit path)
1940    ?~  paz
1941      ~
1942    =/  puz=path  (snoc `path`[pre i.paz] %hoon)
1943    =+  .^(=arch cy+[(scot %p p.bek) q.bek (scot r.bek) puz])
1944    ?^  fil.arch
1945      `puz
1946    $(paz t.paz)
1947  ::  +segments: compute all paths from :path-part, replacing some `/`s with `-`s
1948  ::
1949  ::    For example, when passed a :path-part of 'foo-bar-baz',
1950  ::    the product will contain:
1951  ::    ```
1952  ::    dojo> (segments 'foo-bar-baz')
1953  ::    ~[/foo-bar-baz /foo-bar/baz /foo/bar-baz /foo/bar/baz]
1954  ::    ```
1955  ::
1956  ++  segments
1957    |=  suffix=@tas
1958    ^-  (list path)
1959    =/  parser
1960    (most hep (cook crip ;~(plug ;~(pose low nud) (star ;~(pose low nud)))))
1961    =/  torn=(list @tas)  (fall (rush suffix parser) ~[suffix])
1962    %-  flop
1963    |-  ^-  (list (list @tas))
1964    ?<  ?=(~ torn)
1965    ?:  ?=([@ ~] torn)
1966      ~[torn]
1967    %-  zing
1968    %+  turn  $(torn t.torn)
1969    |=  s=(list @tas)
```

```
1970        ^-  (list (list @tas))
1971        ?>  ?=(^ s)
1972      ~[[i.torn s] [(crip "{(trip i.torn)}-{(trip i.s)}") t.s]]
1973      --  ::clay
1974   ::                                                          ::::
1975   ::::                      ++dill                            :: (1d) console
1976      ::                                                       ::::
1977   ++  dill  ^?
1978      |%
1979      +$  gift                                                 :: out result <-$
1980        $%  [%blit p=(list blit)]                              :: terminal output
1981            [%logo ~]                                          :: logout
1982            [%meld ~]                                          :: unify memory
1983            [%pack ~]                                          :: compact memory
1984            [%trim p=@ud]                                      :: trim kernel state
1985            [%logs =told]                                      :: system output
1986        ==                                                     ::
1987      +$  task                                                 :: in request ->$
1988        $~  [%vega ~]                                          ::
1989        $%  [%boot lit=? p=*]                                  :: weird %dill boot
1990            [%crop p=@ud]                                      :: trim kernel state
1991            [%flog p=flog]                                     :: wrapped error
1992            [%heft ~]                                          :: memory report
1993            $>(%init vane-task)                                :: after gall ready
1994            [%logs p=(unit ~)]                                 :: watch system output
1995            [%meld ~]                                          :: unify memory
1996            [%pack ~]                                          :: compact memory
1997            [%seat =desk]                                      :: install desk
1998            [%shot ses=@tas task=session-task]                 :: task for session
1999            $>(%trim vane-task)                                :: trim state
2000            $>(%vega vane-task)                                :: report upgrade
2001            [%verb ~]                                          :: verbose mode
2002            [%knob tag=term level=?(%hush %soft %loud)]        :: deprecated removeme
2003            session-task                                       :: for default session
2004            told                                               :: system output
2005        ==                                                     ::
2006      ::                                                       ::
2007      +$  session-task                                         :: session request
2008        $%  [%belt p=belt]                                     :: terminal input
2009            [%blew p=blew]                                     :: terminal config
2010            [%flee ~]                                          :: unwatch session
2011            [%hail ~]                                          :: terminal refresh
2012            [%open p=dude:gall q=(list gill:gall)]             :: setup session
2013            [%shut ~]                                          :: close session
2014            [%view ~]                                          :: watch session blits
2015        ==                                                     ::
2016      ::                                                       ::
2017      +$  told                                                 :: system output
2018        $%  [%crud p=@tas q=tang]                              :: error
2019            [%talk p=(list tank)]                              :: tanks (in order)
2020            [%text p=tape]                                     :: tape
2021        ==                                                     ::
2022      ::                                                       ::
2023      ::::                                                     :: (1d2)
2024      ::
2025      +$  blew  [p=@ud q=@ud]                                  :: columns rows
2026      +$  belt                                                 :: client input
2027        $?  bolt                                               :: simple input
```

```
2028          [%mod mod=?(%ctl %met %hyp) key=bolt]      ::  w/ modifier
2029          [%txt p=(list @c)]                         ::  utf32 text
2030          ::TODO  consider moving %hey, %rez, %yow here  ::
2031      ==                                             ::
2032  +$  bolt                                           ::  simple input
2033    $@  @c                                           ::  simple keystroke
2034    $%  [%aro p=?(%d %l %r %u)]                       ::  arrow key
2035        [%bac ~]                                     ::  true backspace
2036        [%del ~]                                     ::  true delete
2037        [%hit x=@ud y=@ud]                           ::  mouse click
2038        [%ret ~]                                     ::  return
2039    ==                                               ::
2040  +$  blit                                           ::  client output
2041    $%  [%bel ~]                                     ::  make a noise
2042        [%clr ~]                                     ::  clear the screen
2043        [%hop p=$@(@ud [x=@ud y=@ud])]               ::  set cursor col/pos
2044        [%klr p=stub]                                ::  put styled
2045        [%mor p=(list blit)]                         ::  multiple blits
2046        [%nel ~]                                     ::  newline
2047        [%put p=(list @c)]                           ::  put text at cursor
2048        [%sag p=path q=*]                            ::  save to jamfile
2049        [%sav p=path q=@]                            ::  save to file
2050        [%url p=@t]                                  ::  activate url
2051        [%wyp ~]                                     ::  wipe cursor line
2052    ==                                               ::
2053  +$  dill-belt                                      ::  arvo input
2054    $%  belt                                         ::  client input
2055        [%cru p=@tas q=(list tank)]                   ::  errmsg (deprecated)
2056        [%hey ~]                                     ::  refresh
2057        [%rez p=@ud q=@ud]                           ::  resize, cols, rows
2058        [%yow p=gill:gall]                           ::  connect to app
2059    ==                                               ::
2060  +$  dill-blit                                      ::  arvo output
2061    $%  blit                                         ::  client output
2062        [%qit ~]                                     ::  close console
2063    ==                                               ::
2064  +$  flog                                           ::  sent to %dill
2065    $%  [%crop p=@ud]                                ::  trim kernel state
2066        $>(%crud told)                               ::
2067        [%heft ~]                                    ::
2068        [%meld ~]                                    ::  unify memory
2069        [%pack ~]                                    ::  compact memory
2070        $>(%text told)                               ::
2071        [%verb ~]                                    ::  verbose mode
2072    ==                                               ::
2073    ::                                               ::
2074  +$  poke                                           ::  dill to userspace
2075    $:  ses=@tas                                     ::  target session
2076        dill-belt                                    ::  input
2077    ==                                               ::
2078  --  ::dill                                         ::
2079  ::                                                 ::::
2080  ::::                        ++eyre                    ::  (1e) http-server
2081  ::                                                 ::::
2082  ++  eyre  ^?                                       
2083  |%                                                 
2084  +$  cache-entry                                    
2085    $:  auth=?                                       
```

```
2086      $=   body
2087      $%   [%payload =simple-payload:http]
2088      ==   ==
2089  +$  gift
2090      $%   ::  ames responses
2091           ::
2092           $>(?(%boon %done) gift:ames)
2093           ::  set-config: configures the external http server
2094           ::
2095           ::      TODO: We need to actually return a (map (unit @t) http-config)
2096           ::      so we can apply configurations on a per-site basis
2097           ::
2098           [%set-config =http-config]
2099           ::  sessions: valid authentication cookie strings
2100           ::
2101           [%sessions ses=(set @t)]
2102           ::  response: response to an event from earth
2103           ::
2104           [%response =http-event:http]
2105           ::  response to a %connect or %serve
2106           ::
2107           ::      :accepted is whether :binding was valid. Duplicate bindings are
2108           ::      not allowed.
2109           ::
2110           [%bound accepted=? =binding]
2111           ::  notification that a cache entry has changed
2112           ::
2113           [%grow =path]
2114      ==
2115      ::
2116  +$  task
2117      $~   [%vega ~]
2118      $%   ::  initializes ourselves with an identity
2119           ::
2120           $>(%init vane-task)
2121           ::  new unix process
2122           ::
2123           $>(%born vane-task)
2124           ::  network request
2125           ::
2126           $>(%plea vane-task)
2127           ::  trim state (in response to memory pressure)
2128           ::
2129           $>(%trim vane-task)
2130           ::  report upgrade
2131           ::
2132           $>(%vega vane-task)
2133           ::  notifies us of the ports of our live http servers
2134           ::
2135           [%live insecure=@ud secure=(unit @ud)]
2136           ::  update http configuration
2137           ::
2138           [%rule =http-rule]
2139           ::  set a base url for eauth, like `'https://sampel.com'
2140           ::
2141           ::      eyre will append /~/eauth to it internally to redirect into eauth
2142           ::
2143           [%eauth-host host=(unit @t)]
```

```
2144        ::    starts handling an inbound http request
2145        ::
2146        [%request secure=? =address =request:http]
2147        ::    starts handling an backdoor http request
2148        ::
2149        [%request-local secure=? =address =request:http]
2150        ::    cancels a previous request
2151        ::
2152        [%cancel-request ~]
2153        ::    connects a binding to an app
2154        ::
2155        [%connect =binding app=term]
2156        ::    connects a binding to a generator
2157        ::
2158        [%serve =binding =generator]
2159        ::    disconnects a binding
2160        ::
2161        ::      This must be called with the same duct that made the binding in
2162        ::      the first place.
2163        ::
2164        [%disconnect =binding]
2165        ::    notifies us that web login code changed
2166        ::
2167        [%code-changed ~]
2168        ::    start responding positively to cors requests from origin
2169        ::
2170        [%approve-origin =origin]
2171        ::    start responding negatively to cors requests from origin
2172        ::
2173        [%reject-origin =origin]
2174        ::    %spew: set verbosity toggle
2175        ::
2176        [%spew veb=@]
2177        ::    remember (or update) a cache mapping
2178        ::
2179        [%set-response url=@t entry=(unit cache-entry)]
2180      ==
2181  ::    +origin: request origin as specified in an Origin header
2182  ::
2183  +$  origin  @torigin
2184  ::    +cors-registry: origins categorized by approval status
2185  ::
2186  +$  cors-registry
2187    $:  requests=(set origin)
2188        approved=(set origin)
2189        rejected=(set origin)
2190      ==
2191  ::    +outstanding-connection: open http connections not fully complete:
2192  ::
2193  ::    This refers to outstanding connections where the connection to
2194  ::    outside is opened and we are currently waiting on an app to
2195  ::    produce the results.
2196  ::
2197  +$  outstanding-connection
2198    $:  ::    action: the action that had matched
2199        ::
2200        =action
2201        ::    inbound-request: the original request which caused this connection
```

```
2202        ::
2203      =inbound-request
2204        ::   session-id: the session associated with this connection
2205        ::   identity:   the identity associated with this connection
2206        ::
2207        ::NOTE  technically the identity is associated with the session (id),
2208        ::        but we may still need to know the identity that was used
2209        ::        after the session proper expires.
2210        ::
2211      [session-id=@uv =identity]
2212        ::   response-header: set when we get our first %start
2213        ::
2214      response-header=(unit response-header:http)
2215        ::   bytes-sent: the total bytes sent in response
2216        ::
2217      bytes-sent=@ud
2218    ==
2219  ::   +authentication-state: state used in the login system
2220  ::
2221  +$   authentication-state
2222    $:   ::   sessions: a mapping of session cookies to session information
2223         ::
2224      sessions=(map @uv session)
2225        ::   visitors: in-progress incoming eauth flows
2226        ::
2227      visitors=(map @uv visitor)
2228        ::   visiting: outgoing eauth state per ship
2229        ::
2230      visiting=(map ship logbook)
2231        ::   endpoint: hardcoded local eauth endpoint for %syn and %ack
2232        ::
2233        ::     user-configured or auth-o-detected, with last-updated timestamp.
2234        ::     both shaped like 'prot://host'
2235        ::
2236      endpoint=[user=(unit @t) auth=(unit @t) =time]
2237    ==
2238  ::   +session: server side data about a session
2239  ::
2240  +$   session
2241    $:   ::   identity: authentication level & id of this session
2242         ::
2243      =identity
2244        ::   expiry-time: when this session expires
2245        ::
2246        ::     We check this server side, too, so we aren't relying on the browser
2247        ::     to properly handle cookie expiration as a security mechanism.
2248        ::
2249      expiry-time=@da
2250        ::   channels: channels opened by this session
2251        ::
2252      channels=(set @t)
2253        ::
2254        ::   TODO: We should add a system for individual capabilities; we should
2255        ::   mint some sort of long lived cookie for mobile apps which only has
2256        ::   access to a single application path.
2257    ==
2258  ::   +visitor: completed or in-progress incoming eauth flow
2259  ::
```

```
2260    ::      duct: boon duct
2261    ::        and
2262    ::      sesh: login completed, session exists
2263    ::        or
2264    ::      pend: awaiting %tune for %keen sent at time, for initial eauth http req
2265    ::      ship: the @p attempting to log in
2266    ::      base: local protocol+hostname the attempt started on, if any
2267    ::      last: the url to redirect to after log-in
2268    ::      toke: authentication secret received over ames or offered by visitor
2269    ::
2270    +$  visitor
2271      $:  duct=(unit duct)
2272      $@  sesh=@uv
2273      $:  pend=(unit [http=duct keen=time])
2274          ship=ship
2275          base=(unit @t)
2276          last=@t
2277          toke=(unit @uv)
2278      ==  ==
2279    ::  +logbook: record of outgoing eauth comms & state
2280    ::
2281    ::      qeu: a queue of nonces for to-be-n/acked pleas
2282    ::      map: per nonce, completed or pending eauth session
2283    ::
2284    +$  logbook  [=(qeu @uv) =(map @uv portkey)]
2285    ::  +portkey: completed or in-progress outgoing eauth flow
2286    ::
2287    ::      made: live since
2288    ::        or
2289    ::      duct: confirm request awaiting redirect
2290    ::      toke: secret to include in redirect, unless aborting
2291    ::
2292    +$  portkey
2293      $@  made=@da           ::  live since
2294      $:  pend=(unit duct)   ::  or await redir
2295          toke=(unit @uv)    ::  with secret
2296      ==
2297    ::  +eauth-plea: client talking to host
2298    ::
2299    +$  eauth-plea
2300      $:  %0
2301      $%  ::  %open: client decided on an attempt, wants to return to url
2302          ::  %shut: client wants the attempt or session closed
2303          ::
2304          [%open nonce=@uv token=(unit @uv)]
2305          [%shut nonce=@uv]
2306      ==  ==
2307    ::  +eauth-boon: host responding to client
2308    ::
2309    +$  eauth-boon
2310      $:  %0
2311      $%  ::  %okay: attempt heard, client to finish auth through url
2312          ::  %shut: host has expired the session
2313          ::
2314          [%okay nonce=@uv url=@t]
2315          [%shut nonce=@uv]
2316      ==  ==
2317    ::  $identity: authentication method & @p
```

```
2318    ::
2319    +$  identity
2320      $~  [%ours ~]
2321      $%  [%ours ~]                              ::  local, root
2322          [%fake who=@p]                         ::  guest id
2323          [%real who=@p]                         ::  authed cross-ship
2324      ==
2325    ::  channel-state: state used in the channel system
2326    ::
2327    +$  channel-state
2328      $:  ::  session: mapping between an arbitrary key to a channel
2329          ::
2330          session=(map @t channel)
2331          ::  by-duct: mapping from ducts to session key
2332          ::
2333          duct-to-key=(map duct @t)
2334      ==
2335    ::  +timer: a reference to a timer so we can cancel or update it.
2336    ::
2337    +$  timer
2338      $:  ::  date: time when the timer will fire
2339          ::
2340          date=@da
2341          ::  duct: duct that set the timer so we can cancel
2342          ::
2343          =duct
2344      ==
2345    ::  channel-event: unacknowledged channel event, vaseless sign
2346    ::
2347    +$  channel-event
2348      $%  $>(%poke-ack sign:agent:gall)
2349          $>(%watch-ack sign:agent:gall)
2350          $>(%kick sign:agent:gall)
2351          [%fact =desk =mark =noun]
2352      ==
2353    ::  channel: connection to the browser
2354    ::
2355    ::    Channels are the main method where a webpage communicates with Gall
2356    ::    apps. Subscriptions and pokes are issues with PUT requests on a path,
2357    ::    while GET requests on that same path open a persistent EventSource
2358    ::    channel.
2359    ::
2360    ::    The EventSource API is a sequence number based API that browser provide
2361    ::    which allow the server to push individual events to the browser over a
2362    ::    connection held open. In case of reconnection, the browser will send a
2363    ::    'Last-Event-Id: ' header to the server; the server then resends all
2364    ::    events since then.
2365    ::
2366    +$  channel
2367      $:  mode=?(%json %jam)
2368          =identity
2369          ::  channel-state: expiration time or the duct currently listening
2370          ::
2371          ::    For each channel, there is at most one open EventSource
2372          ::    connection. A 400 is issues on duplicate attempts to connect to the
2373          ::    same channel. When an EventSource isn't connected, we set a timer
2374          ::    to reap the subscriptions. This timer shouldn't be too short
2375          ::    because the
```

```
2376          ::
2377          state=(each timer duct)
2378          ::  next-id: next sequence number to use
2379          ::
2380          next-id=@ud
2381          ::  last-ack: time of last client ack
2382          ::
2383          ::    used for clog calculations, in combination with :unacked
2384          ::
2385          last-ack=@da
2386          ::  events: unacknowledged events
2387          ::
2388          ::    We keep track of all events where we haven't received a
2389          ::    'Last-Event-Id: ' response from the client or a per-poke {'ack':
2390          ::    ...} call. When there's an active EventSource connection on this
2391          ::    channel, we send the event but we still add it to events because we
2392          ::    can't assume it got received until we get an acknowledgment.
2393          ::
2394          events=(qeu [id=@ud request-id=@ud =channel-event])
2395          ::  unacked: unacknowledged event counts by request-id
2396          ::
2397          ::    used for clog calculations, in combination with :last-ack
2398          ::
2399          unacked=(map @ud @ud)
2400          ::  subscriptions: gall subscriptions by request-id
2401          ::
2402          ::    We maintain a list of subscriptions so if a channel times out, we
2403          ::    can cancel all the subscriptions we've made.
2404          ::
2405          subscriptions=(map @ud [ship=@p app=term =path duc=duct])
2406          ::  heartbeat: sse heartbeat timer
2407          ::
2408          heartbeat=(unit timer)
2409        ==
2410    ::  +binding: A rule to match a path.
2411    ::
2412    ::    A +binding is a system unique mapping for a path to match. A +binding
2413    ::    must be system unique because we don't want two handlers for a path;
2414    ::    what happens if there are two different actions for [~ /]?
2415    ::
2416    +$  binding
2417      $:  ::  site: the site to match.
2418          ::
2419          ::    A ~ will match the Urbit's identity site (your.urbit.org). Any
2420          ::    other value will match a domain literal.
2421          ::
2422          site=(unit @t)
2423          ::  path: matches this prefix path
2424          ::
2425          ::    /~myapp will match /~myapp or /~myapp/longer/path
2426          ::
2427          path=(list @t)
2428      ==
2429    ::  +action: the action to take when a binding matches an incoming request
2430    ::
2431    +$  action
2432      $%  ::  dispatch to a generator
2433          ::
```

```
2434        [%gen =generator]
2435        ::  dispatch to an application
2436        ::
2437        [%app app=term]
2438        ::  internal authentication page
2439        ::
2440        [%authentication ~]
2441        ::  cross-ship authentication handling
2442        ::
2443        [%eauth ~]
2444        ::  internal logout page
2445        ::
2446        [%logout ~]
2447        ::  gall channel system
2448        ::
2449        [%channel ~]
2450        ::  gall scry endpoint
2451        ::
2452        [%scry ~]
2453        ::  respond with the @p the requester is authenticated as
2454        ::
2455        [%name ~]
2456        ::  respond with the @p of the ship serving the response
2457        ::
2458        [%host ~]
2459        ::  respond with the default file not found page
2460        ::
2461        [%four-oh-four ~]
2462      ==
2463  ::  +generator: a generator on the local ship that handles requests
2464  ::
2465  ::    This refers to a generator on the local ship, run with a set of
2466  ::    arguments. Since http requests are time sensitive, we require that the
2467  ::    generator be on the current ship.
2468  ::
2469  +$  generator
2470    $:  ::  desk: desk on current ship that contains the generator
2471        ::
2472        =desk
2473        ::  path: path on :desk to the generator's hoon file
2474        ::
2475        path=(list @t)
2476        ::  args: arguments passed to the gate
2477        ::
2478        args=*
2479    ==
2480  ::  +http-config: full http-server configuration
2481  ::
2482  +$  http-config
2483    $:  ::  secure: PEM-encoded RSA private key and cert or cert chain
2484        ::
2485        secure=(unit [key=wain cert=wain])
2486        ::  proxy: reverse TCP proxy HTTP(s)
2487        ::
2488        proxy=_|
2489        ::  log: keep HTTP(s) access logs
2490        ::
2491        log=?
```

```
2492        :: redirect: send 301 redirects to upgrade HTTP to HTTPS
2493        ::
2494        ::    Note: requires certificate.
2495        ::
2496        redirect=?
2497    ==
2498  :: +http-rule: update configuration
2499  ::
2500  +$  http-rule
2501    $%  :: %cert: set or clear certificate and keypair
2502        ::
2503        [%cert cert=(unit [key=wain cert=wain])]
2504        :: %turf: add or remove established dns binding
2505        ::
2506        [%turf action=?(%put %del) =turf]
2507    ==
2508  ::  +address: client IP address
2509  ::
2510  +$  address
2511    $%  [%ipv4 @if]
2512        [%ipv6 @is]
2513        ::  [%ames @p]
2514    ==
2515  ::  +inbound-request: +http-request and metadata
2516  ::
2517  +$  inbound-request
2518    $:  ::  authenticated: has a valid session cookie
2519        ::
2520        authenticated=?
2521        ::  secure: whether this request was encrypted (https)
2522        ::
2523        secure=?
2524        ::  address: the source address of this request
2525        ::
2526        =address
2527        ::  request: the http-request itself
2528        ::
2529        =request:http
2530    ==
2531  ::
2532  +$  cred                              :: credential
2533    $:  hut=hart                        :: client host
2534        aut=(jug @tas @t)              :: client identities
2535        orx=oryx                       :: CSRF secret
2536        acl=(unit @t)                  :: accept-language
2537        cip=(each @if @is)             :: client IP
2538        cum=(map @tas *)               :: custom dirt
2539    ==                                 ::
2540  +$  epic                              :: FCGI parameters
2541    $:  qix=(map @t @t)                :: query
2542        ced=cred                       :: client credentials
2543        bem=beam                       :: original path
2544    ==                                 ::
2545  ::
2546  +$  hart  [p=? q=(unit @ud) r=host]   :: http sec+port+host
2547  +$  hate  [p=purl q=@p r=moth]        :: semi-cooked request
2548  +$  hiss  [p=purl q=moth]             :: outbound request
2549  +$  host  (each turf @if)             :: http host
```

```
2550    +$  hoke  %+  each  [%localhost ~]              ::  local host
2551             ?(%.0.0.0.0 %.127.0.0.1)              ::
2552    +$  httq                                       ::  raw http request
2553      $:  p=meth                                   ::  method
2554          q=@t                                     ::  unparsed url
2555          r=(list [p=@t q=@t])                     ::  headers
2556          s=(unit octs)                            ::  body
2557      ==                                           ::
2558    +$  httr  [p=@ud q=mess r=(unit octs)]         ::  raw http response
2559    +$  math  (map @t (list @t))                   ::  semiparsed headers
2560    +$  mess  (list [p=@t q=@t])                   ::  raw http headers
2561    +$  meth                                       ::  http methods
2562      $?  %conn                                    ::  CONNECT
2563          %delt                                    ::  DELETE
2564          %get                                     ::  GET
2565          %head                                    ::  HEAD
2566          %opts                                    ::  OPTIONS
2567          %post                                    ::  POST
2568          %put                                     ::  PUT
2569          %trac                                    ::  TRACE
2570      ==                                           ::
2571    +$  moth  [p=meth q=math r=(unit octs)]        ::  http operation
2572    +$  oryx  @t                                   ::  CSRF secret
2573    +$  pork  [p=(unit @ta) q=(list @t)]           ::  fully parsed url
2574    ::  +prox: proxy notification
2575    ::
2576    ::  Used on both the proxy (ward) and upstream sides for
2577    ::  sending/receiving proxied-request notifications.
2578    ::
2579    +$  prox
2580      $:  ::  por: tcp port
2581          ::
2582          por=@ud
2583          ::  sek: secure?
2584          ::
2585          sek=?
2586          ::  non: authentication nonce
2587          ::
2588          non=@uvJ
2589      ==
2590    +$  purf  (pair purl (unit @t))                ::  url with fragment
2591    +$  purl  [p=hart q=pork r=quay]               ::  parsed url
2592    +$  quay  (list [p=@t q=@t])                   ::  parsed url query
2593    ++  quer  |-($@(~ [p=@t q=@t t=$]))            ::  query tree
2594    +$  quri                                       ::  request-uri
2595      $%  [%& p=purl]                              ::  absolute
2596          [%| p=pork q=quay]                       ::  relative
2597      ==                                           ::
2598    ::  +reserved: check if an ipv4 address is in a reserved range
2599    ::
2600    ++  reserved
2601      |=  a=@if
2602      ^-  ?
2603      =/  b  (flop (rip 3 a))
2604      ::  0.0.0.0/8 (software)
2605      ::
2606      ?.  ?=([@ @ @ @ ~] b)  &
2607      ?|  ::  10.0.0.0/8 (private)
```

```
2608            ::
2609            =(10 i.b)
2610            ::    100.64.0.0/10 (carrier-grade NAT)
2611            ::
2612            &(=(100 i.b) (gte i.t.b 64) (lte i.t.b 127))
2613            ::    127.0.0.0/8 (localhost)
2614            ::
2615            =(127 i.b)
2616            ::    169.254.0.0/16 (link-local)
2617            ::
2618            &(=(169 i.b) =(254 i.t.b))
2619            ::    172.16.0.0/12 (private)
2620            ::
2621            &(=(172 i.b) (gte i.t.b 16) (lte i.t.b 31))
2622            ::    192.0.0.0/24 (protocol assignment)
2623            ::
2624            &(=(192 i.b) =(0 i.t.b) =(0 i.t.t.b))
2625            ::    192.0.2.0/24 (documentation)
2626            ::
2627            &(=(192 i.b) =(0 i.t.b) =(2 i.t.t.b))
2628            ::    192.18.0.0/15 (reserved, benchmark)
2629            ::
2630            &(=(192 i.b) |(=(18 i.t.b) =(19 i.t.b)))
2631            ::    192.51.100.0/24 (documentation)
2632            ::
2633            &(=(192 i.b) =(51 i.t.b) =(100 i.t.t.b))
2634            ::    192.88.99.0/24 (reserved, ex-anycast)
2635            ::
2636            &(=(192 i.b) =(88 i.t.b) =(99 i.t.t.b))
2637            ::    192.168.0.0/16 (private)
2638            ::
2639            &(=(192 i.b) =(168 i.t.b))
2640            ::    203.0.113/24 (documentation)
2641            ::
2642            &(=(203 i.b) =(0 i.t.b) =(113 i.t.t.b))
2643            ::    224.0.0.0/8 (multicast)
2644            ::    240.0.0.0/4 (reserved, future)
2645            ::    255.255.255.255/32 (broadcast)
2646            ::
2647            (gte i.b 224)
2648      ==
2649    ::  +ipa: parse ip address
2650    ::
2651    ++  ipa
2652      ;~(pose (stag %ipv4 ip4) (stag %ipv6 ip6))
2653    ::  +ip4: parse ipv4 address
2654    ::
2655    ++  ip4
2656      =+  byt=(ape:ag ted:ab)
2657      (bass 256 ;~(plug byt (stun [3 3] ;~(pfix dot byt))))
2658    ::  +ip6: parse ipv6 address
2659    ::
2660    ++  ip6
2661      %+  bass  0x1.0000
2662      %+  sear
2663        |=  hexts=(list $@(@ [~ %zeros]))
2664        ^-  (unit (list @))
2665        ::  not every list of hextets is an ipv6 address
```

```
2666            ::
2667            =/  legit=?
2668              =+  l=(lent hexts)
2669              =+  c=|=(a=* ?=([~ %zeros] a))
2670              ?|  &((lth l 8) ?=([* ~] (skim hexts c)))
2671                  &(=(8 l) !(lien hexts c))
2672              ==
2673            ?.  legit  ~
2674            %-  some
2675            ::  expand zeros
2676            ::
2677            %-  zing
2678            %+  turn  hexts
2679            |=  hext=$@(@ [~ %zeros])
2680            ?@  hext  [hext]~
2681            (reap (sub 9 (lent hexts)) 0)
2682         ::  parse hextets, producing cell for shorthand zeroes
2683         ::
2684         |^  %+  cook
2685             |=  [a=(list @) b=(list [~ %zeros]) c=(list @)]
2686             :(welp a b c)
2687             ;~  plug
2688             (more col het)
2689             (stun [0 1] cel)
2690             (more col het)
2691             ==
2692         ++  cel  (cold `%zeros ;~(plug col col))
2693         ++  het  (bass 16 (stun [1 4] six:ab))
2694         --
2695       ::
2696       +$  rout  [p=(list host) q=path r=oryx s=path]       ::  http route (new)
2697       +$  user  knot                                        ::  username
2698       --  ::eyre
2699    ::                                                          ::::
2700    ::::                            ++gall                      ::  (1g) extensions
2701       ::                                                       ::::
2702 ++  gall  ^?
2703    |%
2704    +$  gift                                                ::  outgoing result
2705      $%  [%boon payload=*]                                 ::  ames response
2706          [%done error=(unit error:ames)]                   ::  ames message (n)ack
2707          [%flub ~]                                         ::  not ready to handle plea
2708          [%unto p=unto]                                    ::
2709      ==                                                    ::
2710    +$  task                                                ::  incoming request
2711      $~  [%vega ~]                                         ::
2712      $%  [%deal p=sack q=term r=deal]                      ::  full transmission
2713          [%sear =ship]                                     ::  clear pending queues
2714          [%jolt =desk =dude]                               ::  (re)start agent
2715          [%idle =dude]                                     ::  suspend agent
2716          [%load =load]                                     ::  load agent
2717          [%nuke =dude]                                     ::  delete agent
2718          [%doff dude=(unit dude) ship=(unit ship)]         ::  kill subscriptions
2719          [%rake dude=(unit dude) all=?]                    ::  reclaim old subs
2720          $>(%init vane-task)                               ::  set owner
2721          $>(%trim vane-task)                               ::  trim state
2722          $>(%vega vane-task)                               ::  report upgrade
2723          $>(%plea vane-task)                               ::  network request
```

```
2724           [%spew veb=(list verb)]                     ::  set verbosity
2725           [%sift dudes=(list dude)]                   ::  per agent
2726       ==                                              ::
2727   +$  bitt  (map duct (pair ship path))               ::  incoming subs
2728   +$  boat  (map [=wire =ship =term] [acked=? =path])  ::  outgoing subs
2729   +$  boar  (map [=wire =ship =term] nonce=@)          ::  and their nonces
2730   ::
2731   +$  path-state
2732     $:  bob=(unit @ud)
2733         fan=((mop @ud (pair @da (each page @uvI))) lte)
2734     ==
2735   +$  stats                                            ::  statistics
2736     $:  change=@ud                                     ::  processed move count
2737         eny=@uvJ                                       ::  entropy
2738         time=@da                                       ::  current event time
2739     ==
2740   +$  egg                                              ::  migratory agent state
2741     $%  [%nuke sky=(map spur @ud)]                     ::  see /sys/gall $yoke
2742         $:  %live
2743             control-duct=duct
2744             run-nonce=@t
2745             sub-nonce=@
2746             =stats
2747             =bitt
2748             =boat
2749             =boar
2750             code=~
2751             old-state=[%| vase]
2752             =beak
2753             marks=(map duct mark)
2754             sky=(map spur path-state)
2755             ken=(jug spar:ames wire)
2756     ==  ==
2757   +$  egg-any  $%([%15 egg])
2758   +$  bowl                                             ::  standard app state
2759     $:  $:  our=ship                                   ::  host
2760             src=ship                                   ::  guest
2761             dap=term                                   ::  agent
2762             sap=path                                   ::  provenance
2763         ==                                             ::
2764         $:  wex=boat                                   ::  outgoing subs
2765             sup=bitt                                   ::  incoming subs
2766             $=  sky                                    ::  scry bindings
2767             %+  map  path                              ::
2768             ((mop @ud (pair @da (each page @uvI))) lte) ::
2769         ==                                             ::
2770         $:  act=@ud                                    ::  change number
2771             eny=@uvJ                                   ::  entropy
2772             now=@da                                    ::  current time
2773             byk=beak                                   ::  load source
2774     ==  ==                                             ::
2775   +$  dude  term                                       ::  server identity
2776   +$  gill  (pair ship term)                           ::  general contact
2777   +$  load  (list [=dude =beak =agent])                ::  loadout
2778   +$  scar                                             ::  opaque duct
2779     $:  p=@ud                                          ::  bone sequence
2780         q=(map duct bone)                             ::  by duct
2781         r=(map bone duct)                             ::  by bone
```

```
      ==                                        ::
+$  suss  (trel dude @tas @da)                  ::  config report
+$  well  (pair desk term)                      ::
+$  deal
    $%  [%raw-poke =mark =noun]
        task:agent
    ==
+$  unto
    $%  [%raw-fact =mark =noun]
        sign:agent
    ==
::  TODO: add more flags?
::
+$  verb  ?(%odd)
::
::  +agent: app core
::
++  agent
  =<  form
  |%
  +$  step  (quip card form)
  +$  card  (wind note gift)
  +$  note
      $%  [%agent [=ship name=term] =task]
          [%arvo note-arvo]
          [%pyre =tang]
        ::
          [%grow =spur =page]
          [%tomb =case =spur]
          [%cull =case =spur]
      ==
  +$  task
      $%  [%watch =path]
          [%watch-as =mark =path]
          [%leave ~]
          [%poke =cage]
          [%poke-as =mark =cage]
      ==
  +$  gift
      $%  [%fact paths=(list path) =cage]
          [%kick paths=(list path) ship=(unit ship)]
          [%watch-ack p=(unit tang)]
          [%poke-ack p=(unit tang)]
      ==
  +$  sign
      $%  [%poke-ack p=(unit tang)]
          [%watch-ack p=(unit tang)]
          [%fact =cage]
          [%kick ~]
      ==
  ++  form
    $_  ^|
    |_  bowl
    ++  on-init
      *(quip card _^|(..on-init))
    ::
    ++  on-save
      *vase
```

```
2840          ::
2841          ++  on-load
2842          |~  old-state=vase
2843          *(quip card _^|(..on-init))
2844          ::
2845          ++  on-poke
2846          |~  [mark vase]
2847          *(quip card _^|(..on-init))
2848          ::
2849          ++  on-watch
2850          |~  path
2851          *(quip card _^|(..on-init))
2852          ::
2853          ++  on-leave
2854          |~  path
2855          *(quip card _^|(..on-init))
2856          ::
2857          ++  on-peek
2858          |~  path
2859          *(unit (unit cage))
2860          ::
2861          ++  on-agent
2862          |~  [wire sign]
2863          *(quip card _^|(..on-init))
2864          ::
2865          ++  on-arvo
2866          |~  [wire sign-arvo]
2867          *(quip card _^|(..on-init))
2868          ::
2869          ++  on-fail
2870          |~  [term tang]
2871          *(quip card _^|(..on-init))
2872          --
2873      --
2874  --  ::gall
2875  ::  %iris http-client interface
2876  ::
2877  ++  iris  ^?
2878  |%
2879  ::  +gift: effects the client can emit
2880  ::
2881  +$  gift
2882    $%  ::  %request: outbound http-request to earth
2883        ::
2884        ::    TODO: id is sort of wrong for this interface; the duct should
2885        ::    be enough to identify which request we're talking about?
2886        ::
2887        [%request id=@ud request=request:http]
2888        ::  %cancel-request: tell earth to cancel a previous %request
2889        ::
2890        [%cancel-request id=@ud]
2891        ::  %response: response to the caller
2892        ::
2893        [%http-response =client-response]
2894    ==
2895  ::
2896  +$  task
2897    $~  [%vega ~]
```

```
2898      $%  ::  system started up; reset open connections
2899          ::
2900      $>(%born vane-task)
2901          ::  trim state (in response to memory pressure)
2902          ::
2903      $>(%trim vane-task)
2904          ::  report upgrade
2905          ::
2906      $>(%vega vane-task)
2907          ::  fetches a remote resource
2908          ::
2909      [%request =request:http =outbound-config]
2910          ::  cancels a previous fetch
2911          ::
2912      [%cancel-request ~]
2913          ::  receives http data from outside
2914          ::
2915      [%receive id=@ud =http-event:http]
2916    ==
2917  ::  +client-response: one or more client responses given to the caller
2918  ::
2919  +$  client-response
2920    $%  ::  periodically sent as an update on the duct that sent %fetch
2921        ::
2922        $:  %progress
2923            ::  http-response-header: full transaction header
2924            ::
2925            ::    In case of a redirect chain, this is the target of the
2926            ::    final redirect.
2927            ::
2928            =response-header:http
2929            ::  bytes-read: bytes fetched so far
2930            ::
2931            bytes-read=@ud
2932            ::  expected-size: the total size if response had a content-length
2933            ::
2934            expected-size=(unit @ud)
2935            ::  incremental: data received since the last %http-progress
2936            ::
2937            incremental=(unit octs)
2938        ==
2939        ::  final response of a download, parsed as mime-data if successful
2940        ::
2941        [%finished =response-header:http full-file=(unit mime-data)]
2942        ::  canceled by the runtime system
2943        ::
2944        [%cancel ~]
2945    ==
2946  ::  mime-data: externally received but unvalidated mimed data
2947  ::
2948  +$  mime-data
2949    [type=@t data=octs]
2950  ::  +outbound-config: configuration for outbound http requests
2951  ::
2952  +$  outbound-config
2953    $:  ::  number of times to follow a 300 redirect before erroring
2954        ::
2955        ::    Common values for this will be 3 (the limit most browsers use), 5
```

```
2956          ::      (the limit recommended by the http standard), or 0 (let the
2957          ::      requester deal with 300 redirects).
2958          ::
2959          redirects=_5
2960          ::  number of times to retry before failing
2961          ::
2962          ::      When we retry, we'll automatically try to use the 'Range' header
2963          ::      to resume the download where we left off if we have the
2964          ::      'Accept-Range: bytes' in the original response.
2965          ::
2966          retries=_3
2967      ==
2968  ::  +to-httr: adapts to old eyre interface
2969  ::
2970  ++  to-httr
2971    |=  [header=response-header:http full-file=(unit mime-data)]
2972    ^-  httr:eyre
2973    ::
2974    =/  data=(unit octs)
2975      ?~(full-file ~ `data.u.full-file)
2976    ::
2977    [status-code.header headers.header data]
2978    --
2979  ::                                                          ::::
2980  ::::                          ++jael                        ::  (1h) security
2981    ::                                                        ::::
2982  ++  jael  ^?
2983    |%
2984    +$  public-keys-result
2985      $%  [%full points=(map ship point)]
2986          [%diff who=ship =diff:point]
2987          [%breach who=ship]
2988      ==
2989    ::                                                  ::
2990    +$  gift                                            ::  out result <-$
2991      $%  [%done error=(unit error:ames)]               ::  ames message (n)ack
2992          [%boon payload=*]                             ::  ames response
2993          [%private-keys =life vein=(map life ring)]    ::  private keys
2994          [%public-keys =public-keys-result]            ::  ethereum changes
2995          [%turf turf=(list turf)]                      ::  domains
2996      ==                                                ::
2997    ::  +feed: potential boot parameters
2998    ::
2999    +$  feed
3000      $^  [[%1 ~] who=ship kyz=(list [lyf=life key=ring])]
3001      seed
3002    ::  +seed: individual boot parameters
3003    ::
3004    +$  seed  [who=ship lyf=life key=ring sig=(unit oath:pki)]
3005    ::
3006    +$  task                                            ::  in request ->$
3007      $~  [%vega ~]                                     ::
3008      $%  [%dawn dawn-event]                            ::  boot from keys
3009          [%fake =ship]                                 ::  fake boot
3010          [%listen whos=(set ship) =source]             ::  set ethereum source
3011          ::TODO %next for generating/putting new private key
3012          [%meet =ship =life =pass]                     ::  met after breach
3013          [%moon =ship =udiff:point]                    ::  register moon keys
```

```
3014        [%nuke whos=(set ship)]                    ::  cancel tracker from
3015        [%private-keys ~]                          ::  sub to privates
3016        [%public-keys ships=(set ship)]            ::  sub to publics
3017        [%rekey =life =ring]                       ::  update private keys
3018        [%resend ~]                                ::  resend private key
3019        [%ruin ships=(set ship)]                   ::  pretend breach
3020        $>(%trim vane-task)                        ::  trim state
3021        [%turf ~]                                  ::  view domains
3022        $>(%vega vane-task)                        ::  report upgrade
3023        $>(%plea vane-task)                        ::  ames request
3024        [%step ~]                                  ::  reset web login code
3025      ==                                           ::
3026    ::
3027    +$  dawn-event
3028      $:  =seed
3029          spon=(list [=ship point:azimuth-types])
3030          czar=(map ship [=rift =life =pass])
3031          turf=(list turf)
3032          bloq=@ud
3033          node=(unit purl:eyre)
3034      ==
3035    ::
3036    ++  block
3037      =<  block
3038      |%
3039      +$  hash    @uxblockhash
3040      +$  number  @udblocknumber
3041      +$  id      [=hash =number]
3042      +$  block   [=id =parent=hash]
3043      --
3044    ::
3045    ::  Azimuth points form a groupoid, where the objects are all the
3046    ::  possible values of +point and the arrows are the possible values
3047    ::  of (list point-diff).  Composition of arrows is concatenation,
3048    ::  and you can apply the diffs to a +point with +apply.
3049    ::
3050    ::  It's simplest to consider +point as the coproduct of three
3051    ::  groupoids, Rift, Keys, and Sponsor.  Recall that the coproduct
3052    ::  of monoids is the free monoid (Kleene star) of the coproduct of
3053    ::  the underlying sets of the monoids.  The construction for
3054    ::  groupoids is similar.  Thus, the objects of the coproduct are
3055    ::  the product of the objects of the underlying groupoids.  The
3056    ::  arrows are a list of a sum of the diff types of the underlying
3057    ::  groupoids.  Given an arrow=(list diff), you can project to the
3058    ::  underlying arrows with +skim filtering on the head of each diff.
3059    ::
3060    ::  The identity element is ~.  Clearly, composing this with any
3061    ::  +diff gives the original +diff.  Since this is a category,
3062    ::  +compose must be associative (true, because concatenation is
3063    ::  associative).  This is a groupoid, so we must further have that
3064    ::  every +point-diff has an inverse.  These are given by the
3065    ::  +inverse operation.
3066    ::
3067    ++  point
3068      =<  point
3069      |%
3070      +$  point
3071        $:  =rift
```

```
3072              =life
3073              keys=(map life [crypto-suite=@ud =pass])
3074              sponsor=(unit @p)
3075          ==
3076      ::
3077      +$  key-update  [=life crypto-suite=@ud =pass]
3078      ::
3079      ::  Invertible diffs
3080      ::
3081      +$  diffs  (list diff)
3082      +$  diff
3083        $%  [%rift from=rift to=rift]
3084            [%keys from=key-update to=key-update]
3085            [%spon from=(unit @p) to=(unit @p)]
3086        ==
3087      ::
3088      ::  Non-invertible diffs
3089      ::
3090      +$  udiffs  (list [=ship =udiff])
3091      +$  udiff
3092        $:  =id:block
3093        $%  [%rift =rift boot=?]
3094            [%keys key-update boot=?]
3095            [%spon sponsor=(unit @p)]
3096            [%disavow ~]
3097        ==  ==
3098      ::
3099      ++  udiff-to-diff
3100        |=  [=a=udiff =a=point]
3101        ^-  (unit diff)
3102        ?-    +<.a-udiff
3103            %disavow  ~|(%udiff-to-diff-disavow !!)
3104            %spon     `[%spon sponsor.a-point sponsor.a-udiff]
3105            %rift
3106          ?.  (gth rift.a-udiff rift.a-point)
3107            ~
3108          ~?  &(!=(rift.a-udiff +(rift.a-point)) !boot.a-udiff)
3109            [%udiff-to-diff-skipped-rift a-udiff a-point]
3110          `[%rift rift.a-point rift.a-udiff]
3111        ::
3112            %keys
3113          ?.  (gth life.a-udiff life.a-point)
3114            ~
3115          ~?  &(!=(life.a-udiff +(life.a-point)) !boot.a-udiff)
3116            [%udiff-to-diff-skipped-life a-udiff a-point]
3117          :^  ~  %keys
3118            [life.a-point (~(gut by keys.a-point) life.a-point *[@ud pass])]
3119          [life crypto-suite pass]:a-udiff
3120        ==
3121      ::
3122      ++  inverse
3123        |=  diffs=(list diff)
3124        ^-  (list diff)
3125        %-  flop
3126        %+  turn  diffs
3127        |=  =diff
3128        ^-  ^diff
3129        ?-  -.diff
```

```
3130          %rift    [%rift to from]:diff
3131          %keys    [%keys to from]:diff
3132          %spon    [%spon to from]:diff
3133        ==
3134      ::
3135      ++  compose
3136        (bake weld ,[(list diff) (list diff)])
3137      ::
3138      ++  apply
3139        |=  [diffs=(list diff) =a=point]
3140        (roll diffs (apply-diff a-point))
3141      ::
3142      ++  apply-diff
3143        |=  a=point
3144        |:  [*=diff a-point=a]
3145        ^-  point
3146        ?-    -.diff
3147            %rift
3148          ?>  =(rift.a-point from.diff)
3149          a-point(rift to.diff)
3150        ::
3151            %keys
3152          ?>  =(life.a-point life.from.diff)
3153          ?>  =((~(get by keys.a-point) life.a-point) `+.from.diff)
3154          %_  a-point
3155            life  life.to.diff
3156            keys  (~(put by keys.a-point) life.to.diff +.to.diff)
3157          ==
3158        ::
3159            %spon
3160          ?>  =(sponsor.a-point from.diff)
3161          a-point(sponsor to.diff)
3162        ==
3163      --
3164    ::                                              ::
3165    ::::                                            ::
3166      ::                                            ::
3167    +$  source  (each ship term)
3168    +$  source-id  @udsourceid
3169    ::
3170    ::  +state-eth-node: state of a connection to an ethereum node
3171    ::
3172    +$  state-eth-node                              ::  node config + meta
3173      $:  top-source-id=source-id
3174          sources=(map source-id source)
3175          sources-reverse=(map source source-id)
3176          default-source=source-id
3177          ship-sources=(map ship source-id)
3178          ship-sources-reverse=(jug source-id ship)
3179      ==                                            ::
3180    ::                                              ::
3181    ::::                      ++pki:jael            ::  (1h2) certificates
3182      ::                                            ::::
3183    ++  pki  ^?
3184      |%
3185      ::TODO  update to fit azimuth-style keys
3186      ::  the urbit meta-certificate (++will) is a sequence
3187      ::  of certificates (++cert).  each cert in a will
```

```
3188      ::  revokes and replaces the previous cert.  the
3189      ::  version number of a ship is a ++life.
3190      ::
3191      ::  the deed contains an ++arms, a definition
3192      ::  of cosmetic identity; a semi-trusted parent,
3193      ::  which signs the initial certificate and provides
3194      ::  routing services; and a dirty bit.  if the dirty
3195      ::  bit is set, the new life of this ship may have
3196      ::  lost information that the old life had.
3197      ::
3198      +$  hand  @uvH                              ::  128-bit hash
3199      +$  mind  [who=ship lyf=life]               ::  key identifier
3200      +$  name  (pair @ta @t)                     ::  ascii / unicode
3201      +$  oath  @                                 ::  signature
3202      ++  tale                                    ::  urbit-signed *
3203        |$  [typ]                                 ::  payload mold
3204        $:  dat=typ                               ::  data
3205            syg=(map ship (pair life oath))       ::  signatures
3206        ==                                        ::
3207      --  ::  pki
3208    --  ::  jael
3209  ::                                              ::::
3210  ::::                        ++khan              ::  (1i) threads
3211    ::                                            ::::
3212  ++  khan  ^?
3213    |%
3214    +$  gift                                      ::  out result <-$
3215      $%  [%arow p=(avow cage)]                   ::  in-arvo result
3216          [%avow p=(avow page)]                   ::  external result
3217      ==                                          ::
3218    +$  task                                      ::  in request ->$
3219      $~  [%vega ~]                               ::
3220      $%  $>(%born vane-task)                     ::  new unix process
3221          [%done ~]                               ::  socket closed
3222          ::  TODO  mark ignored                  ::
3223          ::                                      ::
3224          [%fard p=(fyrd cage)]                   ::  in-arvo thread
3225          [%fyrd p=(fyrd cast)]                   ::  external thread
3226          [%lard =bear =shed]                     ::  inline thread
3227          $>(%trim vane-task)                     ::  trim state
3228          $>(%vega vane-task)                     ::  report upgrade
3229      ==                                          ::
3230    ::                                            ::
3231    ++  avow  |$  [a]  (each a goof)             ::  $fyrd result
3232    +$  bear  $@(desk beak)                       ::  partial $beak
3233    +$  cast  (pair mark page)                    ::  output mark + input
3234    ++  fyrd  |$  [a]  [=bear name=term args=a]   ::  thread run request
3235    ::                                            ::
3236    +$  shed  _*form:(strand:rand ,vase)          ::  compute vase
3237    --  ::khan
3238  ::                                              ::::
3239  ::::                        ++lick              ::  (1j) IPC
3240    ::                                            ::::
3241  ++  lick  ^?
3242    |%
3243    +$  gift                                      ::  out result <-$
3244      $%  [%spin =name]                           ::  open an IPC port
3245          [%shut =name]                           ::  close an IPC port
```

```
3246          [%spit =name =mark =noun]                    :: spit a noun to the IPC port
3247          [%soak =name =mark =noun]                    :: soak a noun from the IPC port
3248        ==
3249    +$  task                                           :: in request ->$
3250      $~  [%vega ~]                                     ::
3251      $%  $>(%born vane-task)                          :: new unix process
3252          $>(%trim vane-task)                          :: trim state
3253          $>(%vega vane-task)                          :: report upgrade
3254          [%spin =name]                                :: open an IPC port
3255          [%shut =name]                                :: close an IPC port
3256          [%spit =name =mark =noun]                    :: spit a noun to the IPC port
3257          [%soak =name =mark =noun]                    :: soak a noun from the IPC port
3258        ==
3259    ::
3260    +$  name  path
3261    --  ::lick
3262 ::
3263 ++  rand                                              :: computation
3264   |%
3265   +$  card  card:agent:gall
3266   +$  input
3267     $%  [%poke =cage]
3268         [%sign =wire =sign-arvo]
3269         [%agent =wire =sign:agent:gall]
3270         [%watch =path]
3271       ==
3272   +$  strand-input  [=bowl in=(unit input)]
3273   +$  tid    @tatid
3274   +$  bowl
3275     $:  our=ship
3276         src=ship
3277         tid=tid
3278         mom=(unit tid)
3279         wex=boat:gall
3280         sup=bitt:gall
3281         eny=@uvJ
3282         now=@da
3283         byk=beak
3284       ==
3285   ::
3286   ::  cards:  cards to send immediately.  These will go out even if a
3287   ::          later stage of the computation fails, so they shouldn't have
3288   ::          any semantic effect on the rest of the system.
3289   ::          Alternately, they may record an entry in contracts with
3290   ::          enough information to undo the effect if the computation
3291   ::          fails.
3292   ::  wait:  don't move on, stay here.  The next sign should come back
3293   ::         to this same callback.
3294   ::  skip:  didn't expect this input; drop it down to be handled
3295   ::         elsewhere
3296   ::  cont:  continue computation with new callback.
3297   ::  fail:  abort computation; don't send effects
3298   ::  done:  finish computation; send effects
3299   ::
3300   ++  strand-output-raw
3301     |*  a=mold
3302     $~  [~ %done *a]
3303     $:  cards=(list card)
```

```
3304          $=    next
3305          $%    [%wait ~]
3306                [%skip ~]
3307                [%cont self=(strand-form-raw a)]
3308                [%fail err=(pair term tang)]
3309                [%done value=a]
3310          ==
3311      ==
3312    ::
3313    ++  strand-form-raw
3314      |*  a=mold
3315      $-(strand-input (strand-output-raw a))
3316    ::
3317    ::  Abort strand computation with error message
3318    ::
3319    ++  strand-fail
3320      |=  err=(pair term tang)
3321      |=  strand-input
3322      [~ %fail err]
3323    ::
3324    ::  Asynchronous transcaction monad.
3325    ::
3326    ::  Combo of four monads:
3327    ::  - Reader on input
3328    ::  - Writer on card
3329    ::  - Continuation
3330    ::  - Exception
3331    ::
3332    ++  strand
3333      |*  a=mold
3334      |%
3335      ++  output  (strand-output-raw a)
3336      ::
3337      ::  Type of an strand computation.
3338      ::
3339      ++  form  (strand-form-raw a)
3340      ::
3341      ::  Monadic pure.  Identity computation for bind.
3342      ::
3343      ++  pure
3344        |=  arg=a
3345        ^-  form
3346        |=  strand-input
3347        [~ %done arg]
3348      ::
3349      ::  Monadic bind.  Combines two computations, associatively.
3350      ::
3351      ++  bind
3352        |*  b=mold
3353        |=  [m-b=(strand-form-raw b) fun=$-(b form)]
3354        ^-  form
3355        |=  input=strand-input
3356        =/  b-res=(strand-output-raw b)
3357          (m-b input)
3358        ^-  output
3359        :-  cards.b-res
3360        ?-    -.next.b-res
3361          %wait  [%wait ~]
```

```
3362        %skip  [%skip ~]
3363        %cont  [%cont ..$(m-b self.next.b-res)]
3364        %fail  [%fail err.next.b-res]
3365        %done  [%cont (fun value.next.b-res)]
3366      ==
3367    ::
3368    ::  The strand monad must be evaluted in a particular way to maintain
3369    ::  its monadic character.  +take:eval implements this.
3370    ::
3371    ++  eval
3372      |%
3373      ::  Indelible state of a strand
3374      ::
3375      +$  eval-form
3376        $:  =form
3377        ==
3378      ::
3379      ::  Convert initial form to eval-form
3380      ::
3381      ++  from-form
3382        |=  =form
3383        ^-  eval-form
3384        form
3385      ::
3386      ::  The cases of results of +take
3387      ::
3388      +$  eval-result
3389        $%  [%next ~]
3390            [%fail err=(pair term tang)]
3391            [%done value=a]
3392        ==
3393      ::
3394      ++  validate-mark
3395        |=  [in=* =mark =bowl]
3396        ^-  cage
3397        =+  .^  =dais:clay  %cb
3398                /(scot %p our.bowl)/[q.byk.bowl]/(scot %da now.bowl)/[mark]
3399            ==
3400        =/  res  (mule |.((vale.dais in)))
3401        ?:  ?=(%| -.res)
3402          ~|  %spider-mark-fail
3403          (mean leaf+"spider: ames vale fail {<mark>}" p.res)
3404        [mark p.res]
3405      ::
3406      ::  Take a new sign and run the strand against it
3407      ::
3408      ++  take
3409        ::  cards: accumulate throughout recursion the cards to be
3410        ::         produced now
3411        =|  cards=(list card)
3412        |=  [=eval-form =strand-input]
3413        ^-  [[(list card) =eval-result] _eval-form]
3414        =*  take-loop  $
3415        =.  in.strand-input
3416          ?~  in.strand-input  ~
3417          =/  in  u.in.strand-input
3418          ?.  ?=(%agent -.in)        `in
3419          ?.  ?=(%fact -.sign.in)    `in
```

```
3420              ::
3421              :-  ~
3422              :^  %agent  wire.in  %fact
3423              (validate-mark q.q.cage.sign.in p.cage.sign.in bowl.strand-input)
3424          ::  run the strand callback
3425          ::
3426          =/  =output  (form.eval-form strand-input)
3427          ::  add cards to cards
3428          ::
3429          =.  cards
3430            %+  welp
3431              cards
3432            ::  XX add tag to wires?
3433            cards.output
3434          ::  case-wise handle next steps
3435          ::
3436          ?-  -.next.output
3437            %wait  [[cards %next ~] eval-form]
3438            %skip  [[cards %next ~] eval-form]
3439            %fail  [[cards %fail err.next.output] eval-form]
3440            %done  [[cards %done value.next.output] eval-form]
3441            %cont
3442          ::  recurse to run continuation with initialization input
3443          ::
3444            %_  take-loop
3445              form.eval-form  self.next.output
3446              strand-input    [bowl.strand-input ~]
3447            ==
3448          ==
3449        --
3450      --
3451    --  ::strand
3452  ::
3453  +$  gift-arvo                                ::  out result <-$
3454    $~  [%doze ~]
3455    $%  gift:ames
3456        gift:behn
3457        gift:clay
3458        gift:dill
3459        gift:eyre
3460        gift:gall
3461        gift:iris
3462        gift:jael
3463        gift:khan
3464        gift:lick
3465    ==
3466  +$  task-arvo                                ::  in request ->$
3467    $%  task:ames
3468        task:clay
3469        task:behn
3470        task:dill
3471        task:eyre
3472        task:gall
3473        task:iris
3474        task:jael
3475        task:khan
3476        task:lick
3477    ==
```

```
3478  +$  note-arvo                                        ::  out request $->
3479    $~  [%b %wake ~]
3480    $%  [%a task:ames]
3481        [%b task:behn]
3482        [%c task:clay]
3483        [%d task:dill]
3484        [%e task:eyre]
3485        [%g task:gall]
3486        [%i task:iris]
3487        [%j task:jael]
3488        [%k task:khan]
3489        [%l task:lick]
3490        [%$ %whiz ~]
3491        [@tas %meta vase]
3492    ==
3493  ::  full vane names are required in vanes
3494  ::
3495  +$  sign-arvo                                        ::  in result $<-
3496    $%  [%ames gift:ames]
3497        $:  %behn
3498            $%  gift:behn
3499                $>(%wris gift:clay)
3500                $>(%writ gift:clay)
3501                $>(%mere gift:clay)
3502                $>(%unto gift:gall)
3503            ==
3504        ==
3505        [%clay gift:clay]
3506        [%dill gift:dill]
3507        [%eyre gift:eyre]
3508        [%gall gift:gall]
3509        [%iris gift:iris]
3510        [%jael gift:jael]
3511        [%khan gift:khan]
3512        [%lick gift:lick]
3513    ==
3514  ::  $unix-task: input from unix
3515  ::
3516  +$  unix-task                                        ::  input from unix
3517    $~  [%wake ~]
3518    $%  ::  %dill: keyboard input
3519        ::
3520        $>(%belt task:dill)
3521        ::  %dill: configure terminal (resized)
3522        ::
3523        $>(%blew task:dill)
3524        ::  %clay: new process
3525        ::
3526        $>(%boat task:clay)
3527        ::  %behn/%eyre/%iris: new process
3528        ::
3529        $>(%born vane-task)
3530        ::  %eyre: cancel request
3531        ::
3532        [%cancel-request ~]
3533        ::  %dill: reset terminal configuration
3534        ::
3535        $>(%hail task:dill)
```

```
3536    ::    %ames: hear packet
3537    ::
3538    $>(%hear task:ames)
3539    ::    %clay: external edit
3540    ::
3541    $>(%into task:clay)
3542    ::    %clay: synchronous commit
3543    ::
3544    ::      TODO: make $yuki an option for %into?
3545    ::
3546    $>(%park task:clay)
3547    ::    %clay: load blob store
3548    ::
3549    $>(%prep task:clay)
3550    ::    %eyre: learn ports of live http servers
3551    ::
3552    $>(%live task:eyre)
3553    ::    %iris: hear (partial) http response
3554    ::
3555    $>(%receive task:iris)
3556    ::    %eyre: starts handling an inbound http request
3557    ::
3558    $>(%request task:eyre)
3559    ::    %eyre: starts handling an backdoor http request
3560    ::
3561    $>(%request-local task:eyre)
3562    ::    %dill: close session
3563    ::
3564    $>(%shut task:dill)
3565    ::    %behn: wakeup
3566    ::
3567    $>(%wake task:behn)
3568    ==
3569  --  ::
```

Zuse 412K

```
1  ::    /sys/zuse
2  ::    %zuse: arvo library
3  ::
4  =>    ..lull
5  ~%  %zuse  ..part  ~
6  |%
7  ++    zuse  %412
8  ::                                                          ::    ::
9  :::::                                                       ::    ::   (2) engines
10   ::                                                        ::    ::
11  ::                                                         :::::
12  :::::                         ++number                    ::    (2a) number theory
13   ::                                                        :::::
14 ++  number  ^?
15   |%
16    ::                                                       ::    ++fu:number
17   ++  fu                                                    ::    modulo (mul p q)
18    |=   a=[p=@ q=@]
19    =+  b=?:(=([0 0] a) 0 (~(inv fo p.a) (~(sit fo p.a) q.a)))
20    |%
21     ::                                                      ::    ++dif:fu:number
22    ++  dif                                                  ::    subtract
23     |=  [c=[@ @] d=[@ @]]
24     [(~(dif fo p.a) -.c -.d) (~(dif fo q.a) +.c +.d)]
25     ::                                                      ::    ++exp:fu:number
26    ++  exp                                                  ::    exponent
27     |=  [c=@ d=[@ @]]
28     :-  (~(exp fo p.a) (mod c (dec p.a)) -.d)
29     (~(exp fo q.a) (mod c (dec q.a)) +.d)
30     ::                                                      ::    ++out:fu:number
31    ++  out                                                  ::    garner's formula
32     |=   c=[@ @]
33     %+  add   +.c
34     %+  mul   q.a
35     %+  ~(pro fo p.a)  b
36     (~(dif fo p.a) -.c (~(sit fo p.a) +.c))
37     ::                                                      ::    ++pro:fu:number
38    ++  pro                                                  ::    multiply
39     |=  [c=[@ @] d=[@ @]]
40     [(~(pro fo p.a) -.c -.d) (~(pro fo q.a) +.c +.d)]
41     ::                                                      ::    ++sum:fu:number
42    ++  sum                                                  ::    add
43     |=  [c=[@ @] d=[@ @]]
44     [(~(sum fo p.a) -.c -.d) (~(sum fo q.a) +.c +.d)]
45     ::                                                      ::    ++sit:fu:number
46    ++  sit                                                  ::    represent
47     |=   c=@
48     [(mod c p.a) (mod c q.a)]
49    --  ::fu
50   ::                                                        ::    ++pram:number
51   ++  pram                                                  ::    rabin-miller
52    |=  a=@  ^-  ?
53    ?:  ?|  =(0 (end 0 a))
54            =(1 a)
55            =+   b=1
```

```
56          |-   ^-   ?
57          ?:   =(512 b)
58          |
59          ?|(=+(c=+((mul 2 b)) &(!=(a c) =(a (mul c (div a c))))) $(b +(b)))
60        ==
61      |
62    =+   ^=   b
63      =+   [s=(dec a) t=0]
64      |-   ^-   [s=@ t=@]
65      ?:   =(0 (end 0 s))
66        $(s (rsh 0 s), t +(t))
67      [s t]
68    ?>   =((mul s.b (bex t.b)) (dec a))
69    =+   c=0
70    |-   ^-   ?
71    ?:   =(c 64)
72        &
73    =+   d=(~(raw og (add c a)) (met 0 a))
74    =+   e=(~(exp fo a) s.b d)
75    ?&   ?|   =(1 e)
76             =+   f=0
77             |-   ^-   ?
78          ?:   =(e (dec a))
79             &
80          ?:   =(f (dec t.b))
81             |
82          $(e (~(pro fo a) e e), f +(f))
83        ==
84      $(c +(c))
85    ==
86    ::                                           ::  ++ramp:number
87  ++   ramp                                      ::  make r-m prime
88    |=   [a=@ b=(list @) c=@]   ^-   @ux         ::  [bits snags seed]
89    =>   .(c (shas %ramp c))
90    =+   d=*@
91    |-
92    ?:   =((mul 100 a) d)
93      ~|(%ar-ramp !!)
94    =+   e=(~(raw og c) a)
95    ?:   &((levy b |=(f=@ !=(1 (mod e f)))) (pram e))
96        e
97      $(c +(c), d (shax d))
98    ::                                           ::  ++curt:number
99  ++   curt                                      ::  curve25519
100   |=   [a=@ b=@]
101   =>   %=      .
102        +
103     =>   +
104     =+   =+   [p=486.662 q=(sub (bex 255) 19)]
105          =+   fq=~(. fo q)
106        [p=p q=q fq=fq]
107     |%
108     ::                                         ::  ++cla:curt:number
109     ++   cla                                   ::
110       |=   raw=@
111     =+   low=(dis 248 (cut 3 [0 1] raw))
112     =+   hih=(con 64 (dis 127 (cut 3 [31 1] raw)))
113     =+   mid=(cut 3 [1 30] raw)
```

```
114              (can 3 [[1 low] [30 mid] [1 hih] ~])
115          ::                                    ::   ++sqr:curt:number
116          ++  sqr                               ::
117          |=(a=@ (mul a a))
118          ::                                    ::   ++inv:curt:number
119          ++  inv                               ::
120          |=(a=@ (~(exp fo q) (sub q 2) a))
121          ::                                    ::   ++cad:curt:number
122          ++  cad                               ::
123          |=  [n=[x=@ z=@] m=[x=@ z=@] d=[x=@ z=@]]
124          =+  ^=  xx
125            ;:  mul  4   z.d
126              %-  sqr  %-  abs:si
127              %+  dif:si
128                (sun:si (mul x.m x.n))
129                (sun:si (mul z.m z.n))
130            ==
131          =+  ^=  zz
132            ;:  mul  4   x.d
133              %-  sqr  %-  abs:si
134              %+  dif:si
135                (sun:si (mul x.m z.n))
136                (sun:si (mul z.m x.n))
137            ==
138          [(sit.fq xx) (sit.fq zz)]
139          ::                                    ::   ++cub:curt:number
140          ++  cub                               ::
141          |=  [x=@ z=@]
142          =+  ^=  xx
143            %+  mul
144              %-  sqr  %-  abs:si
145              (dif:si (sun:si x) (sun:si z))
146            (sqr (add x z))
147          =+  ^=  zz
148            ;:  mul  4  x  z
149              :(add (sqr x) :(mul p x z) (sqr z))
150            ==
151          [(sit.fq xx) (sit.fq zz)]
152          --  ::
153        ==
154    =+  one=[b 1]
155    =+  i=253
156    =+  r=one
157    =+  s=(cub one)
158    |-
159    ?:  =(i 0)
160      =+  x=(cub r)
161      (sit.fq (mul -.x (inv +.x)))
162    =+  m=(rsh [0 i] a)
163    ?:  =(0 (mod m 2))
164      $(i (dec i), s (cad r s one), r (cub r))
165    $(i (dec i), r (cad r s one), s (cub s))
166  ::                                          ::   ++ga:number
167  ++  ga                                      ::   GF (bex p.a)
168  |=  a=[p=@ q=@ r=@]                         ::   dim poly gen
169  =+  si=(bex p.a)
170  =+  ma=(dec si)
171  =>  |%
```

```
172        ::                                              ::    ++dif:ga:number
173        ++   dif                                        ::    add and sub
174          |=   [b=@ c=@]
175          ~|   [%dif-ga a]
176          ?>   &((lth b si) (lth c si))
177          (mix b c)
178        ::                                              ::    ++dub:ga:number
179        ++   dub                                        ::    mul by x
180          |=   b=@
181          ~|   [%dub-ga a]
182          ?>   (lth b si)
183          ?:   =(1 (cut 0 [(dec p.a) 1] b))
184          (dif (sit q.a) (sit (lsh 0 b)))
185          (lsh 0 b)
186        ::                                              ::    ++pro:ga:number
187        ++   pro                                        ::    slow multiply
188          |=   [b=@ c=@]
189          ?:   =(0 b)
190            0
191          ?:   =(1 (dis 1 b))
192          (dif c $(b (rsh 0 b), c (dub c)))
193          $(b (rsh 0 b), c (dub c))
194        ::                                              ::    ++toe:ga:number
195        ++   toe                                        ::    exp+log tables
196          =+   ^=  nu
197              |=   [b=@ c=@]
198              ^-  (map @ @)
199              =+   d=*(map @ @)
200              |-
201              ?:   =(0 c)
202                d
203              %=   $
204                c  (dec c)
205                d  (~(put by d) c b)
206              ==
207          =+   [p=(nu 0 (bex p.a)) q=(nu ma ma)]
208          =+   [b=1 c=0]
209          |-  ^-  [p=(map @ @) q=(map @ @)]
210          ?:   =(ma c)
211            [(~(put by p) c b) q]
212          %=   $
213            b  (pro r.a b)
214            c  +(c)
215            p  (~(put by p) c b)
216            q  (~(put by q) b c)
217          ==
218        ::                                              ::    ++sit:ga:number
219        ++   sit                                        ::    reduce
220          |=   b=@
221          (mod b (bex p.a))
222        --   ::
223    =+   toe
224    |%
225    ::                                                  ::    ++fra:ga:number
226    ++   fra                                            ::    divide
227      |=   [b=@ c=@]
228      (pro b (inv c))
229    ::                                                  ::    ++inv:ga:number
```

```
230      ++  inv                                  ::  invert
231        |=  b=@
232        ~|  [%inv-ga a]
233        =+  c=(~(get by q) b)
234        ?~  c  !!
235        =+  d=(~(get by p) (sub ma u.c))
236        (need d)
237      ::                                       ::  ++pow:ga:number
238      ++  pow                                  ::  exponent
239        |=  [b=@ c=@]
240        =+  [d=1 e=c f=0]
241        |-
242        ?:  =(p.a f)
243          d
244        ?:  =(1 (cut 0 [f 1] b))
245          $(d (pro d e), e (pro e e), f +(f))
246        $(e (pro e e), f +(f))
247      ::                                       ::  ++pro:ga:number
248      ++  pro                                  ::  multiply
249        |=  [b=@ c=@]
250        ~|  [%pro-ga a]
251        =+  d=(~(get by q) b)
252        ?~  d  0
253        =+  e=(~(get by q) c)
254        ?~  e  0
255        =+  f=(~(get by p) (mod (add u.d u.e) ma))
256        (need f)
257      --  ::ga
258    --  ::number
259 ::                                            ::::
260 ::::                        ++crypto          ::  (2b) cryptography
261   ::                                          ::::
262 ++  crypto  ^?
263   =,  ames
264   =,  number
265   |%
266   ::                                          ::
267   ::::                      ++aes:crypto      ::  (2b1) aes, all sizes
268     ::                                        ::::
269   ++  aes    !.
270     ~%  %aes  ..part  ~
271     |%
272     ::                                        ::  ++ahem:aes:crypto
273     ++  ahem                                  ::  kernel state
274       |=  [nnk=@ nnb=@ nnr=@]
275       =>
276       =+  =>  [gr=(ga 8 0x11b 3) few==>(fe .(a 5))]
277           [pro=pro.gr dif=dif.gr pow=pow.gr ror=ror.few]
278       =>  |%                                  ::
279         ++  cipa  $_  ^?                      ::  AES params
280           |%
281           ++  co  *[p=@ q=@ r=@ s=@]          ::  column coefficients
282           ++  ix  |~(a=@ *@)                  ::  key index
283           ++  ro  *[p=@ q=@ r=@ s=@]          ::  row shifts
284           ++  su  *@                          ::  s-box
285           --  ::cipa
286         --  ::
287         |%
```

```
288        ::                              ::  ++pen:ahem:aes:
289        ++  pen                         ::  encrypt
290        ^-  cipa
291        |%
292        ::                              ::  ++co:pen:ahem:aes:
293        ++  co                          ::  column coefficients
294        [0x2 0x3 1 1]
295        ::                              ::  ++ix:pen:ahem:aes:
296        ++  ix                          ::  key index
297        |~(a=@ a)
298        ::                              ::  ++ro:pen:ahem:aes:
299        ++  ro                          ::  row shifts
300        [0 1 2 3]
301        ::                              ::  ++su:pen:ahem:aes:
302        ++  su                          ::  s-box
303        0x16bb.54b0.0f2d.9941.6842.e6bf.0d89.a18c.
304          df28.55ce.e987.1e9b.948e.d969.1198.f8e1.
305          9e1d.c186.b957.3561.0ef6.0348.66b5.3e70.
306          8a8b.bd4b.1f74.dde8.c6b4.a61c.2e25.78ba.
307          08ae.7a65.eaf4.566c.a94e.d58d.6d37.c8e7.
308          79e4.9591.62ac.d3c2.5c24.0649.0a3a.32e0.
309          db0b.5ede.14b8.ee46.8890.2a22.dc4f.8160.
310          7319.5d64.3d7e.a7c4.1744.975f.ec13.0ccd.
311          d2f3.ff10.21da.b6bc.f538.9d92.8f40.a351.
312          a89f.3c50.7f02.f945.8533.4d43.fbaa.efd0.
313          cf58.4c4a.39be.cb6a.5bb1.fc20.ed00.d153.
314          842f.e329.b3d6.3b52.a05a.6e1b.1a2c.8309.
315          75b2.27eb.e280.1207.9a05.9618.c323.c704.
316          1531.d871.f1e5.a534.ccf7.3f36.2693.fdb7.
317          c072.a49c.afa2.d4ad.f047.59fa.7dc9.82ca.
318          76ab.d7fe.2b67.0130.c56f.6bf2.7b77.7c63
319        --
320        ::                              ::  ++pin:ahem:aes:
321        ++  pin                         ::  decrypt
322        ^-  cipa
323        |%
324        ::                              ::  ++co:pin:ahem:aes:
325        ++  co                          ::  column coefficients
326        [0xe 0xb 0xd 0x9]
327        ::                              ::  ++ix:pin:ahem:aes:
328        ++  ix                          ::  key index
329        |~(a=@ (sub nnr a))
330        ::                              ::  ++ro:pin:ahem:aes:
331        ++  ro                          ::  row shifts
332        [0 3 2 1]
333        ::                              ::  ++su:pin:ahem:aes:
334        ++  su                          ::  s-box
335        0x7d0c.2155.6314.69e1.26d6.77ba.7e04.2b17.
336          6199.5383.3cbb.ebc8.b0f5.2aae.4d3b.e0a0.
337          ef9c.c993.9f7a.e52d.0d4a.b519.a97f.5160.
338          5fec.8027.5910.12b1.31c7.0788.33a8.dd1f.
339          f45a.cd78.fec0.db9a.2079.d2c6.4b3e.56fc.
340          1bbe.18aa.0e62.b76f.89c5.291d.711a.f147.
341          6edf.751c.e837.f9e2.8535.ade7.2274.ac96.
342          73e6.b4f0.cecf.f297.eadc.674f.4111.913a.
343          6b8a.1301.03bd.afc1.020f.3fca.8f1e.2cd0.
344          0645.b3b8.0558.e4f7.0ad3.bc8c.00ab.d890.
345          849d.8da7.5746.155e.dab9.edfd.5048.706c.
```

```
346            92b6.655d.cc5c.a4d4.1698.6886.64f6.f872.
347            25d1.8b6d.49a2.5b76.b224.d928.66a1.2e08.
348            4ec3.fa42.0b95.4cee.3d23.c2a6.3294.7b54.
349            cbe9.dec4.4443.8e34.87ff.2f9b.8239.e37c.
350            fbd7.f381.9ea3.40bf.38a5.3630.d56a.0952
351          --
352      ::                                           ::  ++mcol:ahem:aes:
353      ++  mcol                                     ::
354      |=  [a=(list @) b=[p=@ q=@ r=@ s=@]]
355      ^-  (list @)
356      =+  c=[p=*@ q=*@ r=*@ s=*@]
357      |-  ^-  (list @)
358      ?~  a  ~
359      =>  .(p.c (cut 3 [0 1] i.a))
360      =>  .(q.c (cut 3 [1 1] i.a))
361      =>  .(r.c (cut 3 [2 1] i.a))
362      =>  .(s.c (cut 3 [3 1] i.a))
363      :_  $(a t.a)
364      %+  rep  3
365      %+  turn
366        %-  limo
367        :~  [[p.c p.b] [q.c q.b] [r.c r.b] [s.c s.b]]
368            [[p.c s.b] [q.c p.b] [r.c q.b] [s.c r.b]]
369            [[p.c r.b] [q.c s.b] [r.c p.b] [s.c q.b]]
370            [[p.c q.b] [q.c r.b] [r.c s.b] [s.c p.b]]
371        ==
372      |=  [a=[@ @] b=[@ @] c=[@ @] d=[@ @]]
373      :(dif (pro a) (pro b) (pro c) (pro d))
374      ::                                           ::  ++pode:ahem:aes:
375      ++  pode                                     ::  explode to block
376      |=  [a=bloq b=@ c=@]  ^-  (list @)
377      =+  d=(rip a c)
378      =+  m=(met a c)
379      |-
380      ?:  =(m b)
381        d
382      $(m +(m), d (weld d (limo [0 ~])))
383      ::                                           ::  ++sube:ahem:aes:
384      ++  sube                                     ::  s-box word
385      |=  [a=@ b=@]  ^-  @
386      (rep 3 (turn (pode 3 4 a) |=(c=@ (cut 3 [c 1] b))))
387      --  ::
388  |%
389  ::                                               ::  ++be:ahem:aes:crypto
390  ++  be                                           ::  block cipher
391      |=  [a=? b=@ c=@H]  ^-  @uxH
392      ~|  %be-aesc
393      =>  %=  .
394          +
395        =>  +
396        |%
397        ::                                         ::  ++ankh:be:ahem:aes:
398        ++  ankh                                   ::
399        |=  [a=cipa b=@ c=@]
400        (pode 5 nnb (cut 5 [(mul (ix.a b) nnb) nnb] c))
401        ::                                         ::  ++sark:be:ahem:aes:
402        ++  sark                                   ::
403        |=  [c=(list @) d=(list @)]
```

```
404        ^-  (list @)
405        ?~  c  ~
406        ?~  d  !!
407        [(mix i.c i.d) $(c t.c, d t.d)]
408      ::                                        ::  ++srow:be:ahem:aes:
409      ++  srow                                  ::
410        |=  [a=cipa b=(list @)]  ^-  (list @)
411        =+  [c=0 d=~ e=ro.a]
412        |-
413        ?:  =(c nnb)
414          d
415        :_  $(c +(c))
416        %+  rep  3
417        %+  turn
418          (limo [0 p.e] [1 q.e] [2 r.e] [3 s.e] ~)
419        |=  [f=@ g=@]
420        (cut 3 [f 1] (snag (mod (add g c) nnb) b))
421      ::                                        ::  ++subs:be:ahem:aes:
422      ++  subs                                  ::
423        |=  [a=cipa b=(list @)]  ^-  (list @)
424        ?~  b  ~
425        [(sube i.b su.a) $(b t.b)]
426          --
427        ==
428    =+  [d=?:(a pen pin) e=(pode 5 nnb c) f=1]
429    =>  .(e (sark e (ankh d 0 b)))
430    |-
431    ?.  =(nnr f)
432      =>  .(e (subs d e))
433      =>  .(e (srow d e))
434      =>  .(e (mcol e co.d))
435      =>  .(e (sark e (ankh d f b)))
436      $(f +(f))
437    =>  .(e (subs d e))
438    =>  .(e (srow d e))
439    =>  .(e (sark e (ankh d nnr b)))
440    (rep 5 e)
441  ::                                          ::  ++ex:ahem:aes:crypto
442  ++  ex                                      ::  key expand
443    |=  a=@I  ^-  @
444    =+  [b=a c=0 d=su:pen i=nnk]
445    |-
446    ?:  =(i (mul nnb +(nnr)))
447      b
448    =>  .(c (cut 5 [(dec i) 1] b))
449    =>  ?:  =(0 (mod i nnk))
450          =>  .(c (ror 3 1 c))
451          =>  .(c (sube c d))
452          .(c (mix c (pow (dec (div i nnk)) 2)))
453        ?:  &((gth nnk 6) =(4 (mod i nnk)))
454          .(c (sube c d))
455          .
456    =>  .(c (mix c (cut 5 [(sub i nnk) 1] b)))
457    =>  .(b (can 5 [i b] [1 c] ~))
458    $(i +(i))
459  ::                                          ::  ++ix:ahem:aes:crypto
460  ++  ix                                      ::  key expand, inv
461    |=  a=@  ^-  @
```

```
462        =+  [i=1 j=*@ b=*@ c=co:pin]
463        |-
464        ?:  =(nnr i)
465          a
466        =>  .(b (cut 7 [i 1] a))
467        =>  .(b (rep 5 (mcol (pode 5 4 b) c)))
468        =>  .(j (sub nnr i))
469        %=    $
470          i  +(i)
471           a
472        %+  can  7
473        :~  [i (cut 7 [0 i] a)]
474            [1 b]
475            [j (cut 7 [+(i) j] a)]
476          ==
477        ==
478      --
479    ::                                            ::  ++ecba:aes:crypto
480    ++  ecba                                      ::  AES-128 ECB
481    ~%  %ecba  +>  ~
482    |_  key=@H
483    ::                                            ::  ++en:ecba:aes:crypto
484    ++  en                                        ::  encrypt
485    ~/  %en
486    |=  blk=@H  ^-  @uxH
487    =+  (ahem 4 4 10)
488    =:
489      key  (~(net fe 7) key)
490      blk  (~(net fe 7) blk)
491    ==
492    %-  ~(net fe 7)
493    (be & (ex key) blk)
494    ::                                            ::  ++de:ecba:aes:crypto
495    ++  de                                        ::  decrypt
496    ~/  %de
497    |=  blk=@H  ^-  @uxH
498    =+  (ahem 4 4 10)
499    =:
500      key  (~(net fe 7) key)
501      blk  (~(net fe 7) blk)
502    ==
503    %-  ~(net fe 7)
504    (be | (ix (ex key)) blk)
505    --  ::ecba
506    ::                                            ::  ++ecbb:aes:crypto
507    ++  ecbb                                      ::  AES-192 ECB
508    ~%  %ecbb  +>  ~
509    |_  key=@I
510    ::                                            ::  ++en:ecbb:aes:crypto
511    ++  en                                        ::  encrypt
512    ~/  %en
513    |=  blk=@H  ^-  @uxH
514    =+  (ahem 6 4 12)
515    =:
516      key  (rsh 6 (~(net fe 8) key))
517      blk  (~(net fe 7) blk)
518    ==
519    %-  ~(net fe 7)
```

```
520        (be & (ex key) blk)
521      ::                                        ::  ++de:ecbb:aes:crypto
522      ++    de                                   ::  decrypt
523        ~/  %de
524        |=  blk=@H  ^-  @uxH
525        =+  (ahem 6 4 12)
526        =:
527          key  (rsh 6 (~(net fe 8) key))
528          blk  (~(net fe 7) blk)
529        ==
530        %-  ~(net fe 7)
531        (be | (ix (ex key)) blk)
532      --  ::ecbb
533    ::                                          ::  ++ecbc:aes:crypto
534    ++    ecbc                                  ::  AES-256 ECB
535      ~%  %ecbc  +>   ~
536      |_   key=@I
537      ::                                        ::  ++en:ecbc:aes:crypto
538      ++    en                                  ::  encrypt
539        ~/  %en
540        |=  blk=@H  ^-  @uxH
541        =+  (ahem 8 4 14)
542        =:
543          key  (~(net fe 8) key)
544          blk  (~(net fe 7) blk)
545        ==
546        %-  ~(net fe 7)
547        (be & (ex key) blk)
548      ::                                        ::  ++de:ecbc:aes:crypto
549      ++    de                                  ::  decrypt
550        ~/  %de
551        |=  blk=@H  ^-  @uxH
552        =+  (ahem 8 4 14)
553        =:
554          key  (~(net fe 8) key)
555          blk  (~(net fe 7) blk)
556        ==
557        %-  ~(net fe 7)
558        (be | (ix (ex key)) blk)
559      --  ::ecbc
560    ::                                          ::  ++cbca:aes:crypto
561    ++    cbca                                  ::  AES-128 CBC
562      ~%  %cbca  +>   ~
563      |_   [key=@H prv=@H]
564      ::                                        ::  ++en:cbca:aes:crypto
565      ++    en                                  ::  encrypt
566        ~/  %en
567        |=  txt=@  ^-  @ux
568        =+  pts=?:(=(txt 0) `(list @)`~[0] (flop (rip 7 txt)))
569        =|  cts=(list @)
570        %+  rep  7
571        ::  logically, flop twice here
572        |-  ^-  (list @)
573        ?~  pts
574          cts
575        =+  cph=(~(en ecba key) (mix prv i.pts))
576        %=  $
577          cts  [cph cts]
```

```
578        pts  t.pts
579        prv  cph
580      ==
581    ::                                                    ::  ++de:cbca:aes:crypto
582    ++  de                                                ::  decrypt
583    ~/  %de
584    |=  txt=@  ^-  @ux
585    =+  cts=?:(=(txt 0) `(list @)`~[0] (flop (rip 7 txt)))
586    =|  pts=(list @)
587    %+  rep  7
588    ::  logically, flop twice here
589    |-  ^-  (list @)
590    ?~  cts
591      pts
592    =+  pln=(mix prv (~(de ecba key) i.cts))
593    %=  $
594      pts  [pln pts]
595      cts  t.cts
596      prv  i.cts
597    ==
598  --  ::cbca
599  ::                                                      ::  ++cbcb:aes:crypto
600  ++  cbcb                                                ::  AES-192 CBC
601  ~%  %cbcb  +>  ~
602  |_  [key=@I prv=@H]
603  ::                                                      ::  ++en:cbcb:aes:crypto
604  ++  en                                                  ::  encrypt
605  ~/  %en
606  |=  txt=@  ^-  @ux
607  =+  pts=?:(=(txt 0) `(list @)`~[0] (flop (rip 7 txt)))
608  =|  cts=(list @)
609  %+  rep  7
610  ::  logically, flop twice here
611  |-  ^-  (list @)
612  ?~  pts
613    cts
614  =+  cph=(~(en ecbb key) (mix prv i.pts))
615  %=  $
616    cts  [cph cts]
617    pts  t.pts
618    prv  cph
619  ==
620  ::                                                      ::  ++de:cbcb:aes:crypto
621  ++  de                                                  ::  decrypt
622  ~/  %de
623  |=  txt=@  ^-  @ux
624  =+  cts=?:(=(txt 0) `(list @)`~[0] (flop (rip 7 txt)))
625  =|  pts=(list @)
626  %+  rep  7
627  ::  logically, flop twice here
628  |-  ^-  (list @)
629  ?~  cts
630    pts
631  =+  pln=(mix prv (~(de ecbb key) i.cts))
632  %=  $
633    pts  [pln pts]
634    cts  t.cts
635    prv  i.cts
```

```
636            ==
637        --  ::cbcb
638     ::                                              ::  ++cbcc:aes:crypto
639     ++  cbcc                                         ::  AES-256 CBC
640       ~%  %cbcc  +>   ~
641       |_  [key=@I prv=@H]
642       ::                                            ::  ++en:cbcc:aes:crypto
643       ++  en                                        ::  encrypt
644         ~/  %en
645         |=  txt=@   ^-   @ux
646         =+  pts=?:(=(txt 0) `(list @)`~[0] (flop (rip 7 txt)))
647         =|  cts=(list @)
648         %+  rep  7
649         ::  logically, flop twice here
650         |-  ^-  (list @)
651         ?~  pts
652           cts
653         =+  cph=(~(en ecbc key) (mix prv i.pts))
654         %=  $
655           cts  [cph cts]
656           pts  t.pts
657           prv  cph
658         ==
659       ::                                            ::  ++de:cbcc:aes:crypto
660       ++  de                                        ::  decrypt
661         ~/  %de
662         |=  txt=@   ^-   @ux
663         =+  cts=?:(=(txt 0) `(list @)`~[0] (flop (rip 7 txt)))
664         =|  pts=(list @)
665         %+  rep  7
666         ::  logically, flop twice here
667         |-  ^-  (list @)
668         ?~  cts
669           pts
670         =+  pln=(mix prv (~(de ecbc key) i.cts))
671         %=  $
672           pts  [pln pts]
673           cts  t.cts
674           prv  i.cts
675         ==
676       --  ::cbcc
677     ::                                              ::  ++inc:aes:crypto
678     ++  inc                                         ::  inc. low bloq
679       |=  [mod=bloq ctr=@H]
680       ^-  @uxH
681       =+  bqs=(rip mod ctr)
682       ?~  bqs  0x1
683       %+  rep  mod
684       [(~(sum fe mod) i.bqs 1) t.bqs]
685     ::                                              ::  ++ctra:aes:crypto
686     ++  ctra                                        ::  AES-128 CTR
687       ~%  %ctra  +>   ~
688       |_  [key=@H mod=bloq len=@ ctr=@H]
689       ::                                            ::  ++en:ctra:aes:crypto
690       ++  en                                        ::  encrypt
691         ~/  %en
692         |=  txt=@
693         ^-  @ux
```

```
694        =/   encrypt   ~(en ecba key)
695        =/   blocks  (add (div len 16) ?:(=((^mod len 16) 0) 0 1))
696        ?>   (gte len (met 3 txt))
697        %+   mix  txt
698        %+   rsh   [3 (sub (mul 16 blocks) len)]
699        %+   rep  7
700        =|   seed=(list @ux)
701        |-   ^+  seed
702        ?:   =(blocks 0)  seed
703        %=   $
704          seed    [(encrypt ctr) seed]
705          ctr     (inc mod ctr)
706          blocks  (dec blocks)
707        ==
708      ::                                        ::  ++de:ctra:aes:crypto
709      ++  de                                    ::  decrypt
710        en
711    --  ::ctra
712    ::                                          ::  ++ctrb:aes:crypto
713    ++  ctrb                                    ::  AES-192 CTR
714      ~%  %ctrb  +>  ~
715      |_  [key=@I mod=bloq len=@ ctr=@H]
716      ::                                        ::  ++en:ctrb:aes:crypto
717      ++  en
718        ~/  %en
719        |=  txt=@
720        ^-  @ux
721        =/   encrypt   ~(en ecbb key)
722        =/   blocks  (add (div len 16) ?:(=((^mod len 16) 0) 0 1))
723        ?>   (gte len (met 3 txt))
724        %+   mix  txt
725        %+   rsh   [3 (sub (mul 16 blocks) len)]
726        %+   rep  7
727        =|   seed=(list @ux)
728        |-   ^+  seed
729        ?:   =(blocks 0)  seed
730        %=   $
731          seed    [(encrypt ctr) seed]
732          ctr     (inc mod ctr)
733          blocks  (dec blocks)
734        ==
735      ::                                        ::  ++de:ctrb:aes:crypto
736      ++  de                                    ::  decrypt
737        en
738    --  ::ctrb
739    ::                                          ::  ++ctrc:aes:crypto
740    ++  ctrc                                    ::  AES-256 CTR
741      ~%  %ctrc  +>  ~
742      |_  [key=@I mod=bloq len=@ ctr=@H]
743      ::                                        ::  ++en:ctrc:aes:crypto
744      ++  en                                    ::  encrypt
745        ~/  %en
746        |=  txt=@
747        ^-  @ux
748        =/   encrypt   ~(en ecbc key)
749        =/   blocks  (add (div len 16) ?:(=((^mod len 16) 0) 0 1))
750        ?>   (gte len (met 3 txt))
751        %+   mix  txt
```

```
752        %+  rsh  [3 (sub (mul 16 blocks) len)]
753        %+  rep  7
754        =|  seed=(list @ux)
755        |-  ^+  seed
756        ?:  =(blocks 0)  seed
757        %=  $
758          seed    [(encrypt ctr) seed]
759          ctr     (inc mod ctr)
760          blocks  (dec blocks)
761        ==
762      ::                                            ::  ++de:ctrc:aes:crypto
763      ++  de                                        ::  decrypt
764        en
765      --  ::ctrc
766      ::                                            ::  ++doub:aes:crypto
767      ++  doub                                      ::  double 128-bit
768      |=  ::  string mod finite
769          ::
770          str=@H
771      ::
772      ::  field (see spec)
773      ::
774      ^-  @uxH
775      %-  ~(sit fe 7)
776      ?.  =((xeb str) 128)
777      (lsh 0 str)
778      (mix 0x87 (lsh 0 str))
779      ::                                            ::  ++mpad:aes:crypto
780      ++  mpad                                      ::
781      |=  [oct=@ txt=@]
782      ::
783      ::  pad message to multiple of 128 bits
784      ::  by appending 1, then 0s
785      ::  the spec is unclear, but it must be octet based
786      ::  to match the test vectors
787      ::
788      ^-  @ux
789      =+  pad=(mod oct 16)
790      ?:  =(pad 0)  0x8000.0000.0000.0000.0000.0000.0000.0000
791      (lsh [3 (sub 15 pad)] (mix 0x80 (lsh 3 txt)))
792      ::                                            ::  ++suba:aes:crypto
793      ++  suba                                      ::  AES-128 subkeys
794      |=  key=@H
795      =+  l=(~(en ecba key) 0)
796      =+  k1=(doub l)
797      =+  k2=(doub k1)
798      ^-  [@ux @ux]
799      [k1 k2]
800      ::                                            ::  ++subb:aes:crypto
801      ++  subb                                      ::  AES-192 subkeys
802      |=  key=@I
803      =+  l=(~(en ecbb key) 0)
804      =+  k1=(doub l)
805      =+  k2=(doub k1)
806      ^-  [@ux @ux]
807      [k1 k2]
808      ::                                            ::  ++subc:aes:crypto
809      ++  subc                                      ::  AES-256 subkeys
```

```
810        |=  key=@I
811        =+  l=(~(en ecbc key) 0)
812        =+  k1=(doub l)
813        =+  k2=(doub k1)
814        ^-  [@ux @ux]
815        [k1 k2]
816    ::                                              ::  ++maca:aes:crypto
817    ++  maca                                        ::  AES-128 CMAC
818      ~/  %maca
819      |=  [key=@H oct=(unit @) txt=@]
820      ^-  @ux
821      =+  [sub=(suba key) len=?~(oct (met 3 txt) u.oct)]
822      =+  ^=  pdt
823        ?:  &(=((mod len 16) 0) !=(len 0))
824          [& txt]
825        [| (mpad len txt)]
826      =+  ^=  mac
827        %-  ~(en cbca key 0)
828        %+  mix  +.pdt
829        ?-  -.pdt
830          %&  -.sub
831          %|  +.sub
832        ==
833      ::  spec says MSBs, LSBs match test vectors
834      ::
835      (~(sit fe 7) mac)
836    ::                                              ::  ++macb:aes:crypto
837    ++  macb                                        ::  AES-192 CMAC
838      ~/  %macb
839      |=  [key=@I oct=(unit @) txt=@]
840      ^-  @ux
841      =+  [sub=(subb key) len=?~(oct (met 3 txt) u.oct)]
842      =+  ^=  pdt
843        ?:  &(=((mod len 16) 0) !=(len 0))
844          [& txt]
845        [| (mpad len txt)]
846      =+  ^=  mac
847        %-  ~(en cbcb key 0)
848        %+  mix  +.pdt
849        ?-  -.pdt
850          %&  -.sub
851          %|  +.sub
852        ==
853      ::  spec says MSBs, LSBs match test vectors
854      ::
855      (~(sit fe 7) mac)
856    ::                                              ::  ++macc:aes:crypto
857    ++  macc                                        ::  AES-256 CMAC
858      ~/  %macc
859      |=  [key=@I oct=(unit @) txt=@]
860      ^-  @ux
861      =+  [sub=(subc key) len=?~(oct (met 3 txt) u.oct)]
862      =+  ^=  pdt
863        ?:  &(=((mod len 16) 0) !=(len 0))
864          [& txt]
865        [| (mpad len txt)]
866      =+  ^=  mac
867        %-  ~(en cbcc key 0)
```

```
868        %+  mix  +.pdt
869        ?-  -.pdt
870          %&  -.sub
871          %|  +.sub
872        ==
873      ::  spec says MSBs, LSBs match test vectors
874      ::
875      (~(sit fe 7) mac)
876    ::                                                  ::  ++s2va:aes:crypto
877    ++  s2va                                            ::  AES-128 S2V
878      ~/  %s2va
879      |=  [key=@H ads=(list @)]
880      ?~  ads  (maca key `16 0x1)
881      =/  res  (maca key `16 0x0)
882      %+  maca  key
883      |-  ^-  [[~ @ud] @uxH]
884      ?~  t.ads
885        =/  wyt  (met 3 i.ads)
886        ?:  (gte wyt 16)
887          [`wyt (mix i.ads res)]
888        [`16 (mix (doub res) (mpad wyt i.ads))]
889      %=  $
890        ads  t.ads
891        res  (mix (doub res) (maca key ~ i.ads))
892      ==
893    ::                                                  ::  ++s2vb:aes:crypto
894    ++  s2vb                                            ::  AES-192 S2V
895      ~/  %s2vb
896      |=  [key=@I ads=(list @)]
897      ?~  ads  (macb key `16 0x1)
898      =/  res  (macb key `16 0x0)
899      %+  macb  key
900      |-  ^-  [[~ @ud] @uxH]
901      ?~  t.ads
902        =/  wyt  (met 3 i.ads)
903        ?:  (gte wyt 16)
904          [`wyt (mix i.ads res)]
905        [`16 (mix (doub res) (mpad wyt i.ads))]
906      %=  $
907        ads  t.ads
908        res  (mix (doub res) (macb key ~ i.ads))
909      ==
910    ::                                                  ::  ++s2vc:aes:crypto
911    ++  s2vc                                            ::  AES-256 S2V
912      ~/  %s2vc
913      |=  [key=@I ads=(list @)]
914      ?~  ads  (macc key `16 0x1)
915      =/  res  (macc key `16 0x0)
916      %+  macc  key
917      |-  ^-  [[~ @ud] @uxH]
918      ?~  t.ads
919        =/  wyt  (met 3 i.ads)
920        ?:  (gte wyt 16)
921          [`wyt (mix i.ads res)]
922        [`16 (mix (doub res) (mpad wyt i.ads))]
923      %=  $
924        ads  t.ads
925        res  (mix (doub res) (macc key ~ i.ads))
```

```
926        ==
927      ::                                        ::  ++siva:aes:crypto
928      ++  siva                                   ::  AES-128 SIV
929      ~%  %siva  +>  ~
930      |_  [key=@I vec=(list @)]
931      ::                                         ::  ++en:siva:aes:crypto
932      ++  en                                     ::  encrypt
933      ~/  %en
934      |=  txt=@
935      ^-  (trel @uxH @ud @ux)
936      =+  [k1=(rsh 7 key) k2=(end 7 key)]
937      =+  iv=(s2va k1 (weld vec (limo ~[txt])))
938      =+  len=(met 3 txt)
939      =*  hib  (dis iv 0xffff.ffff.ffff.ffff.7fff.ffff.7fff.ffff)
940      :+
941        iv
942        len
943      (~(en ctra k2 7 len hib) txt)
944      ::                                         ::  ++de:siva:aes:crypto
945      ++  de                                     ::  decrypt
946      ~/  %de
947      |=  [iv=@H len=@ txt=@]
948      ^-  (unit @ux)
949      =+  [k1=(rsh 7 key) k2=(end 7 key)]
950      =*  hib  (dis iv 0xffff.ffff.ffff.ffff.7fff.ffff.7fff.ffff)
951      =+  ^=  pln
952        (~(de ctra k2 7 len hib) txt)
953      ?.  =((s2va k1 (weld vec (limo ~[pln]))) iv)
954        ~
955      `pln
956      --  ::siva
957      ::                                         ::  ++sivb:aes:crypto
958      ++  sivb                                   ::  AES-192 SIV
959      ~%  %sivb  +>  ~
960      |_  [key=@J vec=(list @)]
961      ::                                         ::  ++en:sivb:aes:crypto
962      ++  en                                     ::  encrypt
963      ~/  %en
964      |=  txt=@
965      ^-  (trel @uxH @ud @ux)
966      =+  [k1=(rsh [6 3] key) k2=(end [6 3] key)]
967      =+  iv=(s2vb k1 (weld vec (limo ~[txt])))
968      =*  hib  (dis iv 0xffff.ffff.ffff.ffff.7fff.ffff.7fff.ffff)
969      =+  len=(met 3 txt)
970      :+  iv
971        len
972      (~(en ctrb k2 7 len hib) txt)
973      ::                                         ::  ++de:sivb:aes:crypto
974      ++  de                                     ::  decrypt
975      ~/  %de
976      |=  [iv=@H len=@ txt=@]
977      ^-  (unit @ux)
978      =+  [k1=(rsh [6 3] key) k2=(end [6 3] key)]
979      =*  hib  (dis iv 0xffff.ffff.ffff.ffff.7fff.ffff.7fff.ffff)
980      =+  ^=  pln
981        (~(de ctrb k2 7 len hib) txt)
982      ?.  =((s2vb k1 (weld vec (limo ~[pln]))) iv)
983        ~
```

```
 984          `pln
 985      --  ::sivb
 986    ::                                              ::  ++sivc:aes:crypto
 987    ++  sivc                                        ::  AES-256 SIV
 988    ~%  %sivc  +>  ~
 989    |_  [key=@J vec=(list @)]
 990    ::                                              ::  ++en:sivc:aes:crypto
 991    ++  en                                          ::  encrypt
 992    ~/  %en
 993    |=  txt=@
 994    ^-  (trel @uxH @ud @ux)
 995    =+  [k1=(rsh 8 key) k2=(end 8 key)]
 996    =+  iv=(s2vc k1 (weld vec (limo ~[txt])))
 997    =*  hib  (dis iv 0xffff.ffff.ffff.ffff.7fff.ffff.7fff.ffff)
 998    =+  len=(met 3 txt)
 999    :+
1000      iv
1001      len
1002    (~(en ctrc k2 7 len hib) txt)
1003    ::                                              ::  ++de:sivc:aes:crypto
1004    ++  de                                          ::  decrypt
1005    ~/  %de
1006    |=  [iv=@H len=@ txt=@]
1007    ^-  (unit @ux)
1008    =+  [k1=(rsh 8 key) k2=(end 8 key)]
1009    =*  hib  (dis iv 0xffff.ffff.ffff.ffff.7fff.ffff.7fff.ffff)
1010    =+  ^=  pln
1011      (~(de ctrc k2 7 len hib) txt)
1012    ?.  =((s2vc k1 (weld vec (limo ~[pln]))) iv)
1013      ~
1014      `pln
1015    --  ::sivc
1016  --
1017  ::                                                ::
1018  ::::                        ++ed:crypto            ::  ed25519
1019  ::                                                ::::
1020  ++  ed
1021    =>
1022    =+  =+  [b=256 q=(sub (bex 255) 19)]
1023        =+  fq=~(. fo q)
1024        =+  ^=  l
1025            %+  add
1026              (bex 252)
1027            27.742.317.777.372.353.535.851.937.790.883.648.493
1028        =+  d=(dif.fq 0 (fra.fq 121.665 121.666))
1029        =+  ii=(exp.fq (div (dec q) 4) 2)
1030        [b=b q=q fq=fq l=l d=d ii=ii]
1031    ~%  %coed  ..part  ~
1032    |%
1033    ::                                              ::  ++norm:ed:crypto
1034    ++  norm                                        ::
1035    |=(x=@ ?:(=(0 (mod x 2)) x (sub q x)))
1036    ::                                              ::  ++xrec:ed:crypto
1037    ++  xrec                                        ::  recover x-coord
1038    |=  y=@  ^-  @
1039    =+  ^=  xx
1040        %+  mul  (dif.fq (mul y y) 1)
1041                (inv.fq +:(mul d y y)))
```

```
1042        =+  x=(exp.fq (div (add 3 q) 8) xx)
1043        ?:  !=(0 (dif.fq (mul x x) (sit.fq xx)))
1044          (norm (pro.fq x ii))
1045        (norm x)
1046      ::                                          ::  ++ward:ed:crypto
1047      ++  ward                                    ::  edwards multiply
1048      |=  [pp=[@ @] qq=[@ @]]  ^-  [@ @]
1049      =+  dp=:(pro.fq d -.pp -.qq +.pp +.qq)
1050      =+  ^=  xt
1051        %+  pro.fq
1052          %+  sum.fq
1053            (pro.fq -.pp +.qq)
1054            (pro.fq -.qq +.pp)
1055          (inv.fq (sum.fq 1 dp))
1056      =+  ^=  yt
1057        %+  pro.fq
1058          %+  sum.fq
1059            (pro.fq +.pp +.qq)
1060            (pro.fq -.pp -.qq)
1061          (inv.fq (dif.fq 1 dp))
1062      [xt yt]
1063      ::                                          ::  ++scam:ed:crypto
1064      ++  scam                                    ::  scalar multiply
1065      |=  [pp=[@ @] e=@]  ^-  [@ @]
1066      ?:  =(0 e)
1067        [0 1]
1068      =+  qq=$(e (div e 2))
1069      =>  .(qq (ward qq qq))
1070      ?:  =(1 (dis 1 e))
1071        (ward qq pp)
1072      qq
1073      ::                                          ::  ++etch:ed:crypto
1074      ++  etch                                    ::  encode point
1075      |=  pp=[@ @]  ^-  @
1076      (can 0 ~[[(sub b 1) +.pp] [1 (dis 1 -.pp)]])
1077      ::                                          ::  ++curv:ed:crypto
1078      ++  curv                                    ::  point on curve?
1079      |=  [x=@ y=@]  ^-  ?
1080      .=  0
1081        %+  dif.fq
1082          %+  sum.fq
1083            (pro.fq (sub q (sit.fq x)) x)
1084          (pro.fq y y)
1085        (sum.fq 1 :(pro.fq d x x y y))
1086      ::                                          ::  ++deco:ed:crypto
1087      ++  deco                                    ::  decode point
1088      |=  s=@  ^-  (unit [@ @])
1089      =+  y=(cut 0 [0 (dec b)] s)
1090      =+  si=(cut 0 [(dec b) 1] s)
1091      =+  x=(xrec y)
1092      =>  .(x ?:(!=(si (dis 1 x)) (sub q x) x))
1093      =+  pp=[x y]
1094      ?.  (curv pp)
1095        ~
1096      [~ pp]
1097      ::                                          ::  ++bb:ed:crypto
1098      ++  bb                                      ::
1099      =+  bby=(pro.fq 4 (inv.fq 5))
```

```
1100        [(xrec bby) bby]
1101      --   ::
1102    ~%   %ed   +   ~
1103    |%
1104    ::
1105    ++   point-add
1106      ~/   %point-add
1107      |=  [a-point=@udpoint b-point=@udpoint]
1108      ^-  @udpoint
1109      ::
1110      =/  a-point-decoded=[@ @]   (need (deco a-point))
1111      =/  b-point-decoded=[@ @]   (need (deco b-point))
1112      ::
1113      %-  etch
1114      (ward a-point-decoded b-point-decoded)
1115    ::
1116    ++   scalarmult
1117      ~/   %scalarmult
1118      |=  [a=@udscalar a-point=@udpoint]
1119      ^-  @udpoint
1120      ::
1121      =/  a-point-decoded=[@ @]   (need (deco a-point))
1122      ::
1123      %-  etch
1124      (scam a-point-decoded a)
1125    ::
1126    ++   scalarmult-base
1127      ~/   %scalarmult-base
1128      |=  scalar=@udscalar
1129      ^-  @udpoint
1130      %-  etch
1131      (scam bb scalar)
1132    ::
1133    ++   add-scalarmult-scalarmult-base
1134      ~/   %add-scalarmult-scalarmult-base
1135      |=  [a=@udscalar a-point=@udpoint b=@udscalar]
1136      ^-  @udpoint
1137      ::
1138      =/  a-point-decoded=[@ @]   (need (deco a-point))
1139      ::
1140      %-  etch
1141      %+  ward
1142        (scam bb b)
1143      (scam a-point-decoded a)
1144    ::
1145    ++   add-double-scalarmult
1146      ~/   %add-double-scalarmult
1147      |=  [a=@udscalar a-point=@udpoint b=@udscalar b-point=@udpoint]
1148      ^-  @udpoint
1149      ::
1150      =/  a-point-decoded=[@ @]   (need (deco a-point))
1151      =/  b-point-decoded=[@ @]   (need (deco b-point))
1152      ::
1153      %-  etch
1154      %+  ward
1155        (scam a-point-decoded a)
1156      (scam b-point-decoded b)
1157    ::                                                    ::  ++puck:ed:crypto
```

```
1158    ++   puck                                       ::   public key
1159    ~/   %puck
1160    |=   sk=@I   ^-   @
1161    ?:   (gth (met 3 sk) 32)   !!
1162    =+   h=(shal (rsh [0 3] b) sk)
1163    =+   ^=   a
1164         %+   add
1165           (bex (sub b 2))
1166           (lsh [0 3] (cut 0 [3 (sub b 5)] h))
1167    =+   aa=(scam bb a)
1168    (etch aa)
1169    ::                                               ::   ++suck:ed:crypto
1170    ++   suck                                        ::   keypair from seed
1171    |=   se=@I   ^-   @uJ
1172    =+   pu=(puck se)
1173    (can 0 ~[[b se] [b pu]])
1174    ::                                               ::   ++shar:ed:crypto
1175    ++   shar                                        ::   curve25519 secret
1176    ~/   %shar
1177    |=   [pub=@ sek=@]
1178    ^-   @ux
1179    =+   exp=(shal (rsh [0 3] b) (suck sek))
1180    =.   exp   (dis exp (can 0 ~[[3 0] [251 (fil 0 251 1)]]))
1181    =.   exp   (con exp (lsh [3 31] 0b100.0000))
1182    =+   prv=(end 8 exp)
1183    =+   crv=(fra.fq (sum.fq 1 pub) (dif.fq 1 pub))
1184    (curt prv crv)
1185    ::                                               ::   ++sign:ed:crypto
1186    ++   sign                                        ::   certify
1187    ~/   %sign
1188    |=   [m=@ se=@]   ^-   @
1189    =+   sk=(suck se)
1190    =+   pk=(cut 0 [b b] sk)
1191    =+   h=(shal (rsh [0 3] b) sk)
1192    =+   ^=   a
1193         %+   add
1194           (bex (sub b 2))
1195           (lsh [0 3] (cut 0 [3 (sub b 5)] h))
1196    =+   ^=   r
1197         =+   hm=(cut 0 [b b] h)
1198         =+   ^=   i
1199             %+   can  0
1200             :~   [b hm]
1201                  [(met 0 m) m]
1202             ==
1203         (shaz i)
1204    =+   rr=(scam bb r)
1205    =+   ^=   ss
1206         =+   er=(etch rr)
1207         =+   ^=   ha
1208             %+   can  0
1209             :~   [b er]
1210                  [b pk]
1211                  [(met 0 m) m]
1212             ==
1213         (~(sit fo 1) (add r (mul (shaz ha) a)))
1214    (can 0 ~[[b (etch rr)] [b ss]])
1215    ::                                               ::   ++veri:ed:crypto
```

```
1216    ++  veri                                        ::  validate
1217    ~/  %veri
1218    |=  [s=@ m=@ pk=@]  ^-  ?
1219    ?:  (gth (div b 4) (met 3 s))  |
1220    ?:  (gth (div b 8) (met 3 pk))  |
1221    =+  cb=(rsh [0 3] b)
1222    =+  rr=(deco (cut 0 [0 b] s))
1223    ?~  rr  |
1224    =+  aa=(deco pk)
1225    ?~  aa  |
1226    =+  ss=(cut 0 [b b] s)
1227    =+  ha=(can 3 ~[[cb (etch u.rr)] [cb pk] [(met 3 m) m]])
1228    =+  h=(shaz ha)
1229    =((scam bb ss) (ward u.rr (scam u.aa h)))
1230    --  ::ed
1231  ::                                                 ::
1232  ::::                      ++scr:crypto             ::  (2b3) scrypt
1233    ::                                               ::::
1234  ++  scr
1235    ~%  %scr  ..part  ~
1236    |%
1237    ::                                               ::  ++sal:scr:crypto
1238    ++  sal                                          ::  salsa20 hash
1239    |=  [x=@ r=@]                                    ::  with r rounds
1240    ?>  =((mod r 2) 0)                               ::
1241    =+  few==>(fe .(a 5))
1242    =+  ^=  rot
1243      |=  [a=@ b=@]
1244      (mix (end 5 (lsh [0 a] b)) (rsh [0 (sub 32 a)] b))
1245    =+  ^=  lea
1246      |=  [a=@ b=@]
1247      (net:few (sum:few (net:few a) (net:few b)))
1248    =>  |%
1249        ::                                           ::  ++qr:sal:scr:crypto
1250        ++  qr                                       ::  quarterround
1251          |=  y=[@ @ @ @ ~]
1252          =+  zb=(mix &2.y (rot 7 (sum:few &1.y &4.y)))
1253          =+  zc=(mix &3.y (rot 9 (sum:few zb &1.y)))
1254          =+  zd=(mix &4.y (rot 13 (sum:few zc zb)))
1255          =+  za=(mix &1.y (rot 18 (sum:few zd zc)))
1256          ~[za zb zc zd]
1257        ::                                           ::  ++rr:sal:scr:crypto
1258        ++  rr                                       ::  rowround
1259          |=  [y=(list @)]
1260          =+  za=(qr ~[&1.y &2.y &3.y &4.y])
1261          =+  zb=(qr ~[&6.y &7.y &8.y &5.y])
1262          =+  zc=(qr ~[&11.y &12.y &9.y &10.y])
1263          =+  zd=(qr ~[&16.y &13.y &14.y &15.y])
1264          ^-  (list @)  :~
1265            &1.za   &2.za   &3.za   &4.za
1266            &4.zb   &1.zb   &2.zb   &3.zb
1267            &3.zc   &4.zc   &1.zc   &2.zc
1268            &2.zd   &3.zd   &4.zd   &1.zd   ==
1269        ::                                           ::  ++cr:sal:scr:crypto
1270        ++  cr                                       ::  columnround
1271          |=  [x=(list @)]
1272          =+  ya=(qr ~[&1.x &5.x &9.x &13.x])
1273          =+  yb=(qr ~[&6.x &10.x &14.x &2.x])
```

```
1274          =+  yc=(qr ~[&11.x &15.x &3.x &7.x])
1275          =+  yd=(qr ~[&16.x &4.x &8.x &12.x])
1276          ^-  (list @)  :~
1277            &1.ya  &4.yb  &3.yc  &2.yd
1278            &2.ya  &1.yb  &4.yc  &3.yd
1279            &3.ya  &2.yb  &1.yc  &4.yd
1280            &4.ya  &3.yb  &2.yc  &1.yd  ==
1281        ::                                      ::  ++dr:sal:scr:crypto
1282      ++  dr                                    ::  doubleround
1283        |=  [x=(list @)]
1284        (rr (cr x))
1285        ::                                      ::  ++al:sal:scr:crypto
1286      ++  al                                    ::  add two lists
1287        |=  [a=(list @) b=(list @)]
1288        |-  ^-  (list @)
1289        ?~  a  ~  ?~  b  ~
1290        [i=(sum:few -.a -.b) t=$(a +.a, b +.b)]
1291        --  ::
1292    =+  xw=(rpp 5 16 x)
1293    =+  ^=  ow  |-  ^-  (list @)
1294              ?~  r  xw
1295              $(xw (dr xw), r (sub r 2))
1296    (rep 5 (al xw ow))
1297    ::                                          ::  ++rpp:scr:crypto
1298  ++  rpp                                       ::  rip+filler blocks
1299    |=  [a=bloq b=@ c=@]
1300    =+  q=(rip a c)
1301    =+  w=(lent q)
1302    ?.  =(w b)
1303      ?.  (lth w b)  (slag (sub w b) q)
1304      ^+  q  (weld q (reap (sub b (lent q)) 0))
1305    q
1306    ::                                          ::  ++bls:scr:crypto
1307  ++  bls                                       ::  split to sublists
1308    |=  [a=@ b=(list @)]
1309    ?>  =((mod (lent b) a) 0)
1310    |-  ^-  (list (list @))
1311    ?~  b  ~
1312    [i=(scag a `(list @)`b) t=$(b (slag a `(list @)`b))]
1313    ::                                          ::  ++slb:scr:crypto
1314  ++  slb                                       ::
1315    |=  [a=(list (list @))]
1316    |-  ^-  (list @)
1317    ?~  a  ~
1318    (weld `(list @)`-.a $(a +.a))
1319    ::                                          ::  ++sbm:scr:crypto
1320  ++  sbm                                       ::  scryptBlockMix
1321    |=  [r=@ b=(list @)]
1322    ?>  =((lent b) (mul 2 r))
1323    =+  [x=(snag (dec (mul 2 r)) b) c=0]
1324    =|  [ya=(list @) yb=(list @)]
1325    |-  ^-  (list @)
1326    ?~  b  (flop (weld yb ya))
1327    =.  x  (sal (mix x -.b) 8)
1328    ?~  (mod c 2)
1329      $(c +(c), b +.b, ya [i=x t=ya])
1330    $(c +(c), b +.b, yb [i=x t=yb])
1331    ::                                          ::  ++srm:scr:crypto
```

```
++  srm                                          ::  scryptROMix
|=  [r=@ b=(list @) n=@]
?>  ?&  =((lent b) (mul 2 r))
        =(n (bex (dec (xeb n))))
        (lth n (bex (mul r 16)))
    ==
=+  [v=*(list (list @)) c=0]
=.  v
  |-  ^-  (list (list @))
  =+  w=(sbm r b)
  ?:  =(c n)  (flop v)
  $(c +(c), v [i=[b] t=v], b w)
=+  x=(sbm r (snag (dec n) v))
|-  ^-  (list @)
?:  =(c n)  x
=+  q=(snag (dec (mul r 2)) x)
=+  z=`(list @)`(snag (mod q n) v)
=+  ^=  w  |-  ^-  (list @)
           ?~  x  ~  ?~  z  ~
           [i=(mix -.x -.z) t=$(x +.x, z +.z)]
$(x (sbm r w), c +(c))
::                                               ::  ++hmc:scr:crypto
++  hmc                                          ::  HMAC-SHA-256
|=  [k=@ t=@]
(hml k (met 3 k) t (met 3 t))
::                                               ::  ++hml:scr:crypto
++  hml                                          ::  w+length
|=  [k=@ kl=@ t=@ tl=@]
=>  .(k (end [3 kl] k), t (end [3 tl] t))
=+  b=64
=?  k  (gth kl b)  (shay kl k)
=+  ^=  q  %+  shay  (add b tl)
(add (lsh [3 b] t) (mix k (fil 3 b 0x36)))
%+  shay  (add b 32)
(add (lsh [3 b] q) (mix k (fil 3 b 0x5c)))
::                                               ::  ++pbk:scr:crypto
++  pbk                                          ::  PBKDF2-HMAC-SHA256
~/  %pbk
|=  [p=@ s=@ c=@ d=@]
(pbl p (met 3 p) s (met 3 s) c d)
::                                               ::  ++pbl:scr:crypto
++  pbl                                          ::  w+length
~/  %pbl
|=  [p=@ pl=@ s=@ sl=@ c=@ d=@]
=>  .(p (end [3 pl] p), s (end [3 sl] s))
=+  h=32
::
::  max key length 1GB
::  max iterations 2^28
::
?>  ?&  (lte d (bex 30))
        (lte c (bex 28))
        !=(c 0)
    ==
=+  ^=  l  ?~  (mod d h)
(div d h)
+((div d h))
=+  r=(sub d (mul h (dec l)))
```

```
1390        =+  [t=0 j=1 k=1]
1391        =.  t  |-  ^-  @
1392         ?:  (gth j l)  t
1393         =+  u=(add s (lsh [3 sl] (rep 3 (flop (rpp 3 4 j)))))
1394          =+  f=0  =.  f  |-  ^-  @
1395          ?:  (gth k c)  f
1396          =+  q=(hml p pl u ?:(=(k 1) (add sl 4) h))
1397          $(u q, f (mix f q), k +(k))
1398         $(t (add t (lsh [3 (mul (dec j) h)] f)), j +(j))
1399        (end [3 d] t)
1400    ::                                          ::  ++hsh:scr:crypto
1401    ++  hsh                                     ::  scrypt
1402     ~/  %hsh
1403     |=  [p=@ s=@ n=@ r=@ z=@ d=@]
1404     (hsl p (met 3 p) s (met 3 s) n r z d)
1405    ::                                          ::  ++hsl:scr:crypto
1406    ++  hsl                                     ::  w+length
1407     ~/  %hsl
1408     |=  [p=@ pl=@ s=@ sl=@ n=@ r=@ z=@ d=@]
1409     =|  v=(list (list @))
1410     =>  .(p (end [3 pl] p), s (end [3 sl] s))
1411     =+  u=(mul (mul 128 r) z)
1412     ::
1413     ::  n is power of 2; max 1GB memory
1414     ::
1415     ?>  ?&  =(n (bex (dec (xeb n))))
1416             !=(r 0)  !=(z 0)
1417             %+  lte
1418               (mul (mul 128 r) (dec (add n z)))
1419             (bex 30)
1420             (lth pl (bex 31))
1421             (lth sl (bex 31))
1422         ==
1423     =+  ^=  b  =+  (rpp 3 u (pbl p pl s sl 1 u))
1424       %+  turn  (bls (mul 128 r) -)
1425       |=(a=(list @) (rpp 9 (mul 2 r) (rep 3 a)))
1426     ?>  =((lent b) z)
1427     =+  ^=  q
1428       =+  |-  ?~  b  (flop v)
1429         $(b +.b, v [i=(srm r -.b n) t=v])
1430       %+  turn  `(list (list @))`-
1431       |=(a=(list @) (rpp 3 (mul 128 r) (rep 9 a)))
1432     (pbl p pl (rep 3 (slb q)) u 1 d)
1433    ::                                          ::  ++ypt:scr:crypto
1434    ++  ypt                                     ::  256bit {salt pass}
1435     |=  [s=@ p=@]
1436     ^-  @
1437     (hsh p s 16.384 8 1 256)
1438    --  ::scr
1439  ::                                            ::
1440  ::::                    ++crub:crypto         ::  (2b4) suite B, Ed
1441    ::                                          ::::
1442  ++  crub  !:
1443    ^-  acru
1444    =|  [pub=[cry=@ sgn=@] sek=(unit [cry=@ sgn=@])]
1445    |%
1446    ::                                          ::  ++as:crub:crypto
1447    ++  as                                      ::
```

```
1448        |%
1449        ::                                              ::  ++sign:as:crub:
1450        ++  sign                                         ::
1451          |=  msg=@
1452          ^-  @ux
1453          (jam [(sigh msg) msg])
1454        ::                                              ::  ++sigh:as:crub:
1455        ++  sigh                                         ::
1456          |=  msg=@
1457          ^-  @ux
1458          ?~  sek  ~|  %pubkey-only  !!
1459          (sign:ed msg sgn.u.sek)
1460        ::                                              ::  ++sure:as:crub:
1461        ++  sure                                         ::
1462          |=  txt=@
1463          ^-  (unit @ux)
1464          =+  ;;([sig=@ msg=@] (cue txt))
1465          ?.  (safe sig msg)  ~
1466          (some msg)
1467        ::                                              ::  ++safe:as:crub:
1468        ++  safe
1469          |=  [sig=@ msg=@]
1470          ^-  ?
1471          (veri:ed sig msg sgn.pub)
1472        ::                                              ::  ++seal:as:crub:
1473        ++  seal                                         ::
1474          |=  [bpk=pass msg=@]
1475          ^-  @ux
1476          ?~  sek  ~|  %pubkey-only  !!
1477          ?>  =('b' (end 3 bpk))
1478          =+  pk=(rsh 8 (rsh 3 bpk))
1479          =+  shar=(shax (shar:ed pk cry.u.sek))
1480          =+  smsg=(sign msg)
1481          (jam (~(en siva:aes shar ~) smsg))
1482        ::                                              ::  ++tear:as:crub:
1483        ++  tear                                         ::
1484          |=  [bpk=pass txt=@]
1485          ^-  (unit @ux)
1486          ?~  sek  ~|  %pubkey-only  !!
1487          ?>  =('b' (end 3 bpk))
1488          =+  pk=(rsh 8 (rsh 3 bpk))
1489          =+  shar=(shax (shar:ed pk cry.u.sek))
1490          =+  ;;([iv=@ len=@ cph=@] (cue txt))
1491          =+  try=(~(de siva:aes shar ~) iv len cph)
1492          ?~  try  ~
1493          (sure:as:(com:nu:crub bpk) u.try)
1494        --  ::as
1495      ::                                                ::  ++de:crub:crypto
1496      ++  de                                            ::  decrypt
1497        |=  [key=@J txt=@]
1498        ^-  (unit @ux)
1499        =+  ;;([iv=@ len=@ cph=@] (cue txt))
1500        %^    ~(de sivc:aes (shaz key) ~)
1501           iv
1502         len
1503        cph
1504      ::                                                ::  ++dy:crub:crypto
1505      ++  dy                                            ::  need decrypt
```

```
1506        |=  [key=@J cph=@]
1507        (need (de key cph))
1508      ::                                      ::  ++en:crub:crypto
1509      ++  en                                  ::  encrypt
1510        |=  [key=@J msg=@]
1511        ^-  @ux
1512        (jam (~(en sivc:aes (shaz key)) ~) msg))
1513      ::                                      ::  ++ex:crub:crypto
1514      ++  ex                                  ::  extract
1515        |%
1516        ::                                    ::  ++fig:ex:crub:crypto
1517        ++  fig                               ::  fingerprint
1518          ^-  @uvH
1519          (shaf %bfig pub)
1520        ::                                    ::  ++pac:ex:crub:crypto
1521        ++  pac                               ::  private fingerprint
1522          ^-  @uvG
1523          ?~  sek  ~|  %pubkey-only  !!
1524          (end 6 (shaf %bcod sec))
1525        ::                                    ::  ++pub:ex:crub:crypto
1526        ++  pub                               ::  public key
1527          ^-  pass
1528          (cat 3 'b' (cat 8 sgn.^pub cry.^pub))
1529        ::                                    ::  ++sec:ex:crub:crypto
1530        ++  sec                               ::  private key
1531          ^-  ring
1532          ?~  sek  ~|  %pubkey-only  !!
1533          (cat 3 'B' (cat 8 sgn.u.sek cry.u.sek))
1534        --  ::ex
1535      ::                                      ::  ++nu:crub:crypto
1536      ++  nu                                  ::
1537        |%
1538        ::                                    ::  ++pit:nu:crub:crypto
1539        ++  pit                               ::  create keypair
1540          |=  [w=@ seed=@]
1541          =+  wid=(add (div w 8) ?:(=((mod w 8) 0) 0 1))
1542          =+  bits=(shal wid seed)
1543          =+  [c=(rsh 8 bits) s=(end 8 bits)]
1544          ..nu(pub [cry=(puck:ed c) sgn=(puck:ed s)], sek `[cry=c sgn=s])
1545        ::                                    ::  ++nol:nu:crub:crypto
1546        ++  nol                               ::  activate secret
1547          |=  a=ring
1548          =+  [mag=(end 3 a) bod=(rsh 3 a)]
1549          ~|  %not-crub-seckey  ?>  =('B' mag)
1550          =+  [c=(rsh 8 bod) s=(end 8 bod)]
1551          ..nu(pub [cry=(puck:ed c) sgn=(puck:ed s)], sek `[cry=c sgn=s])
1552        ::                                    ::  ++com:nu:crub:crypto
1553        ++  com                               ::  activate public
1554          |=  a=pass
1555          =+  [mag=(end 3 a) bod=(rsh 3 a)]
1556          ~|  %not-crub-pubkey  ?>  =('b' mag)
1557          ..nu(pub [cry=(rsh 8 bod) sgn=(end 8 bod)], sek ~)
1558        --  ::nu
1559      --  ::crub
1560    ::                                        ::
1561    ::::                      ++crua:crypto   ::  (2b5) suite B, RSA
1562      ::                                      ::::
1563    ++  crua  !!
```

```
1564      ::                                                    ::
1565      ::::                    ++test:crypto                 ::  (2b6) test crypto
1566      ::                                                    ::::
1567  ++  test  ^?
1568      |%
1569      ::                                                    ::  ++trub:test:crypto
1570      ++  trub                                              ::  test crub
1571      |=  msg=@t
1572      ::
1573      ::  make acru cores
1574      ::
1575      =/  ali      (pit:nu:crub 512 (shaz 'Alice'))
1576      =/  ali-pub  (com:nu:crub pub:ex.ali)
1577      =/  bob      (pit:nu:crub 512 (shaz 'Robert'))
1578      =/  bob-pub  (com:nu:crub pub:ex.bob)
1579      ::
1580      ::  alice signs and encrypts a symmetric key to bob
1581      ::
1582      =/  secret-key  %-  shaz
1583      'Let there be no duplicity when taking a stand against him.'
1584      =/  signed-key   (sign:as.ali secret-key)
1585      =/  crypted-key  (seal:as.ali pub:ex.bob-pub signed-key)
1586      ::  bob decrypts and verifies
1587      =/  decrypt-key-attempt  (tear:as.bob pub:ex.ali-pub crypted-key)
1588      =/  decrypted-key   ~|  %decrypt-fail  (need decrypt-key-attempt)
1589      =/  verify-key-attempt  (sure:as.ali-pub decrypted-key)
1590      =/  verified-key    ~|  %verify-fail  (need verify-key-attempt)
1591      ::  bob encrypts with symmetric key
1592      =/  crypted-msg  (en.bob verified-key msg)
1593      ::  alice decrypts with same key
1594      `@t`(dy.ali secret-key crypted-msg)
1595      --  ::test
1596      ::                                                    ::
1597      ::::                    ++keccak:crypto               ::  (2b7) keccak family
1598      ::                                                    ::::
1599  ++  keccak
1600      ~%  %kecc  ..part  ~
1601      |%
1602      ::
1603      ::  keccak
1604      ::
1605      ++  keccak-224  ~/  %k224  |=(a=octs (keccak 1.152 448 224 a))
1606      ++  keccak-256  ~/  %k256  |=(a=octs (keccak 1.088 512 256 a))
1607      ++  keccak-384  ~/  %k384  |=(a=octs (keccak 832 768 384 a))
1608      ++  keccak-512  ~/  %k512  |=(a=octs (keccak 576 1.024 512 a))
1609      ::
1610      ++  keccak  (cury (cury hash keccak-f) padding-keccak)
1611      ::
1612      ++  padding-keccak  (multirate-padding 0x1)
1613      ::
1614      ::  sha3
1615      ::
1616      ++  sha3-224  |=(a=octs (sha3 1.152 448 224 a))
1617      ++  sha3-256  |=(a=octs (sha3 1.088 512 256 a))
1618      ++  sha3-384  |=(a=octs (sha3 832 768 384 a))
1619      ++  sha3-512  |=(a=octs (sha3 576 1.024 512 a))
1620      ::
1621      ++  sha3  (cury (cury hash keccak-f) padding-sha3)
```

```
1622      ::
1623      ++  padding-sha3  (multirate-padding 0x6)
1624      ::
1625      ::  shake
1626      ::
1627      ++  shake-128  |=([o=@ud i=octs] (shake 1.344 256 o i))
1628      ++  shake-256  |=([o=@ud i=octs] (shake 1.088 512 o i))
1629      ::
1630      ++  shake  (cury (cury hash keccak-f) padding-shake)
1631      ::
1632      ++  padding-shake  (multirate-padding 0x1f)
1633      ::
1634      ::  rawshake
1635      ::
1636      ++  rawshake-128  |=([o=@ud i=octs] (rawshake 1.344 256 o i))
1637      ++  rawshake-256  |=([o=@ud i=octs] (rawshake 1.088 512 o i))
1638      ::
1639      ++  rawshake  (cury (cury hash keccak-f) padding-rawshake)
1640      ::
1641      ++  padding-rawshake  (multirate-padding 0x7)
1642      ::
1643      ::  core
1644      ::
1645      ++  hash
1646      ::  per:  permutation function with configurable width.
1647      ::  pad:  padding function.
1648      ::  rat:  bitrate, size in bits of blocks to operate on.
1649      ::  cap:  capacity, bits of sponge padding.
1650      ::  out:  length of desired output, in bits.
1651      ::  inp:  input to hash.
1652      |=  $:  per=$-(@ud $-(@ @))
1653              pad=$-([octs @ud] octs)
1654              rat=@ud
1655              cap=@ud
1656              out=@ud
1657              inp=octs
1658          ==
1659      ^-  @
1660      ::  urbit's little-endian to keccak's big-endian.
1661      =.  q.inp  (rev 3 inp)
1662      %.  [inp out]
1663      (sponge per pad rat cap)
1664      ::
1665      ::NOTE  if ++keccak ever needs to be made to operate
1666      ::        on bits rather than bytes, all that needs to
1667      ::        be done is updating the way this padding
1668      ::        function works. (and also "octs" -> "bits")
1669      ++  multirate-padding
1670      ::  dsb:  domain separation byte, reverse bit order.
1671      |=  dsb=@ux
1672      ?>  (lte dsb 0xff)
1673      |=  [inp=octs mut=@ud]
1674      ^-  octs
1675      =.  mut  (div mut 8)
1676      =+  pal=(sub mut (mod p.inp mut))
1677      =?  pal  =(pal 0)  mut
1678      =.  pal  (dec pal)
1679      :-  (add p.inp +(pal))
```

```
1680      ::  padding is provided in lane bit ordering,
1681      ::  ie, LSB = left.
1682     (cat 3 (con (lsh [3 pal] dsb) 0x80) q.inp)
1683   ::
1684   ++  sponge
1685      ::  sponge construction
1686      ::
1687      ::  preperm:  permutation function with configurable width.
1688      ::  padding:  padding function.
1689      ::  bitrate:  size of blocks to operate on.
1690      ::  capacity: sponge padding.
1691     |=  $:  preperm=$-(@ud $-(@ @))
1692             padding=$-([octs @ud] octs)
1693             bitrate=@ud
1694             capacity=@ud
1695         ==
1696      ::
1697      ::  preparing
1698     =+  bitrate-bytes=(div bitrate 8)
1699     =+  blockwidth=(add bitrate capacity)
1700     =+  permute=(preperm blockwidth)
1701      ::
1702     |=  [input=octs output=@ud]
1703     |^  ^-  @
1704       ::
1705       ::  padding
1706     =.  input   (padding input bitrate)
1707       ::
1708       ::  absorbing
1709     =/  pieces=(list @)
1710       ::  amount of bitrate-sized blocks.
1711       ?>  =(0 (mod p.input bitrate-bytes))
1712       =+  i=(div p.input bitrate-bytes)
1713       |-
1714       ?:  =(i 0)   ~
1715       :_  $(i (dec i))
1716       ::  get the bitrate-sized block of bytes
1717       ::  that ends with the byte at -.
1718       =-  (cut 3 [- bitrate-bytes] q.input)
1719      (mul (dec i) bitrate-bytes)
1720     =/  state=@
1721       ::  for every piece,
1722       %+  roll  pieces
1723       |=  [p=@ s=@]
1724       ::  pad with capacity,
1725       =.  p  (lsh [0 capacity] p)
1726       ::  xor it into the state and permute it.
1727      (permute (mix s (bytes-to-lanes p)))
1728      ::
1729      ::  squeezing
1730     =|  res=@
1731     =|  len=@ud
1732     |-
1733      ::  append a bitrate-sized head of state to the
1734      ::  result.
1735     =.  res
1736       %+  con  (lsh [0 bitrate] res)
1737      (rsh [0 capacity] (lanes-to-bytes state))
```

```
1738        =.  len   (add len bitrate)
1739        ?:  (gte len output)
1740          ::  produce the requested bits of output.
1741          (rsh [0 (sub len output)] res)
1742        $(res res, state (permute state))
1743      ::
1744      ++  bytes-to-lanes
1745        ::  flip byte order in blocks of 8 bytes.
1746        |=  a=@
1747        %^  run  6  a
1748        |=(b=@ (lsh [3 (sub 8 (met 3 b))] (swp 3 b)))
1749      ::
1750      ++  lanes-to-bytes
1751        ::  unflip byte order in blocks of 8 bytes.
1752        |=  a=@
1753        %+  can  6
1754        %+  turn
1755          =+  (rip 6 a)
1756          (weld - (reap (sub 25 (lent -)) 0x0))
1757        |=  a=@
1758        :-  1
1759        %+  can  3
1760        =-  (turn - |=(a=@ [1 a]))
1761        =+  (flop (rip 3 a))
1762        (weld (reap (sub 8 (lent -)) 0x0) -)
1763      --
1764    ::
1765    ++  keccak-f
1766      ::  keccak permutation function
1767      |=  [width=@ud]
1768      ::  assert valid blockwidth.
1769      ?>  =-  (~(has in -) width)
1770          (sy 25 50 100 200 400 800 1.600 ~)
1771      ::  assumes 5x5 lanes state, as is the keccak
1772      ::  standard.
1773      =+  size=5
1774      =+  lanes=(mul size size)
1775      =+  lane-bloq=(dec (xeb (div width lanes)))
1776      =+  lane-size=(bex lane-bloq)
1777      =+  rounds=(add 12 (mul 2 lane-bloq))
1778      |=  [input=@]
1779      ^-  @
1780      =*  a  input
1781      =+  round=0
1782      |^
1783        ?:  =(round rounds)  a
1784        ::
1785        ::  theta
1786        =/  c=@
1787          %+  roll  (gulf 0 (dec size))
1788          |=  [x=@ud c=@]
1789          %+  con  (lsh [lane-bloq 1] c)
1790          %+  roll  (gulf 0 (dec size))
1791          |=  [y=@ud c=@]
1792          (mix c (get-lane x y a))
1793        =/  d=@
1794          %+  roll  (gulf 0 (dec size))
1795          |=  [x=@ud d=@]
```

```
1796        %+  con   (lsh [lane-bloq 1] d)
1797        %+  mix
1798          =-  (get-word - size c)
1799          ?:(=(x 0) (dec size) (dec x))
1800        %^  ~(rol fe lane-bloq)  0  1
1801        (get-word (mod +(x) size) size c)
1802      =.  a
1803        %+  roll  (gulf 0 (dec lanes))
1804        |=  [i=@ud a=_a]
1805        %+  mix  a
1806        %+  lsh
1807          [lane-bloq (sub lanes +(i))]
1808        (get-word i size d)
1809      ::
1810      ::  rho and pi
1811      =/  b=@
1812        %+  roll  (gulf 0 (dec lanes))
1813        |=  [i=@ b=@]
1814        =+  x=(mod i 5)
1815        =+  y=(div i 5)
1816        %+  con  b
1817        %+  lsh
1818          :-  lane-bloq
1819          %+  sub  lanes
1820          %+  add  +(y)
1821          %+  mul  size
1822          (mod (add (mul 2 x) (mul 3 y)) size)
1823        %^  ~(rol fe lane-bloq)  0
1824          (rotation-offset i)
1825        (get-word i lanes a)
1826      ::
1827      ::  chi
1828      =.  a
1829        %+  roll  (gulf 0 (dec lanes))
1830        |=  [i=@ud a=@]
1831        %+  con  (lsh lane-bloq a)
1832        =+  x=(mod i 5)
1833        =+  y=(div i 5)
1834        %+  mix  (get-lane x y b)
1835        %+  dis
1836          =-  (get-lane - y b)
1837          (mod (add x 2) size)
1838        %^  not  lane-bloq  1
1839        (get-lane (mod +(x) size) y b)
1840      ::
1841      ::  iota
1842      =.  a
1843        =+  (round-constant round)
1844        (mix a (lsh [lane-bloq (dec lanes)] -))
1845      ::
1846      ::  next round
1847      $(round +(round))
1848    ::
1849    ++  get-lane
1850      ::  get the lane with coordinates
1851      |=  [x=@ud y=@ud a=@]
1852      =+  i=(add x (mul size y))
1853      (get-word i lanes a)
```

```
1854        ::
1855        ++  get-word
1856          ::  get word {n} from atom {a} of {m} words.
1857          |=  [n=@ud m=@ud a=@]
1858          (cut lane-bloq [(sub m +((mod n m))) 1] a)
1859        ::
1860        ++  round-constant
1861          |=  c=@ud
1862          =-  (snag (mod c 24) -)
1863          ^-  (list @ux)
1864          :~  0x1
1865              0x8082
1866              0x8000.0000.0000.808a
1867              0x8000.0000.8000.8000
1868              0x808b
1869              0x8000.0001
1870              0x8000.0000.8000.8081
1871              0x8000.0000.0000.8009
1872              0x8a
1873              0x88
1874              0x8000.8009
1875              0x8000.000a
1876              0x8000.808b
1877              0x8000.0000.0000.008b
1878              0x8000.0000.0000.8089
1879              0x8000.0000.0000.8003
1880              0x8000.0000.0000.8002
1881              0x8000.0000.0000.0080
1882              0x800a
1883              0x8000.0000.8000.000a
1884              0x8000.0000.8000.8081
1885              0x8000.0000.0000.8080
1886              0x8000.0001
1887              0x8000.0000.8000.8008
1888          ==
1889        ::
1890        ++  rotation-offset
1891          |=  x=@ud
1892          =-  (snag x -)
1893          ^-  (list @ud)
1894          :~   0   1  62  28  27
1895              36  44   6  55  20
1896               3  10  43  25  39
1897              41  45  15  21   8
1898              18   2  61  56  14
1899          ==
1900        --
1901      --  ::keccak
1902    ::                                                          ::
1903    ::::                          ++hmac:crypto                ::  (2b8) hmac family
1904      ::                                                        ::::
1905    ++  hmac
1906      ~%  %hmac  ..part  ~
1907      =,  sha
1908      =>  |%
1909          ++  meet  |=([k=@ m=@] [[(met 3 k) k] [(met 3 m) m]])
1910          ++  flip  |=([k=@ m=@] [(swp 3 k) (swp 3 m)])
1911          --
```

```
1912      |%
1913      ::
1914      ::   use with @
1915      ::
1916      ++  hmac-sha1     (cork meet hmac-sha1l)
1917      ++  hmac-sha256   (cork meet hmac-sha256l)
1918      ++  hmac-sha512   (cork meet hmac-sha512l)
1919      ::
1920      ::   use with @t
1921      ::
1922      ++  hmac-sha1t    (cork flip hmac-sha1)
1923      ++  hmac-sha256t  (cork flip hmac-sha256)
1924      ++  hmac-sha512t  (cork flip hmac-sha512)
1925      ::
1926      ::   use with byts
1927      ::
1928      ++  hmac-sha1l    (cury hmac sha-1l 64 20)
1929      ++  hmac-sha256l  (cury hmac sha-256l 64 32)
1930      ++  hmac-sha512l  (cury hmac sha-512l 128 64)
1931      ::
1932      ::   main logic
1933      ::
1934      ++  hmac
1935      ~/  %hmac
1936      ::  boq: block size in bytes used by haj
1937      ::  out: bytes output by haj
1938      |*  [[haj=$-([@u @] @) boq=@u out=@u] key=byts msg=byts]
1939      ::  ensure key and message fit signaled lengths
1940      =.  dat.key  (end [3 wid.key] dat.key)
1941      =.  dat.msg  (end [3 wid.msg] dat.msg)
1942      ::  keys longer than block size are shortened by hashing
1943      =?  dat.key  (gth wid.key boq)  (haj wid.key dat.key)
1944      =?  wid.key  (gth wid.key boq)  out
1945      ::  keys shorter than block size are right-padded
1946      =?  dat.key  (lth wid.key boq)  (lsh [3 (sub boq wid.key)] dat.key)
1947      ::  pad key, inner and outer
1948      =+  kip=(mix dat.key (fil 3 boq 0x36))
1949      =+  kop=(mix dat.key (fil 3 boq 0x5c))
1950      ::  append inner padding to message, then hash
1951      =+  (haj (add wid.msg boq) (add (lsh [3 wid.msg] kip) dat.msg))
1952      ::  prepend outer padding to result, hash again
1953      (haj (add out boq) (add (lsh [3 out] kop) -))
1954    --  ::  hmac
1955    ::                                              ::
1956    ::::                    ++secp:crypto           ::  (2b9) secp family
1957    ::                                              ::::
1958  ++  secp  !.
1959    ::  TODO: as-octs and hmc are outside of jet parent
1960    =>  :+  ..part
1961        hmc=hmac-sha256l:hmac:crypto
1962      as-octs=as-octs:mimes:html
1963    ~%  %secp  +<  ~
1964    |%
1965    +$  jacobian   [x=@ y=@ z=@]                   ::  jacobian point
1966    +$  point      [x=@ y=@]                       ::  curve point
1967    +$  domain
1968      $:  p=@                                      ::  prime modulo
1969          a=@                                      ::  y^2=x^3+ax+b
```

```
1970          b=@                              ::
1971          g=point                          ::  base point
1972          n=@                              ::  prime order of g
1973        ==
1974    ++  secp
1975      |_  [bytes=@ =domain]
1976      ++  field-p  ~(. fo p.domain)
1977      ++  field-n  ~(. fo n.domain)
1978      ++  compress-point
1979        |=  =point
1980        ^-  @
1981        %+  can  3
1982        :~  [bytes x.point]
1983            [1 (add 2 (cut 0 [0 1] y.point))]
1984        ==
1985      ::
1986      ++  serialize-point
1987        |=  =point
1988        ^-  @
1989        %+  can  3
1990        :~  [bytes y.point]
1991            [bytes x.point]
1992            [1 4]
1993        ==
1994      ::
1995      ++  decompress-point
1996        |=  compressed=@
1997        ^-  point
1998        =/  x=@  (end [3 bytes] compressed)
1999        ?>  =(3 (mod p.domain 4))
2000        =/  fop  field-p
2001        =+  [fadd fmul fpow]=[sum.fop pro.fop exp.fop]
2002        =/  y=@  %+  fpow  (rsh [0 2] +(p.domain))
2003                 %+  fadd  b.domain
2004                 %+  fadd  (fpow 3 x)
2005            (fmul a.domain x)
2006        =/  s=@  (rsh [3 bytes] compressed)
2007        ~|  [`@ux`s `@ux`compressed]
2008        ?>  |(=(2 s) =(3 s))
2009        ::  check parity
2010        ::
2011        =?  y  !=((sub s 2) (mod y 2))
2012          (sub p.domain y)
2013        [x y]
2014      ::
2015      ++  jc                               ::  jacobian math
2016        |%
2017        ++  from
2018          |=  a=jacobian
2019          ^-  point
2020          =/  fop   field-p
2021          =+  [fmul fpow finv]=[pro.fop exp.fop inv.fop]
2022          =/  z  (finv z.a)
2023          :-  (fmul x.a (fpow 2 z))
2024          (fmul y.a (fpow 3 z))
2025        ::
2026        ++  into
2027          |=  point
```

```
2028        ^-  jacobian
2029        [x y 1]
2030      ::
2031      ++  double
2032        |=  jacobian
2033        ^-  jacobian
2034        ?:  =(0 y)  [0 0 0]
2035        =/  fop  field-p
2036        =+  [fadd fsub fmul fpow]=[sum.fop dif.fop pro.fop exp.fop]
2037        =/  s   :(fmul 4 x (fpow 2 y))
2038        =/  m   %+  fadd
2039                  (fmul 3 (fpow 2 x))
2040                  (fmul a.domain (fpow 4 z))
2041        =/  nx  %+  fsub
2042                  (fpow 2 m)
2043                  (fmul 2 s)
2044        =/  ny  %+  fsub
2045                  (fmul m (fsub s nx))
2046                  (fmul 8 (fpow 4 y))
2047        =/  nz  :(fmul 2 y z)
2048        [nx ny nz]
2049      ::
2050      ++  add
2051        |=  [a=jacobian b=jacobian]
2052        ^-  jacobian
2053        ?:  =(0 y.a)  b
2054        ?:  =(0 y.b)  a
2055        =/  fop  field-p
2056        =+  [fadd fsub fmul fpow]=[sum.fop dif.fop pro.fop exp.fop]
2057        =/  u1  :(fmul x.a z.b z.b)
2058        =/  u2  :(fmul x.b z.a z.a)
2059        =/  s1  :(fmul y.a z.b z.b z.b)
2060        =/  s2  :(fmul y.b z.a z.a z.a)
2061        ?:  =(u1 u2)
2062          ?.  =(s1 s2)
2063            [0 0 1]
2064          (double a)
2065        =/  h     (fsub u2 u1)
2066        =/  r     (fsub s2 s1)
2067        =/  h2    (fmul h h)
2068        =/  h3    (fmul h2 h)
2069        =/  u1h2  (fmul u1 h2)
2070        =/  nx    %+  fsub
2071                    (fmul r r)
2072                    :(fadd h3 u1h2 u1h2)
2073        =/  ny    %+  fsub
2074                    (fmul r (fsub u1h2 nx))
2075                    (fmul s1 h3)
2076        =/  nz    :(fmul h z.a z.b)
2077        [nx ny nz]
2078      ::
2079      ++  mul
2080        |=  [a=jacobian scalar=@]
2081        ^-  jacobian
2082        ?:  =(0 y.a)
2083          [0 0 1]
2084        ?:  =(0 scalar)
2085          [0 0 1]
```

```
2086         ?:  =(1 scalar)
2087           a
2088         ?:  (gte scalar n.domain)
2089           $(scalar (mod scalar n.domain))
2090         ?:  =(0 (mod scalar 2))
2091           (double $(scalar (rsh 0 scalar)))
2092         (add a (double $(scalar (rsh 0 scalar))))
2093       --
2094   ++  add-points
2095     |=  [a=point b=point]
2096     ^-  point
2097     =/  j   jc
2098     (from.j (add.j (into.j a) (into.j b)))
2099   ++  mul-point-scalar
2100     |=  [p=point scalar=@]
2101     ^-  point
2102     =/  j   jc
2103     %-  from.j
2104     %+  mul.j
2105       (into.j p)
2106     scalar
2107   ::
2108   ++  valid-hash
2109     |=  has=@
2110     (lte (met 3 has) bytes)
2111   ::
2112   ++  in-order
2113     |=  i=@
2114     ?&  (gth i 0)
2115         (lth i n.domain)
2116       ==
2117   ++  priv-to-pub
2118     |=  private-key=@
2119     ^-  point
2120     ?>  (in-order private-key)
2121     (mul-point-scalar g.domain private-key)
2122   ::
2123   ++  make-k
2124     |=  [hash=@ private-key=@]
2125     ^-  @
2126     ?>  (in-order private-key)
2127     ?>  (valid-hash hash)
2128     =/  v   (fil 3 bytes 1)
2129     =/  k   0
2130     =.  k   %+  hmc  [bytes k]
2131             %-  as-octs
2132             %+  can  3
2133             :~  [bytes hash]
2134                 [bytes private-key]
2135                 [1 0]
2136                 [bytes v]
2137             ==
2138     =.  v   (hmc bytes^k bytes^v)
2139     =.  k   %+  hmc  [bytes k]
2140             %-  as-octs
2141             %+  can  3
2142             :~  [bytes hash]
2143                 [bytes private-key]
```

```
2144                   [1 1]
2145                   [bytes v]
2146                 ==
2147        =.  v  (hmc bytes^k bytes^v)
2148        (hmc bytes^k bytes^v)
2149      ::
2150    ++  ecdsa-raw-sign
2151      |=  [hash=@ private-key=@]
2152      ^-  [r=@ s=@ y=@]
2153      ::  make-k and priv-to pub will validate inputs
2154      =/  k   (make-k hash private-key)
2155      =/  rp  (priv-to-pub k)
2156      =*  r   x.rp
2157      ?<  =(0 r)
2158      =/  fon  field-n
2159      =+  [fadd fmul finv]=[sum.fon pro.fon inv.fon]
2160      =/  s   %+  fmul  (finv k)
2161              %+  fadd  hash
2162              %+  fmul  r
2163              private-key
2164      ?<  =(0 s)
2165      [r s y.rp]
2166      ::  general recovery omitted, but possible
2167      --
2168    ++  secp256k1
2169      ~%  %secp256k1  +  ~
2170      |%
2171      ++  t  :: in the battery for jet matching
2172        ^-  domain
2173        :*  0xffff.ffff.ffff.ffff.ffff.ffff.ffff.ffff.
2174            ffff.ffff.ffff.ffff.ffff.fffe.ffff.fc2f
2175            0
2176            7
2177            :-  0x79be.667e.f9dc.bbac.55a0.6295.ce87.0b07.
2178                029b.fcdb.2dce.28d9.59f2.815b.16f8.1798
2179                0x483a.da77.26a3.c465.5da4.fbfc.0e11.08a8.
2180                fd17.b448.a685.5419.9c47.d08f.fb10.d4b8
2181            0xffff.ffff.ffff.ffff.ffff.ffff.ffff.fffe.
2182            baae.dce6.af48.a03b.bfd2.5e8c.d036.4141
2183        ==
2184      ::
2185    ++  curve             ~(. secp 32 t)
2186    ++  serialize-point   serialize-point:curve
2187    ++  compress-point    compress-point:curve
2188    ++  decompress-point  decompress-point:curve
2189    ++  add-points        add-points:curve
2190    ++  mul-point-scalar  mul-point-scalar:curve
2191    ++  make-k
2192      ~/  %make
2193      |=  [hash=@uvI private-key=@]
2194      ::  checks sizes
2195      (make-k:curve hash private-key)
2196    ++  priv-to-pub
2197      |=  private-key=@
2198      ::  checks sizes
2199      (priv-to-pub:curve private-key)
2200      ::
2201    ++  ecdsa-raw-sign
```

```
2202        ~/  %sign
2203        |=  [hash=@uvI private-key=@]
2204        ^-  [v=@ r=@ s=@]
2205        =/  c   curve
2206        ::  raw-sign checks sizes
2207        =+  (ecdsa-raw-sign.c hash private-key)
2208        =/  rp=point  [r y]
2209        =/  s-high  (gte (mul 2 s) n.domain.c)
2210        =?  s   s-high
2211        (sub n.domain.c s)
2212        =?  rp  s-high
2213        [x.rp (sub p.domain.c y.rp)]
2214        =/  v   (end 0 y.rp)
2215        =?  v   (gte x.rp n.domain.c)
2216        (add v 2)
2217        [v x.rp s]
2218    ::
2219    ++  ecdsa-raw-recover
2220        ~/  %reco
2221        |=  [hash=@ sig=[v=@ r=@ s=@]]
2222        ^-  point
2223        ?>  (lte v.sig 3)
2224        =/  c   curve
2225        ?>  (valid-hash.c hash)
2226        ?>  (in-order.c r.sig)
2227        ?>  (in-order.c s.sig)
2228        =/  x   ?:  (gte v.sig 2)
2229                    (add r.sig n.domain.c)
2230                r.sig
2231        =/  fop   field-p.c
2232        =+  [fadd fmul fpow]=[sum.fop pro.fop exp.fop]
2233        =/  ysq   (fadd (fpow 3 x) b.domain.c)
2234        =/  beta  (fpow (rsh [0 2] +(p.domain.c)) ysq)
2235        =/  y   ?:  =((end 0 v.sig) (end 0 beta))
2236                beta
2237            (sub p.domain.c beta)
2238        ?>  =(0 (dif.fop ysq (fmul y y)))
2239        =/  nz   (sub n.domain.c hash)
2240        =/  j    jc.c
2241        =/  gz   (mul.j (into.j g.domain.c) nz)
2242        =/  xy   (mul.j (into.j x y) s.sig)
2243        =/  qr   (add.j gz xy)
2244        =/  qj   (mul.j qr (inv:field-n.c x))
2245        =/  pub  (from.j qj)
2246        ?<  =([0 0] pub)
2247        pub
2248    ++  schnorr
2249        ~%  %schnorr  ..schnorr  ~
2250        =>  |%
2251        ++  tagged-hash
2252        |=  [tag=@ [l=@ x=@]]
2253        =+  hat=(sha-256:sha (swp 3 tag))
2254        %-  sha-2561:sha
2255        :-  (add 64 l)
2256        (can 3 ~[[l x] [32 hat] [32 hat]])
2257        ++  lift-x
2258        |=  x=@I
2259        ^-  (unit point)
```

```
2260        =/  c  curve
2261        ?.  (lth x p.domain.c)
2262          ~
2263        =/  fop  field-p.c
2264        =+  [fadd fpow]=[sum.fop exp.fop]
2265        =/  cp  (fadd (fpow 3 x) 7)
2266        =/  y  (fpow (rsh [0 2] +(p.domain.c)) cp)
2267        ?.  =(cp (fpow 2 y))
2268          ~
2269        %-  some  :-  x
2270        ?:  =(0 (mod y 2))
2271          y
2272        (sub p.domain.c y)
2273        --
2274    |%
2275    ::
2276    ++  sign                                  ::  schnorr signature
2277      ~/  %sosi
2278      |=  [sk=@I m=@I a=@I]
2279      ^-  @J
2280      ?>  (gte 32 (met 3 m))
2281      ?>  (gte 32 (met 3 a))
2282      =/  c  curve
2283      ::  implies (gte 32 (met 3 sk))
2284      ::
2285      ?<  |(=(0 sk) (gte sk n.domain.c))
2286      =/  pp
2287        (mul-point-scalar g.domain.c sk)
2288      =/  d
2289        ?:  =(0 (mod y.pp 2))
2290          sk
2291        (sub n.domain.c sk)
2292      =/  t
2293        %+  mix  d
2294        (tagged-hash 'BIP0340/aux' [32 a])
2295      =/  rand
2296        %+  tagged-hash  'BIP0340/nonce'
2297        :-  96
2298        (rep 8 ~[m x.pp t])
2299      =/  kp  (mod rand n.domain.c)
2300      ?<  =(0 kp)
2301      =/  rr  (mul-point-scalar g.domain.c kp)
2302      =/  k
2303        ?:  =(0 (mod y.rr 2))
2304          kp
2305        (sub n.domain.c kp)
2306      =/  e
2307        %-  mod
2308        :_  n.domain.c
2309        %+  tagged-hash  'BIP0340/challenge'
2310        :-  96
2311        (rep 8 ~[m x.pp x.rr])
2312      =/  sig
2313        %^  cat  8
2314        (mod (add k (mul e d)) n.domain.c)
2315        x.rr
2316      ?>  (verify x.pp m sig)
2317      sig
```

```
2318          ::
2319          ++  verify                              ::  schnorr verify
2320          ~/  %sove
2321          |=  [pk=@I m=@I sig=@J]
2322          ^-  ?
2323          ?>  (gte 32 (met 3 pk))
2324          ?>  (gte 32 (met 3 m))
2325          ?>  (gte 64 (met 3 sig))
2326          =/  c  curve
2327          =/  pup  (lift-x pk)
2328          ?~  pup
2329            %.n
2330          =/  pp  u.pup
2331          =/  r  (cut 8 [1 1] sig)
2332          ?:  (gte r p.domain.c)
2333            %.n
2334          =/  s  (end 8 sig)
2335          ?:  (gte s n.domain.c)
2336            %.n
2337          =/  e
2338          %-  mod
2339          :_  n.domain.c
2340          %+  tagged-hash  'BIP0340/challenge'
2341          :-  96
2342          (rep 8 ~[m x.pp r])
2343          =/  aa
2344          (mul-point-scalar g.domain.c s)
2345          =/  bb
2346          (mul-point-scalar pp (sub n.domain.c e))
2347          ?:  &(=(x.aa x.bb) !=(y.aa y.bb))       ::  infinite?
2348            %.n
2349          =/  rr  (add-points aa bb)
2350          ?.  =(0 (mod y.rr 2))
2351            %.n
2352          =(r x.rr)
2353          --
2354        --
2355      --
2356    ::
2357    ++  blake
2358      ~%  %blake  ..part  ~
2359      |%
2360      ::TODO  generalize for both blake2 variants
2361      ++  blake2b
2362        ~/  %blake2b
2363        |=  [msg=byts key=byts out=@ud]
2364        ^-  @
2365        ::  initialization vector
2366        =/  iv=@
2367          0x6a09.e667.f3bc.c908.
2368            bb67.ae85.84ca.a73b.
2369            3c6e.f372.fe94.f82b.
2370            a54f.f53a.5f1d.36f1.
2371            510e.527f.ade6.82d1.
2372            9b05.688c.2b3e.6c1f.
2373            1f83.d9ab.fb41.bd6b.
2374            5be0.cd19.137e.2179
2375        ::  per-round constants
```

```
2376        =/  sigma=(list (list @ud))
2377          :~
2378            :~   0   1   2   3   4   5   6   7   8   9  10  11  12  13  14  15  ==
2379            :~  14  10   4   8   9  15  13   6   1  12   0   2  11   7   5   3  ==
2380            :~  11   8  12   0   5   2  15  13  10  14   3   6   7   1   9   4  ==
2381            :~   7   9   3   1  13  12  11  14   2   6   5  10   4   0  15   8  ==
2382            :~   9   0   5   7   2   4  10  15  14   1  11  12   6   8   3  13  ==
2383            :~   2  12   6  10   0  11   8   3   4  13   7   5  15  14   1   9  ==
2384            :~  12   5   1  15  14  13   4  10   0   7   6   3   9   2   8  11  ==
2385            :~  13  11   7  14  12   1   3   9   5   0  15   4   8   6   2  10  ==
2386            :~   6  15  14   9  11   3   0   8  12   2  13   7   1   4  10   5  ==
2387            :~  10   2   8   4   7   6   1   5  15  11   9  14   3  12  13   0  ==
2388            :~   0   1   2   3   4   5   6   7   8   9  10  11  12  13  14  15  ==
2389            :~  14  10   4   8   9  15  13   6   1  12   0   2  11   7   5   3  ==
2390          ==
2391        =>  |%
2392        ++  get-word-list
2393          |=  [h=@ w=@ud]
2394          ^-  (list @)
2395          %-  flop
2396          =+  l=(rip 6 h)
2397          =-  (weld - l)
2398          (reap (sub w (lent l)) 0)
2399        ::
2400        ++  get-word
2401          |=  [h=@ i=@ud w=@ud]
2402          ^-  @
2403          %+  snag  i
2404          (get-word-list h w)
2405        ::
2406        ++  put-word
2407          |=  [h=@ i=@ud w=@ud d=@]
2408          ^-  @
2409          %+  rep  6
2410          =+  l=(get-word-list h w)
2411          %-  flop
2412          %+  weld  (scag i l)
2413          [d (slag +(i) l)]
2414        ::
2415        ++  mod-word
2416          |*  [h=@ i=@ud w=@ud g=$-(@ @)]
2417          (put-word h i w (g (get-word h i w)))
2418        ::
2419        ++  pad
2420          |=  [byts len=@ud]
2421          (lsh [3 (sub len wid)] dat)
2422        ::
2423        ++  compress
2424          |=  [h=@ c=@ t=@ud l=?]
2425          ^-  @
2426          ::  set up local work vector
2427          =+  v=(add (lsh [6 8] h) iv)
2428          ::  xor the counter t into v
2429          =.  v
2430            %-  mod-word
2431            :^  v  12  16
2432            (cury mix (end [0 64] t))
2433          =.  v
```

```
2434        %-  mod-word
2435        :^  v  13  16
2436        (cury mix (rsh [0 64] t))
2437        ::  for the last block, invert v14
2438      =?  v  1
2439        %-  mod-word
2440        :^  v  14  16
2441        (cury mix 0xffff.ffff.ffff.ffff)
2442      ::  twelve rounds of message mixing
2443      =+  i=0
2444      =|  s=(list @)
2445      |^
2446        ?:  =(i 12)
2447          ::  xor upper and lower halves of v into state h
2448          =.  h  (mix h (rsh [6 8] v))
2449          (mix h (end [6 8] v))
2450        ::  select message mixing schedule and mix v
2451        =.  s  (snag (mod i 10) sigma)
2452        =.  v  (do-mix 0 4 8 12 0 1)
2453        =.  v  (do-mix 1 5 9 13 2 3)
2454        =.  v  (do-mix 2 6 10 14 4 5)
2455        =.  v  (do-mix 3 7 11 15 6 7)
2456        =.  v  (do-mix 0 5 10 15 8 9)
2457        =.  v  (do-mix 1 6 11 12 10 11)
2458        =.  v  (do-mix 2 7 8 13 12 13)
2459        =.  v  (do-mix 3 4 9 14 14 15)
2460        $(i +(i))
2461      ::
2462      ++  do-mix
2463        |=  [na=@ nb=@ nc=@ nd=@ nx=@ ny=@]
2464        ^-  @
2465        =-  =.  v  (put-word v na 16 a)
2466            =.  v  (put-word v nb 16 b)
2467            =.  v  (put-word v nc 16 c)
2468                (put-word v nd 16 d)
2469        %-  b2mix
2470        :*  (get-word v na 16)
2471            (get-word v nb 16)
2472            (get-word v nc 16)
2473            (get-word v nd 16)
2474            (get-word c (snag nx s) 16)
2475            (get-word c (snag ny s) 16)
2476        ==
2477      --
2478      ::
2479      ++  b2mix
2480        |=  [a=@ b=@ c=@ d=@ x=@ y=@]
2481        ^-  [a=@ b=@ c=@ d=@]
2482      =.  x  (rev 3 8 x)
2483      =.  y  (rev 3 8 y)
2484      =+  fed=~(. fe 6)
2485      =.  a  :(sum:fed a b x)
2486      =.  d  (ror:fed 0 32 (mix d a))
2487      =.  c  (sum:fed c d)
2488      =.  b  (ror:fed 0 24 (mix b c))
2489      =.  a  :(sum:fed a b y)
2490      =.  d  (ror:fed 0 16 (mix d a))
2491      =.  c  (sum:fed c d)
```

```
2492            =.  b  (ror:fed 0 63 (mix b c))
2493            [a b c d]
2494          --
2495      ::  ensure inputs adhere to contraints
2496      =.  out  (max 1 (min out 64))
2497      =.  wid.msg  (min wid.msg (bex 128))
2498      =.  wid.key  (min wid.key 64)
2499      =.  dat.msg  (end [3 wid.msg] dat.msg)
2500      =.  dat.key  (end [3 wid.key] dat.key)
2501      ::  initialize state vector
2502      =+  h=iv
2503      ::  mix key length and output length into h0
2504      =.  h
2505        %-  mod-word
2506        :^  h  0  8
2507        %+  cury  mix
2508        %+  add  0x101.0000
2509        (add (lsh 3 wid.key) out)
2510      ::  keep track of how much we've compressed
2511      =*  mes  dat.msg
2512      =+  com=0
2513      =+  rem=wid.msg
2514      ::  if we have a key, pad it and prepend to msg
2515      =?  mes  (gth wid.key 0)
2516        (can 3 ~[rem^mes 128^(pad key 128)])
2517      =?  rem  (gth wid.key 0)
2518        (add rem 128)
2519      |-
2520      ::  compress 128-byte chunks of the message
2521      ?:  (gth rem 128)
2522        =+  c=(cut 3 [(sub rem 128) 128] mes)
2523        =.  com  (add com 128)
2524        %_  $
2525          rem  (sub rem 128)
2526          h    (compress h c com |)
2527        ==
2528      ::  compress the final bytes of the msg
2529      =+  c=(cut 3 [0 rem] mes)
2530      =.  com  (add com rem)
2531      =.  c  (pad [rem c] 128)
2532      =.  h  (compress h c com &)
2533      ::  produce output of desired length
2534      %+  rsh  [3 (sub 64 out)]
2535      ::  do some word
2536      %+  rep  6
2537      %+  turn  (flop (gulf 0 7))
2538      |=  a=@
2539      (rev 3 8 (get-word h a 8))
2540    --  ::blake
2541  ::
2542  ++  argon2
2543    ~%  %argon  ..part  ~
2544    |%
2545    ::
2546    ::  structures
2547    ::
2548    +$  argon-type  ?(%d %i %id %u)
2549    ::
```

```
2550      ::   shorthands
2551      ::
2552      ++  argon2-urbit
2553        |=  out=@ud
2554        (argon2 out %u 0x13 4 512.000 1 *byts *byts)
2555      ::
2556      ::  argon2 proper
2557      ::
2558      ::  main argon2 operation
2559      ++  argon2
2560        ::  out:      desired output size in bytes
2561        ::  typ:      argon2 type
2562        ::  version:  argon2 version (0x10/v1.0 or 0x13/v1.3)
2563        ::  threads:  amount of threads/parallelism
2564        ::  mem-cost: kb of memory to use
2565        ::  time-cost: iterations to run
2566        ::  key:      optional secret
2567        ::  extra:    optional arbitrary data
2568        |=  $:  out=@ud
2569                typ=argon-type
2570                version=@ux
2571            ::
2572                threads=@ud
2573                mem-cost=@ud
2574                time-cost=@ud
2575            ::
2576                key=byts
2577                extra=byts
2578            ==
2579        ^-  $-([msg=byts sat=byts] @)
2580        ::
2581        ::  check configuration sanity
2582        ::
2583        ?:  =(0 threads)
2584          ~|  %parallelism-must-be-above-zero
2585          !!
2586        ?:  =(0 time-cost)
2587          ~|  %time-cost-must-be-above-zero
2588          !!
2589        ?:  (lth mem-cost (mul 8 threads))
2590          ~|  :-  %memory-cost-must-be-at-least-threads
2591              [threads %times 8 (mul 8 threads)]
2592          !!
2593        ?.  |(=(0x10 version) =(0x13 version))
2594          ~|  [%unsupported-version version %want [0x10 0x13]]
2595          !!
2596        ::
2597        ::  calculate constants and initialize buffer
2598        ::
2599        ::  for each thread, there is a row in the buffer.
2600        ::  the amount of columns depends on the memory-cost.
2601        ::  columns are split into groups of four.
2602        ::  a single such quarter section of a row is a segment.
2603        ::
2604        ::  blocks:     (m_prime)
2605        ::  columns:    row length (q)
2606        ::  seg-length: segment length
2607        =/  blocks=@ud
```

```
2608        ::  round mem-cost down to the nearest multiple of 4*threads
2609        =+  (mul 4 threads)
2610        (mul (div mem-cost -) -)
2611    =+  columns=(div blocks threads)
2612    =+  seg-length=(div columns 4)
2613    ::
2614    =/  buffer=(list (list @))
2615        (reap threads (reap columns 0))
2616    ::
2617    ::  main function
2618    ::
2619    ::  msg: the main input
2620    ::  sat: optional salt
2621    ~%  %argon2  ..argon2  ~
2622    |=  [msg=byts sat=byts]
2623    ^-  @
2624    ?:  (lth wid.sat 8)
2625      ~|  [%min-salt-length-is-8 wid.sat]
2626      !!
2627    ::
2628    ::  h0: initial 64-byte block
2629    =/  h0=@
2630      =-  (blake2b:blake - 0^0 64)
2631      :-  :(add 40 wid.msg wid.sat wid.key wid.extra)
2632      %+  can  3
2633      =+  (cury (cury rev 3) 4)
2634      :~  (prep-wid extra)
2635          (prep-wid key)
2636          (prep-wid sat)
2637          (prep-wid msg)
2638          4^(- (type-to-num typ))
2639          4^(- version)
2640          4^(- time-cost)
2641          4^(- mem-cost)
2642          4^(- out)
2643          4^(- threads)
2644      ==
2645    ::
2646    ::  do time-cost passes over the buffer
2647    ::
2648    =+  t=0
2649    |-
2650    ?:  (lth t time-cost)
2651      ::
2652      ::  process all four segments in the columns...
2653      ::
2654      =+  s=0
2655      |-
2656      ?.  (lth s 4)  ^$(t +(t))
2657      ::
2658      ::  ...of every row/thread
2659      ::
2660      =+  r=0
2661      |-
2662      ?.  (lth r threads)  ^$(s +(s))
2663      =;  new=_buffer
2664        $(buffer new, r +(r))
2665      %-  fill-segment
```

```
2666          :*  buffer    h0
2667              t         s         r
2668              blocks    columns   seg-length
2669              threads   time-cost  typ          version
2670          ==
2671      ::
2672      ::  mix all rows together and hash the result
2673      ::
2674      =+  r=0
2675      =|  final=@
2676      |-
2677      ?:  =(r threads)
2678        (hash 1.024^final out)
2679      =-  $(final -, r +(r))
2680      %+  mix  final
2681      (snag (dec columns) (snag r buffer))
2682    ::
2683    ::  per-segment computation
2684    ++  fill-segment
2685      |=  $:  buffer=(list (list @))
2686              h0=@
2687              ::
2688              itn=@ud
2689              seg=@ud
2690              row=@ud
2691              ::
2692              blocks=@ud
2693              columns=@ud
2694              seg-length=@ud
2695              ::
2696              threads=@ud
2697              time-cost=@ud
2698              typ=argon-type
2699              version=@ux
2700          ==
2701      ::
2702      ::  fill-segment utilities
2703      ::
2704      =>  |%
2705          ++  put-word
2706            |=  [rob=(list @) i=@ud d=@]
2707            %+  weld  (scag i rob)
2708            [d (slag +(i) rob)]
2709          --
2710      ^+  buffer
2711      ::
2712      ::  rob:   row buffer to operate on
2713      ::  do-i:  whether to use prns from input rather than state
2714      ::  rands: prns generated from input, if we do-i
2715      =+  rob=(snag row buffer)
2716      =/  do-i=?
2717        ?|  ?=(%i typ)
2718            &(?=(%id typ) =(0 itn) (lte seg 1))
2719            &(?=(%u typ) =(0 itn) (lte seg 2))
2720        ==
2721      =/  rands=(list (pair @ @))
2722        ?.  do-i  ~
2723        ::
```

```
2724        ::  keep going until we have a list of :seg-length prn pairs
2725        ::
2726        =+  l=0
2727        =+  counter=1
2728        |-  ^-  (list (pair @ @))
2729        ?:  (gte l seg-length)  ~
2730        =-  (weld - $(counter +(counter), l (add l 128)))
2731        ::
2732        ::  generate pseudorandom block by compressing metadata
2733        ::
2734        =/  random-block=@
2735          %+  compress  0
2736          %+  compress  0
2737          %+  lsh  [3 968]
2738          %+  rep  6
2739          =+  (cury (cury rev 3) 8)
2740          :~  (- counter)
2741              (- (type-to-num typ))
2742              (- time-cost)
2743              (- blocks)
2744              (- seg)
2745              (- row)
2746              (- itn)
2747          ==
2748        ::
2749        ::  split the random-block into 64-bit sections,
2750        ::  then extract the first two 4-byte sections from each.
2751        ::
2752        %+  turn  (flop (rip 6 random-block))
2753        |=  a=@
2754        ^-  (pair @ @)
2755        :-  (rev 3 4 (rsh 5 a))
2756        (rev 3 4 (end 5 a))
2757      ::
2758      ::  iterate over the entire segment length
2759      ::
2760      =+  sin=0
2761      |-
2762      ::
2763      ::  when done, produce the updated buffer
2764      ::
2765      ?:  =(sin seg-length)
2766        %+  weld  (scag row buffer)
2767        [rob (slag +(row) buffer)]
2768      ::
2769      ::  col: current column to process
2770      =/  col=@ud
2771        (add (mul seg seg-length) sin)
2772      ::
2773      ::  first two columns are generated from h0
2774      ::
2775      ?:  &(=(0 itn) (lth col 2))
2776        =+  (app-num (app-num 64^h0 col) row)
2777        =+  (hash - 1.024)
2778        $(rob (put-word rob col -), sin +(sin))
2779      ::
2780      ::  c1, c2: prns for picking reference block
2781      =/  [c1=@ c2=@]
```

```
2782        ?:  do-i  (snag sin rands)
2783        =+  =-  (snag - rob)
2784          ?:  =(0 col)  (dec columns)
2785          (mod (dec col) columns)
2786        :-  (rev 3 4 (cut 3 [1.020 4] -))
2787        (rev 3 4 (cut 3 [1.016 4] -))
2788      ::
2789      ::  ref-row: reference block row
2790      =/  ref-row=@ud
2791        ?:  &(=(0 itn) =(0 seg))  row
2792        (mod c2 threads)
2793      ::
2794      ::  ref-col: reference block column
2795      =/  ref-col=@ud
2796        =-  (mod - columns)
2797        %+  add
2798          ::  starting index
2799          ?:  |(=(0 itn) =(3 seg))  0
2800          (mul +(seg) seg-length)
2801        ::  pseudorandom offset
2802        =-  %+  sub  (dec -)
2803          %+  rsh  [0 32]
2804          %+  mul  -
2805          (rsh [0 32] (mul c1 c1))
2806        ::  reference area size
2807        ?:  =(0 itn)
2808          ?:  |(=(0 seg) =(row ref-row))  (dec col)
2809          ?:  =(0 sin)  (dec (mul seg seg-length))
2810          (mul seg seg-length)
2811        =+  sul=(sub columns seg-length)
2812        ?:  =(ref-row row)  (dec (add sul sin))
2813        ?:  =(0 sin)  (dec sul)
2814        sul
2815      ::
2816      ::  compress the previous and reference block
2817      ::  to create the new block
2818      ::
2819      =/  new=@
2820        %+  compress
2821          =-  (snag - rob)
2822          ::  previous index, wrap-around
2823          ?:  =(0 col)  (dec columns)
2824          (mod (dec col) columns)
2825        ::  get reference block
2826        %+  snag  ref-col
2827        ?:  =(ref-row row)  rob
2828        (snag ref-row buffer)
2829      ::
2830      ::  starting from v1.3, we xor the new block in,
2831      ::  rather than directly overwriting the old block
2832      ::
2833      =?  new  &(!=(0 itn) =(0x13 version))
2834      (mix new (snag col rob))
2835      $(rob (put-word rob col new), sin +(sin))
2836    ::
2837    ::  compression function (g)
2838    ++  compress
2839      ::  x, y: assumed to be 1024 bytes
```

```
2840        |=  [x=@ y=@]
2841        ^-  @
2842        ::
2843        =+  r=(mix x y)
2844        =|  q=(list @)
2845        ::
2846        ::  iterate over rows of r to get q
2847        ::
2848        =+  i=0
2849        |-
2850        ?:  (lth i 8)
2851          =;  p=(list @)
2852            $(q (weld q p), i +(i))
2853          %-  permute
2854          =-  (weld (reap (sub 8 (lent -)) 0) -)
2855          %-  flop
2856          %+  rip  7
2857          (cut 10 [(sub 7 i) 1] r)
2858        ::
2859        ::  iterate over columns of q to get z
2860        ::
2861        =/  z=(list @)  (reap 64 0)
2862        =.  i  0
2863        |-
2864        ::
2865        ::  when done, assemble z and xor it with r
2866        ::
2867        ?.  (lth i 8)
2868          (mix (rep 7 (flop z)) r)
2869        ::
2870        ::  permute the column
2871        ::
2872        =/  out=(list @)
2873          %-  permute
2874          :~  (snag i q)
2875              (snag (add i 8) q)
2876              (snag (add i 16) q)
2877              (snag (add i 24) q)
2878              (snag (add i 32) q)
2879              (snag (add i 40) q)
2880              (snag (add i 48) q)
2881              (snag (add i 56) q)
2882          ==
2883        ::
2884        ::  put the result into z per column
2885        ::
2886        =+  j=0
2887        |-
2888        ?:  =(8 j)  ^$(i +(i))
2889        =-  $(z -, j +(j))
2890        =+  (add i (mul j 8))
2891        %+  weld  (scag - z)
2892        [(snag j out) (slag +(-) z)]
2893      ::
2894      ::  permutation function (p)
2895      ++  permute
2896        ::NOTE  this function really just takes and produces
2897        ::       8 values, but taking and producing them as
```

```
2898      ::       lists helps clean up the code significantly.
2899      |=  s=(list @)
2900      ?>  =(8 (lent s))
2901      ^-  (list @)
2902      ::
2903      ::  list inputs as 16 8-byte values
2904      ::
2905      =/  v=(list @)
2906        %-  zing
2907        ^-  (list (list @))
2908        %+  turn  s
2909        |=  a=@
2910        ::  rev for endianness
2911        =+  (rip 6 (rev 3 16 a))
2912        (weld - (reap (sub 2 (lent -)) 0))
2913      ::
2914      ::  do permutation rounds
2915      ::
2916      =.  v  (do-round v 0 4 8 12)
2917      =.  v  (do-round v 1 5 9 13)
2918      =.  v  (do-round v 2 6 10 14)
2919      =.  v  (do-round v 3 7 11 15)
2920      =.  v  (do-round v 0 5 10 15)
2921      =.  v  (do-round v 1 6 11 12)
2922      =.  v  (do-round v 2 7 8 13)
2923      =.  v  (do-round v 3 4 9 14)
2924      ::  rev for endianness
2925      =.  v  (turn v (cury (cury rev 3) 8))
2926      ::
2927      ::  cat v back together into 8 16-byte values
2928      ::
2929      %+  turn  (gulf 0 7)
2930      |=  i=@
2931      =+  (mul 2 i)
2932      (cat 6 (snag +(-) v) (snag - v))
2933      ::
2934      ::  perform a round and produce updated value list
2935      ++  do-round
2936      |=  [v=(list @) na=@ nb=@ nc=@ nd=@]
2937      ^+  v
2938      =>  |%
2939          ++  get-word
2940          |=  i=@ud
2941          (snag i v)
2942          ::
2943          ++  put-word
2944          |=  [i=@ud d=@]
2945          ^+  v
2946          %+  weld  (scag i v)
2947          [d (slag +(i) v)]
2948          --
2949      =-  =.  v  (put-word na a)
2950          =.  v  (put-word nb b)
2951          =.  v  (put-word nc c)
2952          (put-word nd d)
2953      %-  round
2954      :*  (get-word na)
2955          (get-word nb)
```

```
2956            (get-word nc)
2957            (get-word nd)
2958        ==
2959    ::
2960    ::  perform a round (bg) and produce updated values
2961    ++  round
2962      |=  [a=@ b=@ c=@ d=@]
2963      ^-  [a=@ b=@ c=@ d=@]
2964      ::  operate on 64 bit words
2965      =+  fed=~(. fe 6)
2966      =*  sum   sum:fed
2967      =*  ror   ror:fed
2968      =+  end=(cury end 5)
2969      =.  a  :(sum a b :(mul 2 (end a) (end b)))
2970      =.  d  (ror 0 32 (mix d a))
2971      =.  c  :(sum c d :(mul 2 (end c) (end d)))
2972      =.  b  (ror 0 24 (mix b c))
2973      =.  a  :(sum a b :(mul 2 (end a) (end b)))
2974      =.  d  (ror 0 16 (mix d a))
2975      =.  c  :(sum c d :(mul 2 (end c) (end d)))
2976      =.  b  (ror 0 63 (mix b c))
2977      [a b c d]
2978    ::
2979    ::  argon2 wrapper around blake2b (h')
2980    ++  hash
2981      =,  blake
2982      |=  [byts out=@ud]
2983      ^-  @
2984      ::
2985      ::  msg: input with byte-length prepended
2986      =+  msg=(prep-num [wid dat] out)
2987      ::
2988      ::  if requested size is low enough, hash directly
2989      ::
2990      ?:  (lte out 64)
2991        (blake2b msg 0^0 out)
2992      ::
2993      ::  build up the result by hashing and re-hashing
2994      ::  the input message, adding the first 32 bytes
2995      ::  of the hash to the result, until we have the
2996      ::  desired output size.
2997      ::
2998      =+  tmp=(blake2b msg 0^0 64)
2999      =+  res=(rsh [3 32] tmp)
3000      =.  out  (sub out 32)
3001      |-
3002      ?:  (gth out 64)
3003        =.  tmp  (blake2b 64^tmp 0^0 64)
3004        =.  res  (add (lsh [3 32] res) (rsh [3 32] tmp))
3005        $(out (sub out 32))
3006      %+  add  (lsh [3 out] res)
3007      (blake2b 64^tmp 0^0 out)
3008    ::
3009    ::  utilities
3010    ::
3011    ++  type-to-num
3012      |=  t=argon-type
3013      ?-  t
```

```
3014              %d    0
3015              %i    1
3016              %id   2
3017              %u    10
3018          ==
3019      ::
3020      ++  app-num
3021        |=  [byts num=@ud]
3022        ^-  byts
3023        :-  (add wid 4)
3024        %+  can  3
3025        ~[4^(rev 3 4 num) wid^dat]
3026      ::
3027      ++  prep-num
3028        |=  [byts num=@ud]
3029        ^-  byts
3030        :-  (add wid 4)
3031        %+  can  3
3032        ~[wid^dat 4^(rev 3 4 num)]
3033      ::
3034      ++  prep-wid
3035        |=  a=byts
3036        (prep-num a wid.a)
3037      --
3038    ::
3039    ++  ripemd
3040      ~%  %ripemd  ..part  ~
3041      |%
3042      ++  ripemd-160
3043        ~/  %ripemd160
3044        |=  byts
3045        ^-  @
3046        ::  we operate on bits rather than bytes
3047        =.  wid  (mul wid 8)
3048        ::  add padding
3049        =+  (md5-pad wid dat)
3050        ::  endianness
3051        =.  dat  (run 5 dat |=(a=@ (rev 3 4 a)))
3052        =*  x  dat
3053        =+  blocks=(div wid 512)
3054        =+  fev=~(. fe 5)
3055        ::  initial register values
3056        =+  h0=0x6745.2301
3057        =+  h1=0xefcd.ab89
3058        =+  h2=0x98ba.dcfe
3059        =+  h3=0x1032.5476
3060        =+  h4=0xc3d2.e1f0
3061        ::  i: current block
3062        =+  [i=0 j=0]
3063        =+  *[a=@ b=@ c=@ d=@ e=@]        ::  a..e
3064        =+  *[aa=@ bb=@ cc=@ dd=@ ee=@]   ::  a'..e'
3065        |^
3066          ?:  =(i blocks)
3067            %+  rep  5
3068            %+  turn  `(list @)`~[h4 h3 h2 h1 h0]
3069            ::  endianness
3070            |=(h=@ (rev 3 4 h))
3071          =:  a  h0       aa  h0
```

```
3072              b   h1        bb   h1
3073              c   h2        cc   h2
3074              d   h3        dd   h3
3075              e   h4        ee   h4
3076          ==
3077          ::  j: current word
3078          =+  j=0
3079          |-
3080          ?:  =(j 80)
3081            %=   ^$
3082              i    +(i)
3083              h1   :(sum:fev h2 d ee)
3084              h2   :(sum:fev h3 e aa)
3085              h3   :(sum:fev h4 a bb)
3086              h4   :(sum:fev h0 b cc)
3087              h0   :(sum:fev h1 c dd)
3088            ==
3089          %=  $
3090            j   +(j)
3091          ::
3092            a    e
3093            b    (fn j a b c d e (get (r j)) (k j) (s j))
3094            c    b
3095            d    (rol 10 c)
3096            e    d
3097          ::
3098            aa   ee
3099            bb   (fn (sub 79 j) aa bb cc dd ee (get (rr j)) (kk j) (ss j))
3100            cc   bb
3101            dd   (rol 10 cc)
3102            ee   dd
3103          ==
3104        ::
3105        ++  get  ::  word from x in block i
3106          |=   j=@ud
3107          =+  (add (mul i 16) +(j))
3108          (cut 5 [(sub (mul blocks 16) -) 1] x)
3109        ::
3110        ++  fn
3111          |=  [j=@ud a=@ b=@ c=@ d=@ e=@ m=@ k=@ s=@]
3112          =-  (sum:fev (rol s :(sum:fev a m k -)) e)
3113          =.  j  (div j 16)
3114          ?:  =(0 j)  (mix (mix b c) d)
3115          ?:  =(1 j)  (con (dis b c) (dis (not 0 32 b) d))
3116          ?:  =(2 j)  (mix (con b (not 0 32 c)) d)
3117          ?:  =(3 j)  (con (dis b d) (dis c (not 0 32 d)))
3118          ?:  =(4 j)  (mix b (con c (not 0 32 d)))
3119          !!
3120        ::
3121        ++  rol  (cury rol:fev 0)
3122        ::
3123        ++  k
3124          |=  j=@ud
3125          =.  j  (div j 16)
3126          ?:  =(0 j)  0x0
3127          ?:  =(1 j)  0x5a82.7999
3128          ?:  =(2 j)  0x6ed9.eba1
3129          ?:  =(3 j)  0x8f1b.bcdc
```

```
3130        ?:  =(4 j)  0xa953.fd4e
3131        !!
3132      ::
3133    ++  kk  ::  k'
3134      |=  j=@ud
3135      =.  j  (div j 16)
3136      ?:  =(0 j)  0x50a2.8be6
3137      ?:  =(1 j)  0x5c4d.d124
3138      ?:  =(2 j)  0x6d70.3ef3
3139      ?:  =(3 j)  0x7a6d.76e9
3140      ?:  =(4 j)  0x0
3141      !!
3142      ::
3143    ++  r
3144      |=  j=@ud
3145      %+  snag  j
3146      ^-  (list @)
3147      :~  0   1   2   3   4   5   6   7   8   9   10  11  12  13  14  15
3148          7   4   13  1   10  6   15  3   12  0   9   5   2   14  11  8
3149          3   10  14  4   9   15  8   1   2   7   0   6   13  11  5   12
3150          1   9   11  10  0   8   12  4   13  3   7   15  14  5   6   2
3151          4   0   5   9   7   12  2   10  14  1   3   8   11  6   15  13
3152      ==
3153      ::
3154    ++  rr  ::  r'
3155      |=  j=@ud
3156      %+  snag  j
3157      ^-  (list @)
3158      :~  5   14  7   0   9   2   11  4   13  6   15  8   1   10  3   12
3159          6   11  3   7   0   13  5   10  14  15  8   12  4   9   1   2
3160          15  5   1   3   7   14  6   9   11  8   12  2   10  0   4   13
3161          8   6   4   1   3   11  15  0   5   12  2   13  9   7   10  14
3162          12  15  10  4   1   5   8   7   6   2   13  14  0   3   9   11
3163      ==
3164      ::
3165    ++  s
3166      |=  j=@ud
3167      %+  snag  j
3168      ^-  (list @)
3169      :~  11  14  15  12  5   8   7   9   11  13  14  15  6   7   9   8
3170          7   6   8   13  11  9   7   15  7   12  15  9   11  7   13  12
3171          11  13  6   7   14  9   13  15  14  8   13  6   5   12  7   5
3172          11  12  14  15  14  15  9   8   9   14  5   6   8   6   5   12
3173          9   15  5   11  6   8   13  12  5   12  13  14  11  8   5   6
3174      ==
3175      ::
3176    ++  ss  ::  s'
3177      |=  j=@ud
3178      %+  snag  j
3179      ^-  (list @)
3180      :~  8   9   9   11  13  15  15  5   7   7   8   11  14  14  12  6
3181          9   13  15  7   12  8   9   11  7   7   12  7   6   15  13  11
3182          9   7   15  11  8   6   6   14  12  13  5   14  13  13  7   5
3183          15  5   8   11  14  14  6   14  6   9   12  9   12  5   15  8
3184          8   5   12  9   12  5   14  6   8   13  6   5   15  13  11  11
3185      ==
3186      --
3187    ::
```

```
3188      ++  md5-pad
3189        |=  byts
3190        ^-  byts
3191        =+  (sub 511 (mod (add wid 64) 512))
3192        :-  :(add 64 +(-) wid)
3193        %+  can  0
3194        ~[64^(rev 3 8 wid) +(-)^(lsh [0 -] 1) wid^dat]
3195      --
3196    ::
3197    ++  pbkdf
3198      =>  |%
3199        ++  meet  |=([p=@ s=@ c=@ d=@] [[(met 3 p) p] [(met 3 s) s] c d])
3200        ++  flip  |=  [p=byts s=byts c=@ d=@]
3201                  [wid.p^(rev 3 p) wid.s^(rev 3 s) c d]
3202        --
3203      |%
3204      ::
3205      ::  use with @
3206      ::
3207      ++  hmac-sha1      (cork meet hmac-sha1l)
3208      ++  hmac-sha256    (cork meet hmac-sha256l)
3209      ++  hmac-sha512    (cork meet hmac-sha512l)
3210      ::
3211      ::  use with @t
3212      ::
3213      ++  hmac-sha1t     (cork meet hmac-sha1d)
3214      ++  hmac-sha256t   (cork meet hmac-sha256d)
3215      ++  hmac-sha512t   (cork meet hmac-sha512d)
3216      ::
3217      ::  use with byts
3218      ::
3219      ++  hmac-sha1l     (cork flip hmac-sha1d)
3220      ++  hmac-sha256l   (cork flip hmac-sha256d)
3221      ++  hmac-sha512l   (cork flip hmac-sha512d)
3222      ::
3223      ::  main logic
3224      ::
3225      ++  hmac-sha1d     (cury pbkdf hmac-sha1l:hmac 20)
3226      ++  hmac-sha256d   (cury pbkdf hmac-sha256l:hmac 32)
3227      ++  hmac-sha512d   (cury pbkdf hmac-sha512l:hmac 64)
3228      ::
3229      ++  pbkdf
3230        ::TODO  jet me! ++hmac:hmac is an example
3231        |*  [[prf=$-([byts byts] @) out=@u] p=byts s=byts c=@ d=@]
3232        =>  .(dat.p (end [3 wid.p] dat.p), dat.s (end [3 wid.s] dat.s))
3233        ::
3234        ::  max key length 1GB
3235        ::  max iterations 2^28
3236        ::
3237        ~|  [%invalid-pbkdf-params c d]
3238        ?>  ?&  (lte d (bex 30))
3239                (lte c (bex 28))
3240                !=(c 0)
3241            ==
3242        =/  l
3243          ?~  (mod d out)
3244          (div d out)
3245          +((div d out))
```

```
3246        =+  r=(sub d (mul out (dec l)))
3247        =+  [t=0 j=1 k=1]
3248        =.  t
3249          |-  ^-  @
3250        ?:  (gth j l)  t
3251        =/  u
3252          %+  add  dat.s
3253          %+  lsh  [3 wid.s]
3254          %+  rep  3
3255          (flop (rpp:scr 3 4 j))
3256        =+  f=0
3257        =.  f
3258          |-  ^-  @
3259        ?:  (gth k c)  f
3260        =/  q
3261          %^  rev  3  out
3262          =+  ?:(=(k 1) (add wid.s 4) out)
3263          (prf [wid.p (rev 3 p)] [- (rev 3 - u)])
3264        $(u q, f (mix f q), k +(k))
3265        $(t (add t (lsh [3 (mul (dec j) out)] f)), j +(j))
3266      (rev 3 d (end [3 d] t))
3267    --
3268  --  ::crypto
3269  ::                                                      ::::
3270  ::::                          ++unity                   ::  (2c) unit promotion
3271    ::                                                    ::::
3272  ++  unity  ^?
3273  |%
3274    ::                                                    ::  ++drop-list:unity
3275  ++  drop-list                                           ::  collapse unit list
3276    |*  lut=(list (unit))
3277    ?.  |-  ^-  ?
3278        ?~(lut & ?~(i.lut | $(lut t.lut)))
3279          ~
3280    %-  some
3281    |-
3282    ?~  lut  ~
3283    [i=u:+.i.lut t=$(lut t.lut)]
3284    ::                                                    ::  ++drop-map:unity
3285  ++  drop-map                                            ::  collapse unit map
3286    |*  lum=(map term (unit))
3287    ?:  (~(rep by lum) |=([[@ a=(unit)] b=_|] |(b ?=(~ a))))
3288          ~
3289    (some (~(run by lum) need))
3290    ::                                                    ::  ++drop-pole:unity
3291  ++  drop-pole                                           ::  collapse to tuple
3292    |^  |*  pul=(pole (unit))
3293        ?:  (test-pole pul)  ~
3294        (some (need-pole pul))
3295    ::
3296    ++  test-pole
3297      |*  pul=(pole (unit))
3298      ^-  ?
3299      ?~  pul  &
3300      ?|  ?=(~ -.pul)
3301          ?~(+.pul | (test-pole +.pul))
3302          ==
3303    ::
```

```
3304   ++  need-pole
3305     |*  pul=(pole (unit))
3306     ?~  pul  !!
3307     ?~  +.pul
3308       u:->.pul
3309     [u:->.pul (need-pole +.pul)]
3310     --
3311   --
3312 ::                                                        ::::
3313 :::::                          ++format                    ::  (2d) common formats
3314   ::                                                      ::::
3315 ++  format  ^?
3316   |%
3317   ::  0 ending a line (invalid @t) is not preserved       ::  ++to-wain:format
3318   ++  to-wain                                             ::  cord to line list
3319   ~%  %leer  ..part  ~
3320   |=  txt=cord
3321   ^-  wain
3322   ?~  txt  ~
3323   =/  len=@  (met 3 txt)
3324   =/  cut  =+(cut -(a 3, c 1, d txt))
3325   =/  sub  sub
3326   =|  [i=@ out=wain]
3327   |-  ^+  out
3328   =+  |-  ^-  j=@
3329       ?:  ?|  =(i len)
3330               =(10 (cut(b i)))
3331           ==
3332         i
3333       $(i +(i))
3334   =.  out  :_  out
3335     (cut(b i, c (sub j i)))
3336   ?:  =(j len)
3337     (flop out)
3338   $(i +(j))
3339   ::                                                      ::  ++of-wain:format
3340   ++  of-wain                                             ::  line list to cord
3341   |=  tez=wain  ^-  cord
3342   (rap 3 (join '\0a' tez))
3343   ::                                                      ::  ++of-wall:format
3344   ++  of-wall                                             ::  line list to tape
3345   |=  a=wall  ^-  tape
3346   ?~(a ~ "{i.a}\0a{$(a t.a)}")
3347   ::                                                      ::  json to rn parser
3348   ++  json-rn
3349   %+  knee  *rn  |.
3350     ;~  plug
3351       (easy %d)
3352       ;~(pose (cold | hep) (easy &))
3353       ;~  plug  dim:ag
3354         ;~  pose
3355           ;~  pfix  dot
3356             %+  sear
3357               |=  a=tape
3358               =/  b  (rust a dum:ag)
3359               ?~  b  ~
3360               (some [(lent a) u.b])
3361           (plus (shim '0' '9'))
```

```
3362            ==
3363          (easy [0 0])
3364        ==
3365      ;~  pose
3366        ;~  pfix
3367          (mask "eE")
3368          ;~  plug
3369            ;~(pose (cold | hep) (cold & lus) (easy &))
3370            ;~  pose
3371              ;~(pfix (plus (just '0')) dim:ag)
3372              dim:ag
3373            ==
3374          ==
3375        ==
3376        (easy [& 0])
3377      ==
3378    ==
3379  ==
3380  ::                                          ::  ++enjs:format
3381  ++  enjs  ^?                                 ::  json encoders
3382    |%
3383    ::                                        ::  ++frond:enjs:format
3384    ++  frond                                 ::  object from k-v pair
3385      |=  [p=@t q=json]
3386      ^-  json
3387      [%o [[p q] ~ ~]]
3388    ::                                        ::  ++pairs:enjs:format
3389    ++  pairs                                 ::  object from k-v list
3390      |=  a=(list [p=@t q=json])
3391      ^-  json
3392      [%o (~(gas by *(map @t json)) a)]
3393    ::                                        ::  ++tape:enjs:format
3394    ++  tape                                  ::  string from tape
3395      |=  a=^tape
3396      ^-  json
3397      [%s (crip a)]
3398    ::                                        ::  ++wall:enjs:format
3399    ++  wall                                  ::  string from wall
3400      |=  a=^wall
3401      ^-  json
3402      (tape (of-wall a))
3403    ::                                        ::  ++ship:enjs:format
3404    ++  ship                                  ::  string from ship
3405      |=  a=^ship
3406      ^-  json
3407      [%n (rap 3 '"' (rsh [3 1] (scot %p a)) '"' ~)]
3408    ::                                        ::  ++numb:enjs:format
3409    ++  numb                                  ::  number from unsigned
3410      |=  a=@u
3411      ^-  json
3412      :-  %n
3413      ?:  =(0 a)  '0'
3414      %-  crip
3415      %-  flop
3416      |-  ^-  ^tape
3417      ?:(=(0 a) ~ [(add '0' (mod a 10)) $(a (div a 10))])
3418    ::                                        ::  ++sect:enjs:format
3419    ++  sect                                  ::  s timestamp
```

```
3420        |=  a=^time
3421        (numb (unt:chrono:userlib a))          ::  ++time:enjs:format
3422      ::                                        ::  ms timestamp
3423    ++  time
3424        |=  a=^time
3425        (numb (unm:chrono:userlib a))          ::  ++path:enjs:format
3426      ::                                        ::  string from path
3427    ++  path
3428      |=  a=^path
3429      ^-  json
3430      [%s (spat a)]
3431      ::                                        ::  ++tank:enjs:format
3432    ++  tank                                    ::  tank as string arr
3433      |=  a=^tank
3434      ^-  json
3435      [%a (turn (wash [0 80] a) tape)]
3436    --  ::enjs
3437  ::                                            ::  ++dejs:format
3438  ++  dejs                                      ::  json reparser
3439    =>  |%  ++  grub  *                         ::  result
3440            ++  fist  $-(json grub)             ::  reparser instance
3441        --  ::
3442    |%
3443    ::                                          ::  ++ar:dejs:format
3444    ++  ar                                      ::  array as list
3445      |*  wit=fist
3446      |=  jon=json  ^-  (list _(wit *json))
3447      ?>  ?=([%a *] jon)
3448      (turn p.jon wit)
3449    ::                                          ::  ++as:dejs:format
3450    ++  as                                      ::  array as set
3451      |*  a=fist
3452      (cu ~(gas in *(set _$:a)) (ar a))
3453    ::                                          ::  ++at:dejs:format
3454    ++  at                                      ::  array as tuple
3455      |*  wil=(pole fist)
3456      |=  jon=json
3457      ?>  ?=([%a *] jon)
3458      ((at-raw wil) p.jon)
3459    ::                                          ::  ++at-raw:dejs:format
3460    ++  at-raw                                  ::  array as tuple
3461      |*  wil=(pole fist)
3462      |=  jol=(list json)
3463      ?~  jol  !!
3464      ?-    wil                                 ::  mint-vain on empty
3465          ::  [wit=* t=*]
3466          [* t=*]
3467        =>  .(wil [wit *]=wil)
3468        ?~  t.wil  ?^(t.jol !! (wit.wil i.jol))
3469        [(wit.wil i.jol) ((at-raw t.wil) t.jol)]
3470      ==
3471    ::                                          ::  ++bo:dejs:format
3472    ++  bo                                      ::  boolean
3473      |=(jon=json ?>(?=([%b *] jon) p.jon))
3474    ::                                          ::  ++bu:dejs:format
3475    ++  bu                                      ::  boolean not
3476      |=(jon=json ?>(?=([%b *] jon) !p.jon))
3477    ::                                          ::  ++ci:dejs:format
```

```
3478    ++  ci                                      ::  maybe transform
3479    |*  [poq=gate wit=fist]
3480    |=  jon=json
3481    (need (poq (wit jon)))
3482    ::                                          ::  ++cu:dejs:format
3483    ++  cu                                      ::  transform
3484    |*  [poq=gate wit=fist]
3485    |=  jon=json
3486    (poq (wit jon))
3487    ::                                          ::  ++di:dejs:format
3488    ++  di                                      ::  millisecond date
3489    (cu from-unix-ms:chrono:userlib ni)
3490    ::                                          ::  ++du:dejs:format
3491    ++  du                                      ::  second date
3492    (cu from-unix:chrono:userlib ni)
3493    ::                                          ::  ++mu:dejs:format
3494    ++  mu                                      ::  true unit
3495    |*  wit=fist
3496    |=  jon=json
3497    ?~(jon ~ (some (wit jon)))
3498    ::                                          ::  ++ne:dejs:format
3499    ++  ne                                      ::  number as real
3500    |=  jon=json
3501    ^-  @rd
3502    ?>  ?=([%n *] jon)
3503    (rash p.jon (cook ryld (cook royl-cell:^so json-rn)))
3504    ::                                          ::  ++ni:dejs:format
3505    ++  ni                                      ::  number as integer
3506    |=  jon=json
3507    ?>  ?=([%n *] jon)
3508    (rash p.jon dem)
3509    ::                                          ::  ++ns:dejs:format
3510    ++  ns                                      ::  number as signed
3511    |=  jon=json
3512    ^-  @s
3513    ?>  ?=([%n *] jon)
3514    %+  rash  p.jon
3515    %+  cook  new:si
3516    ;~(plug ;~(pose (cold %| (jest '-')) (easy %&)) dem)
3517    ::                                          ::  ++no:dejs:format
3518    ++  no                                      ::  number as cord
3519    |=(jon=json ?>(?=([%n *] jon) p.jon))
3520    ::                                          ::  ++nu:dejs:format
3521    ++  nu                                      ::  parse number as hex
3522    |=  jon=json
3523    ?>  ?=([%s *] jon)
3524    (rash p.jon hex)
3525    ::                                          ::  ++of:dejs:format
3526    ++  of                                      ::  object as frond
3527    |*  wer=(pole [cord fist])
3528    |=  jon=json
3529    ?>  ?=([%o [@ *] ~ ~] jon)
3530    |-
3531    ?-    wer                                   ::  mint-vain on empty
3532        ::  [[key=@t wit=*] t=*]
3533        [[key=@t *] t=*]
3534      =>  .(wer [[* wit] *]=wer)
3535      ?:  =(key.wer p.n.p.jon)
```

```
3536            [key.wer ~|(key+key.wer (wit.wer q.n.p.jon))]
3537          ?~  t.wer  ~|(bad-key+p.n.p.jon !!)
3538          ((of t.wer) jon)
3539      ==
3540    ::                                              ::  ++ot:dejs:format
3541    ++  ot                                          ::  object as tuple
3542      |*  wer=(pole [cord fist])
3543      |=  jon=json
3544      ?>  ?=([%o *] jon)
3545      ((ot-raw wer) p.jon)
3546    ::                                              ::  ++ot-raw:dejs:format
3547    ++  ot-raw                                      ::  object as tuple
3548      |*  wer=(pole [cord fist])
3549      |=  jom=(map @t json)
3550      ?-      wer                                   ::  mint-vain on empty
3551          ::  [[key=@t wit=*] t=*]
3552          [[key=@t *] t=*]
3553        =>  .(wer [[* wit] *]=wer)
3554        =/  ten  ~|(key+key.wer (wit.wer (~(got by jom) key.wer)))
3555        ?~(t.wer ten [ten ((ot-raw t.wer) jom)])
3556      ==
3557    ::
3558    ++  ou                                          ::  object of units
3559      |*  wer=(pole [cord fist])
3560      |=  jon=json
3561      ?>  ?=([%o *] jon)
3562      ((ou-raw wer) p.jon)
3563    ::                                              ::  ++ou-raw:dejs:format
3564    ++  ou-raw                                      ::  object of units
3565      |*  wer=(pole [cord fist])
3566      |=  jom=(map @t json)
3567      ?-      wer                                   ::  mint-vain on empty
3568          ::  [[key=@t wit=*] t=*]
3569          [[key=@t *] t=*]
3570        =>  .(wer [[* wit] *]=wer)
3571        =/  ten  ~|(key+key.wer (wit.wer (~(get by jom) key.wer)))
3572        ?~(t.wer ten [ten ((ou-raw t.wer) jom)])
3573      ==
3574    ::                                              ::  ++oj:dejs:format
3575    ++  oj                                          ::  object as jug
3576      |*  =fist
3577      ^-  $-(json (jug cord _(fist *json)))
3578      (om (as fist))
3579    ::                                              ::  ++om:dejs:format
3580    ++  om                                          ::  object as map
3581      |*  wit=fist
3582      |=  jon=json
3583      ?>  ?=([%o *] jon)
3584      (~(run by p.jon) wit)
3585    ::                                              ::  ++op:dejs:format
3586    ++  op                                          ::  parse keys of map
3587      |*  [fel=rule wit=fist]
3588      |-  jon=json  ^-  (map _(wonk *fel) _*wit)
3589      =/  jom  ((om wit) jon)
3590      %-  malt
3591      %+  turn  ~(tap by jom)
3592      |*  [a=cord b=*]
3593      =>  .(+< [a b]=+<)
```

```
3594          [(rash a fel) b]
3595        ::                                           ::   ++pa:dejs:format
3596      ++  pa                                          ::   string as path
3597        (su stap)
3598        ::                                           ::   ++pe:dejs:format
3599      ++  pe                                          ::   prefix
3600        |*  [pre=* wit=fist]
3601        (cu |*(* [pre +<]) wit)
3602        ::                                           ::   ++sa:dejs:format
3603      ++  sa                                          ::   string as tape
3604        |=(jon=json ?>(?=([%s *] jon) (trip p.jon)))
3605        ::                                           ::   ++sd:dejs:format
3606      ++  sd                                          ::   string @ud as date
3607        |=  jon=json
3608        ^-  @da
3609        ?>  ?=(%s -.jon)
3610        `@da`(rash p.jon dem:ag)
3611        ::                                           ::   ++se:dejs:format
3612      ++  se                                          ::   string as aura
3613        |=  aur=@tas
3614        |=  jon=json
3615        ?>(?=([%s *] jon) (slav aur p.jon))
3616        ::                                           ::   ++so:dejs:format
3617      ++  so                                          ::   string as cord
3618        |=(jon=json ?>(?=([%s *] jon) p.jon))
3619        ::                                           ::   ++su:dejs:format
3620      ++  su                                          ::   parse string
3621        |*  sab=rule
3622        |=  jon=json  ^+  (wonk *sab)
3623        ?>  ?=([%s *] jon)
3624        (rash p.jon sab)
3625        ::                                           ::   ++uf:dejs:format
3626      ++  uf                                          ::   unit fall
3627        |*  [def=* wit=fist]
3628        |=  jon=(unit json)
3629        ?~(jon def (wit u.jon))
3630        ::                                           ::   ++un:dejs:format
3631      ++  un                                          ::   unit need
3632        |*  wit=fist
3633        |=  jon=(unit json)
3634        (wit (need jon))
3635        ::                                           ::   ++ul:dejs:format
3636      ++  ul                                          ::   null
3637        |=(jon=json ?~(jon ~ !!))
3638        ::
3639      ++  za                                          ::   full unit pole
3640        |*  pod=(pole (unit))
3641        ?~  pod   &
3642        ?~  -.pod  |
3643        (za +.pod)
3644        ::
3645      ++  zl                                          ::   collapse unit list
3646        |*  lut=(list (unit))
3647        ?.  |-  ^-  ?
3648            ?~(lut & ?~(i.lut | $(lut t.lut)))
3649        ~
3650        %-  some
3651        |-
```

```
3652      ?~  lut   ~
3653      [i=u:+.i.lut t=$(lut t.lut)]
3654    ::
3655    ++  zp                                    ::  unit tuple
3656      |*  but=(pole (unit))
3657      ?~  but  !!
3658      ?~  +.but
3659        u:->.but
3660      [u:->.but (zp +.but)]
3661    ::
3662    ++  zm                                    ::  collapse unit map
3663      |*  lum=(map term (unit))
3664      ?:  (~(rep by lum) |=([[@ a=(unit)] b=_|] |(b ?=(~ a))))
3665        ~
3666      (some (~(run by lum) need))
3667    --  ::dejs
3668    ::                                        ::  ++dejs-soft:format
3669  ++  dejs-soft                               ::  json reparse to unit
3670    =,  unity
3671    =>  |%  ++  grub  (unit *)                 ::  result
3672            ++  fist  $-(json grub)            ::  reparser instance
3673          --  ::
3674    ::
3675    ::  XX: this is old code that replaced a rewritten dejs.
3676    ::      the rewritten dejs rest-looped with ++redo.  the old
3677    ::      code is still in revision control -- revise and replace.
3678    ::
3679    |%
3680    ++  ar                                     ::  array as list
3681      |*  wit=fist
3682      |=  jon=json
3683      ?.  ?=([%a *] jon)  ~
3684      %-  zl
3685      |-
3686      ?~  p.jon  ~
3687      [i=(wit i.p.jon) t=$(p.jon t.p.jon)]
3688    ::
3689    ++  at                                     ::  array as tuple
3690      |*  wil=(pole fist)
3691      |=  jon=json
3692      ?.  ?=([%a *] jon)  ~
3693      ?.  =((lent wil) (lent p.jon))  ~
3694      =+  raw=((at-raw wil) p.jon)
3695      ?.((za raw) ~ (some (zp raw)))
3696    ::
3697    ++  at-raw                                 ::  array as tuple
3698      |*  wil=(pole fist)
3699      |=  jol=(list json)
3700      ?~  wil  ~
3701      :-  ?~(jol ~ (-.wil i.jol))
3702      ((at-raw +.wil) ?~(jol ~ t.jol))
3703    ::
3704    ++  bo                                     ::  boolean
3705      |=(jon=json ?.(?=([%b *] jon) ~ [~ u=p.jon]))
3706    ::
3707    ++  bu                                     ::  boolean not
3708      |=(jon=json ?.(?=([%b *] jon) ~ [~ u=!p.jon]))
3709    ::
```

```
3710      ++  ci                                    ::  maybe transform
3711        |*  [poq=gate wit=fist]
3712        |=  jon=json
3713        (biff (wit jon) poq)
3714      ::
3715      ++  cu                                    ::  transform
3716        |*  [poq=gate wit=fist]
3717        |=  jon=json
3718        (bind (wit jon) poq)
3719      ::
3720      ++  da                                    ::  UTC date
3721        |=  jon=json
3722        ?.  ?=([%s *] jon)  ~
3723        (bind (stud:chrono:userlib p.jon) |=(a=date (year a)))
3724      ::
3725      ++  dank                                  ::  tank
3726        ^-  $-(json (unit tank))
3727        %+  re  *tank  |.  ~+
3728        %-  of  :~
3729          leaf+sa
3730          palm+(ot style+(ot mid+sa cap+sa open+sa close+sa ~) lines+(ar dank) ~)
3731          rose+(ot style+(ot mid+sa open+sa close+sa ~) lines+(ar dank) ~)
3732        ==
3733      ::
3734      ++  di                                    ::  millisecond date
3735        (cu from-unix-ms:chrono:userlib ni)
3736      ::
3737      ++  mu                                    ::  true unit
3738        |*  wit=fist
3739        |=  jon=json
3740        ?~(jon (some ~) (bind (wit jon) some))
3741      ::
3742      ++  ne                                    ::  number as real
3743        |=  jon=json
3744        ^-  (unit @rd)
3745        ?.  ?=([%n *] jon)  ~
3746        (rush p.jon (cook ryld (cook royl-cell:^so json-rn)))
3747      ::
3748      ++  ni                                    ::  number as integer
3749        |=  jon=json
3750        ?.  ?=([%n *] jon)  ~
3751        (rush p.jon dem)
3752      ::
3753      ++  no                                    ::  number as cord
3754        |=  jon=json
3755        ?.  ?=([%n *] jon)  ~
3756        (some p.jon)
3757      ::
3758      ++  of                                    ::  object as frond
3759        |*  wer=(pole [cord fist])
3760        |=  jon=json
3761        ?.  ?=([%o [@ *] ~ ~] jon)  ~
3762        |-
3763        ?~  wer  ~
3764        ?:  =(-.-.wer p.n.p.jon)
3765          ((pe -.-.wer +.-.wer) q.n.p.jon)
3766        ((of +.wer) jon)
3767      ::
```

```
3768  ++  ot                                    ::  object as tuple
3769    |*  wer=(pole [cord fist])
3770    |=  jon=json
3771    ?.  ?=([%o *] jon)  ~
3772    =+  raw=((ot-raw wer) p.jon)
3773    ?.((za raw) ~ (some (zp raw)))
3774  ::
3775  ++  ot-raw                                ::  object as tuple
3776    |*  wer=(pole [cord fist])
3777    |=  jom=(map @t json)
3778    ?~  wer  ~
3779    =+  ten=(~(get by jom) -.-.wer)
3780    [?~(ten ~ (+.-.wer u.ten)) ((ot-raw +.wer) jom)]
3781  ::
3782  ++  om                                    ::  object as map
3783    |*  wit=fist
3784    |=  jon=json
3785    ?.  ?=([%o *] jon)  ~
3786    (zm (~(run by p.jon) wit))
3787  ::
3788  ++  op                                    ::  parse keys of map
3789    |*  [fel=rule wit=fist]
3790    %+  cu
3791      |=  a=(list (pair _(wonk *fel) _(need *wit)))
3792      (my:nl a)
3793    %-  ci  :_  (om wit)
3794    |=  a=(map cord _(need *wit))
3795    ^-  (unit (list _[(wonk *fel) (need *wit)]))
3796    %-  zl
3797    %+  turn  ~(tap by a)
3798    |=  [a=cord b=_(need *wit)]
3799    =+  nit=(rush a fel)
3800    ?~  nit  ~
3801    (some [u.nit b])
3802  ::
3803  ++  pe                                    ::  prefix
3804    |*  [pre=* wit=fist]
3805    (cu |*(* [pre +<]) wit)
3806  ::
3807  ++  re                                    ::  recursive reparsers
3808    |*  [gar=* sef=_|.(fist)]
3809    |=  jon=json
3810    ^-  (unit _gar)
3811    ((sef) jon)
3812  ::
3813  ++  sa                                    ::  string as tape
3814    |=  jon=json
3815    ?.(?=([%s *] jon) ~ (some (trip p.jon)))
3816  ::
3817  ++  so                                    ::  string as cord
3818    |=  jon=json
3819    ?.(?=([%s *] jon) ~ (some p.jon))
3820  ::
3821  ++  su                                    ::  parse string
3822    |*  sab=rule
3823    |=  jon=json
3824    ?.  ?=([%s *] jon)  ~
3825    (rush p.jon sab)
```

```
3826        ::
3827        ++  ul    |=(jon=json ?~(jon (some ~) ~))              ::  null
3828        ++  za                                                 ::  full unit pole
3829          |*  pod=(pole (unit))
3830          ?~  pod  &
3831          ?~  -.pod  |
3832          (za +.pod)
3833        ::
3834        ++  zl                                                 ::  collapse unit list
3835          |*  lut=(list (unit))
3836          ?.  |-  ^-  ?
3837              ?~(lut & ?~(i.lut | $(lut t.lut)))
3838            ~
3839          %-  some
3840          |-
3841          ?~  lut  ~
3842          [i=u:+.i.lut t=$(lut t.lut)]
3843        ::
3844        ++  zp                                                 ::  unit tuple
3845          |*  but=(pole (unit))
3846          ?~  but  !!
3847          ?~  +.but
3848            u:->.but
3849          [u:->.but (zp +.but)]
3850        ::
3851        ++  zm                                                 ::  collapse unit map
3852          |*  lum=(map term (unit))
3853          ?:  (~(rep by lum) |=([[@ a=(unit)] b=_|] |(b ?=(~ a))))
3854            ~
3855          (some (~(run by lum) need))
3856        --  ::dejs-soft
3857      ::
3858      ++  klr                                                  ::  styx/stub engine
3859        =,  dill
3860        |%
3861        ++  make                                               ::  stub from styx
3862          |=  a=styx  ^-  stub
3863          =|  b=stye
3864          %+  reel
3865            |-  ^-  stub
3866          %-  zing  %+  turn  a
3867          |=  a=$@(@t (pair styl styx))
3868          ?@  a  [b (tuba (trip a))]~
3869          ^$(a q.a, b (styd p.a b))
3870        ::
3871        |=  [a=(pair stye (list @c)) b=stub]
3872        ?~  b  [a ~]
3873        ?.  =(p.a p.i.b)  [a b]
3874        [[p.a (weld q.a q.i.b)] t.b]
3875        ::
3876        ++  styd                                               ::  stye from styl
3877          |=  [a=styl b=stye]  ^+  b                           ::  with inheritance
3878          :+  ?~  p.a  p.b
3879              ?~  u.p.a  ~
3880              (~(put in p.b) u.p.a)
3881            (fall p.q.a p.q.b)
3882          (fall q.q.a q.q.b)
3883        ::
```

```
3884    ++  lent-char
3885    |=  a=stub  ^-  @
3886    (roll (lnts-char a) add)
3887    ::
3888    ++  lnts-char                                    ::  stub text lengths
3889    |=  a=stub  ^-  (list @)
3890    %+  turn  a
3891    |=  a=(pair stye (list @c))
3892    (lent q.a)
3893    ::
3894    ++  brek                                         ::  index + incl-len of
3895    |=  [a=@ b=(list @)]                             ::  stub pair w/ idx a
3896    =|  [c=@ i=@]
3897    |-  ^-  (unit (pair @ @))
3898    ?~  b  ~
3899    =.  c  (add c i.b)
3900    ?:  (gte c a)
3901    `[i c]
3902    $(i +(i), b t.b)
3903    ::
3904    ++  pact                                         ::  condense stub
3905    |=  a=stub
3906    ^-  stub
3907    ?~  a  ~
3908    ?~  t.a  a
3909    ?.  =(p.i.a p.i.t.a)  [i.a $(a t.a)]
3910    =.  q.i.t.a  (weld q.i.a q.i.t.a)
3911    $(a t.a)
3912    ::
3913    ++  slag                                         ::  slag stub
3914    |=  [a=@ b=stub]
3915    ^-  stub
3916    ?:  =(0 a)  b
3917    ?~  b  ~
3918    =+  c=(lent q.i.b)
3919    ?:  =(c a)  t.b
3920    ?:  (gth c a)
3921    [[p.i.b (^slag a q.i.b)] t.b]
3922    $(a (sub a c), b t.b)
3923    ::
3924    ++  scag                                         ::  scag stub
3925    |=  [a=@ b=stub]
3926    ^-  stub
3927    ?:  =(0 a)  ~
3928    ?~  b  ~
3929    =+  c=(lent q.i.b)
3930    ?:  (gth c a)
3931    [p.i.b (^scag a q.i.b)]~
3932    :-  i.b
3933    $(a (sub a c), b t.b)
3934    ::
3935    ++  swag                                         ::  swag stub
3936    |=  [[a=@ b=@] c=stub]
3937    (scag b (slag a c))
3938    ::
3939    ++  wail                                         ::  overlay stub
3940    |=  [a=stub b=@ c=stub d=@c]
3941    ^-  stub
```

```
3942          ;:    weld
3943            (scag b a)
3944          ::
3945          =+   e=(lent-char a)
3946          ?:  (lte b e)  ~
3947          [*stye (reap (sub b e) d)]~
3948          ::
3949            c
3950            (slag (add b (lent-char c)) a)
3951          ==
3952      --  ::  klr
3953    --
3954  ::    |cloy: clay helpers
3955  ::
3956  ++  cloy
3957    =,  clay
3958    |%
3959    ++  new-desk
3960    |=  [=desk tako=(unit tako) files=(map path page)]
3961    [%c %park desk &/[(drop tako) (~(run by files) (lead %&))] *rang]
3962    --
3963  ::                                                       ::
3964  ::::                              ++differ               ::  (2d) hunt-mcilroy
3965    ::                                                     ::::
3966  ++  differ  ^?
3967    =,  clay
3968    =,  format
3969    |%
3970    ::                                                     ::  ++berk:differ
3971    ++  berk                                               ::  invert diff patch
3972      |*  bur=(urge)
3973      |-  ^+  bur
3974    ?~  bur  ~
3975    :_  $(bur t.bur)
3976    ?-  -.i.bur
3977      %&  i.bur
3978      %|  [%| q.i.bur p.i.bur]
3979    ==
3980    ::                                                     ::  ++loss:differ
3981    ++  loss                                               ::  longest subsequence
3982      ~%  %loss  ..part  ~
3983      |*  [hel=(list) hev=(list)]
3984      |-  ^+  hev
3985      =+  ^=  sev
3986          =+  [inx=0 sev=*(map _i.-.hev (list @ud))]
3987          |-  ^+  sev
3988          ?~  hev  sev
3989          =+  guy=(~(get by sev) i.hev)
3990          %=  $
3991            hev  t.hev
3992            inx  +(inx)
3993            sev  (~(put by sev) i.hev [inx ?~(guy ~ u.guy)])
3994          ==
3995      =|  gox=[p=@ud q=(map @ud [p=@ud q=_hev])]
3996      =<  abet
3997      =<  main
3998      |%
3999      ::                                                   ::  ++abet:loss:differ
```

```
4000    ++  abet                                       ::  subsequence
4001      ^+  hev
4002      ?:  =(0 p.gox)  ~
4003      (flop q:(need (~(get by q.gox) (dec p.gox))))
4004    ::                                             ::  ++hink:loss:differ
4005    ++  hink                                       ::  extend fits top
4006      |=  [inx=@ud goy=@ud]   ^-  ?
4007      ?|  =(p.gox inx)
4008          (lth goy p:(need (~(get by q.gox) inx)))
4009      ==
4010    ::                                             ::  ++lonk:loss:differ
4011    ++  lonk                                       ::  extend fits bottom
4012      |=  [inx=@ud goy=@ud]   ^-  ?
4013      ?|  =(0 inx)
4014          (gth goy p:(need (~(get by q.gox) (dec inx))))
4015      ==
4016    ::                                             ::  ++luna:loss:differ
4017    ++  luna                                       ::  extend
4018      |=  [inx=@ud goy=@ud]
4019      ^+  +>
4020      %_    +>.$
4021          gox
4022        :-  ?:(=(inx p.gox) +(p.gox) p.gox)
4023        %+  ~(put by q.gox)  inx
4024        :+  goy
4025          (snag goy hev)
4026        ?:(=(0 inx)  ~ q:(need (~(get by q.gox) (dec inx))))
4027      ==
4028    ::                                             ::  ++merg:loss:differ
4029    ++  merg                                       ::  merge all matches
4030      |=  gay=(list @ud)
4031      ^+  +>
4032      =+  ^=  zes
4033          =+  [inx=0 zes=*(list [p=@ud q=@ud])]
4034          |-  ^+  zes
4035          ?:  |(?=(~ gay) (gth inx p.gox))  zes
4036          ?.  (lonk inx i.gay)  $(gay t.gay)
4037          ?.  (hink inx i.gay)  $(inx +(inx))
4038          $(inx +(inx), gay t.gay, zes [[inx i.gay] zes])
4039      |-  ^+  +>.^$
4040      ?~(zes +>.^$ $(zes t.zes, +>.^$ (luna i.zes)))
4041    ::                                             ::  ++main:loss:differ
4042    ++  main                                       ::
4043      =+  hol=hel
4044      |-  ^+  +>
4045      ?~  hol  +>
4046      =+  guy=(~(get by sev) i.hol)
4047      $(hol t.hol, +> (merg (flop `(list @ud)`?~(guy ~ u.guy))))
4048      --  ::
4049    ::                                             ::  ++lurk:differ
4050    ++  lurk                                       ::  apply list patch
4051      |*  [hel=(list) rug=(urge)]
4052      ^+  hel
4053      =+  war=`_hel`~
4054      |-  ^+  hel
4055      ?~  rug  (flop war)
4056      ?-    -.i.rug
4057          %&
```

```
4058        %=    $
4059          rug   t.rug
4060          hel   (slag p.i.rug hel)
4061          war   (weld (flop (scag p.i.rug hel)) war)
4062        ==
4063      ::
4064        %|
4065        %=    $
4066          rug   t.rug
4067          hel   =+  gur=(flop p.i.rug)
4068              |-  ^+  hel
4069              ?~  gur  hel
4070              ?>(&(?=(^ hel) =(i.gur i.hel)) $(hel t.hel, gur t.gur))
4071          war   (weld q.i.rug war)
4072        ==
4073      ==
4074    ::                                          ::  ++lusk:differ
4075    ++  lusk                                    ::  lcs to list patch
4076      |*  [hel=(list) hev=(list) lcs=(list)]
4077      =+  ^=  rag
4078          ^-  [$%([%& p=@ud] [%| p=_lcs q=_lcs])]
4079          [%& 0]
4080      =>  .(rag [p=rag q=*(list _rag)])
4081      =<  abet  =<  main
4082      |%
4083      ::                                        ::  ++abet:lusk:differ
4084      ++  abet                                  ::
4085        =?  q.rag  !=([& 0] p.rag)  [p.rag q.rag]
4086        (flop q.rag)
4087      ::                                        ::  ++done:lusk:differ
4088      ++  done                                  ::
4089        |=  new=_p.rag
4090        ^+  rag
4091        ?-  -.p.rag
4092          %|    ?-  -.new
4093                %|  [[%| (weld p.new p.p.rag) (weld q.new q.p.rag)] q.rag]
4094                %&  [new [p.rag q.rag]]
4095              ==
4096          %&    ?-  -.new
4097                %|  [new ?:(=(0 p.p.rag) q.rag [p.rag q.rag])]
4098                %&  [[%& (add p.p.rag p.new)] q.rag]
4099              ==
4100        ==
4101      ::                                        ::  ++main:lusk:differ
4102      ++  main                                  ::
4103        |-  ^+  +
4104        ?~  hel
4105          ?~  hev
4106            ?>(?=(~ lcs) +)
4107          $(hev t.hev, rag (done %| ~ [i.hev ~]))
4108        ?~  hev
4109          $(hel t.hel, rag (done %| [i.hel ~] ~))
4110        ?~  lcs
4111          +(rag (done %| (flop hel) (flop hev)))
4112        ?:  =(i.hel i.lcs)
4113          ?:  =(i.hev i.lcs)
4114            $(lcs t.lcs, hel t.hel, hev t.hev, rag (done %& 1))
4115          $(hev t.hev, rag (done %| ~ [i.hev ~]))
```

```
4116        ?:  =(i.hev i.lcs)
4117          $(hel t.hel, rag (done %| [i.hel ~] ~))
4118          $(hel t.hel, hev t.hev, rag (done %| [i.hel ~] [i.hev ~]))
4119        --  ::
4120      --  ::differ
4121  ::                                                          ::
4122  ::::                              ++html                    ::  (2e) text encodings
4123    ::                                                        ::::
4124  ++  html  ^?  ::  XX rename to web-txt
4125    =,  eyre
4126    |%
4127    ::                                                        ::
4128    ::::                            ++mimes:html              ::  (2e1) MIME
4129      ::                                                      ::::
4130    ++  mimes  ^?
4131    ~%  %mimes  ..part  ~
4132    |%
4133    ::                                                        ::  ++as-octs:mimes:html
4134    ++  as-octs                                               ::  atom to octstream
4135    |=  tam=@  ^-  octs
4136    [(met 3 tam) tam]
4137    ::                                                        ::  ++as-octt:mimes:html
4138    ++  as-octt                                               ::  tape to octstream
4139    |=  tep=tape  ^-  octs
4140    (as-octs (rap 3 tep))
4141    ::                                                        ::  ++en-mite:mimes:html
4142    ++  en-mite                                               ::  mime type to text
4143    |=  myn=mite
4144    %-  crip
4145    |-  ^-  tape
4146    ?~  myn  ~
4147    ?:  =(~ t.myn)  (trip i.myn)
4148    (weld (trip i.myn) `tape`['/' $(myn t.myn)])
4149    ::
4150    ::  |base16: en/decode arbitrary MSB-first hex strings
4151    ::
4152    ++  base16
4153    ~%  %base16  +  ~
4154    |%
4155    ++  en
4156      ~/  %en
4157      |=  a=octs  ^-  cord
4158      (crip ((x-co:co (mul p.a 2)) (end [3 p.a] q.a)))
4159    ::
4160    ++  de
4161      ~/  %de
4162      |=  a=cord  ^-  (unit octs)
4163      (rush a rule)
4164    ::
4165    ++  rule
4166      %+  cook
4167        |=  a=(list @)  ^-  octs
4168        [(add (dvr (lent a) 2)) (rep [0 4] (flop a))]
4169      (star hit)
4170      --
4171    ::  |base64: flexible base64 encoding for little-endian atoms
4172    ::
4173    ++  base64
```

```
4174        =>  |%
4175            +$  byte     @D
4176            +$  word24   @
4177            ::
4178            ++  div-ceil
4179              ::  divide, rounding up.
4180              |=  [x=@ y=@]  ^-  @
4181              ?:  =(0 (mod x y))
4182                (div x y)
4183              +((div x y))
4184            ::
4185            ++  explode-bytes
4186              ::  Explode a bytestring into list of bytes. Result is in LSB order.
4187              |=  =octs  ^-  (list byte)
4188              =/  atom-byte-width  (met 3 q.octs)
4189              =/  leading-zeros    (sub p.octs atom-byte-width)
4190              (weld (reap leading-zeros 0) (rip 3 q.octs))
4191            ::
4192            ++  explode-words
4193              ::  Explode a bytestring to words of bit-width `wid`. Result is in LSW order.
4194              |=  [wid=@ =octs]
4195              ^-  (list @)
4196              =/  atom-bit-width   (met 0 q.octs)
4197              =/  octs-bit-width   (mul 8 p.octs)
4198              =/  atom-word-width  (div-ceil atom-bit-width wid)
4199              =/  rslt-word-width  (div-ceil octs-bit-width wid)
4200              =/  pad              (sub rslt-word-width atom-word-width)
4201              =/  x  (rip [0 wid] q.octs)
4202              %+  weld  x
4203              (reap pad 0)
4204            --
4205          ::
4206          ::  pad: include padding when encoding, require when decoding
4207          ::  url: use url-safe characters '-' for '+' and '_' for '/'
4208          ::
4209          =+  [pad=& url=|]
4210          |%
4211          ::  +en:base64: encode +octs to base64 cord
4212          ::
4213          ::  Encode an `octs` into a base64 string.
4214          ::
4215          ::  First, we break up the input into a list of 24-bit words. The input
4216          ::  might not be a multiple of 24-bits, so we add 0-2 padding bytes at
4217          ::  the end (to the least-significant side, with a left-shift).
4218          ::
4219          ::  Then, we encode each block into four base64 characters.
4220          ::
4221          ::  Finally we remove the padding that we added at the beginning: for
4222          ::  each byte that was added, we replace one character with an = (unless
4223          ::  `pad` is false, in which case we just remove the extra characters).
4224          ::
4225          ++  en
4226            ^-  $-(octs cord)
4227            ::
4228            =/  cha
4229            ?:  url
4230              'ABCDEFGHIJKLMNOPQRSTUVWXYZabcdefghijklmnopqrstuvwxyz0123456789-_'
4231              'ABCDEFGHIJKLMNOPQRSTUVWXYZabcdefghijklmnopqrstuvwxyz0123456789+/'
```

```
4232        ::
4233        |^  |=  bs=octs  ^-  cord
4234          =/  [padding=@ blocks=(list word24)]
4235            (octs-to-blocks bs)
4236          (crip (flop (unpad padding (encode-blocks blocks))))
4237        ::
4238      ++  octs-to-blocks
4239        |=  bs=octs  ^-  [padding=@ud (list word24)]
4240        =/  padding=@ud  (~(dif fo 3) 0 p.bs)
4241        =/  padded=octs  [(add padding p.bs) (lsh [3 padding] (rev 3 bs))]
4242        [padding (explode-words 24 padded)]
4243        ::
4244      ++  unpad
4245        |=  [extra=@ t=tape]  ^-  tape
4246        =/  without  (slag extra t)
4247        ?.  pad  without
4248        (weld (reap extra '=') without)
4249        ::
4250      ++  encode-blocks
4251        |=  ws=(list word24)  ^-  tape
4252        (zing (turn ws encode-block))
4253        ::
4254      ++  encode-block
4255        |=  w=word24  ^-  tape
4256        =/  a  (cut 3 [(cut 0 [0 6] w) 1] cha)
4257        =/  b  (cut 3 [(cut 0 [6 6] w) 1] cha)
4258        =/  c  (cut 3 [(cut 0 [12 6] w) 1] cha)
4259        =/  d  (cut 3 [(cut 0 [18 6] w) 1] cha)
4260        ~[a b c d]
4261      --
4262    ::
4263    ::  +de:base64: decode base64 cord to (unit @)
4264    ::
4265    ++  de
4266      |=  a=cord
4267      ^-  (unit octs)
4268      (rush a parse)
4269    ::  +parse:base64: parse base64 cord to +octs
4270    ::
4271    ++  parse
4272      =<  ^-  $-(nail (like octs))
4273          %+  sear  reduce
4274          ;~  plug
4275            %-  plus  ;~  pose
4276              (cook |=(a=@ (sub a 'A')) (shim 'A' 'Z'))
4277              (cook |=(a=@ (sub a 'G')) (shim 'a' 'z'))
4278              (cook |=(a=@ (add a 4)) (shim '0' '9'))
4279              (cold 62 (just ?:(url '-' '+')))
4280              (cold 63 (just ?:(url '_' '/')))
4281            ==
4282            (stun 0^2 (cold %0 tis))
4283          ==
4284      |%
4285      ::  +reduce:parse:base64: reduce, measure, and swap base64 digits
4286      ::
4287      ++  reduce
4288        |=  [dat=(list @) dap=(list @)]
4289        ^-  (unit octs)
```

```
4290          =/  lat  (lent dat)
4291          =/  lap  (lent dap)
4292          =/  dif  (~(dif fo 4) 0 lat)
4293          ?:  &(pad !=(dif lap))
4294            ::  padding required and incorrect
4295            ~&(%base-64-padding-err-one ~)
4296          ?:  &(!pad !=(0 lap))
4297            ::  padding not required but present
4298            ~&(%base-64-padding-err-two ~)
4299          =/  len  (sub (mul 3 (div (add lat dif) 4)) dif)
4300          :+  ~  len
4301          =/  res  (rsh [1 dif] (rep [0 6] (flop dat)))
4302          =/  amt  (met 3 res)
4303          ::  left shift trailing zeroes in after byte swap
4304          =/  trl  ?:  (lth len amt)  0  (sub len amt)
4305          (lsh [3 trl] (swp 3 res))
4306        --
4307      --
4308    ::
4309    ++  en-base58
4310      |=  dat=@
4311      =/  cha
4312        '123456789ABCDEFGHJKLMNPQRSTUVWXYZabcdefghijkmnopqrstuvwxyz'
4313      %-  flop
4314      |-  ^-  tape
4315      ?:  =(0 dat)  ~
4316      :-  (cut 3 [(mod dat 58) 1] cha)
4317      $(dat (div dat 58))
4318    ::
4319    ++  de-base58
4320      |=  t=tape
4321      =-  (scan t (bass 58 (plus -)))
4322      ;~  pose
4323        (cook |=(a=@ (sub a 56)) (shim 'A' 'H'))
4324        (cook |=(a=@ (sub a 57)) (shim 'J' 'N'))
4325        (cook |=(a=@ (sub a 58)) (shim 'P' 'Z'))
4326        (cook |=(a=@ (sub a 64)) (shim 'a' 'k'))
4327        (cook |=(a=@ (sub a 65)) (shim 'm' 'z'))
4328        (cook |=(a=@ (sub a 49)) (shim '1' '9'))
4329      ==
4330    --  ::mimes
4331  ::                                                ::
4332  ::::                    ++json:html               ::  (2e2) JSON
4333  ::                                                ::::
4334  ++  json  ^?
4335    ~%  %json  ..part  ~
4336    |%
4337    ::                                              ::  ++en:json:html
4338    ++  en                                          ::  encode JSON to cord
4339      ~%  %en  +>+  ~
4340      |^  |=  jon=^json
4341          ^-  cord
4342          (rap 3 (flop (onto jon ~)))
4343      ::                                            ::  ++onto:en:json:html
4344      ++  onto
4345        |=  [val=^json out=(list @t)]
4346        ^+  out
4347        ?~  val  ['null' out]
```

```
4348          ?-     -.val
4349            %a
4350          ?~  p.val  ['[]' out]
4351          =.  out    ['[' out]
4352          !.
4353          |-  ^+  out
4354          =.  out  ^$(val i.p.val)
4355          ?~(t.p.val [']' out] $(p.val t.p.val, out [',' out]))
4356        ::
4357            %b
4358          [?:(p.val 'true' 'false') out]
4359        ::
4360            %n
4361          [p.val out]
4362        ::
4363            %s
4364          [(scap p.val) out]
4365        ::
4366            %o
4367          =/  viz  ~(tap by p.val)
4368          ?~  viz  ['{}' out]
4369          =.  out  ['{' out]
4370          !.
4371          |-  ^+  out
4372          =.  out  ^$(val q.i.viz, out [':' [(scap p.i.viz) out]])
4373          ?~(t.viz ['}' out] $(viz t.viz, out [',' out]))
4374        ==
4375      ::                                      :: ++scap:en:json:html
4376    ++  scap
4377      |=  val=@t
4378      ^-  @t
4379      =/  out=(list @t)  ['"' ~]
4380      =/  len  (met 3 val)
4381      =|  [i=@ud pos=@ud]
4382      |-  ^-  @t
4383      ?:  =(len i)
4384        (rap 3 (flop ['"' (rsh [3 pos] val) out]))
4385      =/  car  (cut 3 [i 1] val)
4386      ?:  ?&  (gth car 0x1f)
4387              !=(car 0x22)
4388              !=(car 0x5C)
4389              !=(car 0x7F)
4390          ==
4391        $(i +(i))
4392      =/  cap
4393        ?+  car  (crip '\\' 'u' ((x-co 4):co car))
4394          %10  '\\n'
4395          %'"'  '\\"'
4396          %'\\'  '\\\\'
4397        ==
4398      $(i +(i), pos +(i), out [cap (cut 3 [pos (sub i pos)] val) out])
4399      --  ::en
4400    ::                                        :: ++de:json:html
4401    ++  de                                    :: parse cord to JSON
4402      ~%  %de  +>+  ~
4403      |^  |=  txt=cord
4404          ^-  (unit ^json)
4405          (rush txt apex)
```

```
4406      ::                                                ::  ++abox:de:json:html
4407      ++  abox                                          ::  array
4408      %+  stag  %a
4409      (ifix [sel (wish ser)] (more (wish com) apex))
4410      ::                                                ::  ++apex:de:json:html
4411      ++  apex                                          ::  any value
4412      %+  knee  *^json  |.  ~+
4413      %+  ifix  [spac spac]
4414      ;~  pose
4415        (cold ~ (jest 'null'))
4416        (stag %b bool)
4417        (stag %s stri)
4418        (cook |=(s=tape [%n p=(rap 3 s)]) numb)
4419        abox
4420        obox
4421      ==
4422      ::                                                ::  ++bool:de:json:html
4423      ++  bool                                          ::  boolean
4424      ;~  pose
4425        (cold & (jest 'true'))
4426        (cold | (jest 'false'))
4427      ==
4428      ::                                                ::  ++esca:de:json:html
4429      ++  esca                                          ::  escaped character
4430      ;~  pfix  bas
4431        =*  loo
4432          =*  lip
4433            ^-  (list (pair @t @))
4434            [b+8 t+9 n+10 f+12 r+13 ~]
4435          =*  wow
4436            ^~
4437            ^-  (map @t @)
4438            (malt lip)
4439          (sear ~(get by wow) low)
4440        ;~(pose doq fas bas loo unic)
4441      ==
4442      ::                                                ::  ++expo:de:json:html
4443      ++  expo                                          ::  exponent
4444      ;~  (comp weld)
4445        (piec (mask "eE"))
4446        (mayb (piec (mask "+-")))
4447        (plus nud)
4448      ==
4449      ::                                                ::  ++frac:de:json:html
4450      ++  frac                                          ::  fraction
4451      ;~(plug dot (plus nud))
4452      ::                                                ::  ++jcha:de:json:html
4453      ++  jcha                                          ::  string character
4454      ;~(pose ;~(less doq bas (shim 32 255)) esca)
4455      ::                                                ::  ++mayb:de:json:html
4456      ++  mayb                                          ::  optional
4457      |*(bus=rule ;~(pose bus (easy ~)))
4458      ::                                                ::  ++numb:de:json:html
4459      ++  numb                                          ::  number
4460      ;~  (comp weld)
4461        (mayb (piec hep))
4462        ;~  pose
4463          (piec (just '0'))
```

```
4464              ;~(plug (shim '1' '9') (star nud))
4465          ==
4466        (mayb frac)
4467        (mayb expo)
4468      ==
4469    ::                                              ::  ++obje:de:json:html
4470    ++  obje                                        ::  object list
4471      %+  ifix  [(wish kel) (wish ker)]
4472      (more (wish com) pear)
4473    ::                                              ::  ++obox:de:json:html
4474    ++  obox                                        ::  object
4475      (stag %o (cook malt obje))
4476    ::                                              ::  ++pear:de:json:html
4477    ++  pear                                        ::  key-value
4478      ;~(plug ;~(sfix (wish stri) (wish col)) apex)
4479    ::                                              ::  ++piec:de:json:html
4480    ++  piec                                        ::  listify
4481      |*  bus=rule
4482      (cook |=(a=@ [a ~]) bus)
4483    ::                                              ::  ++stri:de:json:html
4484    ++  stri                                        ::  string
4485      %+  sear
4486        |=  a=cord
4487        ?.  (sune a)  ~
4488        (some a)
4489      (cook crip (ifix [doq doq] (star jcha)))
4490    ::                                              ::  ++spac:de:json:html
4491    ++  spac                                        ::  whitespace
4492      (star (mask [`@`9 `@`10 `@`13 ' ' ~]))
4493    ::                                              ::  ++unic:de:json:html
4494    ++  unic                                        ::  escaped UTF16
4495      =*  lob  0x0
4496      =*  hsb  0xd800
4497      =*  lsb  0xdc00
4498      =*  hib  0xe000
4499      =*  hil  0x1.0000
4500      |^
4501        %+  cook
4502          |=  a=@
4503          ^-  @t
4504          (tuft a)
4505        ;~  pfix  (just 'u')
4506          ;~(pose solo pair)
4507        ==
4508      ++  quad                                       ::  parse num from 4 hex
4509        (bass 16 (stun [4 4] hit))
4510      ++  meat                                       ::  gen gate for sear:
4511        |=  [bot=@ux top=@ux flp=?]                  ::  accept num in range,
4512        |=  sur=@ux                                  ::  optionally reduce
4513        ^-  (unit @)
4514        ?.  &((gte sur bot) (lth sur top))
4515          ~
4516        %-  some
4517        ?.  flp  sur
4518        (sub sur bot)
4519      ++  solo                                       ::  single valid UTF16
4520        ;~  pose
4521          (sear (meat lob hsb |) quad)
```

```
4522              (sear (meat hib hil |) quad)
4523            ==
4524        ++  pair                                    ::  UTF16 surrogate pair
4525          %+  cook
4526          |=  [hig=@ low=@]
4527            ^-  @t
4528            :(add hil low (lsh [1 5] hig))
4529          ;~  plug
4530            (sear (meat hsb lsb &) quad)
4531            ;~  pfix  (jest '\\u')
4532              (sear (meat lsb hib &) quad)
4533            ==
4534          ==
4535        --
4536      ::                                            ::  ++utfe:de:json:html
4537      ++  utfe                                      ::  UTF-8 sequence
4538        ;~  less  doq  bas
4539          =*  qua
4540          %+  cook
4541          |=  [a=@ b=@ c=@ d=@]
4542          (rap 3 a b c d ~)
4543          ;~  pose
4544            ;~  plug
4545              (shim 241 243)
4546              (shim 128 191)
4547              (shim 128 191)
4548              (shim 128 191)
4549            ==
4550            ;~  plug
4551              (just '\F0')
4552              (shim 144 191)
4553              (shim 128 191)
4554              (shim 128 191)
4555            ==
4556            ;~  plug
4557              (just '\F4')
4558              (shim 128 143)
4559              (shim 128 191)
4560              (shim 128 191)
4561            ==
4562          ==
4563          =*  tre
4564          %+  cook
4565          |=  [a=@ b=@ c=@]
4566          (rap 3 a b c ~)
4567          ;~  pose
4568            ;~  plug
4569              ;~  pose
4570                (shim 225 236)
4571                (shim 238 239)
4572              ==
4573              (shim 128 191)
4574              (shim 128 191)
4575            ==
4576            ;~  plug
4577              (just '\E0')
4578              (shim 160 191)
4579              (shim 128 191)
```

```
4580              ==
4581            ;~  plug
4582              (just '\ED')
4583              (shim 128 159)
4584              (shim 128 191)
4585            ==
4586          ==
4587        =*  dos
4588        %+  cook
4589        |=  [a=@ b=@]
4590          (cat 3 a b)
4591        ;~  plug
4592          (shim 194 223)
4593          (shim 128 191)
4594        ==
4595        ;~(pose qua tre dos)
4596      ==
4597  ::                                    ::  ++wish:de:json:html
4598  ++  wish                              ::  with whitespace
4599  |*(sef=rule ;~(pfix spac sef))
4600  ::  XX: These gates should be moved to hoon.hoon
4601  ::                                    ::  ++sune:de:json:html
4602  ++  sune                              ::  cord UTF-8 sanity
4603  |=  b=@t
4604  ^-  ?
4605  ?:  =(0 b)  &
4606  ?.  (sung b)  |
4607  $(b (rsh [3 (teff b)] b))
4608  ::                                    ::  ++sung:de:json:html
4609  ++  sung                              ::  char UTF-8 sanity
4610  |^  |=  b=@t
4611      ^-  ?
4612      =+  len=(teff b)
4613      ?:  =(4 len)  (quad b)
4614      ?:  =(3 len)  (tres b)
4615      ?:  =(2 len)  (dos b)
4616      (lte (end 3 b) 127)
4617  ::
4618  ++  dos
4619    |=  b=@t
4620    ^-  ?
4621    =+  :-  one=(cut 3 [0 1] b)
4622            two=(cut 3 [1 1] b)
4623    ?&  (rang one 194 223)
4624    (cont two)
4625    ==
4626  ::
4627  ++  tres
4628    |=  b=@t
4629    ^-  ?
4630    =+  :+  one=(cut 3 [0 1] b)
4631            two=(cut 3 [1 1] b)
4632            tre=(cut 3 [2 1] b)
4633    ?&
4634      ?|
4635      ?&  |((rang one 225 236) (rang one 238 239))
4636          (cont two)
4637          ==
```

```
4638              ::
4639              ?&  =(224 one)
4640                  (rang two 160 191)
4641              ==
4642              ::
4643              ?&  =(237 one)
4644                  (rang two 128 159)
4645              ==
4646            ==
4647            ::
4648            (cont tre)
4649          ==
4650        ::
4651    ++  quad
4652        |=  b=@t
4653        ^-  ?
4654        =+  :^  one=(cut 3 [0 1] b)
4655                two=(cut 3 [1 1] b)
4656                tre=(cut 3 [2 1] b)
4657                for=(cut 3 [3 1] b)
4658        ?&
4659          ?|
4660            ?&  (rang one 241 243)
4661                (cont two)
4662            ==
4663            ::
4664            ?&  =(240 one)
4665                (rang two 144 191)
4666            ==
4667            ::
4668            ?&  =(244 one)
4669                (rang two 128 143)
4670            ==
4671          ==
4672          ::
4673          (cont tre)
4674          (cont for)
4675        ==
4676        ::
4677    ++  cont
4678        |=  a=@
4679        ^-  ?
4680        (rang a 128 191)
4681        ::
4682    ++  rang
4683        |=  [a=@ bot=@ top=@]
4684        ^-  ?
4685        ?>  (lte bot top)
4686        &((gte a bot) (lte a top))
4687      --
4688    ::  XX: This +teff should overwrite the existing +teff
4689    ::                                                        ::  ++teff:de:json:html
4690    ++  teff                                                  ::  UTF-8 length
4691      |=  a=@t
4692      ^-  @
4693      =+  b=(end 3 a)
4694      ?:  =(0 b)
4695        ?>  =(`@`0 a)  0
```

```
4696        ?:  (lte b 127)  1
4697        ?:  (lte b 223)  2
4698        ?:  (lte b 239)  3
4699        4
4700     --  ::de
4701   --  ::json
4702   ::                                    ::  ++en-xml:html
4703   ++  en-xml                            ::  xml printer
4704   =<  |=(a=manx `tape`(apex a ~))
4705   |_  _[unq=`?`| cot=`?`|]]
4706   ::                                    ::  ++apex:en-xml:html
4707   ++  apex                              ::  top level
4708   |=  [mex=manx rez=tape]
4709   ^-  tape
4710   ?:  ?=([%$ [[%$ *] ~]] g.mex)
4711     (escp v.i.a.g.mex rez)
4712   =+  man=`mane`n.g.mex
4713   =.  unq  |(unq =(%script man) =(%style man))
4714   =+  tam=(name man)
4715   =+  att=`mart`a.g.mex
4716   :-  '<'
4717   %+  welp  tam
4718   =-  ?~(att rez [' ' (attr att rez)])
4719   ^-  rez=tape
4720   ?:  &(?=(~ c.mex) |(cot ?^(man | (clot man))))
4721     [' ' '/' '>' rez]
4722   :-  '>'
4723   (many c.mex :(weld "</" tam ">" rez))
4724   ::                                    ::  ++attr:en-xml:html
4725   ++  attr                              ::  attributes to tape
4726   |=  [tat=mart rez=tape]
4727   ^-  tape
4728   ?~  tat  rez
4729   =.  rez  $(tat t.tat)
4730   ;:  weld
4731     (name n.i.tat)
4732     "=\""
4733     (escp(unq |) v.i.tat '"' ?~(t.tat rez [' ' rez]))
4734   ==
4735   ::                                    ::  ++escp:en-xml:html
4736   ++  escp                              ::  escape for xml
4737   |=  [tex=tape rez=tape]
4738   ?:  unq
4739     (weld tex rez)
4740   =+  xet=`tape`(flop tex)
4741   !.
4742   |-  ^-  tape
4743   ?~  xet  rez
4744   %=  $
4745     xet  t.xet
4746     rez  ?-  i.xet
4747           %34  ['&' 'q' 'u' 'o' 't' ';' rez]
4748           %38  ['&' 'a' 'm' 'p' ';' rez]
4749           %39  ['&' '#' '3' '9' ';' rez]
4750           %60  ['&' 'l' 't' ';' rez]
4751           %62  ['&' 'g' 't' ';' rez]
4752           *    [i.xet rez]
4753          ==
```

```
4754        ==
4755    ::                                                ::  ++many:en-xml:html
4756    ++   many                                         ::  nodelist to tape
4757    |=   [lix=(list manx) rez=tape]
4758    |-   ^-   tape
4759    ?~   lix  rez
4760    (apex i.lix $(lix t.lix))
4761    ::                                                ::  ++name:en-xml:html
4762    ++   name                                         ::  name to tape
4763    |=   man=mane   ^-   tape
4764    ?@   man  (trip man)
4765    (weld (trip -.man) `tape`[':' (trip +.man)])
4766    ::                                                ::  ++clot:en-xml:html
4767    ++   clot   ~+                                    ::  self-closing tags
4768    %~   has  in
4769    %-   silt   ^-   (list term)   :~
4770      %area  %base  %br  %col  %command  %embed  %hr  %img  %inputt
4771      %keygen  %link  %meta  %param    %source   %track  %wbr
4772        ==
4773    --   ::en-xml
4774    ::                                                ::  ++de-xml:html
4775    ++   de-xml                                       ::  xml parser
4776    =<   |=(a=cord (rush a apex))
4777    |_   ent=_`(map term @t)`[[%apos '\''] ~ ~]
4778    ::                                                ::  ++apex:de-xml:html
4779    ++   apex                                         ::  top level
4780    =+   spa=;~(pose comt whit)
4781    %+   knee  *manx  |.   ~+
4782    %+   ifix
4783      [;~(plug (punt decl) (star spa)) (star spa)]
4784    ;~   pose
4785      %+   sear   |=([a=marx b=marl c=mane] ?.(=(c n.a) ~ (some [a b])))
4786        ;~(plug head many tail)
4787      empt
4788        ==
4789    ::                                                ::  ++attr:de-xml:html
4790    ++   attr                                         ::  attributes
4791    %+   knee  *mart  |.   ~+
4792    %-   star
4793    ;~   plug
4794      ;~(pfix (plus whit) name)
4795      ;~   pose
4796        %+   ifix
4797          :_   doq
4798          ;~(plug (ifix [. .]:(star whit) tis) doq)
4799        (star ;~(less doq escp))
4800        ::
4801        %+   ifix
4802          :_   soq
4803          ;~(plug (ifix [. .]:(star whit) tis) soq)
4804        (star ;~(less soq escp))
4805        ::
4806        (easy ~)
4807        ==
4808        ==
4809    ::                                                ::  ++cdat:de-xml:html
4810    ++   cdat                                         ::  CDATA section
4811    %+   cook
```

```
4812        |=(a=tape ^-(mars ;/(a)))
4813      %+  ifix
4814      [(jest '<![CDATA[') (jest ']]>')]
4815      %-  star
4816      ;~(less (jest ']]>') next)
4817    ::                                          ::  ++chrd:de-xml:html
4818    ++  chrd                                     ::  character data
4819      %+  cook  |=(a=tape ^-(mars ;/(a)))
4820      (plus ;~(pose (just `@`10) escp))
4821    ::                                          ::  ++comt:de-xml:html
4822    ++  comt                                     ::  comments
4823      =-  (ifix [(jest '<!--') (jest '-->')] (star -))
4824      ;~  pose
4825        ;~(less hep prn)
4826        whit
4827        ;~(less (jest '-->') hep)
4828      ==
4829    ::
4830    ++  decl                                     ::  ++decl:de-xml:html
4831      %+  ifix                                   ::  XML declaration
4832      [(jest '<?xml') (jest '?>')]
4833      %-  star
4834      ;~(less (jest '?>') prn)
4835    ::                                          ::  ++escp:de-xml:html
4836    ++  escp                                     ::
4837      ;~(pose ;~(less gal gar pam prn) enty)
4838    ::                                          ::  ++enty:de-xml:html
4839    ++  enty                                     ::  entity
4840      %+  ifix  pam^mic
4841      ;~  pose
4842        =+  def=^+(ent (my:nl [%gt '>'] [%lt '<'] [%amp '&'] [%quot '"'] ~))
4843        %+  sear  ~(get by (~(uni by def) ent))
4844        (cook crip ;~(plug alf (stun 1^31 aln)))
4845        %+  cook  |=(a=@c ?:((gth a 0x10.ffff) '' (tuft a)))
4846        =<  ;~(pfix hax ;~(pose - +))
4847        :-  (bass 10 (stun 1^8 dit))
4848        (bass 16 ;~(pfix (mask "xX") (stun 1^8 hit)))
4849      ==
4850    ::                                          ::  ++empt:de-xml:html
4851    ++  empt                                     ::  self-closing tag
4852      %+  ifix  [gal (jest '/>')]
4853      ;~(plug ;~(plug name attr) (cold ~ (star whit)))
4854    ::                                          ::  ++head:de-xml:html
4855    ++  head                                     ::  opening tag
4856      (ifix [gal gar] ;~(plug name attr))
4857    ::                                          ::  ++many:de-xml:html
4858    ++  many                                     ::  contents
4859      ;~(pfix (star comt) (star ;~(sfix ;~(pose apex chrd cdat) (star comt))))
4860    ::                                          ::  ++name:de-xml:html
4861    ++  name                                     ::  tag name
4862      =+  ^=  chx
4863          %+  cook  crip
4864          ;~  plug
4865            ;~(pose cab alf)
4866            (star ;~(pose cab dot alp))
4867          ==
4868      ;~(pose ;~(plug ;~(sfix chx col) chx) chx)
4869    ::                                          ::  ++tail:de-xml:html
```

```
4870      ++  tail                                          ::  closing tag
4871        (ifix [(jest '</') gar] name)
4872      ::                                                ::  ++whit:de-xml:html
4873      ++  whit                                          ::  whitespace
4874        (mask ~[' ' `@`0x9 `@`0xa])
4875      --  ::de-xml
4876    ::                                                  ::  ++en-urlt:html
4877    ++  en-urlt                                         ::  url encode
4878      |=  tep=tape
4879      ^-  tape
4880      %-  zing
4881      %+  turn  tep
4882      |=  tap=char
4883      =+  xen=|=(tig=@ ?:((gte tig 10) (add tig 55) (add tig '0')))
4884      ?:  ?|  &((gte tap 'a') (lte tap 'z'))
4885              &((gte tap 'A') (lte tap 'Z'))
4886              &((gte tap '0') (lte tap '9'))
4887              =('.' tap)
4888              =('-' tap)
4889              =('~' tap)
4890              =('_' tap)
4891          ==
4892        [tap ~]
4893      ['%' (xen (rsh [0 4] tap)) (xen (end [0 4] tap)) ~]
4894    ::                                                  ::  ++de-urlt:html
4895    ++  de-urlt                                         ::  url decode
4896      |=  tep=tape
4897      ^-  (unit tape)
4898      ?~  tep  [~ ~]
4899      ?:  =('%' i.tep)
4900        ?.  ?=([@ @ *] t.tep)  ~
4901        =+  nag=(mix i.t.tep (lsh 3 i.t.t.tep))
4902        =+  val=(rush nag hex:ag)
4903        ?~  val  ~
4904        =+  nex=$(tep t.t.t.tep)
4905        ?~(nex ~ [~ [`@`u.val u.nex]])
4906      =+  nex=$(tep t.tep)
4907      ?~(nex ~ [~ i.tep u.nex])
4908    ::                                                  ::  ++en-purl:html
4909    ++  en-purl                                         ::  print purl
4910      =<  |=(pul=purl `tape`(apex %& pul))
4911      |%
4912      ::                                                ::  ++apex:en-purl:html
4913      ++  apex                                          ::
4914        |=  qur=quri  ^-  tape
4915        ?-  -.qur
4916          %&  (weld (head p.p.qur) `tape`$(qur [%| +.p.qur]))
4917          %|  ['/' (weld (body p.qur) (tail q.qur))]
4918        ==
4919      ::                                                ::  ++apix:en-purl:html
4920      ++  apix                                          ::  purf to tape
4921        |=  purf
4922        (weld (apex %& p) ?~(q "" `tape`['#' (trip u.q)]))
4923      ::                                                ::  ++body:en-purl:html
4924      ++  body                                          ::
4925        |=  pok=pork  ^-  tape
4926        ?~  q.pok  ~
4927        |-
```

```
4928        =+  seg=(en-urlt (trip i.q.pok))
4929      ?~  t.q.pok
4930        ?~(p.pok seg (welp seg '.' (trip u.p.pok)))
4931      (welp seg '/' $(q.pok t.q.pok))
4932    ::                                          ::  ++head:en-purl:html
4933    ++  head                                    ::
4934      |=  har=hart
4935      ^-  tape
4936      ;:  weld
4937        ?:(&(p.har !?=(hoke r.har)) "https://" "http://")
4938      ::
4939        ?-  -.r.har
4940          %|  (trip (rsh 3 (scot %if p.r.har)))
4941          %&  =+  rit=(flop p.r.har)
4942              |-  ^-  tape
4943              ?~  rit  ~
4944              (weld (trip i.rit) ?~(t.rit "" `tape`['.' $(rit t.rit)])))
4945        ==
4946      ::
4947        ?~(q.har ~ `tape`[':' ((d-co:co 1) u.q.har)])
4948      ==
4949    ::                                          ::  ++tail:en-purl:html
4950    ++  tail                                    ::
4951      |=  kay=quay
4952      ^-  tape
4953      ?:  =(~ kay)   ~
4954      :-  '?'
4955      |-  ^-  tape
4956      ?~  kay  ~
4957      ;:  welp
4958        (en-urlt (trip p.i.kay))
4959        ?~(q.i.kay ~ ['=' (en-urlt (trip q.i.kay))])
4960        ?~(t.kay ~ `tape`['&' $(kay t.kay)])
4961      ==
4962    --  ::
4963    ::                                          ::  ++de-purl:html
4964    ++  de-purl                                 ::  url+header parser
4965      =<  |=(a=cord `(unit purl)`(rush a auri))
4966      |%
4967    ::                                          ::  ++deft:de-purl:html
4968    ++  deft                                    ::  parse url extension
4969      |=  rax=(list @t)
4970      |-  ^-  pork
4971      ?~  rax
4972        [~ ~]
4973      ?^  t.rax
4974        [p.pok [ire q.pok]]:[pok=$(rax t.rax) ire=i.rax]
4975      =/  raf=(like term)
4976        %-  ;~  sfix
4977              %+  sear
4978                |=(a=@ ((sand %ta) (crip (flop (trip a)))))
4979              (cook |=(a=tape (rap 3 ^-((list @) a))) (star aln))
4980            dot
4981          ==
4982        [1^1 (flop (trip i.rax))]
4983      ?~  q.raf
4984        [~ [i.rax ~]]
4985      =+  `[ext=term [@ @] fyl=tape]`u.q.raf
```

```
4986          :-  `ext
4987          ?:(=(~ fyl) ~ [(crip (flop fyl)) ~])
4988          ::                                              ::  ++apat:de-purl:html
4989          ++  apat                                        ::  2396 abs_path
4990            %+  cook  deft
4991            ;~(pfix fas (more fas smeg))
4992          ::                                              ::  ++aurf:de-purl:html
4993          ++  aurf                                        ::  2396 with fragment
4994            %+  cook  |~(a=purf a)
4995            ;~(plug auri (punt ;~(pfix hax (cook crip (star pque)))))
4996          ::                                              ::  ++auri:de-purl:html
4997          ++  auri                                        ::  2396 URL
4998            ;~  plug
4999              ;~(plug htts thor)
5000              ;~(plug ;~(pose apat (easy *pork)) yque)
5001            ==
5002          ::                                              ::  ++auru:de-purl:html
5003          ++  auru                                        ::  2396 with maybe user
5004            %+  cook
5005              |=  $:  a=[p=? q=(unit user) r=[(unit @ud) host]]
5006                      b=[pork quay]
5007                  ==
5008              ^-  (pair (unit user) purl)
5009              [q.a [[p.a r.a] b]]
5010            ::
5011            ;~  plug
5012              ;~(plug htts (punt ;~(sfix urt:ab pat)) thor)
5013              ;~(plug ;~(pose apat (easy *pork)) yque)
5014            ==
5015          ::                                              ::  ++htts:de-purl:html
5016          ++  htts                                        ::  scheme
5017            %+  sear  ~(get by (malt `(list (pair term ?))`[http+| https+& ~]))
5018            ;~(sfix scem ;~(plug col fas fas))
5019          ::                                              ::  ++cock:de-purl:html
5020          ++  cock                                        ::  cookie
5021            %+  most  ;~(plug mic ace)
5022            ;~(plug toke ;~(pfix tis tosk))
5023          ::                                              ::  ++dlab:de-purl:html
5024          ++  dlab                                        ::  2396 domainlabel
5025            %+  sear
5026              |=  a=@ta
5027              ?.(=('-' (rsh [3 (dec (met 3 a))] a)) [~ u=a] ~)
5028            %+  cook  |=(a=tape (crip (cass a)))
5029            ;~(plug aln (star alp))
5030          ::                                              ::  ++fque:de-purl:html
5031          ++  fque                                        ::  normal query field
5032            (cook crip (plus pquo))
5033          ::                                              ::  ++fquu:de-purl:html
5034          ++  fquu                                        ::  optional query field
5035            (cook crip (star pquo))
5036          ::                                              ::  ++pcar:de-purl:html
5037          ++  pcar                                        ::  2396 path char
5038            ;~(pose pure pesc psub col pat)
5039          ::                                              ::  ++pcok:de-purl:html
5040          ++  pcok                                        ::  cookie char
5041            ;~(less bas mic com doq prn)
5042          ::                                              ::  ++pesc:de-purl:html
5043          ++  pesc                                        ::  2396 escaped
```

```
5044        ;~(pfix cen mes)
5045      ::                                              ::  ++pold:de-purl:html
5046      ++  pold                                         ::
5047        (cold ' ' (just '+'))
5048      ::                                              ::  ++pque:de-purl:html
5049      ++  pque                                         ::  3986 query char
5050        ;~(pose pcar fas wut)
5051      ::                                              ::  ++pquo:de-purl:html
5052      ++  pquo                                         ::  normal query char
5053        ;~(pose pure pesc pold fas wut col com)
5054      ::                                              ::  ++pure:de-purl:html
5055      ++  pure                                         ::  2396 unreserved
5056        ;~(pose aln hep cab dot zap sig tar soq pal par)
5057      ::                                              ::  ++psub:de-purl:html
5058      ++  psub                                         ::  3986 sub-delims
5059        ;~  pose
5060          zap  buc  pam  soq  pal  par
5061          tar  lus  com  mic  tis
5062        ==
5063      ::                                              ::  ++ptok:de-purl:html
5064      ++  ptok                                         ::  2616 token
5065        ;~  pose
5066          aln  zap  hax  buc  cen  pam  soq  tar  lus
5067          hep  dot  ket  cab  tic  bar  sig
5068        ==
5069      ::                                              ::  ++scem:de-purl:html
5070      ++  scem                                         ::  2396 scheme
5071        %+  cook  |=(a=tape (crip (cass a)))
5072        ;~(plug alf (star ;~(pose aln lus hep dot)))
5073      ::                                              ::  ++smeg:de-purl:html
5074      ++  smeg                                         ::  2396 segment
5075        (cook crip (star pcar))
5076      ::                                              ::  ++tock:de-purl:html
5077      ++  tock                                         ::  6265 raw value
5078        (cook crip (plus pcok))
5079      ::                                              ::  ++tosk:de-purl:html
5080      ++  tosk                                         ::  6265 quoted value
5081        ;~(pose tock (ifix [doq doq] tock))
5082      ::                                              ::  ++toke:de-purl:html
5083      ++  toke                                         ::  2616 token
5084        (cook crip (plus ptok))
5085      ::                                              ::  ++thor:de-purl:html
5086      ++  thor                                         ::  2396 host+port
5087        %+  cook  |*([* *] [+<+ +<-])
5088        ;~  plug
5089          thos
5090          ;~((bend) (easy ~) ;~(pfix col dim:ag))
5091        ==
5092      ::                                              ::  ++thos:de-purl:html
5093      ++  thos                                         ::  2396 host, no local
5094        ;~  plug
5095          ;~  pose
5096            %+  stag  %&
5097            %+  sear                                    ::  LL parser weak here
5098              |=  a=(list @t)
5099              =+  b=(flop a)
5100              ?>  ?=(^ b)
5101              =+  c=(end 3 i.b)
```

```
5102                ?.(&((gte c 'a') (lte c 'z')) ~ [~ u=b])
5103            (most dot dlab)
5104          ::
5105          %+  stag  %|
5106          =+  tod=(ape:ag ted:ab)
5107          %+  bass  256
5108          ;~(plug tod (stun [3 3] ;~(pfix dot tod)))
5109        ==
5110      ==
5111    ::                                            ::  ++yque:de-purl:html
5112    ++  yque                                      ::  query ending
5113      ;~  pose
5114      ;~(pfix wut yquy)
5115      (easy ~)
5116      ==
5117    ::                                            ::  ++yquy:de-purl:html
5118    ++  yquy                                      ::  query
5119      ;~  pose
5120        ::  proper query
5121        ::
5122        %+  more
5123          ;~(pose pam mic)
5124        ;~(plug fque ;~(pose ;~(pfix tis fquu) (easy '')))
5125        ::
5126        ::  funky query
5127        ::
5128        %+  cook
5129          |=(a=tape [[%$ (crip a)] ~])
5130        (star pque)
5131      ==
5132    ::                                            ::  ++zest:de-purl:html
5133    ++  zest                                      ::  2616 request-uri
5134      ;~  pose
5135      (stag %& (cook |=(a=purl a) auri))
5136      (stag %| ;~(plug apat yque))
5137      ==
5138    --  ::de-purl
5139  ::  +en-turf: encode +turf as a TLD-last domain string
5140  ::
5141  ++  en-turf
5142    |=  =turf
5143    ^-  @t
5144    (rap 3 (flop (join '.' turf)))
5145  ::  +de-turf: parse a TLD-last domain string into a TLD first +turf
5146  ::
5147  ++  de-turf
5148    |=  host=@t
5149    ^-  (unit turf)
5150    %+  rush  host
5151    %+  sear
5152      |=  =host:eyre
5153      ?.(?=(%& -.host) ~ (some p.host))
5154    thos:de-purl:html
5155  ::
5156  ::  MOVEME
5157  ::                                              ::  ++fuel:html
5158  ++  fuel                                        ::  parse urbit fcgi
5159    |=  [bem=beam ced=noun:cred quy=quer]
```

```
5160        ^-  epic
5161        =+  qix=|-(`quay`?~(quy quy [[p q]:quy $(quy t.quy)]))
5162        [(malt qix) ;;(cred ced) bem]
5163    ::
5164    ++  hiss-to-request
5165        |=  =hiss
5166        ^-  request:http
5167        ::
5168        :*  ?-  p.q.hiss
5169              %conn  %'CONNECT'
5170              %delt  %'DELETE'
5171              %get   %'GET'
5172              %head  %'HEAD'
5173              %opts  %'OPTIONS'
5174              %post  %'POST'
5175              %put   %'PUT'
5176              %trac  %'TRACE'
5177            ==
5178        ::
5179        (crip (en-purl:html p.hiss))
5180        ::
5181        ^-  header-list:http
5182        ~!  q.q.hiss
5183        %+  turn  ~(tap by q.q.hiss)
5184        |=  [a=@t b=(list @t)]
5185        ^-  [@t @t]
5186        ?>  ?=(^ b)
5187        [a i.b]
5188        ::
5189        r.q.hiss
5190      ==
5191    --  ::  html
5192  ::                                                    ::
5193  ::::                      ++wired                      ::  wire formatting
5194    ::                                                  ::::
5195  ++  wired  ^?
5196    |%
5197    ::                                                  ::  ++dray:wired
5198    ++  dray                                            ::  load tuple in path
5199      ::
5200      ::  .=  ~[p=~.ack q=~.~sarnel r=~..y]
5201      ::  (dray ~[p=%tas q=%p r=%f] %ack ~sarnel &)
5202      ::
5203      =-  |*  [a=[@tas (pole @tas)] b=*]  ^-  (paf a)
5204          =>  .(b `,(tup -.a +.a)`b)
5205          ?~  +.a  [(scot -.a b) ~]
5206          [(scot -.a -.b) `,(paf +.a)`(..$ +.a +.b)]
5207      :-  paf=|*(a=(pole) ?~(a ,~ ,[(odo:raid ,-.a(. %ta)) ,(..$ +.a)]))
5208      ^=  tup
5209      |*  [a=@tas b=(pole @tas)]
5210      =+  c=(odo:raid a)
5211      ?~(b c ,[c (..$ ,-.b ,+.b)])
5212    ::                                                  ::  ++raid:wired
5213    ++  raid                                            ::  demand path odors
5214      ::
5215      ::  .=  [p=%ack q=~sarnel r=&]
5216      ::  (raid /ack/~sarnel+.y p=%tas q=%p r=%f ~)
5217      ::
```

```
5218        =-    |*   [a=path b=[@tas (pole @tas)]]
5219            =*   fog   (odo -.b)
5220            ?~   +.b   `fog`(slav -.b -.a)
5221            [`fog`(slav -.b -.a) (..$ +.a +.b)]
5222        ^=  odo
5223        |*  a=@tas
5224        |=  b=*
5225        =-  a(, (- b))                        ::  preserve face
5226        ?+  a   @
5227          %c  @c  %da  @da  %dr  @dr  %f   @f   %if  @if  %is  @is  %p   @p
5228          %u  @u  %uc  @uc  %ub  @ub  %ui  @ui  %ux  @ux  %uv  @uv  %uw  @uw
5229          %s  @s  %t   @t   %ta  @ta  %tas @tas
5230        ==
5231  ::  ::                                              ::  ++read:wired
5232  ::  ++  read                                        ::  parse odored path
5233  ::      =<   |*([a=path b=[@tas (pole @tas)]] ((+> b) a))
5234  ::      |*  b=[@tas (pole @tas)]
5235  ::      |=  a=path
5236  ::      ?~  a   ~
5237  ::      =+  hed=(slaw -.b i.a)
5238  ::      =*  fog   (odo:raid -.b)
5239  ::      ?~  +.b
5240  ::        ^-  (unit fog)
5241  ::        ?^(+.a ~ hed)
5242  ::      ^-  (unit [fog _(need *(..^$ +.b))])
5243  ::      (both hed ((..^$ +.b) +.a))
5244    --  ::wired
5245  ::                                                        ::
5246  ::::                              ++title                  ::  (2j) identity
5247    ::                                                        ::::
5248  ++  title
5249  ::  deep core: for vane use, with $roof for scrying
5250  ::
5251  ::      TODO: refactor to share high-level gates like +saxo
5252  ::            among the three cores
5253  ::
5254  =>  |%
5255      ++   sein
5256      |=  [rof=roof pov=path our=ship now=@da who=ship]
5257      ;;  ship
5258      =<  q.q  %-  need  %-  need
5259      (rof ~ pov %j `beam`[[our %sein %da now] /(scot %p who)])
5260      --
5261  ::  middle core: stateless queries for default numeric sponsorship
5262  ::
5263  =>  |%
5264      ::                                          ::  ++clan:title
5265      ++  clan                                    ::  ship to rank
5266      |=  who=ship
5267      ^-  rank
5268      =/  wid   (met 3 who)
5269      ?:  (lte wid 1)    %czar
5270      ?:  =(2 wid)       %king
5271      ?:  (lte wid 4)    %duke
5272      ?:  (lte wid 8)    %earl
5273      ?>  (lte wid 16)   %pawn
5274      ::                                          ::  ++rank:title
5275      +$  rank  ?(%czar %king %duke %earl %pawn)  ::  ship width class
```

```
5276        ::                                    ::   ++name:title
5277        ++   name                             ::   identity
5278        |=   who=ship
5279        ^-   ship
5280        ?.   ?=(%earl (clan who))   who
5281        (sein who)
5282        ::                                    ::   ++saxo:title
5283        ++   saxo                             ::   autocanon
5284        |=   who=ship
5285        ^-   (list ship)
5286        =/   dad   (sein who)
5287        [who ?:(=(who dad) ~ $(who dad))]
5288        ::                                    ::   ++sein:title
5289        ++   sein                             ::   autoboss
5290        |=   who=ship
5291        ^-   ship
5292        =/   mir   (clan who)
5293        ?-   mir
5294        %czar   who
5295        %king   (end 3 who)
5296        %duke   (end 4 who)
5297        %earl   (end 5 who)
5298        %pawn   (end 4 who)
5299        ==
5300        --
5301   ::  surface core: for userspace use, with .^
5302   ::
5303   |%
5304   ::                                         ::   ++cite:title
5305   ++   cite                                  ::   render ship
5306   |=   who=@p
5307   ^-   tape
5308   =/   wid   (met 4 who)
5309   ?:   (lte wid 2)   (scow %p who)
5310   ?:   (lte wid 4)
5311     =/   nom   (scow %p (end 5 who))
5312     :(weld (scag 7 nom) "^" (slag 8 nom))
5313   %-   trip
5314   %+   rap   3
5315   :~   '~'
5316        (tos:po (cut 3 [(dec (mul wid 2)) 1] who))
5317        (tod:po (cut 3 [(mul (dec wid) 2) 1] who))
5318        '_'
5319        (tos:po (cut 3 [1 1] who))
5320        (tod:po (end 3 who))
5321   ==
5322   ::                                         ::   ++saxo:title
5323   ++   saxo                                  ::   autocanon
5324   |=   [our=ship now=@da who=ship]
5325   .^   (list ship)
5326        %j
5327        /(scot %p our)/saxo/(scot %da now)/(scot %p who)
5328   ==
5329   ::                                         ::   ++sein:title
5330   ++   sein                                  ::   autoboss
5331   |=   [our=ship now=@da who=ship]
5332   .^   ship
5333        %j
```

```
5334              /(scot %p our)/sein/(scot %da now)/(scot %p who)
5335        ==
5336     ::   +team was created with two meanings:
5337     ::       A. her / her moon
5338     ::       B. whoever should be able to control her ship
5339     ::
5340     ::   these two things aren't obviously equal anymore,
5341     ::   and it's more important for +team to satisfy B than A,
5342     ::   so now +team just means "her".
5343     ::
5344     ::   (ships can definitely be trusted to control themselves)
5345     ::                                              ::  ++team:title
5346     ++   team                                       ::  her
5347        |=  [her=ship who=ship]
5348        ^-  ?
5349      =(her who)
5350     ::                                              ::  ++moon:title
5351     ++   moon                                       ::  her moon
5352        |=  [her=ship who=ship]
5353        ^-  ?
5354      &(=(%earl (clan who)) =(her (^sein who)))
5355     --   ::title
5356  ::                                                 ::
5357  ::::                    ++milly                    ::  (2k) milliseconds
5358     ::                                              ::::
5359  ++   milly  ^|
5360     |_  now=@da
5361     ::                                              ::  ++around:milly
5362     ++   around                                     ::  relative msec
5363      |=  wen=@da
5364      ^-  @tas
5365      ?:  =(wen now)  %now
5366      ?:  (gth wen now)
5367        (cat 3 (scot %ud (msec (sub wen now))) %ms)
5368      (cat 3 '-' $(now wen, wen now))
5369     ::
5370     ++   about                                      ::  ++about:milly
5371      |=  wun=(unit @da)                             ::  unit relative msec
5372      ^-  @tas
5373      ?~(wun %no (around u.wun))
5374     ::                                              ::  ++mill:milly
5375     ++   mill                                       ::  msec diff
5376      |=  one=@dr
5377      ^-  @tas
5378      ?:  =(`@`0 one)  '0ms'
5379      (cat 3 (scot %ud (msec one)) %ms)
5380     ::                                              ::  ++msec:milly
5381     ++   msec                                       ::  @dr to @ud ms
5382      |=(a=@dr `@ud`(div a (div ~s1 1.000)))
5383     ::                                              ::  ++mull:milly
5384     ++   mull                                       ::  unit msec diff
5385      |=  une=(unit @dr)
5386      ^-  @tas
5387      ?~(une %no (mill u.une))
5388     --
5389  ::
5390  ::::
5391     ::
```

```
5392  ++  contain  ^?
5393  |%
5394  ::  +by-clock: interface core for a cache using the clock replacement algorithm
5395  ::
5396  ::      Presents an interface for a mapping, but somewhat specialized, and with
5397  ::      stateful accessors. The clock's :depth parameter is used as the maximum
5398  ::      freshness that an entry can have. The standard clock algorithm has a depth
5399  ::      of 1, meaning that a single sweep of the arm will delete the entry. For
5400  ::      more scan resistance, :depth can be set to a higher number.
5401  ::
5402  ::      Internally, :clock maintains a :lookup of type
5403  ::      `(map key-type [val=val-type fresh=@ud])`, where :depth.clock is the
5404  ::      maximum value of :fresh. Looking up a key increments its freshness, and a
5405  ::      sweep of the clock arm decrements its freshness.
5406  ::
5407  ::      The clock arm is stored as :queue, which is a `(qeu key-type)`. The head
5408  ::      of the queue represents the position of the clock arm. New entries are
5409  ::      inserted at the tail of the queue. When the clock arm sweeps, it
5410  ::      pops the head off the queue. If the :fresh of the head's entry in :lookup
5411  ::      is 0, remove the entry from the mapping and replace it with the new entry.
5412  ::      Otherwise, decrement the entry's freshness, put it back at the tail of
5413  ::      the queue, and pop the next head off the queue and try again.
5414  ::
5415  ::      Cache entries must be immutable: a key cannot be overwritten with a new
5416  ::      value. This property is enforced for entries currently stored in the
5417  ::      cache, but it is not enforced for previously deleted entries, since we
5418  ::      no longer remember what that key's value was supposed to be.
5419  ::
5420  ++  by-clock
5421    |*  [key-type=mold val-type=mold]
5422    |_  clock=(clock key-type val-type)
5423    ::  +get: looks up a key, marking it as fresh
5424    ::
5425    ++  get
5426      |=  key=key-type
5427      ^-  [(unit val-type) _clock]
5428      ::
5429      =+  maybe-got=(~(get by lookup.clock) key)
5430      ?~  maybe-got
5431        [~ clock]
5432      ::
5433      =.  clock  (freshen key)
5434      ::
5435      [`val.u.maybe-got clock]
5436    ::  +put: add a new cache entry, possibly removing an old one
5437    ::
5438    ++  put
5439      |=  [key=key-type val=val-type]
5440      ^+  clock
5441      ::  do nothing if our size is 0 so we don't decrement-underflow
5442      ::
5443      ?:  =(0 max-size.clock)
5444        clock
5445      ::  no overwrite allowed, but allow duplicate puts
5446      ::
5447      ?^  existing=(~(get by lookup.clock) key)
5448        ::  val must not change
5449        ::
```

```
5450        ?>  =(val val.u.existing)
5451        ::
5452      (freshen key)
5453      ::
5454    =?  clock  =(max-size.clock size.clock)
5455      evict
5456      ::
5457    %_  clock
5458      size    +(size.clock)
5459      lookup  (~(put by lookup.clock) key [val 1])
5460      queue   (~(put to queue.clock) key)
5461    ==
5462  :: +freshen: increment the protection level on an entry
5463  ::
5464  ++  freshen
5465    |=  key=key-type
5466    ^+  clock
5467    %_    clock
5468      lookup
5469    %+  ~(jab by lookup.clock)  key
5470    |=  entry=[val=val-type fresh=@ud]
5471    entry(fresh (min +(fresh.entry) depth.clock))
5472    ==
5473  :: +resize: changes the maximum size, removing entries if needed
5474  ::
5475  ++  resize
5476    |=  new-max=@ud
5477    ^+  clock
5478    ::
5479    =.  max-size.clock  new-max
5480    ::
5481    ?:  (gte new-max size.clock)
5482      clock
5483    ::
5484    (trim (sub size.clock new-max))
5485  ::  +evict: remove an entry from the cache
5486  ::
5487  ++  evict
5488    ^+  clock
5489    ::
5490    =.  size.clock  (dec size.clock)
5491    ::
5492    |-
5493    ^+  clock
5494    ::
5495    =^  old-key  queue.clock  ~(get to queue.clock)
5496    =/  old-entry  (~(got by lookup.clock) old-key)
5497    ::
5498    ?:  =(0 fresh.old-entry)
5499      clock(lookup (~(del by lookup.clock) old-key))
5500    ::
5501    %_    $
5502      lookup.clock
5503    (~(put by lookup.clock) old-key old-entry(fresh (dec fresh.old-entry)))
5504    ::
5505      queue.clock
5506    (~(put to queue.clock) old-key)
5507    ==
```

```
5508    ::    +trim: remove :count entries from the cache
5509    ::
5510    ++  trim
5511      |=  count=@ud
5512      ^+  clock
5513      ?:  =(0 count)
5514        clock
5515      $(count (dec count), clock evict)
5516    ::  +purge: removes all cache entries
5517    ::
5518    ++  purge
5519      ^+  clock
5520      %_  clock
5521        lookup  ~
5522        queue   ~
5523        size    0
5524      ==
5525    --
5526  ::  +to-capped-queue: interface door for +capped-queue
5527  ::
5528  ::    Provides a queue of a limited size where pushing additional items will
5529  ::    force pop the items at the front of the queue.
5530  ::
5531  ++  to-capped-queue
5532    |*  item-type=mold
5533    |_  queue=(capped-queue item-type)
5534    ::  +put: enqueue :item, possibly popping and producing an old item
5535    ::
5536    ++  put
5537      |=  item=item-type
5538      ^-  [(unit item-type) _queue]
5539      ::    are we already at max capacity?
5540      ::
5541      ?.  =(size.queue max-size.queue)
5542        ::  we're below max capacity, so push and increment size
5543        ::
5544        =.  queue.queue  (~(put to queue.queue) item)
5545        =.  size.queue   +(size.queue)
5546        ::
5547        [~ queue]
5548      ::  max is zero, the oldest item to return is the one which just went in.
5549      ::
5550      ?:  =(~ queue.queue)
5551        [`item queue]
5552      ::  we're at max capacity, so pop before pushing; size is unchanged
5553      ::
5554      =^  oldest  queue.queue  ~(get to queue.queue)
5555      =.  queue.queue          (~(put to queue.queue) item)
5556      ::
5557      [`oldest queue]
5558    ::  +get: pop an item off the queue, adjusting size
5559    ::
5560    ++  get
5561      ^-  [item-type _queue]
5562      ::
5563      =.  size.queue           (dec size.queue)
5564      =^  oldest  queue.queue  ~(get to queue.queue)
5565      ::
```

```
5566        [oldest queue]
5567    ::  change the :max-size of the queue, popping items if necessary
5568    ::
5569    ++  resize
5570      =|  pops=(list item-type)
5571      |=  new-max=@ud
5572      ^+  [pops queue]
5573      ::  we're not overfull, so no need to pop off more items
5574      ::
5575      ?:  (gte new-max size.queue)
5576        [(flop pops) queue(max-size new-max)]
5577      ::  we're above capacity; pop an item off and recurse
5578      ::
5579      =^  oldest  queue  get
5580      ::
5581      $(pops [oldest pops])
5582    --
5583  --
5584  ::                                                            ::
5585  ::::                      ++userlib            ::  (2u) non-vane utils
5586  ::                                                            ::::
5587  ++  userlib  ^?
5588  |%
5589  ::                                                            ::
5590  ::::                      ++chrono:userlib      ::  (2uB) time
5591    ::                                                          ::::
5592  ++  chrono  ^?
5593    |%
5594    ::  +from-unix: unix seconds to @da
5595    ::
5596    ++  from-unix
5597      |=  timestamp=@ud
5598      ^-  @da
5599      %+  add  ~1970.1.1
5600      (mul timestamp ~s1)
5601    ::  +from-unix-ms: unix milliseconds to @da
5602    ::
5603    ++  from-unix-ms
5604      |=  timestamp=@ud
5605      ^-  @da
5606      %+  add  ~1970.1.1
5607      (div (mul ~s1 timestamp) 1.000)
5608    ::                                                ::  ++dawn:chrono:
5609    ++  dawn                                          ::  Jan 1 weekday
5610      |=  yer=@ud
5611      =+  yet=(sub yer 1)
5612      %-  mod  :_  7
5613      ;:  add
5614        1
5615        (mul 5 (mod yet 4))
5616        (mul 4 (mod yet 100))
5617        (mul 6 (mod yet 400))
5618      ==
5619    ::                                                ::  ++daws:chrono:
5620    ++  daws                                          ::  date weekday
5621      |=  yed=date
5622      %-  mod  :_  7
5623      %+  add
```

```
5624            (dawn y.yed)
5625            (sub (yawn [y.yed m.yed d.t.yed]) (yawn y.yed 1 1))
5626      ::                                              ::  ++deal:chrono:
5627      ++  deal                                        ::  to leap sec time
5628        |=  yer=@da
5629        =+  n=0
5630        =+  yud=(yore yer)
5631        |-  ^-  date
5632        ?:  (gte yer (add (snag n lef:yu) ~s1))
5633            (yore (year yud(s.t (add n s.t.yud))))
5634        ?:  &((gte yer (snag n lef:yu)) (lth yer (add (snag n lef:yu) ~s1)))
5635            yud(s.t (add +(n) s.t.yud))
5636        ?:  =(+(n) (lent lef:yu))
5637            (yore (year yud(s.t (add +(n) s.t.yud))))
5638        $(n +(n))
5639      ::                                              ::  ++lead:chrono:
5640      ++  lead                                        ::  from leap sec time
5641        |=  ley=date
5642        =+  ler=(year ley)
5643        =+  n=0
5644        |-  ^-  @da
5645        =+  led=(sub ler (mul n ~s1))
5646        ?:  (gte ler (add (snag n les:yu) ~s1))
5647            led
5648        ?:  &((gte ler (snag n les:yu)) (lth ler (add (snag n les:yu) ~s1)))
5649          ?:  =(s.t.ley 60)
5650            (sub led ~s1)
5651          led
5652        ?:  =(+(n) (lent les:yu))
5653            (sub led ~s1)
5654        $(n +(n))
5655      ::                                              ::  ++dust:chrono:
5656      ++  dust                                        ::  print UTC format
5657        |=  yed=date
5658        ^-  tape
5659        =+  wey=(daws yed)
5660        =/  num   (d-co:co 1)  :: print as decimal without dots
5661        =/  pik   |=([n=@u t=wall] `tape`(scag 3 (snag n t)))
5662        ::
5663        "{(pik wey wik:yu)}, ".
5664        "{(num d.t.yed)} {(pik (dec m.yed) mon:yu)} {(num y.yed)} ".
5665        "{(num h.t.yed)}:{(num m.t.yed)}:{(num s.t.yed)} +0000"
5666      ::                                              ::  ++stud:chrono:
5667      ++  stud                                        ::  parse UTC format
5668        =<  |=  a=cord                                ::  expose parsers
5669            %+  biff  (rush a (more sepa elem))
5670            |=  b=(list _(wonk *elem))  ^-  (unit date)
5671            =-  ?.((za:dejs:format -) ~ (some (zp:dejs:format -)))
5672            ^+  =+  [*date u=unit]
5673                *[(u _[a y]) (u _m) (u _d.t) (u _+.t) ~]
5674            :~
5675                |-(?~(b ~ ?.(?=(%y -.i.b) $(b t.b) `+.i.b)))
5676                |-(?~(b ~ ?.(?=(%m -.i.b) $(b t.b) `+.i.b)))
5677                |-(?~(b ~ ?.(?=(%d -.i.b) $(b t.b) `+.i.b)))
5678                |-(?~(b ~ ?.(?=(%t -.i.b) $(b t.b) `+.i.b)))
5679            ==
5680        |%
5681        ::                                            ::  ++snug:stud:chrono:
```

```
5682      ++  snug                                        ::  position in list
5683      |=  a=(list tape)
5684      |=  b=tape
5685      =+  [pos=1 len=(lent b)]
5686      |-  ^-  (unit @u)
5687      ?~  a  ~
5688      ?:  =(b (scag len i.a))
5689        `pos
5690      $(pos +(pos), a t.a)
5691    ::                                                ::  ++sepa:stud:chrono:
5692    ++  sepa                                          ::  separator
5693      ;~(pose ;~(plug com (star ace)) (plus ace))
5694    ::                                                ::  ++elem:stud:chrono:
5695    ++  elem                                          ::  date element
5696      ;~  pose
5697        (stag %t t)  (stag %y y)  (stag %m m)  (stag %d d)
5698        (stag %w w)  (stag %z z)
5699      ==
5700    ::                                                ::  ++y:stud:chrono:
5701    ++  y                                             ::  year
5702      (stag %& (bass 10 (stun 3^4 dit)))
5703    ::                                                ::  ++m:stud:chrono:
5704    ++  m                                             ::  month
5705      (sear (snug mon:yu) (plus alf))
5706    ::                                                ::  ++d:stud:chrono:
5707    ++  d                                             ::  day
5708      (bass 10 (stun 1^2 dit))
5709    ::                                                ::  ++t:stud:chrono:
5710    ++  t                                             ::  hours:minutes:secs
5711      %+  cook  |=([h=@u @ m=@u @ s=@u] ~[h m s])
5712      ;~(plug d col d col d)
5713    ::
5714    ::  XX day of week is currently unchecked, and
5715    ::  timezone outright ignored.
5716    ::                                                ::  ++w:stud:chrono:
5717    ++  w                                             ::  day of week
5718      (sear (snug wik:yu) (plus alf))
5719    ::                                                ::  ++z:stud:chrono:
5720    ++  z                                             ::  time zone
5721      ;~(plug (mask "-+") dd dd)
5722    ::                                                ::  ++dd:stud:chrono:
5723    ++  dd                                            ::  two digits
5724      (bass 10 (stun 2^2 dit))
5725      --  ::
5726    ::                                                ::  ++unm:chrono:userlib
5727    ++  unm                                           ::  Urbit to Unix ms
5728    |=  a=@da
5729    =-  (div (mul - 1.000) ~s1)
5730    (sub (add a (div ~s1 2.000)) ~1970.1.1)
5731    ::                                                ::  ++unt:chrono:userlib
5732    ++  unt                                           ::  Urbit to Unix time
5733    |=  a=@da
5734    (div (sub a ~1970.1.1) ~s1)
5735    ::                                                ::  ++yu:chrono:userlib
5736    ++  yu                                            ::  UTC format constants
5737    |%
5738    ::                                                ::  ++mon:yu:chrono:
5739      ++  mon                                         ::  months
```

```
5740        ^-  (list tape)
5741        :~  "January"  "February"  "March"  "April"  "May"  "June"  "July"
5742            "August"  "September"  "October"  "November"  "December"
5743        ==
5744    ::                                            ::  ++wik:yu:chrono:
5745  ++  wik                                         ::  weeks
5746      ^-  (list tape)
5747      :~  "Sunday"  "Monday"  "Tuesday"  "Wednesday"  "Thursday"
5748          "Friday"  "Saturday"
5749      ==
5750    ::                                            ::  ++lef:yu:chrono:
5751  ++  lef                                         ::  leapsecond dates
5752      ^-  (list @da)
5753      :~  ~2016.12.31..23.59.59    ~2015.6.30..23.59.59
5754          ~2012.6.30..23.59.59     ~2008.12.31..23.59.58
5755          ~2005.12.31..23.59.57    ~1998.12.31..23.59.56
5756          ~1997.6.30..23.59.55     ~1995.12.31..23.59.54
5757          ~1994.6.30..23.59.53     ~1993.6.30..23.59.52
5758          ~1992.6.30..23.59.51     ~1990.12.31..23.59.50
5759          ~1989.12.31..23.59.49    ~1987.12.31..23.59.48
5760          ~1985.6.30..23.59.47     ~1983.6.30..23.59.46
5761          ~1982.6.30..23.59.45     ~1981.6.30..23.59.44
5762          ~1979.12.31..23.59.43    ~1978.12.31..23.59.42
5763          ~1977.12.31..23.59.41    ~1976.12.31..23.59.40
5764          ~1975.12.31..23.59.39    ~1974.12.31..23.59.38
5765          ~1973.12.31..23.59.37    ~1972.12.31..23.59.36
5766          ~1972.6.30..23.59.35
5767      ==
5768    ::
5769    ::  +les:yu:chrono: leapsecond days
5770    ::
5771    ::    https://www.ietf.org/timezones/data/leap-seconds.list
5772    ::
5773  ++  les
5774      ^-  (list @da)
5775      :~  ~2017.1.1  ~2015.7.1  ~2012.7.1  ~2009.1.1  ~2006.1.1  ~1999.1.1
5776          ~1997.7.1  ~1996.1.1  ~1994.7.1  ~1993.7.1  ~1992.7.1  ~1991.1.1
5777          ~1990.1.1  ~1988.1.1  ~1985.7.1  ~1983.7.1  ~1982.7.1  ~1981.7.1
5778          ~1980.1.1  ~1979.1.1  ~1978.1.1  ~1977.1.1  ~1976.1.1  ~1975.1.1
5779          ~1974.1.1  ~1973.1.1  ~1972.7.1
5780      ==
5781  --  ::yu
5782  --  ::chrono
5783  ::                                              ::
5784  ::::                    ++space:userlib          ::  (2uC) file utils
5785  ::                                              ::::
5786 ++  space  ^?
5787  =,  clay
5788  |%
5789  ::                                              ::  ++feel:space:userlib
5790  ++  feel                                        ::  simple file write
5791  |=  [pax=path val=cage]
5792  ^-  miso
5793  =+  dir=.^(arch %cy pax)
5794  ?~  fil.dir  [%ins val]
5795  [%mut val]
5796  ::                                              ::  ++file:space:userlib
5797  ++  file                                        ::  simple file load
```

```
5798      |=  pax=path
5799      ^-  (unit)
5800      =+  dir=.^(arch %cy pax)
5801      ?~(fil.dir ~ [~ .^(* %cx pax)])
5802    ::                                           ::  ++foal:space:userlib
5803    ++  foal                                     ::  high-level write
5804      |=  [pax=path val=cage]
5805      ^-  toro
5806      ?>  ?=([* * *] pax)
5807      [i.t.pax [%& [[[t.t.t.pax (feel pax val)] ~]]]]
5808    ::                                           ::  ++fray:space:userlib
5809    ++  fray                                     ::  high-level delete
5810      |=  pax=path
5811      ^-  toro
5812      ?>  ?=([* * *] pax)
5813      [i.t.pax [%& [[[t.t.t.pax [%del ~]] ~]]]]
5814    ::                                           ::  ++furl:space:userlib
5815    ++  furl                                     ::  unify changes
5816      |=  [one=toro two=toro]
5817      ^-  toro
5818      ~|  %furl
5819      ?>  ?&  =(p.one p.two)                     ::  same path
5820              &(?=(%& -.q.one) ?=(%& -.q.two))   ::  both deltas
5821          ==
5822      [p.one [%& (weld p.q.one p.q.two)]]
5823    --  ::space
5824  ::                                             ::
5825  ::::                      ++unix:userlib        ::  (2uD) unix line-list
5826    ::                                           ::::
5827  ++  unix  ^?
5828    |%
5829    ::                                           ::  ++lune:unix:userlib
5830    ++  lune                                     ::  cord by unix line
5831      ~%  %lune  ..part  ~
5832      |=  txt=@t
5833      ?~  txt
5834        ^-  (list @t)  ~
5835      =+  [byt=(rip 3 txt) len=(met 3 txt)]
5836      =|  [lin=(list @t) off=@]
5837      ^-  (list @t)
5838      %-  flop
5839      |-  ^+  lin
5840      ?:  =(off len)
5841        ~|  %noeol  !!
5842      ?:  =((snag off byt) 10)
5843        ?:  =(+(off) len)
5844          [(rep 3 (scag off byt)) lin]
5845        %=  $
5846          lin  [(rep 3 (scag off byt)) lin]
5847          byt  (slag +(off) byt)
5848          len  (sub len +(off))
5849          off  0
5850        ==
5851      $(off +(off))
5852    ::                                           ::  ++nule:unix:userlib
5853    ++  nule                                     ::  lines to unix cord
5854      ~%  %nule  ..part  ~
5855      |=  lin=(list @t)
```

```
5856        ^-  @t
5857        %+  can  3
5858        %+  turn  lin
5859        |=  t=@t
5860        [+((met 3 t)) (cat 3 t 10)]
5861        --
5862  ::                                              ::
5863  ::::                      ++scanf:userlib        ::  (2uF) exterpolation
5864    ::                                            ::::
5865  ++  scanf
5866    =<  |*  [tape (pole _;/(*[$^(rule tape)]))]   ::  formatted scan
5867        =>  .(+< [a b]=+<)
5868        (scan a (parsf b))
5869    |%
5870    ::                                            ::  ++parsf:scanf:
5871    ++  parsf                                     ::  make parser from:
5872      |*  a=(pole _;/(*[$^(rule tape)]))          ::  ;"chars{rule}chars"
5873      =-  (cook - (boil (norm a)))
5874      |*  (list)
5875      ?~  +<  ~
5876      ?~  t  i
5877      [i $(+< t)]
5878    ::
5879    ::  .=  (boil ~[[& dim] [| ", "] [& dim]]:ag)
5880    ::  ;~(plug dim ;~(pfix com ace ;~(plug dim (easy)))):ag
5881    ::
5882    ::                                            ::  ++boil:scanf:userlib
5883    ++  boil                                      ::
5884      |*  (list (each rule tape))
5885      ?~  +<  (easy ~)
5886      ?:  ?=(%| -.i)  ;~(pfix (jest (crip p.i)) $(+< t))
5887      %+  cook  |*([* *] [i t]=+<)
5888      ;~(plug p.i $(+< t))
5889    ::
5890    ::  .=  (norm [;"{n}, {n}"]:n=dim:ag)  ~[[& dim] [| ", "] [& dim]]:ag
5891    ::
5892    ::                                            ::  ++norm:scanf:userlib
5893    ++  norm                                      ::
5894      |*  (pole _;/(*[$^(rule tape)]))
5895      ?~  +<  ~
5896      =>  .(+< [i=+<- t=+<+])
5897      :_  t=$(+< t)
5898      =+  rul=->->.i
5899      ^=  i
5900      ?~  rul     [%| p=rul]
5901      ?~  +.rul   [%| p=rul]
5902      ?@  &2.rul  [%| p=;;(tape rul)]
5903      [%& p=rul]
5904    --  ::scanf
5905  --
5906  ::  +harden: coerce %soft $hobo or pass-through
5907  ::
5908  ++  harden
5909    |*  task=mold
5910    |=  wrapped=(hobo task)
5911    ^-  task
5912    ?.  ?=(%soft -.wrapped)
5913    wrapped
```

```
5914    ;;(task +.wrapped)
5915  ::
5916  ::
5917  ++  balk
5918    =<  bulk
5919    !:
5920    |%
5921    +$  bulk
5922      $:  [her=ship rif=rift lyf=life]
5923          [van=@ta car=@ta cas=case]
5924          spr=spur
5925      ==
5926    ::
5927    ++  de-part
5928      |=  [=ship =rift =life =(pole knot)]
5929      ^-  (unit bulk)
5930      ?.  ?=([van=@ car=@ cas=@ spr=*] pole)  ~
5931      ?~  cas=(de-case cas.pole)  ~
5932      :-  ~
5933      :*  [ship rift life]
5934          [van.pole car.pole u.cas]
5935          spr.pole
5936      ==
5937    ::
5938    ++  de-path-soft
5939      |=  =(pole knot)
5940      ^-  (unit bulk)
5941      ::  [ship rift life vane care case path]
5942      ?.  ?=([her=@ rif=@ lyf=@ van=@ car=@ cas=@ spr=*] pole)
5943          ~
5944      ?~  her=(slaw %p her.pole)  ~
5945      ?~  rif=(slaw %ud rif.pole)  ~
5946      ?~  lyf=(slaw %ud lyf.pole)  ~
5947      ?~  cas=(de-case cas.pole)  ~
5948      :-  ~
5949      :*  [u.her u.rif u.lyf]
5950          [van.pole car.pole u.cas]
5951          spr.pole
5952      ==
5953    ::
5954    ++  de-path
5955      |=  =path
5956      ^-  bulk
5957      (need (de-path-soft +<))
5958    ::
5959    ++  en-path
5960      |=  =bulk
5961      ^-  path
5962      :*  (scot %p her.bulk)
5963          (scot %ud rif.bulk)
5964          (scot %ud lyf.bulk)
5965          van.bulk
5966          car.bulk
5967          (scot cas.bulk)
5968          spr.bulk
5969      ==
5970    ::
5971    ++  as-omen
```

```
5972      |=  =bulk
5973      ^-  omen
5974      =/  [des=desk pax=path]
5975        ?^  spr.bulk  spr.bulk
5976        [%$ ~]
5977      =/  bem=beam  =,(bulk [[her des cas] pax])
5978      =+  vis=(cat 3 van.bulk car.bulk)
5979      [vis bem]
5980    --
5981  --
```

Ames

```
1  ::    Ames extends Arvo's %pass/%give move semantics across the network.
2  ::
3  ::    Ames receives packets as Arvo events and emits packets as Arvo
4  ::    effects.  The runtime is responsible for transferring the bytes in
5  ::    an Ames packet across a physical network to another ship.
6  ::
7  ::    The runtime tells Ames which physical address a packet came from,
8  ::    represented as an opaque atom.  Ames can emit a packet effect to
9  ::    one of those opaque atoms or to the Urbit address of a galaxy
10 ::    (root node), which the runtime is responsible for translating to a
11 ::    physical address.  One runtime implementation sends UDP packets
12 ::    using IPv4 addresses for ships and DNS lookups for galaxies, but
13 ::    other implementations may overlay over other kinds of networks.
14 ::
15 ::    A local vane can pass Ames a %plea request message.  Ames
16 ::    transmits the message over the wire to the peer ship's Ames, which
17 ::    passes the message to the destination vane.
18 ::
19 ::    Once the peer has processed the %plea message, it sends a
20 ::    message-acknowledgment packet over the wire back to the local
21 ::    Ames.  This ack can either be positive to indicate the request was
22 ::    processed, or negative to indicate the request failed, in which
23 ::    case it's called a "nack".  (Don't confuse Ames nacks with TCP
24 ::    nacks, which are a different concept).
25 ::
26 ::    When the local Ames receives either a positive message-ack or a
27 ::    combination of a nack and naxplanation (explained in more detail
28 ::    below), it gives an %done move to the local vane that had
29 ::    requested the original %plea message be sent.
30 ::
31 ::    A local vane can give Ames zero or more %boon response messages in
32 ::    response to a %plea, on the same duct that Ames used to pass the
33 ::    %plea to the vane.  Ames transmits a %boon over the wire to the
34 ::    peer's Ames, which gives it to the destination vane on the same
35 ::    duct the vane had used to pass the original %plea to Ames.
36 ::
37 ::    %boon messages are acked automatically by the receiver Ames.  They
38 ::    cannot be nacked, and Ames only uses the ack internally, without
39 ::    notifying the client vane that gave Ames the %boon.
40 ::
41 ::    If the Arvo event that completed receipt of a %boon message
42 ::    crashes, Ames instead sends the client vane a %lost message
43 ::    indicating the %boon was missed.
44 ::
45 ::    %plea messages can be nacked, in which case the peer will send
46 ::    both a message-nack packet and a naxplanation message, which is
47 ::    sent in a way that does not interfere with normal operation.  The
48 ::    naxplanation is sent as a full Ames message, instead of just a
49 ::    packet, because the contained error information can be arbitrarily
50 ::    large.  A naxplanation can only give rise to a positive ack --
51 ::    never ack an ack, and never nack a naxplanation.
52 ::
53 ::    Ames guarantees a total ordering of messages within a "flow",
54 ::    identified in other vanes by a duct and over the wire by a "bone":
55 ::    an opaque number.  Each flow has a FIFO queue of %plea requests
56 ::    from the requesting ship to the responding ship and a FIFO queue
```

```
57  ::    of %boon's in the other direction.
58  ::
59  ::    Message order across flows is not specified and may vary based on
60  ::    network conditions.
61  ::
62  ::    Ames guarantees that a message will only be delivered once to the
63  ::    destination vane.
64  ::
65  ::    Ames encrypts every message using symmetric-key encryption by
66  ::    performing an elliptic curve Diffie-Hellman using our private key
67  ::    and the public key of the peer.  For ships in the Jael PKI
68  ::    (public-key infrastructure), Ames looks up the peer's public key
69  ::    from Jael.  Comets (128-bit ephemeral addresses) are not
70  ::    cryptographic assets and must self-attest over Ames by sending a
71  ::    single self-signed packet containing their public key.
72  ::
73  ::    When a peer suffers a continuity breach, Ames removes all
74  ::    messaging state related to it.  Ames does not guarantee that all
75  ::    messages will be fully delivered to the now-stale peer.  From
76  ::    Ames's perspective, the newly restarted peer is a new ship.
77  ::    Ames's guarantees are not maintained across a breach.
78  ::
79  ::    A vane can pass Ames a %heed $task to request Ames track a peer's
80  ::    responsiveness.  If our %boon's to it start backing up locally,
81  ::    Ames will give a %clog back to the requesting vane containing the
82  ::    unresponsive peer's urbit address.  This interaction does not use
83  ::    ducts as unique keys.  Stop tracking a peer by sending Ames a
84  ::    %jilt $task.
85  ::
86  ::    Debug output can be adjusted using %sift and %spew $task's.
87  ::
88  !:
89  =,    ames
90  =*    point                  point:jael
91  =*    public-keys-result    public-keys-result:jael
92  ::    veb: verbosity flags
93  ::
94  =/    veb-all-off
95   :*   snd=`?`%.n  ::  sending packets
96        rcv=`?`%.n  ::  receiving packets
97        odd=`?`%.n  ::  unusual events
98        msg=`?`%.n  ::  message-level events
99        ges=`?`%.n  ::  congestion control
100       for=`?`%.n  ::  packet forwarding
101       rot=`?`%.n  ::  routing attempts
102       kay=`?`%.n  ::  is ok/not responding
103       fin=`?`%.n  ::  remote-scry
104    ==
105 =/    packet-size   13
106 =>
107 ~%    %ames   ..part   ~
108 |%
109 +|    %helpers
110 ::    +trace: print if .verb is set and we're tracking .ship
111 ::
112 ++    trace
113   |=  [mode=?(%ames %fine) verb=? =ship ships=(set ship) print=(trap tape)]
114   ^+  same
```

```
115    ?.  verb
116       same
117    ?.  =>  [ship=ship ships=ships in=in]
118       ~+  |(=(~ ships) (~(has in ships) ship))
119       same
120    (slog leaf/"{(trip mode)}: {(scow %p ship)}: {(print)}" ~)
121 ::  +qos-update-text: notice text for if connection state changes
122 ::
123 ++  qos-update-text
124    |=  [=ship mode=?(%ames %fine) old=qos new=qos k=? ships=(set ship)]
125    ^-  (unit tape)
126    ::
127    =+  trace=(cury trace mode)
128    ?+  [-.old -.new]  ~
129      [%unborn %live]   `"; {(scow %p ship)} is your neighbor"
130      [%dead %live]     ((trace k ship ships |.("is ok")) ~)
131      [%live %dead]     ((trace k ship ships |.("not responding still trying")) ~)
132      [%unborn %dead]   ((trace k ship ships |.("not responding still trying")) ~)
133      [%live %unborn]   `"; {(scow %p ship)} has sunk"
134      [%dead %unborn]   `"; {(scow %p ship)} has sunk"
135    ==
136 ::  +split-message: split message into kilobyte-sized fragments
137 ::
138 ::    We don't literally split it here since that would allocate many
139 ::    large atoms with no structural sharing.  Instead, each
140 ::    static-fragment has the entire message and a counter.  In
141 ::    +encrypt, we interpret this to get the actual fragment.
142 ::
143 ++  split-message
144    ~/  %split-message
145    |=  [=message-num =message-blob]
146    ^-  (list static-fragment)
147    ::
148    =/  num-fragments=fragment-num  (met packet-size message-blob)
149    =|  counter=@
150    ::
151    |-  ^-  (list static-fragment)
152    ?:  (gte counter num-fragments)
153      ~
154    ::
155    :-  [message-num num-fragments counter `@`message-blob]
156    $(counter +(counter))
157 ::  +assemble-fragments: concatenate fragments into a $message
158 ::
159 ++  assemble-fragments
160    ~/  %assemble-fragments
161    |=  [num-fragments=fragment-num fragments=(map fragment-num fragment)]
162    ^-  *
163    ::
164    =|  sorted=(list fragment)
165    =.  sorted
166      =/  index=fragment-num  0
167      |-  ^+  sorted
168      ?:  =(index num-fragments)
169        sorted
170      $(index +(index), sorted [(~(got by fragments) index) sorted])
171    ::
172    (cue (rep packet-size (flop sorted)))
```

```
173  ::  +jim: caching +jam
174  ::
175  ++  jim  |=(n=* ~+((jam n)))
176  ++  spit
177    |=  =path
178    ^-  [pat=@t wid=@ud]
179    =+  pat=(spat path)
180    =+  wid=(met 3 pat)
181    ?>  (lte wid 384)
182    [pat wid]
183  ::  +make-bone-wire: encode ship, rift and bone in wire for sending to vane
184  ::
185  ++  make-bone-wire
186    |=  [her=ship =rift =bone]
187    ^-  wire
188    ::
189    /bone/(scot %p her)/(scot %ud rift)/(scot %ud bone)
190  ::  +parse-bone-wire: decode ship, bone and rift from wire from local vane
191  ::
192  ++  parse-bone-wire
193    |=  =wire
194    ^-  %-  unit
195        $%  [%old her=ship =bone]
196            [%new her=ship =rift =bone]
197        ==
198    ?.  ?|  ?=([%bone @ @ @ ~] wire)
199            ?=([%bone @ @ ~] wire)
200        ==
201      ::  ignore malformed wires
202      ::
203      ~
204    ?+    wire  ~
205        [%bone @ @ ~]
206      `[%old `@p`(slav %p i.t.wire) `@ud`(slav %ud i.t.t.wire)]
207      ::
208        [%bone @ @ @ ~]
209      %-  some
210      :^    %new
211          `@p`(slav %p i.t.wire)
212        `@ud`(slav %ud i.t.t.wire)
213      `@ud`(slav %ud i.t.t.t.wire)
214    ==
215  ::  +make-pump-timer-wire: construct wire for |packet-pump timer
216  ::
217  ++  make-pump-timer-wire
218    |=  [her=ship =bone]
219    ^-  wire
220    /pump/(scot %p her)/(scot %ud bone)
221  ::  +parse-pump-wire: parse .her and .bone from |packet-pump wire
222  ::
223  ++  parse-pump-wire
224    |=  [ship=@ bone=@]
225    ^-  (unit [%pump her=^ship =^bone])
226    ?~  ship=`(unit @p)`(slaw %p ship)
227      ~
228    ?~  bone=`(unit @ud)`(slaw %ud bone)
229      ~
230    `pump/[u.ship u.bone]
```

```
231  ::
232  ++  parse-fine-wire
233    |=  [ship=@ =wire]
234    ^-  (unit [%fine her=^ship =^wire])
235    ?~  ship=`(unit @p)`(slaw %p ship)
236      ~
237    `fine/[u.ship wire]
238  ::  +derive-symmetric-key: $symmetric-key from $private-key and $public-key
239  ::
240  ::    Assumes keys have a tag on them like the result of the |ex:crub core.
241  ::
242  ++  derive-symmetric-key
243    ~/  %derive-symmetric-key
244    |=  [=public-key =private-key]
245    ^-  symmetric-key
246    ::
247    ?>  =('b' (end 3 public-key))
248    =.  public-key  (rsh 8 (rsh 3 public-key))
249    ::
250    ?>  =('B' (end 3 private-key))
251    =.  private-key  (rsh 8 (rsh 3 private-key))
252    ::
253    `@`(shar:ed:crypto public-key private-key)
254  ::  +encode-keys-packet: create key request $packet
255  ::
256  ++  encode-keys-packet
257    ~/  %encode-keys-packet
258    |=  [sndr=ship rcvr=ship sndr-life=life]
259    ^-  shot
260    :*  [sndr rcvr]
261        &
262        &
263        (mod sndr-life 16)
264        `@`1
265        origin=~
266        content=`@`%keys
267    ==
268  ::
269  ++  response-size  13  ::  1kb
270  ::  +sift-roar: assemble scry response fragments into full message
271  ::
272  ++  sift-roar
273    |=  [total=@ud hav=(list have)]
274    ^-  [sig=@ux dat=$@(~ (cask))]
275    =/  mes=@
276    %+  rep  response-size
277    (roll hav |=([=have dat=(list @ux)] [dat.have dat]))
278    =+  sig=(end 9 mes)
279    :-  sig
280    =+  dat=(rsh 9 mes)
281    ?~  dat  ~
282    =/  non  ~|(%fine-cue (cue dat))
283    ~|  [%fine %response-not-cask]
284    ;;((cask) non)
285  ::  +etch-hunk: helper core to serialize a $hunk
286  ::
287  ++  etch-hunk
288    |=  [=ship =life =acru:ames]
```

```
289    |%
290    ::
291    +|  %helpers
292    ::  +show-meow: prepare $meow for printing
293    ::
294    ++  show-meow
295      |=  =meow
296      :*  sig=`@q`(mug sig.meow)
297          num=num.meow
298          dat=`@q`(mug dat.meow)
299      ==
300    ::
301    ++  make-meow
302      |=  [=path mes=@ num=@ud]
303      ^-  meow
304      =/  tot  (met 13 mes)
305      =/  dat  (cut 13 [(dec num) 1] mes)
306      =/  wid  (met 3 dat)
307      :*  sig=(sign-fra path num dat)      ::  fragment signature
308          num=tot                          ::  number of fragments
309          dat=dat                          ::  response data fragment
310      ==
311    ::
312    ++  etch-meow
313      |=  =meow
314      ^-  yowl
315      %+  can  3
316      :~  64^sig.meow
317          4^num.meow
318          (met 3 dat.meow)^dat.meow
319      ==
320    ::
321    +|  %keys
322    ::
323    ++  sign  sigh:as:acru
324    ++  sign-fra
325      |=  [=path fra=@ud dat=@ux]
326      ::~>  %bout.[1 %sign-fra]
327      (sign (jam path fra dat))
328    ::
329    ++  full
330      |=  [=path data=$@(~ (cask))]
331      =/  buf  (jam ship life path data)
332      ::=/  nam  (crip "sign-full {<(met 3 buf)>}")
333      ::~>  %bout.[1 nam]
334      (sign buf)
335    ::
336    +|  %serialization
337    ::
338    ++  etch
339      |=  [=path =hunk data=$@(~ (cask))]
340      ^-  (list yowl)
341      =/  mes=@
342        =/  sig=@  (full path data)
343        ?~  data  sig
344        (mix sig (lsh 9 (jam data)))
345        ::(cat 9 sig (jam data))
346      ::
```

```
347     =/  las   (met 13 mes)
348     =/  tip   (dec (add [lop len]:hunk))
349     =/  top   (min las tip)
350     =/  num   lop.hunk
351     ?>  (lte num top)
352     =|  res=(list yowl)
353     |-  ^+  res
354     ?:  =(num top)
355       =-  (flop - res)
356       (etch-meow (make-meow path mes num))
357     $(num +(num), res :_(res (etch-meow (make-meow path mes num))))
358     --
359   ::  +etch-open-packet: convert $open-packet attestation to $shot
360   ::
361   ++  etch-open-packet
362     ~/  %etch-open-packet
363     |=  [pac=open-packet =acru:ames]
364     ^-  shot
365     :*  [sndr rcvr]:pac
366         req=&  sam=&
367         (mod sndr-life.pac 16)
368         (mod rcvr-life.pac 16)
369         origin=~
370         content=`@`(sign:as:acru (jam pac))
371     ==
372   ::  +sift-open-packet: decode comet attestation into an $open-packet
373   ::
374   ++  sift-open-packet
375     ~/  %sift-open-packet
376     |=  [=shot our=ship our-life=@]
377     ^-  open-packet
378     ::  deserialize and type-check packet contents
379     ::
380     =+  ;;  [signature=@ signed=@]  (cue content.shot)
381     =+  ;;  =open-packet            (cue signed)
382     ::  assert .our and .her and lives match
383     ::
384     ?>  .=         sndr.open-packet  sndr.shot
385     ?>  .=         rcvr.open-packet  our
386     ?>  .=  sndr-life.open-packet  1
387     ?>  .=  rcvr-life.open-packet  our-life
388     ::  only a star can sponsor a comet
389     ::
390     ?>  =(%king (clan:title (^sein:title sndr.shot)))
391     =/  crub  (com:nu:crub:crypto public-key.open-packet)
392     ::  comet public-key must hash to its @p address
393     ::
394     ?>  =(sndr.shot fig:ex:crub)
395     ::  verify signature
396     ::
397     ?>  (safe:as:crub signature signed)
398     open-packet
399   ::  +etch-shut-packet: encrypt and packetize a $shut-packet
400   ::
401   ++  etch-shut-packet
402     ~/  %etch-shut-packet
403     ::  TODO add rift to signed messages to prevent replay attacks?
404     ::
```

```
405    |=  $:  =shut-packet
406            =symmetric-key
407            sndr=ship
408            rcvr=ship
409            sndr-life=@
410            rcvr-life=@
411        ==
412    ^-  shot
413    ::
414    =?   meat.shut-packet
415       ?&  ?=(%& -.meat.shut-packet)
416           (gth (met packet-size fragment.p.meat.shut-packet) 1)
417        ==
418      %_   meat.shut-packet
419        fragment.p
420        (cut packet-size [[fragment-num 1] fragment]:p.meat.shut-packet)
421      ==
422    ::
423    =/  vec  ~[sndr rcvr sndr-life rcvr-life]
424    =/  [siv=@uxH len=@ cyf=@ux]
425      (~(en sivc:aes:crypto (shaz symmetric-key) vec) (jam shut-packet))
426    ::
427    :*  ^=      dyad  [sndr rcvr]
428        ^=      req   ?=(%& -.meat.shut-packet)
429        ^=      sam   &
430        ^=  sndr-tick  (mod sndr-life 16)
431        ^=  sndr-tick  (mod rcvr-life 16)
432        ^=     origin  ~
433        ^=    content  :(mix siv (lsh 7 len) (lsh [3 18] cyf))
434    ==
435  ::  +sift-shut-packet: decrypt a $shut-packet from a $shot
436  ::
437  ++  sift-shut-packet
438    ~/  %sift-shut-packet
439    |=  [=shot =symmetric-key sndr-life=@ rcvr-life=@]
440    ^-  (unit shut-packet)
441    ?.  ?&  =(sndr-tick.shot (mod sndr-life 16))
442            =(rcvr-tick.shot (mod rcvr-life 16))
443        ==
444      ~
445    =/  siv  (end 7 content.shot)
446    =/  len  (end 4 (rsh 7 content.shot))
447    =/  cyf  (rsh [3 18] content.shot)
448    ~|  ames-decrypt+[[sndr rcvr origin]:shot len siv]
449    =/  vec  ~[sndr.shot rcvr.shot sndr-life rcvr-life]
450    %-  some  ;;  shut-packet  %-  cue  %-  need
451    (~(de sivc:aes:crypto (shaz symmetric-key) vec) siv len cyf)
452  ::
453  ++  is-peer-dead
454    |=  [now=@da =peer-state]
455    ^+  peer-state
456    =/  expiry=@da  (add ~s30 last-contact.qos.peer-state)
457    =?  -.qos.peer-state  (gte now expiry)
458      %dead
459    peer-state
460  ::
461  ++  update-peer-route
462    |=  [peer=ship =peer-state]
```

```
463    ^+  peer-state
464    ::    If the peer is not responding, mark the .lane.route as
465    ::    indirect.  The next packets we emit will be sent to the
466    ::    receiver's sponsorship chain in case the receiver's
467    ::    transport address has changed and this lane is no longer
468    ::    valid.
469    ::
470    ::    If .peer is a galaxy, the lane will always remain direct.
471    ::
472    ?.  ?&  ?=(%dead -.qos.peer-state)
473            ?=(^ route.peer-state)
474            direct.u.route.peer-state
475            !=(%czar (clan:title peer))
476        ==
477      peer-state
478    peer-state(direct.u.route %.n)
479  ::
480  +|  %atomics
481  ::
482  +$  private-key      @uwprivatekey
483  +$  signature        @uwsignature
484  ::
485  +|  %kinetics
486  ::  $channel: combined sender and receiver identifying data
487  ::
488  +$  channel
489    $:  [our=ship her=ship]
490        now=@da
491        ::  our data, common to all dyads
492        ::
493        $:  =our=life
494            crypto-core=acru:ames
495            =bug
496        ==
497        ::  her data, specific to this dyad
498        ::
499        $:  =symmetric-key
500            =her=life
501            =her=rift
502            =her=public-key
503            her-sponsor=ship
504    ==  ==
505  ::  $open-packet: unencrypted packet payload, for comet self-attestation
506  ::
507  ::    This data structure gets signed and jammed to form the .contents
508  ::    field of a $packet.
509  ::
510  ::  TODO add rift to prevent replay attacks
511  ::
512  +$  open-packet
513    $:  =public-key
514        sndr=ship
515        =sndr=life
516        rcvr=ship
517        =rcvr=life
518    ==
519  ::  $shut-packet: encrypted packet payload
520  ::
```

```
521  +$   shut-packet
522    $:  =bone
523        =message-num
524        meat=(each fragment-meat ack-meat)
525    ==
526  ::  $fragment-meat: contents of a message-fragment packet
527  ::
528  +$   fragment-meat
529    $:  num-fragments=fragment-num
530        =fragment-num
531        =fragment
532    ==
533  ::  $ack-meat: contents of an acknowledgment packet; fragment or message
534  ::
535  ::      Fragment acks reference the $fragment-num of the target packet.
536  ::
537  ::      Message acks contain a success flag .ok, which is %.n in case of
538  ::      negative acknowledgment (nack), along with .lag that describes the
539  ::      time it took to process the message. .lag is zero if the message
540  ::      was processed during a single Arvo event. At the moment, .lag is
541  ::      always zero.
542  ::
543  +$   ack-meat   (each fragment-num [ok=? lag=@dr])
544  ::  $naxplanation: nack trace; explains which message failed and why
545  ::
546  +$   naxplanation   [=message-num =error]
547  ::
548  +|  %statics
549  ::
550  ::  $ames-state: state for entire vane
551  ::
552  ::      peers:       states of connections to other ships
553  ::      unix-duct:   handle to give moves to unix
554  ::      life:        our $life; how many times we've rekeyed
555  ::      crypto-core: interface for encryption and signing
556  ::      bug:         debug printing configuration
557  ::      snub:        blocklist for incoming packets
558  ::      cong:        parameters for marking a flow as clogged
559  ::      dead:        dead flow consolidation timer and recork timer, if set
560  ::
561  +$   ames-state
562    $+  ames-state
563    $:  peers=(map ship ship-state)
564        =unix=duct
565        =life
566        =rift
567        crypto-core=acru:ames
568        =bug
569        snub=[form=?(%allow %deny) ships=(set ship)]
570        cong=[msg=_5 mem=_100.000]
571        ::
572        $=  dead
573        $:  flow=[%flow (unit dead-timer)]
574            cork=[%cork (unit dead-timer)]
575    ==  ==
576  ::
577  +$   dead-timer        [=duct =wire date=@da]
578  +$   azimuth-state     [=symmetric-key =life =rift =public-key sponsor=ship]
```

```
579  +$  azimuth-state-6  [=symmetric-key =life =public-key sponsor=ship]
580  +$  ames-state-4    ames-state-5
581  +$  ames-state-5
582   $+  ames-state-5
583   $:  peers=(map ship ship-state-5)
584       =unix=duct
585       =life
586       crypto-core=acru-12
587       bug=bug-9
588   ==
589  ::
590  +$  ship-state-4  ship-state-5
591  +$  ship-state-5
592   $+  ship-state-5
593   $%  [%alien alien-agenda-12]
594       [%known peer-state-5]
595   ==
596  ::
597  +$  peer-state-5
598   $+  peer-state-5
599   $:  azimuth-state-6
600       route=(unit [direct=? =lane])
601       =qos
602       =ossuary
603       snd=(map bone message-pump-state-16)
604       rcv=(map bone message-sink-state)
605       nax=(set [=bone =message-num])
606       heeds=(set duct)
607   ==
608  ::
609  +$  bug-9
610   $+  bug-9
611   $:  veb=_[`?`%.n `?`%.n `?`%.n `?`%.n `?`%.n `?`%.n `?`%.n]
612       ships=(set ship)
613   ==
614  ::
615  +$  ames-state-6
616   $+  ames-state-6
617   $:  peers=(map ship ship-state-6)
618       =unix=duct
619       =life
620       crypto-core=acru-12
621       bug=bug-9
622   ==
623  ::
624  +$  ship-state-6
625   $+  ship-state-6
626   $%  [%alien alien-agenda-12]
627       [%known peer-state-6]
628   ==
629  ::
630  +$  peer-state-6
631   $+  peer-state-6
632   $:  azimuth-state
633       route=(unit [direct=? =lane])
634       =qos
635       =ossuary
636       snd=(map bone message-pump-state-16)
```

```
637        rcv=(map bone message-sink-state)
638        nax=(set [=bone =message-num])
639        heeds=(set duct)
640    ==
641 ::
642 +$  ames-state-7
643   $+  ames-state-7
644   $:  peers=(map ship ship-state-7)
645       =unix=duct
646       =life
647       crypto-core=acru-12
648       bug=bug-9
649   ==
650 ::
651 +$  ames-state-8
652   $+  ames-state-8
653   $:  peers=(map ship ship-state-7)
654       =unix=duct
655       =life
656       crypto-core=acru-12
657       bug=bug-9
658       corks=(set wire)
659   ==
660 ::
661 +$  ames-state-9
662   $+  ames-state-9
663   $:  peers=(map ship ship-state-7)
664       =unix=duct
665       =life
666       crypto-core=acru-12
667       bug=bug-9
668       corks=(set wire)
669       snub=(set ship)
670   ==
671 ::
672 +$  ames-state-10
673   $+  ames-state-10
674   $:  peers=(map ship ship-state-7)
675       =unix=duct
676       =life
677       crypto-core=acru-12
678       bug=bug-12
679       corks=(set wire)
680       snub=(set ship)
681   ==
682 ::
683 +$  ship-state-7
684   $+  ship-state-7
685   $%  [%alien alien-agenda-12]
686       [%known peer-state-7]
687   ==
688 ::
689 +$  peer-state-7
690   $+  peer-state-7
691   $:  azimuth-state
692       route=(unit [direct=? =lane])
693       =qos
694       =ossuary
```

```
695       snd=(map bone message-pump-state-16)
696       rcv=(map bone message-sink-state)
697       nax=(set [=bone =message-num])
698       heeds=(set duct)
699       closing=(set bone)
700       corked=(set bone)
701       krocs=(set bone)
702   ==
703 ::
704 +$  ames-state-11
705   $+  ames-state-11
706   $:  peers=(map ship ship-state-7)
707       =unix=duct
708       =life
709       crypto-core=acru-12
710       bug=bug-12
711       corks=(set wire)
712       snub=(set ship)
713       cong=[msg=@ud mem=@ud]
714   ==
715 ::
716 +$  queued-event-11
717   $+  queued-event-11
718   $%  [%call =duct wrapped-task=(hobo task-11)]
719       [%take =wire =duct =sign]
720   ==
721 ::
722 +$  task-11
723   $+  task-11
724   $%  [%snub ships=(list ship)]
725       $<(%snub task)
726   ==
727 ::
728 +$  ames-state-12
729   $+  ames-state-12
730   $:  peers=(map ship ship-state-12)
731       =unix=duct
732       =life
733       crypto-core=acru-12
734       bug=bug-12
735       snub=[form=?(%allow %deny) ships=(set ship)]
736       cong=[msg=@ud mem=@ud]
737   ==
738 ::
739 +$  ship-state-12
740   $+  ship-state-12
741   $%  [%alien alien-agenda-12]
742       [%known peer-state-12]
743   ==
744 ::
745 +$  alien-agenda-12
746   $+  alien-agenda-12
747   $:  messages=(list [=duct =plea])
748       packets=(set =blob)
749       heeds=(set duct)
750   ==
751 ::
752 +$  peer-state-12
```

```
753    $+   peer-state-12
754    $:   azimuth-state
755         route=(unit [direct=? =lane])
756         =qos
757         =ossuary
758         snd=(map bone message-pump-state-16)
759         rcv=(map bone message-sink-state)
760         nax=(set [=bone =message-num])
761         heeds=(set duct)
762         closing=(set bone)
763         corked=(set bone)
764    ==
765    ::
766    +$   bug-12
767    $:   veb=_[`?`%.n `?`%.n `?`%.n `?`%.n `?`%.n `?`%.n `?`%.n `?`%.n]
768         ships=(set ship)
769    ==
770    ::
771    ++   acru-12  $_  ^?
772    |%
773    ++   as  ^?
774      |%  ++  seal  |~([a=pass b=@] *@)
775          ++  sign  |~(a=@ *@)
776          ++  sure  |~(a=@ *(unit @))
777          ++  tear  |~([a=pass b=@] *(unit @))
778      --
779    ++   de  |~([a=@ b=@] *(unit @))
780    ++   dy  |~([a=@ b=@] *@)
781    ++   en  |~([a=@ b=@] *@)
782    ++   ex  ^?
783      |%  ++  fig  *@uvH
784          ++  pac  *@uvG
785          ++  pub  *pass
786          ++  sec  *ring
787      --
788    ++   nu  ^?
789      |%  ++  pit  |~([a=@ b=@] ^?(..nu))
790          ++  nol  |~(a=ring ^?(..nu))
791          ++  com  |~(a=pass ^?(..nu))
792      --
793    --
794    ::
795    +$   ames-state-13
796    $+   ames-state-13
797    $:   peers=(map ship ship-state-13)
798         =unix=duct
799         =life
800         =rift
801         crypto-core=acru:ames
802         =bug
803         snub=[form=?(%allow %deny) ships=(set ship)]
804         cong=[msg=@ud mem=@ud]
805    ==
806    ::
807    +$   ship-state-13
808    $+   ship-state-13
809    $%   [%alien alien-agenda]
810         [%known peer-state-13]
```

```
811    ==
812  ::
813  +$  peer-state-13
814    $+  peer-state-13
815    $:  $:  =symmetric-key
816            =life
817            =rift
818            =public-key
819            sponsor=ship
820        ==
821      route=(unit [direct=? =lane])
822      =qos
823      =ossuary
824      snd=(map bone message-pump-state-16)
825      rcv=(map bone message-sink-state)
826      nax=(set [=bone =message-num])
827      heeds=(set duct)
828      closing=(set bone)
829      corked=(set bone)
830      keens=(map path keen-state-13)
831    ==
832  ::
833  ++  keen-state-13
834    =<  $+  keen-state-13
835        $:  wan=(pha want)   ::  request packts, sent
836            nex=(list want)  ::  request packets, unsent
837            hav=(list have)  ::  response packets, backward
838            num-fragments=@ud
839            num-received=@ud
840            next-wake=(unit @da)
841            listeners=(set duct)
842            metrics=pump-metrics-16
843        ==
844    |%
845    ::  +afx: polymorphic node type for finger trees
846    ::
847    ++  afx
848      |$  [val]
849      $%  [%1 p=val ~]
850          [%2 p=val q=val ~]
851          [%3 p=val q=val r=val ~]
852          [%4 p=val q=val r=val s=val ~]
853      ==
854    ::  +pha: finger tree
855    ::
856    ::    DO NOT USE THIS
857    ::    It's wrong and only kept around for state migration purposes.
858    ::
859    ++  pha
860      |$  [val]
861      $~  [%nul ~]
862      $%  [%nul ~]
863          [%one p=val]
864          [%big p=(afx val) q=(pha val) r=(afx val)]
865      ==
866    ::  +deq: deque
867    ::
868    ::    DO NOT USE THIS
```

```
869  ::      It's wrong and only kept around for state migration purposes.
870  ::
871  ++  deq
872      |*  val=mold
873      |%
874 ::      ::
875 ::      ::  +|  %utilities
876 ::      ::
877 ::      ++  make-afx
878 ::      |=  ls=(list val)
879 ::      ?+  ls  ~|(bad-finger/(lent ls) !!)
880 ::        [* ~]        [%1 ls]
881 ::        [* * ~]      [%2 ls]
882 ::        [* * * ~]    [%3 ls]
883 ::        [* * * * ~]  [%4 ls]
884 ::      ==
885 ::      ++  afx-to-pha
886 ::      |=  =(afx val)
887 ::      ^-  (pha val)
888 ::      (apl *(pha val) +.afx)
889 ::      ::
890 ::      ::  +|  %left-biased-operations
891 ::      ::
892 ::      ::  +pop-left: remove leftmost value from tree
893 ::      ::
894 ::      ++  pop-left
895 ::      |=  a=(pha val)
896 ::      ^-  [val=(unit val) pha=(pha val)]
897 ::      ?-  -.a
898 ::        %nul  ~^a
899 ::      ::
900 ::        %one  [`p.a nul/~]
901 ::      ::
902 ::          %big
903 ::        [`p.p.a (big-left +.+.p.a q.a r.a)]
904 ::      ==
905 ::      ++  apl
906 ::      |=  [a=(pha val) vals=(list val)]
907 ::      ^-  (pha val)
908 ::      =.  vals  (flop vals)
909 ::      |-
910 ::      ?~  vals  a
911 ::      $(a (cons a i.vals), vals t.vals)
912 ::      ::
913 ::      ::
914 ::      ++  dip-left
915 ::      |*  state=mold
916 ::      |=  $:  a=(pha val)
917 ::              =state
918 ::              f=$-([state val] [(unit val) ? state])
919 ::          ==
920 ::      ^+  [state a]
921 ::      =/  acc  [stop=`?`%.n state=state]
922 ::      =|  new=(pha val)
923 ::      |-
924 ::      ?:  stop.acc
925 ::        :: cat new and old
926 ::        [state.acc (weld a new)]
```

```
927  ::        =^  val=(unit val)  a
928  ::          (pop-left a)
929  ::        ?~  val
930  ::          [state.acc new]
931  ::        =^  res=(unit ^val)  acc
932  ::          (f state.acc u.val)
933  ::        ?~  res  $
934  ::        $(new (snoc new u.res))
935  ::      ::
936  ::      ++  big-left
937  ::        |=  [ls=(list val) a=(pha val) sf=(afx val)]
938  ::        ^-  (pha val)
939  ::        ?.  =(~ ls)
940  ::          [%big (make-afx ls) a sf]
941  ::        =/  [val=(unit val) inner=_a]
942  ::          (pop-left a)
943  ::        ?~  val
944  ::          (afx-to-pha sf)
945  ::        [%big [%1 u.val ~] inner sf]
946  ::      ::
947  ::      ++  cons
948  ::        =|  b=(list val)
949  ::        |=  [a=(pha val) c=val]
950  ::        ^-  (pha val)
951  ::        =.  b  [c b]
952  ::        |-
953  ::        ?~  b  a
954  ::        ?-  -.a
955  ::          ::
956  ::            %nul
957  ::          $(a [%one i.b], b t.b)
958  ::          ::
959  ::            %one
960  ::          %=  $
961  ::            b  t.b
962  ::            a  [%big [%1 i.b ~] [%nul ~] [%1 p.a ~]]
963  ::          ==
964  ::          ::
965  ::            %big
966  ::          ?.  ?=(%4 -.p.a)
967  ::            %=  $
968  ::              b  t.b
969  ::            ::
970  ::              a
971  ::              ?-  -.p.a
972  ::                %1  big/[[%2 i.b p.p.a ~] q.a r.a]
973  ::                %2  big/[[%3 i.b p.p.a q.p.a ~] q.a r.a]
974  ::                %3  big/[[%4 i.b p.p.a q.p.a r.p.a ~] q.a r.a]
975  ::              ==
976  ::            ==
977  ::          =/  inner
978  ::            $(a q.a, b ~[s.p.a r.p.a q.p.a])
979  ::          =.  inner
980  ::            $(a inner, b t.b)
981  ::          big/[[%2 i.b p.p.a ~] inner r.a]
982  ::        ==
983  ::      ::
984  ::      ::  +|  %right-biased-operations
```

```
985  ::      ::
986  ::      ::  +snoc: append to end (right) of tree
987  ::      ::
988  ::      ++  snoc
989  ::      |=  [a=(pha val) b=val]
990  ::      ^+  a
991  ::      ?-  -.a
992  ::        %nul  [%one b]
993  ::      ::
994  ::          %one
995  ::        :-  %big
996  ::        :*  [%1 p.a ~]
997  ::            [%nul ~]
998  ::            [%1 b ~]
999  ::        ==
1000 ::      ::
1001 ::          %big
1002 ::        ?-  -.r.a
1003 ::        ::
1004 ::            %1
1005 ::          :-  %big
1006 ::          [p.a q.a [%2 p.r.a b ~]]
1007 ::        ::
1008 ::            %2
1009 ::          :-  %big
1010 ::          [p.a q.a [%3 p.r.a q.r.a b ~]]
1011 ::        ::
1012 ::            %3
1013 ::          :-  %big
1014 ::          [p.a q.a [%4 p.r.a q.r.a r.r.a b ~]]
1015 ::        ::
1016 ::            %4
1017 ::          =/  inner
1018 ::            $(a q.a, b p.r.a)
1019 ::          =.  inner
1020 ::            $(a inner, b q.r.a)
1021 ::          =.  inner
1022 ::            $(a inner, b r.r.a)
1023 ::          :-  %big
1024 ::          :*  p.a
1025 ::              inner
1026 ::              [%2 s.r.a b ~]
1027 ::          ==
1028 ::        ==
1029 ::      ==
1030 ::      ::  +apr: append list to end (right) of tree
1031 ::      ::
1032 ::      ++  apr
1033 ::      |=  [a=(pha val) vals=(list val)]
1034 ::      ^-  (pha val)
1035 ::      ?~  vals  a
1036 ::      $(a (snoc a i.vals), vals t.vals)
1037 ::  ::  +|  %manipulation
1038 ::  ::
1039 ::  ::  +weld: concatenate two trees
1040 ::  ::
1041 ::  ::    O(log n)
1042 ::  ++  weld
```

```
::       =|  c=(list val)
::       |=  [a=(pha val) b=(pha val)]
::       ^-  (pha val)
::       ?-  -.b
::         %nul  (apr a c)
::         %one  (snoc (apr a c) p.b)
::         ::
::           %big
::         ?-  -.a
::           %nul  (apl b c)
::           %one  (cons (apl b c) p.a)
::           ::
::             %big
::           :-  %big
::           =-  [p.a - r.b]
::           $(a q.a, b q.b, c :(welp +.r.a c +.p.b))
::         ==
::       ==
::    ::  +tap: transform tree to list
::    ::
++  tap
  =|  res=(list val)
  |=  a=(pha val)
  !.
  |^  ^+  res
  ?-  -.a
    %nul  ~
    %one  ~[p.a]
    ::
      %big
    =/  fst=_res
      (tap-afx p.a)
    =/  lst=_res
      (tap-afx r.a)
    =/  mid=_res
      $(a q.a)
    :(welp fst mid lst)
  ==
  ++  tap-afx
    |=  ax=(afx val)
    ^+  res
    ?-  -.ax
      %1  +.ax
      %2  +.ax
      %3  +.ax
      %4  +.ax
    ==
  --
  --
--
::
+$  ames-state-14  ames-state-16
+$  ames-state-15  ames-state-16
+$  ames-state-16
  $+  ames-state-16
  $:  peers=(map ship ship-state-16)
      =unix=duct
      =life
```

```
1101        =rift
1102        crypto-core=acru:ames
1103        =bug
1104        snub=[form=?(%allow %deny) ships=(set ship)]
1105        cong=[msg=@ud mem=@ud]
1106      ==
1107  +$  ship-state-16
1108    $+  ship-state-16
1109    $%  [%alien alien-agenda]
1110        [%known peer-state-16]
1111      ==
1112  ::
1113  +$  peer-state-16
1114    $+  peer-state-16
1115    $:  azimuth-state
1116        route=(unit [direct=? =lane])
1117        =qos
1118        =ossuary
1119        snd=(map bone message-pump-state-16)
1120        rcv=(map bone message-sink-state)
1121        nax=(set [=bone =message-num])
1122        heeds=(set duct)
1123        closing=(set bone)
1124        corked=(set bone)
1125        keens=(map path keen-state-16)
1126      ==
1127  ::
1128  +$  keen-state-14  keen-state-16
1129  +$  keen-state-16
1130    $+  keen-state-16
1131    $:  wan=((mop @ud want) lte)
1132        nex=(list want)
1133        hav=(list have)
1134        num-fragments=@ud
1135        num-received=@ud
1136        next-wake=(unit @da)
1137        listeners=(set duct)
1138        metrics=pump-metrics-16
1139      ==
1140  ::
1141  +$  message-pump-state-16
1142    $+  message-pump-state-16
1143    $:  current=_`message-num`1
1144        next=_`message-num`1
1145        unsent-messages=(qeu message-blob)
1146        unsent-fragments=(list static-fragment)
1147        queued-message-acks=(map message-num ack)
1148        packet-pump-state=packet-pump-state-16
1149      ==
1150  ::
1151  +$  packet-pump-state-16
1152    $+  packet-pump-state-16
1153    $:  next-wake=(unit @da)
1154        live=((mop live-packet-key live-packet-val) lte-packets)
1155        metrics=pump-metrics-16
1156      ==
1157  ::
1158  +$  pump-metrics-16
```

```
1159   $+   pump-metrics-16
1160   $:   rto=_~s1
1161        rtt=_~s1
1162        rttvar=_~s1
1163        ssthresh=_10.000
1164        cwnd=_1
1165        num-live=@ud
1166        counter=@ud
1167   ==
1168   ::
1169   +$   queued-event-11-and-16
1170     $+   queued-event-11-and-16
1171     $%   [%call =duct wrapped-task=(hobo task-11-and-16)]
1172          [%take =wire =duct =sign]
1173     ==
1174   ::
1175   +$   task-11-and-16
1176     $+   task-11-and-16
1177     $%   [%kroc dry=?]
1178          [%snub ships=(list ship)]
1179          $<(?(%snub %kroc) task)
1180     ==
1181   ::
1182   +$   queued-event-16
1183     $+   queued-event-16
1184     $%   [%call =duct wrapped-task=(hobo task-16)]
1185          [%take =wire =duct =sign]
1186     ==
1187   ::
1188   +$   task-16
1189     $+   task-16
1190     $%   [%kroc dry=?]
1191          $<(%kroc task)
1192     ==
1193   ::  $bug: debug printing configuration
1194   ::
1195   ::      veb: verbosity toggles
1196   ::      ships: identity filter; if ~, print for all
1197   ::
1198   +$   bug
1199     $:   veb=_veb-all-off
1200          ships=(set ship)
1201     ==
1202   ::
1203   +|   %dialectics
1204   ::
1205   ::  $move: output effect; either request or response
1206   ::
1207   +$   move   [=duct card=(wind note gift)]
1208   ::  $queued-event: event to be handled after initial boot completes
1209   ::
1210   +$   queued-event
1211     $+   queued-event
1212     $%   [%call =duct wrapped-task=(hobo task)]
1213          [%take =wire =duct =sign]
1214     ==
1215   ::  $note: request to other vane
1216   ::
```

```
1217 ::        Ames passes a %plea note to another vane when it receives a
1218 ::        message on a "forward flow" from a peer, originally passed from
1219 ::        one of the peer's vanes to the peer's Ames.
1220 ::
1221 ::        Ames passes a %deep task to itself to handle deferred calls
1222 ::        Ames passes a %private-keys to Jael to request our private keys.
1223 ::        Ames passes a %public-keys to Jael to request a peer's public
1224 ::        keys.
1225 ::
1226 +$  note
1227    $~  [%b %wait *@da]
1228    $%  $:  %a
1229            $>(%deep task:ames)
1230        ==
1231        $:  %b
1232            $>(?(%wait %rest) task:behn)
1233        ==
1234        $:  %c
1235            $>(%warp task:clay)
1236        ==
1237        $:  %d
1238            $>(%flog task:dill)
1239        ==
1240        $:  %g
1241            $>(%deal task:gall)
1242        ==
1243        $:  %j
1244            $>  $?  %private-keys
1245                    %public-keys
1246                    %turf
1247                    %ruin
1248                ==
1249            task:jael
1250        ==
1251        $:  @tas
1252            $>(%plea vane-task)
1253    ==  ==
1254 ::  $sign: response from other vane
1255 ::
1256 +$  sign
1257    $~  [%behn %wake ~]
1258    $%  $:  %behn
1259            $>(%wake gift:behn)
1260        ==
1261        $:  %gall
1262            $>(?(%flub %unto) gift:gall)
1263        ==
1264        $:  %jael
1265            $>  $?  %private-keys
1266                    %public-keys
1267                    %turf
1268                ==
1269            gift:jael
1270        ==
1271        $:  @tas
1272            $>(?(%boon %done) gift:ames)
1273    ==  ==
1274 ::
```

```
1275  ::  $message-pump-task: job for |message-pump
1276  ::
1277  ::    %memo: packetize and send application-level message
1278  ::    %hear: handle receipt of ack on fragment or message
1279  ::    %near: handle receipt of naxplanation
1280  ::    $prod: reset congestion control
1281  ::    %wake: handle timer firing
1282  ::
1283  +$  message-pump-task
1284    $%  [%memo =message-blob]
1285        [%hear =message-num =ack-meat]
1286        [%near =naxplanation]
1287        [%prod ~]
1288        [%wake ~]
1289    ==
1290  ::  $packet-pump-task: job for |packet-pump
1291  ::
1292  ::    %hear: deal with a packet acknowledgment
1293  ::    %done: deal with message acknowledgment
1294  ::    %halt: finish event, possibly updating timer
1295  ::    %wake: handle timer firing
1296  ::    %prod: reset congestion control
1297  ::
1298  +$  packet-pump-task
1299    $%  [%hear =message-num =fragment-num]
1300        [%done =message-num lag=@dr]
1301        [%halt ~]
1302        [%wake current=message-num]
1303        [%prod ~]
1304    ==
1305  ::  $message-sink-task: job for |message-sink
1306  ::
1307  ::    %done: receive confirmation from vane of processing or failure
1308  ::    %drop: clear .message-num from .nax.state
1309  ::    %hear: handle receiving a message fragment packet
1310  ::      .ok: %.y unless previous failed attempt
1311  ::
1312  +$  message-sink-task
1313    $%  [%done ok=?]
1314        [%flub ~]
1315        [%drop =message-num]
1316        [%hear =lane =shut-packet ok=?]
1317    ==
1318  --
1319  ::  external vane interface
1320  ::
1321  |=  our=ship
1322  ::  larval ames, before %born sets .unix-duct; wraps adult ames core
1323  ::
1324  =<  =*  adult-gate   .
1325      =|  queued-events=(qeu queued-event)
1326      =|  $=  cached-state
1327          %-  unit
1328          $%  [%5 ames-state-5]
1329              [%6 ames-state-6]
1330              [%7 ames-state-7]
1331              [%8 ames-state-8]
1332              [%9 ames-state-9]
```

```
1333              [%10 ames-state-10]
1334              [%11 ames-state-11]
1335              [%12 ames-state-12]
1336              [%13 ames-state-13]
1337              [%14 ames-state-14]
1338              [%15 ames-state-15]
1339              [%16 ames-state-16]
1340              [%17 ^ames-state]
1341          ==
1342      ::
1343      |=  [now=@da eny=@ rof=roof]
1344      =*  larval-gate  .
1345      =*  adult-core   (adult-gate +<)
1346      =<  |%
1347          ++  call  ^call
1348          ++  load  ^load
1349          ++  scry  ^scry
1350          ++  stay  ^stay
1351          ++  take  ^take
1352          --
1353      |%
1354      ++  larval-core  .
1355      ::  +call: handle request $task
1356      ::
1357      ++  call
1358      |=  [=duct dud=(unit goof) wrapped-task=(hobo task)]
1359      ::
1360      =/  =task  ((harden task) wrapped-task)
1361      ::  reject larval error notifications
1362      ::
1363      ?^  dud
1364        ~|(%ames-larval-call-dud (mean tang.u.dud))
1365      ::  before processing events, make sure we have state loaded
1366      ::
1367      =^  molt-moves  larval-core  molt
1368      ::
1369      ?:  &(!=(~ unix-duct.ames-state.adult-gate) =(~ queued-events))
1370        =^  moves  adult-gate  (call:adult-core duct dud task)
1371        ~>  %slog.0^leaf/"ames: metamorphosis"
1372      [(weld molt-moves moves) adult-gate]
1373      ::  drop incoming packets until we metamorphose
1374      ::
1375      ?:  ?=(%hear -.task)
1376        [~ larval-gate]
1377      ::  %born: set .unix-duct and start draining .queued-events
1378      ::
1379      ?:  ?=(%born -.task)
1380        ::  process %born using wrapped adult ames
1381        ::
1382        =^  moves  adult-gate  (call:adult-core duct dud task)
1383        =.  moves  (weld molt-moves moves)
1384        ::  kick off a timer to process the first of .queued-events
1385        ::
1386        =.  moves  :_(moves [duct %pass /larva %b %wait now])
1387      [moves larval-gate]
1388      ::  any other event: enqueue it until we have a .unix-duct
1389      ::
1390      ::    XX what to do with errors?
```

```
1391      ::
1392      =.  queued-events  (~(put to queued-events) %call duct task)
1393      [~ larval-gate]
1394    ::  +take: handle response $sign
1395      ::
1396    ++  take
1397      |=  [=wire =duct dud=(unit goof) =sign]
1398      ?^  dud
1399        ~|(%ames-larval-take-dud (mean tang.u.dud))
1400      ::
1401      =^  molt-moves  larval-core  molt
1402      ::
1403      ?:  &(!=(~ unix-duct.ames-state.adult-gate) =(~ queued-events))
1404        =^  moves  adult-gate  (take:adult-core wire duct dud sign)
1405        ~>  %slog.0^leaf/"ames: metamorphosis"
1406        [(weld molt-moves moves) adult-gate]
1407      ::  enqueue event if not a larval drainage timer
1408      ::
1409      ?.  =(/larva wire)
1410        =.  queued-events  (~(put to queued-events) %take wire duct sign)
1411        [~ larval-gate]
1412      ::  larval event drainage timer; pop and process a queued event
1413      ::
1414      ?.  ?=([%behn %wake *] sign)
1415        ~>  %slog.0^leaf/"ames: larva: strange sign"
1416        [~ larval-gate]
1417      ::  if crashed, print, dequeue, and set next drainage timer
1418      ::
1419      ?^  error.sign
1420        ::  .queued-events should never be ~ here, but if it is, don't crash
1421        ::
1422        ?:  =(~ queued-events)
1423          =/  =tang  [leaf/"ames: cursed metamorphosis" u.error.sign]
1424          =/  moves  [duct %pass /larva-crash %d %flog %crud %larva tang]~
1425          [moves adult-gate]
1426        ::  dequeue and discard crashed event
1427        ::
1428        =.  queued-events  +:~(get to queued-events)
1429        ::  .queued-events has been cleared; metamorphose
1430        ::
1431        ?~  queued-events
1432          ~>  %slog.0^leaf/"ames: metamorphosis"
1433          [~ adult-gate]
1434        ::  set timer to drain next event
1435        ::
1436        =/  moves
1437          =/  =tang  [leaf/"ames: larva: drain crash" u.error.sign]
1438          :~  [duct %pass /larva-crash %d %flog %crud %larva tang]
1439              [duct %pass /larva %b %wait now]
1440          ==
1441        [moves larval-gate]
1442      ::  normal drain timer; dequeue and run event
1443      ::
1444      =^  first-event  queued-events  ~(get to queued-events)
1445      =^  moves  adult-gate
1446        ?-  -.first-event
1447          %call  (call:adult-core [duct ~ wrapped-task]:+.first-event)
1448          %take  (take:adult-core [wire duct ~ sign]:+.first-event)
```

```
1449          ==
1450      =.  moves  (weld molt-moves moves)
1451      ::  .queued-events has been cleared; done!
1452      ::
1453      ?~  queued-events
1454        ~>  %slog.0^leaf/"ames: metamorphosis"
1455      [moves adult-gate]
1456      ::  set timer to drain next event
1457      ::
1458      =.  moves  :_(moves [duct %pass /larva %b %wait now])
1459      [moves larval-gate]
1460  ::  lifecycle arms; mostly pass-throughs to the contained adult ames
1461  ::
1462  ++  scry  scry:adult-core
1463  ++  stay  [%17 %larva queued-events ames-state.adult-gate]
1464  ++  load
1465    |=  $=  old
1466        $%  $:  %4
1467            $%  $:  %larva
1468                    events=(qeu queued-event)
1469                    state=ames-state-4
1470                ==
1471                [%adult state=ames-state-4]
1472            ==  ==
1473            $:  %5
1474            $%  $:  %larva
1475                    events=(qeu queued-event)
1476                    state=ames-state-5
1477                ==
1478                [%adult state=ames-state-5]
1479            ==  ==
1480            $:  %6
1481            $%  $:  %larva
1482                    events=(qeu queued-event)
1483                    state=ames-state-6
1484                ==
1485                [%adult state=ames-state-6]
1486            ==  ==
1487            $:  %7
1488            $%  $:  %larva
1489                    events=(qeu queued-event)
1490                    state=ames-state-7
1491                ==
1492                [%adult state=ames-state-7]
1493            ==  ==
1494            $:  %8
1495            $%  $:  %larva
1496                    events=(qeu queued-event)
1497                    state=ames-state-8
1498                ==
1499                [%adult state=ames-state-8]
1500            ==  ==
1501            $:  %9
1502            $%  $:  %larva
1503                    events=(qeu queued-event-11)
1504                    state=ames-state-9
1505                ==
1506                [%adult state=ames-state-9]
```

```
1507            ==   ==
1508            $:   %10
1509            $%   $:   %larva
1510                     events=(qeu queued-event-11-and-16)
1511                     state=ames-state-10
1512                 ==
1513            [%adult state=ames-state-10]
1514            ==   ==
1515            $:   %11
1516            $%   $:   %larva
1517                     events=(qeu queued-event-11-and-16)
1518                     state=ames-state-11
1519                 ==
1520            [%adult state=ames-state-11]
1521            ==   ==
1522            $:   %12
1523            $%   $:   %larva
1524                     events=(qeu queued-event-16)
1525                     state=ames-state-12
1526                 ==
1527            [%adult state=ames-state-12]
1528            ==   ==
1529            $:   %13
1530            $%   $:   %larva
1531                     events=(qeu queued-event-16)
1532                     state=ames-state-13
1533                 ==
1534            [%adult state=ames-state-13]
1535            ==   ==
1536            $:   %14
1537            $%   $:   %larva
1538                     events=(qeu queued-event-16)
1539                     state=ames-state-14
1540                 ==
1541            [%adult state=ames-state-14]
1542            ==   ==
1543            $:   %15
1544            $%   $:   %larva
1545                     events=(qeu queued-event-16)
1546                     state=ames-state-15
1547                 ==
1548            [%adult state=ames-state-15]
1549            ==   ==
1550            $:   %16
1551            $%   $:   %larva
1552                     events=(qeu queued-event-16)
1553                     state=ames-state-16
1554                 ==
1555            [%adult state=ames-state-16]
1556            ==   ==
1557            $:   %17
1558            $%   $:   %larva
1559                     events=(qeu queued-event)
1560                     state=_ames-state.adult-gate
1561                 ==
1562            [%adult state=_ames-state.adult-gate]
1563        ==   ==   ==
1564    |^   ?-   old
```

```
1565          [%4 %adult *]
1566        $(old [%5 %adult (state-4-to-5:load:adult-core state.old)])
1567      ::
1568          [%4 %larva *]
1569      =.  state.old  (state-4-to-5:load:adult-core state.old)
1570      $(-.old %5)
1571      ::
1572          [%5 %adult *]
1573      =.  cached-state  `[%5 state.old]
1574      ~>  %slog.0^leaf/"ames: larva reload"
1575      larval-gate
1576      ::
1577          [%5 %larva *]
1578      ~>  %slog.0^leaf/"ames: larva: load"
1579      =.  cached-state  `[%5 state.old]
1580      =.  queued-events  events.old
1581      larval-gate
1582      ::
1583          [%6 %adult *]
1584      =.  cached-state  `[%6 state.old]
1585      ~>  %slog.0^leaf/"ames: larva reload"
1586      larval-gate
1587      ::
1588          [%6 %larva *]
1589      ~>  %slog.0^leaf/"ames: larva: load"
1590      =.  cached-state  `[%6 state.old]
1591      =.  queued-events  events.old
1592      larval-gate
1593      ::
1594          [%7 %adult *]
1595      =.  cached-state  `[%7 state.old]
1596      ~>  %slog.0^leaf/"ames: larva reload"
1597      larval-gate
1598      ::
1599          [%7 %larva *]
1600      ~>  %slog.0^leaf/"ames: larva: load"
1601      =.  queued-events  events.old
1602      =.  cached-state  `[%7 state.old]
1603      larval-gate
1604      ::
1605          [%8 %adult *]
1606      =.  cached-state  `[%8 state.old]
1607      ~>  %slog.0^leaf/"ames: larva reload"
1608      larval-gate
1609      ::
1610          [%8 %larva *]
1611      ~>  %slog.0^leaf/"ames: larva: load"
1612      =.  cached-state  `[%8 state.old]
1613      =.  queued-events  events.old
1614      larval-gate
1615      ::
1616          [%9 %adult *]
1617      =.  cached-state  `[%9 state.old]
1618      ~>  %slog.0^leaf/"ames: larva reload"
1619      larval-gate
1620      ::
1621          [%9 %larva *]
1622      ~>  %slog.0^leaf/"ames: larva: load"
```

```
1623        =.  cached-state  `[%9 state.old]
1624        =.  queued-events  (event-11-to-12 events.old)
1625        larval-gate
1626      ::
1627          [%10 %adult *]
1628        =.  cached-state  `[%10 state.old]
1629        ~>  %slog.0^leaf/"ames: larva reload"
1630        larval-gate
1631      ::
1632          [%10 %larva *]
1633        ~>  %slog.1^leaf/"ames: larva: load"
1634        =.  cached-state  `[%10 state.old]
1635        =.  queued-events  (event-11-to-17 events.old)
1636        larval-gate
1637      ::
1638          [%11 %adult *]
1639        =.  cached-state  `[%11 state.old]
1640        ~>  %slog.0^leaf/"ames: larva reload"
1641        larval-gate
1642      ::
1643          [%11 %larva *]
1644        ~>  %slog.1^leaf/"ames: larva: load"
1645        =.  cached-state  `[%11 state.old]
1646        =.  queued-events  (event-11-to-17 events.old)
1647        larval-gate
1648      ::
1649          [%12 %adult *]
1650        =.  cached-state  `[%12 state.old]
1651        ~>  %slog.0^leaf/"ames: larva reload"
1652        larval-gate
1653      ::
1654          [%12 %larva *]
1655        ~>  %slog.1^leaf/"ames: larva: load"
1656        =.  cached-state  `[%12 state.old]
1657        =.  queued-events  (event-16-to-17 events.old)
1658        larval-gate
1659      ::
1660          [%13 %adult *]
1661        =.  cached-state  `[%13 state.old]
1662        ~>  %slog.0^leaf/"ames: larva reload"
1663        larval-gate
1664      ::
1665          [%13 %larva *]
1666        ~>  %slog.1^leaf/"ames: larva: load"
1667        =.  cached-state  `[%13 state.old]
1668        =.  queued-events  (event-16-to-17 events.old)
1669        larval-gate
1670      ::
1671          [%14 %adult *]
1672        =.  cached-state  `[%14 state.old]
1673        ~>  %slog.0^leaf/"ames: larva reload"
1674        larval-gate
1675      ::
1676          [%14 %larva *]
1677        ~>  %slog.1^leaf/"ames: larva: load"
1678        =.  cached-state  `[%14 state.old]
1679        =.  queued-events  (event-16-to-17 events.old)
1680        larval-gate
```

```
1681          ::
1682              [%15 %adult *]
1683          =.  cached-state  `[%15 state.old]
1684          ~>  %slog.0^leaf/"ames: larva reload"
1685          larval-gate
1686          ::
1687              [%15 %larva *]
1688          ~>  %slog.1^leaf/"ames: larva: load"
1689          =.  cached-state  `[%15 state.old]
1690          =.  queued-events  (event-16-to-17 events.old)
1691          larval-gate
1692          ::
1693              [%16 %adult *]
1694          =.  cached-state  `[%16 state.old]
1695          ~>  %slog.0^leaf/"ames: larva reload"
1696          larval-gate
1697          ::
1698              [%16 %larva *]
1699          ~>  %slog.1^leaf/"ames: larva: load"
1700          =.  cached-state  `[%16 state.old]
1701          =.  queued-events  (event-16-to-17 events.old)
1702          larval-gate
1703          ::
1704              [%17 %adult *]  (load:adult-core %17 state.old)
1705          ::
1706              [%17 %larva *]
1707          ~>  %slog.1^leaf/"ames: larva: load"
1708          =.  queued-events  events.old
1709          =.  adult-gate    (load:adult-core %17 state.old)
1710          larval-gate
1711      ==
1712      ::
1713      ++  event-11-to-12
1714        |=  events=(qeu queued-event-11)
1715        ^-  (qeu queued-event)
1716        ::  "+rep:in on a +qeu looks strange, but works fine."
1717        ::
1718        %-  ~(rep in events)
1719        |=  [e=queued-event-11 q=(qeu queued-event)]
1720        %-  ~(put to q)  ^-  queued-event
1721        ?.  ?=(%call -.e)  e
1722        =/  task=task-11  ((harden task-11) wrapped-task.e)
1723        %=  e
1724          wrapped-task  ?.(?=(%snub -.task) task [%snub %deny ships.task])
1725        ==
1726      ::
1727      ++  event-11-to-17
1728        |=  events=(qeu queued-event-11-and-16)
1729        ^-  (qeu queued-event)
1730        %-  ~(rep in events)
1731        |=  [e=queued-event-11-and-16 q=(qeu queued-event)]
1732        %-  ~(put to q)  ^-  queued-event
1733        ?.  ?=(%call -.e)  e
1734        =/  task=task-11-and-16  ((harden task-11-and-16) wrapped-task.e)
1735        %=  e
1736          wrapped-task
1737        ?+  -.task  task
1738          %snub  [%snub %deny ships.task]
```

```
1739              %kroc   [%kroc ~]
1740          ==
1741        ==
1742      ::
1743    ++  event-16-to-17
1744      |=  events=(qeu queued-event-16)
1745      ^-  (qeu queued-event)
1746      %-  ~(rep in events)
1747      |=  [e=queued-event-16 q=(qeu queued-event)]
1748      %-  ~(put to q)  ^-  queued-event
1749      ?.  ?=(%call -.e)  e
1750      =/  task=task-16  ((harden task-16) wrapped-task.e)
1751      %=  e
1752        wrapped-task  ?.(?=(%kroc -.task) task [%kroc ~])
1753      ==
1754    --
1755  ::  +molt: re-evolve to adult-ames
1756  ::
1757  ++  molt
1758    ^-  (quip move _larval-core)
1759    ?~  cached-state  [~ larval-core]
1760    ~>  %slog.0^leaf/"ames: molt"
1761    =?  u.cached-state  ?=(%5 -.u.cached-state)
1762      6+(state-5-to-6:load:adult-core +.u.cached-state)
1763    =?  u.cached-state  ?=(%6 -.u.cached-state)
1764      7+(state-6-to-7:load:adult-core +.u.cached-state)
1765    =^  moz  u.cached-state
1766      ?.  ?=(%7 -.u.cached-state)  [~ u.cached-state]
1767      ~>  %slog.0^leaf/"ames: init daily recork timer"
1768      :-  [[/ames]~ %pass /recork %b %wait `@da`(add now ~d1)]~
1769      8+(state-7-to-8:load:adult-core +.u.cached-state)
1770    =?  u.cached-state  ?=(%8 -.u.cached-state)
1771      9+(state-8-to-9:load:adult-core +.u.cached-state)
1772    =?  u.cached-state  ?=(%9 -.u.cached-state)
1773      10+(state-9-to-10:load:adult-core +.u.cached-state)
1774    =?  u.cached-state  ?=(%10 -.u.cached-state)
1775      11+(state-10-to-11:load:adult-core +.u.cached-state)
1776    =?  u.cached-state  ?=(%11 -.u.cached-state)
1777      12+(state-11-to-12:load:adult-core +.u.cached-state)
1778    =?  u.cached-state  ?=(%12 -.u.cached-state)
1779      13+(state-12-to-13:load:adult-core +.u.cached-state)
1780    =?  u.cached-state  ?=(%13 -.u.cached-state)
1781      14+(state-13-to-14:load:adult-core +.u.cached-state)
1782    =?  u.cached-state  ?=(%14 -.u.cached-state)
1783      15+(state-14-to-15:load:adult-core +.u.cached-state)
1784    =?  u.cached-state  ?=(%15 -.u.cached-state)
1785      16+(state-15-to-16:load:adult-core +.u.cached-state)
1786    =^  moz  u.cached-state
1787      ?.  ?=(%16 -.u.cached-state)  [~ u.cached-state]
1788      :_  17+(state-16-to-17:load:adult-core +.u.cached-state)
1789      ?^  moz  moz  ::  if we have just added the timer in state-7-to-8, skip
1790      =;  recork-timer=(list [@da duct])
1791        ?^  recork-timer  ~
1792        ~>  %slog.0^leaf/"ames: init daily recork timer"
1793        [[/ames]~ %pass /recork %b %wait `@da`(add now ~d1)]~
1794      %+  skim
1795        ;;  (list [@da duct])
1796        =<  q.q  %-  need  %-  need
```

```
1797              (rof ~ /ames %bx [[our %$ da+now] /debug/timers])
1798            |=([@da =duct] ?=([[%ames %recork *] *] duct))
1799          ::
1800          ?>  ?=(%17 -.u.cached-state)
1801          =.  ames-state.adult-gate  +.u.cached-state
1802          [moz larval-core(cached-state ~)]
1803          --
1804  ::
1805  =>  ::  |ev: inner event-handling core
1806      ::
1807      ~%  %per-event  ..trace  ~
1808      |%
1809      ++  ev
1810        =|  moves=(list move)
1811        ~%  %event-gate  ..ev  ~
1812        |=  [[now=@da eny=@ rof=roof] =duct =ames-state]
1813        =*  veb  veb.bug.ames-state
1814        =|  cork-bone=(unit bone)  ::  modified by +on-kroc
1815        ~%  %event-core  ..$  ~
1816        |%
1817        +|  %helpers
1818        ::
1819        ++  event-core  .
1820        ++  abet  [(flop moves) ames-state]
1821        ++  emit  |=(=move event-core(moves [move moves]))
1822        ++  emil  |=(mos=(list move) event-core(moves (weld (flop mos) moves)))
1823        ++  channel-state  [life crypto-core bug]:ames-state
1824        ++  trace-fine    (cury trace %fine)
1825        ++  trace-ames    (cury trace %ames)
1826        ++  ev-trace
1827          |=  [verb=? =ship print=(trap tape)]
1828          ^+  same
1829          (trace-ames verb ship ships.bug.ames-state print)
1830        ::  +get-peer-state: lookup .her state or ~
1831        ::
1832        ++  get-peer-state
1833          |=  her=ship
1834          ^-  (unit peer-state)
1835          ::
1836          =-  ?.(?=([~ %known *] -) ~ `+.u)
1837          (~(get by peers.ames-state) her)
1838        ::  +got-peer-state: lookup .her state or crash
1839        ::
1840        ++  got-peer-state
1841          |=  her=ship
1842          ^-  peer-state
1843          ::
1844          ~|  %freaky-alien^her
1845          =-  ?>(?=(%known -<) ->)
1846          (~(got by peers.ames-state) her)
1847        ::  +gut-peer-state: lookup .her state or default
1848        ::
1849        ++  gut-peer-state
1850          |=  her=ship
1851          ^-  peer-state
1852          =/  ship-state  (~(get by peers.ames-state) her)
1853          ?.  ?=([~ %known *] ship-state)
1854            *peer-state
```

```
1855          +.u.ship-state
1856        ::
1857        +|   %tasks
1858        ::  +on-take-flub: vane not ready to process message, pretend it
1859        ::                       was never delivered
1860        ::
1861        ++  on-take-flub
1862          |=  =wire
1863          ^+  event-core
1864          ?~  parsed=(parse-bone-wire wire)
1865            ::  no-op
1866            ::
1867            ~>  %slog.0^leaf/"ames: dropping malformed wire: {(spud wire)}"
1868            event-core
1869          ?>  ?=([@ her=ship *] u.parsed)
1870          =*  her  her.u.parsed
1871          =/  peer-core  (abed-got:pe her)
1872          ?:  ?&  ?=([%new *] u.parsed)
1873                  (lth rift.u.parsed rift.peer-state.peer-core)
1874              ==
1875            ::  ignore events from an old rift
1876            ::
1877          %-  %^  ev-trace  odd.veb  her
1878              |.("dropping old rift wire: {(spud wire)}")
1879            event-core
1880          =/  =bone
1881            ?-(u.parsed [%new *] bone.u.parsed, [%old *] bone.u.parsed)
1882          abet:(on-flub:peer-core bone)
1883        ::  +on-take-done: handle notice from vane that it processed a message
1884        ::
1885        ++  on-take-done
1886          |=  [=wire error=(unit error)]
1887          ^+  event-core
1888          ?~  parsed=(parse-bone-wire wire)
1889            ::  no-op
1890            ::
1891            ~>  %slog.0^leaf/"ames: dropping malformed wire: {(spud wire)}"
1892            event-core
1893          ?>  ?=([@ her=ship *] u.parsed)
1894          =*  her         her.u.parsed
1895          =/  peer-core  (abed-got:pe her)
1896          |^
1897          ?:  ?&  ?=([%new *] u.parsed)
1898                  (lth rift.u.parsed rift.peer-state.peer-core)
1899              ==
1900            ::  ignore events from an old rift
1901            ::
1902          %-  %^  ev-trace  odd.veb  her
1903              |.("dropping old rift wire: {(spud wire)}")
1904            event-core
1905          =/  =bone
1906            ?-(u.parsed [%new *] bone.u.parsed, [%old *] bone.u.parsed)
1907          =?  peer-core  ?=([%old *] u.parsed)
1908            %-  %^  ev-trace  odd.veb  her
1909                |.("parsing old wire: {(spud wire)}")
1910            peer-core
1911        ::  relay the vane ack to the foreign peer
1912        ::
```

```
1913        =<  abet
1914        ?~(error (send-ack bone) (send-nack bone u.error))
1915        ::
1916        ::  if processing succeded, send positive ack packet and exit
1917        ::
1918        ++  send-ack
1919          |=  =bone
1920          ^+  peer-core
1921          ::  handle cork only deals with bones that are in closing
1922          ::
1923          %.  bone
1924          handle-cork:abet:(call:(abed:mi:peer-core bone) %done ok=%.y)
1925        ::  failed; send message nack packet
1926        ::
1927        ++  send-nack
1928          |=  [=bone =^error]
1929          ^+  peer-core
1930          =.  peer-core  abet:(call:(abed:mi:peer-core bone) %done ok=%.n)
1931          ::  construct nack-trace message, referencing .failed $message-num
1932          ::
1933          =/  failed=message-num
1934            last-acked:(~(got by rcv.peer-state.peer-core) bone)
1935          =/  =naxplanation  [failed error]
1936          =/  =message-blob  (jam naxplanation)
1937          ::  send nack-trace message on associated .nack-bone
1938          ::
1939          =/  nack-bone=^bone  (mix 0b10 bone)
1940          abet:(call:(abed:mu:peer-core nack-bone) %memo message-blob)
1941        --
1942      ::  +on-sift: handle request to filter debug output by ship
1943      ::
1944      ++  on-sift
1945        |=  ships=(list ship)
1946        ^+  event-core
1947        =.  ships.bug.ames-state  (sy ships)
1948        event-core
1949      ::  +on-snub: handle request to change ship blacklist
1950      ::
1951      ++  on-snub
1952        |=  [form=?(%allow %deny) ships=(list ship)]
1953        ^+  event-core
1954        =.  snub.ames-state  [form (sy ships)]
1955        event-core
1956      ::  +on-spew: handle request to set verbosity toggles on debug output
1957      ::
1958      ++  on-spew
1959        |=  verbs=(list verb)
1960        ^+  event-core
1961        ::  start from all %.n's, then flip requested toggles
1962        ::
1963        =.  veb.bug.ames-state
1964          %+  roll  verbs
1965          |=  [=verb acc=_veb-all-off]
1966          ^+  veb.bug.ames-state
1967          ?-  verb
1968            %snd  acc(snd %.y)
1969            %rcv  acc(rcv %.y)
1970            %odd  acc(odd %.y)
```

```
            %msg   acc(msg %.y)
            %ges   acc(ges %.y)
            %for   acc(for %.y)
            %rot   acc(rot %.y)
            %kay   acc(kay %.y)
            %fin   acc(fin %.y)
         ==
       event-core
    ::  +on-prod: re-send a packet per flow to each of .ships
    ::
    ++  on-prod
      |=  ships=(list ship)
      ^+  event-core
      =?  ships  =(~ ships)  ~(tap in ~(key by peers.ames-state))
      |^  ^+  event-core
      ?~  ships  event-core
      $(ships t.ships, event-core (prod-peer i.ships))
      ::
      ++  prod-peer
        |=  her=ship
        ^+  event-core
        =/  par  (get-peer-state her)
        ?~  par  event-core
        =/  peer-core  (abed-peer:pe her u.par)
        =/  bones  ~(tap in ~(key by snd.u.par))
        |-  ^+  event-core
        ?~  bones      abet:peer-core
        =.  peer-core  abet:(call:(abed:mu:peer-core i.bones) %prod ~)
        $(bones t.bones)
      --
    ::  +on-cong: adjust congestion control parameters
    ::
    ++  on-cong
      |=  [msg=@ud mem=@ud]
      ^+  event-core
      =.  cong.ames-state  msg^mem
      event-core
    ::  +on-stir: recover from timer desync, setting new timers as needed
    ::
    ::    .arg can be %rift or %dead
    ::
    ++  on-stir
      |=  arg=@t
      ^+  event-core
      |^  ?+  arg  do-stir
            %rift  do-rift
            %dead  do-dead
          ==
      ::
      ++  do-dead
        =/  ded=(unit dead-timer)  +.flow.dead.ames-state
        ?^  ded
          %-  (slog leaf+"ames: turning off dead flow consolidation" ~)
          =.  event-core
            (omit:event-core duct.u.ded %pass wire.u.ded %b %rest date.u.ded)
          (wake-dead-flows:event-core ~)
        ::
        %-  (slog leaf+"ames: switching to dead flow consolidation" ~)
```

```
2029        =;   cor=event-core
2030          set-dead-flow-timer:(wake-dead-flows:cor ~)
2031        %-  ~(rep by peers.ames-state:event-core)
2032        |=  [[=ship =ship-state] core=_event-core]
2033        ^+  event-core
2034        =/  peer-state=(unit peer-state)  (get-peer-state:core ship)
2035        ?~  peer-state  core
2036        %-  ~(rep by snd.u.peer-state)
2037        |=  [[=bone =message-pump-state] cor=_core]
2038        ^+  event-core
2039        =/  next-wake  next-wake.packet-pump-state.message-pump-state
2040        ?.  ?&  =(~m2 rto.metrics.packet-pump-state.message-pump-state)
2041                ?=(^ next-wake)
2042            ==
2043          cor
2044        =/  peer-core  (abed-peer:pe:cor ship u.peer-state)
2045        =/  message-pump  (abed:mu:peer-core bone)
2046        abet:(pu-emit:packet-pump:message-pump %b %rest u.next-wake)
2047      ::
2048      ++  do-rift
2049        =/  =rift
2050          =-  ~|(%no-rift (,@ q.q:(need (need -))))
2051          (rof ~ /ames %j `beam`[[our %rift %da now] /(scot %p our)])
2052        ?:  =(rift rift.ames-state)
2053          event-core
2054        ~&  "ames: fixing rift from {<rift.ames-state>} to {<rift>}"
2055        event-core(ames-state ames-state(rift rift))
2056      ::
2057      ++  do-stir
2058        =/  want=(set [@da ^duct])
2059          %-  ~(rep by peers.ames-state)
2060          |=  [[who=ship s=ship-state] acc=(set [@da ^duct])]
2061          ?.  ?=(%known -.s)  acc
2062          %-  ~(rep by snd.+.s)
2063          |*  [[b=bone m=message-pump-state] acc=_acc]
2064          =*  tim  next-wake.packet-pump-state.m
2065          ?~  tim  acc
2066          %-  ~(put in acc)
2067          [u.tim `^duct`~[ames+(make-pump-timer-wire who b) /ames]]
2068        =.  want
2069          (~(put in want) (add now ~d1) ~[/ames/recork /ames])
2070        ::
2071        =/  have
2072          %-  ~(gas in *(set [@da ^duct]))
2073          =/  tim
2074            ;;  (list [@da ^duct])
2075            =<  q.q  %-  need  %-  need
2076            (rof ~ /ames %bx [[our %$ da+now] /debug/timers])
2077          (skim tim |=([@da hen=^duct] ?=([[%ames ?(%pump %recork) *] *] hen)))
2078        ::
2079        ::  set timers for flows that should have one set but don't
2080        ::
2081        =.  event-core
2082          %-  ~(rep in (~(dif in want) have))
2083          |=  [[wen=@da hen=^duct] this=_event-core]
2084          ?>  ?=([^ *] hen)
2085          (emit:this ~[/ames] %pass t.i.hen %b %wait wen)
2086        ::
```

```
2087        ::  cancel timers for flows that have one set but shouldn't
2088        ::
2089        %-  ~(rep in (~(dif in have) want))
2090        |=  [[wen=@da hen=^duct] this=_event-core]
2091        ?>  ?=([^ *] hen)
2092        (emit:this t.hen %pass t.i.hen %b %rest wen)
2093      --
2094    ::  +on-crud: handle event failure; print to dill
2095    ::
2096    ++  on-crud
2097      |=  =error
2098      ^+  event-core
2099      (emit duct %pass /crud %d %flog %crud error)
2100    ::  +on-heed: handle request to track .ship's responsiveness
2101    ::
2102    ++  on-heed
2103      |=  =ship
2104      ^+  event-core
2105      =/  ship-state  (~(get by peers.ames-state) ship)
2106      ?:  ?=([~ %known *] ship-state)
2107        abet:on-heed:(abed-peer:pe ship +.u.ship-state)
2108      %^  enqueue-alien-todo  ship  ship-state
2109      |=  todos=alien-agenda
2110      todos(heeds (~(put in heeds.todos) duct))
2111    ::  +on-jilt: handle request to stop tracking .ship's responsiveness
2112    ::
2113    ++  on-jilt
2114      |=  =ship
2115      ^+  event-core
2116      =/  ship-state  (~(get by peers.ames-state) ship)
2117      ?:  ?=([~ %known *] ship-state)
2118        abet:on-jilt:(abed-peer:pe ship +.u.ship-state)
2119      %^  enqueue-alien-todo  ship  ship-state
2120      |=  todos=alien-agenda
2121      todos(heeds (~(del in heeds.todos) duct))
2122    ::  +on-dear: handle lane from unix
2123    ::
2124    ++  on-dear
2125      |=  [=ship =lane]
2126      ^+  event-core
2127      ?:  ?=(%.y -.lane)
2128        event-core
2129      =/  ip=@if  (end [0 32] p.lane)
2130      =/  pt=@ud  (cut 0 [32 16] p.lane)
2131      ?:  =(%czar (clan:title ship))
2132        %-  %^  ev-trace  odd.veb  ship
2133            |.("ignoring %dear lane {(scow %if ip)}:{(scow %ud pt)} for galaxy")
2134        event-core
2135      =/  peer-state=(unit peer-state)  (get-peer-state ship)
2136      ?~  peer-state
2137        %-  %^  ev-trace  odd.veb  ship
2138            |.("no peer-state for ship, ignoring %dear")
2139        event-core
2140      %-  %^  ev-trace  rcv.veb  ship
2141          |.("incoming %dear lane {(scow %if ip)}:{(scow %ud pt)]")
2142      abet:(on-dear:(abed-peer:pe ship u.peer-state) lane)
2143    ::  +on-hear: handle raw packet receipt
2144    ::
```

```
++  on-hear
  |=  [l=lane b=blob d=(unit goof)]
  ^+  event-core
  =/  =shot       (sift-shot b)
  ?:  sam.shot  (on-hear-packet l shot d)
  ?:  req.shot  ~|([%fine %request-events-forbidden] !!)
  ::  TODO no longer true
  ::NOTE  we only send requests to ships we know,
  ::        so we should only get responses from ships we know.
  ::        below we assume sndr.shot is a known peer.
  =*  her  sndr.shot
  =+  ?~  d  ~
      %.  ~
      =*  mot  mote.u.d
      %+  slog  leaf+"ames: fine from {<her>} on {<l>} crashed {<mot>}"
      ?.  msg.veb  ~
      tang.u.d
  abet:(on-hear-fine:(abed-got:pe her) l shot)
::  +on-hear-packet: handle mildly processed packet receipt
::
++  on-hear-packet
  ~/  %on-hear-packet
  |=  [=lane =shot dud=(unit goof)]
  ^+  event-core
  %-  (ev-trace rcv.veb sndr.shot |.("received packet"))
  ::
  ?:  =(our sndr.shot)
    event-core
  ?:  .=  =(%deny form.snub.ames-state)
          (~(has in ships.snub.ames-state) sndr.shot)
    %-  (ev-trace rcv.veb sndr.shot |.("snubbed"))
    event-core
  ::
  %.  +<
  ::
  ?.  =(our rcvr.shot)
    on-hear-forward
  ::
  ?:  =(%keys content.shot)
    on-hear-keys
  ?:  ?&  ?=(%pawn (clan:title sndr.shot))
          !?=([~ %known *] (~(get by peers.ames-state) sndr.shot))
      ==
    on-hear-open
  on-hear-shut
::  +on-hear-forward: maybe forward a packet to someone else
::
::    Note that this performs all forwarding requests without
::    filtering.  Any protection against DDoS amplification will be
::    provided by Vere.
::
++  on-hear-forward
  ~/  %on-hear-forward
  |=  [=lane =shot dud=(unit goof)]
  ^+  event-core
  %-  %^  ev-trace  for.veb  sndr.shot
      |.("forward: {<sndr.shot>} -> {<rcvr.shot>}")
  ::  set .origin.shot if it doesn't have one, re-encode, and send
```

```
2203      ::
2204      =?    origin.shot
2205        &(?=(~ origin.shot) !=(%czar (clan:title sndr.shot)))
2206      ?:    ?=(%& -.lane)
2207        ~
2208      ?.  (lte (met 3 p.lane) 6)
2209        ~|  ames-lane-size+p.lane  !!
2210      `p.lane
2211      ::
2212      =/  =blob  (etch-shot shot)
2213      (send-blob for=& rcvr.shot blob (~(get by peers.ames-state) rcvr.shot))
2214      ::  +on-hear-keys: handle receipt of attestion request
2215      ::
2216      ++  on-hear-keys
2217      ~/  %on-hear-keys
2218      |=  [=lane =shot dud=(unit goof)]
2219      =+  %^  ev-trace  msg.veb  sndr.shot
2220          |.("requested attestation")
2221      ?.  =(%pawn (clan:title our))
2222        event-core
2223      =/  =blob  (attestation-packet sndr.shot 1)
2224      (send-blob for=| sndr.shot blob (~(get by peers.ames-state) sndr.shot))
2225      ::  +on-hear-open: handle receipt of plaintext comet self-attestation
2226      ::
2227      ++  on-hear-open
2228      ~/  %on-hear-open
2229      |=  [=lane =shot dud=(unit goof)]
2230      ^+  event-core
2231      =+  %^  ev-trace  msg.veb  sndr.shot
2232          |.("got attestation")
2233      ::  assert the comet can't pretend to be a moon or other address
2234      ::
2235      ?>  ?=(%pawn (clan:title sndr.shot))
2236      ::  if we already know .sndr, ignore duplicate attestation
2237      ::
2238      =/  ship-state  (~(get by peers.ames-state) sndr.shot)
2239      ?:  ?=([~ %known *] ship-state)
2240        event-core
2241      ::
2242      =/  =open-packet  (sift-open-packet shot our life.ames-state)
2243      ::  add comet as an %alien if we haven't already
2244      ::
2245      =?  peers.ames-state  ?=(~ ship-state)
2246        (~(put by peers.ames-state) sndr.shot %alien *alien-agenda)
2247      ::  upgrade comet to %known via on-publ-full
2248      ::
2249      =.  event-core
2250        =/  crypto-suite=@ud  1
2251        =/  keys
2252          (my [sndr-life.open-packet crypto-suite public-key.open-packet]~)
2253        =/  =point
2254          :*  ^=     rift  0
2255              ^=     life  sndr-life.open-packet
2256              ^=     keys  keys
2257              ^=     sponsor  `(^sein:title sndr.shot)
2258          ==
2259        (on-publ / [%full (my [sndr.shot point]~)])
2260      ::  manually add the lane to the peer state
```

```
2261          ::
2262          =.  peers.ames-state
2263            =/  =peer-state  (gut-peer-state sndr.shot)
2264            =.  route.peer-state  `[direct=%.n lane]
2265            (~(put by peers.ames-state) sndr.shot %known peer-state)
2266          ::
2267        event-core
2268      ::  +on-hear-shut: handle receipt of encrypted packet
2269      ::
2270      ++  on-hear-shut
2271        ~/  %on-hear-shut
2272        |=  [=lane =shot dud=(unit goof)]
2273        ^+  event-core
2274        =/  sndr-state  (~(get by peers.ames-state) sndr.shot)
2275        ::  If we don't know them, ask Jael for their keys. If they're a
2276        ::  comet, this will also cause us to request a self-attestation
2277        ::  from the sender. The packet itself is dropped; we can assume it
2278        ::  will be resent.
2279        ::
2280        ?.  ?=([~ %known *] sndr-state)
2281          (enqueue-alien-todo sndr.shot sndr-state |=(alien-agenda +<))
2282        ::  decrypt packet contents using symmetric-key.channel
2283        ::
2284        ::    If we know them, we have a $channel with them, which we've
2285        ::    populated with a .symmetric-key derived from our private key
2286        ::    and their public key using elliptic curve Diffie-Hellman.
2287        ::
2288        =/  =peer-state  +.u.sndr-state
2289        =/  =channel    [[our sndr.shot] now channel-state -.peer-state]
2290        =?  event-core  !=(sndr-tick.shot (mod her-life.channel 16))
2291          %.  event-core
2292          %^  ev-trace  odd.veb  sndr.shot
2293          |.  ^-  tape
2294          =/  sndr  [sndr-tick=sndr-tick.shot her-life=her-life.channel]
2295          "sndr-tick mismatch {<sndr>}"
2296        =?  event-core  !=(rcvr-tick.shot (mod our-life.channel 16))
2297          %.  event-core
2298          %^  ev-trace  odd.veb  sndr.shot
2299          |.  ^-  tape
2300          =/  rcvr  [rcvr-tick=rcvr-tick.shot our-life=our-life.channel]
2301          "rcvr-tick mismatch {<rcvr>}"
2302        ~|  %ames-crash-on-packet-from^her.channel
2303        =/  shut-packet=(unit shut-packet)
2304          (sift-shut-packet shot [symmetric-key her-life our-life]:channel)
2305        ?~  shut-packet
2306          event-core
2307        ::  non-galaxy: update route with heard lane or forwarded lane
2308        ::
2309        =?  route.peer-state  !=(%czar (clan:title her.channel))
2310          ::  if new packet is direct, use that.  otherwise, if the new new
2311          ::  and old lanes are indirect, use the new one.  if the new lane
2312          ::  is indirect but the old lane is direct, then if the lanes are
2313          ::  identical, don't mark it indirect; if they're not identical,
2314          ::  use the new lane and mark it indirect.
2315          ::
2316          ::  if you mark lane as indirect because you got an indirect
2317          ::  packet even though you already had a direct identical lane,
2318          ::  then delayed forwarded packets will come later and reset to
```

```
2319        ::  indirect, so you're unlikely to get a stable direct route
2320        ::  (unless the forwarder goes offline for a while).
2321        ::
2322        ::  conversely, if you don't accept indirect routes with different
2323        ::  lanes, then if your lane is stale and they're trying to talk
2324        ::  to you, your acks will go to the stale lane, and you'll never
2325        ::  time it out unless you reach out to them.  this manifests as
2326        ::  needing to |hi or dotpost to get a response when the other
2327        ::  ship has changed lanes.
2328        ::
2329        ?:  ?=(~ origin.shot)
2330          `[direct=%.y lane]
2331        ?:  ?=([~ %& *] route.peer-state)
2332          ?:  =(lane.u.route.peer-state |+u.origin.shot)
2333            route.peer-state
2334          `[direct=%.n |+u.origin.shot]
2335        `[direct=%.n |+u.origin.shot]
2336      ::  perform peer-specific handling of packet
2337      ::
2338      =<  abet
2339      (~(on-hear-shut-packet pe peer-state channel) [lane u.shut-packet dud])
2340    ::  +on-take-boon: receive request to give message to peer
2341    ::
2342    ++  on-take-boon
2343      |=  [=wire payload=*]
2344      ^+  event-core
2345      ?~  parsed=(parse-bone-wire wire)
2346        ~>  %slog.0^leaf/"ames: dropping malformed wire: {(spud wire)}"
2347        event-core
2348      ::
2349      ?>  ?=([@ her=ship *] u.parsed)
2350      =*  her         her.u.parsed
2351      =/  peer-core   (abed-got:pe her)
2352      ::
2353      ?:  ?&  ?=([%new *] u.parsed)
2354              (lth rift.u.parsed rift.peer-state.peer-core)
2355          ==
2356        ::  ignore events from an old rift
2357        ::
2358        %-  %^  ev-trace  odd.veb  her
2359            |.("dropping old rift wire: {(spud wire)}")
2360        event-core
2361      =/  =bone
2362        ?-(u.parsed [%new *] bone.u.parsed, [%old *] bone.u.parsed)
2363      =?  peer-core   ?=([%old *] u.parsed)
2364        %-  %^  ev-trace  odd.veb  her
2365            |.("parsing old wire: {(spud wire)}")
2366        peer-core
2367      abet:(on-memo:peer-core bone payload %boon)
2368    ::  +on-plea: handle request to send message
2369    ::
2370    ++  on-plea
2371      |=  [=ship =plea]
2372      ^+  event-core
2373      =/  ship-state  (~(get by peers.ames-state) ship)
2374      ::
2375      ?.  ?=([~ %known *] ship-state)
2376        %^  enqueue-alien-todo  ship  ship-state
```

```
2377                |=  todos=alien-agenda
2378                todos(messages [[duct plea] messages.todos])
2379              ::
2380            =+  peer-core=(abed-peer:pe ship +.u.ship-state)
2381            ::  .plea is from local vane to foreign ship
2382              ::
2383            =^  =bone  peer-core  (bind-duct:peer-core duct)
2384          %-  %^  ev-trace  msg.veb  ship
2385              |.  ^-  tape
2386            =/  sndr  [our our-life.channel.peer-core]
2387            =/  rcvr  [ship her-life.channel.peer-core]
2388            "plea {<sndr rcvr bone=bone vane.plea path.plea>}"
2389        abet:(on-memo:peer-core bone plea %plea)
2390      ::  +on-tame: handle request to delete a route
2391      ::
2392      ++  on-tame
2393        |=  =ship
2394        ^+  event-core
2395        ?:  =(%czar (clan:title ship))
2396          %-  %+  slog
2397            leaf+"ames: bad idea to %tame galaxy {(scow %p ship)}, ignoring"
2398            ~
2399          event-core
2400        =/  peer-state=(unit peer-state)  (get-peer-state ship)
2401        ?~  peer-state
2402          %-  (slog leaf+"ames: no peer-state for {(scow %p ship)}, ignoring" ~)
2403          event-core
2404        abet:on-tame:(abed-peer:pe ship u.peer-state)
2405      ::  +on-cork: handle request to kill a flow
2406      ::
2407      ++  on-cork
2408        |=  =ship
2409        ^+  event-core
2410        =/  =plea        [%$ /flow [%cork ~]]
2411        =/  ship-state  (~(get by peers.ames-state) ship)
2412        ?.  ?=([~ %known *] ship-state)
2413          %^  enqueue-alien-todo  ship  ship-state
2414          |=  todos=alien-agenda
2415          todos(messages [[duct plea] messages.todos])
2416        ::
2417        =+  peer-core=(abed-peer:pe ship +.u.ship-state)
2418        =^  =bone  peer-core
2419          ?^  cork-bone  [u.cork-bone peer-core]
2420          (bind-duct:peer-core duct)
2421        ::
2422        ?.  (~(has by by-bone.ossuary.peer-state.peer-core) bone)
2423          %.  event-core
2424          %^  ev-trace  odd.veb  ship
2425          |.("trying to cork {<bone=bone>}, not in the ossuary, ignoring")
2426        ::
2427        %-  %^  ev-trace  msg.veb  ship
2428            |.  ^-  tape
2429          =/  sndr  [our our-life.channel.peer-core]
2430          =/  rcvr  [ship her-life.channel.peer-core]
2431          "cork plea {<sndr rcvr bone=bone vane.plea path.plea>}"
2432        abet:(on-memo:(on-cork-flow:peer-core bone) bone plea %plea)
2433      ::  +on-kroc: cork all stale flows from failed subscriptions
2434      ::
```

```
2435    ++  on-kroc
2436      |=  bones=(list [ship bone])
2437      ^+  event-core
2438      %+  roll  bones
2439      |=  [[=ship =bone] co=_event-core]
2440      (%*(on-cork co cork-bone `bone) ship)
2441    ::  +on-deep: deferred %ames calls from itself
2442    ::
2443    ++  on-deep
2444      |=  =deep
2445      ^+  event-core
2446      ::  currently $deep tasks are all focused on a
2447      ::  particular ship but future ones might not
2448      ::
2449      ?>  ?=([@ =ship *] deep)
2450      =/  ship-state  (~(get by peers.ames-state) ship.deep)
2451      ?>  ?=([~ %known *] ship-state)
2452      =+  peer-core=(abed-peer:pe ship.deep +.u.ship-state)
2453      |^  ?-  -.deep
2454        %nack  abet:(send-nack-trace [nack-bone message-blob]:deep)
2455        %sink  abet:(sink-naxplanation [target-bone naxplanation]:deep)
2456        %drop  abet:(clear-nack [nack-bone message-num]:deep)
2457        %cork  =~((cork-bone bone.deep) (emit duct %give %done ~))
2458        %kill  (kill-bone bone.deep)
2459      ==
2460      ::
2461      ++  send-nack-trace
2462        |=  [=nack=bone =message-blob]
2463        abet:(call:(abed:mu:peer-core nack-bone) %memo message-blob)
2464      ::
2465      ++  sink-naxplanation
2466        |=  [=target=bone =naxplanation]
2467        abet:(call:(abed:mu:peer-core target-bone) %near naxplanation)
2468      ::
2469      ++  clear-nack
2470        |=  [=nack=bone =message-num]
2471        abet:(call:(abed:mi:peer-core nack-bone) %drop message-num)
2472      ::  client ames [%cork as plea] ->  server ames [sinks %cork plea],
2473      ::                                  pass %deep %cork task to self
2474      ::                                  put flow in closing (+cork-bone),
2475      ::                                  and give %done
2476      ::  sink %ack, pass %deep %kill <-  after +on-take-done, ack %cork plea
2477      ::  task to self, and delete the    and delete the flow in +handle-cork
2478      ::  flow (+kill-bone)
2479      ::
2480      ::
2481      ++  cork-bone  |=(=bone abet:(on-cork-flow:peer-core bone))
2482      ++  kill-bone  |=(=bone abet:(on-kill-flow:peer-core bone))
2483      --
2484    ::  +set-dead-flow-timer: set dead flow timer and corresponding ames state
2485    ::
2486    ++  set-dead-flow-timer
2487      ^+  event-core
2488      =.  flow.dead.ames-state.event-core
2489        flow/`[~[/ames] /dead-flow `@da`(add now ~m2)]
2490      (emit:event-core ~[/ames] %pass /dead-flow %b %wait `@da`(add now ~m2))
2491    ::  +wake-dead-flows: call on-wake on all dead flows, discarding any
2492    ::                     ames-state changes
```

```
2493        ::
2494        ++  wake-dead-flows
2495        |=  [error=(unit tang)]
2496        ^+  event-core
2497        %-  ~(rep by peers.ames-state:event-core)
2498        |=  [[=ship =ship-state] core=_event-core]
2499        ^+  event-core
2500        =/  peer-state=(unit peer-state)  (get-peer-state:core ship)
2501        ?~  peer-state  core
2502        =/  peer-core  (abed-peer:pe:core ship u.peer-state)
2503        =<  abort
2504        ^+  peer-core
2505        %-  ~(rep by snd.u.peer-state)
2506        |=  [[=bone =message-pump-state] cor=_peer-core]
2507        ?.  ?&  =(~m2 rto.metrics.packet-pump-state.message-pump-state)
2508                ?=(^ next-wake.packet-pump-state.message-pump-state)
2509            ==
2510          cor
2511        (on-wake:cor bone error)
2512        ::  +on-take-wake: receive wakeup or error notification from behn
2513        ::
2514        ++  on-take-wake
2515        |=  [=wire error=(unit tang)]
2516        ^+  event-core
2517        ?:  ?=([%alien @ ~] wire)
2518          ::  if we haven't received an attestation, ask again
2519          ::
2520          ?^  error
2521            %-  (slog 'ames: attestation timer failed' u.error)
2522            event-core
2523          ?~  ship=`(unit @p)`(slaw %p i.t.wire)
2524            %-  (slog leaf+"ames: got timer for strange wire: {<wire>}" ~)
2525            event-core
2526          =/  ship-state  (~(get by peers.ames-state) u.ship)
2527          ?:  ?=([~ %known *] ship-state)
2528            event-core
2529          (request-attestation u.ship)
2530        ::
2531        ?:  ?=([%dead-flow ~] wire)
2532          set-dead-flow-timer:(wake-dead-flows error)
2533        ::
2534        ?.  ?=([%recork ~] wire)
2535          =/  res=(unit ?([%fine her=ship =^wire] [%pump her=ship =bone]))
2536            ?+  wire   ~
2537              [%pump ship=@ bone=@ ~]  (parse-pump-wire &2.wire &3.wire)
2538              [%fine %behn %wake @ *]  (parse-fine-wire &4.wire t.t.t.t.wire)
2539            ==
2540          ?~  res
2541            %-  (slog leaf+"ames: got timer for strange wire: {<wire>}" ~)
2542            event-core
2543          ::
2544          =/  state=(unit peer-state)  (get-peer-state her.u.res)
2545          ?~  state
2546            %.  event-core
2547            %-  slog
2548            [leaf+"ames: got timer for strange ship: {<her.u.res>}, ignoring" ~]
2549          ::
2550          =/  peer-core  (abed-peer:pe her.u.res u.state)
```

```
2551        ?-  -.u.res
2552          %pump  abet:(on-wake:peer-core bone.u.res error)
2553          ::
2554            %fine
2555          ?.  (~(has by keens.peer-state.peer-core) wire.u.res)
2556            event-core
2557          abet:fi-abet:fi-take-wake:(abed:fi:peer-core wire.u.res)
2558        ==
2559      ::
2560      =.  event-core  (emit duct %pass /recork %b %wait `@da`(add now ~d1))
2561      =.  cork.dead.ames-state
2562        cork/`[~[/ames] /recork `@da`(add now ~d1)]
2563      ::
2564      ?^  error
2565        %-  (slog 'ames: recork timer failed' u.error)
2566        event-core
2567      ::  recork up to one bone per peer
2568      ::
2569      =/  pez  ~(tap by peers.ames-state)
2570      |-  ^+  event-core
2571      ?~  pez  event-core
2572      =+  [her sat]=i.pez
2573      ?.  ?=(%known -.sat)
2574        $(pez t.pez)
2575      $(pez t.pez, event-core abet:recork-one:(abed-peer:pe her +.sat))
2576    ::  +on-init: first boot; subscribe to our info from jael
2577    ::
2578    ++  on-init
2579      ^+  event-core
2580      ::
2581      =~  (emit duct %pass /turf %j %turf ~)
2582          (emit duct %pass /private-keys %j %private-keys ~)
2583          (emit duct %pass /public-keys %j %public-keys [n=our ~ ~])
2584      ==
2585    ::  +on-priv: set our private key to jael's response
2586    ::
2587    ++  on-priv
2588      |=  [=life vein=(map life private-key)]
2589      ^+  event-core
2590      ::
2591      =/  =private-key          (~(got by vein) life)
2592      =.  life.ames-state       life
2593      =.  crypto-core.ames-state  (nol:nu:crub:crypto private-key)
2594      ::  recalculate each peer's symmetric key
2595      ::
2596      =/  our-private-key  sec:ex:crypto-core.ames-state
2597      =.  peers.ames-state
2598        %-  ~(run by peers.ames-state)
2599        |=  =ship-state
2600        ^+  ship-state
2601        ::
2602        ?.  ?=(%known -.ship-state)
2603          ship-state
2604        ::
2605        =/  =peer-state  +.ship-state
2606        =.  symmetric-key.peer-state
2607          (derive-symmetric-key public-key.+.ship-state our-private-key)
2608        ::
```

```
2609                    [%known peer-state]
2610            ::
2611          event-core
2612    ::  +on-publ: update pki data for peer or self
2613    ::
2614    ++  on-publ
2615      |=  [=wire =public-keys-result]
2616      ^+  event-core
2617      ::
2618      |^  ^+  event-core
2619          ::
2620          ?-    public-keys-result
2621              [%diff @ %rift *]
2622            (on-publ-rift [who to.diff]:public-keys-result)
2623          ::
2624              [%diff @ %keys *]
2625            (on-publ-rekey [who to.diff]:public-keys-result)
2626          ::
2627              [%diff @ %spon *]
2628            (on-publ-sponsor [who to.diff]:public-keys-result)
2629          ::
2630              [%full *]
2631            (on-publ-full points.public-keys-result)
2632          ::
2633              [%breach *]
2634            (on-publ-breach who.public-keys-result)
2635          ==
2636      ::  +on-publ-breach: handle continuity breach of .ship; wipe its state
2637      ::
2638      ::    Abandon all pretense of continuity and delete all messaging state
2639      ::    associated with .ship, including sent and unsent messages.
2640      ::    Also cancel all timers related to .ship.
2641      ::
2642      ++  on-publ-breach
2643        |=  =ship
2644        ^+  event-core
2645        ?:  =(our ship)
2646          event-core
2647        ::
2648        =/  ship-state  (~(get by peers.ames-state) ship)
2649        ::  we shouldn't be hearing about ships we don't care about
2650        ::
2651        ?~  ship-state
2652          ~>  %slog.0^leaf/"ames: breach unknown {<our ship>}"
2653          event-core
2654        ::  if an alien breached, this doesn't affect us
2655        ::
2656        ?:  ?=([~ %alien *] ship-state)
2657          ~>  %slog.0^leaf/"ames: breach alien {<our ship>}"
2658          event-core
2659        ~>  %slog.0^leaf/"ames: breach peer {<our ship>}"
2660        ::  a peer breached; drop messaging state
2661        ::
2662        =/  =peer-state  +.u.ship-state
2663        =/  old-qos=qos  qos.peer-state
2664        ::  cancel all timers related to .ship
2665        ::
2666        =.  event-core
```

```
2667        %+    roll   ~(tap by snd.peer-state)
2668        |=    [[=snd=bone =message-pump-state] core=_event-core]
2669        ^+    core
2670        ::
2671        ?~    next-wake=next-wake.packet-pump-state.message-pump-state
2672          core
2673        ::  note: copies +on-pump-rest:message-pump
2674        ::
2675        =/    wire   (make-pump-timer-wire ship snd-bone)
2676        =/    duct   ~[/ames]
2677      (emit:core duct %pass wire %b %rest u.next-wake)
2678    ::  reset all peer state other than pki data
2679    ::
2680      =.    +.peer-state   +:*^peer-state
2681    ::  print change to quality of service, if any
2682    ::
2683      =/    text=(unit tape)
2684        %^    qos-update-text   ship   %ames
2685        [old-qos qos.peer-state kay.veb ships.bug.ames-state]
2686      ::
2687      =?    event-core   ?=(^ text)
2688        (emit duct %pass /qos %d %flog %text u.text)
2689      ::  reinitialize galaxy route if applicable
2690      ::
2691      =?    route.peer-state   =(%czar (clan:title ship))
2692        `[direct=%.y lane=[%& ship]]
2693      ::
2694      =.    peers.ames-state
2695        (~(put by peers.ames-state) ship [%known peer-state])
2696      ::
2697      event-core
2698  ::  +on-publ-rekey: handle new key for peer
2699  ::
2700  ::    TODO: assert .crypto-suite compatibility
2701  ::
2702  ++  on-publ-rekey
2703    |=  $:  =ship
2704            =life
2705            crypto-suite=@ud
2706            =public-key
2707        ==
2708    ^+  event-core
2709    ?:  =(our ship)
2710      event-core
2711    ::
2712    =/  ship-state  (~(get by peers.ames-state) ship)
2713    ?.  ?=([~ %known *] ship-state)
2714      =|  =point
2715      =.  life.point     life
2716      =.  keys.point     (my [life crypto-suite public-key]~)
2717      =.  sponsor.point  `(^^sein:title rof /ames our now ship)
2718      ::
2719      (on-publ-full (my [ship point]~))
2720    ::
2721    =/  =peer-state  !.u.ship-state
2722    =/  =private-key  sec:ex:crypto-core.ames-state
2723    =.  symmetric-key.peer-state
2724      (derive-symmetric-key public-key private-key)
```

```
2725          ::
2726          =.  life.peer-state        life
2727          =.  public-key.peer-state  public-key
2728          ::
2729          =.  peers.ames-state
2730          (~(put by peers.ames-state) ship %known peer-state)
2731        event-core
2732      ::  +on-publ-sponsor: handle new or lost sponsor for peer
2733      ::
2734      ::    TODO: really handle sponsor loss
2735      ::
2736      ++  on-publ-sponsor
2737        |=  [=ship sponsor=(unit ship)]
2738        ^+  event-core
2739        ::
2740        ?:  =(our ship)
2741          event-core
2742        ::
2743        ?~  sponsor
2744          %-  (slog leaf+"ames: {(scow %p ship)} lost sponsor, ignoring" ~)
2745          event-core
2746        ::
2747        =/  state=(unit peer-state)  (get-peer-state ship)
2748        ?~  state
2749          %-  (slog leaf+"ames: missing peer-state, ignoring" ~)
2750          event-core
2751        =.  sponsor.u.state  u.sponsor
2752        =.  peers.ames-state  (~(put by peers.ames-state) ship %known u.state)
2753        event-core
2754      ::  +on-publ-full: handle new pki data for peer(s)
2755      ::
2756      ++  on-publ-full
2757        |=  points=(map ship point)
2758        ^+  event-core
2759        ::
2760        =>  .(points ~(tap by points))
2761        |^  ^+  event-core
2762          ?~  points  event-core
2763          ::
2764          =+  ^-  [=ship =point]  i.points
2765          ::
2766          ?:  =(our ship)
2767            =.  rift.ames-state  rift.point
2768            $(points t.points)
2769          ::
2770          ?.  (~(has by keys.point) life.point)
2771            $(points t.points)
2772          ::
2773          =/  old-ship-state  (~(get by peers.ames-state) ship)
2774          ::
2775          =.  event-core  (insert-peer-state ship point)
2776          ::
2777          =?  event-core  ?=([~ %alien *] old-ship-state)
2778            (meet-alien ship point +.u.old-ship-state)
2779          ::
2780          $(points t.points)
2781        ::
2782        ++  meet-alien
```

```
2783            |=  [=ship =point todos=alien-agenda]
2784            |^  ^+  event-core
2785            ::  if we're a comet, send self-attestation packet first
2786            ::
2787            =?  event-core  =(%pawn (clan:title our))
2788              =/  =blob  (attestation-packet ship life.point)
2789              (send-blob for=| ship blob (~(get by peers.ames-state) ship))
2790            ::  save current duct
2791            ::
2792            =/  original-duct  duct
2793            ::  apply heeds
2794            ::
2795            =.  event-core
2796              %+  roll  ~(tap in heeds.todos)
2797              |=  [=^duct core=_event-core]
2798              (on-heed:core(duct duct) ship)
2799            ::  apply outgoing messages, reversing for FIFO order
2800            ::
2801            =.  event-core
2802              %+  reel  messages.todos
2803              |=  [[=^duct =plea] core=_event-core]
2804              ?:  ?=(%$ -.plea)
2805                (on-cork:core(duct duct) ship)
2806              (on-plea:core(duct duct) ship plea)
2807            ::  apply outgoing packet blobs
2808            ::
2809            =.  event-core
2810              %+  roll  ~(tap in packets.todos)
2811              |=  [=blob core=_event-core]
2812              (send-blob:core for=| ship blob (~(get by peers.ames-state) ship))
2813            ::  apply remote scry requests
2814            ::
2815            =.  event-core  (meet-alien-fine keens.todos)
2816            ::
2817            event-core(duct original-duct)
2818            ::
2819          ++  meet-alien-fine
2820            |=  peens=(jug path ^duct)
2821            ^+  event-core
2822            =+  peer-core=(abed:pe ship)
2823            =<  abet  ^+  peer-core
2824            %-  ~(rep by peens)
2825            |=  [[=path ducts=(set ^duct)] cor=_peer-core]
2826            (~(rep in ducts) |=([=^duct c=_cor] (on-keen:c path duct)))
2827          --
2828        --
2829    ::  on-publ-rift: XX
2830    ::
2831    ++  on-publ-rift
2832      |=  [=ship =rift]
2833      ^+  event-core
2834      ?:  =(our ship)
2835        =.  rift.ames-state  rift
2836        event-core
2837      ?~  ship-state=(~(get by peers.ames-state) ship)
2838        ::  print error here? %rift was probably called before %keys
2839        ::
2840        ~>  %slog.1^leaf/"ames: missing peer-state on-publ-rift"
```

```
2841            event-core
2842        ?:  ?=([%alien *] u.ship-state)
2843          ::  ignore aliens
2844          ::
2845          event-core
2846      =/  =peer-state      +.u.ship-state
2847      =.  rift.peer-state  rift
2848      =.  peers.ames-state
2849        (~(put by peers.ames-state) ship %known peer-state)
2850      event-core
2851      ::
2852    ++  insert-peer-state
2853    |=  [=ship =point]
2854    ^+  event-core
2855      ::
2856    =/  =peer-state     (gut-peer-state ship)
2857    =/  =public-key     pass:(~(got by keys.point) life.point)
2858    =/  =private-key    sec:ex:crypto-core.ames-state
2859    =/  =symmetric-key  (derive-symmetric-key public-key private-key)
2860      ::
2861    =.  qos.peer-state           [%unborn now]
2862    =.  life.peer-state          life.point
2863    =.  rift.peer-state          rift.point
2864    =.  public-key.peer-state    public-key
2865    =.  symmetric-key.peer-state symmetric-key
2866    =.  sponsor.peer-state
2867      ?^  sponsor.point
2868        u.sponsor.point
2869      (^^sein:title rof /ames our now ship)
2870      ::  automatically set galaxy route, since unix handles lookup
2871      ::
2872    =?  route.peer-state  ?=(%czar (clan:title ship))
2873      `[direct=%.y lane=[%& ship]]
2874      ::
2875    =.  peers.ames-state
2876      (~(put by peers.ames-state) ship %known peer-state)
2877      ::
2878    event-core
2879    --
2880  ::  +on-take-turf: relay %turf move from jael to unix
2881  ::
2882  ++  on-take-turf
2883  |=  turfs=(list turf)
2884  ^+  event-core
2885    ::
2886  (emit unix-duct.ames-state %give %turf turfs)
2887  ::  +on-born: handle unix process restart
2888  ::
2889  ++  on-born
2890    ^+  event-core
2891    ::
2892    =.  unix-duct.ames-state  duct
2893    ::
2894    =/  turfs
2895      ;;  (list turf)
2896      =<  q.q  %-  need  %-  need
2897      (rof ~ /ames %j `beam`[[our %turf %da now] /])
2898    ::
```

```
2899      =*  duct  unix-duct.ames-state
2900      ::
2901      =^  cork-moves  cork.dead.ames-state
2902        ?.  ?=(~ +.cork.dead.ames-state)
2903          `cork.dead.ames-state
2904        :-  [~[/ames] %pass /recork %b %wait `@da`(add now ~d1)]~
2905        cork/`[~[/ames] /recork `@da`(add now ~d1)]
2906      ::
2907      %-  emil
2908      %+  weld
2909        cork-moves
2910      ^-  (list move)
2911      :~  [duct %give %turf turfs]
2912          [duct %pass /ping %g %deal [our our /ames] %ping %poke %noun !>(%kick)]
2913      ==
2914    ::  +on-vega: handle kernel reload
2915    ::
2916    ++  on-vega  event-core
2917    ::  +on-trim: handle request to free memory
2918    ::
2919    ::    %ruin comets not seen for six months
2920    ::
2921    ++  on-trim     ::TODO  trim fine parts on high prio
2922      ^+  event-core
2923      =;  rui=(set @p)
2924        (emit duct %pass /ruin %j %ruin rui)
2925      =-  (silt (turn - head))
2926      %+  skim
2927        ~(tap by peers.ames-state)
2928      |=  [=ship s=ship-state]
2929      ?.  &(?=(%known -.s) =(%pawn (clan:title ship)))  %.n
2930      ?&  (gth (sub now ~d180) last-contact.qos.s)
2931          ::
2932          %-  ~(any by snd.s)
2933          |=  m=message-pump-state
2934          !=(~ unsent-fragments.m)
2935      ==
2936    ::
2937    +|  %fine-entry-points
2938    ::
2939    ++  on-keen
2940      |=  spar
2941      ^+  event-core
2942      =+  ~:(spit path)  ::  assert length
2943      =/  ship-state  (~(get by peers.ames-state) ship)
2944      ?:  ?=([~ %known *] ship-state)
2945        abet:(on-keen:(abed-peer:pe ship +.u.ship-state) path duct)
2946      %^  enqueue-alien-todo  ship  ship-state
2947      |=  todos=alien-agenda
2948      todos(keens (~(put ju keens.todos) path duct))
2949    ::
2950    ++  on-cancel-scry
2951      |=  [all=? spar]
2952      ^+  event-core
2953      ?~  ship-state=(~(get by peers.ames-state) ship)
2954        ~|(%cancel-scry-missing-peer^ship^path !!)
2955      ?.  ?=([~ %known *] ship-state)
2956        :: XX delete from alien agenda?
```

```
2957            %.   event-core
2958            %^   trace-fine  fin.veb  ship
2959            [ships.bug.ames-state |.("peer still alien, skip cancel-scry")]
2960         =+  peer=(abed:pe ship)
2961         ?.  (~(has by keens.peer-state.peer) path)
2962            event-core
2963         abet:fi-abet:(fi-unsub:(abed:fi:peer path) duct all)
2964      ::
2965      +|  %implementation
2966      ::  +enqueue-alien-todo: helper to enqueue a pending request
2967      ::
2968      ::    Also requests key and life from Jael on first request.
2969      ::    If talking to a comet, requests attestation packet.
2970      ::
2971      ++  enqueue-alien-todo
2972        |=  $:  =ship
2973                ship-state=(unit ship-state)
2974                mutate=$-(alien-agenda alien-agenda)
2975            ==
2976        ^+  event-core
2977        ::  create a default $alien-agenda on first contact
2978        ::
2979        =+  ^-  [already-pending=? todos=alien-agenda]
2980        ?~  ship-state
2981          [%.n *alien-agenda]
2982        [%.y ?>(?=(%alien -.u.ship-state) +.u.ship-state)]
2983        ::  mutate .todos and apply to permanent state
2984        ::
2985        =.  todos            (mutate todos)
2986        =.  peers.ames-state  (~(put by peers.ames-state) ship %alien todos)
2987        ?:  already-pending
2988          event-core
2989        ::
2990        ?:  =(%pawn (clan:title ship))
2991          (request-attestation ship)
2992        ::  NB: we specifically look for this wire in +public-keys-give in
2993        ::  Jael.  if you change it here, you must change it there.
2994        ::
2995        (emit duct %pass /public-keys %j %public-keys [n=ship ~ ~])
2996      ::  +request-attestation: helper to request attestation from comet
2997      ::
2998      ::    Also sets a timer to resend the request every 30s.
2999      ::
3000      ++  request-attestation
3001        |=  =ship
3002        ^+  event-core
3003        =+  (ev-trace msg.veb ship |.("requesting attestion"))
3004        =.  event-core
3005        =/  =blob  (sendkeys-packet ship)
3006        (send-blob for=| ship blob (~(get by peers.ames-state) ship))
3007        =/  =wire  /alien/(scot %p ship)
3008        (emit duct %pass wire %b %wait (add now ~s30))
3009      ::  +send-blob: fire packet at .ship and maybe sponsors
3010      ::
3011      ::    Send to .ship and sponsors until we find a direct lane,
3012      ::    skipping .our in the sponsorship chain.
3013      ::
3014      ::    If we have no PKI data for a recipient, enqueue the packet and
```

```
3015      ::    request the information from Jael if we haven't already.
3016      ::
3017    ++  send-blob
3018      ~/  %send-blob
3019      |=  [for=? =ship =blob ship-state=(unit ship-state)]
3020      ::
3021      =/  final-ship  ship
3022      %-  (ev-trace rot.veb final-ship |.("send-blob: to {<ship>}"))
3023      |-
3024      |^  ^+  event-core
3025          ?.  ?=([~ %known *] ship-state)
3026            ?:  ?=(%pawn (clan:title ship))
3027              (try-next-sponsor (^sein:title ship))
3028            %^  enqueue-alien-todo  ship  ship-state
3029            |=  todos=alien-agenda
3030            todos(packets (~(put in packets.todos) blob))
3031          ::
3032          =/  =peer-state  +.u.ship-state
3033          ::
3034          ::  XX  routing hack to mimic old ames.
3035          ::
3036          ::    Before removing this, consider: moons when their planet is
3037          ::    behind a NAT; a planet receiving initial acknowledgment
3038          ::    from a star; a planet talking to another planet under
3039          ::    another galaxy.
3040          ::
3041          ?:  ?|  =(our ship)
3042                  ?&  !=(final-ship ship)
3043                      !=(%czar (clan:title ship))
3044                  ==
3045              ==
3046            (try-next-sponsor sponsor.peer-state)
3047          ::
3048          ?:  =(our ship)
3049            ::  if forwarding, don't send to sponsor to avoid loops
3050            ::
3051            ?:  for
3052              event-core
3053            (try-next-sponsor sponsor.peer-state)
3054          ::
3055          ?~  route=route.peer-state
3056            %-  (ev-trace rot.veb final-ship |.("no route to:  {<ship>}"))
3057            (try-next-sponsor sponsor.peer-state)
3058          ::
3059          %-  (ev-trace rot.veb final-ship |.("trying route: {<ship>}"))
3060          =.  event-core
3061            (emit unix-duct.ames-state %give %send lane.u.route blob)
3062          ::
3063          ?:  direct.u.route
3064            event-core
3065          (try-next-sponsor sponsor.peer-state)
3066      ::
3067    ++  try-next-sponsor
3068      |=  sponsor=^ship
3069      ^+  event-core
3070      ::
3071      ?:  =(ship sponsor)
3072        event-core
```

```
3073            ^$(ship sponsor, ship-state (~(get by peers.ames-state) sponsor))
3074        --
3075    ::  +attestation-packet: generate signed self-attestation for .her
3076    ::
3077    ::      Sent by a comet on first contact with a peer.  Not acked.
3078    ::
3079    ++  attestation-packet
3080      |=  [her=ship =her=life]
3081      ^-  blob
3082      %-  etch-shot
3083      %-  etch-open-packet
3084      :_  crypto-core.ames-state
3085      :*  ^=  public-key  pub:ex:crypto-core.ames-state
3086          ^=        sndr  our
3087          ^=   sndr-life  life.ames-state
3088          ^=        rcvr  her
3089          ^=   rcvr-life  her-life
3090      ==
3091    ::  +sendkeys-packet: generate a request for a self-attestation.
3092    ::
3093    ::      Sent by non-comets to comets.  Not acked.
3094    ::
3095    ++  sendkeys-packet
3096      |=  her=ship
3097      ^-  blob
3098      ?>  ?=(%pawn (clan:title her))
3099      %-  etch-shot
3100      (encode-keys-packet our her life.ames-state)
3101    ::
3102    +|  %internals
3103    ::  +pe: create nested |peer-core for per-peer processing
3104    ::
3105    ++  pe
3106      |_  [=peer-state =channel]
3107      +*  veb     veb.bug.channel
3108          her     her.channel
3109          keens   keens.peer-state
3110      ::
3111      +|  %helpers
3112      ::
3113      ++  peer-core  .
3114      ++  pe-emit    |=(move peer-core(event-core (emit +<)))
3115      ++  abed       |=(=ship (abed-peer ship (gut-peer-state ship)))
3116      ++  abed-got   |=(=ship (abed-peer ship (got-peer-state ship)))
3117      ++  abed-peer
3118        |=  [=ship peer=^peer-state]
3119        %_  peer-core
3120          peer-state  peer
3121            channel   [[our ship] now channel-state -.peer]
3122        ==
3123      ::
3124      ++  abort  event-core  :: keeps moves, discards state changes
3125      ++  abet
3126        ^+  event-core
3127        =.  peers.ames-state
3128          (~(put by peers.ames-state) her %known peer-state)
3129        event-core
3130      ::
```

```
3131    ++  pe-trace
3132    |=  [verb=? print=(trap tape)]
3133    ^+  same
3134    (ev-trace verb her print)
3135    ::
3136    ::  +got-duct: look up $duct by .bone, asserting already bound
3137    ::
3138    ++  got-duct
3139    |=  =bone
3140    ^-  ^duct
3141    ~|  %dangling-bone^her^bone
3142    (~(got by by-bone.ossuary.peer-state) bone)
3143    ::
3144    ::  +bind-duct: find or make new $bone for .duct in .ossuary
3145    ::
3146    ++  bind-duct
3147    |=  =^duct
3148    =*  ossa  ossuary.peer-state
3149    ^+  [next-bone.ossa peer-core]
3150    ?^  existing=(~(get by by-duct.ossa) duct)
3151      [u.existing peer-core]
3152    :-  next-bone.ossa
3153    =.  ossa
3154      :+  (add 4 next-bone.ossa)
3155        (~(put by by-duct.ossa) duct next-bone.ossa)
3156      (~(put by by-bone.ossa) next-bone.ossa duct)
3157    peer-core
3158    ::
3159    ++  is-corked
3160    |=  =bone
3161    ?|  (~(has in corked.peer-state) bone)
3162        ?&  =(1 (end 0 bone))
3163            =(1 (end 0 (rsh 0 bone)))
3164            (~(has in corked.peer-state) (mix 0b10 bone))
3165    ==  ==
3166    ::
3167    +|  %tasks
3168    ::
3169    ++  on-heed
3170    peer-core(heeds.peer-state (~(put in heeds.peer-state) duct))
3171    ::
3172    ++  on-jilt
3173    peer-core(heeds.peer-state (~(del in heeds.peer-state) duct))
3174    ::  +update-qos: update and maybe print connection status
3175    ::
3176    ++  update-qos
3177    |=  [mode=?(%ames %fine) =new=qos]
3178    ^+  peer-core
3179    ::
3180    =^  old-qos  qos.peer-state  [qos.peer-state new-qos]
3181    ::  if no update worth reporting, we're done
3182    ::
3183    =/  text
3184      %^  qos-update-text  her  mode
3185      [old-qos new-qos kay.veb ships.bug.ames-state]
3186    ?~  text
3187      peer-core
3188    ::  print message
```

```
3189                ::
3190                =.  peer-core  (pe-emit duct %pass /qos %d %flog %text u.text)
3191                ::  if peer has stopped responding, check if %boon's are backing up
3192                ::
3193                ?.  ?=(?(%dead %unborn) -.qos.peer-state)
3194                  peer-core
3195                check-clog
3196            ::  +on-hear-shut-packet: handle receipt of ack or message fragment
3197            ::
3198            ++  on-hear-shut-packet
3199              |=  [=lane =shut-packet dud=(unit goof)]
3200              ^+  peer-core
3201              ::  update and print connection status
3202              ::
3203              =.  peer-core  (update-qos %ames %live last-contact=now)
3204              ::
3205              =/  =bone   bone.shut-packet
3206              ::
3207              ?:  ?=(%& -.meat.shut-packet)
3208                =+  ?.  &(?=(^ dud) msg.veb)  ~
3209                    %.  ~
3210                    %-  slog
3211                    :_  tang.u.dud
3212                    leaf+"ames: {<her>} fragment crashed {<mote.u.dud>}"
3213                abet:(call:(abed:mi bone) %hear lane shut-packet ?=(~ dud))
3214              ::  benign ack on corked bone
3215              ::
3216              ?:  (is-corked bone)  peer-core
3217              ::  Just try again on error, printing trace
3218              ::
3219              ::    Note this implies that vanes should never crash on %done,
3220              ::    since we have no way to continue using the flow if they do.
3221              ::
3222              =+  ?~  dud  ~
3223                  %.  ~
3224                  %+  slog  leaf+"ames: {<her>} ack crashed {<mote.u.dud>}"
3225                  ?.  msg.veb  ~
3226                  :-  >[bone=bone message-num=message-num meat=meat]:shut-packet<
3227                  tang.u.dud
3228              abet:(call:(abed:mu bone) %hear [message-num +.meat]:shut-packet)
3229            ::
3230            ++  on-flub
3231              |=  =bone
3232              ^+  peer-core
3233              abet:(call:(abed:mi:peer-core bone) %flub ~)
3234            ::  +on-memo: handle request to send message
3235            ::
3236            ++  on-memo
3237              |=  [=bone payload=* valence=?(%plea %boon)]
3238              ^+  peer-core
3239              ?:  ?&  (~(has in closing.peer-state) bone)
3240                      !=(payload [%$ /flow %cork ~])
3241                  ==
3242                ~>  %slog.0^leaf/"ames: ignoring message on closing bone {<bone>}"
3243                peer-core
3244              ?:  (~(has in corked.peer-state) bone)
3245                ~>  %slog.0^leaf/"ames: ignoring message on corked bone {<bone>}"
3246                peer-core
```

```
3247        ::
3248        =/  =message-blob  (dedup-message (jim payload))
3249        =.  peer-core        abet:(call:(abed:mu bone) %memo message-blob)
3250        ::
3251    ?:  ?&  =(%boon valence)
3252            (gte now (add ~s30 last-contact.qos.peer-state))
3253        ==
3254      check-clog
3255    peer-core
3256  ::  +on-wake: handle timer expiration
3257  ::
3258  ++  on-wake
3259    |=  [=bone error=(unit tang)]
3260    ^+  peer-core
3261    ::  if we previously errored out, print and reset timer for later
3262    ::
3263    ::    This really shouldn't happen, but if it does, make sure we
3264    ::    don't brick either this messaging flow or Behn.
3265    ::
3266    ?^  error
3267      =.  peer-core
3268      (pe-emit duct %pass /wake-fail %d %flog %crud %ames-wake u.error)
3269      ::
3270      ?~  message-pump-state=(~(get by snd.peer-state) bone)
3271        peer-core
3272      =*  packet-state  packet-pump-state.u.message-pump-state
3273      ?~  next-wake.packet-state  peer-core
3274      ::  If we crashed because we woke up too early, assume another
3275      ::  timer is already set.
3276      ::
3277      ?:  (lth now.channel u.next-wake.packet-state)
3278        peer-core
3279      ::
3280      =/  =wire  (make-pump-timer-wire her bone)
3281      (pe-emit duct %pass wire %b %wait (add now.channel ~s30))
3282    ::  update and print connection state
3283    ::
3284    =.  peer-core    (update-qos %ames qos:(is-peer-dead now peer-state))
3285    ::  expire direct route if the peer is not responding
3286    ::
3287    =.  peer-state  (update-peer-route her peer-state)
3288    ::  resend comet attestation packet if first message times out
3289    ::
3290    ::    The attestation packet doesn't get acked, so if we tried to
3291    ::    send a packet but it timed out, maybe they didn't get our
3292    ::    attestation.
3293    ::
3294    ::    Only resend on timeout of packets in the first message we
3295    ::    send them, since they should remember forever.
3296    ::
3297    =?  event-core
3298        ?&  ?=(%pawn (clan:title our))
3299            =(1 current:(~(got by snd.peer-state) bone))
3300        ==
3301      =/  =blob  (attestation-packet [her her-life]:channel)
3302      (send-blob for=| her blob `known/peer-state)
3303    ?:  (is-corked bone)
3304      ::  no-op if the bone (or, if a naxplanation, the reference bone)
```

```
3305              ::    was corked, because the flow doesn't exist anymore
3306              ::    TODO: clean up corked bones?
3307              ::
3308            peer-core
3309          ::  maybe resend some timed out packets
3310          ::
3311          abet:(call:(abed:mu bone) %wake ~)
3312        ::
3313        ++  on-hear-fine
3314          |=  [=lane =shot]
3315          ^+  peer-core
3316          ?>  =(sndr-tick.shot (mod life.peer-state 16))
3317          ::  TODO what if the error happened in sift-purr?
3318          ::       does vere discard malformed packets?
3319          =/  [=peep =meow]  (sift-purr `@ux`content.shot)
3320          =/  =path  (slag 3 path.peep)
3321          ::
3322          ?.  (~(has by keens) path)
3323            ~&(dead-response/peep peer-core)
3324          fi-abet:(fi-rcv:(abed:fi path) peep meow lane)
3325        ::
3326        ++  on-keen
3327          |=  [=path =^duct]
3328          ^+  peer-core
3329          ?:  (~(has by keens) path)
3330            ::  TODO use fi-trace
3331            ~>  %slog.0^leaf/"fine: dupe {(spud path)}"
3332            fi-abet:(fi-sub:(abed:fi path) duct)
3333          =.  keens  (~(put by keens) path *keen-state)
3334          fi-abet:(fi-start:(abed:fi path) duct)
3335        ::
3336        ++  on-dear
3337          |=  =lane
3338          ^+  peer-core
3339          peer-core(route.peer-state `[%.y lane])
3340        ::
3341        ++  on-tame
3342          ^+  peer-core
3343          peer-core(route.peer-state ~)
3344        ::  +on-cork-flow: mark .bone as closing
3345        ::
3346        ++  on-cork-flow
3347          |=  =bone
3348          ^+  peer-core
3349          peer-core(closing.peer-state (~(put in closing.peer-state) bone))
3350        ::  +on-kill-flow: delete flow on cork sender side
3351        ::
3352        ++  on-kill-flow
3353          |=  =bone
3354          ^+  peer-core
3355          ?:  (~(has in corked.peer-state) bone)
3356            ~>  %slog.0^leaf/"ames: ignoring kill on corked bone {<bone>}"
3357            peer-core
3358          =.  peer-state
3359            =,  peer-state
3360            %_  peer-state
3361              ::  if the publisher was behind, preemptively remove any nacks
3362              ::
```

```
3363        rcv                 (~(del by (~(del by rcv) bone)) (mix 0b10 bone))
3364        snd                 (~(del by snd) bone)
3365        corked              (~(put in corked) bone)
3366        closing             (~(del in closing) bone)
3367        by-duct.ossuary     (~(del by by-duct.ossuary) (got-duct bone))
3368        by-bone.ossuary     (~(del by by-bone.ossuary) bone)
3369      ==
3370    ::  since we got one cork ack, try the next one
3371    ::
3372    recork-one
3373  ::
3374  +|  %implementation
3375  ::  +dedup-message: replace with any existing copy of this message
3376  ::
3377  ++  dedup-message
3378    |=  =message-blob
3379    ^+  message-blob
3380    ?:  (lte (met 13 message-blob) 1)
3381      message-blob
3382    =/  peers-l=(list [=ship =ship-state])  ~(tap by peers.ames-state)
3383    |-  ^+  message-blob
3384    =*  peer-loop  $
3385    ?~  peers-l
3386      message-blob
3387    ?.  ?=(%known -.ship-state.i.peers-l)
3388      peer-loop(peers-l t.peers-l)
3389    =/  snd-l=(list [=bone =message-pump-state])
3390      ~(tap by snd.ship-state.i.peers-l)
3391    |-  ^+  message-blob
3392    =*  bone-loop  $
3393    ?~  snd-l        peer-loop(peers-l t.peers-l)
3394    =*  unsent-fragments  unsent-fragments.message-pump-state.i.snd-l
3395    =/  blob-l=(list ^message-blob)
3396      ~(tap to unsent-messages.message-pump-state.i.snd-l)
3397    |-  ^+  message-blob
3398    =*  blob-loop  $
3399    ?^  blob-l
3400      ?:  =(i.blob-l message-blob)
3401        i.blob-l
3402      blob-loop(blob-l t.blob-l)
3403    ?~  unsent-fragments  bone-loop(snd-l t.snd-l)
3404    ?:  =(message-blob fragment.i.unsent-fragments)
3405      `@`fragment.i.unsent-fragments
3406    bone-loop(snd-l t.snd-l)
3407  ::  +check-clog: notify clients if peer has stopped responding
3408  ::
3409  ++  check-clog
3410    ^+  peer-core
3411    ::
3412    ::    Only look at response bones.  Request bones are unregulated,
3413    ::    since requests tend to be much smaller than responses.
3414    ::
3415    =/  pumps=(list message-pump-state)
3416      %+  murn  ~(tap by snd.peer-state)
3417      |=  [bone =message-pump-state]
3418      ?:  =(0 (end 0 bone))
3419        ~
3420      `u=message-pump-state
```

```
3421        ::  if clogged, notify client vane
3422        ::
3423        |^  ?.  &(nuf-messages nuf-memory)  peer-core
3424            %+  roll  ~(tap in heeds.peer-state)
3425            |=([d=^duct core=_peer-core] (pe-emit:core d %give %clog her))
3426        ::  +nuf-messages: are there enough messages to mark as clogged?
3427        ::
3428        ++  nuf-messages
3429          =|  num=@ud
3430          |-  ^-  ?
3431          ?~  pumps  |
3432          =.  num
3433            ;:  add  num
3434              (sub [next current]:i.pumps)
3435              ~(wyt in unsent-messages.i.pumps)
3436            ==
3437          ?:  (gte num msg.cong.ames-state)
3438            &
3439          $(pumps t.pumps)
3440        ::  +nuf-memory: is enough memory used to mark as clogged?
3441        ::
3442        ++  nuf-memory
3443          =|  mem=@ud
3444          |-  ^-  ?
3445          ?~  pumps  |
3446          =.  mem
3447            %+  add
3448              %-  ~(rep in unsent-messages.i.pumps)
3449              |=([a=@ b=_mem] (add b (met 3 a)))
3450            ?~  unsent-fragments.i.pumps  0
3451            (met 3 fragment.i.unsent-fragments.i.pumps)
3452          ?:  (gte mem mem.cong.ames-state)
3453            &
3454          $(pumps t.pumps)
3455      --
3456    ::  +send-shut-packet: fire encrypted packet at rcvr and maybe sponsors
3457    ::
3458    ++  send-shut-packet
3459      |=  =shut-packet
3460      ^+  peer-core
3461      ::  swizzle last bone bit before sending
3462      ::
3463      ::    The peer has the opposite perspective from ours about what
3464      ::    kind of flow this is (forward/backward), so flip the bit
3465      ::    here.
3466      ::
3467      =.  event-core
3468        %:  send-blob  for=|  her
3469          %-  etch-shot
3470          %:  etch-shut-packet
3471            shut-packet(bone (mix 1 bone.shut-packet))
3472            symmetric-key.channel
3473            our               her
3474            our-life.channel  her-life.channel
3475        ==
3476        ::
3477        ship-state=`known/peer-state
3478      ==
```

```
3479          peer-core
3480    ::  +recork-one: re-send the next %cork to the peer
3481    ::
3482    ++  recork-one
3483      ^+  peer-core
3484      =/  boz  (sort ~(tap in closing.peer-state) lte)
3485      |-  ^+  peer-core
3486      ?~  boz  peer-core
3487      =/  pum=message-pump-state  (~(got by snd.peer-state) i.boz)
3488      ?.  =(next current):pum
3489        $(boz t.boz)
3490      ::  sanity check on the message pump state
3491      ::
3492      ?.  ?&  =(~ unsent-messages.pum)
3493              =(~ unsent-fragments.pum)
3494              =(~ live.packet-pump-state.pum)
3495          ==
3496        ~>  %slog.0^leaf/"ames: bad pump state {<her i.boz>}"
3497        $(boz t.boz)
3498      ::  no outstanding messages, so send a new %cork
3499      ::
3500      ::  TODO use +trace
3501      ~>  %slog.0^leaf/"ames: recork {<her i.boz>}"
3502      =/  =plea  [%$ /flow [%cork ~]]
3503      (on-memo i.boz plea %plea)
3504    ::  +handle-cork: handle flow kill after server ames has taken %done
3505    ::
3506    ++  handle-cork
3507      |=  =bone
3508      |^  ^+  peer-core
3509      ?.  (~(has in closing.peer-state) bone)  peer-core
3510      =/  pump=message-pump-state
3511        (~(gut by snd.peer-state) bone *message-pump-state)
3512      =?  event-core  ?=(^ next-wake.packet-pump-state.pump)
3513        ::  reset-timer for boons
3514        ::
3515        (reset-timer her bone u.next-wake.packet-pump-state.pump)
3516      =/  nax-bone=^bone  (mix 0b10 bone)
3517      =/  nax-pump=message-pump-state
3518        (~(gut by snd.peer-state) nax-bone *message-pump-state)
3519      =?  event-core  ?=(^ next-wake.packet-pump-state.nax-pump)
3520        %-  %^  ev-trace  odd.veb  her
3521            |.("remove naxplanation flow {<[her bone=nax-bone]>}")
3522        ::  reset timer for naxplanations
3523        ::
3524        (reset-timer her nax-bone u.next-wake.packet-pump-state.nax-pump)
3525      =.  peer-state
3526        =,  peer-state
3527        %_  peer-state
3528          ::  preemptively delete nax flows (e.g. nacks for %watches)
3529          ::
3530          snd      (~(del by (~(del by snd) bone)) nax-bone)
3531          rcv      (~(del by rcv) bone)
3532          corked   (~(put in corked) bone)
3533          closing  (~(del in closing) bone)
3534        ==
3535      peer-core
3536      ::
```

```
3537          ++  reset-timer
3538            |=  [=ship =^bone wake=@da]
3539            (emit [/ames]~ %pass (make-pump-timer-wire ship bone) %b %rest wake)
3540            --
3541          ::
3542        +|  %internals
3543        ::  +mu: constructor for |pump message sender core
3544        ::
3545        ++  mu
3546          |_  [=bone state=message-pump-state]
3547          ::
3548          +|  %helpers
3549          ::
3550          ++  pump  .
3551          ++  abed
3552            |=  b=^bone
3553            pump(bone b, state (~(gut by snd.peer-state) b *message-pump-state))
3554          ++  abet
3555            ::  if the bone was corked, it's been removed from the state,
3556            ::  so we avoid adding it again.
3557            ::
3558            =?  snd.peer-state  !corked  (~(put by snd.peer-state) bone state)
3559            peer-core
3560          ::
3561          ++  packet-pump  (pu packet-pump-state.state)
3562          ++  closing      (~(has in closing.peer-state) bone)
3563          ++  corked       (~(has in corked.peer-state) bone)
3564          ::  +is-message-num-in-range: %.y unless duplicate or future ack
3565          ::
3566          ++  is-message-num-in-range
3567            |=  =message-num
3568            ^-  ?
3569            ::
3570            ?:  (gte message-num next.state)
3571              %.n
3572            ?:  (lth message-num current.state)
3573              %.n
3574            !(~(has by queued-message-acks.state) message-num)
3575          ::
3576          +|  %entry-points
3577          ::  +call: handle a $message-pump-task
3578          ::
3579          ++  call
3580            |=  task=message-pump-task
3581            ^+  pump
3582            ::
3583            =.  pump  =~((dispatch-task task) feed-packets)
3584            =+  top=top-live:packet-pump
3585            ::  sanity check to isolate error cases
3586            ::
3587            ?.  |(?=(~ top) (lte current.state message-num.key.u.top))
3588              ~|([%strange-current current=current.state key.u.top] !!)
3589            ::  maybe trigger a timer based on congestion control calculations
3590            ::
3591            abet:(call:packet-pump %halt ~)
3592          ::
3593          +|  %tasks
3594          ::  +dispatch-task: perform task-specific processing
```

```
3595        ::
3596        ++  dispatch-task
3597          |=  task=message-pump-task
3598          ^+  pump
3599          ::
3600          ?-  -.task
3601            %memo  (on-memo message-blob.task)
3602            %prod  abet:(call:packet-pump %prod ~)
3603            %wake  abet:(call:packet-pump %wake current.state)
3604            %near  %-  on-done
3605                   [[message-num %naxplanation error]:naxplanation.task %&]
3606            %hear
3607              ?-  -.ack-meat.task
3608                %&
3609              (on-hear [message-num fragment-num=p.ack-meat]:task)
3610              ::
3611                %|
3612            =/  cork=?
3613              =+  top=top-live:packet-pump
3614              ::  If we send a %cork and get an ack, we can know by
3615              ::  sequence number that the ack is for the %cork message
3616              ::
3617              ?&  closing
3618                  ?=(^ top)
3619                  =(0 ~(wyt in unsent-messages.state))
3620                  =(0 (lent unsent-fragments.state))
3621                  =(1 ~(wyt by live.packet-pump-state.state))
3622                  =(message-num:task message-num.key.u.top)
3623              ==
3624            =+  [ack msg]=[p.ack-meat message-num]:task
3625            =.  pump
3626              %-  on-done
3627              [[msg ?:(ok.ack [%ok ~] [%nack ~])] cork]
3628            ?.  &(!ok.ack cork)  pump
3629            %.  pump
3630            %+  pe-trace  odd.veb
3631            |.("got nack for %cork {<bone=bone message-num=msg>}")
3632        ==  ==
3633        ::  +on-memo: handle request to send a message
3634        ::
3635        ++  on-memo
3636          |=  blob=message-blob
3637          pump(unsent-messages.state (~(put to unsent-messages.state) blob))
3638        ::  +on-hear: handle packet acknowledgment
3639        ::
3640        ++  on-hear
3641          |=  [=message-num =fragment-num]
3642          ^+  pump
3643          ::  pass to |packet-pump unless duplicate or future ack
3644          ::
3645          ?.  (is-message-num-in-range message-num)
3646            %.  pump
3647            (pe-trace snd.veb |.("hear pump out of range"))
3648          abet:(call:packet-pump %hear message-num fragment-num)
3649        ::  +on-done: handle message acknowledgment
3650        ::
3651        ::  A nack-trace message counts as a valid message nack on the
3652        ::  original failed message.
```

```
3653        ::
3654        ::    This prevents us from having to wait for a message nack packet,
3655        ::    which would mean we couldn't immediately ack the nack-trace
3656        ::    message, which would in turn violate the semantics of backward
3657        ::    flows.
3658        ::
3659    ++  on-done
3660        |=  [[=message-num =ack] cork=?]
3661        ^+  pump
3662        ::  unsent messages from the future should never get acked
3663        ::
3664        ~|  :*  bone=bone
3665                mnum=message-num
3666                next=next.state
3667                unsent-messages=~(wyt in unsent-messages.state)
3668                unsent-fragments=(lent unsent-fragments.state)
3669                any-live=!=(~ live.packet-pump-state.state)
3670            ==
3671        ?>  (lth message-num next.state)
3672        ::  ignore duplicate message acks
3673        ::
3674        ?:  (lth message-num current.state)
3675          %.  pump
3676          %+  pe-trace  snd.veb  |.
3677          "duplicate done {<current=current.state message-num=message-num>}"
3678        ::  ignore duplicate and future acks
3679        ::
3680        ?.  (is-message-num-in-range message-num)
3681          pump
3682        ::  clear and print .unsent-fragments if nonempty
3683        ::
3684        =?    unsent-fragments.state
3685          &(=(current next) ?=(^ unsent-fragments)):state
3686          ::
3687          ~>  %slog.0^leaf/"ames: early message ack {<her>}"
3688          ~
3689        ::  clear all packets from this message from the packet pump
3690        ::
3691        =.  pump  abet:(call:packet-pump %done message-num lag=*@dr)
3692        ::  enqueue this ack to be sent back to local client vane
3693        ::
3694        ::    Don't clobber a naxplanation with just a nack packet.
3695        ::
3696        =?    queued-message-acks.state
3697          =/  old  (~(get by queued-message-acks.state) message-num)
3698          !?=(([~ %naxplanation *] old)
3699          (~(put by queued-message-acks.state) message-num ack)
3700        ::  emit local acks from .queued-message-acks until incomplete
3701        ::
3702        |-  ^+  pump
3703        ::  if .current hasn't been fully acked, we're done
3704        ::
3705        ?~  cur=(~(get by queued-message-acks.state) current.state)
3706          pump
3707        ::  .current is complete; pop, emit local ack, and try next message
3708        ::
3709        =.  queued-message-acks.state
3710          (~(del by queued-message-acks.state) current.state)
```

```
3711        ::  clear all packets from this message from the packet pump
3712        ::
3713        ::    Note we did this when the original packet came in, a few lines
3714        ::    above.  It's not clear why, but it doesn't always clear the
3715        ::    packets when it's not the current message.  As a workaround,
3716        ::    we clear the packets again when we catch up to this packet.
3717        ::
3718        ::    This is slightly inefficient because we run this twice for
3719        ::    each packet and it may emit a few unnecessary packets, but
3720        ::    it's not incorrect.  pump-metrics are updated only once,
3721        ::    at the time when we actually delete the packet.
3722        ::
3723      =.  pump  abet:(call:packet-pump %done current.state lag=*@dr)
3724      ::  give %done to vane if we're ready
3725      ::
3726      ?-    -.u.cur
3727          %ok
3728        =.  peer-core
3729        ::  don't give %done for corks
3730        ::
3731        ?:  cork  (pump-cork current.state)
3732        (pump-done current.state ~)
3733      $(current.state +(current.state))
3734      ::
3735          %nack  pump
3736      ::
3737          %naxplanation
3738        =.  peer-core  (pump-done current.state `error.u.cur)
3739      $(current.state +(current.state))
3740        ==
3741    ::
3742    +|  %implementation
3743    ::  +feed-packets: give packets to |packet-pump until full
3744    ::
3745    ++  feed-packets
3746      ::  if nothing to send, no-op
3747      ::
3748      ?:  &(=(~ unsent-messages) =(~ unsent-fragments)):state
3749        pump
3750      ::  we have unsent fragments of the current message; feed them
3751      ::
3752      ?.  =(~ unsent-fragments.state)
3753        ::  we have unsent fragments of the current message; feed them
3754        ::
3755        =^  unsent  pump  abut:(feed:packet-pump unsent-fragments.state)
3756        =.  unsent-fragments.state    unsent
3757        ::  if it sent all of them, feed it more; otherwise, we're done
3758        ::
3759      ?~(unsent feed-packets pump)
3760      ::  .unsent-messages is nonempty; pop a message off and feed it
3761      ::
3762      =^  =message-blob  unsent-messages.state
3763        ~(get to unsent-messages.state)
3764      ::  break .message into .chunks and set as .unsent-fragments
3765      ::
3766      =.  unsent-fragments.state  (split-message next.state message-blob)
3767      ::  try to feed packets from the next message
3768      ::
```

```
3769            =.  next.state  +(next.state)
3770          feed-packets
3771       ::  +pump-done: handle |message-pump's report of message (n)ack
3772       ::
3773       ++  pump-done
3774         |=  [=message-num error=(unit error)]
3775         ^+  peer-core
3776         ?:  ?&  =(1 (end 0 bone))
3777                 =(1 (end 0 (rsh 0 bone)))
3778                 (~(has in corked.peer-state) (mix 0b10 bone))
3779             ==
3780           %-  %+  pe-trace  msg.veb
3781               =/  dat  [her bone=bone message-num=message-num -.task]
3782               |.("remove naxplanation flow {<dat>}")
3783           ::  we avoid re-adding the bone in abet:mu
3784           ::
3785           =.  snd.peer-state  (~(del by snd.peer-state) bone)
3786         peer-core
3787         ?:  =(1 (end 0 bone))
3788           ::  ack is on "subscription update" message; no-op
3789           ::
3790         ?:  =(0 (end 0 (rsh 0 bone)))  peer-core
3791           ::  nack-trace bone; assume .ok, clear nack from |sink
3792           ::
3793           %+  pe-emit  duct
3794           [%pass /clear-nack %a %deep %drop her (mix 0b10 bone) message-num]
3795         ::  if the bone belongs to a closing flow and we got a
3796         ::  naxplanation, don't relay ack to the client vane
3797         ::
3798         ?:  &(closing ?=(%near -.task))  peer-core
3799         ::  not a nack-trace bone; relay ack to client vane
3800         ::
3801         (pe-emit (got-duct bone) %give %done error)
3802       ::  +pump-cork: handle %cork on the publisher
3803       ::
3804       ++  pump-cork
3805         |=  =message-num
3806         ^+  peer-core
3807         ::  clear all packets from this message from the packet pump
3808         ::
3809         =.  pump  abet:(call:packet-pump %done message-num lag=*@dr)
3810         ?:  corked
3811           %-  %+  pe-trace  odd.veb
3812               |.("trying to delete a corked bone={<bone>}")
3813           peer-core
3814         =/  =wire  (make-bone-wire her her-rift.channel bone)
3815         (pe-emit duct %pass wire %a %deep %kill her bone)
3816       ::  +pu: construct |packet-pump core
3817       ::
3818       ++  pu
3819         |=  state=packet-pump-state
3820         ::
3821         =|  unsent=(list static-fragment)
3822         |%
3823         +|  %helpers
3824         ++  pack  .
3825         ::  +abut: abet with gifts
3826         ::
```

```
3827        ++  abut  [unsent abet]
3828        ++  abet  pump(packet-pump-state.state state)
3829        ++  pu-trace
3830          |=  [verb=? print=(trap tape)]
3831          ^+  same
3832          (trace %ames verb her ships.bug.channel print)
3833        ::
3834        ++  pu-wire  (make-pump-timer-wire her bone)
3835        ++  pu-emit  |=(=note (pe-emit pump-duct %pass pu-wire note))
3836        ::  +packet-queue: type for all sent fragments (order: seq number)
3837        ::
3838        ++  packet-queue
3839          %-  (ordered-map live-packet-key live-packet-val)
3840          lte-packets
3841        ::  +gauge: inflate a |pump-gauge to track congestion control
3842        ::
3843        ++  gauge  (ga metrics.state ~(wyt by live.state))
3844        ::  +to-static-fragment: convenience function for |packet-pump
3845        ::
3846        ++  to-static-fragment
3847          |=  [live-packet-key live-packet-val]
3848          ^-  static-fragment
3849          [message-num num-fragments fragment-num fragment]
3850        ::
3851        ++  pump-duct  ~[/ames]
3852        ++  top-live  (pry:packet-queue live.state)
3853        ::
3854        +|  %entry-points
3855        ::
3856        ++  call
3857          |=  task=packet-pump-task
3858          ^+  pack
3859          ?-  -.task
3860            %hear  (on-hear [message-num fragment-num]:task)
3861            %done  (on-done message-num.task)
3862            %wake  (on-wake current.task)
3863            %prod  on-prod
3864            %halt  set-wake
3865          ==
3866        ::  +feed: try to send a list of packets, returning unsent ones
3867        ::
3868        ++  feed
3869          |=  fragments=(list static-fragment)
3870          ^+  pack
3871          ::  bite off as many fragments as we can send
3872          ::
3873          =/  num-slots  num-slots:gauge
3874          =/  sent      (scag num-slots fragments)
3875          =.  unsent    (slag num-slots fragments)
3876          ::  if nothing to send, we're done
3877          ::
3878          ?~  sent  pack
3879          ::  convert $static-fragment's into +ordered-set [key val] pairs
3880          ::
3881          =/  send-list
3882            %+  turn  sent
3883            |=  static-fragment
3884            ^-  [key=live-packet-key val=live-packet-val]
```

```
3885                     ::
3886                     :-  [message-num fragment-num]
3887                     :-  [sent-date=now.channel tries=1 skips=0]
3888                     [num-fragments fragment]
3889             ::  update .live and .metrics
3890             ::
3891             =.  live.state  (gas:packet-queue live.state send-list)
3892             ::  TMI
3893             ::
3894             =>  .(sent `(list static-fragment)`sent)
3895             ::  emit a $shut-packet for each packet to send
3896             ::
3897             =.  peer-core
3898               %+  roll  sent
3899               |=  [packet=static-fragment core=_peer-core]
3900               (send-shut-packet bone [message-num %& +]:packet)
3901           pack
3902         ::
3903         +|  %tasks
3904         ::  +on-prod: reset congestion control, re-send packets
3905         ::
3906         ++  on-prod
3907           ^+  pack
3908           ?:  =(~ next-wake.state)
3909             pack
3910           ::
3911           =.  metrics.state
3912             %*(. *pump-metrics counter counter.metrics.state)
3913           =.  live.state
3914             %+  run:packet-queue  live.state
3915             |=(p=live-packet-val p(- *packet-state))
3916           ::
3917           =/  sot  (max 1 num-slots:gauge)
3918           =/  liv  live.state
3919           |-  ^+  pack
3920           ?:  =(0 sot)  pack
3921           ?:  =(~ liv)  pack
3922           =^  hed  liv  (pop:packet-queue liv)
3923           =.  peer-core
3924             %+  send-shut-packet  bone
3925             [message-num %& +]:(to-static-fragment hed)
3926           $(sot (dec sot))
3927         ::  +on-wake: handle packet timeout
3928         ::
3929         ++  on-wake
3930           |=  current=message-num
3931           ^+  pack
3932           ::  assert temporal coherence
3933           ::
3934           ?<  =(~ next-wake.state)
3935           =.  next-wake.state  ~
3936           ::  tell congestion control a packet timed out
3937           ::
3938           =.  metrics.state  on-timeout:gauge
3939           =|  acc=(unit static-fragment)
3940           ::  re-send first packet and update its state in-place
3941           ::
3942           =;  [static-fragment=_acc live=_live.state]
```

```
3943        =.  live.state    live
3944        =?  peer-core  ?=(^ static-fragment)
3945          %-  %+  pu-trace   snd.veb
3946              =/  nums  [message-num fragment-num]:u.static-fragment
3947              |.("dead {<nums show:gauge>}")
3948          (send-shut-packet bone [message-num %& +]:u.static-fragment)
3949        pack
3950      ::
3951      %^  (dip:packet-queue _acc)  live.state   acc
3952      |=  $:  acc=_acc
3953              key=live-packet-key
3954              val=live-packet-val
3955          ==
3956      ^-  [new-val=(unit live-packet-val) stop=? _acc]
3957      ::  if already acked later message, don't resend
3958      ::
3959      ?:  (lth message-num.key current)
3960        %.  [~ stop=%.n ~]
3961        %-  slog  :_  ~  :-  %leaf
3962        "ames: strange wake queue, expected {<current>}, got {<key>}"
3963      ::  packet has expired; update it in-place, stop, and produce it
3964      ::
3965      =.  last-sent.val   now.channel
3966      =.  tries.val      +(tries.val)
3967      ::
3968      [`val stop=%.y `(to-static-fragment key val)]
3969    ::  +fast-resend-after-ack: resend timed out packets
3970    ::
3971    ::    After we finally receive an ack, we want to resend all the
3972    ::    live packets that have been building up.
3973    ::
3974    ++  fast-resend-after-ack
3975      |=  [=message-num =fragment-num]
3976      ^+  pack
3977      =;  res=[resends=(list static-fragment) live=_live.state]
3978        =.  live.state  live.res
3979        =.  peer-core
3980          %+  reel  resends.res
3981          |=  [packet=static-fragment core=_peer-core]
3982          (send-shut-packet bone [message-num %& +]:packet)
3983        pack
3984      ::
3985      =/  acc
3986        resends=*(list static-fragment)
3987      ::
3988      %^  (dip:packet-queue _acc)  live.state   acc
3989      |=  $:  acc=_acc
3990              key=live-packet-key
3991              val=live-packet-val
3992          ==
3993      ^-  [new-val=(unit live-packet-val) stop=? _acc]
3994      ?:  (lte-packets key [message-num fragment-num])
3995        [new-val=`val stop=%.n acc]
3996      ::
3997      ?:  (gth (next-expiry:gauge -.val) now.channel)
3998        [new-val=`val stop=%.y acc]
3999      ::
4000      =.  last-sent.val   now.channel
```

```
4001          =.  resends.acc  [(to-static-fragment key val) resends.acc]
4002          [new-val=`val stop=%.n acc]
4003      ::  +on-hear: handle ack on a live packet
4004      ::
4005      ::    If the packet was in our queue, delete it and update our
4006      ::    metrics, possibly re-sending skipped packets. Otherwise, no-op
4007      ::
4008      ++  on-hear
4009      |=  [=message-num =fragment-num]
4010      ^+  pack
4011      ::
4012      =-  ::  if no sent packet matches the ack,
4013          ::  don't apply mutations or effects
4014          ::
4015          ?.  found.-
4016            %-  (pu-trace snd.veb |.("miss {<show:gauge>}"))
4017            pack
4018          ::
4019          =.  metrics.state  metrics.-
4020          =.  live.state     live.-
4021          %-  ?.  ?|  =(0 fragment-num)
4022                      =(0 (mod counter.metrics.state 20))
4023                  ==
4024              same
4025            %+  pu-trace  snd.veb
4026            |.("send: {<fragment=fragment-num show:gauge>}")
4027          ::  .resends is backward, so fold backward and emit
4028          ::
4029          =.  peer-core
4030            %+  reel  resends.-
4031            |=  [packet=static-fragment core=_peer-core]
4032            (send-shut-packet bone [message-num %& +]:packet)
4033          (fast-resend-after-ack message-num fragment-num)
4034      ::
4035      =/  acc
4036        :*  found=`?`%.n
4037            resends=*(list static-fragment)
4038            metrics=metrics.state
4039            num-live=~(wyt by live.state)
4040        ==
4041      ::
4042      ^+  [acc live=live.state]
4043      ::
4044      %^  (dip:packet-queue _acc)  live.state  acc
4045      |=  $:  acc=_acc
4046              key=live-packet-key
4047              val=live-packet-val
4048          ==
4049      ^-  [new-val=(unit live-packet-val) stop=? _acc]
4050      ::
4051      =/  gauge  (ga [metrics num-live]:acc)
4052      ::  is this the acked packet?
4053      ::
4054      ?:  =(key [message-num fragment-num])
4055        ::  delete acked packet, update metrics, and stop traversal
4056        ::
4057        =.     found.acc  %.y
4058        =.   metrics.acc  (on-ack:gauge -.val)
```

```
4059          =.  num-live.acc  (dec num-live.acc)
4060          [new-val=~ stop=%.y acc]
4061        ::  is this a duplicate ack?
4062        ::
4063        ?.  (lte-packets key [message-num fragment-num])
4064          ::  stop, nothing more to do
4065          ::
4066          [new-val=`val stop=%.y acc]
4067        ::  ack was on later packet; mark skipped, tell gauge, & continue
4068        ::
4069          =.  skips.val  +(skips.val)
4070          =^  resend  metrics.acc  (on-skipped-packet:gauge -.val)
4071        ?.  resend
4072          [new-val=`val stop=%.n acc]
4073        ::
4074          =.  last-sent.val  now.channel
4075          =.  tries.val      +(tries.val)
4076          =.  resends.acc    [(to-static-fragment key val) resends.acc]
4077          [new-val=`val stop=%.n acc]
4078      ::  +on-done: apply ack to all packets from .message-num
4079      ::
4080      ++  on-done
4081        |=  =message-num
4082        ^+  pack
4083        ::
4084        =-  =.  metrics.state  metrics.-
4085            =.  live.state     live.-
4086            ::
4087            %.  (fast-resend-after-ack message-num `fragment-num`0)
4088            (pu-trace snd.veb |.("done {<num=message-num show:gauge>}"))
4089        ::
4090        =/  acc  [metrics=metrics.state num-live=~(wyt by live.state)]
4091        ::
4092        ^+  [acc live=live.state]
4093        ::
4094        %^  (dip:packet-queue _acc)  live.state  acc
4095        |=  $:  acc=_acc
4096                key=live-packet-key
4097                val=live-packet-val
4098            ==
4099        ^-  [new-val=(unit live-packet-val) stop=? _acc]
4100        ::
4101        =/  gauge  (ga [metrics num-live]:acc)
4102        ::  if we get an out-of-order ack for a message, skip until it
4103        ::
4104        ?:  (lth message-num.key message-num)
4105          [new-val=`val stop=%.n acc]
4106        ::  if packet was from acked message, delete it and continue
4107        ::
4108        ?:  =(message-num.key message-num)
4109          =.  metrics.acc  (on-ack:gauge -.val)
4110          =.  num-live.acc  (dec num-live.acc)
4111          [new-val=~ stop=%.n acc]
4112        ::  we've gone past the acked message; we're done
4113        ::
4114        [new-val=`val stop=%.y acc]
4115      ::  +set-wake: set, unset, or reset timer, emitting moves
4116      ::
```

```
4117            ++  set-wake
4118             ^+  pack
4119             ::  if nonempty .live, pry at head to get next wake time
4120             ::
4121             =/  new-wake=(unit @da)
4122               ?~  head=(pry:packet-queue live.state)
4123                 ~
4124               `(next-expiry:gauge -.val.u.head)
4125             ::  no-op if no change
4126             ::
4127             ?:  =(new-wake next-wake.state)  pack
4128             ::  unset old timer if non-null
4129             ::
4130             =?  peer-core  !=(~ next-wake.state)
4131               (pu-emit %b %rest (need next-wake.state))
4132             ::  set new timer if non-null and not at at max-backoff
4133             ::
4134             ::  we are using the ~m2 literal instead of max-backoff:gauge
4135             ::  because /app/ping has a special cased maximum backoff of ~s25
4136             ::  and we don't want to consolidate that
4137             ::
4138             =?  peer-core  ?=(^ new-wake)
4139               ?:  ?&(?=(^ +.flow.dead.ames-state) =(~m2 rto.metrics.state))
4140                 peer-core
4141               (pu-emit %b %wait u.new-wake)
4142             ::
4143             =?  next-wake.state  !=(~ next-wake.state)   ~  ::  unset
4144             =?  next-wake.state  ?=(^ new-wake)   new-wake  ::  reset
4145             ::
4146           pack
4147         --
4148       --
4149     ::  +mi: constructor for |sink message receiver core
4150     ::
4151     ++  mi
4152       |_  [=bone state=message-sink-state]
4153       ::
4154       +|  %helpers
4155       ::
4156       ++  sink  .
4157       ++  abed
4158         |=  b=^bone
4159         sink(bone b, state (~(gut by rcv.peer-state) b *message-sink-state))
4160       ++  abet
4161         ::  if the bone was corked, it's been removed from the state,
4162         ::  so we avoid adding it again.
4163         ::
4164         =?  rcv.peer-state  !corked  (~(put by rcv.peer-state) bone state)
4165       peer-core
4166       ::
4167       ++  closing  (~(has in closing.peer-state) bone)
4168       ++  corked   (~(has in corked.peer-state) bone)
4169       ++  received
4170         |=  =^bone
4171         ::    odd bone:                %plea request message
4172         ::    even bone, 0 second bit: %boon response message
4173         ::    even bone, 1 second bit: nack-trace %boon message
4174         ::
```

```
4175          ?:  =(1 (end 0 bone))          %plea
4176          ?:  =(0 (end 0 (rsh 0 bone)))  %boon
4177        %nack
4178      ::
4179    +|  %entry-points
4180    ::  +call: handle a $message-sink-task
4181    ::
4182    ++  call
4183      |=  task=message-sink-task
4184      ^+  sink
4185      ?-    -.task
4186          %drop  sink(nax.state (~(del in nax.state) message-num.task))
4187          %done  (done ok.task)
4188          %flub
4189        %=  sink
4190          last-heard.state        (dec last-heard.state)
4191          pending-vane-ack.state  ~(nap to pending-vane-ack.state)
4192        ==
4193      ::
4194          %hear
4195      |^  ?:  ?|  corked
4196              ?&  %*(corked sink bone (mix 0b10 bone))
4197                  =(%nack (received bone))
4198          ==  ==
4199        ack-on-corked-bone
4200      ::
4201      ?>  ?=(%& -.meat.shut-packet.task)
4202      =+  [num-fragments fragment-num fragment]=+.meat.shut-packet.task
4203      ?:  &(=(num-fragments 1) =(fragment-num 0))
4204        (check-pending-acks fragment)
4205      (hear [lane shut-packet ok]:task)
4206      ::
4207      ++  ack-on-corked-bone
4208        ::  if we %hear a fragment on a corked bone, always ack
4209        ::
4210        =.  peer-core
4211          %+  send-shut-packet  bone
4212          [message-num.shut-packet.task %| %| ok=& lag=*@dr]
4213        %.  sink
4214        %+  pe-trace  odd.veb
4215        |.("hear {<(received bone)>} on corked bone={<bone>}")
4216      ::
4217      ++  check-pending-acks
4218        ::  if this is a %cork %plea and we are still waiting to
4219        ::  hear %acks for previous naxplanations we sent, no-op
4220        ::
4221        |=  frag=@uw
4222        ^+  sink
4223        =/  blob=*  (cue (rep packet-size [frag]~))
4224        =+  pump=(abed:mu (mix 0b10 bone))
4225        ?.  ?&  ?=(^ ;;((soft [%$ path %cork ~]) blob))
4226                ?=(^ live.packet-pump-state.state.pump)
4227            ==
4228          (hear [lane shut-packet ok]:task)
4229        %.  sink
4230        %+  pe-trace  odd.veb
4231        |.("pending ack for naxplanation, skip %cork bone={<bone>}")
4232        --
```

```
4233                  ==
4234              ::
4235              +|  %tasks
4236              ::  +hear: receive message fragment, possibly completing message
4237              ::
4238              ++  hear
4239                |=  [=lane =shut-packet ok=?]
4240                ^+  sink
4241                ::  we know this is a fragment, not an ack; expose into namespace
4242                ::
4243                ?>  ?=(%& -.meat.shut-packet)
4244                =+  [num-fragments fragment-num fragment]=+.meat.shut-packet
4245                ::  seq: message sequence number, for convenience
4246                ::
4247                =/  seq  message-num.shut-packet
4248                ::  ignore messages from far future; limit to 10 in progress
4249                ::
4250                ?:  (gte seq (add 10 last-acked.state))
4251                  %-  %+  pe-trace  odd.veb
4252                      |.("future %hear {<seq=seq last-acked=last-acked.state>}")
4253                  sink
4254                ::
4255                =/  is-last-fragment=?  =(+(fragment-num) num-fragments)
4256                ::  always ack a dupe!
4257                ::
4258                ?:  (lte seq last-acked.state)
4259                  ?.  is-last-fragment
4260                    ::  single packet ack
4261                    ::
4262                    =.  peer-core  (send-shut-packet bone seq %| %& fragment-num)
4263                    %.  sink
4264                    %+  pe-trace  rcv.veb
4265                    |.("send dupe ack {<seq=seq^fragment-num=fragment-num>}")
4266                  ::  whole message (n)ack
4267                  ::
4268                  =/       ok=?  !(~(has in nax.state) seq)
4269                  =.  peer-core  (send-shut-packet bone seq %| %| ok lag=`@dr`0)
4270                  %.  sink
4271                  %+  pe-trace  rcv.veb
4272                  |.("send dupe message ack {<seq=seq>} ok={<ok>}")
4273                ::  last-acked<seq<=last-heard; heard message, unprocessed
4274                ::
4275                ::    Only true if we've heard some packets we haven't acked, which
4276                ::    doesn't happen for boons.
4277                ::
4278                ?:  (lte seq last-heard.state)
4279                  ?:  &(is-last-fragment !closing)
4280                    ::  if not from a closing bone, drop last packet,
4281                    ::  since we don't know whether to ack or nack
4282                    ::
4283                    %-  %+  pe-trace  rcv.veb
4284                        |.  ^-  tape
4285                        =/  data
4286                          :*  her  seq=seq  bone=bone.shut-packet
4287                              fragment-num  num-fragments
4288                              la=last-acked.state  lh=last-heard.state
4289                          ==
4290                        "hear last in-progress {<data>}"
```

```
4291            sink
4292            ::  ack all other packets
4293            ::
4294            =.  peer-core  (send-shut-packet bone seq %| %& fragment-num)
4295            %-  %+  pe-trace  rcv.veb  |.
4296                =/  data
4297                  :*  seq=seq  fragment-num=fragment-num
4298                      num-fragments=num-fragments  closing=closing
4299                  ==
4300                "send ack-1 {<data>}"
4301          sink
4302          ::  last-heard<seq<10+last-heard; this is a packet in a live message
4303          ::
4304          =/  =partial-rcv-message
4305            ::  create default if first fragment
4306            ::
4307            ?~  existing=(~(get by live-messages.state) seq)
4308              [num-fragments num-received=0 fragments=~]
4309            ::  we have an existing partial message; check parameters match
4310            ::
4311            ?>  (gth num-fragments.u.existing fragment-num)
4312            ?>  =(num-fragments.u.existing num-fragments)
4313            ::
4314            u.existing
4315          ::
4316          =/  already-heard-fragment=?
4317            (~(has by fragments.partial-rcv-message) fragment-num)
4318          ::  ack dupes except for the last fragment, in which case drop
4319          ::
4320          ?:  already-heard-fragment
4321            ?:  is-last-fragment
4322              %-  %+  pe-trace  rcv.veb  |.
4323                  =/  data
4324                  [her seq=seq lh=last-heard.state la=last-acked.state]
4325                  "hear last dupe {<data>}"
4326              sink
4327            =.  peer-core  (send-shut-packet bone seq %| %& fragment-num)
4328            %.  sink
4329            %+  pe-trace  rcv.veb
4330            |.("send dupe ack {<her^seq=seq^fragment-num=fragment-num>}")
4331          ::  new fragment; store in state and check if message is done
4332          ::
4333          =.  num-received.partial-rcv-message
4334            +(num-received.partial-rcv-message)
4335          ::
4336          =.  fragments.partial-rcv-message
4337            (~(put by fragments.partial-rcv-message) fragment-num fragment)
4338          ::
4339          =.  live-messages.state
4340            (~(put by live-messages.state) seq partial-rcv-message)
4341          ::  ack any packet other than the last one, and continue either way
4342          ::
4343          =?  peer-core  !is-last-fragment
4344            %-  %+  pe-trace  rcv.veb  |.
4345                =/  data
4346                [seq=seq fragment-num=fragment-num fragments=num-fragments]
4347                "send ack-2 {<data>}"
4348            (send-shut-packet bone seq %| %& fragment-num)
```

```
4349              ::  enqueue all completed messages starting at +(last-heard.state)
4350              ::
4351          |-  ^+  sink
4352              ::  if this is not the next message to ack, we're done
4353              ::
4354          ?.  =(seq +(last-heard.state))
4355            sink
4356              ::  if we haven't heard anything from this message, we're done
4357              ::
4358          ?~  live=(~(get by live-messages.state) seq)
4359            sink
4360              ::  if the message isn't done yet, we're done
4361              ::
4362          ?.  =(num-received num-fragments):u.live
4363            sink
4364              ::  we have whole message; update state, assemble, and send to vane
4365              ::
4366          =.  last-heard.state     +(last-heard.state)
4367          =.  live-messages.state  (~(del by live-messages.state) seq)
4368              ::
4369          %-  %+  pe-trace  msg.veb
4370              |.("hear {<her>} {<seq=seq>} {<num-fragments.u.live>}kb")
4371          =/  message=*  (assemble-fragments [num-fragments fragments]:u.live)
4372          =/  empty=?    =(~ pending-vane-ack.state)
4373              ::  enqueue message to be sent to local vane
4374              ::
4375          =.  pending-vane-ack.state
4376            (~(put to pending-vane-ack.state) seq message)
4377              ::
4378          =?  sink  empty  (handle-sink seq message ok)
4379              ::
4380          $(seq +(seq))
4381        ::  +done: handle confirmation of message processing from vane
4382        ::
4383        ++  done
4384          |=  ok=?
4385          ^+  sink
4386              ::
4387          =^  pending  pending-vane-ack.state
4388            ~(get to pending-vane-ack.state)
4389          =/  =message-num  message-num.p.pending
4390              ::
4391          =.  last-acked.state  +(last-acked.state)
4392          =?  nax.state  !ok  (~(put in nax.state) message-num)
4393              ::
4394          =.  peer-core
4395            (send-shut-packet bone message-num %| %| ok lag=`@dr`0)
4396          ?~  next=~(top to pending-vane-ack.state)  sink
4397          (handle-sink message-num.u.next message.u.next ok)
4398      ::
4399      +|  %implementation
4400      ::  +handle-sink: dispatch message
4401      ::
4402      ++  handle-sink
4403        |=  [=message-num message=* ok=?]
4404        ^+  sink
4405        |^  ?-((received bone) %plea ha-plea, %boon ha-boon, %nack ha-nack)
4406            ::
```

```
4407        ++  ha-plea
4408          ^+  sink
4409          ?:  |(closing corked)  sink
4410          %-  %+  pe-trace  msg.veb
4411              =/  dat  [her bone=bone message-num=message-num]
4412              |.("sink plea {<dat>}")
4413          ?.  ok
4414            =/  nack-bone=^bone  (mix 0b10 bone)
4415            =/  =message-blob    (jam [message-num *error])
4416            =/  =wire  (make-bone-wire her her-rift.channel nack-bone)
4417            ::  send nack-trace with blank .error for security
4418            ::
4419            =.  peer-core
4420              %+  pe-emit  duct
4421              [%pass wire %a %deep %nack her nack-bone message-blob]
4422            ::
4423            (done ok=%.n)
4424          ::
4425          =/  =wire  (make-bone-wire her her-rift.channel bone)
4426          =.  peer-core
4427            =+  ;;  =plea  message
4428            ?.  =(vane.plea %$)
4429              ?+  vane.plea  ~|  %ames-evil-vane^our^her^vane.plea  !!
4430                %c  (pe-emit duct %pass wire %c %plea her plea)
4431                %e  (pe-emit duct %pass wire %e %plea her plea)
4432                %g  (pe-emit duct %pass wire %g %plea her plea)
4433                %j  (pe-emit duct %pass wire %j %plea her plea)
4434              ==
4435            ::  a %cork plea is handled using %$ as the recipient vane to
4436            ::  account for publishers that still handle ames-to-ames %pleas
4437            ::
4438            ?>  &(?=([%cork *] payload.plea) ?=(%flow -.path.plea))
4439            (pe-emit duct %pass wire %a %deep %cork her bone)
4440          sink
4441        ::
4442        ::  +ha-boon: handle response message, acking unconditionally
4443        ::
4444        ::    .bone must be mapped in .ossuary.peer-state, or we crash.
4445        ::    This means a malformed message will kill a flow.  We
4446        ::    could change this to a no-op if we had some sort of security
4447        ::    reporting.
4448        ::
4449        ::    Note that if we had several consecutive packets in the queue
4450        ::    and crashed while processing any of them, the %hole card
4451        ::    will turn *all* of them into losts/nacks.
4452        ::
4453        ::    TODO: This handles a previous crash in the client vane, but
4454        ::    not in %ames itself.
4455        ::
4456        ++  ha-boon
4457          ^+  sink
4458          ?:  |(closing corked)  sink
4459          %-  %+  pe-trace  msg.veb  |.
4460              ::  XX -.task not visible, FIXME
4461              ::
4462              =/  dat  [her bone=bone message-num=message-num]
4463              ?:(ok "sink boon {<dat>}" "crashed on sink boon {<dat>}")
4464          =.  peer-core  (pe-emit (got-duct bone) %give %boon message)
```

```
4465          =?  moves  !ok
4466            ::  we previously crashed on this message; notify client vane
4467            ::
4468          %+  turn  moves
4469          |=  =move
4470          ?.  ?=([* %give %boon *] move)  move
4471          [duct.move %give %lost ~]
4472        ::  send ack unconditionally
4473        ::
4474        (done ok=%.y)
4475      ::
4476      ++  ha-nack
4477        ^+  sink
4478        ::  if we get a naxplanation for a %cork, the publisher hasn't
4479        ::  received the OTA. The /recork timer will retry eventually.
4480        ::
4481        %-  %+  pe-trace  msg.veb
4482          =/  dat  [her bone=bone message-num=message-num]
4483          |.("sink naxplanation {<dat>}")
4484        ::  flip .bone's second bit to find referenced flow
4485        ::
4486        =/  target=^bone  (mix 0b10 bone)
4487        =.  peer-core
4488          ::  will notify |message-pump that this message got naxplained
4489          ::
4490          =/  =wire  (make-bone-wire her her-rift.channel target)
4491          %+  pe-emit  duct
4492          [%pass wire %a %deep %sink her target ;;(naxplanation message)]
4493        ::  ack nack-trace message (only applied if we don't later crash)
4494        ::
4495        (done ok=%.y)
4496      --
4497    --
4498  ::  +fi: constructor for |fine remote scry core
4499  ::
4500  ++  fi
4501    =>  |%
4502      ::  TODO: move +etch-peep/+etch-wail to %lull?
4503      ::
4504      ++  etch-peep
4505        |=  peep
4506        ^-  @
4507        ?>  (lth num ^~((bex 32)))
4508        =+  (spit path)
4509        %+  can  3
4510        :~  4^num        ::  fragment number
4511            2^wid        ::  path size
4512            wid^^@`pat  ::  namespace path
4513        ==
4514      ::
4515      ++  etch-wail
4516        |=  w=wail
4517        ^-  @
4518        ?-  -.w
4519          %0  (lsh 3 (etch-peep +.w))  ::  tag byte
4520        ==
4521      ::
4522      ++  make-shot
```

```
4523              |=  w=wail
4524              ^-  shot
4525              =/  sic  (mod life.ames-state 16)
4526              =/  ric  (mod life.peer-state 16)
4527              [[our her] req=& sam=| sic ric ~ (etch-wail w)]
4528            ::
4529            ::
4530          ++  keys
4531            |%
4532            ++  mess
4533              |=  [=ship life=@ud =path dat=$@(~ (cask))]
4534              (jam +<)
4535            ::
4536            ++  sign  sigh:as:crypto-core.ames-state
4537            ::
4538            ++  veri-fra
4539              |=  [=path fra=@ud dat=@ux sig=@]
4540              (veri sig (jam path fra dat))
4541            ::
4542            ++  veri
4543              |=  [sig=@ dat=@]
4544              ^-  ?
4545              (safe:as:(com:nu:crub:crypto public-key.peer-state) sig dat)
4546            ::
4547            ++  meri
4548              |=  [pax=path sig=@ dat=$@(~ (cask))]
4549              (veri sig (mess her life.peer-state pax dat))
4550            --
4551          --
4552        ::
4553        |_  [=path keen=keen-state]
4554        ::
4555        +|  %helpers
4556        ::
4557        ++  fine  .
4558        ++  abed
4559          |=  p=^path
4560          ~|  no-keen-for-path/p
4561          fine(path p, keen (~(got by keens) p))
4562        ::
4563        ++  fi-abet
4564          ^+  peer-core
4565          ?.  =,  keen
4566              ::  num-fragments is 0 when unknown (i.e. no response yet)
4567              ::  if no-one is listening, kill request
4568              ::
4569              ?|  =(~ listeners.keen)
4570                  &(!=(0 num-fragments) =(num-fragments num-received))
4571              ==
4572            =.  fine  fi-set-wake
4573          peer-core(keens.peer-state (~(put by keens) path keen))  :: XX tack.keens
4574          ::
4575          =?  fine  ?=(^ next-wake.keen)
4576            (fi-rest u.next-wake.keen)
4577          peer-core(keens.peer-state (~(del by keens) path))  :: XX tack.keens
4578        ::
4579        ++  fi-full-path
4580          :^    (scot %p her)
```

```
4581                    (scot %ud rift.peer-state)
4582                   (scot %ud life.peer-state)
4583               path
4584           ::
4585       ++  fi-show
4586         =,  keen
4587         :*  nex=(lent nex)
4588             hav=(lent hav)
4589             num-fragments=num-fragments
4590             num-received=num-received
4591             next-wake=next-wake
4592             metrics=metrics
4593         ==
4594           ::
4595       ++  fi-trace
4596         |=  [verb=? print=(trap tape)]
4597         ^+  same
4598         (trace %fine verb her ships.bug.ames-state print)
4599           ::
4600       ++  fi-emit         |=(move fine(event-core (emit +<)))
4601       ++  fi-mop          ((on @ud want) lte)
4602       ++  fi-gauge        (ga metrics.keen (wyt:fi-mop wan.keen))
4603       ++  fi-wait         |=(tim=@da (fi-pass-timer %b %wait tim))
4604       ++  fi-rest         |=(tim=@da (fi-pass-timer %b %rest tim))
4605           ::
4606       ++  fi-etch-wail
4607         |=(frag=@ud `hoot``@`(etch-shot (make-shot %0 fi-full-path frag)))
4608           ::
4609       ++  fi-send
4610         |=  =blob
4611         fine(event-core (send-blob for=| her blob `known/peer-state))
4612           ::
4613       ++  fi-give-tune
4614         |=  dat=(unit roar)
4615         |=([=^duct =_fine] (fi-emit:fine duct %give %tune [her path] dat))
4616           ::
4617       +|  %entry-points
4618           ::
4619       ++  fi-start
4620         |=  =^duct
4621         %-  (fi-trace fin.veb |.("keen {(spud fi-full-path)}"))
4622         =.  fine  (fi-sub duct)
4623         ?>  =(num-fragments.keen 0)
4624         =/  fra=@      1
4625         =/  req=hoot  (fi-etch-wail fra)
4626         =/     =want  [fra req last=now tries=1 skips=0]
4627         =.  wan.keen  (put:fi-mop ~ [fra .]:want)
4628         (fi-send `@ux`req)
4629           ::
4630       ++  fi-rcv
4631         |=  [[=full=^path num=@ud] =meow =lane:ames]
4632         ^+  fine
4633         =/  og  fine
4634         =.  peer-core  (update-qos %fine %live last-contact=now)
4635         ::  handle empty
4636         ?:  =(0 num.meow)
4637           ?>  =(~ dat.meow)
4638           (fi-done sig.meow ~)
```

```
4639              ::  update congestion, or fill details
4640              ::
4641              =?  fine  =(0 num-fragments.keen)
4642                ?>  =(num 1)
4643                (fi-first-rcv meow)
4644              ::
4645              ?.  ?=([@ @ @ *] full-path)
4646                ~|  fine-path-too-short+full-path
4647                !!
4648              ?.  =(`her (slaw %p i.full-path))
4649                ~|  fine-path-bunk-ship+[full-path her]
4650                !!
4651              ?.  =(`rift.peer-state (slaw %ud i.t.full-path))
4652                ~|  fine-path-bunk-rift+[full-path rift.peer-state]
4653                !!
4654              ?.  =(`life.peer-state (slaw %ud i.t.t.full-path))
4655                ~|  fine-path-bunk-life+[full-path life.peer-state]
4656                !!
4657              ?.  (veri-fra:keys [full-path num [dat sig]:meow])
4658                ~|  fine-purr-fail-signature/num^`@ux`sig.meow
4659                ~|  life.peer-state
4660                !!
4661              ::
4662              =^  found=?  fine  (fi-on-ack num)
4663              ?.  found
4664                (fi-fast-retransmit:og num)
4665              =.  num-received.keen  +(num-received.keen)
4666              =.  hav.keen
4667                ::  insert in reverse order
4668                ::
4669                |-  ^-  (list have)
4670                ?~  hav.keen
4671                  [num meow]~
4672                ?:  (lth num fra.i.hav.keen)
4673                  [i.hav.keen $(hav.keen t.hav.keen)]
4674                [[num meow] hav.keen]
4675              ?.  =(num-fragments num-received):keen
4676                fi-continue
4677              (fi-done [sig dat]:fi-sift-full)
4678            ::
4679            ++  fi-sub
4680              |=(=^duct fine(listeners.keen (~(put in listeners.keen) duct)))
4681            ::  scry is autocancelled in +abet if no more listeners
4682            ::
4683            ++  fi-unsub
4684              |=  [=^duct all=?]
4685              ^+  fine
4686              ?:  all
4687                %-  (fi-trace fin.veb |.("unsub all {<fi-full-path>}"))
4688                =.  fine  (~(rep in listeners.keen) (fi-give-tune ~))
4689                fine(listeners.keen ~)
4690              ::
4691              ?:  (~(has in listeners.keen) duct)
4692                %-  (fi-trace fin.veb |.("unsub {<fi-full-path>} on {<duct>}"))
4693                fine(listeners.keen (~(del in listeners.keen) duct))
4694              ::
4695              %.  fine
4696              (fi-trace fin.veb |.("unknown {<fi-full-path>} {<duct>}"))
```

```
4697        ::
4698        +|  %implementation
4699        ::
4700        ++  fi-on-ack
4701        =|  marked=(list want)
4702        |=  fra=@ud
4703        ^-  [found=? cor=_fine]
4704        =.  fine
4705          =/  first  (pry:fi-mop wan.keen)
4706          ?~  first
4707            fine
4708          ?:  =(fra fra.val.u.first)
4709            fine
4710          =^  resend=?  metrics.keen
4711            (on-skipped-packet:fi-gauge +>.val.u.first)
4712          ?:  !resend
4713            fine
4714          =.  tries.val.u.first  +(tries.val.u.first)
4715          =.  last-sent.val.u.first  now
4716          =.  wan.keen  (put:fi-mop wan.keen u.first)
4717          =.  fine  (fi-send `@ux`hoot.val.u.first)
4718          fine
4719        ::
4720        =/  found  (get:fi-mop wan.keen fra)
4721        ?~  found
4722          [| fine]
4723        =.  metrics.keen  (on-ack:fi-gauge +>.u.found)
4724        =.  wan.keen  +:(del:fi-mop wan.keen fra)
4725        [& fine]
4726        ::
4727        ++  fi-done
4728        |=  [sig=@ data=$@(~ (cask))]
4729        =/  ful  fi-full-path
4730        =/  roar=(unit roar)
4731          ?.  (meri:keys ful sig data)
4732            ~
4733          :+  ~  [ful ?~(data ~ `data)]
4734          [[her [life.peer-state sig]] ~ ~]
4735        ::
4736        %-  (fi-trace fin.veb |.("done {(spud ful)}"))
4737        (~(rep in listeners.keen) (fi-give-tune roar))
4738        ::
4739        ++  fi-first-rcv
4740        |=  =meow
4741        ^+  fine
4742        ::
4743        =;  paz=(list want)
4744          fine(keen keen(num-fragments num.meow, nex (tail paz)))
4745        %+  turn  (gulf 1 num.meow)
4746        |=  fra=@ud
4747        ^-  want
4748        [fra (fi-etch-wail fra) now 0 0]
4749        ::  +fi-continue: send packets based on normal congestion flow
4750        ::
4751        ++  fi-continue
4752        =|  inx=@ud
4753        =|  sent=(list @ud)
4754        =/  max  num-slots:fi-gauge
```

```
4755          |-  ^+  fine
4756          ?:  |(=(~ nex.keen) =(inx max))
4757            fine
4758          =^  =want  nex.keen  nex.keen
4759          =.  last-sent.want  now
4760          =.     tries.want  +(tries.want)
4761          =.       wan.keen  (put:fi-mop wan.keen [fra .]:want)
4762          =.           fine  (fi-send `@ux`hoot.want)
4763          $(inx +(inx))
4764        ::
4765        ++  fi-sift-full
4766          =,  keen
4767          ?.  ?&  =(num-fragments num-received)
4768                  =((lent hav) num-received)
4769              ==
4770            ~|  :-  %frag-mismatch
4771                [have/num-received need/num-fragments path/path]
4772            !!
4773          (sift-roar num-fragments hav)
4774        ::
4775        ++  fi-fast-retransmit
4776          |=  fra=@ud
4777          =;  [cor=_fine wants=_wan.keen]
4778            cor(wan.keen wants)
4779          %^  (dip:fi-mop ,cor=_fine)  wan.keen
4780            fine
4781          |=  [cor=_fine @ud =want]
4782          ^-  [(unit ^want) stop=? cor=_fine]
4783          ?.  (lte fra.want fra)
4784            [`want & cor]
4785          ?:  (gth (next-expiry:fi-gauge:cor +>.want) now)
4786            [`want & cor]
4787          =.  last-sent.want  now
4788          =.  cor  (fi-send:cor `@ux`hoot.want)
4789          [`want | cor]
4790        ::
4791        ++  fi-pass-timer
4792          |=  =note
4793          =/  =wire  (welp /fine/behn/wake/(scot %p her) path)
4794          (fi-emit unix-duct.ames-state %pass wire note)
4795        ::
4796        ++  fi-set-wake
4797          ^+  fine
4798          =/  next-wake=(unit @da)
4799            ?~  want=(pry:fi-mop wan.keen)
4800              ~
4801            `(next-expiry:fi-gauge +>:val.u.want)
4802          ?:  =(next-wake next-wake.keen)
4803            fine
4804          =?  fine  !=(~ next-wake.keen)
4805            =/  old  (need next-wake.keen)
4806            =.  next-wake.keen  ~
4807            (fi-rest old)
4808          =?  fine  ?=(^ next-wake)
4809            =.  next-wake.keen  next-wake
4810            (fi-wait u.next-wake)
4811          fine
4812        ::  +fi-take-wake: handle request packet timeout
```

```
4813            ::
4814            ++  fi-take-wake
4815              ^+  fine
4816              =.  next-wake.keen   ~
4817              =.  peer-core    (update-qos %fine qos:(is-peer-dead now peer-state))
4818              ::  has the direct route expired?
4819              ::
4820              =.  peer-state    (update-peer-route her peer-state)
4821              =.  metrics.keen  on-timeout:fi-gauge
4822              =^  want=(unit want)  wan.keen
4823                ?~  res=(pry:fi-mop wan.keen)  `wan.keen
4824                (del:fi-mop wan.keen key.u.res)
4825              ~|  %took-wake-for-empty-want
4826              ?>  ?=(^ want)
4827              =:      tries.u.want  +(tries.u.want)
4828                  last-sent.u.want  now
4829              ==
4830              =.  wan.keen  (put:fi-mop wan.keen [fra .]:u.want)
4831              (fi-send `@ux`hoot.u.want)
4832            --
4833          ::  +ga: constructor for |pump-gauge congestion control core
4834          ::
4835          ++  ga
4836            |=  [pump-metrics live-packets=@ud]
4837            =*  ship     her
4838            =*  now      now.channel
4839            =*  metrics  +<-
4840            |%
4841            +|  %helpers
4842            ::
4843            ++  ga-trace
4844              |=  [verb=? print=(trap tape)]
4845              ^+  same
4846              (trace %ames verb ship ships.bug.channel print)
4847            ::  +next-expiry: when should a newly sent fresh packet time out?
4848            ::
4849            ::    Use rtt + 4*sigma, where sigma is the mean deviation of rtt.
4850            ::    This should make it unlikely that a packet would time out
4851            ::    from a delay, as opposed to an actual packet loss.
4852            ::
4853            ++  next-expiry
4854              |=  packet-state
4855              ^-  @da
4856              (add last-sent rto)
4857            ::  +num-slots: how many packets can we send right now?
4858            ::
4859            ++  num-slots
4860              ^-  @ud
4861              (sub-safe cwnd live-packets)
4862            ::
4863            ::  +clamp-rto: apply min and max to an .rto value
4864            ::
4865            ++  clamp-rto
4866              |=  rto=@dr
4867              ^+  rto
4868              (min max-backoff (max ^~((div ~s1 5)) rto))
4869            ::  +max-backoff: calculate highest re-send interval
4870            ::
```

```
4871      ::      Keeps pinhole to sponsors open by inspecting the duct (hack).
4872      ::
4873      ++  max-backoff
4874        ^-  @dr
4875        ?:(?=([[%gall %use %ping *] *] duct) ~s25 ~m2)
4876      ::  +in-slow-start: %.y if we're in "slow-start" mode
4877      ::
4878      ++  in-slow-start
4879        ^-  ?
4880        (lth cwnd ssthresh)
4881      ::  +in-recovery: %.y if we're recovering from a skipped packet
4882      ::
4883      ::      We finish recovering when .live-packets finally dips back
4884      ::      down to .cwnd.
4885      ::
4886      ++  in-recovery
4887        ^-  ?
4888        (gth live-packets cwnd)
4889      ::  +sub-safe: subtract with underflow protection
4890      ::
4891      ++  sub-safe
4892        |=  [a=@ b=@]
4893        ^-  @
4894        ?:((lte a b) 0 (sub a b))
4895      ::  +show: produce a printable version of .metrics
4896      ::
4897      ++  show
4898        =/  ms   (div ~s1 1.000)
4899        ::
4900        :*  rto=(div rto ms)
4901            rtt=(div rtt ms)
4902            rttvar=(div rttvar ms)
4903            ssthresh=ssthresh
4904            cwnd=cwnd
4905            num-live=live-packets
4906            counter=counter
4907        ==
4908      ::
4909      +|  %entry-points
4910      ::  +on-ack: adjust metrics based on a packet getting acknowledged
4911      ::
4912      ++  on-ack
4913        |=  =packet-state
4914        ^-  pump-metrics
4915        ::
4916        =.  counter  +(counter)
4917        ::  if below congestion threshold, add 1; else, add avg 1 / cwnd
4918        ::
4919        =.  cwnd
4920          ?:  in-slow-start
4921            +(cwnd)
4922          (add cwnd !=(0 (mod (mug now) cwnd)))
4923        ::  if this was a re-send, don't adjust rtt or downstream state
4924        ::
4925        ?:  (gth tries.packet-state 1)
4926          metrics(rto (clamp-rto (add rtt (mul 4 rttvar))))
4927        ::  rtt-datum: new rtt measurement based on packet roundtrip
4928        ::
```

```
4929        =/  rtt-datum=@dr  (sub-safe now last-sent.packet-state)
4930        ::  rtt-error: difference between this measurement and expected
4931        ::
4932        =/  rtt-error=@dr
4933         ?:  (gte rtt-datum rtt)
4934          (sub rtt-datum rtt)
4935         (sub rtt rtt-datum)
4936        ::  exponential weighting ratio for .rtt and .rttvar
4937        ::
4938        =.  rtt     (div (add rtt-datum (mul rtt 7)) 8)
4939        =.  rttvar  (div (add rtt-error (mul rttvar 7)) 8)
4940        =.  rto     (clamp-rto (add rtt (mul 4 rttvar)))
4941        ::
4942        %.  metrics
4943        %+  ga-trace  ges.veb  |.
4944        "ack update {<show rtt-datum=rtt-datum rtt-error=rtt-error>}"
4945      ::  +on-skipped-packet: handle misordered ack
4946      ::
4947      ++  on-skipped-packet
4948        |=  packet-state
4949        ^-  [resend=? pump-metrics]
4950        ::
4951        =/  resend=?  &((lte tries 1) |(in-recovery (gte skips 3)))
4952        :-  resend
4953        ::
4954        =?  cwnd  !in-recovery (max 2 (div cwnd 2))
4955        %-  %+  ga-trace  snd.veb
4956            |.("skip {<resend=resend in-recovery=in-recovery show>}")
4957        metrics
4958      ::  +on-timeout: (re)enter slow-start mode on packet loss
4959      ::
4960      ++  on-timeout
4961        ^-  pump-metrics
4962        ::
4963        %-  (ga-trace ges.veb |.("timeout update {<show>}"))
4964        =:  ssthresh  (max 1 (div cwnd 2))
4965            cwnd  1
4966            rto   (clamp-rto (mul rto 2))
4967          ==
4968        metrics
4969        --
4970      --
4971    --
4972  --
4973  ::  adult ames, after metamorphosis from larva
4974  ::
4975  =|  =ames-state
4976  |=  [now=@da eny=@ rof=roof]
4977  =*  ames-gate  .
4978  =*  veb  veb.bug.ames-state
4979  |%
4980  ::  +call: handle request $task
4981  ::
4982  ++  call
4983    |=  [=duct dud=(unit goof) wrapped-task=(hobo task)]
4984    ^-  [(list move) _ames-gate]
4985    ::
4986    =/  =task        ((harden task) wrapped-task)
```

```
4987    =/  event-core  (ev [now eny rof] duct ames-state)
4988    ::
4989    =^  moves  ames-state
4990      =<  abet
4991      ::  handle error notifications
4992      ::
4993      ?^  dud
4994        ?+  -.task
4995            (on-crud:event-core -.task tang.u.dud)
4996          %hear  (on-hear:event-core lane.task blob.task dud)
4997        ==
4998      ::
4999      ?-  -.task
5000        %born  on-born:event-core
5001        %hear  (on-hear:event-core [lane blob ~]:task)
5002        %dear  (on-dear:event-core +.task)
5003        %heed  (on-heed:event-core ship.task)
5004        %init  on-init:event-core
5005        %jilt  (on-jilt:event-core ship.task)
5006        %prod  (on-prod:event-core ships.task)
5007        %sift  (on-sift:event-core ships.task)
5008        %snub  (on-snub:event-core [form ships]:task)
5009        %spew  (on-spew:event-core veb.task)
5010        %cong  (on-cong:event-core [msg mem]:task)
5011        %stir  (on-stir:event-core arg.task)
5012        %trim  on-trim:event-core
5013        %vega  on-vega:event-core
5014        %plea  (on-plea:event-core [ship plea]:task)
5015        %cork  (on-cork:event-core ship.task)
5016        %tame  (on-tame:event-core ship.task)
5017        %kroc  (on-kroc:event-core bones.task)
5018        %deep  (on-deep:event-core deep.task)
5019      ::
5020        %keen  (on-keen:event-core +.task)
5021        %yawn  (on-cancel-scry:event-core | +.task)
5022        %wham  (on-cancel-scry:event-core & +.task)
5023      ==
5024    ::
5025    [moves ames-gate]
5026    ::  +take: handle response $sign
5027    ::
5028    ++  take
5029      |=  [=wire =duct dud=(unit goof) =sign]
5030      ^-  [(list move) _ames-gate]
5031      ?^  dud
5032        ~|(%ames-take-dud (mean tang.u.dud))
5033      ::
5034      =/  event-core  (ev [now eny rof] duct ames-state)
5035      ::
5036      =^  moves  ames-state
5037        ?:  ?=([%gall %unto *] sign)
5038          `ames-state
5039        ::
5040        =<  abet
5041        ?-  sign
5042          [@ %done *]  (on-take-done:event-core wire error.sign)
5043          [@ %boon *]  (on-take-boon:event-core wire payload.sign)
5044        ::
```

```
5045        [%behn %wake *]   (on-take-wake:event-core wire error.sign)
5046      ::
5047        [%gall %flub ~]   (on-take-flub:event-core wire)
5048      ::
5049        [%jael %turf *]        (on-take-turf:event-core turf.sign)
5050        [%jael %private-keys *]  (on-priv:event-core [life vein]:sign)
5051        [%jael %public-keys *]   (on-publ:event-core wire public-keys-result.sign)
5052      ==
5053    ::
5054    [moves ames-gate]
5055  ::  +stay: extract state before reload
5056  ::
5057  ++  stay  [%17 %adult ames-state]
5058  ::  +load: load in old state after reload
5059  ::
5060  ++  load
5061    =<  |=  $=  old-state
5062            $%  [%17 ^ames-state]
5063            ==
5064        ^+  ames-gate
5065        ?>  ?=(%17 -.old-state)
5066        ames-gate(ames-state +.old-state)
5067    ::  all state transitions are called from larval ames
5068    ::
5069    |%
5070    ++  our-beam  `beam`[[our %rift %da now] /(scot %p our)]
5071    ++  state-4-to-5
5072      |=  ames-state=ames-state-4
5073      ^-  ames-state-5
5074      =.  peers.ames-state
5075        %-  ~(run by peers.ames-state)
5076        |=  ship-state=ship-state-4
5077        ?.  ?=(%known -.ship-state)
5078          ship-state
5079        =.  snd.ship-state
5080          %-  ~(run by snd.ship-state)
5081          |=  pump=message-pump-state-16
5082          =.  num-live.metrics.packet-pump-state.pump
5083            ~(wyt in live.packet-pump-state.pump)
5084          pump
5085        ship-state
5086      ames-state
5087    ::
5088    ++  state-5-to-6
5089      |=  ames-state=ames-state-5
5090      ^-  ames-state-6
5091      :_  +.ames-state
5092      %-  ~(rut by peers.ames-state)
5093      |=  [=ship ship-state=ship-state-5]
5094      ^-  ship-state-6
5095      ?.  ?=(%known -.ship-state)
5096        ship-state
5097      =/  peer-state=peer-state-5  +.ship-state
5098      =/  =rift
5099        ::  harcoded because %jael doesn't have data about comets
5100        ::
5101        ?:  ?=(%pawn (clan:title ship))  0
5102        ;;  @ud
```

```
5103      =<  q.q  %-  need  %-  need
5104     (rof ~ /ames %j `beam`[[our %rift %da now] /(scot %p ship)])
5105   :-  -.ship-state
5106   :_  +.peer-state
5107   =,  -.peer-state
5108   [symmetric-key life rift public-key sponsor]
5109   ::
5110   ++  state-6-to-7
5111    |=  ames-state=ames-state-6
5112    ^-  ames-state-7
5113    :_  +.ames-state
5114    %-  ~(run by peers.ames-state)
5115    |=  ship-state=ship-state-6
5116    ^-  ship-state-7
5117    ?.  ?=(%known -.ship-state)
5118     ship-state
5119    :-  %known
5120    ^-  peer-state-7
5121    :-  +<.ship-state
5122    [route qos ossuary snd rcv nax heeds ~ ~ ~]:ship-state
5123   ::
5124   ++  state-7-to-8
5125    |=  ames-state=ames-state-7
5126    ^-  ames-state-8
5127    =,  ames-state
5128    :*  peers  unix-duct  life  crypto-core  bug
5129        *(set wire)
5130    ==
5131   ::
5132   ++  state-8-to-9
5133    |=  ames-state=ames-state-8
5134    ^-  ames-state-9
5135    =,  ames-state
5136    :*  peers  unix-duct  life  crypto-core  bug  corks
5137        *(set ship)
5138    ==
5139   ::
5140   ++  state-9-to-10
5141    |=  ames-state=ames-state-9
5142    ^-  ames-state-10
5143    =,  ames-state
5144    :*  peers  unix-duct  life  crypto-core
5145        %=  bug.ames-state
5146          veb  [&1 &2 &3 &4 &5 &6 |6 %.n]:veb.bug
5147        ==
5148        corks  snub
5149    ==
5150   ::
5151   ++  state-10-to-11
5152    |=  ames-state=ames-state-10
5153    ^-  ames-state-11
5154    =,  ames-state
5155    :*  peers  unix-duct  life  crypto-core  bug  corks  snub
5156        ::  5 messages and 100Kb of data outstanding
5157        ::
5158        [msg=5 mem=100.000]
5159    ==
5160   ::
```

```
5161  ++  state-11-to-12
5162    |=  ames-state=ames-state-11
5163    ^-  ames-state-12
5164    :_  =,  ames-state
5165        :*  unix-duct
5166            life
5167            crypto-core
5168            bug
5169            [%deny snub]
5170            cong
5171        ==
5172    ^-  (map ship ship-state-12)
5173    %-  ~(run by peers.ames-state)
5174    |=  ship-state=ship-state-7
5175    ^-  ship-state-12
5176    ?.  ?=(%known -.ship-state)
5177      ship-state
5178    %=  ship-state
5179      +>  [route qos ossuary snd rcv nax heeds closing corked]:+>.ship-state
5180    ==
5181  ::
5182  ++  state-12-to-13
5183    |=  old=ames-state-12
5184    ^-  ames-state-13
5185    =+  !<(=rift q:(need (need (rof ~ /ames %j our-beam))))
5186    =+  pk=sec:ex:crypto-core.old
5187    :*  peers=(~(run by peers.old) ship-state-12-to-13)
5188        unix-duct.old
5189        life.old
5190        rift
5191        ?:(=(*ring pk) *acru:ames (nol:nu:crub:crypto pk))
5192        %=  bug.old
5193          veb  [&1 &2 &3 &4 &5 &6 &7 |7 %.n]:veb.bug.old
5194        ==
5195        snub.old
5196        cong.old
5197    ==
5198  ::
5199  ++  ship-state-12-to-13
5200    |=  old=ship-state-12
5201    ^-  ship-state-13
5202    ?:  ?=(%alien -.old)
5203      old(heeds [heeds.old ~])
5204    old(corked [corked.old ~])
5205  ::
5206  ++  state-13-to-14
5207    |=  old=ames-state-13
5208    ^-  ames-state-14
5209    =-  old(peers -)
5210    %-  ~(run by peers.old)
5211    |=  old=ship-state-13
5212    |^  ?:  ?=(%alien -.old)  old
5213    old(keens (~(run by keens.old) keen-state-13-to-14))
5214    ::
5215    ++  keen-state-13-to-14
5216      |=  old=keen-state-13
5217      ^-  keen-state-14
5218      =-  old(wan -)
```

```
5219        %+  gas:((on @ud want) lte)  ~
5220        %+  turn  (tap:(deq:keen-state-13 want) wan.old)
5221        |=  =want  [fra .]:want
5222      --
5223    ::
5224    ++  state-14-to-15
5225      |=  old=ames-state-14
5226      ^-  ames-state-15
5227      old(rift !<(=rift q:(need (need (rof ~ /ames %j our-beam)))))
5228    ::
5229    ++  state-15-to-16
5230      |=  old=ames-state-15
5231      ^-  ames-state-16
5232      ::  re-initialize default congestion control values, if bunted
5233      ::
5234      old(cong ?.(=(cong.old [0 0]) cong.old [5 100.000]))
5235    ::
5236    ++  state-16-to-17
5237      |=  old=ames-state-16
5238      ^-  ^ames-state
5239      %=    old
5240          cong
5241        :+  cong.old
5242          flow/~
5243        cork/`[~[/ames] /recork `@da`(add now ~d1)]
5244        ::
5245          peers
5246        %-  ~(run by peers.old)
5247        |=  ship-state=ship-state-16
5248        ^-  ^ship-state
5249        ?.  ?=(%known -.ship-state)
5250          ship-state
5251        |^
5252        %=    ship-state
5253          snd    (~(run by snd.ship-state) message-pump-16-to-17)
5254          keens  (~(run by keens.ship-state) keen-state-16-to-17)
5255          rcv    (~(rut by rcv.ship-state) remove-outbound-naxplanations)
5256        ==
5257        ::
5258        ++  message-pump-16-to-17
5259          |=  pump=message-pump-state-16
5260          ^-  message-pump-state
5261          %=    pump
5262              metrics.packet-pump-state
5263            [rto rtt rttvar ssthresh cwnd counter]:metrics.packet-pump-state.pump
5264          ==
5265        ::
5266        ++  keen-state-16-to-17
5267          |=  keen-state=keen-state-16
5268          ^-  ^keen-state
5269          %=  keen-state
5270            metrics  [rto rtt rttvar ssthresh cwnd counter]:metrics.keen-state
5271          ==
5272        ::
5273        ++  remove-outbound-naxplanations
5274          |=  [=bone sink=message-sink-state]
5275          ^+  sink
5276          =/  target=^bone  (mix 0b10 bone)
```

```
5277            ?.  =(%3 (mod target 4))
5278              sink
5279            ?~  pump=(~(get by snd.ship-state) target)
5280              sink
5281            %_    sink
5282              nax
5283            %-  ~(rep in nax.sink)
5284            |=  [=message-num nax=(set message-num)]
5285            ::  we keep messages in the queue that have not been acked.
5286            ::  if the message-num for the naxplanation we sent is
5287            ::  less than the current message, +pump-done:mu had been called,
5288            ::  so the message-num can be safely removed
5289            ::
5290            =?  nax  (gte message-num current.u.pump)
5291              (~(put in nax) message-num)
5292            nax
5293          ==
5294        --
5295      ==
5296    --
5297  ::  +scry: dereference namespace
5298  ::
5299  ++  scry
5300    ^-  roon
5301    |=  [lyc=gang pov=path car=term bem=beam]
5302    ^-  (unit (unit cage))
5303    =*  ren  car
5304    =*  why=shop  &/p.bem
5305    =*  syd  q.bem
5306    =*  lot=coin  $/r.bem
5307    =*  tyl  s.bem
5308    ::
5309    ::  only respond for the local identity, %$ desk, current timestamp
5310    ::
5311    ?.  ?&  =(&+our why)
5312            =([%$ %da now] lot)
5313            =(%$ syd)
5314        ==
5315      ?.  for.veb.bug.ames-state  ~
5316      ~>  %slog.0^leaf/"ames: scry-fail {<why=why lot=lot now=now syd=syd>}"
5317      ~
5318    ::  /ax//whey                    (list mass)
5319    ::  /ax/protocol/version         @
5320    ::  /ax/peers                    (map ship ?(%alien %known))
5321    ::  /ax/peers/[ship]             ship-state
5322    ::  /ax/peers/[ship]/last-contact  (unit @da)
5323    ::  /ax/peers/[ship]/forward-lane  (list lane)
5324    ::  /ax/bones/[ship]             [snd=(set bone) rcv=(set bone)]
5325    ::  /ax/snd-bones/[ship]/[bone]  vase
5326    ::  /ax/snubbed                  (?(%allow %deny) (list ship))
5327    ::  /ax/fine/hunk/[path/...]     (list @ux) scry response fragments
5328    ::  /ax/fine/ducts/[path/]       (list duct)
5329    ::  /ax/rift                     @
5330    ::  /ax/corked/[ship]            (set bone)
5331    ::  /ax/closing/[ship]           (set bone)
5332    ::
5333    ?.  ?=(%x ren)  ~
5334    =>  .(tyl `(pole knot)`tyl)
```

```
5335    ?+    tyl  ~
5336       [%$ %whey ~]
5337    =/  maz=(list mass)
5338       =+  [known alien]=(skid ~(val by peers.ames-state) |=(^ =(%known +<-)))
5339       :~  peers-known+&+known
5340           peers-alien+&+alien
5341       ==
5342    ``mass+!>(maz)
5343    ::
5344       [%protocol %version ~]
5345    ``noun+!>(protocol-version)
5346    ::
5347       [%peers ~]
5348    :^    ~   ~  %noun
5349    !>  ^-  (map ship ?(%alien %known))
5350    (~(run by peers.ames-state) head)
5351    ::
5352       [%peers her=@ req=*]
5353    =/  who  (slaw %p her.tyl)
5354    ?~  who  [~ ~]
5355    =/  peer  (~(get by peers.ames-state) u.who)
5356    ?+    req.tyl  [~ ~]
5357       ~
5358    ?~  peer
5359       [~ ~]
5360    ``noun+!>(u.peer)
5361    ::
5362       [%last-contact ~]
5363    :^    ~   ~  %noun
5364    !>  ^-  (unit @da)
5365    ?.  ?=([~ %known *] peer)
5366       ~
5367    `last-contact.qos.u.peer
5368    ::
5369       [%forward-lane ~]
5370       ::
5371       ::  this duplicates the routing hack from +send-blob:event-core
5372       ::  so long as neither the peer nor the peer's sponsoring galaxy is us,
5373       ::  and the peer has been reached recently:
5374       ::
5375       ::    - no route to the peer, or peer has not been contacted recently:
5376       ::      send to the peer's sponsoring galaxy
5377       ::    - direct route to the peer: use that
5378       ::    - indirect route to the peer: send to both that route and the
5379       ::      the peer's sponsoring galaxy
5380       ::
5381    :^    ~   ~  %noun
5382    !>  ^-  (list lane)
5383    ?:  =(our u.who)
5384       ~
5385    ?.  ?=([~ %known *] peer)
5386       =/  sax  (rof ~ /ames %j `beam`[[our %saxo %da now] /(scot %p u.who)])
5387       ?.  ?=([~ ~ *] sax)
5388          ~
5389       =/  gal  (rear ;;((list ship) q.q.u.u.sax))
5390       ?:  =(our gal)
5391          ~
5392       [%& gal]~
```

```
5393        =;  zar=(trap (list lane))
5394         ?~  route.u.peer  $:zar
5395         =*  rot  u.route.u.peer
5396         ?:(direct.rot [lane.rot ~] [lane.rot $:zar])
5397       ::
5398       |.  ^-  (list lane)
5399       ?:  ?=(%czar (clan:title sponsor.u.peer))
5400         ?:  =(our sponsor.u.peer)
5401           ~
5402         [%& sponsor.u.peer]~
5403       =/  next  (~(get by peers.ames-state) sponsor.u.peer)
5404       ?.  ?=([~ %known *] next)
5405         ~
5406       $(peer next)
5407     ==
5408   ::
5409       [%bones her=@ ~]
5410     =/  who  (slaw %p· her.tyl)
5411     ?~  who  [~ ~]
5412     =/  per  (~(get by peers.ames-state) u.who)
5413     ?.  ?=([~ %known *] per)  [~ ~]
5414     =/  res
5415       =,  u.per
5416       [snd=~(key by snd) rcv=~(key by rcv)]
5417     ``noun+!>(res)
5418   ::
5419       [%snd-bones her=@ bon=@ ~]
5420     =/  who  (slaw %p her.tyl)
5421     ?~  who  [~ ~]
5422     =/  ost  (slaw %ud bon.tyl)
5423     ?~  ost  [~ ~]
5424     =/  per  (~(get by peers.ames-state) u.who)
5425     ?.  ?=([~ %known *] per)  [~ ~]
5426     =/  mps  (~(get by snd.u.per) u.ost)
5427     ?~  mps  [~ ~]
5428     =/  res
5429       u.mps
5430     ``noun+!>(!>(res))
5431   ::
5432       [%snubbed ~]
5433     ``noun+!>([form.snub.ames-state ~(tap in ships.snub.ames-state)])
5434   ::
5435       [%fine %hunk lop=@t len=@t pax=^]
5436     ::TODO  separate endpoint for the full message (instead of packet list)
5437     :: .pax is expected to be a scry path of the shape /vc/desk/rev/etc,
5438     :: so we need to give it the right shape
5439     ::
5440     ?~  blk=(de-path-soft:balk pax.tyl)  ~
5441     ::
5442     ?.  ?&  =(our her.u.blk)
5443             =(rift.ames-state rif.u.blk)
5444             =(life.ames-state lyf.u.blk)
5445         ==
5446       ~&  [%fine-mismatch our=[rift life]:ames-state her=[her rif lyf]:u.blk]
5447       ~
5448     =+  nom=(as-omen:balk u.blk)
5449     ~|  nom
5450     |^
```

```
5451      =/  van  ?@(vis.nom (end 3 vis.nom) way.vis.nom)
5452      ?+    van  ~
5453        %c
5454      =+  pem=(rof lyc /ames nom(vis %cp))
5455      ?.  ?=(^ pem)     ~
5456      ?.  ?=(^ u.pem)   ~
5457      ~|  u.u.pem
5458      =+  per=!<([r=dict:clay w=dict:clay] q.u.u.pem)
5459      ?.  =([%black ~ ~] rul.r.per)  ~
5460      (en-hunk (rof ~ /ames nom))
5461      ::
5462        %e
5463      =/  kyr  ?@(vis.nom (rsh 3 vis.nom) car.vis.nom)
5464      %-  en-hunk
5465      ?+  kyr  ~
5466        %x  (rof ~ /ames nom)
5467      ==
5468      ::
5469        %g
5470      =/  kyr  ?@(vis.nom (rsh 3 vis.nom) car.vis.nom)
5471      %-  en-hunk
5472      ?+  kyr  ~
5473        %x  (rof ~ /ames nom)
5474      ==
5475      ==
5476      ::
5477    ++  en-hunk
5478      |=  res=(unit (unit cage))
5479      ^+  res
5480      ?~  res  ~
5481      =/  =hunk  [(slav %ud lop.tyl) (slav %ud len.tyl)]
5482      ::
5483      =/  hu-co  (etch-hunk our [life crypto-core]:ames-state)
5484      ?-  res
5485        [~ ~]      ``noun+!>((etch:hu-co pax.tyl hunk ~))
5486        [~ ~ *]    ``noun+!>((etch:hu-co pax.tyl hunk [p q.q]:u.u.res))
5487      ==
5488      --
5489    ::
5490      [%fine %ducts pax=^]
5491    ?~  bulk=(de-path-soft:balk pax.tyl)  ~
5492    ?~  peer=(~(get by peers.ames-state) her.u.bulk)
5493      [~ ~]
5494    ?.  ?=([~ %known *] peer)
5495      [~ ~]  :: TODO handle aliens
5496    ?~  spr.u.bulk  [~ ~]
5497    =/  =path  =,(u.bulk [van car (scot cas) spr])
5498    ?~  keen=(~(get by keens.u.peer) path)
5499      [~ ~]
5500    ``noun+!>(listeners:u.keen)
5501    ::
5502      [%rift ~]
5503    ``noun+!>(rift.ames-state)
5504    ::
5505      [%corked her=@ ~]
5506    =/  who  (slaw %p her.tyl)
5507    ?~  who  [~ ~]
5508    =/  per  (~(get by peers.ames-state) u.who)
```

```
5509      ?.   ?=([~ %known *] per)   [~ ~]
5510      ``noun+!>(corked.u.per)
5511   ::
5512        [%closing her=@ ~]
5513    =/   who  (slaw %p her.tyl)
5514    ?~   who  [~ ~]
5515    =/   per  (~(get by peers.ames-state) u.who)
5516    ?.   ?=([~ %known *] per)   [~ ~]
5517    ``noun+!>(closing.u.per)
5518   ==
5519   --
```

Behn 164K

```
1  ::  %behn, just a timer
2  !:
3  !?  164
4  ::
5  =,  behn
6  |=  our=ship
7  =>  |%
8    +$  move  [p=duct q=(wite note gift)]
9    +$  note                                       ::  out request $->
10     $~  [%b %wait *@da]                           ::
11     $%  $:  %b                                    ::    to self
12           $>(%wait task)                          ::  set timer
13         ==                                        ::
14         $:  %d                                    ::    to %dill
15           $>(%flog task:dill)                     ::  log output
16     ==  ==                                        ::
17   +$  sign
18     $~  [%behn %wake ~]
19     $%  [%behn $>(%wake gift)]
20     ==
21   ::
22   +$  behn-state
23     $:  %2
24         timers=(tree [key=@da val=(qeu duct)])
25         unix-duct=duct
26         next-wake=(unit @da)
27         drips=drip-manager
28     ==
29   ::
30   ++  timer-map  ((ordered-map ,@da ,(qeu duct)) lte)
31   ::
32   +$  drip-manager
33     $:  count=@ud
34         movs=(map @ud vase)
35     ==
36   ::
37   +$  timer  [date=@da =duct]
38   --
39  ::
40  =>
41  ~%  %behn  ..part  ~
42  |%
43  ++  per-event
44    =|  moves=(list move)
45    |=  [[now=@da =duct] state=behn-state]
46    ::
47    |%
48    ::
49    +|  %helpers
50    ::
51    ++  this  .
52    ++  emit  |=(m=move this(moves [m moves]))
53    ++  abet
54      ^+  [moves state]
55      ::  moves are statefully pre-flopped to ensure that
56      ::  any prepended %doze is emitted first
```

```
57    ::
58    =.  moves  (flop moves)
59    =/  new=(unit @da)  (bind (pry:timer-map timers.state) head)
60    ::  emit %doze if needed
61    ::
62    =?  ..this
63        ?~  unix-duct.state  |
64        =/  dif=[old=(unit @da) new=(unit @da)]  [next-wake.state new]
65        ?+  dif  ~|([%unpossible dif] !!)
66          [~ ~]  |                      :: no-op
67          [~ ^]  &                      :: set
68          [^ ~]  &                      :: clear
69          [^ ^]  !=(u.old.dif u.new.dif)  :: set if changed
70        ==
71      (emit(next-wake.state new) [unix-duct.state %give %doze new])
72    ::
73    [moves state]
74  ::
75  +|  %entry-points
76  ::
77  ++  call
78  |=  [=task error=(unit tang)]
79  ^+  this
80  ?:  ?&  ?=(^ error)
81          !?=(%wake -.task)
82      ==
83    ::  XX more and better error handling
84    ::
85    ~&  %behn-crud-not-wake^-.task
86    (emit [duct %slip %d %flog %crud -.task u.error])
87  ::
88  ?-  -.task
89    %born  this(next-wake.state ~, unix-duct.state duct)
90    %drip  (drip p.task)
91    %huck  (emit [duct %give %heck syn.task])
92    %rest  this(timers.state (unset-timer [p.task duct]))
93    %trim  this
94    %vega  this
95    %wait  this(timers.state (set-timer [p.task duct]))
96    %wake  (wake(next-wake.state ~) error)
97  ==
98  ::
99  ::  +take-drip: the future is now, %give the deferred move
100 ::
101 ++  take-drip
102 |=  [num=@ud error=(unit tang)]
103 ^+  this
104 =/  drip  (~(got by movs.drips.state) num)
105 %-  emit(movs.drips.state (~(del by movs.drips.state) num))
106 =/  card  [%give %meta drip]
107 ?~  error
108   [duct card]
109 =/  =tang
110   (weld u.error `tang`[leaf/"drip failed" ~])
111 ::  XX we don't know the mote due to the %wake pattern
112 ::
113 [duct %hurl fail/tang card]
114 ::
```

```
115    +|   %tasks
116    ::
117    ::   +drip: enqueue a future gift (as a vase), %pass ourselves a %wait
118    ::
119    ++   drip
120      |=   vax=vase
121      ^+   this
122    %.   [duct %pass /drip/(scot %ud count.drips.state) %b %wait +(now)]
123    %=   emit
124      movs.drips.state   (~(put by movs.drips.state) count.drips.state vax)
125      count.drips.state  +(count.drips.state)
126      ==
127    ::
128    ::   +wake: unix says wake up; process the elapsed timer (or forward error)
129    ::
130    ++   wake
131      |=   error=(unit tang)
132      ^+   this
133      ?:   =(~ timers.state)
134        ::   no-op on spurious but innocuous unix wakeups
135        ::
136        ~?   ?=(^ error)   %behn-wake-no-timer^u.error
137        this
138      =/   [=timer later-timers=_timers.state]   pop-timer
139      ?:   (gth date.timer now)
140        ::   no-op if timer is early, (+abet will reset)
141        ::
142        this
143      ::   pop the first timer and notify client vane,
144      ::   forwarding error if present
145      ::
146      ::     XX %wake errors should be signaled out-of-band
147      ::     [duct.timer %hurl goof %give %wake ~]
148      ::
149      (emit(timers.state later-timers) [duct.timer %give %wake error])
150    ::
151    +|   %implementation
152    ::
153    ::   +pop-timer: dequeue and produce earliest timer
154    ::
155    ++   pop-timer
156      ^+   [*timer timers.state]
157      =^   [date=@da dux=(qeu ^duct)]   timers.state   (pop:timer-map timers.state)
158      =^   dut   dux   ~(get to dux)
159      :-   [date dut]
160      ?:   =(~ dux)
161        timers.state
162      (put:timer-map timers.state date dux)
163    ::   +set-timer: set a timer, maintaining order
164    ::
165    ++   set-timer
166      ~%   %set-timer   ..part   ~
167      |=   t=timer
168      ^+   timers.state
169      =/   found   (find-ducts date.t)
170      (put:timer-map timers.state date.t (~(put to found) duct.t))
171    ::   +find-ducts: get timers at date
172    ::
```

```
173   ::      TODO: move to +ordered-map
174   ::
175   ++  find-ducts
176     |=  date=@da
177     ^-  (qeu ^duct)
178     ?~  timers.state  ~
179     ?:  =(date key.n.timers.state)
180       val.n.timers.state
181     ?:  (lte date key.n.timers.state)
182       $(timers.state l.timers.state)
183     $(timers.state r.timers.state)
184   ::  +unset-timer: cancel a timer; if it already expired, no-op
185   ::
186   ++  unset-timer
187     |=  t=timer
188     ^+  timers.state
189     =/  [found=? dux=(qeu ^duct)]
190       =/  dux  (find-ducts date.t)
191       |-  ^-  [found=? dux=(qeu ^duct)]
192       ?~  dux  |+~
193       ?:  =(duct.t n.dux)  &+~(nip to `(qeu ^duct)`dux)
194       =^  found-left=?  l.dux  $(dux l.dux)
195       ?:  found-left  &+dux
196       =^  found-rite=?  r.dux  $(dux r.dux)
197       [found-rite dux]
198     ?.  found  timers.state
199     ?:  =(~ dux)
200       +:(del:timer-map timers.state date.t)
201     (put:timer-map timers.state date.t dux)
202   --
203   --
204   ::
205   =|  behn-state
206   =*  state  -
207   |=  [now=@da eny=@uvJ rof=roof]
208   =*  behn-gate  .
209   ^?
210   |%
211   ::  +call: handle a +task:behn request
212   ::
213   ++  call
214     ~%  %behn-call  ..part  ~
215     |=  $:  hen=duct
216             dud=(unit goof)
217             wrapped-task=(hobo task)
218         ==
219     ^-  [(list move) _behn-gate]
220     =/  =task  ((harden task) wrapped-task)
221     =/  event-core  (per-event [now hen] state)
222     =^  moves  state
223       abet:(call:event-core task ?~(dud ~ `tang.u.dud))
224     [moves behn-gate]
225   ::  +load: migrate an old state to a new behn version
226   ::
227   ++  load
228     |=  old=behn-state
229     ^+  behn-gate
230     behn-gate(state old)
```

```
231  ::  +scry: view timer state
232  ::
233  ::     TODO: not referentially transparent w.r.t. elapsed timers,
234  ::     which might or might not show up in the product
235  ::
236  ++  scry
237    ^-  roon
238    |=  [lyc=gang pov=path car=term bem=beam]
239    ^-  (unit (unit cage))
240    =*  ren  car
241    =*  why=shop  &/p.bem
242    =*  syd  q.bem
243    =*  lot=coin  $/r.bem
244    =*  tyl  s.bem
245    ::
246    ::  only respond for the local identity, %$ desk, current timestamp
247    ::
248    ?.  ?&  =(&+our why)
249            =([%$ %da now] lot)
250            =(%$ syd)
251        ==
252      ~
253    ::  /bx//whey        (list mass)        memory usage labels
254    ::  /bx/debug/timers  (list [@da duct])  all timers and their ducts
255    ::  /bx/timers       (list @da)         all timer timestamps
256    ::  /bx/timers/next  (unit @da)         the very next timer to fire
257    ::  /bx/timers/[da]  (list @da)         all timers up to and including da
258    ::
259    ?.  ?=(%x ren)  ~
260    ?+  tyl  [~ ~]
261        [%$ %whey ~]
262      =/  maz=(list mass)
263        :~  timers+&+timers.state
264        ==
265      ``mass+!>(maz)
266    ::
267        [%debug %timers ~]
268      :^  ~  ~  %noun
269      !>  ^-  (list [@da duct])
270      %-  zing
271      %+  turn  (tap:timer-map timers)
272      |=  [date=@da q=(qeu duct)]
273      %+  turn  ~(tap to q)
274      |=(d=duct [date d])
275    ::
276        [%timers ~]
277      :^  ~  ~  %noun
278      !>  ^-  (list @da)
279      %-  zing
280      %+  turn  (tap:timer-map timers)
281      |=  [date=@da q=(qeu duct)]
282      (reap ~(wyt in q) date)
283    ::
284        [%timers %next ~]
285      :^  ~  ~  %noun
286      !>  ^-  (unit @da)
287      (bind (pry:timer-map timers) head)
288    ::
```

```
289        [%timers @ ~]
290      ?~  til=(slaw %da i.t.tyl)
291        [~ ~]
292      :^  ~  ~  %noun
293      !>  ^-  (list @da)
294      =/  tiz=(list [date=@da q=(qeu duct)])
295        (tap:timer-map timers)
296      |-  ^-  (list @da)
297      ?~  tiz  ~
298      ?:  (gth date.i.tiz u.til)  ~
299      %+  weld
300        (reap ~(wyt in q.i.tiz) date.i.tiz)
301      $(tiz t.tiz)
302    ==
303  ::
304  ++  stay  state
305  ++  take
306    |=  [tea=wire hen=duct dud=(unit goof) hin=sign]
307    ^-  [(list move) _behn-gate]
308    ?^  dud
309     ~|(%behn-take-dud (mean tang.u.dud))
310    ::
311    ?>  ?=([%drip @ ~] tea)
312    =/  event-core  (per-event [now hen] state)
313    =^  moves  state
314      abet:(take-drip:event-core (slav %ud i.t.tea) error.hin)
315    [moves behn-gate]
316  --
```

Clay

```
1  :: clay (4c), revision control
2  ::
3  :: The way to understand Clay is to take it section-by-section:
4  ::
5  :: - Data structures.  You *must* start here; make sure you understand
6  :: the entire contents of +raft.
7  ::
8  :: - Individual reads.  +aver is the entry point, follow it through
9  :: +read-at-tako to understand each kind of read.
10 ::
11 :: - Subscriptions.  +wake is the center of this mechanism; nothing
12 :: else responds to subscriptions.  +wake has no arguments, which means
13 :: every subscription response happens when something in Clay's *state*
14 :: has changed.  No edge-triggered responses.
15 ::
16 :: - Receiving foreign data.  For individual requests, this is
17 :: +take-foreign-answer.  For sync requests (%many, which is %sing %v
18 :: for a foreign desk), this is +foreign-update.
19 ::
20 :: - Ford.  +ford builds hoon files and gives files their types.
21 :: Read +build-file for the first, and +read-file is the second.
22 ::
23 :: - Writing to a desk.  Every write to a desk goes through +park, read
24 :: it thoroughly.
25 ::
26 :: - Merges.  Control flow starts at +start-merge, then +merge, but
27 :: everything is scaffolding for +merge-by-germ, which is the ideal of
28 :: a merge function: it takes two commits and a merge strategy and
29 :: produces a new commit.
30 ::
31 :: - Tombstoning.  This is in +tomb.
32 ::
33 ::::::::::::::::::::::::::::::::::::::::::::::::::::::::::::::::::::::::::::::::
34 ::
35 :: We use a system of "invariant footnotes", where nonlocal invariants
36 :: are tagged with notes to construct a distributed argument that the
37 :: invariant is maintained.  For example, see [wake].
38 ::
39 :: Each one should be described somewhere, and then it should be
40 :: referenced any time it's touched.  For example, any code which might
41 :: fill a subscription should be tagged with [wake], and if +wake is
42 :: not called by the end of that function, the function itself should
43 :: be tagged with [wake].
44 ::
45 :: The tagged code should constitute an argument that the invariant is
46 :: maintained everywhere.  While this is vulnerable to omission ("I
47 :: forgot that X could fill a subscription", it provides a good minimum
48 :: bar.
49 ::
50 :: Tag the specific line of code which affects the invariant.  You do
51 :: not need to tag every function in a call stack if the invariant is
52 :: guaranteed to be maintained by the time the function returns.
53 ::
54 :: Some invariant references get tagged with whether they "open" or
55 :: "close" the invariant.  For example, adding a commit to the dome
56 :: "opens" the [wake] invariant, while calling +wake closes it.  When
```

```
57  :: an invariant opens, you should be able to scan down and find why it
58  :: closes in each possible flow of control.  For wake, these are
59  :: labeled like this:
60  ::
61  ::    open: [wake] <
62  ::    close: [wake] >
63  ::    open and almost immediately close: [wake] <>
64  ::
65  :: This system is best used for nonlocal invariants and is not
66  :: necessary when a function can guarantee its own invariants.  For
67  :: example, consider a set alongside a @ud representing its size.
68  :: There is an invariant that any time you add or remove an item from
69  :: the set you must update its size.  If you're operating on these
70  :: directly, it could be beneficial to tag each line of code which
71  :: might modify the set and make it clear where the size is modified.
72  ::
73  :: Sometimes code can be restructured so that many fewer tags are
74  :: needed.  In the above example, if the set is modified in many
75  :: places, it may be worth factoring out set+size into a data structure
76  :: with its own arms for put, del, uni, int, etc.  Then the invariant
77  :: only needs to be maintained within that data structure, and call
78  :: sites do not need to be tagged.
79  ::
80  ::::::::::::::::::::::::::::::::::::::::::::::::::::::::::::::::::::::::::
81  ::
82  :: Here are the structures.  `++raft` is the formal arvo state.  It's
83  :: also worth noting that many of the clay-related structures are
84  :: defined in lull.
85  ::
86  ::::::::::::::::::::::::::::::::::::::::::::::::::::::::::::::::::::::::::
87  =/  bud
88    ^~
89    =/  zuse  !>(..zuse)
90    :*  zuse=zuse
91        nave=(slap zuse !,(*hoon nave:clay))
92        cork=(slap zuse !,(*hoon cork))
93        same=(slap zuse !,(*hoon same))
94        mime=(slap zuse !,(*hoon mime))
95        cass=(slap zuse !,(*hoon cass:clay))
96    ==
97  ::
98  |=  our=ship
99  =,  clay
100 =>  |%
101 +$  aeon  @ud                                    :: version number
102 ::
103 :: Part of ++mery, representing the set of changes between the mergebase and
104 :: one of the desks being merged.
105 ::
106 ::  --  `new` is the set of files in the new desk and not in the mergebase.
107 ::  --  `cal` is the set of changes in the new desk from the mergebase except
108 ::      for any that are also in the other new desk.
109 ::  --  `can` is the set of changes in the new desk from the mergebase and that
110 ::      are also in the other new desk (potential conflicts).
111 ::  --  `old` is the set of files in the mergebase and not in the new desk.
112 ::
113 +$  cane
114   $:  new=(map path lobe)
```

```
115      cal=(map path lobe)
116      can=(map path cage)
117      old=(map path ~)
118    ==
119  ::
120  ::   Type of request.
121  ::
122  ::   %d produces a set of desks, %p gets file permissions, %t gets all paths
123  ::   with the specified prefix, %u checks for existence, %v produces a ++dome
124  ::   of all desk data, %w gets @ud and @da variants for the given case, %x
125  ::   gets file contents, %y gets a directory listing, and %z gets a recursive
126  ::   hash of the file contents and children.
127  ::
128  ::   ++   care   ?(%d %p %t %u %v %w %x %y %z)
129  ::
130  ::   Keeps track of subscribers.
131  ::
132  ::   A map of requests to a set of all the subscribers who should be notified
133  ::   when the request is filled/updated.
134  ::
135  +$   cult   (jug wove duct)
136  ::
137  ::   State for ongoing %fuse merges. `con` maintains the ordering,
138  ::   `sto` stores the data needed to merge, and `bas` is the base
139  ::   beak for the merge.
140  ::
141  +$   melt   [bas=beak con=(list [beak germ]) sto=(map beak (unit domo))]
142  ::
143  ::   Domestic desk state.
144  ::
145  ::   Includes subscriber list, dome (desk content), possible commit state (for
146  ::   local changes), possible merge state (for incoming merges), and permissions.
147  ::
148  +$   dojo
149    $:  qyx=cult                              ::  subscribers
150        dom=dome                              ::  desk state
151        per=regs                              ::  read perms per path
152        pew=regs                              ::  write perms per path
153        fiz=melt                              ::  state for mega merges
154    ==
155  ::
156  ::   Over-the-wire backfill request/response
157  ::
158  +$   fill
159    $%  [%0 =desk =lobe]
160        [%1 =desk =lobe]
161    ==
162  ::
163  ::   All except %1 are deprecated
164  ::
165  +$   fell
166    $%  [%direct p=lobe q=page]
167        [%delta p=lobe q=[p=mark q=lobe] r=page]
168        [%dead p=lobe ~]
169        [%1 peg=(unit page)]
170    ==
171  ::
172  ::   New desk data.
```

```
173  ::
174  ::  Sent to other ships to update them about a particular desk.
175  ::  Includes a map of all new aeons to hashes of their commits, the most
176  ::  recent aeon, and sets of all new commits and data.  `bar` is always
177  ::  empty now because we expect you to request any data you don't have
178  ::  yet
179  ::
180  +$  nako                                     ::  subscription state
181    $:  gar=(map aeon tako)                    ::  new ids
182        let=aeon                               ::  next id
183        lar=(set yaki)                         ::  new commits
184        bar=~                                  ::  new content
185    ==                                         ::
186  ::
187  ::
188  ::  Formal vane state.
189  ::
190  ::  --  `rom` is our domestic state.
191  ::  --  `hoy` is a collection of foreign ships where we know something about
192  ::        their clay.
193  ::  --  `ran` is the object store.
194  ::  --  `mon` is a collection of mount points (mount point name to urbit
195  ::        location).
196  ::  --  `hez` is the unix duct that %ergo's should be sent to.
197  ::  --  `cez` is a collection of named permission groups.
198  ::  --  `pud` is an update that's waiting on a kernel upgrade
199  ::
200  +$  raft                                     ::  filesystem
201    $:  rom=room                               ::  domestic
202        hoy=(map ship rung)                    ::  foreign
203        ran=rang                               ::  hashes
204        fad=flow                               ::  ford cache
205        mon=(map term beam)                    ::  mount points
206        hez=(unit duct)                        ::  sync duct
207        cez=(map @ta crew)                     ::  permission groups
208        tyr=(set duct)                         ::  app subs
209        tur=rock:tire                          ::  last tire
210        pud=(unit [=desk =yoki])               ::  pending update
211        sad=(map ship @da)                     ::  scry known broken
212        bug=[veb=@ mas=@]                      ::  verbosity
213    ==                                         ::
214  ::
215  ::  Unvalidated response to a request.
216  ::
217  ::  Like a +$rant, but with a page of data rather than a cage of it.
218  ::
219  +$  rand                                     ::  unvalidated rant
220          $:  p=[p=care q=case r=@tas]         ::  clade release book
221              q=path                           ::  spur
222              r=page                           ::  data
223          ==                                   ::
224  ::
225  ::  Generic desk state.
226  ::
227  ::  --  `lim` is the most recent date we're confident we have all the
228  ::        information for.  For local desks, this is always `now`.  For foreign
229  ::        desks, this is the last time we got a full update from the foreign
230  ::        urbit.
```

```
231  ::  --  `ref` is a possible request manager.  For local desks, this is null.
232  ::      For foreign desks, this keeps track of all pending foreign requests
233  ::      plus a cache of the responses to previous requests.
234  ::  --  `qyx` is the set of subscriptions, with listening ducts. These
235  ::      subscriptions exist only until they've been filled.
236  ::  --  `dom` is the actual state of the filetree.  Since this is used almost
237  ::      exclusively in `++ze`, we describe it there.
238  ::
239  +$  rede                                        ::  universal project
240        $:  lim=@da                               ::  complete to
241            ref=(unit rind)                       ::  outgoing requests
242            qyx=cult                              ::  subscribers
243            dom=dome                              ::  revision state
244            per=regs                              ::  read perms per path
245            pew=regs                              ::  write perms per path
246            fiz=melt                              ::  domestic mega merges
247        ==                                        ::
248  ::
249  ::  Foreign request manager.
250  ::
251  ::  When we send a request to a foreign ship, we keep track of it in here.  This
252  ::  includes a request counter, a map of request numbers to requests, a reverse
253  ::  map of requesters to request numbers, a simple cache of common %sing
254  ::  requests, and a possible nako if we've received data from the other ship and
255  ::  are in the process of validating it.
256  ::
257  +$  rind                                        ::  request manager
258    $:  nix=@ud                                   ::  request index
259        bom=(map @ud update-state)               ::  outstanding
260        fod=(map duct @ud)                        ::  current requests
261        haw=(map mood (unit cage))               ::  simple cache
262    ==                                            ::
263  ::
264  +$  bill  (list dude:gall)
265  ::
266  ::  Active downloads
267  ::
268  +$  update-state
269    $:  =duct
270        =rave
271        have=(map lobe fell)
272        need=(list $@(lobe [=tako =path =lobe]))  ::  opt deets for scry
273        nako=(qeu (unit nako))
274        busy=(unit $@(%ames [kind=@ta =time =path]))  ::  pending request
275    ==
276  ::
277  ::  Domestic ship.
278  ::
279  ::  `hun` is the duct to dill, and `dos` is a collection of our desks.
280  ::
281  +$  room                                        ::  fs per ship
282        $:  hun=duct                              ::  terminal duct
283            dos=(map desk dojo)                   ::  native desk
284        ==                                        ::
285  ::
286  ::  Stored request.
287  ::
288  ::  Like a +$rave but with caches of current versions for %next and %many.
```

```
289  ::  Generally used when we store a request in our state somewhere.
290  ::
291  ::  TODO: remove lobes from %many
292  ::
293  +$  cach  (unit (unit cage))                          ::  cached result
294  +$  wove  [for=(unit [=ship ver=@ud]) =rove]          ::  stored source + req
295  +$  rove                                              ::  stored request
296        $%  [%sing =mood]                               ::  single request
297            [%next =mood aeon=(unit aeon) =cach]        ::  next version of one
298            $:  %mult                                   ::  next version of any
299                =mool                                   ::  original request
300                aeon=(unit aeon)                        ::  checking for change
301                old-cach=(map [=care =path] cach)       ::  old version
302                new-cach=(map [=care =path] cach)       ::  new version
303            ==                                          ::
304            [%many track=? =moat lobes=(map path lobe)] ::  change range
305        ==                                              ::
306  ::
307  ::  Foreign desk data.
308  ::
309  +$  rung
310        $:  rus=(map desk rede)                         ::  neighbor desks
311        ==
312  ::
313  +$  card  (wind note gift)                            ::  local card
314  +$  move  [p=duct q=card]                             ::  local move
315  +$  note                                              ::  out request $->
316    $~  [%b %wait *@da]                                 ::
317    $%  $:  %$                                          ::  to arvo
318            $>(%what waif)                              ::
319        ==                                              ::
320        $:  %a                                          ::  to %ames
321            $>(?(%plea %keen %yawn) task:ames)          ::
322        ==                                              ::
323        $:  %b                                          ::  to %behn
324            $>  $?  %drip                               ::
325                    %rest                               ::
326                    %wait                               ::
327                ==                                      ::
328            task:behn                                   ::
329        ==                                              ::
330        $:  %c                                          ::  to %clay
331            $>  $?  %info                               ::  internal edit
332                    %merg                               ::  merge desks
333                    %fuse                               ::  merge many
334                    %park                               ::
335                    %perm                               ::
336                    %pork                               ::
337                    %warp                               ::
338                    %werp                               ::
339                ==                                      ::
340            task                                        ::
341        ==                                              ::
342        $:  %d                                          ::  to %dill
343            $>  $?  %flog                               ::
344                    %text                               ::
345                ==                                      ::
346            task:dill                                   ::
```

```
347           ==                              ::
348       $:  %g                              ::  to %gall
349           $>  $?  %deal
350                   %jolt
351                   %load
352               ==
353           task:gall
354       ==                                  ::
355       $:  %j                              ::  by %jael
356           $>(%public-keys task:jael)      ::
357   ==  ==                                  ::
358 +$  riot  (unit rant)                     ::  response+complete
359 +$  sign                                  ::  in result $<-
360   $~  [%behn %wake ~]                      ::
361   $%  $:  %ames                            ::
362           $>  $?  %boon                    ::  response
363                   %done                    ::  (n)ack
364                   %lost                    ::  lost boon
365                   %tune                    ::  scry response
366               ==                           ::
367           gift:ames                        ::
368       ==                                  ::
369       $:  %behn                            ::
370           $%  $>(%wake gift:behn)          ::  timer activate
371               $>(%writ gift)               ::
372           ==  ==                           ::
373       $:  %clay                            ::
374           $>  $?  %mere                    ::
375                   %writ                    ::
376                   %wris                    ::
377               ==                           ::
378           gift                             ::
379       ==                                  ::
380       $:  %gall                            ::
381           $>  $?  %unto                    ::
382               ==                           ::
383           gift:gall                        ::
384       ==                                  ::
385       $:  %jael                            ::
386           $>(%public-keys gift:jael)       ::
387   ==  ==                                  ::
388 --  =>
389 ~%  %clay-utilities  ..part  ~
390 ::  %utilities
391 ::
392 |%
393 ++  scry-timeout-time  ~m5
394 ++  scry-retry-time    ~h1
395 ::  +sort-by-head: sorts alphabetically using the head of each element
396 ::
397 ++  sort-by-head
398   |=([a=(pair path *) b=(pair path *)] (aor p.a p.b))
399 ::
400 ::  By convention: paf == (weld pax pat)
401 ::
402 ++  mode-to-commit
403   |=  [hat=(map path lobe) pax=path all=? mod=mode]
404   ^-  [deletes=(set path) changes=(map path cage)]
```

```
405    =/  deletes
406      %-  silt
407      %+  turn
408        ^-  (list path)
409        %+  weld
410          ^-  (list path)
411          %+  murn  mod
412          |=  [pat=path mim=(unit mime)]
413          ^-  (unit path)
414          ?^  mim
415            ~
416          `pat
417        ^-  (list path)
418        ?.  all
419          ~
420        =+  mad=(malt mod)
421        =+  len=(lent pax)
422        =/  descendants=(list path)
423          %+  turn
424          %+  skim  ~(tap by hat)
425          |=  [paf=path lob=lobe]
426          =(pax (scag len paf))
427          |=  [paf=path lob=lobe]
428          (slag len paf)
429        %+  skim
430          descendants
431        |=  pat=path
432        (~(has by mad) pat)
433      |=  pat=path
434      (weld pax pat)
435    ::
436    =/  changes
437      %-  malt
438      %+  murn  mod
439      |=  [pat=path mim=(unit mime)]
440      ^-  (unit [path cage])
441      ?~  mim
442        ~
443      `[(weld pax pat) %mime !>(u.mim)]
444    ::
445    [deletes changes]
446  ::
447  ++  pour-to-mist
448    |=  =pour
449    ^-  mist
450    ?+    -.pour  pour
451        %vale  [%vale path.pour]
452        %arch  [%arch path.pour]
453    ==
454  ::
455  ++  fell-to-page
456    |=  =fell
457    ^-  (unit page)
458    ?-    -.fell
459        %dead    ~
460        %direct  `q.fell
461        %delta   ~
462        %1       peg.fell
```

```
463    ==
464  ::
465  ++  rave-to-rove
466    |=  rav=rave
467    ^-  rove
468    ?-  -.rav
469      %sing  rav
470      %next  [- mood ~ ~]:rav
471      %mult  [- mool ~ ~ ~]:rav
472      %many  [- track moat ~]:rav
473    ==
474  ::
475  ++  rove-to-rave
476    |=  rov=rove
477    ^-  rave
478    ?-  -.rov
479      %sing  rov
480      %next  [- mood]:rov
481      %mult  [- mool]:rov
482      %many  [- track moat]:rov
483    ==
484  --  =>
485  ~%  %clay  +  ~
486  |%
487  ::  Printable form of a wove; useful for debugging
488  ::
489  ++  print-wove
490    |=  =wove
491    :-  for.wove
492    ?-  -.rove.wove
493      %sing  [%sing mood.rove.wove]
494      %next  [%next [mood aeon]:rove.wove]
495      %mult  [%mult [mool aeon]:rove.wove]
496      %many  [%many [track moat]:rove.wove]
497    ==
498  ::
499  ::  Printable form of a cult; useful for debugging
500  ::
501  ++  print-cult
502    |=  =cult
503    %+  turn  ~(tap by cult)
504    |=  [=wove ducts=(set duct)]
505    [ducts (print-wove wove)]
506  ::
507  ++  fusion
508    ~%  %fusion  ..fusion  ~
509    |%
510    ::  +wrap: external wrapper
511    ::
512    ++  wrap
513      |*  [* state:ford]
514      [+<- +<+< +<+>-]  ::  [result cache.state flue]
515    ::
516    ++  with-face  |=([face=@tas =vase] vase(p [%face face p.vase]))
517    ++  with-faces
518      =|  res=(unit vase)
519      |=  vaz=(list [face=@tas =vase])
520      ^-  vase
```

```
521    ?~  vaz  (need res)
522    =/  faz  (with-face i.vaz)
523    =.  res  `?~(res faz (slop faz u.res))
524    $(vaz t.vaz)
525  ::
526  ++  ford
527    !.
528    =>  |%
529      +$  state
530        $:  cache=flow
531            flue
532            cycle=(set mist)
533            drain=(map mist leak)
534            stack=(list (set leak))
535        ==
536      +$  args
537        $:  files=(map path (each page lobe))
538            file-store=(map lobe page)
539            verb=@
540            cache=flow
541            flue
542        ==
543      --
544    ~%  %ford-gate  ..ford  ~
545    |=  args
546    ::  nub: internal mutable state for this computation
547    ::
548    =|  nub=state
549    =.  cache.nub  cache
550    =.  spill.nub  spill
551    =.  sprig.nub  sprig
552    ~%  %ford-core  ..$  ~
553    |%
554    ::  +read-file: retrieve marked, validated file contents at path
555    ::
556    ++  read-file
557      ~/  %read-file
558      |=  =path
559      ^-  [cage state]
560      ~|  %error-validating^path
561      %-  soak-cage
562      %+  gain-sprig  vale+path  |.
563      =.  stack.nub  [~ stack.nub]
564      ?:  (~(has in cycle.nub) vale+path)
565        ~|(cycle+vale+path^cycle.nub !!)
566      =.  cycle.nub  (~(put in cycle.nub) vale+path)
567      %+  gain-leak  vale+path
568      |=  nob=state
569      =.  nub  nob
570      %-  (trace 1 |.("read file {(spud path)}"))
571      =/  file
572        ~|  %file-not-found^path
573        (~(got by files) path)
574      =/  page
575        ?:  ?=(%& -.file)
576          p.file
577        ~|  %tombstoned-file^path^p.file
578        (~(got by file-store) p.file)
```

```
579      =^  =cage  nub  (validate-page path page)
580      [[%cage cage] nub]
581    ::
582    ::  +build-nave: build a statically typed mark core
583    ::
584    ++  build-nave
585      ~/  %build-nave
586      |=  mak=mark
587      ^-  [vase state]
588      ~|  %error-building-mark^mak
589      %-  soak-vase
590      %+  gain-sprig  nave+mak  |.
591      =.  stack.nub  [~ stack.nub]
592      ?:  (~(has in cycle.nub) nave+mak)
593        ~|(cycle+nave+mak^cycle.nub !!)
594      =.  cycle.nub  (~(put in cycle.nub) nave+mak)
595      %-  (trace 1 |.("make mark {<mak>}"))
596      =^  cor=vase  nub  (build-fit %mar mak)
597      =/  gad=vase  (slap cor limb/%grad)
598      ?@  q.gad
599        =+  !<(mok=mark gad)
600        =^  deg=vase  nub  ^$(mak mok)
601        =^  tub=vase  nub  (build-cast mak mok)
602        =^  but=vase  nub  (build-cast mok mak)
603        %+  gain-leak  nave+mak
604        |=  nob=state
605        =.  nub  nob
606        :_  nub  :-  %vase
607        ^-  vase  ::  vase of nave
608        %+  slap
609          (with-faces deg+deg tub+tub but+but cor+cor nave+nave.bud ~)
610        !,  *hoon
611        =/  typ  _+<.cor
612        =/  dif  _*diff:deg
613        ^-  (nave typ dif)
614        |%
615        ++  diff
616          |=  [old=typ new=typ]
617          ^-  dif
618          (diff:deg (tub old) (tub new))
619        ++  form  form:deg
620        ++  join  join:deg
621        ++  mash  mash:deg
622        ++  pact
623          |=  [v=typ d=dif]
624          ^-  typ
625          (but (pact:deg (tub v) d))
626        ++  vale  noun:grab:cor
627        --
628      %+  gain-leak  nave+mak
629      |=  nob=state
630      =.  nub  nob
631      :_  nub  :-  %vase
632      ^-  vase  ::  vase of nave
633      %+  slap  (slop (with-face cor+cor) zuse.bud)
634      !,  *hoon
635      =/  typ  _+<.cor
636      =/  dif  _*diff:grad:cor
```

```
637        ^-  (nave:clay typ dif)
638        |%
639        ++  diff   |=([old=typ new=typ] (diff:~(grad cor old) new))
640        ++  form   form:grad:cor
641        ++  join
642          |=  [a=dif b=dif]
643          ^-  (unit (unit dif))
644          ?:  =(a b)
645            ~
646          `(join:grad:cor a b)
647        ++  mash
648          |=  [a=[=ship =desk =dif] b=[=ship =desk =dif]]
649          ^-  (unit dif)
650          ?:  =(dif.a dif.b)
651            ~
652          `(mash:grad:cor a b)
653        ++  pact   |=([v=typ d=dif] (pact:~(grad cor v) d))
654        ++  vale   noun:grab:cor
655        --
656    ::  +build-dais: build a dynamically typed mark definition
657    ::
658    ++  build-dais
659      ~/  %build-dais
660      |=  mak=mark
661      ^-  [dais state]
662      ~|  %error-building-dais^mak
663      %-  soak-dais
664      %+  gain-sprig  dais+mak  |.
665      =.  stack.nub  [~ stack.nub]
666      ?:  (~(has in cycle.nub) dais+mak)
667        ~|(cycle+dais+mak^cycle.nub !!)
668      =.  cycle.nub  (~(put in cycle.nub) dais+mak)
669      =^  nav=vase  nub  (build-nave mak)
670      %+  gain-leak  dais+mak
671      |=  nob=state
672      =.  nub  nob
673      %-  (trace 1 |.("make dais {<mak>}"))
674      :_  nub  :-  %dais
675      ^-  dais
676      =>  [nav=nav ..zuse]
677      |_  sam=vase
678      ++  diff
679        |=  new=vase
680        (slam (slap nav limb/%diff) (slop sam new))
681      ++  form  !<(mark (slap nav limb/%form))
682      ++  join
683        |=  [a=vase b=vase]
684        ^-  (unit (unit vase))
685        =/  res=vase  (slam (slap nav limb/%join) (slop a b))
686        ?~  q.res     ~
687        ?~  +.q.res   [~ ~]
688        ``(slap res !,(*hoon ?>(?=([~ ~ *] .) u.u)))
689      ++  mash
690        |=  [a=[=ship =desk diff=vase] b=[=ship =desk diff=vase]]
691        ^-  (unit vase)
692        =/  res=vase
693          %+  slam  (slap nav limb/%mash)
694          %+  slop
```

```
695            :(slop [[%atom %p ~] ship.a] [[%atom %tas ~] desk.a] diff.a)
696             :(slop [[%atom %p ~] ship.b] [[%atom %tas ~] desk.b] diff.b)
697          ?~  q.res
698            ~
699          `(slap res !,(*hoon ?>((^ .) u)))
700      ++  pact
701      |=  diff=vase
702      (slam (slap nav limb/%pact) (slop sam diff))
703      ++  vale
704      |:  noun=q:(slap nav !,(*hoon *vale))
705      (slam (slap nav limb/%vale) noun/noun)
706      --
707  ::  +build-cast: produce gate to convert mark .a to, statically typed
708  ::
709  ++  build-cast
710  ~/  %build-cast
711  |=  [a=mark b=mark]
712  ^-  [vase state]
713  ~|  error-building-cast+[a b]
714  %-  soak-vase
715  %+  gain-sprig  cast+a^b  |.
716  =.  stack.nub  [~ stack.nub]
717  ?:  (~(has in cycle.nub) cast+[a b])
718    ~|(cycle+cast+[a b]^cycle.nub !!)
719  ?:  =(a b)
720    %+  gain-leak  cast+a^b
721    |=  nob=state
722    %-  (trace 4 |.("identity shortcircuit"))
723    =.  nub  nob
724    :_(nub vase+same.bud)
725  ?:  =([%mime %hoon] [a b])
726    %-  (trace 4 |.("%mime -> %hoon shortcircuit"))
727    :_(nub [%vase =>(..zuse !>(|=(m=mime q.q.m)))])
728  ::  try +grow; is there a +grow core with a .b arm?
729  ::
730  %-  (trace 1 |.("make cast {<a>} -> {<b>}"))
731  =^  old=vase  nub  (build-fit %mar a)
732  ?:  =/  ram  (mule |.((slap old !,(*hoon grow))))
733      ?:  ?=(%| -.ram)  %.n
734      =/  lab  (mule |.((slob b p.p.ram)))
735      ?:  ?=(%| -.lab)  %.n
736      p.lab
737    ::  +grow core has .b arm; use that
738    ::
739    %+  gain-leak  cast+a^b
740    |=  nob=state
741    %-  (trace 4 |.("{<a>} -> {<b>}: +{(trip b)}:grow:{(trip a)}"))
742    =.  nub  nob
743    :_  nub  :-  %vase
744    %+  slap  (with-faces cor+old ~)
745    ^-  hoon
746    :+  %brcl  !,(*hoon v=+<.cor)
747    :+  %tsgl  limb/b
748    !,(*hoon ~(grow cor v))
749  ::  try direct +grab
750  ::
751  =^  new=vase  nub  (build-fit %mar b)
752  =/  rab  (mule |.((slap new tsgl/[limb/a limb/%grab])))
```

```
753      ?:  &(?=(%& -.rab) ?=(^ q.p.rab))
754        %+  gain-leak  cast+a^b
755        |=  nob=state
756        %-  (trace 4 |.("{<a>} -> {<b>}: +{(trip a)}:grab:{(trip b)}"))
757        =.  nub  nob
758        :_(nub vase+p.rab)
759      ::  try +jump
760      ::
761      =/  jum  (mule |.((slap old tsgl/[limb/b limb/%jump])))
762      ?:  ?=(%& -.jum)
763        =/  via  !<(mark p.jum)
764        %-  (trace 4 |.("{<a>} -> {<b>}: via {<via>} per +jump:{(trip a)}"))
765        (compose-casts a via b)
766      ?:  ?=(%& -.rab)
767        =/  via  !<(mark p.rab)
768        %-  (trace 4 |.("{<a>} -> {<b>}: via {<via>} per +grab:{(trip b)}"))
769        (compose-casts a via b)
770      ?:  ?=(%noun b)
771        %+  gain-leak  cast+a^b
772        |=  nob=state
773        %-  (trace 4 |.("{<a>} -> {<b>} default"))
774        =.  nub  nob
775        :_(nub vase+same.bud)
776      ~|(no-cast-from+[a b] !!)
777      ::
778    ++  compose-casts
779      |=  [x=mark y=mark z=mark]
780      ^-  [soak state]
781      =^  uno=vase  nub  (build-cast x y)
782      =^  dos=vase  nub  (build-cast y z)
783      %+  gain-leak  cast+x^z
784      |=  nob=state
785      =.  nub  nob
786      :_  nub  :-  %vase
787      %+  slap
788      (with-faces uno+uno dos+dos ~)
789      !,(*hoon |=(_+<.uno (dos (uno +<))))
790    ::  +build-tube: produce a $tube mark conversion gate from .a to .b
791    ::
792    ++  build-tube
793      |=  [a=mark b=mark]
794      ^-  [tube state]
795      ~|  error-building-tube+[a b]
796      %-  soak-tube
797      %+  gain-sprig  tube+a^b  |.
798      =.  stack.nub  [~ stack.nub]
799      ?:  (~(has in cycle.nub) tube+[a b])
800        ~|(cycle+tube+[a b]^cycle.nub !!)
801      =^  gat=vase  nub  (build-cast a b)
802      %+  gain-leak  tube+a^b
803      |=  nob=state
804      =.  nub  nob
805      %-  (trace 1 |.("make tube {<a>} -> {<b>}"))
806      :_(nub [%tube =>([gat=gat ..zuse] |=(v=vase (slam gat v)))])
807    ::
808    ++  validate-page
809      |=  [=path =page]
810      ^-  [cage state]
```

```
811        ~|    validate-page-fail+path^from+p.page
812        =/    mak=mark  (head (flop path))
813        ?:    =(mak p.page)
814          (page-to-cage page)
815        =^    [mark vax=vase]  nub  (page-to-cage page)
816        =^    =tube  nub  (build-tube p.page mak)
817        :_(nub [mak (tube vax)])
818      ::
819      ++  page-to-cage
820        |=  =page
821        ^-  [cage state]
822        ?:    =(%hoon p.page)
823          :_(nub [%hoon [%atom %t ~] q.page])
824        ?:    =(%mime p.page)
825          :_(nub [%mime =>([;;(mime q.page) ..zuse] !>(-))])
826        =^    =dais  nub  (build-dais p.page)
827        :_(nub [p.page (vale:dais q.page)])
828      ::
829      ++  cast-path
830        |=  [=path mak=mark]
831        ^-  [cage state]
832        =/    mok  (head (flop path))
833        ~|    error-casting-path+[path mok mak]
834        =^    cag=cage  nub  (read-file path)
835        ?:    =(mok mak)
836          [cag nub]
837        =^    =tube  nub  (build-tube mok mak)
838        ~|    error-running-cast+[path mok mak]
839        :_(nub [mak (tube q.cag)])
840      ::
841      ++  run-pact
842        |=  [old=page diff=page]
843        ^-  [cage state]
844        ?:    ?=(%hoon p.old)
845          =/    txt=wain  (to-wain:format ;;(@t q.old))
846          =+    ;;(dif=(urge cord) q.diff)
847          =/    new=@t  (of-wain:format (lurk:differ txt dif))
848          :_(nub [%hoon =>([new ..zuse] !>(-))])
849        =^    dys=dais  nub  (build-dais p.old)
850        =^    syd=dais  nub  (build-dais p.diff)
851        :_(nub [p.old (~(pact dys (vale:dys q.old)) (vale:syd q.diff))])
852      ::
853      ++  prelude
854        |=  =path
855        ^-  vase
856        =^    cag=cage  nub  (read-file path)
857        ?>    =(%hoon p.cag)
858        =/    tex=tape  (trip !<(@t q.cag))
859        =/    =pile  (parse-pile path tex)
860        =.    hoon.pile  !,(*hoon .)
861        =^    res=vase  nub  (run-prelude pile)
862        res
863      ::
864      ++  build-dependency
865        ~/    %build-dep
866        |=  dep=(each [dir=path fil=path] path)
867        ^-  [vase state]
868        =/    =path
```

```
869        ?:(?=(%| -.dep) p.dep fil.p.dep)
870      ~|  %error-building^path
871      %-  soak-vase
872      %+  gain-sprig  file+path  |.
873      =.  stack.nub  [~ stack.nub]
874      %-  (trace 1 |.("make file {(spud path)}"))
875      ?:  (~(has in cycle.nub) file+path)
876        ~|(cycle+file+path^cycle.nub !!)
877      =.  cycle.nub  (~(put in cycle.nub) file+path)
878      =^  cag=cage  nub  (read-file path)
879      ?>  =(%hoon p.cag)
880      =/  tex=tape  (trip !<(@t q.cag))
881      =/  =pile  (parse-pile path tex)
882      =^  sut=vase  nub  (run-prelude pile)
883      %+  gain-leak  file+path
884      |=  nob=state
885      =.  nub  nob
886      =/  res=vase  (slap sut hoon.pile)
887      [[%vase res] nub]
888    ::
889    ++  build-file
890      |=  =path
891      (build-dependency |+path)
892    ::  +build-directory: builds files in top level of a directory
893    ::
894    ::    this excludes files directly at /path/hoon,
895    ::    instead only including files in the unix-style directory at /path,
896    ::    such as /path/file/hoon, but not /path/more/file/hoon.
897    ::
898    ++  build-directory
899      |=  =path
900      ^-  [(map @ta vase) state]
901      %-  soak-arch
902      %+  gain-sprig  arch+path  |.
903      =.  stack.nub  [~ stack.nub]
904      %+  gain-leak  arch+path
905      |=  nob=state
906      =.  nub  nob
907      =/  fiz=(list @ta)
908        =/  len  (lent path)
909        %+  murn  ~(tap by files)
910        |=  [pax=^path *]
911        ^-  (unit @ta)
912        ?.  =(path (scag len pax))
913          ~
914        =/  pat  (slag len pax)
915        ?:  ?=([@ %hoon ~] pat)
916          `i.pat
917        ~
918      ::
919      =|  rez=(map @ta vase)
920      |-
921      ?~  fiz
922        [[%arch rez] nub]
923      =*  nom=@ta    i.fiz
924      =/  pax=^path  (weld path nom %hoon ~)
925      =^  res  nub  (build-dependency &+[path pax])
926      $(fiz t.fiz, rez (~(put by rez) nom res))
```

```
927      ::
928      ++  run-prelude
929        |=  =pile
930        =/  sut=vase   zuse.bud
931        =^  sut=vase   nub   (run-tauts sut %sur sur.pile)
932        =^  sut=vase   nub   (run-tauts sut %lib lib.pile)
933        =^  sut=vase   nub   (run-raw sut raw.pile)
934        =^  sut=vase   nub   (run-raz sut raz.pile)
935        =^  sut=vase   nub   (run-maz sut maz.pile)
936        =^  sut=vase   nub   (run-caz sut caz.pile)
937        =^  sut=vase   nub   (run-bar sut bar.pile)
938        [sut nub]
939      ::
940      ++  parse-pile
941        ~/  %parse-pile
942        |=  [pax=path tex=tape]
943        ^-  pile
944        =/  [=hair res=(unit [=pile =nail])]
945          %-  road  |.
946          ((pile-rule pax) [1 1] tex)
947        ?^  res   pile.u.res
948        %-  mean
949        =/  lyn  p.hair
950        =/  col  q.hair
951        ^-  (list tank)
952        :~  leaf+"syntax error at [{<lyn>} {<col>}] in {<pax>}"
953            ::
954            =/  =wain  (to-wain:format (crip tex))
955            ?:  (gth lyn (lent wain))
956              '<<end of file>>'
957            (snag (dec lyn) wain)
958          ::
959            leaf+(runt [(dec col) '-'] "^")
960        ==
961      ::
962      ++  pile-rule
963        |=  pax=path
964        %-  full
965        %+  ifix
966          :_  gay
967          ::  parse optional /? and ignore
968          ::
969          ;~(plug gay (punt ;~(plug fas wut gap dem gap)))
970        |^
971        ;~  plug
972          %+  cook   (bake zing (list (list taut)))
973          %+  rune   hep
974          (most ;~(plug com gaw) taut-rule)
975        ::
976          %+  cook   (bake zing (list (list taut)))
977          %+  rune   lus
978          (most ;~(plug com gaw) taut-rule)
979        ::
980          %+  rune  tis
981          ;~(plug sym ;~(pfix gap stap))
982        ::
983          %+  rune  sig
984          ;~((glue gap) sym wyde:vast stap)
```

```
985        ::
986          %+  rune  cen
987          ;~(plug sym ;~(pfix gap ;~(pfix cen sym)))
988        ::
989          %+  rune  buc
990          ;~  (glue gap)
991            sym
992            ;~(pfix cen sym)
993            ;~(pfix cen sym)
994          ==
995        ::
996          %+  rune  tar
997          ;~  (glue gap)
998            sym
999            ;~(pfix cen sym)
1000           ;~(pfix stap)
1001         ==
1002       ::
1003         %+  stag  %tssg
1004         (most gap tall:(vang & pax))
1005       ==
1006       ::
1007     ++  pant
1008       |*  fel=^rule
1009       ;~(pose fel (easy ~))
1010       ::
1011     ++  mast
1012       |*  [bus=^rule fel=^rule]
1013       ;~(sfix (more bus fel) bus)
1014       ::
1015     ++  rune
1016       |*  [bus=^rule fel=^rule]
1017       %-  pant
1018       %+  mast  gap
1019       ;~(pfix fas bus gap fel)
1020       --
1021   ::
1022   ++  taut-rule
1023     %+  cook  |=(taut +<)
1024     ;~  pose
1025     (stag ~ ;~(pfix tar sym))
1026     ;~(plug (stag ~ sym) ;~(pfix tis sym))
1027     (cook |=(a=term [`a a]) sym)
1028     ==
1029   ::
1030   ++  run-tauts
1031     |=  [sut=vase wer=?(%lib %sur) taz=(list taut)]
1032     ^-  [vase state]
1033     ?~  taz  [sut nub]
1034     =^  pin=vase  nub  (build-fit wer pax.i.taz)
1035     =?  p.pin  ?=(^ face.i.taz)  [%face u.face.i.taz p.pin]
1036     $(sut (slop pin sut), taz t.taz)
1037   ::
1038   ++  run-raw
1039     |=  [sut=vase raw=(list [face=term =path])]
1040     ^-  [vase state]
1041     ?~  raw  [sut nub]
1042     =^  pin=vase  nub  (build-file (snoc path.i.raw %hoon))
```

```
1043        =.  p.pin  [%face face.i.raw p.pin]
1044      $(sut (slop pin sut), raw t.raw)
1045    ::
1046    ++  run-raz
1047      |=  [sut=vase raz=(list [face=term =spec =path])]
1048      ^-  [vase state]
1049      ?~  raz  [sut nub]
1050      =^  res=(map @ta vase)  nub
1051        (build-directory path.i.raz)
1052      =;  pin=vase
1053        =.  p.pin  [%face face.i.raz p.pin]
1054        $(sut (slop pin sut), raz t.raz)
1055      ::
1056      =/  =type  (~(play ut p.sut) [%kttr spec.i.raz])
1057      ::  ensure results nest in the specified type,
1058      ::  and produce a homogenous map containing that type.
1059      ::
1060      :-  %-  ~(play ut p.sut)
1061          [%kttr %make [%wing ~[%map]] ~[[%base %atom %ta] spec.i.raz]]
1062      |-
1063      ?~  res  ~
1064      ?.  (~(nest ut type) | p.q.n.res)
1065        ~|  [%nest-fail path.i.raz p.n.res]
1066        !!
1067      :-  [p.n.res q.q.n.res]
1068      [$(res l.res) $(res r.res)]
1069    ::
1070    ++  run-maz
1071      |=  [sut=vase maz=(list [face=term =mark])]
1072      ^-  [vase state]
1073      ?~  maz  [sut nub]
1074      =^  pin=vase  nub  (build-nave mark.i.maz)
1075      =.  p.pin  [%face face.i.maz p.pin]
1076      $(sut (slop pin sut), maz t.maz)
1077    ::
1078    ++  run-caz
1079      |=  [sut=vase caz=(list [face=term =mars])]
1080      ^-  [vase state]
1081      ?~  caz  [sut nub]
1082      =^  pin=vase  nub  (build-cast mars.i.caz)
1083      =.  p.pin  [%face face.i.caz p.pin]
1084      $(sut (slop pin sut), caz t.caz)
1085    ::
1086    ++  run-bar
1087      |=  [sut=vase bar=(list [face=term =mark =path])]
1088      ^-  [vase state]
1089      ?~  bar  [sut nub]
1090      =^  =cage  nub  (cast-path [path mark]:i.bar)
1091      =.  p.q.cage  [%face face.i.bar p.q.cage]
1092      $(sut (slop q.cage sut), bar t.bar)
1093    ::
1094    ::  +build-fit: build file at path, maybe converting '-'s to '/'s in path
1095    ::
1096    ++  build-fit
1097      |=  [pre=@tas pax=@tas]
1098      ^-  [vase state]
1099      (build-file (fit-path pre pax))
1100    ::
```

```
1101    ::    +fit-path: find path, maybe converting '-'s to '/'s
1102    ::
1103    ::        Try '-' before '/', applied left-to-right through the path,
1104    ::        e.g. 'a-foo/bar' takes precedence over 'a/foo-bar'.
1105    ::
1106    ++  fit-path
1107      |=  [pre=@tas pax=@tas]
1108      ^-  path
1109      =/  paz  (segments pax)
1110      |-  ^-  path
1111      ?~  paz
1112        ~_(leaf/"clay: no files match /{(trip pre)}/{(trip pax)}/hoon" !!)
1113      =/  pux=path  pre^(snoc i.paz %hoon)
1114      ?:  (~(has by files) pux)
1115        pux
1116      $(paz t.paz)
1117    ::
1118    ++  all-fits
1119      |=  [=term suf=term]
1120      ^-  (list path)
1121      %+  turn  (segments suf)
1122      |=  seg=path
1123      [term (snoc seg %hoon)]
1124    ::
1125    ::  Gets a map of the data at the given path and all children of it.
1126    ::
1127    ::      i.e. +dip:of for a map, except doesn't shorten paths
1128    ::
1129    ++  dip-hat
1130      |=  pax=path
1131      ^-  (map path (each page lobe))
1132      %-  malt
1133      %+  skim  ~(tap by files)
1134      |=  [p=path *]
1135      ?|  ?=(~ pax)
1136          ?&  !?=(~ p)
1137              =(-.pax -.p)
1138              $(p +.p, pax +.pax)
1139      ==  ==
1140    ::
1141    ++  trace
1142      |=  [pri=@ print=(trap tape)]
1143      (^trace verb pri print)
1144    ::
1145    ++  mist-to-pour
1146      |=  =mist
1147      ^-  pour
1148      ?+    -.mist  mist
1149          %vale
1150        :+  %vale  path.mist
1151        ~|  %file-not-found-mist^path.mist
1152        =/  lob  (~(got by files) path.mist)
1153        ?-  -.lob
1154          %&  (page-to-lobe p.lob)
1155          %|  p.lob
1156        ==
1157      ::
1158          %arch
```

```
1159      =/  dip  (dip-hat path.mist)
1160      :+  %arch  path.mist
1161      %-  ~(run by dip)
1162      |=  file=(each page lobe)
1163      ?-  -.file
1164        %&  (page-to-lobe p.file)
1165        %|  p.file
1166      ==
1167    ==
1168  ::
1169  ++  soak-cage  |=([s=soak n=state] ?>(?=(%cage -.s) [cage.s n]))
1170  ++  soak-vase  |=([s=soak n=state] ?>(?=(%vase -.s) [vase.s n]))
1171  ++  soak-dais  |=([s=soak n=state] ?>(?=(%dais -.s) [dais.s n]))
1172  ++  soak-tube  |=([s=soak n=state] ?>(?=(%tube -.s) [tube.s n]))
1173  ++  soak-arch  |=([s=soak n=state] ?>(?=(%arch -.s) [dir.s n]))
1174  ::
1175  ++  gain-sprig
1176    |=  [=mist next=(trap [soak state])]
1177    ^-  [soak state]
1178    ?~  got=(~(get by sprig.nub) mist)
1179      $:next
1180    =?  stack.nub  ?=(^ stack.nub)
1181      stack.nub(i (~(put in i.stack.nub) leak.u.got))
1182    [soak.u.got nub]
1183  ::
1184  ++  gain-leak
1185    |=  [=mist next=$-(state [soak state])]
1186    ^-  [soak state]
1187    =^  top=(set leak)  stack.nub  stack.nub
1188    =/  =leak  [(mist-to-pour mist) top]
1189    =.  cycle.nub  (~(del in cycle.nub) mist)
1190    =?  stack.nub  ?=(^ stack.nub)
1191      stack.nub(i (~(put in i.stack.nub) leak))
1192    =/  spilt  (~(has in spill.nub) leak)
1193    =^  =soak  nub
1194      ?^  got=(~(get by cache.nub) leak)
1195        %-  %+  trace  3  |.
1196            =/  refs    ?:(spilt 0 1)
1197            %+  welp  "cache {<pour.leak>}: adding {<refs>}, "
1198            "giving {<(add refs refs.u.got)>}"
1199        =?  cache.nub  !spilt
1200        (~(put by cache.nub) leak [+(refs.u.got) soak.u.got])
1201        [soak.u.got nub]
1202      %-  (trace 2 |.("cache {<pour.leak>}: creating"))
1203      =^  =soak  nub  (next nub)
1204      =.  cache.nub  (~(put by cache.nub) leak [1 soak])
1205      ::  If we're creating a cache entry, add refs to our dependencies
1206      ::
1207      =/  deps  ~(tap in deps.leak)
1208      |-
1209      ?~  deps
1210        [soak nub]
1211      =/  got  (~(got by cache.nub) i.deps)
1212      %-  %+  trace  3  |.
1213          %+  welp  "cache {<pour.leak>} for {<pour.i.deps>}"
1214          ": bumping to ref {<refs.got>}"
1215      =.  cache.nub  (~(put by cache.nub) i.deps got(refs +(refs.got)))
1216      $(deps t.deps)
```

```
1217      ?:  spilt
1218        [soak nub]
1219      %-  (trace 3 |.("spilt {<mist>}"))
1220      =:  spill.nub  (~(put in spill.nub) leak)
1221          sprig.nub  (~(put by sprig.nub) mist leak soak)
1222          ==
1223      [soak nub]
1224      --
1225    ::
1226    ++  lose-leak
1227      |=  [verb=@ fad=flow =leak]
1228      ^-  flow
1229      ?~  got=(~(get by fad) leak)
1230        %-  (trace verb 0 |.("lose missing leak {<leak>}"))
1231        fad
1232      ?:  (lth 1 refs.u.got)
1233        %-  (trace verb 3 |.("cache {<pour.leak>}: decrementing from {<refs.u.got>}"))
1234        =.  fad  (~(put by fad) leak u.got(refs (dec refs.u.got)))
1235        fad
1236      =+  ?.  =(0 refs.u.got)  ~
1237          ((trace verb 0 |.("lose zero leak {<leak>}")) ~)
1238      %-  (trace verb 2 |.("cache {<pour.leak>}: freeing"))
1239      =.  fad  (~(del by fad) leak)
1240      =/  leaks  ~(tap in deps.leak)
1241      |-  ^-  flow
1242      ?~  leaks
1243        fad
1244      =.  fad  ^$(leak i.leaks)
1245      $(leaks t.leaks)
1246    ::
1247    ++  lose-leaks
1248      |=  [verb=@ fad=flow leaks=(set leak)]
1249      ^-  flow
1250      =/  leaks  ~(tap in leaks)
1251      |-
1252      ?~  leaks
1253        fad
1254      $(fad (lose-leak verb fad i.leaks), leaks t.leaks)
1255    ::
1256    ++  trace
1257      |=  [verb=@ pri=@ print=(trap tape)]
1258      ?:  (lth verb pri)
1259        same
1260      (slog leaf+"ford: {(print)}" ~)
1261    --
1262  ::::::::::::::::::::::::::::::::::::::::::::::::::::::::::::::::::::::::::
1263  ::  section 4cA, filesystem logic
1264  ::
1265  ::  This core contains the main logic of clay.  Besides `++ze`, this directly
1266  ::  contains the logic for commiting new revisions (local urbits), managing
1267  ::  and notifying subscribers (reactivity), and pulling and validating content
1268  ::  (remote urbits).
1269  ::
1270  ::  The state includes:
1271  ::
1272  ::  --  local urbit `our`
1273  ::  --  current time `now`
1274  ::  --  current duct `hen`
```

```
1275  ::  --  scry handler `ski`
1276  ::  --  all vane state `++raft` (rarely used, except for the object store)
1277  ::  --  target urbit `her`
1278  ::  --  target desk `syd`
1279  ::
1280  ::  For local desks, `our` == `her` is one of the urbits on our pier.  For
1281  ::  foreign desks, `her` is the urbit the desk is on and `our` is the local
1282  ::  urbit that's managing the relationship with the foreign urbit.  Don't mix
1283  ::  up those two, or there will be wailing and gnashing of teeth.
1284  ::
1285  ::  While setting up `++de`, we check if `our` == `her`. If so, we get
1286  ::  the desk information from `dos.rom`.  Otherwise, we get the rung from
1287  ::  `hoy` and get the desk information from `rus` in there.  In either case,
1288  ::  we normalize the desk information to a `++rede`, which is all the
1289  ::  desk-specific data that we utilize in `++de`.  Because it's effectively
1290  ::  a part of the `++de` state, let's look at what we've got:
1291  ::
1292  ::  --  `lim` is the most recent date we're confident we have all the
1293  ::      information for.  For local desks, this is always `now`.  For foreign
1294  ::      desks, this is the last time we got a full update from the foreign
1295  ::      urbit.
1296  ::  --  `ref` is a possible request manager.  For local desks, this is null.
1297  ::      For foreign desks, this keeps track of all pending foreign requests
1298  ::      plus a cache of the responses to previous requests.
1299  ::  --  `qyx` is the set of subscriptions, with listening ducts. These
1300  ::      subscriptions exist only until they've been filled.
1301  ::  --  `dom` is the actual state of the filetree.  Since this is used almost
1302  ::      exclusively in `++ze`, we describe it there.
1303  ::
1304  ::::::::::::::::::::::::::::::::::::::::::::::::::::::::::::::::::::::::::::
1305  ++  de                                             :: per desk
1306    ~%  %de  ..de  ~
1307    |=  [now=@da rof=roof hen=duct raft]
1308    ~/  %de-in
1309    |=  [her=ship syd=desk]
1310    ::  NB: ruf=raft crashes in the compiler
1311    ::
1312    =*  ruf  |3.+6.^$
1313    =|  [mow=(list move) hun=(unit duct) rede]
1314    =*  red=rede  ->+
1315    =<  apex
1316    ~%  %de-core  ..$  ~
1317    |%
1318    ++  abet                                         :: resolve
1319      ^-  [(list move) raft]
1320      :-  (flop mow)
1321      ?.  =(our her)
1322        ::  save foreign +rede
1323        ::
1324      =/  run  (~(gut by hoy.ruf) her *rung)
1325      =/  rug  (~(put by rus.run) syd red)
1326      ruf(hoy (~(put by hoy.ruf) her run(rus rug)))
1327    ::  save domestic +room
1328    ::
1329    %=  ruf
1330      hun.rom  (need hun)
1331      dos.rom  (~(put by dos.rom.ruf) syd [qyx dom per pew fiz]:red)
1332    ==
```

```
1333    ::
1334    ++  apex
1335      ^+  ..park
1336      ?.  =(our her)
1337        ::  no duct, foreign +rede or default
1338        ::
1339        =.  mow
1340          ?:  (~(has by hoy.ruf) her)
1341            ~
1342          [hun.rom.ruf %pass /sinks %j %public-keys (silt her ~)]~
1343        =.  hun  ~
1344        =.  |2.+6.park
1345          =/  rus  rus:(~(gut by hoy.ruf) her *rung)
1346          %+  ~(gut by rus)  syd
1347          [lim=~2000.1.1 ref=`*rind qyx=~ dom=*dome per=~ pew=~ fiz=*melt]
1348        ..park
1349      ::  administrative duct, domestic +rede
1350      ::
1351      =.  mow  ~
1352      =.  hun  `hun.rom.ruf
1353      =.  |2.+6.park
1354        =/  jod  (~(gut by dos.rom.ruf) syd *dojo)
1355        [lim=now ref=*(unit rind) [qyx dom per pew fiz]:jod]
1356      ..park
1357    ::
1358    ::  Handle `%sing` requests
1359    ::
1360    ++  aver
1361      |=  [for=(unit ship) mun=mood]
1362      ^-  [(unit (unit cage)) _..park]
1363      =+  ezy=?~(ref ~ (~(get by haw.u.ref) mun))
1364      ?^  ezy
1365        [`u.ezy ..park]
1366      ?:  ?=([%s [%ud *] %late *] mun)
1367        :_  ..park
1368        ^-  (unit (unit cage))
1369        :+  ~  ~
1370        ^-  cage
1371        :-  %cass
1372        ?~  let.dom
1373          !>([0 *@da])
1374        !>([let.dom t:(~(got by hut.ran) (~(got by hit.dom) let.dom))])
1375      =+  tak=(case-to-tako case.mun)
1376      ?:  ?=([%s case %case ~] mun)
1377        ::  case existence check
1378        [``[%flag !>(!=(~ tak))] ..park]
1379      ?~(tak [~ ..park] (read-at-tako:ze for u.tak mun))
1380    ::
1381    ::  Queue a move.
1382    ::
1383    ++  emit
1384      |=  mof=move
1385      %_(+> mow [mof mow])
1386    ::
1387    ::  Queue a list of moves
1388    ::
1389    ++  emil
1390      |=  mof=(list move)
```

```
1391        %_(+> mow (weld (flop mof) mow))
1392    ::
1393    ::  Queue a list of moves, to be emitted before the rest
1394    ::
1395    ++  lime
1396        |=  mof=(list move)
1397        %_(+> mow (weld mow (flop mof)))
1398    ::
1399    ::  Set timer.
1400    ::
1401    ++  bait
1402        |=  [hen=duct tym=@da]
1403        (emit hen %pass /tyme/(scot %p her)/[syd] %b %wait tym)
1404    ::
1405    ::  Cancel timer.
1406    ::
1407    ++  best
1408        |=  [hen=duct tym=@da]
1409        (emit hen %pass /tyme/(scot %p her)/[syd] %b %rest tym)
1410    ::
1411    ::  Give %writ, or slip a drip if foreign desk
1412    ::
1413    ++  writ
1414        |=  res=(unit [=mood =cage])
1415        ^-  card
1416        =/  =riot
1417          ?~  res
1418            ~
1419          `[[care.mood case.mood syd] path.mood cage]:[u.res syd=syd]
1420        ?~  ref
1421          [%give %writ riot]
1422        [%pass /drip %b %drip !>([%writ riot])]
1423    ::
1424    ++  case-to-date
1425        |=  =case
1426        ^-  @da
1427        ::  if the case is already a date, use it.
1428        ::
1429        ?:  ?=([%da *] case)
1430          p.case
1431        ::  translate other cases to dates
1432        ::
1433        =/  aey  (case-to-aeon-before lim case)
1434        ?~  aey  `@da`0
1435        ?:  =(0 u.aey)  `@da`0
1436        t:(aeon-to-yaki:ze u.aey)
1437    ::
1438    ++  case-to-aeon  (cury case-to-aeon-before lim)
1439    ::
1440    ::  Reduce a case to an aeon (version number)
1441    ::
1442    ::  We produce null if we can't yet reduce the case for whatever
1443    ::  resaon (usually either the time or aeon hasn't happened yet or
1444    ::  the label hasn't been created).
1445    ::
1446    ++  case-to-aeon-before
1447        |=  [lim=@da lok=case]
1448        ^-  (unit aeon)
```

```
1449      ?-    -.lok
1450        %tas  (~(get by lab.dom) p.lok)
1451        %ud   ?:((gth p.lok let.dom) ~ [~ p.lok])
1452        %uv   `(tako-to-aeon:ze p.lok)
1453        %da
1454      ?:  (gth p.lok lim)  ~
1455      |-  ^-  (unit aeon)
1456      ?:  =(0 let.dom)  [~ 0]                         ::  avoid underflow
1457      ?:  %+  gte  p.lok
1458          =<  t
1459          ~|  [%letdom let=let.dom hit=hit.dom hut=~(key by hut.ran)]
1460          ~|  [%getdom (~(get by hit.dom) let.dom)]
1461          %-  aeon-to-yaki:ze
1462          let.dom
1463        [~ let.dom]
1464      $(let.dom (dec let.dom))
1465      ==
1466    ::
1467    ++  case-to-tako
1468      |=  lok=case
1469      ^-  (unit tako)
1470      ?:  ?=(%uv -.lok)
1471        ?:((~(has by hut.ran) p.lok) `p.lok ~)
1472      (bind (case-to-aeon-before lim lok) aeon-to-tako:ze)
1473    ::
1474    ::  Create a ford appropriate for the aeon
1475    ::
1476    ::  Don't forget to call +tako-flow!
1477    ::
1478    ++  tako-ford
1479      |=  tak=tako
1480      %-  ford:fusion
1481      :-  (~(run by q:(tako-to-yaki:ze tak)) |=(=lobe |+lobe))
1482      [lat.ran veb.bug fad ?:(=(tak (aeon-to-tako:ze let.dom)) fod.dom [~ ~])]
1483    ::  Produce ford cache appropriate for the aeon
1484    ::
1485    ++  tako-flow
1486      |*  [tak=tako res=* fud=flow fod=flue]
1487      :-  res
1488      ^+  ..park
1489      ?:  &(?=(~ ref) =((aeon-to-tako:ze let.dom) tak))
1490        ..park(fad fud, fod.dom fod)
1491      :: if in the past, don't update ford cache, since any results have
1492      :: no roots
1493      ::
1494      ..park
1495    ::
1496    ++  request-wire
1497      |=  [kind=@ta =ship =desk index=@ud]
1498      /[kind]/(scot %p ship)/[desk]/(scot %ud index)
1499    ::
1500    ::  Transfer a request to another ship's clay.
1501    ::
1502    ++  send-over-ames
1503      |=  [=duct =ship index=@ud =riff]
1504      ^+  +>
1505      ::
1506      =/  =desk  p.riff
```

```
1507      =/  =wire  (request-wire %warp-index ship desk index)
1508      =/  =path  [%question desk (scot %ud index) ~]
1509      (emit duct %pass wire %a %plea ship %c path `riff-any`[%1 riff])
1510    ::
1511    ++  send-over-scry
1512      |=  [kind=@ta =duct =ship index=@ud =desk =mood]
1513      ^-  [[timeout=@da =path] _..send-over-scry]
1514      =/  =time  (add now scry-timeout-time)
1515      =/  =wire  (request-wire kind ship desk index)
1516      =/  =path
1517        =,  mood
1518        [%c care (scot case) desk path]
1519      :-  [time path]
1520      %-  emil
1521      :~  [hen %pass wire %a %keen ship path]
1522          [hen %pass wire %b %wait time]
1523      ==
1524    ::
1525    ++  cancel-scry-timeout
1526      |=  inx=@ud
1527      ~|  [%strange-timeout-cancel-no-scry-request her syd inx]
1528      ?>  ?=(^ ref)
1529      =/  sat=update-state  (~(got by bom.u.ref) inx)
1530      ?>  ?=([~ ^] busy.sat)
1531      =/  =wire  (request-wire kind.u.busy.sat her syd inx)
1532      (emit hen %pass wire %b %rest time.u.busy.sat)
1533    ::
1534    ++  foreign-capable
1535      |=  =rave
1536      |^
1537      ?-    -.rave
1538          %many  &
1539          %sing  (good-care care.mood.rave)
1540          %next  (good-care care.mood.rave)
1541          %mult
1542        %-  ~(all in paths.mool.rave)
1543        |=  [=care =path]
1544        (good-care care)
1545      ==
1546      ::
1547      ++  good-care
1548        |=  =care
1549        (~(has in ^~((silt `(list ^care)`~[%q %u %w %x %y %z]))) care)
1550      --
1551    ::
1552    ::  Build and send agents to gall
1553    ::
1554    ::  Must be called at the end of a commit, but only while Clay is in a
1555    ::  fully-consistent state (eg not in the middle of a kelvin upgrade).
1556    ::
1557    ++  goad
1558      ^+  ..park
1559      =^  moves-1  ruf   abet
1560      =^  moves-2  ruf   abet:goad:(lu now rof hen ruf)
1561      =.  ..park  apex
1562      (emil (weld moves-1 moves-2))
1563    ::
1564    ::  Notify subscribers of changes to tire
```

```
1565    ::
1566    ::  Must be called any time tire could have changed, unless you called
1567    ::  goad (which calls tare internally).
1568    ::
1569    ++  tare
1570      ^+  ..park
1571      =^  moves-1  ruf  abet
1572      =^  moves-2  ruf  abet:tare:(lu now rof hen ruf)
1573      =.  ..park  apex
1574      (emil (weld moves-1 moves-2))
1575    ::
1576    ::  Create a request that cannot be filled immediately.
1577    ::
1578    ::  If it's a local request, we just put in in `qyx`, setting a timer if it's
1579    ::  waiting for a particular time.  If it's a foreign request, we add it to
1580    ::  our request manager (ref, which is a ++rind) and make the request to the
1581    ::  foreign ship.
1582    ::
1583    ++  duce                                          ::  produce request
1584      |=  wov=wove
1585      ^+  +>
1586      =.  wov  (dedupe wov)
1587      =.  qyx  (~(put ju qyx) wov hen)
1588      ?~  ref
1589        ::  [wake] at @da must check if subscription was fulfilled
1590        ::
1591        (run-if-future rove.wov |=(@da (bait hen +<)))
1592      |-  ^+  +>+.$
1593      =/  =rave  (rove-to-rave rove.wov)
1594      =?  rave  ?=([%sing %v *] rave)
1595      [%many %| [%ud let.dom] case.mood.rave path.mood.rave]
1596      ::
1597      ?.  (foreign-capable rave)
1598        ~|([%clay-bad-foreign-request-care rave] !!)
1599      ::
1600      =+  inx=nix.u.ref
1601      =.  +>+.$
1602        =<  ?>(?=(^ ref) .)
1603        (send-over-ames hen her inx syd `rave)
1604      %=  +>+.$
1605        nix.u.ref  +(nix.u.ref)
1606        bom.u.ref  (~(put by bom.u.ref) inx [hen rave ~ ~ ~ ~])
1607        fod.u.ref  (~(put by fod.u.ref) hen inx)
1608      ==
1609    ::
1610    ::  If a similar request exists, switch to the existing request.
1611    ::
1612    ::  "Similar" requests are those %next and %many requests which are the same
1613    ::  up to starting case, but we're already after the starting case.  This
1614    ::  stacks later requests for something onto the same request so that they
1615    ::  all get filled at once.
1616    ::
1617    ++  dedupe                                         ::  find existing alias
1618      |=  wov=wove
1619      ^-  wove
1620      =;  won=(unit wove)  (fall won wov)
1621      =*  rov  rove.wov
1622      ?-    -.rov
```

```
1623        %sing  ~
1624        %next
1625    =+  aey=(case-to-aeon case.mood.rov)
1626    ?~  aey   ~
1627    %-  ~(rep in ~(key by qyx))
1628    |=  [haw=wove res=(unit wove)]
1629    ?^  res  res
1630    ?.  =(for.wov for.haw)  ~
1631    =*  hav  rove.haw
1632    =-  ?:(- `haw ~)
1633    ?&  ?=(%next -.hav)
1634        =(mood.hav mood.rov(case case.mood.hav))
1635      ::
1636      ::  only a match if this request is before
1637      ::  or at our starting case.
1638      =+  hay=(case-to-aeon case.mood.hav)
1639      ?~(hay | (lte u.hay u.aey))
1640    ==
1641  ::
1642        %mult
1643    =+  aey=(case-to-aeon case.mool.rov)
1644    ?~  aey   ~
1645    %-  ~(rep in ~(key by qyx))
1646    |=  [haw=wove res=(unit wove)]
1647    ?^  res  res
1648    ?.  =(for.wov for.haw)  ~
1649    =*  hav  rove.haw
1650    =-  ?:(- `haw ~)
1651    ?&  ?=(%mult -.hav)
1652        =(mool.hav mool.rov(case case.mool.hav))
1653      ::
1654      ::  only a match if this request is before
1655      ::  or at our starting case, and it has been
1656      ::  tested at least that far.
1657      =+  hay=(case-to-aeon case.mool.hav)
1658      ?&  ?=(^ hay)
1659          (lte u.hay u.aey)
1660          ?=(^ aeon.hav)
1661          (gte u.aeon.hav u.aey)
1662      ==
1663    ==
1664  ::
1665        %many
1666    =+  aey=(case-to-aeon from.moat.rov)
1667    ?~  aey   ~
1668    %-  ~(rep in ~(key by qyx))
1669    |=  [haw=wove res=(unit wove)]
1670    ?^  res  res
1671    ?.  =(for.wov for.haw)  ~
1672    =*  hav  rove.haw
1673    =-  ?:(- `haw ~)
1674    ?&  ?=(%many -.hav)
1675        =(hav rov(from.moat from.moat.hav))
1676      ::
1677      ::  only a match if this request is before
1678      ::  or at our starting case.
1679      =+  hay=(case-to-aeon from.moat.hav)
1680      ?~(hay | (lte u.hay u.aey))
```

```
1681          ==
1682        ==
1683      ::
1684      ++  set-norm
1685        |=  =norm
1686        =.  nor.dom  norm
1687        ..park
1688      ::
1689      ++  set-worn
1690        |=  [=tako =norm]
1691        ?:  &(=(our her) =(tako (aeon-to-tako:ze let.dom)))
1692          (mean leaf+"clay: can't set norm for current commit in {<syd>}" ~)
1693        =.  tom.dom  (~(put by tom.dom) tako norm)
1694        ..park
1695      ::
1696      ::  Attach label to aeon
1697      ::
1698      ++  label
1699        |=  [bel=@tas aey=(unit aeon)]
1700        ^+  ..park
1701        =/  yon  ?~(aey let.dom u.aey)
1702        =/  yen  (~(get by lab.dom) bel)  :: existing aeon?
1703        ::  no existing aeon is bound to this label
1704        ::
1705        ?~  yen
1706          =.  lab.dom  (~(put by lab.dom) bel yon)           ::  [wake] <>
1707          wake
1708        ::  an aeon is bound to this label,
1709        ::  but it is the same as the existing one, so we no-op
1710        ::
1711        ?:  =(u.yen yon)
1712          ~&  "clay: tried to rebind existing label {<bel>} to equivalent aeon {<yon>}"
1713          ..park
1714        ::  an existing aeon bound to the label
1715        ::  that is distinct from the requested one.
1716        ::  rewriting would violate referential transparency
1717        ::
1718        ~|  %tried-to-rewrite-existing-label
1719        ~|  "requested aeon: {<yon>}, existing aeon: {<u.yen>}"
1720        !!
1721      ::
1722      ::  Porcelain commit
1723      ::
1724      ++  info
1725        ~/  %info
1726        |=  [deletes=(set path) changes=(map path cage)]
1727        ^+  ..park
1728        ?:  =(0 let.dom)
1729          ?>  ?=(~ deletes)
1730          =/  data=(map path (each page lobe))
1731            (~(run by changes) |=(=cage &+[p q.q]:cage))
1732          (park | & &+[~ data] *rang)
1733        ::
1734        =/  parent-tako=tako  (aeon-to-tako:ze let.dom)
1735        =/  data=(map path (each page lobe))
1736          =/  parent-yaki  (tako-to-yaki:ze parent-tako)
1737          =/  after-deletes
1738            %-  ~(dif by q.parent-yaki)
```

```
1739          (malt (turn ~(tap in deletes) |=(=path [path *lobe]))))
1740       =/  after=(map path (each page lobe))
1741         (~(run by after-deletes) |=(=lobe |+lobe))
1742       %-  ~(uni by after)
1743       ^-  (map path (each page lobe))
1744      (~(run by changes) |=(=cage &+[p q.q]:cage))
1745    ::
1746    =/  =yuki  [~[parent-tako] data]
1747    (park | & &+yuki *rang)
1748  ::
1749  ::  Unix commit
1750  ::
1751  ++  into
1752    ~/  %into
1753    |=  [pax=path all=? mod=(list [pax=path mim=(unit mime)])]
1754    ^+  ..park
1755    ::  filter out unchanged, cached %mime values
1756    ::
1757    =.  mod
1758      %+  skip  mod
1759      |=  [pax=path mim=(unit mime)]
1760      ?~  mim
1761        |
1762      ?~  mum=(~(get by mim.dom) pax)
1763        |
1764      ::  TODO: check mimetype
1765      ::
1766      =(q.u.mim q.u.mum)
1767    =/  =yaki
1768      ?:  =(0 let.dom)
1769        *yaki
1770      (~(got by hut.ran) (~(got by hit.dom) let.dom))
1771    (info (mode-to-commit q.yaki pax all mod))
1772  ::
1773  ::  Plumbing commit
1774  ::
1775  ::    Guaranteed to finish in one event.
1776  ::
1777  ::    updated: whether we've already completed sys upgrade
1778  ::    goat: whether we should call +goad at the end.  Only false
1779  ::      during kelvin upgrade so that all commits can happen before
1780  ::      the +goad.
1781  ::    yoki: new commit
1782  ::    rang: any additional objects referenced
1783  ::
1784  ::    [goad] < if goat is false, then the caller is responsible to
1785  ::    call +goad.
1786  ::
1787  ::    TODO: needs to check tako in rang
1788  ::
1789  ++  park
1790    =/  check-sane  |
1791    |^
1792    |=  [updated=? goat=? =yoki =rang]
1793    ^+  ..park
1794    =:  hut.ran  (~(uni by hut.rang) hut.ran)
1795        lat.ran  (~(uni by lat.rang) lat.ran)
1796      ==
```

```
1797        =/  new-data=(map path (each page lobe))
1798          ?-  -.yoki
1799            %&  q.p.yoki
1800            %|  (~(run by q.p.yoki) |=(=lobe |+lobe))
1801          ==
1802        ?.  %-  ~(all in new-data)  :: use +all:in so we get the key
1803            |=  [=path tum=(each page lobe)]
1804            ?:  |(?=(%& -.tum) (~(has by lat.ran) p.tum))
1805              &
1806          =-  (mean leaf/- ~)
1807          "clay: commit failed, file tombstoned: {<path>} {<`@uv`p.tum>}"
1808          !!
1809        ::  find desk kelvin
1810        ::
1811        =/  kel=(set weft)  (waft-to-wefts (get-kelvin yoki))
1812        ?.  ?|  (~(has in kel) zuse+zuse)                   :: kelvin match
1813                ?&  !=(%base syd)                           :: best-effort compat
1814                    %-  ~(any in kel)
1815                    |=  =weft
1816                    &(=(%zuse lal.weft) (gth num.weft zuse))
1817                ==
1818                ?&  =(%base syd)                            ::  ready to upgrade
1819                %+  levy  ~(tap by tore:(lu now rof hen ruf))
1820                |=  [=desk =zest wic=(set weft)]
1821                ?|  =(%base desk)
1822                    !?=(%live zest)
1823                    !=(~ (~(int in wic) kel))
1824                ==
1825            ==
1826        ==
1827        ?:  (~(all in kel) |=(=weft (gth num.weft zuse)))
1828          %-  (slog leaf+"clay: old-kelvin, {<[need=zuse/zuse have=kel]>}" ~)
1829          ..park
1830        =.  wic.dom                                 ::  [tare] <
1831          %+  roll  ~(tap in kel)
1832          |:  [weft=*weft wic=wic.dom]
1833          (~(put by wic) weft yoki)
1834        =?  ..park  !?=(%base syd)  wick            ::  [wick]
1835        %-  (slog leaf+"clay: wait-for-kelvin, {<[need=zuse/zuse have=kel]>}" ~)
1836        tare                                        ::  [tare] >
1837      =.  wic.dom
1838        %-  ~(gas by *(map weft ^yoki))
1839        %+  skip  ~(tap by wic.dom)
1840        |=  [w=weft ^yoki]
1841        (gte num.w zuse)
1842      ::
1843      =/  old-yaki
1844        ?:  =(0 let.dom)
1845          *yaki
1846        (aeon-to-yaki:ze let.dom)
1847      =/  old-kel=(set weft)
1848        ?:  =(0 let.dom)
1849          [zuse+zuse ~ ~]
1850        (waft-to-wefts (get-kelvin %| old-yaki))
1851      =/  [deletes=(set path) changes=(map path (each page lobe))]
1852        (get-changes q.old-yaki new-data)
1853      ~|  [from=let.dom deletes=deletes changes=~(key by changes)]
1854      ::
```

```
1855    ::  promote ford cache
1856    ::  promote and fill in mime cache
1857    ::
1858    =/  invalid  (~(uni in deletes) ~(key by changes))
1859    ::  if /sys updated in %base, defer to arvo and return early
1860    ::
1861    ?:  &(=(%base syd) !updated (~(any in invalid) is-kernel-path))
1862      (sys-update yoki new-data)
1863    ::  after this point, there must be no early return except if it's a
1864    ::  complete no-op.  any error conditions must crash.  since we're
1865    ::  changing state, we may need to call +wake, +goad, etc, which
1866    ::  happens at the end of the function.
1867    ::
1868    ::  [wick] if this commit added compatibility to a future kelvin,
1869    ::  then we might have unblocked a kelvin upgrade.
1870    ::
1871    ::  or, if *this* is a kelvin upgrade, it's possible that another
1872    ::  kelvin upgrade will immediately be ready.  for example, this
1873    ::  could be the case if all desks but one are ready for the next
1874    ::  two kelvins, and then that desk is suspended or receives a
1875    ::  commit with compatiblity with both kelvins.
1876    ::
1877    ::  in any of these cases, we finish the current commit but call
1878    ::  +wick so that we try to execute the kelvin upgrade afterward.
1879    ::  we want this commit to persist even if the subsequent kelvin
1880    ::  upgrade fails.
1881    ::
1882    =.  ..park  wick
1883    =.  wic.dom                                    ::  [tare] <
1884      %+  roll  ~(tap in kel)
1885      |:  [weft=*weft wic=wic.dom]
1886      ?:  (gte num.weft zuse)
1887        wic
1888      (~(put by wic) weft yoki)
1889    ::
1890    =+  ?.  (did-kernel-update invalid)  ~
1891        ((slog 'clay: kernel updated' ~) ~)
1892    =?  updated  updated  (did-kernel-update invalid)
1893    =>  ?.  updated  .
1894        ~>(%slog.0^leaf/"clay: rebuilding {<syd>} after kernel update" .)
1895    ::  clear caches if zuse reloaded
1896    ::
1897    =/  old-fod  fod.dom
1898    =.  fod.dom
1899      ?:  updated  [~ ~]
1900      (promote-ford fod.dom invalid)
1901    =.  fad
1902      (lose-leaks:fusion veb.bug fad (~(dif in spill.old-fod) spill.fod.dom))
1903    =?  changes  updated  (changes-for-upgrade q.old-yaki deletes changes)
1904    ::
1905    =/  files
1906      =/  original=(map path (each page lobe))
1907        (~(run by q.old-yaki) |=(=lobe |+lobe))
1908      %-  ~(dif by (~(uni by original) changes))
1909      %-  ~(gas by *(map path (each page lobe)))
1910      (turn ~(tap in deletes) |=(=path [path |+*lobe]))
1911    =/  =args:ford:fusion  [files lat.ran veb.bug fad fod.dom]
1912    ::
```

```
1913    =^    change-cages  args  (checkout-changes args changes)
1914    =/    sane-continuation  (sane-changes changes change-cages)
1915    =/    new-pages=(map lobe page)
1916      %-   malt
1917      %+   turn  ~(tap by change-cages)
1918      |=   [=path =lobe =cage]
1919      [lobe [p q.q]:cage]
1920    =/    data=(map path lobe)
1921      %-   ~(urn by new-data)
1922      |=   [=path value=(each page lobe)]
1923      ?-   -.value
1924        %|   p.value
1925        %&   lobe:(~(got by change-cages) path)
1926      ==
1927    ::  if we didn't change the data and it's not a merge commit, abort
1928    ::
1929    ?:    &(=([r.old-yaki ~] p.p.yoki) =(data q.old-yaki))
1930      ::  [tare] > if no changes, then commits-in-waiting could not have
1931      ::  changed.
1932      ::
1933      ..park
1934    =/    =yaki
1935      ?-   -.yoki
1936        %&   (make-yaki p.p.yoki data now)
1937        %|   ?>  =(data q.p.yoki)
1938             p.yoki
1939      ==
1940    ::  [wake] < [ergo] < [goad] <
1941    ::
1942    =:    let.dom  +(let.dom)
1943          hit.dom  (~(put by hit.dom) +(let.dom) r.yaki)
1944          hut.ran  (~(put by hut.ran) r.yaki yaki)
1945          lat.ran  (~(uni by new-pages) lat.ran)
1946      ==
1947    =.    file-store.args  lat.ran
1948    ::
1949    =/    mem  (want-mime 0)
1950    =/    res=[mum=(map path (unit mime)) mim=_mim.dom args=_args]
1951      ?.   mem  [~ ~ args]
1952      =^   mum  args  (checkout-mime args deletes ~(key by changes))
1953      [mum (apply-changes-to-mim mim.dom mum) args]
1954    =.    mim.dom  mim.res
1955    =.    args     args.res
1956    ::
1957    =.    fod.dom  [spill sprig]:args
1958    =.    fad      cache.args
1959    =.    ..park   (emil (print q.old-yaki data))
1960    ::  if upgrading kelvin and there's a commit-in-waiting, use that
1961    ::
1962    =?    ..park  &(=(%base syd) !=(old-kel kel))
1963      =/   desks=(list [=desk =dojo])  ~(tap by dos.rom)
1964      =^   moves-1  ruf  abet
1965      =|   moves-2=(list move)
1966      |-   ^+  ..park
1967      ?~   desks
1968        =.   ..park  apex
1969        (emil (weld moves-1 moves-2))
1970      ?.   ?=(%live liv.dom.dojo.i.desks)
```

```
1971        $(desks t.desks)
1972      ?:  ?=(%base desk.i.desks)
1973        $(desks t.desks)
1974      ?~  wat=(~(get by wic.dom.dojo.i.desks) zuse+zuse)
1975        (mean (cat 3 'clay: missing commit-in-waiting on ' desk.i.desks) ~)
1976      =/  den  ((de now rof hen ruf) our desk.i.desks)
1977      ::  [goad] < call without goading so that we apply all the commits
1978      ::  before trying to compile all desks to send to gall.
1979      ::
1980      =^  moves-3  ruf  abet:(park:den | | u.wat *^rang)
1981      =.  moves-2  (weld moves-2 moves-3)
1982        $(desks t.desks)
1983    ::  tell gall to try to run agents if %held
1984    ::
1985    ::  [goad] > if goat or desk not running.  %held uses park-held to
1986    ::  defer the goad into a new event, to attempt to revive the desk.
1987    ::  Note that %base will always be %live.
1988    ::
1989    =.  ..park
1990      ?-  liv.dom
1991        %held  (emit hen %pass /park-held/[syd] %b %wait now)
1992        %dead  ..park
1993        %live  ?:(goat goad ..park)
1994      ==
1995    ::  notify unix and subscribers
1996    ::
1997    =?  ..park  mem  (ergo 0 mum.res)                    ::  [ergo] >
1998    wake:tare                                            ::  [wake] > [tare] >
1999    ::
2000    ::  +is-kernel-path: should changing .pax cause a kernel or vane reload?
2001    ::
2002    ++  is-kernel-path  |=(pax=path ?=([%sys *] pax))
2003    ::
2004    ++  did-kernel-update
2005      |=  invalid=(set path)
2006      ?.  =(%base syd)
2007        |
2008      %-  ~(any in invalid)
2009      |=(p=path &((is-kernel-path p) !?=([%sys %vane *] p)))
2010    ::
2011    ::  +get-kelvin: read the desk's kernel version from /sys/kelvin
2012    ::
2013    ++  get-kelvin
2014      |=  =yoki
2015      ^-  waft
2016      |^  ?-    -.yoki
2017                %|
2018        %-  lobe-to-waft
2019        ~>  %mean.(cat 3 'clay: missing /sys/kelvin on ' syd)
2020        ~|  ~(key by q.p.yoki)
2021        (~(got by q.p.yoki) /sys/kelvin)
2022      ::
2023                %&
2024      =/  fil=(each page lobe)
2025        ~>  %mean.(cat 3 'clay: missing /sys/kelvin on ' syd)
2026        ~|  ~(key by q.p.yoki)
2027        (~(got by q.p.yoki) /sys/kelvin)
2028      ?-    -.fil
```

```
2029              %&   (page-to-waft p.fil)
2030              %|   (lobe-to-waft p.fil)
2031            ==
2032          ==
2033      ::
2034    ++  lobe-to-waft
2035      |=  =lobe
2036      ^-  waft
2037      =/  peg=(unit page)  (~(get by lat.ran) lobe)
2038      ?~  peg  ~|([%sys-kelvin-tombstoned syd] !!)
2039      (page-to-waft u.peg)
2040      ::
2041    ++  page-to-waft
2042      |=  =page
2043      ^-  waft
2044      ?+    p.page  ~|(clay-bad-kelvin-mark/p.page !!)
2045        %kelvin  ;;(waft q.page)
2046        %mime    (cord-to-waft q.q:;;(mime q.page))
2047      ==
2048      --
2049    ::
2050    ::  Find which files changed or were deleted
2051    ::
2052    ++  get-changes
2053      |=  [old=(map path lobe) new=(map path (each page lobe))]
2054      ^-  [deletes=(set path) changes=(map path (each page lobe))]
2055      =/  old=(map path (each page lobe))
2056        (~(run by old) |=(=lobe |+lobe))
2057      :*  %-  silt  ^-  (list path)
2058          %+  murn  ~(tap by (~(uni by old) new))
2059          |=  [=path *]
2060          ^-  (unit ^path)
2061          =/  a  (~(get by new) path)
2062          =/  b  (~(get by old) path)
2063          ?:  |(=(a b) !=(~ a))
2064            ~
2065          `path
2066        ::
2067          %-  malt  ^-  (list [path (each page lobe)])
2068          %+  murn  ~(tap by (~(uni by old) new))
2069          |=  [=path *]
2070          ^-  (unit [^path (each page lobe)])
2071          =/  a  (~(get by new) path)
2072          =/  b  (~(get by old) path)
2073          ?:  |(=(a b) ?=(~ a))
2074            ~
2075          `[path u.a]
2076      ==
2077    ::  Find all files for full desk rebuild
2078    ::
2079    ++  changes-for-upgrade
2080      |=  $:  old=(map path lobe)
2081              deletes=(set path)
2082              changes=(map path (each page lobe))
2083          ==
2084      ^+  changes
2085      =.  old
2086        %+  roll  ~(tap in deletes)
```

```
2087        |=  [pax=path old=_old]
2088        (~(del by old) pax)
2089      =/  pre=_changes  (~(run by old) |=(lob=lobe |+lob))
2090      (~(uni by pre) changes)
2091    ::
2092    ++  promote-ford
2093      |=  [fod=flue invalid=(set path)]
2094      ^-  flue
2095      =/  old=(list leak)  ~(tap in spill.fod)
2096      =|  new=flue
2097      |-  ^-  flue
2098      ?~  old
2099        new
2100      =/  invalid
2101        |-  ^-  ?
2102        ?|  ?+    -.pour.i.old  %|
2103                %vale  (~(has in invalid) path.pour.i.old)
2104                %arch
2105            ::  TODO: overly conservative, should be only direct hoon
2106            ::  children
2107            ::
2108            =/  len  (lent path.pour.i.old)
2109            %-  ~(any in invalid)
2110            |=  =path
2111            =(path.pour.i.old (scag len path))
2112          ==
2113        ::
2114          =/  deps  ~(tap in deps.i.old)
2115          |-  ^-  ?
2116          ?~  deps
2117            %|
2118          ?|  ^$(i.old i.deps)
2119              $(deps t.deps)
2120          ==
2121        ==
2122      =?  new  !invalid
2123        :-  (~(put in spill.new) i.old)
2124        =/  =mist  (pour-to-mist pour.i.old)
2125        ?~  got=(~(get by sprig.fod) mist)
2126          sprig.new
2127        (~(put by sprig.new) mist u.got)
2128      $(old t.old)
2129    ::
2130    ++  page-to-cord
2131      |=  =page
2132      ^-  @t
2133      ?+  p.page  ~|([%sys-bad-mark p.page] !!)
2134        %hoon  ;;(@t q.page)
2135        %mime  q.q:;;(mime q.page)
2136      ==
2137    ::
2138    ++  lobe-to-cord
2139      |=  =lobe
2140      ^-  @t
2141      =/  peg=(unit page)  (~(get by lat.ran) lobe)
2142      ?~  peg
2143        ~|([%lobe-to-cord-tombstoned syd lobe] !!)
2144      ;;(@t q.u.peg)
```

```
2145       ::
2146       ::  Updated q.yaki
2147       ::
2148       ++  checkout-changes
2149       |=  [=ford-args:ford:fusion changes=(map path (each page lobe))]
2150       ^-  [(map path [=lobe =cage]) args:ford:fusion]
2151       %+  roll  `(list [path (each page lobe)])`~(tap by changes)
2152       |=  $:  [=path change=(each page lobe)]
2153               [built=(map path [lobe cage]) cache=_ford-args]
2154           ==
2155       ^+  [built ford-args]
2156       =.  ford-args  cache
2157       =/  [=cage fud=flow fod=flue]
2158         ::  ~>  %slog.[0 leaf/"clay: validating {(spud path)}"]
2159         %-  wrap:fusion
2160         (read-file:(ford:fusion ford-args) path)
2161       =.  cache.ford-args  fud
2162       =.  spill.ford-args  spill.fod
2163       =.  sprig.ford-args  sprig.fod
2164       =/  =lobe
2165         ?-  -.change
2166           %|  p.change
2167           ::  Don't use p.change.i.cans because that's before casting to
2168           ::  the correct mark.
2169           ::
2170           %&  (page-to-lobe [p q.q]:cage)
2171         ==
2172       [(~(put by built) path [lobe cage]) ford-args]
2173       ::
2174       ::  Print notification to console
2175       ::
2176       ++  print
2177       |=  [old=(map path lobe) new=(map path lobe)]
2178       ^-  (list move)
2179       =/  [deletes=(set path) upserts=(map path (each page lobe))]
2180         (get-changes old (~(run by new) |=(=lobe |+lobe)))
2181       =/  upsert-set  ~(key by upserts)
2182       =/  old-set     ~(key by old)
2183       =/  changes=(set path)    (~(int in upsert-set) old-set)
2184       =/  additions=(set path)  (~(dif in upsert-set) old-set)
2185       ?~  hun
2186         ~
2187       ?:  (lte let.dom 1)
2188         ~
2189       |^
2190       ;:  weld
2191         (paths-to-notes '-' deletes)
2192         (paths-to-notes ':' changes)
2193         (paths-to-notes '+' additions)
2194       ==
2195       ::
2196       ++  paths-to-notes
2197       |=  [prefix=@tD paths=(set path)]
2198       %+  turn  ~(tap in paths)
2199       |=  =path
2200       ^-  move
2201       [u.hun %pass /note %d %text prefix ' ' ~(ram re (path-to-tank path))]
2202       ::
```

```
2203    ++  path-to-tank
2204      |=  =path
2205      =/  pre=^path  ~[(scot %p our) syd (scot %ud let.dom)]
2206      :+  %rose  ["/" "/" ~]
2207      %+  turn  (weld pre path)
2208      |=  a=cord
2209      ^-  tank
2210      ?:  ((sane %ta) a)
2211        [%leaf (trip a)]
2212      [%leaf (dash:us (trip a) '\'' ~)]
2213    --
2214    ::
2215    ::  Check sanity
2216    ::
2217    ++  sane-changes
2218      |=  $:  changes=(map path (each page lobe))
2219              change-cages=(map path [lobe cage])
2220          ==
2221      ^-  (unit [(map path [lobe cage]) args:ford:fusion])
2222      ?.  check-sane
2223        ~
2224      =/  tak=(unit tako)  (~(get by hit.dom) let.dom)
2225      ?~  tak
2226        ~
2227      =/  =yaki  (~(got by hut.ran) u.tak)
2228      ::  Assert all pages hash to their lobe
2229      ::
2230      =/  foo
2231        %-  ~(urn by lat.ran)
2232        |=  [=lobe =page]
2233        =/  actual-lobe=^lobe  `@uv`(page-to-lobe page)
2234        ~|  [%bad-lobe have=lobe need=actual-lobe]
2235        ?>  =(lobe actual-lobe)
2236        ~
2237      ::  Assert we calculated the same change-cages w/o cache
2238      ::
2239      ::  ? remove deletes
2240      ::
2241      =/  all-changes=(map path (each page lobe))
2242        =/  original=(map path (each page lobe))
2243          (~(run by q.yaki) |=(=lobe |+lobe))
2244        (~(uni by original) changes)
2245      =/  =args:ford:fusion  [all-changes lat.ran veb.bug ~ ~ ~]
2246      =^  all-change-cages  args  (checkout-changes args all-changes)
2247      =/  ccs=(list [=path =lobe =cage])  ~(tap by change-cages)
2248      |-  ^+  *sane-changes
2249      ?^  ccs
2250        ?.  =(`[lobe cage]:i.ccs (~(get by all-change-cages) path.i.ccs))
2251          ~|  not-same-cages+path.i.ccs
2252          !!
2253        $(ccs t.ccs)
2254      `[all-change-cages args]
2255    ::
2256    ::  Delay current update until sys update is complete
2257    ::
2258    ++  sys-update
2259      |=  $:  =yoki
2260              data=(map path (each page lobe))
```

```
2261                  ==
2262          ^+   ..park
2263          ?>   =(~ pud)
2264          =.   pud   `[syd yoki]
2265          |^   %.   [hen %slip %c %pork ~]
2266              emit:(pass-what files)
2267          ::
2268          ++   files
2269            ^-   (list (pair path (cask)))
2270            %+   murn
2271              ~(tap by data)
2272            |=   [pax=path dat=(each page lobe)]
2273            ^-   (unit (pair path (cask)))
2274            =/   xap   (flop pax)
2275            ?>   ?=(^ xap)
2276            ?.   ?=(%hoon i.xap)   ~
2277            :^   ~   (flop t.xap)   %hoon
2278            ~|   [pax=pax p.dat]
2279            ?-   -.dat
2280              %&   (page-to-cord p.dat)
2281              %|   (lobe-to-cord p.dat)
2282            ==
2283          ::
2284          ++   pass-what
2285            |=   fil=(list (pair path (cask)))
2286            ^+   ..park
2287            (emit hen %pass /what %$ what/fil)
2288          --
2289        --
2290      ::
2291      ::  [goad] Try to revive desk, but if it fails crash the event.
2292      ::
2293      ++   take-park-held
2294        |=   err=(unit tang)
2295        ^+   ..park
2296        ?^   err
2297        ((slog leaf+"clay: desk {<syd>} failed to unsuspend" u.err) ..park)
2298        =.   liv.dom   %live
2299        goad
2300      ::
2301      ::  We always say we're merging from 'ali' to 'bob'.  The basic steps,
2302      ::  not all of which are always needed, are:
2303      ::
2304      ::  --   fetch ali's desk, async in case it's remote
2305      ::  --   diff ali's desk against the mergebase
2306      ::  --   diff bob's desk against the mergebase
2307      ::  --   merge the diffs
2308      ::  --   commit
2309      ::
2310      ++   start-merge
2311        |=   [=ali=ship =ali=desk =case =germ]
2312        ^+   ..start-merge
2313        =/   =wire   /merge/[syd]/(scot %p ali-ship)/[ali-desk]/[germ]
2314        (emit hen %pass wire %c %warp ali-ship ali-desk `[%sing %v case /])
2315      ::
2316      ++   make-melt
2317        |=   [bas=beak con=(list [beak germ])]
2318        ^-   melt
```

```
2319      :+  bas  con
2320      %-  ~(gas by *(map beak (unit domo)))
2321      :-  [bas *(unit domo)]
2322      (turn con |=(a=[beak germ] [-.a *(unit domo)]))
2323    ::
2324    ++  start-fuse
2325      |=  [bas=beak con=(list [beak germ])]
2326      ^+  ..start-fuse
2327      =/  moves=(list move)
2328        %+  turn
2329          [[bas *germ] con]
2330        |=  [bec=beak germ]
2331        ^-  move
2332        =/  wir=wire  /fuse/[syd]/(scot %p p.bec)/[q.bec]/(scot r.bec)
2333        [hen %pass wir %c %warp p.bec q.bec `[%sing %v r.bec /]]
2334      ::
2335      ::  We also want to clear the state (fiz) associated with this
2336      ::  merge and print a warning if it's non trivial i.e. we're
2337      ::  starting a new fuse before the previous one terminated.
2338      ::
2339      =/  err=tang
2340        ?~  con.fiz
2341          ~
2342        =/  discarded=tang
2343          %+  turn
2344            ~(tap in sto.fiz)
2345          |=  [k=beak v=(unit domo)]
2346          ^-  tank
2347          =/  received=tape  ?~(v "missing" "received")
2348          leaf+"{<(en-beam k ~)>} {received}"
2349        :_  discarded
2350        leaf+"fusing into {<syd>} from {<bas>} {<con>} - overwriting prior fuse"
2351      =.  fiz  (make-melt bas con)
2352      ((slog err) (emil moves))
2353    ::
2354    ++  take-fuse
2355      |^
2356      ::
2357      |=  [bec=beak =riot]
2358      ^+  ..take-fuse
2359      ?~  riot
2360        ::
2361        ::  By setting fiz to *melt the merge is aborted - any further
2362        ::  responses we get for the merge will cause take-fuse to crash
2363        ::
2364        =.  fiz  *melt
2365        =/  msg=tape  <(en-beam bec ~)>
2366        ((slog [leaf+"clay: fuse failed, missing {msg}"]~) ..take-fuse)
2367      ?.  (~(has by sto.fiz) bec)
2368        =/  msg=tape  <(en-beam bec ~)>
2369        ((slog [leaf+"clay: got strange fuse response {<msg>}"]~) ..take-fuse)
2370      =.  fiz
2371        :+  bas.fiz  con.fiz
2372        (~(put by sto.fiz) bec `!<(domo q.r.u.riot))
2373      =/  all-done=flag
2374        %-  ~(all by sto.fiz)
2375        |=  res=(unit domo)
2376        ^-  flag
```

```
2377        !=(res ~)
2378      ?.  all-done
2379        ..take-fuse
2380      =|  rag=rang
2381      =/  clean-state  ..take-fuse
2382      =/  initial-dome=domo  (need (~(got by sto.fiz) bas.fiz))
2383      =/  next-yaki=yaki
2384        (~(got by hut.ran) (~(got by hit.initial-dome) let.initial-dome))
2385      =/  parents=(list tako)  ~[(~(got by hit.initial-dome) let.initial-dome)]
2386      =/  merges  con.fiz
2387      |-
2388      ^+  ..take-fuse
2389      ?~  merges
2390        =.  ..take-fuse  (done-fuse clean-state %& ~)
2391        (park | & [%| next-yaki(p (flop parents))] rag)
2392      =/  [bec=beak g=germ]  i.merges
2393      =/  ali-dom=domo  (need (~(got by sto.fiz) bec))
2394      =/  result  (merge-helper p.bec q.bec g ali-dom `next-yaki)
2395      ?-    -.result
2396          %|
2397        =/  failing-merge=tape  "{<bec>} {<g>}"
2398        (done-fuse clean-state %| %fuse-merge-failed leaf+failing-merge p.result)
2399      ::
2400          %&
2401        =/  merge-result=(unit merge-result)  +.result
2402        ?~  merge-result
2403          ::
2404          :: This merge was a no-op, just continue
2405          ::
2406          $(merges t.merges)
2407        ?^  conflicts.u.merge-result
2408          ::
2409          :: If there are merge conflicts send the error and abort the merge
2410          ::
2411          (done-fuse clean-state %& conflicts.u.merge-result)
2412        =/  merged-yaki=yaki
2413          ?-    -.new.u.merge-result
2414              %|  +.new.u.merge-result
2415              %&
2416            ::
2417            :: Convert the yuki to yaki
2418            ::
2419            =/  yuk=yuki  +.new.u.merge-result
2420            =/  lobes=(map path lobe)
2421              %-  ~(run by q.yuk)
2422              |=  val=(each page lobe)
2423              ^-  lobe
2424              ?-  -.val
2425                %&  (page-to-lobe +.val)
2426                %|  +.val
2427              ==
2428          (make-yaki p.yuk lobes now)
2429        ==
2430        %=  $
2431          next-yaki  merged-yaki
2432          merges     t.merges
2433          hut.ran    (~(put by hut.ran) r.merged-yaki merged-yaki)
2434          lat.rag    (~(uni by lat.u.merge-result) lat.rag)
```

```
2435          lat.ran     (~(uni by lat.u.merge-result) lat.ran)
2436          parents     [(~(got by hit.ali-dom) let.ali-dom) parents]
2437        ==
2438      ==
2439    ::  +done-fuse: restore state after a fuse is attempted, whether it
2440    ::  succeeds or fails.
2441    ::
2442    ++  done-fuse
2443      |=  [to-restore=_..take-fuse result=(each (set path) (pair term tang))]
2444      ^+  ..take-fuse
2445      =.  fiz.to-restore  *melt
2446      (done:to-restore result)
2447      --
2448    ::
2449    ++  done
2450      |=  result=(each (set path) (pair term tang))
2451      ^+  ..merge
2452      (emit hen %give %mere result)
2453    ::
2454    ++  merge
2455      |=  [=ali=ship =ali=desk =germ =riot]
2456      ^+  ..merge
2457      ?~  riot
2458        (done %| %ali-unavailable ~[>[ali-ship ali-desk germ]<])
2459      =/  ali-dome=domo
2460        ?:  &(?=(@ -.q.q.r.u.riot) !=(~ -.q.q.r.u.riot))
2461          !<(domo q.r.u.riot)
2462        +:!<([* domo] q.r.u.riot)
2463      =/  result=(each (unit merge-result) (pair term tang))
2464        (merge-helper ali-ship ali-desk germ ali-dome ~)
2465      ?-    -.result
2466          %|  (done %| +.result)
2467          %&
2468      =/  mr=(unit merge-result)  +.result
2469      ?~  mr
2470        (done %& ~)
2471      =.  ..merge  (done %& conflicts.u.mr)
2472      (park | & new.u.mr ~ lat.u.mr)
2473      ==
2474    ::
2475    +$  merge-result  [conflicts=(set path) new=yoki lat=(map lobe page)]
2476    ::
2477    ++  merge-helper
2478      |=  [=ali=ship =ali=desk =germ ali-dome=domo next-yaki=(unit yaki)]
2479      ^-  (each (unit merge-result) [term tang])
2480      |^
2481      ^-  (each (unit merge-result) [term tang])
2482      =/  ali-yaki=yaki  (~(got by hut.ran) (~(got by hit.ali-dome) let.ali-dome))
2483      =/  bob-yaki=(unit yaki)
2484        ?~  next-yaki
2485          ?~  let.dom
2486            ~
2487          (~(get by hut.ran) (~(got by hit.dom) let.dom))
2488        next-yaki
2489      =/  res  (mule |.((merge-by-germ ali-yaki bob-yaki)))
2490      ?-  -.res
2491        %&  &+p.res
2492        %|  |+merge-failed+p.res
```

```
2493        ==
2494        ::
2495    ++  merge-by-germ
2496      |=  [=ali=yaki bob-yaki=(unit yaki)]
2497      ^-  (unit merge-result)
2498      ::
2499      ::  If this is an %init merge, we set the ali's commit to be
2500      ::  bob's.
2501      ::
2502      ?:  ?=(%init germ)
2503        ?>  ?=(~ bob-yaki)
2504        `[conflicts=~ new=|+ali-yaki lat=~]
2505      ::
2506      =/  bob-yaki  (need bob-yaki)
2507      |^
2508      ^-  (unit merge-result)
2509      ?-    germ
2510      ::
2511      ::  If this is a %only-this merge, we check to see if ali's and bob's
2512      ::  commits are the same, in which case we're done.
2513      ::  Otherwise, we create a new commit with bob's data plus ali and
2514      ::  bob as parents.
2515      ::
2516          %only-this
2517        ?:  =(r.ali-yaki r.bob-yaki)
2518          ~
2519        :*  ~
2520            conflicts=~
2521            new=&+[[r.bob-yaki r.ali-yaki ~] (to-yuki q.bob-yaki)]
2522            lat=~
2523        ==
2524      ::
2525      ::  If this is a %only-that merge, we check to see if ali's and bob's
2526      ::  commits are the same, in which case we're done.  Otherwise, we
2527      ::  create a new commit with ali's data plus ali and bob as
2528      ::  parents.
2529      ::
2530          %only-that
2531        ?:  =(r.ali-yaki r.bob-yaki)
2532          ~
2533        :*  ~
2534            conflicts=~
2535            new=&+[[r.bob-yaki r.ali-yaki ~] (to-yuki q.ali-yaki)]
2536            lat=~
2537        ==
2538      ::
2539      ::  Create a merge commit with exactly the contents of the
2540      ::  destination desk except take any files from the source commit
2541      ::  which are not in the destination desk.
2542      ::
2543          %take-this
2544        ?:  =(r.ali-yaki r.bob-yaki)
2545          ~
2546        =/  new-data  (~(uni by q.ali-yaki) q.bob-yaki)
2547        :*  ~
2548            conflicts=~
2549            new=&+[[r.bob-yaki r.ali-yaki ~] (to-yuki new-data)]
2550            lat=~
```

```
2551          ==
2552      ::
2553      ::  Create a merge commit with exactly the contents of the source
2554      ::  commit except preserve any files from the destination desk
2555      ::  which are not in the source commit.
2556      ::
2557          %take-that
2558      ?:  =(r.ali-yaki r.bob-yaki)
2559          ~
2560      =/  new-data  (~(uni by q.bob-yaki) q.ali-yaki)
2561      :*  ~
2562          conflicts=~
2563          new=&+[[r.bob-yaki r.ali-yaki ~] (to-yuki new-data)]
2564          lat=~
2565      ==
2566      ::
2567      ::  If this is a %fine merge, we check to see if ali's and bob's
2568      ::  commits are the same, in which case we're done.  Otherwise, we
2569      ::  check to see if ali's commit is in the ancestry of bob's, in
2570      ::  which case we're done.  Otherwise, we check to see if bob's
2571      ::  commit is in the ancestry of ali's.  If not, this is not a
2572      ::  fast-forward merge, so we error out.  If it is, we add ali's
2573      ::  commit to bob's desk and checkout.
2574      ::
2575          %fine
2576      ?:  =(r.ali-yaki r.bob-yaki)
2577          ~
2578      ?:  (~(has in (reachable-takos:ze r.bob-yaki)) r.ali-yaki)
2579          ~
2580      ?.  (~(has in (reachable-takos:ze r.ali-yaki)) r.bob-yaki)
2581        ~_  %bad-fine-merge
2582        ~|  "tried fast-forward but is not ancestor or descendant"
2583        !!
2584      `[conflicts=~ new=|+ali-yaki lat=~]
2585      ::
2586          ?(%meet %mate %meld %meet-this %meet-that)
2587      ?:  =(r.ali-yaki r.bob-yaki)
2588          ~
2589      ?:  (~(has in (reachable-takos:ze r.bob-yaki)) r.ali-yaki)
2590          ~
2591      ?:  (~(has in (reachable-takos:ze r.ali-yaki)) r.bob-yaki)
2592        $(germ %fine)
2593      =/  merge-points  (find-merge-points ali-yaki bob-yaki)
2594      ?~  merge-points
2595        ~_  %merge-no-merge-base
2596        ~|  "consider a %this or %that merge to get a mergebase"
2597        !!
2598      =/  merge-point=yaki  n.merge-points
2599      ?:  ?=(?(%mate %meld) germ)
2600        =/  ali-diffs=cane  (diff-base ali-yaki bob-yaki merge-point)
2601        =/  bob-diffs=cane  (diff-base bob-yaki ali-yaki merge-point)
2602        =/  bof=(map path (unit cage))
2603        (merge-conflicts can.ali-diffs can.bob-diffs)
2604      (build ali-yaki bob-yaki merge-point ali-diffs bob-diffs bof)
2605      =/  ali-diffs=cane  (calc-diffs ali-yaki merge-point)
2606      =/  bob-diffs=cane  (calc-diffs bob-yaki merge-point)
2607      =/  both-diffs=(map path *)
2608        %-  %~  int  by
```

```
2609              %-  ~(uni by `(map path *)`new.ali-diffs)
2610              %-  ~(uni by `(map path *)`cal.ali-diffs)
2611              %-  ~(uni by `(map path *)`can.ali-diffs)
2612              `(map path *)`old.ali-diffs
2613          %-  ~(uni by `(map path *)`new.bob-diffs)
2614          %-  ~(uni by `(map path *)`cal.bob-diffs)
2615          %-  ~(uni by `(map path *)`can.bob-diffs)
2616          `(map path *)`old.bob-diffs
2617      ?:  &(?=(%meet germ) !=(~ both-diffs))
2618        ~_  %meet-conflict
2619        ~|  [~(key by both-diffs) "consider a %mate merge"]
2620        !!
2621    =/  both-done=(map path lobe)
2622        |^
2623      ?-  germ
2624        %meet       ~
2625        %meet-this  (resolve (~(uni by new.bob-diffs) cal.bob-diffs))
2626        %meet-that  (resolve (~(uni by new.ali-diffs) cal.ali-diffs))
2627      ==
2628      ++  resolve
2629        |=  news=(map path lobe)
2630        %-  malt  ^-  (list [path lobe])
2631        %+  murn  ~(tap by both-diffs)
2632        |=  [=path *]
2633        ^-  (unit [^path lobe])
2634        =/  new  (~(get by news) path)
2635        ?~  new
2636          ~
2637        `[path u.new]
2638      --
2639    ::
2640    =/  deleted
2641      %-  ~(dif by (~(uni by old.ali-diffs) old.bob-diffs))
2642      (~(run by both-done) |=(* ~))
2643    =/  not-deleted=(map path lobe)
2644      %+  roll  ~(tap by deleted)
2645      =<  .(not-deleted q.merge-point)
2646      |=  [[pax=path ~] not-deleted=(map path lobe)]
2647      (~(del by not-deleted) pax)
2648    =/  hat=(map path lobe)
2649      %-  ~(uni by not-deleted)
2650      %-  ~(uni by new.ali-diffs)
2651      %-  ~(uni by new.bob-diffs)
2652      %-  ~(uni by cal.ali-diffs)
2653      cal.bob-diffs
2654    :*  ~
2655        conflicts=~
2656        new=&+[[r.bob-yaki r.ali-yaki ~] (to-yuki hat)]
2657        lat=~
2658    ==
2659  ==
2660  ::
2661  ++  to-yuki
2662    |=  m=(map path lobe)
2663    ^-  (map path (each page lobe))
2664    (~(run by m) |=(=lobe |+lobe))
2665  ::
2666  ::  The set of changes between the mergebase and one of the desks
```

```
2667        ::  being merged
2668        ::
2669        ::  --  `new` is the set of files in the new desk and not in the
2670        ::  mergebase.
2671        ::  --  `cal` is the set of changes in the new desk from the
2672        ::  mergebase except for any that are also in the other new desk.
2673        ::  --  `can` is the set of changes in the new desk from the
2674        ::  mergebase that are also in the other new desk (potential
2675        ::  conflicts).
2676        ::  --  `old` is the set of files in the mergebase and not in the
2677        ::  new desk.
2678        ::
2679        +$  cane
2680          $:  new=(map path lobe)
2681              cal=(map path lobe)
2682              can=(map path cage)
2683              old=(map path ~)
2684          ==
2685        ::
2686        ::  Calculate cane knowing there are no files changed by both
2687        ::  desks
2688        ::
2689        ++  calc-diffs
2690          |=  [hed=yaki bas=yaki]
2691          ^-  cane
2692          :*  %-  molt
2693              %+  skip  ~(tap by q.hed)
2694              |=  [pax=path lob=lobe]
2695              (~(has by q.bas) pax)
2696            ::
2697              %-  molt
2698              %+  skip  ~(tap by q.hed)
2699              |=  [pax=path lob=lobe]
2700              =+  (~(get by q.bas) pax)
2701              |(=(~ -) =([~ lob] -))
2702            ::
2703              ~
2704            ::
2705              %-  malt  ^-  (list [path ~])
2706              %+  murn  ~(tap by q.bas)
2707              |=  [pax=path lob=lobe]
2708              ^-  (unit (pair path ~))
2709              ?.  =(~ (~(get by q.hed) pax))
2710                ~
2711              `[pax ~]
2712          ==
2713        ::
2714        ::  Diff yak against bas where different from yuk
2715        ::
2716        ++  diff-base
2717          |=  [yak=yaki yuk=yaki bas=yaki]
2718          ^-  cane
2719          =/  new=(map path lobe)
2720            %-  malt
2721            %+  skip  ~(tap by q.yak)
2722            |=  [=path =lobe]
2723            (~(has by q.bas) path)
2724          ::
```

```
2725        =/  cal=(map path lobe)
2726          %-  malt  ^-  (list [path lobe])
2727          %+  murn  ~(tap by q.bas)
2728          |=  [pax=path lob=lobe]
2729          ^-  (unit (pair path lobe))
2730          =+  a=(~(get by q.yak) pax)
2731          =+  b=(~(get by q.yuk) pax)
2732          ?.  ?&  ?=(^ a)
2733                  !=([~ lob] a)
2734                  =([~ lob] b)
2735              ==
2736            ~
2737          `[pax +.a]
2738        ::
2739        =/  can=(map path cage)
2740          %-  malt
2741          %+  murn  ~(tap by q.bas)
2742          |=  [=path =lobe]
2743          ^-  (unit [^path cage])
2744          =/  in-yak  (~(get by q.yak) path)
2745          ?~  in-yak
2746            ~
2747          ?:  =(lobe u.in-yak)
2748            ~
2749          =/  in-yuk  (~(get by q.yuk) path)
2750          ?~  in-yuk
2751            ~
2752          ?:  =(lobe u.in-yuk)
2753            ~
2754          ?:  =(u.in-yak u.in-yuk)
2755            ~
2756          =/  cug=(unit cage)  (diff-lobes lobe u.in-yak)
2757          ?~  cug
2758            ~_  %tombstoned-mergebase
2759            ~|  path
2760            ~|  "consider a 2-way merge such as %only-this or %only-that"
2761            !!
2762          `[path u.cug]
2763        ::
2764      =/  old=(map path ~)
2765          %-  malt  ^-  (list [path ~])
2766          %+  murn  ~(tap by q.bas)
2767          |=  [pax=path lob=lobe]
2768          ?.  =(~ (~(get by q.yak) pax))
2769            ~
2770          (some pax ~)
2771        ::
2772      [new cal can old]
2773    ::
2774    ::  These can/should save their caches
2775    ::
2776    ++  lobe-to-cage
2777      |=  =lobe
2778      ^-  (unit cage)
2779      =/  peg=(unit page)  (~(get by lat.ran) lobe)
2780      ?~  peg
2781        ~
2782      =/  [=cage *]
```

```
2783            %-  wrap:fusion
2784            (page-to-cage:(tako-ford (~(got by hit.dom) let.dom)) u.peg)
2785          `cage
2786        ::
2787      ++  get-dais
2788        |=  =mark
2789        ^-  dais
2790        =/  [=dais *]
2791            %-  wrap:fusion
2792            (build-dais:(tako-ford (~(got by hit.dom) let.dom)) mark)
2793        dais
2794        ::
2795        ::  Diff two files on bob-desk
2796        ::
2797      ++  diff-lobes
2798        |=  [a=lobe =b=lobe]
2799        ^-  (unit cage)
2800        =/  a-cage  (lobe-to-cage a-lobe)
2801        =/  b-cage  (lobe-to-cage b-lobe)
2802        ?:  |(?=(~ a-cage) ?=(~ b-cage))
2803          ~
2804        ?>  =(p.u.a-cage p.u.b-cage)
2805        =/  =dais  (get-dais p.u.a-cage)
2806        `[form:dais (~(diff dais q.u.a-cage) q.u.b-cage)]
2807        ::
2808        ::  Merge diffs that are on the same file.
2809        ::
2810      ++  merge-conflicts
2811        |=  [ali-conflicts=(map path cage) bob-conflicts=(map path cage)]
2812        ^-  (map path (unit cage))
2813        %-  ~(urn by (~(int by ali-conflicts) bob-conflicts))
2814        |=  [=path *]
2815        ^-  (unit cage)
2816        =/  cal=cage  (~(got by ali-conflicts) path)
2817        =/  cob=cage  (~(got by bob-conflicts) path)
2818        =/  =mark
2819          =+  (slag (dec (lent path)) path)
2820          ?~(- %$ i.-)
2821        =/  =dais  (get-dais mark)
2822        =/  res=(unit (unit vase))  (~(join dais *vale:dais) q.cal q.cob)
2823        ?~  res
2824          `[form:dais q.cob]
2825        ?~  u.res
2826          ~
2827        `[form:dais u.u.res]
2828        ::
2829        ::  Apply the patches in bof to get the new merged content.
2830        ::
2831        ::  Gather all the changes between ali's and bob's commits and the
2832        ::  mergebase.  This is similar to the %meet of ++merge, except
2833        ::  where they touch the same file, we use the merged versions.
2834        ::
2835      ++  build
2836        |=  $:  ali=yaki
2837                bob=yaki
2838                bas=yaki
2839                dal=cane
2840                dob=cane
```

```
2841                      bof=(map path (unit cage))
2842              ==
2843          ^-  (unit merge-result)
2844          =/  both-patched=(map path cage)
2845          %-  malt
2846          %+  murn  ~(tap by bof)
2847          |=  [=path cay=(unit cage)]
2848          ^-  (unit [^path cage])
2849          ?~  cay
2850              ~
2851          :+  ~  path
2852          =+  (~(get by q.bas) path)
2853          ?~  -
2854              ~|  %mate-strange-diff-no-base
2855              !!
2856          ::  +need ok because we would have crashed in +diff-base
2857          ::
2858          =/  =cage  ~|([%build-need path] (need (lobe-to-cage u.-)))
2859          =/  =dais  (get-dais p.cage)
2860          ?>  =(p.u.cay form.dais)
2861          :-  p.cage
2862          (~(pact dais q.cage) q.u.cay)
2863          =/  con=(map path *)                      ::  2-change conflict
2864          %-  molt
2865          %+  skim  ~(tap by bof)
2866          |=([pax=path cay=(unit cage)] ?=(~ cay))
2867          =/  cab=(map path lobe)                   ::  conflict base
2868          %-  ~(urn by con)
2869          |=  [pax=path *]
2870          (~(got by q.bas) pax)
2871          =.  con                                   ::  change+del conflict
2872          %-  ~(uni by con)
2873          %-  malt  ^-  (list [path *])
2874          %+  skim  ~(tap by old.dal)
2875          |=  [pax=path ~]
2876          ?:  (~(has by new.dob) pax)
2877            ~|  %strange-add-and-del
2878            !!
2879          (~(has by can.dob) pax)
2880          =.  con                                   ::  change+del conflict
2881          %-  ~(uni by con)
2882          %-  malt  ^-  (list [path *])
2883          %+  skim  ~(tap by old.dob)
2884          |=  [pax=path ~]
2885          ?:  (~(has by new.dal) pax)
2886            ~|  %strange-del-and-add
2887            !!
2888          (~(has by can.dal) pax)
2889          =.  con                                   ::  add+add conflict
2890          %-  ~(uni by con)
2891          %-  malt  ^-  (list [path *])
2892          %+  skip  ~(tap by (~(int by new.dal) new.dob))
2893          |=  [pax=path *]
2894          =((~(got by new.dal) pax) (~(got by new.dob) pax))
2895          ?:  &(?=(%mate germ) ?=(^ con))
2896            =+  (turn ~(tap by `(map path *)`con) |=([path *] >[+<-]<))
2897            ~_  %mate-conflict
2898            ~|  (turn ~(tap by `(map path *)`con) |=([path *] +<-))
```

```
2899              !!
2900          =/  old=(map path lobe)                            ::  oldies but goodies
2901          %+  roll  ~(tap by (~(uni by old.dal) old.dob))
2902          =<  .(old q.bob)
2903          |=  [[pax=path ~] old=(map path lobe)]
2904          (~(del by old) pax)
2905          =/  [hot=(map path lobe) lat=(map lobe page)]    ::  new content
2906          %+  roll  ~(tap by both-patched)
2907          |=  [[pax=path cay=cage] hat=(map path lobe) lat=(map lobe page)]
2908          =/  =page   [p q.q]:cay
2909          =/  =lobe   (page-to-lobe page)
2910          :-  (~(put by hat) pax lobe)
2911          ?:  (~(has by lat) lobe)
2912            lat
2913          (~(uni by (malt [lobe page] ~)) lat)
2914          =/  hat=(map path lobe)                           ::  all the content
2915          %-  ~(uni by old)
2916          %-  ~(uni by new.dal)
2917          %-  ~(uni by new.dob)
2918          %-  ~(uni by cal.dal)
2919          %-  ~(uni by cal.dob)
2920          %-  ~(uni by hot)
2921            cab
2922          =/  del=(map path ?)
2923          (~(run by (~(uni by old.dal) old.dob)) |=(~ %|))
2924          =/  new  &+[[r.bob r.ali ~] (~(run by hat) |=(=lobe |+lobe))]
2925          :*  ~
2926            (silt (turn ~(tap by con) head))
2927            new
2928            lat
2929          ==
2930        --
2931      --
2932    ::
2933    ::  Find the most recent common ancestor(s).
2934    ::
2935    ::    For performance, this depends on +reachable-takos being
2936    ::    memoized.
2937    ::
2938    ++  find-merge-points
2939      |=  [=ali=yaki =bob=yaki]
2940      ^-  (set yaki)
2941      ::  Loop through ancestors breadth-first, lazily generating ancestry
2942      ::
2943      =/  ali-takos  (reachable-takos:ze r.ali-yaki)
2944      ::  Tako worklist
2945      ::
2946      =/  takos=(qeu tako)  [r.bob-yaki ~ ~]
2947      ::  Mergebase candidates.  Have proven they're common ancestors, but
2948      ::  not that they're a most recent
2949      ::
2950      =|  bases=(set tako)
2951      ::  Takos we've already checked or are in our worklist
2952      ::
2953      =|  done=(set tako)
2954      |-  ^-  (set yaki)
2955      =*  outer-loop  $
2956      ::  If we've finished our worklist, convert to yakis and return
```

```
2957        ::
2958        ?:  =(~ takos)
2959          (silt (turn ~(tap in bases) ~(got by hut.ran)))
2960        =^  =tako  takos  ~(get to takos)
2961        =.  done  (~(put in done) tako)
2962        ::  If this is a common ancestor, stop recursing through our
2963        ::  parentage.  Check if it's comparable to any existing candidate.
2964        ::
2965        ?:  (~(has in ali-takos) tako)
2966          =/  base-list  ~(tap in bases)
2967          |-  ^-  (set yaki)
2968          =*  bases-loop  $
2969          ?~  base-list
2970            ::  Proven it's not an ancestor of any previous candidate.
2971            ::  Remove all ancestors of new candidate and add it to the
2972            ::  candidate list.
2973            ::
2974            =.  bases
2975              =/  new-reachable  (reachable-takos:ze tako)
2976              (~(put in (~(dif in bases) new-reachable)) tako)
2977            outer-loop
2978          ::  If it's an ancestor of another candidate, this is not most
2979          ::  recent, so skip and try next in worklist.
2980          ::
2981          =/  base-reachable  (reachable-takos:ze i.base-list)
2982          ?:  (~(has in base-reachable) tako)
2983            outer-loop
2984          bases-loop(base-list t.base-list)
2985        ::  Append parents to list and recurse
2986        ::
2987        =/  bob-yaki  (~(got by hut.ran) tako)
2988        =/  new-candidates  (skip p.bob-yaki ~(has in done))
2989        %_  outer-loop
2990          done  (~(gas in done) new-candidates)
2991          takos  (~(gas to takos) new-candidates)
2992        ==
2993      ::
2994      ++  want-mime
2995        |=  yon=aeon
2996        %-  ~(any by mon)
2997        |=  =beam
2998        &(=(p.beam her) =(q.beam syd) =(r.beam ud+yon))
2999      ::
3000      ::  Update mime cache
3001      ::
3002      ++  checkout-mime
3003        |=  $:  =ford=args:ford:fusion
3004                deletes=(set path)
3005                changes=(set path)
3006            ==
3007        ^-  [(map path (unit mime)) args:ford:fusion]
3008        =/  mim=(map path (unit mime))
3009          =/  dels=(list path)  ~(tap by deletes)
3010          |-  ^-  (map path (unit mime))
3011          ?~  dels
3012            ~
3013          (~(put by $(dels t.dels)) i.dels ~)
3014        =/  cans=(list path)  ~(tap by changes)
```

```
3015      |-  ^-  [(map path (unit mime)) args:ford:fusion]
3016      ?~  cans
3017        [mim ford-args]
3018      =/  [=cage fud=flow fod=flue]
3019        ~|  mime-cast-fail+i.cans
3020        (wrap:fusion (cast-path:(ford:fusion ford-args) i.cans %mime))
3021      =.  cache.ford-args  fud
3022      =.  spill.ford-args  spill.fod
3023      =.  sprig.ford-args  sprig.fod
3024      =^  mim  ford-args  $(cans t.cans)
3025      [(~(put by mim) i.cans `!<(mime q.cage)) ford-args]
3026    ::
3027    ::  Add or remove entries to the mime cache
3028    ::
3029    ++  apply-changes-to-mim
3030      |=  [mim=(map path mime) changes=(map path (unit mime))]
3031      ^-  (map path mime)
3032      =/  changes-l=(list [pax=path change=(unit mime)])
3033        ~(tap by changes)
3034      |-  ^-  (map path mime)
3035      ?~  changes-l
3036        mim
3037      ?~  change.i.changes-l
3038        $(changes-l t.changes-l, mim (~(del by mim) pax.i.changes-l))
3039      $(changes-l t.changes-l, mim (~(put by mim) [pax u.change]:i.changes-l))
3040    ::
3041    ::  Emit update to unix sync
3042    ::
3043    ::  [ergo] Must be called any time the set of files changes that must
3044    ::  be mirrored to unix.  +want-mime may optionally be used to cheaply
3045    ::  check if a version of a desk is mirrored to unix (and so +ergo
3046    ::  must be called).
3047    ::
3048    ++  ergo
3049      |=  [yon=aeon mim=(map path (unit mime))]
3050      ^+  ..park
3051      =/  must  (must-ergo yon mon (turn ~(tap by mim) head))
3052      %-  emil
3053      %+  turn  ~(tap by must)
3054      |=  [pot=term len=@ud pak=(set path)]
3055      :*  (need hez)  %give  %ergo  pot
3056          %+  turn  ~(tap in pak)
3057          |=  pax=path
3058          [(slag len pax) (~(got by mim) pax)]
3059      ==
3060    ::
3061    ::  Output is a map of mount points to {length-of-mounted-path set-of-paths}.
3062    ::
3063    ++  must-ergo
3064      |=  [yon=aeon mon=(map term beam) can=(list path)]
3065      ^-  (map term (pair @ud (set path)))
3066      %-  malt  ^-  (list (trel term @ud (set path)))
3067      %+  murn  ~(tap by mon)
3068      |=  [nam=term bem=beam]
3069      ^-  (unit (trel term @ud (set path)))
3070      =-  ?~(- ~ `[nam (lent s.bem) (silt `(list path)`-)])
3071      %+  skim  can
3072      |=  pax=path
```

```
3073      &(=(p.bem her) =(q.bem syd) =(r.bem ud+yon) =(s.bem (scag (lent s.bem) pax)))
3074      ::
3075      ::  Mount a beam to unix
3076      ::
3077      ++  mount
3078        |=  [pot=term =case =spur]
3079        ^+  ..mount
3080        =/  old-mon  (~(get by mon) pot)
3081        ?^  old-mon
3082          %-  (slog >%already-mounted< >u.old-mon< ~)
3083          ..mount
3084        =/  yon  (case-to-aeon case)
3085        ?~  yon
3086          %-  (slog >%unknown-case< >[her syd case spur]< ~)
3087          ..mount
3088        =/  for-yon  ?:(=(let.dom u.yon) 0 u.yon)
3089        =.  mon                                             ::  [ergo]
3090          (~(put by mon) pot [her syd ud+for-yon] spur)
3091        =/  =yaki  (~(got by hut.ran) (~(got by hit.dom) u.yon))
3092        =/  files  (~(run by q.yaki) |=(=lobe |+lobe))
3093        =/  =args:ford:fusion
3094          [files lat.ran veb.bug fad ?:(=(yon let.dom) fod.dom [~ ~])]
3095        =^  mim  args
3096          (checkout-mime args ~ ~(key by files))
3097        =.  mim.dom  (apply-changes-to-mim mim.dom mim)
3098        (ergo for-yon mim)
3099      ::
3100      ::  Unmount a beam
3101      ::
3102      ++  unmount
3103        |=  [pot=term =case =spur]
3104        ^+  ..unmount
3105        ?>  ?=(^ hez.ruf)
3106        =.  mon  (~(del by mon) pot)                        ::  [ergo]
3107        =?  mim.dom  !(want-mime 0)  ~
3108        (emit u.hez.ruf %give %ogre pot)
3109      ::
3110      ::  Set permissions for a node.
3111      ::
3112      ++  perm
3113        |=  [pax=path rit=rite]
3114        ^+  +>
3115        =/  mis=(set @ta)
3116          %+  roll
3117          =-  ~(tap in -)
3118          ?-  -.rit
3119            %r   who:(fall red.rit *rule)
3120            %w   who:(fall wit.rit *rule)
3121            %rw  (~(uni in who:(fall red.rit *rule)) who:(fall wit.rit *rule))
3122          ==
3123          |=  [w=whom s=(set @ta)]
3124          ?:  |(?=(%& -.w) (~(has by cez) p.w))  s
3125          (~(put in s) p.w)
3126        ?^  mis
3127          ::  TODO remove this nasty hack
3128          ::
3129          ?.  ?=([[[%a *] *] hen)
3130            +>.$
```

```
3131        =-  (emit hen %give %done `[%perm-fail [%leaf "No such group(s): {-}"]~])
3132        %+  roll  ~(tap in `(set @ta)`mis)
3133        |=  [g=@ta t=tape]
3134        ?~  t  (trip g)
3135        :(weld t ", " (trip g))
3136    ::   TODO remove this nasty hack
3137    ::
3138    =<  ?.  ?=([[[%a *] *] hen)
3139        .
3140        (emit hen %give %done ~)
3141    ::
3142    ?-  -.rit                                    ::  [wake] <>
3143      %r   wake(per (put-perm per pax red.rit))
3144      %w   wake(pew (put-perm pew pax wit.rit))
3145      %rw  wake(per (put-perm per pax red.rit), pew (put-perm pew pax wit.rit))
3146    ==
3147  ::
3148  ++  put-perm
3149    |=  [pes=regs pax=path new=(unit rule)]
3150    ?~  new  (~(del by pes) pax)
3151    (~(put by pes) pax u.new)
3152  ::
3153  ::  Remove a group from all rules.
3154  ::
3155  ::  [wake] <
3156  ::
3157  ++  forget-crew
3158    |=  nom=@ta
3159    %=  +>                                      ::  [wake] < +call
3160      per  (forget-crew-in nom per)
3161      pew  (forget-crew-in nom pew)
3162    ==
3163  ::
3164  ++  forget-crew-in
3165    |=  [nom=@ta pes=regs]
3166    %-  ~(run by pes)
3167    |=  r=rule
3168    r(who (~(del in who.r) |+nom))
3169  ::
3170  ++  set-rein                                  ::  [goad] <
3171    |=  [ren=(map dude:gall ?)]
3172    ^+  ..park
3173    ..park(ren.dom ren)
3174  ::
3175  ++  set-zest                                  ::  [goad] <
3176    |=  liv=zest
3177    =?  liv  =(%base syd)  %live
3178    ..park(liv.dom liv)
3179  ::
3180  ++  rise                                      ::  [goad] <
3181    |=  [=dude:gall on=(unit ?)]
3182    ?<  =(%base syd)
3183    %_    ..park
3184        ren.dom
3185      ?~  on
3186        (~(del by ren.dom) dude)
3187      (~(put by ren.dom) dude u.on)
3188    ==
```

```
3189      ::
3190      ++  stay
3191        |=  ver=(unit weft)
3192        ^+  ..park
3193        =.  wic.dom                                    ::  [tare] <>
3194          ?~  ver
3195            ~
3196          (~(del by wic.dom) u.ver)
3197        tare
3198      ::
3199      ::  Try to apply highest-versioned %base commit-in-waiting
3200      ::
3201      ::  [wick] Must be called whenever we might have unblocked a kelvin
3202      ::  upgrade.  This is move-order agnostic because it defers the
3203      ::  upgrade into a new event.
3204      ::
3205      ++  wick
3206        ^+  ..park
3207        (emit hen %pass /wick %b %wait now)
3208      ::
3209      ++  take-wick
3210        |=  err=(unit tang)
3211        ^+  ..park
3212        ?^  err
3213          ((slog leaf+"clay: failed to upgrade kelvin (wick)" u.err) ..park)
3214        ?>  ?=(%base syd)
3215        =/  wis=(list [weft =yoki])
3216          %+  sort  ~(tap by wic.dom)
3217          |=  [a=[weft yoki] b=[weft yoki]]
3218          (gth num.a num.b)
3219        =.  wis  (skip wis |=([[* a=@ud] *] (gte a zuse)))
3220        ?~  wis  ::  Every commit bottoms out here ?
3221          ..park
3222        (park | & yoki.i.wis *rang)
3223      ::
3224      ::  Cancel a request.
3225      ::
3226      ::  For local requests, we just remove it from `qyx`.  For foreign requests,
3227      ::  we remove it from `ref` and tell the foreign ship to cancel as well.
3228      ::
3229      ++  cancel-request                              ::    release request
3230        ^+  ..cancel-request
3231        =^  wos=(list wove)  qyx
3232          :_  (~(run by qyx) |=(a=(set duct) (~(del in a) hen)))
3233          %-  ~(rep by qyx)
3234          |=  [[a=wove b=(set duct)] c=(list wove)]
3235          ?:((~(has in b) hen) [a c] c)
3236        ::
3237        ?~  ref
3238          =>  .(ref `(unit rind)`ref)
3239          ?:  =(~ wos)  ..cancel-request            ::   TODO handle?
3240          |-  ^+  ..cancel-request
3241          ?~  wos  ..cancel-request
3242          =.  ..cancel-request  (run-if-future rove.i.wos |=(@da (best hen +<)))
3243          $(wos t.wos)
3244        ::
3245        ?~  nux=(~(get by fod.u.ref) hen)
3246          ..cancel-request(ref `(unit rind)`ref)  ::   XX TMI
```

```
3247    =/  sat  (~(got by bom.u.ref) u.nux)
3248    =:  fod.u.ref  (~(del by fod.u.ref) hen)
3249        bom.u.ref  (~(del by bom.u.ref) u.nux)
3250      ==
3251    ::  cancel the request as appropriate
3252    ::
3253    ?.  ?=([~ ^] busy.sat)
3254      %.  [hen her u.nux [syd ~]]
3255      send-over-ames(ref `(unit rind)`ref)     ::  XX TMI
3256    %-  emil
3257    =*  bus  u.busy.sat
3258    =/  =wire  (request-wire kind.bus her syd u.nux)
3259    ~&  %cancel-request-yawn
3260    :~  [hen %pass wire %a %yawn her path.bus]
3261        [hen %pass wire %b %rest time.bus]
3262      ==
3263    ::
3264    ::  Handles a request.
3265    ::
3266    ::  `%sing` requests are handled by ++aver.  `%next` requests are handled by
3267    ::  running ++aver at the given case, and then subsequent cases until we find
3268    ::  a case where the two results aren't equivalent.  If it hasn't happened
3269    ::  yet, we wait.  `%many` requests are handled by producing as much as we can
3270    ::  and then waiting if the subscription range extends into the future.
3271    ::
3272    ++  start-request
3273      |=  [for=(unit [ship @ud]) rav=rave]
3274      ^+  ..start-request
3275      ?:  &(?=(^ for) !(foreign-capable rav))
3276        ~&  [%bad-foreign-request-care from=for rav]
3277        ..start-request
3278      =^  [new-sub=(unit rove) cards=(list card)]  ..start-request
3279        (try-fill-sub for (rave-to-rove rav))
3280      =.  ..start-request  (send-cards cards [hen ~ ~])
3281      ?~  new-sub
3282        ..start-request
3283      (duce for u.new-sub)
3284    ::
3285    ::  +retry-with-ames: we tried scrying. now try with ames instead.
3286    ::
3287    ++  retry-with-ames
3288      |=  [kind=@ta inx=@ud]
3289      ^+  ..retry-with-ames
3290      ~|  [%retry-with-ames kind]
3291      ?>  ?=(%back-index kind)
3292      ~|  [%strange-retry-no-request her syd inx]
3293      ?>  ?=(^ ref)
3294      =/  sat=update-state  (~(got by bom.u.ref) inx)
3295      ::  mark her as having broken scry comms
3296      ::
3297      =.  sad  (~(put by sad) her now)
3298      ::  clean up scry request & timer
3299      ::
3300      =.  ..retry-with-ames
3301        =<  ?>(?=(^ ref) .)
3302        ~|  [%strange-retry-not-scry her syd inx busy.sat -.rave.sat]
3303        =/  bus  ?>(?=([~ ^] busy.sat) u.busy.sat)
3304        =/  =wire  (request-wire kind her syd inx)
```

```
3305        %-  emil
3306        ~&  %retry-with-ames-yawn
3307        :~  [hen %pass wire %b %rest time.bus]
3308            [hen %pass wire %a %yawn her path.bus]
3309        ==
3310      ::  re-send over ames
3311      ::
3312      =.  bom.u.ref  (~(put by bom.u.ref) inx sat(busy ~))
3313      abet:work:(foreign-update inx)
3314    ::
3315    ::  Called when a foreign ship answers one of our requests.
3316    ::
3317    ::  If it's a `%many` request, process in +take-foreign-update
3318    ::
3319    ::  After updating ref (our request manager), we handle %x, %w, and %y
3320    ::  responses.  For %x, we call ++validate-x to validate the type of
3321    ::  the response.  For %y, we coerce the result to an arch.
3322    ::
3323    ++  take-foreign-answer                          ::  external change
3324    |=  [inx=@ud rut=(unit rand)]
3325    ^+  +>
3326    ?>  ?=(^ ref)
3327    =+  ruv=(~(get by bom.u.ref) inx)
3328    ?~  ruv
3329      ~&  %bad-answer
3330      +>.$
3331    =/  rav=rave  rave.u.ruv
3332    ?:  ?=(%many -.rav)
3333      abet:(apex:(foreign-update inx) rut)
3334    ?~  rut
3335      ::  nothing here, so cache that
3336      ::
3337      %_    wake                                 ::  [wake] <>
3338          haw.u.ref
3339        ?.  ?=(%sing -.rav)  haw.u.ref
3340        (~(put by haw.u.ref) mood.rav ~)
3341      ==
3342    |^
3343    =/  result=(unit cage)  (validate u.rut)
3344    =/  =mood  [p.p q.p q]:u.rut
3345    =:  haw.u.ref  (~(put by haw.u.ref) mood result)    ::  [wake] <>
3346        bom.u.ref  (~(del by bom.u.ref) inx)
3347        fod.u.ref  (~(del by fod.u.ref) hen)
3348      ==
3349    wake
3350    ::  something here, so validate
3351    ::
3352    ++  validate
3353      |=  =rand
3354      ^-  (unit cage)
3355      ?-    p.p.rand
3356          %a  ~|  %no-big-ford-builds-across-network-for-now  !!
3357          %b  ~|  %i-guess-you-ought-to-build-your-own-marks  !!
3358          %c  ~|  %casts-should-be-compiled-on-your-own-ship  !!
3359          %d  ~|  %totally-temporary-error-please-replace-me  !!
3360          %e  ~|  %yes-naves-also-shouldnt-cross-the-network  !!
3361          %f  ~|  %even-static-casts-should-be-built-locally  !!
3362          %p  ~|  %requesting-foreign-permissions-is-invalid  !!
```

```
3363        %r   ~|   %no-cages-please-they-are-just-way-too-big   !!
3364        %s   ~|   %please-dont-get-your-takos-over-a-network    !!
3365        %t   ~|   %requesting-foreign-directory-is-vaporware    !!
3366        %v   ~|   %weird-shouldnt-get-v-request-from-network    !!
3367        %q   `[p %noun q]:r.rand
3368        %u   `(validate-u r.rand)
3369        %w   `(validate-w r.rand)
3370        %x   (validate-x [p.p q.p q r]:rand)
3371        %y   `[p.r.rand !>(;;(arch q.r.rand))]
3372        %z   `(validate-z r.rand)
3373      ==
3374    ::
3375    ::  Make sure the incoming data is a %u response
3376    ::
3377    ++  validate-u
3378      |=  =page
3379      ^-  cage
3380      ?>  ?=(%flag p.page)
3381      :-  p.page
3382      !>  ;;(? q.page)
3383    ::
3384    ::  Make sure the incoming data is a %w response
3385    ::
3386    ++  validate-w
3387      |=  =page
3388      ^-  cage
3389      :-  p.page
3390      ?+  p.page  ~|  %strange-w-over-nextwork  !!
3391        %cass  !>(;;(cass q.page))
3392        %null  [[%atom %n ~] ~]
3393        %nako  !>(~|([%molding [&1 &2 &3]:q.page] ;;(nako q.page)))
3394      ==
3395    ::
3396    ::  Make sure that incoming data is of the mark it claims to be.
3397    ::
3398    ++  validate-x
3399      |=  [car=care cas=case pax=path peg=page]
3400      ^-  (unit cage)
3401      =/  vale-result
3402        %-  mule  |.
3403        %-  wrap:fusion
3404        ::  Use %base's marks to validate, so we don't have to build the
3405        ::  foreign marks
3406        ::
3407        =/  base-dome  dom:(~(got by dos.rom) %base)
3408        =/  f
3409          %-  %*(. tako-ford dom base-dome)
3410          (~(got by hit.base-dome) let.base-dome)
3411        (page-to-cage:f peg)
3412      ?:  ?=(%| -.vale-result)
3413        %-  (slog >%validate-x-failed< p.vale-result)
3414        ~
3415      `-.p.vale-result
3416    ::
3417    ::  Make sure the incoming data is a %z response
3418    ::
3419    ++  validate-z
3420      |=  =page
```

```
3421        ^-    cage
3422        ?>    ?=(%uvi p.page)
3423        :-    p.page
3424        !>    ;;(@uvI q.page)
3425      --
3426    ::
3427    ::  Respond to backfill request
3428    ::
3429    ::  Maybe should verify the requester is allowed to access this lobe?
3430    ::
3431    ++  give-backfill
3432      |=  [ver=?(%0 %1) =lobe]
3433      ^+  ..give-backfill
3434      =/  peg=(unit page)  (~(get by lat.ran) lobe)
3435      =/  res
3436        ?-  ver
3437          %0  ?~(peg [%1 ~] [%direct lobe u.peg])
3438          %1  [%1 peg]
3439        ==
3440      (emit hen %give %boon res)
3441    ::
3442    ::  Ingest foreign update, requesting missing lobes if necessary
3443    ::
3444    ++  foreign-update
3445      |=  inx=@ud
3446      ?>  ?=(^ ref)
3447      =/  [sat=update-state lost=?]
3448        =/  ruv  (~(get by bom.u.ref) inx)
3449        ?~  ruv
3450          ~&  [%clay-foreign-update-lost her syd inx]
3451          [*update-state &]
3452        [u.ruv |]
3453      =/  done=?  |
3454      =.  hen  duct.sat
3455      |%
3456      ++  abet
3457        ^+  ..foreign-update
3458        ?:  lost
3459          ..foreign-update
3460        ?:  done
3461          =:  bom.u.ref  (~(del by bom.u.ref) inx)
3462              fod.u.ref  (~(del by fod.u.ref) hen)
3463            ==
3464          =<(?>(?=(^ ref) .) wake)
3465        =.  bom.u.ref  (~(put by bom.u.ref) inx sat)
3466        ..foreign-update
3467      ::
3468      ++  apex
3469        |=  rut=(unit rand)
3470        ^+  ..abet
3471        ?:  lost  ..abet
3472        ?~  rut
3473          =.  nako.sat  (~(put to nako.sat) ~)
3474          work
3475        ?>  ?=(%nako p.r.u.rut)
3476        =/  nako  ;;(nako q.r.u.rut)
3477        ::  must be appended because we delete off front
3478        ::
```

```
3479        =.  need.sat  (welp need.sat (missing-lobes nako))
3480        =.  nako.sat  (~(put to nako.sat) ~ nako)
3481        work
3482      ::
3483      ++  missing-lobes
3484        |=  =nako
3485        ^-  (list [tako path lobe])
3486        =|  miss=(set lobe)
3487        =/  let-tako  (~(got by gar.nako) let.nako)
3488        =/  yakis  ~(tap in lar.nako)
3489        |-  ^-  (list [tako path lobe])
3490        =*  yaki-loop  $
3491        ?~  yakis
3492          ~
3493        =/  =norm
3494          ::  Always try to fetch the entire last commit, because often we
3495          ::  want to merge from it.
3496          ::
3497          ?:  =(let-tako r.i.yakis)
3498            *norm:clay
3499          (~(gut by tom.dom) r.i.yakis nor.dom)
3500        =/  lobes=(list [=path =lobe])  ~(tap by q.i.yakis)
3501        |-  ^-  (list [tako path lobe])
3502        =*  blob-loop  $
3503        ?~  lobes
3504          yaki-loop(yakis t.yakis)
3505        =*  lobe  lobe.i.lobes
3506        ?:  ?|  (~(has by lat.ran) lobe)
3507                =([[~ %|] +:(~(fit of norm) path.i.lobes))
3508                (~(has in miss) lobe)
3509            ==
3510          blob-loop(lobes t.lobes)
3511        :-  [r.i.yakis i.lobes]
3512        blob-loop(lobes t.lobes, miss (~(put in miss) lobe))
3513      ::
3514      ::  Receive backfill response
3515      ::
3516      ++  take-backfill
3517        |=  =fell
3518        ^+  ..abet
3519        ?:  lost  ..abet
3520        =?  need.sat  ?=(^ need.sat)  t.need.sat
3521        =.  ..park  =>((take-fell fell) ?>(?=(^ ref) .))
3522        work(busy.sat ~)
3523      ::
3524      ::  Fetch next lobe
3525      ::
3526      ++  work
3527        ^+  ..abet
3528        ?.  =(~ busy.sat)  ::NOTE  tmi
3529          ..abet
3530        |-  ^+  ..abet
3531        ?~  need.sat
3532          ::  NB: if you change to release nakos as we get enough lobes
3533          ::  for them instead of all at the end, you *must* store the
3534          ::  `lim` that should be applied after the nako is complete and
3535          ::  not use the one in the rave, since that will apply to the
3536          ::  end of subscription.
```

```
3537            ::
3538            |-  ^+  ..abet
3539            ?:  =(~ nako.sat)
3540              ..abet
3541            =^  next=(unit nako)  nako.sat  ~(get to nako.sat)
3542            ?~  next
3543              ..abet(done &)
3544            =.  ..abet  =>((apply-foreign-update u.next) ?>(?=(~ need.sat) .))
3545            =.  ..foreign-update  =<(?>(?=(^ ref) .) wake)  ::  [wake] >
3546            $
3547       ::  This used to be what always removed an item from `need`.  Now,
3548       ::  we remove in +take-backfill, but in the meantime we could have
3549       ::  received the next data from elsewhere (such as another desk
3550       ::  updating).  Additionally, this is needed for backward
3551       ::  compatibility with old /backfill wires.
3552       ::
3553       =/  =lobe
3554         ?@  i.need.sat  i.need.sat
3555         lobe.i.need.sat
3556       ?:  (~(has by lat.ran) lobe)
3557         $(need.sat t.need.sat)
3558       ::  otherwise, fetch the next blob (aka fell)
3559       ::
3560       =^  scry=(unit [@ta @da path])  ..foreign-update
3561         =<  ?>(?=(^ ref) .)
3562         ::  if we know a revision & path for the blob,
3563         ::  and :ship's remote scry isn't known to be broken,
3564         ::  or we learned it was broken more than an hour ago,
3565         ::
3566         ?:  ?&  ?=(^ i.need.sat)
3567             ?|  !(~(has by sad) her)
3568                 (gth now (add scry-retry-time (~(got by sad) her)))
3569             ==  ==
3570           ::  make the request over remote scry
3571           ::
3572           =/  =mood  [%q uv+tako path]:i.need.sat
3573           =<  [`[%back-index -] +]
3574           (send-over-scry %back-index hen her inx syd mood)
3575         ::  otherwise, request over ames
3576         ::
3577         :-  ~
3578         =/  =wire  (request-wire %back-index her syd inx)
3579         =/  =path  [%backfill syd (scot %ud inx) ~]
3580         ::  TODO: upgrade to %1 when most ships have upgaded
3581         =/  =fill  [%0 syd lobe]
3582         (emit hen %pass wire %a %plea her %c path fill)
3583       ..abet(busy.sat ?~(scry `%ames scry))
3584    ::
3585    ::  When we get a %w foreign update, store this in our state.
3586    ::
3587    ::  We get the commits from the nako and add them to our object
3588    ::  store, then we update the map of aeons to commits and the latest
3589    ::  aeon.
3590    ::
3591    ::  [wake] <
3592    ::
3593    ++  apply-foreign-update
3594      |=  =nako
```

```
3595        ^+   ..abet
3596        ::   hit: updated commit-hashes by @ud case
3597        ::   nut: new commit-hash/commit pairs
3598        ::   hut: updated commits by hash
3599        ::
3600        =/   hit   (~(uni by hit.dom) gar.nako)
3601        =/   nut   (turn ~(tap in lar.nako) |=(=yaki [r.yaki yaki]))
3602        =/   hut   (~(uni by (malt nut)) hut.ran)
3603        ::   traverse updated state and sanity check
3604        ::
3605        =+   ~|   :*  %bad-foreign-update
3606                     [gar=gar.nako let=let.nako nut=(turn nut head)]
3607                     [hitdom=hit.dom letdom=let.dom]
3608                ==
3609        ?:   =(0 let.nako)
3610          ~
3611        =/  =aeon  1
3612        |-  ^-  ~
3613        =/  =tako
3614          ~|  [%missing-aeon aeon]  (~(got by hit) aeon)
3615        =/  =yaki
3616          ~|  [%missing-tako tako]  (~(got by hut) tako)
3617        ?:  =(let.nako aeon)
3618          ~
3619        $(aeon +(aeon))
3620        ::   produce updated state
3621        ::
3622        =/  =rave  rave:(~(got by bom.u.ref) inx)
3623        ?>  ?=(%many -.rave)
3624        ::   [ergo] We do not call +ergo here, but if we wanted to support
3625        ::   keeping a foreign mounted desk up-to-date, this would open
3626        ::   that invariant.
3627        ::
3628        ::   [goad] Same for +goad -- if we supported running agents off
3629        ::   foreign desks at an up-to-date revision, we would need to call
3630        ::   +goad here.
3631        ::
3632        =:  let.dom    (max let.nako let.dom)            ::  [wake] < +work
3633            hit.dom    hit
3634            hut.ran    hut
3635            ::  Is this correct?  Seeems like it should only go to `to` if
3636            ::  we've gotten all the way to the end.  Leaving this
3637            ::  behavior unchanged for now, but I believe it's wrong.
3638            ::
3639            lim        ?.(?=(%da -.to.moat.rave) lim p.to.moat.rave)
3640          ==
3641        ..abet
3642      --
3643   ::
3644   ++  seek
3645     |=  =cash
3646     ^+  ..park
3647     ?>  ?=(^ ref)
3648     =/  =tako
3649       ?:  ?=(%tako -.cash)
3650         p.cash
3651       (aeon-to-tako:ze (need (case-to-aeon cash)))
3652     =/  =yaki  (tako-to-yaki:ze tako)
```

```
3653      =/  lobes=(list lobe)
3654        %+  murn  ~(tap by q.yaki)
3655        |=  [=path =lobe]
3656        ?:  (~(has by lat.ran) lobe)
3657              ~
3658          `lobe
3659      %-  emil
3660      %+  turn  lobes
3661      |=  =lobe
3662      ::  TODO: upgrade to %1 when most ships have upgaded
3663      ::
3664      =/  =fill  [%0 syd lobe]
3665      =/  =wire  /seek/(scot %p her)/[syd]
3666      =/  =path  [%backfill syd ~]
3667      [hen %pass wire %a %plea her %c path fill]
3668    ::
3669    ++  take-fell
3670      |=  =fell
3671      ^+  ..park
3672      ?>  ?=(^ ref)
3673      =/  peg=(unit page)  (fell-to-page fell)
3674      =?  lat.ran  ?=(^ peg)
3675        (~(uni by (malt [(page-to-lobe u.peg) u.peg] ~)) lat.ran)
3676      ..park
3677    ::
3678    ::  fire function if request is in future
3679    ::
3680    ++  run-if-future
3681      |=  [rov=rove fun=$-(@da _.)]
3682      ^+  +>.$
3683      =/  date=(unit @da)
3684        ?-      -.rov
3685            %sing
3686          ?.  ?=(%da -.case.mood.rov)  ~
3687          `p.case.mood.rov
3688        ::
3689            %next  ~
3690            %mult  ~
3691            %many
3692        %^  hunt  lth
3693          ?.  ?=(%da -.from.moat.rov)    ~
3694          ?.  (lth now p.from.moat.rov)  ~
3695          [~ p.from.moat.rov]
3696        ?.  ?=(%da -.to.moat.rov)  ~
3697        `(max now p.to.moat.rov)
3698        ==
3699      ?~  date
3700        +>.$
3701      (fun u.date)
3702    ::
3703    ++  send-cards
3704      |=  [cards=(list card) ducts=(set duct)]
3705      ^+  ..park
3706      %-  emil
3707      %-  zing
3708      %+  turn  cards
3709      |=  =card
3710      %+  turn  ~(tap by ducts)
```

```
3711      |=  =duct
3712      [duct card]
3713      ::
3714      ::  Loop through open subscriptions and check if we can fill any of
3715      ::  them.
3716      ::
3717      ::  [wake] This must be called any time something might have changed
3718      ::  which fills a subscription or changes the set of subscriptions.
3719      ::
3720      ::  It is safe to call this multiple times, because it updates the
3721      ::  subscription state to reflect that it's responded.  Usually this
3722      ::  means deleting the subscription, but %many can respond multiple
3723      ::  times.
3724      ::
3725      ::  One way of describing this invariant is that if you called +wake
3726      ::  on every desk at the end of every +call/+take, it would always
3727      ::  no-op.
3728      ::
3729      ++  wake
3730        ^+  .
3731        =/  subs=(list [=wove ducts=(set duct)])  ~(tap by qyx)
3732        =|  qux=cult
3733        |-  ^+  ..wake
3734        ?~  subs
3735          ..wake(qyx qux)
3736        ?:  =(~ ducts.i.subs)
3737          $(subs t.subs)
3738        =^  [new-sub=(unit rove) cards=(list card)]  ..park
3739          (try-fill-sub wove.i.subs)
3740        =.  ..wake  (send-cards cards ducts.i.subs)
3741        =?  qux  ?=(^ new-sub)
3742          =/  =wove  [for.wove.i.subs u.new-sub]
3743          %+  ~(put by qux)  wove
3744          (~(uni in ducts.i.subs) (~(get ju qux) wove))
3745        $(subs t.subs)
3746      ::
3747      ::  Try to fill a subscription
3748      ::
3749      ++  try-fill-sub
3750        |=  [far=(unit [=ship ver=@ud]) rov=rove]
3751        ^-  [[(unit rove) (list card)] _..park]
3752        =/  for=(unit ship)  ?~(far ~ `ship.u.far)
3753        ?-    -.rov
3754            %sing
3755          =/  cache-value=(unit (unit cage))
3756            ?~(ref ~ (~(get by haw.u.ref) mood.rov))
3757          ?^  cache-value
3758            ::  if we have a result in our cache, produce it
3759            ::
3760            :_  ..park  :-  ~  :_  ~
3761            (writ ?~(u.cache-value ~ `[mood.rov u.u.cache-value]))
3762          ::  else, check to see if rove is for an aeon we know
3763          ::
3764          =/  tako=(unit tako)  (case-to-tako case.mood.rov)
3765          ?~  tako
3766            [[`rov ~] ..park]
3767          ::  we have the appropriate tako, so read in the data
3768          ::
```

```
3769        =^  value=(unit (unit cage))  ..park
3770          (read-at-tako:ze for u.tako mood.rov)
3771        ?~  value
3772          ::  we don't have the data directly.  how can we fetch it?
3773          ::
3774          ?:  =(0v0 u.tako)
3775            ~&  [%clay-sing-indirect-data-0 `path`[syd '0' path.mood.rov]]
3776            [[~ ~] ..park]
3777          ~&  [%clay-sing-indirect-data desk=syd mood=mood.rov tako=u.tako]
3778          [[`rov ~] ..park]
3779        ::  we have the data, so produce the results
3780        ::
3781        :_  ..park  :-  ~  :_  ~
3782        %-  writ
3783        ?~  u.value
3784          ~
3785        `[mood.rov u.u.value]
3786      ::
3787      ::  %next is just %mult with one path, so we pretend %next = %mult here.
3788      ::
3789        ?(%next %mult)
3790      ?.  ?=(~ for)
3791      ::  reject if foreign (doesn't work over the network)
3792        ::
3793        [[~ ~] ..park]
3794      ::  because %mult requests need to wait on multiple files for each
3795      ::  revision that needs to be checked for changes, we keep two
3796      ::  cache maps.  {old} is the revision at {(dec aeon)}, {new} is
3797      ::  the revision at {aeon}.  if we have no {aeon} yet, that means
3798      ::  it was still unknown last time we checked.
3799        ::
3800      =*  vor  rov
3801      |^
3802      =/  rov=rove
3803        ?:  ?=(%mult -.vor)  vor
3804        :*  %mult
3805            [case [[care path] ~ ~]]:mood.vor
3806            aeon.vor
3807            [[[care.mood.vor path.mood.vor] cach.vor] ~ ~]
3808            ~
3809        ==
3810      ?>  ?=(%mult -.rov)
3811      ::  recurse here on next aeon if possible/needed.
3812        ::
3813      |-
3814      ::  if we don't have an aeon yet, see if we have one now.
3815        ::
3816      ?~  aeon.rov
3817        =/  aeon=(unit aeon)  (case-to-aeon case.mool.rov)
3818        ::  if we still don't, wait.
3819        ::
3820        ?~  aeon  [(store rov) ..park]
3821        ::  if we do, update the request and retry.
3822        ::
3823        $(aeon.rov `+(u.aeon), old-cach.rov ~, new-cach.rov ~)
3824      ::  if old isn't complete, try filling in the gaps.
3825        ::
3826      =^  o  ..park
```

```
3827      ?:  (complete old-cach.rov)
3828        [old-cach.rov ..park]
3829      (read-unknown mool.rov(case [%ud (dec u.aeon.rov)]) old-cach.rov)
3830    =.  old-cach.rov  o
3831    ::  if the next aeon we want to compare is in the future, wait again.
3832    ::
3833    =/  next-aeon=(unit aeon)  (case-to-aeon [%ud u.aeon.rov])
3834    ?~  next-aeon  [(store rov) ..park]
3835    ::  if new isn't complete, try filling in the gaps.
3836    ::
3837    =^  n  ..park
3838      ?:  (complete new-cach.rov)
3839        [new-cach.rov ..park]
3840      (read-unknown mool.rov(case [%ud u.aeon.rov]) new-cach.rov)
3841    =.  new-cach.rov  n
3842    ::  if new still isn't complete, wait again.
3843    ::
3844    ?.  (complete new-cach.rov)
3845      [(store rov) ..park]
3846    ::  if old not complete, give a result (possible false positive).
3847    ::
3848    ?:  !(complete old-cach.rov)
3849      :_  ..park
3850      %-  respond
3851      %-  malt
3852      %+  murn  ~(tap in paths.mool.rov)
3853      |=  [=care =path]
3854      ^-  (unit [mood (unit cage)])
3855      =/  cached  (~(get by new-cach.rov) [care path])
3856      ?.  ?=([~ ~ *] cached)
3857        %-  (slog 'clay: strange new-cache' >[care path cached]< ~)
3858        ~
3859      `u=[[care [%ud let.dom] path] u.u.cached]
3860    ::  both complete, so check if anything has changed
3861    ::
3862    =/  changes=(map mood (unit cage))
3863      %+  roll  ~(tap by old-cach.rov)
3864      |=  $:  [[car=care pax=path] old-cach=cach]
3865              changes=(map mood (unit cage))
3866          ==
3867      =/  new-cach=cach  (~(got by new-cach.rov) car pax)
3868      ?<  |(?=(~ old-cach) ?=(~ new-cach))
3869      =/  new-entry=(unit (pair mood (unit cage)))
3870        =/  =mood  [car [%ud u.aeon.rov] pax]
3871        ?~  u.new-cach
3872        ::  if new does not exist, always notify
3873        ::
3874        `[mood ~]
3875        ?~  u.old-cach
3876        ::  added
3877        ::
3878        `[mood `u.u.new-cach]
3879        ?:  =([p q.q]:u.u.new-cach [p q.q]:u.u.old-cach)
3880        ::  unchanged
3881        ::
3882          ~
3883        ::  changed
3884        ::
```

```
3885              `[mood `u.u.new-cach]
3886          ::  if changed, save the change
3887          ::
3888          ?~  new-entry
3889            changes
3890          (~(put by changes) u.new-entry)
3891        ::  if there are any changes, send response. if none, move on to
3892        ::  next aeon.
3893        ::
3894        ?^  changes  [(respond changes) ..park]
3895        $(u.aeon.rov +(u.aeon.rov), new-cach.rov ~)
3896        ::
3897        ::  check again later
3898        ::
3899        ++  store
3900          |=  rov=rove
3901          ^-  [(unit rove) (list card)]
3902          =/  new-rove=rove
3903            ?>  ?=(%mult -.rov)
3904            ?:  ?=(%mult -.vor)  rov
3905            ?>  ?=([* ~ ~] old-cach.rov)
3906            =*  one  n.old-cach.rov
3907            [%next [care.p.one case.mool.rov path.p.one] aeon.rov q.one]
3908          [`new-rove ~]
3909        ::
3910        ::  send changes
3911        ::
3912        ++  respond
3913          |=  res=(map mood (unit cage))
3914          ^-  [(unit rove) (list card)]
3915          :-  ~
3916          ?:  ?=(%mult -.vor)
3917            :_  ~
3918            =/  moods  ~(key by res)
3919            =/  cas
3920              ?>  ?=(^ moods)
3921              [%da (case-to-date case.n.moods)]
3922            =/  res
3923              (~(run in moods) |=(m=mood [care.m path.m]))
3924            =/  gift  [%wris cas res]
3925            ?:  ?=(^ ref)
3926              [%pass /drip %b %drip !>(gift)]  :: XX s/b [%behn %wris ...] in $sign?
3927            [%give gift]
3928          ?>  ?=([* ~ ~] res)
3929          :_  ~
3930          %-  writ
3931          ?~  q.n.res
3932            ~
3933          `[p u.q]:n.res
3934        ::
3935        ::  no unknowns
3936        ::
3937        ++  complete
3938          |=  hav=(map (pair care path) cach)
3939          ?&  !=(~ hav)
3940              (levy ~(tap by hav) know)
3941          ==
3942        ::
```

```
3943    ::  know about file in cach
3944    ::
3945    ++  know  |=([(pair care path) c=cach] ?=(^ c))
3946    ::
3947    ::  fill in the blanks
3948    ::
3949    ++  read-unknown
3950    |=  [=mool hav=(map (pair care path) cach)]
3951    ^-  [_hav _..park]
3952    =?  hav  ?=(~ hav)
3953      %-  malt  ^-  (list (pair (pair care path) cach))
3954      %+  turn
3955        ~(tap in paths.mool)
3956      |=  [c=care p=path]
3957      ^-  [[care path] cach]
3958      [[c p] ~]
3959    |-  ^+  [hav ..park]
3960    ?~  hav  [hav ..park]
3961    =^  lef  ..park  $(hav l.hav)
3962    =.  l.hav  lef
3963    =^  rig  ..park  $(hav r.hav)
3964    =.  r.hav  rig
3965    =/  [[=care =path] =cach]  n.hav
3966    ?^  cach
3967      [hav ..park]
3968    =^  q  ..park  (aver for care case.mool path)
3969    =.  q.n.hav  q
3970    [hav ..park]
3971    --
3972    ::
3973        %many
3974    :_  ..park
3975    ?.  |(?=(~ for) (allowed-by:ze u.for path.moat.rov per.red))
3976      [~ ~]
3977    =/  from-aeon  (case-to-aeon from.moat.rov)
3978    ?~  from-aeon
3979      ::  haven't entered the relevant range, so do nothing
3980      ::
3981      [`rov ~]
3982    =/  to-aeon  (case-to-aeon to.moat.rov)
3983    ::  TODO: shouldn't skip if tracking
3984    ::
3985    =/  up-to  ?~(to-aeon let.dom u.to-aeon)
3986    =/  ver  ?~(far %1 ver.u.far)
3987    =.  from.moat.rov  [%ud +(let.dom)]
3988    =/  =card
3989      =/  =cage
3990        ?:  track.rov
3991          [%null [%atom %n ~] ~]
3992        [%nako !>((make-nako:ze ver u.from-aeon up-to))]
3993      (writ ~ [%w ud+let.dom /] cage)
3994    ?~  to-aeon
3995      ::  we're in the middle of the range, so produce what we can,
3996      ::  but don't end the subscription
3997      ::
3998      [`rov card ~]
3999    ::  we're past the end of the range, so end subscription
4000    ::
```

```
4001        [~ [card (writ ~) ~]]
4002      ==
4003    ::
4004    :::::::::::::::::::::::::::::::::::::::::::::::::::::::::::::::::::::::::::
4005    ::
4006    ::  This core has no additional state, and the distinction exists purely for
4007    ::  documentation.  The overarching theme is that `++de` directly contains
4008    ::  logic for metadata about the desk, while `++ze` is composed primarily
4009    ::  of helper functions for manipulating the desk state (`++dome`) itself.
4010    ::  Functions include:
4011    ::
4012    ::  --  converting between cases, commit hashes, commits, content hashes,
4013    ::      and content
4014    ::  --  creating commits and content and adding them to the tree
4015    ::  --  finding which data needs to be sent over the network to keep the
4016    ::      other urbit up-to-date
4017    ::  --  reading from the file tree through different `++care` options
4018    ::  --  the `++me` core for merging.
4019    ::
4020    ::  The dome is composed of the following:
4021    ::
4022    ::  --  `let` is the number of the most recent revision.
4023    ::  --  `hit` is a map of revision numbers to commit hashes.
4024    ::  --  `lab` is a map of labels to revision numbers.
4025    ::
4026    :::::::::::::::::::::::::::::::::::::::::::::::::::::::::::::::::::::::::::
4027    ::
4028    ::
4029    ::  Other utility functions
4030    ::
4031    ++  ze
4032      |%
4033      ::  These convert between aeon (version number), tako (commit hash),
4034      ::  and yaki (commit data structure)
4035      ::
4036      ++  aeon-to-tako  |=(=aeon ?:(=(0 aeon) 0v0 (~(got by hit.dom) aeon)))
4037      ++  aeon-to-yaki  |=(=aeon (tako-to-yaki (aeon-to-tako aeon)))
4038      ++  tako-to-yaki  ~(got by hut.ran)
4039      ::
4040      ++  tako-to-aeon
4041        |=  tak=tako
4042        ^-  aeon  ~+
4043        ?:  =(0v0 tak)  0
4044        =/  a=aeon  1
4045        |-
4046        ?:  (gth a let.dom)  ~|([%tako-mia tak] !!)
4047        ?:  (~(has in (reachable-takos (~(got by hit.dom) a))) tak)  a
4048        $(a +(a))
4049      ::
4050      ::  Creates a nako of all the changes between a and b.
4051      ::
4052      ++  make-nako
4053        |=  [ver=@ud a=aeon b=aeon]
4054        ^-  nako
4055        :+  ?>  (lte b let.dom)
4056            |-
4057        ?:  =(b let.dom)
4058          hit.dom
```

```
4059          ::  del everything after b
4060          $(hit.dom (~(del by hit.dom) let.dom), let.dom (dec let.dom))
4061        b
4062      ?:  =(0 b)
4063      [~ ~]
4064    =/  excludes=(set tako)
4065        =|  acc=(set tako)
4066        =/  lower=@ud  1
4067        |-
4068        ::  a should be excluded, so wait until we're past it
4069        ?:  (gte lower +(a))
4070          acc
4071        =/  res=(set tako)  (reachable-takos (~(got by hit.dom) lower))
4072        $(acc (~(uni in acc) res), lower +(lower))
4073    =/  includes=(set tako)
4074        =|  acc=(set tako)
4075        =/  upper=@ud  b
4076        |-
4077        ?:  (lte upper a)
4078          acc
4079        =/  res=(set tako)  (reachable-takos (~(got by hit.dom) upper))
4080        $(acc (~(uni in acc) res), upper (dec upper))
4081    [(~(run in (~(dif in includes) excludes)) tako-to-yaki) ~]
4082  ::  Traverse parentage and find all ancestor hashes
4083  ::
4084  ++  reachable-takos                                ::  reachable
4085    |=  p=tako
4086    ^-  (set tako)
4087    ~+
4088    =|  s=(set tako)
4089    |-  ^-  (set tako)
4090    =.  s  (~(put in s) p)
4091    =+  y=(tako-to-yaki p)
4092    |-  ^-  (set tako)
4093    ?~  p.y
4094      s
4095    ?:  (~(has in s) i.p.y)
4096      $(p.y t.p.y)
4097    =.  s  ^$(p i.p.y)
4098    $(p.y t.p.y)
4099  ::
4100  ++  read-a
4101    !.
4102    |=  [=tako =path]
4103    ^-  [(unit (unit cage)) _..park]
4104    =^  =vase  ..park
4105      ~_  leaf/"clay: %a build failed {<[syd tako path]>}"
4106      %+  tako-flow   tako
4107      %-  wrap:fusion
4108      (build-file:(tako-ford tako) path)
4109    :_(..park [~ ~ %vase !>(vase)])
4110  ::
4111  ++  read-b
4112    !.
4113    |=  [=tako =path]
4114    ^-  [(unit (unit cage)) _..park]
4115    ?.  ?=([@ ~] path)
4116      [[~ ~] ..park]
```

```
4117        =^  =dais  ..park
4118        %+  tako-flow  tako
4119        %-  wrap:fusion
4120        (build-dais:(tako-ford tako) i.path)
4121      :_(..park [~ ~ %dais !>(dais)])
4122    ::
4123    ++  read-c
4124      !.
4125      |=  [=tako =path]
4126      ^-  [(unit (unit cage)) _..park]
4127      ?.  ?=([@ @ ~] path)
4128        [[~ ~] ..park]
4129      =^  =tube  ..park
4130        %+  tako-flow  tako
4131        %-  wrap:fusion
4132        (build-tube:(tako-ford tako) [i i.t]:path)
4133      :_(..park [~ ~ %tube !>(tube)])
4134    ::
4135    ++  read-e
4136      !.
4137      |=  [=tako =path]
4138      ^-  [(unit (unit cage)) _..park]
4139      ?.  ?=([@ ~] path)
4140        [[~ ~] ..park]
4141      =^  =vase  ..park
4142        %+  tako-flow  tako
4143        %-  wrap:fusion
4144        (build-nave:(tako-ford tako) i.path)
4145      :_(..park [~ ~ %nave vase])
4146    ::
4147    ++  read-f
4148      !.
4149      |=  [=tako =path]
4150      ^-  [(unit (unit cage)) _..park]
4151      ?.  ?=([@ @ ~] path)
4152        [[~ ~] ..park]
4153      =^  =vase  ..park
4154        %+  tako-flow  tako
4155        %-  wrap:fusion
4156        (build-cast:(tako-ford tako) [i i.t]:path)
4157      :_(..park [~ ~ %cast vase])
4158    ::
4159    ::  TODO move to +read-buc
4160    ::
4161    ++  read-d
4162      !.
4163      |=  [=tako =path]
4164      ^-  (unit (unit cage))
4165      ~&  [%clay %d-on-desk-deprecated desk=syd %use-empty-desk]
4166      ?.  =(our her)
4167        [~ ~]
4168      ?^  path
4169        ~&(%no-cd-path [~ ~])
4170      [~ ~ %noun !>(~(key by dos.rom.ruf))]
4171    ::
4172    ::  Gets the permissions that apply to a particular node.
4173    ::
4174    ::  If the node has no permissions of its own, we use its parent's.
```

```
4175    ::  If no permissions have been set for the entire tree above the node,
4176    ::  we default to fully private (empty whitelist).
4177    ::
4178    ++  read-p
4179      |=  pax=path
4180      ^-  (unit (unit cage))
4181      =-  [~ ~ %noun !>(-)]
4182      :-  (read-p-in pax per.red)
4183      (read-p-in pax pew.red)
4184    ::
4185    ++  read-p-in
4186      |=  [pax=path pes=regs]
4187      ^-  dict
4188      =/  rul=(unit rule)  (~(get by pes) pax)
4189      ?^  rul
4190        :+  pax  mod.u.rul
4191        %-  ~(rep in who.u.rul)
4192        |=  [w=whom out=(pair (set ship) (map @ta crew))]
4193        ?:  ?=([%& @p] w)
4194          [(~(put in p.out) +.w) q.out]
4195        =/  cru=(unit crew)  (~(get by cez.ruf) +.w)
4196        ?~  cru  out
4197        [p.out (~(put by q.out) +.w u.cru)]
4198      ?~  pax  [/ %white ~ ~]
4199      $(pax (scag (dec (lent pax)) `path`pax))
4200    ::
4201    ++  may-read
4202      |=  [who=ship car=care tak=tako pax=path]
4203      ^-  ?
4204      ?+  car
4205        (allowed-by who pax per.red)
4206          ::
4207          %p
4208        =(who our)
4209          ::
4210          ?(%y %z)
4211        =+  yak=(tako-to-yaki tak)
4212        =+  len=(lent pax)
4213        =-  (levy ~(tap in -) |=(p=path (allowed-by who p per.red)))
4214        %+  roll  ~(tap in (~(del in ~(key by q.yak)) pax))
4215        |=  [p=path s=(set path)]
4216        ?.  =(pax (scag len p))  s
4217        %-  ~(put in s)
4218        ?:  ?=(%z car)  p
4219        (scag +(len) p)
4220      ==
4221    ::
4222    ++  may-write
4223      |=  [w=ship p=path]
4224      (allowed-by w p pew.red)
4225    ::
4226    ++  allowed-by
4227      |=  [who=ship pax=path pes=regs]
4228      ^-  ?
4229      =/  rul=real  rul:(read-p-in pax pes)
4230      =/  in-list/?
4231        ?|  (~(has in p.who.rul) who)
4232            ::
```

```
4233            %-  ~(rep by q.who.rul)
4234            |=  [[@ta cru=crew] out=_|]
4235            ?:  out  &
4236            (~(has in cru) who)
4237          ==
4238      ?:  =(%black mod.rul)
4239        !in-list
4240      in-list
4241  ::  +content-hash: get hash of contents (%cz hash)
4242  ::
4243  ++  content-hash
4244    |=  [=yaki pax=path]
4245    ^-  @uvI
4246    =+  len=(lent pax)
4247    =/  descendants=(list (pair path lobe))
4248        %+  turn
4249          %+  skim  ~(tap by (~(del by q.yaki) pax))
4250          |=  [paf=path lob=lobe]
4251          =(pax (scag len paf))
4252        |=  [paf=path lob=lobe]
4253        [(slag len paf) lob]
4254    =+  us=(~(get by q.yaki) pax)
4255    ?:  &(?=(~ descendants) ?=(~ us))
4256      *@uvI
4257    %+  roll
4258      ^-  (list (pair path lobe))
4259      [[~ ?~(us *lobe u.us)] descendants]
4260    |=([[path lobe] @uvI] (shax (jam +<)))
4261  ::  +read-q: typeless %x
4262  ::
4263  ::  useful if the marks can't be built (eg for old marks built
4264  ::  against an incompatible standard library).  also useful if you
4265  ::  don't need the type (eg for remote scry) because it's faster.
4266  ::
4267  ++  read-q
4268    |=  [tak=tako pax=path]
4269    ^-  (unit (unit cage))
4270    ?:  =(0v0 tak)
4271      [~ ~]
4272    =+  yak=(tako-to-yaki tak)
4273    =+  lob=(~(get by q.yak) pax)
4274    ?~  lob
4275      [~ ~]
4276    =/  peg=(unit page)  (~(get by lat.ran) u.lob)
4277    ::  if tombstoned, nothing to return
4278    ::
4279    ?~  peg
4280      ~
4281    ``[p.u.peg %noun q.u.peg]
4282  ::  +read-r: %x wrapped in a vase
4283  ::
4284  ++  read-r
4285    |=  [tak=tako pax=path]
4286    ^-  [(unit (unit cage)) _..park]
4287    =^  x  ..park  (read-x tak pax)
4288    :_  ..park
4289    ?~  x    ~
4290    ?~  u.x  [~ ~]
```

```
4291        ``[p.u.u.x !>(q.u.u.x)]
4292    ::  +read-s: produce miscellaneous
4293    ::
4294    ++  read-s
4295      |=  [tak=tako pax=path =case]
4296      ^-  (unit (unit cage))
4297      ?:  ?=([%subs ~] pax)
4298        ?.  =([%da now] case)  ~
4299        =|  sus=(set ship)
4300        =/  doj=(unit dojo)  (~(get by dos.rom) syd)
4301        ?~  doj
4302          ``noun+!>(sus)
4303        =/  wos  ~(tap in ~(key by qyx.u.doj))
4304        |-
4305        ?~  wos
4306          ``noun+!>(sus)
4307        ?~  for.i.wos
4308          $(wos t.wos)
4309        %=  $
4310          wos  t.wos
4311          sus  (~(put in sus) ship.u.for.i.wos)
4312        ==
4313      ?:  ?=([%bloc ~] pax)
4314        :^  ~  ~  %noun
4315        :-  -:!>(*(map lobe page))
4316        ^-  (map lobe page)
4317        %-  %~  rep  in
4318            |-  ^-  (set tako)
4319            =/  ts=(set tako)
4320              %-  reachable-takos
4321              (~(got by hit.dom) let.dom)
4322            ?:  (lte let.dom 1)  ts
4323            (~(uni in ts) $(let.dom (dec let.dom)))
4324        |=  [t=tako o=(map lobe page)]
4325        %-  ~(gas by o)
4326        %+  turn
4327          ~(val by q:(~(got by hut.ran) t))
4328          |=(l=lobe [l (~(got by lat.ran) l)])
4329      ?.  ?=([@ * *] pax)
4330        `~
4331      ?+    i.pax  `~
4332          %tako
4333        ``tako+[-:!>(*tako) tak]
4334      ::
4335          %yaki
4336        =/  yak=(unit yaki)  (~(get by hut.ran) (slav %uv i.t.pax))
4337        ?~  yak
4338          ~
4339        ``yaki+[-:!>(*yaki) u.yak]
4340      ::
4341          %blob
4342        =/  peg=(unit page)  (~(get by lat.ran) (slav %uv i.t.pax))
4343        ?~  peg
4344          ~
4345        ``blob+[-:!>(*page) u.peg]
4346      ::
4347          %hash
4348        =/  yak=(unit yaki)  (~(get by hut.ran) (slav %uv i.t.pax))
```

```
4349            ?~  yak
4350              ~
4351            ``uvi+[-:!>(*@uvI) (content-hash u.yak /)]
4352        ::
4353          %cage
4354        ::  should save ford cache
4355        ::
4356        =/  =lobe  (slav %uv i.t.pax)
4357        =/  peg=(unit page)  (~(get by lat.ran) lobe)
4358        ?~  peg
4359          ~
4360        =/  [=cage *]
4361          %-  wrap:fusion
4362          (page-to-cage:(tako-ford tak) u.peg)
4363        ``cage+[-:!>(*^cage) cage]
4364        ::
4365          %open  ``open+!>(prelude:(tako-ford tak))
4366          %late  !!  :: handled in +aver
4367          %case  !!  :: handled in +aver
4368          %base-tako
4369        ::  TODO this ignores the given beak
4370        ::  maybe move to +aver?
4371        ?>  ?=(^ t.t.pax)
4372        :^  ~  ~  %uvs  !>
4373        ^-  (list @uv)
4374        =/  tako-a  (slav %uv i.t.pax)
4375        =/  tako-b  (slav %uv i.t.t.pax)
4376        =/  yaki-a  (~(got by hut.ran) tako-a)
4377        =/  yaki-b  (~(got by hut.ran) tako-b)
4378        %+  turn    ~(tap in (find-merge-points yaki-a yaki-b))
4379        |=  =yaki
4380        r.yaki
4381        ::
4382          %base
4383        ?>  ?=(^ t.t.pax)
4384        :^  ~  ~  %uvs  !>
4385        ^-  (list @uv)
4386        =/  him  (slav %p i.t.pax)
4387        =/  other  dom:((de now rof hen ruf) him i.t.t.pax)
4388        ?:  =(0 let.other)
4389          ~
4390        =/  our-yaki  (~(got by hut.ran) tak)
4391        =/  other-yaki  (~(got by hut.ran) (~(got by hit.other) let.other))
4392        %+  turn  ~(tap in (find-merge-points other-yaki our-yaki))
4393        |=  =yaki
4394        r.yaki
4395      ==
4396    ::  +read-t: produce the list of paths within a yaki with :pax as prefix
4397    ::
4398    ++  read-t
4399      |=  [tak=tako pax=path]
4400      ^-  (unit (unit [%file-list (hypo (list path))]))
4401      ::  if asked for version 0, produce an empty list of files
4402      ::
4403      ?:  =(0v0 tak)
4404        ``[%file-list -:!>(*(list path)) *(list path)]
4405      ::  look up the yaki snapshot based on the version
4406      ::
```

```
4407      =/  yak=yaki  (tako-to-yaki tak)
4408      ::  calculate the path length once outside the loop
4409      ::
4410      =/  path-length  (lent pax)
4411      ::
4412      :^  ~   ~  %file-list
4413      :-  -:!>(*(list path))
4414      ^-  (list path)
4415      ::  sort the matching paths alphabetically
4416      ::
4417      =-  (sort - aor)
4418      ::  traverse the filesystem, filtering for paths with :pax as prefix
4419      ::
4420      %+  skim  ~(tap in ~(key by q.yak))
4421      |=(paf=path =(pax (scag path-length paf)))
4422    ::
4423    ::  Checks for existence of a node at an aeon.
4424    ::
4425    ::  This checks for existence of content at the node, and does *not* look
4426    ::  at any of its children.
4427    ::
4428    ++  read-u
4429      |=  [tak=tako pax=path]
4430      ^-  (unit (unit [%flag (hypo ?)]))
4431      ::  if asked for version 0, that never exists, so always give false
4432      ::
4433      ?:  =(0v0 tak)
4434        ``[%flag -:!>(*?) |]
4435      ::  look up the yaki snapshot based on the version
4436      ::
4437      =/  yak=yaki  (tako-to-yaki tak)
4438      ::  produce the result based on whether or not there's a file at :pax
4439      ::
4440      ``[%flag -:!>(*?) (~(has by q.yak) pax)]
4441    ::
4442    ::  Gets the dome (desk state) at a particular aeon.
4443    ::
4444    ++  read-v
4445      |=  [tak=tako pax=path]
4446      ^-  (unit (unit [%dome (hypo domo:clay)]))
4447      =/  yon=aeon  (tako-to-aeon:ze tak)
4448      ?:  (lth yon let.dom)
4449        :*  ~   ~  %dome  -:!>(*domo)
4450            ^-  domo
4451        :*  let=yon
4452            hit=(molt (skim ~(tap by hit.dom) |=([p=@ud *] (lte p yon))))
4453            lab=(molt (skim ~(tap by lab.dom) |=([* p=@ud] (lte p yon))))
4454        ==  ==
4455      ?:  (gth yon let.dom)
4456        ~
4457      ``[%dome -:!>(*domo) [let hit lab]:dom]
4458    ::
4459    ::  Gets all cases refering to the same revision as the given case.
4460    ::
4461    ::  For the %da case, we give just the canonical timestamp of the revision.
4462    ::
4463    ++  read-w
4464      |=  tak=tako
```

```
4465        ^-  (unit (unit cage))
4466        =-  [~ ~ %cass !>(-)]
4467        ^-  cass  ::TODO  should include %uv case
4468        :-  (tako-to-aeon tak)
4469        ?:  =(0v0 tak)  `@da`0
4470      t:(tako-to-yaki tak)
4471    ::
4472    ::  Get the data at a node.
4473    ::
4474    ::  Use ford to read the file.  Note this special-cases the hoon
4475    ::  mark for bootstrapping purposes.
4476    ::
4477    ++  read-x
4478      |=  [tak=tako pax=path]
4479      ^-  [(unit (unit cage)) _..park]
4480      =/  q  (read-q tak pax)
4481      ?~  q    `..park
4482      ?~  u.q  [[~ ~] ..park]
4483      ::  should convert any lobe to cage
4484      ::
4485      =^  =cage  ..park
4486        %+  tako-flow  tak
4487        %-  wrap:fusion
4488        (page-to-cage:(tako-ford tak) p.u.u.q q.q.u.u.q)
4489      [``cage ..park]
4490    ::
4491    ::  Gets an arch (directory listing) at a node.
4492    ::
4493    ++  read-y
4494      |=  [tak=tako pax=path]
4495      ^-  (unit (unit [%arch (hypo arch)]))
4496      ?:  =(0v0 tak)
4497        ``[%arch -:!>(*arch) *arch]
4498      =+  yak=(tako-to-yaki tak)
4499      =+  len=(lent pax)
4500      :^  ~  ~  %arch
4501      ::  ~&  cy+pax
4502      :-  -:!>(*arch)
4503      ^-  arch
4504      :-  (~(get by q.yak) pax)
4505      ^-  (map knot ~)
4506      %-  molt  ^-  (list (pair knot ~))
4507      %+  turn
4508        ^-  (list (pair path lobe))
4509        %+  skim  ~(tap by (~(del by q.yak) pax))
4510        |=  [paf=path lob=lobe]
4511        =(pax (scag len paf))
4512      |=  [paf=path lob=lobe]
4513      =+  pat=(slag len paf)
4514      [?>(?=(^ pat) i.pat) ~]
4515    ::
4516    ::  Gets a recursive hash of a node and all its children.
4517    ::
4518    ++  read-z
4519      |=  [tak=tako pax=path]
4520      ^-  (unit (unit [%uvi (hypo @uvI)]))
4521      ?:  =(0v0 tak)
4522        ``uvi+[-:!>(*@uvI) *@uvI]
```

```
4523        [~ ~ %uvi [%atom %'uvI' ~] (content-hash (tako-to-yaki tak) pax)]
4524      ::
4525      ::  Get a value at an aeon.
4526      ::
4527      ::  Value can be either null, meaning we don't have it yet, [null null],
4528      ::  meaning we know it doesn't exist, or [null null cage],
4529      ::  meaning we either have the value directly or a content hash of the
4530      ::  value.
4531      ::
4532      ++  read-at-tako                              ::    read-at-tako:ze
4533        |=  [for=(unit ship) tak=tako mun=mood]      ::  seek and read
4534        ^-  [(unit (unit cage)) _..park]
4535        ::  non-zero commits must be known, and reachable from within this desk
4536        ::
4537        ?.  ?|  =(0v0 tak)
4538            ?&  (~(has by hut.ran) tak)
4539                ?|  (~(any by hit.dom) |=(=tako =(tak tako)))  ::  fast-path
4540                    |-  ^-  ?
4541                    ?:  (lte let.dom 1)
4542                      %.n
4543                    ?|  (~(has in (reachable-takos (aeon-to-tako:ze let.dom))) tak)
4544                        $(let.dom (dec let.dom))
4545                    ==
4546                ==
4547                |(?=(~ for) (may-read u.for care.mun tak path.mun))
4548            ==  ==
4549          [~ ..park]
4550        ::  virtualize to catch and produce deterministic failures
4551        ::
4552        |^  =/  res  (mule |.(read))
4553            ?:  ?=(%& -.res)  p.res
4554            %.  [[~ ~] ..park]
4555            (slog leaf+"clay: read-at-tako fail {<[desk=syd mun]>}" p.res)
4556        ::
4557        ++  read
4558          ^-  [(unit (unit cage)) _..park]
4559          ?-  care.mun
4560            %a  (read-a tak path.mun)
4561            %b  (read-b tak path.mun)
4562            %c  (read-c tak path.mun)
4563            %d  [(read-d tak path.mun) ..park]
4564            %e  (read-e tak path.mun)
4565            %f  (read-f tak path.mun)
4566            %p  [(read-p path.mun) ..park]
4567            %q  [(read-q tak path.mun) ..park]
4568            %r  (read-r tak path.mun)
4569            %s  [(read-s tak path.mun case.mun) ..park]
4570            %t  [(read-t tak path.mun) ..park]
4571            %u  [(read-u tak path.mun) ..park]
4572            %v  [(read-v tak path.mun) ..park]
4573            %w  [(read-w tak) ..park]
4574            %x  (read-x tak path.mun)
4575            %y  [(read-y tak path.mun) ..park]
4576            %z  [(read-z tak path.mun) ..park]
4577          ==
4578        --
4579      --
4580    --
```

```
4581  ::  userspace agent management
4582  ::
4583  ++  lu
4584    |=  [now=@da rof=roof hen=duct raft]
4585    =*  ruf  |3.+<.$
4586    =|  mow=(list move)
4587    |%
4588    ++  abet
4589      ^-  [(list move) raft]
4590      [(flop mow) ruf]
4591    ::
4592    ++  emit
4593      |=  mof=move
4594      %_(+> mow [mof mow])
4595    ::
4596    ++  emil
4597      |=  mof=(list move)
4598      %_(+> mow (weld (flop mof) mow))
4599    ::  +ford: init ford
4600    ::
4601    ++  ford
4602      |=  [her=ship syd=desk yon=(unit aeon)]
4603      =/  den  ((de now rof hen ruf) her syd)
4604      %-  tako-ford:den
4605      ::TODO  is this +got after +got semantically correct?
4606      (~(got by hit.dom:(~(got by dos.rom) syd)) ?~(yon let.dom:den u.yon))
4607    ::  +wrap: save ford cache
4608    ::
4609    ++  wrap
4610      |*  [her=ship syd=desk yon=(unit aeon) res=* =state:ford:fusion]
4611      =^  moves  ruf
4612        =/  den  ((de now rof hen ruf) her syd)
4613        =/  tak  (aeon-to-tako:ze:den ?~(yon let.dom:den u.yon))
4614        abet:+:(tako-flow:den tak res cache.state &2.state)
4615      [res (emil moves)]
4616    ::
4617    ++  trace
4618      |=  [pri=@ print=(trap tape)]
4619      ?:  (lth veb.bug pri)
4620        same
4621      (slog leaf+"goad: {(print)}" ~)
4622    ::  +goad: emit %load move for all desks, applying $rein's
4623    ::
4624    ::  [goad] Must be called any time the set of running agents changes.
4625    ::  This is whenever an agent is started, stopped, or updated.
4626    ::
4627    ::  This is not move-order agnostic -- you must be careful of
4628    ::  reentrancy as long as arvo's move order is depth-first.
4629    ::
4630    ::  [tare] >
4631    ::
4632    ++  goad
4633      ^+  ..abet
4634      =^  sat=(list [=desk =bill])  ..abet
4635        =/  desks=(list desk)  ~(tap in ~(key by dos.rom))
4636        |-  ^-  [(list [desk bill]) _..abet]
4637        ?~  desks
4638          [~ ..abet]
```

```
4639        =/  den   ((de now rof hen ruf) our i.desks)
4640        ?.  =(%live liv.dom.den)
4641          %-  (trace 2 |.("{<i.desks>} is not live"))
4642          $(desks t.desks)
4643        =^  res  den  (aver:den ~ %x da+now /desk/bill)
4644        =.  ruf  +:abet:den
4645        ?.  ?=([~ ~ *] res)
4646          $(desks t.desks)
4647        =/  bill  ~|  [%building-bill i.desks]  !<(bill q.u.u.res)
4648        =/  rid  (override bill ren.dom.den)
4649        %-  %+  trace  2  |.
4650            "{<i.desks>} has bill {<bill>} and rein {<ren.dom.den>}, so {<rid>}"
4651        =^  sats  ..abet  $(desks t.desks)
4652        [[[i.desks rid] sats] ..abet]
4653      ::
4654    =.  sat  (apply-precedence sat)
4655    =+  ?:  (lth veb.bug 1)  ~
4656        %.  ~  %-  slog
4657        %+  turn  sat
4658        |=  [=desk =bill]
4659        leaf+"goad: output: {<desk>}: {<bill>}"
4660    =^  agents  ..abet  (build-agents sat)
4661    ::  TODO: enable if we can reduce memory usage
4662    ::
4663    ::  =.  ..abet
4664    ::  (build-marks (turn (skip sat |=([desk =bill] =(bill ~))) head))
4665    ::
4666    =.  ..abet  tare                                    ::  [tare] >
4667    (emit hen %pass /lu/load %g %load agents)
4668  ::  +override: apply rein to bill
4669  ::
4670  ++  override
4671    |=  [duz=bill ren=(map dude:gall ?)]
4672    ^-  bill
4673    =.  duz
4674      %+  skip  duz
4675      |=  =dude:gall
4676      =(`| (~(get by ren) dude))
4677    ::
4678    =/  dus  (sy duz)
4679    =.  duz
4680      %+  weld  duz
4681      %+  murn  ~(tap by ren)
4682      |=  [=dude:gall on=?]
4683      ?:  &(?=(%& on) !(~(has in dus) dude))
4684        `u=dude
4685      ~
4686    duz
4687  ::  +apply-precedence: resolve conflicts between $bill's
4688  ::
4689  ::    policy is to crash if multiple desks are trying to run the same
4690  ::    agent.
4691  ::
4692  ++  apply-precedence
4693    |=  sat=(list [=desk =bill])
4694    ^+  sat
4695    ::  sort desks in alphabetical order with %base first
4696    ::
```

```
4697    =.  sat  (sort sat sort-desks)
4698    ::  for each desk
4699    ::
4700    =|  done=(set dude:gall)
4701    |-  ^+  sat
4702    ?~  sat
4703        ~
4704    ::  for each agent
4705    ::
4706    =/  bil  bill.i.sat
4707    =^  this  done
4708      |-  ^-  [bill (set dude:gall)]
4709      ?~  bil
4710        [~ done]
4711      ::
4712      ?:  (~(has in done) i.bil)
4713        ~>  %mean.(cat 3 'clay: cannot run app from two desks: %' i.bil)
4714        !!
4715      =.  done  (~(put in done) i.bil)
4716      =^  next  done  $(bil t.bil)
4717      [[i.bil next] done]
4718    [[desk.i.sat this] $(sat t.sat)]
4719  ::
4720  ++  sort-desks
4721    |=  [a=[=desk *] b=[=desk *]]
4722    ^-  ?
4723    ?:  =(%base desk.a)  &
4724    ?:  =(%base desk.b)  |
4725    (aor desk.a desk.b)
4726  ::  build-file for each dude
4727  ::
4728  ++  build-agents
4729    |=  sat=(list [=desk =bill])
4730    ^-  [load:gall _..abet]
4731    =|  lad=load:gall
4732    |-  ^-  [load:gall _..abet]
4733    ?~  sat
4734      [lad ..abet]
4735    =/  f  (ford our desk.i.sat ~)
4736    =^  new=load:gall  ..abet
4737      %-  wrap  :^  our  desk.i.sat  ~
4738      |-  ^-  [load:gall state:ford:fusion]
4739      ?~  bill.i.sat
4740        [~ nub.f]
4741      =^  =vase  nub.f  (build-file:f /app/[i.bill.i.sat]/hoon)
4742      =/  agent  ~|  [%building-app bill.i.sat]  !<(agent:gall vase)
4743      =^  lid  nub.f  $(bill.i.sat t.bill.i.sat)
4744      [[[[i.bill.i.sat [our desk.i.sat da+now] agent] lid] nub.f]
4745    =.  lad  (weld lad new)
4746    $(sat t.sat)
4747  ::  build-dais for each mark
4748  ::
4749  ++  build-marks
4750    |=  desks=(list desk)
4751    ^+  ..abet
4752    ?~  desks
4753      ..abet
4754    =/  f  (ford our i.desks ~)
```

```
4755      =^  null  ..abet
4756        %-  wrap  :^  our  i.desks  ~
4757        =^  marks=(list mark)  nub.f
4758          =/  pax=path  /
4759          |-  ^-  [(list mark) _nub.f]
4760          =/  den  ((de now rof hen ruf) our i.desks)
4761          =^  res  den  (aver:den ~ %y da+now mar+pax)
4762          ?.  ?=([~ ~ *] res)
4763            [~ nub.f]
4764          =/  arch  ~|  [%building-arch i.desks]  !<(arch q.u.u.res)
4765          =/  m1=(list mark)
4766            ?.  ?&  ?=(^ fil.arch)
4767                    ?=(^ pax)
4768                    =(/hoon (slag (dec (lent pax)) `path`pax))
4769                ==
4770                  ~
4771            :_  ~
4772            ?~  t.pax
4773              ''
4774            |-  ^-  mark
4775            ?~  t.t.pax
4776              i.pax
4777            (rap 3 i.pax '-' $(pax t.pax) ~)
4778          ::
4779          =^  m2  nub.f
4780            |-  ^-  [(list mark) _nub.f]
4781            ?~  dir.arch
4782              [~ nub.f]
4783            =^  n1  nub.f  ^$(pax (weld pax /[p.n.dir.arch]))
4784            =^  n2  nub.f  $(dir.arch l.dir.arch)
4785            =^  n3  nub.f  $(dir.arch r.dir.arch)
4786            [:(weld n1 n2 n3) nub.f]
4787          [(weld m1 m2) nub.f]
4788        ::
4789        |-  ^-  [~ state:ford:fusion]
4790        ?~  marks
4791          [~ nub.f]
4792        =^  =dais  nub.f  (build-dais:f i.marks)
4793        $(marks t.marks)
4794      $(desks t.desks)
4795    ::
4796    ++  tore
4797      ^-  rock:tire
4798      %-  ~(run by dos.rom)
4799      |=  =dojo
4800      [liv.dom.dojo ~(key by wic.dom.dojo)]
4801    ::
4802    ::  [tare] Must be called any time the zest or commits-in-waiting
4803    ::  might have changed for a desk.  +goad calls this uncondtionally,
4804    ::  but if you're not calling +goad, you may need to call this.
4805    ::
4806    ++  tare
4807      ?:  =(~ tyr)
4808        ..abet
4809      =/  tor  tore
4810      =/  waves=(list wave:tire)  (walk:tire tur tor)
4811      ?~  waves
4812        ..abet
```

```
4813      =.  tur  tor
4814      %-  emil
4815      %-  zing
4816      %+  turn  ~(tap in tyr)
4817      |=  =duct
4818      ^-  (list move)
4819      %+  turn  waves
4820      |=  =wave:tire
4821      ^-  move
4822      [duct %give %tire %| wave]
4823      --
4824    --
4825    ::::::::::::::::::::::::::::::::::::::::::::::::::::::::::::::::::::::::::::
4826    ::                    section 4cA, filesystem vane
4827    ::
4828    ::  This is the arvo interface vane.  Our formal state is a `++raft`, which
4829    ::  has five components:
4830    ::
4831    ::  --  `rom` is the state for all local desks.
4832    ::  --  `hoy` is the state for all foreign desks.
4833    ::  --  `ran` is the global, hash-addressed object store.
4834    ::  --  `mon` is the set of mount points in unix.
4835    ::  --  `hez` is the duct to the unix sync.
4836    ::
4837    ::::::::::::::::::::::::::::::::::::::::::::::::::::::::::::::::::::::::::::
4838    =|                                              ::  instrument state
4839        $:  ver=%14                                 ::  vane version
4840            ruf=raft                                ::  revision tree
4841        ==                                          ::
4842    |=  [now=@da eny=@uvJ rof=roof]                 ::  current invocation
4843    ~%  %clay-top  ..part  ~
4844    |%                                              ::
4845    ++  call                                        ::  handle request
4846      ~/  %clay-call
4847      |=  $:  hen=duct
4848              dud=(unit goof)
4849              wrapped-task=(hobo task)
4850          ==
4851      ^-  [(list move) _..^$]
4852      ::
4853      =/  req=task  ((harden task) wrapped-task)
4854      ::
4855      ::  TODO handle error notifications
4856      ::
4857      ?^  dud
4858        [[[hen %slip %d %flog %crud [-.req tang.u.dud]] ~] ..^$]
4859      ::
4860      ?-    -.req
4861          %boat
4862        :_  ..^$
4863        [hen %give %hill (turn ~(tap by mon.ruf) head)]~
4864      ::
4865          %cred
4866        =.  cez.ruf
4867          ?~  cew.req  (~(del by cez.ruf) nom.req)
4868          (~(put by cez.ruf) nom.req cew.req)
4869        ::  wake all desks, a request may have been affected.
4870        =|  mos=(list move)
```

```
4871    =/  des  ~(tap in ~(key by dos.rom.ruf))
4872    |-
4873    ?~  des  [[[hen %give %done ~] mos] ..^^$]
4874    =/  den  ((de now rof hen ruf) our i.des)
4875    =^  mor  ruf
4876      =<  abet:wake                                    ::  [wake] >
4877      ?:  ?=(^ cew.req)  den
4878      (forget-crew:den nom.req)
4879    $(des t.des, mos (weld mos mor))
4880    ::
4881        %crew
4882    [[hen %give %cruz cez.ruf]~ ..^$]
4883    ::
4884        %crow
4885    =/  des  ~(tap by dos.rom.ruf)
4886    =|  rus=(map desk [r=regs w=regs])
4887    |^
4888      ?~  des  [[hen %give %croz rus]~ ..^^$]
4889      =+  per=(filter-rules per.q.i.des)
4890      =+  pew=(filter-rules pew.q.i.des)
4891      =?  rus  |(?=(^ per) ?=(^ pew))
4892        (~(put by rus) p.i.des per pew)
4893      $(des t.des)
4894    ::
4895    ++  filter-rules
4896      |=  pes=regs
4897      ^+  pes
4898      =-  (~(gas in *regs) -)
4899      %+  skim  ~(tap by pes)
4900      |=  [p=path r=rule]
4901      (~(has in who.r) |+nom.req)
4902    --
4903    ::
4904        %drop
4905    ~&  %clay-idle
4906    [~ ..^$]
4907    ::
4908        %info
4909    ?:  ?=(%| -.dit.req)
4910      =/  bel=@tas         p.dit.req
4911      =/  aey=(unit aeon)  q.dit.req
4912      =^  mos  ruf
4913        =/  den  ((de now rof hen ruf) our des.req)
4914        abet:(label:den bel aey)
4915      [mos ..^$]
4916    =/  [deletes=(set path) changes=(map path cage)]
4917      =/  =soba  p.dit.req
4918      =|  deletes=(set path)
4919      =|  changes=(map path cage)
4920      |-  ^+  [deletes changes]
4921      ?~  soba
4922        [deletes changes]
4923      ?-  -.q.i.soba
4924        %del  $(soba t.soba, deletes (~(put in deletes) p.i.soba))
4925        %ins  $(soba t.soba, changes (~(put by changes) [p p.q]:i.soba))
4926        %mut  $(soba t.soba, changes (~(put by changes) [p p.q]:i.soba))
4927        %dif  ~|(%dif-not-implemented !!)
4928      ==
```

```
4929        =^  mos  ruf
4930          =/  den  ((de now rof hen ruf) our des.req)
4931          abet:(info:den deletes changes)
4932        [mos ..^$]
4933      ::
4934          %init
4935        [~ ..^$(hun.rom.ruf hen)]
4936      ::
4937          %into
4938        =.  hez.ruf  `hen
4939        =+  bem=(~(get by mon.ruf) des.req)
4940        ?:  &(?=(~ bem) !=(%$ des.req))
4941          ~|([%bad-mount-point-from-unix des.req] !!)
4942        =/  bem=beam
4943            ?^  bem
4944              u.bem
4945            [[our %base %ud 1] ~]  ::  TODO: remove this fallback?
4946        =/  dos  (~(get by dos.rom.ruf) q.bem)
4947        ?~  dos
4948          !!  ::  fire next in queue
4949        =^  mos  ruf
4950          =/  den  ((de now rof hen ruf) our q.bem)
4951          abet:(into:den s.bem all.req fis.req)
4952        [mos ..^$]
4953      ::
4954          %merg                                        ::  direct state up
4955        ?:  =(%$ des.req)
4956          ~|(%merg-no-desk !!)
4957        ?.  ((sane %tas) des.req)
4958          ~|([%merg-bad-desk-name des.req] !!)
4959        =^  mos  ruf
4960          =/  den  ((de now rof hen ruf) our des.req)
4961          abet:(start-merge:den her.req dem.req cas.req how.req)
4962        [mos ..^$]
4963      ::
4964          %fuse
4965        ?:  =(%$ des.req)
4966          ~|(%fuse-no-desk !!)
4967        ?.  ((sane %tas) des.req)
4968          ~|([%fuse-bad-desk-name des.req] !!)
4969        =^  mos  ruf
4970          =/  den  ((de now rof hen ruf) our des.req)
4971          abet:(start-fuse:den bas.req con.req)
4972        [mos ..^$]
4973      ::
4974          %mont
4975        =.  hez.ruf  ?^(hez.ruf hez.ruf `[[%$ %sync ~] ~])
4976        =^  mos  ruf
4977          =/  den  ((de now rof hen ruf) p.bem.req q.bem.req)
4978          abet:(mount:den pot.req r.bem.req s.bem.req)
4979        [mos ..^$]
4980      ::
4981          %dirk
4982        ?~  hez.ruf
4983          ~&  %no-sync-duct
4984          [~ ..^$]
4985        ?.  (~(has by mon.ruf) pot.req)
4986          ~&  [%not-mounted pot.req]
```

```
4987          [~ ..^$]
4988          [~[[u.hez.ruf %give %dirk pot.req]] ..^$]
4989     ::
4990          %ogre
4991      ?:  =(~ hez.ruf)
4992      ~&  %no-sync-duct
4993          [~ ..^$]
4994      =*  pot  pot.req
4995      =/  bem=(list [pot=term beam])
4996        ?@  pot
4997          ?~  got=(~(get by mon.ruf) pot)
4998            ~&  [%not-mounted pot]
4999              ~
5000          [pot u.got]~
5001      %+  skim  ~(tap by mon.ruf)
5002      |=  [=term =beam]
5003      =(pot beam)
5004    |-  ^-  [(list move) _..^^$]
5005    ?~  bem
5006        [~ ..^^$]
5007    =^  moves-1  ruf
5008      =/  den  ((de now rof hen ruf) p.i.bem q.i.bem)
5009      abet:(unmount:den pot.i.bem r.i.bem s.i.bem)
5010    =^  moves-2  ..^^$  $(bem t.bem)
5011    [(weld moves-1 moves-2) ..^^$]
5012     ::
5013          %park
5014      ?.  ((sane %tas) des.req)
5015        ~|([%park-bad-desk des.req] !!)
5016      =^  mos  ruf
5017        =/  den  ((de now rof hen ruf) our des.req)
5018        abet:(park:den | & [yok ran]:req)
5019      [mos ..^$]
5020     ::
5021          %pork
5022      =/  [syd=desk =yoki]  (need pud.ruf)
5023      =.  pud.ruf  ~
5024      =^  mos  ruf
5025        =/  den  ((de now rof hen ruf) our syd)
5026        abet:(park:den & & yoki *rang)
5027      [mos ..^$]
5028     ::
5029          %prep
5030      [~ ..^$(lat.ran.ruf (~(uni by lat.req) lat.ran.ruf))]
5031     ::
5032          %perm
5033      =^  mos  ruf
5034        =/  den  ((de now rof hen ruf) our des.req)
5035        abet:(perm:den pax.req rit.req)
5036      [mos ..^$]
5037     ::
5038          %rein
5039      =^  m1  ruf
5040        =/  den  ((de now rof hen ruf) our des.req)
5041        abet:(set-rein:den ren.req)
5042      =^  m2  ruf  abet:goad:(lu now rof hen ruf)          ::  [goad] >
5043      [(weld m1 m2) ..^$]
5044     ::
```

```
5045        %stir
5046    ?+    arg.req  ~|(%strange-stir !!)
5047        [%verb @]   [~ ..^$(veb.bug.ruf +.arg.req)]
5048        [%mass @]   [~ ..^$(mas.bug.ruf +.arg.req)]
5049        [%goad ~]
5050    =^  mos  ruf  abet:goad:(lu now rof hen ruf)
5051    [mos ..^$]
5052    ::
5053        [%rise =desk =dude:gall on=(unit ?)]
5054    =^  m1  ruf
5055      =/  den  ((de now rof hen ruf) our desk.arg.req)
5056      abet:(rise:den dude.arg.req on.arg.req)
5057    =^  m2  ruf  abet:goad:(lu now rof hen ruf)        ::  [goad] <
5058    [(weld m1 m2) ..^$]
5059    ::
5060        [%stay =desk ver=(unit weft)]
5061    =^  moves  ruf
5062      =/  den  ((de now rof hen ruf) our desk.arg.req)
5063      abet:(stay:den ver.arg.req)
5064    [moves ..^$]
5065    ::
5066        [%trim ~]
5067    =:    fad.ruf       *flow
5068          dos.rom.ruf
5069        %-  ~(run by dos.rom.ruf)
5070        |=  =dojo
5071        dojo(fod.dom *flue)
5072        ::
5073          hoy.ruf
5074        %-  ~(run by hoy.ruf)
5075        |=  =rung
5076        %=      rung
5077          rus
5078        %-  ~(run by rus.rung)
5079        |=  =rede
5080        rede(fod.dom *flue)
5081        ==
5082      ==
5083    [~ ..^$]
5084    ::
5085        [%fine ~]
5086    ~&  "clay: resetting fine state.  old:"
5087    ~&  sad.ruf
5088    `..^$(sad.ruf ~)
5089    ==
5090  ::
5091    %tire
5092    ?~  p.req
5093    =.  tyr.ruf  (~(del in tyr.ruf) hen)
5094    `..^$
5095  =.  tyr.ruf  (~(put in tyr.ruf) hen)
5096  :_  ..^$
5097  [hen %give %tire %& tore:(lu now rof hen ruf)]~
5098  ::
5099    %tomb  (tomb-clue:tomb hen clue.req)
5100    %trim  [~ ..^$]
5101    %vega
5102  ::  wake all desks, then send pending notifications
```

```
5103      ::
5104      =^  wake-moves  ..^$
5105        =/  desks=(list [=ship =desk])
5106          %+  welp
5107            (turn ~(tap by dos.rom.ruf) |=([=desk *] [our desk]))
5108          %-  zing
5109          %+  turn  ~(tap by hoy.ruf)
5110          |=  [=ship =rung]
5111          %+  turn  ~(tap by rus.rung)
5112          |=  [=desk *]
5113          [ship desk]
5114        |-  ^+  [*(list move) ..^^$]
5115        ?~  desks
5116          [~ ..^^$]
5117        =^  moves-1  ..^^$  $(desks t.desks)
5118        =^  moves-2  ruf  abet:wake:((de now rof hen ruf) [ship desk]:i.desks)
5119        [(weld moves-1 moves-2) ..^^$]
5120      [wake-moves ..^$]
5121      ::
5122        ?(%warp %werp)
5123      :: capture whether this read is on behalf of another ship
5124      ::  for permissions enforcement
5125      ::
5126      =^  for  req
5127        ?:  ?=(%warp -.req)
5128          [~ req]
5129        ::  ?:  =(our who.req)
5130        ::    [~ [%warp wer.req rif.req]]
5131        :-  ?:(=(our who.req) ~ `[who.req -.rif.req])
5132        [%warp wer.req riff.rif.req]
5133      ::
5134      ?>  ?=(%warp -.req)
5135      =*  rif  rif.req
5136      =^  mos  ruf
5137        =/  den  ((de now rof hen ruf) wer.req p.rif)
5138        =<  abet
5139        ?~  q.rif
5140          cancel-request:den
5141        (start-request:den for u.q.rif)
5142      [mos ..^$]
5143      ::
5144        %wick
5145      =^  mos  ruf
5146        abet:wick:((de now rof hen ruf) our %base)          ::  [wick]
5147      [mos ..^$]
5148      ::
5149        %zeal
5150      =^  m1  ruf
5151        =|  mos=(list move)
5152        |-  ^+  [mos ruf]
5153        ?~  lit.req
5154          [mos ruf]
5155        =/  den  ((de now rof hen ruf) our desk.i.lit.req)
5156        =^  mos-new  ruf  abet:(set-zest:den zest.i.lit.req)
5157        $(mos (weld mos mos-new), lit.req t.lit.req)
5158      =^  m2  ruf
5159        abet:wick:((de now rof hen ruf) our %base)
5160      =^  m3  ruf  abet:goad:(lu now rof hen ruf)
```

```
5161       [:(weld m1 m2 m3) ..^$]
5162   ::
5163         %zest
5164       =^  m1  ruf
5165       =/  den  ((de now rof hen ruf) our des.req)
5166       ::  [wick] could be suspending the last blocking desk
5167       ::
5168       abet:wick:(set-zest:den liv.req)
5169       =^  m2  ruf  abet:goad:(lu now rof hen ruf)
5170       [(weld m1 m2) ..^$]
5171   ::
5172         %plea
5173       =*  her  ship.req
5174       =*  pax  path.plea.req
5175       =*  res  payload.plea.req
5176       ::
5177       ?:  ?=([%backfill *] pax)
5178         =+  ;;(=fill res)
5179         =^  mos  ruf
5180         =/  den  ((de now rof hen ruf) our desk.fill)
5181         abet:(give-backfill:den -.fill lobe.fill)
5182       [[[hen %give %done ~] mos] ..^$]
5183       ?>  ?=([%question *] pax)
5184       =+  ryf=;;(riff-any res)
5185       :_  ..^$
5186       :~  [hen %give %done ~]
5187         =/  =wire
5188           [%foreign-warp (scot %p her) t.pax]
5189         [hen %pass wire %c %werp her our ryf]
5190       ==
5191     ==
5192   ::
5193 ++  load
5194   =>  |%
5195       +$  raft-any
5196         $%  [%14 raft-14]
5197             [%13 raft-13]
5198             [%12 raft-12]
5199             [%11 raft-11]
5200             [%10 raft-10]
5201             [%9 raft-9]
5202             [%8 raft-8]
5203             [%7 raft-7]
5204             [%6 raft-6]
5205         ==
5206       ::  We redefine the latest raft with * for the the ford caches.
5207       ::  +clear-cache upgrades to +raft
5208       ::
5209       +$  raft-14
5210         $+  raft-14
5211         $:  rom=room-13
5212             hoy=(map ship rung-14)
5213             ran=rang
5214             fad=*
5215             mon=(map term beam)
5216             hez=(unit duct)
5217             cez=(map @ta crew)
5218             tyr=(set duct)
```

```
5219              tur=rock:tire
5220              pud=(unit [=desk =yoki])
5221              sad=(map ship @da)
5222              bug=[veb=@ mas=@]
5223          ==
5224      +$  rung-14
5225        $:  rus=(map desk rede-14)
5226          ==
5227      +$  rede-14
5228        $:  lim=@da
5229            ref=(unit rind-14)
5230            qyx=cult
5231            dom=dome-13
5232            per=regs
5233            pew=regs
5234            fiz=melt
5235          ==
5236      +$  rind-14
5237        $:  nix=@ud
5238            bom=(map @ud update-state)
5239            fod=(map duct @ud)
5240            haw=(map mood (unit cage))
5241          ==
5242      ::
5243      +$  raft-13
5244        $+  raft-13
5245        $:  rom=room-13
5246            hoy=(map ship rung-13)
5247            ran=rang
5248            fad=*
5249            mon=(map term beam)
5250            hez=(unit duct)
5251            cez=(map @ta crew)
5252            tyr=(set duct)
5253            tur=rock:tire
5254            pud=(unit [=desk =yoki])
5255            bug=[veb=@ mas=@]
5256          ==
5257      +$  room-13
5258        $:  hun=duct
5259            dos=(map desk dojo-13)
5260          ==
5261      +$  dojo-13
5262        $:  qyx=cult
5263            dom=dome-13
5264            per=regs
5265            pew=regs
5266            fiz=melt
5267          ==
5268      +$  dome-13
5269        $:  let=aeon
5270            hit=(map aeon tako)
5271            lab=(map @tas aeon)
5272            tom=(map tako norm)
5273            nor=norm
5274            mim=(map path mime)
5275            fod=*
5276            wic=(map weft yoki)
```

```
5277              liv=zest
5278              ren=rein
5279          ==
5280      +$  rung-13
5281        $:  rus=(map desk rede-13)
5282          ==
5283      +$  rede-13
5284        $:  lim=@da
5285            ref=(unit rind-11)
5286            qyx=cult
5287            dom=dome-13
5288            per=regs
5289            pew=regs
5290            fiz=melt
5291          ==
5292      ::
5293      +$  raft-12
5294        $+  raft-12
5295        $:  rom=room-11
5296            hoy=(map ship rung-11)
5297            ran=rang
5298            fad=*
5299            mon=(map term beam)
5300            hez=(unit duct)
5301            cez=(map @ta crew)
5302            pud=(unit [=desk =yoki])
5303            bug=[veb=@ mas=@]
5304          ==
5305      +$  raft-11
5306        $+  raft-11
5307        $:  rom=room-11
5308            hoy=(map ship rung-11)
5309            ran=rang
5310            fad=*
5311            mon=(map term beam)
5312            hez=(unit duct)
5313            cez=(map @ta crew)
5314            pud=(unit [=desk =yoki])
5315          ==
5316      +$  room-11
5317        $+  room-11
5318        $:  hun=duct
5319            dos=(map desk dojo-11)
5320          ==
5321      +$  dojo-11
5322        $+  dojo-11
5323        $:  qyx=cult
5324            dom=dome-11
5325            per=regs
5326            pew=regs
5327            fiz=melt
5328          ==
5329      +$  dome-11
5330        $+  dome-11
5331        $:  let=aeon
5332            hit=(map aeon tako)
5333            lab=(map @tas aeon)
5334            tom=(map tako norm)
```

```
5335              nor=norm
5336              mim=(map path mime)
5337              fod=*
5338          ==
5339      +$  rung-11
5340        $+  rung-11
5341        $:  rus=(map desk rede-11)
5342          ==
5343      +$  rede-11
5344        $+  rede-11
5345        $:  lim=@da
5346            ref=(unit rind-11)
5347            qyx=cult
5348            dom=dome-11
5349            per=regs
5350            pew=regs
5351            fiz=melt
5352          ==
5353      +$  rind-11
5354        $+  rind-11
5355        $:  nix=@ud
5356            bom=(map @ud update-state-11)
5357            fod=(map duct @ud)
5358            haw=(map mood (unit cage))
5359          ==
5360      +$  update-state-11
5361        $+  update-state-11
5362        $:  =duct
5363            =rave
5364            need=(list lobe)
5365            nako=(qeu (unit nako))
5366            busy=_|
5367          ==
5368      +$  raft-10
5369        $+  raft-10
5370        $:  rom=room-10
5371            hoy=(map ship rung-10)
5372            ran=rang-10
5373            mon=(map term beam)
5374            hez=(unit duct)
5375            cez=(map @ta crew)
5376            pud=(unit [=desk =yoki])
5377            dist-upgraded=_|
5378          ==
5379      +$  rang-10
5380        $:  hut=(map tako yaki)
5381            lat=(map lobe blob-10)
5382          ==
5383      +$  blob-10
5384        $%  [%delta p=lobe q=[p=mark q=lobe] r=page]
5385            [%direct p=lobe q=page]
5386            [%dead p=lobe ~]
5387          ==
5388      +$  room-10
5389        $:  hun=duct
5390            dos=(map desk dojo-10)
5391          ==
5392      +$  dojo-10
```

```
5393        $:  qyx=cult-10
5394            dom=dome-10
5395            per=regs
5396            pew=regs
5397            fiz=melt-10
5398        ==
5399    +$  dome-10
5400        $:  ank=ankh-10
5401            let=aeon
5402            hit=(map aeon tako)
5403            lab=(map @tas aeon)
5404            mim=(map path mime)
5405            fod=*
5406        ==
5407    +$  ankh-10  (axal [p=lobe q=cage])
5408    +$  rung-10
5409        $:  rus=(map desk rede-10)
5410        ==
5411    +$  rede-10
5412        $:  lim=@da
5413            ref=(unit rind-10)
5414            qyx=cult-10
5415            dom=dome-10
5416            per=regs
5417            pew=regs
5418            fiz=melt-10
5419        ==
5420    +$  rind-10
5421        $:  nix=@ud
5422            bom=(map @ud update-state-10)
5423            fod=(map duct @ud)
5424            haw=(map mood (unit cage))
5425        ==
5426    +$  update-state-10
5427        $:  =duct
5428            =rave
5429            have=(map lobe blob-10)
5430            need=(list lobe)
5431            nako=(qeu (unit nako-10))
5432            busy=_|
5433        ==
5434    +$  nako-10
5435        $:  gar=(map aeon tako)
5436            let=aeon
5437            lar=(set yaki)
5438            bar=(set blob-10)
5439        ==
5440    +$  melt-10
5441    [bas=beak con=(list [beak germ]) sto=(map beak (unit dome-clay-10))]
5442    +$  dome-clay-10
5443        $:  ank=ankh-10
5444            let=@ud
5445            hit=(map @ud tako)
5446            lab=(map @tas @ud)
5447        ==
5448    +$  cult-10  (jug wove-10 duct)
5449    +$  wove-10  [for=(unit [=ship ver=@ud]) =rove-10]
5450    +$  rove-10
```

```
5451      $%  [%sing =mood]
5452          [%next =mood aeon=(unit aeon) =cach-10]
5453          $:  %mult
5454              =mool
5455              aeon=(unit aeon)
5456              old-cach=(map [=care =path] cach-10)
5457              new-cach=(map [=care =path] cach-10)
5458          ==
5459          [%many track=? =moat lobes=(map path lobe)]
5460      ==
5461  +$  cach-10  (unit (unit (each cage lobe)))
5462  +$  raft-9
5463    $+  raft-9
5464    $:  rom=room-10
5465        hoy=(map ship rung-10)
5466        ran=rang-10
5467        mon=(map term beam)
5468        hez=(unit duct)
5469        cez=(map @ta crew)
5470        pud=(unit [=desk =yoki])
5471    ==
5472  +$  raft-8
5473    $+  raft-8
5474    $:  rom=room-8
5475        hoy=(map ship rung-8)
5476        ran=rang-10
5477        mon=(map term beam)
5478        hez=(unit duct)
5479        cez=(map @ta crew)
5480        pud=(unit [=desk =yoki])
5481    ==
5482  +$  room-8
5483    $:  hun=duct
5484        dos=(map desk dojo-8)
5485    ==
5486  +$  rung-8
5487    $:  rus=(map desk rede-8)
5488    ==
5489  +$  dojo-8
5490    $:  qyx=cult-10
5491        dom=dome-8
5492        per=regs
5493        pew=regs
5494        fiz=melt-10
5495    ==
5496  +$  dome-8
5497    $:  ank=ankh-10
5498        let=aeon
5499        hit=(map aeon tako)
5500        lab=(map @tas aeon)
5501        mim=(map path mime)
5502        fod=*
5503        fer=*  ::  reef cache, obsolete
5504    ==
5505  +$  rede-8
5506    $:  lim=@da
5507        ref=(unit rind-10)
5508        qyx=cult-10
```

```
5509            dom=dome-8
5510            per=regs
5511            pew=regs
5512            fiz=melt-10
5513          ==
5514      +$  raft-7
5515        $+  raft-7
5516        $:  rom=room-7
5517            hoy=(map ship rung-7)
5518            ran=rang-10
5519            mon=(map term beam)
5520            hez=(unit duct)
5521            cez=(map @ta crew)
5522            pud=(unit [=desk =yoki])
5523          ==
5524      +$  room-7
5525        $:  hun=duct
5526            dos=(map desk dojo-7)
5527          ==
5528      +$  rung-7
5529        $:  rus=(map desk rede-7)
5530          ==
5531      +$  dojo-7
5532        $:  qyx=cult-10
5533            dom=dome-8
5534            per=regs
5535            pew=regs
5536          ==
5537      +$  rede-7
5538        $:  lim=@da
5539            ref=(unit rind-10)
5540            qyx=cult-10
5541            dom=dome-8
5542            per=regs
5543            pew=regs
5544          ==
5545      +$  raft-6
5546        $+  raft-6
5547        $:  rom=room-6
5548            hoy=(map ship rung-6)
5549            ran=rang-10
5550            mon=(map term beam)
5551            hez=(unit duct)
5552            cez=(map @ta crew)
5553            pud=(unit [=desk =yoki])
5554          ==
5555      +$  room-6  [hun=duct dos=(map desk dojo-6)]
5556      +$  dojo-6
5557        $:  qyx=cult-10
5558            dom=dome-6
5559            per=regs
5560            pew=regs
5561          ==
5562      +$  dome-6
5563        $:  ank=ankh-10
5564            let=aeon
5565            hit=(map aeon tako)
5566            lab=(map @tas aeon)
```

```
5567              mim=(map path mime)
5568              fod=*
5569              fer=*
5570          ==
5571      +$  rung-6
5572        $:  rus=(map desk rede-6)
5573        ==
5574      +$  rede-6
5575        $:  lim=@da
5576            ref=(unit rind-10)
5577            qyx=cult-10
5578            dom=dome-6
5579            per=regs
5580            pew=regs
5581        ==
5582      --
5583  |=  old=raft-any
5584  |^
5585  =?  old  ?=(%6 -.old)    7+(raft-6-to-7 +.old)
5586  =?  old  ?=(%7 -.old)    8+(raft-7-to-8 +.old)
5587  =?  old  ?=(%8 -.old)    9+(raft-8-to-9 +.old)
5588  =?  old  ?=(%9 -.old)    10+(raft-9-to-10 +.old)
5589  =?  old  ?=(%10 -.old)   11+(raft-10-to-11 +.old)
5590  =?  old  ?=(%11 -.old)   12+(raft-11-to-12 +.old)
5591  =?  old  ?=(%12 -.old)   13+(raft-12-to-13 +.old)
5592  =?  old  ?=(%13 -.old)   14+(raft-13-to-14 +.old)
5593  ?>  ?=(%14 -.old)
5594  ..^^$(ruf (clear-cache +.old))
5595  ::
5596  :: We clear the ford cache so we don't have to know how to upgrade
5597  :: the types, which are complicated and eg contravariant in +hoon.
5598  :: Also, many of the results would be different if zuse is different.
5599  ::
5600  ++  clear-cache
5601    |=  raf=raft-14
5602    ^-  raft
5603    %=    raf
5604        fad  *flow
5605        dos.rom
5606      %-  ~(run by dos.rom.raf)
5607      |=  doj=dojo-13
5608      ^-  dojo
5609      doj(fod.dom *flue)
5610    ::
5611        hoy
5612      %-  ~(run by hoy.raf)
5613      |=  =rung-14
5614      %-  ~(run by rus.rung-14)
5615      |=  =rede-14
5616      ^-  rede
5617      rede-14(dom dom.rede-14(fod *flue))
5618    ==
5619  :: +raft-6-to-7: delete stale ford caches (they could all be invalid)
5620  ::
5621  ++  raft-6-to-7
5622    |=  raf=raft-6
5623    ^-  raft-7
5624    %=    raf
```

```
5625          dos.rom
5626      %-  ~(run by dos.rom.raf)
5627      |=  doj=dojo-6
5628      ^-  dojo-7
5629      doj(fod.dom **)
5630    ::
5631          hoy
5632      %-  ~(run by hoy.raf)
5633      |=  =rung-6
5634      %-  ~(run by rus.rung-6)
5635      |=  =rede-6
5636      rede-6(dom dom.rede-6(fod **))
5637    ==
5638  ::  +raft-7-to-8: create bunted melts in each dojo/rede
5639  ::
5640  ++  raft-7-to-8
5641    |=  raf=raft-7
5642    ^-  raft-8
5643    %=  raf
5644          dos.rom
5645      %-  ~(run by dos.rom.raf)
5646      |=  doj=dojo-7
5647      ^-  dojo-8
5648      [qyx.doj dom.doj per.doj pew.doj *melt-10]
5649    ::
5650          hoy
5651      %-  ~(run by hoy.raf)
5652      |=  =rung-7
5653      %-  ~(run by rus.rung-7)
5654      |=  r=rede-7
5655      ^-  rede-8
5656      [lim.r ref.r qyx.r dom.r per.r pew.r *melt-10]
5657    ==
5658  ::  +raft-8-to-9: remove reef cache
5659  ::
5660  ++  raft-8-to-9
5661    |=  raf=raft-8
5662    ^-  raft-9
5663    %=  raf
5664          dos.rom
5665      %-  ~(run by dos.rom.raf)
5666      |=  =dojo-8
5667      ^-  dojo-10
5668      =/  dom  dom.dojo-8
5669      dojo-8(dom [ank.dom let.dom hit.dom lab.dom mim.dom *flow])
5670    ::
5671          hoy
5672      %-  ~(run by hoy.raf)
5673      |=  =rung-8
5674      %-  ~(run by rus.rung-8)
5675      |=  =rede-8
5676      ^-  rede-10
5677      =/  dom  dom.rede-8
5678      rede-8(dom [ank.dom let.dom hit.dom lab.dom mim.dom *flow])
5679    ==
5680  ::  +raft-9-to-10: add .dist-upgraded
5681  ::
5682  ++  raft-9-to-10
```

```
5683      |=  raf=raft-9
5684      ^-  raft-10
5685    raf(pud [pud.raf dist-upgraded=|])
5686  ::
5687  ::    +raft-10-to-11:
5688  ::
5689  ::      add tom and nor to dome
5690  ::      remove parent-mark from delta blobs
5691  ::      change blobs to pages
5692  ::      remove have from update-state
5693  ::      remove bar from nako
5694  ::      remove ankh
5695  ::      set cases in mon to ud+0
5696  ::      add fad
5697  ::      change fod type in dom
5698  ::      change bom type in dom
5699  ::
5700  ++  raft-10-to-11
5701    |=  raf=raft-10
5702    |^
5703    ^-  raft-11
5704    %=    raf
5705        dos.rom
5706      %-  ~(run by dos.rom.raf)
5707      |=  =dojo-10
5708      ^-  dojo-11
5709      %=    dojo-10
5710          fiz  *melt
5711          qyx  (cult-10-to-cult qyx.dojo-10)
5712          dom
5713        :*  let.dom.dojo-10
5714            hit.dom.dojo-10
5715            lab.dom.dojo-10
5716            ~
5717            *norm
5718            mim.dom.dojo-10
5719            [~ ~]
5720        ==
5721      ==
5722    ::
5723        hoy
5724      %-  ~(run by hoy.raf)
5725      |=  =rung-10
5726      %-  ~(run by rus.rung-10)
5727      |=  =rede-10
5728      ^-  rede-11
5729      %=    rede-10
5730          fiz      *melt
5731          qyx      (cult-10-to-cult qyx.rede-10)
5732          dom
5733        :*  let.dom.rede-10
5734            hit.dom.rede-10
5735            lab.dom.rede-10
5736            ~
5737            *norm
5738            mim.dom.rede-10
5739            [~ ~]
5740        ==
```

```
5741          ::
5742            ref
5743        ?~  ref.rede-10
5744            ~
5745        %=      ref.rede-10
5746            bom.u
5747          %-  ~(run by bom.u.ref.rede-10)
5748          |=  =update-state-10
5749          ^-  update-state-11
5750          %=      update-state-10
5751             |2
5752          ^-  [(list lobe) (qeu (unit nako)) _|]
5753          %=      |3.update-state-10
5754             nako
5755            %-  ~(gas to *(qeu (unit nako)))
5756            %+  turn  ~(tap to nako.update-state-10)
5757            |=  nak=(unit nako-10)
5758            ?~  nak  ~
5759            `u.nak(bar ~)
5760          ==
5761        ==
5762      ==
5763    ==
5764    ::
5765      lat.ran
5766    %-  ~(gas by *(map lobe page))
5767    %+  murn  ~(tap by lat.ran.raf)
5768    |=  [=lobe =blob-10]
5769    ^-  (unit [^lobe page])
5770    ?-  -.blob-10
5771      %delta  ((slog 'clay: tombstoning delta!' ~) ~)
5772      %dead   ~
5773      %direct  `[lobe q.blob-10]
5774    ==
5775    ::
5776      |3
5777    ^+  |3:*raft-11
5778    :-  *flow
5779    %=  |3.raf
5780      mon  (~(run by mon.raf) |=(=beam beam(r ud+0)))
5781      |3  pud.raf
5782    ==
5783  ==
5784  ::
5785  ++  cult-10-to-cult
5786    |=  qyx=cult-10
5787    ^-  cult
5788    =/  qux=(list [=wove-10 ducts=(set duct)])  ~(tap by qyx)
5789    %-  malt
5790    |-  ^-  (list [wove (set duct)])
5791    ?~  qux
5792      ~
5793    :_  $(qux t.qux)
5794    %=  i.qux
5795      rove-10.wove-10
5796      ?-    -.rove-10.wove-10.i.qux
5797        %sing  rove-10.wove-10.i.qux
5798        %many  rove-10.wove-10.i.qux
```

```
5683      |=  raf=raft-9
5684      ^-  raft-10
5685    raf(pud [pud.raf dist-upgraded=|])
5686    ::
5687    ::  +raft-10-to-11:
5688    ::
5689    ::    add tom and nor to dome
5690    ::    remove parent-mark from delta blobs
5691    ::    change blobs to pages
5692    ::    remove have from update-state
5693    ::    remove bar from nako
5694    ::    remove ankh
5695    ::    set cases in mon to ud+0
5696    ::    add fad
5697    ::    change fod type in dom
5698    ::    change bom type in dom
5699    ::
5700    ++  raft-10-to-11
5701      |=  raf=raft-10
5702      |^
5703      ^-  raft-11
5704      %=    raf
5705          dos.rom
5706      %-  ~(run by dos.rom.raf)
5707      |=  =dojo-10
5708      ^-  dojo-11
5709      %=    dojo-10
5710          fiz  *melt
5711          qyx  (cult-10-to-cult qyx.dojo-10)
5712          dom
5713        :*  let.dom.dojo-10
5714            hit.dom.dojo-10
5715            lab.dom.dojo-10
5716            ~
5717            *norm
5718            mim.dom.dojo-10
5719            [~ ~]
5720        ==
5721      ==
5722      ::
5723          hoy
5724      %-  ~(run by hoy.raf)
5725      |=  =rung-10
5726      %-  ~(run by rus.rung-10)
5727      |=  =rede-10
5728      ^-  rede-11
5729      %=    rede-10
5730          fiz     *melt
5731          qyx     (cult-10-to-cult qyx.rede-10)
5732          dom
5733        :*  let.dom.rede-10
5734            hit.dom.rede-10
5735            lab.dom.rede-10
5736            ~
5737            *norm
5738            mim.dom.rede-10
5739            [~ ~]
5740        ==
```

```
    ::
        ref
      ?~  ref.rede-10
        ~
      %=    ref.rede-10
          bom.u
        %-  ~(run by bom.u.ref.rede-10)
        |=  =update-state-10
        ^-  update-state-11
        %=    update-state-10
            |2
          ^-  [(list lobe) (qeu (unit nako)) _|]
          %=    |3.update-state-10
              nako
            %-  ~(gas to *(qeu (unit nako)))
            %+  turn  ~(tap to nako.update-state-10)
            |=  nak=(unit nako-10)
            ?~  nak  ~
            `u.nak(bar ~)
          ==
        ==
      ==
    ==
    ::
        lat.ran
      %-  ~(gas by *(map lobe page))
      %+  murn  ~(tap by lat.ran.raf)
      |=  [=lobe =blob-10]
      ^-  (unit [^lobe page])
      ?-  -.blob-10
        %delta  ((slog 'clay: tombstoning delta!' ~) ~)
        %dead   ~
        %direct  `[lobe q.blob-10]
      ==
    ::
        |3
      ^+  |3:*raft-11
      :-  *flow
      %=  |3.raf
        mon  (~(run by mon.raf) |=(=beam beam(r ud+0)))
        |3   pud.raf
      ==
    ==
    ::
    ++  cult-10-to-cult
      |=  qyx=cult-10
      ^-  cult
      =/  qux=(list [=wove-10 ducts=(set duct)])  ~(tap by qyx)
      %-  malt
      |-  ^-  (list [wove (set duct)])
      ?~  qux
        ~
      :_  $(qux t.qux)
      %=  i.qux
        rove-10.wove-10
        ?-    -.rove-10.wove-10.i.qux
          %sing  rove-10.wove-10.i.qux
          %many  rove-10.wove-10.i.qux
```

```
5799              %next
5800            %=  rove-10.wove-10.i.qux
5801              cach-10  (cach-10-to-cach cach-10.rove-10.wove-10.i.qux)
5802            ==
5803        ::
5804              %mult
5805            %=  rove-10.wove-10.i.qux
5806              old-cach  (caches-10-to-caches old-cach.rove-10.wove-10.i.qux)
5807              new-cach  (caches-10-to-caches new-cach.rove-10.wove-10.i.qux)
5808            ==
5809          ==
5810        ==
5811      ::
5812      ++  cach-10-to-cach
5813        |=  =cach-10
5814        ^-  cach
5815        ?~  cach-10
5816          ~
5817        ?~  u.cach-10
5818          [~ ~]
5819        ?-  -.u.u.cach-10
5820          %&  ``p.u.u.cach-10
5821          %|  ~
5822        ==
5823      ::
5824      ++  caches-10-to-caches
5825        |=  caches-10=(map [=care =path] cach-10)
5826        ^-  (map [=care =path] cach)
5827        (~(run by caches-10) cach-10-to-cach)
5828      --
5829    ::  +raft-11-to-12: add bug
5830    ::
5831    ++  raft-11-to-12
5832      |=  raf=raft-11
5833      ^-  raft-12
5834      raf(pud [pud.raf 0 0])
5835    ::  +raft-12-to-13:
5836    ::
5837    ::    add .liv and .ren to $dome's
5838    ::    add .tyr and .tur to $raft
5839    ::
5840    ++  raft-12-to-13
5841      |=  raf=raft-12
5842      |^  ^-  raft-13
5843      ::  turn on %base desk  ::  TODO handle other desks somehow
5844      ::                      ::  maybe have kiln send one-time list of desks
5845      ::
5846      =;  rof
5847        rof(dos.rom (~(jab by dos.rom.rof) %base |=(d=dojo-13 d(liv.dom %live))))
5848      ^-  raft-13
5849      %=  raf
5850        dos.rom  (~(run by dos.rom.raf) dojo-11-to-13)
5851        hoy      (~(run by hoy.raf) rung-11-to-13)
5852        |6       [&7.raf ~ ~ |7.raf]
5853      ==
5854      ::
5855      ++  dojo-11-to-13
5856        |=  doj=dojo-11
```

```
5857        ^-  dojo-13
5858        doj(dom (dome-11-to-13 dom.doj))
5859      ::
5860    ++  rung-11-to-13
5861      |=  rug=rung-11
5862      ^-  rung-13
5863      rug(rus (~(run by rus.rug) rede-11-to-13))
5864      ::
5865    ++  rede-11-to-13
5866      |=  red=rede-11
5867      ^-  rede-13
5868      red(dom (dome-11-to-13 dom.red))
5869      ::
5870    ++  dome-11-to-13
5871      |=  dom=dome-11
5872      ^-  dome-13
5873      dom(fod [fod.dom ~ liv=%dead ren=~])
5874      --
5875    ::
5876    ::  +raft-13-to-14: add sad, change busy
5877    ::
5878    ++  raft-13-to-14
5879      |=  raf=raft-13
5880      ^-  raft-14
5881      %=    raf
5882        bug  [~ bug.raf]
5883      ::
5884          hoy
5885        %-  ~(run by hoy.raf)
5886        |=  =rung-13
5887        %-  ~(run by rus.rung-13)
5888        |=  =rede-13
5889        ^-  rede-14
5890        %=    rede-13
5891            ref
5892          ?~  ref.rede-13
5893            ~
5894          %=    ref.rede-13
5895              bom.u
5896            %-  ~(run by bom.u.ref.rede-13)
5897            |=  update-state-11
5898            ^-  update-state
5899            =/  busy  ?:(busy `%ames ~)
5900            [duct rave ~ need nako busy]
5901          ==
5902        ==
5903      ==
5904    --
5905  ::
5906  ++  scry                                  ::  inspect
5907    ~/  %clay-scry
5908    ^-  roon
5909    |=  [lyc=gang pov=path car=term bem=beam]
5910    ^-  (unit (unit cage))
5911    =*  scry-loop  $
5912    |^
5913    =*  ren  car
5914    =/  why=shop  &/p.bem
```

```
5915    =*   syd   q.bem
5916    =/   lot=coin  $/r.bem
5917    =*   tyl   s.bem
5918    ::
5919    ?.   ?=(%& -.why)   ~
5920    =*   his   p.why
5921    ::
5922    ?:   &(?=(%x ren) =(tyl //whey))
5923      ``mass+!>(whey)
5924    ::
5925    ::   ~&   scry+[ren `path`[(scot %p his) syd ~(rent co lot) tyl]]
5926    ::   =-   ~&   %scry-done   -
5927    =+   luk=?.(?=(%$ -.lot) ~ ((soft case) p.lot))
5928    ?~   luk   [~ ~]
5929    ?:   =(%$ ren)
5930      [~ ~]
5931    =+   run=((soft care) ren)
5932    ?~   run   [~ ~]
5933    ::TODO  if it ever gets filled properly, pass in the full fur.
5934    ::
5935    =/   for=(unit ship)  ?~(lyc ~ ?~(u.lyc ~ `n.u.lyc))
5936    ?:   &(=(our his) ?=(?(%d %x) ren) =(%$ syd) =([%da now] u.luk))
5937      ?-   ren
5938        %d  (read-buc-d tyl)
5939        %x  (read-buc-x tyl)
5940      ==
5941    =/   den   ((de now rof [/scryduct ~] ruf) his syd)
5942    =/   result  (mule |.(-:(aver:den for u.run u.luk tyl)))
5943    ?:   ?=(%| -.result)
5944      %-  (slog >%clay-scry-fail< p.result)
5945      ~
5946    p.result
5947    ::
5948    ++   read-buc-d
5949      |=  =path
5950      ^-  (unit (unit cage))
5951      ?^  path  ~&(%no-cd-path [~ ~])
5952      [~ ~ %noun !>(~(key by dos.rom.ruf))]
5953    ::
5954    ++   read-buc-x
5955      |=  =path
5956      ^-  (unit (unit cage))
5957      ?~  path
5958        ~
5959      ?+    i.path  ~
5960        %sweep  ``[%sweep !>(sweep)]
5961        %rang   ``[%rang !>(ran.ruf)]
5962        %tomb   ``[%flag !>((tomb t.path))]
5963        %cult   ``[%cult !>((cult t.path))]
5964        %flow   ``[%flow !>(fad.ruf)]
5965        %domes  domes
5966        %tire   ``[%tire !>(tore:(lu now rof *duct ruf))]
5967        %tyre   ``[%tyre !>(tyr.ruf)]
5968      ==
5969    ::
5970    ++   domes
5971      =/   domes
5972        %-  ~(gas by *cone)
```

```
5973        %+  turn  ~(tap by dos.rom.ruf)
5974        |=  [=desk =dojo]
5975        [[our desk] dom.dojo]
5976    =.  domes
5977      %-  ~(uni by domes)
5978      %-  ~(gas by *cone)
5979      ^-  (list [[ship desk] dome])
5980      %-  zing
5981      ^-  (list (list [[ship desk] dome]))
5982      %+  turn  ~(tap by hoy.ruf)
5983      |=  [=ship =rung]
5984      ^-  (list [[^ship desk] dome])
5985      %+  turn  ~(tap by rus.rung)
5986      |=  [=desk =rede]
5987      [[ship desk] dom.rede]
5988    ``[%domes !>(`cone`domes)]
5989  ::
5990  ++  cult
5991    |=  =path
5992    ^-  (set [@p rave])
5993    %-  %~  run  in
5994        %~  key  by
5995        ?~  path  *^cult
5996        qyx:(~(gut by dos.rom.ruf) i.path *dojo)
5997    |=  wove
5998    :-  ship:(fall for [ship=our @ud])
5999    ?-  -.rove
6000      %sing  rove
6001      %next  [%next mood.rove]
6002      %mult  [%mult mool.rove]
6003      %many  [%many [track moat]:rove]
6004    ==
6005  ::
6006  ::  True if file is accessible
6007  ::
6008  ++  tomb
6009    |=  =path
6010    ^-  ?
6011    =/  bem  (de-beam path)
6012    ?~  bem       %|
6013    =/  cay  scry-loop(car %y, bem u.bem)
6014    ?~  cay       %|
6015    ?~  u.cay     %|
6016    =+  !<(=arch q.u.u.cay)
6017    ?~  fil.arch  %|
6018    (~(has by lat.ran.ruf) u.fil.arch)
6019  ::
6020  ::  Check for refcount errors
6021  ::
6022  ++  sweep
6023    ^-  (list [need=@ud have=@ud leak])
6024    =/  marked=(map leak [need=@ud have=@ud])
6025      (~(run by fad.ruf) |=([refs=@ud *] [0 refs]))
6026    =.  marked
6027      =/  items=(list [=leak *])  ~(tap by fad.ruf)
6028      |-  ^+  marked
6029      ?~  items
6030        marked
```

```
6031      =/  deps  ~(tap in deps.leak.i.items)
6032      |-  ^+  marked
6033      ?~  deps
6034        ^$(items t.items)
6035      =.  marked
6036        %+  ~(put by marked)  i.deps
6037        =/  gut  (~(gut by marked) i.deps [0 0])
6038        [+(-.gut) +.gut]
6039      $(deps t.deps)
6040    ::
6041    =/  spills=(list (set leak))
6042      %+  welp
6043        %+  turn  ~(tap by dos.rom.ruf)
6044        |=  [* =dojo]
6045        spill.fod.dom.dojo
6046      %-  zing
6047      %+  turn  ~(tap by hoy.ruf)
6048      |=  [* =rung]
6049      %+  turn  ~(tap by rus.rung)
6050      |=  [* =rede]
6051      spill.fod.dom.rede
6052    ::
6053    =.  marked
6054      |-
6055      ?~  spills
6056        marked
6057      =/  leaks  ~(tap in i.spills)
6058      |-
6059      ?~  leaks
6060        ^$(spills t.spills)
6061      =.  marked
6062        %+  ~(put by marked)  i.leaks
6063        =/  gut  (~(gut by marked) i.leaks [0 0])
6064        [+(-.gut) +.gut]
6065      $(leaks t.leaks)
6066    ::
6067    %+  murn  ~(tap by marked)
6068    |=  [=leak need=@ud have=@ud]
6069    ?:  =(need have)
6070      ~
6071    `u=[need have leak]
6072  --
6073  ::
6074  ::  We clear the ford cache by replacing it with its bunt as a literal,
6075  ::  with its singleton type.  This nests within +flow and +flue without
6076  ::  reference to +type, +hoon, or anything else in the sample of cache
6077  ::  objects.  Otherwise we would be contravariant in those types, which
6078  ::  makes them harder to change.
6079  ::
6080  ++  stay
6081    ^-  raft-any:load
6082    =/  flu  [~ ~]
6083    =+  `flue`flu
6084    =/  flo  ~
6085    =+  `flow`flo
6086    :-  ver
6087    ^-  raft-14:load
6088    %=  ruf
```

```
6089        fad  flo
6090        dos.rom
6091    %-   ~(run by dos.rom.ruf)
6092    |=   =dojo
6093    dojo(fod.dom flu)
6094  ::
6095        hoy
6096    %-   ~(run by hoy.ruf)
6097    |=   =rung
6098    %=      rung
6099          rus
6100      %-   ~(run by rus.rung)
6101      |=   =rede
6102      rede(fod.dom flu)
6103      ==
6104    ==
6105  ::
6106  ++   take                                          ::  accept response
6107  ~/  %clay-take
6108  |=  [tea=wire hen=duct dud=(unit goof) hin=sign]
6109  ^+  [*(list move) ..^$]
6110  ?^  dud
6111    ?+    tea
6112    ~|(%clay-take-dud (mean tang.u.dud))
6113    ::
6114        [%drip ~]
6115    %.  [~ ..^$]
6116    %-  slog
6117    ^-  tang
6118    :*  'clay: drip fail'
6119        [%rose [": " "" ""] 'bail' mote.u.dud ~]
6120        tang.u.dud
6121    ==
6122    ==
6123  ::
6124  ::  pseudo %slip on %drip
6125  ::
6126  ?:  ?=([%drip ~] tea)
6127    ?>  ?=([?(%behn %clay) ?(%writ %wris) *] hin)
6128    [[`move`[hen %give +.hin] ~] ..^$]
6129  ::
6130  ?:  ?=([%lu %load *] tea)
6131    ?>  ?=(%unto +<.hin)
6132    ?>  ?=(%poke-ack -.p.hin)
6133    ?~  p.p.hin
6134      [~ ..^$]
6135    =+  ((slog 'clay: reloading agents failed' u.p.p.hin) ~)
6136    !!
6137  ::
6138  ?:  ?=([%merge @ @ @ @ ~] tea)
6139    ?>  ?=(%writ +<.hin)
6140    =*  syd  i.t.tea
6141    =/  ali-ship  (slav %p i.t.t.tea)
6142    =*  ali-desk  i.t.t.t.tea
6143    =/  germ  (germ i.t.t.t.t.tea)
6144    =^  mos  ruf
6145      =/  den  ((de now rof hen ruf) our syd)
6146      abet:(merge:den ali-ship ali-desk germ p.hin)
```

```
6147        [mos ..^$]
6148      ::
6149      ?:   ?=([%fuse @ @ @ @ ~] tea)
6150        ?>   ?=(%writ +<.hin)
6151        =*   syd   i.t.tea
6152        =/   ali-ship=@p   (slav %p i.t.t.tea)
6153        =*   ali-desk=desk   i.t.t.t.tea
6154        =/   ali-case   (rash i.t.t.t.t.tea nuck:so)
6155        ?>   ?=([%$ *] ali-case)
6156        =^   mos   ruf
6157          =/   den   ((de now rof hen ruf) our syd)
6158          abet:(take-fuse:den [ali-ship ali-desk (case +.ali-case)] p.hin)
6159        [mos ..^$]
6160      ::
6161      ?:   ?=([%park-held @ ~] tea)
6162        ?>   ?=(%wake +<.hin)
6163        =*   syd   i.t.tea
6164        =^   mos   ruf
6165          =/   den   ((de now rof hen ruf) our syd)
6166          abet:(take-park-held:den error.hin)
6167        [mos ..^$]
6168      ::
6169      ?:   ?=([%wick ~] tea)
6170        ?>   ?=(%wake +<.hin)
6171        =^   mos   ruf
6172          =/   den   ((de now rof hen ruf) our %base)
6173          abet:(take-wick:den error.hin)
6174        [mos ..^$]
6175      ::
6176      ?:   ?=([%foreign-warp *] tea)
6177        ?:   ?=(%wris +<.hin)   ~&   %dropping-wris   `..^$
6178        ?>   ?=(%writ +<.hin)
6179        :_   ..^$
6180        [hen %give %boon `(unit rand)`(bind `riot`p.hin rant-to-rand)]~
6181      ::
6182      ?:   ?=([%warp-index @ @ @ ~] tea)
6183        ?+   +<.hin   ~|   %clay-warp-index-strange   !!
6184          %done
6185        ?~   error.hin
6186          [~ ..^$]
6187        ::   TODO better error handling
6188        ::
6189        ~&   %clay-take-warp-index-error^our^tea^tag.u.error.hin
6190        %-   (slog tang.u.error.hin)
6191        [~ ..^$]
6192      ::
6193          %lost
6194        %-   (slog leaf+"clay: lost warp from {<tea>}" ~)
6195        [~ ..^$]
6196      ::
6197          %boon
6198        =/   her=ship     (slav %p i.t.tea)
6199        =/   =desk        (slav %tas i.t.t.tea)
6200        =/   index=@ud    (slav %ud i.t.t.t.tea)
6201        ::
6202        =^   mos   ruf
6203          =+   ;;(res=(unit rand) payload.hin)
6204          =/   den   ((de now rof hen ruf) her desk)
```

```
6205        abet:(take-foreign-answer:den index res)
6206      [mos ..^$]
6207    ==
6208  ::
6209  ?:  ?=([%back-index @ @ @ *] tea)
6210    ?+    +<.hin  ~|  %clay-backfill-index-strange  !!
6211      %done
6212    ?~   error.hin
6213      [~ ..^$]
6214    ::  TODO better error handling
6215    ::
6216    ~&  %clay-take-backfill-index-error^our^tea^tag.u.error.hin
6217    %-  (slog tang.u.error.hin)
6218    [~ ..^$]
6219  ::
6220      %lost
6221    %-  (slog leaf+"clay: lost backfill from {<tea>}" ~)
6222    [~ ..^$]
6223  ::
6224      ?(%boon %tune)
6225    =/  her=ship   (slav %p i.t.tea)
6226    =/  =desk      (slav %tas i.t.t.tea)
6227    =/  index=@ud  (slav %ud i.t.t.t.tea)
6228    ::
6229    =/  fell=(unit fell)
6230      ?:  ?=(%boon +<.hin)  `;;(fell payload.hin)
6231      ?~  roar.hin  ~
6232      ?~  q.dat.u.roar.hin  ~
6233      `[%1 `u.q.dat.u.roar.hin]
6234    ::
6235    =^  mos  ruf
6236      =/  den  ((de now rof hen ruf) her desk)
6237      ?~  fell
6238        ::  We shouldn't get back null on any of the fine requests we
6239        ::  make unless they're out of date
6240        ::
6241        %-  (slog leaf+"clay: got null from {<her>}, falling back to ames" ~)
6242        abet:(retry-with-ames:den %back-index index)
6243      =?  den  ?=(%tune +<.hin)
6244        (cancel-scry-timeout:den index)
6245      abet:abet:(take-backfill:(foreign-update:den index) u.fell)
6246    [mos ..^$]
6247  ::
6248      %wake
6249    ?^  error.hin
6250      [[hen %slip %d %flog %crud %wake u.error.hin]~ ..^$]
6251    =/  her=ship   (slav %p i.t.tea)
6252    =/  =desk      (slav %tas i.t.t.tea)
6253    =/  index=@ud  (slav %ud i.t.t.t.tea)
6254    =^  mos  ruf
6255      =/  den  ((de now rof hen ruf) her desk)
6256      abet:(retry-with-ames:den %back-index index)
6257    [mos ..^$]
6258    ==
6259  ::
6260  ?:  ?=([%seek @ @ ~] tea)
6261    ?+    +<.hin  ~|  %clay-seek-strange  !!
6262      %done
```

```
6263      ?~   error.hin
6264        [~ ..^$]
6265      %-  (slog leaf+"clay: seek nack from {<tea>}" u.error.hin)
6266        [~ ..^$]
6267    ::
6268        %lost
6269      %-  (slog leaf+"clay: lost boon from {<tea>}" ~)
6270        [~ ..^$]
6271    ::
6272        %boon
6273      =+   ;;  =fell  payload.hin
6274      ::
6275      =/  her=ship  (slav %p i.t.tea)
6276      =/  =desk      (slav %tas i.t.t.tea)
6277      =^   mos   ruf
6278        =/  den  ((de now rof hen ruf) her desk)
6279        abet:(take-fell:den fell)
6280      [mos ..^$]
6281    ==
6282  ::
6283  ?:  ?=([%sinks ~] tea)
6284    ?>  ?=(%public-keys +<.hin)
6285    ?.  ?=(%breach -.public-keys-result.hin)
6286      [~ ..^$]
6287    =/  who  who.public-keys-result.hin
6288    ?:  =(our who)
6289      [~ ..^$]
6290    ::  Cancel subscriptions
6291    ::
6292    =/  foreign-desk=(unit rung)
6293      (~(get by hoy.ruf) who)
6294    ?~  foreign-desk
6295      [~ ..^$]
6296    =/  cancel-ducts=(list duct)
6297      %-  zing  ^-  (list (list duct))
6298      %+  turn  ~(tap by rus.u.foreign-desk)
6299      |=  [=desk =rede]
6300      ^-  (list duct)  %-  zing  ^-  (list (list duct))
6301      %+  turn  ~(tap by qyx.rede)
6302      |=  [=wove ducts=(set duct)]
6303      ::  ~&  [%sunk-wove desk (print-wove wove) ducts]
6304      ~(tap in ducts)
6305    =/  cancel-moves=(list move)
6306      %+  turn  cancel-ducts
6307      |=(=duct [duct %pass /drip %b %drip !>([%writ ~])])
6308    ::  delete local state of foreign desk
6309    ::
6310    =.  hoy.ruf  (~(del by hoy.ruf) who)
6311    [cancel-moves ..^$]
6312  ::
6313  ?-    -.+.hin
6314      %public-keys  ~|([%public-keys-raw tea] !!)
6315    ::
6316      %mere
6317    ?:  ?=(%& -.p.+.hin)
6318      ~&  'initial merge succeeded'
6319      [~ ..^$]
6320    ~>  %slog.
```

```
6321          :^  0  %rose  [" " "[" "]"]
6322          :^     leaf+"initial merge failed"
6323            leaf+"my most sincere apologies"
6324          >p.p.p.+.hin<
6325          q.p.p.+.hin
6326       [~ ..^$]
6327    ::
6328       %wake
6329    ::  TODO: handle behn errors
6330    ::
6331    ?^  error.hin
6332      [[hen %slip %d %flog %crud %wake u.error.hin]~ ..^$]
6333    ::
6334    ?.  ?=([%tyme @ @ ~] tea)
6335      ~&  [%clay-strange-timer tea]
6336      [~ ..^$]
6337    ::  [wake] when requested time passes, call +wake
6338    ::
6339    =/  her  (slav %p i.t.tea)
6340    =/  syd  (slav %tas i.t.t.tea)
6341    =^  mos  ruf
6342      =/  den  ((de now rof hen ruf) her syd)
6343      abet:wake:den
6344    [mos ..^$]
6345    ::
6346      ::  handled in the wire dispatcher
6347      ::
6348      %boon  !!
6349      %tune  !!
6350      %lost  !!
6351      %unto  !!
6352      %wris  ~&  %strange-wris  !!
6353      %writ
6354    %-  (slog leaf+"clay: strange writ (expected on upgrade to Fusion)" ~)
6355      [~ ..^$]
6356    ::
6357       %done
6358    ?~  error=error.hin
6359      [~ ..^$]
6360    %-  (slog >%clay-lost< >tag.u.error< tang.u.error)
6361      [~ ..^$]
6362    ==
6363  ::
6364  ++  rant-to-rand
6365    |=  rant
6366    ^-  rand
6367  [p q [p q.q]:r]
6368  ::  +whey: produce memory usage report
6369  ::
6370  ++  whey
6371    ^-  (list mass)
6372    ?:  (gth mas.bug.ruf 0)
6373      =/  domestic
6374        %+  turn  (sort ~(tap by dos.rom.ruf) aor)
6375        |=  [=desk =dojo]
6376        :+  desk  %|
6377        :~  mime+&+mim.dom.dojo
6378            flue+&+fod.dom.dojo
```

```
6379              dojo+&+dojo
6380          ==
6381      :~  :+  %object-store  %|
6382          :~  commits+&+hut.ran.ruf
6383              :+  %pages  %|
6384              %+  turn  ~(tap by lat.ran.ruf)
6385              |=  [=lobe =page]
6386              [(scot %uv lobe) %& page]
6387          ==
6388          domestic+|+domestic
6389          foreign+&+hoy.ruf
6390          ford-cache+&+fad.ruf
6391      ==
6392  =/  domestic
6393      %+  turn  (sort ~(tap by dos.rom.ruf) aor)
6394      |=  [=desk =dojo]
6395      :+  desk  %|
6396      :~  mime+&+mim.dom.dojo
6397          flue+&+fod.dom.dojo
6398          dojo+&+dojo
6399      ==
6400      :~  :+  %object-store  %|
6401          :~  commits+&+hut.ran.ruf
6402              pages+&+lat.ran.ruf
6403          ==
6404          domestic+|+domestic
6405          foreign+&+hoy.ruf
6406          ford-cache+&+fad.ruf
6407  ==
6408  ::
6409  ++  tomb
6410    |%
6411    ::  +tomb-clue: safely remove objects
6412    ::
6413    ++  tomb-clue
6414      |=  [=duct =clue]
6415      ^-  [(list move) _..^$]
6416      ?-    -.clue
6417          %lobe  `(tomb-lobe lobe.clue &)
6418          %all
6419        =/  lobes=(list [=lobe =page])  ~(tap by lat.ran.ruf)
6420        |-
6421        ?~  lobes
6422          `..^^$
6423        =.  ..^^$  (tomb-lobe lobe.i.lobes &)
6424        $(lobes t.lobes)
6425      ::
6426          %pick  pick
6427          %norm
6428        =^  mos  ruf
6429          =/  den  ((de now rof duct ruf) ship.clue desk.clue)
6430          abet:(set-norm:den norm.clue)
6431        [mos ..^$]
6432      ::
6433          %worn
6434        =^  mos  ruf
6435          =/  den  ((de now rof duct ruf) ship.clue desk.clue)
6436          abet:(set-worn:den tako.clue norm.clue)
```

```
6437        [mos ..^$]
6438      ::
6439          %seek
6440        =^  mos  ruf
6441          =/  den  ((de now rof duct ruf) ship.clue desk.clue)
6442          abet:(seek:den cash.clue)
6443        [mos ..^$]
6444      ==
6445    ::  +tomb-lobe: remove specific lobe
6446    ::
6447    ++  tomb-lobe
6448      |=  [lob=lobe veb=?]
6449      ^+  ..^$
6450      =/  peg=(unit page)  (~(get by lat.ran.ruf) lob)
6451      ?~  peg
6452        (noop veb leaf+"clay: file already tombstoned" ~)
6453      ::
6454      =/  used=(unit beam)
6455        =/  desks=(list [=desk =dojo])  ~(tap by dos.rom.ruf)
6456        |-
6457        =*  desk-loop  $
6458        ?~  desks
6459          ~
6460        ?:  =(0 let.dom.dojo.i.desks)
6461          desk-loop(desks t.desks)
6462        =/  =yaki
6463          %-  ~(got by hut.ran.ruf)
6464          %-  ~(got by hit.dom.dojo.i.desks)
6465          let.dom.dojo.i.desks
6466        =/  paths=(list [=path =lobe])  ~(tap by q.yaki)
6467        |-
6468        =*  path-loop  $
6469        ?~  paths
6470          desk-loop(desks t.desks)
6471        ?:  =(lob lobe.i.paths)
6472          `[[our desk.i.desks ud+let.dom.dojo.i.desks] path.i.paths]
6473        path-loop(paths t.paths)
6474      ::
6475      ?^  used
6476        (noop veb leaf+"clay: file used in {<(en-beam u.used)>}" ~)
6477      ::
6478      =.  lat.ran.ruf  (~(del by lat.ran.ruf) lob)
6479      (noop veb leaf+"clay: file successfully tombstoned" ~)
6480    ::
6481    ++  noop
6482      |=  [veb=? =tang]
6483      ?.  veb
6484        ..^$
6485      ((slog tang) ..^$)
6486    ::
6487    ++  draw-raft
6488      ^-  (set [norm yaki])
6489      =/  room-yakis
6490        =/  rooms=(list [=desk =dojo])  ~(tap by dos.rom.ruf)
6491        |-  ^-  (set [norm yaki])
6492        ?~  rooms
6493          ~
6494        (~(uni in $(rooms t.rooms)) (draw-dome %& dom.dojo.i.rooms))
```

```
6495    =/  rung-yakis
6496      =/  rungs=(list [=ship =rung])  ~(tap by hoy.ruf)
6497      |-  ^-  (set [norm yaki])
6498      ?~  rungs
6499        ~
6500      %-  ~(uni in $(rungs t.rungs))
6501      =/  redes=(list [=desk =rede])  ~(tap by rus.rung.i.rungs)
6502      |-  ^-  (set [norm yaki])
6503      ?~  redes
6504        ~
6505      (~(uni in $(redes t.redes)) (draw-dome %| dom.rede.i.redes))
6506    (~(uni in room-yakis) rung-yakis)
6507    ::
6508    ++  draw-dome
6509    |=  [domestic=? =dome]
6510    ^-  (set [norm yaki])
6511    =/  =aeon  1
6512    |-  ^-  (set [norm yaki])
6513    ?:  (lth let.dome aeon)
6514      ~
6515    =/  =tako  (~(got by hit.dome) aeon)
6516    =/  yakis=(set [norm yaki])
6517      ?.  &(=(let.dome aeon) domestic)
6518        ~
6519      [[*norm (~(got by hut.ran.ruf) tako)] ~ ~]
6520    %-  ~(uni in yakis)
6521    %-  ~(uni in (draw-tako tom.dome nor.dome tako))
6522    $(aeon +(aeon))
6523    ::
6524    ++  draw-tako
6525    |=  [tom=(map tako norm) nor=norm =tako]
6526    ^-  (set [norm yaki])
6527    ~+
6528    =/  =norm  (~(gut by tom) tako nor)
6529    =/  =yaki  (~(got by hut.ran.ruf) tako)
6530    =/  takos
6531      |-  ^-  (set [^norm ^yaki])
6532      ?~  p.yaki
6533        ~
6534      (~(uni in $(p.yaki t.p.yaki)) ^$(tako i.p.yaki))
6535    (~(put in takos) norm yaki)
6536    ::
6537    ::  +pick: copying gc based on norms
6538    ::
6539    ++  pick
6540    =|  lat=(map lobe page)
6541    =|  sen=(set [norm (map path lobe)])
6542    |^
6543    =.  ..pick-raft  pick-raft
6544    =.  lat.ran.ruf  lat
6545    `..^$
6546    ::
6547    ++  pick-raft
6548      ^+  ..pick-raft
6549    =/  yakis=(list [=norm =yaki])  ~(tap in draw-raft)
6550    |-  ^+  ..pick-raft
6551    ?~  yakis
6552      ..pick-raft
```

```
6553      ::    ~&  >  [%picking [norm r.yaki]:i.yakis]
6554        $(yakis t.yakis, ..pick-raft (pick-yaki i.yakis))
6555      ::
6556      ::  NB: recurring tree-wise with the `sen` cache provides
6557      ::  approximately a 100x speedup on a mainnet moon in 4/2022
6558      ::
6559    ++  pick-yaki
6560      |=  [=norm =yaki]
6561      ^+  ..pick-raft
6562      |-  ^+  ..pick-raft
6563      ?~  q.yaki
6564        ..pick-raft
6565      ?:  (~(has in sen) norm q.yaki)
6566        ..pick-raft
6567      =.  sen  (~(put in sen) norm q.yaki)
6568      =/  peg=(unit page)  (~(get by lat.ran.ruf) q.n.q.yaki)
6569      ::  ~&  >>  [%picking-lobe ?=(^ peg) +:(~(fit of norm) p.n.q.yaki) n.q.yaki]
6570      =?  lat  &(?=(^ peg) !=([~ %|] +:(~(fit of norm) p.n.q.yaki)))
6571        (~(uni by `(map lobe page)`[[q.n.q.yaki u.peg] ~ ~]) lat)
6572      =.  ..pick-raft  $(q.yaki l.q.yaki)
6573      $(q.yaki r.q.yaki)
6574    --
6575  --
6576 --
```

Dill

```
1   !:
2   ::  dill (4d), terminal handling
3   ::
4   |=  our=ship
5   =,  dill
6   =>  |%
7   +$  gill  (pair ship term)                      ::  interface tiles
8   --                                              ::  general contact
9   =>  |%                                          ::
10  +$  axle                                        ::  console protocol
11    $:  %7                                        ::
12      hey=(unit duct)                             ::  default duct
13      dug=(map @tas axon)                         ::  conversations
14      eye=(jug @tas duct)                         ::  outside observers
15      ear=(set duct)                              ::  syslog listeners
16      lit=?                                       ::  boot in lite mode
17      egg=_|                                      ::  see +take, removeme
18    ==                                            ::
19  +$  axon                                        ::  dill session
20    $:  ram=term                                  ::  console program
21      tem=(unit (list dill-belt))                 ::  pending, reverse
22      wid=_80                                      ::  terminal width
23    ==                                            ::
24  +$  log-level  ?(%hush %soft %loud)             ::  none, line, full
25  --  =>                                          ::
26  |%                                              ::  protocol outward
27  +$  mess                                        ::
28    $%  [%dill-poke p=(hypo poke)]                ::
29    ==                                            ::
30  +$  move  [p=duct q=(wind note gift)]           ::  local move
31  +$  note                                        ::  out request $->
32    $~  [%d %verb ~]                              ::
33    $%  $:  %$                                    ::
34          $>(?(%verb %whey) waif)                 ::
35        ==                                        ::
36        $:  %c                                    ::
37          $>  $?  %merg                           ::  merge desks
38                  %perm                           ::  change permissions
39                  %warp                           ::  wait for clay hack
40                  %zest                           ::
41              ==                                  ::
42          task:clay                               ::
43        ==                                        ::
44        $:  %d                                    ::
45          $>  $?  %crud                           ::
46                  %heft                           ::
47                  %text                           ::
48                  %verb                           ::
49              ==                                  ::
50          task:dill                               ::
51        ==                                        ::
52        $:  %g                                    ::
53          $>(%deal task:gall)                     ::
54        ==                                        ::
55        $:  %j                                    ::
56          $>  $?  %dawn                           ::
```

```
57                    %fake                           ::
58                    ==                              ::
59            task:jael                               ::
60      ==  ==                                        ::
61  +$  sign                                          :: in result $<-
62    $~  [%dill %blit ~]                             ::
63    $%  $:  %behn                                   ::
64            $%  $>(%writ gift:clay)                 :: XX %slip
65                $>(%mere gift:clay)                 :: XX %slip
66            ==  ==                                  ::
67        $:  %clay                                   ::
68            $>  $?  %mere                           ::
69                    %writ                           ::
70                ==                                  ::
71            gift:clay                               ::
72        ==                                          ::
73        $:  %dill                                   ::
74            $>(%blit gift:dill)                     ::
75        ==                                          ::
76        $:  %gall                                   ::
77            $>(%unto gift:gall)                     ::
78    ==  ==                                          ::
79  ::::::::                                          :: dill tiles
80  --
81  =|  all=axle
82  |=  [now=@da eny=@uvJ rof=roof]                   :: current invocation
83  =>  ~%  %dill  ..part  ~
84    |%
85    ++  as                                          :: per cause
86    =|  moz=(list move)
87    |_  [hen=duct ses=@tas axon]
88    ++  abet                                        :: resolve
89      ^-  [(list move) axle]
90      [(flop moz) all(dug (~(put by dug.all) ses +<+>))]
91    ::
92    ++  call                                        :: receive input
93      |=  kyz=task
94      ^+  +>
95      ?+    -.kyz  ~&  [%strange-kiss -.kyz]  +>
96        %hail  (send %hey ~)
97        %belt  (send `dill-belt`p.kyz)
98        %blew  (send(wid p.p.kyz) %rez p.p.kyz q.p.kyz)
99        %heft  (pass /whey %$ whey/~)
100       %meld  (dump kyz)
101       %pack  (dump kyz)
102       %crop  (dump trim+p.kyz)
103       %verb  (pass /verb %$ kyz)
104     ::
105         %seat
106       %^  pass  /seat  %g
107       :+  %deal  [our our /dill]
108       [%hood %poke %kiln-install !>([desk.kyz our desk.kyz])]
109       ==
110     ::
111    ++  crud                                       ::
112      |=  [err=@tas tac=tang]
113      =-  +>.$(moz (weld - moz))
114      %+  turn
```

```
115        ~(tap in ear.all)
116      (late %give %logs %crud err tac)
117    ::
118    ++  dump                               ::  pass down to hey
119      |=  git=gift
120      ?>  ?=(^ hey.all)
121      +>(moz [[u.hey.all %give git] moz])
122    ::
123    ++  done                               ::  gift to viewers
124      |=  git=gift
125      =-  +>.$(moz (weld - moz))
126      %+  turn
127        ~(tap in (~(get ju eye.all) ses))
128      |=(=duct [duct %give git])
129    ::
130    ++  deal                               ::  pass to %gall
131      |=  [=wire =deal:gall]
132      (pass wire [%g %deal [our our /dill] ram deal])
133    ::
134    ++  pass                               ::  pass note
135      |=  [=wire =note]
136      +>(moz :_(moz [hen %pass wire note]))
137    ::
138    ++  from                               ::  receive blit
139      |=  bit=dill-blit
140      ^+  +>
141      ?:  ?=(%qit -.bit)
142        (dump %logo ~)
143      ::TODO  so why is this a (list blit) again?
144      (done %blit bit ~)
145    ::
146    ++  sponsor
147      ^-  ship
148      =/  dat=(unit (unit cage))
149        (rof `[our ~ ~] /dill j/[[our sein/da/now] /(scot %p our)])
150      ;;(ship q.q:(need (need dat)))
151    ::
152    ++  init                               ::  initialize
153      (pass /merg/base [%c %merg %kids our %base da+now %init])
154    ::
155    ++  mere                               ::  continue init
156      ^+  .
157      =/  myt  (flop (fall tem ~))
158      =.  tem  ~
159      =.  ..mere  (pass /zest %c %zest %base %live)
160      =.  ..mere  (show-desk %kids)
161      =.  ..mere  (open ~)
162      |-  ^+  ..mere
163      ?~  myt  ..mere
164      $(myt t.myt, ..mere (send i.myt))
165    ::
166    ++  into                               ::  preinitialize
167      |=  gyl=(list gill)
168      =.  tem  `(turn gyl |=(a=gill [%yow a]))
169      (pass / [%c %warp our %base `[%sing %y [%ud 1] /]])
170    ::
171    ++  open
172      |=  gyl=(list gill)
```

```
173      ::TODO  should allow handlers from non-base desks
174      ::TODO  maybe ensure :ram is running?
175      =.  +>  peer
176      %+  roll  gyl
177      |=  [g=gill _..open]
178      (send [%yow g])
179    ::
180    ++  send                                    ::  send action
181      |=  bet=dill-belt
182      ^+  +>
183      ?^  tem
184        +>(tem `[bet u.tem])
185      (deal /send/[ses] [%poke [%dill-poke !>([ses bet])]])
186    ::
187    ++  peer
188      (deal /peer/[ses] %watch /dill/[ses])
189    ::
190    ++  pull
191      (deal /peer/[ses] %leave ~)
192    ::
193    ++  show-desk                               ::  permit reads on desk
194      |=  des=desk
195      (pass /show [%c %perm des / r+`[%black ~]])
196    ::
197    ++  take                                    ::  receive
198      |=  [tea=wire sih=sign]
199      ^+  +>
200      ?-  sih
201          [%gall %unto *]
202        ::  ~&  [%take-gall-unto +>.sih]
203        ?-    -.+>.sih
204          %raw-fact   !!
205          %kick       peer
206          %poke-ack   ?~(p.p.+>.sih +>.$ (crud %coup u.p.p.+>.sih))
207          %watch-ack
208        ?~  p.p.+>.sih
209          +>.$
210        (dump:(crud %reap u.p.p.+>.sih) %logo ~)
211        ::
212          %fact
213        ?.  ?=(%dill-blit p.cage.p.+>.sih)
214          +>.$
215        (from ;;(dill-blit q.q.cage.p.+>.sih))
216        ==
217        ::
218        [?(%behn %clay) %writ *]
219      init
220        ::
221        [?(%behn %clay) %mere *]
222      ?:  ?=(%& -.p.sih)
223        mere
224      (mean >%dill-mere-fail< >p.p.p.sih< q.p.p.sih)
225        ::
226        [%dill %blit *]
227      (done +.sih)
228      ==
229    --
230  ::
```

```
231    ++  ax                                         ::  make ++as from name
232    |=  [hen=duct ses=@tas]
233    ^-  (unit _as)
234    =/  nux  (~(get by dug.all) ses)
235    ?~  nux  ~
236    (some ~(. as hen ses u.nux))
237    ::
238    ++  aw                                         ::  make ++as from wire
239    |=  [hen=duct wir=wire]
240    ^-  (unit _as)
241    %+  ax  hen
242    ?+  wir  %$
243      [?(%peer %send) @ *]  i.t.wir
244    ==
245  --
246  |%                                               ::  poke+peek pattern
247  ++  call                                         ::  handle request
248  |=  $:  hen=duct
249          dud=(unit goof)
250          wrapped-task=(hobo task)
251      ==
252  ^+  [*(list move) ..^$]
253  =/  task=task
254    ~|  wrapped-task
255    ((harden task) wrapped-task)
256  ~|  -.task
257  ::  unwrap session tasks, default to session %$
258  ::
259  =^  ses=@tas  task
260    ?:(?=(%shot -.task) +.task [%$ task])
261  ::  error notifications "downcast" to %crud
262  ::
263  =?  task  ?=(^ dud)
264    ~|  %crud-in-crud
265    ?<  ?=(%crud -.task)
266    [%crud -.task tang.u.dud]
267  ::
268  ::  the boot event passes thru %dill for initial duct distribution
269  ::
270  ?:  ?=(%boot -.task)
271    ?>  ?=(?(%dawn %fake) -.p.task)
272    ?>  =(~ hey.all)
273    =.  hey.all  `hen
274    =/  boot
275      ((soft $>($?(%dawn %fake) task:jael)) p.task)
276    ?~  boot
277      ~&  %dill-no-boot
278      ~&  p.task
279      ~|  invalid-boot-event+hen  !!
280    =.  lit.all  lit.task
281    [[hen %pass / %j u.boot]~ ..^$]
282  ::  we are subsequently initialized.
283  ::
284  ?:  ?=(%init -.task)
285    ?>  =(~ dug.all)
286    ::  configure new terminal, setup :hood and %clay
287    ::
288    =*  duc  (need hey.all)
```

```
289    =/  app  %hood
290    =/  say  (tuba "<awaiting {(trip app)}, this may take a minute>")
291    =/  zon=axon  [app input=[~ ~] width=80]
292    ::
293    =^  moz  all  abet:(~(into as duc %$ zon) ~)
294    =.  eye.all  (~(put ju eye.all) %$ duc)
295    [moz ..^$]
    ::  %flog tasks are unwrapped and sent back to us on our default duct
296
297    ::
298    ?:  ?=(%flog -.task)
299      ?~  hey.all
300        [~ ..^$]
301      ::  this lets lib/helm send %heft a la |mass
302      ::
303      =?  p.task  ?=([%crud %hax-heft ~] p.task)  [%heft ~]
304      ::
305      $(hen u.hey.all, wrapped-task p.task)
    ::  %vega and %trim notifications come in on an unfamiliar duct
306
307    ::
308    ?:  ?=(?(%trim %vega) -.task)
309      [~ ..^$]
    ::  %knob used to set a verbosity level for an error tag,
310
    ::  but dill no longer prints errors itself, so implementing %knob
311
    ::  has become a recommendation to error printers (like drum).
312
    ::  remove this when %knob gets removed from lull, next kelvin release.
313
314    ::
315    ?:  ?=(%knob -.task)
316      ~&  [%dill %knob-deprecated]
317      [~ ..^$]
    ::  %open opens a new dill session
318
319    ::
320    ?:  ?=(%open -.task)
321      ?:  (~(has by dug.all) ses)
322        ::TODO  should we allow, and just send the %yow blits?
323        ~|  [%cannot-open-existing ses]
324        !!
325      =/  zon=axon  [p.task ~ width=80]
326      =^  moz  all  abet:(~(open as hen ses zon) q.task)
327      =.  eye.all  (~(put ju eye.all) ses hen)
328      [moz ..^$]
    ::  %shut closes an existing dill session
329
330    ::
331    ?:  ?=(%shut -.task)
332      ?:  =(%$ ses)
333        ~|  %cannot-shut-default-session
334        !!
335      =/  nus
336        ~|  [%no-session ses]
337        (need (ax hen ses))
    ::NOTE  we do deletion from state outside of the core,
338
    ::      because +abet would re-insert.
339    ::
    ::TODO  send a %bye blit? xx
340
341      =^  moz  all  abet:pull:nus
342      =.  dug.all  (~(del by dug.all) ses)
343      =.  eye.all  (~(del by eye.all) ses)
344      [moz ..^$]
    ::  %view opens a subscription to the target session, on the current duct
345
346    ::
```

```
347    ?:  ?=(%view -.task)
348      =/  nus
349        ::  crash on viewing non-existent session
350        ::
351        ~|  [%no-session ses]
352        (need (ax hen ses))
353      ::  register the viewer and send a %hey so they get the full screen
354      ::
355      =^  moz  all
356        abet:(send:nus %hey ~)
357      :-  moz
358      ..^$(eye.all (~(put ju eye.all) ses hen))
359    ::  %flee closes a subscription to the target session, from the current duct
360    ::
361    ?:  ?=(%flee -.task)
362      :-  ~
363      ..^$(eye.all (~(del ju eye.all) ses hen))
364    ::  %logs opens or closes a subscription to system output
365    ::
366    ?:  ?=(%logs -.task)
367      =.  ear.all
368        ?~  p.task  (~(del in ear.all) hen)
369        (~(put in ear.all) hen)
370      [~ ..^$]
371    ::  if we were $told something, give %logs to all interested parties
372    ::
373    ?:  ?=(?(%crud %talk %text) -.task)
374      :_  ..^$
375      (turn ~(tap in ear.all) (late %give %logs task))
376    ::
377    =/  nus
378    (ax hen ses)
379    ?~  nus
380      ::  session :ses does not exist
381      ::  could be before %boot (or %boot failed)
382      ::
383      ~&  [%dill-call-no-session ses hen -.task]
384      [~ ..^$]
385    ::
386    =^  moz  all  abet:(call:u.nus task)
387    [moz ..^$]
388    ::
389    ++  load                                    ::  import old state
390      =<  |=  old=any-axle
391      ?-  -.old
392        %7  ..^$(all old)
393        %6  $(old (axle-6-to-7 old))
394        %5  $(old (axle-5-to-6 old))
395        %4  $(old (axle-4-to-5 old))
396      ==
397    |%
398    +$  any-axle  $%(axle axle-6 axle-5 axle-4)
399    ::
400    +$  axle-6
401      $:  %6
402          hey=(unit duct)
403          dug=(map @tas axon)
404          eye=(jug @tas duct)
```

```
405          lit=?
406          veb=(map @tas log-level)
407          egg=_|
408      ==
409    ::
410    ++  axle-6-to-7
411      |=  a=axle-6
412      ^-  axle
413      [%7 hey dug eye ~ lit egg]:a
414    ::
415    +$  axle-5
416      $:  %5
417          hey=(unit duct)                    ::  default duct
418          dug=(map @tas axon)                ::  conversations
419          eye=(jug @tas duct)                ::  outside listeners
420          lit=?                              ::  boot in lite mode
421          veb=(map @tas log-level)
422      ==
423    ::
424    ++  axle-5-to-6
425      |=  a=axle-5
426      ^-  axle-6
427      ::  [%6 hey `(map @tas axon)`dug eye lit veb |]
428      a(- %6, veb [veb.a &])
429    ::
430    +$  axle-4
431      $:  %4
432          hey=(unit duct)
433          dug=(map duct axon-4)
434          eye=(jug duct duct)
435          lit=?
436          veb=(map @tas log-level)
437      ==
438    ::
439    +$  axon-4
440      $:  ram=term
441          tem=(unit (list dill-belt-4))
442          wid=_80
443          pos=$@(@ud [@ud @ud])
444          see=$%([%lin (list @c)] [%klr stub])
445      ==
446    ::
447    +$  dill-belt-4
448      $%  [%ctl p=@c]
449          [%met p=@c]
450          dill-belt
451      ==
452    ::
453    ++  axle-4-to-5
454      |=  axle-4
455      ^-  axle-5
456      :-  %5
457      =-  [hey nug nay lit veb]
458      %+  roll  ~(tap by dug)
459      |=  [[=duct =axon-4] nug=(map @tas axon) nay=(jug @tas duct)]
460      =/  ses=@tas
461        ~|  [%unexpected-duct duct]
462        ?>(=([//term/1]~ duct) %$)
```

```
463      :-  (~(put by nug) ses (axon-4-to-5 axon-4))
464      %+  ~(put by nay) ses
465      (~(put in (~(get ju eye) duct)) duct)
466    ::
467    ++  axon-4-to-5
468      |=  axon-4
469      ^-  axon
470      =;  tem  [ram tem wid]
471      ?~  tem  ~
472      %-  some
473      %+  turn  u.tem
474      |=  b=dill-belt-4
475      ^-  dill-belt
476      ?.  ?=(?(%ctl %met) -.b)  b
477      [%mod -.b p.b]
478      --
479    ::
480    ++  scry
481      ^-  roon
482      |=  [lyc=gang pov=path car=term bem=beam]
483      ^-  (unit (unit cage))
484      =*  ren  car
485      =*  why=shop  &/p.bem
486      =*  syd  q.bem
487      =*  lot=coin  $/r.bem
488      =*  tyl  s.bem
489    ::
490      ?.  ?=(%& -.why)  ~
491      =*  his  p.why
492    ::
493    ::  only respond for the local identity, %$ desk, current timestamp
494    ::
495      ?.  ?&  =(&+our why)
496              =([%$ %da now] lot)
497              =(%$ syd)
498          ==
499      ~
500    ::  /%x//whey          (list mass)    memory usage labels
501    ::  /dy/sessions       (set @tas)     all existing sessions
502    ::  /du/sessions/[ses]  ?             does session ses exist?
503    ::
504      ?+  [ren tyl]  ~
505      [%x %$ %whey ~]     =-  ``mass+!>(`(list mass)`-)
506                         [hey+&+hey.all dug+&+dug.all ~]
507    ::
508      [%y %sessions ~]    ``noun+!>(~(key by dug.all))
509      [%u %sessions @ ~]  ``noun+!>((~(has by dug.all) (snag 1 tyl)))
510      ==
511    ::
512    ++  stay  all
513    ::
514    ++  take                                        :: process move
515      |=  [tea=wire hen=duct dud=(unit goof) hin=sign]
516      ^+  [*(list move) ..^$]
517      ?^  dud
518      ~|(%dill-take-dud (mean tang.u.dud))
519    ::
520      =;  [moz=(list move) lax=_..^$]
```

```
521   =?  moz  egg.all.lax
522     ::  dill pre-release (version %5) in some cases ended up in a state
523     ::  where it had both an old-style and new-style subscription open
524     ::  for the default session. here, we obliterate both and establish
525     ::  only the new-style subscription.
526     ::
527     =/  hey  (need hey.all.lax)
528     =/  =sack  [our our /dill]
529     :*  [hey %pass / %g %deal sack %hood %leave ~]
530         [hey %pass [%peer %$ ~] %g %deal sack %hood %leave ~]
531         [hey %pass [%peer %$ ~] %g %deal sack %hood %watch [%dill %$ ~]]
532         moz
533     ==
534   =.  egg.all.lax  |
535   [moz lax]
536   ::
537   =/  nus  (aw hen tea)
538   ?~  nus
539     ::  :tea points to an unrecognized session
540     ::
541     ~&  [%dill-take-no-session tea -.hin +<.hin]
542     [~ ..^$]
543   =^  moz  all  abet:(take:u.nus tea hin)
544   [moz ..^$]
545 --
```

Eyre

```
1  !:
2  ::  lighter than eyre
3  ::
4  |=  our=ship
5  =,  eyre
6  ::  internal data structures
7  ::
8  =>  =~
9  ::
10 ::  internal data structures that won't go in zuse
11 ::
12 |%
13 +$  move
14    ::
15    $:  ::  duct: request identifier
16        ::
17        =duct
18        ::
19        ::
20        card=(wind note gift)
21    ==
22 ::  +note: private request from eyre to another vane
23 ::
24 +$  note
25    $%  [%a $>(?(%plea %keen %yawn) task:ames)]
26        [%b $>(?(%rest %wait) task:behn)]
27        [%c $>(%warp task:clay)]
28        [%d $>(%flog task:dill)]
29        [%g $>(%deal task:gall)]
30    ==
31 ::  +sign: private response from another vane to eyre
32 ::
33 +$  sign
34    $%  [%ames $>(?(%done %boon %lost %tune) gift:ames)]
35        [%behn $>(%wake gift:behn)]
36        [%gall gift:gall]
37        [%clay gift:clay]
38    ==
39 --
40 ::  more structures
41 ::
42 |%
43 ++  axle
44    $:  ::  date: date at which http-server's state was updated to this data structure
45        ::
46        date=%~2023.5.15
47        ::  server-state: state of inbound requests
48        ::
49        =server-state
50    ==
51 ::  +server-state: state relating to open inbound HTTP connections
52 ::
53 +$  server-state
54    $:  ::  bindings: actions to dispatch to when a binding matches
55        ::
56        ::    Eyre is responsible for keeping its bindings sorted so that it
```

```
57      ::      will trigger on the most specific binding first. Eyre should send
58      ::      back an error response if an already bound binding exists.
59      ::
60      ::      TODO: It would be nice if we had a path trie. We could decompose
61      ::      the :binding into a (map (unit @t) (trie knot =action)).
62      ::
63      bindings=(list [=binding =duct =action])
64      ::  cache: mapping from url to versioned entry
65      ::
66      cache=(map url=@t [aeon=@ud val=(unit cache-entry)])
67      ::  cors-registry: state used and managed by the +cors core
68      ::
69      =cors-registry
70      ::  connections: open http connections not fully complete
71      ::
72      connections=(map duct outstanding-connection)
73      ::  auth: state managed by the +authentication core
74      ::
75      auth=authentication-state
76      ::  channel-state: state managed by the +channel core
77      ::
78      =channel-state
79      ::  domains: domain-names that resolve to us
80      ::
81      domains=(set turf)
82      ::  http-config: our server configuration
83      ::
84      =http-config
85      ::  ports: live servers
86      ::
87      ports=[insecure=@ud secure=(unit @ud)]
88      ::  outgoing-duct: to unix
89      ::
90      outgoing-duct=duct
91      ::  verb: verbosity
92      ::
93      verb=@
94  ==
95  ::  channel-request: an action requested on a channel
96  ::
97  +$  channel-request
98    $%  ::  %ack: acknowledges that the client has received events up to :id
99        ::
100       [%ack event-id=@ud]
101       ::  %poke: pokes an application, validating :noun against :mark
102       ::
103       [%poke request-id=@ud ship=@p app=term mark=@tas =noun]
104       ::  %poke-json: pokes an application, translating :json to :mark
105       ::
106       [%poke-json request-id=@ud ship=@p app=term mark=@tas =json]
107       ::  %watch: subscribes to an application path
108       ::
109       [%subscribe request-id=@ud ship=@p app=term =path]
110       ::  %leave: unsubscribes from an application path
111       ::
112       [%unsubscribe request-id=@ud subscription-id=@ud]
113       ::  %delete: kills a channel
114       ::
```

```
115          [%delete ~]
116      ==
117  ::   clog-timeout: the delay between acks after which clog-threshold kicks in
118  ::
119  ++   clog-timeout      ~s30
120  ::   clog-threshold: maximum per-subscription event buildup, after clog-timeout
121  ::
122  ++   clog-threshold    50
123  ::   channel-timeout: the delay before a channel should be reaped
124  ::
125  ++   channel-timeout   ~h12
126  ::   session-timeout: the delay before an idle session expires
127  ::
128  ++   session-timeout   ~d7
129  --
130  ::   utilities
131  ::
132  |%
133  ::   +combine-octs: combine multiple octs into one
134  ::
135  ++   combine-octs
136    |=  a=(list octs)
137    ^-  octs
138    :-  %+  roll  a
139        |=  [=octs sum=@ud]
140        (add sum p.octs)
141    (can 3 a)
142  ::   +prune-events: removes all items from the front of the queue up to :id
143  ::
144  ::      also produces, per request-id, the amount of events that have got acked,
145  ::      for use with +subtract-acked-events.
146  ::
147  ++   prune-events
148    =|  acked=(map @ud @ud)
149    |=  [q=(qeu [id=@ud @ud channel-event]) id=@ud]
150    ^+  [acked q]
151    ::  if the queue is now empty, that's fine
152    ::
153    ?:  =(~ q)
154      [acked ~]
155    ::
156    =/  next=[item=[id=@ud request-id=@ud channel-event] _q]  ~(get to q)
157    ::  if the head of the queue is newer than the acknowledged id, we're done
158    ::
159    ?:  (gth id.item.next id)
160      [acked q]
161    ::  otherwise, note the ack, and check next item
162    ::
163    %_  $
164      q  +:next
165    ::
166        acked
167      =,  item.next
168      %+  ~(put by acked)  request-id
169      +((~(gut by acked) request-id 0))
170    ==
171  ::   +subtract-acked-events: update the subscription map's pending ack counts
172  ::
```

```
173  ++    subtract-acked-events
174  |=    [acked=(map @ud @ud) unacked=(map @ud @ud)]
175  ^+    unacked
176  %+    roll   ~(tap by acked)
177  |=    [[rid=@ud ack=@ud] unacked=_unacked]
178  ?~    sus=(~(get by unacked) rid)
179      unacked
180  %+    ~(put by unacked)  rid
181  ?:    (lte u.sus ack)  0
182  (sub u.sus ack)
183  ::    +find-channel-mode: deduce requested mode from headers
184  ::
185  ++    find-channel-mode
186  |=    [met=method:http hes=header-list:http]
187  ^-    ?(%json %jam)
188  =+    ^-   [hed=@t jam=@t]
189      ?:    ?=(%'GET' met)   ['x-channel-format' 'application/x-urb-jam']
190      ['content-type' 'application/x-urb-jam']
191  =+    typ=(bind (get-header:http hed hes) :(cork trip cass crip))
192  ?:(=(`jam typ) %jam %json)
193  ::    +parse-channel-request: parses a list of channel-requests
194  ::
195  ++    parse-channel-request
196  |=    [mode=?(%json %jam) body=octs]
197  ^-    (each (list channel-request) @t)
198  ?-    mode
199      %json
200    ?~   maybe-json=(de:json:html q.body)
201    |+'put body not json'
202    ?~   maybe-requests=(parse-channel-request-json u.maybe-json)
203    |+'invalid channel json'
204    &+u.maybe-requests
205  ::
206      %jam
207    ?~   maybe-noun=(bind (slaw %uw q.body) cue)
208    |+'invalid request format'
209    ?~   maybe-reqs=((soft (list channel-request)) u.maybe-noun)
210    ~&   [%miss u.maybe-noun]
211    |+'invalid request data'
212    &+u.maybe-reqs
213  ==
214  ::    +parse-channel-request-json: parses a json list of channel-requests
215  ::
216  ::    Parses a json array into a list of +channel-request. If any of the items
217  ::    in the list fail to parse, the entire thing fails so we can 400 properly
218  ::    to the client.
219  ::
220  ++    parse-channel-request-json
221  |=    request-list=json
222  ^-    (unit (list channel-request))
223  ::    parse top
224  ::
225  =,    dejs-soft:format
226  =-    ((ar -) request-list)
227  ::
228  |=    item=json
229  ^-    (unit channel-request)
230  ::
```

```
231    ?~  maybe-key=((ot action+so ~) item)
232      ~
233    ?:  =('ack' u.maybe-key)
234      ((pe %ack (ot event-id+ni ~)) item)
235    ?:  =('poke' u.maybe-key)
236      %.  item
237      %+  pe  %poke-json
238      (ot id+ni ship+(su fed:ag) app+so mark+(su sym) json+some ~)
239    ?:  =('subscribe' u.maybe-key)
240      %.  item
241      %+  pe  %subscribe
242      (ot id+ni ship+(su fed:ag) app+so path+(su stap) ~)
243    ?:  =('unsubscribe' u.maybe-key)
244      %.  item
245      %+  pe  %unsubscribe
246      (ot id+ni subscription+ni ~)
247    ?:  =('delete' u.maybe-key)
248      `[%delete ~]
249    ::  if we reached this, we have an invalid action key. fail parsing.
250    ::
251      ~
252  ::  +auth-styling: css for login and eauth pages
253  ::
254  ++  auth-styling
255      '''
256      @import url("https://rsms.me/inter/inter.css");
257      @font-face {
258          font-family: "Source Code Pro";
259          src: url("https://storage.googleapis.com/media.urbit.org/fonts/scp-regular.woff");
260          font-weight: 400;
261          font-display: swap;
262      }
263      :root {
264        --red-soft: #FFEFEC;
265        --red: #FF6240;
266        --gray-100: #E5E5E5;
267        --gray-400: #999999;
268        --gray-800: #333333;
269        --white: #FFFFFF;
270      }
271      html {
272        font-family: Inter, sans-serif;
273        height: 100%;
274        margin: 0;
275        width: 100%;
276        background: var(--white);
277        color: var(--gray-800);
278        -webkit-font-smoothing: antialiased;
279        line-height: 1.5;
280        font-size: 16px;
281        font-weight: 600;
282        display: flex;
283        flex-flow: row nowrap;
284        justify-content: center;
285      }
286      body {
287        display: flex;
288        flex-flow: column nowrap;
```

```
289    justify-content: center;
290    max-width: 300px;
291    padding: 1rem;
292    width: 100%;
293  }
294  body.local #eauth,
295  body.eauth #local {
296    display: none;
297    min-height: 100%;
298  }
299  #eauth input {
300    /*NOTE dumb hack to get approx equal height with #local */
301    margin-bottom: 15px;
302  }
303  body nav {
304    background: var(--gray-100);
305    border-radius: 2rem;
306    display: flex;
307    justify-content: space-around;
308    overflow: hidden;
309    margin-bottom: 1rem;
310  }
311  body nav div {
312    width: 50%;
313    padding: 0.5rem 1rem;
314    text-align: center;
315    cursor: pointer;
316  }
317  body.local nav div.local,
318  body.eauth nav div.eauth {
319    background: var(--gray-800);
320    color: var(--white);
321    cursor: default;
322  }
323  nav div.local {
324    border-right: none;
325    border-top-right-radius: 0;
326    border-bottom-right-radius: 0;
327  }
328  nav div.eauth {
329    border-left: none;
330    border-top-left-radius: 0;
331    border-bottom-left-radius: 0;
332  }
333  body > *,
334  form > input {
335    width: 100%;
336  }
337  form {
338    display: flex;
339    flex-flow: column;
340    align-items: flex-start;
341  }
342  input {
343    background: var(--gray-100);
344    border: 2px solid transparent;
345    padding: 0.5rem;
346    border-radius: 0.5rem;
```

```
347    font-size: inherit;
348    color: var(--gray-800);
349    box-shadow: none;
350    width: 100%;
351  }
352  input:disabled {
353    background: var(--gray-100);
354    color: var(--gray-400);
355  }
356  input:focus {
357    outline: none;
358    background: var(--white);
359    border-color: var(--gray-400);
360  }
361  input:invalid:not(:focus) {
362    background: var(--red-soft);
363    border-color: var(--red);
364    outline: none;
365    color: var(--red);
366  }
367  button[type=submit] {
368    margin-top: 1rem;
369  }
370  button[type=submit], a.button {
371    font-size: 1rem;
372    padding: 0.5rem 1rem;
373    border-radius: 0.5rem;
374    background: var(--gray-800);
375    color: var(--white);
376    border: none;
377    font-weight: 600;
378    text-decoration: none;
379  }
380  input:invalid ~ button[type=submit] {
381    border-color: currentColor;
382    background: var(--gray-100);
383    color: var(--gray-400);
384    pointer-events: none;
385  }
386  span.guest, span.guest a {
387    color: var(--gray-400);
388  }
389  span.failed {
390    display: flex;
391    flex-flow: row nowrap;
392    height: 1rem;
393    align-items: center;
394    margin-top: 0.875rem;
395    color: var(--red);
396  }
397  span.failed svg {
398    height: 1rem;
399    margin-right: 0.25rem;
400  }
401  span.failed path {
402    fill: transparent;
403    stroke-width: 2px;
404    stroke-linecap: round;
```

```
405      stroke: currentColor;
406    }
407    .mono {
408      font-family: 'Source Code Pro', monospace;
409    }
410    @media all and (prefers-color-scheme: dark) {
411    :root {
412      --white: #000000;
413      --gray-800: #E5E5E5;
414      --gray-400: #808080;
415      --gray-100: #333333;
416      --red-soft: #7F1D1D;
417    }
418    }
419    @media screen and (min-width: 30em) {
420      html {
421        font-size: 14px;
422      }
423    }
424    '''
425  ::  +login-page: internal page to login to an Urbit
426  ::
427  ++  login-page
428    |=  [redirect-url=(unit @t) our=@p =identity eauth=(unit ?) failed=?]
429    ^-  octs
430    =+  redirect-str=?~(redirect-url "" (trip u.redirect-url))
431    %-  as-octs:mimes:html
432    %-  crip
433    %-  en-xml:html
434    =/  favicon  %+
435      weld  "<svg width='10' height='10' viewBox='0 0 10 10' xmlns='http://www.w3.org/2000/svg'>"
436            "<circle r='3.09' cx='5' cy='5' /></svg>"
437    ;html
438      ;head
439        ;meta(charset "utf-8");
440        ;meta(name "viewport", content "width=device-width, initial-scale=1, shrink-to-fit=no");
441        ;link(rel "icon", type "image/svg+xml", href (weld "data:image/svg+xml;utf8," favicon));
442        ;title:"Urbit"
443        ;style:"{(trip auth-styling)}"
444        ;style:"{?^(eauth "" "nav \{ display: none; }")}"
445        ;script:"our = '{(scow %p our)}';"
446        ;script:'''
447            let name, pass;
448            function setup(isEauth) {
449              name = document.getElementById('name');
450              pass = document.getElementById('pass');
451              if (isEauth) goEauth(); else goLocal();
452            }
453            function goLocal() {
454              document.body.className = 'local';
455              pass.focus();
456            }
457            function goEauth() {
458              document.body.className = 'eauth';
459              name.focus();
460            }
461            function doEauth() {
462              console.log('mb get value from event', event);
```

```
463            console.log('compare', name.value, our);
464            if (name.value == our) {
465              event.preventDefault();
466              goLocal();
467            }
468          }
469          '''
470      ==
471    ;body
472      =class    "{?:(=(`& eauth) "eauth" "local")}"
473      =onload   "setup({?:(=(`& eauth) "true" "false")})"
474      ;nav
475        ;div.local(onclick "goLocal()"):"Local"
476        ;div.eauth(onclick "goEauth()"):"EAuth"
477      ==
478      ;div#local
479        ;p:"Urbit ID"
480        ;input(value "{(scow %p our)}", disabled "true", class "mono");
481        ;+  ?:  =(%ours -.identity)
482            ;div
483              ;p:"Already authenticated"
484              ;a.button/"{(trip (fall redirect-url '/'))}":"Continue"
485            ==
486        ;form(action "/~/login", method "post", enctype "application/x-www-form-urlencoded")
487          ;p:"Access Key"
488          ;input
489          =type     "password"
490          =name     "password"
491          =id       "pass"
492          =placeholder  "sampel-ticlyt-migfun-falmel"
493          =class    "mono"
494          =required "true"
495          =minlength "27"
496          =maxlength "27"
497          =pattern  "((?:[a-z]\{6}-)\{3}(?:[a-z]\{6}))";
498          ;input(type "hidden", name "redirect", value redirect-str);
499          ;+  ?.  failed  ;span;
500            ;span.failed
501              ;svg(xmlns "http://www.w3.org/2000/svg", viewBox "0 0 16 16")
502                ;path(d "m8 8 4-4M8 8 4 4m4 4-4 4m4-4 4 4");
503              ==
504            Key is incorrect
505            ==
506          ;button(type "submit"):"Continue"
507        ==
508      ==
509      ;div#eauth
510        ;form(action "/~/login", method "post", onsubmit "return doEauth()")
511          ;p:"Urbit ID"
512          ;input.mono
513          =name "name"
514          =id     "name"
515          =placeholder  "{(scow %p our)}"
516          =required "true"
517          =minlength "4"
518          =maxlength "57"
519          =pattern    "~(((([a-z]\{6})\{1,2}-\{0,2})+|[a-z]\{3})";
520          ;p
```

```
521              ; You will be redirected to your own web interface to authorize
522              ; logging in to
523              ;span.mono:"{(scow %p our)}"
524              ; .
525            ==
526          ;input(type "hidden", name "redirect", value redirect-str);
527          ;button(name "eauth", type "submit"):"Continue"
528        ==
529      ==
530    ;*  ?:   ?=(%ours -.identity)  ~
531      =+  id=(trim 29 (scow %p who.identity))
532      =+  as="proceed as{?:(?=(%fake -.identity) " guest" "")}"
533      ;+  ;span.guest.mono
534          ; Or
535          ;a/"{(trip (fall redirect-url '/'))}":"{as}"
536          ; :
537          ;br;
538          ; {p.id}
539          ;br;
540          ; {q.id}
541        ==
542    ==
543    ;script:'''
544          var failSpan = document.querySelector('.failed');
545          if (failSpan) {
546            document.querySelector("input[type=password]")
547              .addEventListener('keyup', function (event) {
548                failSpan.style.display = 'none';
549            });
550          }
551          '''
552    ==
553 ::  +eauth-error-page: render an eauth error reporting page
554 ::
555 ::    optionally redirects the user back to either the login page if we're
556 ::    acting as server, or the host if we're the client.
557 ::
558 ++  eauth-error-page
559  |=  $=  return
560      $?  ~                     ::  no known return target
561          [%server last=@t]  ::  we are the host, return to login
562          [%client goal=@t]  ::  we are the client, return to host
563      ==
564  ^-  octs
565  %-  as-octs:mimes:html
566  %-  crip
567  %-  en-xml:html
568  =/  return=(unit @t)
569    ?-  return
570      ~                     ~
571      [%server *]  %-  some
572                   %^  cat 3  '/~/login?eauth&redirect='
573                   (crip (en-urlt:html (trip last.return)))
574      [%client *]  `goal.return  ::TODO  plus nonce? or abort?
575    ==
576  =/  favicon  %+
577    weld  "<svg width='10' height='10' viewBox='0 0 10 10' xmlns='http://www.w3.org/2000/svg'>"
578          "<circle r='3.09' cx='5' cy='5' /></svg>"
```

```
579  =/  msg=tape
580    ?~  return  "Something went wrong!"
581    "Something went wrong! You will be redirected back..."
582  ;html
583    ;head
584      ;*  ?~  return  ~
585          :_  ~
586          ;meta(http-equiv "Refresh", content "5; url={(trip u.return)}");
587      ;meta(charset "utf-8");
588      ;meta(name "viewport", content "width=device-width, initial-scale=1, shrink-to-fit=no");
589      ;link(rel "icon", type "image/svg+xml", href (weld "data:image/svg+xml;utf8," favicon));
590      ;title:"Urbit"
591      ;style:'''
592              @import url("https://rsms.me/inter/inter.css");
593              :root {
594                --black60: rgba(0,0,0,0.6);
595                --white: rgba(255,255,255,1);
596              }
597              html {
598                font-family: Inter, sans-serif;
599                height: 100%;
600                margin: 0;
601                width: 100%;
602                background: var(--white);
603                color: var(--black60);
604                -webkit-font-smoothing: antialiased;
605                line-height: 1.5;
606                font-size: 12px;
607                display: flex;
608                flex-flow: row nowrap;
609                justify-content: center;
610              }
611              body {
612                display: flex;
613                flex-flow: column nowrap;
614                justify-content: center;
615                max-width: 300px;
616                padding: 1rem;
617                width: 100%;
618              }
619              '''
620      ==
621    ;body:"{msg}"
622  ==
623  ::  +render-tang-to-marl: renders a tang and adds <br/> tags between each line
624  ::
625  ++  render-tang-to-marl
626    |=  [wid=@u tan=tang]
627    ^-  marl
628    =/  raw=(list tape)  (zing (turn tan |=(a=tank (wash 0^wid a))))
629    ::
630    |-  ^-  marl
631    ?~  raw  ~
632    [;/(i.raw) ;br; $(raw t.raw)]
633  ::  +render-tang-to-wall: renders tang as text lines
634  ::
635  ++  render-tang-to-wall
636    |=  [wid=@u tan=tang]
```

```
637    ^-  wall
638    (zing (turn tan |=(a=tank (wash 0^wid a))))
639  ::  +wall-to-octs: text to binary output
640  ::
641  ++  wall-to-octs
642    |=  =wall
643    ^-  (unit octs)
644    ::
645    ?:  =(~ wall)
646      ~
647    ::
648    :-  ~
649    %-  as-octs:mimes:html
650    %-  crip
651    %-  zing  ^-  ^wall
652    %-  zing  ^-  (list ^wall)
653    %+  turn  wall
654    |=  t=tape
655    ^-  ^wall
656    ~[t "\0a"]
657  ::  +internal-server-error: 500 page, with a tang
658  ::
659  ++  internal-server-error
660    |=  [authorized=? url=@t t=tang]
661    ^-  octs
662    %-  as-octs:mimes:html
663    %-  crip
664    %-  en-xml:html
665    ;html
666      ;head
667        ;title:"500 Internal Server Error"
668      ==
669      ;body
670        ;h1:"Internal Server Error"
671        ;p:"There was an error while handling the request for {(trip url)}."
672        ;*  ?:  authorized
673              ;=
674                ;code:"*{(render-tang-to-marl 80 t)}"
675              ==
676            ~
677      ==
678    ==
679  ::  +error-page: error page, with an error string if logged in
680  ::
681  ++  error-page
682    |=  [code=@ud authorized=? url=@t t=tape]
683    ^-  octs
684    ::
685    =/  code-as-tape=tape  (format-ud-as-integer code)
686    =/  message=tape
687      ?+  code  "{(scow %ud code)} Error"
688        %400  "Bad Request"
689        %403  "Forbidden"
690        %404  "Not Found"
691        %405  "Method Not Allowed"
692        %500  "Internal Server Error"
693      ==
694    ::
```

```
695    %-  as-octs:mimes:html
696    %-  crip
697    %-  en-xml:html
698    ;html
699      ;head
700        ;title:"{code-as-tape} {message}"
701      ==
702      ;body
703        ;h1:"{message}"
704        ;p:"There was an error while handling the request for {(trip url)}."
705        ;*  ?:  authorized
706              ;=
707                ;code:"{t}"
708              ==
709            ~
710      ==
711    ==
712  ::  +format-ud-as-integer: prints a number for consumption outside urbit
713  ::
714  ++  format-ud-as-integer
715    |=  a=@ud
716    ^-  tape
717    ?:  =(0 a)  ['0' ~]
718    %-  flop
719    |-  ^-  tape
720    ?:(=(0 a) ~ [(add '0' (mod a 10)) $(a (div a 10))])
721  ::  +host-matches: %.y if the site :binding should be used to handle :host
722  ::
723  ++  host-matches
724    |=  [binding=(unit @t) host=(unit @t)]
725    ^-  ?
726    ::  if the binding allows for matching anything, match
727    ::
728    ?~  binding
729      %.y
730    ::  if the host is ~, that means we're trying to bind nothing to a real
731    ::  binding. fail.
732    ::
733    ?~  host
734      %.n
735    ::  otherwise, do a straight comparison
736    ::
737    =(u.binding u.host)
738  ::  +find-suffix: returns [~ /tail] if :full is (weld :prefix /tail)
739  ::
740  ++  find-suffix
741    |=  [prefix=path full=path]
742    ^-  (unit path)
743    ?~  prefix
744      `full
745    ?~  full
746      ~
747    ?.  =(i.prefix i.full)
748      ~
749    $(prefix t.prefix, full t.full)
750  ::  +simplified-url-parser: returns [(each @if @t) (unit port=@ud)]
751  ::
752  ++  simplified-url-parser
```

```
753      ;~    plug
754        ;~    pose
755          %+    stag    %ip
756          =+    tod=(ape:ag ted:ab)
757          %+    bass    256
758          ;~(plug tod (stun [3 3] ;~(pfix dot tod)))
759          ::
760          (stag %site (cook crip (star ;~(pose dot alp))))
761        ==
762        ;~    pose
763          (stag ~ ;~(pfix col dim:ag))
764          (easy ~)
765        ==
766      ==
767    ::    +host-sans-port: strip the :<port> from a host string
768    ::
769    ++    host-sans-port
770      ;~    sfix
771        %+    cook    crip
772        %-    star
773        ;~    less
774          ;~(plug col (punt dem) ;~(less next (easy ~)))
775          next
776        ==
777        (star next)
778      ==
779    ::    +per-server-event: per-event server core
780    ::
781    ++    per-server-event
782      ~%    %eyre-per-server-event    ..part    ~
783      ::    gate that produces the +per-server-event core from event information
784      ::
785      |=    [[eny=@ =duct now=@da rof=roof] state=server-state]
786      =/    eyre-id    (scot %ta (cat 3 'eyre_' (scot %uv (sham duct))))
787      |%
788      ::    +request-local: bypass authentication for local lens connections
789      ::
790      ++    request-local
791        |=    [secure=? =address =request:http]
792        ^-    [(list move) server-state]
793        ::
794        =/    act    [%app app=%lens]
795        ::
796        =/    connection=outstanding-connection
797          [act [& secure address request] [*@uv [%ours ~]] ~ 0]
798        ::
799        =.    connections.state
800          %.    (~(put by connections.state) duct connection)
801          (trace 2 |.("{<duct>} creating local"))
802        ::
803        (request-to-app [%ours ~] app.act inbound-request.connection)
804      ::    +request: starts handling an inbound http request
805      ::
806      ++    request
807        |=    [secure=? =address =request:http]
808        ^-    [(list move) server-state]
809        =*    headers    header-list.request
810        ::    for requests from localhost, respect the "forwarded" header
```

```
811    ::
812    =/  [secure=? =^address]
813      =*  same  [secure address]
814      ?.  =([%ipv4 .127.0.0.1] address)        same
815      ?~  forwards=(forwarded-params headers)  same
816      :-  (fall (forwarded-secure u.forwards) secure)
817      (fall (forwarded-for u.forwards) address)
818    ::
819    =/  host  (get-header:http 'host' headers)
820    =/  [=action suburl=@t]
821      (get-action-for-binding host url.request)
822    ::
823    ::TODO  we might want to mint new identities only for requests that end
824    ::       up going into userspace, not the ones that get handled by eyre.
825    ::       perhaps that distinction, where userspace requests are async, but
826    ::       eyre-handled requests are always synchronous, provides a fruitful
827    ::       angle for refactoring...
828    =^  [suv=@uv =identity som=(list move)]  state
829      (session-for-request:authentication request)
830    =;  [moz=(list move) sat=server-state]
831      [(weld som moz) sat]
832    ::
833    =/  authenticated  ?=(%ours -.identity)
834    ::  if we have no eauth endpoint yet, and the request is authenticated,
835    ::  deduce it from the hostname
836    ::
837    =?  endpoint.auth.state
838        ?&  authenticated
839            ?=(^ host)
840            ?=(~ auth.endpoint.auth.state)
841        ==
842      %-  (trace 2 |.("eauth: storing endpoint at {(trip u.host)}"))
843      :+  user.endpoint.auth.state
844        `(cat 3 ?:(secure 'https://' 'http://') u.host)
845      now
846    ::  record that we started an asynchronous response
847    ::
848    =/  connection=outstanding-connection
849      [action [authenticated secure address request] [suv identity] ~ 0]
850    =.  connections.state
851      ::  NB: required by +handle-response and +handle-request:authentication.
852      ::  XX optimize, not all requests are asynchronous
853      ::
854      (~(put by connections.state) duct connection)
855    ::  redirect to https if insecure, redirects enabled
856    ::  and secure port live
857    ::
858    ?:  ?&  !secure
859            redirect.http-config.state
860            ?=(^ secure.ports.state)
861        ==
862      =/  location=@t
863        %+  rap  3
864        :~  'https://'
865            (rash (fall host '') host-sans-port)
866            ?:  =(443 u.secure.ports.state)
867                ''
868            (crip ":{(a-co:co u.secure.ports.state)}")
```

```
869        ?:  ?=([[~ ~] ~] (parse-request-line url.request))
870          '/'
871          url.request
872      ==
873    %-  handle-response
874    :*  %start
875        :-  status-code=301
876        headers=['location' location]~
877        data=~
878        complete=%.y
879    ==
880  ::  figure out whether this is a cors request,
881  ::  whether the origin is approved or not,
882  ::  and maybe add it to the "pending approval" set
883  ::
884  =/  origin=(unit origin)
885    (get-header:http 'origin' headers)
886  =^  cors-approved  requests.cors-registry.state
887    =,  cors-registry.state
888    ?~  origin                        [| requests]
889    ?:  (~(has in approved) u.origin)  [& requests]
890    ?:  (~(has in rejected) u.origin)  [| requests]
891    [| (~(put in requests) u.origin)]
892  ::  if this is a cors preflight request from an approved origin
893  ::  handle it synchronously
894  ::
895  ?:  &(?=(^ origin) cors-approved ?=(%'OPTIONS' method.request))
896    %-  handle-response
897    =;  =header-list:http
898      [%start [204 header-list] ~ &]
899    ::  allow the method and headers that were asked for,
900    ::  falling back to wildcard if none specified
901    ::
902    ::NOTE  +handle-response will add the rest of the headers
903    ::
904    :~  :-  'Access-Control-Allow-Methods'
905        =-  (fall - '*')
906        (get-header:http 'access-control-request-method' headers)
907      ::
908      :-  'Access-Control-Allow-Headers'
909        =-  (fall - '*')
910        (get-header:http 'access-control-request-headers' headers)
911    ==
912  ::  handle requests to the cache
913  ::
914  =/  entry  (~(get by cache.state) url.request)
915  ?:  &(?=(^ entry) ?=(%'GET' method.request))
916    (handle-cache-req authenticated request val.u.entry)
917  ::
918  ?-  -.action
919    %gen
920  =/  bek=beak  [our desk.generator.action da+now]
921  =/  sup=spur  path.generator.action
922  =/  ski       (rof ~ /eyre %ca bek sup)
923  =/  cag=cage  (need (need ski))
924  ?>  =(%vase p.cag)
925  =/  gat=vase  !<(vase q.cag)
926  =/  res=toon
```

```
927        %-  mock  :_  (look rof ~ /eyre)
928        :_  [%9 2 %0 1]  |.
929        %+  slam
930          %+  slam  gat
931          !>([[now=now eny=eny bek=bek] ~ ~])
932          ::TODO  should get passed the requester's identity
933          !>([authenticated request])
934      ?:  ?=(%2 -.res)
935        =+  connection=(~(got by connections.state) duct)
936        %^  return-static-data-on-duct  500  'text/html'
937        %:  internal-server-error
938            authenticated.inbound-request.connection
939            url.request.inbound-request.connection
940            leaf+"generator crashed"
941            p.res
942        ==
943      ?:  ?=(%1 -.res)
944        =+  connection=(~(got by connections.state) duct)
945        %^  return-static-data-on-duct  500  'text/html'
946        %:  internal-server-error
947            authenticated.inbound-request.connection
948            url.request.inbound-request.connection
949            leaf+"scry blocked on"
950            (fall (bind (bind ((soft path) p.res) smyt) (late ~)) ~)
951        ==
952      =/  result  ;;(simple-payload:http +.p.res)
953      ::  ensure we have a valid content-length header
954      ::
955      ::  We pass on the response and the headers the generator produces, but
956      ::  ensure that we have a single content-length header set correctly in
957      ::  the returned if this has a body, and has no content-length if there
958      ::  is no body returned to the client.
959      ::
960      =.  headers.response-header.result
961        ?~  data.result
962        (delete-header:http 'content-length' headers.response-header.result)
963        ::
964        %^  set-header:http  'content-length'
965        (crip (format-ud-as-integer p.u.data.result))
966        headers.response-header.result
967      ::
968      %-  handle-response
969      ^-  http-event:http
970      :*  %start
971          response-header.result
972          data.result
973          complete=%.y
974      ==
975    ::
976        %app
977      (request-to-app identity app.action inbound-request.connection)
978    ::
979        %authentication
980      (handle-request:authentication secure host address [suv identity] request)
981    ::
982        %eauth
983      (on-request:eauth:authentication [suv identity] request)
984    ::
```

```
985         %logout
986       (handle-logout:authentication [suv identity] request)
987     ::
988         %channel
989       (handle-request:by-channel [suv identity] address request)
990     ::
991         %scry
992       (handle-scry authenticated address request(url suburl))
993     ::
994         %name
995       (handle-name identity request)
996     ::
997         %host
998     %^  return-static-data-on-duct  200  'text/plain'
999     (as-octs:mimes:html (scot %p our))
1000    ::
1001        %four-oh-four
1002    %^  return-static-data-on-duct  404  'text/html'
1003    (error-page 404 authenticated url.request ~)
1004   ==
1005  ::  +handle-name: respond with the requester's @p
1006  ::
1007  ++  handle-name
1008   |=  [=identity =request:http]
1009   ^-  (quip move server-state)
1010   ?.  =(%'GET' method.request)
1011     %^  return-static-data-on-duct  405  'text/html'
1012     (error-page 405 & url.request "may only GET name")
1013   %^  return-static-data-on-duct  200  'text/plain'
1014   =/  nom=@p
1015     ?+(-.identity who.identity %ours our)
1016   (as-octs:mimes:html (scot %p nom))
1017  ::  +handle-cache-req: respond with cached value, 404 or 500
1018  ::
1019  ++  handle-cache-req
1020   |=  [authenticated=? =request:http entry=(unit cache-entry)]
1021   |^  ^-  (quip move server-state)
1022   ?~  entry
1023     (error-response 404 "cache entry for that binding was deleted")
1024   ?:  &(auth.u.entry !authenticated)
1025     (error-response 403 ~)
1026   =*  body  body.u.entry
1027   ?-    -.body
1028       %payload
1029     %-  handle-response
1030     :*  %start
1031     response-header.simple-payload.body
1032     data.simple-payload.body
1033     complete=%.y
1034   ==
1035   ==
1036   ::
1037  ++  error-response
1038   |=  [status=@ud =tape]
1039   ^-  (quip move server-state)
1040   %^  return-static-data-on-duct  status  'text/html'
1041   (error-page status authenticated url.request tape)
1042   --
```

```
1043    ::  +handle-scry: respond with scry result, 404 or 500
1044    ::
1045    ++  handle-scry
1046      |=  [authenticated=? =address =request:http]
1047      |^  ^-  (quip move server-state)
1048      ?.  authenticated
1049      (error-response 403 ~)
1050      ?.  =(%'GET' method.request)
1051      (error-response 405 "may only GET scries")
1052      ::  make sure the path contains an app to scry into
1053      ::
1054      =+  req=(parse-request-line url.request)
1055      ?.  ?=(^ site.req)
1056      (error-response 400 "scry path must start with app name")
1057      ::  attempt the scry that was asked for
1058      ::
1059      =/  res=(unit (unit cage))
1060      (do-scry %gx i.site.req (snoc t.site.req (fall ext.req %mime)))
1061      ?~  res     (error-response 500 "failed scry")
1062      ?~  u.res   (error-response 404 "no scry result")
1063      =*  mark    p.u.u.res
1064      =*  vase    q.u.u.res
1065      ?:  =(%mime mark)
1066        =/  =mime  !<(mime vase)
1067        %^  return-static-data-on-duct   200
1068        (rsh 3 (spat p.mime))  q.mime
1069      ::  attempt to find conversion gate to mime
1070      ::
1071      =/  tub=(unit [tub=tube:clay mov=move])
1072      (find-tube i.site.req mark %mime)
1073      ?~  tub  (error-response 500 "no tube from {(trip mark)} to mime")
1074      ::  attempt conversion, then send results
1075      ::
1076      =/  mym=(each mime tang)
1077      (mule |.(!<(mime (tub.u.tub vase))))
1078      =^  cards  state
1079        ?-  -.mym
1080          %|  (error-response 500 "failed tube from {(trip mark)} to mime")
1081          %&  %+  return-static-data-on-duct   200
1082              [(rsh 3 (spat p.p.mym)) q.p.mym]
1083        ==
1084      [[mov.u.tub cards] state]
1085      ::
1086      ++  find-tube
1087        |=  [dap=term from=mark to=mark]
1088        ^-  (unit [tube:clay move])
1089        =/  des=(unit (unit cage))
1090        (do-scry %gd dap /$)
1091        ?.  ?=([~ ~ *] des)   ~
1092        =+  !<(=desk q.u.u.des)
1093        =/  tub=(unit (unit cage))
1094        (do-scry %cc desk /[from]/[to])
1095        ?.  ?=([~ ~ %tube *] tub)  ~
1096        :-  ~
1097        :-  !<(tube:clay q.u.u.tub)
1098        :^  duct  %pass  /conversion-cache/[from]
1099        [%c %warp our desk `[%sing %c da+now /[from]/[to]]]
1100      ::
```

```
1101    ++  do-scry
1102      |=  [care=term =desk =path]
1103      ^-  (unit (unit cage))
1104      (rof ~ /eyre care [our desk da+now] path)
1105      ::
1106    ++  error-response
1107      |=  [status=@ud =tape]
1108      ^-  (quip move server-state)
1109      %^  return-static-data-on-duct  status  'text/html'
1110      (error-page status authenticated url.request tape)
1111      --
1112    ::  +request-to-app: subscribe to app and poke it with request data
1113    ::
1114    ++  request-to-app
1115      |=  [=identity app=term =inbound-request:eyre]
1116      ^-  (quip move server-state)
1117      ::  if the agent isn't running, we synchronously serve a 503
1118      ::
1119      ?.  !<(? q:(need (need (rof ~ /eyre %gu [our app da+now] /$))))
1120        %^  return-static-data-on-duct  503  'text/html'
1121        %:  error-page
1122          503
1123          ?=(%ours -.identity)
1124          url.request.inbound-request
1125          "%{(trip app)} not running"
1126        ==
1127      ::  otherwise, subscribe to the agent and poke it with the request
1128      ::
1129      :_  state
1130      :~  %+  deal-as
1131            /watch-response/[eyre-id]
1132          [identity our app %watch /http-response/[eyre-id]]
1133          ::
1134          %+  deal-as
1135            /run-app-request/[eyre-id]
1136          :^  identity  our  app
1137          :+  %poke  %handle-http-request
1138          !>(`[@ta inbound-request:eyre]`[eyre-id inbound-request])
1139      ==
1140    ::  +cancel-request: handles a request being externally aborted
1141    ::
1142    ++  cancel-request
1143      ^-  [(list move) server-state]
1144      ::
1145      ?~  connection=(~(get by connections.state) duct)
1146        ::  nothing has handled this connection
1147        ::
1148        [~ state]
1149      ::
1150      =.  connections.state  (~(del by connections.state) duct)
1151      ::
1152      ?-    -.action.u.connection
1153          %gen  [~ state]
1154          %app
1155        :_  state
1156        :_  ~
1157        =,  u.connection
1158        %-  (trace 1 |.("leaving subscription to {<app.action>}"))
```

```
1159        (deal-as /watch-response/[eyre-id] identity our app.action %leave ~)
1160      ::
1161          ?(%authentication %eauth %logout)
1162        ::NOTE  expiry timer will clean up cancelled eauth attempts
1163        [~ state]
1164      ::
1165          %channel
1166        on-cancel-request:by-channel
1167      ::
1168          ?(%scry %four-oh-four %name %host)
1169        ::  it should be impossible for these to be asynchronous
1170        ::
1171        !!
1172      ==
1173    ::  +return-static-data-on-duct: returns one piece of data all at once
1174    ::
1175    ++  return-static-data-on-duct
1176      |=  [code=@ content-type=@t data=octs]
1177      ^-  [(list move) server-state]
1178      ::
1179      %-  handle-response
1180      :*  %start
1181          :-  status-code=code
1182          ^=  headers
1183            :~  ['content-type' content-type]
1184                ['content-length' (crip (format-ud-as-integer p.data))]
1185            ==
1186          data=[~ data]
1187          complete=%.y
1188      ==
1189    ::  +authentication: per-event authentication as this Urbit's owner
1190    ::
1191    ::    Right now this hard codes the authentication page using the old +code
1192    ::    system, but in the future should be pluggable so we can use U2F or
1193    ::    WebAuthn or whatever is more secure than passwords.
1194    ::
1195    ++  authentication
1196      |%
1197      ::  +handle-request: handles an http request for the login page
1198      ::
1199      ++  handle-request
1200        |=  [secure=? host=(unit @t) =address [session-id=@uv =identity] =request:http]
1201        ^-  [(list move) server-state]
1202        ::  parse the arguments out of request uri
1203        ::
1204        =+  request-line=(parse-request-line url.request)
1205        =/  redirect     (get-header:http 'redirect' args.request-line)
1206        =/  with-eauth=(unit ?)
1207          ?:  =(~ eauth-url:eauth)  ~
1208          `?=(^ (get-header:http 'eauth' args.request-line))
1209        ::  if we received a simple get: show the login page
1210        ::
1211        ::NOTE  we never auto-redirect, to avoid redirect loops with apps that
1212        ::        send unprivileged users to the login screen
1213        ::
1214        ?:  =('GET' method.request)
1215          %^  return-static-data-on-duct  200  'text/html'
1216          (login-page redirect our identity with-eauth %.n)
```

```
1217        ::  if we are not a post, return an error
1218        ::
1219        ?.  =('POST' method.request)
1220          %^  return-static-data-on-duct  405  'text/html'
1221          (login-page ~ our identity with-eauth %.n)
1222        ::  we are a post, and must process the body type as form data
1223        ::
1224        ?~  body.request
1225          %^  return-static-data-on-duct  400  'text/html'
1226          (login-page ~ our identity with-eauth %.n)
1227        ::
1228        =/  parsed=(unit (list [key=@t value=@t]))
1229          (rush q.u.body.request yquy:de-purl:html)
1230        ?~  parsed
1231          %^  return-static-data-on-duct  400  'text/html'
1232          (login-page ~ our identity with-eauth %.n)
1233        ::
1234        =/  redirect=(unit @t)  (get-header:http 'redirect' u.parsed)
1235        ?^  (get-header:http 'eauth' u.parsed)
1236          ?~  ship=(biff (get-header:http 'name' u.parsed) (cury slaw %p))
1237            %^  return-static-data-on-duct  400  'text/html'
1238            (login-page redirect our identity `& %.n)
1239          ::TODO  redirect logic here and elsewhere is ugly
1240          =/  redirect  (fall redirect '')
1241          =/  base=(unit @t)
1242            ?~  host  ~
1243            `(cat 3 ?:(secure 'https://' 'http://') u.host)
1244          (start:server:eauth u.ship base ?:(=(redirect '') '/' redirect))
1245        ::
1246        =.  with-eauth  (bind with-eauth |=(? |))
1247        ?~  password=(get-header:http 'password' u.parsed)
1248          %^  return-static-data-on-duct  400  'text/html'
1249          (login-page redirect our identity with-eauth %.n)
1250        ::  check that the password is correct
1251        ::
1252        ?.  =(u.password code)
1253          %^  return-static-data-on-duct  400  'text/html'
1254          (login-page redirect our identity with-eauth %.y)
1255        ::  clean up the session they're changing out from
1256        ::
1257        =^  moz  state
1258          (close-session session-id |)
1259        ::  initialize the new session
1260        ::
1261        =^  fex  state  (start-session %local)
1262        ::  associate the new session with the request that caused the login
1263        ::
1264        ::    if we don't do this here, +handle-response will include the old
1265        ::    session's cookie, confusing the client.
1266        ::
1267        =.  connections.state
1268          %+  ~(jab by connections.state)  duct
1269          |=  o=outstanding-connection
1270          o(session-id session.fex)
1271        ::  store the hostname used for this login, later reuse it for eauth
1272        ::
1273        =?  endpoint.auth.state  ?=(^ host)
1274          %-  (trace 2 |.("eauth: storing endpoint at {(trip u.host)}"))
```

```
1275        :+  user.endpoint.auth.state
1276          `(cat 3 ?:(secure 'https://' 'http://') u.host)
1277        now
1278      ::
1279      =;  out=[moves=(list move) server-state]
1280        out(moves [give-session-tokens :(weld moz moves.fex moves.out)])
1281      ::NOTE  that we don't provide a 'set-cookie' header here.
1282      ::       +handle-response does that for us.
1283      ?~  redirect
1284        (handle-response %start 204^~ ~ &)
1285      =/  actual-redirect  ?:(=(u.redirect '') '/' u.redirect)
1286      (handle-response %start 303^['location' actual-redirect]~ ~ &)
1287    ::  +handle-logout: handles an http request for logging out
1288    ::
1289    ++  handle-logout
1290      |=  [[session-id=@uv =identity] =request:http]
1291      ^-  [(list move) server-state]
1292      ::  whatever we end up doing, we always respond with a redirect
1293      ::
1294      =/  response=$>(%start http-event:http)
1295        =/  redirect=(unit @t)
1296          %+  get-header:http  'redirect'
1297          args:(parse-request-line url.request)
1298        :*  %start
1299            response-header=[303 ['location' (fall redirect '/~/login')]~]
1300            data=~
1301            complete=%.y
1302        ==
1303      ::  read options from the body
1304      ::  all: log out all sessions with this identity?
1305      ::  sid: which session do we log out? (defaults to requester's)
1306      ::  hos: host to log out from, for eauth logins (sid signifies the nonce)
1307      ::
1308      =/  arg=header-list:http
1309        ?~  body.request  ~
1310        (fall (rush q.u.body.request yquy:de-purl:html) ~)
1311      =/  all=?
1312      ?=(^ (get-header:http 'all' arg))
1313      =/  sid=(unit @uv)
1314        ?.  ?=(%ours -.identity)  `session-id
1315        ?~  sid=(get-header:http 'sid' arg)  `session-id
1316        ::  if you provided the parameter, but it doesn't parse, we just
1317        ::  no-op. otherwise, a poorly-implemented frontend might result in
1318        ::  accidental log-outs, which would be very annoying.
1319        ::
1320        (slaw %uv u.sid)
1321      =/  hos=(unit @p)
1322        ?.  ?=(%ours -.identity)  ~
1323        (biff (get-header:http 'host' arg) (cury slaw %p))
1324      ?~  sid
1325        (handle-response response)
1326      ::  if this is an eauth remote logout, send the %shut
1327      ::
1328      =*  auth  auth.state
1329      ?:  ?=(^ hos)
1330        =^  moz   state  (handle-response response)
1331        :-  [(send-plea:client:eauth u.hos %0 %shut u.sid) moz]
1332        =/  book  (~(gut by visiting.auth) u.hos *logbook)
```

```
1333        =.  qeu.book  (~(put to qeu.book) u.sid)
1334        =.  visiting.auth  (~(put by visiting.auth) u.hos book)
1335        state
1336      ::  if the requester is logging themselves out, make them drop the cookie
1337      ::
1338      =?  headers.response-header.response  =(u.sid session-id)
1339        :_  headers.response-header.response
1340        ['set-cookie' (session-cookie-string session-id |)]
1341      ::  close the session as requested, then send the response
1342      ::
1343      =^  moz1  state  (close-session u.sid all)
1344      =^  moz2  state  (handle-response response)
1345    [[give-session-tokens (weld moz1 moz2)] state]
1346  ::  +session-id-from-request: attempt to find a session cookie
1347  ::
1348  ++  session-id-from-request
1349    |=  =request:http
1350    ^-  (unit @uv)
1351    ::  are there cookies passed with this request?
1352    ::
1353    =/  cookie-header=@t
1354      %+  roll  header-list.request
1355      |=  [[key=@t value=@t] c=@t]
1356      ?.  =(key 'cookie')
1357        c
1358      (cat 3 (cat 3 c ?~(c 0 '; ')) value)
1359    ::  is the cookie line valid?
1360    ::
1361    ?~  cookies=(rush cookie-header cock:de-purl:html)
1362      ~
1363    ::  is there an urbauth cookie?
1364    ::
1365    ?~  urbauth=(get-header:http (crip "urbauth-{(scow %p our)}") u.cookies)
1366      ~
1367    ::  if it's formatted like a valid session cookie, produce it
1368    ::
1369    `(unit @)`(rush u.urbauth ;~(pfix (jest '0v') viz:ag))
1370  ::  +request-is-logged-in: checks to see if the request has non-guest id
1371  ::
1372  ++  request-is-logged-in
1373    |=  =request:http
1374    ^-  ?
1375    ?~  session-id=(session-id-from-request request)
1376      |
1377    ?~  session=(~(get by sessions.auth.state) u.session-id)
1378      |
1379    &(!?=(%fake -.identity.u.session) (lte now expiry-time.u.session))
1380  ::  +request-is-authenticated: checks to see if the request is "us"
1381  ::
1382  ::    We are considered authenticated if this request has an urbauth
1383  ::    Cookie for the local identity that is not expired.
1384  ::
1385  ++  request-is-authenticated
1386    |=  =request:http
1387    ^-  ?
1388    ::  does the request pass a session cookie?
1389    ::
1390    ?~  session-id=(session-id-from-request request)
```

```
1391            %.n
1392      ::    is this a session that we know about?
1393      ::
1394      ?~    session=(~(get by sessions.auth.state) `@uv`u.session-id)
1395            %.n
1396      ::    does this session have our id, and is it still valid?
1397      ::
1398      &(?=(%ours -.identity.u.session) (lte now expiry-time.u.session))
1399    ::  +start-session: create a new session with %local or %guest identity
1400    ::
1401    ++  start-session
1402      |=  kind=?(%local %guest [%eauth who=@p])
1403      ^-  [[session=@uv =identity moves=(list move)] server-state]
1404      =;  [key=@uv sid=identity]
1405        :-  :+  key  sid
1406            ::    if no session existed previously, we must kick off the
1407            ::    session expiry timer
1408            ::
1409            ?^  sessions.auth.state  ~
1410            [duct %pass /sessions/expire %b %wait (add now session-timeout)]~
1411        =-  state(sessions.auth -)
1412        %+  ~(put by sessions.auth.state)  key
1413        [sid (add now session-timeout) ~]
1414      ::  create a new session with a fake identity
1415      ::
1416      =/  sik=@uv  new-session-key
1417      :-  sik
1418      ?:  ?=(%local kind)        [%ours ~]
1419      ?:  ?=([%eauth @] kind)    [%real who.kind]
1420      :-  %fake
1421      ::  pre-scramble our ship name into its displayed value, and
1422      ::  truncate it to be at most moon-length, so that we can overlay
1423      ::  it onto the end of a comet name for visual consistency.
1424      ::  to prevent escalation, make sure the guest identity isn't ours.
1425      ::
1426      |-
1427      =;  nom=@p
1428        ?.  =(our nom)  nom
1429        $(eny (shas %next-name eny))
1430      %+  end  3^16
1431      %^  cat  3
1432        (end 3^8 (fein:ob our))
1433      (~(raw og (shas %fake-name eny)) 128)
1434    ::  +session-for-request: get the session details for the request
1435    ::
1436    ::    creates a guest session if the request does not have a valid session.
1437    ::    there is no need to call +give-session-tokens after this, because
1438    ::    guest session do not make valid "auth session" tokens.
1439    ::
1440    ++  session-for-request
1441      |=  =request:http
1442      ^-  [[session=@uv =identity moves=(list move)] server-state]
1443      =*  new  (start-session %guest)
1444      ?~  sid=(session-id-from-request request)
1445        new
1446      ?~  ses=(~(get by sessions.auth.state) u.sid)
1447        new
1448      ?:  (gth now expiry-time.u.ses)
```

```
1449            new
1450          [[u.sid identity.u.ses ~] state]
1451      ::  +close-session: delete a session and its associated channels
1452      ::
1453      ::    if :all is true, deletes all sessions that share the same identity.
1454      ::    if this closes an %ours session, the caller is responsible for
1455      ::    also calling +give-session-tokens afterwards.
1456      ::
1457      ++  close-session
1458        |=  [session-id=@uv all=?]
1459        ^-  [(list move) server-state]
1460        ?~  ses=(~(get by sessions.auth.state) session-id)
1461          [~ state]
1462        ::  delete the session(s) and find the associated ids & channels
1463        ::
1464        =^  [siz=(list @uv) channels=(list @t)]  sessions.auth.state
1465          =*  sessions  sessions.auth.state
1466          ::  either delete just the specific session and its channels,
1467          ::
1468          ?.  all
1469            :-  [[session-id]~ ~(tap in channels.u.ses)]
1470            (~(del by sessions) session-id)
1471          ::  or delete all sessions with the identity from :session-id
1472          ::
1473          %+  roll  ~(tap by sessions)
1474          |=  $:  [sid=@uv s=session]
1475                  [[siz=(list @uv) caz=(list @t)] sez=(map @uv session)]
1476          ==
1477          ^+  [[siz caz] sez]
1478          ?.  =(identity.s identity.u.ses)
1479            ::  identity doesn't match, so re-store this session
1480            ::
1481            [[siz caz] (~(put by sez) sid s)]
1482          ::  identity matches, so register this session as closed
1483          ::
1484          [[[sid siz] (weld caz ~(tap in channels.s))] sez]
1485        ::  close all affected channels and send their responses
1486        ::
1487        =|  moves1=(list move)
1488        |-  ^-  (quip move server-state)
1489        ?^  channels
1490          %-  %+  trace  1
1491              |.("{(trip i.channels)} discarding channel due to closed session")
1492          =^  moz    state
1493            (discard-channel:by-channel i.channels |)
1494          $(moves1 (weld moves1 moz), channels t.channels)
1495        ::  lastly, %real sessions require additional cleanup
1496        ::
1497        ?.  ?=(%real -.identity.u.ses)  [moves1 state]
1498        =^  moves2  visitors.auth.state
1499          %+  roll  ~(tap by visitors.auth.state)
1500          |=  [[nonce=@uv visa=visitor] [moz=(list move) viz=(map @uv visitor)]]
1501          ?^  +.visa  [moz (~(put by viz) nonce visa)]
1502          :_  viz
1503          %+  weld  moz
1504          ?~  duct.visa  ~
1505          [(send-boon:server:eauth(duct u.duct.visa) %0 %shut nonce)]~
1506        [(weld `(list move)`moves1 `(list move)`moves2) state]
```

```
1507      ::   +code: returns the same as |code
1508      ::
1509      ++  code
1510        ^-  @ta
1511        =/  res=(unit (unit cage))
1512          (rof ~ /eyre %j [our %code da+now] /(scot %p our))
1513        (rsh 3 (scot %p ;;(@ q.q:(need (need res)))))
1514      ::  +session-cookie-string: compose session cookie
1515      ::
1516      ++  session-cookie-string
1517        |=  [session=@uv extend=?]
1518        ^-  @t
1519        %-  crip
1520        =;  max-age=tape
1521          "urbauth-{(scow %p our)}={(scow %uv session)}; Path=/; Max-Age={max-age}"
1522        %-  format-ud-as-integer
1523        ?.  extend  0
1524        (div (msec:milly session-timeout) 1.000)
1525      ::
1526      ::
1527      ++  eauth
1528        =*  auth  auth.state
1529        |%
1530        ++  server
1531          |%
1532          ::  +start: initiate an eauth login attempt for the :ship identity
1533          ::
1534          ++  start
1535            |=  [=ship base=(unit @t) last=@t]
1536            ^-  [(list move) server-state]
1537            %-  (trace 2 |.("eauth: starting eauth into {(scow %p ship)}"))
1538            =/  nonce=@uv
1539              |-
1540              =+  n=(~(raw og (shas %eauth-nonce eny)) 64)
1541              ?.  (~(has by visitors.auth) n)  n
1542              $(eny (shas %try-again n))
1543            =/  visit=visitor  [~ `[duct now] ship base last ~]
1544            =.  visitors.auth  (~(put by visitors.auth) nonce visit)
1545            :_  state
1546            ::  we delay serving an http response until we receive a scry %tune
1547            ::
1548            :~  (send-keen %keen ship nonce now)
1549                (start-timeout /visitors/(scot %uv nonce))
1550            ==
1551          ::  +on-tune: receive a client-url remote scry result
1552          ::
1553          ++  on-tune
1554            |=  [ship=@p nonce=@uv url=@t]
1555            ^-  [(list move) server-state]
1556            %-  (trace 2 |.("eauth: %tune from {(scow %p ship)}"))
1557            ::  guarantee the ship still controls the nonce
1558            ::
1559            =/  visa=visitor  (~(got by visitors.auth) nonce)
1560            ?>  &(?=(^ +.visa) =(ship ship.visa))
1561            ::  redirect the visitor to their own confirmation page
1562            ::
1563            =.  visitors.auth  (~(put by visitors.auth) nonce visa(pend ~))
1564            %-  handle-response(duct http:(need pend.visa))
```

```
1565        =;  url=@t  [%start 303^['location' url]~ ~ &]
1566        %+  rap  3
1567        :~  url
1568            '?server='  (scot %p our)
1569            '&nonce='   (scot %uv nonce)
1570        ==
1571    ::  +on-plea: receive an eauth network message from a client
1572    ::
1573    ++  on-plea
1574      |=  [=ship plea=eauth-plea]
1575      ^-  [(list move) server-state]
1576      %-  (trace 2 |.("eauth: {(trip +<.plea)} from {(scow %p ship)}"))
1577      =;  res=[(list move) server-state]
1578        =^  moz  state  res
1579        [[[duct %give %done ~] moz] state]
1580      ?-  +<.plea
1581          %open
1582        ::  this attempt may or may not have been started in +start yet
1583        ::
1584        =/  visa=visitor
1585          %+  ~(gut by visitors.auth)  nonce.plea
1586          [~ ~ ship ~ '/' ~]
1587        ?>  ?=(^ +.visa)
1588        ?>  =(ship ship.visa)
1589        ::NOTE  that token might still be empty, in which case the http
1590        ::      client will probably signal an abort when they return
1591        ::
1592        =.  duct.visa      `duct
1593        =.  toke.visa      token.plea
1594        =.  visitors.auth  (~(put by visitors.auth) nonce.plea visa)
1595        ::  if the eauth attempt was started on our side, we may know the
1596        ::  specific base url the user used; make sure they go back there
1597        ::
1598        =/  url=@t
1599          %-  need
1600          ?~  base.visa  eauth-url
1601          eauth-url(user.endpoint.auth base.visa)
1602        [[(send-boon %0 %okay nonce.plea url)]~ state]
1603      ::
1604          %shut
1605        ::  the visitor wants the associated session gone
1606        ::
1607        ?~  visa=(~(get by visitors.auth) nonce.plea)  [~ state]
1608        =.  visitors.auth  (~(del by visitors.auth) nonce.plea)
1609        =?  sessions.auth  ?=(@ +.u.visa)
1610          (~(del by sessions.auth) sesh.u.visa)
1611        [[(send-boon %0 %shut nonce.plea)]~ state]
1612      ==
1613    ::  +cancel: the client aborted the eauth attempt, so clean it up
1614    ::
1615    ++  cancel
1616      |=  [nonce=@uv last=@t]
1617      ^-  [(list move) server-state]
1618      ::  if the eauth attempt doesn't exist, or it was already completed,
1619      ::  we cannot cancel it
1620      ::
1621      ?~  visa=(~(get by visitors.auth) nonce)  [~ state]
1622      ?@  +.u.visa  [~ state]
```

```
1623        ::  delete the attempt, and go back to the login page
1624        ::
1625        %-  (trace 2 |.("eauth: cancelling login"))
1626        =.  visitors.auth  (~(del by visitors.auth) nonce)
1627        =^  moz  state
1628          =/  url=@t
1629            %^  cat  3  '/~/login?eauth&redirect='
1630            (crip (en-urlt:html (trip last)))
1631          (handle-response %start 303^['location' url]~ ~ &)
1632        :_  state
1633        %+  weld  moz
1634        ?~  duct.u.visa  ~
1635        [(send-boon(duct u.duct.u.visa) %0 %shut nonce)]~
1636    ::  +expire: host-side cancel an eauth attempt if it's still pending
1637    ::
1638    ++  expire
1639      |=  nonce=@uv
1640      ^-  [(list move) server-state]
1641      ?~  visa=(~(get by visitors.auth) nonce)
1642        [~ state]
1643      ?@  +.u.visa  [~ state]
1644      %-  (trace 2 |.("eauth: expiring"))
1645      =^  moz  state
1646        ?~  pend.u.visa  [~ state]
1647        %-  return-static-data-on-duct(duct http.u.pend.u.visa)
1648        [503 'text/html' (eauth-error-page %server last.u.visa)]
1649      =?  moz  ?=(^ pend.u.visa)
1650        [(send-keen %yawn ship.u.visa nonce keen.u.pend.u.visa) moz]
1651      =.  visitors.auth  (~(del by visitors.auth) nonce)
1652      :_  state
1653      %+  weld  moz
1654      ?~  duct.u.visa  ~
1655      [(send-boon(duct u.duct.u.visa) %0 %shut nonce)]~
1656    ::  +finalize: eauth attempt was approved: mint the client a new session
1657    ::
1658    ::      gives the http response on the current duct
1659    ::
1660    ++  finalize
1661      |=  [=plea=^duct nonce=@uv =ship last=@t]
1662      ^-  [(list move) server-state]
1663      %-  (trace 2 |.("eauth: finalizing login for {(scow %p ship)}"))
1664      ::  clean up the session they're changing out from,
1665      ::  mint the new session,
1666      ::  associate it with the nonce,
1667      ::  and the finalization request,
1668      ::  and send the visitor the cookie + final redirect
1669      ::
1670      =^  moz1  state
1671        (close-session session-id:(~(got by connections.state) duct) |)
1672      =^  [sid=@uv * moz2=(list move)]  state
1673        (start-session %eauth ship)
1674      =.  visitors.auth
1675        %+  ~(jab by visitors.auth)  nonce
1676        |=(v=visitor v(+ sid))
1677      =.  connections.state
1678        %+  ~(jab by connections.state)  duct
1679        |=  o=outstanding-connection
1680        o(session-id sid)
```

```
1681          =^  moz3  state
1682            =;  hed  (handle-response %start 303^hed ~ &)
1683            :~  ['location' last]
1684                ['set-cookie' (session-cookie-string sid &)]
1685            ==
1686          [:(weld moz1 moz2 moz3) state]
1687        ::  +on-fail: we crashed or received an empty %tune, clean up
1688        ::
1689        ++  on-fail
1690          |=  [=ship nonce=@uv]
1691          ^-  [(list move) server-state]
1692          ::  if the eauth attempt doesn't exist, or it was already completed,
1693          ::  we can no-op here
1694          ::
1695          ?~  visa=(~(get by visitors.auth) nonce)  [~ state]
1696          ?@  +.u.visa  [~ state]
1697          ::  delete the attempt, and go back to the login page
1698          ::
1699          %-  (trace 2 |.("eauth: failed login"))
1700          =.  visitors.auth  (~(del by visitors.auth) nonce)
1701          =^  moz  state
1702            ?~  pend.u.visa  [~ state]
1703            %-  return-static-data-on-duct(duct http.u.pend.u.visa)
1704            [503 'text/html' (eauth-error-page %server last.u.visa)]
1705          :_  state
1706          %+  weld  moz
1707          ?~  duct.u.visa  ~
1708          [(send-boon(duct u.duct.u.visa) %0 %shut nonce)]~
1709        ::
1710        ::TODO  +on-request?
1711        ::
1712        ++  send-keen
1713          |=  [kind=?(%keen %yawn) =ship nonce=@uv =time]
1714          ^-  move
1715          %-  (trace 2 |.("eauth: %{(trip kind)} into {(scow %p ship)}"))
1716          ::  we round down the time to make it more likely to hit cache,
1717          ::  at the expense of not working if the endpoint changed within
1718          ::  the last hour.
1719          ::
1720          =/  =wire       /eauth/keen/(scot %p ship)/(scot %uv nonce)
1721          =.  time        (sub time (mod time ~h1))
1722          =/  =spar:ames  [ship /e/x/(scot %da time)//eauth/url]
1723          [duct %pass wire %a ?-(kind %keen keen+spar, %yawn yawn+spar)]
1724        ::
1725        ++  send-boon
1726          |=  boon=eauth-boon
1727          ^-  move
1728          %-  (trace 2 |.("eauth: sending {(trip +<.boon)}"))
1729          [duct %give %boon boon]
1730        --
1731      ::
1732      ++  client
1733        |%
1734        ::  +start: as the client, approve or abort an eauth attempt
1735        ::
1736        ::    assumes the duct is of an incoming eauth start/approve request
1737        ::
1738        ++  start
```

```
1739      |=  [host=ship nonce=@uv grant=?]
1740      ^-  [(list move) server-state]
1741      =/  token=@uv  (~(raw og (shas %eauth-token eny)) 128)
1742      ::  we always send an %open, because we need to redirect the user
1743      ::  back to the host. and we always set a timeout, because we may
1744      ::  not get a response quickly enough.
1745      ::
1746      :-  :~  (send-plea host %0 %open nonce ?:(grant `token ~))
1747              (start-timeout /visiting/(scot %p host)/(scot %uv nonce))
1748          ==
1749      ::  make sure we aren't attempting with this nonce already,
1750      ::  then remember the secret so we can include it in the redirect
1751      ::
1752      =/  book  (~(gut by visiting.auth) host *logbook)
1753      ?<  (~(has by map.book) nonce)
1754      =.  visiting.auth
1755        %+  ~(put by visiting.auth)  host
1756        :-  (~(put to qeu.book) nonce)
1757        (~(put by map.book) nonce [`duct ?:(grant `token ~)])
1758      state
1759    ::  +on-done: receive n/ack for plea we sent
1760    ::
1761    ++  on-done
1762      |=  [host=ship good=?]
1763      ^-  [(list move) server-state]
1764      %-  %-  trace
1765          ?:  good
1766          [2 |.("eauth: ack from {(scow %p host)}")]
1767          [1 |.("eauth: nack from {(scow %p host)}")]
1768      =/  book  (~(gut by visiting.auth) host *logbook)
1769      ?~  ~(top to qeu.book)
1770        %.  [~ state]
1771        (trace 0 |.("eauth: done on empty queue from {(scow %p host)}"))
1772      =^  nonce=@uv  qeu.book  ~(get to qeu.book)
1773      ?:  good
1774        =.  visiting.auth
1775          ?:  =([~ ~] book)
1776          (~(del by visiting.auth) host)
1777          (~(put by visiting.auth) host book)
1778        [~ state]
1779      =/  port  (~(get by map.book) nonce)
1780      ?~  port  [~ state]
1781      ::  delete the attempt/session, serve response if needed
1782      ::
1783      =.  visiting.auth
1784        =.  map.book
1785        (~(del by map.book) nonce)
1786        ?:  =([~ ~] book)
1787        (~(del by visiting.auth) host)
1788        (~(put by visiting.auth) host book)
1789      ::
1790      ?@  u.port      [~ state]
1791      ?~  pend.u.port  [~ state]
1792      %^  return-static-data-on-duct(duct u.pend.u.port)  503  'text/html'
1793      (eauth-error-page ~)
1794    ::  +on-boon: receive an eauth network response from a host
1795    ::
1796    ::    crashes on unexpected circumstances, in response to which we
```

```
1797        ::      should abort the eauth attempt
1798        ::
1799        ++  on-boon
1800        |=  [host=ship boon=eauth-boon]
1801        ^-  [(list move) server-state]
1802        %-  (trace 2 |.("eauth: %{(trip +<.boon)} from {(scow %p host)}"))
1803        ?-  +<.boon
1804            %okay
1805        =/  book  (~(got by visiting.auth) host)
1806        =/  port  (~(got by map.book) nonce.boon)
1807        ?>  ?=(^ port)
1808        ?>  ?=(^ pend.port)
1809        ::  update the outgoing sessions map, deleting if we aborted
1810        ::
1811        =.  visiting.auth
1812          ?^  toke.port
1813            %+  ~(put by visiting.auth)  host
1814            :-  qeu.book
1815            ::NOTE  optimistic
1816            (~(put by map.book) nonce.boon now)
1817          =.  map.book
1818            (~(del by map.book) nonce.boon)
1819          ?:  =([~ ~] book)
1820            (~(del by visiting.auth) host)
1821          (~(put by visiting.auth) host book)
1822        ::  always serve a redirect, with either the token, or abort signal
1823        ::
1824        =;  url=@t
1825          %-  handle-response(duct u.pend.port)
1826          [%start 303^['location' url]~ ~ &]
1827        %+  rap  3
1828        :*  url.boon
1829            '?nonce='  (scot %uv nonce.boon)
1830            ?~  toke.port  ['&abort']~
1831            ~['&token='  (scot %uv u.toke.port)]
1832        ==
1833        ::
1834            %shut
1835        ::  the host has deleted the corresponding session
1836        ::
1837        =.  visiting.auth
1838          =/  book
1839            (~(gut by visiting.auth) host *logbook)
1840          =.  map.book
1841            (~(del by map.book) nonce.boon)
1842          ?:  =([~ ~] book)
1843            (~(del by visiting.auth) host)
1844          (~(put by visiting.auth) host book)
1845        [~ state]
1846        ==
1847        ::
1848        ++  expire
1849        |=  [host=ship nonce=@uv]
1850        ^-  [(list move) server-state]
1851        =/  book  (~(gut by visiting.auth) host *logbook)
1852        =/  port  (~(get by map.book) nonce)
1853        ::  if the attempt was completed, we don't expire it
1854        ::
```

```
1855      ?~  port      [~ state]
1856      ?@  u.port    [~ state]
1857      ::  delete pending attempts, serve response if needed
1858      ::
1859      %-  %+  trace  1
1860          |.("eauth: attempt into {(scow %p host)} expired")
1861      =.  visiting.auth
1862        =.  map.book
1863          (~(del by map.book) nonce)
1864        ?:  =([~ ~] book)
1865          (~(del by visiting.auth) host)
1866        (~(put by visiting.auth) host book)
1867      ::
1868      ?~  pend.u.port  [~ state]
1869      %^  return-static-data-on-duct(duct u.pend.u.port)  503  'text/html'
1870      (eauth-error-page ~)
1871  ::
1872  ++  send-plea
1873    |=  [=ship plea=eauth-plea]
1874    ^-  move
1875    ::NOTE  no nonce in the wire, to avoid proliferating flows
1876    =/  =wire  /eauth/plea/(scot %p ship)
1877    %-  (trace 2 |.("eauth: {(trip +<.plea)} into {(scow %p ship)}"))
1878    [[/eyre/eauth/synthetic]~ %pass wire %a %plea ship %e /eauth/0 plea]
1879  ::
1880  ++  confirmation-page
1881    |=  [server=ship nonce=@uv]
1882    ^-  octs
1883    %-  as-octs:mimes:html
1884    %-  crip
1885    %-  en-xml:html
1886    =/  favicon  %+
1887      weld  "<svg width='10' height='10' viewBox='0 0 10 10' xmlns='http://www.w3.org/2000/svg'>"
1888            "<circle r='3.09' cx='5' cy='5' /></svg>"
1889    ;html
1890      ;head
1891        ;meta(charset "utf-8");
1892        ;meta(name "viewport", content "width=device-width, initial-scale=1, shrink-to-fit=no");
1893        ;link(rel "icon", type "image/svg+xml", href (weld "data:image/svg+xml;utf8," favicon));
1894        ;title:"Urbit"
1895        ;style:"{(trip auth-styling)}"
1896        ;style:'''
1897            form {
1898              border: 1px solid var(--black20);
1899              border-radius: 4px;
1900              padding: 1rem;
1901              align-items: stretch;
1902              font-size: 14px;
1903            }
1904            .red {
1905              background: var(--black05) !important;
1906              color: var(--black60) !important;
1907              border: 1px solid var(--black60) !important;
1908            }
1909            code {
1910              font-weight: bold;
1911              font-family: "Source Code Pro", monospace;
1912            }
```

```
1913                         button {
1914                           display: inline-block;
1915                         }
1916                         '''
1917             ==
1918           ;body
1919             ;form(action "/~/eauth", method "post")
1920               ; Hello, {(scow %p our)}.
1921               ; You are trying to log in to:
1922               ;code:"{(scow %p server)}"
1923               ;input(type "hidden", name "server", value (scow %p server));
1924               ;input(type "hidden", name "nonce", value (scow %uv nonce));
1925               ;button(type "submit", name "grant", value "grant"):"approve"
1926               ;button(type "submit", name "reject", class "red"):"reject"
1927             ==
1928         ==
1929       ==
1930     --
1931   :: +on-request: http request to the /~/eauth endpoint
1932   ::
1933   ++  on-request
1934     |=  [[session-id=@uv =identity] =request:http]
1935     ^-  [(list move) server-state]
1936     ::  we may need the requester to log in before proceeding
1937     ::
1938     =*  login
1939       =;  url=@t  (handle-response %start 303^['location' url]~ ~ &)
1940       %^  cat  3  '/~/login?redirect='
1941       (crip (en-urlt:html (trip url.request)))
1942     ::  or give them a generic, static error page in unexpected cases
1943     ::
1944     =*  error  %^  return-static-data-on-duct  400  'text/html'
1945                (eauth-error-page ~)
1946     ::  GET requests either render the confirmation page,
1947     ::  or finalize an eauth flow
1948     ::
1949     ?:  ?=(%'GET' method.request)
1950       =/  args=(map @t @t)  (malt args:(parse-request-line url.request))
1951       =/  server=(unit @p)  (biff (~(get by args) 'server') (cury slaw %p))
1952       =/  nonce=(unit @uv)  (biff (~(get by args) 'nonce') (cury slaw %uv))
1953       =/  token=(unit @uv)  (biff (~(get by args) 'token') (cury slaw %uv))
1954       =/  abort=?           (~(has by args) 'abort')
1955       ::
1956       ?~  nonce  error
1957       ::
1958       ?^  server
1959         ::  request for confirmation page
1960         ::
1961         ?.  ?=(%ours -.identity)  login
1962         =/  book  (~(gut by visiting.auth) u.server *logbook)
1963         =/  door  (~(get by map.book) u.nonce)
1964         ?~  door
1965           ::  nonce not yet used, render the confirmation page as normal
1966           ::
1967           %^  return-static-data-on-duct  200  'text/html'
1968           (confirmation-page:client u.server u.nonce)
1969         ::  if we're still awaiting a redirect target, we choose to serve
1970         ::  this latest request instead
```

```
1971              ::
1972              ?@  u.door        error
1973              ?~  pend.u.door   error
1974              =.  map.book      (~(put by map.book) u.nonce u.door(pend `duct))
1975              =.  visiting.auth  (~(put by visiting.auth) u.server book)
1976              %-  return-static-data-on-duct(duct u.pend.u.door)
1977              [202 'text/plain' (as-octs:mimes:html 'continued elsewhere...')]
1978          ::  important to provide an error response for unexpected states
1979          ::
1980          =/  visa=(unit visitor)  (~(get by visitors.auth) u.nonce)
1981          ?~  visa         error
1982          ?@  +.u.visa      error
1983          =*  error  %^  return-static-data-on-duct  400  'text/html'
1984                      (eauth-error-page %server last.u.visa)
1985          ::  request for finalization, must either abort or provide a token
1986          ::
1987          ::NOTE  yes, this means that unauthenticated clients can abort
1988          ::        any eauth attempt they know the nonce for, but that should
1989          ::        be pretty benign
1990          ?:  abort  (cancel:^server u.nonce last.u.visa)
1991          ?~  token  error
1992          ::  if this request provides a token, but the client didn't, complain
1993          ::
1994          ?~  toke.u.visa  error
1995          ::  verify the request
1996          ::
1997          ?.  =(u.token u.toke.u.visa)
1998            %-  (trace 1 |.("eauth: token mismatch"))
1999            error
2000          ?~  duct.u.visa  error
2001          (finalize:^server u.duct.u.visa u.nonce ship.u.visa last.u.visa)
2002        ::
2003        ?.  ?=(%'POST' method.request)
2004          %^  return-static-data-on-duct  405  'text/html'
2005          (eauth-error-page ~)
2006        ?.  =(%ours -.identity)  login
2007        ::  POST requests are always submissions of the confirmation page
2008        ::
2009        =/  args=(map @t @t)
2010          (malt (fall (rush q:(fall body.request *octs) yquy:de-purl:html) ~))
2011        =/  server=(unit @p)   (biff (~(get by args) 'server') (cury slaw %p))
2012        =/  nonce=(unit @uv)   (biff (~(get by args) 'nonce') (cury slaw %uv))
2013        =/  grant=?            =(`'grant' (~(get by args) 'grant'))
2014        ::
2015        =*  error   %^  return-static-data-on-duct  400  'text/html'
2016                     (eauth-error-page ~)
2017        ?~  server  error
2018        ?~  nonce   error
2019        =/  book    (~(gut by visiting.auth) u.server *logbook)
2020        ?:  (~(has by map.book) u.nonce)  error
2021        (start:client u.server u.nonce grant)
2022      ::
2023      ++  eauth-url
2024        ^-  (unit @t)
2025        =/  end=(unit @t)  (clap user.endpoint.auth auth.endpoint.auth head)
2026        ?~  end  ~
2027        `(cat 3 u.end '/~/eauth')
2028      ::
```

```
2029        ++  start-timeout
2030          |=  =path
2031          ^-  move
2032          [duct %pass [%eauth %expire path] %b %wait (add now ~m5)]
2033        --
2034      --
2035  ::  +channel: per-event handling of requests to the channel system
2036  ::
2037  ::    Eyre offers a remote interface to your Urbit through channels, which
2038  ::    are persistent connections on the server which can be disconnected and
2039  ::    reconnected on the client.
2040  ::
2041  ++  by-channel
2042    ::  moves: the moves to be sent out at the end of this event, reversed
2043    ::
2044    =|  moves=(list move)
2045    |%
2046    ::  +handle-request: handles an http request for the subscription system
2047    ::
2048    ++  handle-request
2049      |=  [[session-id=@uv =identity] =address =request:http]
2050      ^-  [(list move) server-state]
2051      ::  parse out the path key the subscription is on
2052      ::
2053      =+  request-line=(parse-request-line url.request)
2054      ?.  ?=([@t @t @t ~] site.request-line)
2055        ::  url is not of the form '/~/channel/'
2056        ::
2057        %^  return-static-data-on-duct  400  'text/html'
2058        (error-page 400 & url.request "malformed channel url")
2059      ::  channel-id: unique channel id parsed out of url
2060      ::
2061      =+  channel-id=i.t.t.site.request-line
2062      ::
2063      ?:  =('PUT' method.request)
2064        ::  PUT methods starts/modifies a channel, and returns a result immediately
2065        ::
2066        (on-put-request channel-id identity request)
2067      ::
2068      ?:  =('GET' method.request)
2069        (on-get-request channel-id [session-id identity] request)
2070      ?:  =('POST' method.request)
2071        ::  POST methods are used solely for deleting channels
2072        (on-put-request channel-id identity request)
2073      ::
2074      ((trace 0 |.("session not a put")) `state)
2075    ::  +on-cancel-request: cancels an ongoing subscription
2076    ::
2077    ::    One of our long lived sessions just got closed. We put the associated
2078    ::    session back into the waiting state.
2079    ::
2080    ++  on-cancel-request
2081      ^-  [(list move) server-state]
2082      ::  lookup the session id by duct
2083      ::
2084      %-  (trace 1 |.("{<duct>} moving channel to waiting state"))
2085      ::
2086      ?~  maybe-channel-id=(~(get by duct-to-key.channel-state.state) duct)
```

```
2087        ((trace 0 |.("{<duct>} no channel to move")) `state)
2088      ::
2089      =/  maybe-session
2090        (~(get by session.channel-state.state) u.maybe-channel-id)
2091      ?~  maybe-session
2092        ((trace 1 |.("{<maybe-session>} session doesn't exist")) `state)
2093      ::
2094      =/  heartbeat-cancel=(list move)
2095        ?~  heartbeat.u.maybe-session  ~
2096        :~  %^  cancel-heartbeat-move
2097              u.maybe-channel-id
2098            date.u.heartbeat.u.maybe-session
2099          duct.u.heartbeat.u.maybe-session
2100        ==
2101      ::
2102      =/  expiration-time=@da  (add now channel-timeout)
2103      ::
2104      :-  %+  weld  heartbeat-cancel
2105        [(set-timeout-move u.maybe-channel-id expiration-time) moves]
2106      %_    state
2107          session.channel-state
2108        %+  ~(jab by session.channel-state.state)  u.maybe-channel-id
2109        |=  =channel
2110        ::  if we are canceling a known channel, it should have a listener
2111        ::
2112        ?>  ?=([%| *] state.channel)
2113        channel(state [%& [expiration-time duct]], heartbeat ~)
2114      ::
2115          duct-to-key.channel-state
2116        (~(del by duct-to-key.channel-state.state) duct)
2117      ==
2118  ::  +update-timeout-timer-for: sets a timeout timer on a channel
2119  ::
2120  ::    This creates a channel if it doesn't exist, cancels existing timers
2121  ::    if they're already set (we cannot have duplicate timers), and (if
2122  ::    necessary) moves channels from the listening state to the expiration
2123  ::    state.
2124  ::
2125  ++  update-timeout-timer-for
2126    |=  [mode=?(%json %jam) =identity channel-id=@t]
2127    ^+  ..update-timeout-timer-for
2128    ::  when our callback should fire
2129    ::
2130    =/  expiration-time=@da  (add now channel-timeout)
2131    ::  if the channel doesn't exist, create it and set a timer
2132    ::
2133    ?~  maybe-channel=(~(get by session.channel-state.state) channel-id)
2134      ::
2135      %_    ..update-timeout-timer-for
2136          session.channel-state.state
2137        %+  ~(put by session.channel-state.state)  channel-id
2138        [mode identity [%& expiration-time duct] 0 now ~ ~ ~]
2139      ::
2140          moves
2141        [(set-timeout-move channel-id expiration-time) moves]
2142      ==
2143    ::  if the channel has an active listener, we aren't setting any timers
2144    ::
```

```
2145      ?:  ?=([%| *] state.u.maybe-channel)
2146        ..update-timeout-timer-for
2147      ::  we have a previous timer; cancel the old one and set the new one
2148      ::
2149      %_    ..update-timeout-timer-for
2150        session.channel-state.state
2151      %+  ~(jab by session.channel-state.state)  channel-id
2152      |=  =channel
2153      channel(state [%& [expiration-time duct]])
2154      ::
2155        moves
2156      :*  (cancel-timeout-move channel-id p.state.u.maybe-channel)
2157        (set-timeout-move channel-id expiration-time)
2158        moves
2159      ==
2160    ==
2161    ::
2162    ++  set-heartbeat-move
2163      |=  [channel-id=@t heartbeat-time=@da]
2164      ^-  move
2165      :^  duct  %pass  /channel/heartbeat/[channel-id]
2166      [%b %wait heartbeat-time]
2167    ::
2168    ++  cancel-heartbeat-move
2169      |=  [channel-id=@t heartbeat-time=@da =^duct]
2170      ^-  move
2171      :^  duct  %pass  /channel/heartbeat/[channel-id]
2172      [%b %rest heartbeat-time]
2173    ::
2174    ++  set-timeout-move
2175      |=  [channel-id=@t expiration-time=@da]
2176      ^-  move
2177      [duct %pass /channel/timeout/[channel-id] %b %wait expiration-time]
2178    ::
2179    ++  cancel-timeout-move
2180      |=  [channel-id=@t expiration-time=@da =^duct]
2181      ^-  move
2182      :^  duct  %pass  /channel/timeout/[channel-id]
2183      [%b %rest expiration-time]
2184    ::  +on-get-request: handles a GET request
2185    ::
2186    ::    GET requests connect to a channel for the server to send events to
2187    ::    the client in text/event-stream format.
2188    ::
2189    ++  on-get-request
2190      |=  [channel-id=@t [session-id=@uv =identity] =request:http]
2191      ^-  [(list move) server-state]
2192      ::  if the channel doesn't exist, we cannot serve it.
2193      ::  this 404 also lets clients know if their channel was reaped since
2194      ::  they last connected to it.
2195      ::
2196      ?.  (~(has by session.channel-state.state) channel-id)
2197        %^  return-static-data-on-duct  404  'text/html'
2198        (error-page 404 | url.request ~)
2199      ::
2200      =/  mode=?(%json %jam)
2201        (find-channel-mode %'GET' header-list.request)
2202      =^  [exit=? =wall moves=(list move)]  state
```

```
2203        ::  the request may include a 'Last-Event-Id' header
2204        ::
2205    =/  maybe-last-event-id=(unit @ud)
2206      ?~  maybe-raw-header=(get-header:http 'last-event-id' header-list.request)
2207        ~
2208      (rush u.maybe-raw-header dum:ag)
2209    =/  channel
2210      (~(got by session.channel-state.state) channel-id)
2211    ::  we put some demands on the get request, and may need to do some
2212    ::  cleanup for prior requests.
2213    ::
2214    ::  find the channel creator's identity, make sure it matches
2215    ::
2216    ?.  =(identity identity.channel)
2217      =^  mos  state
2218        %^  return-static-data-on-duct  403  'text/html'
2219        (error-page 403 | url.request ~)
2220      [[& ~ mos] state]
2221    ::  make sure the request "mode" doesn't conflict with a prior request
2222    ::
2223    ::TODO  or could we change that on the spot, given that only a single
2224    ::        request will ever be listening to this channel?
2225    ?.  =(mode mode.channel)
2226      =^  mos  state
2227        %^  return-static-data-on-duct  406  'text/html'
2228        =;  msg=tape  (error-page 406 %.y url.request msg)
2229        "channel already established in {(trip mode.channel)} mode"
2230      [[& ~ mos] state]
2231    ::  when opening an event-stream, we must cancel our timeout timer
2232    ::  if there's no duct already bound. else, kill the old request,
2233    ::  we will replace its duct at the end of this arm
2234    ::
2235    =^  cancel-moves  state
2236      ?:  ?=([%& *] state.channel)
2237        :_  state
2238        (cancel-timeout-move channel-id p.state.channel)^~
2239      =.  duct-to-key.channel-state.state
2240        (~(del by duct-to-key.channel-state.state) p.state.channel)
2241      =/  cancel-heartbeat
2242        ?~  heartbeat.channel  ~
2243        :_  ~
2244        %+  cancel-heartbeat-move  channel-id
2245        [date duct]:u.heartbeat.channel
2246      =-  [(weld cancel-heartbeat -<) ->]
2247      (handle-response(duct p.state.channel) [%cancel ~])
2248    ::  flush events older than the passed in 'Last-Event-ID'
2249    ::
2250    =?  state  ?=(^ maybe-last-event-id)
2251      (acknowledge-events channel-id u.maybe-last-event-id)
2252    ::TODO  that did not remove them from the channel queue though!
2253    ::        we may want to account for maybe-last-event-id, for efficiency.
2254    ::        (the client _should_ ignore events it heard previously if we do
2255    ::        end up re-sending them, but _requiring_ that feels kinda risky)
2256    ::
2257    ::  combine the remaining queued events to send to the client
2258    ::
2259    =;  event-replay=wall
2260      [[| - cancel-moves] state]
```

```
2261        %-  zing
2262        %-  flop
2263        =/  queue  events.channel
2264        =|  events=(list wall)
2265        |-
2266        ^+  events
2267        ?:  =(~ queue)
2268          events
2269        =^  head  queue  ~(get to queue)
2270        =,  p.head
2271        ::NOTE  these will only fail if the mark and/or json types changed,
2272        ::       since conversion failure also gets caught during first receive.
2273        ::       we can't do anything about this, so consider it unsupported.
2274        =/  said
2275          (channel-event-to-tape channel request-id channel-event)
2276        ?~  said  $
2277        $(events [(event-tape-to-wall id +.u.said) events])
2278    ?:  exit  [moves state]
2279    ::  send the start event to the client
2280    ::
2281    =^  http-moves  state
2282      %-  handle-response
2283      :*  %start
2284          :-  200
2285          :~  ['content-type' 'text/event-stream']
2286              ['cache-control' 'no-cache']
2287              ['connection' 'keep-alive']
2288          ==
2289          (wall-to-octs wall)
2290          complete=%.n
2291      ==
2292    ::  associate this duct with this session key
2293    ::
2294    =.  duct-to-key.channel-state.state
2295      (~(put by duct-to-key.channel-state.state) duct channel-id)
2296    ::  associate this channel with the session cookie
2297    ::
2298    =.  sessions.auth.state
2299      %+  ~(jab by sessions.auth.state)
2300        session-id
2301      |=  =session
2302      session(channels (~(put in channels.session) channel-id))
2303    ::  initialize sse heartbeat
2304    ::
2305    =/  heartbeat-time=@da  (add now ~s20)
2306    =/  heartbeat  (set-heartbeat-move channel-id heartbeat-time)
2307    ::  record the mode & duct for future output,
2308    ::  and record heartbeat-time for possible future cancel
2309    ::
2310    =.  session.channel-state.state
2311      %+  ~(jab by session.channel-state.state)  channel-id
2312      |=  =channel
2313      %_  channel
2314        mode      mode
2315        state     [%| duct]
2316        heartbeat  (some [heartbeat-time duct])
2317      ==
2318    ::
```

```
2319        [[heartbeat :(weld http-moves moves)] state]
2320    ::  +acknowledge-events: removes events before :last-event-id on :channel-id
2321    ::
2322    ++  acknowledge-events
2323    |=  [channel-id=@t last-event-id=@u]
2324    ^-  server-state
2325    %_    state
2326        session.channel-state
2327    %+  ~(jab by session.channel-state.state)  channel-id
2328    |=  =channel
2329    ^+  channel
2330    =^  acked  events.channel
2331        (prune-events events.channel last-event-id)
2332    =.  unacked.channel
2333        (subtract-acked-events acked unacked.channel)
2334    channel(last-ack now)
2335    ==
2336    ::  +on-put-request: handles a PUT request
2337    ::
2338    ::    PUT requests send commands from the client to the server. We receive
2339    ::    a set of commands in JSON format in the body of the message.
2340    ::    channels don't exist until a PUT request is sent. it's valid for
2341    ::    this request to contain an empty list of commands.
2342    ::
2343    ++  on-put-request
2344    |=  [channel-id=@t =identity =request:http]
2345    ^-  [(list move) server-state]
2346    ::  if the channel already exists, and is not of this identity, 403
2347    ::
2348    ::    the creation case happens in the +update-timeout-timer-for below
2349    ::
2350    ?:  ?~  c=(~(get by session.channel-state.state) channel-id)  |
2351        !=(identity identity.u.c)
2352      %^  return-static-data-on-duct  403  'text/html'
2353      (error-page 403 | url.request ~)
2354    ::  error when there's no body
2355    ::
2356    ?~  body.request
2357      %^  return-static-data-on-duct  400  'text/html'
2358      (error-page 400 %.y url.request "no put body")
2359    ::
2360    =/  mode=?(%json %jam)
2361      (find-channel-mode %'PUT' header-list.request)
2362    ::  if we cannot parse requests from the body, give an error
2363    ::
2364    =/  maybe-requests=(each (list channel-request) @t)
2365      (parse-channel-request mode u.body.request)
2366    ?:  ?=(%| -.maybe-requests)
2367      %^  return-static-data-on-duct  400  'text/html'
2368      (error-page 400 & url.request (trip p.maybe-requests))
2369    ::  check for the existence of the channel-id
2370    ::
2371    ::    if we have no session, create a new one set to expire in
2372    ::    :channel-timeout from now. if we have one which has a timer, update
2373    ::    that timer.
2374    ::
2375    =.  ..on-put-request  (update-timeout-timer-for mode identity channel-id)
2376    ::  for each request, execute the action passed in
```

```
2377        ::
2378    =+  requests=p.maybe-requests
2379        ::  gall-moves: put moves here first so we can flop for ordering
2380        ::  errors: if we accumulate any, discard the gall-moves and revert
2381        ::
2382    =|  gall-moves=(list move)
2383    =|  errors=(map @ud @t)
2384    =/  og-state  state
2385    =/  from=ship
2386      ?+(-.identity who.identity %ours our)
2387    |-
2388        ::
2389    ?~  requests
2390      ?:  =(~ errors)
2391        ::  everything succeeded, mark the request as completed
2392        ::
2393        =^  http-moves  state
2394          %-  handle-response
2395          :*  %start
2396              [status-code=204 headers=~]
2397              data=~
2398              complete=%.y
2399          ==
2400        ::
2401        [:(weld (flop gall-moves) http-moves moves) state]
2402      ::  some things went wrong. revert all operations & give 400
2403      ::
2404      %-  (trace 1 |.("{<channel-id>} reverting due to errors"))
2405      =.  state  og-state
2406      =^  http-moves  state
2407        %^  return-static-data-on-duct  400  'text/html'
2408        %-  as-octs:mimes:html
2409        %+  rap  3
2410        %+  turn  (sort ~(tap by errors) dor)
2411        |=  [id=@ud er=@t]
2412        (rap 3 (crip (a-co:co id)) ': ' er '<br/>' ~)
2413      [(weld http-moves moves) state]
2414    ::
2415    ?-    -.i.requests
2416        %ack
2417      ::  client acknowledges that they have received up to event-id
2418      ::
2419      %_  $
2420        state     (acknowledge-events channel-id event-id.i.requests)
2421        requests  t.requests
2422      ==
2423    ::
2424        ?(%poke %poke-json)
2425      =,  i.requests
2426      ::
2427      ?.  |(=(from our) =(ship our))
2428        =+  [request-id 'non-local operation']
2429        $(errors (~(put by errors) -), requests t.requests)
2430      ::
2431      =.  gall-moves
2432        =/  =wire  /channel/poke/[channel-id]/(scot %ud request-id.i.requests)
2433        :_  gall-moves
2434        ^-  move
```

```
2435        %+   deal-as
2436          /channel/poke/[channel-id]/(scot %ud request-id)
2437        :^  from  ship  app
2438        ^-  task:agent:gall
2439        :+  %poke-as  mark
2440        ?-  -.i.requests
2441          %poke        [%noun !>(noun)]
2442          %poke-json   [%json !>(json)]
2443        ==
2444      ::
2445      $(requests t.requests)
2446    ::
2447        %subscribe
2448      =,  i.requests
2449      ::
2450      ?.  |(=(from our) =(ship our))
2451        =+  [request-id 'non-local operation']
2452        $(errors (~(put by errors) -), requests t.requests)
2453      ::
2454      ::TODO  could error if the subscription is a duplicate
2455      =.  gall-moves
2456        :_  gall-moves
2457        ^-  move
2458        %-  (trace 1 |.("subscribing to {<app>} on {<path>}"))
2459        %+  deal-as
2460          (subscription-wire channel-id request-id from ship app)
2461        [from ship app %watch path]
2462      ::
2463      =.  session.channel-state.state
2464        %+  ~(jab by session.channel-state.state)  channel-id
2465        |=  =channel
2466        =-  channel(subscriptions -)
2467        %+  ~(put by subscriptions.channel)
2468          request-id
2469        [ship app path duct]
2470      ::
2471      $(requests t.requests)
2472    ::
2473        %unsubscribe
2474      =,  i.requests
2475      ::
2476      ?.  |(=(from our) =(ship our))
2477        =+  [request-id 'non-local operation']
2478        $(errors (~(put by errors) -), requests t.requests)
2479      ::
2480      =/  usession  (~(get by session.channel-state.state) channel-id)
2481      ?~  usession
2482        $(requests t.requests)
2483      =/  subscriptions  subscriptions:u.usession
2484      ::
2485      ?~  maybe-subscription=(~(get by subscriptions) subscription-id)
2486        ::  the client sent us a weird request referring to a subscription
2487        ::  which isn't active.
2488        ::
2489        %.  $(requests t.requests)
2490        =*  msg=tape  "{(trip channel-id)} {<subscription-id>}"
2491        (trace 0 |.("missing subscription in unsubscribe {msg}"))
2492      ::
```

```
2493        =.  gall-moves
2494          :_  gall-moves
2495          ^-  move
2496          =,  u.maybe-subscription
2497          %-  (trace 1 |.("leaving subscription to {<app>}"))
2498          %+  deal-as
2499            (subscription-wire channel-id subscription-id from ship app)
2500          [from ship app %leave ~]
2501        ::
2502        =.  session.channel-state.state
2503          %+  ~(jab by session.channel-state.state)  channel-id
2504          |=  =channel
2505          %_  channel
2506            subscriptions  (~(del by subscriptions.channel) subscription-id)
2507            unacked        (~(del by unacked.channel) subscription-id)
2508          ==
2509        ::
2510        $(requests t.requests)
2511      ::
2512        %delete
2513        %-  (trace 1 |.("{<channel-id>} discarding due to %delete PUT"))
2514        =^  moves  state
2515          (discard-channel channel-id |)
2516        =.  gall-moves
2517          (weld gall-moves moves)
2518        $(requests t.requests)
2519      ::
2520    ==
2521  ::  +on-gall-response: sanity-check a gall response, send as event
2522  ::
2523  ++  on-gall-response
2524    |=  [channel-id=@t request-id=@ud extra=wire =sign:agent:gall]
2525    ^-  [(list move) server-state]
2526    ::  if the channel doesn't exist, we should clean up subscriptions
2527    ::
2528    ::    this is a band-aid solution. you really want eyre to have cleaned
2529    ::    these up on-channel-delete in the first place.
2530    ::    until the source of that bug is discovered though, we keep this
2531    ::    in place to ensure a slightly tidier home.
2532    ::
2533    ?.  ?&  !(~(has by session.channel-state.state) channel-id)
2534            ?=(?(%fact %watch-ack) -.sign)
2535            ?=([@ @ *] extra)
2536        ==
2537      (emit-event channel-id request-id sign)
2538    =/  =ship    (slav %p i.extra)
2539    =*  app=term  i.t.extra
2540    =*  msg=tape  "{(trip channel-id)} {(trip app)}"
2541    %-  (trace 0 |.("removing watch for non-existent channel {msg}"))
2542    :_  state
2543    :_  ~
2544    ^-  move
2545    =/  [as=@p old=?]
2546      ?+  t.t.extra  ~|([%strange-wire extra] !!)
2547        ~    [our &]
2548        [@ ~]  [(slav %p i.t.t.extra) |]
2549      ==
2550    =/  =wire  (subscription-wire channel-id request-id as ship app)
```

```
2551      %+  deal-as
2552        ::NOTE  we previously used a wire format that had the local identity
2553        ::         implicit, instead of explicit at the end of the wire. if we
2554        ::         detect we used the old wire here, we must re-use that format
2555        ::         (without id in the wire) for sending the %leave.
2556        ?:(old (snip wire) wire)
2557      [as ship app %leave ~]
2558    ::  +emit-event: records an event occurred, possibly sending to client
2559    ::
2560    ::    When an event occurs, we need to record it, even if we immediately
2561    ::    send it to a connected browser so in case of disconnection, we can
2562    ::    resend it.
2563    ::
2564    ::    This function is responsible for taking the event sign and converting
2565    ::    it into a text/event-stream. The :sign then may get sent, and is
2566    ::    stored for later resending until acknowledged by the client.
2567    ::
2568    ++  emit-event
2569      |=  [channel-id=@t request-id=@ud =sign:agent:gall]
2570      ^-  [(list move) server-state]
2571      ::
2572      =/  channel=(unit channel)
2573        (~(get by session.channel-state.state) channel-id)
2574      ?~  channel
2575        :_  state  :_  ~
2576        [duct %pass /flog %d %flog %crud %eyre-no-channel >id=channel-id< ~]
2577      ::  it's possible that this is a sign emitted directly alongside a fact
2578      ::  that triggered a clog & closed the subscription. in that case, just
2579      ::  drop the sign.
2580      ::  poke-acks are not paired with subscriptions, so we can process them
2581      ::  regardless.
2582      ::
2583      ?:  ?&  !?=(%poke-ack -.sign)
2584              !(~(has by subscriptions.u.channel) request-id)
2585          ==
2586        [~ state]
2587      ::  attempt to convert the sign to json.
2588      ::  if conversion succeeds, we *can* send it. if the client is actually
2589      ::  connected, we *will* send it immediately.
2590      ::
2591      =/  maybe-channel-event=(unit channel-event)
2592        (sign-to-channel-event sign u.channel request-id)
2593      ?~  maybe-channel-event  [~ state]
2594      =/  =channel-event  u.maybe-channel-event
2595      =/  said=(unit (quip move tape))
2596        (channel-event-to-tape u.channel request-id channel-event)
2597      =?  moves  ?=(^ said)
2598        (weld moves -.u.said)
2599      =*  sending  &(?=([%| *] state.u.channel) ?=(^ said))
2600      ::
2601      =/  next-id  next-id.u.channel
2602      ::  if we can send it, store the event as unacked
2603      ::
2604      =?  events.u.channel  ?=(^ said)
2605        %-  ~(put to events.u.channel)
2606        [next-id request-id channel-event]
2607      ::  if it makes sense to do so, send the event to the client
2608      ::
```

```
2609        =?  moves   sending
2610          ^-  (list move)
2611          :_  moves
2612          ::NOTE  assertions in this block because =* is flimsy
2613          ?>  ?=([%| *] state.u.channel)
2614          :+  p.state.u.channel  %give
2615          ^-  gift
2616          :*  %response  %continue
2617          ::
2618              ^=  data
2619              %-  wall-to-octs
2620              (event-tape-to-wall next-id +:(need said))
2621          ::
2622              complete=%.n
2623          ==
2624        =?  next-id  ?=(^ said)  +(next-id)
2625        ::  update channel's unacked counts, find out if clogged
2626        ::
2627        =^  clogged  unacked.u.channel
2628          ::  only apply clog logic to facts.
2629          ::  and of course don't count events we can't send as unacked.
2630          ::
2631          ?:  ?|  !?=(%fact -.sign)
2632                  ?=(~ said)
2633              ==
2634            [| unacked.u.channel]
2635          =/  num=@ud
2636            (~(gut by unacked.u.channel) request-id 0)
2637          :_  (~(put by unacked.u.channel) request-id +(num))
2638          ?&  (gte num clog-threshold)
2639              (lth (add last-ack.u.channel clog-timeout) now)
2640          ==
2641        ::  if we're clogged, or we ran into an event we can't serialize,
2642        ::  kill this gall subscription.
2643        ::
2644        =*  msg=tape  "on {(trip channel-id)} for {(scow %ud request-id)}"
2645        =/  kicking=?
2646          ?:  clogged
2647            ((trace 0 |.("clogged {msg}")) &)
2648          ?.  ?=(~ said)  |
2649            ((trace 0 |.("can't serialize event, kicking {msg}")) &)
2650        =?  moves       kicking
2651          :_  moves
2652          ::NOTE  this shouldn't crash because we
2653          ::        - never fail to serialize subscriptionless signs (%poke-ack),
2654          ::        - only clog on %facts, which have a subscription associated,
2655          ::        - and already checked whether we still have that subscription.
2656          =+  (~(got by subscriptions.u.channel) request-id)
2657          %-  (trace 1 |.("leaving subscription to {<app>}"))
2658          %+  deal-as
2659            (subscription-wire channel-id request-id identity.u.channel ship app)
2660          [identity.u.channel ship app %leave ~]
2661        ::  update channel state to reflect the %kick
2662        ::
2663        =?  u.channel  kicking
2664          %_  u.channel
2665            subscriptions  (~(del by subscriptions.u.channel) request-id)
2666            unacked        (~(del by unacked.u.channel) request-id)
```

```
2667        events          %-  ~(put to events.u.channel)
2668                         :+  next-id
2669                           request-id
2670                         (need (sign-to-channel-event [%kick ~] u.channel request-id))
2671        ==
2672    ::  if a client is connected, send the kick event to them
2673    ::
2674    =?  moves  &(kicking ?=([%| *] state.u.channel))
2675      :_  moves
2676      :+  p.state.u.channel  %give
2677      ^-  gift
2678      :*  %response  %continue
2679      ::
2680          ^=  data
2681          %-  wall-to-octs
2682          %+  event-tape-to-wall  next-id
2683          +:(need (channel-event-to-tape u.channel request-id %kick ~))
2684      ::
2685          complete=%.n
2686        ==
2687    =?  next-id  kicking  +(next-id)
2688    ::
2689    :-  (flop moves)
2690    %_      state
2691        session.channel-state
2692      %+  ~(put by session.channel-state.state)  channel-id
2693      u.channel(next-id next-id)
2694    ==
2695  ::  +sign-to-channel-event: strip the vase from a sign:agent:gall
2696  ::
2697  ++  sign-to-channel-event
2698    |=  [=sign:agent:gall =channel request-id=@ud]
2699    ^-  (unit channel-event)
2700    ?.  ?=(%fact -.sign)  `sign
2701    ?~  desk=(app-to-desk channel request-id)  ~
2702    :-  ~
2703    [%fact u.desk [p q.q]:cage.sign]
2704  ::  +app-to-desk
2705  ::
2706  ++  app-to-desk
2707    |=  [=channel request-id=@ud]
2708    ^-  (unit desk)
2709    =/  sub  (~(get by subscriptions.channel) request-id)
2710    ?~  sub
2711      ((trace 0 |.("no subscription for request-id {(scow %ud request-id)}")) ~)
2712    =/  des=(unit (unit cage))
2713    (rof ~ /eyre %gd [our app.u.sub da+now] /$)
2714    ?.  ?=([~ ~ *] des)
2715      ((trace 0 |.("no desk for app {<app.u.sub>}")) ~)
2716    `!<(=desk q.u.u.des)
2717  ::  +channel-event-to-tape: render channel-event from request-id in specified mode
2718  ::
2719  ++  channel-event-to-tape
2720    |=  [=channel request-id=@ud =channel-event]
2721    ^-  (unit (quip move tape))
2722    ?-  mode.channel
2723      %json  %+  bind  (channel-event-to-json channel request-id channel-event)
2724             |=((quip move json) [+<- (trip (en:json:html +<+))])
```

```
2725        %jam    =-   `[~ (scow %uw (jam -))]
2726               [request-id channel-event]
2727      ==
2728  ::   +channel-event-to-json: render channel event as json channel event
2729  ::
2730  ++  channel-event-to-json
2731    ~%  %eyre-channel-event-to-json  ..part  ~
2732    |=  [=channel request-id=@ud event=channel-event]
2733    ^-  (unit (quip move json))
2734    ::  for facts, we try to convert the result to json
2735    ::
2736    =/  [from=(unit [=desk =mark]) jsyn=(unit sign:agent:gall)]
2737      ?.  ?=(%fact -.event)          [~ `event]
2738      ?:  ?=(%json mark.event)
2739        ?~  jsin=((soft json) noun.event)
2740          %.  [~ ~]
2741          (slog leaf+"eyre: dropping fake json for {(scow %ud request-id)}" ~)
2742        [~ `[%fact %json !>(u.jsin)]]
2743      ::  find and use tube from fact mark to json
2744      ::
2745      ::
2746      =*  have=mark  mark.event
2747      =/  convert=(unit vase)
2748        =/  cag=(unit (unit cage))
2749          (rof ~ /eyre %cf [our desk.event da+now] /[have]/json)
2750        ?.  ?=([~ ~ *] cag)  ~
2751        `q.u.u.cag
2752      ?~  convert
2753        ((trace 0 |.("no convert from {(trip have)} to json")) [~ ~])
2754      ~|  "conversion failed from {(trip have)} to json"
2755      [`[desk.event have] `[%fact %json (slym u.convert noun.event)]]
2756    ?~  jsyn  ~
2757    %-  some
2758    :-  ?~  from  ~
2759        :_  ~
2760        :^  duct  %pass  /conversion-cache/[mark.u.from]
2761        [%c %warp our desk.u.from `[%sing %f da+now /[mark.u.from]/json]]
2762    =*  sign  u.jsyn
2763    =,  enjs:format
2764    %-  pairs
2765    ^-  (list [@t json])
2766    :-  ['id' (numb request-id)]
2767    ?-    -.sign
2768        %poke-ack
2769      :~  ['response' [%s 'poke']]
2770          ::
2771          ?~  p.sign
2772            ['ok' [%s 'ok']]
2773          ['err' (wall (render-tang-to-wall 100 u.p.sign))]
2774      ==
2775    ::
2776        %fact
2777      :+  ['response' [%s 'diff']]
2778        :-  'json'
2779        ~|  [%unexpected-fact-mark p.cage.sign]
2780        ?>  =(%json p.cage.sign)
2781        !<(json q.cage.sign)
2782      ::
```

```
          ?~  from    ~
          ['mark' [%s mark.u.from]]~
      ::
          %kick
          ['response' [%s 'quit']]~
      ::
          %watch-ack
        :~  ['response' [%s 'subscribe']]
          ::
            ?~  p.sign
              ['ok' [%s 'ok']]
            ['err' (wall (render-tang-to-wall 100 u.p.sign))]
        ==
      ==
  ::
  ++  event-tape-to-wall
    ~%  %eyre-tape-to-wall  ..part  ~
    |=  [event-id=@ud =tape]
    ^-  wall
    :~  (weld "id: " (format-ud-as-integer event-id))
        (weld "data: " tape)
        ""
    ==
  ::
  ++  on-channel-heartbeat
    |=  channel-id=@t
    ^-  [(list move) server-state]
    ::
    =/  res
      %-  handle-response
      :*  %continue
          data=(some (as-octs:mimes:html ':\0a'))
          complete=%.n
      ==
    =/  http-moves  -.res
    =/  new-state  +.res
    =/  heartbeat-time=@da  (add now ~s20)
    :_  %_    new-state
            session.channel-state
          %+  ~(jab by session.channel-state.state)  channel-id
          |=  =channel
          channel(heartbeat (some [heartbeat-time duct]))
        ==
    (snoc http-moves (set-heartbeat-move channel-id heartbeat-time))
  ::  +discard-channel: remove a channel from state
  ::
  ::    cleans up state, timers, and gall subscriptions of the channel
  ::
  ++  discard-channel
    |=  [channel-id=@t expired=?]
    ^-  [(list move) server-state]
    ::
    =/  usession=(unit channel)
      (~(get by session.channel-state.state) channel-id)
    ?~  usession
      [~ state]
    =/  session=channel  u.usession
    ::
```

```
2841        :_  %_    state
2842              session.channel-state
2843            (~(del by session.channel-state.state) channel-id)
2844          ::
2845              duct-to-key.channel-state
2846            ?.  ?=(%| -.state.session)  duct-to-key.channel-state.state
2847            (~(del by duct-to-key.channel-state.state) p.state.session)
2848          ==
2849      =/  heartbeat-cancel=(list move)
2850        ?~  heartbeat.session  ~
2851        :~  %^  cancel-heartbeat-move
2852              channel-id
2853            date.u.heartbeat.session
2854          duct.u.heartbeat.session
2855        ==
2856      =/  expire-cancel=(list move)
2857        ?:  expired  ~
2858        ?.  ?=(%& -.state.session)  ~
2859        =,  p.state.session
2860        [(cancel-timeout-move channel-id date duct)]~
2861      %+  weld  heartbeat-cancel
2862      %+  weld  expire-cancel
2863      ::  produce a list of moves which cancels every gall subscription
2864      ::
2865      %+  turn  ~(tap by subscriptions.session)
2866      |=  [request-id=@ud ship=@p app=term =path duc=^duct]
2867      ^-  move
2868      %-  (trace 1 |.("{<channel-id>} leaving subscription to {<app>}"))
2869      %+  deal-as
2870        (subscription-wire channel-id request-id identity.session ship app)
2871      [identity.session ship app %leave ~]
2872      --
2873    ::  +handle-gall-error: a call to +poke-http-response resulted in a %coup
2874    ::
2875    ++  handle-gall-error
2876      |=  =tang
2877      ^-  [(list move) server-state]
2878      ::
2879      ?~  connection-state=(~(get by connections.state) duct)
2880        %.  `state
2881        (trace 0 |.("{<duct>} error on invalid outstanding connection"))
2882      =*  connection  u.connection-state
2883      =/  moves-1=(list move)
2884        ?.  ?=(%app -.action.connection)
2885          ~
2886        :_  ~
2887        =,  connection
2888        %-  (trace 1 |.("leaving subscription to {<app.action>}"))
2889        (deal-as /watch-response/[eyre-id] identity our app.action %leave ~)
2890      ::
2891      =^  moves-2  state
2892        %^  return-static-data-on-duct  500  'text/html'
2893        ::
2894        %-  internal-server-error  :*
2895          authenticated.inbound-request.connection
2896          url.request.inbound-request.connection
2897          tang
2898        ==
```

```
2899        [(weld moves-1 moves-2) state]
2900    ::  +handle-response: check a response for correctness and send to earth
2901    ::
2902    ::      All outbound responses including %http-server generated responses need to go
2903    ::      through this interface because we want to have one centralized place
2904    ::      where we perform logging and state cleanup for connections that we're
2905    ::      done with.
2906    ::
2907    ++  handle-response
2908      |=  =http-event:http
2909      ^-  [(list move) server-state]
2910      ::  verify that this is a valid response on the duct
2911      ::
2912      ?~  connection-state=(~(get by connections.state) duct)
2913        ((trace 0 |.("{<duct>} invalid outstanding connection")) `state)
2914      ::
2915      |^  ^-  [(list move) server-state]
2916          ::
2917          ?-    -.http-event
2918          ::
2919            %start
2920          ?^  response-header.u.connection-state
2921            ((trace 0 |.("{<duct>} error multiple start")) error-connection)
2922          ::  extend the request's session's + cookie's life
2923          ::
2924          =^  response-header  sessions.auth.state
2925            =,  authentication
2926            =*  session-id  session-id.u.connection-state
2927            =*  sessions    sessions.auth.state
2928            =*  inbound     inbound-request.u.connection-state
2929            ::
2930            ?.  (~(has by sessions) session-id)
2931              ::  if the session has expired since the request was opened,
2932              ::  tough luck, we don't create/revive sessions here
2933              ::
2934              [response-header.http-event sessions]
2935            :_  %+  ~(jab by sessions)  session-id
2936                |=  =session
2937                session(expiry-time (add now session-timeout))
2938            =-  response-header.http-event(headers -)
2939            %^  set-header:http  'set-cookie'
2940              (session-cookie-string session-id &)
2941            headers.response-header.http-event
2942          ::
2943          =*  connection  u.connection-state
2944          ::
2945          ::  if the request was a simple cors request from an approved origin
2946          ::  append the necessary cors headers to the response
2947          ::
2948          =/  origin=(unit origin)
2949            %+  get-header:http  'origin'
2950            header-list.request.inbound-request.connection
2951          =?  headers.response-header
2952              ?&  ?=(^ origin)
2953                  (~(has in approved.cors-registry.state) u.origin)
2954              ==
2955            %^  set-header:http  'Access-Control-Allow-Origin'        u.origin
2956            %^  set-header:http  'Access-Control-Allow-Credentials'  'true'
```

```
2957                    headers.response-header
2958              ::
2959              =.  response-header.http-event  response-header
2960              =.  connections.state
2961                ?:  complete.http-event
2962                  :: XX  optimize by not requiring +put:by in +request
2963                  ::
2964                  (~(del by connections.state) duct)
2965                ::
2966                %-  (trace 2 |.("{<duct>} start"))
2967                %+  ~(put by connections.state)  duct
2968                %=  connection
2969                  response-header  `response-header
2970                  bytes-sent  ?~(data.http-event 0 p.u.data.http-event)
2971                ==
2972              ::
2973            pass-response
2974          ::
2975              %continue
2976          ?~  response-header.u.connection-state
2977            %.  error-connection
2978            (trace 0 |.("{<duct>} error continue without start"))
2979          ::
2980          =.  connections.state
2981            ?:  complete.http-event
2982              %-  (trace 2 |.("{<duct>} completed"))
2983              (~(del by connections.state) duct)
2984            ::
2985            %-  (trace 2 |.("{<duct>} continuing"))
2986            ?~  data.http-event
2987              connections.state
2988            ::
2989            %+  ~(put by connections.state)  duct
2990            =*  size  p.u.data.http-event
2991            =*  conn  u.connection-state
2992            conn(bytes-sent (add size bytes-sent.conn))
2993          ::
2994        pass-response
2995      ::
2996          %cancel
2997      :: todo: log this differently from an ise.
2998      ::
2999      ((trace 1 |.("cancel http event")) error-connection)
3000        ==
3001  ::
3002  ++  pass-response
3003    ^-  [(list move) server-state]
3004    [[duct %give %response http-event]~ state]
3005  ::
3006  ++  error-connection
3007    :: todo: log application error
3008    ::
3009    :: remove all outstanding state for this connection
3010    ::
3011    =.  connections.state
3012    (~(del by connections.state) duct)
3013    :: respond to outside with %error
3014    ::
```

```
3015        ^-  [(list move) server-state]
3016        :_  state
3017        :-  [duct %give %response %cancel ~]
3018        ?.  ?=(%app -.action.u.connection-state)
3019              ~
3020        :_  ~
3021        =,  u.connection-state
3022        %-  %+  trace  1
3023            |.("leaving subscription to {<app.action>}")
3024        (deal-as /watch-response/[eyre-id] identity our app.action %leave ~)
3025      --
3026  ::  +set-response: remember (or update) a cache mapping
3027  ::
3028  ++  set-response
3029    |=  [url=@t entry=(unit cache-entry)]
3030    ^-  [(list move) server-state]
3031    =/  aeon  ?^(prev=(~(get by cache.state) url) +(aeon.u.prev) 1)
3032    =.  cache.state  (~(put by cache.state) url [aeon entry])
3033    :_  state
3034    [outgoing-duct.state %give %grow /cache/(scot %ud aeon)/(scot %t url)]~
3035  ::  +add-binding: conditionally add a pairing between binding and action
3036  ::
3037  ::    Adds =binding =action if there is no conflicting bindings.
3038  ::
3039  ++  add-binding
3040    |=  [=binding =action]
3041    ^-  [(list move) server-state]
3042    =^  success  bindings.state
3043      ::  prevent binding in reserved namespaces
3044      ::
3045      ?:  ?|  ?=([%'~' *] path.binding)    ::  eyre
3046              ?=([%'~_~' *] path.binding)  ::  runtime
3047          ==
3048        [| bindings.state]
3049      [& (insert-binding [binding duct action] bindings.state)]
3050    :_  state
3051    [duct %give %bound & binding]~
3052  ::  +remove-binding: removes a binding if it exists and is owned by this duct
3053  ::
3054  ++  remove-binding
3055    |=  =binding
3056    ::
3057    ^-  server-state
3058    %_    state
3059        bindings
3060      %+  skip  bindings.state
3061      |=  [item-binding=^binding item-duct=^duct =action]
3062      ^-  ?
3063      &(=(item-binding binding) =(item-duct duct))
3064    ==
3065  ::  +get-action-for-binding: finds an action for an incoming web request
3066  ::
3067  ++  get-action-for-binding
3068    |=  [raw-host=(unit @t) url=@t]
3069    ^-  [=action suburl=@t]
3070    ::  process :raw-host
3071    ::
3072    ::    If we are missing a 'Host:' header, if that header is a raw IP
```

```
3073    ::    address, or if the 'Host:' header refers to [our].urbit.org, we want
3074    ::    to return ~ which means we're unidentified and will match against any
3075    ::    wildcard matching.
3076    ::
3077    ::    Otherwise, return the site given.
3078    ::
3079    =/  host=(unit @t)
3080      ?~  raw-host
3081        ~
3082      ::  Parse the raw-host so that we can ignore ports, usernames, etc.
3083      ::
3084      =+  parsed=(rush u.raw-host simplified-url-parser)
3085      ?~  parsed
3086        ~
3087      ::  if the url is a raw IP, assume default site.
3088      ::
3089      ?:  ?=([%ip *] -.u.parsed)
3090        ~
3091      ::  if the url is "localhost", assume default site.
3092      ::
3093      ?:  =([%site 'localhost'] -.u.parsed)
3094        ~
3095      ::  render our as a tape, and cut off the sig in front.
3096      ::
3097      =/  with-sig=tape  (scow %p our)
3098      ?>  ?=(^ with-sig)
3099      ?:  =(u.raw-host (crip t.with-sig))
3100        ::  [our].urbit.org is the default site
3101        ::
3102        ~
3103      ::
3104      raw-host
3105    ::  url is the raw thing passed over the 'Request-Line'.
3106    ::
3107    ::    todo: this is really input validation, and we should return a 500 to
3108    ::    the client.
3109    ::
3110    =/  request-line  (parse-request-line url)
3111    =/  parsed-url=(list @t)  site.request-line
3112    =?  parsed-url  ?=([%'~' %channel-jam *] parsed-url)
3113      parsed-url(i.t %channel)
3114    ::
3115    =/  bindings  bindings.state
3116    |-
3117    ::
3118    ?~  bindings
3119      [[%four-oh-four ~] url]
3120    ::
3121    ?.  (host-matches site.binding.i.bindings raw-host)
3122      $(bindings t.bindings)
3123    ?~  suffix=(find-suffix path.binding.i.bindings parsed-url)
3124      $(bindings t.bindings)
3125    ::
3126    :-  action.i.bindings
3127    %^  cat  3
3128    %+  roll
3129      ^-  (list @t)
3130      (join '/' (flop ['' u.suffix]))
```

```
3131        (cury cat 3)
3132      ?~  ext.request-line  ''
3133      (cat 3 '.' u.ext.request-line)
3134  ::  +give-session-tokens: send valid local session tokens to unix
3135  ::
3136  ++  give-session-tokens
3137      ^-  move
3138      :-  outgoing-duct.state
3139      :+  %give  %sessions
3140      %-  sy
3141      %+  murn  ~(tap by sessions.auth.state)
3142      |=  [sid=@uv session]
3143      ?.  ?=(%ours -.identity)  ~
3144      (some (scot %uv sid))
3145  ::  +new-session-key
3146  ::
3147  ++  new-session-key
3148      |-  ^-  @uv
3149      =/  candidate=@uv  (~(raw og (shas %session-key eny)) 128)
3150      ?.  (~(has by sessions.auth.state) candidate)
3151        candidate
3152      $(eny (shas %try-again candidate))
3153  ::
3154  ++  deal-as
3155      |=  [=wire identity=$@(@p identity) =ship =dude:gall =task:agent:gall]
3156      ^-  move
3157      =/  from=@p
3158      ?@  identity  identity
3159      ?+(-.identity who.identity %ours our)
3160      [duct %pass wire %g %deal [from ship /eyre] dude task]
3161  ::
3162  ++  trace
3163      |=  [pri=@ print=(trap tape)]
3164      ?:  (lth verb.state pri)  same
3165      (slog leaf+"eyre: {(print)}" ~)
3166      --
3167  ::
3168  ++  forwarded-params
3169    |=  =header-list:http
3170    ^-  (unit (list (map @t @t)))
3171    %+  biff
3172      (get-header:http 'forwarded' header-list)
3173    unpack-header:http
3174  ::
3175  ++  forwarded-for
3176    |=  forwards=(list (map @t @t))
3177    ^-  (unit address)
3178    ?.  ?=(^ forwards)  ~
3179    =*  forward  i.forwards
3180    ?~  for=(~(get by forward) 'for')  ~
3181  ::NOTE  per rfc7239, non-ip values are also valid. they're not useful
3182    ::      for the general case, so we ignore them here. if needed,
3183    ::      request handlers are free to inspect the headers themselves.
3184    ::
3185    %+  rush  u.for
3186    ;~  sfix
3187      ;~(pose (stag %ipv4 ip4) (stag %ipv6 (ifix [sel ser] ip6)))
3188      ;~(pose ;~(pfix col dim:ag) (easy ~))
```

```
3189    ==
3190  ::
3191  ++  forwarded-secure
3192    |=  forwards=(list (map @t @t))
3193    ^-  (unit ?)
3194    ?.  ?=(^ forwards)  ~
3195    =*  forward  i.forwards
3196    ?~  proto=(~(get by forward) 'proto')  ~
3197    ?+  u.proto  ~
3198      %http   `|
3199      %https  `&
3200    ==
3201  ::
3202  ++  parse-request-line
3203    |=  url=@t
3204    ^-  [[ext=(unit @ta) site=(list @t)] args=(list [key=@t value=@t])]
3205    (fall (rush url ;~(plug apat:de-purl:html yque:de-purl:html)) [[~ ~] ~])
3206  ::  +insert-binding: add a new binding, replacing any existing at its path
3207  ::
3208  ++  insert-binding
3209    |=  $:  new=[=binding =duct =action]
3210            bindings=(list [=binding =duct =action])
3211        ==
3212    ^+  bindings
3213    ?~  bindings  [new]~
3214    =*  bid  binding.i.bindings
3215    ::  replace already bound paths
3216    ::
3217    ?:  =([site path]:bid [site path]:binding.new)
3218      ~>  %slog.[0 leaf+"eyre: replacing existing binding at {<`path`path.bid>}"]
3219      [new t.bindings]
3220    ::  if new comes before bid, prepend it.
3221    ::  otherwise, continue our search.
3222    ::
3223    =;  new-before-bid=?
3224      ?:  new-before-bid  [new bindings]
3225      [i.bindings $(bindings t.bindings)]
3226    ?:  =(site.binding.new site.bid)
3227      (aor path.bid path.binding.new)
3228    (aor (fall site.bid '') (fall site.binding.new ''))
3229  ::
3230  ++  channel-wire
3231    |=  [channel-id=@t request-id=@ud]
3232    ^-  wire
3233    /channel/subscription/[channel-id]/(scot %ud request-id)
3234  ::
3235  ++  subscription-wire
3236    |=  [channel-id=@t request-id=@ud as=$@(@p identity) =ship app=term]
3237    ^-  wire
3238    =/  from=@p
3239      ?@  as  as
3240      ?+(-.as who.as %ours our)
3241    %+  weld  (channel-wire channel-id request-id)
3242    ::NOTE  including the originating identity is important for the band-aid
3243    ::        solution currently present in +on-gall-response, where we may
3244    ::        need to issue a %leave after we've forgotten the identity with
3245    ::        which the subscription was opened.
3246    /(scot %p ship)/[app]/(scot %p from)
```

```
3247  --
3248  ::  end the =~
3249  ::
3250  .  ==
3251  ::  begin with a default +axle as a blank slate
3252  ::
3253  =|  ax=axle
3254  ::  a vane is activated with current date, entropy, and a namespace function
3255  ::
3256  |=  [now=@da eny=@uvJ rof=roof]
3257  ::  allow jets to be registered within this core
3258  ::
3259  ~%  %http-server  ..part  ~
3260  |%
3261  ++  call
3262    ~/  %eyre-call
3263    |=  [=duct dud=(unit goof) wrapped-task=(hobo task)]
3264    ^-  [(list move) _http-server-gate]
3265    ::
3266    =/  task=task  ((harden task) wrapped-task)
3267    ::
3268    ::  XX handle more error notifications
3269    ::
3270    ?^  dud
3271      :_  http-server-gate
3272      ::  always print the error trace
3273      ::
3274      :-  [duct %slip %d %flog %crud [-.task tang.u.dud]]
3275      ^-  (list move)
3276      ::  if a request caused the crash, respond with a 500
3277      ::
3278      ?.  ?=(?(%request %request-local) -.task)  ~
3279      ^~
3280      =/  data  (as-octs:mimes:html 'crud!')
3281      =/  head
3282        :~  ['content-type' 'text/html']
3283            ['content-length' (crip (a-co:co p.data))]
3284        ==
3285      [duct %give %response %start 500^head `data &]~
3286    ::  %init: tells us what our ship name is
3287    ::
3288    ?:  ?=(%init -.task)
3289      ::  initial value for the login handler
3290      ::
3291      =.  bindings.server-state.ax
3292        =-  (roll - insert-binding)
3293        ^-  (list [binding ^duct action])
3294        :~  [[~ /~/login] duct [%authentication ~]]
3295            [[~ /~/eauth] duct [%eauth ~]]
3296            [[~ /~/logout] duct [%logout ~]]
3297            [[~ /~/channel] duct [%channel ~]]
3298            [[~ /~/scry] duct [%scry ~]]
3299            [[~ /~/name] duct [%name ~]]
3300            [[~ /~/host] duct [%host ~]]
3301        ==
3302      [~ http-server-gate]
3303    ::  %trim: in response to memory pressure
3304    ::
```

```
3305    ::      Cancel all inactive channels
3306    ::      XX cancel active too if =(0 trim-priority) ?
3307    ::
3308    ?:  ?=(%trim -.task)
3309      =*  event-args    [[eny duct now rof] server-state.ax]
3310      =*  by-channel    by-channel:(per-server-event event-args)
3311      =*  channel-state  channel-state.server-state.ax
3312      ::
3313      =/  inactive=(list @t)
3314        =/  full=(set @t)  ~(key by session.channel-state)
3315        =/  live=(set @t)
3316        (~(gas in *(set @t))  ~(val by duct-to-key.channel-state))
3317        ~(tap in (~(dif in full) live))
3318      ::
3319      ?:  =(~ inactive)
3320        [~ http-server-gate]
3321      ::
3322      =/  len=tape  (scow %ud (lent inactive))
3323      ~>  %slog.[0 leaf+"eyre: trim: closing {len} inactive channels"]
3324      ::
3325      =|  moves=(list (list move))
3326      |-  ^-  [(list move) _http-server-gate]
3327      =*  channel-id  i.inactive
3328      ?~  inactive
3329        [(zing (flop moves)) http-server-gate]
3330      :: discard channel state, and cancel any active gall subscriptions
3331      ::
3332      =^  mov  server-state.ax  (discard-channel:by-channel channel-id |)
3333      $(moves [mov moves], inactive t.inactive)
3334    ::
3335    :: %vega: notifies us of a completed kernel upgrade
3336    ::
3337    ?:  ?=(%vega -.task)
3338      [~ http-server-gate]
3339    :: %born: new unix process
3340    ::
3341    ?:  ?=(%born -.task)
3342      :: close previously open connections
3343      ::
3344      ::     When we have a new unix process, every outstanding open connection is
3345      ::     dead. For every duct, send an implicit close connection.
3346      ::
3347      =^  closed-connections=(list move)  server-state.ax
3348        =/  connections=(list [=^duct *])
3349          ~(tap by connections.server-state.ax)
3350        ::
3351        =|  closed-connections=(list move)
3352        |-
3353        ?~  connections
3354          [closed-connections server-state.ax]
3355        ::
3356        =/  event-args
3357          [[eny duct.i.connections now rof] server-state.ax]
3358        =/  cancel-request  cancel-request:(per-server-event event-args)
3359        =^  moves  server-state.ax  cancel-request
3360        ::
3361        $(closed-connections (weld moves closed-connections), connections t.connections)
3362      :: save duct for future %give to unix
```

```
3363       ::
3364       =.  outgoing-duct.server-state.ax  duct
3365       ::  send all cache mappings to runtime
3366       ::
3367       =/  cache-moves=(list move)
3368         %+  turn  ~(tap by cache.server-state.ax)
3369         |=  [url=@t cache-val=[aeon=@ud val=(unit cache-entry)]]
3370       [duct %give %grow /cache/(scot %u aeon.cache-val)/(scot %t url)]
3371       ::
3372       :_  http-server-gate
3373       :*  ::  hand back default configuration for now
3374           ::
3375           [duct %give %set-config http-config.server-state.ax]
3376           ::  provide a list of valid auth tokens
3377           ::
3378           =<  give-session-tokens
3379           (per-server-event [eny duct now rof] server-state.ax)
3380         ::
3381           (zing ~[closed-connections cache-moves])
3382       ==
3383     ::
3384     ?:  ?=(%code-changed -.task)
3385       ~>  %slog.[0 leaf+"eyre: code-changed: throwing away local sessions"]
3386       =*  event-args  [[eny duct now rof] server-state.ax]
3387       ::  find all the %ours sessions, we must close them
3388       ::
3389       =/  siz=(list @uv)
3390         %+  murn  ~(tap by sessions.auth.server-state.ax)
3391         |=  [sid=@uv session]
3392         ?:(?=(%ours -.identity) (some sid) ~)
3393       =|  moves=(list (list move))
3394       |-  ^-  [(list move) _http-server-gate]
3395       ?~  siz
3396       [(zing (flop moves)) http-server-gate]
3397       ::  discard the session, clean up its channels
3398       ::
3399       =^  mov  server-state.ax
3400         (close-session:authentication:(per-server-event event-args) i.siz |)
3401       $(moves [mov moves], siz t.siz)
3402     ::
3403     ?:  ?=(%eauth-host -.task)
3404       =.  user.endpoint.auth.server-state.ax  host.task
3405       =.  time.endpoint.auth.server-state.ax  now
3406       [~ http-server-gate]
3407     ::
3408     ::  all other commands operate on a per-server-event
3409     ::
3410     =/  event-args  [[eny duct now rof] server-state.ax]
3411     =/  server  (per-server-event event-args)
3412     ::
3413     ?-    -.task
3414         ::  %live: notifies us of the ports of our live http servers
3415         ::
3416         %live
3417       =.  ports.server-state.ax  +.task
3418       ::  enable http redirects if https port live and cert set
3419       ::
3420       =.  redirect.http-config.server-state.ax
```

```
3421        &(?=(^ secure.task) ?=(^ secure.http-config.server-state.ax))
3422      [~ http-server-gate]
3423        ::  %rule: updates our http configuration
3424        ::
3425        %rule
3426      ?-  -.http-rule.task
3427          ::  %cert: install tls certificate
3428          ::
3429          %cert
3430        =*  config  http-config.server-state.ax
3431        ?:  =(secure.config cert.http-rule.task)
3432        [~ http-server-gate]
3433        =.  secure.config  cert.http-rule.task
3434        =.  redirect.config
3435          ?&  ?=(^ secure.ports.server-state.ax)
3436              ?=(^ cert.http-rule.task)
3437          ==
3438        :_  http-server-gate
3439        =*  out-duct  outgoing-duct.server-state.ax
3440        ?~  out-duct  ~
3441      [out-duct %give %set-config config]~
3442          ::  %turf: add or remove domain name
3443          ::
3444          %turf
3445        =*  domains  domains.server-state.ax
3446        =/  mod=(set turf)
3447          ?:  ?=(%put action.http-rule.task)
3448            (~(put in domains) turf.http-rule.task)
3449          (~(del in domains) turf.http-rule.task)
3450        ?:  =(domains mod)
3451        [~ http-server-gate]
3452        =.  domains  mod
3453        :_  http-server-gate
3454        =/  cmd
3455          [%acme %poke `cage`[%acme-order !>(mod)]]
3456        [duct %pass /acme/order %g %deal [our our /eyre] cmd]~
3457      ==
3458    ::
3459        %plea
3460      ~|  path.plea.task
3461      ?>  ?=([%eauth %'0' ~] path.plea.task)
3462      =+  plea=;;(eauth-plea payload.plea.task)
3463      =^  moves  server-state.ax
3464        (on-plea:server:eauth:authentication:server ship.task plea)
3465      [moves http-server-gate]
3466    ::
3467        %request
3468      =^  moves  server-state.ax  (request:server +.task)
3469      [moves http-server-gate]
3470    ::
3471        %request-local
3472      =^  moves  server-state.ax  (request-local:server +.task)
3473      [moves http-server-gate]
3474    ::
3475        %cancel-request
3476      =^  moves  server-state.ax  cancel-request:server
3477      [moves http-server-gate]
3478    ::
```

```
3479        %connect
3480    =^  moves  server-state.ax
3481      %+  add-binding:server  binding.task
3482      [%app app.task]
3483    [moves http-server-gate]
3484  ::
3485        %serve
3486    =^  moves  server-state.ax
3487      %+  add-binding:server  binding.task
3488      [%gen generator.task]
3489    [moves http-server-gate]
3490  ::
3491        %disconnect
3492    =.  server-state.ax  (remove-binding:server binding.task)
3493    [~ http-server-gate]
3494  ::
3495        %approve-origin
3496    =.  cors-registry.server-state.ax
3497      =,  cors-registry.server-state.ax
3498      :+  (~(del in requests) origin.task)
3499        (~(put in approved) origin.task)
3500      (~(del in rejected) origin.task)
3501    [~ http-server-gate]
3502  ::
3503        %reject-origin
3504    =.  cors-registry.server-state.ax
3505      =,  cors-registry.server-state.ax
3506      :+  (~(del in requests) origin.task)
3507        (~(del in approved) origin.task)
3508      (~(put in rejected) origin.task)
3509    [~ http-server-gate]
3510  ::
3511        %spew
3512    =.  verb.server-state.ax  veb.task
3513    `http-server-gate
3514  ::
3515        %set-response
3516    =^  moves  server-state.ax  (set-response:server +.task)
3517    [moves http-server-gate]
3518    ==
3519  ::
3520  ++  take
3521    ~/  %eyre-take
3522    |=  [=wire =duct dud=(unit goof) =sign]
3523    ^-  [(list move) _http-server-gate]
3524    =>  %=    .
3525            sign
3526          ?:  ?=(%gall -.sign)
3527            ?>  ?=(%unto +<.sign)
3528            sign
3529          sign
3530        ==
3531    ::  :wire must at least contain two parts, the type and the build
3532    ::
3533    ?>  ?=([@ *] wire)
3534    ::
3535    |^  ^-  [(list move) _http-server-gate]
3536        ::
```

```
3537        ?:  ?=(%eauth i.wire)
3538          eauth
3539        ?^  dud
3540          ~|(%eyre-take-dud (mean tang.u.dud))
3541        ?+  i.wire
3542          ~|([%bad-take-wire wire] !!)
3543        ::
3544          %run-app-request    run-app-request
3545          %watch-response     watch-response
3546          %sessions           sessions
3547          %channel            channel
3548          %acme               acme-ack
3549          %conversion-cache   `http-server-gate
3550        ==
3551    ::
3552    ++  run-app-request
3553      ::
3554      ?>  ?=([%gall %unto *] sign)
3555      ::
3556      ::
3557      ?>  ?=([%poke-ack *] p.sign)
3558      ?>  ?=([@ *] t.wire)
3559      ?~  p.p.sign
3560        ::  received a positive acknowledgment: take no action
3561        ::
3562        [~ http-server-gate]
3563      ::  we have an error; propagate it to the client
3564      ::
3565      =/  event-args  [[eny duct now rof] server-state.ax]
3566      =/  handle-gall-error
3567        handle-gall-error:(per-server-event event-args)
3568      =^  moves  server-state.ax
3569        (handle-gall-error u.p.p.sign)
3570      [moves http-server-gate]
3571    ::
3572    ++  watch-response
3573      ::
3574      =/  event-args  [[eny duct now rof] server-state.ax]
3575      ::
3576      ?>  ?=([@ *] t.wire)
3577      ?:  ?=([%gall %unto %watch-ack *] sign)
3578        ?~  p.p.sign
3579          ::  received a positive acknowledgment: take no action
3580          ::
3581          [~ http-server-gate]
3582        ::  we have an error; propagate it to the client
3583        ::
3584        =/  handle-gall-error
3585          handle-gall-error:(per-server-event event-args)
3586        =^  moves  server-state.ax  (handle-gall-error u.p.p.sign)
3587        [moves http-server-gate]
3588      ::
3589      ?:  ?=([%gall %unto %kick ~] sign)
3590        =/  handle-response  handle-response:(per-server-event event-args)
3591        =^  moves  server-state.ax
3592          (handle-response %continue ~ &)
3593        [moves http-server-gate]
3594      ::
```

```
3595    ?>  ?=([%gall %unto %fact *] sign)
3596    =/  =mark  p.cage.p.sign
3597    =/  =vase  q.cage.p.sign
3598    ?.  ?=  ?(%http-response-header %http-response-data %http-response-cancel)
3599        mark
3600      =/  handle-gall-error
3601        handle-gall-error:(per-server-event event-args)
3602      =^  moves  server-state.ax
3603        (handle-gall-error leaf+"eyre bad mark {(trip mark)}" ~)
3604      [moves http-server-gate]
3605    ::
3606    =/  =http-event:http
3607      ?-  mark
3608        %http-response-header  [%start !<(response-header:http vase) ~ |]
3609        %http-response-data    [%continue !<((unit octs) vase) |]
3610        %http-response-cancel  [%cancel ~]
3611      ==
3612    =/  handle-response  handle-response:(per-server-event event-args)
3613    =^  moves  server-state.ax
3614      (handle-response http-event)
3615    [moves http-server-gate]
3616  ::
3617  ++  channel
3618    ::
3619    =/  event-args  [[eny duct now rof] server-state.ax]
3620    ::  channel callback wires are triples.
3621    ::
3622    ?>  ?=([@ @ @t *] wire)
3623    ::
3624    ?+  i.t.wire
3625      ~|([%bad-channel-wire wire] !!)
3626    ::
3627      %timeout
3628    ?>  ?=([%behn %wake *] sign)
3629    ?^  error.sign
3630      [[duct %slip %d %flog %crud %wake u.error.sign]~ http-server-gate]
3631    =*  id  i.t.t.wire
3632    %-  %+  trace:(per-server-event event-args)  1
3633      |.("{(trip id)} cancelling channel due to timeout")
3634    =^  moves  server-state.ax
3635      (discard-channel:by-channel:(per-server-event event-args) id &)
3636    [moves http-server-gate]
3637    ::
3638      %heartbeat
3639    =/  on-channel-heartbeat
3640      on-channel-heartbeat:by-channel:(per-server-event event-args)
3641    =^  moves  server-state.ax
3642      (on-channel-heartbeat i.t.t.wire)
3643    [moves http-server-gate]
3644    ::
3645      ?(%poke %subscription)
3646    ?>  ?=([%gall %unto *] sign)
3647    ~|  eyre-sub=wire
3648    ?>  ?=([@ @ @t @ *] wire)
3649    ?<  ?=(%raw-fact -.p.sign)
3650    =*  channel-id  i.t.t.wire
3651    =*  request-id  i.t.t.t.wire
3652    =*  extra-wire  t.t.t.t.wire
```

```
3653        =/  on-gall-response
3654          on-gall-response:by-channel:(per-server-event event-args)
3655        ::  ~&  [%gall-response sign]
3656        =^  moves  server-state.ax
3657          %-  on-gall-response
3658          [channel-id (slav %ud request-id) extra-wire p.sign]
3659        [moves http-server-gate]
3660      ==
3661    ::
3662    ++  sessions
3663      ::
3664      ?>  ?=([%behn %wake *] sign)
3665      ::
3666      ?^  error.sign
3667        [[duct %slip %d %flog %crud %wake u.error.sign]~ http-server-gate]
3668      ::NOTE  we are not concerned with expiring channels that are still in
3669      ::      use. we require acks for messages, which bump their session's
3670      ::      timer. channels have their own expiry timer, too.
3671      ::  remove cookies that have expired
3672      ::
3673      =*  sessions  sessions.auth.server-state.ax
3674      =.  sessions.auth.server-state.ax
3675        %-  ~(gas by *(map @uv session))
3676        %+  skip  ~(tap in sessions)
3677        |=  [cookie=@uv session]
3678        (lth expiry-time now)
3679      ::  if there's any cookies left, set a timer for the next expected expiry
3680      ::
3681      ^-  [(list move) _http-server-gate]
3682      :_  http-server-gate
3683      :-  =<  give-session-tokens
3684          (per-server-event [eny duct now rof] server-state.ax)
3685      ?:  =(~ sessions)  ~
3686      =;  next-expiry=@da
3687        [duct %pass /sessions/expire %b %wait next-expiry]~
3688      %+  roll  ~(tap by sessions)
3689      |=  [[@uv session] next=@da]
3690      ?:  =(*@da next)  expiry-time
3691      (min next expiry-time)
3692    ::
3693    ++  eauth
3694      =*  auth  auth.server-state.ax
3695      =*  args  [[eny duct now rof] server-state.ax]
3696      ^-  [(list move) _http-server-gate]
3697      ~|  [wire +<.sign]
3698      ?+  t.wire  !!
3699          [%plea @ ~]
3700        =/  =ship  (slav %p i.t.t.wire)
3701        ::
3702        ?:  |(?=(^ dud) ?=([%ames %lost *] sign))
3703          %-  %+  trace:(per-server-event args)  0
3704            ?~  dud  |.("eauth: lost boon from {(scow %p ship)}")
3705            |.("eauth: crashed on %{(trip +<.sign)} from {(scow %p ship)}")
3706        ::NOTE  when failing on pending attempts, we just wait for the timer
3707        ::      to clean up. when failing on live sessions, well, we should
3708        ::      just be careful not to crash when receiving %shut boons.
3709        ::      (we do not want to have the nonce in the wire, so this is the
3710        ::      best handling we can do. the alternative is tracking)
```

```
3711        [~ http-server-gate]
3712      ::
3713    ?:  ?=([%ames %done *] sign)
3714      =^  moz  server-state.ax
3715        %.  [ship ?=(~ error.sign)]
3716        on-done:client:eauth:authentication:(per-server-event args)
3717      [moz http-server-gate]
3718      ::
3719    ?>  ?=([%ames %boon *] sign)
3720      =/  boon  ;;(eauth-boon payload.sign)
3721      =^  moz  server-state.ax
3722        %.  [ship boon]
3723        on-boon:client:eauth:authentication:(per-server-event args)
3724      [moz http-server-gate]
3725  ::
3726      [%keen @ @ ~]
3727    =/  client=@p  (slav %p i.t.t.wire)
3728    =/  nonce=@uv  (slav %uv i.t.t.t.wire)
3729      ::
3730    ?^  dud
3731      =^  moz  server-state.ax
3732        %.  [client nonce]
3733        on-fail:server:eauth:authentication:(per-server-event args)
3734      [moz http-server-gate]
3735      ::
3736    ?>  ?=([%ames %tune *] sign)
3737    ?>  =(client ship.sign)
3738    =/  url=(unit @t)
3739      ?~  roar.sign  ~
3740      ?~  q.dat.u.roar.sign  ~
3741      ;;((unit @t) q.u.q.dat.u.roar.sign)
3742    =^  moz  server-state.ax
3743      ?~  url
3744        %.  [client nonce]
3745        on-fail:server:eauth:authentication:(per-server-event args)
3746      %.  [client nonce u.url]
3747      on-tune:server:eauth:authentication:(per-server-event args)
3748      [moz http-server-gate]
3749  ::
3750      [%expire %visiting @ @ ~]
3751    ?>  ?=([%behn %wake *] sign)
3752    =/  server=@p  (slav %p i.t.t.wire)
3753    =/  nonce=@uv  (slav %uv i.t.t.t.wire)
3754    =^  moz  server-state.ax
3755      %.  [server nonce]
3756      expire:client:eauth:authentication:(per-server-event args)
3757      [~ http-server-gate]
3758      ::
3759      [%expire %visitors @ ~]
3760    =/  nonce=@uv  (slav %uv i.t.t.t.wire)
3761    =^  moz  server-state.ax
3762      (expire:server:eauth:authentication:(per-server-event args) nonce)
3763      [moz http-server-gate]
3764    ==
3765  ::
3766  ++  acme-ack
3767    ?>  ?=([%gall %unto *] sign)
3768      ::
```

```
3769      ?>   ?=([%poke-ack *] p.sign)
3770      ?~   p.p.sign
3771       ::   received a positive acknowledgment: take no action
3772       ::
3773       [~ http-server-gate]
3774      ::  received a negative acknowledgment: XX do something
3775      ::
3776      [((slog u.p.p.sign) ~) http-server-gate]
3777    --
3778  ::
3779  ++  http-server-gate  ..$
3780  ::  +load: migrate old state to new state (called on vane reload)
3781  ::
3782  ++  load
3783    =>   |%
3784       +$  axle-any
3785        $%  [date=%~2020.10.18 server-state=server-state-0]
3786            [date=%~2022.7.26 server-state=server-state-0]
3787            [date=%~2023.2.17 server-state=server-state-1]
3788            [date=%~2023.3.16 server-state=server-state-2]
3789            [date=%~2023.4.11 server-state-3]
3790            [date=%~2023.5.15 server-state]
3791        ==
3792       ::
3793       +$  server-state-0
3794        $:  bindings=(list [=binding =duct =action])
3795            =cors-registry
3796            connections=(map duct outstanding-connection-3)
3797            auth=authentication-state-3
3798            channel-state=channel-state-2
3799            domains=(set turf)
3800            =http-config
3801            ports=[insecure=@ud secure=(unit @ud)]
3802            outgoing-duct=duct
3803        ==
3804       ::
3805       +$  server-state-1
3806        $:  bindings=(list [=binding =duct =action])
3807            =cors-registry
3808            connections=(map duct outstanding-connection-3)
3809            auth=authentication-state-3
3810            channel-state=channel-state-2
3811            domains=(set turf)
3812            =http-config
3813            ports=[insecure=@ud secure=(unit @ud)]
3814            outgoing-duct=duct
3815            verb=@                                      ::  <-  new
3816        ==
3817       ::
3818       +$  server-state-2
3819        $:  bindings=(list [=binding =duct =action])
3820            cache=(map url=@t [aeon=@ud val=(unit cache-entry)])  ::  <-  new
3821            =cors-registry
3822            connections=(map duct outstanding-connection-3)
3823            auth=authentication-state-3
3824            channel-state=channel-state-2
3825            domains=(set turf)
3826            =http-config
```

```
3827              ports=[insecure=@ud secure=(unit @ud)]
3828              outgoing-duct=duct
3829              verb=@
3830          ==
3831      +$  channel-state-2
3832        $:  session=(map @t channel-2)
3833            duct-to-key=(map duct @t)
3834        ==
3835      +$  channel-2
3836        $:  state=(each timer duct)
3837            next-id=@ud
3838            last-ack=@da
3839            events=(qeu [id=@ud request-id=@ud channel-event=channel-event-2])
3840            unacked=(map @ud @ud)
3841            subscriptions=(map @ud [ship=@p app=term =path duc=duct])
3842            heartbeat=(unit timer)
3843        ==
3844      +$  channel-event-2
3845        $%  $>(%poke-ack sign:agent:gall)
3846            $>(%watch-ack sign:agent:gall)
3847            $>(%kick sign:agent:gall)
3848            [%fact =mark =noun]
3849        ==
3850    ::
3851      +$  server-state-3
3852        $:  bindings=(list [=binding =duct =action])
3853            cache=(map url=@t [aeon=@ud val=(unit cache-entry)])
3854            =cors-registry
3855            connections=(map duct outstanding-connection-3)
3856            auth=authentication-state-3
3857            channel-state=channel-state-3
3858            domains=(set turf)
3859            =http-config
3860            ports=[insecure=@ud secure=(unit @ud)]
3861            outgoing-duct=duct
3862            verb=@
3863        ==
3864      +$  outstanding-connection-3
3865        $:  =action
3866            =inbound-request
3867            response-header=(unit response-header:http)
3868            bytes-sent=@ud
3869        ==
3870      +$  authentication-state-3  sessions=(map @uv session-3)
3871      +$  session-3
3872        $:  expiry-time=@da
3873            channels=(set @t)
3874        ==
3875      +$  channel-state-3
3876        $:  session=(map @t channel-3)
3877            duct-to-key=(map duct @t)
3878        ==
3879      +$  channel-3
3880        $:  mode=?(%json %jam)
3881            state=(each timer duct)
3882            next-id=@ud
3883            last-ack=@da
3884            events=(qeu [id=@ud request-id=@ud =channel-event])
```

```
3885              unacked=(map @ud @ud)
3886              subscriptions=(map @ud [ship=@p app=term =path duc=duct])
3887              heartbeat=(unit timer)
3888          ==
3889        --
3890    |=  old=axle-any
3891    ^+  http-server-gate
3892    ?-    -.old
3893    ::
3894    ::  adds /~/name
3895    ::
3896        %~2020.10.18
3897      %=  $
3898          date.old  %~2022.7.26
3899        ::
3900          bindings.server-state.old
3901        %+  insert-binding
3902          [[~ /~/name] outgoing-duct.server-state.old [%name ~]]
3903          bindings.server-state.old
3904      ==
3905    ::
3906    ::  enables https redirects if certificate configured
3907    ::  inits .verb
3908    ::
3909        %~2022.7.26
3910      =.  redirect.http-config.server-state.old
3911        ?&  ?=(^ secure.ports.server-state.old)
3912            ?=(^ secure.http-config.server-state.old)
3913        ==
3914      $(old [%~2023.2.17 server-state.old(|8 [|8 verb=0]:server-state.old)])
3915    ::
3916    ::  inits .cache
3917    ::
3918        %~2023.2.17
3919      $(old [%~2023.3.16 [bindings ~ +]:server-state.old])
3920    ::
3921    ::  inits channel mode and desks in unacked events
3922    ::
3923        %~2023.3.16
3924    ::
3925    ::  Prior to this desks were not part of events.channel.
3926    ::  When serializing we used to rely on the desk stored in
3927    ::  subscriptions.channel, but this state is deleted when we clog.
3928    ::  This migration adds the desk to events.channel, but we can not
3929    ::  scry in +load to populate the desks in the old events,
3930    ::  so we just kick all subscriptions on all channels.
3931      %=    $
3932          date.old  %~2023.4.11
3933        ::
3934          server-state.old
3935        %=  server-state.old
3936            session.channel-state
3937          %-  ~(run by session.channel-state.server-state.old)
3938          |=  c=channel-2
3939          =;  new-events
3940            :-  %json
3941            c(events new-events, unacked ~, subscriptions ~)
3942          =|  events=(qeu [id=@ud request-id=@ud =channel-event])
```

```
3943        =/  1  ~(tap in ~(key by subscriptions.c))
3944        |-
3945        ?~  1  events
3946        %=  $
3947          1              t.1
3948          next-id.c  +(next-id.c)
3949          events       (~(put to events) [next-id.c i.1 %kick ~])
3950        ==
3951      ==
3952    ==
3953    ::
3954    ::  guarantees & stores a session for each request, and a @p identity for
3955    ::  each session and channel
3956    ::
3957        %~2023.4.11
3958    %=  $
3959    date.old  %~2023.5.15
3960    ::
3961        connections.old
3962    %-  ~(run by connections.old)
3963    |=  outstanding-connection-3
3964    ^-  outstanding-connection
3965    [action inbound-request [*@uv [%ours ~]] response-header bytes-sent]
3966    ::
3967        auth.old
3968    :_  [~ ~ [~ ~ now]]
3969    %-  ~(run by sessions.auth.old)
3970    |=  s=session-3
3971    ^-  session
3972    [[%ours ~] s]
3973    ::
3974        session.channel-state.old
3975    %-  ~(run by session.channel-state.old)
3976    |=  c=channel-3
3977    ^-  channel
3978    [-.c [%ours ~] +.c]
3979    ::
3980        bindings.old
3981    %+  insert-binding  [[~ /~/host] outgoing-duct.old [%host ~]]
3982    %+  insert-binding  [[~ /~/eauth] outgoing-duct.old [%eauth ~]]
3983    bindings.old
3984    ==
3985    ::
3986        %~2023.5.15
3987    http-server-gate(ax old)
3988    ==
3989 ::  +stay: produce current state
3990 ::
3991 ++  stay  `axle`ax
3992 ::  +scry: request a path in the urbit namespace
3993 ::
3994 ++  scry
3995  ~/  %eyre-scry
3996  ^-  roon
3997  |=  [lyc=gang pov=path car=term bem=beam]
3998  ^-  (unit (unit cage))
3999  =*  ren  car
4000  =*  why=shop  &/p.bem
```

```
4001    =*  syd  q.bem
4002    =/  lot=coin  $/r.bem
4003    =*  tyl  s.bem
4004    ::
4005    ?.  ?=(%& -.why)
4006      ~
4007    =*  who  p.why
4008    ::
4009    ?.  ?=(%$ -.lot)
4010      [~ ~]
4011    ?.  =(our who)
4012      ?.  =([%da now] p.lot)
4013        [~ ~]
4014      ~&  [%r %scry-foreign-host who]
4015      ~
4016    ?:  &(?=(%x ren) ?=(%$ syd))
4017      =,  server-state.ax
4018      ?+  tyl  [~ ~]
4019        [%$ %whey ~]            =-  ``mass+!>(`(list mass)`-)
4020                                :~  bindings+&+bindings.server-state.ax
4021                                    auth+&+auth.server-state.ax
4022                                    connections+&+connections.server-state.ax
4023                                    channels+&+channel-state.server-state.ax
4024                                    axle+&+ax
4025                                ==
4026      ::
4027        [%cors ~]             ``noun+!>(cors-registry)
4028        [%cors %requests ~]  ``noun+!>(requests.cors-registry)
4029        [%cors %approved ~]  ``noun+!>(approved.cors-registry)
4030        [%cors %rejected ~]  ``noun+!>(rejected.cors-registry)
4031      ::
4032          [%cors ?(%approved %rejected) @ ~]
4033        =*  kind  i.t.tyl
4034        =*  orig  i.t.t.tyl
4035        ?~  origin=(slaw %t orig)  [~ ~]
4036        ?-  kind
4037          %approved  ``noun+!>((~(has in approved.cors-registry) u.origin))
4038          %rejected  ``noun+!>((~(has in rejected.cors-registry) u.origin))
4039        ==
4040      ::
4041          [%eauth %url ~]
4042        =*  endpoint  endpoint.auth.server-state.ax
4043        ?.  ?=(%da -.p.lot)  [~ ~]
4044        ::  we cannot answer for something prior to the last set time,
4045        ::  or something beyond the present moment.
4046        ::
4047        ?:  ?|  (lth q.p.lot time.endpoint)
4048                (gth q.p.lot now)
4049            ==
4050          ~
4051        :^  ~  ~  %noun
4052        !>  ^-  (unit @t)
4053        =<  eauth-url:eauth:authentication
4054        (per-server-event [eny *duct now rof] server-state.ax)
4055      ::
4056          [%authenticated %cookie @ ~]
4057        ?~  cookies=(slaw %t i.t.t.tyl)  [~ ~]
4058        :^  ~  ~  %noun
```

```
4059        !>   ^-  ?
4060        %-  =<  request-is-authenticated:authentication
4061            (per-server-event [eny *duct now rof] server-state.ax)
4062        %*(. *request:http header-list ['cookie' u.cookies]~)
4063     ::
4064        [%cache @ @ ~]
4065        ?~  aeon=(slaw %ud i.t.tyl)          [~ ~]
4066        ?~  url=(slaw %t i.t.t.tyl)          [~ ~]
4067        ?~  entry=(~(get by cache) u.url)    [~ ~]
4068        ?.  =(u.aeon aeon.u.entry)           [~ ~]
4069        ?~  val=val.u.entry                  [~ ~]
4070        ``noun+!>(u.val)
4071     ==
4072   ?.  ?=(%$ ren)
4073     [~ ~]
4074   ?+  syd  [~ ~]
4075     %bindings              ``noun+!>(bindings.server-state.ax)
4076     %connections           ``noun+!>(connections.server-state.ax)
4077     %authentication-state  ``noun+!>(auth.server-state.ax)
4078     %channel-state         ``noun+!>(channel-state.server-state.ax)
4079   ::
4080       %host
4081   %-  (lift (lift |=(a=hart:eyre [%hart !>(a)])))
4082   ^-  (unit (unit hart:eyre))
4083   =.  p.lot  ?.(=([%da now] p.lot) p.lot [%tas %real])
4084   ?+  p.lot
4085     [~ ~]
4086   ::
4087       [%tas %fake]
4088   ``[& [~ 8.443] %& /localhost]
4089   ::
4090       [%tas %real]
4091   =*  domains  domains.server-state.ax
4092   =*  ports  ports.server-state.ax
4093   =/  =host:eyre  [%& ?^(domains n.domains /localhost)]
4094   =/  port=(unit @ud)
4095     ?.  ?=(^ secure.ports)
4096       ?:(=(80 insecure.ports) ~ `insecure.ports)
4097     ?:(=(443 u.secure.ports) ~ secure.ports)
4098   ``[?=(^ secure.ports) port host]
4099     ==
4100   ==
4101 --
```

Gall 163K

```
1   !:
2   ::   ::  %gall, agent execution
3   !?  163
4   ::
5   ::::
6   |=  our=ship
7   ::  veb: verbosity flags
8   ::
9   =/  veb-all-off
10    ::  TODO: add more flags?
11    ::
12    :*  odd=`?`%.n  ::  unusual events
13    ==
14  =,  gall
15  =>
16  |%
17  +|  %helpers
18  ::  +trace: print if .verb is set and we're tracking .dude
19  ::
20  ++  trace
21    |=  [verb=? =dude dudes=(set dude) print=tang]
22    ^+  same
23    ?.  verb
24      same
25    ?.  =>  [dude=dude dudes=dudes in=in]
26      ~+  |(=(~ dudes) (~(has in dudes) dude))
27      same
28    (slog print)
29  ::
30  ::  $bug: debug printing configuration
31  ::
32  ::    veb: verbosity toggles
33  ::    dudes: app filter; if ~, print for all
34  ::
35  +$  bug
36    $:  veb=_veb-all-off
37        dudes=(set dude)
38    ==
39  ::
40  +|  %main
41  ::
42  ::  $move: Arvo-level move
43  ::
44  +$  move  [=duct move=(wind note-arvo gift-arvo)]
45  ::  $state-15: overall gall state, versioned
46  ::
47  +$  state-15  [%15 state]
48  ::  $state: overall gall state
49  ::
50  ::    system-duct: TODO document
51  ::    outstanding: outstanding request queue
52  ::    contacts: other ships we're in communication with
53  ::    yokes: running agents
54  ::    blocked: moves to agents that haven't been started yet
55  ::    bug: debug printing configuration
56  ::    leaves: retry nacked %leaves timer, if set
```

```
57  ::
58  +$  state
59    $:  system-duct=duct
60        outstanding=(map [wire duct] (qeu remote-request))
61        contacts=(set ship)
62        yokes=(map term yoke)
63        blocked=(map term (qeu blocked-move))
64        =bug
65        leaves=(unit [=duct =wire date=@da])
66    ==
67  ::  $routes: new cuff; TODO: document
68  ::
69  +$  routes
70    $:  disclosing=(unit (set ship))
71        attributing=[=ship =path]
72    ==
73  ::  $yoke: agent runner state
74  ::
75  ::    control-duct: TODO document
76  ::    run-nonce: unique for each rebuild
77  ::    sub-nonce: app-wide global %watch nonce
78  ::    stats: TODO document
79  ::    bitt: incoming subscriptions
80  ::    boat: outgoing subscriptions
81  ::    boar: and their nonces
82  ::    code: most recently loaded code
83  ::    agent: agent core
84  ::    beak: compilation source
85  ::    marks: mark conversion requests
86  ::    sky: scry bindings
87  ::    ken: open keen requests
88  ::
89  +$  yoke
90    $%  [%nuke sky=(map spur @ud)]
91        $:  %live
92            control-duct=duct
93            run-nonce=@t
94            sub-nonce=_1
95            =stats
96            =bitt
97            =boat
98            =boar
99            code=*
100           agent=(each agent vase)
101           =beak
102           marks=(map duct mark)
103           sky=(map spur path-state)
104           ken=(jug spar:ames wire)
105   ==  ==
106 ::
107 ++  on-path  ((on @ud (pair @da (each page @uvI))) lte)
108 ::  $blocked-move: enqueued move to an agent
109 ::
110 +$  blocked-move  [=duct =routes move=(each deal unto)]
111 ::
112 +$  ames-response
113   $%  [%d =mark noun=*]
114       [%x ~]
```

```
115      ==
116  ::    $ames-request: network request (%plea)
117  ::
118  ::       %m: poke
119  ::       %l: watch-as
120  ::       %s: watch
121  ::       %u: leave
122  ::
123  +$  ames-request-all
124    $%  [%0 ames-request]
125      ==
126  +$  ames-request
127    $%  [%m =mark noun=*]
128        [%l =mark =path]
129        [%s =path]
130        [%u ~]
131      ==
132  ::    $remote-request: kinds of agent actions that can cross the network
133  ::
134  ::       Used in wires to identify the kind of remote request we made.
135  ::       Bijective with the tags of $ames-request.
136  ::
137  +$  remote-request
138    $?  %watch
139        %watch-as
140        %poke
141        %leave
142        %missing
143      ==
144  ::    |migrate: data structures for upgrades
145  ::
146  +|  %migrate
147  ::
148  ::    $spore: structures for update, produced by +stay
149  ::
150  ::    remember to duplicate version tag changes here to $egg-any:gall in lull
151  ::
152  +$  spore
153    $:  %15
154        system-duct=duct
155        outstanding=(map [wire duct] (qeu remote-request))
156        contacts=(set ship)
157        eggs=(map term egg)
158        blocked=(map term (qeu blocked-move))
159        =bug
160        leaves=(unit [=duct =wire date=@da])
161      ==
162  --
163  ::  adult gall vane interface, for type compatibility with pupa
164  ::
165  =|  state=state-15
166  |=  [now=@da eny=@uvJ rof=roof]
167  =*  gall-payload  .
168  ~%  %gall-top  ..part  ~
169  |%
170  ::  +mo: Arvo-level move handling
171  ::
172  ::       An outer core responsible for routing moves to and from Arvo; it calls
```

```
173  ::      an inner core, +ap, to route internal moves to and from agents.
174  ::
175  ++  mo
176  ~%  %gall-mo  +>  ~
177  |_  [hen=duct moves=(list move)]
178  ::
179  ++  trace
180  |=  [verb=? =dude print=tang]
181  ^+  same
182  (^trace verb dude dudes.bug.state print)
183  ::
184  ::  +mo-abed: initialise state with the provided duct
185  ::  +mo-abet: finalize, reversing moves
186  ::  +mo-pass: prepend a standard %pass to the current list of moves
187  ::  +mo-give: prepend a standard %give to the current list of moves
188  ::  +mo-talk: build task to print config report or failure trace
189  ::
190  ++  mo-core  .
191  ++  mo-abed  |=(hun=duct mo-core(hen hun))
192  ++  mo-abet  [(flop moves) gall-payload]
193  ++  mo-emit  |=(=move mo-core(moves [move moves]))
194  ++  mo-give  |=(=gift (mo-emit hen give+gift))
195  ++  mo-talk
196  |=  rup=(each suss tang)
197  ^-  [wire note-arvo]
198  :+  /sys/say  %d
199  ^-  task:dill
200  ?-  -.rup
201     %&  [%text "gall: {(t q)}ed %{(t p)}":[t=trip p.rup]]
202     %|  [%talk leaf+"gall: failed" (flop p.rup)]
203  ==
204  ++  mo-pass  |=(p=[wire note-arvo] (mo-emit hen pass+p))
205  ++  mo-slip  |=(p=note-arvo (mo-emit hen slip+p))
206  ++  mo-past
207  |=  =(list [wire note-arvo])
208  ?~  list
209    mo-core
210  =.  mo-core  (mo-pass i.list)
211  $(list t.list)
212  ::  +mo-jolt: (re)start agent
213  ::
214  ++  mo-jolt
215  |=  [dap=term =ship =desk]
216  ^+  mo-core
217  =/  =wire  /sys/cor/[dap]/(scot %p ship)/[desk]
218  ..mo-core
219  ::  XX  (mo-pass wire %c %jolt dap ship desk)
220  ::  +mo-doff: kill all outgoing subscriptions
221  ::
222  ++  mo-doff
223  |=  [prov=path dude=(unit dude) ship=(unit ship)]
224  ^+  mo-core
225  =/  apps=(list (pair term yoke))
226    ?~  dude  ~(tap by yokes.state)
227    (drop (bind (~(get by yokes.state) u.dude) (lead u.dude)))
228  |-  ^+  mo-core
229  ?~  apps  mo-core
230  ?:  ?=(%nuke -.q.i.apps)  $(apps t.apps)
```

```
231      =/  ap-core  (ap-yoke:ap p.i.apps [~ our prov] q.i.apps)
232      $(apps t.apps, mo-core ap-abet:(ap-doff:ap-core ship))
233  ::  +mo-rake: send %cork's for old subscriptions if needed
234  ::
235  ++  mo-rake
236    |=  [prov=path dude=(unit dude) all=?]
237    ^+  mo-core
238    =/  apps=(list (pair term yoke))
239      ?~  dude  ~(tap by yokes.state)
240      (drop (bind ~(get by yokes.state) u.dude) (lead u.dude)))
241    |-  ^+  mo-core
242    ?~  apps  mo-core
243    ?:  ?=(%nuke -.q.i.apps)  $(apps t.apps)
244    =/  ap-core  (ap-yoke:ap p.i.apps [~ our prov] q.i.apps)
245    $(apps t.apps, mo-core ap-abet:(ap-rake:ap-core all))
246  ::  +mo-receive-core: receives an app core built by %ford.
247  ::
248  ::    Presuming we receive a good core, we first check to see if the agent
249  ::    is already running.  If so, we update its beak in %gall's state,
250  ::    initialise an +ap core for the agent, install the core we got from
251  ::    %ford, and then resolve any moves associated with it.
252  ::
253  ::    If we're dealing with a new agent, we create one using the result we
254  ::    got from %ford, add it to the collection of agents %gall is keeping
255  ::    track of, and then do more or less the same procedure as we did for the
256  ::    running agent case.
257  ::
258  ++  mo-receive-core
259    ~/  %mo-receive-core
260    |=  [prov=path dap=term bek=beak =agent]
261    ^+  mo-core
262    ::
263    =/  yak  (~(get by yokes.state) dap)
264    =/  tex=(unit tape)
265      ?~  yak  `"installing"
266      ?:  ?=(%nuke -.u.yak)  `"unnuking"  ::TODO good message here?
267      ?-    -.agent.u.yak
268          %|  `"reviving"
269          %&
270        ?:  =(code.u.yak agent)
271          ~
272        `"reloading"
273      ==
274    =+  ?~  tex  ~
275        ~>  %slog.[0 leaf+"gall: {u.tex} {<dap>}"]  ~
276    ::
277    ?:  ?=([~ %live *] yak)
278      ?:  &(=(q.beak.u.yak q.bek) =(code.u.yak agent) =(-.agent.u.yak &))
279        mo-core
280      ::
281      =.  yokes.state
282        (~(put by yokes.state) dap u.yak(beak bek, code agent))
283      =/  ap-core  (ap-abed:ap dap [~ our prov])
284      =.  ap-core  (ap-reinstall:ap-core agent)
285      =.  mo-core  ap-abet:ap-core
286      (mo-clear-queue dap)
287    ::
288    =.  yokes.state
```

```
289      %+  ~(put by yokes.state)  dap
290      %*    .  *$>(%live yoke)
291        control-duct  hen
292        beak          bek
293        code          agent
294        agent         &+agent
295        run-nonce     (scot %uw (end 5 (shas %yoke-nonce eny)))
296        sky
297      ?~  yak  ~
298      (~(run by sky.u.yak) (corl (late ~) (lead ~)))
299      ==
300    ::
301    =/  old  mo-core
302    =/  wag
303      =/  ap-core  (ap-abed:ap dap [~ our prov])
304      (ap-upgrade-state:ap-core ~)
305    ::
306    =/  maybe-tang  -.wag
307    =/  ap-core  +.wag
308    ?^  maybe-tang
309      =.  mo-core  old
310      (mo-pass (mo-talk %.n u.maybe-tang))
311    ::
312    =.  mo-core  ap-abet:ap-core
313    =.  mo-core  (mo-clear-queue dap)
314    =/  =suss  [dap %boot now]
315    (mo-pass (mo-talk %.y suss))
316  ::  +mo-send-foreign-request: handle local request to .ship
317  ::
318  ++  mo-send-foreign-request
319    ~/  %mo-send-foreign-request
320    |=  [=ship foreign-agent=term =deal]
321    ^+  mo-core
322    ::
323    =.  mo-core  (mo-track-ship ship)
324    ?<  ?=(?(%raw-poke %poke-as) -.deal)
325    =/  =ames-request-all
326      :-  %0
327      ?-  -.deal
328        %poke      [%m p.cage.deal q.q.cage.deal]
329        %leave     [%u ~]
330        %watch-as  [%l [mark path]:deal]
331        %watch     [%s path.deal]
332      ==
333    ::
334    =/  wire
335      /sys/way/(scot %p ship)/[foreign-agent]
336    ::
337    =/  =note-arvo
338      =/  =path  /ge/[foreign-agent]
339      [%a %plea ship %g path ames-request-all]
340    ::
341    =.  outstanding.state
342      =/  stand
343      (~(gut by outstanding.state) [wire hen] *(qeu remote-request))
344      (~(put by outstanding.state) [wire hen] (~(put to stand) -.deal))
345    (mo-pass wire note-arvo)
346  ::  +mo-track-ship: subscribe to ames and jael for notices about .ship
```

```
347  ::
348  ++  mo-track-ship
349    |=  =ship
350    ^+  mo-core
351    ::  if already contacted, no-op
352    ::
353    ?:  (~(has in contacts.state) ship)
354      mo-core
355    ::  first contact; update state and subscribe to notifications
356    ::
357    =.  contacts.state  (~(put in contacts.state) ship)
358    ::  ask ames to track .ship's connectivity
359    ::
360    =.  moves  [[system-duct.state %pass /sys/lag %a %heed ship] moves]
361    ::  ask jael to track .ship's breaches
362    ::
363    =/  =note-arvo  [%j %public-keys (silt ship ~)]
364    =.  moves
365      [[system-duct.state %pass /sys/era note-arvo] moves]
366    mo-core
367  ::  +mo-untrack-ship: cancel subscriptions to ames and jael for .ship
368  ::
369  ++  mo-untrack-ship
370    |=  =ship
371    ^+  mo-core
372    ::  if already canceled, no-op
373    ::
374    ?.  (~(has in contacts.state) ship)
375      mo-core
376    ::  delete .ship from state and kill subscriptions
377    ::
378    =.  contacts.state  (~(del in contacts.state) ship)
379    ::
380    =.  moves  [[system-duct.state %pass /sys/lag %a %jilt ship] moves]
381    ::
382    =/  =note-arvo  [%j %nuke (silt ship ~)]
383    =.  moves
384      [[system-duct.state %pass /sys/era note-arvo] moves]
385    mo-core
386  ::  +mo-breach: ship breached, so forget about them
387  ::
388  ++  mo-breach
389    |=  [prov=path =ship]
390    ^+  mo-core
391    =.  mo-core  (mo-untrack-ship ship)
392    =.  mo-core  (mo-filter-queue ship)
393    =/  agents=(list [name=term =yoke])  ~(tap by yokes.state)
394    =.  outstanding.state
395      %-  malt
396      %+  skip  ~(tap by outstanding.state)
397      |=  [[=wire duct] (qeu remote-request)]
398      =(/sys/way/(scot %p ship) (scag 3 wire))
399    ::
400    |-  ^+  mo-core
401    ?~  agents
402      mo-core
403    =?  mo-core  ?=(%live -.yoke.i.agents)
404      =/  =routes  [disclosing=~ attributing=[ship prov]]
```

```
405       =/  app  (ap-abed:ap name.i.agents routes)
406       ap-abet:(ap-breach:app ship)
407     $(agents t.agents)
408   ::  +mo-handle-sys: handle a +sign incoming over /sys.
409   ::
410   ::    (Note that /sys implies the +sign should be routed to a vane.)
411   ::
412   ++  mo-handle-sys
413   ~/  %mo-handle-sys
414   |=  [=wire =sign-arvo]
415   ^+  mo-core
416   ::
417   ?+  -.wire  !!
418     %lyv  ..mo-core  ::  vestigial
419     %cor  ..mo-core  ::  vestigial
420     %era  (mo-handle-sys-era wire sign-arvo)
421     %lag  (mo-handle-sys-lag wire sign-arvo)
422     %req  (mo-handle-sys-req wire sign-arvo)
423     %way  (mo-handle-sys-way wire sign-arvo)
424   ==
425   ::  +mo-handle-sys-era: receive update about contact
426   ::
427   ++  mo-handle-sys-era
428   |=  [=wire =sign-arvo]
429   ^+  mo-core
430   ?>  ?=([%jael %public-keys *] sign-arvo)
431   ?>  ?=([%era ~] wire)
432   ?.  ?=(%breach -.public-keys-result.sign-arvo)
433     mo-core
434   (mo-breach /jael who.public-keys-result.sign-arvo)
435   ::  +mo-handle-sys-lag: handle an ames %clog notification
436   ::
437   ++  mo-handle-sys-lag
438   |=  [=wire =sign-arvo]
439   ^+  mo-core
440   ::
441   ?>  ?=([%lag ~] wire)
442   ?>  ?=([%ames %clog *] sign-arvo)
443   ::
444   =/  agents=(list [=dude =yoke])  ~(tap by yokes.state)
445   |-  ^+  mo-core
446   ?~  agents  mo-core
447   ::
448   =?  mo-core  ?=(%live -.yoke.i.agents)
449     =/  app  (ap-abed:ap dude.i.agents [~ our /ames])
450     ap-abet:(ap-clog:app ship.sign-arvo)
451   ::
452   $(agents t.agents)
453   ::  +mo-handle-sys-req: TODO description
454   ::
455   ::    TODO: what should we do if the remote nacks our %pull?
456   ++  mo-handle-sys-req
457   |=  [=wire =sign-arvo]
458   ^+  mo-core
459   ::
460   ?>  ?=([%req @ @ ~] wire)
461   =/  him  (slav %p i.t.wire)
462   =/  dap  i.t.t.wire
```

```
463      ::
464      ?>    ?=([?(%gall %behn) %unto *] sign-arvo)
465      =/    =unto   +>.sign-arvo
466      ::
467      ?-       -.unto
468          %raw-fact   ~|([%gall-raw-req wire] !!)
469          %poke-ack
470        =/   err=(unit error:ames)
471          ?~   p.unto   ~
472          `[%poke-ack u.p.unto]
473        (mo-give %done err)
474      ::
475          %fact
476        =+  [mark noun]=[p q.q]:cage.unto
477        (mo-give %boon %d mark noun)
478      ::
479          %kick
480        (mo-give %boon %x ~)
481      ::
482          %watch-ack
483        =/   err=(unit error:ames)
484          ?~   p.unto   ~
485          `[%watch-ack u.p.unto]
486        (mo-give %done err)
487      ==
488    ::  +mo-handle-sys-way: handle response to outgoing remote request
489    ::
490    ++  mo-handle-sys-way
491      |=  [=wire =sign-arvo]
492      ^+  mo-core
493      ?>  ?=([%way @ @ $@(~ [@ ~])] wire)
494      =/  =ship         (slav %p i.t.wire)
495      =/  foreign-agent   i.t.t.wire
496      ::
497      ?+    sign-arvo   !!
498          [%ames %done *]
499        =/   err=(unit tang)
500          ?~   error=error.sign-arvo
501            ~
502          `[[%leaf (trip tag.u.error)] tang.u.error]
503        =^   remote-request   outstanding.state
504        ?~   t.t.t.wire
505          =/   full-wire   sys+wire
506          =/   stand
507            (~(gut by outstanding.state) [full-wire hen] ~)
508          ::
509          ::  default is to send both ack types; should only hit if
510          ::  cleared queue in +load 3-to-4 or +load-4-to-5
511          ::
512          =?   stand   ?=(~ stand)
513            ~&   [%gall-missing wire hen]
514            (~(put to *(qeu remote-request)) %missing)
515          ~|  [full-wire=full-wire hen=hen stand=stand]
516          =^   rr   stand   ~(get to stand)
517          :-   rr
518          ?:   =(~ stand)
519            ::   outstanding leaves are only deleted when acked
520            ::
```

```
521          ?:  &(?=(^ err) ?=(%leave rr))
522            outstanding.state
523          (~(del by outstanding.state) [full-wire hen])
524        (~(put by outstanding.state) [full-wire hen] stand)
525      ::  non-null case of wire is old, remove on next breach after
526      ::  2019/12
527      ::
528      [;;(remote-request i.t.t.t.wire) outstanding.state]
529    ::  send a %cork if we get a %nack upon initial subscription
530    ::
531    =?  mo-core
532        &(?=(^ err) |(?=(%watch-as remote-request) ?=(%watch remote-request)))
533      (mo-pass sys+wire %a %cork ship)
534    ::
535    ?-  remote-request
536      %watch-as  (mo-give %unto %watch-ack err)
537      %watch     (mo-give %unto %watch-ack err)
538      %poke      (mo-give %unto %poke-ack err)
539      %missing   ~>(%slog.[3 'gall: missing'] mo-core)
540      ::
541        %leave
542      ::  if we get an %ack for a %leave, send %cork. otherwise,
543      ::  the /nacked-leaves timer will re-send the %leave eventually.
544      ::
545      ?~  err
546        (mo-pass sys+wire %a %cork ship)
547      ::  if first time hearing a %nack for a %leave, after upgrade
548      ::  or if all outstanding %leaves have been handled, set up timer
549      ::
550      =?  mo-core  ?=(~ leaves.state)
551        (mo-emit [/gall]~ %pass /nacked-leaves %b %wait `@da`(add now ~m2))
552      =?  leaves.state  ?=(~ leaves.state)
553        `[[/gall]~ /nacked-leaves `@da`(add now ~m2)]
554      mo-core
555    ==
556  ::
557    [%ames %boon *]
558  ?^  t.t.t.wire
559    ::  kill subscriptions which use the old wire format
560    ::
561    !!
562  =/  =ames-response  ;;(ames-response payload.sign-arvo)
563  ::  %d: diff; ask clay to validate .noun as .mark
564  ::  %x: kick; tell agent the publisher canceled the subscription, and
565  ::      cork; tell ames to close the associated flow.
566  ::
567  ?-  -.ames-response
568    %d (mo-give %unto %raw-fact mark.ames-response noun.ames-response)
569    %x =.  mo-core  (mo-give %unto %kick ~)
570       =/  key  [[%sys wire] hen]
571       =?  outstanding.state  =(~ (~(gut by outstanding.state) key ~))
572         (~(del by outstanding.state) key)
573       (mo-pass [%sys wire] %a %cork ship)
574    ==
575  ::
576    [%ames %lost *]
577    ::  note this should only happen on reverse bones, so only facts
578    ::  and kicks
```

```
579        ::
580        ::  TODO: %drip %kick so app crash can't kill the remote %pull
581        ::
582        =.  mo-core  (mo-send-foreign-request ship foreign-agent %leave ~)
583        =.  mo-core  (mo-give %unto %kick ~)
584      mo-core
585    ==
586  ::  +mo-handle-use: handle a typed +sign incoming on /use.
587  ::
588  ::    (Note that /use implies the +sign should be routed to an agent.)
589  ::
590  ::    Initialises the specified agent and then performs an agent-level
591  ::    +take on the supplied +sign.
592  ::
593  ++  mo-handle-use
594    ~/  %mo-handle-use
595    |=  [=wire =sign-arvo]
596    ^+  mo-core
597    ::
598    ?.  ?=([@ @ @ *] wire)
599      ~&  [%mo-handle-use-bad-wire wire]
600      !!
601    ::
602    =/  dap=term  i.wire
603    =/  yoke  (~(get by yokes.state) dap)
604    ?.  ?=([~ %live *] yoke)
605      %-  (slog leaf+"gall: {<dap>} dead, got {<+<.sign-arvo>}" ~)
606      mo-core
607    ?.  =(run-nonce.u.yoke i.t.wire)
608      %-  (slog leaf+"gall: got old {<+<.sign-arvo>} for {<dap>}" ~)
609      mo-core
610    ::
611    ?.  ?=([?(%gall %behn) %unto *] sign-arvo)
612      ?:  ?=(%| -.agent.u.yoke)
613        %-  (slog leaf+"gall: {<dap>} dozing, dropping {<+<.sign-arvo>}" ~)
614        mo-core
615      =/  app
616        =/  =ship  (slav %p i.t.t.wire)
617        =/  =routes  [disclosing=~ attributing=[ship /[-.sign-arvo]]]
618        (ap-abed:ap dap routes)
619      ::
620      =.  app  (ap-generic-take:app t.t.t.wire sign-arvo)
621      ap-abet:app
622    ?>  ?=([%out @ @ *] t.t.wire)
623    =/  =ship  (slav %p i.t.t.t.wire)
624    =/  other-agent  i.t.t.t.t.wire
625    =/  prov=path  ?.(=(ship our) *path /gall/[other-agent])
626    =/  =routes  [disclosing=~ attributing=[ship prov]]
627    =/  =unto  +>.sign-arvo
628    ?:  ?=(%| -.agent.u.yoke)
629      =/  blocked=(qeu blocked-move)
630        =/  waiting  (~(get by blocked.state) dap)
631        =/  deals  (fall waiting *(qeu blocked-move))
632        =/  deal  [hen routes |+unto]
633        (~(put to deals) deal)
634      ::
635      %-  (slog leaf+"gall: {<dap>} dozing, got {<-.unto>}" ~)
636      %_  mo-core
```

```
637          blocked.state  (~(put by blocked.state) dap blocked)
638        ==
639    =/  app  (ap-abed:ap dap routes)
640    =.  app
641      (ap-specific-take:app t.t.wire unto)
642    ap-abet:app
643  ::  +mo-clear-queue: clear blocked tasks from the specified running agent.
644  ::
645  ++  mo-clear-queue
646    |=  dap=term
647    ^+  mo-core
648    ?.  (~(has by yokes.state) dap)
649      mo-core
650    ?~  maybe-blocked=(~(get by blocked.state) dap)
651      mo-core
652    =/  blocked=(qeu blocked-move)  u.maybe-blocked
653    |-  ^+  mo-core
654    ?:  =(~ blocked)
655      =.  blocked.state  (~(del by blocked.state) dap)
656      mo-core
657    =^  [=duct =routes blocker=(each deal unto)]  blocked
658      ~(get to blocked)
659    ?:  ?=(%| -.blocker)  $
660    =/  =move
661      =/  =sack  [ship.attributing.routes our path.attributing.routes]
662      =/  card  [%slip %g %deal sack dap p.blocker]
663      [duct card]
664    $(moves [move moves])
665  ::  +mo-filter-queue: remove all blocked tasks from ship.
666  ::
667  ++  mo-filter-queue
668    |=  =ship
669    =/  agents=(list [name=term blocked=(qeu blocked-move)])
670      ~(tap by blocked.state)
671    =|  new-agents=(map term (qeu blocked-move))
672    |-  ^+  mo-core
673    ?~  agents
674      mo-core(blocked.state new-agents)
675    =|  new-blocked=(qeu blocked-move)
676    |-  ^+  mo-core
677    ?:  =(~ blocked.i.agents)
678      ?~  new-blocked
679        ^$(agents t.agents)
680      %=  ^$
681        agents        t.agents
682        new-agents    (~(put by new-agents) name.i.agents new-blocked)
683      ==
684    =^  mov=blocked-move  blocked.i.agents  ~(get to blocked.i.agents)
685    =?  new-blocked  !=(ship ship.attributing.routes.mov)
686      (~(put to new-blocked) mov)
687    $
688  ::  +mo-idle: put agent to sleep
689  ::
690  ++  mo-idle
691    |=  [prov=path dap=dude]
692    ^+  mo-core
693    =/  yoke=(unit yoke)  (~(get by yokes.state) dap)
694    ?:  |(?=(~ yoke) ?=(%nuke -.u.yoke))
```

```
695      ~>  %slog.0^leaf/"gall: ignoring %idle for {<dap>}, not running"
696      mo-core
697    ap-abet:ap-idle:(ap-abed:ap dap [~ our prov])
698  ::  +mo-nuke: delete agent completely
699  ::
700  ++  mo-nuke
701    |=  [prov=path dap=dude]
702    ^+  mo-core
703    =/  yoke=(unit yoke)  (~(get by yokes.state) dap)
704    ?:  |(?=(~ yoke) ?=(%nuke -.u.yoke))
705      ~>  %slog.0^leaf/"gall: ignoring %nuke for {<dap>}, not running"
706      mo-core
707    ~>  %slog.0^leaf/"gall: nuking {<dap>}"
708    =.  mo-core  ap-abet:ap-nuke:(ap-abed:ap dap [~ our prov])
709    =-  mo-core(yokes.state -)
710    %+  ~(jab by yokes.state)  dap
711    |=  =^yoke
712    ?:  ?=(%nuke -.yoke)  yoke
713    :-  %nuke
714    %-  ~(run by sky.yoke)
715    |=  path-state
716    (fall (clap bob (bind (ram:on-path fan) head) max) 0)
717  ::  +mo-load: install agents
718  ::
719  ++  mo-load
720    |=  [prov=path agents=(list [=dude =beak =agent])]
721    =.  mo-core
722      |-  ^+  mo-core
723      ?~  agents  mo-core
724      =/  [=dude =desk]  [dude q.beak]:i.agents
725      ::  ~>  %slog.0^leaf/"gall: starting {<dude>} on {<desk>}"
726      $(agents t.agents, mo-core (mo-receive-core prov i.agents))
727    ::
728    =/  kil
729      =/  lol
730        (skim ~(tap by yokes.state) |=([* y=yoke] &(?=(%live -.y) -.agent.y)))
731      =/  mol  (~(gas by *(map term yoke)) lol)
732      =/  sol  ~(key by mol)
733      =/  new  (silt (turn agents head))
734      ~(tap in (~(dif in sol) new))
735    |-  ^+  mo-core
736    ?~  kil  mo-core
737    ~>  %slog.0^leaf/"gall: stopping {<i.kil>}"
738    $(kil t.kil, mo-core (mo-idle prov i.kil))
739  ::  +mo-peek:  call to +ap-peek (which is not accessible outside of +mo).
740  ::
741  ++  mo-peek
742    ~/  %mo-peek
743    |=  [veb=? dap=term =routes care=term =path]
744    ^-  (unit (unit cage))
745    ::
746    ?.  ?=([~ %live *] (~(get by yokes.state) dap))  [~ ~]
747    =/  app  (ap-abed:ap dap routes)
748    (ap-peek:app veb care path)
749  ::
750  ++  mo-apply
751    |=  [dap=term =routes =deal]
752    ^+  mo-core
```

```
753        ?-    -.deal
754          ?(%watch %watch-as %leave %poke)
755        (mo-apply-sure dap routes deal)
756        ::
757          %raw-poke
758        ::  don't validate %noun pokes, for performance
759        ::
760        ?:  =(%noun mark.deal)
761          (mo-apply-sure dap routes [%poke %noun %noun noun.deal])
762        =/  =case  da+now
763        =/  yok  (~(got by yokes.state) dap)
764        =/  =desk  q.beak:?>(?=(%live -.yok) yok)  ::TODO acceptable assertion?
765        =/  sky  (rof ~ /gall %cb [our desk case] /[mark.deal])
766        ?-    sky
767          ?(~ [~ ~])
768        =/  ror  "gall: raw-poke fail :{(trip dap)} {<mark.deal>}"
769        (mo-give %unto %poke-ack `[leaf+ror]~)
770        ::
771          [~ ~ *]
772        =+  !<(=dais:clay q.u.u.sky)
773        =/  res  (mule |.((vale:dais noun.deal)))
774        ?:  ?=(%| -.res)
775          =/  ror  "gall: raw-poke vale fail :{(trip dap)} {<mark.deal>}"
776          (mo-give %unto %poke-ack `[leaf+ror p.res])
777        =.  mo-core
778          %+  mo-pass  /nowhere
779          [%c %warp our desk ~ %sing %b case /[mark.deal]]
780        (mo-apply-sure dap routes [%poke mark.deal p.res])
781        ==
782        ::
783          %poke-as
784        =/  =case      da+now
785        =/  =mars:clay  [p.cage mark]:deal
786        =/  mars-path  /[a.mars]/[b.mars]
787        =/  yok  (~(got by yokes.state) dap)
788        =/  =desk  q.beak:?>(?=(%live -.yok) yok)  ::TODO acceptable assertion?
789        =/  sky  (rof ~ /gall %cc [our desk case] mars-path)
790        ?-    sky
791          ?(~ [~ ~])
792        =/  ror  "gall: poke cast fail :{(trip dap)} {<mars>}"
793        (mo-give %unto %poke-ack `[leaf+ror]~)
794        ::
795          [~ ~ *]
796        =+  !<(=tube:clay q.u.u.sky)
797        =/  res  (mule |.((tube q.cage.deal)))
798        ?:  ?=(%| -.res)
799          =/  ror  "gall: poke-as cast fail :{(trip dap)} {<mars>}"
800          (mo-give %unto %poke-ack `[leaf+ror p.res])
801        =.  mo-core
802          %+  mo-pass  /nowhere
803          [%c %warp our desk ~ %sing %c case /[a.mars]/[b.mars]]
804        (mo-apply-sure dap routes [%poke mark.deal p.res])
805        ==
806        ==
807    ::
808  ++  mo-apply-sure
809      |=  [dap=term =routes =deal]
810      ^+  mo-core
```

```
811      =/  app  (ap-abed:ap dap routes)
812      =.  app  (ap-apply:app deal)
813    ap-abet:app
814  ::  +mo-handle-local: handle locally.
815  ::
816  ::      If the agent is not running or blocked, assign it the supplied
817  ::      +deal.  Otherwise simply apply the action to the agent.
818  ::
819  ++  mo-handle-local
820    |=  [prov=path =ship agent=term =deal]
821    ^+  mo-core
822    ::
823    =/  =routes  [disclosing=~ attributing=[ship prov]]
824    =/  running  (~(get by yokes.state) agent)
825    =/  is-running  &(?=([~ %live *] running) ?=(%& -.agent.u.running))
826    =/  is-blocked  (~(has by blocked.state) agent)
827    ::  agent is running; deliver move normally
828    ::
829    ?.  |(!is-running is-blocked)
830      (mo-apply agent routes deal)
831    ::
832    =/  blocked=(qeu blocked-move)
833      =/  waiting  (~(get by blocked.state) agent)
834      =/  deals  (fall waiting *(qeu blocked-move))
835      =/  deal  [hen routes &+deal]
836      (~(put to deals) deal)
837    ::
838    %-  (slog leaf+"gall: not running {<agent>} yet, got {<-.deal>}" ~)
839    %_  mo-core
840      blocked.state  (~(put by blocked.state) agent blocked)
841    ==
842  ::  +mo-handle-ames-request: handle %ames request message.
843  ::
844  ++  mo-handle-ames-request
845    |=  [=ship agent-name=term =ames-request]
846    ^+  mo-core
847    ::  %u/%leave gets automatically acked
848    ::
849    =.  mo-core  (mo-track-ship ship)
850    =?  mo-core  ?=(%u -.ames-request)  (mo-give %done ~)
851    ::
852    =/  yok=(unit yoke)  (~(get by yokes.state) agent-name)
853    ?~  yok
854      (mo-give %flub ~)
855    ?:  ?=(%nuke -.u.yok)
856      (mo-give %flub ~)
857    ?:  ?=(%.n -.agent.u.yok)
858      (mo-give %flub ~)
859    ::
860    =/  =wire  /sys/req/(scot %p ship)/[agent-name]
861    ::
862    =/  =deal
863      ?-  -.ames-request
864        %m  [%raw-poke [mark noun]:ames-request]
865        %l  [%watch-as [mark path]:ames-request]
866        %s  [%watch path.ames-request]
867        %u  [%leave ~]
868      ==
```

```
869        (mo-pass wire %g %deal [ship our /] agent-name deal)
870    ::  +mo-spew: handle request to set verbosity toggles on debug output
871    ::
872    ++  mo-spew
873      |=  verbs=(list verb)
874      ^+  mo-core
875      ::  start from all %.n's, then flip requested toggles
876      ::
877      =.  veb.bug.state
878        %+  roll  verbs
879        |=  [=verb acc=_veb-all-off]
880        ^+  veb.bug.state
881        ?-  verb
882          %odd  acc(odd %.y)
883        ==
884      mo-core
885    ::  +mo-sift: handle request to filter debug output by agent
886    ::
887    ++  mo-sift
888      |=  dudes=(list dude)
889      ^+  mo-core
890      =.  dudes.bug.state  (sy dudes)
891      mo-core
892      ::
893    ++  mo-handle-nacked-leaves
894      |=  =wire
895      ^+  mo-core
896      ?>  ?=([%sys %way @ @ ~] wire)
897      (mo-pass wire %a %plea (slav %p &3.wire) %g /ge/[&4.wire] %0 %u ~)
898    ::
899    ::  +ap: agent engine
900    ::
901    ::    An inner, agent-level core.  The sample refers to the agent we're
902    ::    currently focused on.
903    ::
904    ++  ap
905      ~%  %gall-ap  +>  ~
906      |_  $:  agent-name=term
907              agent-routes=routes
908              agent-duct=duct
909              agent-moves=(list move)
910              agent-config=(list (each suss tang))
911              =$>(%live yoke)
912          ==
913      ::
914      ++  trace
915        |=  [verb=? print=tang]
916        ^+  same
917        (^trace verb agent-name print)
918      ::
919      ++  ap-nonce-wire
920        |=  [=wire =dock]
921        ^+  wire
922        =/  nonce=@  (~(got by boar.yoke) wire dock)
923        ?:  =(0 nonce)  wire
924        [(scot %ud nonce) wire]
925      ::
926      ++  ap-core  .
```

```
927  ::  +ap-abed: initialise state for an agent, with the supplied routes.
928  ::
929  ::      The agent must already be running in +gall -- here we simply update
930  ::      +ap's state to focus on it.
931  ::
932  ++  ap-abed
933    ~/  %ap-abed
934    |=  [dap=term =routes]
935    ^+  ap-core
936    %^  ap-yoke  dap  routes
937    =<  ?>(?=(%live -) .)
938    (~(got by yokes.state) dap)
939  ::  +ap-yoke: initialize agent state, starting from a $yoke
940  ::
941  ++  ap-yoke
942    |=  [dap=term =routes yak=$>(%live ^yoke)]
943    ^+  ap-core
944    =.  stats.yak
945      :+  +(change.stats.yak)
946        (shaz (mix (add dap change.stats.yak) eny))  ::  TODO: so bad, use +og
947      now
948    =.  agent-name  dap
949    =.  agent-routes  routes
950    =.  yoke  yak
951    =.  agent-duct  hen
952    ap-core
953  ::  +ap-abet: resolve moves.
954  ::
955  ++  ap-abet
956    ^+  mo-core
957    ::
958    =/  running  (~(put by yokes.state) agent-name yoke)
959    =/  moves
960      =/  talker  |=(report=(each suss tang) [hen %pass (mo-talk report)])
961      =/  from-suss  (turn agent-config talker)
962      :(weld agent-moves from-suss moves)
963    ::
964    %_  mo-core
965      yokes.state  running
966      moves        moves
967    ==
968  ::
969  ++  ap-yawn-all
970    ^-  (list card:agent)
971    %-  zing
972    %+  turn  ~(tap by ken.yoke)
973    |=  [=spar:ames wyz=(set wire)]
974    %+  turn  ~(tap in wyz)
975    |=  =wire
976    [%pass wire %arvo %a %yawn spar]
977  ::
978  ++  ap-idle
979    ^+  ap-core
980    ?:  ?=(%| -.agent.yoke)  ap-core
981    =>  [ken=ken.yoke (ap-ingest ~ |.([ap-yawn-all p.agent.yoke]))]
982    ap-core(ken.yoke ken, agent.yoke |+on-save:ap-agent-core)
983  ::
984  ++  ap-nuke
```

```
985        ^+  ap-core
986      =/  inbound-paths=(set path)
987        %-  silt
988        %+  turn  ~(tap by bitt.yoke)
989        |=  [=duct =ship =path]
990        path
991      =/  will=(list card:agent)
992        ;:  welp
993        ?:  =(~ inbound-paths)
994          ~
995          [%give %kick ~(tap in inbound-paths) ~]~
996        ::
997        %+  turn  ~(tap by boat.yoke)
998        |=  [[=wire =dock] ? =path]
999        [%pass wire %agent dock %leave ~]
1000        ::
1001        ap-yawn-all
1002      ==
1003    =^  maybe-tang ap-core  (ap-ingest ~ |.([will *agent]))
1004    ap-core
1005  ::  +ap-grow: bind a path in the agent's scry namespace
1006  ::
1007  ++  ap-grow
1008    |=  [=spur =page]
1009    ^+  ap-core
1010    =-  ap-core(sky.yoke -)
1011    %+  ~(put by sky.yoke)  spur
1012    =/  ski  (~(gut by sky.yoke) spur *path-state)
1013    =-  ski(fan (put:on-path fan.ski -< -> &/page))
1014    ?~  las=(ram:on-path fan.ski)
1015      [(fall bob.ski 0) now]
1016    :_  (max now +(p.val.u.las))
1017    ?~(bob.ski +(key.u.las) +((max key.u.las u.bob.ski)))
1018  ::  +ap-tomb: tombstone -- replace bound value with hash
1019  ::
1020  ++  ap-tomb
1021    |=  [=case =spur]
1022    ^+  ap-core
1023    =-  ap-core(sky.yoke -)
1024    =/  yon  ?>(?=(%ud -.case) p.case)
1025    =/  old  (~(get by sky.yoke) spur)
1026    ?~  old  ::  no-op if nonexistent
1027      %.  sky.yoke
1028      %+  trace  odd.veb.bug.state
1029      [leaf+"gall: {<agent-name>}: tomb {<[case spur]>} no sky"]~
1030    =/  val  (get:on-path fan.u.old yon)
1031    ?~  val  ::  no-op if nonexistent
1032      %.  sky.yoke
1033      %+  trace  odd.veb.bug.state
1034      [leaf+"gall: {<agent-name>}: tomb {<[case spur]>} no val"]~
1035    ?-      -.q.u.val
1036        %|  ::  already tombstoned, no-op
1037      %.  sky.yoke
1038      %+  trace  odd.veb.bug.state
1039      [leaf+"gall: {<agent-name>}: tomb {<[case spur]>} no-op"]~
1040      ::
1041        %&  ::  replace with hash
1042      %+  ~(put by sky.yoke)  spur
```

```
1043          u.old(fan (put:on-path fan.u.old yon u.val(q |/(shax (jam p.q.u.val)))))
1044        ==
1045    ::  +ap-cull: delete all bindings up to and including .case
1046    ::
1047    ::      Also store .case as the high water mark for .spur
1048    ::      to prevent any deleted cases from being re-bound later.
1049    ::
1050    ++  ap-cull
1051      |=  [=case =spur]
1052      ^+  ap-core
1053      =-  ap-core(sky.yoke -)
1054      =/  yon  ?>(?=(%ud -.case) p.case)
1055      =/  old  (~(get by sky.yoke) spur)
1056      ?~  old  ::  no-op if nonexistent
1057        %.  sky.yoke
1058        %+  trace  odd.veb.bug.state
1059        [leaf+"gall: {<agent-name>}: cull {<[case spur]>} no-op"]~
1060      %+  ~(put by sky.yoke)  spur  ::  delete all older paths
1061      [`yon (lot:on-path fan.u.old `+(yon) ~)]
1062    ::  +ap-from-internal: internal move to move.
1063    ::
1064    ::      We convert from cards to duct-indexed moves when resolving
1065    ::      them in Arvo.
1066    ::
1067    ::      We accept %huck to "fake" being a message to a ship but
1068    ::      actually send it to a vane.
1069    ::
1070    +$  carp  $+  carp  (wind neet gift:agent)
1071    +$  neet  $+  neet
1072      $<  ?(%grow %tomb %cull)
1073      $%  note:agent
1074          [%agent [=ship name=term] task=[%raw-poke =mark =noun]]
1075          [%huck [=ship name=term] =note-arvo]
1076      ==
1077    ::
1078    ++  ap-from-internal
1079      ~/  %ap-from-internal
1080      |=  card=carp
1081      ^-  (list move)
1082      ::
1083      ?-    -.card
1084          %slip  !!
1085      ::
1086          %give
1087        =/  =gift:agent  p.card
1088        ?:  ?=(%kick -.gift)
1089          =/  ducts=(list duct)  (ap-ducts-from-paths paths.gift ship.gift)
1090          %+  turn  ducts
1091          |=  =duct
1092          ~?  &(=(duct system-duct.state) !=(agent-name %hood))
1093            [%agent-giving-on-system-duct agent-name -.gift]
1094          [duct %give %unto %kick ~]
1095        ::
1096        ?.  ?=(%fact -.gift)
1097          [agent-duct %give %unto gift]~
1098        ::
1099        =/  ducts=(list duct)  (ap-ducts-from-paths paths.gift ~)
1100        =/  =cage  cage.gift
```

```
1101        %-  zing
1102        %+  turn  ducts
1103        |=  =duct
1104        ^-  (list move)
1105        ~?  &(=(duct system-duct.state) !=(agent-name %hood))
1106          [%agent-giving-on-system-duct agent-name -.gift]
1107        =/  =mark  (~(gut by marks.yoke) duct p.cage)
1108        ::
1109        ?:  =(mark p.cage)
1110          [duct %give %unto %fact cage.gift]~
1111        =/  =mars:clay  [p.cage mark]
1112        =/  =case       da+now
1113        =/  bek=beak    [our q.beak.yoke case]
1114        =/  mars-path  /[a.mars]/[b.mars]
1115        =/  sky  (rof ~ /gall %cc bek mars-path)
1116        ?-    sky
1117            ?(~ [~ ~])
1118          %-  (slog leaf+"watch-as fact conversion find-fail" >sky< ~)
1119          (ap-kill-up-slip duct)
1120        ::
1121            [~ ~ *]
1122          =+  !<(=tube:clay q.u.u.sky)
1123          =/  res  (mule |.((tube q.cage)))
1124          ?:  ?=(%| -.res)
1125            %-  (slog leaf+"watch-as fact conversion failure" p.res)
1126            (ap-kill-up-slip duct)
1127          :~  :*  duct %pass /nowhere %c %warp  our  q.beak.yoke  ~
1128                  %sing %c  case  mars-path
1129              ==
1130              [duct %give %unto %fact b.mars p.res]
1131          ==
1132      ==
1133    ::
1134        %pass
1135      =/  =duct  system-duct.state
1136      =/  =wire  p.card
1137      =/  =neet  q.card
1138      ?:  ?=(%pyre -.neet)
1139        %:  mean
1140          leaf/"gall: %pyre from {<agent-name>}, killing event"
1141          leaf/"wire: {<wire>}"
1142          tang.neet
1143        ==
1144      =.  wire
1145        :^  %use  agent-name  run-nonce.yoke
1146        ?-  -.neet
1147          %agent  [%out (scot %p ship.neet) name.neet wire]
1148          %huck   [%out (scot %p ship.neet) name.neet wire]
1149          %arvo   [(scot %p ship.attributing.agent-routes) wire]
1150        ==
1151      ::
1152      =/  =note-arvo
1153        =/  prov=path  /gall/[agent-name]
1154        ?-  -.neet
1155          %arvo  ?.  ?=([[%l *] +.neet)
1156                   +.neet
1157                 ?+  +.neet
1158                   ~|(%nope !!)
```

```
1159                        [%l ?(%spin %shut) *]   +.neet(name [agent-name name.+.neet])
1160                        [%l %spit *]            +.neet(name [agent-name name.+.neet])
1161                   ==
1162         %huck   note-arvo.neet
1163         %agent  [%g %deal [our ship.neet prov] [name task]:neet]
1164       ==
1165     [duct %pass wire note-arvo]~
1166   ==
1167 ::  +ap-breach: ship breached, so forget about them
1168 ::
1169 ++  ap-breach
1170   |=  =ship
1171   ^+  ap-core
1172   =/  in=(list [=duct =^ship =path])  ~(tap by bitt.yoke)
1173   |-  ^+  ap-core
1174   ?^  in
1175     =?  ap-core  =(ship ship.i.in)
1176       =/  core  ap-load-delete(agent-duct duct.i.in)
1177       core(agent-duct agent-duct)
1178     $(in t.in)
1179   ::
1180   =/  out=(list [=wire =^ship =term])
1181     ~(tap ^in ~(key by boat.yoke))
1182   |-  ^+  ap-core
1183   ?~  out
1184     ap-core
1185   =?  ap-core  =(ship ship.i.out)
1186     =/  core
1187       =.  agent-duct  system-duct.state
1188       =.  wire.i.out  (ap-nonce-wire i.out)
1189       =/  way         [%out (scot %p ship) term.i.out wire.i.out]
1190       (ap-specific-take way %kick ~)
1191     core(agent-duct agent-duct)
1192   $(out t.out)
1193 ::  +ap-clog: handle %clog notification from ames
1194 ::
1195 ::    Kills subscriptions from .ship in both directions:
1196 ::      - notifies local app that subscription is dead
1197 ::      - gives remote %quit to notify subscriber ship
1198 ::    TODO: %drip local app notification for error isolation
1199 ::
1200 ++  ap-clog
1201   |=  =ship
1202   ^+  ap-core
1203   ::
1204   =/  in=(list [=duct =^ship =path])  ~(tap by bitt.yoke)
1205   |-  ^+  ap-core
1206   ?~  in  ap-core
1207   ::
1208   =?  ap-core  =(ship ship.i.in)
1209     =/  core  ap-kill-up(agent-duct duct.i.in)
1210     core(agent-duct agent-duct)
1211   $(in t.in)
1212 ::  +ap-agent-core: agent core with current bowl and state
1213 ::
1214 ++  ap-agent-core
1215   ?>  ?=(%& -.agent.yoke)
1216   ~(. p.agent.yoke ap-construct-bowl)
```

```
1217      ::    +ap-ducts-from-paths: get ducts subscribed to paths
1218      ::
1219      ++  ap-ducts-from-paths
1220        |=  [target-paths=(list path) target-ship=(unit ship)]
1221        ^-  (list duct)
1222        ?~  target-paths
1223          ?~  target-ship
1224            ~[agent-duct]
1225          %+  murn  ~(tap by bitt.yoke)
1226          |=  [=duct =ship =path]
1227          ^-  (unit ^duct)
1228          ?:  =(target-ship `ship)
1229            `duct
1230          ~
1231        %-  zing
1232        %+  turn  target-paths
1233        |=  =path
1234        (ap-ducts-from-path path target-ship)
1235      ::    +ap-ducts-from-path: get ducts subscribed to path
1236      ::
1237      ++  ap-ducts-from-path
1238        |=  [target-path=path target-ship=(unit ship)]
1239        ^-  (list duct)
1240        %+  murn  ~(tap by bitt.yoke)
1241        |=  [=duct =ship =path]
1242        ^-  (unit ^duct)
1243        ?:  ?&  =(target-path path)
1244                |(=(target-ship ~) =(target-ship `ship))
1245            ==
1246          `duct
1247        ~
1248      ::    +ap-apply: apply effect.
1249      ::
1250      ++  ap-apply
1251        |=  =deal
1252        ^+  ap-core
1253        ?-  -.deal
1254          %watch-as  (ap-subscribe-as +.deal)
1255          %poke      (ap-poke +.deal)
1256          %watch     (ap-subscribe +.deal)
1257          %raw-poke  !!
1258          %poke-as   !!
1259          %leave     ap-load-delete
1260        ==
1261      ::    +ap-peek: peek.
1262      ::
1263      ++  ap-peek
1264        ~/  %ap-peek
1265        |=  [veb=? care=term tyl=path]
1266        ^-  (unit (unit cage))
1267        ::  take trailing mark off path for %x scrys
1268        ::
1269        =^  want=mark  tyl
1270          ?.  ?=(%x care)  [%$ tyl]
1271          =.  tyl  (flop tyl)
1272          [(head tyl) (flop (tail tyl))]
1273        ::  call the app's +on-peek, producing [~ ~] if it crashes
1274        ::
```

```
1275      =/  peek-result=(each (unit (unit cage)) tang)
1276        (ap-mule-peek |.((on-peek:ap-agent-core [care tyl])))
1277      ?:  ?=(%| -.peek-result)
1278        ?.  veb  [~ ~]
1279        ((slog leaf+"peek bad result" p.peek-result) [~ ~])
1280      ::  for non-%x scries, or failed %x scries, or %x results that already
1281      ::  have the requested mark, produce the result as-is
1282      ::
1283      ?.  ?&  ?=(%x care)
1284              ?=([~ ~ *] p.peek-result)
1285              !=(want p.u.u.p.peek-result)
1286          ==
1287        p.peek-result
1288      ::  for %x scries, attempt to convert to the requested mark if needed
1289      ::
1290      =*  have  p.u.u.p.peek-result
1291      =*  vase  q.u.u.p.peek-result
1292      =/  tub=(unit tube:clay)
1293        ?:  =(have want)  `(bake same ^vase)
1294        =/  tuc=(unit (unit cage))
1295          (rof ~ /gall %cc [our q.beak.yoke da+now] /[have]/[want])
1296        ?.  ?=([~ ~ *] tuc)  ~
1297        `!<(tube:clay q.u.u.tuc)
1298      ?~  tub
1299        ((slog leaf+"peek no tube from {(trip have)} to {(trip want)}" ~) ~)
1300      =/  res  (mule |.((u.tub vase)))
1301      ?:  ?=(%& -.res)
1302        ``want^p.res
1303      ((slog leaf+"peek failed tube from {(trip have)} to {(trip want)}" ~) ~)
1304  ::  +ap-move: send move
1305  ::
1306  ++  ap-move
1307    |=  =(list move)
1308    ap-core(agent-moves (weld (flop list) agent-moves))
1309  ::  +ap-give: return result.
1310  ::
1311  ++  ap-give
1312    |=  =gift:agent
1313    (ap-move (ap-from-internal %give gift))
1314  ::  +ap-pass: request action.
1315  ::
1316  ++  ap-pass
1317    |=  [=path =neet]
1318    (ap-move (ap-from-internal %pass path neet))
1319  ::  +ap-construct-bowl: set up bowl.
1320  ::
1321  ++  ap-construct-bowl
1322    ^-  bowl
1323    :*  :*  our                               ::  host
1324            ship.attributing.agent-routes     ::  guest
1325            agent-name                        ::  agent
1326            path.attributing.agent-routes     ::  provenance
1327        ==                                    ::
1328        :*  wex=boat.yoke                     ::  outgoing
1329            sup=bitt.yoke                     ::  incoming
1330            sky=(~(run by sky.yoke) tail)     ::  bindings
1331        ==                                    ::
1332        :*  act=change.stats.yoke             ::  tick
```

```
1333              eny=eny.stats.yoke           ::  nonce
1334              now=time.stats.yoke          ::  time
1335              byk=beak.yoke                ::  source
1336        ==  ==
1337    ::  +ap-reinstall: reinstall.
1338    ::
1339    ++  ap-reinstall
1340      ~/  %ap-reinstall
1341      |=  =agent
1342      ^+  ap-core
1343      =/  old-state=vase
1344        ?:  ?=(%& -.agent.yoke)
1345          on-save:ap-agent-core
1346        p.agent.yoke
1347      =?  ap-core  &(?=(%| -.agent.yoke) ?=(^ ken.yoke))
1348        =-  +:(ap-ingest ~ |.([+< agent]))
1349        %-  zing
1350        %+  turn  ~(tap by `(jug spar:ames wire)`ken.yoke)
1351        |=  [=spar:ames wyz=(set wire)]
1352        (turn ~(tap in wyz) |=(=wire [%pass wire %arvo %a %keen spar]))
1353      =^  error  ap-core
1354        (ap-install(agent.yoke &+agent) `old-state)
1355      ?~  error
1356        ap-core
1357      (mean >%load-failed< u.error)
1358    ::  +ap-subscribe-as: apply %watch-as.
1359    ::
1360    ++  ap-subscribe-as
1361      |=  [=mark =path]
1362      ^+  ap-core
1363      =.  marks.yoke  (~(put by marks.yoke) agent-duct mark)
1364      (ap-subscribe path)
1365    ::  +ap-subscribe: apply %watch.
1366    ::
1367    ++  ap-subscribe
1368      ~/  %ap-subscribe
1369      |=  pax=path
1370      ^+  ap-core
1371      =/  incoming   [ship.attributing.agent-routes pax]
1372      =.  bitt.yoke  (~(put by bitt.yoke) agent-duct incoming)
1373      =^  maybe-tang  ap-core
1374        %+  ap-ingest  %watch-ack  |.
1375        (on-watch:ap-agent-core pax)
1376      ?^  maybe-tang
1377        ap-silent-delete
1378      ap-core
1379    ::  +ap-poke: apply %poke.
1380    ::
1381    ++  ap-poke
1382      ~/  %ap-poke
1383      |=  =cage
1384      ^+  ap-core
1385      =^  maybe-tang  ap-core
1386        %+  ap-ingest  %poke-ack  |.
1387        (on-poke:ap-agent-core cage)
1388      ap-core
1389    ::  +ap-error: pour error.
1390    ::
```

```
1391    ++  ap-error
1392      |=  [=term =tang]
1393      ^+  ap-core
1394      =/  form  |=(=tank [%rose [~ "! " ~] tank ~])
1395      =^  maybe-tang  ap-core
1396        %+  ap-ingest  ~  |.
1397        (on-fail:ap-agent-core term (turn tang form))
1398      ap-core
1399    ::  +ap-generic-take: generic take.
1400    ::
1401    ++  ap-generic-take
1402      ~/  %ap-generic-take
1403      |=  [=wire =sign-arvo]
1404      ^+  ap-core
1405      =?  sign-arvo  ?=([%lick *] sign-arvo)
1406        ?+  sign-arvo
1407          ~|(%nope !!)
1408        ::
1409          [%lick %soak *]
1410        =-  sign-arvo(name -)
1411        ?>  &(?=(^ name.sign-arvo) =(agent-name i.name.sign-arvo))
1412        t.name.sign-arvo
1413      ==
1414      =^  maybe-tang  ap-core
1415        %+  ap-ingest  ~  |.
1416        (on-arvo:ap-agent-core wire sign-arvo)
1417      =?  ken.yoke  ?=([%ames %tune spar=* *] sign-arvo)
1418        (~(del ju ken.yoke) spar.sign-arvo wire)
1419      ?^  maybe-tang
1420        (ap-error %arvo-response u.maybe-tang)
1421      ap-core
1422    ::  +ap-specific-take: specific take.
1423    ::
1424    ++  ap-specific-take
1425      |=  [=wire =unto]
1426      ^+  ap-core
1427      ~|  wire=wire
1428      ?>  ?=([%out @ @ *] wire)
1429      =/  other-ship  (slav %p i.t.wire)
1430      =/  other-agent  i.t.t.wire
1431      =/  =dock  [other-ship other-agent]
1432      =/  agent-wire  t.t.t.wire
1433      =/  nonce=@  0
1434      ::
1435      =^  =sign:agent  ap-core
1436        ?.  ?=(%raw-fact -.unto)
1437          [unto ap-core]
1438        =/  =case  da+now
1439        ?:  ?=(%spider agent-name)
1440          :-  [%fact mark.unto !>(noun.unto)]
1441          ap-core
1442        =/  sky  (rof ~ /gall %cb [our q.beak.yoke case] /[mark.unto])
1443        ?.  ?=([~ ~ *] sky)
1444          (mean leaf+"gall: ames mark fail {<mark.unto>}" ~)
1445        ::
1446        =+  !<(=dais:clay q.u.u.sky)
1447        =/  res  (mule |.((vale:dais noun.unto)))
1448        ?:  ?=(%| -.res)
```

```
1449            (mean leaf+"gall: ames vale fail {<mark.unto>}" p.res)
1450        :-  [%fact mark.unto p.res]
1451    %-  ap-move  :_  ~
1452        :^  hen  %pass  /nowhere
1453        [%c %warp our q.beak.yoke ~ %sing %b case /[mark.unto]]
1454    |^  ^+  ap-core
1455        ::  %poke-ack has no nonce; ingest directly
1456        ::
1457        ?:  ?=(%poke-ack -.sign)
1458          ingest-and-check-error
1459        ::  if .agent-wire matches, it's an old pre-nonce subscription
1460        ::
1461        ?:  (~(has by boat.yoke) sub-key)
1462          run-sign
1463        ::  if an app happened to use a null wire, no-op
1464        ::
1465        ?:  =(~ agent-wire)
1466          on-missing
1467        =/  has-nonce=(unit @ud)  (slaw %ud (head agent-wire))
1468        ?:  &(?=(~ has-nonce) ?=(%kick -.sign))
1469          on-weird-kick
1470        ::  pop nonce off .agent-wire and match against stored subscription
1471        ::
1472        ?>  ?=(^ has-nonce)
1473        =:  nonce        u.has-nonce
1474            agent-wire  (tail agent-wire)
1475          ==
1476        ?~  got=(~(get by boar.yoke) sub-key)
1477          on-missing
1478        ?:  =(nonce.u.got nonce)
1479          run-sign
1480        (on-bad-nonce nonce.u.got)
1481        ::
1482    ++  sub-key  [agent-wire dock]
1483    ++  ingest   (ap-ingest ~ |.((on-agent:ap-agent-core agent-wire sign)))
1484    ++  run-sign
1485      ?-    -.sign
1486          %poke-ack  !!
1487          %fact
1488        =^  tan  ap-core  ingest
1489        ?~  tan  ap-core
1490        =.  ap-core  (ap-kill-down sub-key)
1491        (ap-error -.sign leaf/"take %fact failed, closing subscription" u.tan)
1492        ::
1493          %kick
1494        =:  boar.yoke  (~(del by boar.yoke) sub-key)
1495            boat.yoke  (~(del by boat.yoke) sub-key)
1496          ==
1497        ingest-and-check-error
1498        ::
1499          %watch-ack
1500        ?.  (~(has by boat.yoke) sub-key)
1501        %.  ap-core
1502        %+  trace  odd.veb.bug.state  :~
1503          leaf+"{<agent-name>}: got ack for nonexistent subscription"
1504          leaf+"{<dock>}: {<agent-wire>}"
1505          >wire=wire<
1506        ==
```

```
1507        =?  boar.yoke   ?=(^ p.sign)   (~(del by boar.yoke) sub-key)
1508        ::
1509        =.  boat.yoke
1510          ?^  p.sign   (~(del by boat.yoke) sub-key)
1511          ::
1512        %+  ~(jab by boat.yoke)  sub-key
1513        |=  val=[acked=? =path]
1514        %.  val(acked &)
1515        %^  trace  &(odd.veb.bug.state acked.val)
1516        leaf/"{<agent-name>} 2nd watch-ack on {<val>}"  ~
1517        ::
1518        ingest-and-check-error
1519      ==
1520    ::
1521    ++  on-missing
1522      %.  ap-core
1523      %+  trace  odd.veb.bug.state  :~
1524        leaf+"{<agent-name>}: got {<-.sign>} for nonexistent subscription"
1525        leaf+"{<dock>}: {<[nonce=nonce agent-wire]>}"
1526        >wire=wire<
1527      ==
1528    ::
1529    ++  on-weird-kick
1530      %.  run-sign
1531      %+  trace  odd.veb.bug.state  :~
1532        leaf+"{<agent-name>}: got %kick for nonexistent subscription"
1533        leaf+"{<dock>}: {<agent-wire>}"
1534        >wire=wire<
1535      ==
1536    ::
1537    ++  on-bad-nonce
1538      |=  stored-nonce=@
1539      %.  ap-core
1540      %+  trace  odd.veb.bug.state  :~
1541        =/  nonces  [expected=stored-nonce got=nonce]
1542        =/  ok  |(?=(?(%fact %kick) -.sign) =(~ p.sign))
1543        leaf+"{<agent-name>}: stale {<-.sign>} {<nonces>} ok={<ok>}"
1544        ::
1545        leaf+"{<dock>}: {<agent-wire>}"
1546        >wire=wire<
1547      ==
1548    ::
1549    ++  ingest-and-check-error
1550      ^+  ap-core
1551      =^  tan ap-core  ingest
1552      ?~(tan ap-core (ap-error -.sign leaf/"take {<-.sign>} failed" u.tan))
1553    --
1554  ::  +ap-install: install wrapper.
1555  ::
1556  ++  ap-install
1557    |=  old-agent-state=(unit vase)
1558    ^-  [(unit tang) _ap-core]
1559    ::
1560    =^  maybe-tang  ap-core  (ap-upgrade-state old-agent-state)
1561    ::
1562    =.  agent-config
1563      :_  agent-config
1564      ^-  (each suss tang)
```

```
1565            ?^  maybe-tang
1566              |/u.maybe-tang
1567            &/[agent-name ?~(old-agent-state %boot %bump) now]
1568          ::
1569        [maybe-tang ap-core]
1570    ::  +ap-upgrade-state: low-level install.
1571    ::
1572    ++  ap-upgrade-state
1573      ~/  %ap-upgrade-state
1574      |=  maybe-vase=(unit vase)
1575      ^-  [(unit tang) _ap-core]
1576      ::
1577      =^  maybe-tang  ap-core
1578        %+  ap-ingest  ~
1579        ?~  maybe-vase
1580          |.  on-init:ap-agent-core
1581        |.  (on-load:ap-agent-core u.maybe-vase)
1582      [maybe-tang ap-core]
1583    ::  +ap-silent-delete: silent delete.
1584    ::
1585    ++  ap-silent-delete
1586      ^+  ap-core
1587      ap-core(bitt.yoke (~(del by bitt.yoke) agent-duct))
1588    ::  +ap-load-delete: load delete.
1589    ::
1590    ++  ap-load-delete
1591      ^+  ap-core
1592      ::
1593      =/  maybe-incoming  (~(get by bitt.yoke) agent-duct)
1594      ?~  maybe-incoming
1595        ap-core
1596      ::
1597      =/  incoming  u.maybe-incoming
1598      =.  bitt.yoke  (~(del by bitt.yoke) agent-duct)
1599      ::
1600      =^  maybe-tang  ap-core
1601        %+  ap-ingest  ~  |.
1602        (on-leave:ap-agent-core q.incoming)
1603      ?^  maybe-tang
1604        (ap-error %leave u.maybe-tang)
1605      ap-core
1606    ::  +ap-kill-up: 2-sided kill from publisher side
1607    ::
1608    ++  ap-kill-up
1609      ^+  ap-core
1610      ::
1611      =>  ap-load-delete
1612      (ap-give %kick ~ ~)
1613    ::  +ap-kill-up-slip: 2-sided kill from publisher side by slip
1614    ::
1615    ::  +ap-kill-up is reentrant if you call it in the
1616    ::  middle of processing another deal
1617    ::
1618    ::  Should probably call +ap-error with error message
1619    ::
1620    ++  ap-kill-up-slip
1621      |=  =duct
1622      ^-  (list move)
```

```
1623    ::
1624    =/  =sack  [our our /gall/[agent-name]]
1625    :~  [duct %slip %g %deal sack agent-name %leave ~]
1626        [duct %give %unto %kick ~]
1627    ==
1628    ::  +ap-kill-down: 2-sided kill from subscriber side
1629    ::
1630    ::    Must process leave first in case kick handler rewatches.
1631    ::
1632    ++  ap-kill-down
1633      |=  [sub-wire=wire =dock]
1634      ^+  ap-core
1635      =.  ap-core
1636        ::  we take care to include the nonce in the "kernel-facing" wire
1637        ::
1638        (ap-pass (ap-nonce-wire sub-wire dock) %agent dock %leave ~)
1639      (ap-pass sub-wire %huck dock %b %huck `sign-arvo`[%gall %unto %kick ~])
1640    ::  +ap-doff: kill old-style outgoing subscriptions
1641    ::
1642    ++  ap-doff
1643      |=  ship=(unit ship)
1644      ^+  ap-core
1645      =/  subs  ~(tap in ~(key by boat.yoke))
1646      |-  ^+  ap-core
1647      ?~  subs  ap-core
1648      =+  [wyr dok]=i.subs
1649      ?:  &(?=(^ ship) !=(u.ship ship.dok))
1650        $(subs t.subs)
1651      ::  if we haven't created new-style (nonced) subscriptions yet,
1652      ::  kick the old-style (nonceless) one that's in use right now.
1653      ::
1654      ::NOTE  yes, still safe for pre-release ships with nonce=1,
1655      ::       this makes a new flow but cleans it up right away.
1656      ::
1657      =?  ap-core  (gte 1 (~(got by boar.yoke) wyr dok))
1658        (ap-pass wyr %agent dok %leave ~)
1659      $(subs t.subs)
1660    ::  +ap-rake: clean up the dead %leave's
1661    ::
1662    ++  ap-rake
1663      |=  all=?
1664      =/  subs  ~(tap in ~(key by boat.yoke))
1665      |^  ^+  ap-core
1666      ?~  subs  ap-core
1667      =/  [=wire =dock]  i.subs
1668      =/  non  (~(got by boar.yoke) wire dock)
1669      ?:  &(!all =(0 non))
1670        $(subs t.subs)
1671      ?~  per=(scry-peer-state p.dock)
1672        $(subs t.subs)
1673      ::
1674      =/  dud=(set duct)
1675        =/  mod=^wire
1676          :*  %gall  %use  agent-name  run-nonce.yoke
1677              %out  (scot %p p.dock)  q.dock
1678              '0'  wire
1679          ==
1680        %-  ~(rep by by-duct.ossuary.u.per)
```

```
1681        |=  [[=duct =bone] out=(set duct)]
1682        ^+  out
1683        ?.  ?&  ?=([* [%gall %use @ @ %out @ @ @ *] *] duct)
1684                =(mod i.t.duct(i.t.t.t.t.t.t.t '0'))
1685            ==
1686          out
1687        ?:  (~(has in closing.u.per) bone)  out
1688        ~>  %slog.0^leaf+"gall: rake {<i.t.duct>}"
1689        (~(put in out) duct)
1690      ::
1691      %-  ap-move
1692      (turn ~(tap in dud) |=(d=duct [+.d %pass -.d %a %cork p.dock]))
1693      ::
1694      ++  scry-peer-state
1695        |=  her=ship
1696        ~+  ^-  (unit peer-state:ames)
1697        =/  sky  (rof [~ ~] /gall %ax [our %$ da+now] /peers/(scot %p her))
1698        ?:  |(?=(~ sky) ?=(~ u.sky))
1699          ~
1700        =/  sat  !<(ship-state:ames q.u.u.sky)
1701        ?>(?=(%known -.sat) (some +.sat))
1702      --
1703    ::  +ap-mule: run virtualized with intercepted scry, preserving type
1704    ::
1705    ::    Compare +mute and +mule.  Those pass through scry, which
1706    ::    doesn't allow us to catch crashes due to blocking scry.  If
1707    ::    you intercept scry, you can't preserve the type
1708    ::    polymorphically.  By monomorphizing, we are able to do so
1709    ::    safely.
1710    ::
1711    ++  ap-mule
1712      |=  run=_^?(|.(*step:agent))
1713      ^-  (each step:agent tang)
1714      =/  res  (mock [run %9 2 %0 1] (look rof ~ /gall/[agent-name]))
1715      ?-  -.res
1716        %0  [%& !<(step:agent [-:!>(*step:agent) p.res])]
1717        %1  [%| (smyt ;;(path p.res)) ~]
1718        %2  [%| p.res]
1719      ==
1720    ::  +ap-mule-peek: same as +ap-mule but for (unit (unit cage))
1721    ::
1722    ++  ap-mule-peek
1723      |=  run=_^?(|.(*(unit (unit cage))))
1724      ^-  (each (unit (unit cage)) tang)
1725      =/  res  (mock [run %9 2 %0 1] (look rof ~ /gall/[agent-name]))
1726      ?-  -.res
1727        %0  [%& !<((unit (unit cage)) [-:!>(*(unit (unit cage))) p.res])]
1728        %1  [%| (smyt ;;(path p.res)) ~]
1729        %2  [%| p.res]
1730      ==
1731    ::  +ap-ingest: call agent arm
1732    ::
1733    ::    Handle acks here because they need to be emitted before the
1734    ::    rest of the moves.
1735    ::
1736    ++  ap-ingest
1737      |=  [ack=?(%poke-ack %watch-ack ~) run=_^?(|.(*step:agent))]
1738      ^-  [(unit tang) _ap-core]
```

```
1739      =/  result  (ap-mule run)
1740      =^  new-moves  ap-core  (ap-handle-result result)
1741      =/  maybe-tang=(unit tang)
1742        ?:  ?=(%& -.result)
1743          ~
1744        `p.result
1745      =/  ack-moves=(list move)
1746        %-  zing
1747        %-  turn  :_  ap-from-internal
1748        ^-  (list carp)
1749        ?-  ack
1750          ~        ~
1751          %poke-ack   [%give %poke-ack maybe-tang]~
1752          %watch-ack  [%give %watch-ack maybe-tang]~
1753        ==
1754      ::
1755      =.  agent-moves
1756        :(weld (flop new-moves) ack-moves agent-moves)
1757      [maybe-tang ap-core]
1758    ::  +ap-handle-result: handle result.
1759    ::
1760    ++  ap-handle-result
1761      ~/  %ap-handle-result
1762      |=  result=(each step:agent tang)
1763      ^-  [(list move) _ap-core]
1764      ?:  ?=(%| -.result)
1765        `ap-core
1766      ::
1767      =.  agent.yoke  &++.p.result
1768      =^  fex  ap-core  (ap-handle-sky -.p.result)
1769      =.  ken.yoke   (ap-handle-ken fex)
1770      =/  moves      (zing (turn fex ap-from-internal))
1771      =.  bitt.yoke   (ap-handle-kicks moves)
1772      (ap-handle-peers moves)
1773    ::  +ap-handle-sky: apply effects to the agent's scry namespace
1774    ::
1775    ++  ap-handle-sky
1776      =|  fex=(list carp)
1777      |=  caz=(list card:agent)
1778      ^+  [fex ap-core]
1779      ?~  caz  [(flop fex) ap-core]
1780      ?-  i.caz
1781        [%pass * %grow *]  $(caz t.caz, ap-core (ap-grow +.q.i.caz))
1782        [%pass * %tomb *]  $(caz t.caz, ap-core (ap-tomb +.q.i.caz))
1783        [%pass * %cull *]  $(caz t.caz, ap-core (ap-cull +.q.i.caz))
1784        [%pass * ?(%agent %arvo %pyre) *]  $(caz t.caz, fex [i.caz fex])
1785        [%give *]  $(caz t.caz, fex [i.caz fex])
1786        [%slip *]  !!
1787      ==
1788    ::  +ap-handle-ken
1789    ::
1790    ++  ap-handle-ken
1791      |=  fex=(list carp)
1792      ^+  ken.yoke
1793      %+  roll  fex
1794      |=  [=carp ken=_ken.yoke]
1795      ?+  carp  ken
1796        [%pass * %arvo %a %keen spar=*]  (~(put ju ken) [spar.q p]:carp)
```

```
1797            [%pass * %arvo %a %yawn spar=*]  (~(del ju ken) [spar.q p]:carp)
1798          ==
1799      ::  +ap-handle-kicks: handle cancels of bitt.watches
1800      ::
1801      ++  ap-handle-kicks
1802        ~/  %ap-handle-kicks
1803        |=  moves=(list move)
1804        ^-  bitt
1805        =/  quits=(list duct)
1806          %+  murn  moves
1807          |=  =move
1808          ^-  (unit duct)
1809          ?.  ?=([* %give %unto %kick *] move)
1810            ~
1811          `duct.move
1812        ::
1813        =/  quit-map=bitt
1814          (malt (turn quits |=(=duct [duct *[ship path]])))
1815        (~(dif by bitt.yoke) quit-map)
1816      ::  +ap-handle-peers: handle new boat.watches
1817      ::
1818      ++  ap-handle-peers
1819        ~/  %ap-handle-peers
1820        |=  moves=(list move)
1821        ^-  [(list move) _ap-core]
1822        =|  new-moves=(list move)
1823        |-  ^-  [(list move) _ap-core]
1824        ?~  moves
1825          [(flop new-moves) ap-core]
1826        =/  =move  i.moves
1827        ?:  ?=([* %pass * %g %deal * * %leave *] move)
1828          =/  =wire  p.move.move
1829          ?>  ?=([%use @ @ %out @ @ *] wire)
1830          =/  =dock            [q.p q]:q.move.move
1831          =/  sys-wire=^wire  (scag 6 `^wire`wire)
1832          =/  sub-wire=^wire  (slag 6 `^wire`wire)
1833          ::
1834          ?.  (~(has by boat.yoke) sub-wire dock)
1835            %.  $(moves t.moves)
1836            %^  trace  odd.veb.bug.state
1837            leaf/"gall: {<agent-name>} missing subscription, got %leave"  ~
1838          =/  nonce=@  (~(got by boar.yoke) sub-wire dock)
1839          =.  p.move.move
1840            %+  weld  sys-wire
1841            (ap-nonce-wire sub-wire dock)
1842          =:  boat.yoke  (~(del by boat.yoke) [sub-wire dock])
1843              boar.yoke  (~(del by boar.yoke) [sub-wire dock])
1844            ==
1845          :: if nonce = 0, this was a pre-nonce subscription so later
1846          :: subscriptions need to start subscribing on the next nonce
1847          ::
1848          =?  sub-nonce.yoke  =(nonce 0)  +(sub-nonce.yoke)
1849          $(moves t.moves, new-moves [move new-moves])
1850        ?.  ?=([* %pass * %g %deal * * ?(%watch %watch-as) *] move)
1851          $(moves t.moves, new-moves [move new-moves])
1852        =/  =wire  p.move.move
1853        ?>  ?=([%use @ @ %out @ @ *] wire)
1854        =/  sys-wire=^wire  (scag 6 `^wire`wire)
```

```
1855        =/  sub-wire=^wire  (slag 6 `^wire`wire)
1856        =/  [=dock =deal]  [[q.p q] r]:q.move.move
1857        ::
1858        ?:  (~(has by boat.yoke) sub-wire dock)
1859          =.  ap-core
1860            =/  =tang
1861              ~[leaf+"subscribe wire not unique" >agent-name< >sub-wire< >dock<]
1862            =/  have  (~(got by boat.yoke) sub-wire dock)
1863            %-  (slog >out=have< tang)
1864            (ap-error %watch-not-unique tang)  ::  reentrant, maybe bad?
1865          $(moves t.moves)
1866        ::
1867        ::NOTE  0-check guards against pre-release bug
1868        =?  p.move.move  !=(0 sub-nonce.yoke)
1869          (weld sys-wire [(scot %ud sub-nonce.yoke) sub-wire])
1870        %_      $
1871          moves              t.moves
1872          new-moves      [move new-moves]
1873          sub-nonce.yoke  +(sub-nonce.yoke)
1874        ::
1875          boat.yoke
1876        %+  ~(put by boat.yoke)  [sub-wire dock]
1877        :-  acked=|
1878        path=?+(-.deal !! %watch path.deal, %watch-as path.deal)
1879        ::
1880          boar.yoke
1881        (~(put by boar.yoke) [sub-wire dock] sub-nonce.yoke)
1882      ==
1883    --
1884  --
1885  ::  +call: request
1886  ::
1887  ++  call
1888    ~%  %gall-call  +>    ~
1889    |=  [=duct dud=(unit goof) hic=(hobo task)]
1890    ^-  [(list move) _gall-payload]
1891    ?^  dud
1892      ~|(%gall-call-dud (mean tang.u.dud))
1893    ::
1894    ~|  [%gall-call-failed duct hic]
1895    =/  =task  ((harden task) hic)
1896    =/  prov=path
1897      ?:  ?=(%deal -.task)
1898        ?.(=(p.p.task our) *path r.p.task)
1899      ?.  ?&  ?=([^ *] duct)
1900              ?=  $?  %ames  %behn  %clay
1901                      %dill  %eyre  %gall
1902                      %iris  %jael  %khan
1903                  ==
1904              i.i.duct
1905          ==
1906        *path
1907      /[i.i.duct]
1908    ::
1909    =/  mo-core  (mo-abed:mo duct)
1910    ?-    -.task
1911        %deal
1912      =/  [=sack =term =deal]  [p q r]:task
```

```
1913      ?.  =(q.sack our)
1914        ?>  =(p.sack our)
1915      mo-abet:(mo-send-foreign-request:mo-core q.sack term deal)
1916    mo-abet:(mo-handle-local:mo-core prov p.sack term deal)
1917  ::
1918      %init  [~ gall-payload(system-duct.state duct)]
1919      %plea
1920    =/  =ship  ship.task
1921    =/  =path  path.plea.task
1922    =/  =noun  payload.plea.task
1923    ::
1924    ~|  [ship=ship plea-path=path]
1925    ?>  ?=([%ge @ ~] path)
1926    =/  agent-name  i.t.path
1927    ::
1928    =+  ;;(=ames-request-all noun)
1929    ?>  ?=(%0 -.ames-request-all)
1930    =>  (mo-handle-ames-request:mo-core ship agent-name +.ames-request-all)
1931    mo-abet
1932  ::
1933      %sear  mo-abet:(mo-filter-queue:mo-core ship.task)
1934      %jolt  mo-abet:(mo-jolt:mo-core dude.task our desk.task)
1935      %idle  mo-abet:(mo-idle:mo-core prov dude.task)
1936      %load  mo-abet:(mo-load:mo-core prov +.task)
1937      %nuke  mo-abet:(mo-nuke:mo-core prov dude.task)
1938      %doff  mo-abet:(mo-doff:mo-core prov +.task)
1939      %rake  mo-abet:(mo-rake:mo-core prov +.task)
1940      %spew  mo-abet:(mo-spew:mo-core veb.task)
1941      %sift  mo-abet:(mo-sift:mo-core dudes.task)
1942      %trim  [~ gall-payload]
1943      %vega  [~ gall-payload]
1944    ==
1945  ::  +load: recreate vane; note, only valid if called from pupa
1946  ::
1947  ++  load
1948    |^  |=  old=spore-any
1949        =?  old  ?=(%7 -.old)   (spore-7-to-8 old)
1950        =?  old  ?=(%8 -.old)   (spore-8-to-9 old)
1951        =?  old  ?=(%9 -.old)   (spore-9-to-10 old)
1952        =?  old  ?=(%10 -.old)  (spore-10-to-11 old)
1953        =?  old  ?=(%11 -.old)  (spore-11-to-12 old)
1954        =?  old  ?=(%12 -.old)  (spore-12-to-13 old)
1955        =?  old  ?=(%13 -.old)  (spore-13-to-14 old)
1956        =?  old  ?=(%14 -.old)  (spore-14-to-15 old)
1957        ?>  ?=(%15 -.old)
1958      gall-payload(state old)
1959    ::
1960    +$  spore-any
1961      $%  spore
1962          spore-7
1963          spore-8
1964          spore-9
1965          spore-10
1966          spore-11
1967          spore-12
1968          spore-13
1969          spore-14
1970      ==
```

```
1971  +$  spore-14
1972    $:  %14
1973        system-duct=duct
1974        outstanding=(map [wire duct] (qeu remote-request))
1975        contacts=(set ship)
1976        eggs=(map term egg)
1977        blocked=(map term (qeu blocked-move))
1978        =bug
1979    ==
1980  +$  spore-13
1981    $:  %13
1982        system-duct=duct
1983        outstanding=(map [wire duct] (qeu remote-request))
1984        contacts=(set ship)
1985        eggs=(map term egg)
1986        blocked=(map term (qeu blocked-move-13))
1987        =bug
1988    ==
1989  +$  blocked-move-13  [=duct routes=routes-13 move=(each deal unto)]
1990  +$  routes-13
1991    $:  disclosing=(unit (set ship))
1992        attributing=ship
1993    ==
1994  +$  spore-12
1995    $:  %12
1996        system-duct=duct
1997        outstanding=(map [wire duct] (qeu remote-request))
1998        contacts=(set ship)
1999        eggs=(map term egg-12)
2000        blocked=(map term (qeu blocked-move-13))
2001        =bug
2002    ==
2003  +$  egg-12
2004    $%  [%nuke sky=(map spur @ud)]
2005        $:  %live
2006            control-duct=duct
2007            run-nonce=@t
2008            sub-nonce=@
2009            =stats
2010            =bitt
2011            =boat
2012            =boar
2013            code=~
2014            old-state=[%| vase]
2015            =beak
2016            marks=(map duct mark)
2017            sky=(map spur path-state)
2018    ==  ==
2019  +$  spore-11
2020    $:  %11
2021        system-duct=duct
2022        outstanding=(map [wire duct] (qeu remote-request))
2023        contacts=(set ship)
2024        eggs=(map term egg-11)
2025        blocked=(map term (qeu blocked-move-13))
2026        =bug
2027    ==
2028  +$  egg-11
```

```
2029        $:  control-duct=duct
2030            run-nonce=@t
2031            sub-nonce=@
2032            =stats
2033            =bitt
2034            =boat
2035            =boar
2036            code=~
2037            old-state=[%| vase]
2038            =beak
2039            marks=(map duct mark)
2040        ==
2041    +$  spore-10
2042      $:  %10
2043            system-duct=duct
2044            outstanding=(map [wire duct] (qeu remote-request))
2045            contacts=(set ship)
2046            eggs=(map term egg-10)
2047            blocked=(map term (qeu blocked-move-13))
2048            =bug
2049        ==
2050    +$  egg-10
2051      $:  control-duct=duct
2052            run-nonce=@t
2053            sub-nonce=@
2054            live=?
2055            =stats
2056            =bitt
2057            =boat
2058            =boar
2059            old-state=(each vase vase)
2060            =beak
2061            marks=(map duct mark)
2062        ==
2063    +$  spore-9
2064      $:  %9
2065            system-duct=duct
2066            outstanding=(map [wire duct] (qeu remote-request-9))
2067            contacts=(set ship)
2068            eggs=(map term egg-10)
2069            blocked=(map term (qeu blocked-move-13))
2070            =bug
2071        ==
2072    ::
2073    +$  remote-request-9  ?(remote-request %cork)
2074    ::
2075    +$  spore-8
2076      $:  %8
2077            system-duct=duct
2078            outstanding=(map [wire duct] (qeu remote-request-9))
2079            contacts=(set ship)
2080            eggs=(map term egg-8)
2081            blocked=(map term (qeu blocked-move-13))
2082        ==
2083    +$  egg-8
2084      $:  control-duct=duct
2085            run-nonce=@t
2086            live=?
```

```
          =stats
          watches=watches-8
          old-state=(each vase vase)
          =beak
          marks=(map duct mark)
      ==
  ==
+$  watches-8  [inbound=bitt outbound=boat-8]
+$  boat-8  (map [wire ship term] [acked=? =path])
+$  spore-7
  $:  %7
      wipe-eyre-subs=_|  ::NOTE  band-aid for #3196
      system-duct=duct
      outstanding=(map [wire duct] (qeu remote-request-9))
      contacts=(set ship)
      eggs=(map term egg-8)
      blocked=(map term (qeu blocked-move-13))
  ==
::
++  spore-7-to-8
  |=  old=spore-7
  ^-  spore-8
  :-  %8
  =.  eggs.old
    %-  ~(urn by eggs.old)
    |=  [a=term e=egg-8]
    ::  kiln will kick off appropriate app revival
    ::
    e(old-state [%| p.old-state.e])
  +>.old
::
++  spore-8-to-9
  |=  old=spore-8
  ^-  spore-9
  =-  old(- %9, eggs -, blocked [blocked.old *bug])
  %-  ~(run by eggs.old)
  |=  =egg-8
  ^-  egg-10
  =/  [=bitt =boat =boar]  (watches-8-to-9 watches.egg-8)
  :*  control-duct.egg-8
      run-nonce.egg-8
      sub-nonce=1
      live.egg-8
      stats.egg-8
      bitt  boat  boar
      [old-state beak marks]:egg-8
  ==
::
++  watches-8-to-9
  |=  watches-8
  ^-  [bitt boat boar]
  [inbound outbound (~(run by outbound) |=([acked=? =path] nonce=0))]
::
::  remove %cork
::
++  spore-9-to-10
  |=  old=spore-9
  =-  old(- %10, outstanding -)
  %-  ~(run by outstanding.old)
```

```
2145      |=  q=(qeu remote-request-9)
2146      %-  ~(gas to *(qeu remote-request))
2147      %+  murn  ~(tap to q)
2148      |=(r=remote-request-9 ?:(?=(%cork r) ~ `r))
2149    ::
2150    ::  removed live
2151    ::  changed old-state from (each vase vase) to [%| vase]
2152    ::  added code
2153    ::
2154    ++  spore-10-to-11
2155      |=  old=spore-10
2156      ^-  spore-11
2157      %=    old
2158        -  %11
2159        eggs
2160      %-  ~(urn by eggs.old)
2161      |=  [a=term e=egg-10]
2162      ^-  egg-11
2163      e(|3 |4.e(|4 `|8.e(old-state [%| p.old-state.e])))
2164      ==
2165    ::
2166    ::  added sky
2167    ::
2168    ++  spore-11-to-12
2169      |=  old=spore-11
2170      ^-  spore-12
2171      %=    old
2172        -  %12
2173        eggs
2174      %-  ~(urn by eggs.old)
2175      |=  [a=term e=egg-11]
2176      ^-  egg-12
2177      live/e(marks [marks.e sky:*$>(%live egg)])
2178      ==
2179    ::
2180    ::  added ken
2181    ::
2182    ++  spore-12-to-13
2183      |=  old=spore-12
2184      ^-  spore-13
2185      %=    old
2186        -  %13
2187        eggs
2188      %-  ~(urn by eggs.old)
2189      |=  [a=term e=egg-12]
2190      ^-  egg
2191      ?:  ?=(%nuke -.e)  e
2192      e(sky [sky.e ken:*$>(%live egg)])
2193      ==
2194    ::  added provenance path to routes
2195    ::
2196    ++  spore-13-to-14
2197      |=  old=spore-13
2198      ^-  spore-14
2199      %=    old
2200        -  %14
2201        ::
2202        blocked
```

```
2203        ^-  (map term (qeu blocked-move))
2204        %-  ~(run by blocked.old)
2205        |=  q=(qeu blocked-move-13)
2206        %-  ~(gas to *(qeu blocked-move))
2207        %+  turn  ~(tap to q)
2208        |=  blocked=blocked-move-13
2209        ^-  blocked-move
2210        %=  blocked
2211          attributing.routes  [ship=attributing.routes.blocked path=/]
2212        ==
2213      ==
2214    ::  added nacked-leaves timer
2215    ::
2216    ++  spore-14-to-15
2217      |=  old=spore-14
2218      ^-  spore
2219      old(- %15, bug [bug.old ~])
2220    --
2221  ::  +scry: standard scry
2222  ::
2223  ++  scry
2224    ~/  %gall-scry
2225    ^-  roon
2226    |=  [lyc=gang pov=path care=term bem=beam]
2227    ^-  (unit (unit cage))
2228    =*  ship  p.bem
2229    =*  dap   q.bem
2230    =/  =coin  $/r.bem
2231    =*  path  s.bem
2232    ::
2233    ?:  ?&  ?=(%da -.r.bem)
2234            (gth p.r.bem now)
2235        ==
2236      ~
2237    ::
2238    ?.  ?=([%$ *] path)  ::  [%$ *] is for the vane, all else is for the agent
2239      ?.  ?&  =(our ship)
2240              =([%$ %da now] coin)
2241          ==                          ~
2242      ?.  (~(has by yokes.state) dap)  [~ ~]
2243      ?.  ?=(^ path)                  ~
2244      =/  =routes  [~ ship pov]
2245      (mo-peek:mo & dap routes care path)
2246    ::
2247    =>  .(path t.path)
2248    ::
2249    ?:  ?&  =(%u care)
2250            =(~ path)
2251            =([%$ %da now] coin)
2252            =(our ship)
2253        ==
2254      =;  hav=?
2255      [~ ~ noun+!>(hav)]
2256      =/  yok=(unit yoke)  (~(get by yokes.state) dap)
2257      &(?=([~ %live *] yok) -.agent.u.yok)
2258    ::
2259    ?:  ?&  =(%d care)
2260            =(~ path)
```

```
2261            =([%$ %da now] coin)
2262            =(our ship)
2263          ==
2264      =/  yok=(unit yoke)  (~(get by yokes.state) dap)
2265      ?.  ?=([~ %live *] yok)
2266        [~ ~]
2267      [~ ~ desk+!>(q.beak.u.yok)]
2268    ::
2269    ?:  ?&  =(%e care)
2270            =(~ path)
2271            =([%$ %da now] coin)
2272            =(our ship)
2273          ==
2274      :+  ~  ~
2275      :-  %apps  !>  ^-  (set [=dude live=?])
2276      =*  syd=desk  dap
2277      %+  roll  ~(tap by yokes.state)
2278      |=  [[=dude =yoke] acc=(set [=dude live=?])]
2279      ?.  ?&  ?=(%live -.yoke)
2280              =(syd q.beak.yoke)
2281            ==
2282        acc
2283      (~(put in acc) [dude -.agent.yoke])
2284    ::
2285    ?:  ?&  =(%f care)
2286            =(~ path)
2287            =([%$ %da now] coin)
2288            =(our ship)
2289          ==
2290      :+  ~  ~
2291      :-  %nonces  !>  ^-  (map dude @)
2292      %-  malt  %+  murn  ~(tap by yokes.state)
2293      |=  [=dude =yoke]
2294      ?:  ?=(%nuke -.yoke)  ~  `[dude sub-nonce.yoke]
2295    ::
2296    ?:  ?&  =(%n care)
2297            ?=([@ @ ^] path)
2298            =([%$ %da now] coin)
2299            =(our ship)
2300          ==
2301      =/  yok  (~(get by yokes.state) dap)
2302      ?.  ?=([~ %live *] yok)
2303        [~ ~]
2304      =/  [=^ship =term =wire]
2305        [(slav %p i.path) i.t.path t.t.path]
2306      ?~  nonce=(~(get by boar.u.yok) [wire ship term])
2307        [~ ~]
2308      [~ ~ atom+!>(u.nonce)]
2309    ::
2310    ?:  ?&  =(%v care)
2311            =([%$ %da now] coin)
2312            =(our ship)
2313          ==
2314      =/  yok  (~(get by yokes.state) dap)
2315      ?.  ?=([~ %live *] yok)
2316        [~ ~]
2317      =/  =egg
2318        %=    u.yok
```

```
2319              code    ~
2320              agent
2321           :-   %|
2322         ?:   ?=(%|  -.agent.u.yok)
2323            p.agent.u.yok
2324         on-save:p.agent.u.yok
2325              ==
2326       ``noun+!>([-:*spore egg])
2327   ::
2328   ?:   ?&  =(%w care)
2329             =([%$ %da now] coin)
2330             =(our ship)
2331            ==
2332     =/  yok  (~(get by yokes.state) q.bem)
2333     ?.   ?=([~ %live *] yok)          [~ ~]
2334     ?~   ski=(~(get by sky.u.yok) path)  [~ ~]
2335     ?~   las=(ram:on-path fan.u.ski)    [~ ~]
2336       ``case/!>(ud/key.u.las)
2337   ::
2338   ?:   ?=(%x care)
2339     ?.   =(p.bem our)   ~
2340       ::
2341     ?:   ?=(%$ q.bem)   :: app %$ reserved
2342       ?+    path   ~
2343          [%whey ~]
2344          =/  blocked
2345             =/  queued   (~(run by blocked.state) |=((qeu blocked-move) [%.y +<]))
2346          (sort ~(tap by queued) aor)
2347            ::
2348          =/  running
2349             %+  turn  (sort ~(tap by yokes.state) aor)
2350             |=  [dap=term =yoke]
2351             ^-  mass
2352             =/  met=(list mass)
2353               =/  dat  (mo-peek:mo | dap [~ ship pov] %x /whey/mass)
2354               ?:  ?=(?(~ [~ ~]) dat)   ~
2355               (fall ((soft (list mass)) q.q.u.u.dat) ~)
2356             ?~  met
2357               dap^&+yoke
2358             dap^|+(welp met dot+&+yoke ~)
2359            ::
2360          =/  maz=(list mass)
2361             :~  [%foreign %.y contacts.state]
2362                 [%blocked %.n blocked]
2363                 [%active %.n running]
2364             ==
2365          ``mass+!>(maz)
2366        ==
2367     ::
2368     ?~  yok=(~(get by yokes.state) q.bem)  ~
2369     ?:  ?=(%nuke -.u.yok)  ~
2370     =/  ski  (~(get by sky.u.yok) path)
2371     ?~  ski  ~
2372     =/  res=(unit (each page @uvI))
2373       ?+    -.r.bem  ~
2374          %ud  (bind (get:on-path fan.u.ski p.r.bem) tail)
2375          %da
2376       %-  head
```

```
2377          %^      (dip:on-path (unit (each page @uvI)))
2378              fan.u.ski
2379          ~
2380          |=  [res=(unit (each page @uvI)) @ud =@da val=(each page @uvI)]
2381          ^-  [new=(unit [@da _val]) stop=? res=(unit _val)]
2382          :-  `[da val]
2383          ?:((lte da p.r.bem) |/`val &/res)
2384        ==
2385    ?.  ?=([~ %& *] res)  ~
2386    ``p.u.res(q !>(q.p.u.res))
2387    ::
2388    ?:  ?&  =(%t care)
2389            =([%$ %da now] coin)
2390            =(our ship)
2391        ==
2392    =/  yok  (~(get by yokes.state) q.bem)
2393    ?.  ?=([~ %live *] yok)  ~
2394    :^  ~  ~  %file-list  !>  ^-  (list ^path)
2395    %+  skim  ~(tap in ~(key by sky.u.yok))
2396    |=  =spur
2397    ?&  =(path (scag (lent path) spur))
2398        !=(path spur)
2399    ==
2400    ::
2401    ?:  ?&  =(%z care)
2402            =(our ship)
2403        ==
2404    =/  yok  (~(get by yokes.state) q.bem)
2405    ?.  ?=([~ %live *] yok)      ~
2406    ?~  ski=(~(get by sky.u.yok) path)  ~
2407    =/  res=(unit (pair @da (each noun @uvI)))
2408      ?+  -.r.bem  ~
2409        %ud  (get:on-path fan.u.ski p.r.bem)
2410        %da  ?.(=(p.r.bem now) ~ (bind (ram:on-path fan.u.ski) tail))
2411      ==
2412    ?+  res  ~
2413      [~ @ %| *]  ``noun/!>(p.q.u.res)
2414      [~ @ %& *]  ``noun/!>(`@uvI`(shax (jam p.q.u.res)))
2415    ==
2416    ~
2417  ::  +stay: save without cache; suspend non-%base agents
2418  ::
2419  ::    TODO: superfluous? see +molt
2420  ::
2421  ++  stay
2422    ^-  spore
2423    =;  eggs=(map term egg)  state(yokes eggs)
2424    %-  ~(run by yokes.state)
2425    |=  =yoke
2426    ^-  egg
2427    ?:  ?=(%nuke -.yoke)  yoke
2428    %=      yoke
2429        code  ~
2430        agent
2431      :-  %|
2432      ?:  ?=(%| -.agent.yoke)
2433        p.agent.yoke
2434      on-save:p.agent.yoke
```

```
2435      ==
2436 ::   +take: response
2437 ::
2438 ++   take
2439   ~/  %gall-take
2440   |=  [=wire =duct dud=(unit goof) syn=sign-arvo]
2441   ^-  [(list move) _gall-payload]
2442   ?^  dud
2443     ~&(%gall-take-dud ((slog tang.u.dud) [~ gall-payload]))
2444   ?:  =(/nowhere wire)
2445     [~ gall-payload]
2446   ?:  =(/clear-huck wire)
2447     =/  =gift  ?>(?=([%behn %heck %gall *] syn) +>+.syn)
2448     [[duct %give gift]~ gall-payload]
2449   ::
2450   ?:  ?=([%nacked-leaves ~] wire)
2451     =;  core=_mo-core:mo
2452       :: next time a %leave gets nacked, the state and timer will be set again.
2453       ::
2454       mo-abet:core(leaves.state ~)
2455     %-  ~(rep by outstanding.state)
2456     |=  [[[=^wire =^duct] stand=(qeu remote-request)] core=_mo-core:mo]
2457     ?:  =(~ stand)  core
2458     =^  rr  stand   ~(get to stand)
2459     :: sanity check in the outstanding queue:
2460     :: if there's a %leave, that should be the only request
2461     ::
2462     ~?  >>>  &(?=(%leave rr) =(^ stand))
2463       "outstanding queue not empty [{<wire>} {<duct>} {<stand>}]"
2464     =?  core  &(?=(%leave rr) =(~ stand))
2465       (mo-handle-nacked-leaves:(mo-abed:core duct) wire)
2466     core
2467   ::
2468   ~|  [%gall-take-failed wire]
2469   ?>  ?=([?(%sys %use) *] wire)
2470   =<  mo-abet
2471   %.  [t.wire ?:(?=([%behn %heck *] syn) syn.syn syn)]
2472   ?-  i.wire
2473     %sys  mo-handle-sys:(mo-abed:mo duct)
2474     %use  mo-handle-use:(mo-abed:mo duct)
2475   ==
2476 --
```

Iris

```
1  !:
2  ::  http-client
3  ::
4  |=  our=ship
5  =,  iris
6  ::
7  ::
8  ::  internal data structures
9  ::
10 =>  =~
11 ::
12 ::  internal data structures that won't go in zuse
13 ::
14 |%
15 +$  move
16   ::
17   $:  ::  duct: request identifier
18       ::
19       =duct
20       ::
21       ::
22       card=(wind note gift)
23   ==
24 ::  +note: private request from light to another vane
25 ::
26 +$  note
27   $%  ::  %d: to dill
28       ::
29       $:  %d
30           ::
31           ::
32       $%  [%flog =flog:dill]
33   ==  ==  ==
34 --
35 ::  more structures
36 ::
37 |%
38 +$  axle
39   $:  ::  date: date at which light's state was updated to this data structure
40       ::
41       date=%~2019.2.8
42       ::
43       ::
44       =state
45   ==
46 ::  +state:client: state relating to open outbound HTTP connections
47 ::
48 +$  state
49   $:  ::  next-id: monotonically increasing id number for the next connection
50       ::
51       next-id=@ud
52       ::  connection-by-id: open connections to the
53       ::
54       connection-by-id=(map @ud [=duct =in-progress-http-request])
55       ::  connection-by-duct: used for cancellation
56       ::
```

```
57        connection-by-duct=(map duct @ud)
58        ::  outbound-duct: the duct to send outbound requests on
59        ::
60        outbound-duct=duct
61    ==
62 ::  +in-progress-http-request: state around an outbound http
63 ::
64 +$  in-progress-http-request
65    $:  ::  remaining-redirects: http limit of number of redirects before error
66        ::
67        remaining-redirects=@ud
68        ::  remaining-retries: number of times to retry the request
69        ::
70        remaining-retries=@ud
71        ::  response-header: the response headers from the %start packet
72        ::
73        ::      We send the response headers with each %http-progress, so we must
74        ::      save them.
75        ::
76        response-header=(unit response-header:http)
77        ::  chunks: a list of partial results returned from unix
78        ::
79        ::      This list of octs must be flopped before it is composed as the
80        ::      final response, as we want to be able to quickly insert.
81        ::
82        chunks=(list octs)
83        ::  bytes-read: the sum of the size of the :chunks
84        ::
85        bytes-read=@ud
86        ::  expected-size: the expected content-length of the http request
87        ::
88        expected-size=(unit @ud)
89    ==
90 --
91 ::
92 |%
93 ::  +combine-octs: combine multiple octs into one
94 ::
95 ++  combine-octs
96    |=  a=(list octs)
97    ^-  octs
98    :-  %+  roll  a
99        |=  [=octs sum=@ud]
100       (add sum p.octs)
101   (can 3 a)
102 ::  +per-client-event: per-event client core
103 ::
104 ++  per-client-event
105   |=  [[eny=@ =duct now=@da rof=roof] =state]
106   |%
107   ::  +request: makes an external web request
108   ::
109   ++  request
110     |=  [=request:http =outbound-config]
111     ^-  [(list move) ^state]
112     ::  if there's already a request on this duct, abort
113     ::
114     ?:  (~(has by connection-by-duct.state) duct)
```

```
115        ~&   %cant-send-second-http-client-request-on-same-duct
116        [~ state]
117    ::   get the next id for this request
118    ::
119    =^   id   next-id.state   [next-id.state +(next-id.state)]
120    ::   add a new open session
121    ::
122    =.   connection-by-id.state
123      %+   ~(put by connection-by-id.state)   id
124      =,   outbound-config
125      [duct [redirects retries ~ ~ 0 ~]]
126    ::   keep track of the duct for cancellation
127    ::
128    =.   connection-by-duct.state
129      (~(put by connection-by-duct.state) duct id)
130    ::   start the download
131    ::
132    ::   the original eyre keeps track of the duct on %born and then sends a
133    ::   %give on that duct. this seems like a weird inversion of
134    ::   responsibility, where we should instead be doing a pass to unix. the
135    ::   reason we need to manually build ids is because we aren't using the
136    ::   built in duct system.
137    ::
138    ::   email discussions make it sound like fixing that might be hard, so
139    ::   maybe i should just live with the way it is now?
140    ::
141    :-   [outbound-duct.state %give %request id request]~
142    state
143  ::   +cancel: client cancels an outstanding request
144  ::
145  ++   cancel
146      ^-   [(list move) ^state]
147      ::
148      ?~   cancel-id=(~(get by connection-by-duct.state) duct)
149        ~&   %iris-invalid-cancel
150        [~ state]
151      ::
152      :-   [outbound-duct.state %give %cancel-request u.cancel-id]~
153      (cleanup-connection u.cancel-id)
154  ::   +receive: receives a response to an http-request we made
155  ::
156  ::      TODO: Right now, we are not following redirect and not handling retries
157  ::      correctly. We need to do this.
158  ::
159  ++   receive
160      |=   [id=@ud =http-event:http]
161      ^-   [(list move) ^state]
162      ::   ensure that this is a valid receive
163      ::
164      ?~   connection=(~(get by connection-by-id.state) id)
165        ~&   [%eyre-unknown-receive id]
166        [~ state]
167      ::
168      ?-   -.http-event
169        %start
170      ::   TODO: Handle redirects and retries here, before we start dispatching
171      ::      back to the application.
172      ::
```

```
173      ::   record data from the http response that only comes from %start
174      ::
175      =.  connection-by-id.state
176       %+  ~(jab by connection-by-id.state)  id
177       |=  [duct=^duct =in-progress-http-request]
178       ::
179       =.  expected-size.in-progress-http-request
180         ?~  str=(get-header:http 'content-length' headers.response-header.http-event)
181           ~
182         ::
183         (rush u.str dum:ag)
184       ::
185       =.  response-header.in-progress-http-request
186        `response-header:http-event
187       ::
188       [duct in-progress-http-request]
189     ::
190     ?:  complete.http-event
191       (send-finished id data.http-event)
192     ::
193     (record-and-send-progress id data.http-event)
194   ::
195       %continue
196     ?:  complete.http-event
197       (send-finished id data.http-event)
198     ::
199     (record-and-send-progress id data.http-event)
200   ::
201       %cancel
202     ::  we have received a cancel from outside; pass it on to our requester
203     ::
204     :_  (cleanup-connection id)
205     ^-  (list move)
206     :_  ~
207     :*  duct.u.connection
208     %give
209     %http-response
210     %cancel
211       ~
212     ==
213   ==
214 ::  +record-and-send-progress: save incoming data and send progress report
215 ::
216 ++  record-and-send-progress
217   |=  [id=@ud data=(unit octs)]
218   ^-  [(list move) ^state]
219   ::
220   =.  connection-by-id.state
221    %+  ~(jab by connection-by-id.state)  id
222    |=  [duct=^duct =in-progress-http-request]
223    ::  record the data chunk and size, if it exists
224    ::
225    =?  chunks.in-progress-http-request
226      ?=(^ data)
227    [u.data chunks.in-progress-http-request]
228    =?  bytes-read.in-progress-http-request
229      ?=(^ data)
230    (add bytes-read.in-progress-http-request p.u.data)
```

```
231      ::
232          [duct in-progress-http-request]
233    ::
234    =/  connection  (~(got by connection-by-id.state) id)
235    :_  state
236    ^-  (list move)
237    :_  ~
238    :*  duct.connection
239          %give
240          %http-response
241          %progress
242          (need response-header.in-progress-http-request.connection)
243          bytes-read.in-progress-http-request.connection
244          expected-size.in-progress-http-request.connection
245          data
246      ==
247    ::  +send-finished: sends the %finished, cleans up the session state
248    ::
249    ++  send-finished
250      |=  [id=@ud data=(unit octs)]
251      ^-  [(list move) ^state]
252      ::
253    =/  connection  (~(got by connection-by-id.state) id)
254    ::  reassemble the octs that we've received into their final form
255      ::
256    =/  data=octs
257      %-  combine-octs
258      %-  flop
259      ::
260      ?~  data
261        chunks.in-progress-http-request.connection
262      [u.data chunks.in-progress-http-request.connection]
263    ::
264    =/  response-header=response-header:http
265      (need response-header.in-progress-http-request.connection)
266    ::
267    =/  mime=@t
268      ?~  mime-type=(get-header:http 'content-type' headers.response-header)
269        'application/octet-stream'
270      u.mime-type
271      ::
272    :_  (cleanup-connection id)
273    :~  :*  duct.connection
274            %give
275            %http-response
276            %finished
277            response-header
278            ?:(=(0 p.data) ~ `[mime data])
279      ==  ==
280    ::
281    ++  cleanup-connection
282      |=  id=@ud
283      ^-  ^state
284    ?~  con=(~(get by connection-by-id.state) id)
285      state
286    %_    state
287      connection-by-id    (~(del by connection-by-id.state) id)
288      connection-by-duct  (~(del by connection-by-duct.state) duct.u.con)
```

```
289      ==
290    --
291  --
292  ::  end the =~
293  ::
294  .  ==
295  ::  begin with a default +axle as a blank slate
296  ::
297  =|  ax=axle
298  ::  a vane is activated with current date, entropy, and a namespace function
299  ::
300  |=  [now=@da eny=@uvJ rof=roof]
301  ::  allow jets to be registered within this core
302  ::
303  ~%  %http-client  ..part  ~
304  |%
305  ++  call
306    |=  [=duct dud=(unit goof) wrapped-task=(hobo task)]
307    ^-  [(list move) _light-gate]
308    ::
309    =/  task=task  ((harden task) wrapped-task)
310    ::
311    ::  XX handle error notifications
312    ::
313    ?^  dud
314      =/  moves=(list move)
315        [[duct %slip %d %flog %crud [-.task tang.u.dud]] ~]
316      [moves light-gate]
317    ::  %trim: in response to memory pressure
318    ::
319    ?:  ?=(%trim -.task)
320      [~ light-gate]
321    ::  %vega: notifies us of a completed kernel upgrade
322    ::
323    ?:  ?=(%vega -.task)
324      [~ light-gate]
325    ::
326    =/  event-args  [[eny duct now rof] state.ax]
327    =/  client  (per-client-event event-args)
328    ?-    -.task
329    ::
330        %born
331      ::  create a cancel for each outstanding connection
332      ::
333      ::    TODO: We should gracefully retry on restart instead of just sending a
334      ::    cancel.
335      ::    TODO  we might not want to do that though!
336      ::
337      =/  moves=(list move)
338        %+  turn  ~(tap by connection-by-duct.state.ax)
339        |=  [=^duct @ud]
340        ^-  move
341        [duct %give %http-response %cancel ~]
342      ::  reset all connection state on born
343      ::
344      =:  next-id.state.ax              0
345          connection-by-id.state.ax    ~
346          connection-by-duct.state.ax  ~
```

```
347          outbound-duct.state.ax        duct
348    ==
349    ::
350    [moves light-gate]
351  ::
352      %request
353    =^  moves  state.ax  (request:client +.task)
354    [moves light-gate]
355  ::
356      %cancel-request
357    =^  moves  state.ax  cancel:client
358    [moves light-gate]
359  ::
360      %receive
361    =^  moves  state.ax  (receive:client +.task)
362    [moves light-gate]
363    ==
364  ::  http-client issues no requests to other vanes
365  ::
366  ++  take
367    |=  [=wire =duct dud=(unit goof) sign=*]
368    ^-  [(list move) _light-gate]
369    ?<  ?=(^ dud)
370    !!
371  ::
372  ++  light-gate  ..$
373  ::  +load: migrate old state to new state (called on vane reload)
374  ::
375  ++  load
376    |=  old=axle
377    ^+  ..^$
378    ::
379    ~!  %loading
380    ..^$(ax old)
381  ::  +stay: produce current state
382  ::
383  ++  stay  `axle`ax
384  ::  +scry: request a path in the urbit namespace
385  ::
386  ++  scry
387    ^-  roon
388    |=  [lyc=gang pov=path car=term bem=beam]
389    ^-  (unit (unit cage))
390    =*  ren  car
391    =*  why=shop  &/p.bem
392    =*  syd  q.bem
393    =*  lot=coin  $/r.bem
394    =*  tyl  s.bem
395    ::
396    ?.  ?=(%& -.why)  ~
397    =*  his  p.why
398    ?:  &(?=(%x ren) =(tyl //whey))
399      =/  maz=(list mass)
400        :~  nex+&+next-id.state.ax
401            outbound+&+outbound-duct.state.ax
402            by-id+&+connection-by-id.state.ax
403            by-duct+&+connection-by-duct.state.ax
404            axle+&+ax
```

```
405        ==
406        ``mass+!>(maz)
407    [~ ~]
408    --
```

Jael 150K

```
1  !:                                           ::  /vane/jael
2  ::                                           ::  %reference/0
3  !?  150
4  ::
5  ::
6  ::  %jael: secrets and promises.
7  ::
8  ::  todo:
9  ::
10 ::    - communication with other vanes:
11 ::      - actually use %behn for expiring secrets
12 ::      - report %ames propagation errors to user
13 ::
14 ::    - nice features:
15 ::      - scry namespace
16 ::      - task for converting invites to tickets
17 ::
18 |=  our=ship
19 =,  pki:jael
20 =,  jael
21 =,  crypto
22 =,  jael
23 =,  ethereum-types
24 =,  azimuth-types
25 =,  point=point:jael
26 ::                                           :::::
27 ::::                    # models             ::  data structures
28   ::                                         :::::
29 ::  the %jael state comes in two parts: absolute
30 ::  and relative.
31 ::
32 ::  ++state-relative is subjective, denormalized and
33 ::  derived.  it consists of all the state we need to
34 ::  manage subscriptions efficiently.
35 ::
36 =>  |%
37 +$  state-2
38   $:  %2
39      pki=state-pki-2
40      etn=state-eth-node                       ::  eth connection state
41   ==                                          ::
42 +$  state-pki-2                               ::  urbit metadata
43   $:  $=  own                                 ::  vault (vein)
44     $:  yen=(set duct)                        ::  trackers
45        sig=(unit oath)                        ::  for a moon
46        tuf=(list turf)                        ::  domains
47        fak=_|                                 ::  fake keys
48        lyf=life                               ::  version
49        step=@ud                               ::  login code step
50        jaw=(map life ring)                    ::  private keys
51     ==                                        ::
52     $=  zim                                   ::  public
53     $:  yen=(jug duct ship)                   ::  trackers
54        ney=(jug ship duct)                    ::  reverse trackers
55        nel=(set duct)                         ::  trackers of all
56        dns=dnses                              ::  on-chain dns state
```

```
57            pos=(map ship point)              ::  on-chain ship state
58         ==                                   ::
59    ==                                         ::
60  +$  message-all
61    $%  [%0 message]
62    ==
63  +$  message                                 ::  message to her jael
64    $%  [%nuke whos=(set ship)]               ::  cancel trackers
65        [%public-keys whos=(set ship)]        ::  view ethereum events
66    ==                                         ::
67  +$  message-result
68    $%  [%public-keys-result =public-keys-result]  ::  public keys boon
69    ==
70  +$  card                                     ::  i/o action
71    (wind note gift)                           ::
72  ::                                           ::
73  +$  move                                     ::  output
74    [p=duct q=card]                            ::
75  ::                                           ::
76  +$  note                                     ::  out request $->
77    $~  [%a %plea *ship *plea:ames]            ::
78    $%  $:  %a                                 ::     to %ames
79            $>(%plea task:ames)                ::  send request message
80        ==                                     ::
81        $:  %b                                 ::     to %behn
82            $>(%wait task:behn)                ::  set timer
83        ==                                     ::
84        $:  %e                                 ::     to %eyre
85            [%code-changed ~]                  ::  notify code changed
86        ==                                     ::
87        $:  %g                                 ::     to %gall
88            $>(%deal task:gall)                ::  talk to app
89        ==                                     ::
90        $:  %j                                 ::     to self
91            $>(%listen task)                   ::  set ethereum source
92        ==                                     ::
93        $:  @tas                               ::
94    $%  $>(%init vane-task)                    ::  report install
95    ==  ==  ==                                 ::
96  ::                                           ::
97  +$  sign                                     ::  in result $<-
98    $~  [%behn %wake ~]                        ::
99    $%  $:  %ames                              ::
100           $%  $>(%boon gift:ames)            ::  message response
101               $>(%done gift:ames)            ::  message (n)ack
102               $>(%lost gift:ames)            ::  lost boon
103       ==  ==                                 ::
104       $:  %behn                              ::
105           $>(%wake gift:behn)                ::
106       ==                                     ::
107       $:  %gall                              ::
108           $>(%unto gift:gall)                ::
109       ==                                     ::
110   ==                                         ::
111 --  ::                                       ::
112 ::                                           ::::
113 ::::                      # light            ::  light cores
114   ::                                         ::::
```

```
115  =>   |%
116  ::
117  ::::                          ## ethereum^light        ::   ++ez
118  ::                                                     ::   wallet algebra
119  ++  ez                                                 ::::
120  ::   simple ethereum-related utility arms.
121  ::
122  |%
123  ::
124  ::   +order-events: sort changes by block and log numbers
125  ::
126  ++  order-events
127  |=  loz=(list (pair event-id diff-azimuth))
128  ^+  loz
129  %+  sort  loz
130  ::   sort by block number, then by event log number,
131  ::TODO  then by diff priority.
132  |=  [[[b1=@ud l1=@ud] *] [[b2=@ud l2=@ud] *]]
133  ?.  =(b1 b2)  (lth b1 b2)
134  ?.  =(l1 l2)  (lth l1 l2)
135  &
136  --
137  --
138  ::                                                      ::::
139  ::::                          #  heavy                  ::   heavy engines
140  ::                                                      ::::
141  =>
142  ~%  %jael  ..part  ~
143  |%
144  ::                                                      ::   ++of
145  ::::                          ## main^heavy             ::   main engine
146  ::                                                      ::::
147  ++  of
148  ::   this core handles all top-level %jael semantics,
149  ::   changing state and recording moves.
150  ::
151  ::   logically we could nest the ++su core within it, but
152  ::   we keep them separated for clarity.  the ++curd and
153  ::   ++cure arms complete relative and absolute effects,
154  ::   respectively, at the top level.
155  ::
156  ::   XX doc
157  ::
158  ::   a general pattern here is that we use the ++et core
159  ::   to generate absolute effects (++change), then invoke
160  ::   ++su to calculate the derived effect of these changes.
161  ::
162  ::   for ethereum-related events, this is preceded by
163  ::   invocation of ++et, which produces ethereum-level
164  ::   changes (++chain). these get turned into absolute
165  ::   effects by ++cute.
166  ::
167  ::   arvo issues: should be merged with the top-level
168  ::   vane interface when that gets cleaned up a bit.
169  ::
170  =|  moz=(list move)
171  =|  $:  $:  ::  now: current time
172          ::  eny: unique entropy
```

```
173              ::
174              now=@da
175              eny=@uvJ
176          ==
177          ::  all vane state
178          ::
179          state-2
180      ==
181  ::  lex: all durable state
182  ::  moz: pending actions
183  ::
184  =*  lex  ->
185  |%
186  ::                                              ::  ++abet:of
187  ++  abet                                        ::  resolve
188    [(flop moz) lex]
189  ::                                              ::  ++sein:of
190  ++  emit
191    |=  =move
192    +>.$(moz [move moz])
193  ::
194  ++  poke-watch
195    |=  [hen=duct app=term =purl:eyre]
196    %-  emit
197    :*  hen
198        %pass
199        /[app]/poke
200        %g
201        %deal
202        [our our /jael]
203        app
204        %poke
205        %azimuth-poke
206        !>([%watch (crip (en-purl:html purl)) %default])
207    ==
208  ::
209  ++  sein                                        ::  sponsor
210    |=  who=ship
211    ^-  ship
212    ::  XX save %dawn sponsor in .own.sub, check there
213    ::
214    =/  pot  (~(get by pos.zim.pki) who)
215    ?:  ?&  ?=(^ pot)
216            ?=(^ sponsor.u.pot)
217        ==
218      u.sponsor.u.pot
219    (^sein:title who)
220  ::                                              ::  ++saxo:of
221  ++  saxo                                        ::  sponsorship chain
222    |=  who=ship
223    ^-  (list ship)
224    =/  dad  (sein who)
225    [who ?:(=(who dad) ~ $(who dad))]
226  ::                                              ::  ++call:of
227  ++  call                                        ::  invoke
228    |=  $:  ::  hen: event cause
229            ::  tac: event data
230            ::
```

```
231              hen=duct
232              tac=task
233          ==
234    ^+   +>
235    ?-      -.tac
236    ::
237    ::  boot from keys
238    ::    $:  %dawn
239    ::        =seed
240    ::        spon=ship
241    ::        czar=(map ship [=rift =life =pass])
242    ::        turf=(list turf)
243    ::        bloq=@ud
244    ::        node=purl
245    ::    ==
246    ::
247        %dawn
248    ::  single-homed
249    ::
250    ~|  [our who.seed.tac]
251    ?>  =(our who.seed.tac)
252    ::  save our parent signature (only for moons)
253    ::
254    =.  sig.own.pki  sig.seed.tac
255    ::  load our initial public key
256    ::
257    =/  spon-ship=(unit ship)
258      =/  flopped-spon  (flop spon.tac)
259      ?~(flopped-spon ~ `ship.i.flopped-spon)
260    =.  pos.zim.pki
261      =/  cub  (nol:nu:crub:crypto key.seed.tac)
262      %+  ~(put by pos.zim.pki)
263        our
264        [0 lyf.seed.tac (my [lyf.seed.tac [1 pub:ex:cub]] ~) spon-ship]
265    ::  our initial private key
266    ::
267    =.  lyf.own.pki  lyf.seed.tac
268    =.  jaw.own.pki  (my [lyf.seed.tac key.seed.tac] ~)
269    ::  XX save sponsor in .own.pki
270    ::  XX reconcile with .dns.eth
271    ::  set initial domains
272    ::
273    =.  tuf.own.pki  turf.tac
274    ::  our initial galaxy table as a +map from +life to +public
275    ::
276    =/  spon-points=(list [ship point])
277      %+  turn  spon.tac
278      |=  [=ship az-point=point:azimuth-types]
279      ~|  [%sponsor-point az-point]
280      ?>  ?=(^ net.az-point)
281      :*  ship
282          continuity-number.u.net.az-point
283          life.u.net.az-point
284          (malt [life.u.net.az-point 1 pass.u.net.az-point] ~)
285          ?.  has.sponsor.u.net.az-point
286              ~
287            `who.sponsor.u.net.az-point
288      ==
```

```
289      =/  points=(map =ship =point)
290        %-  ~(run by czar.tac)
291        |=  [=a=rift =a=life =a=pass]
292        ^-  point
293        [a-rift a-life (malt [a-life 1 a-pass] ~) ~]
294      =.  points
295        (~(gas by points) spon-points)
296      =.  +>.$
297        %-  curd  =<  abet
298        (public-keys:~(feel su hen now pki etn) pos.zim.pki %full points)
299      ::
300      ::  start subscriptions
301      ::
302      =.  +>.$
303        %^  poke-watch  hen  %azimuth
304        %+  fall  node.tac
305        (need (de-purl:html 'http://eth-mainnet.urbit.org:8545'))
306      ::
307      =.  moz
308        %+  weld  moz
309        ::  order is crucial!
310        ::
311        ::    %dill must init after %gall
312        ::    the %give init (for unix) must be after %dill init
313        ::    %jael init must be deferred (makes http requests)
314        ::
315        ^-  (list move)
316        :~  [hen %slip %e %init ~]
317            [hen %slip %d %init ~]
318            [hen %slip %g %init ~]
319            [hen %slip %c %init ~]
320            [hen %slip %a %init ~]
321        ==
322      +>.$
323    ::
324    ::  boot fake
325    ::    [%fake =ship]
326    ::
327      %fake
328    ::  single-homed
329    ::
330    ?>  =(our ship.tac)
331    ::  fake keys are deterministically derived from the ship
332    ::
333    =/  cub  (pit:nu:crub:crypto 512 our)
334    ::  our initial public key
335    ::
336    =.  pos.zim.pki
337      %+  ~(put by pos.zim.pki)
338        our
339      [rift=0 life=1 (my [`@ud`1 [`life`1 pub:ex:cub]] ~) `(^sein:title our)]
340    ::  our private key
341    ::
342    ::    Private key updates are disallowed for fake ships,
343    ::    so we do this first.
344    ::
345    =.  lyf.own.pki  1
346    =.  jaw.own.pki  (my [1 sec:ex:cub] ~)
```

```
347        ::   set the fake bit
348        ::
349        =.  fak.own.pki  &
350        ::   initialize other vanes per the usual procedure
351        ::
352        ::      Except for ourselves!
353        ::
354        =.  moz
355          %+  weld  moz
356          ^-  (list move)
357          :~  [hen %slip %e %init ~]
358              [hen %slip %d %init ~]
359              [hen %slip %g %init ~]
360              [hen %slip %c %init ~]
361              [hen %slip %a %init ~]
362          ==
363        +>.$
364      ::
365      ::  set ethereum source
366      ::     [%listen whos=(set ship) =source]
367      ::
368          %listen
369        ::  %-  (slog leaf+"jael: listen {<whos.tac>} {<source.tac>}" ~)
370        %-  curd  =<  abet
371        (sources:~(feel su hen now pki etn) [whos source]:tac)
372      ::
373      ::  cancel all trackers from duct
374      ::     [%nuke whos=(set ship)]
375      ::
376          %nuke
377        =/  ships=(list ship)
378          %~  tap  in
379          %-  ~(int in whos.tac)
380          (~(get ju yen.zim.pki) hen)
381        =.  ney.zim.pki
382          |-  ^-  (jug ship duct)
383          ?~  ships
384            ney.zim.pki
385          (~(del ju $(ships t.ships)) i.ships hen)
386        =.  yen.zim.pki
387          |-  ^-  (jug duct ship)
388          ?~  ships
389            yen.zim.pki
390          (~(del ju $(ships t.ships)) hen i.ships)
391        =?  nel.zim.pki  ?=(~ whos.tac)
392          (~(del in nel.zim.pki) hen)
393        ?^  whos.tac
394          +>.$
395        %_  +>.$
396          yen.own.pki  (~(del in yen.own.pki) hen)
397        ==
398      ::
399      ::  update private keys
400      ::
401          %rekey
402        %-  curd  =<  abet
403        (private-keys:~(feel su hen now pki etn) life.tac ring.tac)
404      ::
```

```
405    ::  resend private key to subscribers
406    ::
407        %resend
408    %-  curd  =<  abet
409    %-  ~(exec su hen now pki etn)
410    [yen.own.pki [%give %private-keys [lyf jaw]:own.pki]]
411    ::
412    ::  register moon keys
413    ::
414        %moon
415    ?.  =(%earl (clan:title ship.tac))
416      ~&  [%not-moon ship.tac]
417      +>.$
418    ?.  =(our (^sein:title ship.tac))
419      ~&  [%not-our-moon ship.tac]
420      +>.$
421    %-  curd  =<  abet
422    (~(new-event su hen now pki etn) [ship udiff]~:tac)
423    ::
424    ::  rotate web login code
425    ::
426        %step
427    %=  +>.$
428      step.own.pki  +(step.own.pki)
429      moz           [[hen %pass / %e %code-changed ~] moz]
430    ==
431    ::
432    ::  watch public keys
433    ::     [%public-keys ships=(set ship)]
434    ::
435        %public-keys
436    %-  curd  =<  abet
437    (~(public-keys ~(feed su hen now pki etn) hen) ships.tac)
438    ::
439    ::  seen after breach
440    ::     [%meet our=ship who=ship]
441    ::
442        %meet
443    +>.$
444    ::
445    ::  XX should be a subscription
446    ::  XX reconcile with .dns.eth
447    ::  request domains
448    ::     [%turf ~]
449    ::
450        %turf
451    ::  ships with real keys must have domains,
452    ::  those with fake keys must not
453    ::
454    ~|  [fak.own.pki tuf.own.pki]
455    ?<  =(fak.own.pki ?=(^ tuf.own.pki))
456    +>.$(moz [[hen %give %turf tuf.own.pki] moz])
457    ::
458    ::  learn of kernel upgrade
459    ::     [%vega ~]
460    ::
461        %vega
462    +>.$
```

```
463      ::
464      ::  in response to memory pressure
465      ::      [%trim p=@ud]
466      ::
467        %trim
468      +>.$
469      ::
470      ::  watch private keys
471      ::      [%private-keys ~]
472      ::
473        %private-keys
474      (curd abet:~(private-keys ~(feed su hen now pki etn) hen))
475      ::
476      ::  authenticated remote request
477      ::      [%west p=ship q=path r=*]
478      ::
479        %plea
480      =*  her   ship.tac
481      =+  ;;(=message-all payload.plea.tac)
482      ?>  ?=(%0 -.message-all)
483      =/  =message  +.message-all
484      ?-    -.message
485      ::
486      ::  cancel trackers
487      ::      [%nuke whos=(set ship)]
488      ::
489        %nuke
490      =.  moz  [[hen %give %done ~] moz]
491      $(tac message)
492      ::
493      ::  view ethereum events
494      ::      [%public-keys whos=(set ship)]
495      ::
496        %public-keys
497      =.  moz  [[hen %give %done ~] moz]
498      $(tac message)
499      ==
500      ::
501      ::  pretend ships breached
502      ::      [%ruin ships=(set ship)]
503      ::
504        %ruin
505      ::NOTE  we blast this out to _all_ known ducts, because the common
506      ::        use case for this is comets, about who nobody cares.
507      =/  dus  (~(uni in nel.zim.pki) ~(key by yen.zim.pki))
508      =/  sus  ~(. su hen now pki etn)
509      =/  sis  ~(tap in ships.tac)
510      |-
511      ?~  sis  (curd abet:sus)
512      =.  sus  (exec:sus dus %give %public-keys %breach i.sis)
513      $(sis t.sis)
514      ==
515      ::
516      ++  take
517      |=  [tea=wire hen=duct hin=sign]
518      ^+  +>
519      ?-  hin
520          [%ames %done *]
```

```
521      ?~  error.hin  +>.$
522      ~&  [%done-bad tag.u.error.hin]
523      %-  (slog tang.u.error.hin)
524      ::TODO  fail:et
525      +>.$
526    ::
527        [%ames %boon *]
528      =+  ;;  [%public-keys-result =public-keys-result]  payload.hin
529      %-  curd  =<  abet
530      (public-keys:~(feel su hen now pki etn) pos.zim.pki public-keys-result)
531    ::
532        [%ames %lost *]
533      ::  TODO: better error handling
534      ::
535      ~|  %jael-ames-lost
536      !!
537    ::
538        [%behn %wake *]
539      ?^  error.hin
540        %-  %+  slog
541            leaf+"jael unable to resubscribe, run :azimuth|listen"
542          u.error.hin
543        +>.$
544      ?>  ?=([%breach @ ~] tea)
545      =/  =source-id  (slav %ud i.t.tea)
546      =/  =source  (~(got by sources.etn) source-id)
547      =/  ships  (~(get ju ship-sources-reverse.etn) source-id)
548      %-  curd  =<  abet
549      (sources:~(feel su hen now pki etn) ships source)
550    ::
551        [%gall %unto *]
552      ?-      +>-.hin
553          %raw-fact  !!
554      ::
555          %kick
556        ?>  ?=([@ *] tea)
557        =*  app  i.tea
558        ::NOTE  we expect azimuth-tracker to be kill
559        ?:  =(%azimuth-tracker app)  +>.$
560        ~|([%jael-unexpected-quit tea hin] !!)
561      ::
562          %poke-ack
563        ?~  p.p.+>.hin
564          +>.$
565        %-  (slog leaf+"jael-bad-coup" u.p.p.+>.hin)
566        +>.$
567      ::
568          %watch-ack
569        ?~  p.p.+>.hin
570          +>.$
571        %-  (slog u.p.p.+>.hin)
572        ~|([%jael-unexpected-reap tea hin] +>.$)
573      ::
574          %fact
575        ?>  ?=([@ *] tea)
576        =*  app  i.tea
577        =+  ;;(=udiffs:point q.q.cage.p.+>.hin)
578        %-  curd  =<  abet
```

```
579            (~(new-event su hen now pki etn) udiffs)
580          ==
581        ==
582      ::                                                      ::  ++curd:of
583      ++  curd                                                ::  relative moves
584        |=  $:  moz=(list move)
585                pki=state-pki-2
586                etn=state-eth-node
587            ==
588        +>(pki pki, etn etn, moz (weld (flop moz) ^moz))
589      --
590    ::                                                        ::  ++su
591    ::::                        ## relative^heavy             ::  subjective engine
592      ::                                                      ::::
593    ++  su
594        ::  the ++su core handles all derived state,
595        ::  subscriptions, and actions.
596        ::
597        ::  ++feed:su registers subscriptions.
598        ::
599        ::  ++feel:su checks if a ++change should notify
600        ::  any subscribers.
601        ::
602    =|  moz=(list move)
603    =|  $:  hen=duct
604            now=@da
605            state-pki-2
606            state-eth-node
607        ==
608    ::  moz: moves in reverse order
609    ::  pki: relative urbit state
610    ::
611    =*  pki   ->+<
612    =*  etn   ->+>
613    |%
614    ++  this-su  .
615    ::                                                        ::  ++abet:su
616    ++  abet                                                  ::  resolve
617      [(flop moz) pki etn]
618    ::                                                        ::  ++exec:su
619    ++  emit
620      |=  =move
621      +>.$(moz [move moz])
622    ::
623    ++  exec                                                  ::  mass gift
624      |=  [yen=(set duct) cad=card]
625      =/  noy  ~(tap in yen)
626      |-  ^+  this-su
627      ?~  noy  this-su
628      $(noy t.noy, moz [[i.noy cad] moz])
629    ::
630    ++  emit-peer
631      |=  [app=term =path]
632      %-  emit
633      :*  hen
634          %pass
635          [app path]
636          %g
```

```
637          %deal
638          [our our /jael]
639          app
640          %watch
641          path
642      ==
643    ::
644    ++  peer
645      |=  [app=term whos=(set ship)]
646      ?:  =(~ whos)
647        (emit-peer app /)
648      =/  whol=(list ship)  ~(tap in whos)
649      |-  ^+  this-su
650      ?~  whol  this-su
651      =.  this-su  (emit-peer app /(scot %p i.whol))
652      $(whol t.whol)
653    ::
654    ++  public-keys-give
655      |=  [yen=(set duct) =public-keys-result]
656      |^
657      =+  yez=(sort ~(tap in yen) sorter)
658      |-  ^+  this-su
659      ?~  yez  this-su
660      =*  d  i.yez
661      =.  this-su
662        ?.  &(?=([[%ames @ @ *] *] d) !=(%public-keys i.t.i.d))
663          %-  emit
664        [d %give %public-keys public-keys-result]
665        %-  emit
666      [d %give %boon %public-keys-result public-keys-result]
667      $(yez t.yez)
668      ::
669      ::  We want to notify Ames, then Clay, then Gall.  This happens to
670      ::  be alphabetical, but this is mostly a coincidence.
671      ::
672      ++  sorter
673        |=  [a=duct b=duct]
674        ?.  ?=([[@ *] *] a)
675          |
676        ?.  ?=([[@ *] *] b)
677          &
678        (lth (end 3 i.i.a) (end 3 i.i.b))
679      --
680    ::
681    ++  get-source
682      |=  who=@p
683      ^-  source
684      =/  ship-source  (~(get by ship-sources.etn) who)
685      ?^  ship-source
686        (~(got by sources) u.ship-source)
687      ?:  =((clan:title who) %earl)
688        [%& (^sein:title who)]
689      (~(got by sources) default-source.etn)
690    ::
691    ++  get-source-id
692      |=  =source
693      ^-  [source-id _this-su]
694      =/  source-reverse  (~(get by sources-reverse) source)
```

```
695      ?^  source-reverse
696        [u.source-reverse this-su]
697      :-  top-source-id.etn
698      %_  this-su
699        top-source-id.etn     +(top-source-id.etn)
700        sources.etn           (~(put by sources) top-source-id.etn source)
701        sources-reverse.etn   (~(put by sources-reverse) source top-source-id.etn)
702      ==
703    ::
704    ++  new-event
705      |=  =udiffs:point
706      ^+  this-su
707      =/  original-pos  pos.zim.pki
708      |-  ^+  this-su
709      ?~  udiffs
710        this-su
711      =/  a-point=point  (~(gut by pos.zim.pki) ship.i.udiffs *point)
712      =/  a-diff=(unit diff:point)  (udiff-to-diff:point udiff.i.udiffs a-point)
713      =?  this-su  ?=(^ a-diff)
714        =?    this-su
715            ?&  =(our ship.i.udiffs)
716                ?=(%keys -.u.a-diff)
717                (~(has by jaw.own) life.to.u.a-diff)
718            ==
719          ::  if this about our keys, and we already know these, start using them
720          ::
721          =.  lyf.own  life.to.u.a-diff
722          ::  notify subscribers (ames) to start using our new private keys
723          ::
724          (exec yen.own [%give %private-keys [lyf jaw]:own])
725        ::
726        (public-keys:feel original-pos %diff ship.i.udiffs u.a-diff)
727      $(udiffs t.udiffs)
728    ::
729    ++  subscribers-on-ship
730      |=  =ship
731      ^-  (set duct)
732      ::  union of general and ship-specific subs
733      ::
734      %-  ~(uni in nel.zim)
735      (~(get ju ney.zim) ship)
736    ::
737    ++  feed
738      |_  ::  hen: subscription source
739          ::
740          hen=duct
741      ::
742      ::  Handle subscription to public-keys
743      ::
744      ++  public-keys
745        |=  whos=(set ship)
746        ?:  fak.own.pki
747          (public-keys:fake whos)
748        ::  Subscribe to parent of moons
749        ::
750        =.  ..feed
751          =/  moons=(jug ship ship)
752            %-  ~(gas ju *(jug spon=ship who=ship))
```

```
753      %+  murn  ~(tap in whos)
754      |=  who=ship
755      ^-  (unit [spon=ship child=ship])
756      ?.  =(%earl (clan:title who))
757        ~
758      ?:  (~(has by ship-sources) who)
759        ~
760      `[(^sein:title who) who]
761    =/  moonl=(list [spon=ship ships=(set ship)])
762      ~(tap by moons)
763    |-  ^+  ..feed
764    ?~  moonl
765      ..feed
766    ?:  =(our spon.i.moonl)
767      $(moonl t.moonl)
768    =.  ..feed  (sources:feel ships.i.moonl [%& spon.i.moonl])
769    $(moonl t.moonl)
770  ::  Add to subscriber list
771  ::
772  =.  ney.zim
773    =/  whol=(list ship)  ~(tap in whos)
774    |-  ^-  (jug ship duct)
775    ?~  whol
776      ney.zim
777    (~(put ju $(whol t.whol)) i.whol hen)
778  =.  yen.zim
779    %-  ~(gas ju yen.zim)
780    %+  turn  ~(tap in whos)
781    |=  who=ship
782    [hen who]
783  =?  nel.zim  ?=(~ whos)
784    (~(put in nel.zim) hen)
785  ::  Give initial result
786  ::
787  =/  =public-keys-result
788    :-  %full
789    ?:  =(~ whos)
790      pos.zim
791    %-  my  ^-  (list (pair ship point))
792    %+  murn
793      ~(tap in whos)
794    |=  who=ship
795    ^-  (unit (pair ship point))
796    =/  pub  (~(get by pos.zim) who)
797    ?~  pub  ~
798    ?:  =(0 life.u.pub)  ~
799    `[who u.pub]
800  =.  ..feed  (public-keys-give (sy hen ~) public-keys-result)
801  ..feed
802  ::
803  ::  Handle subscription to private-keys
804  ::
805  ++  private-keys
806    %_  ..feed
807      moz      [[hen %give %private-keys [lyf jaw]:own] moz]
808      yen.own  (~(put in yen.own) hen)
809    ==
810  ::
```

```
811    ++  fake
812      ?>  fak.own.pki
813      |%
814      ++  public-keys
815        |=  whos=(set ship)
816        =/  whol=(list ship)  ~(tap in whos)
817        =/  passes
818          |-  ^-  (list [who=ship =pass])
819          ?~  whol
820            ~
821          =/  cub  (pit:nu:crub:crypto 512 i.whol)
822          :-  [i.whol pub:ex:cub]
823          $(whol t.whol)
824        =/  points=(list (pair ship point))
825        %+  turn  passes
826        |=  [who=ship =pass]
827        ^-  [who=ship =point]
828        [who [rift=0 life=1 (my [1 1 pass] ~) `(^sein:title who)]]
829        =.  moz  [[hen %give %public-keys %full (my points)] moz]
830        ..feel
831      --
832    --
833    ::
834    ++  feel
835      |%
836      ::
837      ::  Update public-keys
838      ::
839      ++  public-keys
840        |=  [original=(map ship point) =public-keys-result]
841        ^+  ..feel
842        ?:  ?=(%full -.public-keys-result)
843          =/  pointl=(list [who=ship =point])
844            ~(tap by points.public-keys-result)
845          |-  ^+  ..feel
846          ?~  pointl
847            ..feel(pos.zim (~(uni by pos.zim) points.public-keys-result))
848          ::  if changing rift upward and we already had keys for them,
849          ::  then signal a breach
850          ::
851          =?  ..feel
852            =/  point
853              (~(get by pos.zim) who.i.pointl)
854            ?&  (~(has by original) who.i.pointl)
855              ?=(^ point)
856              (gth rift.point.i.pointl rift.u.point)
857            ==
858          =.  ..feel
859            %+  public-keys-give
860              (subscribers-on-ship who.i.pointl)
861            [%breach who.i.pointl]
862          =/  sor  (~(get by sources-reverse) %& who.i.pointl)
863          ?~  sor
864            ..feel
865          ::  delay resubscribing because Ames is going to clear any
866          ::  messages we send now.
867          ::
868          (emit hen %pass /breach/(scot %ud u.sor) %b %wait now)
```

```
869      ::
870      =.  ..feel
871        %+  public-keys-give
872          (subscribers-on-ship who.i.pointl)
873          [%full (my i.pointl ~)]
874        $(pointl t.pointl)
875    ::
876    ?:  ?=(%breach -.public-keys-result)
877      :: we calculate our own breaches based on our local state
878      ::
879      ..feel
880    =*  who  who.public-keys-result
881    =/  a-diff=diff:point  diff.public-keys-result
882    =/  maybe-point  (~(get by pos.zim) who)
883    =/  =point  (fall maybe-point *point)
884    ::  if changing rift upward and we already had keys for them, then
885    ::  signal a breach
886    ::
887    =?   ..feel
888         ?&  (~(has by original) who)
889             ?=(^ maybe-point)
890             ?=(%rift -.a-diff)
891             (gth to.a-diff rift.point)
892         ==
893      =.  ..feel
894        %+  public-keys-give
895          (subscribers-on-ship who)
896          [%breach who]
897      =/  sor  (~(get by sources-reverse) %& who)
898      ?~  sor
899        ..feel
900      :: delay resubscribing because Ames is going to clear any
901      :: messages we send now.
902      ::
903      (emit hen %pass /breach/(scot %ud u.sor) %b %wait now)
904    ::
905    =.  point
906      ?-  -.a-diff
907        %spon  point(sponsor to.a-diff)
908        %rift  point(rift to.a-diff)
909        %keys
910      %_  point
911          life  life.to.a-diff
912          keys
913        %+  ~(put by keys.point)
914          life.to.a-diff
915          [crypto-suite pass]:to.a-diff
916        ==
917      ==
918    ::
919    =.  pos.zim  (~(put by pos.zim) who point)
920    %+  public-keys-give
921      (subscribers-on-ship who)
922    ?~  maybe-point
923      [%full (my [who point]~)]
924    [%diff who a-diff]
925  ::
926  ::  Update private-keys
```

```
927      ::
928      ++  private-keys
929        |=  [=life =ring]
930        ^+  ..feel
931        ?:  &(=(lyf.own life) =((~(get by jaw.own) life) `ring))
932          ..feel
933        ::  only eagerly update lyf if we were behind the chain life
934        ::
935        =?  lyf.own
936            ?|  ?=(%earl (clan:title our))
937                ?&  (gth life lyf.own)
938                ::
939                    =+  pon=(~(get by pos.zim) our)
940                    ?~  pon  |
941                    (lth lyf.own life.u.pon)
942            ==  ==
943          life
944        =.  jaw.own  (~(put by jaw.own) life ring)
945        (exec yen.own [%give %private-keys lyf.own jaw.own])
946      ::
947      ::  Change sources for ships
948      ::
949      ++  sources
950        |=  [whos=(set ship) =source]
951        ^+  ..feel
952        =^  =source-id  this-su  (get-source-id source)
953        =.  ..feed
954          ?~  whos
955            ..feed(default-source.etn source-id)
956          =/  whol=(list ship)  ~(tap in `(set ship)`whos)
957          =.  ship-sources.etn
958            |-  ^-  (map ship ^source-id)
959            ?~  whol
960              ship-sources.etn
961            (~(put by $(whol t.whol)) i.whol source-id)
962          =.  ship-sources-reverse.etn
963            %-  ~(gas ju ship-sources-reverse.etn)
964            (turn whol |=(=ship [source-id ship]))
965          ..feed
966        ::
967        ?:  ?=(%& -.source)
968          %-  emit
969          =/  =message-all  [%0 %public-keys whos]
970          [hen %pass /public-keys %a %plea p.source %j /public-keys message-all]
971        (peer p.source whos)
972      --
973    ::
974    ::  No-op
975    ::
976    ++  meet
977      |=  [who=ship =life =pass]
978      ^+  +>
979      +>.$
980    --
981  --
982  ::                                                            ::::
983  ::::                        #  vane                           ::  interface
984    ::                                                          ::::
```

```
985   ::
986   :: lex: all durable %jael state
987   ::
988   =| lex=state-2
989   |= $: :: now: current time
990          :: eny: unique entropy
991          :: rof: namespace resolver
992          ::
993          now=@da
994          eny=@uvJ
995          rof=roof
996      ==
997   ^?
998   |%
999   ::                                          :: ++call
1000  ++ call                                     :: request
1001    |= $: :: hen: cause of this event
1002           :: hic: event data
1003           ::
1004           hen=duct
1005           dud=(unit goof)
1006           hic=(hobo task)
1007        ==
1008    ^- [(list move) _..^$]
1009    ?^ dud
1010      ~|(%jael-call-dud (mean tang.u.dud))
1011    ::
1012    =/ =task ((harden task) hic)
1013    =^ did lex
1014      abet:(~(call of [now eny] lex) hen task)
1015    [did ..^$]
1016  ::                                          :: ++load
1017  ++ load                                     :: upgrade
1018    => |%
1019         ::
1020         +$ any-state $%(state-1 state-2)
1021         +$ state-1
1022           $: %1
1023              pki=state-pki-1
1024              etn=state-eth-node
1025           ==
1026         +$ state-pki-1
1027           $: $= own
1028              $: yen=(set duct)
1029                 sig=(unit oath)
1030                 tuf=(list turf)
1031                 boq=@ud
1032                 nod=purl:eyre
1033                 fak=_|
1034                 lyf=life
1035                 step=@ud
1036                 jaw=(map life ring)
1037              ==
1038              $= zim
1039              $: yen=(jug duct ship)
1040                 ney=(jug ship duct)
1041                 nel=(set duct)
1042                 dns=dnses
```

```
1043                     pos=(map ship point)
1044            ==        ==
1045        --
1046    |=   old=any-state
1047    ^+   ..^$
1048    =?   old   ?=(%1 -.old)
1049      %=   old
1050        -            %2
1051        own.pki  own.pki.old(+>+ +>.+>+.own.pki.old)
1052      ==
1053    ?>   ?=(%2 -.old)
1054    ..^$(lex old)
1055    ::                                              ::   ++scry
1056    ++   scry                                       ::   inspect
1057    ^-   roon
1058    |=   [lyc=gang pov=path car=term bem=beam]
1059    ^-   (unit (unit cage))
1060    =*   ren   car
1061    =*   why=shop   &/p.bem
1062    =*   syd   q.bem
1063    =*   lot=coin   $/r.bem
1064    =*   tyl   s.bem
1065    ::
1066    ::   XX review for security, stability, cases other than now
1067    ::
1068    ?.   =(lot [%$ %da now])   ~
1069    ::
1070    ?:   &(?=(%x ren) =(tyl //whey))
1071      =/   maz=(list mass)
1072        :~   pki+&+pki.lex
1073             etn+&+etn.lex
1074        ==
1075      ``mass+!>(maz)
1076    ::
1077    ?.   =(%$ ren)   [~ ~]
1078    ?+   syd
1079      ~
1080    ::
1081        %step
1082    ?.   ?=([@ ~] tyl)   [~ ~]
1083    ?.   =([%& our] why)
1084      [~ ~]
1085    =/   who   (slaw %p i.tyl)
1086    ?~   who   [~ ~]
1087    ``[%noun !>(step.own.pki.lex)]
1088    ::
1089        %code
1090    ?.   ?=([@ ~] tyl)   [~ ~]
1091    ?.   =([%& our] why)
1092      [~ ~]
1093    =/   who   (slaw %p i.tyl)
1094    ?~   who   [~ ~]
1095    =/   sec   (~(got by jaw.own.pki.lex) lyf.own.pki.lex)
1096    =/   sal   (add %pass step.own.pki.lex)
1097    ``[%noun !>((end 6 (shaf sal (shax sec))))]
1098    ::
1099        %fake
1100    ?.   ?=(~ tyl)   [~ ~]
```

```
1101      ?.  =([%& our] why)
1102        [~ ~]
1103      ``[%noun !>(fak.own.pki.lex)]
1104    ::
1105        %life
1106      ?.  ?=([@ ~] tyl)  [~ ~]
1107      ?.  =([%& our] why)
1108        [~ ~]
1109    =/  who  (slaw %p i.tyl)
1110    ?~  who  [~ ~]
1111    ::  fake ships always have life=1
1112    ::
1113    ?:  fak.own.pki.lex
1114      ``[%atom !>(1)]
1115    ?:  =(u.who p.why)
1116      ``[%atom !>(lyf.own.pki.lex)]
1117    =/  pub  (~(get by pos.zim.pki.lex) u.who)
1118    ?~  pub  ~
1119    ``[%atom !>(life.u.pub)]
1120    ::
1121        %lyfe                                    ::  unitized %life
1122      ?.  ?=([@ ~] tyl)  [~ ~]
1123      ?.  =([%& our] why)
1124        [~ ~]
1125    =/  who  (slaw %p i.tyl)
1126    ?~  who  [~ ~]
1127    ::  fake ships always have life=1
1128    ::
1129    ?:  fak.own.pki.lex
1130      ``[%noun !>((some 1))]
1131    ?:  =(u.who p.why)
1132      ``[%noun !>((some lyf.own.pki.lex))]
1133    =/  pub  (~(get by pos.zim.pki.lex) u.who)
1134    ?~  pub  ``[%noun !>(~)]
1135    ``[%noun !>((some life.u.pub))]
1136    ::
1137        %rift
1138      ?.  ?=([@ ~] tyl)  [~ ~]
1139      ?.  =([%& our] why)
1140        [~ ~]
1141    =/  who  (slaw %p i.tyl)
1142    ?~  who  [~ ~]
1143    ::  fake ships always have rift=0
1144    ::
1145    ?:  fak.own.pki.lex
1146      ``[%atom !>(0)]
1147    =/  pos  (~(get by pos.zim.pki.lex) u.who)
1148    ?~  pos  ~
1149    ``[%atom !>(rift.u.pos)]
1150    ::
1151        %ryft                                    ::  unitized %rift
1152      ?.  ?=([@ ~] tyl)  [~ ~]
1153      ?.  =([%& our] why)
1154        [~ ~]
1155    =/  who  (slaw %p i.tyl)
1156    ?~  who  [~ ~]
1157    ::  fake ships always have rift=0
1158    ::
```

```
1159    ?:  fak.own.pki.lex
1160      ``[%noun !>((some 0))]
1161    =/  pos  (~(get by pos.zim.pki.lex) u.who)
1162    ?~  pos  ``[%noun !>(~)]
1163      ``[%noun !>((some rift.u.pos))]
1164    ::
1165        %vein
1166    ?.  ?=([@ ~] tyl)  [~ ~]
1167    ?.  &(?=(%& -.why) =(p.why our))
1168      [~ ~]
1169    =/  lyf  (slaw %ud i.tyl)
1170    ?~  lyf  [~ ~]
1171    ::
1172    ?~  r=(~(get by jaw.own.pki.lex) u.lyf)
1173      [~ ~]
1174    ::
1175    [~ ~ %noun !>(u.r)]
1176    ::
1177        %vile
1178    =*  life  lyf.own.pki.lex
1179    =/  =seed  [our life (~(got by jaw.own.pki.lex) life) ~]
1180    [~ ~ %atom !>((jam seed))]
1181    ::
1182        %deed
1183    ?.  ?=([@ @ ~] tyl)  [~ ~]
1184    ?.  &(?=(%& -.why) =(p.why our))
1185      [~ ~]
1186    =/  who  (slaw %p i.tyl)
1187    =/  lyf  (slaw %ud i.t.tyl)
1188    ?~  who  [~ ~]
1189    ?~  lyf  [~ ~]
1190    ::
1191    ?:  fak.own.pki.lex
1192      =/  cub  (pit:nu:crub:crypto 512 u.who)
1193      :^  ~  ~  %noun
1194      !>  [1 pub:ex:cub ~]
1195    ::
1196    =/  rac  (clan:title u.who)
1197    ?:  ?=(%pawn rac)
1198      ?.  =(u.who p.why)
1199        [~ ~]
1200      ?.  =(1 u.lyf)
1201        [~ ~]
1202      =/  sec  (~(got by jaw.own.pki.lex) u.lyf)
1203      =/  cub  (nol:nu:crub:crypto sec)
1204      =/  sig  (sign:as:cub (shaf %self (sham [u.who 1 pub:ex:cub])))
1205      :^  ~  ~  %noun
1206      !>  [1 pub:ex:cub `sig]
1207    ::
1208    =/  pub  (~(get by pos.zim.pki.lex) u.who)
1209    ?~  pub
1210      ~
1211    ?:  (gth u.lyf life.u.pub)
1212      ~
1213    =/  pas  (~(get by keys.u.pub) u.lyf)
1214    ?~  pas
1215      ~
1216    :^  ~  ~  %noun
```

```
1217      !>  [u.lyf pass.u.pas ~]
1218    ::
1219        %earl
1220      ?.  ?=([@ @ ~] tyl)  [~ ~]
1221      ?.  =([%& our] why)
1222        [~ ~]
1223      =/  who  (slaw %p i.tyl)
1224      =/  lyf  (slaw %ud i.t.tyl)
1225      ?~  who  [~ ~]
1226      ?~  lyf  [~ ~]
1227      ?:  (gth u.lyf lyf.own.pki.lex)
1228        ~
1229      ?:  (lth u.lyf lyf.own.pki.lex)
1230        [~ ~]
1231      :: XX check that who/lyf hasn't been booted
1232      ::
1233      =/  sec  (~(got by jaw.own.pki.lex) u.lyf)
1234      =/  moon-sec  (shaf %earl (sham our u.lyf sec u.who))
1235      =/  cub  (pit:nu:crub:crypto 128 moon-sec)
1236      =/  =seed  [u.who 1 sec:ex:cub ~]
1237      ``[%seed !>(seed)]
1238    ::
1239        %sein
1240      ?.  ?=([@ ~] tyl)  [~ ~]
1241      ?.  =([%& our] why)
1242        [~ ~]
1243      =/  who  (slaw %p i.tyl)
1244      ?~  who  [~ ~]
1245      :^  ~  ~  %atom
1246      !>  ^-  ship
1247      (~(sein of [now eny] lex) u.who)
1248    ::
1249        %saxo
1250      ?.  ?=([@ ~] tyl)  [~ ~]
1251      ?.  =([%& our] why)
1252        [~ ~]
1253      =/  who  (slaw %p i.tyl)
1254      ?~  who  [~ ~]
1255      :^  ~  ~  %noun
1256      !>  ^-  (list ship)
1257      (~(saxo of [now eny] lex) u.who)
1258    ::
1259        %subscriptions
1260      ?.  ?=([@ ~] tyl)  [~ ~]
1261      ?.  =([%& our] why)
1262        [~ ~]
1263      :^  ~  ~  %noun
1264      !>([yen ney nel]:zim.pki.lex)
1265    ::
1266        %sources
1267      ?.  ?=(~ tyl)  [~ ~]
1268      :^  ~  ~  %noun  !>
1269      etn.lex
1270    ::
1271        %turf
1272      ?.  ?=(~ tyl)  [~ ~]
1273      [~ ~ %noun !>(tuf.own.pki.lex)]
1274    ==
```

```
1275  ::                                              ::  ++stay
1276  ++  stay                                        ::  preserve
1277    lex
1278  ::                                              ::  ++take
1279  ++  take                                        ::  accept
1280    |=  $:  ::  tea: order
1281            ::  hen: cause
1282            ::  hin: result
1283            ::
1284          tea=wire
1285          hen=duct
1286          dud=(unit goof)
1287          hin=sign
1288        ==
1289    ^-  [(list move) _..^$]
1290    ?^  dud
1291      ~|(%jael-take-dud (mean tang.u.dud))
1292    ::
1293    =^  did  lex  abet:(~(take of [now eny] lex) tea hen hin)
1294    [did ..^$]
1295  --
```

Khan 164K

```
1   ::  %khan, thread runner
2   ::
3   ::  this vane presents a command/response interface for running
4   ::  threads. two modes are supported: %fard for intra-arvo
5   ::  requests (i.e. within the same kernel space) and %fyrd for
6   ::  external requests (e.g. from the unix control plane.)
7   ::
8   ::  both modes take a thread start request consisting of a
9   ::  namespace, thread name, and input data; they respond over the
10  ::  same duct with either success or failure. %fard takes its
11  ::  input arguments as a cage and produces %arow, which contains
12  ::  a cage on success (or tang on failure). %fyrd takes an output
13  ::  mark and input page; it produces %avow, which contains a page
14  ::  on success.
15  ::
16  ::  threads currently expect input and produce output as vase,
17  ::  not cage. %fard/%arow use cage instead since this is the
18  ::  eventual desired thread API; however, the input mark is
19  ::  currently ignored, and the output mark is always %noun. (for
20  ::  forward compatibility, it is safe to specify %noun as the
21  ::  input mark.)
22  ::
23  ::  %fyrd does mark conversion on both ends, and additionally
24  ::  lifts its input into a $unit. this second step is done
25  ::  because threads conventionally take their input as a unit,
26  ::  with ~ for the case of "no arguments".
27  ::
28  ::  n.b. the current convention for threads is to use !< to
29  ::  unpack their input vase. !< imposes the requirement that the
30  ::  input type nests within the specified type. this limits %fyrd
31  ::  to threads with inputs for which a named mark exists; it is
32  ::  impossible to use %noun in general since it does not nest.
33  ::  threads written against the current vase-based API could use
34  ::  ;; instead of !< to unpack their input, thus allowing the
35  ::  use of %fyrd with %noun. however the eventual solution is
36  ::  probably to make threads consume and produce cages, and do
37  ::  mark conversion where appropriate.
38  !:
39  !?  164
40  ::
41  =,  khan
42  |=  our=ship
43  =>  |%                                        ::  %khan types
44  +$  move  [p=duct q=(wite note gift)]         ::
45  +$  note                                      ::    out request $->
46    $~  [%g %deal *sack *term *deal:gall]       ::
47    $%  $:  %g                                  ::      to %gall
48            $>(%deal task:gall)                 ::  full transmission
49        ==                                      ::
50        $:  %k                                  ::      to self
51            $>(%fard task)                      ::  internal thread
52    ==  ==                                      ::
53  +$  sign                                      ::    in response $<-
54    $%  $:  %gall                               ::    from %gall
55            $>(%unto gift:gall)                 ::  update
56        ==                                      ::
```

```
57            $:  %khan                              ::      from self
58            $>(?(%arow %avow) gift)                ::    thread result
59          ==  ==                                   ::
60      +$  khan-state                               ::
61        $:  %0                                     ::      state v0
62            hey=duct                               ::    unix duct
63            tic=@ud                                ::    tid counter
64          ==                                       ::
65      --                                           ::
66  =>
67  |%
68  ++  get-beak
69    |=  [=bear now=@da]
70    ?@(bear [our bear %da now] bear)
71  ::
72  ++  get-dais
73    |=  [=beak =mark rof=roof]
74    ^-  dais:clay
75    ?~  ret=(rof ~ /khan %cb beak /[mark])
76      ~|(mark-unknown+mark !!)
77    ?~  u.ret
78      ~|(mark-invalid+mark !!)
79    ?>  =(%dais p.u.u.ret)
80    !<(dais:clay q.u.u.ret)
81  ::
82  ++  get-tube
83    |=  [=beak =mark =out=mark rof=roof]
84    ^-  tube:clay
85    ?~  ret=(rof ~ /khan %cc beak /[mark]/[out-mark])
86      ~|(tube-unknown+[mark out-mark] !!)
87    ?~  u.ret
88      ~|(tube-invalid+[mark out-mark] !!)
89    ?>  =(%tube p.u.u.ret)
90    !<(tube:clay q.u.u.ret)
91  ::
92  ++  make-wire
93    |=  [=beak =mark]
94    ^-  wire
95    [%fyrd (en-beam beak mark ~)]
96  ::
97  ++  read-wire
98    |=  =wire
99    ^-  (pair beak mark)
100   ~|  khan-read-wire+wire
101   ?>  ?=([%fyrd ^] wire)
102   =/  =beam  (need (de-beam t.wire))
103   ?>(?=([@ ~] s.beam) beam(s i.s.beam))
104 ::
105 ++  poke-spider
106   |=  [hen=duct =cage]
107   ^-  move
108   [hen %pass //g %g %deal [our our /khan] %spider %poke cage]
109 ::
110 ++  watch-spider
111   |=  [hen=duct =path]
112   ^-  move
113   [hen %pass //g %g %deal [our our /khan] %spider %watch path]
114 --
```

```
115  =|  khan-state
116  =*  state  -
117  |=  [now=@da eny=@uvJ rof=roof]
118  =*  khan-gate  .
119  ^?
120  |%
121  ::  +call: handle a +task request
122  ::
123  ++  call
124    |=  $:  hen=duct
125            dud=(unit goof)
126            wrapped-task=(hobo task)
127        ==
128    ^-  [(list move) _khan-gate]
129    ::
130    =/  =task  ((harden task) wrapped-task)
131    ?^  dud
132      ~|(%khan-call-dud (mean tang.u.dud))
133    ?+  -.task  [~ khan-gate]
134      %born
135    [~ khan-gate(hey hen, tic 0)]
136      ::
137      %fard  (bard hen 'khan-fyrd--' bear.p.task %| [name args]:p.task)
138      %lard  (bard hen 'khan-lard--' bear.task %& shed.task)
139      %fyrd
140    =*  fyd        p.task
141    =/  =beak      (get-beak bear.fyd now)
142    =/  =wire      (make-wire beak p.args.fyd)
143    =/  =dais:clay (get-dais beak p.q.args.fyd rof)
144    =/  =vase
145      (slap (vale.dais q.q.args.fyd) !,(*hoon [~ u=.]))
146    =-  [[hen %pass wire -]~ khan-gate]
147    [%k %fard bear.fyd name.fyd p.q.args.fyd vase]
148    ==
149  ::
150  ++  bard
151    |=  [hen=duct prefix=@ta =bear payload=(each shed [name=term args=cage])]
152    ^-  [(list move) _khan-gate]
153    =/  =tid:rand  (cat 3 prefix (scot %uv (sham (mix tic eny))))
154    =/  =beak      (get-beak bear now)
155    =/  =cage
156      ?-  -.payload
157      %&  [%spider-inline !>([~ `tid beak p.payload])]
158      %|  [%spider-start !>([~ `tid beak [name q.args]:p.payload])]
159      ==
160    =.  tic  +(tic)
161    :_  khan-gate
162    :~  (watch-spider hen /thread-result/[tid])
163      (poke-spider hen cage)
164    ==
165  ::
166  ::  +load: migrate an old state to a new khan version
167  ::
168  ++  load
169    |=  old=khan-state
170    ^+  khan-gate
171  khan-gate(state old)
172  ::  +scry: nothing to see as yet
```

```
173  ::
174  ++    scry
175     ^-    roon
176     |=   [lyc=gang pov=path car=term bem=beam]
177     ^-   (unit (unit cage))
178     ~
179  ++    stay    state
180  ::    +take: handle responses.
181  ::
182  ++    take
183     |=   [tea=wire hen=duct dud=(unit goof) hin=sign]
184     ^-   [(list move) _khan-gate]
185     ?^   dud
186       ~|(%khan-take-dud (mean tang.u.dud))
187     :_    khan-gate
188     ?-      -.hin
189         %gall
190     ?+      -.p.hin  ~
191           ?(%poke-ack %watch-ack)
192         ?~   p.p.hin  ~
193         %-   (slog 'khan-ack' u.p.p.hin)
194         [hen %give %arow %| -.p.hin u.p.p.hin]~
195       ::
196           %fact
197       =*   cag   cage.p.hin
198       ?+     p.cag   ~&(bad-fact+p.cag !!)
199           %thread-fail
200         =/   =tang  !<(tang q.cag)
201         ::   %-   (slog 'khan-fact' tang)
202         [hen %give %arow %| p.cag tang]~
203       ::
204           %thread-done
205         [hen %give %arow %& %noun q.cag]~
206         ==
207       ==
208     ::
209         %khan
210     ?.   ?=(%arow +<.hin)    ~
211     ?.   ?=([%fyrd *] tea)   ~
212     =*   row   p.hin
213     ?.   ?=(%& -.row)
214       [hen %give %avow row]~
215     =/   [=beak =mark]   (read-wire tea)
216     =/   =tube:clay       (get-tube beak p.p.row mark rof)
217     =/   =vase            (tube q.p.row)
218     [hen %give %avow %& mark q.vase]~
219     ==
220  --
```

Lick 164K

```
1  ::  %lick
2  !:
3  !?  164
4  ::
5  =,  lick
6  |=  our=ship
7  =>  |%
8      +$  move  [p=duct q=(wite note gift)]
9      +$  note  ~                                      ::  out request $->
10     +$  sign  ~
11     ::
12     +$  lick-state
13       $:  %0
14           unix-duct=_`duct`[//lick ~]
15           owners=(map name duct)
16       ==
17     ::
18     +$  name    path
19     --
20  ::
21  ~%  %lick  ..part  ~
22  ::
23  =|  lick-state
24  =*  state   -
25  |=  [now=@da eny=@uvJ rof=roof]
26  =*  lick-gate  .
27  ^?
28  |%
29  ::  +register: Create a move to register an agent with vere
30  ::
31  ++  register
32    |=  =name
33    ^-  move
34    [unix-duct.state %give [%spin name]]
35  ::  +disconnect: Create Move to send a disconnect soak to am agent
36  ::
37  ++  disconnect
38    |=  =name
39    ^-  move
40    =/  =duct  (~(get by owners) name)
41    [+.duct %give [%soak name %disconnect ~]]
42  ::  +call: handle a +task:lick request
43  ::
44  ++  call
45    |=  $:  hen=duct
46            dud=(unit goof)
47            wrapped-task=(hobo task)
48        ==
49    ^-  [(list move) _lick-gate]
50    ::
51    =/  =task  ((harden task) wrapped-task)
52    ?+  -.task  [~ lick-gate]
53        %born    :: need to register devices with vere and send disconnect soak
54      :-  %+  weld
55          (turn ~(tap in ~(key by owners.state)) register)
56          (turn ~(tap in ~(key by owners.state)) disconnect)
```

```
57      lick-gate(unix-duct hen)
58      ::
59        %spin      :: A gall agent wants to spin a communication line
60      :-  ~[(register name.task)]
61      lick-gate(owners (~(put by owners) name.task hen))
62      ::
63        %shut      :: shut down a communication line
64      :-  [unix-duct.state %give [%shut name.task]]~
65      lick-gate(owners (~(del by owners) name.task))
66      ::
67        %soak      :: push a soak to the ipc's owner
68      =/  ner=duct  (~(get by owners.state) name.task)
69      :_  lick-gate
70      [+.ner %give [%soak name.task mark.task noun.task]]~
71      ::
72        %spit      :: push a spit to ipc
73      :_  lick-gate
74      [unix-duct.state %give [%spit name.task mark.task noun.task]]~
75      ==
76  ::  +load: migrate an old state to a new lick version
77  ::
78  ++  load
79    |=  old=lick-state
80    ^+  lick-gate
81    lick-gate(state old)
82  ::  +scry: view state
83  ::
84  ::  %a  scry out a list of all ipc ports
85  ::  %d  get the owner of an ipc port
86  ++  scry
87    ^-  roon
88    |=  [lyc=gang pov=path car=term bem=beam]
89    ^-  (unit (unit cage))
90    |^
91    ::  only respond for the local identity, current timestamp
92    ::
93    ?.  ?&  =(our p.bem)
94            =(%$ q.bem)
95            =([%da now] r.bem)
96        ==
97      ~
98    ?+  car  ~
99      %a  read-a
100     %d  read-d
101     %u  read-u
102   ==
103   ::  +read-a: scry our list of ports
104   ::
105   ++  read-a
106     ^-  (unit (unit cage))
107     =/  ports=(list name)  ~(tap in ~(key by owners))
108     ``[%noun !>(ports)]
109   ::  +read d: get ports owner
110   ::
111   ++  read-d
112     ^-  (unit (unit cage))
113     =/  devs=(unit duct)  (~(get by owners) s.bem)
114     ?~  devs  [~ ~]
```

```
115      ``[%noun !>(devs)]
116   ::  +read u: does a port exist
117   ::
118   ++  read-u
119     ^-  (unit (unit cage))
120       ``[%noun !>((~(has by owners) s.bem))]
121   ::
122   --
123  ::
124  ++  stay
125    state
126  ++  take
127   |=  [tea=wire hen=duct dud=(unit goof) hin=sign]
128   ^-  [(list move) _lick-gate]
129   ?^  dud
130     ~|(%lick-take-dud (mean tang.u.dud))
131   ::
132   [~ lick-gate]
133  --
```

Milton Keynes UK
Ingram Content Group UK Ltd.
UKHW051058220424
441551UK00016B/1070